UNDERSTANDING FAMILIES INTO THE NEW MILLENIUM: A DECADE IN REVIEW

Understanding Families Into the New Millenium:

A Decade in Review

Edited by Robert M. Milardo

NCFR

National Council on Family Relations

Contents

ROBERT M. MILARDO, EDITOR
University of Maine

The Decade in Review

Good science has difficulty with compliance, in that innovation derives from noncompliance. Given the symbolic ending of a millennium, we do have an interesting opportunity to explore noncompliance and innovation. This volume is assembled to both review advances of the last decade, as well as to move beyond this scope and consider a broader time horizon, both across the distant past and within the glimmer of the future.

The volume is designed to address two essential goals. The first is to assess how we conduct the discovery and interpretation of knowledge about families without regard for reviewing specific substantive areas or advances over a specific period of time. Toward this end, I commissioned 6 articles where authors were charged with assessing the generation and accumulation of knowledge in family studies. They were asked to think like a mountain (or at least a vast range of foothills), review significant advances over the near and distant past as well as significant areas of underdevelopment, and to consider ways to reframe the future fields of inquiry. Their contributions were originally published in the February, May, and August 2000 issues of the journal and are reprinted here.

Our second goal is to take stock of the field of family studies and to review recent advances. These "decade reviews" composed the November 2000 issue of the journal and are reprinted here. There have been three previous decade reviews including the initial one edited by Carlfred Broderick, which actually spanned three issues of the journal (November, 1970; February and May, 1971), one edited by Felix Berardo (November, 1980), and the most recent edited by Alan Booth (November, 1990). All have had a similar purpose and have been highly influential in guiding the next generation of scholars and their scholarship.

Planning for the decade reviews began in November 1997 at the annual meeting of the National Council on Family Relations and proceeded in several stages. I first established a purpose as noted above and identified the major topics included in the two previous decade reviews. The initial plan was presented to the editorial board and subsequently revised. In defining the scope of the project, I excluded topics better dealt with in other arenas (e.g., child development, or family therapy), as well as issues having to do with methodology or analytical procedures. Advances in the methods of family research was the subject of a recent issue of the journal (November, 1995) edited by Marilyn Coleman, and will likely form the basis of a future issue of the journal.

Early in 1998, the full board was mailed a revised planning document and a questionnaire that listed the topics featured in previous decade reviews, asking members to rate each topic in terms of priority and needed coverage. Topics with the highest ratings were those that, in the opinion of the rater, saw considerable growth and investment over the previous decade. Raters were encouraged to suggest additional topics not included in the previous decade reviews or to suggest new ways of reorganizing or reconceptualizing topics, and they did so on all counts.

Fifty-four board members responded to this survey (a 77% response rate), and they often provided very detailed commentary. From their ratings and suggestions I identified topics that were clearly highly rated and seen as important areas of continuing inquiry, innovation, and growth (e.g., marital quality and interaction, work and family, divorce and its consequences), as well as areas that were relatively new and rapidly advancing (e.g., fatherhood, biosocial perspectives on families).

Some areas covered in past reviews received consistently low ratings, indicating they were viewed as witnessing relatively little growth over the decade. These included the areas of mate selection, religion and family life, family enrichment, power, and kinship. With the exception of religion and kinship, which seem to be neglected topics, the other areas are best viewed as areas undergoing dynamic shifts in their conceptualization. Mate selection, far from being entirely neglected, has merged into the more general field of close relationships; family power continues to be of interest to many, especially those in the field of family violence, although often under the guise of "control" (see Johnson & Ferraro, this volume). Research on kinship has certainly changed in focus, with research on caregiving among the elderly and grandparenting seeing growth (see Allen, Blieszner, & Roberto, this volume), while otherwise being largely neglected as a form of relationship or context in which families develop. Family enrichment is another area receiving low ratings although this probably represents the limits of the journal's purpose, rather than a comment on the area's vitality (see Bradbury, Fincham, & Beach, this volume).

Parallel with the evaluations of the editorial board, I conducted a content analysis of articles published following the last decade review. This analysis presents another way to judge whether the topics initially selected for consideration actually appear in the journal with some frequency. There should be substantial overlap in the content analysis and the results of the survey of the board members, and this was in fact the case.

One issue of the journal from each year of publication (1991–1998) was randomly selected, yielding a sample of 163 articles (excluding "feedback items"). And, for those interested in the minutiae: 60% of first authors were female; 28% of articles were single-authored; 89% used interview or survey methods, typically with large samples; 10% were based on the National Survey of Families and Households and 5% on the National Longitudinal Study of Youth; 4% were based solely on qualitative methods (a proportion

that is increasing); 2% represented theory or review (a surprisingly low percentage and one that surely needs to increase); 3% were based on observational research, and none on experimental designs.

All 163 articles were categorized based upon their titles and abstracts. Where an article clearly fell into two categories and could not be fairly represented in one or the other, I recorded it in both, and this resulted in 172 entries. Topics in the top quartile included: family structure with marital status or relational types as the independent or dependent variable (19 articles); parenting and parent child relations (15); divorce (13); marital quality with most treating quality as a dependent variable (10); violence between intimates (9 concerning spouses or adult partners, and one concerning siblings); work and family (10); child or adolescent development in the context of family relations (9); caregiving and the elderly (8); family or marital interaction (7); and families and their adolescent children (7). The remaining articles were dispersed over 20 areas, although the topics of adolescent development and parenting, single mothers, mother-child relations, stepfamilies, and elderly families were all represented well by five to six articles each.

The overlap between these methods of identifying key areas of growth was substantial and all became areas for which, with the counsel of the journal's deputy editors, I later solicited reviews. The process did permit some unanticipated insights about the journal as it represents scholarship on family issues. Much of our knowledge is generated by survey designs, and on the distinct variety of measures, and hence knowledge, with which those designs excel. Undoubtedly, important advances will come from more specialized survey designs that permit distinctions between groups (e.g., cultural, ethnic, class, race or sexual orientation) (see Marks, this volume; Walker, this volume). A representative sample of a nation or metropolitan area is a fine place to begin inquiry, but it does not yield the kind of precision we require for successful theory or application. For instance, the effects of divorce may depend as much on the type of marriage terminated as the simple fact that the marriage ended (see Amato, this volume). The representation of known groups is paradoxically burdened with the lack of representation of any particular individual.

The National Survey of Families and Households presents an illustration. In this mass survey, respondents were asked: "During the past 12 months, how often did you see any of your full brothers or sisters?" Reponses ranged along the usual 6-points from not at all to several times per week. This is an interesting question, and I wonder what the answer might be; however, the responses to this question as phrased will not tell us—the meaning of responses is unknown. They may as well represent beliefs rather than behaviors, evaluations of closeness regarding a favorite sibling, or feelings of obligation to all siblings in general. On the other hand, the NSFH asks a variety of questions regarding the number of full-, step-, and half-siblings and their residential proximity to respondents. Here questions are concrete; the meaning is clear. In these instances mass surveys excel.

We need additional work on the internal character of relationships, not only in terms of the psychological character of participants, but also in terms of what they actually do with one another. The essays by Huston on the social ecology of marriage, Walker on the construction and communication of knowledge, and Gottman and Nottarius on the marital interaction literature, are especially pertinent in suggesting a suitable conceptual design to frame our current and future inquiries and locate the sometimes quite startling discoveries of the last decade.

Twenty-three articles were commissioned for the decade reviews and each was charged with summarizing in some detail the recent advances in the field. These reviews are intended to be comprehensive and integrative of advances in theory and research, to cross disciplinary boundaries where appropriate, and to forecast future needs. With a broad mix of authors representing the fields of inquiry so familiar to our readers, and some not so familiar, we hope to water the vigorous seedlings of innovation. This should not be terribly difficult. There have been extraordinary advances in the last decade in theory, research design and measurement, and in the sophistication of analytic techniques, both empirical and qualitative. They are not typically discontinuous innovations, or sudden drifts from usual practice, but rather represent a continuous growth centered and built upon what has been reported in the immediate past. One has only to observe topics that appeared in earlier editions of this journal to appreciate the continuity in development. For instance, the first decade reviews of the 1960s included articles on marital happiness and satisfaction, parent-child relations, family policy, minority families, sexuality, aging and the elderly, and kinship. In all, 7 of the 14 featured topics included in the 1960s review are featured in the 2000 review. This growth, precisely because of its continuity, because of its subtle drift of increasing sophistication, requires acknowledgement and celebration lest we fail to notice the subtlety in its utter breadth and profound importance. In the very first issues of the journal, Ernest Burgess wrote about predicting marital success, while others penned studies of parenting, individual development, and social structural influences on families; we find these fundamental issues continue to confront the field and yield innovations in all regards.

As a complement to the reviews that appear in this volume, I do want to call attention to the classic book reviews published in the August 2000 issue of the journal. Marc Baranowski, our book review editor, designed this feature to call attention to the more influential volumes published in the twentieth century (but prior to 1990). Forty-two classic books were nominated by the JMF deputy editors and editorial board, and from these Marc selected 15 to be reviewed. These are volumes that had a major impact on the field of family studies, and very often on allied fields as well. Each is reviewed anew with the intention of reflecting on why that particular book figured so prominently, the nature of that impact, and its current level of influence. In calling attention to these classic works, we hope to provide a secure foundation for evaluating the growth of the field and its central conerstones.

We simply know a good deal about people and their close personal relationships, and more importantly we know a good deal about how to think about families (i.e., theory) and how to apply that thinking (i.e., methodology). My only prediction for the next millennium is that there will always be more to know, and while this should humble us it should not detract from celebrating the accumulation of fine scholarship in the production of practical knowledge.

JETSE SPREY   *Case Western Reserve University*

Theorizing in Family Studies: Discovering Process

This paper makes the case that theorizing in family studies might be different if scholars asked the types of questions that now are asked in the physical sciences. Initial efforts to move toward a more abstract explanatory level in family studies led to inventorying and verification. This paper argues that the recognition of a realm of discovery, allowing for the creative and disciplinary use of imagination and metaphor, would extend the scope and quality of questioning. To ground the argument, the paper focuses on the problematics associated with the conceptualization of process in marriages and families.

> We say, "The wind is blowing," as if the wind were actually a thing at rest which, at a given point in time, begins to move and blow ... as if a wind could exist which did not blow.
>
> (Norbert Elias, 1978, p. 112)

More than two decades ago the sociologist Robert Nisbet (1976) argued that many social scientists fail to recognize the important difference between the "logic of discovery" and that of "demonstration" (p. 5). Only the latter, in his view, is subject to a set of strict methodological rules. It was "demonstration," he suggested, "in all its nineteenth century certitude, determinism, and mechanism, that seems to have had the greatest impact on those who, like Comte and Mill, were seeking

37410 Beech Hills Drive, Willoughby Hills, OH 44094.

Key Words: discovery, process, theory.

the absolute, final, and irrefutable science of man" (p. 16). He considered his book, *Sociology as an Art Form,* "as a kind of prophylaxis against, not science, but *scientism,* which is science with the spirit of discovery and creation left out" (p. 4).

Following Nisbet's conceptual distinction between two realms of explanation, discovery and verification, my focus in this essay is primarily on the former. I see discovery as a process in which the initial images needed to guide further questioning take shape. In this realm, metaphors give rise to concepts, whereas tacit knowing may be fashioned into working hypotheses. In that setting both imagination and creativity play an important role.

Discovery, as an intellectual component of explanatory practice in family studies, is lagging behind the rapid progress that marks its verificational counterpart. The reason for this will be considered in a later section of this paper. No attempt is made, however, to present a complete overview of discovery in our field. Instead, its complexity and ambiguity are highlighted through a close look at the conceptualization of the elusive idea of "process" as reflected in the contemporary literature on marriage and family. To begin, however, a brief review of our not-too-distant past seems in order.

LOOKING BACK

Even a cursory look at early key publications in family studies draws attention to some broad generalizations about the nature of marriage and family in society at large. Such statements often were theoretical in intent in that they touched on both the "hows" and "whys" of the origin, the course,

1

and the future of these institutions. Consider, for example, the way in which Burgess and Locke prefaced their influential book, *The Family: From Institution to Companionship* (1945):

> The central thesis of this volume is that the family in historical times has been, and at present is, in transition from an institution to a companionship. In the past the important factors unifying the family have been external. At present, in the new emerging form of the companionship family, its unity inheres less and less in community pressures and more and more in such interpersonal relations as the mutual affection, the sympathetic understanding, and the comradeship of its members. . . . The emphasis in this volume, then, is upon the family as a unity of interacting persons (1) that shapes the personality development of its members and (2) that is adaptable to social change. (p. vii)

The above statement seems "theoretical" more in intent than in form or substance, while its factual content may no longer pass without amendments (Coontz, 1992). What matters here, however, is not so much the empirical adequacy or the theoretical validity of what was stated, but rather the "beginnings" it contained. There is, for example, the conception of marriage and family as integral parts of society but also the recognition that the forms and the cultural values they reflect are not carved in stone. There is the recognition of the impact of "social forces" on the "inside" of specific marriages and families. Throughout the 800 pages of the book, the authors presented a reasoned and well-documented picture of two major institutions in transition and a specter of a social order that provided a foundation and a challenge for questioning about and research on the "macro" and the "micro" manifestations of marriage and family processes.

Propitious beginnings, however, do not guarantee orderly progress. Instead, they may give rise to scattered lines of questioning accompanied by a wide range of data gathering. Family studies, as it evolved during the 1950s, did not altogether escape this fate. Not surprisingly, then, more than a decade later, Hill and Hansen (1960) in a trendsetting paper on the need for "conceptual frameworks" observed:

> We have been so busy researching, piling finding on finding, that the essential task of inventorying has been badly neglected. We have lagged in developing a technology for coping with the range and quantity of research findings which would enable us to sift reliable from unreliable generalizations and note the extent to which findings

from different conceptual approaches can be integrated into accretive theory. (p. 299)

In their view, such frameworks would provide a necessary step toward the genesis of "an inventory of research propositions on marriage and the family" that, even when still incomplete, would open the door to the "development of numerous potentials in the inventory" and offer "tools of value to marriage and family students, researchers, and theory builders" (p. 310).

Family scholars heeded this advice. Throughout the 1960s and 1970s, a number of conceptual schemes were introduced (Burr, Hill, Nye, & Reiss, 1979; Christensen, 1964; Nye and Berardo, 1966). Several of these gained sufficient recognition to become embedded in the explanatory lore of family studies. Furthermore, conceptual reasoning per se increasingly was recognized as an integral part of explanatory practice.

Throughout the 1980s and 1990s, some frameworks grew into "perspectives," or analytic vocabularies linked to a set of more or less coherent assumptions about the entities and processes in specific domains of scholarly interest. Consequently, such schemes became more flexible and more useful as intellectual tools in the analysis of phenomena of interest to students of marriage and family. Two references illustrate this point. The authors of a recent publication on fatherhood (Doherty, Kouneski, & Erickson, 1998), aimed to examine "the concept of responsible fathering, summarize findings from the major areas of research on responsible fathering, and offer a conceptual framework to guide future research and program development" (p. 278). Their stated goal was "one of synthesis and theory development rather than comprehensive documentation." In a similar vein, Amato and Booth (1997), in their recent book, *A Generation at Risk: Growing Up in an Era of Family Upheaval,* singled out the "life-course perspective" as providing "an organizing framework" for their book. At the end of this century, theory development remains a promise, but both the content and the aims of both these efforts clearly reach beyond Hill's and Hansen's seminal contribution.

Even with the adoption and improved use of conceptual reasoning, however, the domain of discovery in family studies is ripe for further exploration. Much published work in the family field carefully documents the "what" of specific phenomena or events but limits its explanation to an account of "how" they came about. Why things happened in a given manner often is explained inductively, that is, by means of post facto or ad hoc conclusions. This practice is neither wrong nor misplaced. It may provide a first step to further, more theoretically focused research. Moreover, its findings may be quite helpful to clinicians or policymakers.

The danger in this practice is that a growing interest and investment in questioning the "whats" and "hows" of marriage and family may lead to the demise of "why" questioning or its delegation to domains such as philosophy, history, or the supernatural. "Unexplained," "error variance," or both terms may then become more or less permanent fixtures of explanatory statements in our field. Queries such as why marriage? why family? and why parenthood? would remain unasked or merely answered by a reference to the whims of the supernatural or Mother Nature.

Asking why things happen in a certain way requires, in Nisbet's phrase (1976), a "spirit of discovery and creation," and this implies a domain in which the use of imagination becomes a legitimate option in explanatory reasoning. This may seem too risky to some empirically minded researchers. In fact, Nisbet's argument does little to counter reasonable doubts, as is evident from the following: "What else is imagination but the moving around in the mind, restlessly, compulsively, so often randomly, of *images* with which to express and to maintain some aspect of perceived reality?" (p. 13).

Do those who cannot or will not curb their restless or random thoughts deserve to be heard? The "creative" use of one's imagination is not subject to the rules and prescriptions that discipline the process of verification. Instead the former primarily depends on controls from within. In other words, risk, subjectivity, and ambiguity remain aspects of discovery in family studies.

In view of this, how do we move from the what and the how to the why without losing track of the "real" world? This question plagues many scholarly disciplines, not just our own. Nisbet, as indicated in the title of his book, looks to the arts as source of inspiration and companionship in his quest for wisdom. I prefer to see how scholars in the natural sciences handle the risks associated with discovery. My impression is that they simply decided to live with it. The following brief quote, taken from a book on theoretical physics, illustrates this point. Its author views further progress in physical theory as a continuing process of reformulation

. . . in terms that are more and more fundamental and at the same time farther and farther from everyday experience. How can we hope to make a theory based on observables when no aspect of our experience—perhaps not even space and time—appears at the most fundamental level of our theories. (Weinberg, 1993, p. 184)

Theorizing in the natural sciences is no longer totally constrained by what can be observed or measured directly. Its practitioners can afford a disciplined use of the imagination while the necessity of verification is not discarded but merely left behind. There seems the awareness that without the use of "terms that are more and more fundamental" (Weinberg, 1993, p. 184) the growth of theoretical explanation may come to a halt. Scientists, such as Weinberg and Hawking (1998), seem disinclined to let this happen.

Of course, family studies differs drastically from physics and theoretical biology. Its scholarly capital may not be sufficient to allow much speculation or overly ambitious risk taking. Nonetheless, I see the gap between the "capital" of the natural sciences and our own as one of degree rather than of kind. I doubt that the vulnerability of our discipline warrants either a neglect or the exclusion of "discovery" from its explanatory enterprise. Without denying the crucial importance of verification, my focus in what follows is on discovery, a process from which a clear and unambiguous "methodology" seems absent.

POINTS OF VIEW

To avoid potential ambiguity and confusion, some of the main ideas that underpin this essay's case are discussed briefly in this section.

Explanation

Explanations answer questions that, in turn, may be phrased on various levels of abstraction. Inquiries beginning with either "what" or "how," for instance, generally can be dealt with both empirically and conclusively. "Why" questions, on the other hand, call for answers in which facts and ideas conjointly reach beyond the immediate setting of what is to be explained.

My questioning reflects an image of a "layered" world in which different realities may require explanations that cannot necessarily be reduced to each other. That a group is more than the sum of its parts illustrates this point, one expressed well by Stephen Gould, a prominent student of evolution, who sees the real world as

> ... constructed not as a smooth continuum, permitting simple extrapolation from the lowest level to the highest, but as a series of ascending levels, each bound to the one below it in some ways and independent in others. Discontinuities and seams characterize the transitions; "emergent" features, not implicit in the operation of processes at lower levels, may control events at higher levels. The basic processes ... may enter into explanations on all levels ... but they work in different ways on the characteristic material of diverse levels. (Gould, 1987, p. 116)

Studying marriage and family, then means looking for linkages, causal or otherwise, between what we perceives as their macro, micro, and perhaps other "realities." Potential "seams" and "discontinuities," however, may not be assumed without good reason or evidence.

Reductionism

If we conceive of a living process as both dynamic and in some way bounded, its most relevant attribute

> ... is not complexity, per se, but organization. The complex processes that occur are of a cooperative nature, thus endowing the organism with a coherent identity as a whole. It is this impression that the organism is somehow harnessing the blind and purposeless forces of physics and arranging them ... as part of a plan or project, that seems baffling. What is the source of this "purpose without purpose"? (Davies, 1989, p. 101)

"Organization," then, concerns the ongoing relationships among the constituent parts of a process. It involves not only the elements in and by themselves, but also the nature of their interdependence. The processes Davies had in mind are biological, but they do not differ qualitatively from those of marriage and family. His comment deserves our attention because it underlines both the "wholeness" of process and the relevance of its order.

Current treatments of marriage and family process often are "reductionist" in that they focus, almost exclusively, on individuals as they perform their respective roles. Terms such as "spouse," which derives its meaning from a tie to a unique partner, and "generation," which makes sense only because of other generations, tend to lose much of their meaning after being reduced to attributes of individuals. We know this, of course, but that does not prevent frequent exclusively reductionist reasoning in our field. A short reference to a recent research report illustrates this point: "The dependent variable implicit in many discussions of change in marriage is the trajectory of marital satisfaction, or the full course of spouses' feelings about their relationship from the beginning of the marriage" (Karney & Bradbury, 1997, p. 1086).

Because marital satisfaction is measured at the individual level, the above covers two trajectories, one for each spouse. This muddles the interpretation of "the full course of spouses' feelings." What does it stand for? A summation of two sets of personal scores? A computed average of two scores? What happens if spouses strongly disagree? Do their measured feelings cancel each other, or signal the existence of one asymmetrical relationship? Davies (1989) made this point:

> Because living organisms are nonlinear (for a start!) any attempts to explain their qualities as wholes by the use of analysis is doomed to failure ... this is not to denigrate the very important work of molecular biologists who carefully unravel the chemical processes that take place in living systems, only to recognize that understanding such processes will not alone explain the collective organizational properties of the organism. (p. 102)

Substituting the word "psychologist" for "molecular biologist" clearly illustrates both the strength and the limitations of purely reductionist reasoning in family studies. Its focus on individuals who happen to live in marriages or families is, by itself, not sufficient to explain what goes on between spouses, between parents and children and, for that matter, between siblings in specific households. This is not to say that a holistic approach will provide better information. It will, however, furnish significant additional insight and understanding, an issue to be taken up again in this essay.

Alternatives to Reductionism

This section puts forward two explanatory approaches that, each in its own way, augment—or, if desired, substitute for—what may be seen as overly reductionist reasoning. The first one, the concept of social forces, is most suitable to the holistic analysis of social process. The second one, the use of historical data, expertise, or both may augment rather than replace traditional social-science-oriented approaches.

The concept of social forces or conditions directs questioning away from the intentions, emotions, and attitudes of individuals, as in this example: "Social structures of discrimination are not reducible to socially created constructs; we believe that they have an independent reality and influence beyond the construction processes of those in disadvantaged positions" (Boss, Doherty, LaRossa, Schumm, & Steinmetz, 1993, p. 18).

The "independent realities" alluded to above allow the process itself, that is, its course and structuring, to be the major focus of attention. The "independent reality" of such "forces," however, is a consequence, not of what they actually are, but of the fact that they are experienced as real. To avoid "vitalism," the belief that living entities are driven by a "life force," any explanation incorporating the concept of "social forces" must distinguish between their intentionality and their outcomes. Whatever initiates a social process may strongly influence its course but does not necessarily determine the nature of its ending.

Process is a social phenomenon that cannot be conceived of separately from the march of time. In view of this, a brief comment on the possible use of historical information as a potential resource in its explanation seems warranted. Humans, unique in their nature, reflect on their past and continually produce revised accounts of it. Depending on their accuracy, such stories may furnish a true account of what happened, but they do not tell us what else could have occurred. Does this mean that historical knowledge is no more than a special brand of fiction? Perhaps, but to me its value lies not in its factual truth but rather in the contextual quality of its questioning. Good history transforms the "setting" of events into an integral part of what went on at a given time and place. Thus, historians are eminently qualified to remind family scholars that the "context" of what takes place is far more than a mere external setting:

> I would implore a historical social science in which considerations of context could challenge our sense of our situation. I would entreat a more active construction of context, in which it actually impinged on our agendas themselves. I would wish a history that was ingredient to our analytic purchase on our problems rather than merely a repository of antecedents and illustrations. (Zuckerman, 1993, p. 232)

Michael Zuckerman was addressing an audience of other historians and developmental psychologists, but his observation is equally relevant to all students of marriage and family. Reclaiming the lives of women from the past, for instance, does not explain them, but it allows us to recognize them as fundamentally different from those of men. Moreover, such knowledge underscores a view of human existence as a process of continued and, at times, seemingly chaotic change.

IN SEARCH OF PROCESS

Used metaphorically, the term "process" connotes an image of movement and change. As such, its use facilitates thinking about what remains a familiar but also elusive phenomenon. Deeper questioning, however, demands at least a serious attempt to define what is to be explained. In this essay, "process" is defined as all that happens, did happen, or reasonably may be expected to happen on all levels of marriage and family realities.

Metaphorically, a social process seems to resemble a river, a familiar phenomenon to most of us. As known to science, rivers are "self-organizing, dynamic, systems; complex, but analyzable" (Yates, 1987, p. 33). As another scientist puts it,

> One way to imitate these characteristics of a river system is to scribe a sand pile so that run-off begins in channels. But as channels are carved and silt up, they begin to meander, and the network that evolves adapts to the rain water supply and to the nature of the land. This adaptation by changing form becomes increasingly prominent if the supply flow is fluctuating, or impulsive, rather than constant. (Iberall, 1987, p. 34)

Defining process in this manner means to see its flow not as something it does but rather as what it is. Or, to paraphrase Piaget's conception of structuring, any process comprises the attributes of wholeness, change, and self-regulation" (1971, p. 5–6).

Tapping the river metaphor once again, its stream is more than the sum of its currents because its flow is constrained by, but also shapes, its banks. Furthermore, its final destination does not cause its flow, it merely provides an ending. The force driving real rivers is gravity. At this point, our metaphor breaks down. Real rivers do not plan, but because humans do, it is tempting to substitute the notion of "intentionality" for that of "gravitation" as the driving "force" in human processes. This would solve one conceptual problem but create others, as is well illustrated in a final comment to a discussion of mate selection as a "social transition to marriage" (Surra & Huston, 1987):

> Of course, there is always the possibility that the objective conditions necessary to promote stability are present without the partners' knowing it. . . . Nevertheless it is probably difficult to sustain inaccurate subjective assessments over the long run. As the objective evidence accumulates during the course of married life, and as spouses become less motivated to idealize their situation, they may change their initial assessments. Consequently, commitment will fluctuate as the balance is struck between objective and subjective reality. (p. 117)

A river is unaware that its banks affect its flow, and therefore those who study it do not need to translate "objective" evidence into "subjective" assessments. Social scientists do not share this privilege. Surra and Huston appear to consider all spousal assessments of their joint existence—accurate or not—as "subjective," which implies that so-far-unknown "objective forces" simply do not exist. If their consequences are felt, they will be assigned, inaccurately, to other "causes." Regardless of the ways in which so-called "objective" reality is experienced, its assessment by those involved is as subjective as it is real. In my view, the misleading "subjective-objective" dichotomy only exists in the minds of scholars who may equate—at times, wrongly—the experienced reality of specific consequences with their presumed causality. The important "balance" to be "struck between objective and subjective reality" referred to in Surra and Huston's statement does not exist and, as such, defies conceptualization. What does exist is a process in perpetual reciprocity with the experienced "realities" of its external environment. Analogous to a river's flow, it is guided by, but also shapes, its banks.

In the above context, the undeniable presence and influence of human "intentionality" may well play an important role, but not one directly analogous to that of gravity in the physical world. Personally, I see its explanatory role more as a variable than as an attribute in attempts to understand the velocity and course of processes such as those in marriage and family. On the institutional level, for example, the idea of "intent" seems even more ambiguous than on its micro counterpart. On the former level, the idea of "momentum" makes more sense to me.

Time and Place

Recently, I watched a performance by a group of rock musicians. While they played, these folks were not just "passing" time, they were "making" time. As a process, their show equaled time. After the music stopped, that time was up, and a new stage underway. Considering process as a whole requires the inclusion of time and space into its course. In a recent book on "complexification" the mathematician Casti (1995) defined time "as the manifestation of relations between events":

> The alternate view, in which space is given a priori and objects are "things" that merely sit in it, rose to popularity with Descartes and forms the basis of Newtonian science. . . . In this "scientific" view of temporal matters, time is a kind of cosmic wastebasket, sitting there waiting for events to be deposited into it. (pp. 199–200)

He subscribes to the Aristotelian view of time "as the measure of change with respect to before and after." This is what I have in mind. "Change," as the wind in the epigram at the onset of this essay, cannot be imagined, certainly not explained, without a "before and after." The same holds for process as it is generated in time.

Onset, Direction, Ending

How do we conceptualize the onset, the direction, and the end of social processes such as marriage and family? Any process tends to be seen as beginning at some time, as then moving on, and finally as coming to its end. A specific marriage, then, starts with some type of ceremony and subsequently proceeds to its termination. A family, in turn, usually begins at the arrival of the first child. One might ask, however, do these processes move away from their beginnings? Or are they somehow directed toward their respective endings? The answer is clear: A "living" process has no option but to move away from its onset and then to continue to what may turn out to be its end. To return to the pre-onset is out of the question. Contemporary chaos theory (e.g., Hall, 1992; Peak & Frame, 1994) supports the premise that for any process—a weather system, a river, or a family—precise knowledge about its beginnings provides important clues to its further course. Predicting the nature of its ending, however, remains an educated guess at best. Most marriages in our society actually originate before their legal inception (e.g., Orbuch, Veroff, & Holmberg, 1993). The decision to cohabit also tends to follow a previous period of exploration (Bumpass, Sweet, & Cherlin, l991). Families, in turn, rarely originate on the spur of the moment. Much research on marital quality, family quality, or both overlooks these crucial preludes, whereas studies of premarital relations often come to a halt at the door of the courthouse.

No marriage or family lasts forever. A considerable proportion ends when one spouse dies; others end because of some other type of dissolution. During the past decade, the concept of "divorce process," indicating a nonrandom series of events leading or "cascading" (Gottman, 1994) to a legal dissolution, gained ground in family studies (e.g., Ahrons & Rodgers, 1987; Kitson & Holmes, 1992). To label the course of a given process with its outcome, however, simply states that a divorce process is one that ends in a divorce. In this context, the death of a spouse is not used to name its antecedent process. Is this because students of marriage and family still tacitly assume that death remains the "natural" way to end a marriage or a family? It is acceptable, of course, to hold this view, as long as it is understood that it echoes a religious rather than a rational premise. Many reproductive and caring processes in the animal world do not last till the death of one or both parents, a fact that does not make them less "loving" or efficient. It is reasonable at least to imagine such a scenario for the world of Homo sapiens.

A better understanding of the potential linkages between a given process's origin, velocity, and direction seems crucial to our ability to understand how and where it is to end. In this context, it may help, for example, to conceive of its course as either "passive" or "driven," a distinction made by students of long-range evolutionary trends (Gould, l987; McShea, 1994). "Passivity," describes a diffuse move away from a beginning but without a clear destination. Its label directs attention to "currents in the stream" without losing complete sight of the river.

"Mate selection," in my view, qualifies as such a "passive process." It appears no longer to be headed toward any goal in particular but merely moves away from childhood and early adolescence or from being single, leaving these processes behind. A quote from of a comprehensive review of the mate selection literature published during the l980s underlined this: "Throughout the review, I use the term mate selection loosely, for choosing a spouse is only one of the many forms that close heterosexual relationships take . . . the

term is outdated for describing the variety of premarital relationship experiences" (Surra, l990, p. 844).

In addition to being outdated, the term is confusing because it still implies a destination rather than just an ending. In fact, given the current decline in legal marriage, even the label "premarital," unless stretched to include some forms of cohabitation, is beginning to lose much of its original meaning.

A "driven" process is seen as "biased" in the sense that its course is influenced by the workings of "natural selection" (McShea, 1994, p. 1748). Among humans such a bias might indicate the influence of external forces or conditions but also the intended conduct of those who constitute a given process. The authors of a study of "commitment" processes in premarital relationships (Surra & Hughes, l997), for example, did distinguish between "relationship-driven" and "event-driven" processes. The two were found to differ on "stability of commitment over time; on the individuals own understanding of why they became committed; and on relationship dimensions" (p. 17). Which one was most likely to end in marriage was not established so that a possible selective "bias" is yet undiscovered. This notwithstanding, the author's conclusion is relevant enough to warrant comment:

> Over the long run, we expect that the negative qualities of event-driven relationships will overshadow the attractions of a dramatic courtship and that the stronger bases of relationship-driven commitments will lead to more satisfying interaction and more positive outcomes for these partners. (p. 19)

Surra and Hughes clearly saw a connection between the nature of premarital commitment and the ensuing marital process. Moreover, they favored a commitment powered from "within." In the choice between a process driven by "love" and one driven by necessity or, in relational terms, by love and *Kameradschaft,* the authors voted for love. I prefer to abstain.

Although, the above commitment processes are not mutually exclusive, their relationship raises questions: Do they add up to one? And, if so, to what degree and how? Do two relation-driven commitments become one "extrapowerful" one? Would a relation-driven course complement an event-driven one or compete with it? Does it make conceptual sense, then, to predict marital success or failure before such questions have been answered? I am not sure it does, because I doubt that an exact "match" of commitments is essential to the proper functioning of a social process. Information provided by the authors of a recent report on "how couples maintain marriages" (Weigel & Ballard-Reisch, 1999) is pertinent to this point:

> [I]t is possible that behaviors designed to maintain the marital relationship may have different meanings for wives and husbands. While wives' use of maintenance behaviors may be more influenced by dynamics within the relationship, husbands, may be more influenced by aspects external to the relationship. (1999, p. 268)

In other words, the personal commitments and meanings with which potential partners enter a presumably lasting relationship, may well be dissimilar and remain that way as long as such differences can be managed effectively. I suspect that many enduring marital and family bonds are asymmetrical in a variety of ways. Totally identical commitment processes may or may not be a bonus to the course of a process. The collective ability to negotiate and live with asymmetries and even inequities, however, seems a necessary condition for the stability of human processes.

Few couples are likely to enter a marriage or start a family with the intention of parting. What happens, then, if dissolution changes from a mere option to a real choice? A few studies provide insight into the "how" of such a transition (e.g., Vaughan, 1986), but none, to my knowledge really gets to the why of it. A study of marital satisfaction by Karney and Bradbury (1997), however, is of interest here. The authors compared a decline of satisfaction between spousal categories reporting respectively higher and lower levels of initial satisfaction. It was found that "higher levels of satisfaction are, in fact, associated with less steep declines in marital satisfaction over time" (p. 1084). High-starters, of course, cannot increase, but the relatively small magnitude of their decline is interesting. Does it mean, for example, that those who start high bring a relatively strong "momentum" into their marriage? Would it make sense, theoretically, to link the onset of this momentum to the premarital stage of their relationship? Perhaps, but this must be demonstrated rather than assumed. Also worthy of asking, is why the lower-starters decided to marry at all? Are the premarital trajectories of these high and lower scorers really comparable? I doubt it.

Orderly Process

Contemporary thinking in family studies, as in classical physics (Nicolis & Prigogine, 1977), remains focused on the notions of permanence and stability. In fact, the former generally is used to define the latter. In that context, lack of permanence, diversity, and even complexity tend to be considered challenges to the "natural" course of events. In contrast, I see them as equally predictable aspects of marriage and family processes. Because of this, the idea of "self-organization" attains considerable explanatory relevance.

To clarify this let me return to my original metaphor. Even though rivers are both "adaptive" and "impulsive" in shaping their trajectories, their flow can be orderly and self-maintaining despite periods of severe turbulence. To show the relevance of this for human systems, I begin with a statement by the editor of a massive volume on self-organization:

> Broadly speaking, self-organization describes the ability of systems comprising many units and subject to constraints, to organize themselves in various spatial, temporal or spatiotemporal activities. These emerging properties are pertinent to the system as a whole and cannot be seen in units which comprise the system. (Babloyantz, 1991, p. ix)

Many processes, biological and human, "exhibit high spontaneous order" (Kaufman, 1989, p. 67). Scientists use this idea of self-organization to bypass the narrow conceptual dichotomy between "static" and "dynamic:"

> We contemplate some of the most remarkable processes of which we are aware: energy transforming into matter transforming into life; sperm and egg becoming a human being; rivers sculpting continents; molecules arranging for their own preservation.... In all these activities the processes of self-organization, self-maintenance, or self-repair appear to be fundamental. Order is emergent, created out of materials, potentials, fluxes, and principles at hand. (Yates, 1987, p. 2)

Because marriage and family may well be less stable than other human processes, it seems reasonable to aim for a conceptual vocabulary that offers access to ideas such as complexity, order, and emergence. "Complexity," for one, means more than mere complication. As a feature of a process, it describes not just what is but also what may be. A triad, for example, is more complex than a dyad because it allows, but does not determine, three possible two-against-one alliances. In a similar vein, a five-person household allows 10 different dyads. Increasing its size by one member opens the door to 15 such combinations. "Complexity" increases significantly under such conditions, but the consequences for the "order" of those processes is unknown because this is a question that few have asked.

The logical opposite of "order" is randomness rather than mere disharmony. In family studies, however, "order" often remains equated with stability, durability, or both. Because of this, the notion of "orderly chaos" may strike some family scholars as a contradiction in terms. Our colleagues in the natural sciences take a different view. In reference to what he called "the burgeoning theory of deterministic chaos," Davies (1989) wrote:

> It turns out that more or less all nonlinear systems possess parameter regimes wherein the dynamics is essentially random. Although these are deterministic systems, their behavior is so sensitive to their initial conditions that predictability is impossible.... Chaotic systems in the real world include the weather, the motion of the conical pendulum, three-body motion and certain fish and insect populations. (Davies, 1989, p. 106)

Human institutions are not listed in the above array of nonlinear processes. I suggest that students of marriage and family consider conceptualizing both these processes as basically nonlinear and, therefore, encompassing phenomena whose dynamics can be situational and thus generally unpredictable. Doing this, takes one beyond a mere shift in focus. It would mean a departure from some "givens" in our scholarly past. Divorce, for example, could be seen on the institutional level as a newly integrated potential in contemporary marriage and family, rather than as a destructive, essentially outside force. As an institutional component of marriage and family, it could be seen metaphorically as analogous to a severe thunderstorm serving to restore a balance rather than destroying what happens to be in its path. Heavy weather may cause considerable local damage, but it also clears the air.

The notion of "self-organization" calls up an image of the family car. When moving, it develops "momentum" which, in turn, tends to resist, at least temporarily, any change in direction. According to its professionals, the stock market, too, may either gain or lose momentum. So what about process in marriage and family? It may be analytically useful to search for analogues to momentum in such processes. Would it be passive, or could it be seen to drive a given process to resist external contingencies?

Webster's *New Riverside University Dictionary* (1984) defines "emergence" as "coming into existence." As an intrinsic attribute of process or time it further adds a connotation of "renewal," one of continuing reemergence and change. Just as the wind derives its identity from its velocity, the idea that a process lacks emergence makes no sense. The idea of emergence, however, does not offer insight into the nature or cause of a given process's ending. It does not help us understand when, how, or why an ending turns into either a destination or an "attractor" that draws a process toward a specific resolution. We have known this for a long time, as is well illustrated in the following literary passage:

> "Read them", said the King. The White Rabbit put on his spectacles. "Where shall I begin, please your Majesty?" he asked. "Begin at the beginning," the King said gravely," and go on till the end: then stop." (Carroll, 1865/1949, p. 142)

Questions and Answers

Earlier, I suggested that the starting images underpinning questioning affect what is asked and the kind of answers sought. The family field harbors clinicians, policymakers, and scholars from different academic disciplines. This heterogeneity is reflected in its literature and also in the standards of those whose personal and professional interests guide its various research endeavors. In what follows, my comments may at times reflect a difference in premises or interest. They are not designed to be critical but to show the interdependence between the exact nature of questioning and the knowledge contained in its answers.

In a recent publication, Gottman, Coan, Carrere, & Swanson (1998) reported findings from a study "designed to explore marital interaction processes that are predictive of divorce or marital stability, processes that further discriminated between happily and unhappily stable couples" (p. 5). In it they defined and investigated seven "process models," ranging from "anger as a dangerous emotion" to "physiological soothing of the male" (p. 5). A single process model of marriage did not evolve, however. Instead, the authors showed that some of these strategies worked, but others turned out to be predictors of instability, divorce, or both. In a paragraph addressed to therapists, they advised the use of two specific clinical strategies (p. 20). This serves as an example of research that remains in close touch with what is "observable," and does not leave the real world behind. Not surprisingly, then, the authors argue that the use of an inductively tested "prediction model," may prove "to be superior to building an intervention by imagining what target populations in trouble may need or by imagining it according to some theoretical position" (p. 5). I have no quarrel with this approach as long as it is understood that it precludes a range of questioning of interest to me. I wonder, for example, why some of these seven models are functional and others are not. Why do some spouses become "locked" into a process of reciprocal destructiveness? Game theorists observed long ago that certain couples see their existence as analogous to a "zero-sum game," while others perceive it as a "non-zero-sum" game. (Epstein & Santa Barbara, 1975; Montoro, 1994). How does this come about? Finally, what happens if we approach marriage and family processes holistically, as an ongoing interplay between conflicting strategies and relationships, rather than between individuals? In that framework, concepts such as balancing and negotiation become attributes of relationships instead of individuals.

A different approach to questioning, one that incorporates the idea of social forces, can be found in Elder's well-known *Children of the Great Depression* (1974/1999), a book presenting a thorough account of the lives of a sample of children during The Depression. It also illustrates both the strengths and limitations of a developmental, and basically reductionist, line of questioning. In a new chapter, added to the book's reissue (1999), Elder commented on the fate of the children he studied:

> Their historical location placed them at risk of this deprivational event. Some were exposed to severe hardships through the family, whereas others managed to avoid them altogether. These contrasting situations . . . established an "experiment of nature" with empirical holdings that support *a principle of historical time and place.* (1999, p. 304, emphasis in original)

Elder's idea of "historical time" is insightful but remains that of a "basket" into which the children's lives are deposited. His selection of path analysis, a statistical technique resting on the assumptions of "linearity, addition, and asymme-

try" (p. 174), supports this view. Time, defined as such, serves primarily as a reminder that life was different in the past but fails to transplant actual experience into the present. Even the use of documents dating from the past does not bring this about. Historical writing, regardless of its documentation, always represents hindsight because those who interpret it know how things worked out. Even the best, most realistic accounts miss the day-to-day uncertainty, fear, or hope that color living in the shadow of tomorrow.

Elder's book is titled *Children of the Great Depression,* but its subjects were not *of* that depression, they *were* that depression. Theoretically, there is insufficient reason to assume that in a future depression children, and adults, would experience things in the ways described in the author's study. There may be similarities, of course, but even they would need explanation. I doubt that in our rapidly changing society the past is likely to repeat itself.

My second comment reaches beyond the confines of Elder's important study. "Developmentalism" is psychological in orientation and thus tends to focus on the individual rather than on the group to which he or she belongs. Families, however, tend to consist of parents as well as siblings. The same holds for the households they constitute. Crises and other contingencies affect all the relationships that constitute their process. How, then, did the depression of the 1930s influence the ties among the members of the "deprived" families in Elder's study? What happened to those between brothers and sisters, between fathers and daughters, between mothers and sons? Did deprivation change sibling rivalries? If so, how? Did it alter the bonding between "first-borns" and "later-borns," to borrow a dichotomy from a lengthy report on sibling relationships (Sulloway, 1996)? Much information is lost when families or households are reduced to mere aggregates of individuals. Even Amato and Booth, in their book, *A Generation at Risk* (1997), did not escape the limitations imposed by life-course thinking. As part of their introduction (pp. 15–22), they presented a brief section called "sons versus daughters" (pp. 21–22). It begins by stating that "sons and daughters experience family life differently" (p. 21). Indeed they do, but they also experience it together. Within the complex structuring of a family process, the denotation "sons versus daughters" may make sense, but it remains only one among others, such as sons versus daughters, daughters versus daughters, or sons versus sons, to mention just a few.

In the view of its proponents, life-course theory tells us "how lives are socially organized in biological, social, and historical time and guides explanations of how the resulting social pattern affects the way we think, feel, and act" (Elder, 1999, p. 333). Considered biologically all human life is "social" by definition. Its sociability, however, does not take place over time; it generates time. I do not question the value of the life-course perspective as a major "organizing" frame of reference, but neither do I see it as theoretical in its own right. A closer look at the process of "childhood" may help clarify this point.

On the cover of the 25th anniversary edition of Elder's book is a photo of 12 children. Regardless of whether they belonged to his sample, they resemble children being photographed: a bit solemn, intent, and expectant. So, apart from the photographer, what are they looking at? The future? I doubt it, because childhood, as a process, has no future. As a river's subsidiary, it simply disappears into a new and different process. Thus, to be a well-functioning child, during a depression or during a booming economy, means letting the future take care of itself while concentrating on one's life in the here and now. This, I suggest, is exactly what the young subjects of Elder's research were doing throughout the Great Depression. As children, they were as much a part of it as it was of their lives and those of their families. I do not doubt that the attitudes and skills they acquired during their youth are likely to have entered into their adult lives, but only to the degree that this made sense. This "sense making," however, in turn depends as much on their experience as grown-ups in a better economy as on the ways in which they, as children, were a part of the Great Depression.

As an afterthought, then, I would like to offer a somewhat different, admittedly speculative, view of childhood, a process that still primarily seems defined by adults for the benefit of their world. A caterpillar is "destined" to become a butterfly; I suggest, however, that its main goal in life is to be a well-functioning caterpillar, rather than a "junior" butterfly. Of course, the human childhood process differs greatly from the larvae stage in insect societies, but by how much? Is that difference one of degree or kind? Does it make sense to judge the childhood process as a mere stage designed to feed into a different, more important one? I doubt it.

How, then, do we expect children to behave, as well-adjusted caterpillars or as "minors" in a world of butterflies? Clearly, and perhaps fortunately, the process of human development avoids a caterpillar stage. Instead, we have a process that serves as an end in itself to those who live it and as a means to an end to those who control it, a situation that, as I see it, defies a conception of the life course as either continuous or linear.

The foregoing commentaries—different as they may be—both address research aimed at the "microlevel" of marital and family existence. Even a brief look at the content of recent *Decade Reviews* of the journals in our field reveals that most research in family studies, except that by demographers and historians, focuses on this level.

Macrovariables, if perceived as such, often are treated as "external" factors that, in one way or another, condition what happens "inside" marriages, families, or households. Consequently, such factors do little more than offer an outside context to what is explained, a point alluded to during my brief discussion of the potential contributions of historians to family studies. My comments on macrolevel explanation are brief and focussed largely on its potential linkages to its micro counterpart.

Some family scholars, and many outside commentators, see the present and future state of marriage and family—as institutions—as directly linked to what takes place on their respective micro-levels of existence. At the onset of this paper, however, I proposed a "layered" image of human sociability, one in which each level may be causally linked to the one "above" or "below" but also may be independent in some ways. Many of my colleagues clearly have rejected this point of view. Popenoe (1996), for example, argued that:

> In the industrial nations today, marriage is becoming deinstitutionalized. Growing numbers of people are cohabiting outside of marriage. The assigned roles for husband and wife are endlessly negotiated, especially with regard to the allocation of work and child care responsibilities. (p. 247)

I do not dispute these facts, but I interpret them differently. Because marriage's basic function is a "negentropic" or "ordering" one, its prime "enemy" is reproductive promiscuity or random mating rather than mere diversification. Newly appearing monogamous and presumably lasting arrangements, such as same-sex unions and forms of contractual cohabitation, are likely to empower rather than weaken the marriage institution. If we see the function of family as "caring," some of its alternate forms, for example, single-parent, and even polygamous parents, also may reinforce rather than damage the institution. Personally, I do not favor the introduction of polygamy on our current family scene, but my rationale is cultural and political, not sociological.

I agree with the contention that lifelong marriage, as a one-and-only form, seems to be losing ground, but I see no reason for it to disappear. Marriage, as a form, is changing rather than de-institutionalizing. I expect it to survive in a variety of socially sanctioned forms. On a closely related front, I agree with Amato's and Booth's claim (1997) that we are witnessing a period of "family upheaval," but I am not sure that our *youth* needs to be singled out as a "generation at risk." I suggested elsewhere (Sprey, 1999, pp. 683–684) that all of us currently are "at risk," each generation facing its own special demons. The risk confronting the increasing number of unmarried youth seems associated with the absence of choices: There are, as of yet, not enough meaningful alternatives to traditional marriage and family, a situation that may encourage young people to make inappropriate decisions.

As social institutions the current and future course of marriage and family cannot be adequately explained "from the bottom up." Rather, it requires a careful assessment of their relations to and dependence on other institutions and society at large. How, for example, are marriage and family linked to and controlled by the church, the world of work, formal education, and the political system? Who decides, for example, the fate of the so-called "marriage tax" in our society? Who decides the nature of child support or the mandatory bussing of young children? What about the increasing intrusion of the "public realm," especially the media into the "privacy" of a system that derives much of its "specialness" from its exclusion of outsiders?

Because families are held responsible for the care of their children, it does make sense to ask if a divorce will harm its caring capacity. Amato and Booth's research (1997), for example, did show that in "low-conflict" processes children, as a category, are likely to suffer after their parents' divorce. Parental remarriage also may be seen as a potential risk. And so forth. To argue, however, that divorce, as such, endangers the institutions of marriage and family remains to be demonstrated. To offer a mundane comparison, car accidents of-

ten harm individuals, but they are not necessarily indicative of traffic problems. Neither are "drunk drivers," for that matter. To bring in Stephen Gould's comment (1987) again, the macro and micro realities of marriage and family must be seen as interconnected in some ways and independent in others. It is up to family scholars to identify the linkages but also to discover and explain the independent features.

In Conclusion

This paper has been about the "images" that allow students of marriage and family to raise the questions they wish to ask. In fact, these preconceptions neither are nor need to be unbiased. They simply reflect the accumulated knowledge which, at the moment, is considered to be valid or within reason. "Verification," I argue, is concerned with the documentation of what passes for truth at a given time. "Discovery," aims to establish what reasonably can be seen as possible. This, in turn, accounts for its need for a disciplined use of imagination.

Apart from the above summary, this essay does not really need a conclusion. Its argument is presented throughout its narrative. This, then, allows for a few, self-consciously speculative comments. At one point in his absorbing book, *A Brief History of Time* (1996), Stephen Hawking asked, "why do we remember the past but not the future?" He answered by invoking the second law of thermodynamics, which says that in any closed system disorder, or entropy, always increases with time. He then continued: "The increase of disorder or entropy with time is one example of what is called the arrow of time, something that distinguishes the past from the future, giving a direction to time" (p. 149).

This helped my contemplation of two elusive issues, to wit, (a) the direction of process and (b) the problem of order. Time, as we live it, is by definition "directional," it moves, like an arrow, away from its beginning, somewhere in the past, to its yet unknown destination at some point in the future. No wonder, then, that we are tempted to define the direction of a process by its outcome, which leads to my second issue, the problem of order. Hawking suggested that "disorder," or randomness, increases with time:

> Suppose a system starts out in one of the small number of ordered states. As time goes by, the system will evolve according to the laws of science and its state will change. At a later time, it

is more probable that the system will be in a disordered state than in an ordered one because there are more disordered states. Thus disorder will tend to increase with time if the system obeys an initial condition of high order. (p. 150)

Recall, with reference to the above, that of the seven "interaction processes" listed in the previously cited study by Gottman, Coan, Carrere, & Swanson (1998), only two appeared to be functional; the other five became predictors of instability or divorce. If we consider a marriage, at its inception, a process in a state of "high order" it will, statistically considered, be far more likely to move to "disorder" than to remain orderly. Hawking reminded us that in the world of nature, a state of disorder is far more probable than a state of order. This reminds me of the saying that there are far more ways to be unhappy than happy in a close relationship. In this context, then, marital "satisfaction" becomes not only a rare experience, but one that requires continuous review and renegotiation. Which leads me, again, to the issue of "intentionality."

Years ago, I asked the students in my family course if, given the rising divorce rate, they foresaw divorce and a second marriage in their future. Not surprisingly, few of them did. One young woman, however, suggested that my question was unrealistic. When asked why, she said, "If I knew I would get a divorce, I would marry my second husband first." I have not forgotten that answer, because it was so eminently rational. It makes no sense to marry if you expect a divorce. Where, then, does this leave "intentionality," or "commitment," or a trial marriage, for that matter? On the road to Hell, the one paved with good intentions?

Many or perhaps most contemporary couples do not marry, much less plan a family, with their eyes closed. Yet, marriage and family, as lifelong bonds, are becoming less common. Good intentions alone, then, seem not enough to counter the simple fact that there probably are many more ways to move away from "satisfaction" than toward it. "Order," especially in long-term relationships, may well become an increasingly rare phenomenon in modern societies. In that case, the quest for "orderly" but less permanent alternatives may, by necessity, become more generally accepted in our culture.

Which introduces my final, perhaps most outrageous, comment. It begins with a quote:

Life without Lucille? Unfathomable, to contemplate how quiet and still my home would be, and how much less laughter there'd be, and how much less tenderness, and how unanchored I'd feel without her presence, the simple constancy of it. (Knapp, 1998, p. 6)

Lucille is a two-year-old dog, owned by the author of *Pack of Two* (1998), an interesting book about the relationships between humans and their dogs. Knapp reported, among other things, that roughly one third of all Americans live with dogs these days and that a sizable proportion of them view their pet as a member of the family or household (p. 13). I guess that comparable statistics on cat ownership would not be substantially different. In view of this, it is amazing how few data on pet ownership appear in the data banks that aim to document all aspects of marriage and family in our society. Perhaps it is because the terms "family" and "household" remain poorly differentiated in our literature. I can only guess, therefore, how many singles in our society may decide that a dog or a cat may provide better companionship or love than another human being. By the same token, I can only guess to what extent the presence of dogs, cats, birds, or other pets may alleviate the problematics of joint living in contemporary households. Perhaps we should stop guessing and find out.

REFERENCES

Ahrons, C. R., & Rodgers, R. C. (1987). *Divorced families*. New York: Norton.

Amato, P. R., & Booth, A. (1997). *A generation at risk; Growing up in an era of family upheaval* Cambridge, MA: Harvard University Press.

Babloyantz, A. (Ed.). (1991). *Self-organization, emerging properties and learning*. New York: Plenum.

Boss, P. G., Doherty, W. J., LaRossa, R., Schumm, W. R., & Steinmetz, S. K., (Eds.). (1993). *Sourcebook of family theories and methods: A contextual approach*. New York: Plenum.

Bumpass, L. L., Sweet, J. A., & Cherlin, A. (1991). The role of cohabitation in declining rates of marriage. *Journal of Marriage and the Family, 53,* 913–927.

Burgess, E. W., & Locke, J. (1945). *The family, from institution to companionship*. New York: American Book.

Burr, W. R., Hill, R., Nye, F. I., & Reiss, I. L. (Eds.). (1979). *Contemporary theories about the family* (Vol. 2). New York: Free Press.

Carroll, L. (1865/1949). *Alice's adventures in wonderland.* Great Britain: Harmonsworth.

Casti, J. L. (1995). *Complexification.* New York: Harper Perennial.

Christensen, H. T. (Ed.). (1964). *Handbook of marriage and the family.* Chicago: Rand McNally.

Coontz, S. (1992). *The way we never were.* New York: Basic Books.

Davies, P. C. W. (1989). The physics of complex organization. In B. Goodwin & P. Saunders (Eds.), *Theoretical biology* (pp.101–111). Edinburgh, Scotland: Edinburgh University Press.

Doherty, W. J., Kouneski, E. F., & Erickson, M. F. (1998). Responsible fathering: An overview and conceptual framework. *Journal of Marriage and the Family, 60,* 277–292.

Elder, G. H., Jr. (1974/1999). *Children of the great depression* (25th anniversary edition). Boulder, CO: Westview Press.

Elias, N. (1978). *What is sociology?* New York: Columbia University Press.

Epstein, N. B., & Santa Barbara, J. (1975). Conflict behavior in clinical couples: Interpersonal perceptions and stable outcomes. *Family Process, 14,* 51–66.

Gottman, J. M. (1994). *What predicts divorce?* Hillsdale, NJ: Erlbaum.

Gottman, J. M., Coan, J., Carrere, S., & Swanson, C. (1998). Predicting marital happiness and stability from newlywed interactions. *Journal of Marriage and the Family, 60,* 5–22.

Gould, S. J. (1987). Is a new and general theory of evolution emerging? In F. E. Yates, A. Garfinkel, D. O. Walter, & G. B. Yates (Eds.), *Self-organizing systems. The emergence of order* (pp.113–130). New York: Plenum Press.

Hall, N. (Ed.). (1992). *The new scientist guide to chaos.* New York: Penguin Books.

Hawking, S. (1996). *A brief history of time.* (Updated and expanded ed.). New York: Bantam Books.

Hill, R., & Hansen, D. A. (1960). The identification of conceptual frameworks utilized in family study. *Marriage and Family Living, 22,* 299–311.

Iberall, A. S. (1987). On rivers. In F. E. Yates, A. Garfinkel, D. O. Walter, & G. B. Yates (Eds.), *Self-organizing systems: The emergence of order* (pp. 33–47). New York: Plenum Press.

Karney, B.R, & Bradbury, T. N. (1997). Neuroticism, marital interaction, and the trajectory of marital satisfaction. *Journal of Personality and Social Psychology, 72,* 1075–1092.

Kaufman, S. A. (1989). Origins of order in evolution: Self-organization and selection. In B. Goodwin & P. Saunders (Eds.), *Theoretical biology* (pp. 67–88). Edinburgh, Scotland: Edinburgh University Press.

Kitson, G. C., & Holmes, W. A. (1992). *Portrait of divorce.* New York: Guilford Press.

Knapp, C. (1998). *Pack of two: The intricate bond between people and dogs.* New York: Delta Press.

McShea, D. W. (1994). Mechanisms of large-scale evolutionary trends. *Evolution, 48,* 1747–1763.

Montoro, J. (1994). *Cooperation and competition among aged parents and adult children.* Unpublished doctoral dissertation, Case Western University. Cleveland, Ohio.

Nicolis, G., & Prigogine, I. (Eds.). (1977). *Self-organization in nonequilibrium systems.* New York: John Wiley.

Nisbet, R. (1976). *Sociology as an art form.* New York: Oxford University Press.

Nye, F. I., & Berardo, F. (Eds.). (1966). *Emerging conceptual frameworks in family analysis.* New York: MacMillan.

Orbuch, T. L., Veroff, J., & Holmberg, D. (1993). Becoming a married couple: The emergence of meaning in the first years of marriage. *Journal of Marriage and the Family, 55,* 815–826.

Peak, D., & Frame, M. (1994). *Chaos under control. The art and science of complexity.* New York: W. H. Freeman.

Piaget, J. (1971). *Structuralism.* New York: Harper Torchbooks.

Popenoe, D. (1996). Modern marriage: Revising the cultural script. In D. Popenoe, J. B. Elshtain, & D. Blankenhorn (Eds.), *Promises to keep: Decline and renewal of marriage in America* (pp. 247–269). Langham, MD: Rowman & Littlefield.

Riverside. (1984). *Webster's II new Riverside university dictionary.* Boston: Author.

Sprey, J. (1999). Family dynamics: An essay on conflict and power. In M. B. Sussman, S. K. Steinmetz, & G. Peterson (Eds.), *Handbook of marriage and the family* (2nd rev. ed., pp. 667–685). New York: Plenum.

Sulloway, F. J. (1996). *Born to rebel. Birth order, family dynamics, and creative lives* New York: Pantheon Books.

Surra, C. A. (1990). Research and theory on mate selection and premarital relationships in the 1980s. *Journal of Marriage and the Family, 52,* 844–865

Surra, C. A., & Hughes, D. K. (1997). Commitment processes in accounts of the development of premarital relationships. *Journal of Marriage and the Family, 59,* 5–21

Surra, C. A., & Huston, T. L. (1987). Mate selection as a social transition. In D. Perlman & S. Duck (Eds.), *Intimate relationships: Development, dynamics, and deterioration* (pp. 88–120). Newbury Park, CA: Sage.

Vaughan, D. (1986). *Uncoupling.* New York: Oxford University Press.

Weigel, D. J., & Ballard-Reisch, D. S. (1999). How couples maintain marriages: A closer look at self and spouse influences upon the use of maintenance behaviors in marriages. *Family Relations, 48,* 263–269.

Weinberg, S. (1993). *Dreams of a final theory.* New York: Vintage Books.

Yates, F. E., Garfinkel, A., Walter, D. O., & Yates, G. B. (Eds.). (1987). *Self-organizing systems; The emergence of order.* New York: Plenum Press.

Zuckerman, M. (1993). History and developmental psychology, a dangerous liaison: A historian's perspective. In G. H. Elder, J. Modell, & R. D. Parker, (Eds.), *Children in time and place: Developmental and historical insights* (pp. 230–240). New York: Cambridge University Press.

TED L. HUSTON   *University of Texas at Austin*

The Social Ecology of Marriage and Other Intimate Unions

This article provides an interdisciplinary framework for studying marital and other intimate relationships. Three levels of analysis are distinguished: (a) the society, characterized in terms of both macrosocietal forces and the ecological niches within which particular spouses and couples function; (b) the individual spouses, including their psychosocial and physical attributes, as well as the attitudes and beliefs they have about each other and their relationship; and (c) the marriage relationship, viewed as a behavioral system embedded within a larger network of close relationships. The discussion focuses primarily on the interplay between the spouses and their marriage, emphasizing the importance of distinguishing, both analytically and operationally, the individual from the dyadic (or group) levels of analysis. It is also argued that in order to appreciate how marriages work, social scientists must understand not only how these 2 levels of analysis interpenetrate each other but also how macrosocietal forces and the ecological niches within which couples live impinge on partners and their marital relationship.

This article sets forth an ecological framework that can be used to examine the marital system, considered as a whole, or to examine any particular marital behavior pattern, such as division of

Department of Human Ecology (A2700), University of Texas at Austin, Austin, TX 78712 (huston@mail.utexas.edu).

Key Words: commitment, marriage, social ecology.

labor, companionship, the expression of affection and hostility, patterns of conflict resolution, and sexual activity. My analysis is intended to apply to any marriage-like union, regardless of its gender composition or whether the partners live under the same roof. The framework could readily be expanded to encompass friendships, or even plural marriages, such as exist among subpopulations of Mormons in Utah who practice polygyny (Altman & Ginat, 1996). My goal is to provide a broad prolegomenon for research, rather than to summarize past research or to show how cultural, interpersonal, and psychological factors combine to create distinctive lifestyles. The terms *marriage* and *union* will be used interchangeably, and *mate, spouse,* and *partner* will be used alternately to designate the individuals who constitute the marital pair.

The historical, multilayered, interdependent causal pathways that produce, maintain, and modify marital behavior create enormous analytic problems that must be overcome by scholars who wish to understand why marriages function the way they do. The present framework distinguishes three broad levels of analysis: (a) the society, characterized in terms of both macrosocietal forces and the ecological niches within which particular spouses and couples function; (b) the individual spouses, including their psychosocial and physical attributes, as well as the attitudes and beliefs they have about each other and their relationship; and (c) the marriage relationship, viewed as a behavioral system embedded within a larger network of close relationships (Bates & Harvey,

1975; Berscheid, 1998; Hinde, 1987; Kelley et al., 1983; Levinger, 1994). These three types of factors—societal, individual, and marital—interpenetrate each other, and they operate together in a complex, interdependent fashion. The framework offered here, much like a framework put forth by Kelley and his colleagues, is intended to provide a conceptual blueprint, one that provides a sense of the types of questions that would be asked about marriage from an ecological perspective. As with the framework of Kelley et al., the approach "transcends any one specific theory, disciplinary approach, and any single relationship phenomenon" (p. 15). Nonetheless, the framework is intended to challenge social scientists to build their research programs during the 21st century with a greater appreciation of four fundamental ideas: (a) that marriages are interpersonal systems (and hence must be studied as small groups), (b) that spouses' psychological and physical qualities shape their individual and collective efforts to maintain a successful union, (c) that both marriage relationships and the partners themselves are dynamic (i.e., they change by context and they evolve over time), and (d) that marital unions are embedded in a social context.

The portraits of marriage that social scientists create often tell us as much about the person behind the camera (i.e., the reporter) as they do about the relationship; many relationship portraits provide such a blurred image that they give us little more than a fuzzy sense of the quality of the marriage, or a general sense of marital behavior patterns. Other portraits, which are taken at close range, are clearly focused; they provide a wonderful, richly drawn view of a specific interactional phenomena—such as how a couple resolves a problem in a particular setting. They usually include little information, however, about the psychological, social, and environmental contexts within which the interaction is embedded. The propensity of researchers to use either an unfocused lens or to zero in on narrow and isolated slices of the larger marital terrain has produced a literature on marriage that provides limited insight into how marriages actually work. Such a state of affairs also has undermined the development of sophisticated theories designed to link the qualities and dispositions of the spouses to features of their marriage relationship and has hindered efforts to examine how the ecological context influences the details of couples' day-to-day married life. The framework outlined below describes the kinds of data needed, maps out the larger terrain

of marriage, and draws attention to the kinds of distinctions researchers need to make to conduct sound research. It is offered with the hope that it will provide a set of operating principles that will help improve the quality of research during the first few years of the 21st century.

The conceptualization outlined below is ecological, in the sense that marital behavior patterns are seen as a reflection of the environmental context within which they are embedded, and social psychological, in that the goal is to relate the qualities of the individual spouses to the characteristics of their marriage relationship. Figure 1 provides a schematic view of the interplay among the macroenvironmental context (box A), the characteristics of the individuals who constitute the marital pair (box B), and the marital relationship as a behavioral system (box C; cf. Hinde, 1987; Kelley et al., 1983; Levinger, 1994; Robins, 1990). It is important to keep in mind, of course, that the macroenvironment, the individuals who make up the marital system, and spouses' marital behavior influence each other continuously over time.

This article considers three issues that can be illustrated in the boxes of Figure 1. First, I focus on conceptual issues associated with describing marital behavior in its context. Second, I take up issues pertaining to the interplay between individuals and the marriage relationships they create (box B→C). Third, I show how the macroenvironment within which marriage relationships are embedded affects the individuals (box A→B) and the marital microsystem (box A→C) and how the decisions that individuals and couples make affect the context of their own marriage and, in aggregate, contribute to stability or change in macrosocietal patterns (both B & C→A).

Many writings on marriage and other intimate relationships blur the distinction between the individual (Figure 1, box B) and the marriage relationship (Figure 1, box C; cf. Fincham & Bradbury, 1987; Kelley et al., 1983; Thompson & Walker, 1982). The significance of this confusion for research on marriage, however, has not been fully appreciated because if it had been, omnibus measures of marital quality and satisfaction—such as the Locke-Wallace scale (Locke & Wallace, 1959) and the Dyadic Adjustment Scale (Spanier, 1976)—would have fallen out of favor years ago. These omnibus scales combine spouses' general evaluations of their marriage (e.g., whether they are happy-unhappy), their beliefs about how similar they are to each other with regard to various matters (e.g., how they handle such matters as fi-

FIGURE 1. A THREE-LEVEL MODEL FOR VIEWING MARRIAGE

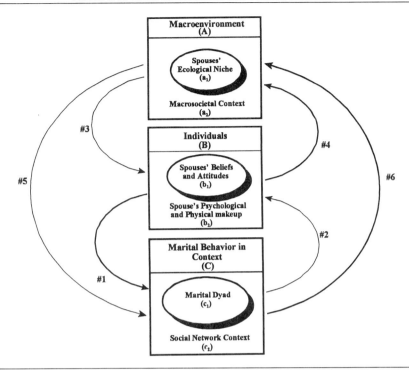

nances or their leisure interests), and their characterizations of marital behavioral patterns (e.g., how affectionate or companionate the spouses are with each other or how well they get along). Researchers need to recognize that how spouses feel about their marriage—how happy they are, how much they love each other—undoubtedly affects both their characterizations of how similar they are to each other and their beliefs about how well they get along. It is also likely that spouses who believe that they are of like mind or who characterize their marriage as highly affectionate infer from these ratings that they are happy. Suppose we want to use the Locke-Wallace scale to examine connections between marital happiness (an individual-level variable) and how marital couples interact with each other in a laboratory problem-solving situation (i.e., behavioral patterns). This is problematic; given that some items on the Locke-Wallace scale require spouses to characterize how well they get along, what do we conclude, for example, when analyses based on observational data show that couples who are responsive to each other's ideas score higher on the scale? Are they happier with their marriage? Or are they merely able to characterize, in general terms, how well

they actually do get along? Thus, because it is important to understand the roots of marital satisfaction, researchers should discard standard measures of satisfaction in favor of measures that are purely evaluative (see Fincham & Bradbury, 1987).

MARRIAGE AS A BEHAVIORAL ECOSYSTEM

The box at the bottom of Figure 1 (box C) shows the marital dyad as a sphere (c_1) embedded within a larger box representing the social network (c_2), or the other individuals who constitute the immediate social environment within which marital activities and interactions are embedded. *Marital behavior* is the foundation on which careful descriptions of marriage relationships can be built. Figure 1 (box C) points to the idea that marital activities and interactions (c_1) often take place in the presence of other family members and friends (c_2). Usually, however, researchers focusing on the dynamics of marital interaction study couples as two-person units, as if they rarely spent time together as part of a social group (see Gottman & Notarius, in press, for a review of the marital interaction literature). However, the presence or absence of others can have an important impact on the types of behavior spouses exhibit. Some kinds of marital behavior rarely occur in public settings (e.g., sexual intercourse or physical aggression). Parenthood not only changes the extent and nature of the time spouses spend with each other, it also affects how frequently they pursue activities with friends and kin (Huston & Vangelisti, 1995). Couples who have young children schedule regular "dates," just so they can spend some time periodically doing something fun together as a couple. Moreover, it is important to keep in mind that some features of marriage—such as the propensity of either of the spouses to seek support from friends or kin (Surra & Milardo, 1991), the proclivity of individual partners to form coalitions with their children to influence their mate (Gilbert, Christensen, & Margolin, 1984), or the inclination of spouses to flirt with others in front of their partner—can only be understood when couples are studied in group settings. Finally, the centrality of the spouses in each other's day-to-day lives, as well as their joint and independent involvement with friends and kin, may reveal much about the nature of the spouses' marital relationship.

Both a wide-angle and a close-up lens must be used to create a rich, comprehensive portrait of a marriage relationship. The use of a wide-angle lens brings macrobehavioral patterns into view and shows how couples spend their time—what they do together and apart. The use of a close-up lens brings into focus microbehavioral patterns—the details of husband-wife interaction. Sociologists (Bernard, 1964; Bott, 1971; Burgess & Locke, 1945) typically write about macrobehavioral patterns (such as division of labor and companionship), whereas psychologists and communications scholars usually study microbehavioral patterns, seeking to understand the interpersonal patterns that lead to distress and divorce (Gottman, 1994; Gottman & Krokoff, 1989; Noller, 1984; Wills, Weiss, & Patterson, 1974).

Taking a Wide-Angle View of Marriage: Describing Molar Behavior Patterns

"Time, like money, is a scarce resource that can be spent in different ways" (Medrich, Roizen, Rubin, & Buckley, 1982, p. 14), and the way spouses use their time reveals much about the nature of their marital relationship. Couples must garner economic resources, maintain a household, care for children (if they become parents), maintain connections with friends and relatives, and

manage their joint and individual leisure time. When social scientists write about matters such as the division of labor, marital companionship, and the ties spouses maintain with friends and kin, they often have time use patterns in mind. Marriages thus can be distinguished in terms of what the spouses do with their time, who they do various activities with, and details of the give-and-take that make up the interpersonal dialogues they have with each other.

How might a social scientist, interested in creating an ecologically valid description of marriage as a behavioral system, proceed? Ideally, one would follow husbands and wives over a representative sample of days, unobtrusively recording details of their activities and interactions. The movement of individual spouses from activity to activity consists of sequences of behavior with beginnings, endings, and transition points. Here is a portrayal in such terms of a day in the life of a married couple, John and Cindy:

> John and Cindy rise early Friday morning and *pack lunches* for the family, after which John *prepares breakfast;* meanwhile, Cindy wakes up their daughter, Jessica, and *helps her get dressed* for school. The family *eats breakfast* and *talks* about their plans for the day. Cindy showers and gets dressed for work, while John *puts away the dishes.* John then showers and gets dressed for work while Cindy *drives* Jessica to school. John and Cindy begin *working* at their separate offices around 8 a.m. They *chat* briefly on the telephone and decide to go for a walk in the park during their lunch hour. They enjoy a leisurely *walk* at noon and, as they *eat lunch, discuss* their evening plans. They both return to work; at midafternoon, John leaves to *retrieve Jessica* from school to take her to a piano lesson. After work, Cindy *stops by the bank* and then *goes to the grocery store.* While Cindy and John get ready to go out, Cindy's mother stops by their home to pick up Jessica and *visits* for a few minutes before returning home. John and Cindy meet another couple for *dinner* before going to a *concert.* They drive home, and their evening draws to a close after they *have sex* and drift off to sleep.

The decisions that wives and husbands—like Cindy and John—make as they move from one activity to another and from one day to another cumulate to create macrobehavioral marital patterns (Huston & Rempel, 1989; Levinger & Huston, 1990). If spouses' mundane activities are tracked over a representative sample of days, their marital lifestyle comes into focus. We are then able to map how they divide up household work, how involved they are in child care activities,

TABLE 1.　SUMMARY OF DIARY DATA FROM A DAY IN THE LIFE OF JOHN AND CINDY: SPOUSES' DAY (OVERALL)

Spouse	Total No. of Expressions of Affection (As Reported by Spouse)	Total No. of Negative Behaviors (as Reported by Spouse)	Total No. of Conflicts	Daily Marital Satisfaction (1 = *dissatisfied*, 7 = *satisfied*)	Daily Hassles (1 = *relaxed*, 7 = *hassled*)
John	6	1	1	6	4
Cindy	7	0	1	5	3

what leisure activities they do together, and the character of the interpersonal ties they maintain, together and separately, with others (Huston, Robins, Atkinson, & McHale, 1987). These kinds of macrobehavioral activity patterns have been the staples out of which social scientists have built portraits of marital lifestyles (e.g., Bernard, 1964).

Obtaining diary data. The portrait of John and Cindy's day was intended to foreshadow a telephone diary approach my colleagues and I have developed and refined over many years to obtain reliable and valid data about couples' marital lifestyles (Huston & Rempel, 1989; Huston et al., 1987). We presumed that the characteristics and distinguishing features of couples' marital lifestyles would come into sharp focus if we gathered data about their activities and interactions over a number of days, rather than a single day.

The telephone diary procedure tracks spouses' comings and goings over a representative series of days, yielding a rich multidimensional portrait of the multiple facets of married life. Rather than obtaining open-ended reports of spouses' activities—which we knew would produce data of highly uneven quality—we created a highly structured interview in which we queried each of the spouses about a comprehensive list of the kinds of activities husbands and wives do when they are not at work (Huston et al., 1987). To secure representative information about each couples' day-to-day life together, we telephoned spouses on multiple occasions, spaced over a 2- to 3-week period; during each telephone interview, we obtained from each of the spouses systematic information about their participation in activities and their interactions with each other over the 24-hour period ending at 5 p.m. the day of the call. Spouses reported their own participation in specific activities pertaining to household work, child care, leisure, and conversations—and indicated for each activity whether they did the activity with their spouse or independently. They were also asked to report who, if anyone, other than the spouse was involved with them in the activity. We have recently

elaborated the telephone diary procedure to obtain spouses' ratings of how they felt while doing each activity, using a 7-point scale anchored by a frowning and a happy face.

Spouses were asked to indicate the frequency with which their partner enacted several specific positive and negative behaviors during the 24-hour period, as well as the total number of conflicts they had during the period covered by the telephone interview. Finally, at the end of each daily interview, spouses reported how they felt about their marriage that day and how hassled or relaxed the day had been. This telephone procedure for collecting diary data, though labor intensive, produces high-quality data that overcome many of the limitations of self-report data (Huston et al., 1987; see Reis & Gable, in press, for a broader discussion of diary methods).

Summarizing diary data. Spouses' activities during each day can be summarized by interdigitating the diary data generated from both partners, yielding a record of their day, much like that shown for Cindy and John in Tables 1 and 2. Table 1 provides total counts of some phenomena (e.g., amount of affection), as well as evaluations of the day (e.g., of marital satisfaction). Table 2 illustrates the kinds of summary data that can be obtained on a day-to-day basis from participants. The particular information researchers might choose to capture using telephone diary interviews will undoubtedly vary, of course, depending on investigators' ideas and interests. The record of John and Cindy's activities, as portrayed in Table 2, thus is intended to be illustrative rather than proscriptive. Each activity is shown as a row; the information that was gathered about each activity is shown in columns. The specific activities in which John and Cindy engaged— what they did (the italicized words in the paragraph above)—are shaded in Table 2. The two columns to the left of the activity show when the activity was done. The column to the immediate right of the activity shows how the macrobehavior might be categorized more generally (e.g., as a household task, child care activity, or leisure pursuit). The

Table 2. Summary of Diary Data from a Day in the Life of John and Cindy: Chronology of Activities

Beginning Time	Duration (min)	Activity	Type of Activity	Participant(s)				Affect (1 = negative, 7 = positive)	
				Husband	Wife	Child	Others	Husband	Wife
6:45 a.m.	10	Pack lunches	Household	✓	✓	—	—	4	3
6:55 a.m.	15	Prepare breakfast	Household	✓		—	—	4	—
7:00 a.m.	10	Help child dress	Child care		✓	✓	—	—	4
7:10 a.m.	20	Eat breakfast	Eat, conversation	✓	✓	✓	—	6	6
7:30 a.m.	10	Do dishes	Household	✓		—	—	5	—
7:30 a.m.	15	Drop off child	Household		✓	✓	—	—	4
8:00 a.m.	240	At work	Paid work	✓		—	—	4	—
8:00 a.m.	240	At work	Paid work	✓	✓	—	—	5	4
11:00 a.m.	5	Talk on phone	Conversation	✓	✓	—	—	7	5
12:00 p.m.	35	Go for a walk/talk	Leisure, conversation	✓	✓	—	—	3	6
12:35 p.m.	15	Eat lunch	Eat a meal	✓	✓	—	—	3	2
1:00 p.m.	150	At work	Paid work	✓		—	—	—	—
1:00 p.m.	240	At work	Paid work	✓	✓	—	—	4	4
3:30 p.m.	15	Pick up child	Child care	✓		✓	—	4	—
3:45 p.m.	60	Take child to a lesson	Child care		✓	✓	—	—	—
5:00 p.m.	10	Go to bank	Household		✓	—	—	—	4
5:10 p.m.	20	Pick up groceries	Household		✓	—	—	—	4
6:30 p.m.	15	Visit	Leisure		✓	—	Wife's mom	—	5
7:00 p.m.	120	Go to dinner	Leisure, conversation	✓	✓	—	Cpl friends	6	6
9:00 p.m.	180	Go to a concert	Leisure	✓	✓	—	Cpl friends	7	6
12:00 a.m.	45	Sexual intercourse	Leisure, socioemotional behavior	✓	✓	—	—	7	7

Note: Personal grooming was omitted from table activities.

next column shows who participated in the activity: the husband, wife, child, and other members of the family's social network. The coding scheme we use also allows us to make finer distinctions among those others, differentiating, for example, activities done with the husband's relatives from those done with the wife's relatives. The last set of columns provides information about John's and Cindy's reported affect while engaging in each activity. Many aspects of spouses' phenomenological experience could be indexed, such as excited-bored, relaxed-nervous, and cooperative-competitive; we show ratings of the affect they reportedly experienced because writings about marital success emphasize the importance of affective experiences (e.g., Larson & Richards, 1994). Affective experiences, because they are apt to vary depending on the activity and the social context within which they are embedded, may provide insight into spouses' more general feelings about each other and their relationship. Thus, for example, spouses who are high in levels of romantic love, compared with those spouses who are less enamored, may experience elevated levels of positive affect when they do activities together. What we see on the macrobehavioral surface of marriage may reflect the patterns of affect spouses experience when they are together. Thus, if the time spouses spend in leisure activity together is not particularly enjoyable (compared with the time they spend in such pursuits alone or with others), they may begin to spend less time together.

Profiling marital lifestyles. Profiles of couples' marriages can be built from telephone diary data when such data are gathered from spouses over several days (see Huston et al., 1987). By aggregating the data over a representative sample of days, it is possible to create summary indices of various aspects of marriage, including (a) marital *role patterns* (as shown by spouses' participation in household and child care activities); (b) marital *companionship* (as reflected in the extent to which spouses talk to each other and spend leisure time together); (c) *socioemotional patterns* (as evident in how affectionate spouses are with each other, how often they express negativity, and the frequency with which they have sexual intercourse); and (d) *spouses' involvement with friends and kin* (as reflected in the amount of time they spend engaging in recreational activities and conversation).

My own program of research illustrates how the diverse and rich data generated by the telephone diary technique make it possible to study a variety of aspects of marriage. We have used such

diary data to create typologies of marital lifestyles (Johnson, Huston, Gaines, & Levinger, 1992) and to study a variety of specific aspects of marriage—such as the division of labor (Atkinson & Huston, 1984), the expression of positive and negative feelings in marriage (Huston & Vangelisti, 1991), and factors that predict the amount of time spouses spend with friends and kin (Huston & Geis, 1993). Because we gathered diary data yearly over the early years of marriage, we have been able to track how marital behavior patterns change over time. These data show that marriages typically lose some of their romantic intensity over the first year, evolving away from a romantic, recreational relationship toward more of a working partnership (Huston, McHale, & Crouter, 1986). More specifically, couples show less affection and spend proportionately more of their joint time doing chores (rather than recreational pursuits); their feelings of romantic love also tend to become weaker with time. Because couples differ in whether or not they become parents and, if they do, in how long they wait, we have also been able to separate analytically normative changes in marriage from changes associated with parenthood (Crawford & Huston, 1993; MacDermid, Huston, & McHale, 1990). When couples become parents, their division of labor becomes more gender differentiated (MacDermid et al., 1990); parenthood also alters the extent to which husbands and wives engage in leisure activities, together and separately, that they enjoy (Crawford & Huston, 1993). Moreover, recently, we obtained long-term follow-up data on couples whom we had studied during their early years of marriage using telephone diary methods. These data indicated, among other things, that couples who subsequently divorced showed sharper declines in their level of affection over the first 2 years compared with couples who stayed married (Huston, Caughlin, Houts, Smith, & George, in press).

An important strength of diary-type data is that they can be aggregated in a variety of ways, depending on the investigator's purpose (see Herbst, 1965). The basic macrobehavioral unit—an activity—can be characterized in terms of both the social context within which it takes place, as well as in terms of the actor's psychological state (e.g., emotions); thus, it is possible to examine, for instance, the significance of particular types of activities and activity patterns as sources of pleasure and displeasure in a marriage. Because multiple activities take place each day and because those activities differ from day to day, it is possible to identify the kinds of activities and events that co-vary, for example, with day-to-day fluctuations in marital satisfaction. Moreover, when diary data are gathered from both partners, the importance of each partner's activities for the other spouse can also be assessed.

Additional uses of diary-type data to study marriage. Whereas my colleagues and I have used diary data to create portraits of marriage relationships, others have used diary data to examine how contextual variables affect marital experiences. Because diary procedures are designed to preserve information concerning the context within which activity occurs, they are particularly suitable for studying the interplay between day-to-day events, emotions, and behaviors. Some diary techniques require the spouses to record their behavior at either the first opportunity or at the end of the day (Almeida, Wethington, & Chandler, 1999; Thompson & Bolger, 1999; Wills et al., 1974); others use a beeper technique to obtain reports on what spouses are doing and how they are feeling during randomly selected moments throughout the day (Larson & Richards, 1994). Usually, these strategies yield data that are of insufficient scope to produce multidimensional profiles of marriage. Nonetheless, such diary approaches have yielded interesting findings concerning how spouses experience their day-to-day life. They have been used to examine the interpersonal circumstances that give rise to positive and negative emotions and the conditions under which emotions are transmitted from one spouse to another (Gable & Reis, 1999; Larson & Almeida, 1999). Thompson and Bolger (1999), for example, used diary data gathered from spouses over several days as one of the partners moved closer to taking an important examination (the New York State Bar). Examinees' depressed mood on a given day became less strongly related to their partners' daily feelings about their relationship as the exam day approached, indicating that partners increasingly made allowances for examinees' negative affect. Using the beeper technique, Larson and Richards (1994) showed that the extent to which married partners reported that positive affect was elevated when they were doing things together, compared with their baseline level, depended on their overall level of marital satisfaction.

Strengths of diary data over other techniques. Because gathering diary data is time consuming, why not simply ask spouses to characterize how

household work is divided, how companionate they and their partner are, or how their partner reacts on days when they are stressed? Several problems associated with using survey-type questions for obtaining data about these marital patterns are behind the appeal of diary-type data. First, many factors other than spouses' actual marital patterns or experiences in marriage influence global summary reports; some of these factors also systematically bias such reports (Huston & Robins, 1982; Noller & Guthrie, 1991; Reis & Gable, in press; Robins, 1990; Schwarz, 1990; Sudman, Bradburn, & Schwartz, 1996). When spouses are asked to provide accurate summary reports of division of labor, for instance, they have to decide what to include in the domain of household labor. Is mowing the lawn or shoveling snow to be included in the equation? Researchers have solved this problem by providing spouses with a list of household activities and asking them to indicate, for each, who takes primary responsibility. Even when this is done, however, and even if we assume that spouses are sufficiently motivated to answer the questions accurately, problems remain. Spouses must have kept track of both their own contribution and that of their mate; they must also be able to retrieve the information from memory when asked; furthermore, they must select a time frame to apply to the task and decide what weight to give the various chores—they could use the amount of time spent, the number of chores done, or any of a number of other criteria; finally, they must calculate how the behavior pattern relates to the options available on the scale. Most spouses, when faced with survey-type questions, no doubt report their general impressions. These impressions may be influenced by relationship schema (e.g., their beliefs about appropriate marital roles), how much in love or how satisfied they are with their marriage, or their sensitivities (e.g., a spouse philosophically committed to equally sharing responsibility for household duties may keep better track of each partner's contributions). Some of the shortcomings of global self-report data can be overcome by creating a latent variable based on the reports of both spouses (and others), but consideration must be given to the possibility that the reports are biased in the same way. Spouses who are both deeply in love, for instance, may characterize their own and each other's behavior in rosy terms.

However, even when participant reports of general patterns are accurate, they are limited because they focus on overall patterns of behavior, rather than on how behavior fluctuates by context and on a day-by-day basis. Diary data can be aggregated in a variety of ways, making it possible, for example, to examine how fluctuations in husbands' and wives' work around the house affects their day-to-day ratings of marital satisfaction; thus, for example, are wives happier on days when their husband performs more household tasks than he usually does? Is marital well-being enhanced the more spouses do household work together, as a team, rather than independently?

In spite of my reservations about questionnaire data, I would argue that social scientists ought to continue obtaining global reports of marital patterns but should also view such reports as reflecting the spouses' beliefs about their marriage (Figure 1, box B), rather than as capturing relationship properties (Figure 1, box C). Such beliefs may, in turn, affect how they act in marriage or react to their spouse's behavior. Partners who see their mate as more affectionate than diary or interactional data suggest, may perhaps be happier with their marriage than those who seem to have more accurate views of their relationship. The idea that dating couples and newly married spouses idealize each other (Huston et al., in press), for instance, might be usefully studied by examining how well people are able to sustain a positive image of their partner when it is inconsistent with the day-to-day reality of their experiences in the relationship.

Diary data is most frequently used, however, to depict molar behavior. John and Cindy's day seemed almost choreographed in that family members' movements from one activity to another appear well coordinated. The portrait provides little sense, however, of how John and Cindy interacted with each other when they were together: How responsive were they to each other's ideas during their lunch hour conversation? More generally, how effective are they at solving problems together? How do they respond to each other's criticisms or expressions of anger? Although diary reports can provide information about macrobehavioral patterns and the overall affective tenor of the day-to-day life of the couple, the give-and-take that makes up episodes of interaction cannot be investigated effectively without using direct observation techniques.

Using a Close-Up Lens: Describing Microbehavioral Marital Behavior

Directly observing spouses as they ruminate together about their day or as they work toward re-

solving a disagreement, provides much richer data about marital interaction than does daily diary data (see Gottman & Notarius, in press). Microbehaviorally oriented researchers, for instance, have coded face-to-face interaction in terms of the content of what people say, the affect in their voices, their facial expressions while they speak, and the expressions on the faces of the spouses as they listen to each other. The daily diary reports of affect, shown in Table 2, associated with each activity suggest that John and Cindy's day went well, except for their lunch together, which both John and Cindy found unpleasant. Suppose, for purposes of illustration, we had tracked that lunch hour conversation between John and Cindy using a coding system like those developed by researchers who have studied the nuances of marital interaction (Markman & Notarius, 1987). We would have seen John attempt to beg off taking Jessica to her piano lesson, citing pressing business matters. Cindy might have responded, perhaps with sarcasm in her voice, that his business concerns seem more important to him on days when he has family responsibilities. As Cindy lodged her accusation, John's face might have become more tense, and his body might have pulled away from Cindy. Observational data, by capturing communication on multiple levels, has been used to identify behavioral causes and manifestations of marital distress (Figure 1, link 2; Karney & Bradbury, 1995). Particular interaction styles, for example, defensiveness, stubbornness, high levels of criticism, the tendency to reciprocate negativity, and withdrawal during conflict, have been found both to covary with satisfaction and to predict decreases in satisfaction in marriage (Gottman, 1990, 1994; Gottman & Krokoff, 1989; Markman, 1981; Markman, Floyd, Stanley, & Storaasli, 1998).

Macrobehavioral and microbehavioral patterns are usually examined in isolation from one another. Macrobehavioral activities, however, provide the larger ecological context within which microbehavioral marital behaviors are played out. Thus, microbehavioral activities can be seen as intermittent interpersonal gatherings, punctuating the spouses' day and sometimes redirecting them as they move across their environment, pursuing various activities. Little is known, however, about how patterns of activity affect the details of marital interaction or how the particulars of marital interaction serve to alter the terrain that couples travel. Until the linkages between macro- and microbehavioral patterns are explored, the contributions that either of the two camps make to understanding marriage will be limited.

The Psychological Infrastructure
of Marriage

John and Cindy appear to have worked out a generally successful modus vivendi, or what Burgess (1926) might have called a "well-adjusted" marriage, if we can take the day we tracked them as representative of their life together. Their activities are smoothly coordinated (Berscheid, 1985), joint pursuits generally produce positive affect in both of them (Kelley, 1979), and their interactions are peppered primarily by positive rather than negative affect (Karney & Bradbury, 1995). The morning proceeded such that each spouse's activities played smoothly off the other's. Had John, Cindy, or Jessica failed to perform specific activities in a timely fashion, the tuneful harmony of their morning might well have turned dissonant—perhaps creating disappointment, anger, or overt conflict (Berscheid, 1983). The rest of the day also unfolds smoothly, with the exception of their negative exchange at lunch.

Why were John and Cindy able to work out such a successful set of understandings? The portrait of John's and Cindy's day contains no more than clues about John and Cindy's motivations—why they do what they do and why they respond to each other in particular ways. We can sense that they are both close and on common ground because their plans and activities are well articulated. Their marriage also appears to be embedded in a supportive and friendly network of kin and friendship alliances. I now turn to an examination of the psychological infrastructure of marriage—the meshing of the psychological proclivities of the spouses, their feelings about each other, and the understandings they have developed—that might lie beneath the surface of marriages like that of John and Cindy.

Marriage was seen as a "unity of interacting personalities" by Burgess (1926) who, in taking *personality* to mean the spouses' total sense of themselves and their partner in the relationship, placed issues of marital adjustment and adaptation at the very heart of marriage. "A well adjusted marriage," wrote Burgess and Cottrell (1939) 13 years later, may be defined as "a marriage in which the attitudes and actions of each of the partners produce[s] an environment which is highly favorable to the proper functioning of the personality structures of each primary, particularly in the sphere of relationships." The idea that marriage involves a continuing give-and-take between spouses has been noted at periodic intervals by

family scientists (e.g., Bernard, 1964; Waller, 1938). Waller, in his usual colorful fashion, suggests (p. 308):

> The social form created by marriage must find its way in a sort of tentative process; it must grow as a grapevine grows, blindly reaching out its tendrils, making many false starts but attaining at last to light and solidity... each member must try out many patterns of behavior in the new situation. Some patterns will appear highly successful; these will stabilize in the form of powerful habits. Other patterns of behavior will be penalized by conflict or other forms of failure; it is thus that the limits of interaction are defined.

This section of the article focuses on the two interrelated matters that Burgess (1926), Waller (1938), and Bernard (1964) took as central to understanding marriage: First, marital adjustment is a process that takes place over time through which spouses seek to adapt to each other. Second, these adaptations, though they continue throughout the course of marriage, vary in their success, thereby producing unions that differ in closeness, satisfactoriness, and stability.

Marital Adjustment as an Adaptation Process

The three-dimensional, layered character of Figure 2 is intended to convey the idea that husbands' and wives' psychological proclivities lie beneath the surface of their day-to-day life together (cf. Bradbury & Fincham, 1988; Huston & Robins, 1982; Robins, 1990). Spouses' proclivities shape their activities and anchor their reactions to each other. The two-headed arrows connecting marital interaction and behavior to the spouses is intended to convey the idea that married partners are themselves changed by their experiences in marriage. Marital interaction is shown in the foreground of the figure as a sequence of interwoven subjective events and overt behaviors (see Kelley et al., 1983). Figure 2 portrays "states of being" as lying beneath the surface of marital activities and interactions. The embeddedness of each spouse's activities and marital interaction in states of being, as shown in Figure 2, is intended to suggest that such states are experienced in context and that they change, both in response to spouses' own behavior and that of others. Such states regulate spouses' movements from one activity to another, as well as direct their functioning during interaction. Marital interaction is intermittent, and thus it punctuates at various intervals each spouse's on-

FIGURE 2. THE PSYCHOLOGICAL INFRASTRUCTURE OF MARRIAGE

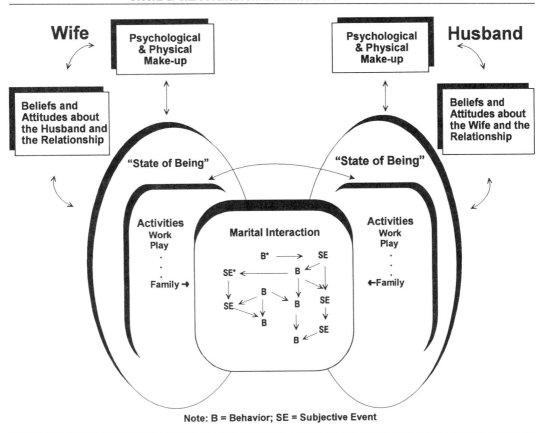

Note: B = Behavior; SE = Subjective Event

going, day-to-day activities. What spouses have been doing, are doing as they interact, or plan to do later often structures their discussions. The figure also points to the idea that spouses influence each other, both directly in terms of the activities they choose to enact when they are together (shown in the foreground as marital interaction) as well as indirectly, as when one spouse prepares breakfast while the other reads the paper (see Peplau, 1983). Thus, the two-headed arrow that connects husbands' and wives' activities serves to remind us both that what each spouse does, even when the spouses are apart, often matters to the other and that spouses' activities are coordinated (in varying degrees).

The processes depicted in Figure 2 stand in front of an implied background consisting of the sociocultural environment and the ecological niches in the society within which particular married couples function. The spouses who constitute the marital pair both live within and have been raised in a specific living environment or, more likely, in

a series of such environments (households, neighborhoods, etc.), and their lives span a specific series of historical eras (e.g., the Great Depression, the Vietnam War). These settings and experiences shape individuals' dispositions, values, psychological states, and habits of thought, which are then brought into their marriage (Figure 1, link 3). Thus, for example, spouses' prior experiences may lead them to bring patriarchal or egalitarian values to their marriage, to have particular social values, political leanings, and leisure interests, to be invested in varying degrees in the welfare of others in their life (e.g., parents, siblings, friends), or to feel either secure or insecure about their relationships with significant others.

A general model of marital adjustment. The model portrayed in Figure 2 can be summarized in terms of ten interrelated axioms. The first axiom, implicit in Waller's (1938) depiction of marital adjustment processes, is that husbands and wives bring stable social, physical, and psychological attributes to marriage that bear upon how they behave and what they seek from each other. A husband who holds patriarchal values, for instance, will behave very differently in marriage compared with one who holds egalitarian attitudes. Some qualities—such as psychological expressiveness—make spouses easy to be around (Huston & Geis, 1993; Lamke, 1989), whereas other qualities—such as moodiness and emotional lability—produce conflict and undermine marital satisfaction (Caughlin, Huston, and Houts, in press).

The second axiom is that these relatively stable, general proclivities are latent until they are activated in situ. Psychological causes always operate locally, even though they may be rooted in the distant past (see Cook & Campbell, 1979). Thus, to account for a spouse's behavior in marriage, researchers need to pay equal attention to his or her general proclivities and to the situations that activate them. A person who is high strung or who is high in trait anxiety might be expected to show more anger and hostility in marriage in general, but his or her propensity toward negativity may increase under stress. Thus, the actual amount of negativity that spouses express toward their mate should be a conjoint function of their trait anxiety and the frequency with which they are confronted with environmental stressors. Figure 2 thus shows that a spouse's state of being (i.e., thoughts and emotions at a particular time)—whether it be anger, jealousy, tenderness, obligation, or some other state—results from a confluence of dispositions and circumstances and suggests that states of being are manifest in terms of specific types of activities and behavior.

This brings me to the third axiom, namely that spouses are interdependent, such that what each spouse says and does influences the other, both immediately and over time. This influence process, of course, lies at the heart of theoretical writings about marital adjustment (e.g., Bernard, 1964; Waller, 1938). The reader might recall the conflict over lunch between John and Cindy: John quickly reversed field when Cindy strongly resisted, and he backed off his proposal that Cindy leave work to take Jessica to her piano lesson. The lunch hour conflict might have gone seriously awry had either spouse been anger-prone or if John had pushed Cindy hard to comply with his request. Even though the conflict appears to have been resolved reasonably amicably, the exchange was seen as unpleasant by both of the spouses (as shown in Table 1). The dialogue also affected how John and Cindy spent at least part

of their afternoon; also, the feelings and thoughts generated during the exchange may have resurfaced later, perhaps in another context. The placement of spouses' subjective states underneath their activities and interactions in Figure 2 is designed to remind us that subjective states not only feed into behavior, as noted earlier, but are also altered as a result. Moreover, depending on the kinds of thoughts and emotions stimulated by an activity or an exchange, spouses may refine their views and evaluations of each other and the marriage.

Thus, the fourth axiom is that on the basis of their experiences in the relationship, spouses refashion the following: (a) their beliefs about each other's personality, values, interests, and attitudes; (b) their schemas and understandings about the nature of their marital relationship; and (c) their evaluations of each other and the marriage. Of course, newlyweds develop ideas about each other and their relationship during courtship, and these ideas reflect, at least to some extent, knowledge of each other's relatively stable psychological attributes. Thus, even though newlyweds continue to chisel out an experientially based understanding of each other, this chiseling is not done in marriage either dispassionately or anew.

The fifth axiom parallels the second one, except the focus shifts to spouses' beliefs and attitudes about their partner and the relationship rather than being on their more general psychological qualities and dispositions. Relationship-specific knowledge structures and dispositions are latent until they are activated in a specific situation. Once they are activated, they affect spouses' behavior and their reactions to each other's behavior. The phrase "beliefs and attitudes" (shown in Figure 2) is intended as a general moniker that includes spouses' working models, their schemas, and their evaluations that are specific to the partner and the relationship. Such relationship-specific cognitions and evaluations are shown in Figure 2 as feeding into spouses' states of being, which, in turn, are shown as lying beneath the surface of their overt behavior. Thus, even though Cindy may love John, her love for him may be latent until circumstances actuate her love; when her love is actuated, a collection of thoughts and emotions surfaces (a subjective state), which, in turn, channel her to express her love toward John.

The next axiom, the sixth, is that spouses' stable psychological qualities, as well as their working models, schemas, and evaluations of each other and the relationship, affect how they respond to each other's behavior and to marital patterns of behavior, over time. Cindy's negative reaction to John's proposal that she take Jessica to the piano lesson, for example, may have been rooted in her sense that the proposal was inappropriate, given both her own ideas about gender roles in marriage and her belief that they had an understanding about how to handle this kind of situation.

The seventh axiom is that spouses' behavior reflects, in varying degrees, not only their own dispositional tendencies but also, indirectly, those of their mate. Thus, John's level of participation in household work may be anchored in both his own and Cindy' ideas about gender roles. Similarly, their joint leisure pursuits may reflect an equal compromise between their individual interests, or they may be weighted toward one or the other spouse's interests. The exploration of *partner effects,* or the influence of one partner's dispositions on the other's behavior, is rare in research on marriage, but now that the statistical tools are available, such research will become increasingly common (cf. Kenny & Cook, 1999). Finally, when influence is examined over time, it is possible to ferret out the extent to which each spouse's ideas about such matters as household responsibilities or leisure interests change toward the views of the partner.

The eighth axiom, somewhat implicit in the seventh one, is that marital partners' psychological makeup, as well as their working models and their schemas, fit together in varying degrees. Compatibility theory (Huston & Houts, 1998; Levinger & Rands, 1985) and interdependence theory (Kelley, 1979) both suggest that certain combinations of psychological attributes that combine to promote marital harmony, rather than conflict, are apt to create a sense of marital well-being. Such well-being, in turn, ought to encourage partners to become increasingly invested in each other's well-being. (Harmonious relationships, of course, are not necessarily healthy or close [cf. Berscheid, 1998]. Alcoholics may reinforce each other's drinking, but hasten themselves to premature deaths, and couples who have very traditional ideas about marital roles and few leisure interests in common may spend little time in each other's company.)

This brings me to the ninth and tenth axioms, which I will treat in tandem. Spouses' working models, schemas, and evaluations change as a result of their experiences in the marriage (axiom 9); these changes, in turn, may lead them to alter the physical and social environment (axiom 10).

These changes in the individuals and in the context of their marriage (Berscheid & Lopes, 1997; Kelley, 1983) may increase or decrease marital harmony and stability. The focus of research, up to now, has been on interpersonal factors that change spouses' marital satisfaction. The dominance of the social learning tradition in behavioral research on marriage has led most researchers to assume that changes in how spouses feel about their marriage are accretive, reflecting patterns of rewards and costs (see Karney & Bradbury, 1995), and that these changes affect marital interaction. Spouses who are uncertain they can trust their mate may, for instance, try to reduce the opportunities their mate might have to betray their trust. Moreover, some changes in spouses' views of each other may be abrupt rather than accretive; trust may take a dramatic plunge when a spouse feels betrayed by his or her mate's indiscretion. The concentration of research on marital satisfaction leaves us with information about how spouses come to believe their marriage is egalitarian or about how spouses come to see their partner as having moral fiber or as being resilient. Thus, spouses' views of each other's character, and hence their attraction, may depend, in part, on how well they handle crises, on their ability to meet their responsibilities, and on how they interact with children. The roots of these changes that occur in the heads of the spouses, which are rarely studied, may provide the basis for a strengthened alliance or may move the couple toward disenchantment and, perhaps, divorce.

These ten axioms, when considered together, suggest that the individual partners and the marriage relationship affect each other continuously over time. The psychological and physical characteristics spouses bring to their day-to-day life together set the stage for their interpersonal dialogues, but the nature of these dialogues depends partly on particular behaviors (or patterns of behavior) that take place and on the fact that the same behavior can be interpreted and evaluated (or coded) in a variety of ways. Thus, spouses' expressions of anger may be rooted, for example, in their personality traits, situational stress, the behavior of their mate, misunderstandings, a violation of agreed upon relationship norms, their mate's personality, or marital dissatisfaction. Moreover, each spouse's behavior may have either positive or negative consequences for either or both of the partners. These consequences are sometimes anticipated and intended, but spouses do not always think about the consequences of their actions. Finally, the same behavior (or pattern of behavior) may be viewed differently by the spouses, as when they disagree about whether a spouse whose behavior has negative consequences for his or her mate meant to do harm. As noted earlier, the idea that marriage involves a continuing dialogue between the spouses has been noted periodically (e.g., Bernard, 1964; Waller, 1938), but rarely have researchers intensively studied couples from courtship through the early years of marriage, even though it is during this period that marital relationships take on much of their social form (cf. Bradbury, 1998).

Social scientists interested in linking the spouses' psychological qualities to marital behavior patterns have proceeded intuitively rather than systematically. As a consequence, few efforts have been made to distinguish various types of attributes and to specify the psychological and interpersonal mechanisms through which they affect marital adjustment. In the following subsections, I identify key concepts and processes that researchers studying the interplay between spousal qualities and their marital activities and interactions need to think through. In addition to marital satisfaction, researchers need to examine such matters as how spouses come to understand their power in the relationship, how they develop and lose respect for each other, or how they maintain strong feelings of love.

Spouses as architects of their marriage. The movement of spouses from activity to activity through the course of the day is volitional, even though people may not pause to think about what to do. Although spouses' actions—even seemingly spontaneous ones—are rooted in their states of being, they do not always actively contemplate the alternatives before them at each choice point. John and Cindy's choreographed morning script certainly has a routine feel to it. Social psychologists suggest that habits, which are defined as propensities to behave in particular ways given a familiar context, are often embedded in volitional and intentional action systems (see Ouellette & Wood, 1998). Self-consciousness and introspection often betray the conflicting nature of the psychological forces toward and away from engaging in a particular action; similarly, reflection might occur when people are drawn toward doing something that is taboo or when they become aware that pursuing their own interests might undermine the interests of others. People motivated to maintain a balance between their role commitments may of-

ten be faced with trying to balance conflicting demands (cf. Marks & MacDermid, 1996).

When we move to marital interaction, behavior that seems spontaneous nonetheless is viewed as reflecting particular actors' subjective states. Gottman (1994), for instance, identifies *criticism* as reflecting disapproval, *complaint* as rooted in aggrievement, *defensiveness* as resulting from an attempt to avoid blame, *contempt* as a manifestation of disdain, and *stonewalling* as reflecting hostile, closed-off feelings. It is easy to imagine that these thoughts and behaviors are more likely to be activated when the actor's immediate goals are frustrated or at times when the actor is under stress. Such behavioral proclivities toward the partner can be stable or transient, and if stable, they can reflect the psychological makeup of the spouse or how they think and feel about their spouse (or others; Gottman, 1994). A sense of self-importance, for example, may cause a husband to show contempt toward his wife, or such contempt may reflect a well-earned lack of respect. Unfortunately, behavioral researchers have rarely attempted to trace the psychological reasons why spouses feel and behave in particular ways toward their partner during interaction. We know little more than that spouses who are distressed about their marriage express negativity more often and show greater reciprocity in negativity than happy couples. But the question of why unhappy spouses feel and show contempt or disapproval or feel potentially blameworthy is largely left unanswered (cf. Karney & Bradbury, 1995).

A particular line of action or way of behaving toward one's mate may be characterized and experienced by actors in a number of ways. The nature of the act, the context within which the act occurs, and the consequences the act has for the actor and for others all play a part in the motives attributed to the spouse who acts. Thus, acts can be seen as reflecting the actor's needs, sense of morality, unconscious drives, goals, or purposes (Wegner & Vallacher, 1986). How acts are characterized, both by the actor and others, serves to define how spouses see each other and their marriage relationship.

Lewin's (1948) analysis of voluntary action, as applied to marriage, suggests that potential activities and behaviors, situated in particular social and environmental contexts, are often evaluated in terms of the relative strength of the valences associated with them (cf. Herbst, 1952, 1953; Levinger & Huston, 1990). The notion that spouses' choices depend on the valences of various lines of activity suggests the importance of identifying factors that affect such valences. It is also important to keep in mind that when the valences associated with a particular line of action are highly and consistently positive, actors will develop particular habits of behavior. Thus, an extrovert may gravitate toward social gatherings, rather than toward solitary pursuits, even though he or she may not identify his actions in terms of this proclivity. It is easier to identify the valences associated with lines of action when actors' alternatives have similar values or when the consequences of the choices for the self and for other people are salient. A wife who is behind in her work at the office may be confronted with a choice between staying late to clean up her desk and returning home for dinner. The decision she reaches is no doubt rooted, at least in part, in her values, attitudes, and the like, as well as in the expectations of her coworkers, superiors, and family.

The valences of alternative activities and behaviors, according to Lewin's (1948) analysis, differ in both quality (positive or negative) and strength. Thus, an actor's ambivalence and uncertainty intensify if the valence changes when the line of action is examined from different perspectives. Although Lewin (1948) did not distinguish between types of factors that might affect valences, Heider (1958) suggested that self-regulated behavior is generally seen as reflecting, in varying degrees, what (a) actors seem to *want*, *need*, or *desire*; (b) what they feel they *ought* to do; and (c) what they believe they have the *ability* to do. These three types of psychological forces may be internal or general and thus reflect actors' psychological makeup; or, they may be situationally or relationship specific, as when partners negotiate a set of understandings regarding their rights and responsibilities for particular types of situations.

The importance of distinguishing matters such as what people want to do (or desire to do) from what they feel they ought to do and what they feel competent to do has a number of important implications for researchers studying marriage. First, the pertinence of the three facets of spouses' psychological makeup for marriage may depend on the activity or behavior under consideration. Spouses are generally seen to do household work primarily because they feel they ought to do it, whereas they are thought to pursue recreation largely for pleasure. Whether the motives associated with these various types of activities are indeed empirically reducible in these ways should not be assumed. My colleagues and I made this mistake when we failed to inquire about how much spouses would enjoy or dislike doing various household and child care tasks and focused, instead, on their beliefs about which partner ought to do each task and their ideas about how well they each could do the tasks (Atkinson and Huston, 1984; McHale & Huston, 1984).

Second, sociologists have tended to focus on the idea that spouses' behavior in marriage is regulated by their understanding of what they ought to do. This reflects sociologists' long-standing interest in social structure, power, and roles (e.g., Bates & Harvey, 1975). Psychologists, with their interest in the hedonic basis of behavior, turn to actors' basic wants, needs, or desires or to their love and attraction as causes of behavior. Third, what people want to do, feel they ought to do, and believe they have the ability to do are not always aligned within a particular individual. Spouses may restrain themselves from doing something they want to do because they feel it is morally wrong or because they are not sure how to go about doing it (McHale & Huston, 1984). Fourth, the three types of considerations may differ in importance from one person to another. A person who seeks pleasure wherever it can be found, with little internal moral constraint or concern for others, might be characterized as self-absorbed or, perhaps, narcissistic. A person who has a considerable range of competencies and who places only moderate importance on matters of social correctness might be characterized as a competent pragmatist. When marriage partners' actions toward each other and their commentaries about each other's behavior resonate to issues of right and wrong, their relationship may take on the overtones of a morality play.

Figures 1 and 2 distinguish between what might be thought of as personological factors that affect marital dynamics and the beliefs and attitudes spouses develop about each other and the relationship. The idea that a person's psychological makeup affects marital dynamics has a long history (Auhagen & Hinde, 1997). Terman and his colleagues (1938), for example, suggested the following:

> Whether by nature or nurture, there are persons so lacking in qualities which make for compatibility that they would be incapable of finding happiness in any marriage. There are others, less extreme, who could find it only under the most favorable circumstances; and still others whose dispositions and outlooks upon life would preserve them from acute unhappiness however unfortunately they were mated (p. 110).

Any quality that a mate brings to marriage that might affect how spouses either behave in marriage or react to each other's behavior fits within what I mean when I speak of spouses' psychological makeup and physical makeup. Personality traits, values, interests, social attitudes, and physical qualities exemplify features of spouses' makeup that might affect marital dynamics. These relatively durable qualities also include spouses' core values: their sense of identity, their attitudes (e.g., about politics, hunting, the opera, or the institution of marriage), their stereotypes (e.g., implicit theories about men and women), their intelligence, their skills, their temperament, their passions, and their ideas about what they want in a marriage or in a partner. Spouses may enter marriage with particular ideas or knowledge structures about how relationships work, such as believing that relationships cannot work without love, or that men and women must equally share household chores (Fletcher & Kinmouth, 1992). To the extent that these preferences precede marriage and endure once couples marry, they may affect how couples structure their marriage and how they come to evaluate each other and their marriage.

Moreover, because these features of a person's psychological makeup are thought to reflect general and stable proclivities, they bear upon how people react to a variety of situations. People who are moody or tense, by nature, may react more strongly to stressors than others. A man with a love of fishing, for instance, relates to the world, in part, through a fisherman's eyes, a man who thinks of himself as the primary breadwinner may be feel threatened when he is out of work, and a woman who thinks of herself as intelligent will likely become angry if she is patronized.

These general, stable attributes and proclivities can be distinguished from those that are specific to the partner or the relationship. Spouses love, admire, and trust one another in varying degrees, and these kinds of attitudes both shape and are shaped by how spouses relate to one another. Other in-the-head phenomena specific to the partner and the marriage include satisfaction with the marriage, the understandings that partners develop about appropriate behavior, beliefs they have about their marriage (e.g., who is dominant, how household work is divided, or the centrality of the marriage in each of the partner's lives), and ideas the spouses have about each other's psychological makeup (e.g., their goals, values, interests, or personality).

These attitudes and beliefs need to be distinguished from spouses' psychological and physical makeup for two primary reasons. First, they develop and change as a consequence of the relationship and thus both shape and are shaped by the marriage relationship. Second, such specific attitudes and evaluations develop out of the interplay between spouses' general dispositions and the history of the spouses in their relationship. A spouse thus may trust his or her mate, at first, because the spouse generally believes people are trustworthy. This initial trust, in turn, may cause the trusting individual to behave in ways that encourage trustworthy behavior. Thus, a generalized trust in others may foreshadow the development of trust in particular relationships. A similar kind of process may link attachment styles, as general dispositions, to how spouses come to feel about a particular intimate partner. Regardless of how much trust or security a person feels initially, such trust or security is apt to give way quickly should it be violated. Thus, it is particularly important when examining emergent, relationship-specific beliefs and evaluations to recognize that they are apt to result from the interplay between psychological and interpersonal forces. Although it makes sense to treat stable personality dispositions as exogenous variables in models of marital adjustment, relationship-specific beliefs and attitudes are more usefully modeled as both causes and consequences of marital activities and behavior.

Affect, cognition, and changes in spouse's beliefs and attitudes about each other. This impact of participation in a marriage on the spouses is shown in Figure 2 as the upward element of the arrows emanating from each spouses' state of being. We know very little about how spouses' experiences in the marriage affect their attitudes and beliefs about each other and the relationship or about how these internal changes, in turn, produce changes in marital patterns. A husband who enters marriage with the general idea that women ought to be "put on a pedestal," for instance, may initially be comfortable making decisions for the two of them without seeking his wife's input. This combination of values and behavior may be reinforced or undermined over time, depending on whether his wife wants to be put on a pedestal in such a fashion. If she is uncomfortable with such a role (perhaps because she has different ideas about gender roles or perhaps because he tends to make poor decisions), she may confront him. She may keep her concerns to herself, however, if she believes he will not be open to them. Thus, depending on the spouses' psychological makeup and how their interactions unfold, spouses may deal with situations in which the husband makes decisions for the couple with any number of thoughts and feelings that, in turn, affect how they see each other and the world within which they function.

Most research on marriage has focused primarily on marital satisfaction. The roots of other attitudes and beliefs, such as how spouses' sense of trust, love, or respect develops in marriage, is poorly understood. We know precious little about the conditions that sustain feelings of love or lead a spouse to admire his or her mate, or about what experiences encourage a spouse to develop a superior attitude. My sense is that the focus of recent research on the affective substrate of marital interaction will prove less useful when researchers shift their attention from studying the antecedents of marital satisfaction to examining the marital patterns that give rise to some of these other beliefs and evaluations. Researchers will no doubt need to know something about the spouses' psychological qualities—their values, role preferences, and the like—as well as something about macrobehavioral activities to account for such matters as whether spouses feel household tasks are divided equitably or whether they feel their partner is worthy of admiration. A wife may come to admire her husband, for example, largely by such matters as his willingness to make time for his mother or his children, by his ability to handle stress, or by his success in the occupational world.

Just as it is important to recognize that particular behaviors can reflect a variety of underlying motives, researchers need to take into account that they may produce varied reactions, depending on how the behavior is interpreted. Behavior that actually reflects an actor's disapproval, for instance, may produce varying degrees of discomfort in its target, depending on whether the disapproval is seen as emanating from the communicant's critical nature, whether the disapproval is seen as reflecting a loss of affection, or whether the target feels the disapproval is well deserved. Spouses thus react not only to each other's behavior in terms of whether it supports their interests but also to the attitudes and beliefs that seem to lie beneath the behavior (cf. Kelley, 1979). Indeed, when partners in intimate relationships are asked to identify specific behaviors they would like their partner to change, they often report, instead, more global complaints that center on their partner's person-

ality, character, or attitudes about the relationship (Kelley, 1979).

Because husbands' and wives' psychological makeup, knowledge structures, and attitudes are reflected in their behavior (as well as in their reactions to each other's behavior), spouse's dispositions play off one another. A wife who is ambivalent about her marriage, for example, may express little or intermittent affection toward her husband, which, in turn, may trigger a strong reaction from him, particularly if he is insecure. Spouses relate to each other's personality as it is manifest in the relationship. A person who is prone to emotional ups and downs, for example, may be harder to live with on a day-to-day basis compared with someone who is even tempered (Caughlin et al., in press). Selfishness, depression, and aggressiveness no doubt undermine marriage (Kitson, 1992), whereas qualities like warmth and openness appear to enhance marriage relationships (Lamke, 1989). The extent to which married partners' psychological qualities fit together ought to relate to the degree to which the partners are able to establish a harmonious, mutually satisfying marriage bond, according to compatibility theories of marriage (Huston & Houts, 1998). Thus, over time, the images, attitudes, and feelings the spouses develop about each other reflect the psychological qualities that lie beneath the surface of their behavior.

Spouses develop new understandings, their motivations to behave in particular ways become stronger or weaker, and individuals acquire, sharpen, or lose their sense of skill with regard to particular matters. Each spouse provides a context for the other, and both partners are influenced, individually and jointly, by events outside the relationship that impinge on them. Thus, although husbands and wives come to their relationships with beliefs about appropriate ways to behave, inclinations to act in particular ways, and a package of skills, these initial propensities, rooted in their personality and values (or more generally, in their psychological makeup) are often muted or amplified in the context of the marriage relationship. Spouses who have a strong bond with one another may increasingly internalize each other's ideas about appropriate behavior. A husband who is tough-minded, in general, may be tenderhearted when it comes to his wife. Partners' dispositions toward each other in the relationship are themselves causally interdependent (Kelley, 1979, 1983). Thus, for example, the inclination of one partner to show love will be dampened if it is not, over time, reciprocated. Similarly, a competitive spouse who makes choices that preempt the partner may indirectly encourage the partner to seek similar advantage.

A few observations can be made to conclude this section, using Figure 2 as a point of reference. If we are to effectively meet Burgess's (1926) challenge of studying marriage as a "unity of interacting personalities," we need to recognize first that spouses' marital behavior, when examined in its totality, is anchored in a mix of the spouses' behavioral dispositions. The amalgam of psychological forces that regulate marital behavior is mediated through the spouses' states of being, which, in turn, are partly anchored both in the spouses' psychological makeup and in their beliefs and attitudes about each other and the marriage. Marital behavior is too often studied as if its significance to the actors can be understood apart from the history of the spouses' relationship with each other; the propensity of researchers to disembody marital behavior from the spouses' psychological characteristics has made it difficult to trace the deeper psychological roots of marital interaction and the roots of distress.

Second, because behavior is the medium through which dispositions are expressed, researchers need to gather data not only about what people do and how they act when they are together but also data that bear on why people do what they do and act as they do. Third, spouses influence each other, and this influence extends over time; thus, longitudinal research carried out with couples that examines how the spouses' ideas about each other and their motives both shape and are shaped by their history together is sorely needed.

Marital Success and Stability

Up to now, my focus has been on marital adjustment as a process. As noted earlier, marital adjustment is also used as a summary evaluation of the quality of the marriage relationship at a particular time in its history. I question two assumptions that appear to underlie the focus on marital satisfaction as the primary cause of marital stability. First, as Karney and Bradbury (1995) recently pointed out, "the magnitude of the linkage [between satisfaction and divorce] has not been large" (p. 25). Second, satisfaction typically has been used as the sole indicant of the extent to which spouses are drawn to each other and, hence, motivated to stay married.

Johnson's (1991, 1999) model of commitment points to the idea that the decisions spouses make to stay married or divorce reflect, in varying degrees, not only the extent to which the spouses want to stay married (what Johnson calls *personal commitment*) but also the extent to which they feel they *ought* to stay married (Johnson's *moral commitment*) and the degree to which they think they *have* to stay married (*structural commitment*). The moral obligation that people feel to stay married may reflect, in one degree or another, relatively stable values about the morality of divorce anchored in their upbringing, spouses' concerns about the welfare of their children, understandings spouses have reached with each other about the permanence of their union, and the degree to which they see themselves as steadfast in keeping their commitments. Moral commitment, thus, is rooted partly in a person's values and personality, and partly in the marriage itself. Structural commitment, in contrast to both personal and moral commitment, is experienced as emanating from the outside. People may feel they have to stay in a relationship because of financial concerns, because they lack the opportunity to form competing relationships, or because they worry about negative social sanctions. The root causes of structural commitment can generally be located in the spouse's social network or ecological niche. Spouses who are very strongly drawn to each other, according to Johnson, may rarely think about moral and structural constraints, but if their personal commitment declines, moral and structural barriers are apt to become more salient.

The reasons why spouses are committed to staying married, according to Johnson (1991, 1999), undoubtedly affects how spouses relate to one another, how much time they spend together, and whether they pursue other relationships that might compete with the marriage. Spouses who no longer want to stay married but do so out of a sense of obligation or external constraint, for example, may show little interest in and affection toward their mate. Research linking configurations of commitment to marital behavior, however, has yet to be undertaken.

The second problem with the focus on marital satisfaction is that it provides only a pale representation of the total constellation of psychological forces that draw spouses toward one another. Love, admiration, a sense of being compatible, and trust are probably just as important, if not more important, than satisfaction in accounting for spouses' desire to stay married (cf. Lamm, Wiesmann, & Keller, 1998). These various assessments also are rooted in a variety of marital experiences and as such, they reinforce the importance of researchers moving beyond focusing on how spouses communicate at a randomly selected time in their relationship. Marital satisfaction clearly resonates to the affective character of marital interaction (see Gottman & Notarius, in press). Factors that generate and sustain love, admiration, and trust, however, are apt to be anchored in how spouses respond to particular kinds of situations—such as those in which spouses help each other, solve a problem together, overcome a difficulty, or resist temptation—rather than be rooted in the kinds of features of communication styles commonly studied in marital interaction research.

Researchers have just begun to examine changes in spouses' evaluations of their marriage at multiple points in time, beginning with the newlywed years, rather than focusing on single cross-sectional snapshots of couples who have been married varied lengths of time (see Bradbury, 1998). We found in a recent longitudinal study, for instance, that declines in love over the first 2 years of marriage foreshadowed divorce, whereas newlywed differences in love that were stable over the first 2 years of marriage predicted marital satisfaction 13 years into marriage among the couples who stay married (Huston et al., in press). Thus, if researchers are to study disaffection as a process (Kayser, 1993), they need to obtain evaluations from spouses on multiple occasions.

THE MACROENVIRONMENTAL CONTEXT OF MARRIAGE

The macrosocietal context (Figure 1, box A) includes features of the society, culture, and physical environment within which an aggregate of individuals and couples live. Had I opened this article with a thumbnail sketch of marriage in contemporary Japanese culture, where the divorce rate is less than half that of the United States, I would have described a society in which the macrosocietal sanctions against divorce are so strong as to render the feelings the spouses have toward one another largely irrelevant to marital stability. Although Japanese culture is changing, spouses generally begin marriage with the expectation that marriage requires considerable patience and tolerance. According to a 37-nation survey recently carried out by Japanese researchers (Kristol, 1996), Japanese couples are remarkably incompatible, more so than couples almost anywhere in

the world. The patriarchal value system within which marriage relationships in Japan are embedded puts pressure on wives, rather than husbands, to accommodate, and it provides little social support for marriage patterns that deviate from the norm. This brief characterization points to differences between cultures in the extent to which marital behavior is regulated by factors that arise outside the marriage.

Figure 1 schematically shows the linkages between the macroenvironment, the individual spouses, and marital behavior patterns. I subdivide the macroenvironment into the macrosocietal context (a_1) and the spouses' ecological niche (a_2) within the macroenvironment. At the macrocosmic level, nations, subcultures, and neighborhoods can be described in terms of societal conditions, in terms of historical events, and in terms of the belief systems that members of a cultural or subcultural group hold about various matters and the way that particular societal institutions ought to function. When belief systems are widely shared within a society or group, they are often internalized as moral imperatives. Such imperatives are often codified into law, and they affect the way societal institutions function. The opportunities and constraints placed on various categories of people—for example, men and women—affect the kinds of skills they acquire and the extent to which societal institutions provide incentives to encourage or discourage particular types of behavior. Spouses' ideas about marital roles and their understandings of the rules that regulate the behavior of wives and husbands in the culture reflect, at least to some extent, macrosocietal forces. In rural Japan, for instance, couples contemplating divorce would be hard-pressed to find support for taking such an action (Kristol, 1996); such support could be found more readily, however, in major urban centers in Japan. Societies and subcultures differ, of course, in the pluralism of the members' values, as well as in how much contact is encouraged between subgroups holding different values. The pluralistic nature of the macrosociety within which inhabitants of the United States currently live, in contrast to societies that are more homogeneous, makes it possible for couples to fashion a network supportive of a wide range of marital lifestyles or of divorcing for a variety of reasons.

The particular ecological niche, defined as a constellation of behavior settings within which spouses function on a day-to-day basis, affects both the spouses and the marriage relationship.

Couples who live in poor, urban neighborhoods must deal with very different issues than those who live in metropolitan suburbs, small towns, or rural areas (Burton & Jarrett, in press). The behavior settings within which a dual-worker couple with two young children live out their lives are very different from those of a retired elderly couple, whose children were married and moved away years ago.

The behavior settings within which people function also provide the medium through which cultural values are articulated, reinforced, or undermined. The link between societal conditions and the marital relationship (Figure 1, link 5) suggests that the embeddedness of the marriage in a macrosocietal milieu can directly affect husband-wife interaction. For example, the economic depression of the 1930s put people out of work and created economically pressed households, often populated by members of a nuclear family, their extended family, and friends.

Macrosocietal changes can affect marital and family dynamics (e.g., Conger & Elder, 1994; Elder, 1964) by altering the ecological niches within which subsets of the population function. What happens in behavior settings outside the home can, and often does, affect the internal dynamics of the marriage relationship. The effects of features of a couples' environmental niche on marital interaction, however, are often mediated through their effects on the husband, the wife, or both partners (in Figure 1, link 3, followed by link 1). Work-related stress may be transported by the worker into the home and thereby create conflict in the marital relationship (Bolger, DeLongis, Kessler, & Wethington, 1989; Crouter, Perry-Jenkins, Huston, & Crawford, 1989; Halford, Gravestock, Lowe, & Scheldt, 1992). Economic hardship, for example, tends to produce anxiety and depression (Figure 1, link 3), which, in turn, is associated with marital conflict (link 1; Conger, Reuter, & Elder, 1999). Qualities of the husband and wife, however, may also either amplify or diminish (i.e., moderate) the impact of macroenvironmental conditions. The impact of economic hardship on marital conflict, for example, may be buffered by the amount of social support spouses provide one another (Conger et al., 1999), or may be intensified if either the husband or wife has a psychological propensity toward moodiness or irascibility, or if either spouse is already distressed about the marriage.

CONCLUSIONS

The ecological model described in this paper focuses on issues pertaining to causal processes that cut across the three prime units of analysis. Most theories about marriage and other intimate relationships focus attention on only part of the whole causal system. Biologically oriented social scientists ordinarily start with the attributes of husbands and wives—their physical appearance, health status, and temperament—and examine how these qualities are reflected in the spouses' proclivities relevant to marital relationships (Figure 1, link 5) or, more rarely, to marital interaction (link 3). Evolutionary theorists take an essentialist view of sex differences, seeking to explain gender differences in intimate relationships in terms of the principles of natural selection (link 1). Sociologists, particularly feminists, take a constructivist view of gender, seeing it as a social category, the significance of which depends on the social and cultural context. Thus, for example, power differences experienced in marriage are traced to patriarchal macrosocietal structures (links 3 and 5). Symbolic interactionists (e.g., McCall & Simmons, 1978) suggest that people are gratified by, and hence become attached to, others who validate their identity (i.e., their general sense of themselves; links 1 and 2). Sociologists and developmental psychologists suggest that the ecological niches within which the spouses were raised affect their marital proclivities (link 3), which, in turn, affect marital patterns (link 1; Tallman, Gray, Kullberg, & Henderson, 1999).

Role theorists (e.g, Bates & Harvey, 1975) invoke "culture" to explain the recurrence of similar patterns of activity by different sets of actors in marriage, as well as the stability of such patterns over time. Once a norm is learned and established, it becomes a part of the personality of the actors in the relationship, serving both as an internal rudder regulating the spouses' behavior and as a basis for sanctioning behavior that deviates from normative prescriptions. Sociologists and family social scientists also have examined the interplay between kin and friendship networks and the marital relationships (within box C of Figure 1, the link between c_1 and c_2). Behavioral psychologists often focus on the interplay between marital interaction and marital satisfaction (Figure 1, links 1 and 2). Social psychologists often begin with the attributes of the individual spouses (e.g., personality, values, compatibility) and seek to link these to marital behavior and, ultimately, to the attitudes and beliefs spouses develop toward each other (Figure 1, links 1 and 2).

The ecological study of marriage also requires researchers to link constructs across the levels—societal, individual, and marital—recognizing that each level provides the context for the others. The macrosocietal context within which marriage relationships are embedded is affected by the mix of decisions individual spouses and married couples make; similarly, individual spouses not only shape the contours of their marriage but are shaped by it, as well. The circular patterns of cause and effect, when examined with the idea that these cause-effect relationships also depend on contextual factors, imply that no single effort to understand the interplay between marriage and context can capture more than a sliver of the dynamic and circular processes involved. New ways of analyzing data that simultaneously take into account individual-, dyadic-, and group-level effects make ecologically sensitive research easier to do than was heretofore possible (see Kashy & Grotevant, 1999). Moreover, if researchers working on subparts of the larger reciprocal causal system are aware of what their colleagues are doing in related disciplines, our collective efforts to understand marriage will show remarkable advances in the 21st century.

NOTE

The author would like to thank Laura George for her help in thinking through the broad outlines of the ecological model and to thank Gilbert Geis, Sylvia Niehuis, Shanna Smith, Paul Miller, and Christopher Rasmussen for their thoughtful reflections on an earlier draft of this manuscript. Work on this article was supported by grants from the National Science Foundation (SBR-9311846) and the National Institute of Mental Health (MH 33938).

REFERENCES

Almeida, D., Wethington, E., & Chandler, A. L. (1999) Daily transmission of tensions between marital dyads and parent-child dyads. *Journal of Marriage and the Family, 61,* 49–61.

Altman, I., & Ginat, J. (1996) *Polygamous families in contemporary society.* New York: Cambridge University Press.

Atkinson, J., & Huston, T. L. (1984) Sex role orientation and division of labor early in marriage. *Journal of Personality and Social Psychology, 46,* 330–345.

Auhagen, A. E., & Hinde, R. A. (1997) Individual characteristics and personal relationships. *Personal Relationships, 4,* 63–84.

Bates, F. L., & Harvey, C. C. (1975) *The structure of social systems.* New York: Gardner.

Bernard, J. (1964) The adjustment of married mates. In

H. T. Christensen (Ed.), *Handbook of marriage and the family* (pp. 675–739). Chicago: Rand McNally.

Berscheid, E. (1983) Emotion. In H. H. Kelley, E. Berscheid, A. Christensen, J. H. Harvey, T. L. Huston, L. A. Peplau, & D. R. Peterson (Eds.), *Close relationships* (pp. 110–168). New York: Freeman.

Berscheid, E. (1985) Compatibility, interdependence, and emotion. In W. Ickes (Ed.), *Compatible and incompatible relationships* (pp. 143–162). New York: Springer-Verlag.

Berscheid, E. (1998) A social psychological view of marital dysfunction and stability. In T. N. Bradbury (Ed.), *The developmental course of marital dysfunction* (pp. 441–459). New York: Cambridge University Press.

Berscheid, E., & Lopes, J. (1997) A temporal model of relationship satisfaction and stability. In R. J. Sternberg & M. Hojjat (Eds.), *Satisfaction in close relationships* (pp. 129–159). New York: Plenum Press.

Bolger, N., DeLongis, A., Kessler, R. C., & Wethington, E. (1989) The contagion of stress across multiple roles. *Journal of Marriage and the Family, 51,* 175–183.

Bott, E. (1971) *Family and the social network: Roles, norms, and external relationships in ordinary urban families* (2nd ed.). New York: Free Press.

Bradbury, T. N. (Ed.) (1998) *The developmental course of marital dysfunction.* New York: Cambridge University Press.

Bradbury, T. N., & Fincham, F. D. (1988) Individual difference variables in close relationships: A contextual model of marriage as an integrative framework. *Journal of Personality and Social Psychology, 54,* 713–721.

Burgess, E. W. (1926) The family as a system of interacting personalities. *Family, 7,* 3–9.

Burgess, E. W., & Cottrell, L. (1939) *Predicting success or failure in marriage.* Englewood Cliffs, NJ: Prentice-Hall.

Burgess, E. W., & Locke, H. J. (1945) *The family: From institution to companionship.* New York: American Book.

Burton, L., & Jarrett, R. L. (in press). In the mix, yet on the margins: The place of families in urban neighborhood and child development research. *Journal of Marriage and the Family.*

Caughlin, J. P., Huston, T. L., & Houts, R. M. (2000) How does personality matter in marriage? An examination of trait anxiety, interpersonal negativity, and marital satisfaction. *Journal of Personality and Social Psychology, 78,* 326–336.

Conger, R., & Elder, G. (1994) *Families in troubled times: Adapting to change in rural America.* New York: Aldine deGruyer.

Conger, R. D., Reuter, M. A., & Elder, G. (1999) Couple resilience to economic pressure. *Journal of Personality and Social Psychology, 76,* 54–71.

Cook, T. D., & Campbell, D. T. (1979) *Quasi-experimentation: Design and analysis issues for field settings.* Chicago: Rand McNally.

Crawford, D. W., & Huston, T. L. (1993) The impact of the transition to parenthood on marital leisure. *Personality and Social Psychology Bulletin, 18,* 39–46.

Crouter, A., Perry-Jenkins, M., Huston, T. L., & Crawford, D. (1989) The influence of work-induced psychological states on behavior at home. *Basic and Applied Social Psychology, 10,* 273–292.

Elder, G. (1964) *Children of the depression.* Berkeley, CA: University of California Press.

Fincham, F. D., & Bradbury, T. N. (1987) The assessment of marital quality: A reevaluation. *Journal of Marriage and the Family, 49,* 797–809.

Fletcher, G. J. O., & Kinmouth, L. (1992) Measuring relationship beliefs: An individual differences measure. *Journal of Research in Personality, 26,* 371–397.

Gable, S. L., & Reis, H. T. (1999) Now and then, them and us, this and that: Studying relationships across time, partner, context, and person. *Personal Relationships, 6,* 415–432.

Gilbert, R., Christensen, A., & Margolin, G. (1984) Patterns of alliances in nondistressed and multiproblem families. *Family Process, 23,* 75–876.

Gottman, J. M. (1990) How marriages change. In G. R. Patterson (Ed.) *Depression and aggression in family interaction* (pp. 75–101). Hillsdale, NJ: Erlbaum.

Gottman, J. M. (1994) *What predicts divorce? The relationship between marital processes and marital outcomes.* Hillsdale, NJ: Erlbaum.

Gottman, J. M., & Krokoff, L. J. (1989) The relationship between marital interaction and marital satisfaction: A longitudinal view. *Journal of Consulting and Clinical Psychology, 57,* 47–52.

Gottman, J., & Notarius, C. I. (in press). Observing marital interaction. *Journal of Marriage and the Family.*

Halford, W. K., Gravestock, F. M., Lowe, R., & Scheldt, S. (1992) Toward a behavioral ecology of stressful marital interactions. *Behavioral Assessment, 14,* 199–217.

Heider, F. (1958) *The psychology of interpersonal relations.* New York: Wiley.

Herbst, P. (1952) The measurement of family relationships. *Human Relations, 5,* 3–35.

Herbst, P. (1953) Analysis and measurement of a situation: The child in the family. *Human Relations, 6,* 113–140.

Herbst, P. (1965) Problems of theory and method in the integration of the behavioural sciences. *Human Relations, 18,* 351–359.

Hinde, R. (1987) *Individuals, relationships, and culture.* New York: Cambridge University Press.

Huston, T. L., Caughlin, J. P., Houts, R. M., Smith, S. E., & George, L. (in press). The connubial crucible: Newlywed years as predictors of marital delight, distress, and divorce. *Journal of Personality and Social Psychology.*

Huston, T. L., & Geis, G. (1993) In what ways do gender-related attributes and beliefs affect marriage? *Journal of Social Issues, 49,* 87–106.

Huston, T. L., & Houts, R. (1998) The psychological infrastructure of courtship and marriage: The role pf personality and compatibility in the evolution of romantic relationships. In T. N. Bradbury (Ed.), *The developmental course of marital dysfunction* (pp. 114–151). New York: Cambridge University Press.

Huston, T. L., McHale, S. M., & Crouter, A. (1986) When the honeymoon's over: Changes in the marriage relationship over the first year. In R. Gilmour & S. Duck (Eds.), *Theoretical frameworks for personal relationships* (pp. 109–132). Hillsdale, NJ: Erlbaum.

Huston, T. L., & Rempel, J. (1989) Interpersonal attitudes, dispositions, and behavior in family and other close relationships. *Journal of Family Psychology, 3,* 177–198.

Huston, T. L., & Robins, E. (1982) Conceptual and methodological issues in studying close relationships. *Journal of Marriage and the Family, 44,* 901–925.

Huston, T. L., Robins, E., Atkinson, J., & McHale, S. (1987) Surveying the landscape of marital behavior: A behavioral self-report approach to studying marriage. In S. Oskamp (Ed.), *Family processes and problems: Social psychological aspects* (pp. 45–71). Beverly Hills, CA: Sage.

Huston, T. L., & Vangelisti, A. (1991) Socioemotional behavior and satisfaction in marital relationships: A longitudinal study. *Journal of Personality and Social Psychology, 61,* 721–733.

Huston, T. L., & Vangelisti, A. (1995) How parenthood affects marriage. In M. Fitzpatrick & A. Vangelisti (Eds.), *Perspectives on family communication* (pp. 147–176). Newbury Park, CA: Sage.

Johnson, M. P. (1991) Commitment to personal relationships. In W. H. Jones & D. Perlman (Eds.), *Advances in personal relationships* (Vol. 3, pp. 117–143). London: Jessica Kingsley.

Johnson, M. P. (1999) Personal, moral, and structural commitment to relationships: Experiences of choice and constraint. In W. H. Jones & J. M. Adams (Eds.), *Handbook of interpersonal commitment and relationship stability* (pp. 73–87). New York: Kluwer Academic-Plenum Press.

Johnson, M. P., Huston, T. L., Gaines, S. O., & Levinger, G. (1992) Patterns of married life among young couples. *Journal of Personal and Social Relationships, 9,* 343–364.

Karney B. R., & Bradbury, T. N. (1995) The longitudinal course of marital quality and stability: A review of theory, method, and research. *Psychology Bulletin, 118,* 3–34.

Kashy, D. A., & Grotevant, H. D. (1999) Methodological and data analytic advances in the study of interpersonal relationships: Introduction to the special issue. *Personal Relationships, 6,* 411–413.

Kayser, K. (1993) *When love dies: The process of marital disaffection.* New York: Guilford Press.

Kelley, H. H. (1979) *Personal relationships: Their structures and processes.* Hillsdale, NJ: Erlbaum.

Kelley, H. H. (1983) Epilogue. In H. H. Kelley, E. Berscheid, A. Christensen, J. H. Harvey, T. L. Huston, G. Levinger, E. McClintock, L. A. Peplau, & D. R. Peterson (Eds.), *Close relationships* (pp. 486–503). New York: Academic Press.

Kelley, H. H., Berscheid, E., Christensen, A., Harvey, J. H., Huston, T. L., Levinger, G., McClintock, E., Peplau, L. A., & Peterson, D. R., (1983) *Close relationships.* New York: Freeman.

Kenny, D. A., & Cook, W. (1999) Partner effects in relationship research: conceptual issues, analytic difficulties, and illustrations. *Personal Relationships, 6,* 433–458.

Kitson, G. C. (1992) *Portrait of divorce: Adjustment to marital breakdown.* New York: Guilford Press.

Kristol, N. D. (1996, February 11) Who needs love? In Japan, many couples don't. *The New York Times,* pp. 1, 6.

Lamke, L. K. (1989) Marital adjustment among rural

couples: The role of expressiveness. *Sex Roles, 21,* 579–590.

Lamm, H., Wiesmann, U., & Keller, K. (1998) Subjective determinants of attraction: Self-perceived causes of the rise and decline of liking, love, and being in love. *Personal Relationships, 5,* 91–104.

Larson, R., & Almeida, D. (1999) Emotional transmission in the daily lives of families: A new paradigm for studying family process. *Journal of Marriage and the Family, 61,* 5–20.

Larson, R., & Richards, M. H. (1994) *Divergent realities: The emotional lives of mothers, fathers, and adolescents.* New York: Basic Books.

Levinger, G. (1994) Figure versus ground: Micro- and macroperspectives on the social psychology of personal relationships. In R. Erber & R. Gilmour (Eds.), *Theoretical frameworks for personal relationships.* Hillsdale, NJ: Erlbaum.

Levinger, G., & Huston, T. L. (1990) The social psychology of marriage. In F. D. Fincham & T. N. Bradbury (Eds.), *The psychology of marriage: Conceptual, empirical, and applied perspectives* (pp. 19–58). New York: Guilford Press.

Levinger, G., & Rands, M. (1985) Compatibility in marriage and other close relationships. In W. Ickes (Ed.), *Compatible and incompatible relationships* (pp. 309–331). New York: Springer-Verlag.

Lewin, K. (1948) *Field theory in social science.* New York: Harper.

Locke, H. J., & Wallace, K. M. (1959) Short marital adjustment and prediction tests: Their reliability and validity. *Marriage and Family Living, 21,* 251–255.

MacDermid, S., Huston, T. L., & McHale, S. M. (1990) Changes in marriage associated with the transition to parenthood: Individual differences as a function of sex role attitudes and changes in the division of household labor. *Journal of Marriage and the Family, 52,* 475–486.

Malle, B. (1999) How people explain behavior: A new theoretical approach. *Personality and Social Psychology Review, 3,* 23–48.

Markman, H. J. (1981) Prediction of marital distress: A 5-year follow-up. *Journal of Consulting and Clinical Psychology, 49,* 760–762.

Markman, H. J., Floyd, F. J., Stanley, S. M., & Storaasli, R. D. (1988) Prevention of marital distress: A longitudinal investigation. *Journal of Consulting and Clinical Psychology, 56,* 210–217.

Markman, H. J., & Notarius, C. I. (1987) Coding marital and family interaction: Current status. In T. Jacob (Ed.), *Family interaction and psychopathology: Theories, methods, and findings* (pp. 325–390). New York: Plenum Press.

Marks, S. R., & MacDermid, S. M. (1996) Multiple roles and the self: A theory of role balance. *Journal of Marriage and the Family, 58,* 417–432.

McCall, G. J., & Simmons, J. L. (1978) *Identities and interactions* (Rev. ed.). New York: Free Press.

McHale, S. M. & Huston, T. L. (1984) Men and women as parents: Sex role orientations, employment, and parental roles with infants. *Child Development, 55,* 1349–1361.

Medrich, E., Roizen, J. A., Rubin, V., & Buckley, S. (1982) *The serious business of growing up: A study of children's lives outside school.* Berkeley, CA: University of California Press.

Noller, P. (1984) *Nonverbal communication and marital interaction.* Elmsford, NY: Pergamon Press.

Noller, P., & Guthrie, D. (1991) Studying communication in marriage: An integration and critical evaluation. In W. H. Jones & D. Perlman (Eds.), *Advances in personal relationships* (Vol. 3, pp. 37–73). London: Jessica Kingsley.

Ouellette, J. A., & Wood, W. (1998) Habit and intention in everyday life: The multiple processes by which past behavior predicts future behavior. *Psychological Bulletin, 124,* 54–74.

Peplau, L. A. (1983) Roles and gender. In H. H. Kelley et al., *Close relationships* (pp. 220–264). New York: Freeman.

Reis, H. T., & Gable, S. L. (in press). Methods for studying daily experience. In H. T. Reis & C. M. Judd (Eds.), *Handbook of research methods in social psychology.* New York: Cambridge University Press.

Robins, E. (1990) The study of interdependence in marriage. In F. D. Fincham & T. N. Bradbury (Eds.), *The psychology of marriage: Basic issues and applications* (pp. 59–86). New York: Guilford Press.

Schwarz, N. (1990) Assessing frequency reports of mundane behaviors: Contributions of cognitive psychology to questionnaire construction. In C. Hendrick & M. S. Clark (Eds.), *Research methods in personality and social psychology* (pp. 98–119). Newbury Park, CA: Sage.

Spanier, G. B. (1976) Measuring dyadic adjustment: New scales for assessing the quality of marriage and similar dyads. *Journal of Marriage and the Family, 38,* 15–38.

Sudman, S., Bradburn, N. M., & Schwarz, N. (1996) *Thinking about answers: The application of cognitive processes to survey methodology.* San Francisco: Jossey-Bass.

Surra, C. A., & Milardo, R. M. (1991) The social psychological context of developing relationships: Interactive and psychological networks. In W. H. Jones & D. Perlman (Eds.), *Advances in personal relationships* (Vol. 3, pp. 1–36). London: Jessica Kingsley.

Tallman, I., Gray, L. M., Kullberg, V., & Henderson, D. (1999) The intergenerational transmission of marital conflict: Testing a process model. *Social Psychology Quarterly, 62,* 219–239.

Terman, L. W., Buttenwieser, P., Ferguson, L. W., Johnson, W. B., & Wilson, D. P. (1938) *Psychological factors in marital happiness.* New York: McGraw-Hill.

Thompson, A. & Bolger, N. (1999) Emotional transmission in couples under emotional distress. *Journal of Marriage and the Family, 61,* 38–48.

Thompson, L., & Walker, A. J. (1982) The dyad as a unit of analysis: conceptual and methodological issues. *Journal of Marriage and the Family, 44,* 889–900.

Wegner, D. M., & Vallacher, R. R. (1986) Action identification. In R. M. Sorrentino & F. T. Higgins (Eds.), *Handbook of motivation and cognition* (pp. 550–581). New York: Guilford Press.

Wills, T. A., Weiss, R. L., & Patterson, G. R. (1974) A behavioral analysis of the determinants of marital satisfaction. *Journal of Consulting and Clinical Psychology, 42,* 802–811.

KATHERINE R. ALLEN *Virginia Polytechnic Institute and State University*

A Conscious and Inclusive Family Studies

I argue that family scholars must take bolder steps to engage the tensions between our heritage of positivist science and its postmodern challenges. I also argue that constructing theories, utilizing research methods, and examining substantive issues should be relevant to the diversity of the families we study and to ourselves as members of families. I offer examples of developing an informed reflexive consciousness to broaden the rationalist foundation that dominates family scholarship. For a more inclusive, balanced, and invigorated family studies, our subjective experiences and commitments as researchers should be acknowledged, confronted, and integrated. A family studies that is responsible to our readers, students, selves, and the people whose lives we study requires that we engage the critical intersections of race, class, gender, sexual orientation, and age as they define family diversity.

Recently, I noticed that I have two pictures of my father in a tuxedo. The first was taken in 1951, when he was 18 years old, the month his own beloved father died, and days before he and my mother realized they would have to get married. My father's arms are draped around my mother in a pose for his senior prom—a picture of innocence, demonstrating their love for each other. There would be no tuxedo at their hurried wedding a few months later. Five children and five grandchildren later, I have a new picture of my

Department of Human Development, Virginia Polytechnic Institute and State University, Blacksburg, VA 24061 (kallen@vt.edu).

Key Words: critical consciousness, diversity, family science, feminism, inclusivity, reflection, subjectivity.

father in a tuxedo. At 63, he was the best man in my 40-year-old cousin's first wedding—to a younger woman of a different race who has a child from a previous relationship. Reflecting on the temporal space between these two photographs, I picture a process that intrigues me as a scholar: the demographic, economic, and social changes that have affected family life in the 20th century. I can literally see who is standing by my father's side, then and now. The comparison of these photographs evokes the complexities of both personal relationships and structural transformations in adult life. The pictures in my living room are linked to larger images of how families are changing in a postmodern world. The pictures are a touchstone reminding me about ways my experiences are similar to and different from others with whom I live, work, or study.

In addition to the hypotheses I generate about family change by examining these photographs, I am aware of something deeply emotional, tapping into my private, subjective experience and offering opportunities for a fuller understanding of social change. The pictures are charged with powerful feelings about my life history, my relationship with my family of origin, my desire to be a good daughter, and, at the same time, my struggle to be honest about what family life has been like for me—a sometimes confusing mix of loss and pain, but more often than not, a celebration of forgiveness and renewal. These two ways of looking at the pictures, experientially and analytically, inform my passionate commitment to understanding family structure and process in an historical context. I need both perspectives to make sense of what captures my attention and encourages my imagination as a human being and as a family scholar.

I make two arguments in this essay. First, I argue that the notion of objectivity is too often used as a shield behind which people in positions of power to shape discourse and practice in family studies (e.g., those who publish in mainstream journals, including myself) hide ideologically driven commitments. Consciously reflecting on how our personal life history and values are relevant to a particular inquiry in which we are engaged is a way to improve our ability to critically analyze the knowledge we produce because we make as transparent as we can all the ideas that guide a study. Second, I argue that acknowledging, confronting, and integrating the ambiguities and complexities of our subjective experiences can help us generate a more inclusive family studies that can deal with the family diversity we, as scholars, are trying to understand and represent. We cannot ignore the prevalence of family diversity any longer, but reflection, of course, is not enough to help us deal with this diversity in our scholarly procedures. We also have to listen to and heed the voices of marginalized individuals and families, including our own.

SELF-CONSCIOUSNESS IN FAMILY STUDIES

Objectivity Is Not Objective

Family scholars need to "come to our senses" (Berman, 1989) to consciously acknowledge how our private experience of being in the world affects our public statements regarding the work we do (Reason, 1994). The status quo requires social scientists to intellectualize, but too often, this endeavor presents only the appearance and not the reality of objectivity. The unexamined belief that a study is objective because it upholds the scientific method keeps many of us from accurately representing and understanding the diversities that characterize family life. Family scholars must take bold steps away from the universalizing impulse that dominates much of the mainstream quantitative research on families. Like other scholars who have published in the *Journal of Marriage and the Family* (e.g., Miller, 1993; Sprey, 1988; Thompson, L., 1992), I argue that we should move toward an understanding of knowledge about families as constructed, partial, contested, and contingent on ever-changing historical variations. This movement requires us to expand our repertoire of what counts as legitimate empirical knowledge to include emotional sensitivity, intuitive understanding, and reflective awareness as a

way to improve the validity of our research practices and products. We can no longer rely solely on those who experience marginalization as individuals and as families to challenge the injustice of this distortion (Dilworth-Anderson, Burton, & Johnson, 1993). We each need to be responsible for representing and understanding family diversity.

Despite numerous challenges from radical-critical, feminist, or postmodern theorists (Agger, 1998; Cheal, 1991; Doherty, Boss, LaRossa, Schumm, & Steinmetz, 1993; Osmond, 1987; Osmond & Thorne, 1993; Sprey, 1988; Thorne, 1982), the interdisciplinary area of family studies promotes a conservative academic discourse in which the central positivist core once articulated by Christensen (1964) remains intact. The dominant discourse about families prevails in our mainstream journals, long after critiques of the absence of radical-critical theories (Osmond) and feminist interpretations of published scholarship (Thompson & Walker, 1989, 1995) have been widely circulated. Meta-analyses of family scholarship have also appeared in the *Journal of Marriage and the Family,* citing the exclusion and distortion of racial diversities, particularly with regard to black families (Demos, 1990). However, race continues to be treated as a binary category (as in White/Black or White/other), if at all, in most investigations of families, and not as a social construction within varied cultural contexts (Dilworth-Anderson et al., 1993; Johnson, 1988; Marks & Leslie, 2000). Sexual orientation is almost completely ignored in prestigious, mainstream journals that publish family studies content (Allen & Demo, 1995). Rather than being objective, the mainstream view of families is biased, because the pervasiveness of family diversity today and historically (Coontz, 1992; D'Emilio & Freedman, 1997) has yet to replace the dominant ideology of "The Standard North American Family" (Smith, D. E., 1993). Even more telling, this version of "The Family" excludes the diverse families in which many family scholars actually live.

By denying or ignoring our selves in the research process, we sanitize research reports (Stanley, 1990). Our identities, feelings, thoughts, ideologies, and political commitments as authors are literally written out of the research report, obscuring the fact that research reports are social constructions (Miller, 1993). The postpositivist, and now the postmodern, turn in social science calls into question the positivist notion of objective truth. Research practice has shifted from "the presumption of neutral description to engaged communication" (Bochner, Ellis, & Tillmann-Healy, 1997, p. 309). Many family scholars may be frightened that this shift could throw out the standards we rely on—as authors, reviewers, and editors—to evaluate theories and knowledge in a fair, objective manner. Daly (1997) argued persuasively, however, that the skepticism about a singular truth does not mean we must abandon practices associated with science (e.g., theory construction, empirical rigor, substantiated truth claims, and awareness of bias). Instead, the postmodern challenge requires us to be more honest and realistic about where our ideas and analyses come from. Otherwise, we create false oppositions (e.g., feminine-masculine, qualitative-quantitative, scholar-practitioner, secular-religious) and sustain these constructions as if they were real things that could be categorized and prioritized, as in male is better than female, White is better than Black, quantitative is better than qualitative, and so on.

My experiences as a writer and editor remind me that these bifurcations are easily reduced to stereotypic labels. Reducing another person or idea to a label is a distortion I have participated in when I disagreed with or did not understand another's perspective. Not wanting to be seen as weak or foolish by admitting my lack of understanding, a label makes it easy to disguise my confusion. If I disapprove of another's ideology, I can hide my disapproval in an epistemological or methodological argument. Because my intellectual community tends to reject vulnerability and humility as research processes, I am expected to locate my disagreement in a socially acceptable manner. As Boler (1999) argued, to object on the basis of personal identity or feeling is to commit a faux pas, and women are particularly in danger of being dismissed for speaking about "emotion in the hallowed halls of academe" (p. xvi). Instead, I was taught to rationalize and find something wrong with a theory or method. The postmodern turn in social science now challenges this convention that allows us to obscure our differences (Fine, 1994; Lincoln, 1997). When taking the role of editor and reviewer of others' manuscripts, family scholars also should be explicit and accountable for stating the assumptions that go into our own ideas about the ideas of others.

Rigor is compromised when we ignore an important part of the scholarly mode of production: examining our commitment to our own work. Core disagreements about the very nature of families characterize our discipline. (See, for example,

Cheal, 1991; Glenn, 1993; Scanzoni, Polonko, Teachman, & Thompson, 1989; Stacey, 1996.) Yet, few of us hold ourselves accountable for revealing how our ideas are rooted in our own history, experience, and values. As we give up the search for theoretical uniformity, we will have to work with and not gloss over the tensions in our disparate viewpoints (Sprey, 1995). Family studies is an exciting location for intellectual discourse and social change when we can take on our own ideas critically and engage each other with respect, care, and rigor. We can also look for what we find useful in another's work, thereby reframing the process of knowledge generation and critique as a co-construction (Marks, 1996; Nespor & Barber, 1995). Critique can be an activity of mutual exploration, not simple confrontation; let us appreciate how difficult it is to step outside the mainstream of conventional quantitative practice. In this essay, I engage the practice of self-conscious research to generate an inclusive family studies so that the process of creating knowledge is more sensible and relevant to the families we study.

Practicing Reflexivity

What kind of permission do we need to give each other to take public chances and expose our private commitments as a way to deepen the kinds of complex issues we are willing to study? In what ways are we limited by a process of critique in which there must be winners and losers—published or rejected, tenured or fired—without an invitation to be innovative and engaged? There is a story behind every paper we present or publish; we could learn more about the author's interpretation and how to evaluate the scholarship if we knew more about why and how the knowledge was created. Like the feminist research narratives collected by Sollie and Leslie (1994), it is easier to constructively engage our differences the more writers, readers, and reviewers are willing to explicitly name their theoretical assumptions, methodological choices, and value orientations. Although social scientists are increasingly exposed to constructivist ways of understanding the world (Miller, 1993), mainstream family studies is still undergirded by positivist psychology and sociology (Agger, 1998; Bochner et al., 1997). It is never too late to catch up to where many of our students already are and to share the leadership for dealing with the complexities that we face as chroniclers, interpreters, and interventionists of and for families.

I am not arguing for a simple declaration of our situatedness, as if the mere act of stating my social address (Bronfenbrenner & Crouter, 1983) at the beginning or end of a research report (e.g., "I am a White, middle-class mother of two") is enough to illuminate my research orientation. I am not advocating that we merely replace one elite discourse (e.g., positivist, quantitative science), with another (e.g., postpositivist or postmodern qualitative narrative analysis) (Nespor & Barber, 1995). Rather, I ask family scholars directly to be explicit about who we are and what we assume, and I also give examples of how to participate in developing an informed reflexive consciousness. Below, I use a narrative strategy of placing my experience in the center of analysis to make a case for what others have called "an informed consciousness" (Thompson, B., 1996, p. 104), "a critical subjectivity" (Reason, 1994, p. 327), and "a reflective search for self-understanding" (Klein & Jurich, 1993, p. 31). Using stories from my own life, I work through the thoughts, feelings, and actions of each episode to illustrate how I struggle to engage current challenges to traditional research practice.

My experiences as a qualitative researcher and a theorist engaged with life-course, feminist, and postmodern ideas have brought to the fore many questions about scientific legitimacy. In a discipline where objectivity still holds great power in how research is funded and evaluated, qualitative researchers (e.g., ethnographers, grounded theorists, intensive interviewers, life-history narrators) have struggled with financing and publishing our work in prestigious outlets (LaRossa & Wolf, 1985). Precisely because qualitative researchers tend to believe that the researcher is the instrument (see Denzin & Lincoln, 1994), we have developed ways of acknowledging and wrestling with personal biases, thereby resisting premature conclusions that distort or simplify others' experiences (Allen & Walker, 2000). Critical awareness of self, a primary strategy used by qualitative researchers, is essential for producing valuable analyses from textual data (Bateson, 1984). I propose that more family scholars learn some of the skills and sensitivities to lived experience that qualitative researchers from other disciplines have developed. (See Banks, 2000; Boss, 1999; Collins, 1990; Daly, 1997; Emerson, Fretz, & Shaw, 1995; Gilgun, 1995; Lewin & Leap, 1996, for examples of tracking how subjectivity influences ways in which data and empirical generalizations are represented.)

Knowledge is not pure but comes from some partial perspective (Thomas & Wilcox, 1987). Influenced by critical and feminists theories, I believe family-studies knowledge must be useful for ourselves and for the people we study (Osmond & Thorne, 1993; Smith, D. E., 1987). Through narrative practice, we can teach ourselves and each other to become aware of the perspectives that guide our research and the biases embedded in what we do and how we live (White & Epston, 1990). Narrative, or storytelling, is integral in Western life and culture. Storytelling is "a critical means by which we make ourselves intelligible within the social world" (Gergen & Gergen, 1988, p. 17). The narrative method is an interaction with one's audience, who comprise a trusted partner in the creation of scholarship:

> Writing for an imagined readership that you trust and respect . . . allows the fullest testing of your writing capacities, the freshest and most honest arguments, the least bluff, defence and ventriloquism, the most play, the least condescension. Writing to a trusted reader is . . . an invitation to a dance, offering a sympathetic partner the chance to play with your text, to hear its harmonies, to note its dissonances, to make it part of their own experience, to put it in motion, to realise its possibilities. (Game & Metcalfe, 1996, p. 33)

To make my case in this essay, I build on the interdisciplinary scholarship of race, class, and gender that has been articulated most thoroughly and persuasively by Black and Latina feminist scholars (e.g., Baca Zinn & Dill, 1996; Collins, 1986, 1990; Dill, 1983; hooks, 1989, 1994; Hull, Scott, & Smith, 1982; Lorde, 1984; Morrison, 1992), by antiracist White feminists (e.g., Fine, Weis, Powell, & Wong, 1997; Frankenberg, 1993; McIntosh, 1993; Thompson & Tyagi, 1996), by interdisciplinary scholars in gay, lesbian, and queer studies (e.g., Fuss, 1991; Parker & Gagnon, 1995; Weston, 1991), by liberatory educational scholars (e.g., Boler, 1999; Freire, 1970; Greene, 1988; McLaren, 1997), and by qualitative social scientists who locate their subjectivity as researchers and theorists in the center of analysis (e.g., Belenky, Clinchy, Goldberger, & Tarule, 1986; Daly, 1997; Game & Metcalfe, 1996; Kleinman & Copp, 1993; Krieger, 1991, 1996; Lather, 1991; Richardson, 1997; Stacey, 1990). My argument is also informed by feminist philosophers of science, who are grounded in science as a rational enterprise but at the same time see science as an historical and political entity that silently champions patriarchal values of emotional remoteness and hierarchical control (Boler, 1999; Harding, 1987; Keller & Longino, 1996; McCaughey, 1993, 1997). Acknowledging and minimizing bias is a good thing, but I also want to call attention to the inadequate practice of relegating the discussion of bias in research reports to a brief "limitations" section. The conventions we adhere to in reporting research allow us to silence a full discussion of the biases (e.g., perspectives) that infuse the research process. We shortchange knowledge by only talking about bias in socially acceptable ways.

STRATEGIES FOR A CONSCIOUS AND INCLUSIVE FAMILY STUDIES

There has been a grave imbalance in our field created by reliance on outdated notions of positivist science that even the physicists who created it have abandoned (Capra, 1991; Hawking, 1996). Gone are the days when family scholars could hide behind the shield of objectivity as a defense for the legitimacy of our methods and results. In recent examinations of critical and postpositivist theorizing in family studies, Osmond (1987) and Thomas and Wilcox (1987) concluded that the goal of a value-free social science articulated by Christensen (1964) is impossible to achieve. Despite the recognition by family scholars about abandoning the search for the discovery of a single universal truth in favor of allowing for multiple truths, most of the research we publish in the mainstream journals is rooted in the 19th-century orthodoxy of positivist science (Agger, 1998; Osmond, 1987). All scientific claims are saturated with localized meaning; as many philosophers of science now argue, "no orthodoxy—or skepticism—can be totally stable, no theoretical closure complete, no incommensurability absolute" (Smith, B. H., 1993, p. 95). All theoretical formulations are contingent and loaded with the acknowledged and the implicit perspectives of the observer. Being explicit in what ideas, theories, and personal commitments we use to construct our arguments will help us know more clearly and honestly about where we actually disagree.

However, at a time when other disciplines are experimenting with the virtues and limitations of alternative forms of data representation, quantitative science continues to dominate the discourse and practice of family studies (Sprey, 1988;

Thompson & Walker, 1995). Even Donald Campbell, whose monograph (Campbell & Stanley, 1966) on quasi-experimental and experimental research design laid out the methodological ideal many social scientists still follow, raised challenging questions about accepted research practice (Eisner, 1997). Although qualitative, naturalistic methods are now the "favored approach for doing educational research among doctoral students" (Eisner, p. 5), family studies still privileges quantitative scientific research, with its illusion of objectivity. Noting a similar problem in psychology and sociology, Bochner et al. (1997) saw hope in the new generation of social scientists, who are being exposed to interpretive and postmodern forms of data representation.

Family studies was founded by those with an applied motivation to improve family life, but, in the interest of gaining scientific legitimacy, a more detached view of science supplanted earlier advocacy and activist aims (Christensen, 1964). Scholars such as C. Wright Mills (1959) and Jessie Bernard (1981) have made towering arguments about public and private connections, but despite the esteem in which these visionaries are held in family studies, most investigations are still characterized by what Mills criticized as studies of "one small milieu after another" (p. 224). This practice has been challenged by renewed calls for moral responsibility in our work. (See Boler, 1999, and Doherty, 1995, for recent examples in educational research and family therapy, respectively.) Social scientists are increasingly taking value stances, as in the publication of Glenn's (1997) examination of marriage and family textbooks in a mainstream family journal, *Family Relations*. This work was commissioned by a conservative think tank (Institute for American Values, 1997), and as the textbook authors' rejoinders to Glenn's critique indicated, it is not value-free or objective (Glenn, 1993).

If our goal is to study social structures and processes related to families, we need ways to include more realistic understandings of the diversity of people's lives in our investigations. These ways require us to explicitly name our assumptions, standpoints, and biases and to grapple with their inconsistencies, their ambiguities, and their effect on others. To be more accountable to families who have been ignored or marginalized, we must be willing to risk stating what we really believe and what really motivates our work.

Expanding Our Science to Include Ourselves: A Critical Reflection

It is easier to evaluate ideas when the assumptions are stated explicitly (Lavee & Dollahite, 1991). As I listened to a male colleague in another discipline lecture recently about children of divorce, I filtered the content through my own standpoint as a mother, divorced from my former husband, and now raising two sons with my female partner. I was aware of the partiality of the speaker's truth claims, and I was aware of the pain and embarrassment of hearing a man talk so casually and dismissively about the "problem" of mother-only families, a family type in which I live.

When the speaker concluded his speech by proposing marriage (presumably, he meant heterosexual marriage) as the best solution to the problems children face in single-parent or divorced families, the audience grumbled. Sensing their dismay, the speaker said, "When I was young, I couldn't imagine saying this, but now that my kids are older, I want them to be more responsible than I was." I had a hunch that despite his one-word solution (i.e., marriage) to the complexity of issues he had just described, he was probably in his second marriage. After his talk was over, I asked him about his marital history. He said, "Yes, I'm in my second marriage, but what does that matter?" Well, it matters greatly to me when men who have been divorced tell women they should not be single mothers, especially if those men are not engaged in the day-to-day realities of raising children. Part of how I trust the validity of another scholar's argument is in the way she or he substantiates research claims and conclusions. I found myself doubting this scholar's conclusions about his research because despite self-disclosing about his own children, he did not reflect critically on his assumptions about marriage, divorce, and children's lives. Instead, he allowed his personal experience to seep, unreflexively, into his research and conclusions. He packaged his solution to the alleged problem of mother-only families in a narrow, socially sanctioned admonition that fit the status quo of his academic peer group. From my feminist lens, I was critical of his lack of pragmatic strategies for social change. He also failed to answer questions that students in the audience raised about the dilemmas and ambiguities of intimate relationships.

The conversation following his speech would have been different if he had explicitly used an informed, reflexive approach. Instead of concluding with an offhand summary that marriage is the solution to today's family problems, more discussion of how gender shapes women's and men's lives and creates difficulties for sustaining long-term relationships (Risman & Johnson-Sumerford, 1998; Thompson & Walker, 1989), for example, would have informed the audience's desire to engage the relational complexities they raised. Instead of speaking of marriage as a unitary phenomenon, he could have emphasized the contradictions and trade-offs of marriage, particularly for women (Schwartz, 1994), the multiple ways in which long-term couples structure marriage (Cuber & Harroff, 1965), and the challenge of creating intimacy with a partner over many years (Schnarch, 1998), inviting the young adults in the room to engage in a realistic discussion of their fears, concerns, and desires to succeed as intimate partners. He could also have addressed oppressive conditions linked to marriage, such as the fact that marriage is legally denied to same-sex partners in all 50 states (Eskridge, 1996) or that intersections among race, class, and gender have reduced opportunities for marriage among Black Americans (Tucker & Taylor, 1989). I also doubted what my colleague was saying because he did not acknowledge how the ideologies embedded in his private experience were silently informing his research presentation.

Using critical reflection instead of lacking awareness about his privileged position, he could have deconstructed his vulnerabilities about his children and used these feelings to inform his solutions. As Miller (1993) and Walker (1996) have done in the *Journal of Marriage and the Family,* he could have made his ideology available for others' scrutiny. It is easier to judge the merit of what people say if they expose the ideological commitments they hold. An informed critical consciousness is a better way to debate the issues that divide our field. Furthermore, such dialogue gives opportunities for marginalized voices to be heard and to co-construct our research products with multiple audiences (Nespor & Barber, 1995).

Listening to the students in the room reminded me that those I have taught crave examples of how to deal with their personal lives in their research. Not only do they want guidance on choosing appropriate theories and methods, they also want open conversations about pursuing an engaged and passionate scholarly life. They want to observe and read successful examples of this invisible part of knowledge production, particularly because we are in a field in which we also live as private citizens (Miller, 1993). Qualitative researchers caution against sanitizing methods by cleansing the data of errors before publication (Stanley, 1990). Students, as well, benefit from explicit exposure to how scholars construct an argument, select among an array of methods, and fashion a vast amount of information into publications that are worth reading. Most important, students want knowledge that is meaningful; they want "an education that is healing to the uninformed, unknowing spirit" (hooks, 1994, p. 19). When a researcher informs her scholarship with critical reflection about the influence of her private experience and ideological commitments, vitality and validity infuse the work. This is the kind of research that people want to read, understand, critique, revise, and use (Mills, 1959).

Integrating Critical Reflection and Personal Narrative Into Family Studies

In most mainstream journal articles, we disembody ourselves as knowers, discussing theory, methodology, and findings as distinct entities. This fragmentation denies the interconnections of emotions and cognitions and denigrates personal experience as irrelevant and inferior. Academics state the theoretical or methodological strategies guiding our work, but few of us know how to name the private investments and family experiences that implicitly inform and direct the research process. Learning to be reflexive is a strategy for improving the quality of our scholarship by embodying ourselves in our work.

Reflection is a process of interrogating intellectual ideas with personal experience. Rooted in critical and feminist perspectives on oppression, it is a postpositivist strategy that values both subjectivity and science, reconnecting the emotional and the rational as tools for generating contextualized knowledge (Du Bois, 1983; Kleinman & Copp, 1993; Krieger, 1991). The impetus for my earlier research on lifelong single women, for example, came from a dissatisfaction with how "spinsters" were characterized in the empirical literature as deviant and bereft of family connections (Allen & Pickett, 1987). My emotional and subjective reactions to the empirical literature I was reading gave me the energy and confidence to challenge the received (i.e., published) wisdom and to chart a different course. I never let my image of my own "spinster aunt," a woman in her 70s for whom I was named, fade as I pursued this study (Allen, 1994). The stereotypes I read

about older women who never married did not fit the complexity and diversity that characterized her adulthood. Intense emotional responses can empower women and men who feel excluded, silenced, co-opted, and ill-used (Lorde, 1984). Letting in what had been screened out in the literature helped me to critique this distortion of knowledge by open dialogue with my aunt and with my colleagues.

Reflexive work involves emotional *and* empirical knowledge, as I recently experienced in a discussion group of Black and White women to which I belong. Nine women on my campus formed our group as a way to understand how race and gender are linked, particularly in light of recent racial tensions involving Black and White students. Our powerful exchanges about race, gender, class, and sexual orientation have transformed my view of myself and my relationships with others, reminded me of my marginalized status as a lesbian woman, and have helped me challenge my race and class privilege as a White, middle-class, educated professional. I tell this story to demonstrate how critical reflection in the company of peers from diverse social locations informs consciousness.

Initially, the White women came together to interrogate our racial privilege, knowing that Whites must initiate the process of deepening our color consciousness and the invisible privileges of majority status in the presence of each other (Fine et al., 1997; Frankenberg, 1993; Thompson, B., 1996). We wanted a safe space in which to raise questions and learn how to take responsibility for our own internalization of race prejudice, without adding to other women's painful history of racial oppression.

Eventually, we were joined by several Black women and began the difficult work of learning to listen to each other and ask previously silenced questions. As activists on our campus, we also had a tangible goal that focused our discussions: We were scheduled to interpret our conversations at a women's studies conference (Allen et al., 1996). The performance, "Color Conversations," revealed our stories, emotions, and actions toward one another. To prepare for our presentation, we spent months talking about things we had felt, observed, and even believed but had not been able to ask each other because of internalized racial barriers dividing us. We asked each other questions such as, "Why do so many Black women reject feminism?" "Why are so many White women submissive to men?" We discovered differences in our personal and professional ways of relating to each other. We learned that the Black women relied on each other, saying, "I've got your back." The Black women had been to each others' homes, but the White women's linkages with each other were strictly professional. Noting divisions and isolation from one another within and across racial lines, we explored our distrust during many conversations, eventually deciding to rotate meetings at each other's homes.

One evening, in my living room, our group exploded over the topic of the Black women's hurt when Black men choose White women as partners. In one exchange, feeling guilty and helpless, but equally angry at the stereotyping of White women as submissive, I resorted to a defensive posture of positioning myself as an "expert" on the subject of intimate relationships. Quoting a hodgepodge of demographic facts about interracial relationships, gendered violence, and the like, my heart was pounding as these thoughts were running through my head and out of my mouth. What happened next provided the crucible needed to break through polite disagreements with each other and deepen critical consciousness.

Fearful that I talked too much, that I would be accused of bringing up my own painful history of marginalization and thereby derailing the conversation about race with a corollary discussion of sexual orientation, gender, and other issues I confront daily, I retreated from my fear by hiding behind the role of "expert on the family." My colleagues did not indulge this bluff. With fingers pointing at me, they said I was making a grab for power by intellectualizing—switching into a heady space to cover my own feelings of marginalization.

I passed this insight through my filter of self-knowledge, wondering about my constructions of self in relation to their challenging observation. I defended myself at first, easily finding words to say that my ideas were "simply" an offering to help us build a political coalition (Reagon, 1983) at our university. Reflecting further, and cradled by the insistent yet collaborative confrontation and dialogic process (Collins, 1990), I realized the value of my colleagues' critique: I *was* more comfortable bringing an intellectual product, rather than my full self, to the group. As an academic, I have been required to privilege intellectual over experiential knowledge. Upon more reflection, I could admit to myself (often my strongest critic) that what I was really worried about was having my mothering judged by other women. I was un-

comfortable about the other women observing me in my home, making (potential) judgments about the way I raise my children, scrutinizing me as a mother, not as a scholar. I also uncovered some illogical and formerly unknown stereotypes about Black women that I had adopted sometime in the past. So, that was it: I was creating an uninformed bifurcation and acting on this false belief that, as a White woman, I was a permissive parent, and the Black women, by definition, were authoritarian.

In the company of colleagues with whom I was critically engaged, I made conscious a previously unconscious and totalizing prejudice that Black women are less submissive than White women and that they are better disciplinarians as parents. This epiphany helped me see how one of my beliefs was shaped by distortions in my knowledge of "Black motherhood." I saw how illogical my reduction was. I admitted to myself and my colleagues the arrogance, ignorance, and fear behind my unexamined beliefs that were infiltrating our interaction. Subjecting myself to others' scrutiny, and giving myself permission not to pull away and hide behind the so-called facts of mainstream family studies, gave me an opportunity to develop a critical analysis of how much more comfortable it is to stay in the world of ideas, disconnected from the whirl of feelings present in the company of others whose experience I was claiming to know something "scholarly" about. Naming and subsequently understanding my intellectualization was a way to work through complex feelings to something better, something informed by academic *and* experiential knowledge. I now know I can expect more from all of these women than I once thought and that they are willing to engage in deepening conversation with me because of new layers of trust that come from respectfully and reflectively challenging unnamed assumptions.

Despite its potential to deepen knowledge, however, reflection is often perceived as self-absorbed, collapsing into egotism, confession, or exploitation of one's private life (Lofland & Lofland, 1995). Relegated to the female world (Bernard, 1981), emotional expression and subjective knowledge are devalued. Ironically, now that marginalized groups are finding their voices, public intellectuals decry the loss of civility in public discourse (Stacey, 1996). I agree with Polanyi (1958) that tacit knowledge is a valid way to know. Like Boss' (1987) reliance on intuition in her research on boundary ambiguity, I have taught myself to trust reflective insights from my own life, using touchstones of personal experience to inform my scholarship. Reflexive practice is a process of self-critique, not self-absorption. Its effects multiply when reflection includes collaborative engagement with others who are working together to change the status quo (Boler, 1999; Collins, 1990).

In a research report, then, I would like to know what are the ways in which private life intersects with research aims and findings? How are we, as researchers, constrained by the place in which we live and work? What are the economic and political cultures that shape what we study, how we study it, and how we respond to others? How do we balance respecting our individual heritage and coming together for the causes and problems different groups share? I suggest we experiment with reflexive writing and research reporting. No doubt we will falter, saying too much or too little, but we will be more honest than to pretend that some distanced observer conducted our work. The way we work with ourselves, each other, and the people we study must be reshaped "so that groups previously marginalized and represented by others can become representers of their own experience. This implies a simultaneous redefinition of both authorship and of audience" (Nespor & Barber, 1995, p. 51).

Becoming More Inclusive of Diversity in Family Studies

The original interests on which family studies was based (e.g., sociology, social work, education, and marriage counseling; Christensen, 1964) and the emerging trends that contribute to its vitality (e.g., contextualism, feminism, and multiculturalism; Doherty et al., 1993) share a concern with understanding social problems, easing family tensions, and contributing to social change. Yet, contemporary family research is often distanced from these activist, participatory aims. We still rely on a rationalist discourse that privileges a White male researcher and his family. By discouraging subjectivity and inclusivity, we deny the reality of family complexity and diversity and thereby stigmatize difference.

Several decades ago, in writing about how stigma emerges from the general values of a society, Erving Goffman (1963) described the ideal of perfection against which every man [sic] is measured and against which every man, to some degree, fails. His analysis revealed the linkage of domination and subordination that undergirds the value

system of U.S. society and that is consciously and unconsciously promoted in our broader social institutions. People conforming to these standards have more privilege than those who do not:

> there is only one complete unblushing male in America: a young, married, white, urban, northern, heterosexual Protestant father of college education, fully employed, of good complexion, weight, and height, and a recent record in sports. Every American male tends to look out upon the world from this perspective, this constituting one sense in which one can speak of a common value system in America. Any male who fails to qualify in any one of these ways is likely to view himself—during moments at least—as unworthy, incomplete, and inferior (p. 128).

This perfect man, evidently, heads up the perfect family, at least in many family studies texts. In presuming the primacy of the heterosexual, two-parent, middle-class, White nuclear family, we deny our knowledge of plurality in family life (Scanzoni, 1999). I think this discourse is really about whether men are in charge of women and families. Like men who deviate from the ideal of manhood that Goffman so eloquently sketched, the ideal of family often promoted today privileges a group of people in which fathers are in charge. The entrenched ideology of the traditional family inhibits efforts to expand legitimate modes of discourse about families (Stacey, 1996). Even more insidious, the ideology of the White, well-off, heterosexual nuclear family as superior to all other families inhibits the visioning of alternatives to disempowered circumstances: Some women do not leave abusive relationships because they are financially dependent on their partners or may fear for their safety.

In her critique of social science, hooks (1994) analyzed why those who benefit from the status quo are reluctant to hear the truth about others' lives. She explains that people with greater amounts of privilege are ashamed when exposed to another's difference or pain. The disadvantages others face remind people with greater privilege of their own inadequacy, as individuals, to fix the conditions that make life difficult for others. But, without conscious reflection and collective action about subjective experiences of diversity (Boler, 1999), scholars can deceive themselves about the validity of experience that departs from the status quo (Reason, 1994). There are also threats to our livelihood and reputation when deviating from accepted practice by including the researcher's standpoint, as Sussman (1986) described in his editorial about publishing articles that were rejected by mainstream marriage and family journals. Challenging the dominating systems that contaminate thinking, feeling, and acting can seem hopeless, futile, and certainly not profitable when one main discourse prevails.

On the other hand, using personal experiences as a bridge to connect us to other human beings opens us to new theoretical and methodological possibilities. As a mother and a lesbian, for example, I am forced to attend to the potential harm my children could be subjected to because of my status in a society hostile to families headed by two women. As a parent, I consciously develop webs of influence with others, to help them see my children through my own caring eyes (Ruddick, 1989). Confronting the potential hurdles my children face allows me to think empathically about other children, other mothers and fathers, and other families in disadvantaged or diverse circumstances. This connection increases my ability to see others as fully human and to disrupt the dehumanizing impulse to devalue those on the margins. As Jaffe and Miller (1994) described, it is a way of linking the microlevel of social interaction, which integrates one's emotional experiences and social locations, with the macrolevel of social, economic, and political structures. Being marginalized means that one is "in and of our society but in important ways also not 'of' it" (Du Bois, 1983, p. 111). The insider-outsider experience creates a double consciousness, rendering an awareness of stigma and a knowledge about the behavior of those who have more power than those who occupy an oppressed status (Collins, 1986; Merton, 1972). Cultivating a critical consciousness is important, especially for those of us who benefit, even inadvertently, from the status quo.

As a starting point, family scholars must recognize the relative forces of privilege and oppression operating in family life. Second, we must insist on complex, inclusive perspectives that examine the intersections of race, class, and gender without reducing them to a stereotype or a variable. Third, we must be more modest in our truth claims (Miller, 1993), remembering that all knowledge is partial and subject to distortion. Marks' (1996) metaphor of companion planting, "how to have a science of families that is truly welcoming to all its potential constituents," reveals a plan for inclusivity: "This does not mean merely leaving room for variety; it means working out the garden plan so that very different com-

ponents can fully thrive *because* of their proximity to each other" (p. 570). Finally, a critical consciousness requires collective social action to create knowledge that moves people, in practical and passionate ways, to make necessary changes in the way they treat their own and others' lives as respectable subjects for scientific understanding.

CONCLUSION

In this paper, I ask colleagues to grapple with, integrate, and communicate in public about our private investments in the work we do. Autobiography, subjectivity, and reflexivity have a place in the research process. They offer partial insights into a scholar's interest in a subject. They provide the energy to search for fuller understandings than what existing theories and research methods allow. The practice of critical reflection allows us to make informed assessments of our own and others' arguments. We can acknowledge and deal with our subjectivity without obscuring or overwhelming the goals of rigorous empiricism and theory construction or critical assessment.

The larger strategy is to integrate epistemology, methodology, and ontology by making the intersections across gender, race, class, sexual orientation, and age—our own and others'—evident in our investigations. Studying families reflexively and critically opens us to ideas, feelings, and actions that challenge and change us. Rather than shutting down or turning off to differences beyond our private experience, paying attention to diversity in family structures and processes is a way to deepen our perceptions about families and improve the validity of our understanding. A family studies informed by critical consciousness is more accountable to the people we study, the students we teach, and the readers we engage.

How knowledge gets constructed is not self-evident. We must openly engage the underlying commitments that inform our work. In this essay, I join other scholars in saying that our academic investigations come from our private investments. Unless we kindly take each other on, we lose the ability to affect each others' work in ways that make the best use of our differences. If we ignore the contested ground on which we work, we accumulate facts but fail to truly influence how others study and understand families, including those families of which we are a part. When quantitative precision is valued over imagination and depth, we lose the safety to be visionary. The more we carry on the process of critical reflection and research practice in public—open to respectful peer scrutiny and with a commitment to the generative role of teaching students how to create scholarship that matters—the more invigorated and vital family studies will be.

Our assumptions, values, feelings, and histories shape the scholarship we propose, the findings we generate, and the conclusions we draw. Our insights about family processes and structures are affected by our membership in particular families, by the lives of those we study, and by what we care about knowing and explaining. I want to see changes in the sexist, racist, classist, heterosexist, and ageist biases of our field. I am also eager for discussion and challenge because I want to improve the arguments I make, and I want to more fully understand the arguments of others with whom I think I disagree. We are embedded in the power dynamics that shape our scholarship. Coming to our senses through informed critical reflection on where we have been and where we want to go will help us create a family studies capable of making intentional differences in our complex world.

NOTE

Many colleagues helped me shape the ideas presented in this paper. I am grateful to Rosemary Blieszner, Megan Boler, David Demo, Karen Roberto, Kusum Singh, Tamara Stone, Jay Teachman, Alexis Walker, and Lynn White for their generous support and constructive comments, and to Elizabeth Bounds, Mark Fine, Ann Kilkelly, and Martha McCaughey for their multiple readings of this paper. I thank Alan Acock, Joan Aldous, and Barbara Settles, organizer, discussant, and moderator, respectively, for the 1996 Special Session of the Theory Construction and Research Methods Workshop, held at the Annual Meeting of the National Council on Family Relations, Kansas City, Missouri, where these ideas were first presented. Finally, I am indebted to Pauline Boss and Kerry Daly for their careful insights and attention.

REFERENCES

Agger, B. (1998). *Critical social theories.* Boulder, CO: Westview.

Allen, K. R. (1994). Feminist reflections on lifelong single women. In D. L. Sollie & L. A. Leslie (Eds.), *Gender, families, and close relationships: Feminist research journeys* (pp. 97–119). Thousand Oaks, CA: Sage.

Allen, K. R., Bounds, E., Carlisle, B., Cain, C., Pendergrass, B., Plaut, L., Scott, D., Watford, B., & Williams-Green, J. (1996, September). *Color conversations.* Plenary session, Racialization, Gender, and the Academy Conference, Virginia Women's Studies Association and Fourth Annual Feminist Research and Pedagogy Conference, Roanoke, VA.

Allen, K. R., & Demo, D. H. (1995). The families of lesbians and gay men: A new frontier in family research. *Journal of Marriage and the Family, 57,* 111–127.

Allen, K. R., & Pickett, R. S. (1987). Forgotten streams in the family life course: Utilization of qualitative retrospective interviews in the analysis of lifelong single women's family careers. *Journal of Marriage and the Family, 49,* 517–526.

Allen, K. R., & Walker, A. J. (2000). Qualitative research. In C. Hendrick & S. S. Hendrick (Eds.), *Close relationships: A sourcebook.* Thousand Oaks, CA: Sage.

Baca Zinn, M., & Dill, B. T. (1996). Theorizing difference from multiracial feminism. *Feminist Studies, 22,* 321–332.

Banks, I. (2000). *Hair matters: Beauty, power, and black women's consciousness.* New York: New York University Press.

Bateson, M. C. (1984). *With a daughter's eye: A memoir of Margaret Mead and Gregory Bateson.* New York: HarperCollins.

Belenky, M. F., Clinchy, B. M., Goldberger, N. R., & Tarule, J. M. (1986). *Women's ways of knowing: The development of self, voice, and mind.* New York: Basic.

Berman, M. (1989). *Coming to our senses: Body and spirit in the hidden history of the West.* New York: Simon & Schuster.

Bernard, J. (1981). *The female world.* New York: Free Press.

Bochner, A. P., Ellis, C., & Tillmann-Healy, L. M. (1997). Relationships as stories. In S. Duck (Ed.), *Handbook of personal relationships* (pp. 307–324). New York: John Wiley.

Boler, M. (1999). *Feeling power: Emotions and education.* New York: Routledge.

Boss, P. G. (1987). The role of intuition in family research: Three issues of ethics. *Contemporary Family Therapy, 9,* 146–159.

Boss, P. G. (1999). *Ambiguous loss: Learning to live with unresolved grief.* Cambridge, MA: Harvard University Press.

Bronfenbrenner, U., & Crouter, A. C. (1983). The evolution of environmental models in developmental research. In P. H. Mussen (Ed.), *Handbook of child psychology* (4th ed., pp. 357–414). New York: Wiley.

Campbell, D. T., & Stanley, J. C. (1966). *Experimental and quasi-experimental designs for research.* Chicago: Rand McNally.

Capra, F. (1991). *The tao of physics* (3rd ed.) Boston: Shambhala.

Cheal, D. (1991). *Family and the state of theory.* Toronto, Canada: University of Toronto Press.

Christensen, H. T. (1964). Development of the family field of study. In H. T. Christensen (Ed.), *Handbook of marriage and the family* (p. 3–32). Chicago: Rand McNally.

Collins, P. H. (1986). Learning from the outsider within: The sociological significance of black feminist thought. *Social Problems, 33(6),* 14–32.

Collins, P. H. (1990). *Black feminist thought: Knowledge, consciousness and the politics of empowerment.* Boston: Unwin Hyman.

Coontz, S. (1992). *The way we never were: American families and the nostalgia trap.* New York: Basic.

Cuber, J. F., & Harroff, P. B. (1965). *The significant Americans.* New York: Appleton-Century.

Daly, K. (1997). Re-placing theory in ethnography: A postmodern view. *Qualitative Inquiry, 3,* 343–365.

D'Emilio, J., & Freedman, E. B. (1997). *Intimate matters: A history of sexuality in America* (2nd ed.). Chicago: University of Chicago Press.

Demos, V. (1990). Black family studies in *Journal of Marriage and the Family* and the issue of distortion: A trend analysis. *Journal of Marriage and the Family, 52,* 603–612.

Denzin, N. K., & Lincoln, Y. S. (Eds.). (1994). *Handbook of qualitative research.* Thousand Oaks, CA: Sage.

Dill, B. T. (1983). Race, class, and gender: Prospects for an all-inclusive sisterhood. *Feminist Studies, 9,* 131–150.

Dilworth-Anderson, P., Burton, L. M., & Johnson, L. B. (1993). Reframing theories for understanding race, ethnicity, and families. In P. G. Boss, W. J. Doherty, R. LaRossa, W. R. Schumm, & S. K. Steinmetz (Eds.), *Sourcebook of family theories and methods* (pp. 627–646). New York: Plenum.

Doherty, W. J. (1995). *Soul searching: Why psychotherapists must promote moral responsibility.* New York: Basic.

Doherty, W. J., Boss, P. G., LaRossa, R., Schumm, W. R., & Steinmetz, S. K. (1993). Family theories and methods: A contextual approach. In P. G. Boss, W. J. Doherty, R. LaRossa, W. R. Schumm, & S. K. Steinmetz (Eds.), *Sourcebook of family theories and methods* (pp. 3–30). New York: Plenum.

Du Bois, B. (1983). Passionate scholarship: Notes on values, knowing and method in feminist social science. In G. Bowles & R. D. Klein (Eds.), *Theories of women's studies* (pp. 105–116). London: Routledge.

Eisner, E. W. (1997). The promise and perils of alternative forms of data representation. *Educational Researcher, 26(6),* 4–10.

Emerson, R. M., Fretz, R. I., & Shaw, L. L. (1995). *Writing ethnographic fieldnotes.* Chicago: University of Chicago Press.

Eskridge, W. N., Jr. (1996). *The case for same sex marriage.* New York: Free Press.

Fine, M. (1994). Working the hyphens: Reinventing self and other in qualitative research. In N. K. Denzin & Y. S. Lincoln (Eds.), *Handbook of qualitative research* (pp. 70–82). Thousand Oaks, CA: Sage.

Fine, M., Weis, L., Powell, L. C., & Wong, L. M. (Eds.). (1997). *Off white: Readings on race, power, and society.* New York: Routledge.

Frankenberg, R. (1993). *White women, race matters: The social construction of whiteness.* Minneapolis, MN: University of Minnesota Press.

Freire, P. (1970). *Pedagogy of the oppressed.* New York: Herder & Herder.

Fuss, D. (Ed.). (1991). *Inside/out: Lesbian theories, gay theories.* New York: Routledge.

Game, A., & Metcalfe, A. (1996). *Passionate sociology.* London: Sage.

Gergen, K. J., & Gergen, M. M. (1988). Narrative and the self as relationship. In L. Berkowitz (Ed.), *Advances in experimental social psychology* (pp. 17–56). San Diego, CA: Academic.

Gilgun, J. F. (1995). We shared something special: The moral discourse of incest perpetrators. *Journal of Marriage and the Family, 75,* 265–281.

Glenn, N. D. (1993). A plea for objective assessment of the notion of family decline. *Journal of Marriage and the Family, 55,* 542–544.

Glenn, N. D. (1997). A critique of twenty family and marriage and the family textbooks. *Family Relations, 46,* 197–208.

Goffman, E. (1963). *Stigma: Notes on the management of spoiled identity.* New York: Simon & Schuster.

Greene, M. (1988). *The dialectic of freedom.* New York: Teachers College Press.

Harding, S. (1987). Introduction: Is there a feminist method? In S. Harding (Ed.), *Feminism & methodology* (pp. 1–14). Bloomington, IN: Indiana University Press.

Hawking, S. (1996). *A brief history of time* (2nd ed.). New York: Bantam.

hooks, b. (1989). *Talking back: Thinking feminist, thinking black.* Boston: South End Press.

hooks, b. (1994). *Teaching to transgress: Education as the practice of freedom.* New York: Routledge.

Hull, G. T., Scott, P. B., & Smith, B. (Eds.). (1982). *All the women are white, all the blacks are men, but some of us are brave: Black women's studies.* Old Westbury, NY: Feminist Press.

Institute for American Values. (1997). *Closed hearts, closed minds: The textbook story of marriage.* New York: Author.

Jaffe, D. J., & Miller, E. M. (1994). Problematizing meaning. In J. F. Gubrium & A. Sankar (Eds.), *Qualitative methods in aging research* (pp. 51–64). Thousand Oaks, CA: Sage.

Johnson, L. B. (1988). Perspectives on Black family empirical research: 1965–1978. In H. P. McAdoo (Ed.), *Black families* (2nd ed., pp. 91–106). Newbury Park, CA: Sage.

Keller, E. F., & Longino, H. E. (Eds.). (1996). *Feminism & science.* Oxford, U.K.: Oxford University Press.

Klein, D. M., & Jurich, J. A. (1993). Metatheory and family studies. In P. G. Boss, W. J. Doherty, R. LaRossa, W. R. Schumm, & S. K. Steinmetz (Eds.), *Sourcebook of family theories and methods* (pp. 31–67). New York: Plenum.

Kleinman, S., & Copp, M. A. (1993). *Emotions and fieldwork.* Newbury Park, CA: Sage.

Krieger, S. (1991). *Social science and the self: Personal essays on an art form.* New Brunswick, NJ: Rutgers University Press.

Krieger, S. (1996). *The family silver: Essays on relationships among women.* Berkeley, CA: University of California Press.

LaRossa, R., & Wolf, J. H. (1985). On qualitative family research. *Journal of Marriage and the Family, 47,* 531–541.

Lather, P. (1991). *Getting smart: Feminist research and pedagogy with/in the postmodern.* New York: Routledge.

Lavee, Y., & Dollahite, D. C. (1991). The linkage between theory and research in family science. *Journal of Marriage and the Family, 53,* 361–373.

Lewin, E., & Leap, W. L. (Eds.). (1996). *Out in the field: Reflections of lesbian and gay anthropologists.* Urbana, IL: University of Illinois Press.

Lincoln, Y. S. (1997). Self, subject, audience, text: Living at the edge, writing in the margins. In W. G. Tierney & Y. S. Lincoln (Eds.), *Representation and the text: Reframing the narrative voice* (pp. 37–55). Albany, NY: State University of New York Press.

Lofland, J., & Lofland, L. H. (1995). *Analyzing social settings* (3rd ed.). Belmont, CA: Wadsworth.

Lorde, A. (1984). *Sister outsider*. Freedom, CA: Crossing Press.

Marks, S. R. (1996). The problem and politics of wholeness in family studies. *Journal of Marriage and the Family, 58,* 565–571.

Marks, S. R., & Leslie, L. A. (2000). Family diversity and intersecting categories: Toward a richer approach to multiple roles. In D. H. Demo, K. R. Allen, & M. A. Fine (Eds.), *Handbook of family diversity.* (pp. 402–423). New York: Oxford University Press.

McCaughey, M. (1993). Redirecting feminist critiques of science. *Hypatia, 8,* 72–84.

McCaughey, M. (1997). *Real knockouts: The physical feminism of women's self-defense.* New York: New York University Press.

McIntosh, P. (1993). White privilege and male privilege: A personal account of coming to see correspondences through work in Women's Studies. In A. Minas (Ed.), *Gender basics* (pp. 30–38). Belmont, CA: Wadsworth.

McLaren, P. (1997). *Revolutionary multiculturalism: Pedagogies of dissent for the new millennium.* Boulder, CO: Westview.

Merton, R. K. (1972). Insiders and outsiders: A chapter in the sociology of knowledge. *American Journal of Sociology, 78,* 9–47.

Miller, B. C. (1993). Families, science, and values: Alternative views of parenting effects and adolescent pregnancy. *Journal of Marriage and the Family, 55,* 7–21.

Mills, C. W. (1959). *The sociological imagination.* London: Oxford University Press.

Morrison, T. (Ed.). (1992). *Race-ing justice, en-gendering power.* New York: Pantheon.

Nespor, J., & Barber, L. (1995). Audience and the politics of narrative. In J. A. Hatch & R. Wisniewski (Eds.), *Life history and narrative* (pp. 49–62). London: Falmer.

Osmond, M. W. (1987). Radical-critical theories. In M. B. Sussman & S. K. Steinmetz (Eds.), *Handbook of marriage and the family* (pp. 103–124). New York: Plenum.

Osmond, M. W., & Thorne, B. (1993). Feminist theories: The social construction of gender in families and society. In P. G. Boss, W. J. Doherty, R. LaRossa, W. R. Schumm, & S. K. Steinmetz (Eds.), *Sourcebook of family theories and methods* (pp. 591–623). New York: Plenum.

Parker, R. G., & Gagnon, J. H. (Eds.). (1995). *Conceiving sexuality: Approaches to sex research in a postmodern world.* New York: Routledge.

Polanyi, M. (1958). *Personal knowledge: Towards a post-critical philosophy.* Chicago: University of Chicago Press.

Reagon, B. J. (1983). Coalition politics: Turning the century. In B. Smith (Ed.), *Home girls: A black feminist anthology* (pp. 356–368). New York: Kitchen Table Press.

Reason, P. (1994). Three approaches to participative inquiry. In N. K. Denzin & Y. S. Lincoln (Eds.), *Hand-*

book of qualitative research (pp. 324–339). Thousand Oaks, CA: Sage.

Richardson, L. (1997). *Fields of play: Constructing an academic life.* New Brunswick, NJ: Rutgers University Press.

Risman, B. J., & Johnson-Sumerford, D. (1998). Doing it fairly: A study of postgender marriages. *Journal of Marriage and the Family, 60,* 23–40.

Ruddick, S. (1989). *Maternal thinking: Toward a politics of peace.* Boston: Beacon.

Scanzoni, J. (1999). *Designing families: The search for self and community in the information age.* Thousand Oaks, CA: Pine Forge Press.

Scanzoni, J., Polonko, K., Teachman, J., & Thompson, L. (1989). *The sexual bond: Rethinking families and close relationships.* Newbury Park, CA: Sage.

Schnarch, D. M. (1998). *Passionate marriage.* New York: Henry Holt.

Schwartz, P. (1994). *Peer marriage.* New York: Free Press.

Smith, B. H. (1993). Unloading the self-refutation charge. *Common Knowledge, 2,* 81–95.

Smith, D. E. (1987). *The everyday world as problematic: A feminist sociology.* Boston: Northeastern University Press.

Smith, D. E. (1993). The standard North American family: SNAF as an ideological code. *Journal of Family Issues, 14,* 50–65.

Sollie, D. L., & Leslie, L. A. (Eds.). (1994). *Gender, families, and close relationships: Feminist research journeys.* Thousand Oaks, CA: Sage.

Sprey, J. (1988). Current theorizing on the family: An appraisal. *Journal of Marriage and the Family, 50,* 875–890.

Sprey, J. (1995). Explanatory practice in family studies. *Journal of Marriage and the Family, 57,* 867–878.

Stacey, J. (1990). *Brave new families: Stories of domestic upheaval in late twentieth century America.* New York: Basic.

Stacey, J. (1996). *In the name of the family: Rethinking family values in the postmodern age.* Boston: Beacon Press.

Stanley, L. (1990). Feminist praxis and the academic mode of production: An editorial introduction. In L. Stanley (Ed.), *Feminist praxis: Research, theory and epistemology in feminist sociology* (pp. 3–19). London: Routledge.

Sussman, M. B. (1986). The Charybdis of publishing in academia. *Marriage and Family Review, 10,* 1–9.

Thomas, D. L., & Wilcox, J. E. (1987). The rise of family theory: A historical and critical analysis. In M. B. Sussman & S. K. Steinmetz (Eds.), *Handbook of marriage and the family* (pp. 81–102). New York: Plenum.

Thompson, B. (1996). Time traveling and border crossing: Reflections on white identity. In B. Thompson & S. Tyagi (Eds.), *Names we call home* (pp. 93–109). New York: Routledge.

Thompson, B., & Tyagi, S. (Eds.). (1996). *Names we call home: Autobiography on racial identity.* New York: Routledge.

Thompson, L. (1992). Feminist methodology for family studies. *Journal of Marriage and the Family, 54,* 3–18.

Thompson, L., & Walker, A. J. (1989). Gender in families: Women and men in marriage, work, and parenthood. *Journal of Marriage and the Family, 51,* 845–871.

Thompson, L., & Walker, A. J. (1995). The place of feminism in family studies. *Journal of Marriage and the Family, 57,* 847–865.

Thorne, B. (1982). Feminist rethinking of the family. In B. Thorne & M. Yalom (Eds.), *Rethinking the family: Some feminist questions* (pp. 1–24). New York: Longman.

Tucker, M. B., & Taylor, R. J. (1989). Demographic correlates of relationship status among Black Americans. *Journal of Marriage and the Family, 51,* 655–665.

Walker, A. J. (1996). Couples watching television: Gender, power, and the remote control. *Journal of Marriage and the Family, 58,* 813–823.

Weston, K. (1991). *Families we choose: Lesbians, gays, kinship.* New York: Columbia University Press.

White, M., & Epston, D. (1990). *Narrative means to therapeutic ends.* New York: Norton.

ALEXIS J. WALKER   *Oregon State University*

Refracted Knowledge: Viewing Families Through the Prism of Social Science

I reinforce a vision for family science in which we routinely step back from our research to consider the fit of the empirical world with the reality of everyday life. This vision suggests that we pursue the methodological advances of the past decade but remain mindful of the limitations of the scientific approach. Such mindfulness will help us attend to both similarity and variability in families and in family-life experience. A responsible social science also requires that we attend to rhetoric or how we communicate. I reflect on the practice of humility as a way to achieve these goals.

Each year, I teach a course designed to provide an overview of the state of the field of family science. Over the course of 10 weeks, through readings, discussion, and assignments, the graduate students and I "review significant advances. . . and significant areas of underdevelopment and . . . consider ways to reframe the future fields of inquiry" (Milardo, 2000). It is both an exhilarating and an exasperating experience. It is exhilarating because, in preparation, I have the pleasure of reading provocative and inspiring research from across the landscape of the field and from many disciplinary perspectives, demonstrating that we understand families better every day. It is exhilarating as well because bringing this work to

Human Development and Family Sciences, 322 Milam Hall, Oregon State University, Corvallis OR 97330–5102 (walkera@orst.edu).

Key Words: audience, conceptualization, knowledge, methods, science, scientific writing.

students sometimes sparks in them a flame of desire that will grow into a powerful source of light and energy in the pursuit of knowledge.

It is exasperating—in a minor way—because it is so terribly difficult to select from many impressive articles the handful that can be read, studied, and interrogated over an academic quarter. It is exasperating, too, because there are some areas about which we know very little, but I will have more to say about that later. The major way in which it is exasperating is in the cursory attention we give to the limitations of our knowledge and of our scientific practice.

In some ways, assessing the discipline, as we do every 10 years in the pages of this journal, is the task we face when training graduate students who hope to become the next generation of family scholars. We must educate them about what is known and demonstrate what is noteworthy in the literature, in subject, in method, in analysis, and in implications. Some work in our discipline is extraordinary in all of these areas. More commonly, however, the practice of social science reflects smaller achievements and a good bit of incremental change in our understanding of families.

In addition to the highlights and achievements, we also must educate students about the limitations of our knowledge. On the one hand, we have everyday life as it is lived in families at the beginning of the 21st century. On the other hand, we have the scientific method that can only approximate family life, dealing as it does in theory, representation, operationalization, probability, estimation, and interpretation. Stellar achievements, significant advancements, underdeveloped domains, and missing areas of study are all inevitable when we overlay the practice of social science against the reality of family life.

In assessing the state of the field for this essay, I take the same path I follow in teaching graduate students. I begin by celebrating exemplars, work that illustrates just how far we have come by employing scientific ways of knowing. I follow with cautionary notes about the limitations of our knowledge and ideas about the way in which our work can be strengthened by paying more attention to those limitations. I argue for greater disclosure about these limitations as a way of producing better family scholarship, practice, and policy. I conclude with a statement about how humility in the practice of science can move us toward these goals.

SIGNIFICANT ADVANCES: HOW FAR WE HAVE COME

In assessing the achievements of the field over the past decade, I celebrate four journal articles. Certainly there were more than four articles worth noting in the past 10 years, as well as significant chapters and books. Most of these noteworthy publications will be highlighted in the fourth issue of this volume (November, 2000) in which authors describe the major advances in particular domains within the study of families. Because my purpose is a more global one, I chose instead to identify a handful of articles that have implications for the discipline as a whole, rather than within given areas of study.

These articles are significant in that they call attention to our ways of thinking and of knowing. They provide a vantage point from which we can pay more attention to what we do. Because they have implications for how we think, they carry with them the potential to help us become better scholars, better teachers, and better communicators. In chronological order, I briefly describe each, identifying the research question, the method, the results, and then the implications for the field.

FAMILY RESPONSES TO EARLY MOTHERHOOD IN AN URBAN, AFRICAN AMERICAN COMMUNITY

Early in the decade, in *Family Relations,* Nancy Apfel and Victoria Seitz (1991) documented varying ways in which African American adolescent mothers approach parenthood in the context of their relationships with their own mothers. Their research question: What role do African American grandmothers play in their daughters' early transition to motherhood? They recruited more than three quarters of the population of first-time, African American mothers, aged 18 or younger, in New Haven, Connecticut, and their mothers or othermothers (Hill Collins, 1991). They interviewed each of these 119 women and the 103 of their mothers or othermothers, asking them typical questions about household composition, child-care tasks, and parenting practices. They also did something different: They asked about the details of daily routines, about what happened in emergencies, about who helped the young mother, and how she was helped. Most important, they asked both mothers and grandmothers to describe all of the information they could provide about a typical day.

From these detailed descriptions of everyday life, they constructed four models of family response to the early motherhood of an adolescent daughter in African American families. For each model, they identified both potential benefits and potential risks to the grandchild, the mother, the grandmother, and their cross-generation relationships. They articulated how each model, each way of responding, actually reflected two dimensions: the extent to which the adolescent mother was involved in direct child care and underlying belief systems about the nature of parenthood and whether parenting is learned.

The implications of Apfel and Seitz's (1991) work are profound. Their findings alerted us to the folly of unquestioned assumptions, such as (a) the presence of other adults in the household guarantees help and support for a young mother, and (b) adolescent mothers who live alone do not have access to help from family members. They confirmed, yet again, the tremendous variability in the ways individuals and family members respond to a seemingly stressful situation. One of the most striking aspects of their work is that they did not problematize any of the models they identified. Instead, they illustrated the ways in which each *might* be problematic and each *might* be successful. Through this thoughtful and careful exercise, they demonstrated how the nature of outcomes depends a great deal on where and on whom one focuses one's attention. They explained, for example, how a positive outcome for one family member may not necessarily be a positive outcome for another. They were clear throughout about the limitations of their research in terms of the nature of their sample, their inability to attend to changes over time, and so on. They were appropriately cautious in drawing implications from what they had learned.

Why should this article matter to the pursuit of family science? Apfel and Seitz's (1991) work is exemplary in several ways. Notably, they focused on a poorly understood area of concern in an understudied and underserved population. They presumed nothing about the family relationships and behavior of the women in their sample. They began this new area of investigation in the most appropriate way: with a blank slate. They asked the women to tell them everything that happens in a typical day in their lives. They did not ask only about a particular time of day, about interaction only with a particular person, or about only one domain of activity. They did not foreclose on any possibility.

Theirs is a textbook approach to investigation of an area about which little is known. As students, we learned about the need to begin new domains of research with methods that are open to the widest range of possibilities. Our research, however, only rarely follows this model of beginning at the beginning. Instead, we begin in the middle, having already decided where to focus, foreclosing other possibilities. No wonder that some of what we discover adds little to our understanding and has minimal potential to influence practice and policy. Empirical inquiry that begins before an area is adequately conceptualized cannot represent well the domain of study.

MARRIAGE AND SOCIAL ATTACHMENT

Midway through the decade, Catherine Ross (1995) "reconceptualized marital status" (p. 27) in the pages of the *Journal of Marriage and the Family*. Ross's research focus was the association of marital status and well-being. Why is it, she puzzled, that married people have higher well-being than unmarried people do? Is it marriage per se, or is it something correlated with marriage that explains this relation? Ross deconstructed marital status into the dimensions presumed to be concomitant with it: social integration, social support, economic well-being, and emotional support. Further, she arrayed intimate connections into what she called a "continuum of social attachment," ranging from low to high: no partner, a noncoresidential partner, a live-in partner, and a coresident married partner.

Ross pursued her question by randomly drawing a national probability sample of persons aged 18 or older in the United States. She performed a series of multiple regression analyses to explain psychological well-being, controlling for gender, race, and age, all of which are known to be associated with the dependent variable. She began by examining the influence of the continuum of attachment. With each subsequent model, she added as a predictor one of the dimensions presumed to covary with marital status.

Her discovery: Much of what we attribute to being married actually results from social attachment, social support, and economic well-being. When all variables were included in the model, marital status (except for widowhood) had no influence on well-being. Individuals who did not have a partner indeed were at a disadvantage, but those who had a nonmarital partner and who had the benefits that come with partnership were as well off as those who were married. In other words, social attachment is a better predictor of psychological well-being than is marital status.

Why have other studies shown that unmarried people, on average, are more distressed than married people? Because unmarried people are more likely than are married people to have low social attachment and low emotional support, not because they are unmarried. They are not certain to have lower levels of these key dimensions, just more likely. Why are divorced women, on average, more distressed than married women? Because they are more likely than married women to face economic hardship. Why are divorced men, on average, more distressed then married men? Because they are more likely than married men to have low social support. Being married, however, does not guarantee social attachment, emotional support, or financial support.

Ross (1995) compared the well-being of individuals in four groups: happy partnerships, moderately happy partnerships, unhappy partnerships, and without partners. Her findings? Persons in happy relationships, regardless of marital status, had the highest well-being of all. Individuals in unhappy partnerships had the lowest well-being, significantly lower than that of the other three groups. Being in an unhappy relationship is worse for your well-being than not having a partner at all.

Why should this article matter to the pursuit of family science? Ross (1995) provided compelling evidence that treating marriage as a unidimensional construct is problematic. Marriage is, at best, an imperfect proxy for other dimensions of social attachment. Her findings confirmed what many individuals know from their own experience: Marriage does not always enhance one's well-being, and there are other partnerships that provide the benefits presumed to be associated only with marriage. It is not surprising, then, that the institution of marriage became somewhat less enticing to people over the last decades of the 20th century. At a minimum, we need to be cautious in our presumptions about marriage and about what marriage means. We should be cautious as well in the way we think about the relationships of people who are not married. How many other dimensions in our field of study are actually indicators of something else? As Ross suggested, we need to measure these component dimensions directly.

Ross's (1995) study also calls into question the meaning of dichotomous demographic variables. Some unmarried individuals are similar to married individuals in social attachment, social support, and financial support. Some married individuals are not socially attached. Except from a legal position, married and unmarried are not mutually exclusive categories. Nor, except legally, is each category internally consistent.

I do not mean to suggest that we should never employ statistical controls in our analyses. Instead, I draw attention to what such controls mean and the way we think about them. A statistical control is a tool, and, in the case of marital status, a crude and imprecise one. When we use it, we need to be cautious of how the married-unmarried dichotomy artificially distinguishes between categories that, in some ways, have more within-group than between-group diversity. Conceptually, the married-unmarried dichotomy downplays within-group differences and treats as real some differences between the two groups that are only apparent. As I note later in this essay, the limitations of such controls should be evident up front in reports of our research and should extend through our conclusions and implications.

Single Mothers and Welfare

In 1997, Kathryn Edin and Laura Lein published in *American Sociological Review* their study of survival strategies of single mothers in low-wage jobs or on public assistance. Their research questions: How do single mothers survive when neither their jobs nor welfare provide sufficient income. What are the implications of these necessary survival strategies for leaving welfare? Their approach was to conduct multiple, in-depth interviews with mothers in four U.S. cities that varied in geographic location, size, racial-ethnic make up, level of public assistance provided, average wage, cost of living, viability of the local economy, nature of the informal and underground economy, and enforcement of child support.

Edin and Lein (1997) enumerated how women on welfare or in low-wage jobs survived despite insufficient funds: They generated additional income through a variety of strategies, depending on the quality of their social support systems and the social-structural characteristics where they lived. Women on welfare worked for pay at side jobs and received financial aid from some of the members of their social networks and from community groups. "Employed" mothers actually found it more difficult to meet their expenses. Without Medicaid and given the substantial expenses they incurred because they had jobs, they also had less time to take on additional waged labor or to solicit support from community agencies and groups. Those employed women who were successful had low expenses (this was unusual), obtained significant financial support from the people they knew, or both.

Edin and Lein (1997) found that some noncustodial fathers provided child support directly to the child's mother rather than through official channels. These fathers were retained on public records as noncompliant with child-support orders. Getting this hidden aid was a strategy custodial mothers used to maximize their income. Hiding it kept them from losing public aid equivalent to the child support they received.

Edin and Lein (1997) also demonstrated that mothers in the labor force were in a better position than were mothers on public assistance to reduce the costs of paid work (e.g., child care), in part because they relied on social-network members who were better off and could provide more and steady financial help. One reason women were on public assistance, then, was that they did not have the sort of personal safety net that would enable them to survive despite low-wage employment. A strong, supportive social network, not side employment or agency help, is necessary to move from public assistance to low-wage work. Although women on public assistance endorsed the work ethic, they knew that paid work was not a viable option for them.

Why does Edin and Lein's (1997) research matter to the pursuit of family science? Their thoughtful and careful sampling and recruitment strategies meant that they obtained information from a group of women who are seriously under-represented in studies of low-income families and families on public assistance. Their strategy of using comparison groups refrained from problematizing and marginalizing women on welfare. Furthermore, their relentless approach to developing rapport meant that they obtained previously hidden information. Across the four cities, from 2% to 19% of women on public assistance reported that their survival strategies, such as selling sex, drugs, or stolen materials, violated laws, the rules of public assistance, or both. From 27% to 41% received cash assistance from a child's father. Before this study, our knowledge of strategies for women in low-wage jobs or on public assistance was anecdotal, incomplete, and unreliable. These two aspects of their work, recruitment and rapport, are remarkable on their own, particularly given their focus on a population researchers may see as "uncooperative."

By linking the survival strategies women used to the social-structural context in which they lived, Edin and Lein (1997) demonstrated women's agency and rationality in providing for their families. In each city, women pursued different ways to "make ends meet." For example, women on public assistance were more likely to engage in side employment in larger cities, where such work was less likely to be detected. In cities with large illegal immigrant populations, it was easier to obtain false identity cards, which also helped women pursue waged labor. Women got more help from the fathers of their children in cities with stricter enforcement of child-support policies. Rather than passive recipients of public support, then, women on welfare are active in meeting their own needs and those of their children. The implications for policies and programs are evident. The findings raise serious questions about the consequences of removing from welfare women who do not have a supportive, financially healthy social network. The strategy of pursuing their work in four unique cities also reminds us that what we learn through research is situated in a particular sociohistorical context and location.

Intergenerational Aid in African American and White Families

In 1998, the *Journal of Family Issues* published an article by Rukmalie Jayakody comparing financial aid across generations in African American and White families. Jayakody's work was in response to studies suggesting that African American parents give less aid to their adult children than do White parents. She speculated that this pattern of findings occurred because investigators had considered either children's needs or parents' resources, but not both. Her work is in the finest tradition of social science. When we overlay empirical evidence onto the map of social reality, we see that some research findings provide a relatively poor fit with real life. A poor fit should be troubling to all family scholars and should act as a catalyst for further research, as it seems to have done for Jayakody.

Jayakody (1998) pursued her question using the Panel Study of Income Dynamics (PSID) and the Time and Money Transfer file, a 1998 PSID supplement. Her findings demonstrated that, considering both children's needs and parents' resources, White children receive more aid only in the lowest income group: those earning less than $15,000 annually. There were no differences between African Americans and Whites in the receipt of aid among adult children earning $15,000 or more. Both children's needs and parents' resources matter. If children have less income, controlling for parents' resources, they are more likely to receive financial aid. If parents have more income, controlling for children's need, children get more aid. The findings suggest that the poorest Black families are unable to provide much in the way of financial help to their adult children in need. That limitation, and not attitudes or values, accounts for the distinction between African Americans and Whites at the lowest income level, a distinction that disappears at or above annual income levels of $15,000.

The importance of her study is self-evident, but I draw attention to Jayakody's (1998) work primarily because of the tremendous care she exercised in cautioning the reader about what the findings mean. Throughout the article, not only in the methods section, Jayakody reminded us about respondents who were excluded from the sample (e.g., cohabitors, students), problems with the measures (e.g., data on parents' income were provided by adult children), problems with analysis (e.g., missing data), and so on.

Jayakody (1998) placed particular emphasis on the way aid from parents is measured. In the PSID, aid of less than $100 is not recorded. Other surveys have similar approaches. The aid threshold in the National Longitudinal Survey of Youth (NLSY), for example, is half or more of the aid recipient's income. Jayakody cautioned that these levels may be unrealistically high, particularly for low-income African Americans for whom small amounts of aid are significant. High thresholds place low-income families at a disadvantage, and these families are disproportionately people of color. Because other data sets employ similarly high levels of financial aid as a baseline, researchers have begun to conclude that, other things being equal, Whites give more aid to their adult children than comparable Blacks. Indeed, it is this conclusion that seems to have motivated Jayakody to conduct this research.

Jayakody (1998) did not limit her concerns to the baseline level of aid received. Other issues were identified as well: "Existing survey measures are not fully responsive to the objective of determining the prevalence of financial exchange, and as a consequence, likely underestimate the number of families who receive money from their parents" (p. 528). For example, survey questions about aid are ambiguous as to referent. Do they mean all aid during a given time period, she asked, or do they inquire only about a single transfer? Respondents do not receive instructions about how to answer these questions. In Jayakody's view, such lack of clarity may put some families at a particular disadvantage relative to others.

Jayakody's (1998) results were significant, but she was quick to point out that problems remain. Although race effects were still present at the lowest income level, for example, these effects may not be independent of socioeconomic influences. Because only parents' income was measured, other important parental resources, such as savings, investments, and home ownership, were not considered. In Jayakody's view, studies that focus on the transfer of aid should measure wealth. Because there is no income level among African Americans that even comes close to 50% of the median net wealth for Whites in the same income category, she argued that any remaining race differences could be due to this wealth differential. Poor Blacks simply are less able than poor Whites to provide financial aid. Better resource measures, then, could further diminish race findings.

HOW FAR WE HAVE COME

These four articles say a great deal about where we stand in the study of families. Each reflects a novel conceptualization of an important domain in the field, one that overcomes previous limitations. These studies, and similar work throughout

the decade not highlighted here, moved our understanding forward beyond the incremental levels more characteristic of everyday social science. When students read and discuss these papers, you can see both their enthusiasm for the study of families and their determination to engage in it themselves.

On a more prosaic level, the authors of these papers reminded us that we have available a variety of research designs, not all of which are suited to investigate a certain research question. One could not have deconstructed marital status without a large-scale survey, for example, but we would have learned very little from a nationwide telephone survey of low-income employed women, women on public assistance, and inner-city adolescent mothers. A highly structured interview served Ross's (1995) purpose, a less structured interview served Edin and Lein's (1997) purpose, and an unstructured interview served Apfel and Seitz's (1991) purpose. Edin and Lein drew samples from various locations, while diverse urban locations were not important to Apfel and Seitz's study.

All four studies demonstrated variability in the ways individuals meet their needs and those of other family members, and the authors drew attention to that variability. Finally, authors in all four papers were careful to point out the limitations of their work, for example, what the studies were unable to tell us and how certain findings were, in part, an artifact of method. They exercised caution in conclusions, interpretation, and in application. In particular, Jayakody's (1998) work is a model for attending to audience in considering the limitations of the research enterprise.

EMPIRICAL REALITY VERSUS EVERYDAY LIFE: LIMITATIONS OF SOCIAL SCIENCE

When writing about research, we should keep both our audience and the limitations of science in the forefront. Typically, however, we pay far less attention to both than we should. Consider the advice of Ramage and Bean (1997) concerning audience:

> Before you can decide what to say about content, you need to ask: Who am I writing for and why? What does my audience already know (and not know) about my topic? . . . What effect do I want my writing to have on that audience? (p. 11)

PAYING ATTENTION TO THE AUDIENCE

Much of the debate about the way we pursue the study of individuals and families takes place in the written record. This record, consisting primarily of journal articles, stands on its own. Authors do not follow their articles around to answer questions, to clarify points, or to urge caution. A rigorous process of review by peers and editors helps to ensure that the work is of high quality. In some ways, however, journal articles are written as if the limitations of research are self-evident. This practice is not without consequence. Ultimately, it has the potential to harm both our status as a science and our understanding of family life. In part, this is because of the way such articles are read.

There are myriad ways in which individuals approach a journal article. Some read only the abstract. Some read the introduction, skip the methods and results, and then move forward to the discussion and conclusion. After having read the abstract, others examine the tables and peruse the results but dispense with the introduction and the discussion. Dare we hope that even a minority read them from the first word of the title through the last word of the discussion? Ultimately, all writing is for the reader, and the most effective writer pays attention to the audience (Ramage & Bean, 1997). How readers approach our research reports matter. Readers who only read the abstract or the introduction and conclusions risk making more of the findings than they should because they may have missed key qualifications. One may see this as an error on the part of the reader, but the consequences extend into family practice and policy with implications for people's lives.

In addition to variability in *how* journal articles and other reports of research are read, there is variability as well in *why* they are read. My beginning graduate students mostly read journal articles in response to an assignment. As a researcher, I read articles to help shape a research question, to identify an appropriate measure, or to understand fully what is known about a particular area of study. As an instructor, I read them to learn about some aspect of family life that I will then pass on to others. Certainly there are other motives. Journalists may read them to obtain information that will be communicated to a nonacademic audience. Practitioners may read them to inform social policies or to shape interventions with families. Some among these audiences have neither the scientific background nor the experience to judge empirical reports.

Trained as scientists and well schooled in reading journal articles, we have learned to read between the lines of empirical reports. We know how to look for consistency across the various aspects of the research enterprise: theoretical background and conceptualization, research design, sample and sampling procedures, measurement, and analytic techniques. We raise questions if the separate parts do not fit into a logical whole, that is, if the conceptualization is unrelated to the population sampled or to the way key variables are measured. We consider the evidence in support of the author's position and generate alternative explanations for the research findings.

Even scientists, however, lack the background to judge certain studies. Reading between the lines of empirical reports has become somewhat more difficult as the field has become larger and more sophisticated. We now must have expertise in sampling, narrative analysis, confirmatory factor analysis, hierarchical linear models, and structural equation modeling, as just a few examples. Methodological developments have enhanced our knowledge and our ability to pursue it, but they also have made things more difficult even for the scientific reader.

There is, then, both an increasing sophistication in the field and a decreasing likelihood that any individual family scholar will have the necessary expertise to understand the literature fully. Therefore, I ask that we pay more attention to the readers of our journals and the purposes for which journal articles are read. Outside of one's area of expertise, scientists do bring to their reading a healthy skepticism developed through years of reading and conducting research. It is folly, however, to assume that students, practitioners, and other audiences, who do not (yet) share our tradition of skepticism and critical analysis, do the same. These audiences are particularly vulnerable to both misunderstanding and misinformation. We owe it to them, to our colleagues, and to ourselves to exercise caution in writing about our research. Failing to note caveats, concerns, and contexts violates fundamental research principals (e.g., Babbie, 1995; Gamson, 1999; see also Stacey, 1999; Walker & McGraw, 2000) and places a needless burden on readers, particularly those not trained in social science. It may even burden those with scientific training. My knowledge of sampling strategies, measurement problems, specialized analyses, techniques for handling missing data, and so on, is limited at best. It would help me if

I were told what was useful about a particular approach and what remained of concern.

We need to be sure to support our assertions with evidence to avoid reviewing only the literature in favor or our position, to place no more confidence in existing findings than is justified, and to refrain from overgeneralizing beyond the population sampled or the domain of study. The complexity of everyday life and the inadequacies of social science require us to be cautious and careful in our work and in the telling of it. Particularly when addressing areas that may influence people directly, we need to be sure that our interpretation of our work is consistent with reality (e.g., Demo & Acock, 1996; Entwisle & Alexander, 1996).

In considering families in poverty, for example, we need to be sure readers understand that poverty and family structure are not perfectly correlated. Although Puerto Rican and African American families in poverty are disproportionately unmarried mothers and their children, for example, the same is not true for Whites, Mexicans, and Cuban Americans (Lichter & Landale, 1995). Nearly half of all poor Mexican American children live in married-couple households. In fact, rates of poverty for single-mother households vary considerably by race and ethnicity: Among single-mother households, African Americans, Mexican Americans, and Puerto Ricans have poverty rates that are almost twice as high as those of Whites (Manning & Smock, 1997).

We need to be clear when we describe children in single-parent households that many of these children, especially those who are African American, Mexican American, Puerto Rican, and Asian American, live with only one parent but also with other adults (e.g., Aquilino, 1996; Manning & Smock, 1997; Smock, 2000). According to Manning and Smock, estimates of adult coresidence are artificially low because we rely primarily on static measures of household composition. In any case, just as marital status is a weak proxy for social attachment, family structure is a weak proxy for internal family dynamics (Solomon & Marx, 1995).

When examining the relationship between marital disruption and child outcomes, we need to acknowledge that the best assessments of this relationship do not stop at a parent's marital status. Instead, they acknowledge that divorce is at once a status and a process (R. M. Milardo, personal communication, August 30, 1999); it is both an interpersonal event and a subjective condition (Huston & Robins, 1982). When examining the influence of divorce on children, which of the three is the focus? For many children, divorce is a weak proxy for economic deprivation (McLanahan & Sandefur, 1994), which, itself, leads to high residential mobility, changes between schools, moves into poorer neighborhoods, and other effects of downward mobility. As Furstenberg (1999) argued, because the decline in family relations that almost inevitably precedes divorce is not usually accounted for in studies of how divorce influences children, one cannot reliably attribute child outcomes to the divorce itself.

In the literature, we use divorce as a proxy for a variety of things. Rarely is it conceptualized as a specific event. Commonly, it is an option within the categorical variable of marital status. It is also, however, a proxy for an unspecified process of marital decline influencing the family environment, as well as a set of outcomes tied to reduced income, residential mobility, decreased interaction with a nonresidential parent, and interaction with a residential, emotionally distressed parent. As Ross (1995) argued, we need to measure influences directly, not with inadequate and underconceptualized proxies.

In our training as researchers, we learned about the need for designs appropriate to research questions, to minimize threats to internal validity and maximize external validity, to be aware of the limitations in one's approach, and so on. We may have this knowledge, but we air too little of it in the written reports of our research. This is why Jayakody's (1998) article is so striking. It is a rare paper in which the researcher so carefully points out the limitations of what she has done. It may be common for researchers to note sampling and measurement problems in the methods section of an article, but cautions throughout the remainder of the paper are missing all too frequently.

Paying attention to the limitations of what we do is useful because it helps us to practice good science and to hold ourselves accountable for what we are doing (see also Allen, 2000; Miller, 1993). It makes us think about how our peers, our students, and others may make use of our work. It acknowledges our responsibility as researchers and as communicators.

THE LIMITATIONS OF SOCIAL SCIENCE

Below, I highlight some specific limitations of social science that require us to pay more attention to what we do and how we do it. Doing so will help us to become better scholars and better communicators, regardless of how or why people read our work.

Sampling Issues

One major advance in the past decade was the availability of national data sets designed specifically with family scholars in mind. These data sets have multiple advantages in that they include representative samples, oversamples of underrepresented groups, and some measures with established properties of reliability and validity. Some also include reports from more than one family member and are longitudinal in design.

Available data, however, are not always appropriate for certain research questions. In writing about research with these data sets, authors should make clear why the survey was reasonable for investigating the question at hand. More than 30 years ago, Herbert Blumer (1969, p. 25) decried the tendency to rely on only one approach to gathering data rather that to determine one's method by "the nature of the data to be sought." Although not intended by their originators, publicly available data sets contribute to this problem. Because of the representative nature of their samples, their large numbers, their valued position in social science, and the difficulty in securing financial support for data collection, researchers may be tempted to use these data to address questions for which they are inappropriate. There are many reasons why such data may not be the most useful for answering certain research questions.

Sampling is one reason. Data sets have samples with particular characteristics. The NLSY, for example, began appropriately with a young sample. Studies using the NLSY to examine longitudinally the influence of parents on children may be problematic because the children with the most years of data are those whose mothers were very young at the time of their birth. Younger mothers are more likely than are older mothers to have less education and lower income and are less likely to be married to the child's father. These characteristics are not unrelated to children's outcomes. The National Survey of Families and Households (NSFH) has a younger adult sample than the Health and Retirement Survey. The sample characteristics of these data sets are important constraints on the nature of the questions that can be addressed with them, or, at a minimum, the limitations of any conclusions drawn from research in which they are used.

A major advantage of several of the national data sets is the oversampling of some groups, particularly people of color. Important differences by geography within minority communities, however, may be underidentified in such samples. People of color who participate in national surveys generally reside in areas with high concentrations of minorities (Connell & Gibson, 1997; Norgard & Rodgers, 1997). Such communities also have differential access to services, so research questions tied to service use might be particularly problematic with survey data.

Despite having been oversampled, some groups are notably underrepresented in national data sets, increasingly so with longitudinal data. African Americans, Hispanics, younger respondents, renters, and those with lower income and less education are even less likely to be included in second and later waves than in initial samples (Myers & Booth, 1996). Sorenson (1997) studied nonresident fathers using two data sets: the NSFH and the Survey of Income and Program Participation (SIPP). She was able to identify 78% of nonresident fathers in the population from the SIPP but only 56% from the NSFH. Nonresident fathers who were missing from these data sets, in comparison with those who were included, disproportionately were non-White, under 30 years of age, had less than a high school education, had poor employment histories, were institutionalized or otherwise living in group settings, and were more likely to have additional children who lived in a different location from those referred to in the survey. Unlike many others, Sorenson was careful to remind the reader of this limitation throughout her article.

Scientists who use a nationally representative data set draw from it a subsample, consistent with the aims of their research. These subsamples include certain respondents but tell us little about the individuals omitted because of one or another of the subsample criteria. Stephens (1996) used the NSFH to study postdivorce contact between children and their nonresidential fathers including only children born during a first marriage whose primary residence was more than half of the year with mothers. These criteria enabled her to include 85% of all divorced households in the survey. Throughout her article, Stephens was careful to remind the reader of the missing 15%.

Michael Johnson's (1995) thoughtful analysis of contradictions in the literature on couple violence demonstrated anew the critical nature of sampling in social science. Quantitative mass surveys present one perspective, whereas qualitative studies of shelter populations present a very different perspective. Johnson argued that each captures a different type of violence. Conducting couple violence research while relying on only one type of sample will result in a distorted understanding of family life.

Every design produces a sample with both distinctive and unintended characteristics. Karney and his colleagues (1995) argued that because sampling strategies influence who responds and who does not, researchers should include in articles all details about sampling procedures in addition to information about the population and rates of nonresponse. Further, they suggested that researchers consider whether strategies to improve rates of participation could create or exacerbate recruitment and response bias. We need to learn as much as we can about sampling practices and their consequences and systematically alert ourselves and our readers to the potential implications of the practices we employ.

Measurement Issues

Measurement is a complex domain with many potential areas of concern. Nonresponse is an area related to measurement that complicates scientific practice. Individuals who participate in surveys but who do not respond to all items may differ systematically from those who do. In Wave I of the NSFH, for example, 38% of husbands aged 55 to 72 did not respond to "female" items in the household task measures, and 33% did not respond to "male" items (Szinovacz & Harpster, 1994). Nonresponding husbands tend to have characteristics similar to those of husbands who do less household work (Ishii-Kuntz & Coltrane, 1992; Szinovacz & Harpster). Thus, studies of household labor using men in this age group from the NSFH that fail to address nonresponse in their analyses systematically bias the family work of husbands in a positive direction. Readers need to know about this bias.

Even when participants respond to items, measurement problems exist when scales are developed before the domain of the construct is conceptualized adequately. Measures of household labor are conspicuous examples. That individuals "dovetail" tasks (e.g., prepare meals while washing clothes) has plagued this area of study for many years (Berheide, 1984). Furthermore, much of the family labor that is invisible, such as management and emotion work, is excluded from most measures (for discussion, see Demo & Acock, 1993; DeVault, 1991; Erickson, 1993; Mederer, 1993). Family work is one of a number of areas in which we should think about the fit between social science and everyday life.

Try to imagine answering a question such as, "How much time do you spend each week washing dishes?" First, I would have to consider whether I do them myself or have help. If I have help only part of the time, I have to determine how much time is saved by whatever amount of help is available. I also need to think about how much cooking is usually done—lots of cooking means many more dishes—and what kinds of things are cooked—how dirty are those pots and pans? How often do I dry dishes and put them away, and how often do I leave them to dry on their own? Because doing dishes is not one of my favorite tasks, I may be likely to overestimate the time I spend in this activity. How systematic is my overestimation? Then again, I am generally a poor estimator of the passage of time. How systematic is my poor estimation? It is not a simple task to produce these numbers. And this is before I perform any mathematical operation, such as adding times together, subtracting times with help, multiplying to project an average day across a week or month. It would be useful to ask people how they go about answering questions such as these so as to clarify what the numbers mean.

Dressel and Clark (1990) drew our attention to the complexity of tasks such as family care. Family work is a tangled web of thinking and doing, and our measures seem to fall far short of this intricacy (see also DeVault, 1991). Furthermore, we have yet to determine the utility of standardized measures, in this and in other areas, across individuals varying in race, ethnicity, culture, class, and geographic region (e.g., McCulloch, 1995). We need to pay more attention to measurement.

A minor but still significant measurement concern is one I call *insufficiently determined data.* These data are unclear in their referent. For example, an increasingly popular domain of study is the relationships between adult children and their parents. Some data sets ask adult children about help they receive from their parents, but, as Aquilino (1994) noted, they do not distinguish whether the help they receive is from mothers or fathers. Others ask mothers and fathers about their interaction or relationships with adult children, but it is unclear whether the findings are relevant only to a specific child or represent an "average" relationship for a parent and all of her or his children.

Research on intergenerational ties is challenging, in part, because parents have different numbers of children, some parents are widowed, and some parents—and children—are remarried. Furthermore, relationships between adult children and their parents vary by gender, race, marital status, social class, and so on (Rossi & Rossi, 1990; Silverstein & Bengtson, 1997). The inability to distinguish between parents and among children compromises our understanding of intergenerational bonds. It flattens the unique character of ties between mothers and daughters, mothers and sons, fathers and daughters, and fathers and son. Similar problems occur with data about parents and young children. For example, Cooksey and Fondell (1996) noted that when parent-child interaction is assessed globally or on average, researchers are unable to link outcomes for a specific child to that child's interactions with a parent.

Another way in which data are insufficiently determined is that certain measures are unavailable in some data sets or are included in ways reflecting a limited conceptualization of the variable's domain. The Asset and Health Dynamics among the oldest old (AHEAD) data set was designed to examine physical and cognitive health status of aging persons, and family structure, assets, transfers, and family caregiving (Soldo, Hurd, Rodgers, & Wallace, 1997). Unlike some of the data sets described above, AHEAD provides specific information for every individual family member. For example, it includes information on aid given and aid received identified to specific children or children-in-law. Only instrumental aid was assessed, however. There are no data on socioemotional exchanges. One can, and should, use the AHEAD to examine intergenerational exchanges, but should point to the limitations resulting from the inability to link aid exchange to the socioemotional context of a particular relationship.

A related aspect of measurement to consider is how categories are conceptualized for purposes of analysis. How do researchers handle outliers, persons whose scores are three standard deviations beyond the mean? Collapsing outliers into the highest or lowest category obscures potentially important information. Although some outliers may be at the extreme as a result of random error, others are significant in their own right. Despite their small numbers, they merit scientific attention. Rather than the central tendency that is often

our major focus, they have something to say about variability, the people we often miss in our research. The presence of individuals whose scores do not seem to fit with those of any "natural" groupings should always make us step back and think about the relation between the practice of science and the reality of social life. When is it justified to group together for analytic reasons individuals who are conceptually distinct? We need to pay more attention to the small numbers of respondents who do not seem to fit our predesigned response categories. Such individuals should pique our interest, and we should learn more about them before we decide whether it is appropriate to combine them with others. And we should always communicate to our audience details about how outliers were handled and the implications of our decisions.

The Significance and Meaning of Research Findings

Being well aware of the limitations of social science to explain social life, we are satisfied when quantitative studies can account for only a small portion of variance in the dependent variable of interest, the vast majority of the outcome remaining unexplained (see Mangen, 1995). In a recent newsletter article, Alan Acock (1999) wrote passionately about the need for caution in interpretation even of significant results. Findings may be significant, he argued, but trivial or of limited substantive value. The availability of data sets with very large samples and the ability to analyze them on desktop computers have had two effects, according to Acock: (a) the strengthening of quantitative research and (b) the production of results of "profound unimportance" (p. 12). Trained scientists know that sample size is at fault here, but Acock argued that "readers trained before we had these data sets are blinded by this" (p. 12). Readers should read the methods sections of articles, he argued, and researchers should provide understandable information about the importance of any identified effects. I argue further that researchers should provide this information, not only in methods sections, but also in the discussion, conclusions, and implications.

Paying Attention to Our Subject Matter

I began this essay with several statements about the ways in which assessing the field—and teaching others about it—are exhilarating and exasperating. One final way in which taking stock of the field is exasperating is that we sometimes have very little to say worth noting on subjects of tremendous importance to the lived experience of family members (Allen, 2000; Smock, 2000). Any one of us could generate a list of these subjects: in-laws and in-law relationships, for example. They are a major feature of everyday life, and they merit very little attention in our journals. Step-kin and former kin, is another example. Millions of individuals have adult stepsiblings, stepparents, and stepgrandparents, as well as former mothers-in-law, fathers-in-law, sisters-in-law, and brothers-in-law. Millions of others are in cohabiting heterosexual or gay and lesbian relationships, and they, too, have quasi-kin connections (Allen; Allen & Demo, 1995; Smock). Other examples are the death of a parent; marriage and other intimate partnerships among couples in their 70s, 80s, and 90s; and leisure in families. This is not to say that there is no work in these areas, only that there is far less than there should be, particularly given their importance in the daily life of individuals and families.

I hardly know what to say when my students ask about these subjects. Although there were many advances in the last decade, we really need to pay more attention to what families are like today and bring our search for knowledge more closely in line with that reality (Allen, 2000). This is a concern that scholars of color and feminists in our field have been raising for a long time. Obviously, it bears repeating. In my graduate class, these missing topics prompt a discussion of possible ideas for thesis research. The same opportunity lies before us with this volume of the *Journal of Marriage and the Family*. The missing topics of today should be prominent features of the landscape of the discipline when we look back over the past 10 years.

HUMILITY

From 1958 through 1966, I attended Sacred Heart School in Tarentum, Pennsylvania, under the stern, exacting, and sometimes kind supervision of the Sisters of Divine Providence. Despite the baby boom, two grades per classroom, and enrollment worthy of Roman Catholic parents fully committed to the sacrament of procreation, I rarely felt out of range of those alert and vigilant women while in elementary school. Relentlessly, Sister Natalie, Sister Rose Ellen, Sister Georgeann, and then Sister Ancilla swooped in on us amid their yards of black cloth and clattering rosary beads to identify transgressions and demand correction and atonement.

Having written at length about how we need to pay more attention to responsible science, I risk the appearance of hovering over my colleagues, swooping in to point out errors and to demand modification and repentance. Fortunately, the written word is neither as overbearing nor as onerous as the physical presence of those heavily shrouded, impossibly large figures of my childhood. Furthermore, although the sisters carried with them both the temporary transfer of parental control and the weight of papal authority, my status is far less powerful. Rather than authority, I rely on the community of social scientists who have agreed, in principle and in practice, to subject our work to review, testing, and amendment by our peers (e.g., Furstenberg, 1999). I fall back on our self-critical tradition (e.g., Allen, 2000), and, from this location, draw attention to the ways in which, despite notable and illuminating accomplishments in the 1990s, we failed to adhere to our own standards and practices.

Humility was a virtue prized by the sisters, many of whom demonstrated it in their daily lives. Although it is not one of the cardinal principles of scientific inquiry, we would do well to cultivate a more humble approach to both research and its subjects (Ruddick, 1982). A sense of humility might help alleviate or avoid some of the problems that arise in our work. It might also help us to think about our readers and about how our research might be used.

In pointing out problems in our research and the way we write about it, I in no way intend to diminish the achievements of the past 10 years. The successes of the decade compel us to remember how important it is that we each play an active role in maintaining high standards of scholarship. In doing so, we obviate the need for a monitoring body as imposing and unyielding as the Sisters of Divine Providence.

NOTE

I thank Katherine Allen, Sally Gallagher, Stephen Marks, and Lori McGraw for their careful reading and thoughtful comments.

REFERENCES

Acock, A. (1999, December). Practitioners should use caution when applying quantitative research. *National Council on Family Relations Report, 44* (4),11–12.

Allen, K. R. (2000). A conscious and inclusive family

studies. *Journal of Marriage and the Family, 62,* 4–17.

Allen, K. R., & Demo, D. H. (1995). The families of lesbians and gay men: A new frontier in family research. *Journal of Marriage and the Family, 57,* 111–127.

Apfel, N. H., & Seitz, V. (1991). Four models of adolescent mother-grandmother relationships in Black inner-city families. *Family Relations, 40,* 421–429.

Aquilino, W. S. (1994). Later life parental divorce and widowhood: Impact on young adults' assessment of parent-child relations. *Journal of Marriage and the Family, 56,* 908–922.

Aquilino, W. S. (1996). The life course of children born to unmarried mothers: Childhood living arrangements and young adult outcomes. *Journal of Marriage and the Family, 58,* 293–310.

Babbie, E. (1995). *The practice of social research* (7th ed.). Belmont, CA: Wadsworth.

Berheide, C. W. (1984). Women's work in the home: Seems like old times. *Marriage and Family Review, 7* (3/4), 37–55.

Blumer, H. (1969). *Symbolic interactionism: Perspective and method.* Englewood Cliffs, NJ: Prentice-Hall.

Connell, C. M., & Gibson, G. D. (1997). Racial, ethnic, and cultural differences in dementia caregiving: Review and analysis. *The Gerontologist, 37,* 355–364.

Cooksey, E. C., & Fondell, M. M. (1996). Spending time with his kids: Effects of family structure on fathers' and children's lives. *Journal of Marriage and the Family, 58,* 693–707.

Demo, D. H., & Acock, A. C. (1993). Family diversity and the division of labor: How much have things really changed? *Family Relations, 42,* 323–331.

Demo, D. H., & Acock, A. C. (1996). Singlehood, marriage, and remarriage: The effects of family structure and family relationships on mothers' well-being. *Journal of Family Issues, 17,* 388–407.

DeVault, M. L. (1991). *Feeding the family: The social organization of caring as gendered work.* Chicago: University of Chicago Press.

Dressel, P. L., & Clark, A. (1990). A critical look at family care. *Journal of Marriage and the Family, 52,* 769–782.

Edin, K., & Lein, L. (1997). Work, welfare, and single mothers' economic survival strategies. *American Sociological Review, 62,* 253–266.

Entwisle, D. R., & Alexander, K. L. (1996). Family type and children's growth in reading and math over the primary grades. *Journal of Marriage and the Family, 58,* 341–355.

Erickson, R. J. (1993). Reconceptualizing family work: The effect of emotion work on perceptions of marital quality. *Journal of Marriage and the Family, 55,* 888–900.

Furstenberg, F. F., Jr. (1999). Children and family change: Discourse between social scientists and the media. *Contemporary Sociology: A Journal of Reviews, 28,* 10–17.

Gamson, W. A. (1999). Beyond the science-versus-advocacy distinction. *Contemporary Sociology: A Journal of Reviews, 28,* 23–26.

Hill Collins, P. (1991). The meaning of motherhood in Black culture and Black mother-daughter relationships. In P. Bell-Scott, B. Guy-Sheftall, J. J. Royster, J. Sims-Wood, M. DeCosta-Willis, & L. Fultz (Eds.), *Double stitch: Black women write about mothers and daughters* (pp. 42–60). Boston: Beacon Press.

Huston, T. L., & Robins, E. (1982). Conceptual and methodological issues in studying close relationships. *Journal of Marriage and the Family, 44,* 901–925.

Ishii-Kuntz, M., & Coltrane, S. (1992). Remarriage, stepparenting, and household labor. *Journal of Family Issues, 13,* 215–233.

Jayakody, R. (1998). Race differences in intergenerational financial assistance: The needs of children and the resources of parents. *Journal of Family Issues, 19,* 508–533.

Johnson, M. P. (1995). Patriarchal terrorism and common couple violence: Two forms of violence against women. *Journal of Marriage and the Family, 57,* 283–294.

Karney, B. R., Davila, J., Cohan, C. L., Sullivan, K. T., Johnson, M. D., & Bradbury, T. N. (1995). An empirical investigation of sampling strategies in marital research. *Journal of Marriage and the Family, 57,* 909–920.

Lichter, D. T., & Landale, N. S. (1995). Parental work, family structure, and poverty among Latino children. *Journal of Marriage and the Family, 57,* 346–354.

Mangen, D. J. (1995). Methods and analysis of family data. In R. Blieszner & V. H. Bedford (Eds.), *Handbook of aging and the family* (pp. 148–177). Westport, CT: Greenwood.

Manning, W. D., & Smock, P. J. (1997). Children's living arrangements in unmarried-mother families. *Journal of Family Issues, 18,* 526–544.

McCulloch, B. J. (1995). Aging and kinship in a rural context. In R. Blieszner & V. H. Bedford (Eds.), *Handbook of aging and the family* (pp. 332–354). Westport, CT: Greenwood.

McLanahan, S., & Sandefur, G. (1994). *Growing up with a single parent: What hurts, what helps.* Cambridge, MA: Harvard University Press.

Mederer, H. (1993). Division of labor in two-earner homes: Task accomplishment versus household management as critical variables in perceptions about family work. *Journal of Marriage and the Family, 55,* 133–145.

Milardo, R. M. (2000). The year 2000 volume: A decade or more in review. *Journal of Marriage and the Family, 62,* 1–3.

Miller, B. C. (1993). Families, science, and values: Alternative views of parenting effects and adolescent pregnancy. *Journal of Marriage and the Family, 55,* 7–21.

Myers, S. M., & Booth, A. (1996). Men's retirement and marital quality. *Journal of Family Issues, 17,* 336–357.

Norgard, T. M., & Rodgers, W. L. (1997). Patterns of in-home care among elderly Black and White Americans. *Journals of Gerontology, 52B,* 93–101.

Ramage, J. D., & Bean, J. C. (1997). *The Allyn and Bacon guide to writing.* Boston: Allyn and Bacon.

Ross, C. E. (1995). Reconceptualizing marital status as a continuum of social attachment. *Journal of Marriage and the Family, 57,* 129–140.

Rossi, A. S., & Rossi, P. H. (1990). *Of human bonding: Parent-child relations across the life course.* New York: Aldine de Gruyter.

Ruddick, S. (1982). *Maternal thinking: Toward a politics of peace.* Boston: Beacon.

Silverstein, M., & Bengtson, V. L. (1997). Intergenerational solidarity and the structure of adult child-parent relationships in American families. *American Sociological Review, 103,* 429–460.

Smock, P. J. (2000). Cohabitation in the United States: An appraisal of research themes, findings, and implications. *Annual Review of Sociology, 26* (in press).

Soldo, B. J., Hurd, M. D., Rodgers, W. L., & Wallace, R. B. (1997). Asset and health dynamics among the oldest old: An overview of the AHEAD study. *Journals of Gerontology, 52B* (special issue),1–20.

Solomon, J. C., & Marx, J. (1995). "To grandmother's house we go": Health and school adjustment of children raised solely by grandparents. *The Gerontologist, 35,* 386–394.

Sorenson, E. (1997). A national profile of nonresident fathers and their ability to pay child support. *Journal of Marriage and the Family, 59,* 785–797.

Stacey, J. (1999). Virtual truth with a vengeance. *Contemporary Sociology: A Journal of Reviews, 28,* 18–23.

Stephens, L. S. (1996). Will Johnny see Daddy this week? An empirical test of three theoretical perspectives of postdivorce contact. *Journal of Family Issues, 17,* 466–494.

Szinovacz, M., & Harpster, P. (1994). Couples' employment/retirement status and the division of household labor. *Journal of Gerontology: Social Sciences, 49,* S125–S136.

Walker, A. J., & McGraw, L. A. (2000). Who is responsible for responsible fathering? *Journal of Marriage and the Family, 62,* 563–570.

STEPHEN R. MARKS   *University of Maine*

Teasing Out the Lessons of the 1960s: Family Diversity and Family Privilege

The tumult of the 1960s brought new strains of cultural relativism. I survey the continuing impact of some of these strains on family studies, focusing especially on the study of family diversity as an offshoot of the relativistic project. A dominant discourse still drives much of our work, however, and I illustrate it with some recent examples. The diversity agenda is hampered too often by unintended erasures of large categories of people in nondominant family arrangements. As a corrective to this tendency, I propose an agenda to study family privilege and entitlement, that is, to treat it as a "social problem" much as we treat poverty or juvenile delinquency. I illustrate with my own narrative of how I learned privilege and entitlement growing up male in a White, Jewish, upper-middle-class family. I end with some recommendations about how we might bring this agenda into our research and writing.

A new millennium is an occasion for some stocktaking, and this essay begins with the 1960s as the last great watershed of the 20th century. The tumult of the 1960s compressed a myriad of sometimes-contradictory social forces into a few explosive years, including a new surge of cultural relativism. I begin with an overview of some of these currents, focusing particularly on the emerging relativization of ideas and interests of the dominant groups. I then turn to the impact of this challenge on family studies and consider some contemporary lapses in meeting the challenge effectively. My point of departure is that the attempt within family studies to deal with the diversity of North American family patterns often is marred by unintended erasures of too much of that very diversity. I draw on two recent studies to illustrate how the assumptions that constitute a "dominant discourse" (Collins, 1998, p. 295) can shape the way family scholars conduct their research. I mean no blame here; my own research has been likewise too little cognizant of how these blind spots have shaped my work. As a corrective, I suggest that family scholars from the dominant groups begin to spotlight family privilege—beginning with our own—as something worthy of our research efforts. The core of this paper is my own such contribution: a personal narrative about growing up male in a White, Jewish, upper-middle-class family. I end with an agenda for further relativizing the diversity agenda.

THE 1960S WATERSHED

The 1960s currents of cultural relativism exploded into popular awareness in large part through the invention of television news, which had penetrated American homes only a little more than a decade before. If the early 20th century relativism was more academically focused on the diversity among distant or exotic cultures, the new lessons trained squarely on the more familiar but forgotten diversity here at home. Critically scrutinizing central

Department of Sociology, 5728 Fernald Hall, University of Maine, Orono, ME 04469–5728 (marks@maine.maine.edu).

Key Words: cultural relativism, diversity, gender, privilege, race, social class.

features of Euro-American culture, the lessons were delivered first in the streets and only later in textbooks and classrooms. Racist traditions at home and anticommunist policies in Vietnam were challenged as wrongheaded products of American imperialism. The interests of affluent, White, heterosexual males lay exposed, contested, and relativized from every direction, as numerous social movements broke through the complacency of the post–World War II era. The image of America as a great "melting pot" was challenged. Whereas most European groups eventually had been welcomed into the pot, other groups had been categorically displaced, excluded, and subjugated. Native Americans, African Americans, Latinos, White women who had not linked their fate to a White husband, married White women who lacked the gender privileges of their husbands, gays and lesbians—these and other categories clamored for a redress of inequities and for a recognition of their unique historical experiences.

Even within the dominant White middle class, sharp lines of division split the generations, as millions of youth began to challenge the "establishment" their parents had created. Vietnam became America's first thoroughly unpopular war. Political protesters and hippie "flower children" were strange bedfellows, but both groups were centered largely on college campuses, both were often the children of G.I. Bill beneficiaries, and both took a dim view of the future their parents had mapped out for them, especially insofar as a stay in Vietnam was no longer avoidable through student "deferments" of military service to attend college. Popular culture abounded with the energy of social upheaval. Dustin Hoffman's role in the 1967 film *The Graduate* typified the sense of absurdity of preparing to enter White, middle-class life-as-usual. "Make love, not war," advised a ubiquitous bumper sticker. "Never trust anyone over 30," admonished another one. "Tune in, turn on, drop out," Timothy Leary counseled, not long after he was fired from Harvard University for experimenting with the psychedelic drug LSD.

One of the biggest impacts of the 1960s watershed was the transformation of self-awareness it inspired. In absolute numbers, few people marched with Dr. King, burned draft cards, or descended on Haight-Ashbury in San Francisco for the 1967 "Summer of Love," but millions participated vicariously and talked endlessly with their friends about the irresistibility of this tidal wave of change, and they began to imagine themselves different than they were before. Negroes became

Blacks and then African Americans, and slogans like "Black is Beautiful" began to transform what Black people saw when they looked in the mirror. Homosexuals became gays and lesbians, distinguishable from "straights" as an alternate sexual orientation. "Miss" and "Mrs." merged into "Ms.," a term more closely parallel to "Mr." No longer could nationalism be a comfortable identity hook, nor could middle-class achievement or marriage insofar as the likely female outcome would be that "dwindling into wives" against which Jessie Bernard (1972) warned women.

Social Movements, Family Diversity, and Family Studies

As the 1970s unfolded, the upheaval spread into the social sciences, bringing into the academy that spirit of critical questioning and sense of unlimited potential that had awakened outside the "ivory tower" as if from a deep sleep. The discipline of family studies was no less influenced than the other social sciences. Intentional communities (e.g., Twin Oaks in Virginia and The Farm in Tennessee) now dotted the American landscape, and discussing them in family courses was almost obligatory. In many respects, the communes were White, middle-class translations of some of the social movements that spawned them. They were antiwar, anticapitalist, and hostile to nuclear families, which they saw as repressive training grounds for the empty privatism of their parents. Studies of social class and race challenged White nuclear familism from another angle. Stack's (1974) study of low-income Black families documented households that are joined together as networks of pooled resources, implicitly exposing as a White, middle-class bias the conviction that isolated nuclear families are *the* unit of child care and adult nurturing.

The institution of marriage itself came under vigorous assault. Hippies attacked the sexual possessiveness of monogamy as an institution, and White married people themselves drew on a popular book called *Open Marriage* (O'Neill & O'Neill, 1972) to dignify an unfettered expansion of their sexual options. *Bob and Carol and Ted and Alice,* a 1969 period film, featured two White couples who deal with their marital struggles by thoroughly indulging their cross-couple attractions.

The politics of marriage-as-usual were also challenged at the grass roots by White feminist "consciousness-raising" groups in which perhaps millions of middle-class women learned that their silently held resentments toward male partners—assumptions about who does the housework and child care, makes the decisions, and gets their overall needs attended to within the relationship—were not at all isolated. All it took was some frank opening up of private experiences to throw the commonality into bold relief (Messer-Davidow, 1995). Once again, the academy followed suit, and a close scrutiny of gender issues began to enter the social science curriculum. Women's Studies programs increasingly won academic legitimacy, as White feminists convinced some of their colleagues that the traditional curriculum had excluded women's voices, perspectives, and unique history.

Now 30 years later, we are still teasing out the lessons of the 1960s. As we enter the new millennium, our yearnings for wholeness are informed more than ever before by a knowledge of structural inequality—the unequal distribution of advantages and disadvantages by race, gender, social class, sexual orientation, and other social categories. The idea that America is a pure meritocracy was long ago challenged as a myth. The newer knowledge suggests that some categories of people have a head start, whereas others are beset with nearly insurmountable obstacles that block the path to the starting line. If individual achievement is a race, that race is not a fair one.

Theorizing Diversity: Whose Standpoint?

This awareness of inequality and diversity will continue to shape social science in the 21st century. To be sure, most family scholars continue to be White, heterosexual, married persons such as myself. The research published in the *Journal of Marriage and the Family* and elsewhere will, as always, reflect the interests of those who do the studies. But the composition of these doers has been changing as more and more women, people of color, lesbians and gays, and scholars from working-class backgrounds compose the academy. These scholars have challenged their exclusion by discourses that are presented as generic family reality, and some of us from the dominant groups who earlier saw families in a White, male, middle-class image have been listening and learning.

As the interests of family scholars break free of the insular confines from which they originally sprung, awareness of multiple family realities will continue to broaden. Recent qualitative studies with a comparative focus have been especially useful in providing an insider view of some of this diversity. Seccombe, James, and Walters' (1998) study of African American and White welfare mothers, and Uttal's (1999) study of some differences among African American, Anglo American, and Mexican American employed women's use of relatives for child care are excellent examples of this genre. Quantitative studies have also become more inclusive as researchers are striving to bring diversity into their sampling strategies, if not always into their theoretical foundations. Amato's (2000) study of single parents is a model of how to enrich research findings through a careful consideration of racial-ethnic family diversity. Drawing both on census data and on the 1987–1988 National Survey of Families and Households (NSFH), Amato weaved together a complex story of differences *and* similarities among African American, Latino, and White single parents.

The Dominant Discourse: Problems of Erasure and Exclusion

Much research, however, continues to reflect elements of a dominant discourse in ways that are surely not intended (Allen, 2000). I shall illustrate with two studies, both of which begin with a keen alertness to social diversity. Both are thoughtful and well executed, and both add important contributions to our knowledge base. But as their studies proceed, one of them erases important elements of the diversity with which it started, and the other is seriously compromised by an important exclusion.

In a study of parents' school involvement and children's grades, Bogenschneider (1997) drew on a diverse sample of approximately 10,000 high school students in nine public schools in California and Wisconsin. "The schools were selected to ensure a heterogeneous population of urban, suburban, and rural adolescents from diverse ethnic and socioeconomic backgrounds" (p. 722). The results reveal a strong relationship between parental involvement and children's grades, and with few exceptions this pattern holds regardless of parents' gender and education, child's gender, or family structure and race. Bogenschneider thus started by allowing for diverse family contexts to affect an outcome and ended by suggesting that in this case, a "proximal process" (parental school involvement) has "cross-contextual" validity in driving the outcome (children's grades): "Contextually driven analyses are a vital first step, but are even more illuminating if complemented with the next step—demonstrating the possibility of universal processes that cut across gender, education, ethnicity, and family structure" (p. 731).

The problem is that the case for universality is seriously compromised by the erasure of some of the diversity with which Bogenschneider started. Owing to considerations of statistical power, the analysis of parents' school involvement and children's grades across different racial-ethnic groups is confined to families with biological mothers and fathers. Most African American families are ruled out by this procedure because only 38% of Black children in 1990 lived with two parents, and the percent living with two biological parents had to be smaller still (O'Hare, Pollard, Mann, & Kent, 1991). Similarly, Bogenschneider's analysis of how "more stable, resource-rich environments" affect the impact of mothers' school involvement on children is not relevant to most African American families. The results show that children who live with both biological parents benefit from mothers' greater involvement, regardless of these mothers' level of education. Children who live with their mother and a stepfather also benefit from the mother's involvement, but only if the mother is in the high-education group. Again, these two-parent family structures do not apply to the majority of African Americans. Raising children in the context of a marriage (for those preferring to do so) is largely a White woman's privilege (Jarrett, 1994), as fully 79% of White children in 1990 lived with two parents—more than twice the percentage for Black children (O'Hare et al.).

One finding from this study does apply to most African American children and their mothers: In single-mother families, children's grades benefit from school-involved mothers regardless of mothers' level of education. In fact, when less educated single mothers are school involved, their children benefit even more than do those children who live with both biological parents and have a school-involved mother.

Note, however, that only 20% of single mothers were highly school-involved, compared with 51% of mothers in biological two-parent families (Bogenschneider, 1997, p. 729). Despite this much slimmer likelihood of involvement among single mothers, Bogenschneider lays her emphasis on the good impact on a child's grades when mothers do get school involved. She thus calls for "broad-based school and workplace polices that facilitate opportunities for parents to be involved in the

schooling of offspring as old as adolescents" (p. 732).

Even granting such opportunities for more school involvement, this is a tall order for African American single mothers, 61% of whom have incomes below poverty (O'Hare et al., 1991) and for whom sheer survival must surely be the paramount issue. Moreover, this analysis leaves all the burden of involvement in children's schooling on the single mother, and it sidesteps the structural issues (e.g., Black male incarceration, jobs that do not pay Black men a living wage, etc.) that stand in the way of heterosexual Black women finding viable marriage partners to provide companionship and to help with monitoring the child's education. Finally, it ignores the tendency of many Black parent-child relationships to become embedded in extended kinship networks, including "othermothers" (Collins, 1990) and surrogate fathers (Allen & Connor, 1997), some of whom may actively provide the school involvement that Bogenschneider only surveyed within the nuclear unit (see also Johnson, 1995). Indeed, Entwisle and Alexander (2000) have found that children in mother-grandmother families have a significant advantage in their transition to school (as seen in their first reading mark) compared with children living in other types of single-mother families. (For a similar kind of erasure, see Amato and Rivera, 1999, who found that the salutary impact of father involvement on children's problem behaviors holds for both biological fathers and for stepfathers and across Black, White, and Latino families. In limiting the sample to households with a married couple and children, the authors eliminate most African American mothers, fathers, and children, leaving only those whose household composition is most similar to that of White families. This erasure of the majority of contemporary Black family experiences is done without comment.)

Another instance of diversity compromised is found in Upchurch, Anshensel, Sucoff, and Levy-Storms (1999), who analyze adolescent sexual activity in relation to diverse neighborhood and family contexts. Here we find exclusion compounded by total erasure. In a sample of 870 Los Angeles adolescents that is remarkable for its careful attention to racial-ethnic diversity, the authors explore contextual accompaniments of the transition to a first sexual experience between the 8th and the 10th grades. Their procedure was to gain consent both from the parent(s) and the targeted individual and to conduct the interview either at the teenager's home or in some other private location chosen by the teenager. The interview process carefully builds rapport, asking the teenager a variety of questions about personal life, stress, and mental health. Only midway through this process does the interviewer pop the question of whether the respondent has "ever had sexual intercourse, and if so, how many months ago they had first had sex" (Upchurch, Levy-Storms, Sucoff, & Aneshensel, 1998, pp. 122–123).

Now, consider a 16-year-old adolescent who has had sexual feelings for (or activity with) a same-sex person, and this within the fiercely heterosexual climate of high school, and imagine the level of uncertainty and self-doubt attending these feelings or actions. Then imagine this individual sitting in the interview, taking in the question about having had "sexual intercourse," and understanding full well that this is the rhetorical stock-in-trade of heterosexuality. Surely, she or he will be effectively silenced, and yet, using a conservative estimate of 5%, a sample of 870 should harbor some 44 such individuals.

Perhaps some already had refused to be interviewed (the refusal rate of the 8th graders was 6%, and there was a further 23% attrition for the 10th-grade reinterviews; Upchurch et al., 1998). More than likely, however, some did stumble their way into the first or into both interviews, and these teenagers are a hidden factor in the findings, neither planned for nor recognized, their potential "contamination" of the data never signaled as a limitation of the study. Exclusion was here compounded by full erasure. Could any of the researchers (or the journal reviewers, friendly readers, or editors) have been gay, lesbian, or bisexual? Somehow, the error has been missed, heteronormative thinking has prevailed, and researchers have pushed some teenagers deeper into the closet. It is as if the heterosexual police were patrolling the neighborhoods, knocking on doors, and warning the deviants to stay inside. (See Whitbeck, Yoder, Hoyt, & Conger, 1999, for another study of adolescent sexuality using the same "sexual intercourse" question without qualification.)

Unpacking the Research Gaze of the Privileged

As Jarrett (1994, p. 45) affirmed, "researchers should look seriously at alternative family arrangements and cease to assume the superiority of mainstream family patterns." These two agendas are complementary, not identical. Looking seriously at alternative family arrangements (which is increasingly happening within family studies) will not erode the dominant discourse as long as mainstream-centric assumptions remain suppressed or unexamined. I have an image of a tourist bus pausing at an inner-city ghetto, its well-heeled tourists peering out at the locals from behind tinted one-way windows. The image then shifts to a more interactive mode, as some of the tourists exit the bus to mix with the locals. The more adventurous tourists coax invitations into nearby homes, their hosts providing family history accounts and stories about their hardships. The image ends with the tourists reboarding the bus and returning to their own homes and families.

If social science is unavoidably part tourism, then the task at hand is to make the tour more systematic and complete, and this means critically including ourselves (and people like us) in the sights that are seen. The research gaze must be turned now and again 180 degrees onto the gazers. As academic research professionals, we too easily forget that we are a highly privileged group in comparison with people in other strata of society, regardless of our social origins, our categorical differences, and the real impact of these differences on the allocation of academic rewards. When our research gaze trains on people in families with less "advantages" than we have, we can lose sight of the systemic nature of the structures of social stratification within which we, too, are embedded. Overclasses thrive in relation to the languishing of underclasses (Gans, 1999); the "advantaged" are implicated in the fortunes or misfortunes of the "disadvantaged." To focus our research gaze on the problematics only within one of these two poles is to leave the myth of the meritocracy unchallenged, as if all it takes is some reform at the bottom to render the system fair. The recent appearance of a *Handbook of Family Diversity* (Demo, Allen, & Fine, 2000) is a case in point. "Poverty and Economic Hardship" (Rank, 2000) are well documented, both in the chapter bearing that title and in other chapters addressing this topic, but the volume offers no treatment of privileged families, whose economic and cultural hegemony in part constitutes much of the diversity that is so well detailed by many of the authors. Privileged families are part of family diversity; they do not stand outside of it.

Studies of groups at the margins conducted by researchers from dominant groups—even the work of very caring scholars—may all too easily degenerate into an idle celebration of diversity, followed by a call for policy changes that might help "them," the people at the margins. We the researchers then reenact the dualistic thinking that creates hierarchy in the first place (Frankenberg, 1993; Hurtado & Stewart, 1997; West & Fenstermaker, 1995a, 1995b). Discursively, we position ourselves as the advantaged ones, and we restore "them," the disadvantaged, as an "other," different from and less fortunate than people like us. This is mainstream superiority, pure and simple, whether its gaze trains on family patterns, education, jobs, or anything else.

Celebrating diversity and working for appropriate policy changes are of course important priorities. My concern here is with the other step of this complex tangle: Until we in the dominant group begin to "unpack [the] invisible knapsack" of privileges (McIntosh, 1988) that accrue to our race, class, gender, and sexual orientation, our progress on all the other fronts will be retarded or stalled. We will slip back, without awareness, into White-think, middle-class-think, men-think, hetero-think or some combination of these, and the erasure of key components of the everyday experience of people in nondominant family arrangements will be inevitable.

THE INTERGENERATIONAL TRANSMISSION OF ENTITLEMENT: AN AGENDA FOR FAMILY STUDIES

Families and households are places where categorical memberships get constituted, solidified, celebrated, or held in contempt. "It is [in families]," hooks (1996, p. 72) wrote, "that most of us learn our ideas about race, gender, and class." To be sure, families are not the only such sites. Schools are virtual think tanks for new ways of perpetuating old social categories and for the creation of new ones, and peers may undo even the most deliberate instruction that parents pass on to their children. The same is true of television and the other mass media. Properly qualified, however, hooks's point merits notice, as families are usually a child's first introduction to social categories and the point of departure for revisions coming from other social locations.

Although family scholars have generated countless studies of parents and children, it is one of the oddities within family studies that the exploration of how people learn the entitlements that accrue to their social categories (with the partial exception of gender) has been deferred. Why has this kind of inquiry not found its way into family studies? Part of the problem is that opportunity is only seen as problematic when some group or category does not have it. Rarely is the *presence* of opportunity the target of critical scrutiny. That is, we tend to see the continuum as ranging from advantage to disadvantage. Perhaps we should see the endpoints as overadvantage and underadvantage, for then the systemic interconnections between the two poles appear less opaque, and the excesses within the "over" side become more transparent.

Another reason for the inattention to what is learned in families about categories is that some of the writers (e.g., Hill Collins, Baca Zinn) who have done the most to alert us to issues of systemic inequality have, unfortunately, discredited a family socialization perspective as a proper vehicle for analyzing these issues. There are good historical reasons for this, crystallized within the academy by the reaction to the Moynihan Report (1965), which essentially blamed the "tangle of pathology" of Black poverty on the *culture* of poverty learned within Black homes. Critics countered this kind of victim-blaming analysis with a structural focus, arguing that the macrostructure of differential economic opportunity, not family and community culture, should be the focus of any attempt to understand and contest inequality.

It is time to call a halt to the "either-or" mentality that would have us choose between macrostructural and cultural approaches to inequality (see Collins et al., 1995; West & Fenstermaker, 1995a, 1995b). The culture of the home and local network surely do make a difference. As Entwisle and Alexander (2000) have shown, children whose parents expect them to do better in school do so, and those same parents are more likely to take actions on behalf of their children's education. Bogenschneider's (1997) finding discussed earlier does deserve notice: Even relatively uneducated single mothers can make a big difference when they get more involved in their child's education. "Family values," expectations, and opinions do matter, *and* oppressive macrostructures can make it extremely difficult to dare to reach for very much, even for one's children. Studying family culture and socialization need not lead to blaming this or that type of family. But the charge of victim blaming will be deserved as long as the research gaze peers exclusively at the family culture of those who have been displaced to the margins. The corrective is to study family culture more thoroughly, not to avoid studying it at all, and one way to do this is to focus on the family culture of the overprivileged.

In the next several sections, I offer a narrative account of how I learned categorical privileges, and I stress the process of intergenerational transmission within my family of origin. In this effort, I stand on the shoulders of writers outside family studies who have provided invaluable guidance about undertaking analyses of this sort (Fine, Weis, Powell, & Wong, 1997; Frankenberg, 1993; McIntosh, 1988; Thompson & Tyagi, 1996). Regarding White privilege, Roman (1997) has warned that "it is difficult to discern the difference between ritual enactments of confession and genuine self-/social criticism," adding that "reflexivity has often given way to uncritical narratives of redemption" (p. 271). Heeding this admonition, my purpose is to begin to turn the social reproduction of privilege into the same kind of critical object of inquiry as more familiar topical objects, such as poverty, welfare, and crime.

Jewish Insiders, "Goyisha" Outsiders

I grew up in an "isolated nuclear family" in Miami Beach in the 1940s and 1950s. The world presented to me consisted of insiders and outsiders. There were Jews like us, who comprised perhaps a majority of the people who lived in Miami Beach, and there were gentiles, who were referred to anonymously as "the goyim." Concerning the goyim world, further distinctions were salient in my household. A Jewish boy like me will marry a nice Jewish girl, not a shikza—a non-Jewish woman. Shikza was probably one of my first exposures to intersecting categories. I often heard this word in my childhood, especially in sentences such as, "He's going out with a shikza," or worse yet, "He married a shikza." I cannot remember ever hearing the word "shagitz," a non-Jewish man. Perhaps it is because shagitzes were less dangerous. Although a Jewish woman who marries a shagitz is doing a very unfortunate thing, her children will still be Jewish. But a Jewish man involved with a shikza is a more serious matter. He is a man, he has agency, and he should know better. If he marries a shikza and she is unwilling to convert to Judaism, his children cannot be Jewish. Jews are chosen people, I was taught through the myriad implicit messages and the intonations that accompanied informal talk, so no one of sound mind would deprive his children of their privileged heritage.

Marriage, Divorce, Widowhood, Singlehood, and Heterosexuality

Note that in my household, marriage was the default setting, the normal state for an adult. Whom you marry, not whether you marry, was the matter of moment. Divorce was a disgrace. Widowhood was a misfortune. Remaining single was clearly deviant, although that deviance was gendered. The measured way my father occasionally declared of someone, "She's a *spinster*" (he emphasized it for effect), conveyed a clear notion of something fundamentally undesirable or problematic about her, whereas "bachelor" status for males was more likely to evoke mere curiosity.

Notice, too, that heterosexuality was likewise the default setting in the language of my household. Whereas marriage was a marked category (it was one among several recognized possibilities, albeit inferior ones), heterosexuality was unmarked; that is, it was the *only* possibility in the discursive repertoire of my household. There was no such thing as a person's "sexual orientation."

Upper-Middle-Class Socialization

I also learned about social classes. Early on I learned that there are rich people, poor people, and people like us who were trying to get wealthy. My father grew up poor, and he endlessly regaled my sister and me with stories of having worked his way through college and medical school. Raised in Chicago by a widowed mother, his achievement as a physician was held up to us as an almost Godly accomplishment. That success, however, was tempered by his experience of the Depression years, and my childhood was replete with cautions about "knowing the value of a dollar," and warnings that "we'll wind up in the poorhouse if we're not careful." At times, I almost believed that we were one step from poverty, but my father's medical practice and real estate investments were thriving, and it would have been difficult to sustain the idea that we were almost poor.

Within this overall framework in which wealth was pitted against poverty as if in mortal combat, I learned a set of upper-middle-class entitlements presented almost as axioms about how my life will unfold. I will be a doctor like my father, or failing that, a lawyer. The world of occupations was presented as a hierarchy, with medicine at the very top. Osteopaths and dentists were failed doctors "who couldn't make the grade," and chiropractors were "quacks." I was certain I would be a doctor until I almost flunked out of college. Before then, there was never any doubt in my family that I would become any kind of professional I chose to be (in the most unlikely event of my deciding not to be a doctor). I learned to assume that the ultimate function of education is to prepare you for a prestigious profession; that work in your job will be stimulating, enjoyable, socially important, even fun; and that very ample income—far more than "enough to support your family"—is a mere byproduct of this important work you do (see also Connell, 1998). Perhaps most important, I learned that there are no externally imposed constraints to arriving at your chosen profession. Frequently warned about anti-Semitism, we were protected from it by living in Miami Beach, and by attending Jewish summer camps "up North" from the time we were young children. Under these sheltered circumstances, the only barrier to success was seen to be your own lack of gumption.

My gumption short-circuited in my early adolescence. Conflicts with my father accelerated, my grades in public school deteriorated, and I was hanging around with the "wrong element." Here is the flavor of it: I periodically went with one or more of these friends late at night to the school grounds, where we gathered rock-like baby coconuts and fired them through the classroom windows of those teachers we hated the most, smirking triumphantly the next morning when the principal lamented that "vandals once again struck Nautilus Junior High School." I hated school. My father's response to my declining grades was first to blame my mother and then to send me away in 1957 to a New England prep school, where he hoped I would "get some discipline." There, when it became clear that I was in danger of failing geometry, my father called the headmaster and demanded to know how I could have barely opened my geometry book; after all, he was spending a lot of money to send his son to private school. The result was an arrangement for him to pay extra money for special tutoring, and I passed the course.

Upper-Middle-Class White Deviance

Adolescent rebellions are of course commonplace in American culture. My own defiance, marked by surfeits of self-assertion and secret sabotage against any authority figures who had power over me, was surely not unusual, and it reflected my race, class, and gender privileges. I never noticed the privileges I already enjoyed or the ones that were mapped out for my future. On the contrary, I focused on pushing through any limits I encountered. I fancied that there should be no barriers to my full expansion within anything I wanted to do, whether that was weaving in and out of traffic at breakneck speed on my bicycle, tearing up the golf course greens of the country club at which no Jews were allowed, or hiding in the bushes to hurl plastic water bags at passing cars.

All of this was class, race, and gender-entitled acting out (Chambliss, 1997). I was filled with the hot air of my station and my father's aura of self-importance. One might say that my petty rule breaking and defiant mentality were subsidized by upper-middle-class White male privilege. From a young age, I was primed for success. I was given to the belief that any difficulties I encountered should yield quickly to my efforts to surmount them and that life was an opportunity to express myself. At times when I might have faltered, my father's money and the resources and skills he could buy for me—speech therapists to attend to the aftermath of my cleft palate, a "nose job" to "correct" my "Jewish nose," Miami Beach residence and Jewish summer camps up North to protect against anti-Semitism, prep school, tutors when I needed them, college tuition and all my living expenses at a small, private liberal arts college—these were like a steady wind at my back blowing me forward, fueling the illusion that I was an individual creating my own destiny. My father's money, my family's Whiteness, and my maleness were a triumvirate of capital I could rely on without becoming aware of how they were subsidizing me.

Learning Gender

My mother's scant presence in this account thus far is not an oversight. I grew up in a patriarchy. My mother devoted herself almost entirely to meeting my father's unrelenting needs, interests, and demands, and except for rare occasions when she opposed something he wanted (e.g., another real estate purchase that would add too egregiously to her already considerable management burden), his decisions were the ones that moved our family in matters both large and small. He had an ever-expanding list of things for her to do, and he became impatient and angry with her when they were not done promptly and to his satisfaction. When he wanted her to work in his office and hire domestic workers to look after the house and my sister and me, she did so. When he wanted her to type a letter or edit and type his medical papers, she dropped everything else to do so. He frequently required her ego-boosting services, which she provided. If they went somewhere, he was the one who insisted on it. Except for her fantasies, her periods of psychotherapy, and her love of reading, which she could do only in the interstices of his demands, she did not have a life of her own. Nor do I think she wanted one, at least most of the time. It was a fairly benign arrangement, as patriarchies go. Along with his imperialism, my father had a knack for creating an aura of drama around the facets of his life, and my mother was more than willing for him to pull her into that energy. There was some levity and mirth. They could laugh uproariously together, and there were spontaneous eruptions of singing and dancing in my household at those times when my father wanted that to happen.

Levity notwithstanding, this was a lopsided arrangement, resulting in that skewed pattern of male entitlement and female subservience described so astutely by many modern feminists (e.g., Dinnerstein, 1976; Frye, 1983). I surely would have embraced the same model, had my father shown more of an interest in the internals of my world and had he not been so stingy with his approval. Instead, I identified intensely with my mother, seeking her alliance against my father's peremptory ways and drawn to that same readiness to nurture that must have drawn my father to her. It took me a long time to begin to work through the contradictions. On one hand, I came to my marriage with a yearning to have my own needs anticipated, attended to, and satisfied; on the other, I saw clearly the folly of expecting to be waited on, and I knew unequivocally that both people in a partnership should be able to have a life of their own. As a young adult, then, I was primed to recognize some problematic elements of male entitlement, and when feminism resurfaced in the late 1960s, I was ready (however ambivalently at first) to grapple with it.

Learning Whiteness

In my youth I quickly picked up a nonreflexive knowledge of White supremacy. As I wrote elsewhere (Marks & Leslie, 2000):

> the official belief system of my family was that public racial segregation was an unmitigated evil

and . . . skin color should make no difference in the way people are treated. In everyday informal talk, however, the racial divide was as big as the Grand Canyon. There were White people and there were *Schvartzas*—African American people, whom I encountered only in their apparent function of working for people like us." (p. 404)

We usually had a maid. Live-in maids had to be White because Black maids were not permitted to sleep in our house, nor did I know of any who slept in my friends' houses. As a form of intended humor, my father would sometimes say of my mother, in her presence, "Golda has some Negro blood." I later understood this humor to be one of the variety of forms through which my father put my mother in her place beneath him, as "Negroes" were presumed to be our inferiors.

Throughout my childhood, racial segregation was a legally enforced fact of life. Riding on city busses, I learned early on that Blacks were required to sit in the back of the bus and Whites could sit anywhere else, and I also learned that this was a terrible thing. But the rules of segregation seemed merely confusing to me, something I occasionally bumped into and never at the expense of my own convenience. I have a vivid childhood memory of being in downtown Miami (a rare event) and needing to find a public bathroom somewhere. I remember peering over the labels on four different doors: "Men," "Women," "Colored Men," "Colored Women." Never having seen this before, I stood there immobilized. My need was urgent enough, but these labels referenced something momentous, and I did not want to make a mistake. Back at home in Miami Beach, it never occurred to me that these confusing signs were absent simply because African Americans had no rightful claim even to segregated public spaces there. They came across the causeways from "Colortown," and although their bodily needs might be privately accommodated by us Whites who employed them, no allowance was made for the existence of these people other than through their service to us and our families.

We Jewish White folks, I learned, were the true center of Miami Beach; everyone else was either an outsider or an employee, particularly African Americans. We—my parents, my friends, my school, and I—had no awareness that this entire racial system rested on the legacy of slavery, which continued to subsidize our privileges.

Until I was sent away to prep school, I had no Black schoolmates. African American peers were so alien to my experience that they may as well have lived in a different country. At the same time, however, they were symbolically and discursively present. On the playground in Miami Beach, a male might call out to a male friend, "Hey, Schvartz" (dropping the final "a" in "Schvartza"), intended as the kind of joking "put-down" that expresses intimacy and caring. You bond by demonstrating that you are close enough to refer to someone in the language of an inferior category, knowing that he will know that you do not really "mean" it, and thereby reinforcing each others' brotherhood within the superior category. You are both White, and you are both Jewish; and you know that he will know what "Schvartz" means. (Calling someone a "queer" or a "faggot" was a still more common way of achieving the same solidarity.)

Perhaps 20% of the students at my prep school were African Americans. It took some time for me to see these classmates as normal humans, not because I felt hostile but because they represented such an alien "other" in my experience that I was ill prepared to see anything about them as being the same as myself. I remember wanting to find out if a dark-skinned schoolmate's penis was the same color as the rest of him. I have a fainter recollection of stealing a look in the toilet before he flushed it, eager to find out if his feces were a different color than my own. Again, racism may thrive on sheer ignorance; it does not require felt hostility to rear its head. The first evening at prep school, when another African American schoolmate admired one of my sport jackets and asked me if he could wear it to dinner, I felt reluctant. What did he really want? Was he going to steal it from me? I said, "Okay, but don't get it dirty." In my experience, African Americans always had been inferiors. Although Black females had often fed me and cared for me when I was child, I still thought that Black bodies were dirtier than White ones, and I feared that the dirt of a Black body might rub off on my new sport jacket.

Small wonder, as hooks (1996) noted, that the liveliest question African American parents have had about a newborn was not whether the child was a girl or a boy but how dark or light the child's skin color was: "To be born light meant that one was born with an advantage, recognized by everyone. To be born dark was to start life handicapped, with a serious disadvantage" (p. 121). And small wonder, too, that back at prep school in 1958, I recall an occasion when Tim, an African American male peer, holding out his light-skinned arm for all those present to behold, declared: "I like to think I just have a nice suntan." The lessons learned in my family and then on the playground were simply being reflected here on the other side of the color line. Ignorant racist beliefs about the dirtiness of Black bodies on one side, unacceptability and hatred of black skin color or on the other.

The fact is, I came to prep school from a family and community in which no one took responsibility for our White-skin–privileges. My parents were liberal democrats from Chicago, living in Miami Beach. They voted democratic in part because they believed that government should "help the poor" and should do more to dismantle the racial segregation laws. Conveniently, there was an amorphous group of "deep South" Whites in places like Alabama, Mississippi, and upstate Florida who called Negroes "Niggers" and who did explicit things or said specific words that conveyed "prejudice." Prejudiced White southerners outside our community then became the repository for the twin demons of prejudice and discrimination, and we could maintain the illusion that racism was a form of victimization in which the villains were faraway outsiders who had nothing to do with us. Bad people were prejudiced, and we were good people. So when African American domestic workers insisted on entering and leaving our home through the back door and steadfastly declined invitations to sit at the dinner table with us, my parents could feel how terrible it was that prejudiced bigots had contaminated these people's sense of self-worth—without, however, any understanding of our own complicity with the system. (Our meals, for example, were ritually served to us in courses, and the sequence of responsibilities engendered a show of *readiness* to serve that was anything but compatible with eating when we ate. Of course, why should "they" want to eat with "us?")

My internal reaction to Tim's "suntan" comment was thus continuous with my family training. Poor Tim, filled with internalized racism, damaged by that prejudice coming from faraway bigots! Instead of crediting Tim with making his way through a system whose White majority constructed his otherness at every turn, I got to position myself as superior again—superior both to the faraway bigots who "caused" Tim to mirror a racist construction about skin color and to Tim himself for not being powerful enough to resist and contest the construction. Instead of scrutinizing the White tradition of enhancing *my* appearance through darkening my skin up to the point of not getting "*too* tan"), I could enter a condescending internal dialogue in which the focus trained on how Tim dealt with *his* skin color in the face of bad White people who are "prejudiced." Instead of taking a reflexive turn to recognize my own complicity with the White supremacy he was mirroring, I used the opportunity to internally restore my dominance.

By the time I graduated from prep school in 1960, the racial divide still loomed large in my awareness. I had shed my initial uncertainty about whether Black bodies worked the same way White ones did, and I had become friendly with several African American peers, but I had not dispelled my core sensibility that African Americans were essentially different from me, and they had a handicap that had nothing to do with good people like me. I retained the sense that they, not I, were the ones in whom a difference resided, just as I believed that other people, not I, were the ones who responded to this "difference" with prejudice and discrimination, resulting in African Americans having needless obstacles in the way of becoming more like me, with all my advantages. And I carefully contextualized the African Americans who had become my peers as being somehow apart from the millions of African Americans outside the insular confines of my prep school world. These outside people were still an alien "other," and I had not yet found a reason to shake that perception, nor had anyone ever encouraged me to do so.

Around that time, I went to Chicago to visit my sister. While there, returning from a visit alone to a relative, I got off the train at the wrong stop—Englewood instead of Ingleside—and I found myself in the middle of a Black neighborhood. Not realizing how far I was from my sister's apartment in Hyde Park, I began to walk in what I thought was the right direction, and now aware that the only faces I was seeing were Black ones, I quickly became fearful and my steps became faster. Soon, my fear turned to terror and my accelerating pace broke into a quick jog and then a full run, propelled by fantasies of gangs of Blacks who would kill me because I was White. I ran for blocks and blocks, scrutinizing every street corner and every space between buildings for the grave danger lurking there. Hopelessly lost, I wound up the only white-skinned person on a bus. I recall sitting halfway out of my seat, surveying the faces, hyper-vigilant, wanting to get an edge on whatever peril could be there riding with me. Clearly, the peril was in myself.

Bell Hooks (1996) triggered this Chicago memory from 35 years past. She recalled the place of her own youth, "where black folks associated whiteness with the terrible, the terrifying, the terrorizing" (p. 39), and again I become painfully aware of the mirroring effect. The racial socialization in my White family meshes tightly with that in Black families. Both are reflections of the legacy of White supremacy, but the Black side of it is firmly rooted in historical realities, whereas the White terror has lost touch with its own origins. Create the racial hierarchy, create the terror, forget that we Whites created it (or worse yet, assume that others created it and that we ourselves do nothing to recreate it), and then reappropriate it as mortal danger to our own White selves. "Those who are significantly endangered come to be defined as inherently dangerous" Kaye/Kantrowitz (1996, p. 125) wrote. The fear in Whites, hooks (1996, pp. 267–268) added, "is the first sign of the internalization in the white psyche of white supremacist sentiments. It serves to mask white power and privilege." The terrible conclusion is that when White entitlement flows so readily into fear of Blacks, then redoubled acts of White terror (done in the name of self-protection) can never be far behind.

DISCUSSION

Implications of the Narrative

Privilege and the way people learn it in families needs to become a research topic, or "object of inquiry," perhaps a "social problem" on the level of "poverty" or "juvenile delinquency." The legacy of my own youth was an intricately crafted entitlement complex that I learned how to keep invisible to myself. My parents mediated to me an elaborate package of insiders and outsiders. They chose a community and created a home world in which our race and class privileges could not only thrive but remain (with the exception of our Jewish heritage) unmarked. The people whose categories were discursively marked were the "less fortunate" others stationed around us. These outsider "others" then provided some important material support for our privileges, as well as constant symbolic reminders of how much "better off" we were (see Morrison, 1992). As do all children, I internalized much of this world and learned how to reproduce it. Our family was pulled by the lumbering locomotive of my father's professional achievement and self-distinction, and the trip was not designed for sustained reflexivity about the passing territory. A "dominant discourse" pervaded my sensibilities—not yet the formalized version of the academy but the more insidious kind that frames one's assumptions about everyday life.

I suggest that teasing out the lessons of the 1960s in family studies will mean extending the relativizing currents that marked that era. This will not be easy, and as long as people from the dominant groups (such as myself) make up the vast majority of family scholars, we will need a dual confrontation with the institutional practices of hierarchy. First, we need to redouble our efforts to keep hearing the voices of nondominant others clearly enough to get ourselves decentered. Reading their works—repetitively, so that they become integral to how we see the world—is one way to move in that direction. Second, the topic of family privilege itself needs to become a prominent research focus, and I end with some thoughts about how this project might unfold.

Strategies for Spotlighting Family Privilege and Entitlement

Merely altering our written and spoken language could make a major contribution to relativizing the centrality of dominant groups in our discourse and in our mind's eye. The success in moving toward less sexist language shows that this can be done, and these gains should be extended to race, social class, and sexual orientation. When respondents are all White or all some other dominant category, it is not enough to signal this fact only in describing the sample and in noting the limitations of the study. Appropriate qualifiers should be inserted throughout, and they may make a difference in the way a reader's perspective and research imagination get triggered by the discourse. For example, in the discussion section of a recent study of early sexuality among rural Whites, we should not have to wait until the 5th paragraph to be reminded that it is *White* rural people we are learning about (Whitbeck et al., 1999). In contrast, consider the discussion section of a recent article about sibling relationships in rural African American families (Brody, Stoneman, Smith, & Gibson, 1999). Here, we are reminded nearly in every paragraph that we are reading about African Americans, and we are alerted repeatedly to possible differences from the patterns of Whites. Notice, too, that the title of the first article is utterly generic ("Early Adolescent Sexual Activity: A De-

velopmental Study"), whereas the title of the second article is contextually specific ("Sibling Relationships in Rural African American Families"). When we universalize our presentation of dominant categories but clearly signal the specifics of nondominant categories, we perpetuate the tendency to mark the latter as an "other" and to foster an "in-group"–"out-group" mentality. The solution, again, is to focus the research gaze more prominently on the categorical attributes of dominance by marking the dominant categories at least as repetitively as we mark the nondominant categories.

We need to turn narratives of privilege into a new research motif. It is not clear how this genre might unfold, and I know of no models in family studies other than my own attempt. Moreover, for students in contemporary classrooms, narratives such as mine may be met by distancing moves that are all too convenient. The 1940s and 1950s crudeness of some of my material too readily lends itself to dismissive and distancing reactions on the part of youthful readers, much like the "prejudiced" White southerners of my youth provided me with a convenient foil in which I could hide my own racism. Accordingly, we need some narratives of learned entitlement generated by people who came of age in the 1970s and 1980s. We need to hear female as well as male voices, and we need to know how learned entitlements may change their contours in accordance with different religious backgrounds and from within a variety of ethnic groups.

Although I have advocated for an informed and critical "family socialization" perspective for the study of learned entitlement, I also suggested earlier that schools in general and peer groups in particular are important vehicles for the consolidation of entitled self-concepts. Gubrium and Holstein (1990) have argued cogently against any narrowly geographic exploration of family phenomena, suggesting that to privilege the household as *the* authentic site of family construction and maintenance is altogether arbitrary. Family, they insist, is to be found wherever consistent claims about it become organized, defended, and enforced.

The practical research implications of this view are enormous, for it expands the array of possibilities for studying family privilege, whether through narrative or through some other strategy. When a parent or parents purchase a home, for example, they typically act so as to preserve, perpetuate, or extend whatever social class and race privileges they already have. The sense of entitlement they bring to this process might be explored through narratives in which respondents who have children (or intend to have them) talk about how they select one neighborhood instead of another, and one home rather than another within their neighborhood of choice. Equally revealing would be narratives generated from real estate agents, perhaps tape-recorded conversations with their clients. Buying a home is buying into overadvantage or underadvantage, depending on one's resources, as there is a clear and direct link from property taxes to the funding of public education and the quality of local schools (Kozol, 1991). A school in a wealthy district may spend double or triple the amount per student that a school in a poor district spends. Fully cognizant of this connection, people in privileged statuses never stumble into home-buying decisions, and real estate agents are not unlike school guidance counselors insofar as both have the job of steering their respective clients into the slots in which they "belong," based on appearance, language and rhetoric, demeanor, skin color, and other cues that can help profile people about whom little is really known.

It thus becomes arbitrary to see the origin of children's sense of entitlement only in the messages they hear from their parents. To be sure, these messages remain an excellent conduit of this phenomenon and therefore should be studied. But, we can also study it in schools, in real estate offices, on playgrounds, and elsewhere, for in selecting a neighborhood and a house in which children can grow up, privileged families set up the conditions for the transmission and reproduction of their privileges. Their children then inherit these conditions, including the best of educational facilities and teachers, as well as like-minded peers who will usually help to keep them on course. Like the opening of automatic doors, the whole process is set up in such a way that it may become virtually unnoticed by those who are its beneficiaries, and it therefore may require some intricately crafted research strategies to bring these family entitlement processes to light.

NOTE

Many people have offered me valuable support and feedback at various phases of this work. I am especially grateful to Katherine Allen, Michael Brown, Susan Cassano, Kimberly Cook, Jane Gilgun, Joan Marks, Peter Marks, Peggy McIntosh, and Alexis Walker.

REFERENCES

Allen, K. R. (2000). A conscious and inclusive family studies. *Journal of Marriage and the Family, 62,* 4–17.

Allen, W. D., & Connor, M. (1997). An African American perspective on generative fathering. In A. J. Hawkins & D. C. Dollahite (Eds.), *Generative fathering: Beyond deficit perspectives* (pp. 52–70). Newbury Park, CA: Sage.

Amato, P. R. (2000). Diversity within single-parent families. In Demo, D. H., Allen, K. R., & Fine, M. A. (Eds.), *Handbook of family diversity* (pp. 149–172). New York: Oxford University Press.

Amato, P. R., & Rivera, F. (1999). Parental involvement and children's behavior problems. *Journal of Marriage and the Family, 61,* 375–384.

Bernard, J. (1972). *The future of marriage.* New York: World.

Bogenschneider, K. (1997). Parental involvement in adolescent schooling: A proximal process with transcontextual validity. *Journal of Marriage and the Family, 59,* 718–733.

Brody, G. H., Stoneman, Z., Smith, T., & Gibson, N. M. (1999). Sibling relationships in rural African American families. *Journal of Marriage and the Family, 61,* 1046–1057.

Chambliss, W. J. (1997). The saints and the roughnecks. In J. M. Henslin (Ed.), *Down to earth sociology: Introductory readings* (pp. 246–260). New York: Free Press.

Collins, P. H. (1990). *Black feminist thought: Knowledge, consciousness, and the politics of empowerment.* New York: Routledge.

Collins, P. H. (1998). Shifting the center: Race, class, and feminist theorizing about motherhood. In S. J. Ferguson (Ed.), *Shifting the center: Understanding contemporary families* (pp. 291–310). Mountain View, CA: Mayfield.

Collins, P. H., Maldonado, L. A., Takagi, D. Y., Thorne, B., Weber, L., & Winant, H. (1995). Symposium on West and Fenstermaker's "Doing Difference." *Gender & Society, 9,* 491–506.

Connell, R. W. (1998). Disruptions: Improper masculinities and schooling. In M. S. Kimmel & M. A. Messner (Eds.), *Men's lives* (4th ed., pp. 141–154). Boston: Allyn and Bacon.

Demo, D. H., Allen, K. R., & Fine, M. A. (Eds.). (2000). *Handbook of family diversity.* New York: Oxford University Press.

Dinnerstein, D. (1976). *The mermaid and the minotaur: Sexual arrangements and human malaise.* New York: Harper Colophon.

Entwisle, D. R., & Alexander, K. L. (2000). Diversity in family structure: Effects on schooling. In D. H. Demo, K. R. Allen, & M. A. Fine (Eds.), *Handbook of family diversity* (pp. 316–337). New York: Oxford University Press.

Fine, M., Weis, L., Powell, L. C., & L. M. Wong (Eds.). (1997). *Off white: Readings on race, power, and society.* New York: Routledge.

Frankenberg, R. (1993). *White women, race matters: The social construction of whiteness.* Minneapolis, MN: University of Minnesota Press.

Frye, M. (1983). *The politics of reality.* Trumansburg, NY: Crossing Press.

Gans, H. J. (1999). Positive functions of the undeserving poor: Uses of the underclass in America. In S. J. Ferguson (Ed.), *Mapping the social landscape: Readings in sociology* (2nd ed., pp. 288–302). Mountain View, CA: Mayfield.

Gubrium, J. F., & Holstein, J. A. (1990). *What is family?* Mountain View, CA: Mayfield.

hooks, b. (1996). *Killing rage.* New York: Owl Books.

Hurtado, A., & Stewart, A. I. (1997). Through the looking glass: Implications of studying whiteness for feminist methods. In M. Fine, L. Weis, L. C. Powell, & L. M. Wong (Eds.), *Off white: Readings on race, power, and society* (pp. 297–311). New York: Routledge.

Jarrett, R. (1994). Living poor: Family life among single parent African American women. *Social Problems, 41,* 30–49.

Johnson, M. (1995). Maternal agency vs. the brotherhood of males. In J. K. Gardiner (Ed.), *Provoking agents: Gender and agency in theory and practice* (pp. 152–166). Urbana: University of Illinois Press.

Kaye-Kantrowitz, M. (1996). Jews in the U.S.: The rising costs of Whiteness. In B. Thompson & S. Tyagi (Eds.), *Names we call home: Autobiography on racial identity* (pp. 120–137). New York: Routledge.

Kozol, J. (1991). *Savage inequalities: Children in America's schools.* New York: Harper.

Marks, S. R., & Leslie, L. A. (2000). Family diversity and intersecting categories: Toward a richer approach to multiple roles. In D. H. Demo, K. R. Allen, & M. A. Fine (Eds.), *Handbook of family diversity* (pp. 402–423). New York: Oxford University Press.

McIntosh, P. (1988). *White privilege and male privilege: A personal account of coming to see correspondences through work in women's studies.* Working paper 189, Wellesley College Center for Research on Women, Wellesley, MA.

Messer-Davidow, E. (1995). Acting otherwise. In J. K. Gardiner (Ed.), *Provoking agents: Gender and agency in theory and practice* (pp. 23–51). Urbana: University of Illinois Press.

Morrison, T. (1992). *Playing in the dark.* New York: Vintage.

Moynihan, D. (1965). *The Negro family: The case for national action.* Washington, DC: Office of Policy Planning and Research, U.S. Department of Labor.

O'Hare, W. P., Pollard, K. M., Mann, T. L., & Kent, M. M. (Eds.) (1991). African Americans in the 1990s. *Population Bulletin, 46* (1)..

O'Neill, N., & O'Neill, G. (1972). *Open marriage.* New York: Avon.

Rank, M. R. (2000). Poverty and economic hardship in families. In D. H. Demo, K. R. Allen, & M. A. Fine (Eds.), *Handbook of family diversity* (pp. 293–315). New York: Oxford University Press.

Roman, L. G. (1997). Denying (white) racial privilege: Redemption discourses and the uses of fantasy. In M. Fine, L. Weis, L. C. Powell, & L. M. Wong (Eds.), *Off white: Readings on race, power, and society* (pp. 270–282). New York: Routledge.

Seccombe, K., James, D., & Walters, K. B. (1998). "They think you ain't much of nothing": The social construction of the welfare mother. *Journal of Marriage and the Family, 60,* 849–865.

Stack, C. (1974). *All our kin.* New York: Harper and Row.

Thompson, B., & Tyagi, S. (Eds.). (1996). *Names we call home: Autobiography on racial identity.* New York: Routledge.

Upchurch, D. M., Levy-Storms, L., Sucoff, C. A., & Aneshensel, C. S. (1998). Gender and ethnic differences in the timing of sexual activity. *Family Planning Perspectives, 30,* 121–127.

Upchurch, D. M., Anshensel, C. S., Sucoff, C. A., & Levy-Storms, L. (1999). Neighborhood and family contexts of adolescent sexual activity. *Journal of Marriage and the Family, 61,* 920–933.

Uttal, L. (1999). Using kin for child care: Embedment in the socioeconomic networks of extended families. *Journal of Marriage and the Family, 61,* 845–857.

West, C., & Fenstermaker, S. (1995a). Doing difference. *Gender & Society, 9,* 8–37.

West, C., & Fenstermaker, S. (1995b). Reply: (Re)Doing difference. *Gender & Society, 9,* 506–513.

Whitbeck, L. B., Yoder, K. A., Hoyt, D. R., & Conger, R. D. (1999). Early adolescent sexual activity: A developmental study. *Journal of Marriage and the Family, 61,* 934–946.

STEPHANIE COONTZ   *The Evergreen State College*

Historical Perspectives on Family Studies

This article explores the relationship of historical research to contemporary family studies. Family history was influenced greatly by fields such as sociology and anthropology, leading it to make several contributions to those fields in turn. The continuing collaboration of these disciplines can significantly enrich current family research, practice, and policy making. History's specific contribution lies in its attention to context. Although historical research confirms sociologic and ethnographic findings on the diversity of family forms, for example, it also reveals that all families are not created equal. The advantage of any particular type of family at any particular time is constructed out of contingent and historically variable social relationships. Historical research allows researchers to deepen their analysis of family diversity and family change by challenging widespread assumptions about what is and what is not truly new in family life. Such research complicates generalizations about the impact of family change and raises several methodological cautions about what can be compared and controlled for in analyzing family variations and outcomes.

When I was invited to contribute an article summarizing recent work and new directions in historical research on families, my first thought was to focus on the contributions of historians to the understanding of contemporary families. Almost immediately, however, I realized that the most

Family Studies and History, Evergreen State College, Olympia, WA 98502 (coontzs@hotmail.com).

Key Words: class, comparative family forms and functions, family history, family methodology, family diversity, gender and age relations, marriage.

striking feature of family history until recently has been its enormous debt to other disciplines. In consequence, I decided to discuss what historians have learned from other fields and to suggest a few areas where we may be able to repay our debts.

For years, historians treated families either as natural, taken-for-granted backdrops to "real" history or as mere epiphenomena, sets of interpersonal relationships far too individualized to accommodate systematic historical analysis. Only gradually did historians learn from sociologists, demographers, and economists to see families as social institutions in which variations could be related to socioeconomic pressures, cultural conflicts, and political transformations.

Initially, historians often drew outdated lessons from these other disciplines, citing early sociologists, for example, on how modernization and industrialization caused the decline of the "traditional" extended family. During the 1960s, however, the Cambridge Group for the History of Population and Social Structure discovered that from the 16th through the 19th centuries, mean household size had remained fairly constant, averaging about 4.75, and that even the largest households contained relatively few kin. Other researchers found that industrialization actually increased the incidence of extended family coresidence in many regions.

Some historians then went to the other extreme, suggesting that the distinctive feature of Western European and American history was the early and long-standing predominance of nuclear families. Later research, however, demonstrated an important kernel of truth in earlier generalizations about the decline of extended families. Because life spans were shorter in the past, comparatively few families had enough living members to potentially reside as a multigenerational household. Even a small number of extended-family households represented a high proportion of all such potential arrangements. Today, by contrast, even large numbers of coresident extended families embody but a tiny fraction of potential multigenerational households, indicating a major shift in preferred living arrangements. Similarly, idealization of nuclear family privacy was a fairly recent historical alternative to a system in which servants, boarders, lodgers, or visiting distant kin moved more freely in and out of the household and in which little value was placed on constructing a special sphere of interaction for the married couple and their children (Hareven, 1987, 1996; Ruggles, 1994).

Nevertheless, as historians returned to their own training—making more precise distinctions among regions, diverse class or cultural patterns, and situational differences in family life and sexuality—their research continued to challenge unilineal generalizations about the impact of modernization on families. Thomas Bender, for example, used ethnographies along with history to complicate older ideas about a transition from "gemeinschaft" to "gesellschaft" relations. Bender suggested that researchers study the tension, interaction, and sometimes mutual dependence of those modes of social behavior, pointing out that the spread of contractual relations in some areas of life has sometimes strengthened communal relations in another (Bender, 1982).

Other historians demonstrated the fallacy of postulating linear transitions from one family "type" to another. In the ancient Mediterranean world, households and groupings of relatives were so disparate that a single meaning for family could not be discerned. Family membership has since contracted and expanded in different periods, places, and social classes. Averaging out these trends hides the fact that changes in one group often went in opposing directions to changes in another, which makes it difficult to privilege one set of changes as inherently more modern. Thus, historical research on families supports criminologist Michael Maltz's caution about the problems that arise when the field of statistics is viewed as the study of averages rather than as the study of variation (Davidoff, Doolittle, Fink, & Holden, 1999; Herlihy, 1985; Maltz, 1994; Seccombe, 1993).

By the 1970s, influenced by family systems theory, historians also began to investigate the processes that have linked family members to each other and to external social institutions. Several researchers pioneered the study of the life cycle, and later of the life course, examining the intersection between individual life histories, family needs, and historical forces. Such collaboration produced studies such as Glen Elder's investigation of how the family behaviors of individuals were affected by having grown up during the Great Depression and William Tuttle's study of the effects of World War II (Elder, 1974; Elder, Modell, & Parke, 1993; Hareven, 1987, 1996; Tuttle, 1993). Discussion of family "strategies" gradually has replaced older portrayals of families as passive objects of historical change. This concept was further refined when feminists noted that families have not only joint interests, but also internal conflicts over resources, power, autonomy, and choices (Davidoff et al., 1999).

Historians were among the pioneers of gender studies and developed a rich body of work in this area quite early. Initially, however, many contrasted such "social history" with traditional political and economic narratives, as though the two were unconnected. More recent historical work, taking a cue from anthropology and sociology, has investigated the role of "private" gender and sexual relations in producing public political and economic institutions, rituals, and conflicts (Freedman, 1997; Gordon, 1997; Koven & Michel, 1993).

Early historical work was somewhat naive in its attempt to generate overarching assertions about changing family priorities, power differentials, and relationships. Some historians argued that, in general, parents were uncaring and marriages were loveless before the advent of "affective individualism." Closer historical examination revealed that such generalizations rested on ethnocentric misreadings of evidence. This led to a spate of studies attempting to establish the essential continuity of family ties and emotions (Graff, 1995; Pollock, 1983; Walter, 1989).

More nuanced investigations, however, revealed that although people in the past were probably not more or less caring than they are today, the object, form, and meaning of their family affections have all varied tremendously. Some of the most interesting new historical work has been on the history of childhood and the variability of parenting practices. Equally provocative has been the finding that contemporary assumptions about sexual identity or orientation seriously distort the very different mix of romantic and sensual conventions that prevailed in family life as recently as the 19th century. (Freedman, 1997; Graff, 1995; Glenn, Chang, & Chauncy, 1994; Hansen, 1995; Hawes & Hiner, 1991; Katz, 1995; Rothman, 1984; Szreter, 1996).

Other historical research has shown that despite some nearly universal family roles in both social and biological reproduction, nuclear families were less central to people's identity in the past than often is assumed. Sentimentalization of family ties, for instance, is a comparatively recent phenomenon. Older definitions of family seldom distinguished the nuclear unit from unrelated household residents, and neighbors were sometimes preferred over kin as sources of aid. Antebellum American evangelists, in sharp contrast to many modern religious definitions of family values, defined character as the willingness to stand against "social sins," such as slavery, in opposition to one's family if necessary (Coontz, 1988, 2000; Dayton, 1992; Epstein, 1996; Mintz & Kellogg, 1988).

Similarly, many of the family rituals and festivities we now think of as traditional developed comparatively recently. Until the late 19th century, civic festivals and Fourth of July parades were more important occasions for celebration and strong emotion than were most family holidays. The sit-down family meal, with its set hours and its high expectations of familial communication, was a mid-nineteenth-century invention (Caplow et al., 1982; Gillis, 1996).

FRUITS OF COLLABORATION: HISTORICAL STUDIES OF FAMILY DIVERSITY AND THE SOCIAL CONSTRUCTION OF PRIVILEGE

One of the richest results of the interchange between sociology, anthropology, and history has been the huge outpouring of work on family diversity since the late 1980s. Historians of racial-ethnic families have demonstrated that the concept of Whiteness, including "White" family patterns, emerged only slowly in the United States. The Irish, for example, were originally considered a non-White race and in some circles were treated with even more contempt than were African-Americans. In the 19th century, however, the Irish won reclassification as Whites, becoming an ethnic group rather than a racial one. Italians and Greeks were not granted "White" status until the early 20th century (Barrett & Roediger, 1997; Jacobson, 1998; Roediger, 1988).

Such findings have interesting implications for internal family roles and processes because the creation and preservation of racial categories historically has involved special controls over women's reproductive behavior and sexual image. They also support claims by many scholars of race and ethnicity that when Whiteness is taken as the norm, and "people of color" are studied as an addition or variation, the study of "diversity" perpetuates a Eurocentric and ahistorical world view (Liu, 1994).

Like race, ethnicity also was socially constructed in a dialectic between dominant groups and successive immigrants to America. The family "traditions" of such ethnic groups were not merely passed down from older generations' memories of their native culture. Rather, different groups drew selectively from cultural resources, often creating new "traditions" as they adapted to or resisted changing economic or political constraints and opportunities. Chinese immigrants to the United States, for example, moved successively through three different "cultural preferences" for family organization as they adjusted to changing historical conditions. Other groups used family ties differently (and frequently more extensively) than they had in their native lands (Coontz, Parson, & Raley, 1999; Glenn, 1999; Sanchez, 1993).

Such historical studies have helped to challenge the multicultural buffet approach to diversity, which records "variations" by race and class rather than examining interactions, conflicts, and mutual influences. The cult of full-time motherhood and protected childhood among the native-born, White middle class of the 19th century, for instance, cannot be understood merely as a distinctive cultural value or even a privilege of higher income per se. It was a historically specific class and ethnic relationship that depended on a supply of cheap labor to take over the tasks that used to occupy the bulk of a middle-class housewife's time. That supply of labor was created by a particular mix of class, race, and ethnic relations. Thus, the secluded domestic family of the middle class was constructed in tandem with child labor in the field and factories and with extended-family household production in the "sweated trades" (Coontz, 2000; Dill and Zinn, 1994).

Similarly, dual-earner families in the contemporary United States depend on a global economy in which many of their consumer goods are produced by families who do not rely primarily on paid employment. The ways in which U.S. middle-class families organize child care and marital relations, including gender equity at home, are often contingent on the availability of low-wage female workers, many without husbands of their own, to take over middle-class wives' customary household work (Buvinic, 1998; Chang, 1999; Risman, 1998).

Investigation of such interdependencies has aligned historians with sociologists and anthropologists who challenge culture-bound or essentialist assumptions about the "right" way to organize family relations and who refute catastrophic claims about collapse of "the" family. Nonetheless, history does not support the conclusion that "anything goes" in family life. If many conservatives distort the historical record in claiming the universal superiority of a particular family form or value set, some liberals distort it in the other direction. It does not follow that people can simply shrug off the weight of historical sediment that has been deposited all around them to freely create new family relations and values.

Almost every known society has had a legally, economically, and culturally privileged family form that confers significant advantages on those who live within it, even if those advantages are not evenly distributed or are accompanied by high costs for certain family members. Individuals who cannot or will not participate in the favored family form face powerful stigmas and handicaps. History provides no support for the notion that all families are created equal in any specific time and place. Rather, history highlights the social construction of family forms and the privileges that particular kinds of families confer.

For example, women's economic dependence on marriage and the consequent association of single-mother households with deprivation are not immutable. In many foraging societies, women traditionally contributed 60% to 90% of calories, and they were often in charge of household food distribution. They gained access to other resources, such as game brought home from group hunts, through kin redistribution networks rather than through marital ones. In such cases, a man often was more disadvantaged by single status than a woman was (Coontz & Henderson, 1986; Dahlberg, 1981). Colin Turnbull (1962) recounted noticing an emaciated, unkempt man among the Mbuti, normally an egalitarian society. When he asked why the man seemed in such dire straits, he was told that the man was too bad-tempered to keep a wife.

High rates of separation had few ill effects on women and children in band-level foraging societies in which the ethos was to share food and childrearing with everyone in camp. Even in less egalitarian societies, such as those organized on principles of patrilocal kinship, marriage is not always the main source of protection for women. Often a woman has more call on her brother's resources than on her husband's, and higher status as a sister than as a wife (Amadiume, 1987; Bilge & Kaufman, 1982; Ogbomo, 1997; Sacks, 1979).

Most historians, anthropologists, and economists agree that the eclipse of extended kinship as the main mechanism of production and distribution limited the claims of individuals on resources beyond the household, whereas the development of plow agriculture, along with increased militarization, made women more dependent on men's productive activities. Somewhat later, the early growth of day labor further reduced the economic contribution of women in relation to men. Marriage, however unequal in its burdens and benefits, then became the main form of income redistribution to non–wage-earning individuals, resulting in substantial penalties for women and children not encased in that institution (Acker, 1988; Honeyman & Goodman, 1991; Humphries, 1990; Laslett, 1988).

In some such marital systems, children's labor or wages are redistributed to parents, making mothers a beneficiary, albeit a junior one, of children's work. In others, men redistribute wages to both women and children, but women frequently transform those wages into goods and services that would cost more to buy on the open market than the amount of the initial male contribution.

The historical record shows that the effectiveness of marriage in redistributing the products of wage labor varies, then, according to gender and age relations. In the United States today, women and children generally have a higher standard of living within marriage than they do outside it, although married women with children tend to do more household work than their cohabiting or single-mother counterparts. In other parts of the world, the redistributional role of marriage is severely limited by high levels of male dominance. In several Third World countries, children receive a greater proportion of family resources and get their nutritional needs met more efficiently when the woman rather than the man is the main household earner. Many scholars of Third World development, as well as students of urban poverty in the United States, suggest that higher wages for women therefore would be a more effective strategy than increasing marriage rates for combating the impoverishment of women and children (Chafetz & Hagan, 1996; Dwyer & Bruce, 1988; Horton & Miller, 1987; Ishii-Kuntz, 1994; Kabeer, 1994).

The redistributional functions of marriage also vary by community context. Among poor women, for example, single parenthood reflects painful dilemmas unacknowledged by those who exhort them to escape poverty by getting married. Certainly, a stable, employed, cooperative husband would improve such women's economic prospects and make childrearing easier. On the other hand, getting married can be risky, cutting the woman off from other support networks and linking her fate to a man who may be economically or emotionally unstable. In the absence of a rock-solid marriage and a husband with a job, a poor woman may have more access to support if she remains enmeshed in kin and friendship networks, with the flexibility to switch sexual partners—even if such behavior further limits her long-term prospects for attaining a stable marriage. This may explain in part why some research indicates that infant mortality rates are lower and children's reading scores higher among impoverished young mothers when they remain single than when they marry the child's father (Albrecht, Miller, & Clarke, 1994; Chant, 1985; Cooksey, 1997; Kabeer, 1994).

The organization of the state further complicates the redistributional role of marriage. In many ancient societies, emerging state systems reinforced women's and children's dependence on marriage by explicitly restricting their older claims on a wider kinship network. The ancient Greek state, for example, strove to reduce the authority of the clan (*genos*) and elevate that of the household (*oikos*). Such states also introduced new social and economic penalties for female adultery and for "illegitimacy."

Other types of states, however, organize redistribution and social citizenship in ways that reduce the dependence of women and children on marriage. Countries with a smaller proportion of low-wage jobs or with more extensive child-support systems, for example, have lower levels of female and child poverty. In the United States, according to a 1995 study, 57.9% of female-headed families with children were poor, compared with a rate of 16.5% in the United Kingdom and 7.9% in the Netherlands (Rainwater, 1995).

CHANGE AND CONTINUITY IN HISTORICAL PERSPECTIVE

Thus far, I have discussed areas in which history, sociology, and anthropology have refined each other's generalizations about patterns of change to take better account of variation, nuance, and diversity. The benefits of collaboration also extend to contemporary studies of family life.

One of the most exciting results of the growth in family research over the past few decades has been the accumulation of longitudinal studies of families. These data sets have enriched immensely the resources of historians. In turn, historians can offer perspective on how representative decade-by-decade variations may be. To a historian, for instance, a 20-year longitudinal study—or even a 40-year study—is relatively short term.

Consider the data that show a decline since the early 1970s in several indicators of child well-being. In 1997, 19.9% of all Americans under age 18 lived below the poverty level, compared with 14% in 1969, 15.1% in 1970 and 14.4% in 1973. But the period from 1969 through 1973 was the low point of child poverty in the entire 20th century because of the unique combination of the Great Society welfare programs coming on top of a period of prolonged rising real wages, high rates of unionization, and low unemployment. The child poverty rate was 27.3% in 1959 and even higher at the turn of the century (Rawlings, 1998, p. 211).

Another area in which historical perspective helps is the evaluation of reports that parents spend less time with their children than they did in the 1970s. This claim should be taken with a grain of salt because many estimates are made simply on the basis that women have increased their work hours and thus have fewer potential hours to spend with their children. But even if there has been a decrease since the 1970s, that decade's practices were far from any "traditional" norm.

In colonial America, families routinely sent young children and adolescents to live in other people's homes as servants, apprentices, or simply as dependent kin. In the early 1900s, thousands of children worked away from their parents in mines, mills, or factories, whereas many others spent more time on the streets than in the family home. Even many middle-class families of the past spent surprisingly little time interacting with their children because they had more children, more time-consuming household tasks, and far lower expectations of quality parenting. In the late 1970s, researchers returned to the "Middletown" studied by Robert and Helen Lynd in the 1920s and found that 1970s parents spent much more time with their children than had parents in the 1920s (Bahr, 1980; Calvert, 1992; Caplow et al., 1982; Coontz, 2000; Kain, 1990; Mintz & Kellogg, 1988; O'Day, 1994). Yet the children raised in those "uninvolved" 1920s families managed to cope with the Great Depression and fight World War II.

Even in comparison with the 1970s, I know of no studies documenting a decline in parents' assistance with children's schoolwork. In oral histories that my research assistants, Margaret Sinclair and Mary Wright-Croes, currently are compiling, informants who reared children in the 1930s, 1940s, and 1950s consistently report spending less time supervising homework than did their adult children or grandchildren in the 1980s and 1990s (Sinclair, 1999; Wright-Croes, 1999).

Comparisons of contemporary families with those of the 1950s are especially misleading. As many historians and sociologists have demonstrated, the 1950s family was atypical even for the 20th century. For the first time in 80 years, the age of marriage fell sharply, fertility rates increased, and the proportion of never-married individuals plummeted. The values attached to nuclear-family living, including the rejection of "interference" by extended kin and the expectation that family life should be people's main source of personal gratification, were also new—and their hegemony even at the time should not be exaggerated. Furthermore, historian Jessica Weiss recently has demonstrated that what we now call "the" 1950s family was only a single and temporary stage in the family cycle of the generation that formed families during and immediately after World War II (Coontz, 1997, 2000; May, 1988; Meyerowitz, 1994; Weiss, 2000).

In 1950, only 16% of all children had mothers who worked full-time for wages outside the home. Today, 59% of children, including a majority of preschoolers, have mothers who are employed (Spain & Bianchi, 1996). This is a dramatic change in a comparatively short period of time, posing many challenges to existing values and childrearing practices. Nonetheless, exclusive child care by mothers and sole breadwinning by fathers have been exceedingly rare in history. It is far more typical for women to have combined production and reproduction than to have specialized in one or the other.

In 19th-century England and America, child labor was an essential part of the family economy, with the ironic result that when wives did work outside the home, they did so when their children were extremely young, withdrawing only when the children became able to contribute to family finances. It was not until the 1920s that a bare majority of children in the United States grew up in a home in which the father went out to work, the mother stayed at home and was not heavily involved in running a farm or household business, and the children were at home or in school rather than at work. In the 1950s, about 60% of children grew up in this family form, a higher percentage than before or since (Creighton, 1996; Hernandez, 1993; Robinson, 1995; Rotella & Alter, 1993).

What Is Truly New

These examples should not be taken to mean that the more things change, the more they remain the same. Rather, by showing what is not new in a long-range perspective, historians throw into sharper focus the qualitative and unprecedented changes that are occurring in families.

Take the question of whether marriage is a dying institution. In 1999, a report issued by the National Marriage Project declared that the marriage rate had fallen by 43% since 1960 (Popenoe & Whitehead, 1999). This dramatic drop in marriage rates, which they calculated on the basis of how many single women aged 15 years and older get married each year, is partly an artifact of the rising age of marriage. In 1960, the median age at first marriage for women was 20.4 years. By 1998, it was 25. The fact that a lower proportion of all women aged 15 and older are getting married each year than in the past does not necessarily mean that a lower proportion of all women will ever get married. As of March 1998, 20.5% of all women aged 18 years and older had never married, compared with 13.1% in 1960. On the other hand, of women aged 35 and older, 7.7 were never married in 1998, compared with 7.2% in 1960 (U.S. Bureau of the Census, 1998, 1975).

This statistic probably overrepresents the proportion of women who are marrying today because it includes earlier generations who were more likely to get married. On the other hand, more and more women are marrying for the first time at age 40 or older. At any rate, a long-range perspective makes recent increases in nonmarriage rates seem much less dramatic. The percentage of unmarried women aged 18 and older in 1998

(20.5%) is much closer to the rate of singlehood in 1900, when 20.4% of women aged 20 and older had never married, than it is to the rate at the end of the 1950s (U.S. Bureau of the Census, 1975).

Marriage, then, is not a doomed institution, contrary to some predictions. Nonetheless, it is certainly a transformed institution. Over the course of the 20th century, marriage has come to occupy and organize a smaller and smaller portion of people's lives, as well as to be far less permanent once entered. This is partly because of long-range demographic change, partly because of new cultural norms making divorce and nonmarriage more acceptable, and partly because the state and the market have taken over many family functions that used to make marriage more essential for individuals.

The average age of marriage for contemporary women is now 2 years higher than its previous U.S. peak in 1890 and 4 years higher than it was in the 1950s. Meanwhile, rates of nonmarriage for African American women approach world-historic highs (Teachman, Tedrow, & Crowder, in press). Despite periodic fluctuations in the number of adult children residing with parents, the tradition of youths remaining in the parental home until marriage is dead. Even apart from divorce, this means that young people experience a protracted period of life outside marriage, either their parents' or their own. Meanwhile, the bewildering array of family relations made possible by reproductive technology—along with the new prevalence of divorce, cohabitation, and unwed motherhood and the new visibility of gay and lesbian couples—has separated childrearing from marriage and challenged customary definitions of parental rights. The eclipse of sequencing, which was the typical way that 20th-century women balanced their growing labor force participation with their continued responsibility for childrearing, has created a crisis in the way that child care has been organized for most of the century.

This decline in the role of marriage and gender specialization in organizing people's lives, which is also occurring in most other parts of the world, may be seen as part of a major economic and political revolution in redistribution and care-giving mechanisms (Acker, 1988; Coontz 1997). Historical perspective is helpful in assessing the causes and consequences, both pro and con, of this revolution. For example, before we bemoan the declining commitment of parents to children, we should recognize that the role of families in co-ordinating the education, health care, and training of youth is now much more complex than it was in the past and extends over a longer life span.

Once children were considered insurance for parents' old age, and children's earnings frequently were what enabled parents to buy a home. Today, parents provide insurance for their children's entry into or maintenance of middle-class status. This often includes help with home buying or subsidized boarding in the parental home, as well as an increasingly prolonged and expensive investment in education.

Additionally, technology now enables (and health insurance requires) families to provide an enormous amount of medical care at home, much of which formerly would have been provided by doctors or nurses. Fewer people are put in nursing homes, and hospital stays are shorter. In 1997, 21 million people were providing free care to a family member or friend, up from seven million in 1987. As medical ethicist Carol Levine commented, this is "a quantum leap for the responsibilities of families" (Fisher, 1998).

Also unprecedented is the responsibility that adult children bear for their parents, who in previous generations were unlikely to live long enough to require substantial and prolonged assistance. There is little evidence that children's altruism toward parents was greater in the past; witness the elaborate wills that were drawn up in colonial days to prevent neglect of a surviving parent. Until the expansion of Social Security and Medicare in the 1960s and 1970s, elders were more likely than any other age group to live in poverty. There is no evidence that government programs have lessened adult children's commitment to elders. Today one in four U.S. workers gives 11 hours or more unpaid care per week to an aging family friend or relative, and almost 50% say they expect to do so within the next 10 years (Finch, 1994; Shore, 1998).

Nor does history suggest that the distinctive feature of today's changing care-giving patterns involves children's premature exposure to adult roles and knowledge. I have already noted the prevalence of child labor, both in and out of the home, in the past. In preindustral societies, youths were integrated into—or at least intimately exposed to—most adult activities. In colonial America, children were often in the same room (sometimes the same bed) in which adult sexual activity took place. During the 19th century, middle-class and "respectable" working-class families increasingly sheltered their girls from sexual knowledge, but prostitution was much more widespread than it is today. As late as 1896, the "age of consent" was 12 or under in the majority of states (Coontz, 1997, 2000; D'Emilio & Freedman, 1988; Pivar, 1974).

What does seem new is that youth today are more excluded from productive roles than they were in the past, but at the same time, they are much more fully integrated into consumer roles. With the age of sexual maturity falling and the age of economic and educational independence rising, young people have developed a youth culture that crosses geographic borders, as well as some racial, class, and gender boundaries. Part of the convergence in the life course and social outlook of youth (bearing in mind the countervailing trend of intensification of child labor in some parts of the world) results from adolescents' lengthened period of economic dependence in the industrial world, as extended education becomes the primary route to finding a job that provides a livable wage. This convergence also results from the new independence teens have in their access to information, consumer goods (or at least consumer images) and to a global mass entertainment and advertising culture. Although transnational and multicultural alliances have resulted from some of these changes in the experience of youths, some young people attempt to use their class, race, gender, or heterosexual privileges to compensate for or strike out against the constraints of age inequality, venting their frustrations with the adult world on other youth (Wyn & White, 1997). This changing historical context, not merely the individual characteristics of different families, should form the backdrop to discussion of contemporary youth issues, including the new forms and targets of youthful violence.

Racial and ethnic diversity among families is certainly not new. But Michael Omi and Howard Winant argue that racial hierarchies, once imposed primarily through coercion, now rest on "a complex system of compromises, legitimizing ideologies . . . political rules and bureaucratic regulations" (Omi & Winant, 1994, pp. 75–76). Despite the persistence of racial discrimination and the concentration of poverty among inner-city African Americans, racism is no longer monolithic. The fact that there are some arenas in which African Americans or other historically oppressed groups can "play the race card" should not obscure the fact that the odds in the race game still favor Whites, but it does change the ways in which White racial power is exercised. The new diversity of Latin American and Asian immigrants, along with their rapid population growth, has further muddied older racial hierarchies, with complex consequences for family experiences (Coontz, Parson, & Raley, 1999; Rubin, 1994). The result is a "messy racial hegemony," marked by contradictory, conflicted, and ambiguous relationships.

The concept of a "messy" hegemony also applies to changing gender relations, both in society at large and within individual families. Both economically and culturally, it is now easier than in the past for the average woman to survive outside of marriage. Between 1980 and 1994, the wages of women who were not mothers rose from 72% to 95% of men's wages. Occupational segregation has fallen dramatically. Women now comprise nearly half of all midlevel managers, up from 17% in 1970 (Blau & Ehrenberg, 1997), while the cultural acceptance of women's rights, at least as an abstract principle, is unprecedented.

On the other hand, approximately half of women's wage improvement relative to men has come from declines in real wages for low-income men. Since the 1970s, it has also become more difficult to support a family on one salary than in the two decades following World War II. The burdens of child care and housework still fall disproportionately on women, and women are less likely than are men to have access to parent-friendly work policies. Partly in consequence, mothers' wages are only 75% of men's (Blau & Ehrenberg, 1997; Hernandez, 1993; Lewin, 1997; Shore, 1998; Spain & Bianchi, 1996). Meanwhile, young women wrestle with a changing but still persistent sexual double standard, and women still suffer disproportionately from sexual harassment on the job and violence in the home.

Labeling these unequal relations as patriarchy, however, conceals important variations in the form, content, and consequences of male dominance. Most historians would reserve the term patriarchy to describe a family system in which male control over property intersects with the household head's control over the labor of women and children, a situation that historically produced much closer congruence in forms of political, economic, and interpersonal domination than prevails in today's complex and fluid tangle of power relations and gender norms.

EVALUATING FAMILY CHANGE

Few historians are morally or ethically neutral about these rearrangements in family life and gender roles, but most of us are skeptical of either "optimistic" or "pessimistic" assessments of such change. Historical case studies show clearly that change is seldom unitary in its effects and that it almost invariably involves trade-offs rather than unambiguous gains or losses. Just as some researchers argue that ambivalence is built into most contemporary relationships, history suggests that ambiguity and inconsistency are built into social change and family transitions. The "good" dynamic in many transformations is often inseparable from the "bad," and their combined outcome can seldom by interpreted as a clear-cut "step forward" or "fall back" (Coontz, 1996; Luescher & Pillemer, 1998; Walter, 1989).

In early America, for instance, the traditional insistence on hierarchy, inequality, and the forcible subordination of "inferiors" to "superiors" was undermined by the spread of democratic ideology, resulting in important restrictions on the prerogatives of elites but also producing more insidiously paternalistic and protectionist justifications for social inequality. In the case of women, a new essentialist definition of female vulnerability and domesticity set limits on patriarchal prerogatives and led to a softening of husband-wife relations. Nonetheless, it also reduced the instances in which women could act as "deputy husbands" or *femmes sole.*

Women gained new protections and reverence in their roles as wife or mother, but prejudice against their participation in public life mounted, and women were excluded from several occupations, such as printing and tavern keeping, in which they had formerly been well represented. Yet the essentialist ideology that defined women as qualitatively different from men also created a sense of sisterhood that helped inspire some women to organize the women's rights movement. As Nancy Cott (1977) has put it, the bonds that held women down also linked them together, although the reverse was also true (Coontz, 1988; Gordon, 1997; Gundersen, 1996; Hall, 1992).

It is not just that the "good" features of any change are hopelessly entangled with the "bad." They frequently help create "the bad," and vice versa. In addition, they constantly transform the institution, idea, or relationship that originally gave them birth. The more I study history, the more value I find in a conceptual tool utilized by both Hegel and Marx: the notion of contradiction. In families, as well as in social formations, the same processes that are essential to maintain a particular relationship or institution simultaneous-

ly create oppositions that eventually transform, undermine, or even destroy it.

For example, the American Revolution, which eventually spurred industrialization, initially delayed the development of a distinct manufacturing sector by stimulating rural enterprises and household production. Yet in late–18th- and early–19th-century America, family mechanisms designed to maximize self-sufficiency and reproduce a household economy helped create the very dependence on wage labor and markets that transformed the preindustrial household. The families most likely to be drawn into wage work and commerce were the ones who tried to preserve their traditional household economies by dividing the inheritance, living in close residential proximity, and encouraging supplementary crafts or seasonal wage work of children in their search for self-sufficiency (Clark, 1990; Henretta, 1991).

Similarly, however one judges 1950s family arrangements and values, it is clear that they had built-in tendencies toward self-transformation. The romanticization of family life that pervaded the mass media in that era sanctioned increasing consumerism by families, and eventually by individuals, creating pressures for wives to "supplement" their husbands' wages. As women rushed to get married at an earlier age, the decreasing proportion of single women in the population practically forced employers to change their attitudes toward hiring married women. Even families who moved to the suburbs in pursuit of a nuclear-family oasis helped make households more dependent on the market by removing themselves from kin networks and neighborly exchanges. In the meanwhile, the unprecedented focus on a child-centered family encouraged couples to embrace family planning, paving the way for a recreational sexuality increasingly separated from reproductive constraints (Coontz, 2000; Smith, 1987).

THE IMPORTANCE OF CONTEXT: IMPLICATIONS FOR FAMILY METHODOLOGY

Such complicated interactions provide examples of why historical perspective adds an important dimension to the reevaluation of causality and methodology that is now going on in family studies (Allen, 2000; Marks, in press). This is because history is, in E. P. Thompson's (1972) words, "above all the discipline of context," in which any fact "can be given meaning only within an ensemble of other meanings" (p. 45). Historians can provide countless examples of how any given phenomenon or "fact" can become something remarkably different, depending on what it is paired with, surrounded by, or opposed to. Our work thus reinforces the cautions that careful researchers have always raised about what generalizations may be drawn from quantitative analysis.

Historians have benefited tremendously from the increasing sophistication of the statistical tools of the social sciences: A content analysis of the *Journal of Family History* over the 1980s found that 75% of the articles used statistical analysis (Schvaneveldt, Pickett, & Young, 1993), and recent historical work continues along the same lines.

Yet history also reminds us that the things we easily can count are not always the things that count the most for families. Thompson (1963) noted that when we survey any society at any given point, we see "simply a multitude of individuals" with a multitude of incomes, years in school, and personal experiences. To find meaningful patterns, Thompson insisted, we must look not at structures, categories, or any easily measured attributes of individuals or institutions, but at the larger relationships among those structures, individuals, and institutions (pp. 9, 11).

When historians use the word "relationships" in this context, we do not mean the habitual or intentional interactions and exchanges between groups or individuals. Rather, the word refers to the mutually constitutive positions that different groups and individuals occupy in the prevailing system of production, distribution, rights, obligations, and legitimacy. There is no such thing as a White person in the absence of the social category of a Black person, and vice versa. Being White or Black is not something that is defined by actual complexion or genetic inheritance, but by a historical relationship between two groups.

As physicist David Bohm (1999, p. 39) notes of science, the task is not just to investigate separate factors, nor even their random collisions and occasional interactions. We must identify those "effectively constant relationships" that structure social interactions in any given social formation even as they transform the participants and the social formation itself.

Such structural relationships are likely to be the most persistent source of conflict and dynamism in a society, but they often operate only as a conditioner of other, more contingent factors that may be more frequent initiators of specific variations. Sometimes, then, what we can measure and

count may be only those comparatively marginal differences that can be distinguished over the huge background noise of the social context.

A relationship that frequently operates in this way is that of class, and this is not easily captured by the kind of controls commonly used to identify socioeconomic status, necessary though such controls may be. As a historian, my experience leads me to see class not merely as a particular income, occupation, or level of educational attainment but as a set of long-term options, privileges, and vulnerabilities that can be defined only in relation to those of other groups. Class involves engagement in a historically specific pattern of interaction with other socioeconomic and political groups or institutions, or with different tiers of the same institutions. To take a minor example of the measurement problems this raises, 4 years at Harvard often represents an entirely different set of experiences and social relations than does 6 years at a state college.

Class status creates, results from, and interacts with other mechanisms of distributing power and resources. In combination, these mechanisms produce complex interactions that cannot be understood by simply adding or subtracting one or another factor. Few societies have constructed material class inequalities without use of racial or ethnic hierarchies. Gender dynamics also help produce class differences. In turn, the experience of gender and race varies by class.

Class therefore involves multifaceted relationships both with economic and political institutions and with prevailing ideologies of difference, including race, ethnicity, religion, gender, and sexuality, to create historically and regionally specific "social locations" where families and individuals fashion their strategies and meanings (Lamphere, Zavella, & Gonzales, 1993, p. 4). Such social locations are not themselves static. As Renato Rosaldo (1989) pointed out, "our everyday lives are crisscrossed by border zones, pockets, and eruptions of all kinds" (p. 207). Social borders are constantly redrawn by historical processes that involve people in shifting identities, conflicts, and alliances.

The historical changes that have the biggest impact on family organization and values often emerge when incremental and quantitative changes suddenly produce something qualitatively new. This is precisely when we need to be most suspicious of the commensurability of data that we may be able to collect. As Thompson (1972) cautions fellow historians, "Where the influence of the social sciences is undoubtedly most fruitful, it is, at exactly the same point, most treacherous: . . . at the point where these 17th-century families become the nuclear family; where these 13th-century Russian peasants and these 19th-century Irish cotters become the peasantry; where these Chartist Plug rioters and those communards become violence in industrial society" (p. 46)—or where the male-breadwinner family system becomes something else entirely.

In my own research, for instance, I am currently grappling with how to usefully compare today's 15-year-olds with those of the 1950s, even after taking into account the different class and racial-ethnic distribution of young people then and now. Can one learn much about "youth" by equating either of these population subsets to 15-year-olds in the early 18th century, when among a host of other differences, the median age of the population was just a year or two older than 15? Youth is not just a biological, chronological, or psychological category, but a historically constructed relationship to families, schools, courts, police, political institutions, public space, adults, and younger children. Commonalities of youth status vary in different periods, and they are always refracted through prevailing hierarchies of gender, race, ethnicity, sexuality, and class (Wyn & White, 1997).

Or consider the question of how to interpret what people say about the satisfactions of marriage and family life. On one hand, attention to context reminds us that varying linguistic conventions often imperfectly reflect the actual mix of affectionate and instrumental interactions in families. Peasant and working-class patterns of communication, for example, tend to reinforce social solidarities and identities by translating individualized emotions into the language of custom, interest, and duty. Individuals' tender feelings may be disguised by "tough terms," because of the fear that intense individual ties may be experienced as a threat by the larger group. In other periods or classes, the opposite distortion may occur, as group interests and power claims are expressed in a language of individualized, voluntary affection (Medick & Sabine, 1984).

On the other hand, emotions derive from intellectual and ideological judgments about social and personal relationships (Solomon, 1978). As such, contrasting emotional expressions may exemplify more than linguistic differences. They may represent an actual metamorphosis in social relationships and world views. Elaine Tyler May

(1980, 1988) suggested that rising divorce rates in the early 1900s reflected heightened expectations of marriage; yet she has also shown how women in the 1950s labeled their marriages as very happy even while they detailed discontents that would lead a modern observer to rate their marriages far less positively. Lillian Rubin's research reveals that definitions of what constitutes a good marriage and a lovable husband have changed dramatically among working-class women since the 1970s (Hammerton, 1992; Rubin, 1976/1992).

Historians, of course, are not the only researchers who stress the importance of context, witness the nuanced analysis of ethnographies such as *Brave New Families* (Stacey, 1998) or *Down on Their Luck* (Anderson & Snow, 1985). Many statisticians are also conscious of the limits as well as the benefits of their methods (Maltz, 1994). Still as Marks (in press) points out, this remains an ongoing problem even for researchers committed to recognizing variation. Constructing a sample that has comparable categories (e.g., two-parent households) may involve studying only an unrepresentative cross section of one group or ignoring data that would help us understand the distal causes of the correlations we find. For example, Marks (in press) reviewed one study showing that "involved fathers" make a tremendous difference for children's well-being in all racial and socioeconomic groups. This is an important and potentially useful finding, but it is easy to then ignore the racial and class dynamics that affect the distribution of involved fathers, as well as to overlook smaller patterns that allow some children with uninvolved fathers to succeed.

Similar cautions are raised by the growing evidence from many different disciplines that the impact of poverty or unemployment on people's family behaviors (as well as the impact of family behaviors on poverty or unemployment) depends on so many interacting contextual factors that it is difficult to make useful generalizations about correlations, much less overarching causes. Unemployment has a different meaning in cities today than it did during the Great Depression. Even during the 1930s, people reacted to job loss differently just after the Wall Street crash than when the sit-down strikes were going on in urban factories. Historian Roger Lane (1997) suggested that in some poor neighborhoods during the 19th century, better pay or more regular work may have led to more homicides, by increasing people's alcohol consumption. In other periods, unemployment and relative deprivation have increased violent crime (Dawley, 1991; Katz, 1993; Lane; Sugrue, 1996).

Similarly, urban historians join many sociologists in arguing that poverty in today's central cities plays a qualitatively different role than it did in the past. Once it was a way of disciplining new workers to the rhythms and demands of industrial labor. Today, it serves to exclude residents from access to work. People's reactions to poverty seem to depend not just on the character of the neighborhood, but that of nearby neighborhoods, as well as the interaction among neighborhoods and the concentration of affluence and poverty. Families' behavior, values, and range of choices also vary depending on the amount of their confidence in public institutions, the social messages that people receive or generate about the reasons for poverty and wealth, and prior trends in poverty, which affect perceptions about whether life is improving or deteriorating (Anderson, 1990; Katz, 1993; Lane, 1997; Massey, 1996).

All these considerations complicate our notion of what constitutes an "at-risk" behavior or status for families or individuals. Being prudent in an impoverished or homeless environment may mean passing up chances for long-term betterment, whereas behaviors that are judicious in a middle-class, professional environment can be very risky for lower-class individuals. Aspirations that would reflect unrealistic fantasizing about fame or quick riches in a middle-class youth might represent a realistic assessment by a lower-class individual of what offers as good a long shot as any for escaping his or her environment. What is risky sexual behavior for a girl with good education and employment prospects may be a rational way of negotiating race, class, and gender power relations for a young woman with fewer options, even if it often reinforces her lack of power in the long run. From another angle, what is called deferred gratification in middle-class youth (going on to college; avoiding marriage or childbirth) may, in fact, be a socially rewarded way of following the easiest, most gratifying path (Rubin, 1976/1992; Snow & Anderson, 1993; Stack, 1974; Willis, 1977; Wyn & White, 1997).

Attention to context enriches qualitative research, as well as quantitative research, challenging broad generalizations about "adaptive" or "dysfunctional" behaviors and abstract characterizations of culture or "style." Historian Robin D. G. Kelley (1997), for example, has written a withering critique of recent ethnographic descriptions of African American culture. He argues that many

authors not only ignore the "diverse and contradictory range of practices, attitudes, and relationships that are dynamic, historically situated, and ethnically hybrid," but also completely miss the role of irony and humor in the behaviors and "rituals" they record (p. 9).

Understanding the specificity of social location and the importance of context does not necessarily produce the relativism that has been associated with some versions of "postmodernist" theorizing. Rather, it directs our attention to the tension between the institutional or historical constraints under which people operate and the tool kit of personal, cultural, and social resources they use to make choices about how to adapt to or resist those constraints, along with the complex interactions that produce unanticipated outcomes to such choices. It also should remind us of the need to balance our interests as researchers with our obligations as citizens.

Both as researchers and as citizens, we need a continuing dialogue among historians, ethnographers, and social scientists about ways to cut across the overgeneralizations and simplistic interpretation of correlations that currently deform so much of the public discussion of families. Interdisciplinary collaboration, especially between family studies and history, is not only intellectually rewarding, but practically useful as well. It helps the families we study and the audiences we write for to better interpret their lives and assess their choices for the future.

NOTE

The author would like to thank Steven Mintz and Philip and Carolyn Cowan for their thoughtful comments on an earlier draft.

REFERENCES

Acker, J. (1988). Class, gender, and the relations of distribution. *Signs, 13,* 473–497.

Albrecht, S., Miller, M., & Clarke, L. (1994). Assessing the importance of family structure in understanding birth outcomes. *Journal of Marriage and the Family, 56,* 987–1003.

Allen, K. R. (2000). A conscious and inclusive family studies. *Journal of Marriage and the Family 62,* 4–17.

Amadiume, I. (1987). *Male daughters, female husbands: Gender and sex in an African society.* London: Zed Books.

Anderson, E. (1990). *Streetwise: Race, class, and change in an urban community.* Chicago: University of Chicago Press.

Bahr, H. (1980). Changes in family life in middletown, 1924–77. *Public Opinion Quarterly, 44,* 35–52.

Barrett, J., & Roediger, D. (1997). Inbetween peoples:

Race, nationality and the "new immigrant" working class. *Journal of American Ethnic History, 16,* 3–44.

Bender, T. (1982). *Community and social change in America.* Baltimore: Johns Hopkins University Press.

Bilge, B., & Kaufman, G. (1983). Children of divorce and one-parent families: Cross-cultural perspectives. *Family Relations, 32,* 59–71.

Blau, F., & Ehrenberg, R., (Eds.). (1997). *Gender and family issues in the workplace.* New York: Sage.

Bohm, D. (1999). *Causality and chance in modern physics.* Philadelphia: University of Pennsylvania.

Buvinic, M. (1998). Women in poverty: A new global underclass. *Foreign Policy, 108,* 38–53.

Calvert, K. (1992). *Children in the house.* Boston: Northeastern.

Caplow, T., Bahr, H. M., Chadwick, B. A., Hill, R., & Williamson, M. H. (1982). *Middletown families: Fifty years of change and continuity.* Minneapolis, MN: University of Minnesota.

Chafetz, J., & Hagan, J. (1996). The gender division of labor and family change in industrial societies: A theoretical accounting. *Journal of Comparative Family Studies, 27,* 187–219.

Chang, G. (1999). Global exchange: The World Bank, "welfare reform," and the global trade in Filipina workers. In S. Coontz, M. Parson, & G. Raley (Eds.), *American families: A multicultural reader.* New York: Routledge.

Chant, S. (1985). Single-parent families: Choice or constraint? The formation of female-headed households in Mexican shanty towns. *Development and Change, 16,* 41–59.

Chauncy, G. (1994). *Gay New York: Gender, urban culture, and the making of the gay urban world, 1890–1940.* New York. Basic Books.

Clark, C. (1990). *The roots of rural capitalism: western Massachusetts, 1780–1800.* Ithaca, NY: Cornell University Press.

Cooksey, E. (1997). Consequences of young Mothers' marital histories for children's cognitive development. *Journal of Marriage and the Family, 59,* 245–261.

Coontz, S. (1988). *The social origins of private life: A history of American families, 1600–1900.* London: Verso.

Coontz, S. (1997). *The way we really are: Coming to terms with America's changing families.* New York: Basic Books.

Coontz, S. (2000). *The way we never were: American families and the nostalgia trap.* New York: Basic Books.

Coontz, S., & Henderson, P. (1986). Property forms, political power, and female labour in the origins of class and state systems. In S. Coontz & P. Henderson (Eds.), *Women's work, men's property: On the origins of gender and class.* New York: Verso.

Coontz, S., Parson, M., & Raley, G. (1999). *American families: A multicultural reader.* New York: Routledge.

Cott, N. (1977). *The bonds of womanhood: "Woman's sphere" in New England, 1780–1835.* New Haven: Yale University Press.

Creighton, C. (1996). The rise of the male breadwinner family: A reappraisal. *Comparative Studies in Society and History, 38,* 310–337.

Dahlberg, F. (Ed.). (1981). *Woman the gatherer.* New Haven: Yale University Press.

Davidoff, L., Doolittle, M., Fink, F., & Holden, K. (1999). *The family story: Blood, contract and intimacy, 1830–1960.* London: Longman.

Dawley, A. (1991). *Struggles for justice: Social responsibility and the liberal state.* Cambridge, MA: Belknap.

Dayton, D. (1992). *Discovering an evangelical heritage.* Columbus, OH: Hendrickson.

D'Emilio, J., & Freedman, E. (1988). *Intimate matters: A history of sexuality in America.* New York: Harper and Row.

Dill, B. (1999). Fictive kin, paper sons, and compadrazgo: Women of color and the struggle for family survival. In S. Coontz, M. Parson, & G. Raley (Eds.). *American families: A multicultural reader.* New York: Routledge.

Dill, B., & Zinn, M. (1994). *Women of color in U.S. society.* Philadelphia, PA: Temple University Press.

Dwyer, D., & Bruce, J. (Eds.). (1988). *A house divided: Woman and income in the Third World.* Stanford, CA: Stanford University Press.

Elder, G. (1974). *Children of the Great Depression: Social change in life experience.* Chicago: University of Chicago Press.

Elder G., Modell, J., & Parke, R. D. (Eds.). (1993). *Children in time and space: Developmental and historical insights.* New York: Cambridge University Press.

Epstein, S. A. (1996). The Medieval family: A place of refuge and sorrow. In *Portraits of Medieval and Renaissance living: Essays in memory of David Herlihy.* S. Cohn & S. Epstein (Eds.), Ann Arbor, MI: University of Michigan.

Finch, J. (1994). Do families support each other more or less than in the past? In M. Drake (Ed.), *Time, family and community: Perspectives on community history.* Oxford, UK: Blackwell.

Fisher, I. (1998, June 7). Families provide medical care, tubes and all. *The New York Times,* p. A1.

Franklin, D. (1997). *Ensuring inequality: The structural transformation of the African American family.* New York: Oxford University Press.

Freedman, E. (1997). *The history of the family and the history of sexuality.* Washington, DC: American Historical Association.

Gillis, J. (1996). *A world of their own making: Myth, ritual, and the quest for family values.* New York: Basic.

Glenn, E. N. (1991). Cleaning up/kept down: A historical perspective on racial inequality in women's work. *Stanford Law Review, 43,* 1333–1357.

Glenn, E. N. (1999). Split household, small producer, and dual wage earner: An analysis of Chinese-American family strategies. In S. Coontz, M. Parson, & G. Raley (1999). *American families: A multicultural reader.* New York: Routledge.

Glenn, E. N., Chang, G., & Forcey, L. R. (1994). *Mothering: Ideology, experience, and agency.* New York: Routledge.

Graff, H. (1995). *Conflicting paths: Growing up in America.* Cambridge, MA: Harvard University Press.

Gordon, L. (1997). *U. S. women's history.* Washington, DC: American Historical Association.

Gundersen, J. (1996). *To be useful to the world: Women*

in revolutionary America, 1740–1790. New York: Twayne.

Hall, C. (1992). The early formation of Victorian domestic ideology. In C. Hall (Ed.), *White, male, and middle class: Explorations in feminism and history.* London: Polity Press.

Hammerton, A. J. (1992). *Cruelty and companionship: Conflict in nineteenth-century married life.* New York: Routledge.

Hansen, K. (1995). No kisses is like youres: An erotic friendship between two African American women during the mid-nineteenth century. *Gender and History, 7,* 153–182.

Hareven, T. (1987). Historical analysis of the family. In M. Sussman & S. Steinmetz (Eds.), *Handbook of marriage and the family.* New York: Plenum Press.

Hareven, T. (1996). What difference does it make?; *Social Science History, 20,* 317–344.

Hawes, J., & Hiner, N. R., (Eds.). (1991). *Children in historical and comparative perspective.* Westport, CT: Greenwood Press.

Herlihy, D. (1985). *Medieval households.* Cambridge, MA: Harvard University Press.

Henretta, J. (1991). *The origins of American capitalism: Collected essays.* Boston: Northeastern University Press.

Hernandez, D. (1993). *America's children: Resources from family, government, and the economy.* New York: Sage.

Honeyman, K., & Goodman, J. (1991). Women's work, gender conflict, and labour markets in Europe, 1500–1900. *Economic History Review, XLIV,* 608–628.

Humphries, J. (1990). Enclosures, common rights, and women: The proletarianization of families in the late eighteenth and early nineteenth centuries. *The Journal of Economic History, L,* pp. 17–43.

Ishii-Kuntz, M. (1994). Work and family life: Findings from international research and suggestions for future study. *Journal of Family Issues, 15,* 490–506.

Jacobson, M. (1998). *Whiteness of a different color: European immigrants and the alchemy of race.* Cambridge, MA: Harvard University Press.

Kabeer, N. (1994). *Reversed realities: Gender hierarchies in development thought.* London: Verso.

Kain, E. (1990). *The myth of family decline: Understanding families in a world of rapid social change.* Lexington, MA: Heath.

Katz, J. (1995). *The invention of heterosexuality.* New York: Dutton.

Katz, M. (Ed.). (1993). *The "underclass" debate: Views from history.* Princeton, NJ: Princeton University Press.

Katz, M. (1995). *Improving poor people: The welfare state, the "underclass," and urban schools as history.* Princeton, NJ: Princeton University Press.

Kelley, R. (1997). *Yo' mama's disfunctional! Fighting the culture wars in urban America.* Boston: Beacon Press.

Koven, S., & Michel, S. (Eds.). (1993). *Mothers of a new world: Maternalist politics and the origins of welfare states.* New York: Routledge.

Lamphere, L., Zavella, P., & Gonzales, F., with Evans, P. (1993). *Sunbelt working mothers: Reconciling family and factory.* Ithaca, NY: Cornell University Press.

Lane, R. (1997). *Murder in America: A history.* Columbus, OH: Ohio State University Press.

Laslett, P. (1988). Family, kinship and collectivity as systems of support in pre-industrial Europe: A consideration of the "nuclear-hardship" hypothesis. *Continuity and Change, 3,* 153–175.

Lewin, T. (1997, September 15). Women losing ground to men in widening income difference. *The New York Times,* p. A12.

Liu, T. (1994). Teaching the differences among women from a historical perspective. In V. Ruiz & E. Dubois (Eds.), *Unequal sisters: A multicultural reader in U.S. women's history.* New York: Routledge.

Luescher, L., & Pillemer, K. (1998). Intergenerational ambivalence: A new approach to the study of parent-child relations in later life. *Journal of Marriage and the Family, 60,* 413–425.

Maltz, M. (1994). Deviating from the mean: The declining significance of significance. *Journal of Research in Crime and Delinquency, 31,* 434–463.

Marks, S. (in press). Teasing out the lessons of the sixties: Family diversity and family privilege. *Journal of Marriage and the Family.*

Massey, D. (1996). The age of extremes: Concentrated affluence and poverty in the twenty-first century. *Demography 33,* 395–412.

May, E. (1980). *Great expectations: Marriage and divorce in post-Victorian America.* Chicago: University of Chicago Press.

May, E. (1988). *Homeward bound: American families in the Cold War era.* New York: Basic Books.

Medick, H., & Sabine, D. (1984). *Interest and emotion: Essays on the study of family and kinship.* New York: Cambridge University Press.

Meyerowitz, J., (Ed.). (1994). *Not June Cleaver: Women and gender in postwar America, 1945–1960.* Philadelphia: Temple University Press.

Mintz, S., & Kellogg, S. (1988). *Domestic revolutions: A social history of American family life.* New York: Free Press.

Mullings, L. (1997). *On our own terms: Race, class, and gender in the lives of African-American Women.* New York: Routledge.

O'Day, R. (1994). *The family and family relationships. 1500–1900: England, France and the United States of America.* New York: St. Martin's.

Ogbomo, O. (1997). *When men and woman mattered: A history of gender relations among the Owan of Nigeria.* Rochester, NY: University of Rochester Press.

Omi, M., & Winant, H. (1994). *Racial formation in the United States: From the 1960s to the 1990s.* New York: Routledge.

Pivar, D. (1974). *Purity crusade: Sexual Morality and Social Control, 1868–1900.* Westport, CT: Greenwood Press.

Pollock, L. (1983). *Forgotten children: Parent-child relations from 1500–1900.* Cambridge, England: Cambridge University Press.

Popenoe, D., & Whitehead, B. D. (1999, June). *The state of our unions, 1999* New Brunswick, NJ: The National Marriage Project.

Rainwater, L. (1995). Poverty and the income packaging of working parents: The United States in comparative perspective. *Children and Youth Services Review, 17,* 11–41.

Rawlings, L. (1998). *Poverty and income trends: 1997.* Washington, DC: Center on Budget and Policy Priorities.

Risman, B. (1998). *Gender vertigo: American families in transition.* New Haven, CT: Yale University Press.

Robinson, R. (1995). Family economic strategies in nineteenth- and early twentieth-century Indianapolis. *Journal of Family History, 20,* 1–22.

Roediger, D. (1988). *The wages of whiteness: Race and the making of the American working class.* London: Verso.

Rosaldo, R. (1989). *Culture and truth: The remaking of social analysis.* Boston: Beacon Press.

Rotella, E., & Alter, G. (1993). Working-class debt in the late nineteenth century United States. *Journal of Family History, 18,* 111–134.

Rothman, E. (1984). *Hands and hearts: A history of courtship in America.* New York: Basic Books.

Rubin, L. (1976/1992). *Worlds of pain: Life in the working-class family.* New York: Basic Books.

Rubin, L. (1994). *Families on the fault line.* New York: Basic Books.

Ruggles, S. (1994). The transformation of American family structure. *American Historical Review, 99,* 103–128.

Sacks, K. (1979). Sisters and wives: The past and future of sexual equality. Westport, CT: Greenwood Press.

Sanchez, G. (1993). *Becoming Mexican American: Ethnicity, culture, and identity in Chicano Los Angeles, 1900–1945.* New York: Oxford University Press.

Schvaneveldt, J., Pickett, R., & Young, M. (1993). Historical methods in family research. In P. Boss et al. (Eds.), *Sourcebook of family theories and methods: A contextual approach.* New York: Plenum Press.

Seccombe, W. (1993). *Weathering the storm: Working-class families from the industrial revolution to the fertility decline.* London: Verso.

Shore, R. (1998). *Ahead of the curve: Why America's leading employers are addressing the needs of new and expectant parents.* New York: Families and Work Institute.

Sinclair, M. (1999). *Changing patterns in three generations of eight families: A brief ethnography.* Unpublished manuscript, The Evergreen State College, Olympia, WA.

Smith, J. (1987). Transforming households: Working-class women and economic crisis. *Social Problems, 34,* 416–436.

Snow, D., & Anderson, L. (1993). *Down on their luck: A study of homeless street people.* Berkeley, CA: University of California Press.

Solomon, R. (1978). Emotion and anthropology: The logic of emotional world views. *Inquiry, 21,* 111–136.

Spain, D., & Bianchi, S. M. (1996). *Balancing act: Motherhood, marriage, and employment among American women.* New York: Sage.

Stacey, J. (1998). *Brave new families: stories of domestic upheaval in late-twentieth-century America.* Berkeley, CA: University of California Press.

Stack, C. (1974). *All our kin: Strategies for survival in a black community.* New York: Harper and Row.

Stack, C. (1993). Cultural perspectives on child welfare. In M. Minow (Ed.), *Family matters: Readings on family lives and the law.* New York: New Press.

Sugrue, T. (1996). *The origins of the urban crisis: Race and inequality in postwar Detroit.* Princeton, NJ: Princeton University Press.

Szreter, S. (1996). Victorian Britain, 1867–1963: Towards a social history of sexuality. *Journal of Victorian Culture, 1,* 31–52.

Teachman, J. D., Tedrow, L. M., & Crowder, K. D. (in press). The changing demography of America's families. *Journal of Marriage and the Family.*

Thompson, E. P. (1963). *The making of the English working class.* New York: Vintage.

Thompson, E. P. (1972). Anthropology and the discipline of historical context. *Midland History, 3,* 41–55.

Turnbull, C. (1962). *The forest people.* New York: Simon & Schuster.

Tuttle, W. M., Jr. (1993). *Daddy's gone to war: The Second World War in the lives of America's children.* New York: Oxford University Press.

U.S. Bureau of the Census. (1975). *Marital Status of the Population, by Age and Series: 1890–1970. Historical Statistics of the United States: Colonial Times to 1970* (Series A 160–171; pp. 20–21). Washington, DC: U.S. Government Publishing Office.

U.S. Bureau of the Census. (1998). *Marital Status and Living Arrangements of Adults 18 Years Old and Over:* March 1998, Table B, and *Marital Status and Living Arrangements, Table MS-2* (Current Population Reports, Series P20–514, March 1998 update). Washington, DC: U.S. Government Publishing Office.

Walter, H. (1989). Who are they? When is then? Comparison in histories of the Western family. *Journal of Comparative Family Studies, 20,* 159–173.

Weiss, J. (2000). *To have and to hold: Marriage, the baby boom, and social change.* Chicago: University of Chicago Press.

Willis, P. (1977). *Learning to labor: How working-class kids get working-class jobs.* New York: Columbia University Press.

Wright-Croes, M. (1999). *Family routine in seven American families: A three generation perspective.* Unpublished manuscript, The Evergreen State College, Olympia, WA.

Wrigley, E. A. et al. (1997). *English population history from family reconstitution, 1580–1837.* New York: Cambridge University Press.

Wyn, J., & White, R. (1997). *Rethinking youth.* London: Sage.

Zinn, M. B. (1994). Feminist thinking from racial-ethnic families. In M. B. Zinn & B. D. Dill, (Eds.), *Women of color in U.S. society.* Philadelphia: Temple University Press.

DAVID H. DEMO   *The University of North Carolina—Greensboro*

MARTHA J. COX   *University of North Carolina—Chapel Hill**

Families With Young Children: A Review of Research in the 1990s

Research conducted in the past decade on families with young children concentrated on 5 broad topics: (a) the transition to parenthood; (b) the importance of maternal sensitivity for children's attachment security and subsequent adjustment and social competence; (c) the effectiveness of particular parenting styles and practices; (d) interparental, familial, and broader societal factors influencing parenting behaviors and child adjustment; and (e) the impact of family structure and household composition on children's well-being. Our review documents substantial diversity in family structures, parenting arrangements, and child-rearing values and practices both within and across ethnic and racial groups. Collectively, the evidence suggests that in most families with young children, parents and children seem to be doing well. We conclude that substantial work is required to expand the study of families with young children beyond mother-child dyads in White, middle-class, two-parent, first-marriage families.

Families with young children remained a vital concern of researchers and practitioners in the

Department of Human Development and Family Studies, The University of North Carolina at Greensboro, P.O. Box 26170, Greensboro, NC 27402-6170.

*Frank Porter Graham Child Development Center, University of North Carolina at Chapel Hill, Chapel Hill, NC 27599-8180.

Key Words: child adjustment, family diversity, parent-child relations, parenting.

1990s. Reflecting the larger society, American families in this category are characterized by rich diversity on several dimensions, including household configuration and family structure, racial and ethnic heritage, socioeconomic resources, and number, gender, ages, and sibling structure of children.

The objective of this review is to summarize, critique, and reflect on research conducted in the 1990s on families with children in the first decade of life. We also include in our review a number of studies employing samples that include age ranges spanning middle or late childhood into early adolescence. Several methods were used to identify relevant journal articles and books, but most of the studies were identified through a systematic analysis of every issue of seven premier journals published in the 1990s: *Journal of Marriage and the Family, Child Development, Developmental Psychology, Journal of Family Psychology, Development and Psychopathology, Family Relations,* and *Journal of Family Issues.* We also devote most of our attention to topics receiving the most research attention. In the past decade, there was substantial interest in early childhood attachment relationships and in children's outcomes associated with various parenting practices and family structures. Our review, like most of the research on families with young children in the past decade, is guided by several theoretical frameworks: life-course, family systems, developmental, ecological, and feminist theories.

Families with young children continue to confront many challenges and stressors, including pressures associated with parental employment and working conditions, underemployment, unemployment, economic hardship, and alarming rates of child poverty. Even in more advantaged middle-income families, everyday economic realities impinge on parents as they work longer hours than ever before and incur the expenses of all-day or part-time child care. Another sobering development is public disinvestment in children. The social and political climate in the United States over the past 3 decades has led to severe cutbacks in federal, local, and private support for services for families with young children. Historian Stephanie Coontz (1997) noted that since the mid-1970s, politicians, employers, and nonparents have grown increasingly indifferent toward the needs of the next generation, as "governments and corporations have transferred more and more of the costs of raising, educating, and training children back onto parents" (p. 142).

High rates of marital dissolution and nonmarital childbearing over the past few decades have led to dramatic decreases in the proportions of White, African American, and Hispanic children living with two parents. From 1970 to 1994, the percentages fell from 90% to less than 80% among White children, from 60% to 33% among African American children, and from 80% to 65% among Hispanic children (Teachman, 2000). Further, because these percentages are based on cross-sectional snapshots of the population, they significantly underestimate the proportion of children who spend periods of their childhood in single-parent households. It is also important in understanding the context of children's lives that five of every six single-parent households are headed by a mother (U.S. Bureau of the Census, 1998). Women's high investments in child care and other unpaid family labor, wage discrimination against women, and lack of compliance with and enforcement of child support payments contribute to post-divorce economic plight for many single mothers and their children and the feminization of poverty.

The last 2 decades have been characterized by growing inequality in the income of American families, stagnant wages for white men and declining wages for African American men, and very modest gains in family income (Teachman, 2000). Children are more likely than any other age group to experience poverty in the United States, comprising 40% of the poor population. In arguably the most affluent nation in the world, one of four American children live in poverty, the highest rate across 17 developed nations (Rank, 2000). Children living in female-headed families, Native American children living on reservations, African American children, and Hispanic children are especially likely both to live in poverty and to suffer the most severe and long-lasting episodes of poverty. At greatest risk are children at the intersection of two or more dimensions of minority status. For example, 70% of African American children under age 6 living in single-parent households have family incomes below the poverty level (Rank). Duration and severity of poverty impair infants' and young children's physical and mental growth, academic ability, and socioemotional well-being (Duncan & Brooks-Gunn, 1997), inhibit effective parenting, and increase the chances that children will attend inferior schools and live in high-risk environments (Rank).

For families with young children, the familial context and ecology typically involves middle-aged parents, the children's grandparents, and other relatives, with each member experiencing the family from a unique developmental and historical vantage point. In this context, many families fare quite well. Most parents care deeply about, support, nurture, and appropriately control their children, especially considering their many other obligations (Demo, 1992). Without dismissing legitimate concerns surrounding problematic behavior among many parents and children, research suggests that most children seem to be doing well and that many are remarkably resilient in the face of family misfortune or disruption (Haggerty, Sherrod, Garmezy, & Rutter, 1994).

PARENTING AND PARENT-CHILD RELATIONS

The Transition to Parenthood

In the 1990s, there has been continued interest in understanding early family formation and the transition to first-time parenthood. Whereas much of the research in earlier decades was retrospective and self-report, many studies in the past decade are longitudinal, following couples before and after the birth of the first child. Although early writing on the transition to parenthood focused on the "crisis" of parenthood for young couples, recent longitudinal studies have focused on understanding the variability in couples' adjustment to parenthood and the factors associated with that variability. In line with our conclusion that most children seem to be doing well, it appears that after an initial disruption, most couples also seem to be doing well. Early studies examined couples before and after the transition to parenthood and found that, in the aggregate, marital satisfaction declined precipitously after the birth of a child. Belsky and Rovine (1990) noted the importance of examining variability within groups and found four distinct patterns of change, however: accelerating decline, linear decline, no change, and modest positive increase. Other studies have illuminated factors that are associated with these patterns of change. Wallace and Gotlib (1990) found, not surprisingly, that the best single predictor of postpartum marital adjustment was prenatal marital adjustment. Cox, Paley, Burchinal, and Payne (1999) observed that among couples who showed an increase or no change in marital satisfaction during the 2 years following the birth, neither spouse had high depressive symptoms, at least one of the spouses showed good problem-solving communication before the birth of the child, and the first-born was more likely to be a male child. For most couples, however, significant declines in negativity began about the first year after the child's birth, a finding replicated by Gable, Belsky, & Crnic (1995).

Other investigators observed that adjustment to parenthood was more difficult for women who expected (before parenthood) that things would be better at 1 year after birth than they actually were, and that high expectations regarding child-care assistance from the spouse and the extended family were associated with a more difficult adjustment for women (Kalmuss, Davidson, & Cushman, 1992). This perhaps reflects the fact that parents' activities become more instrumental and child-oriented after the birth of a child and the division of tasks becomes more gender-based (Cowan & Cowan, 2000). Levy-Schiff (1994) found that fathers' positive caregiving behaviors were strong predictors of marital satisfaction among both husbands and wives in the 9 months after the first child's birth.

Belsky and Rovine (1990) proposed that the couple's adjustment to parenthood is influenced by the child's temperament. In turn, the quality of marital adjustment appears to influence parenting practices and the development of the child. Some studies suggest that fathers' parenting behavior, compared with that of mothers, may be more influenced by the coparental relationship (Doherty, Kouneski, & Erickson, 1998), although the find-

ings are mixed and may depend on the specific parenting behaviors observed and the age of the child. Belsky, Youngblade, Rovine, and Volling (1991) found that more negative paternal behavior and more negative child behavior were present in families in which marriages were deteriorating in quality. For mothers there was some evidence of a compensatory process such that more negative marriages were associated with slightly more positive maternal behavior. In contrast, Cox, Paley, Payne, and Burchinal (1999) found that mothers who had shown more withdrawal in marital interactions prenatally showed less sensitivity, warmth, and involvement with their 3-month-olds even when controlling for symptoms of depression and the negative mood of the child. For fathers, there was a similar, but less strong, effect of marital withdrawal.

As with many areas of the study of families, we know more about women and their transitions than about men. How men are changed by becoming parents and how their behaviors and attitudes affect their families are still vastly understudied areas. This is also evident in the literature examining young children's early attachments, in which the nearly exclusive focus has been on mothers and their children.

Early Childhood Attachment Relationships

Thompson (1998) claimed that Freud's emphasis on the infant-mother relationship as unique and as the first love object and prototype of all later love objects has led to the general consideration of the child's relationship with the mother as a foundation for personality growth. He further noted that although psychobiological, learning, and psychoanalytic explanations have been influential, research in the last decade on infant-parent attachment relationships has been guided by ethological attachment theory elaborated by Bowlby (1951, 1958) and Ainsworth (Ainsworth, Blehar, Waters, & Wall, 1978). Bowlby argued that the infant's attachment to the caregiver arises from species-typical behavioral systems, evolved to promote infant survival, thus motivating infants to seek protective proximity of adults, especially when distressed, alarmed, or in danger (Thompson).

The most frequently used assessment of attachment involves the measurement of infant-parent attachment in the Strange Situation (Ainsworth et al., 1978). The assessment is comprised of a series of episodes in which the baby experiences separations from and reunions with the parent. Infants who are classified as securely attached (Group B, about 65% of infants) use the parent as a secure base during the procedure and respond positively to the parent's return either with smiling or contact and proximity seeking. Infants who are insecure-avoidant (Group A, about 20% of infants) avoid the parent on reunions and at other points in the procedure. Infants who are insecure-resistant (Group C, about 15% of infants) show combinations of resistance, anger, and distress.

Attachment theory raises some of the most important questions of the decade, and indeed of earlier decades: How important are early experiences for psychosocial growth? How flexible are social attachment behaviors once learned? Under what conditions is there stability over childhood and into adulthood in social behavior and social relationships, and under what conditions is there instability? In the 1990s, many studies (Cox, Owen, Henderson, & Margand, 1992; National Institute of Child Health and Human Development [NICHD] Early Child Care Research Network, 1997) and a meta-analysis (DeWolff & Van-Ijzendoorn, 1997) have demonstrated that, as predicted by theory, maternal sensitivity is associated with infant attachment security. Seifer, Schiller, Sameroff, Resnick, and Riordan (1996), however, who failed to find the association, cautioned that other factors besides maternal sensitivity need to be studied in the explanation of variability in attachment security of 1-year-olds. This sentiment is echoed by DeWolff and VanIjzendoorn, whose meta-analysis of 66 studies finds a moderately strong positive association between maternal sensitivity and attachment security. The authors noted that other influences seem to interact with sensitivity to determine attachment security, and they suggested that further study needs to consider the complex interactions between context and maternal sensitivity in unstable and stressful settings. Much attachment research has been conducted with advantaged middle-class American samples, providing limited understanding of the way in which cultural or socioeconomic context moderates the relationship between maternal sensitivity and security of attachment. Cowan (1997) argued further that the attachment focus on maternal behavior ignores the family system.

In the last decade, the study of attachment security has expanded to the infant-father relationship and the examination of attachment relationships at later ages. Major questions have been whether paternal sensitivity to the infant during the first year predicts infant-father security of at-

tachment and whether maternal sensitivity is related to attachment assessed at ages beyond infancy. Some studies find that paternal sensitivity is associated with infant-father attachment (Cox et al., 1992) and a meta-analysis of the association between paternal sensitivity and infant-father attachment found a significant, but weak, relation (De Wolff & Van Ijzendoorn, 1997). Belsky (1996) considered the broader social context of the infant-father relationship and found that fathers of secure infants were more extraverted and agreeable, tended to have more positive marriages, and experienced more positive spillover between work and family than fathers of insecure infants.

Waters and Deane (1985) developed an alternative measure to the Strange Situation that can be used at 12 months up to 5 years (Vaughn & Waters, 1990). Based on Q-sort methodology, the Attachment Q-Set (AQS) requires observers to describe mother-child interaction in a naturalistic setting, or parents sort cards to describe their child's behavior. Several studies report significant correlations between AQS security scores and attachment classifications from the Strange Situation (Seifer et al., 1996; Vaughn & Waters, 1990), while others do not. Other studies (Seifer et al.; Teti et al., 1991) have reported that Q-sort security scores were related positively to observed sensitive mothering.

In the last decade, new procedures have been developed to evaluate the security of attachment in older children, generally 4.5 to 6 years, using observations of children in extended separation and reunion procedures similar to the Strange Situation (Crittendon, 1992). These procedures, although interesting and promising, have not been as thoroughly validated as the Strange Situation (Thompson, 1998), but some studies show an expected association between attachment classifications and maternal style (e.g., Stevenson-Hinde & Shouldice, 1995).

Additional issues involve the stability of attachment over time and the extent to which children who show early secure attachment also show competent social adaptation at later ages. Thompson (1998) summarized the work on stability of the Strange Situation over the last 2 decades and found wide variety from study to study in terms of the proportions of infants who maintained stable classifications. Generally, secure patterns show far more stability over time than insecure patterns, and higher income samples show more stability than lower income samples. Investigating the stability of the AQS and separation-reunion paradigms with older children, Youngblade, Park, and Belsky (1993) observed moderate stability between parent-sorted AQS scores at 12 and 36 months. Wartner, Grossman, Fremmer-Bombik, and Suess (1994) reported that more than 80% of children seen in the Strange Situation as infants obtained the same classification from a 6-year-old separation-reunion procedure. Howes and Hamilton (1992) indicated that attachments between preschoolers and their teachers were stable over a 6- to 12-month period using an observer-sorted AQS.

It seems that both stability and change may be lawful, but important questions remain concerning the processes associated with stability and change. Teti, Wolfe Sakin, Kucera, and Corns (1996) suggested that certain events may lead to the reorganization of the mother-child relationship. Using the AQS, they found that security scores of firstborns dropped after the birth of a new sibling, and the most dramatic drop was for those children whose mothers had high scores on depression, anxiety, or hostility.

Other work during the last decade has focused on understanding disorders of attachment (Zeanah, Mammen, & Lieberman, 1993). This work has been stimulated by research on the social behavior of infants reared in conditions not regarded as species-typical, such as infants raised in institutions or in foster care or children subjected to maltreatment. Disorders of attachment then represent more profound and pervasive disturbances in the child's feeling of safety and security than the patterns of attachment discussed earlier. Zeanah et al. proposed five categories of attachment disorders, but there is little research on the utility, etiology, or long-term implications of these diagnostic categories. A disoriented, disorganized pattern of attachment has been identified as occurring with greater frequency among children adopted later in infancy (Chisholm, 1998), maltreated children and children living in extreme poverty (Carlson, 1998), and families in which parents show some form of psychopathology (Teti, Gelfand, Messinger, & Russell, 1995). Thus, increased rates of disordered attachment seem to occur in situations that deviate too far from what are species-typical rearing conditions for young children, and disordered attachment seems to be associated with higher rates of maladjusted behavior in children. Nonetheless, these studies suggest wide variability in outcomes for children who seemingly suffer similarly deprived environments, suggesting that we need much more information concerning the conditions under which these disorders occur and the variety of pathways to outcomes for children.

Parenting in Middle and Late Childhood and Child Adjustment

A large literature before the 1990s established the benefits to children of authoritative parenting—generally characterized by high levels of parental warmth, support, and control—in contrast to permissive or authoritarian parenting. Research conducted in the last decade provides further evidence linking authoritative parenting with positive child adjustment and relating power-assertive techniques to child maladjustment. Recent studies have sought to further specify the dimensions and correlates of authoritative and authoritarian parenting and to assess the generalizability of these constructs beyond White middle-class families in the United States. Dekovic and Gerris (1992), for example, found that, among Dutch parents, higher and more complex parental reasoning predicted home observations of authoritative childrearing, indirect positive control, warmth, acceptance, and support. Studying families in the West Indies, Rohner, Kean, and Cournoyer (1991) found that physical punishment by parents substantially impairs children's psychological adjustment, particularly when the punishment is frequent and severe, in large part because it contributes to children's feelings of being rejected by parents.

Important questions have emerged, however, regarding the desirability and effectiveness of authoritative practices in lower income and minority families. Partly because of chronic financial stress and negative life events, poor mothers in both White and Black families are more likely than their affluent counterparts to value obedience, to issue commands, to be restrictive, and to use physical punishment in disciplining their children (Hoff-Ginsberg & Tardif, 1995; McLoyd, 1990). The occurrence and severity of child abuse are also related to low family income, parental unemployment or underemployment, and economic decline (Belsky, 1993; National Research Council, 1993). Although empirical evidence is limited, poor African American parents, and particularly fathers, appear to be less involved and less emotionally expressive than socioeconomically advantaged parents, but the former feel an important parental responsibility to keep their children "in line" and out of trouble (McLoyd). Similarly, in a study of three racial groups, Leadbeater and Bishop (1994) found that African American mothers were the most protective, strict, and vigilant, followed by Puerto Rican mothers and Anglo-American mothers.

Clearly, there is substantial variability among low income Black parents in their parenting styles and their attitudes toward physical punishment. Bluestone and Tamis-LeMonda (1999) found that working- and middle-class African American mothers of children aged 5 to 12 were most likely to use reasoning and other child-centered approaches to discipline and least likely to use physical punishment. Kelley, Power, and Wimbush (1992) reported that Black parents who use power-assertive techniques are as likely as other parents to reason with their children and to consider the children's perspectives. Interestingly, Avenevoli, Sessa, and Steinberg (1999) found that among African American adolescents, authoritative parenting is related to higher levels of delinquent behavior. Chao (1994) argued that the concepts *authoritative* and *authoritarian* parenting are ethnocentric and that Chinese and other Asian childrearing patterns are better described as emphasizing indigenous Confucian training ideologies that blend parental love, concern, involvement, and physical closeness with firm control, governance, and teaching of the child. Among European American parents, "training" was perceived negatively and associated with strict, rigid, militaristic practices (Chao). Collectively, these findings underscore the sociohistorical and cultural specificity of childrearing values and behaviors and suggest that much greater attention be devoted to the conceptualization, interpretation, and empirical investigation of parenting practices among marginalized and minority families in diverse contexts.

A substantial body of research conducted before the 1990s, predominantly involving White families, demonstrated the importance of socioeconomic resources for effective parenting. Extending Elder's (1974; Elder, Nguyen, & Caspi, 1985) model, McLoyd's (1990) influential review documented systematic evidence that poverty and near-poor living conditions in African American families bear a direct association with children's impaired socioemotional functioning and that much of the adverse effect of chronic economic hardship on children is due to its impact on parents' psychological distress and their behavior toward the child. Persistent poverty and financial distress erode parents' ability to provide consistent

involvement, support, nurturance, empathy, and discipline; increase the occurrence of coercive and punitive parental behavior; and weaken marital and other interparental bonds (McLoyd). Social networks lessen the strains on parents by providing valuable interpersonal and economic resources, such as collaborative child care, informational support, and role modeling.

Subsequent research has replicated these patterns among a variety of socioeconomically disadvantaged groups. Among depressed or psychologically distressed African American mothers who currently or formerly received welfare, employment reduced the frequency of spanking (Jackson, Gyamfi, Brooks-Gunn, & Blake, 1998). Other conditions shown to inhibit parents' ability to provide consistent warmth and support and effective discipline include family economic hardship (Bank, Forgatch, Patterson, & Fetrow, 1993; Dodge, Pettit, & Bates, 1994; McLoyd, 1990), neighborhood poverty (Klebanov, Brooks-Gunn, & Duncan, 1994), marital conflict (Patterson, Reid, & Dishion, 1992), and maternal antisocial qualities (Bank et al., 1993; Belsky, 1993). A number of studies involving both White and racial and ethnic minority families suggest that the effects on child and adolescent adjustment of a range of risk factors and stressful conditions, including economic hardship, interparental conflict, and maternal depression, are mediated by consistent parental support and discipline (Dumka, Roosa, & Jackson, 1997; Luster & McAdoo, 1991; McLoyd).

Although researchers have made significant progress in including minority participants in their samples, few studies have explicitly focused on the conceptualization and explanation of parent-child relationships in racial and ethnic minority families (Graham, 1992). Reflecting the pervasive oppression and marginalization of minority families in American society, prominent issues in the scholarship on racial and ethnic minority and immigrant families are (a) the extendedness of such families and their adaptive strategies, (b) biculturalism and acculturation, (c) heterogeneity in family form and process within and across racial and ethnic groups, and (d) the challenges and burdens associated with economic deprivation.

Extended families are highly valued among ethnic minorities. They typically extend across households, geographical boundaries, and multiple generations; they involve relationships among affinal, consanguine, and fictive or chosen kin; and, relative to nuclear families, they are characterized by higher levels of interaction and close-ness (Harrison, Wilson, Pine, Chan, & Buriel, 1990; Mott, 1990). Yet there is tremendous diversity both across and within ethnic groups in the form and function of extended family networks. Mexican American extended families become stronger and more elaborate as they become acculturated, actively displaying their familism through ongoing social exchanges, frequent communication and visiting, and family celebrations (Baca Zinn & Wells, 2000). Dumka et al. (1997) found that, among low-income Mexican immigrant and Mexican American families, more highly acculturated mothers were more consistent in disciplining. The authors suggested that more acculturated parents may adopt more restrictive parenting practices to protect their children from the threats of high-risk urban environments.

Among extended as well as nuclear African American families, egalitarian family dynamics are more common than they are in White families. Owing to both cultural factors (e.g., shared values) and historical experiences (notably slavery), role sharing, flexibility, reciprocity, and complementarity are widely observed in African American families, providing adaptive responses to more rigid, gender-based, and patriarchal patterns (Billingsley, 1992; Collins, 1990; Taylor, 2000). Consistent with earlier studies, Tolson and Wilson (1990) characterize the environment of African American families as being higher than average on achievement orientation, moral-religious emphasis, organization, and control, but exhibiting lower levels of expressiveness, conflict, independence, intellectual-cultural orientation, and active-recreational orientation. Although substantially more research is necessary to understand variation in family processes across African American families, there is also evidence of meaningful strains in multigenerational households and diminished parenting effectiveness when economic hardship intersects with early mothering and early grandmothering (Chase-Lansdale, Brooks-Gunn, & Zamsky, 1994).

Childrearing Values and Practices

Mainstream American culture in the late 20th century placed a strong value on individualism, competition, independence, self-development and self-satisfaction, and parents' childrearing behaviors generally emphasized the development of children's autonomy (Alwin, 1990). There is consistent evidence, however, that ethnic minority chil-dren, in comparison with White children, are more likely to be socialized to value cooperation, sharing, reciprocity, obligation, and interdependence (Harrison et al., 1990). African American parents, in comparison with White parents, tend to be more egalitarian in childrearing, emphasizing traits such as assertiveness, independence, and self-confidence in both boys and girls, although contradictory messages within the family and the larger society become more prevalent and powerful as Black children move into adolescence and young adulthood (Taylor, 2000). From the time they are born, Mexican American children are socialized in a context of "thick" social relations characterized by frequent interaction across extensive kinship networks, and they are taught to value cooperation, family unity, and solidarity over competition and individual achievement (Baca Zinn & Wells, 2000). Asian American children are socialized to value and comply with familial authority to the point of relinquishing personal desires and interests (Ishii-Kuntz, 2000). Chinese and Chinese American children are taught Confucian traditions that emphasize harmonious relations with others, loyalty and respect to elders, and subordination in hierarchical relationships, particularly in father-son, husband-wife, and older brother-younger brother relationships (Chao, 1994). Asian American parents typically exercise control over their children's friendship choices, clothing, and extracurricular activities and retain this control through their children's high school years (Ishii-Kuntz). Japanese American children tend to be closely supervised by their parents, who simultaneously teach them two different but overlapping sets of values—one rooted in Japanese culture and the other facilitating assimilation into mainstream American culture (Ishii-Kuntz).

Within and across ethnic and racial minority groups, there is considerable variation in parents' strategies for transmitting norms, values, and beliefs and in trying to inculcate racial pride and self-respect in their children. Boykin and Toms (1985) discussed a "triple quandry" confronting African American parents who must choose between (a) socializing their children into the mainstream (largely sacrificing their cultural heritage), (b) stressing their oppressed minority status, or (c) teaching culturally valued behaviors in the black community. Consistent with theories emphasizing the importance of parental socialization and interpersonal relationships in Black families (McAdoo, 1978; Stack, 1974), feelings of closeness to other Blacks and positive evaluations of Blacks as a group are associated with socialization messages promoting racial awareness, integration, and assertiveness (Demo & Hughes, 1990).

Adding to ethnic and racial diversity, family relationships and children's socialization vary by children's gender, although the nature of the differences is a matter of debate and interpretation. Recent reviews (Fagot, 1995; Lytton & Romney, 1991) corroborate earlier conclusions (Maccoby & Jacklin, 1974) that there are few areas in which parents' behavior toward boys and girls can be differentiated. Parents interact similarly with sons and daughters on such dimensions as amount of time spent together, parental warmth, supervision, disciplining techniques, parental reasoning and communication styles, and encouragement of achievement and independence (Lytton & Romney; Peterson, Bodman, Bush, & Madden-Derdich, 2000). However, parents tend to encourage gender-typed clothing, activities, toys, and environments (Crouter, Manke, & McHale, 1995; Fagot). Parents' rules and expectations for household labor also vary by children's gender. Across diverse single-parent, two-parent, single-earner, and dual-earner family structures, daughters, especially teenage daughters, perform significantly more housework than sons (Demo & Acock, 1993; Goldscheider & Waite, 1991), and the tasks they are assigned tend to correspond with stereotypical definitions of gender-appropriate responsibilities (Benin & Edwards, 1990; Blair, 1992). As a consequence, fundamentally gendered aspects of family relationships are transmitted from one generation to the next.

Family Relationships Over Time

More longitudinal studies and more studies guided by life span and life course frameworks were positive developments in the 1990s. Clarifying earlier findings based largely on cross-sectional studies of married couples with children living in the United States, Stattin and Klackenberg (1992) employed a prospective design to chart the trajectories of marital, mother-child, and father-child relations in Swedish families over the years from the child's birth to age 18. They found that, at any one point in time, the vast majority of parents describe their marriages, as well as mother-child and father-child relationships, in favorable terms. Following families over time, however, it is clear that disharmonious marital and parent-child relationships increase gradually but steadily as children get older, peaking at ages 10 to 12. Discord in father-child relations exhibits a similar pattern, but the downward trajectory continues in an almost linear form throughout adolescence. Marked stabilities were observed over time, with parent-child discord when the child was aged 4 to 6 significantly predicting discord when the child was 13 to 15.

Research indicates substantial stability in parenting behaviors, values, and interparental conflict from middle childhood through adolescence (Acock & Demo, 1999; McNally, Eisenberg, & Harris, 1991). Among both mothers and fathers, parenting satisfaction is highly stable over time, is strongly associated with perceived marital quality, and is predictive of increases in marital quality (Rogers & White, 1998). Fathers report significantly lower satisfaction with parenting than do mothers, and parents of stepchildren report much less satisfaction than those with only biological children (Rogers & White, 1998).

Marital Relationships and Child Development

Before the 1990s, a considerable body of research documented the association between marital relationships, particularly marital conflict, and emotional and behavioral problems in children. These studies defined marital discord in a variety of ways, from overall self-report of marital quality to overt conflict, with most studies simply documenting an association between such constructs and child adjustment, without proposing mechanisms that may account for the association. Recent research has established critical differences between "constructive" and "destructive" conflict, raising some important questions: What kinds of conflict are associated with what child outcome, under what conditions and through what processes does conflict undermine child development, and when is conflict more benign or even facilitative of healthy development in families (Cox & Brooks-Gunn, 1999)?

In the 1990s, a "second generation" of research advanced this literature by beginning to clarify when and why this linkage exists between marital conflict and children's behavior problems (Fincham, 1994). This research suggests that overt marital conflict is more strongly related to disrupted parenting and child adjustment than is overall marital satisfaction or quality (Coiro & Emery, 1998). Katz and Gottman (1993) found that mutually hostile marital patterns when children were 5 years old predicted externalizing behavior problems when children were age 8, whereas husbands' angry and withdrawn behavior predicted later internalizing behavior problems. Marital satisfaction and child temperament were unrelated to behavior problem outcomes, however.

Studies suggest that for children who are old enough to understand and interpret the conflict, intense verbal conflicts that are child-related and poorly resolved have more direct negative effects than do conflicts that do not concern children and are resolved constructively and nonaggressively (Fincham, Grych, & Osborne, 1994). Jouriles, Norwood, McDonald, Vincent, and Mahoney (1996) empirically link physical marital violence and other forms of marital aggression with externalizing and internalizing problems in children. Long-term effects are suggested by McNeal and Amato (1998), who find that parents' reports of marital violence when children were in adolescence or preadolescence predicted offsprings' later reports of negative outcomes in early adulthood. When conflicts are resolved or dealt with constructively, however, they are not necessarily negative for children (Easterbrooks, Cummings, & Emde, 1994). In fact, constructive conflict can help children learn appropriate ways to handle interpersonal difficulties (Cummings & Wilson, 1999).

Much of the theorizing about the processes through which marital conflict affects children assumes that one route may be through the effect of conflict on parenting. Again, interparental conflict may not always result in more negative parenting. Because conflict can be a way to work out differences that may cause resentment, anger, or withdrawal (Gottman, 1994), parents who engage in constructive conflict may actually be better able to parent than those who withdraw from conflict (Cox, Paley, Payne, et al., 1999). There is evidence, however, that hostile, angry affect experienced in the marital relationship can "spill over" into the parent-child relationship (Coiro & Emery, 1998; Erel & Burman, 1995). Parents who are angry, exhausted, or demoralized from marital conflict may simply be less emotionally available or attuned to their children and experience more tension in their interactions with their children (Margolin, Christensen, & John, 1996). The anger and withdrawal engendered by marital conflict may lead parents to be actively rejecting, hostile, or physically aggressive with their children, and this may be particularly true for fathers (Crockenberg & Covey, 1991). Clearly, marital conflict can lead to parent-child conflict, and vice-versa, but parent-child conflict appears to be a more proximate and

stronger influence on children's adjustment than interparental conflict, particularly in adolescence (Acock & Demo, 1999).

Recent research has also considered the importance of children's individual appraisals of the marital conflict and their own coping strategies (Davies & Cummings, 1994; Grych & Fincham, 1990). These models emphasize that children do not just react to the conflict itself, but to its meaning for them. Cummings and his colleagues (Cummings & Wilson, 1999; Davies & Cummings) have advanced the "emotional security hypothesis," suggesting that the emotional impact of marital conflict on the child varies depending on the appraisal the child makes of the implications of the conflict for herself and for her family. Long-term exposure to unresolved and highly negative conflict seems to sensitize children to the occurrence of conflict, and their appraisals of the conflict tend to be more negative. Variations in children's coping strategies also have been investigated. O'Brien, Margolin, and John (1995) found that children who used coping strategies that involved them in their parents' conflict had higher levels of maladjustment, whereas children who distanced themselves from parents' conflict or who had coping strategies that activated social support had lower levels of maladjustment.

Siblings and Sibling Relations

Relations among siblings traditionally have received little attention in the family and developmental literatures, but in the 1990s, there was an increase in sibling research. This research has focused on a wide array of issues including sibling conflict, the impact on a child of a sibling's birth, differential treatment of siblings in families, age changes in sibling relationships, and the effects of sibling relationships on development.

Research suggests striking differences in sibling relationships across families (Dunn, 1993). A number of factors related to family functioning appear to influence the quality of sibling relationships and, as family systems theories posit, parent-child dyads influence sibling dyads. Equal treatment by fathers, family harmony during family discussions, and parents' perceptions of family cohesiveness are related to levels of sibling conflict (Brody, Stoneman, McCoy, & Forehand, 1992). Volling and Belsky (1992) also implicated father's treatment in finding that facilitative and affectionate fathering was associated with more prosocial sibling interaction. In that study, higher sibling conflict and aggression were related to higher levels of conflict between the mother and the two children at 6 years, intrusive and overcontrolling mothering at 3 years, and insecure infant-mother attachments. Brody, Stoneman, and McCoy (1994) documented that interparental conflict, children's difficult temperament, and differential negativity in parent-sibling relationships also predict low sibling relationship quality.

Other studies indicate that differential parental treatment of siblings is related to the quality of sibling relationships. McHale et al. (1995) find that differential treatment in which one parent reports being closer to one child and the other parent reports being equally close to the children is associated with poorer marital relationships. Erel et al. (1998) found that an older sibling's negative behavior in sibling interaction is linked to negative dimensions of marital and mother-child relationships; this link seems to be mediated by the mother's power assertion with the older sibling.

Burmester and Furman (1990) noted that information about age changes in sibling relations is scarce. From their study of children in grades 3, 6, 9, and 12, they suggested that relationships become progressively more egalitarian and less intense with age. Other research suggests that the assumption that warmer, closer, and less conflicted sibling relationships are better may not be warranted. Raffaelli (1992) considered sibling conflict among preadolescents and early adolescents and suggested that sibling conflict may provide a context in which age appropriate issues of individuation and differentiation are played out. Positive effects of conflict may only occur when the conflict is moderate, however. Stormshak, Bellanti, and Bierman (1996) identified 3 types of sibling dyads among aggressive first and second grade children: conflictual (high conflict, low warmth), involved (moderate conflict and warmth), and supportive (low conflict, high warmth). Children in involved sibling relationships showed better adjustment than did children in conflictual relationships.

Siblings may be important for development on many levels. Perner, Ruffman, and Leekam (1994) found that 3- to 4-year-old children from larger families, when compared with children from smaller families, were better able to predict a story character's mistaken, false-belief-based action. They suggested that sibling interaction provides a rich database for building a "theory of mind." Youngblade and Dunn (1995) supported this contention, finding that child-sibling pretense play was related to the child's performance on an affective understanding task. The authors interpreted their findings as supporting the importance of children's interactions with their siblings for the development of understanding of "other minds."

In some respects, however, the birth of a sibling may place some children at a disadvantage, at least initially. Baydar, Greek, and Brooks-Gunn (1997) found that the younger child's birth results in fewer positive interactions between the mother and the older child, especially if the birth interval is short and if the mother adopts a controlling style. These changes result in lower verbal ability in the older child and, about 2.5 years after the birth of the sibling, negative effects are seen on achievement and socioemotional adjustment. Although some positive effects attributable to the birth of a sibling are evident in peer relations, Baydar, Hyle, and Brooks-Gunn (1997) reported temporary increases in behavior problems of older children, lower reading recognition scores, and lower self-perceptions, especially among the children of economically disadvantaged families.

The presence of siblings changes the context of an older child's development in the family. It appears that some aspects of those changes are beneficial for development, whereas other aspects may be deleterious, especially in families with few financial resources to divide among children.

FAMILY STRUCTURE, HOUSEHOLD COMPOSITION, AND CHILDREN'S LIVING ARRANGEMENTS

Research in the 1990s demonstrated substantial diversity and fluidity in children's living arrangements, and numerous studies examined children's adjustment in different family structures. Investigators typically define family structure as number of parents present in the household, parents' marital status, and more recently, parents' sexual orientation. Most commonly, children living in "intact" families with two biological parents in their first marriage are considered the benchmark and compared to children living in some other arrangement. This body of research has yielded a great deal of valuable information. But a major limitation of this work has been a tendency to combine all single-parent families into one category (and all two-parent families in a second category), obscuring variability in resources and outcomes within family types. A related limitation is an overreliance on comparisons of mean ratings across groups. Furthermore, most of the research linking family structure and child well-being continues to rely on one-point-in-time classifications of parents' marital status as the central explanatory variable. Such measures typically ignore the sequencing, duration, and quality of involvement of parents, stepparents, grandparents, and other kin, thus minimizing the influence of a variety of parental and nonparental family members on child development.

Although much work in this area is atheoretical, the implicit reasoning in most studies involves socialization and family stress arguments. From a socialization viewpoint, it is typically assumed that children are advantaged if they live with two heterosexual parents in their first marriage because (a) the parents provide both same-sex and other-sex role models, and (b) the children should benefit from the social, emotional, and economic resources of two parents. A family stress explanation posits that changes in living arrangements (e.g., parents exiting the household and changes in neighborhood, school, and peer groups) are disruptive and stressful for children and weaken parent-child bonds.

Researchers have been energetic in studying family structure and attempting to identify family environments that facilitate or inhibit children's development and well-being. The consistent pattern, however, is that family structure per se tells us little about children's adjustment. Amato and Keith's (1991) meta-analysis of 92 (mostly North American) studies found a small advantage favoring children in two-parent families over their peers in divorced single-parent families, with a median effect size of .14 of a standard deviation. A comprehensive review of studies conducted in the United Kingdom, Australia, and New Zealand (Rodgers & Pryor, 1998) documents similarly small differences across children living in various family structures. Examining data from the first wave of the National Survey of Families and Households, Acock and Demo (1994) found few statistically significant differences in mothers' reports of children's well-being across first-married, divorced, remarried, and continuously single-parent families. Where differences existed, children in first married families tended to fare slightly better on measures of socioemotional adjustment and academic performance. Similarly, Hawkins and Eggebeen (1991) found no differences in the verbal and intellectual functioning of children in intact families and that of children living in five types of maritally disrupted family structures.

One reason that family structure alone does not explain much is that even careful classifications of parents' marital status do not tell us much about family relationships, histories, and trajectories. Illustrating the limitations of classifications made at any single point in time, Wojtkiewicz (1992) found that most children who are classified as living in a "nonintact" family at age 15 have lived in a variety of single-parent and two-parent households for intervals during their childhood and adolescence. Aquilino's (1996) analysis of a nationally representative sample of children born to unmarried mothers demonstrates that the household configurations and life trajectories of such children are characterized by tremendous diversity. Only one in five lived exclusively in single-parent households throughout their childhood, and nearly half had other relatives who lived with them for periods during their childhood. Importantly, variations in kin involvement and in the timing and sequencing of changes in children's living arrangements had profound consequences for educational attainment, home-leaving, and employment outcomes. For example, children experiencing multiple transitions, experiencing them later in childhood, and those living in stepfamilies fared poorly in comparison with those living their entire childhood in stable single-parent families or moving into two-parent families with biological or adoptive parents. Other studies show benefits of stable single-parent living arrangements for children's socioemotional adjustment and global well-being (Acock & Demo, 1994), and deleterious effects of multiple transitions (Capaldi & Patterson, 1991; Kurdek, Fine, & Sinclair, 1995), supporting a life-stress perspective.

A second limitation of relying on family structure as a predictor of children's adjustment is that there are many similarities in the dynamics of parent-child relationships across diverse household configurations. Parents have similar rules and expectations for their children across first married, divorced, continuously single, and remarried family structures, with most parents strongly endorsing culturally valued guidelines for their children's behavior (Acock & Demo, 1994). Mothers in all of these family types reported having enjoyable times with their children almost daily, and there were no differences in the frequency of their reading or homework activities with children or in their own or their husbands' difficulties with children. Studies also document consistency in maternal control and high levels of maternal support across family types (Acock & Demo; Simons & Associates, 1996). There are, however, some small but noteworthy differences, with mothers in first married families reporting somewhat more pleasant and less stressful relationships with their children, less yelling at and spanking of their children, and higher levels of involvement in various school-related, religious, and community activities (Acock & Demo). Relative to differences in parent-child interaction by family type, there are much larger differences by parents' gender, with many fathers minimally involved in their children's lives, regardless of the father's residential status (Parke & Sterns, 1993). In postdivorce families, although there is wide variation in fathers' involvement, contact tends to be infrequent, diminishes over time (King, 1994; Maccoby & Mnookin, 1992), and decreases further as a stepfather enters the children's lives (Seltzer, 1991).

Important differences across and within racial groups represent further diversity in children's experience of family structure. African American children are much more likely than White children to live in and benefit from extended family arrangements. Recent analyses indicate that one in five African American families are extended, compared with 1 in 10 White families (Glick, 1997). Clearly, Black families are not a homogeneous group, and variations in their structural configuration are associated with variations in family climate. For example, Tolson and Wilson (1990) reported higher levels of organization and lower levels of moral-religious emphasis in families headed by one adult caregiver than in those headed by two adults. Charting the evolution of African American children's living arrangements from first grade through adolescence, Hunter and Ensminger (1992) observed substantial diversity and fluidity in family structure over time, with both parents and nonparents moving in and out of the household and in and out of central childrearing roles. Studying the Woodlawn community in Chicago, they distinguished 86 different combinations of adults living in households with first graders, and 35 different extended family configurations, illustrating the limitations of conventional classifications of children's family living arrangements and leading the researchers to conclude that the term "female-headed household" is inadequate for understanding the realities and complexities of urban African American families. Indeed, parenting, in the true sense of the word, is being done by more than one adult family member in most of these households, often involving members of multiple generations and most often including close, supportive relations between children, their mothers, and coresidential grandmothers.

Although aggregate analyses show that fathers tend to be less involved in children's lives than are mothers, a common assumption is that father-absent residential arrangements translate into infrequent paternal contact with children. This assumption reflects an ideology that privileges two-parent families and pathologizes single-parent families. Careful demographic analyses reveal that many nonresidential fathers maintain routine interaction with their children, however (King & Heard, 1999; Mott, 1990), and Maccoby and Mnookin's (1992) repeated observations of families over several years illustrate that many children move from one household to another to live with a different parent. Fathers also report more frequent paternal contact than mothers report (Braver, 1998; Manning & Smock, 1999).

There are some encouraging developments in this line of research. Over the past decade, greater attention has been devoted to identifying family formation, dissolution, and reformation trajectories and how they relate to children's adjustment. Second, research conducted in the 1990s on children's development in diverse family structures has paid much more careful attention to the dynamics of parent-child and interparental relationships. Few researchers, however, have employed more sophisticated person-process-context-time models to the study of family structure and child well-being.

Children's Experience of Parental Divorce

Evaluating the results of 180 studies on children's adjustment to divorce, Amato (1993) concluded that empirical evidence strongly suggests that interparental conflict is a risk factor in the life course of children. Accumulating evidence indicates that many children in first-married families endure high levels of interparental conflict and marital unhappiness throughout their childhood, with prolonged exposure directly and indirectly impairing their well-being. Some informative longitudinal and prospective studies of divorce and parent-child relationships illustrate that problems in parent-child relationships are elevated as early as 8 to 12 years before parental divorce and that poor marital relationships and high marital discord account for many of the problems in postdivorce parent-child relationships, including reduced parent-child affection (Amato & Booth, 1996). Kline, Johnston, and Tschann (1991) found that clinical ratings of marital conflict at the time of filing for divorce were directly related to children's problematic emotional and behavioral adjustment 2 years later; marital conflict also had indirect effects through poor mother-child relationships and heightened postdivorce hostilities between parents. In addition to interparental conflict, there are strong indications that other factors that predate divorce, such as ineffective and inconsistent parenting, parent-child conflict, and child adjustment problems (Cherlin et al., 1991) contribute to problems experienced by children of divorce.

Following divorce, there is considerable variability both in children's residential arrangements and in the nature of coparenting relationships (Maccoby & Mnookin, 1992). In the second year postseparation, one fourth of divorced couples have a cooperative coparenting relationship, one third are conflicted, nearly one third are disengaged, and a smaller, fourth group is "mixed" in that they are somewhat cooperative but also conflicted. Residential arrangements are unrelated to coparenting conflict, but preseparation interparental hostility is a strong predictor of subsequent coparenting conflict.

Divorce appears to weaken fathers', but not mothers' affection for their children (Amato & Booth, 1996) and inhibits paternal contact. Seltzer's (1991) analysis of the National Survey of Families and Households, and King's (1994) analysis of the National Longitudinal Survey of Youth yield remarkably similar estimates of paternal involvement among fathers living apart from their children: more than one fourth of such children did not see their fathers at all in the previous year, only 27% saw their fathers at least weekly, and less than one third of children who see their nonresident fathers had the opportunity to spend extended periods of time with them. More than half of fathers exerted no influence in childrearing decisions, and just under half paid any child support in the previous year (Seltzer, 1991). Fathers who are more involved with their children postdivorce tend to be those who were closer to their children prior to divorce, live near their children, and have joint custody (Arditti & Keith, 1993).

Undesirable life events that commonly occur to children of divorce have been linked with children's postdivorce adjustment in both cross-sectional (Sandler, Wolchik, Braver, & Fogas, 1991) and prospective longitudinal studies (Sandler, Tein, & West, 1994). Studying a sample of 7- to 13-year-olds whose parents had divorced within the past 2 years, the researchers found that children use a variety of coping strategies, including active coping (problem solving and cognitive restructuring), avoidance, support seeking, and distraction, and that using these techniques reduces children's postdivorce internalizing and conduct problems.

Children in Stepfamilies

Throughout the 1990s, a small group of researchers continued to trace the influence of stepfamily structure on children's adjustment. These studies consistently report that children in stepfamilies, in comparison with those in first-married families, are more likely to experience a broad range of adjustment problems. Comparisons of mean adjustment levels across groups typically yield modest differences, including poorer academic achievement, lower socioemotional adjustment, and more behavioral problems (Acock & Demo, 1994; Capaldi & Patterson, 1991; Hetherington & Stanley-Hagan, 2000). Considering the demographic growth of children in stepfamilies, it is encouraging that the adjustment problems they experience appear to diminish with time since transition and that more recent studies, and studies using stronger methodologies, suggest smaller disadvantages (Amato & Keith, 1991; Hetherington & Stanley-Hagan). Thus, children may be most vulnerable during the family dissolution and reformation periods, but most children are quite resilient, adapting to their new living arrangements and exhibiting normal ranges of adjustment within 2 or 3 years of stepfamily formation (Emery & Forehand, 1994). Children's resilience is likely to be related to the stabilization in stepfamily relationships that occurs within 2 years following stepfamily formation, by which time there are few differences in parent-child relationships and family functioning between stepfamilies and first-marriage families (Ganong & Coleman, 1994; Hetherington & Clingempeel, 1992). African American stepfamilies have received little empirical attention, perhaps partly because African Americans are substantially less likely than Whites to remarry (Staples & Johnson, 1993). One study using a national sample indicates that both child and adult adjustment in African American stepfather families is similar to that in African American first married families and White stepfather families (Fine, McKenry, Donnelly, & Voydanoff, 1992).

CONCLUSIONS

Research in the past decade substantiates and clarifies earlier evidence indicating the importance of family relationships and resources for children's development and well-being. Although investigators devoted far greater attention to children and their adjustment than to the experience of parenthood and parents' adjustment, researchers in the 1990s were much more diligent than earlier scholars in studying the influence of parents' emotional well-being in shaping children's development. Across families of diverse racial and socioeconomic backgrounds, it is clear that parents' emotional well-being, positive interparental relations, and consistent parental support, sensitivity, and discipline facilitate children's well-being, often to the point of compensating for economic hardship, family disruption, and other adverse life circumstances. Within and across racial groups, however, there are notable differences in parenting practices and values, urging caution in generalizing about the desirability and effectiveness of particular parenting strategies.

We know more about the early experience of parenthood than about later stages or trajectories. For many adults, the initial transition to parenthood is disruptive, but among those who are married, marital negativity appears to subside during the second year. Evidence also documents variability across groups of parents during the first few years, but longer term trajectories spanning the first decade of children's lives remain unexplored. Similarly, in the 1990s, studies of attachment relationships extended later into childhood, providing glimpses of parents' attachments with their children as late as ages 5 and 6. It will be important to replicate and extend these studies to chart the course of mother-child and father-child relationship trajectories through childhood, to observe multiple children and their relationships within a family system, and to examine how these behaviors correlate with children's and parents' adjustment. Other studies suggest considerable stability in parent-child relations, parenting behaviors, and parenting values through late childhood and adolescence.

Family researchers and child developmentalists need to move beyond a preoccupation with conventional classifications of family structure to explore the rich variety of family members, kin support networks, and neighborhood resources impacting on children's development. Living with grandparents or other relatives as supplemental parents provides socialization benefits through enhanced attention to and supervision of children and is associated with better transitions to school, work habits, and educational attainment (Aquili-

no, 1996; Entwisle & Alexander, 2000). Grandmothers' coresidence may be far more beneficial when mothers are very young (i.e., early or middle adolescents), however, and thus burdened by developmental challenges (Chase-Lansdale et al., 1994). There is also evidence that having grandparents and other relatives serve as custodial, adoptive, or substitute parents diminishes the chances of high school completion and accelerates home-leaving (Aquilino, 1996). Beyond the household, characteristics of the neighborhood context influence the quality of family relationships. Even after controlling for family poverty and other family conditions, neighborhood poverty is associated with less maternal warmth and responsiveness and worse home environments for children (Klebanov et al., 1994). Klebanov and colleagues speculated that living in a socially isolated and impoverished neighborhood depletes mothers of their personal warmth, but much further study is required. Future research should examine family structure in combination with family interaction and over time, examining the effects of timing (child's age at parenting transition), time since transition (Amato, 1993), and the patterning of transitions involving nonparent family members (Hunter & Ensminger, 1992). We also need to redouble our efforts to understand childrearing in its ethnic and cultural context and investigate the likely consequences for parents and children of the diminishing availability of kin among African Americans, Chicanos, and Puerto Ricans (Dilworth-Anderson, 1999; Rochelle, 1997).

Some important issues are emerging in the study of families with children. One relatively new line of inquiry is the development and adjustment of children living in families headed by lesbian, gay, or bisexual parents. Several careful reviews (Patterson, 1992; Savin-Williams & Esterberg, 2000) and a recent meta-analysis (Allen & Burrell, 1996) demonstrate no significant differences between children reared by heterosexual parents and those reared by lesbian or gay parents regarding gender identity, self-concept, intelligence, personality characteristics, emotional adjustment, behavioral problems, or peer relations. A persistent limitation of these studies, however, is that most rely on small samples of White, middle-class, previously married lesbians and their children. As a result, we cannot be confident concerning the generalizability of many of the findings, particularly with regard to children who have multiple risk factors (e.g., poor, ethnic or racial minority children who have experienced parental divorce) or children of other rarely studied household configurations (e.g., children living with gay fathers). Many scholars question the usefulness of a deficit-comparison approach and the accompanying focus on documenting differences in children's adjustment as a function of parents' sexual orientation, however (Savin-Williams & Esterberg; Stacey, 1996).

Something researchers have yet to determine, and that in our opinion offers a very important and timely area for study, is how multiple dimensions of stratification or family diversity intersect with one another. For example, as indicated earlier, there is evidence that children reared in lesbian and gay households fare very well and in some cases better than children in two-heterosexual-parent households. An important question is how children fare when parents' sexual minority status, parental divorce, and other "social addresses" interact with risk factors such as economic hardship, preexisting behavior problems, or high-crime neighborhoods. We suggest that little will be gained from further examination of family structure differences without sufficient attention to important variation within such classifications, including critical information on family processes and the larger contexts within which children live.

A number of important methodological and theoretical challenges confront researchers studying families with young children in the new millennium. Through the 1990s, the conventional practice was to focus on a specific dyad within the family, typically the mother and a target child, ignoring the presence of and dynamics among other family members. As a result, we know little about how families function as a whole or as a system (e.g., alliances). Further, the conceptualization and analytic strategy underlying most studies involves an assumption that parental behaviors bear a linear relationship with child outcomes, such that more parental support, control, supervision, time spent with child, and other desirable behaviors, are posited to be associated with higher child well-being. This is not always the case, however. Kurdek and Fine (1994), for example, show that although family acceptance and control are positively related to children's adjustment, a curvilinear relationship better explains the association between control and adjustment. Interpretations of biological parents' influence on children's behavior also tend to be exaggerated and need to be much more sensitive to genotype-environment correlations or to the tendency for similarities in parental and child behavior to be due in part to

their sharing both heredity and environment (Plomin, 1994). Finally, much of what we know about families continues to be based on mothers' perceptions of family relations. What does the family look like from the father's perspective, the daughter's perspective, and the son's perspective? How do men experience the transition to parenthood, early attachment, and subsequent involvement with their daughters and sons? We will need to accept and confront these challenges if we are to understand the rich diversity of families with young children.

NOTE

We thank Leigh Ann Carr, Roger Goodman, Sheryl Scrimsher, and Robbyn Wood for their bibliographic assistance.

REFERENCES

Acock, A. C., & Demo, D. H. (1994). *Family diversity and well-being.* Thousand Oaks, CA: Sage.

Acock, A. C., & Demo, D. H. (1999). Dimensions of family conflict and their influence on child and adolescent adjustment. *Sociological Inquiry, 69,* 641–658.

Ainsworth, M. D. S., Blehar, M. C., Waters, E., & Wall, S. (1978). *Patterns of attachment.* Hillsdale, NJ: Erlbaum.

Allen, M., & Burrell, N. (1996). Comparing the impact of homosexual and heterosexual parents on children: Meta-analysis of existing research. *Journal of Homosexuality, 32,* 19–35.

Alwin, D. F. (1990). Cohort replacement and changes in parental socialization values. *Journal of Marriage and the Family, 52,* 347–360.

Amato, P. R. (1993). Children's adjustment to divorce: Theories, hypotheses, and empirical support. *Journal of Marriage and the Family, 55,* 23–38.

Amato, P. R., & Booth, A. (1996). A prospective study of divorce and parent-child relationships. *Journal of Marriage and the Family, 58,* 356–365.

Amato, P. R., & Keith, B. (1991). Parental divorce and the well-being of children: A meta-analysis. *Psychological Bulletin, 110,* 26–46.

Aquilino, W. S. (1996). The life course of children born to unmarried mothers: Childhood living arrangements and young adult outcomes. *Journal of Marriage and the Family, 58,* 293–310.

Arditti, J. A., & Keith, T. Z. (1993). Visitation frequency, child support payment, and the father-child relationship postdivorce. *Journal of Marriage and the Family, 55,* 699–712.

Avenevoli, S., Sessa, F. M., & Steinberg, L. (1999). Family structure, parenting practices, and adolescent adjustment: An ecological examination. In E. M. Hetherington (Ed.), *Coping with divorce, single parenting, and remarriage* (pp. 65–90). Mahwah, NJ: Erlbaum.

Baca Zinn, M., & Wells, B. (2000). Diversity within Latino families: New lessons for family social science. In D. H. Demo, K. R. Allen, & M. A. Fine

(Eds.), *The handbook of family diversity* (pp. 252–273). New York: Oxford University Press.

Bank, L., Forgatch, M. S., Patterson, G. R., & Fetrow, R. A. (1993). Parenting practices of single mothers: Mediators of negative contextual factors. *Journal of Marriage and the Family, 55,* 371–384.

Baydar, N., Greek, A., & Brooks-Gunn, J. (1997). A longitudinal study of the effects of the birth of a sibling during the first 6 years of life. *Journal of Marriage and the Family, 59,* 939–956.

Baydar, N., Hyle, D., & Brooks-Gunn, J. (1997). A longitudinal study of the effects of the birth of a sibling during preschool and early grade school years. *Journal of Marriage and the Family, 59,* 957–965.

Belsky, J. (1993). Etiology of child maltreatment: A developmental-ecological analysis. *Psychological Bulletin, 114,* 413–434.

Belsky, J. (1996). Parent, infant, and social-contextual antecedents of father-son attachment security. *Developmental Psychology, 32(5),* 905–913.

Belsky, J., & Rovine, M. (1990). Patterns of marital change across the transition to parenthood: Pregnancy to three years postpartum. *Journal of Marriage and the Family, 52,* 5–19.

Belsky, J., Youngblade, C., Rovine, M., & Volling, B. (1991). Patterns of marital change and parent-child interaction. *Journal of Marriage and the Family, 53,* 487–498.

Benin, M. H., & Edwards, D. (1990). Adolescents' chores: The difference between dual and single-earner families. *Journal of Marriage and the Family, 52,* 361–373.

Billingsley, A. (1992). *Climbing Jacob's ladder: The enduring legacy of African American families.* New York: Simon and Schuster.

Blair, S. L. (1992). Sex-typing of children's housework. *Youth and Society, 23,* 178–203.

Bluestone, C., & Tamis-LeMonda, C. S. (1999). Correlates of parenting styles in predominantly working- and middle-class African American mothers. *Journal of Marriage and the Family, 61,* 881–893.

Bowlby, J. (1951). Maternal care and child health. Geneva, Switzerland: World Health Organization.

Bowlby, J. (1958). The nature of the child's tie to his mother. *International Journal of Psychoanalysis, 39,* 350–373.

Boykin, A. W., & Toms, F. D. (1985). Black child socialization: A conceptual framework. In H. P. McAdoo & J. L. McAdoo (Eds.), *Black children: Social, educational, and parental environments* (pp. 33–51). Beverly Hills, CA: Sage.

Braver, S. L. (1998). *Divorced dads: Shattering the myths.* New York: Tarcher Putnam.

Brody, G. H., Stoneman, Z., & McCoy, J. K. (1994). Forecasting sibling relationships in early adolescence from child temperaments and family processes in middle childhood. *Child Development, 65,* 771–784.

Brody, G. H., Stoneman, Z., McCoy, J. K., & Forehand, R. (1992). Contemporaneous and longitudinal associations of sibling conflict with family relationship assessments and family discussions about sibling problem. *Child Development, 63,* 391–400.

Buhrmester, D., & Furman, W. (1990). Perceptions of sibling relationships during middle childhood and adolescence. *Child Development, 61,* 1387–1398.

Capaldi, D. M., & Patterson, G. R. (1991). Relations of parental transitions to boys' adjustment problems: I. A linear hypothesis. II. Mothers at risk for transitions and unskilled parenting. *Developmental Psychology, 27,* 489–504.

Carlson, E. A. (1998). A prospective longitudinal study of attachment disorganization/disorientation. *Child Development, 69,* 1107–1128.

Chao, R. K. (1994). Beyond parental control and authoritarian parenting style: Understanding Chinese parenting through the cultural notion of training. *Child Development, 65,* 1111–1119.

Chase-Lansdale, P. L., Brooks-Gunn, J., & Zamsky, E. S. (1994). Young African-American multigenerational families in poverty: Quality of mothering and grandmothering. *Child Development, 65,* 373–393.

Cherlin, A. J., Furstenberg, F. F., Jr., Chase-Lansdale, L. P., Kiernan, K. E., Robins, P. K., Morrison, D. R., & Teitler, J. O. (1991). Longitudinal effects of divorce in Great Britain and the United States. *Science, 252,* 1386–1389.

Chisholm, K. (1998). A three year follow-up of attachment and indiscriminate friendliness in children adopted from Romanian orphanages. *Child Development, 69,* 1092–1106.

Coiro, M. J., & Emery, R. E. (1998). Do marriage problems affect fathering more than mothering? A quantitative and qualitative review. *Clinical Child and Family Psychology Review, 1,* 23–40.

Collins, P. (1990). *Black feminist thought.* Boston, MA: Unwin Hyman.

Coontz, S. (1997). *The way we really are: Coming to terms with America's changing families.* New York: Basic Books.

Cowan, C. P., & Cowan, P. A. (2000). *When partners become parents: The big life change for couples.* Mahwah, NJ: Erlbaum.

Cowan, P. A. (1997). Beyond meta-analysis: A plea for a family systems view of attachment. *Child Development, 68* (4), 601–603.

Cox, M., Owen, M., Henderson, V. K., & Margand, N. A. (1992). Prediction of infant-father and infant-mother attachment. *Developmental Psychology, 28,* 474–483.

Cox, M. J., & Brooks-Gunn, J. (1999). Studying conflict and cohesion in families: An overview. In M. Cox & J. Brooks-Gunn (Eds.) *Conflict and cohesion in families: Causes and consequences.* The advances in family research series. (pp. 321–344). Mahwah, NJ: Erlbaum.

Cox, M. J., Paley, B., Burchinal, M., & Payne, C. C. (1999). Marital perceptions and interactions across the transition to parenthood. *Journal of Marriage and the Family, 61,* 611–625.

Cox, M. J., Paley, B., Payne, C. C., & Burchinal, M. (1999). The transition to parenthood: Marital conflict and withdrawal and parent-infant interactions. In M. J. Cox & J. Brooks-Gunn (Eds.) *Conflict and cohesion in families: Causes and consequences* (pp. 87–104), Mahwah, NJ: Erlbaum.

Crittendon, P. M. (1992). Quality of attachment in the preschool years. *Development and Psychopathology 4,* 209–241.

Crockenberg, S. L., & Covey, S. (1991). Marital conflict and externalizing behavior in children. In D. Cicchetti & S. Toth (Eds.), *Rochester symposium on developmental psychopathology: Vol. 3: Models and integra-*

tions (pp. 235–260). Rochester, NY: University of Rochester Press.

Crouter, A. C., Manke, B. A., & McHale, S. M. (1995). The family context of gender intensification in early adolescence. *Child Development, 66,* 317–329.

Cummings, E. M., & Wilson, A. (1999). Contexts of marital conflict and children's emotional security: Exploring the distinction between constructive and destructive conflict from the children's perspective. In M. Cox & J. Brooks-Gunn (Eds.), *Conflict and closeness in families: Causes and consequences* (pp. 105–129). Mahwah, NJ: Erlbaum.

Davies, P. T., & Cummings, E. M. (1994). Marital conflict and child adjustment: An emotional security hypothesis. *Psychological Bulletin, 116,* 387–411.

Dekovic, M., & Gerris, J. R. M. (1992). Parental reasoning complexity, social class, and child-rearing behaviors. *Journal of Marriage and the Family, 54,* 675–685.

Demo, D. H. (1992). Parent-child relations: Assessing recent changes. *Journal of Marriage and the Family, 54,* 104–117.

Demo, D. H., & Acock, A. C. (1993). Family diversity and the division of domestic labor: How much have things really changed? *Family Relations, 42,* 323–331.

Demo, D. H., & Hughes, M. (1990). Socialization and racial identity among Black Americans. *Social Psychology Quarterly, 53,* 364–374.

DeWolff, M. S., & Van Ijzendoorn, M. H. (1997). Sensitivity and attachment: A meta-analysis on parental antecedents of infant attachment. *Child Development, 68,* 571–591.

Dilworth-Anderson, P. (1999, November). *Shifting paradigms in the study of contemporary American families: Issues of race, culture, and ethnicity.* Marie Peters Award Address, presented at the annual meeting of the National Council on Family Relations, Irvine, CA.

Dodge, K. A., Pettit, G. S., & Bates, J. E. (1994). Socialization mediators of the relation between socioeconomic status and child conduct problems. *Child Development, 65,* 649–665.

Doherty, W. J., Kouneski, E. F., & Erickson, M. F. (1998). Responsible fathering: An overview and conceptual framework. *Journal of Marriage and the Family, 60,* 277–292.

Dumka, L. E., Roosa, M. W., & Jackson, K. M. (1997). Risk, conflict, mothers' parenting, and children's adjustment in low-income, Mexican immigrant, and Mexican American families. *Journal of Marriage and the Family, 59,* 309–323.

Duncan, G. J., & Brooks-Gunn, J. (1997). *Consequences of growing up poor.* New York: Russell Sage Foundation.

Dunn, J. (1993). *Young children's close relationships: Beyond attachment.* Newbury Park, CA: Sage.

Easterbrooks, M. A., Cummings, E. M., & Emde, R. N. (1994). Young children's responses to constructive marital disputes. *Journal of Family Psychology, 8,* 160–169.

Elder, G. H. (1974). *Children of the Great Depression.* Chicago: University of Chicago Press.

Elder, G. H., Nguyen, T., & Caspi, A. (1985). Linking family hardship to children's lives. *Child Development, 56,* 361–375.

Emery, R. E., & Forehand, R. (1994). Parental divorce and children's well-being: A focus on resilience. In R. J. Haggerty, L. R. Sherrod, N. Garmezy, & M. Rutter (Eds.), *Stress, risk, and resilience in children and adolescents* (pp. 64–99). Cambridge, U.K.: Cambridge University Press.

Entwisle, D. R., & Alexander, K. L. (2000). Diversity in family structure: Effects on schooling. In D. H. Demo, K. R. Allen, & M. A. Fine (Eds.), *Handbook of family diversity* (pp. 316–337). New York: Oxford University Press.

Erel, O., & Burman, B. (1995). Interrelatedness of marital relations and parent-child relations: A meta-analytic review. *Psychological Bulletin, 118,* 108–132.

Erel, O., Margolin, G., & John, R. S. (1998). Observed sibling interactions: Links with the marital and the mother-child relationship. *Developmental Psychology, 34,* 288–298.

Fagot, B. I. (1995). Parenting boys and girls. In M. H. Bornstein (Ed.), *Handbook of parenting: Vol. 1. Children and parenting* (pp. 163–183). Hillsdale, NJ: Erlbaum.

Fincham, F. D. (1994). Understanding the association between marital conflict and child adjustment: An overview. *Journal of Family Psychology, 8,* 123–127.

Fincham, F. D., Grych, J. H., & Osborne, L. N. (1994). Does marital conflict cause child maladjustment? Directions and challenges for longitudinal research. *Journal of Family Psychology, 8,* 128–140.

Fine, M. A., McKenry, P. C., Donnelly, B. W., & Voydanoff, P. (1992). Perceived adjustment of parents and children: Variations by family structure, race, and gender. *Journal of Marriage and the Family, 54,* 118–127.

Gable, S., Belsky, J., & Crnic, K. (1995). Coparenting during the child's 2nd year: A descriptive account. *Journal of Marriage and the Family, 57,* 609–616.

Ganong, L. H., & Coleman, M. (1994). *Remarried family relationships.* Thousand Oaks, CA: Sage.

Glick, P. (1997). Demographic pictures of African American families. In H. McAdoo (Ed.), *Black families* (3rd ed., pp. 118–138). Thousand Oaks, CA: Sage.

Goldscheider, F. K., & Waite, L. J. (1991). *New families, no families? The transformation of the American home.* Berkeley: University of California Press.

Gottman, J. M. (1994). *What predicts divorce.* Hillsdale, NJ: Erlbaum.

Graham, S. (1992). Most of the subjects were White and middle class: Trends in published research on African Americans in selected APA journals, 1970–1989. *American Psychologist, 47,* 629–639.

Grych, J. H., & Fincham, F. D. (1990). Marital conflict and children's adjustment: A cognitive-contextual framework. *Psychological Bulletin, 108,* 267–290.

Haggerty, R. J., Sherrod, L. R., Garmezy, N., & Rutter, M. (Eds.). (1994). *Stress, risk, and resilience in children and adolescents.* Cambridge, U.K.: Cambridge University Press.

Harrison, A. O., Wilson, M. N., Pine, C. J., Chan, S. Q., & Buriel, R. (1990). Family ecologies of ethnic minority children. *Child Development, 61,* 347–362.

Hawkins, A. J., & Eggebeen, D. (1991). Are fathers fungible? Patterns of coresident adult men in maritally disrupted families and young children's well-being. *Journal of Marriage and the Family, 53,* 958–972.

Hetherington, E. M., & Clingempeel, W. (1992). Coping with marital transitions: A family systems perspective. *Monographs of the Society for Research on Child Development, 57* (2/3, Serial no. 227).

Hetherington, E. M., & Stanley-Hagan, M. (2000). Diversity among stepfamilies. In D. H. Demo, K. R. Allen, & M. A. Fine (Eds.), *Handbook of family diversity* (pp. 173–196). New York: Oxford University Press.

Hoff-Ginsberg, E., & Tardif, T. (1995). Socioeconomic status and parenting. In M. Bornstein (Ed.), *Handbook of parenting* (Vol. 2, pp. 161–188). Mahwah, NJ: Erlbaum.

Howes, C., & Hamilton, C. E. (1992). Children's relationships with child care teachers: Stability and concordance with parental attachments. *Child Development, 63,* 867–878.

Hunter, A. G., & Ensminger, M. E. (1992). Diversity and fluidity in children's living arrangements: Family transitions in an urban Afro-American community. *Journal of Marriage and the Family, 54,* 418–426.

Ishii-Kuntz, M. (2000). Diversity within Asian American families. In D. H. Demo, K. R. Allen, & M. A. Fine (Eds.), *The handbook of family diversity* (pp. 274–292). New York: Oxford University Press.

Jackson, A. P., Gyamfi, P., Brooks-Gunn, J., & Blake, M. (1998). Employment status, psychological well-being, social support, and physical discipline practices of single Black mothers. *Journal of Marriage and the Family, 60,* 894–902.

Jouriles, E. N., Norwood, W. D., McDonald, R., Vincent, J. P., & Mahoney, A. (1996). Physical violence and other forms of marital aggression: Links with children's behavior problems. *Journal of Family Psychology, 10,* 223–234.

Kalmuss, D., Davidson, A., & Cushman, L. (1992). Parenting expectations, experiences, and adjustment to parenthood: A test of the violated expectations framework. *Journal of Marriage and the Family, 54,* 516–526.

Katz, L., & Gottman, J. (1993). Patterns of marital conflict predict children's internalizing and externalizing behaviors. *Developmental Psychology, 29,* 940–950.

Kelley, M. L., Power, T. G., & Wimbush, D. D. (1992). Determinants of disciplinary practices in low-income Black mothers. *Child Development, 63,* 573–582.

King, V. (1994). Nonresident father involvement and child well-being: Can dads make a difference? *Journal of Family Issues, 15,* 78–96.

King, V., & Heard, H. E. (1999). Nonresident father visitation, parental conflict, and mothers' satisfaction: What's best for child well-being? *Journal of Marriage and the Family, 61,* 385–396.

Klebanov, P. K., Brooks-Gunn, J., & Duncan, G. J. (1994). Does neighborhood and family poverty affect mothers' parenting, mental health, and social support. *Journal of Marriage and the Family, 56,* 441–455.

Kline, M., Johnston, J. R., & Tschann, J. M. (1991). The long shadow of marital conflict: A model of children's postdivorce adjustment. *Journal of Marriage and the Family, 53,* 297–309.

Kurdek, L. A., & Fine, M. A. (1994). Family acceptance and family control as predictors of adjustment in

young adolescents: Linear, curvilinear, or interactive effects. *Child Development, 65,* 1137–1146.

Kurdek, L. A., Fine, M. A., & Sinclair, R. J. (1995). School adjustment in sixth graders: Parenting transitions, family climate, and peer norm effects. *Child Development, 66,* 430–445.

Leadbeater, B. J., & Bishop, S. J. (1994). Predictors of behavior problems in preschool children of inner city Afro-American and Puerto Rican adolescent mothers. *Child Development, 65,* 638–648.

Levy-Schiff, R. (1994). Individual and contextual correlates of marital change across the transition to parenthood. *Developmental Psychology, 30,* 591–601.

Luster, T., & McAdoo, H. P. (1991). Factors related to the achievement and adjustment of young African American children. *Child Development, 65,* 1080–1094.

Lytton, H., & Romney, D. M. (1991). Parents' differential socialization of boys and girls: A meta-analysis. *Psychological Bulletin, 109,* 267–296.

Maccoby, E. E., & Jacklin, C. N. (1974). *The psychology of sex differences.* Stanford, CA: Stanford University Press.

Maccoby, E. E., & Mnookin, R. H. (1992). *Dividing the child: Social and legal dilemmas of custody.* Cambridge, MA: Harvard University Press.

Manning, W. D., & Smock, P. J. (1999). New families and nonresident father-child visitation. *Social Forces, 78,* 87–116.

Margolin, G., Christensen, A., & John, R. S. (1996). The continuance and spillover of everyday tensions in distressed and nondistressed families. *Journal of Family Psychology, 10,* 304–321.

McAdoo, H. P. (1978). Factors related to stability in upwardly mobile black families. *Journal of Marriage and the Family, 40,* 762–778.

McHale, S. M., Crouter, A. C., McGuire, S. A., & Updegraff, K. A. (1995). Congruence between mothers' and fathers' differential treatment of siblings: Links with family relations and children's well-being. *Child Development, 66,* 116–128.

McLoyd, V. C. (1990). The impact of economic hardship on Black families and children: Psychological distress, parenting, and socioemotional development. *Child Development, 61,* 311–346.

McNally, S., Eisenberg, N., & Harris, J. D. (1991). Consistency and change in maternal child-rearing practices and values: A longitudinal study. *Child Development, 62,* 190–198.

McNeal, C., & Amato, P. R. (1998). Parents' marital violence: Long-term consequences for children. *Journal of Family Issues, 19,* 123–139.

Mott, F. L. (1990). When is a father really gone? Paternal-child contact in father-absent homes. *Demography, 27,* 499–517.

National Research Council, Panel on Research on Child Abuse and Neglect. (1993). *Understanding child abuse and neglect.* Washington, DC: National Academy Press.

NICHD Early Child Care Research Network. (1997). The effects of infant child care on infant-mother attachment security: Results of the NICHD Study of Early Child Care. *Child Development, 68,* 860–879.

O'Brien, M., Margolin, G., & John, R. S. (1995). Relation among marital conflict, child coping, and child adjustment. *Journal of Clinical Child Psychology, 24,* 346–361.

Parke, R. D., & Sterns, P. N. (1993). Fathers and child rearing. In G. H. Elder, Jr., J. Modell, & R. D. Parke (Eds.), *Children in time and place: Developmental and historical insights* (pp. 147–170). New York: Cambridge University Press.

Patterson, C. J. (1992). Children of lesbian and gay parents. *Child Development, 63,* 1025–1042.

Patterson, G. R., Reid, J. B., & Dishion, T. (1992). *Antisocial boys.* Eugene, OR: Castalia.

Perner, J., Ruffman, T., & Leekam, S. R. (1994). Theory of mind is contagious: You catch it from your sibs. *Child Development, 65,* 1228–1238.

Peterson, G. W., Bodman, D. A., Bush, K. R., & Madden-Derdich, D. (2000). Gender and parent-child relationships. In D. H. Demo, K. R. Allen, & M. A. Fine (Eds.), *The handbook of family diversity* (pp. 82–104). New York: Oxford University Press.

Plomin, R. (1994). *Genetics and experience: The interplay between nature and nurture.* Thousand Oaks, CA: Sage.

Raffaelli, M. (1992). Sibling conflict in early adolescence. *Journal of Marriage and the Family, 54,* 652–663.

Rank, M. R. (2000). Poverty and economic hardship in families. In D. H. Demo, K. R. Allen, & M. A. Fine (Eds.), *The handbook of family diversity* (pp. 293–315). New York: Oxford University Press.

Rochelle, A. (1997). *No more kin: Exploring race, class, and gender in family networks.* Thousand Oaks, CA: Sage.

Rodgers, B., & Pryor, J. (1998). *Divorce and separation: The outcomes for children.* York: Rowntree Foundation.

Rogers, S. J., & White, L. K. (1998). Satisfaction with parenting: The role of marital happiness, family structure, and parents' gender. *Journal of Marriage and the Family, 60,* 293–308.

Rohner, R. P., Kean, K. J., & Cournoyer, D. E. (1991). Effects of corporal punishment, perceived caretaker warmth, and cultural beliefs on the psychological adjustment of children in St. Kitts, West Indies. *Journal of Marriage and the Family, 53,* 681–693.

Sandler, I. N., Tein, J., & West, S. G. (1994). Coping, stress, and psychological symptoms of children of divorce: A cross-sectional and longitudinal study. *Child Development, 65,* 1744–1763.

Sandler, I. N., Wolchik, S. A., Braver, S. L., & Fogas, B. (1991). Stability and quality of life events and psychological symptomatology of children of divorce. *American Journal of Community Psychology, 19,* 501–520.

Savin-Williams, R. C., & Esterberg, K. G. (2000). Lesbian, gay, and bisexual families. In D. H. Demo, K. R. Allen, & M. A. Fine (Eds.), *The handbook of family diversity* (pp. 197–215). New York: Oxford University Press.

Seifer, R., Schiller, M., Sameroff, A. J., Resnick, S., & Riordan, K. (1996). Attachment, maternal sensitivity, and infant temperament during the first year of life. *Developmental Psychology, 32,* 12–25.

Seltzer, J. A. (1991). Relationships between fathers and children who live apart: The father's role after separation. *Journal of Marriage and the Family, 53,* 79–101.

Simons, R. L. & Associates. (1996). *Understanding differences between divorced and intact families: Stress, interaction, and child outcome.* Thousand Oaks, CA: Sage.

Stacey, J. (1996). *In the name of the family: Rethinking family values in the postmodern age.* Boston: Beacon Press.

Stack, C. (1974). *All our kin.* New York: Harper and Row.

Staples, R., & Johnson, L. B. (1993). *Black families at the crossroads.* San Francisco, CA: Jossey-Bass.

Stattin, H., & Klackenberg, G. (1992). Discordant family relations in intact families: Developmental tendencies over 18 years. *Journal of Marriage and the Family, 54,* 940–956.

Stevenson-Hinde, J., & Shouldice, A. (1995). Maternal interactions and self-reports related to attachment classifications at 4.5 years. *Child Development, 66,* 583–596.

Stormshak, E. A., Bellanti, C. J., & Bierman, K. L., & the Conduct Problems Prevention Research Group (1996). The quality of sibling relationships and the development of social competence and behavioral control in aggressive children. *Developmental Psychology, 32,* 79–89.

Taylor, R. L. (2000). Diversity within African American families. In D. H. Demo, K. R. Allen, & M. A. Fine (Eds.), *The handbook of family diversity* (pp. 232–251). New York: Oxford University Press.

Teachman, J. D. (2000). Diversity of family structure: Economic and social influences. In D. H. Demo, K. R. Allen, & M. A. Fine (Eds.), *The handbook of family diversity* (pp. 32–58). New York: Oxford University Press.

Teti, D. M., Gelfand, D. M., Messinger, D. S., Russell, I. (1995). Maternal depression and the quality of early attachment: An examination of infants, preschoolers, and their mothers. *Developmental Psychology, 31,* 364–376.

Teti, D. M., Nakagawa, M., Das, R., & Wirth, O. (1991). Security of attachment between preschoolers and their mothers: Relations among social interaction, parenting stress, and mothers' sorts of the Attachment Q-Set. *Developmental Psychology, 27,* 440–447.

Teti, D., Wolfe Sakin, J., Kucera, E., & Corns, K. (1996). And baby makes four: Predictors of attachment security among preschool-age first borns during the transition to siblinghood. *Child Development, 67,* 579–596.

Thompson, R. A. (1998). Early sociopersonality development. In W. Damon & N. Eisenberg (Eds), *Handbook of child psychology* (Vol. 3, 5th ed., pp. 25–104) New York: Wiley.

Tolson, T. F. J., & Wilson, M. N. (1990). The impact of two- and three-generational Black family structure on perceived family climate. *Child Development, 61,* 416–428.

U.S. Bureau of the Census. (1998). *Household and family characteristics: March, 1997* (pp. 20–509). Washington, DC.

Vaughn, B., & Waters, E. (1990). Attachment behavior at home and in the laboratory: Q-Sort observations and Strange Situation classifications of one-year-olds. *Child Development, 61,* 1965–1990.

Volling, B. L., & Belsky, J. (1992). The contribution of mother-child and father-child relationships to the quality of sibling interaction: A longitudinal study. *Child Development, 63,* 1209–1222.

Wallace, P. M., & Gotlib, I. H. (1990). Marital adjustment during the transition to parenthood: Stability and predictors of change. *Journal of Marriage and the Family, 52,* 21–29.

Wartner, U. G., Grossman, K., Fremmer-Bombik, E., & Suess, G. (1994). Attachment patterns at age six in South Germany: Predictability from infancy and implications for preschool behavior. *Child Development, 65,* 1014–1027.

Waters, E., & Deane, K. E. (1985). Defining and assessing individual differences in attachment relationships: Q-methodology and the organization of behavior in infancy and early childhood. In I. Bretherton & E. Waters (Eds.), Growing points for attachment theory and research. *Monographs of the Society for Research in Child Development, 50(1/2, Serial No. 209),* 41–65.

Wojtkiewicz, R. A. (1992). Diversity in experiences of parental structure during childhood and adolescence. *Demography, 29,* 59–68.

Youngblade, L. M., & Dunn, J. (1995). Individual differences in young children's pretend play with mother and sibling: Links to relationships and understanding of other people's feelings and beliefs. *Child Development, 66,* 1472–1492.

Youngblade, L. M., Park, K. A., & Belsky, J. (1993). Measurement of young children's close friendships: A comparison of two independent assessment systems and their association with attachment security. *International Journal of Behavioral Development, 16,* 563–587.

Zeanah, C. H., Mammen, O. K., & Lieberman, A. F. (1993). Disorders of attachment. In C. H. Zeanah (Ed.), *Handbook of infant mental health* (pp. 332–349) New York: Guilford Press.

FRANK F. FURSTENBERG   *University of Pennsylvania*

The Sociology of Adolescence and Youth in the 1990s: A Critical Commentary

The 1990s saw considerable advances in the state of research on adolescence and youth. This article provides a critical commentary on a subset of this research, focusing on the causes and consequences of the lengthened period in which the transition to adulthood occurs. It provides a brief history of adolescence research, identifying a select set of topics, themes, and research problems that will guide research on adolescence and youth over the next decade. These research foci, which include peer group relations, biological influences on adolescence, employment experiences, increased autonomy, and racial and gender differences, are described as representing either continuities or advances in adolescence research. The strengths and shortcomings of this research are detailed. The paper concludes by suggesting promising areas for future research and by providing guidelines for undertaking such research.

Research on adolescence flourished in the final decades of the 20th century. So extensive is the literature in the fields of sociology, demography, and developmental psychology that it is simply not possible to credit all the advances that have occurred even in the last decade. (see Crockett & Crouter, 1995; Settersten, 1999.) This omission is compounded because I will virtually neglect the

Department of Sociology, University of Pennsylvania, 3718 Locust Walk, Philadelphia, PA 19104 (fff@pop.upenn.edu).

Key Words: adolescence, multiple contexts, 1990s, social science research, transition to adulthood.

burgeoning areas of research in history, health sciences, law, and public policy—to mention but a few of the fields in which significant work has been written during the past decade (see Feldman & Elliott, 1990; Lerner, Peterson, & Brooks-Gunn, 1991). So with apologies to the readers of this volume and the authors of this rich literature, rather than attempting to produce a systematic overview in this essay, I have set myself the more modest task of identifying a selected set of promising topics, themes, and research problems that have the potential to illuminate the sociology of adolescence and youth during the next decade.

The emphasis will be on the links between the adolescent years and the transition to adulthood, an area of scholarship that has come into its own during the past decade but one in which developmentalists have not yet begun to play a major role (Settersten, 1999; Sherrod, 1993). As such, I will give relatively less emphasis to the important contribution of researchers whose work has focused on the links between late childhood and early adolescence. This work is separately summarized in the multiple volumes of the Carnegie Commission that appeared in the first half of the 1990s (Carnegie Council on Adolescent Development, 1995; Lerner, 1993).

The topic of the transition to adulthood has been the subject of considerable investigation by economists and social demographers because of its policy significance. In the coming years, it also should attract more interest among sociologists and psychologists, if only because of the extension of adolescence beyond the teen years. I will show how the increasing prominence of adolescence is rooted in global structural forces that have extended the period of youth. This review then considers some of the consequences of the prolongation of adulthood on young people, their parents, and the larger society.

A Brief History of Adolescence: Research and Researchers

It is impossible to chart new directions without taking stock of where we have been in the recent past. Although it is not surprising that the adolescence literature has grown over the last several decades, it is more interesting to report that many of the themes identified in the early literature endure. The themes set out by Hall, who is credited with establishing the field of adolescence research with the appearance of his two-volume text on adolescence in 1904, continue to define the scope of the field nearly a century later (Petersen, 1991). The scholarly culture of adolescence studies has been remarkably persistent (Lerner, Peterson, & Brooks-Gunn, 1991; Mirel, 1991). Many of the focal concerns in Hall's classic text were pursued by his early followers in psychology and sociology. Then as now, scholars continue to place a strong emphasis on adolescence as a problematic life stage in modern society.

This theme remained throughout the postwar period, which ironically is now enshrined as the golden era of family harmony (Coontz, 1992; Skolnick, 1991). Of course, the existence of adolescence and youth antedated the 20th century, as social historians such as Kett (1977), Demos (1986), and Katz (1975) have convincingly demonstrated. Unemployment, the extension of education, and the decline of the family-based farm began to create a social class of people who were neither children nor adults. As such, these people enjoyed a lengthy period of semiautonomy. This stage typically began after early childhood and stretched through the transition to adulthood, a stage that frequently endured into the third decade of life.

Adolescence only emerged as a discrete life stage in the middle decades of the 20th century, when the transition from childhood to adulthood became (at least temporarily) more predictable, rapidly accomplished, and socially organized (Evans & Heinz, 1993; Feldman & Elliott, 1990; Furstenberg, Modell, & Hershberg, 1976; George, 1993; Modell, 1989). As a rule, adolescence becomes culturally defined as a life stage when full-time education replaces full-time employment as the primary activity of young people. This transformation typically happens in societies with advanced economies, in which a greater premium is placed on education and training. Considerable variation exists across Western nations in the policies and programs that integrate education with entrance to the labor force, as shall be discussed later in this review. Nonetheless, youth in these nations, in one form or another, have been simultaneously pushed out of the labor market and sheltered from the adult world (Mulder & Manting, 1994; Shavit & Müller, 1998; Zelizer, 1985). This phase of the life course establishes a youth-based social world that is age segregated, partially buffered from adult control, and relatively turned in on itself. This transformation encourages the development of a youth culture that is impelled to distinguish itself from adulthood and can establish its own system of rewards (Berger, 1972; Coleman, 1974; Eckert, 1989; Flacks, 1971). To a great degree, the problematic features of adolescence and the transition to adulthood are structurally created and maintained by social institutions that isolate youth from adults; ironically, this is done to prepare them for future roles. Culturally, youth are simultaneously indulged and castigated—allowed or even encouraged to seek their own company yet reproached for being self-centered, irresponsible, and occupied with self-destructive or socially destructive behaviors (Farkas & Johnson, 1997). A good deal of the literature written since the 1960s, when studies of adolescence and early adulthood became a large-scale endeavor, concerns this central paradox: Advanced industrial societies create adolescence and early adulthood as life stages in ways that inevitably render them problematic. In one way or another, much of the social science research on adolescence has been dominated by this cultural contradiction.

Biological Influences in Adolescence

Ever since Mead (1928) published her famous study, *Coming of Age in Samoa,* scholars from different disciplines have disagreed over the extent to which adolescence—as a life stage or as a developmental period—is biologically programmed. Something akin to adolescence has been observed by animal ethologists studying the departure of primates from their family, the organization and stratification of peer-dominated age groups, and "acting out" behaviors of youthful primates. Maccoby (1998) devoted a portion of her elegant review of the origins of gender differences to the empirical evidence garnered from animal biology, especially the superb descriptive studies of Suomi and his collaborators (Berman, Rasmussen, & Suomi, 1994).

Maccoby made a strong case that the origins of gender behavior are shaped by biological traits that are reinforced in early peer-directed play. During the past decade, Brooks-Gunn and her collaborators (Brooks-Gunn & Graber, 1994; Graber et al., 1996) have made substantial contributions to the hormone-behavior links that trigger changes in girls and their psychological and social development. Like Maccoby, this line of research demonstrates how biological and social factors interact and complement one another to shape gender differences during adolescence. For years, sociologist Udry (1994), among others, has cautioned researchers that they ignore the biological bases of sexual behavior among adolescents at their own peril. He and his collaborators have shown that the timing of sexual behavior is targeted by biological changes, although the context and content of sexual expression is surely socially negotiated. Finally, it should not be forgotten that Simmons and Blyth (1987) conducted a pioneering study on how biological changes accompanying puberty may have different consequences in different social contexts.

Gradually, sociologists, whose disciplinary biases make us attend almost exclusively to the forces of culture and social structure, are beginning to accept the notion that biology matters in a variety of ways for both individual and interpersonal processes (Rowe & Rodgers, 1997). Following the lead of Plomin and his collaborators, researchers have become increasingly aware of how much children's temperament influences sibling responses to family environments and perceptions of the world outside the household (Dunn & Plomin, 1991; Plomin, 1990). These research developments are encouraging. Even so, ignorance of biological science makes many social scientists vulnerable to simple-minded and reductionist explanations (Herrnstein & Murray, 1994; Popenoe, 1996). The controversies over how genetic and biological influences condition and constrain social behavior during adolescence is likely to be clarified by researchers in the decades ahead. It seems more than likely that complete explanations will take fuller account of the interactions between biological, psychological, and social conditions.

THE DEMOGRAPHY OF ADOLESCENCE AND YOUTH

By all accounts, adolescence became a more distinctive and culturally marked life stage during the second third of this century. During this period, adolescence also became more protracted and less orderly than it was at midcentury (Rindfuss, 1991). In the 1950s, nearly half of all women were married by age 20 and men by age 23. Typically, marriage was the central event that orchestrated the many aspects of the passage to adulthood, including school departure; entrance to the labor force; the onset of sexual relations (although evidence indicates that pregnancy commonly precipitated unions and sexual initiation frequently occurred just before couples entered marriage); and departure from the natal household. Closely intertwined and interdependent, these events typically occurred in the late teens and early 20s for a large portion of the population. The close interrelationship of these life events began to unravel in the late 1960s; at the century's end, the transition to adulthood extended well into the third decade of life and is not completed by a substantial fraction of young adults until their 30s (as was the case at the beginning of the century; Buchmann, 1989; Cavalli & Galland, 1995; Crouter, 1998; Rindfuss; Veevers, Gee, & Wister, 1996; White & Lacy, 1997).

The events that make up the transition to adulthood have generally been studied separately rather than in conjunction with one another. Nonetheless, all of the discrete indicators have risen substantially over the past several decades with a single exception—the age of onset of sexual relations (Billy, Tanfer, Grady, & Klepinger, 1993; Warner et al., 1998). The median age of departure from school has risen by about 3 years since 1960: fewer than two fifths (38%) of all youth aged 18 and 19 were enrolled in school in 1960, compared with 62% in 1996 (Ventura, 1995). The median age of school exit is now close to 21, and a higher number of students in their 20s and early 30s are returning to school than ever before (Jacobs & Stoner-Eby, 1998).

Data are not readily available on the age at which youth enter the labor force full time, but a recent report by the American Youth Policy Forum (Halperin, 1998) showed the diminishing likelihood that younger workers will earn sufficient income to support a family. Citing the work of Bernhardt and her colleagues (1998), who compared two cohorts of young White men in the National Longitudinal Surveys who came of age in the period from 1966 to 1981 and a more recent cohort who entered the labor force between 1979 and 1994, the report concluded that "the transition to permanent employment is taking longer." By age 30, only 57% of the more recent cohort had worked for 2 or more years in a full-time, year-round job (compared to 63% of the earlier cohort). Obviously, the figures for African American and other disadvantaged minorities would be much lower.

Needless to say, these changes carry profound implications for the timing of marriage and the formation of families. The median age of marriage for women has risen from 20.3 in 1960 to 24.8 in 1996. A similar rise has occurred among men, whose median age of marriage climbed to 27.1 in 1996, 4.3 years later than it had been in 1960 (U.S. Bureau of the Census, 1996). Even though the age at first intercourse leveled off or possibly even declined in the early 1990s, the gap between onset of sexual activity and marriage now is huge compared with what it was in the 1950s. About half of all women today have sexual relations by age 18, more than 5 years earlier than the median age of marriage. Similarly, departure from the natal household now occurs well before marriage for many young people, who leave home to pursue schooling or after they enter the labor force, even though young adults are more likely to remain in their parents' household into their early 20s (Goldscheider & Goldscheider, 1994; White, 1994; White & Rogers, 1997).

Despite the considerable attention devoted to early parenthood, the total level of fertility among teenagers is much lower now than it was at mid-century (Alan Guttmacher Institute, 1994; Elo, King, & Furstenberg, 1999). In large measure, this decline has accompanied the rising age of marriage. Birth rates for teenagers and for women in their early 20s are significantly lower than were levels in the 1960s. At the same time, the high proportion of unmarried women and growing prevalence of nonmarital sexual behavior resulted in rising rates and ratios of out-of-wedlock births among teenagers and women in their early 20s. Recently, this upward trend has leveled off; among Black women, the rate of out-of-wedlock births dropped substantially by the 1990s. None-theless, because of the steeper decline of marital than nonmarital births, the ratio of out-of-wedlock births to marital births for youth has continued to climb (Smith, Morgan, & Koropeckyj-Cox, 1996). Even so, some of these nonmarital births occur in

cohabiting unions that may either eventuate in marriage or remain relatively stable units.

In the 1990s, marriage is less normative during late adolescence or even early adulthood, no doubt in part because it is more difficult for couples to achieve. Gaining economic security in an uncertain and often unrewarding labor market is a part of the problem (Cready & Fossett, 1997; Lichter, Kephart, McLaughlin, & Landry, 1992; Mare & Winship, 1991; Wallulis, 1998). It seems also likely that marital instability in the parental generation may introduce a note of caution to young couples, many of whom are reluctant to make a matrimonial commitment when they can hedge their bets by cohabiting (Edin, 1998; Furstenberg, 1995). Apparently, both changes in social structure and culture have encouraged a growing portion of youth to delay family formation to gain more education and labor market experience. In recent decades, these trends have meant that young adults more frequently reside in their parents' households, at least episodically, while they attempt to gain a foothold in the labor market (Cavalli & Galland, 1995; Goldscheider & Waite, 1991; Schnaiberg & Goldenberg, 1989). This pattern of later "nest leaving" by young adults is far less practiced by adolescents in stepfamilies, presumably because of the child's less cohesive relationship with the stepparent (Goldscheider & Goldscheider, 1994).

In sum, these demographic patterns suggest that the transition to adulthood is now occurring over a longer span of years than was the case during the middle of the 20th century. Accordingly, youth, a period that spans late adolescence and early adulthood, has become a more prominent stage of the life course. Relatively little in-depth or even survey data on the processes of identity and the establishment of goals and commitments is available that would complement these demographic data (Arnett, 1998; Brown & Booth, 1996; Cordon, 1997; Grotevant, 1997; Grotevant & Cooper, 1988; Hagan & Wheaton, 1993). Just how young people construct adult identities in a world in which attaining the traditional markers of adult status has become more difficult (or at least considerably delayed) is an issue worth pursuing in future research. (An interesting variant of this question examines the special situation of immigrant youth, which has begun to receive more attention in the past decade; Rumbaut, 1999). A mounting set of studies indicates that these diverse pathways to achieving success in adulthood exist among different Hispanic and Asian American nationalities (Hurtado, Carter, & Spuler, 1996; McLoyd & Steinberg, 1998; Padilla, 1997; Saetermoe, Beneli, & Busch, 1999).

SUCCESSFUL ADOLESCENCE AND THE TRANSITION TO ADULTHOOD

As indicated earlier, the vast majority of articles and studies of youth are focused on the problematic features of adolescence and explicitly on problem behavior. A review of the leading journals on adolescence indicated that at least half of all articles were principally about youthful misbehavior and maladjustment: delinquency and violence, substance abuse, school problems, mental health, and the like. This focus is especially prominent in the literature on early adolescence when youth engage in more behaviors defined as "high risk" (Bahr, Maughan, Marcos, & Li, 1998; Barber, 1992; Bogenschneider, Wu, Raffaelli, & Tsay, 1998; Buehler et al., 1998; Christopher, Madura, & Weaver, 1998; Dryfoos, 1998; Hoffman & Johnson, 1998; Perkins, Luster, Villarruel, & Small, 1998; Veneziano & Rohner, 1998). A far smaller share of the literature concerns measures of conventional behaviors (Crockett & Crouter, 1995) to adolescent success or to adult roles. One could argue that the two realms of behavior are simply opposite sides of a common coin. Nonetheless, such an approach inevitably treats successful adolescents and young adults as escape artists who manage to dodge the hazards of growing up, rather than focusing on the ways that young people acquire and master skills, construct positive identities, and learn how to negotiate social roles simultaneously in the youth culture and adult world (Graber et al., 1996).

This perspective avoids drawing a sharp line between "good" and "bad" behaviors because most youth (like many adults) engage in behaviors that may have more complex meanings depending on both their context and consequences (Becker, 1973). Why should learning to drive safely be regarded as a positive development, whereas learning to drink responsibly is seen as a negative event? Both driving and drinking have the potential to be deadly, but both can also signify learning to manage potentially harmful actions, can serve as a measure of increased autonomy, and can be ways of socially promoting trust and signaling maturity. Interestingly, driving has become a standard rite of passage during adolescence, whereas drinking remains an, albeit widely practiced, underground activity, not socially sanctioned, and by

all accounts poorly managed (Crowe, Philbin, Richards, & Crawford, 1998; Harford & Grant, 1987; Johnston, O'Malley, & Bachman, 1999).

Along the same lines, countless articles have been written on the ostensibly perilous transition from virginity to sexual activity, which for the vast majority of young people occurs sometime between the ages of 14 and 21 (Rodgers, 1999; Small & Luster, 1994). In fact, this transition assumes a highly orderly form that looks rather similar for men and women, although it begins slightly later for women. In other words, if we know the age at which the first 10% of the population has sex, we can predict the age at which the next 80% will have sex with amazing precision. Nonetheless, scores of articles are published every year on the psychosocial and contextual determinants of onset of intercourse (Grunseit al., 1997). By contrast, little research has evaluated the reasons that sexual intercourse is regarded as a form of problem behavior in the United States (Luker, 1997; Nathanson, 1992). This is not to say that the transition does not have problematic features; it surely does, but so, too, do the transitions to driving, changing residential location, going to a weekly summer camp, and entering the labor force, none of which are viewed as inherently dangerous or even pathological. Suppose we treated these so-called risky behaviors more even handedly. We might then begin to construct a sociology of adolescence that more clearly reveals the ways in which social institutions and culture create and reinforce patterns problematic to promotion of successful development in any given society or at different historical moments in the same society (National Research Council, 1993).

All too little work provides a thick description of how adolescence appears to those going through it (Medrich, Roizen, Rubin, & Buckley, 1982). Relatively few ethnographies are carried out on the ways that young people experience, perceive, and organize the social world, but there are some important exceptions. Over the past decade or so, several excellent accounts have described the activities of low-income youth in ways that reveal the logic of young people's involvement in illegal activities. For example, Sullivan (1989) showed how youth acquire different roles afforded by varying social opportunities. Several compelling accounts of the lives of Black teenage mothers have also been written during the past decade (Anderson, 1999; Horowitz, 1999; Kaplan, 1997). Unfortunately, we have fewer studies of the lives of working-class youth or middle-class, college-bound teens and even fewer studies of privileged adolescents (Gerson, 1985, 1993; Holland & Eisenhart, 1990). Moreover, the volumes that segregate youth into different categories by gender and ethnicity fail to provide a comparative description of adolescence that crosses conventional sociological categories. Thus, we have the impression that the issues, practices, and identities of youth in different social locations are highly dissimilar, a proposition that calls for further investigation using comparative ethnographic data (Edin & Lein, 1997; Newman, 1999a; Phelan, Davidson, & Yu, 1998; Sullivan, 1989).

One potentially interesting data source providing descriptive information on youth—time-use studies—has not been adequately mined (Bryant & Zick, 1996). Both national and international surveys of time use provide a wealth of information on the attitudes and behavior of teenagers and young adults. One of the most creative studies of the decade employed helpers to explore how families construct common realities in the face of conflicting and competing demands (Larson & Richards, 1994). Larson and Verma (1998) have recently provided an excellent summary of the extant surveys showing how time-use data reveal age, class, and gender differences. A growing number of researchers are beginning to exploit time-use data to examine the lives of adolescents, employing cross-national data sets on time use in various nations (Fuligni & Stevenson, 1995; Gauthier, 1999). This line of research allows us to explore how, with whom, and where adolescents and young adults spend their time (Larson, 1997; Larson, Richards, Moneta, Holmbeck, & Duckett, 1996). Thus, comparative work of this type may begin to shed some light on how the course of development changes as children move through and beyond the adolescent years and how that experience may be changing as a result of educational and employment opportunities (Bianchi & Robinson, 1997).

ADOLESCENCE IN MULTIPLE CONTEXTS: PARENTS, PEERS, AND NEIGHBORHOODS

Considerable attention has been devoted in the sociological and developmental literature to changes in the settings in which adolescents spend time: at home, with peers, in school, in the community, and at work. It is generally acknowledged that time spent outside the household increases at the expense of family time (Aquilino, 1997; Rossi & Rossi, 1990). This means that direct parental supervision declines, whereas contact with peers increases; thus, adolescents, at least in American society, tend to spend a growing amount of time outside the control of adults (Baumrind, 1991; Bryant & Zick, 1996; Bulcroft, Carmody, & Bulcroft, 1996). This phenomenon is taken as a matter of course and may even be considered desirable by some adults. Yet most surveys indicate that Americans believe that parents provide too little supervision (National Commission on Children, 1991). Even parents hold that view, although they tend to believe it is true more for other parents than for themselves (Furstenberg, 1999). It seems that we place a high value on autonomy among our young but at the same time worry about its consequences (Alwin, 1988; Owens, Mortimer, & Finch, 1996).

Beliefs regarding levels of parental supervision notwithstanding, most surveys of both parents and their offspring indicate that parents generally keep reasonably close tabs on their younger teens. The techniques of control generally change during the course of adolescence, however (Larson & Richards, 1994; Steinberg, Lamborn, Darling, Mounts, & Dornbusch, 1994; Steinberg, Lamborn, Dornbusch, & Darling, 1992). Direct monitoring declines, and parents typically relax rules for older adolescents, believing that they can count on their children to follow their directives, although such rules vary by race and ethnicity (Bulcroft, Carmody, & Bulcroft, 1996; Furstenberg, Cook, Eccles, Elder, & Sameroff, 1999). Of course, youth usually do follow their directives, but certainly less so than most parents believe. No doubt, parents often underreport their own children's use of alcohol and drugs, school problems, and sexual behavior (Bogenschneider et al., 1998). Indeed, it could be said that a developmental task of adolescents is learning what not to tell parents and how not to tell them.

In general, however, most studies show that these so-called adolescent problem behaviors occur episodically and experimentally (Jessor, 1993; Osgood, Johnston, O'Malley, & Bachman, 1988). During adolescence, youth are learning to deal with potentially risky behaviors. This stage, not coincidentally, occurs at the same time peer influence increases. In effect, as many studies have shown, peers either comanage or take over the management of adultlike behaviors (Bogenschneider et al., 1998; Cohen, 1991; Hartup, 1993). Of course, peer groups themselves have different standards, which in some circumstances may be more conservative than parents would tolerate for themselves, but typically are more permissive than parents would advocate for their children (Millstein, Petersen, & Nightingale, 1993).

How parents read and interpret their children's behavior has for some time been a topic of interest to developmental psychologists and family sociologists (Barber & Eccles, 1992). Nonetheless, we still know all too little about how parents manage children's behaviors outside the home through indirect techniques not involving face-to-face supervision. For example, by their choice of neighborhoods and schools or involvement in functional communities, principally churches and voluntary organizations, parents attempt to situate their children in settings that affect the likelihood of exposure to conforming peers (Furstenberg et al., 1999; Phelan et al., 1998).

In a much publicized book, Harris (1998) asserted that the influence of parents is much overrated. Parental effects, she argued, are overstated because they fail to take account of heritable traits. Moreover, drawing on the work of behavioral genetics (Rowe & Rodgers, 1997), Harris claimed that peer influence easily outweighs the impact of families. This may yet turn out to be true, but her argument missed the indirect influence of families through management strategies that do not involve face-to-face interactions. Although the choice of peers is not exclusively under the oversight of families, parents do have a great deal of control over peer choice, especially when they have the resources to select the environments in which their children spend time (Demo, 1992; Lareau, 1997; Saporito & Lareau, 1999; Wynn, 1995).

Of course, children become more active in the selection of peers, especially when they reach adolescence (Frønes, 1995; Phelan, Yu, & Davidson, 1994). A long tradition of research stretching back to the Chicago School of Sociology has explored the issue of peer group processes, including youths' movements in and out of friendship networks, informal social groups, gangs, and voluntary organizations (Sampson, 1992; Tannenbaum, 1938; Thrasher, 1927). Over the past decade, the study of social networks has become more sophisticated as researchers have begun to examine longitudinal data on the relationship between network changes and behavioral patterns (Cairns, Leung, Buchanan, & Cairns, 1995; Ennett & Bauman, 1996). Multilevel statistical models that permit more accurate assessments of contextual effects can now be applied to peer groups, using data sources that take dense samples of class-

rooms, schools, or neighborhoods (Bryk & Raudenbush, 1992; Cook, Herman, Phillips, & Settersten, 1999).

During the 1990s, a huge outpouring of studies has occurred among researchers interested in both schools and neighborhoods (Brooks-Gunn, Duncan, & Aber, 1997; Entwisle & Alexander, 1993; Ryan, Adams, Gullotta, Weissberg, & Hampton, 1995). School transitions have been a popular topic, as have been school choice, tracking, and the influence of small learning communities. A number of studies have demonstrated how the school system shapes the course of academic and social development (Wigfield, Eccles, & Rodriguez, 1998). The overlap between these topical areas in the sociology of education and adolescent development could be even greater. For example, it would be useful to explore how adolescents negotiate school transitions; how gender and ethnic affiliations and identities are altered in different school settings; and how gender, ethnicity, and racial status are consolidated or reinforced by placement in school. Much more attention has been given to the earlier school transitions (out of primary school and through middle school) than to the transitions that take place during and following high school. A lacuna exists, especially for lower-income youth who move into community college, but even the transition to college has not yet been adequately researched (Kane & Rouse, 1999; Pascarelli, Edison, Nora, Hagedorn, & Terenzini, 1998; Terenzini et al., 1994).

Neighborhood studies are in vogue again, stimulated by the interest in the so-called urban underclass (Jencks & Peterson, 1991). Over the past decade, a number of studies have been conducted on the direct and indirect effects of growing up in areas of concentrated poverty. Using multilevel models to examine for neighborhood influences on adolescent behaviors has not shown a strong impact of the quality of neighborhoods, independent of the demographic characteristics of the resident families (Cook, Shagle, & Degirmencioglu, 1997; Furstenberg et al., 1999). Rather, impacts of each context are modest and additive. It seems that adolescent development is shaped and directed by the combination of contexts rather than demonstrated by any single setting. In an examination of families, schools, and neighborhoods in Prince Georges County, Maryland, Cook and his collaborators have explored this proposition (Cook et al., in press). They have shown that contexts in this suburban community are relatively independent of one another. Families that function well do not always send their children to high-quality schools or live in socially cohesive neighborhoods. In sum, the effects of each of these contexts alone is modest, but when they are all positive or negative, their effect on developmental trajectories can be powerful.

Elder and his colleagues have explored the impact of multiple and changing contexts in rural communities in Iowa (Elder, King, & Conger, 1996). Their research points to the role of farming and farming traditions in shaping the values and behaviors of youth. The breakdown of farm communities appears to contribute to family problems, different styles of parenting, and lower levels of prosocial behavior among the youth whose families leave the farm. This work suggests that youth become disengaged from the community as their families become less embedded occupationally and socially in what was once a tightly integrated social setting (Elder & Conger, 2000).

EMPLOYMENT EXPERIENCE AND ADOLESCENT DEVELOPMENT

Earlier in this century, work experience constituted a major, if not the major, activity during the adolescent years. Whether they went to work on farms, at trades, or in factories, most youth were employed by their midteens. Surprisingly, labor force participation for young men between the ages of 16 and 19 has remained remarkably steady throughout the century and has actually increased for young women (U.S. Bureau of the Census, 1976, 1996). Of course, the nature of work has changed drastically; it is more likely to be part time or seasonal, as more youth are balancing work and school activities simultaneously.

The costs and benefits of work for youth have been hotly debated in this and in the two previous decades. One group of researchers has pointed to the harmful effects of work on school performance and educational commitment, whereas others have noted the potential benefits of employment for gaining skills, maturity, and social contacts (Greenberger & Steinberg, 1986; Mortimer, Pimentel, Ryu, Nash, & Lee, 1996). Some common ground between these conflicting perspectives has been discovered during the 1990s. Many researchers now agree that long hours, dangerous settings, and the absence of adult supervision contribute to the negative effects of work (Dunn, Runyan, Cohen, & Schulman, 1998; Markel & Frone, 1998; Mihalic & Elliott, 1997; Singh, 1998). On the other hand, employment can

promote positive development if working conditions are favorable (Mortimer et al., 1996; Newman, 1996b). Certainly, it seems that the absence of employment experience for adolescents can be costly. Learning to master work demands and manage work roles promotes responsibility and self-respect and may help youth clarify future goals.

There is growing interest in the developmental benefits of unpaid or volunteer jobs as well, although data on the consequences of community service are less systematic (Flanagan & Sherrod, 1998; Johnson, Beebe, Mortimer, & Snyder, 1998). A U. S. Department of Labor study showed that approximately one out of every eight adolescents and young adults spent an average of 4 hours a week in a volunteer activity. A promising area of research would be to examine the social processes that lead to these changing patterns, as well as their consequences for later life social involvement. Similarly, we know little about the role of extracurricular activities in the development of social skills and competencies that may increase self-regard and help widen social contacts. The building of human, cultural, and social capital is ripe for further exploration among adolescents and young adults (Aschaffenburg & Maas, 1997; Stanton-Salazar, 1997; Teachman, Paasch, & Carver, 1997).

As I noted earlier in this essay, too little recognition has been accorded to the obvious fact that most adolescents make it to adulthood relatively unscathed and prepared to accept and assume adult roles. Despite the popular perception that youth are neglected, troubled, and ill-prepared to enter adulthood, it seems that not all patterns during adolescence are negative. Interestingly, a volume issued by the U.S. Department of Health and Human Services (1999) showing that many indices of well-being among youth (e.g., academic achievement, lower poverty, or declining teenage childbearing) were rising hardly garnered any attention.

CROSS-NATIONAL STUDIES OF ADOLESCENCE AND YOUTH

Considering the exalted place the United States enjoys in the global economy, only a trickle of explicitly comparative studies have appeared in the 1990s (Goldscheider, 1997; Kerkhoff & Macrae, 1992; Silverberg, Vazsonyi, Schlegel, & Schmidt, 1998). Moreover, only a few of those studies have exploited the many extant data sources that include identical or similar data on youth from a large number of countries (Buchmann, 1989; Chisolm, Buchner, Kruger, & du Bois-Reymond, 1995; Hurrelmann & Hamilton, 1996). Thus, it has been difficult to relate national contexts to the welfare of youth or the course of adolescent development.

Current efforts by a committee sponsored by the Society for Research on Adolescence under the direction of Reed Larson is attempting to redress this problem. Prior research has focused on isolated institutional comparisons, such as the ways that different countries manage the transition to sexuality, to draw lessons about better or worse ways of preparing youth to take responsibility for sexual behavior (Jones et al., 1985). Among others, Hamilton (1994) has pointed out striking differences in the arrangement of the transition from school into the labor force in countries that have a tradition of providing apprenticeships as part of the schooling system (Hamilton & Lempert, 1996). Some research is also being carried out on different patterns of family formation among nations with developed economies (Blossfeld, 1995; Knudsen & Waerness, 1999). Similarly, there is some modest work on how different cultures cultivate citizenship responsibilities (Torney-Purta & Amadeo, 1999). All of these promising topics, as well as other areas of cross-national research, are at a relatively primitive stage.

DISCUSSION AND CONCLUSION

Imagine when, some time in the 21st century, scholars will look back at this final decade review of the *Journal of Marriage and the Family* to see what captured the interests of family scholars at the conclusion of the 20th century. In research on youth, will the themes that have endured throughout this century still be familiar, or will they be quaint remembrances of a different era? Looking at the early studies of adolescence in the first half of the 20th century, it is easy to see the continuities that have persisted: the emphasis on growing autonomy from family, peer group relations, and, most of all, a pervasive focus on the problematic aspects of youth. We have seen some shifts in attention from a concentration on social class differences to more work on race and ethnic variations, and gender has become a much larger topic of scholarly concern (Portes, 1996). It is difficult to imagine that these areas of study will disappear altogether. It is almost an axiom of research on youth that adults inevitably find things to worry

about in regard to the cohorts who are coming of age. Usually, adult concerns for the next generation resemble the same issues their own parents worried about. It may be the one constant in intergenerational studies (Rossi & Rossi, 1990).

I speculate that at least some of this anxiety is unjustified and that scholars have spent too little time trying to understand how things operate well or adequately in the course of growing up in American society or in Western society more generally. With some reluctance, I have not addressed the growing literature on adolescence in developing countries, not because it is unimportant, but simply because the subject deserves a separate essay. I have, however, contended that U.S. scholars need to become less parochial if we are to achieve a firm grasp of which aspects of adolescence are peculiar to our culture and social system and which are more general or even universal. Surely, historians of the field in the next century will criticize American researchers for their single-minded attention to the United States while neglecting other areas of the world. Although this ethnocentric focus is slowly giving way to a more comparative approach, we are still in the early stages of this transformation. Scholarly isolationism cannot be tolerated for much longer.

Some other limitations of the current literature are equally apparent. Researchers have been much more attentive in looking at adolescence in single rather than multiple contexts. Most of our studies focus on the influence of families or schools or peers or neighborhoods; only recently have investigators begun to examine multiple contexts in a single study. If we are to gain a more complete understanding of when, how, and why different contexts shape the trajectories of development, we cannot continue to study one context at a time. There is strong reason to believe that contexts operate in tandem even when their effects are relatively independent of one another. The degree to which negative and positive contexts are clustered for youth in different positions in society is itself a topic of considerable importance in this era of growing inequality.

One promising development during the past decade has been the greater availability of large-scale surveys, especially longitudinal studies that follow children through adolescence into early adulthood (Anderson, 1993; Aquilino, 1996; Brooks-Gunn, Duncan, Klebanov, & Sealand, 1993; Duncan, 1994; Goodman, 1999; Lee, Burkham, Zimiles, & Ladewski, 1994; Lewis, Ross, & Mirowsky, 1999; Lye, Klepinger, Hyle, & Nelson,

1995; Powell & Parcel, 1999; Resnick et al., 1997; Sui-Chu & Willms, 1996).

We have not done as well in conducting systematic qualitative studies of how youth and their parents, teachers, and mentors construct the world and negotiate the processes that lead to success and failure. Indeed, the social construction of success at different ages and in disparate locations of society is another topic that deserves more attention than it has received from the research community. The prevailing variable-centered approach to examining success and failure often favors hairsplitting precision over more holistic understanding. Again, there is some cause for optimism because survey and qualitative researchers are beginning to collaborate on ways of cross-walking between methods of research. Integrating surveys and qualitative research will surely help reduce another type of academic segregation—the study of single domains of success or failure—and move us closer to a deeper understanding of how adolescents and their families think of growing up, in terms of the complex processes of managing different and sometimes competing demands. Specialization in areas of cognitive, affective, and social arenas need not be abandoned, but specialized studies could certainly benefit from more work exploring these different domains together.

As I commented at the beginning of this essay, our disciplines have drawn artificial boundaries that are not extant in the natural world. Many disciplines have left biology out of the picture and have acted as if individual differences do not matter. Others have focused on individual differences while neglecting culture and social structure. This balkanized approach to the study of adolescence serves us poorly. One of the most commendable developments in the past decade has been the formation of the Society on Research of Adolescence, which has begun to publish its own journal and is making considerable headway toward an intellectual reunification. In addition, *Journal of Marriage and the Family* welcomes the contributions of scholarly work from a broader number of disciplines. These promising trends are a welcome prelude to research in the 21st century.

NOTE

This research was supported by the MacArthur Foundation Research Network on Successful Adolescent Development in High-Risk Settings, The MacArthur Foundation Research Network on the Transitions to Adulthood, as well as the Zellerbach Family Fund.

REFERENCES

Alan Guttmacher Institute. (1994). *Sex and America's teenagers.* New York: Author.

Alwin, D. (1988). From obedience to autonomy: Changes in traits desired in children. *The Public Opinion Quarterly, 52,* 33–52.

Anderson, D. K. (1993). Adolescent mothers drop out. *American Sociological Review, 58,* 735–738.

Anderson, E. (1999). *Code of the street: Decency, violence, and the moral life of the inner city.* New York: W. W. Norton.

Aquilino, W. S. (1996). The life course of children born to unmarried mothers: Childhood living arrangements and young adult outcomes. *Journal of Marriage and the Family, 58,* 293–310.

Aquilino, W. S. (1997). From adolescent to young adult: A prospective study of parent-child relations during the transition to adulthood. *Journal of Marriage and the Family, 59,* 670–686.

Arnett, J. J. (1998). Learning to stand alone: The contemporary American transition to adulthood in cultural and historical context. *Human Development, 41,* 295–315.

Aschaffenburg, K., & Maas, I. (1997). Cultural and educational careers: The dynamics of social reproduction. *American Sociological Review, 62,* 573–587.

Bahr, S. J., Maughan, S. L., Marcos, A. C., & Li, B. (1998). Family, religiosity, and the risk of adolescent drug use. *Journal of Marriage and the family, 60,* 979–992.

Barber, B. K. (1992). Family, personality, and adolescent problem behaviors. *Journal of Marriage and the Family, 54,* 69–79.

Barber, B. L., & Eccles, J. S. (1992). Long-term influence of divorce and single parenting on adolescent family- and work-related values, behaviors, and aspirations. *Psychological Bulletin, 1,* 108–126.

Baumrind, D. (1991). Parenting styles and adolescent development. In R. M. Lerner, A. C. Petersen, & J. Brooks-Gunn (Eds.), *Encyclopedia of adolescence.* New York: Garland.

Becker, H. S. (1973). *Outsiders, studies in the sociology of deviance.* New York: Free Press.

Berger, B. M. (1972). On the youthfulness of youth cultures. In P. K. Manning & M. Truzzi (Eds.), *Youth and sociology* (pp. 52–68). Englewood Cliffs, NJ: Prentice-Hall.

Berman, C. M., Rasmussen, K. L. R., & Suomi, S. J. (1994). Responses of free-ranging rhesus-monkeys to a natural form of social separation. 1. Parallels with mother-infant separation in captivity. *Child Development, 69,* 1672–1688.

Bernhardt, A., Morris, M., Handcock, M., & Scott, M. (1998). Summary of findings: Work and opportunity in the post-industrial labor market. New York: Institute on Education and the Economy, Teachers College, Columbia University.

Bianchi, S. M., & Robinson, J. (1997). What did you do today? Children's use of time, family composition, and the acquisition of social capital. *Journal of Marriage and the Family, 59,* 332–344.

Billy, J. O. G., Tanfer, K., Grady, W. R., & Klepinger, D. H. (1993). The sexual behavior of men in the United States. *Family Planning Perspectives, 25,* 52–60.

Blossfeld, H. P. (Ed.). (1995). *The new role of women:*

Family formation in modern societies. Boulder, CO: Westview Press.

Bogenschneider, K., Wu, M., Raffaelli, M., Tsay, J. C. (1998). "Other teens drink, but not my kid": Does parental awareness of adolescent alcohol use protect adolescents from risky consequences? *Journal of Marriage and the Family, 60,* 356–373.

Brooks-Gunn, J., Duncan, G. J., & Aber, J. L. (Eds.). (1997). *Neighborhood poverty* (Vols. I–II). New York: Russell Sage.

Brooks-Gunn, J., Duncan, G. J., Klebanov, P. K., & Sealand, N. (1993). Do neighborhoods influence child and adolescent development? *American Journal of Sociology, 99,* 353–395.

Brooks-Gunn, J., & Graber, J. A. (1994). Puberty as a biological and social event: Implications for research on pharmacology. *Journal of Adolescent Health, 15,* 663–671.

Brown, S. L., & Booth, A. (1996). Cohabitation versus marriage: A comparison of relationship quality. *Journal of Marriage and the Family, 58,* 668–678.

Bryant, W. K., & Zick, C. D. (1996). An examination of parent-child shared time. *Journal of Marriage and the Family, 58,* 227–237.

Bryk, A. S., & Raudenbush, S. W. (1992). *Hierarchical linear models: Applications and data analysis methods.* Newbury Park, CA: Sage.

Buchmann, M. (1989). *The script of life in modern society.* Chicago: University of Chicago Press.

Buehler, C., Krishnakumar, A., Stone, G., Anthony, C., Pemberton, S., Gerard, J., & Barber, B. K. (1998). *Journal of Marriage and the Family, 60,* 119–132.

Bulcroft, R. A., Carmody, D. C., & Bulcroft, K. A. (1996). Patterns of parental independence giving to adolescents: Variations by race, age, and gender of child. *Journal of Marriage and the Family, 58,* 866–883.

Cairns, R. B., Leung, M. C., Buchanan, L., & Cairns, B. D. (1995). Friendships and social networks in childhood and adolescence: Fluidity, reliability, and interrelations. *Child Development, 66,* 1330–1345.

Carnegie Council on Adolescent Development. (1995). *Great transitions: Preparing adolescents for a new century.* New York: Carnegie.

Cavalli, A., & Galland, O. (Eds.). (1995). *Youth in Europe.* London: Pinter.

Chisolm, L., Buchner, P., Kruger, H. H., & du Bois-Reymond, M. (1995). *Growng up in Europe: Contemporary horizons in childhood and youth studies.* Berlin: Walter de Gruyter.

Christopher, F. S., Madura, M., & Weaver, L. (1998). Premarital sexual aggressors: A multivariate analysis of social, rational, and individual variables. *Journal of Marriage and the Family, 60,* 56–59.

Cohen, J. M. (1991). *Age and influence in adolescence: Parents versus* [Association paper]. Washington, DC: American Sociological Association.

Coleman, J. S. (1974). *Youth: Transition to adulthood.* Report of the Panel on Youth of the President's Science Advisory Committee. Chicago: University of Chicago Press.

Cook, T. D., Habib, F., Phillips, M, Settersten, R. A., Shagle, S. C., & Degirmencioglu, S. M. (in press). Comer's school development program: A theory-based evaluation. *American Educational Research Journal.*

Cook, T. D., Herman, M. R., Phillips, M., & Settersten, R. A., Jr. (1999). *How neighborhoods, families, peer groups, and schools jointly affect changes in early adolescent development.* Unpublished manuscript.

Cook, T. D., Shagle, S. C., & Degirmencioglu, S. M. (1997). Capturing social process for testing mediational models of neighborhood effects. In J. Brooks-Gunn, G. J. Duncan, & J. L. Aber (Eds.), *Neighborhood poverty* (Vol. II, pp. 94–119). New York: Russell Sage.

Coontz, S. (1992). *The way we never were: American families and the nostalgia trap.* New York: Basic Books.

Cordon, J. A. F. (1997). Youth residential independence and autonomy—A comparative study. *Journal of Family Issues, 18,* 576–607.

Cready, C. M., & Fossett, M. A. (1997). Mate availability and African American family structure in the U. S. nonmetropolitan south, 1960–1990. *Journal of Marriage and the Family, 59,* 192–203.

Crockett, L. J., & Crouter, A. C. (Eds.). (1995). *Pathways through adolescence: Individual development in relation to social contexts.* Mahwah, NJ: Erlbaum.

Crouter, A. C. (1998). Leaving home: Understanding the transition to adulthood. *International Journal of Behavioral Development, 22,* 219–221.

Crowe, P. A., Philbin, J., Richards, M. H., & Crawford, I. (1998). Adolescent alcoholic involvement and the experience of social environments. *Journal of Research on Adolescence, 8,* 403–422.

Demo, D. (1992). Parent-child relations: Assessing recent changes. *Journal of Marriage and the Family, 54,* 104–117.

Demos, J. (1986). *Past, present, and personal: The family and the life course in American history.* New York: Oxford University Press.

Dryfoos, J. (1998). *Safe passage: Making it through adolescence in a risky society.* New York: Oxford University Press.

Duncan, G. J. (1994). Families and neighbors as sources of disadvantage in the schooling decisions of White and Black adolescents. *American Journal of Education, 103,* 20–53.

Dunn, J., & Plomin, R. (1991). Why are siblings so different? The significance of differences in sibling experiences within the family. *Family Process, 30,* 271–283.

Dunn, K. A., Runyan, C. W., Cohen, L. R., & Schulman, M. D. (1998). Teens at work: A statewide study of jobs, hazards, and injuries. *Journal of Adolescent Health, 22,* 19–25.

Eckert, P. (1989). *Jocks and burnouts: Social categories and identity in the high school.* New York: Teachers College, Columbia University.

Edin, K. (1998, May). *Why don't poor single mothers get married (or remarried)?* Paper presented at the Russell Sage Foundation, New York, NY.

Edin, K., & Lein, L. (1997). *Making ends meet: How single mothers survive welfare and low-wage work.* New York: Russell Sage.

Elder, G. H., Jr., & Conger R. D. (2000). *Children of the land: Adversity and success in rural America.* Chicago: University of Chicago Press.

Elder, G. H., Jr., King, V., & Conger, R. D. (1996). Intergenerational continuity and change in rural lives:

Historical and developmental insights. *International Journal of Behavioral Development, 19,* 433–455.

Elo, I. T., King, R. B., & Furstenberg, F. F. (1999). Adolescent females: Their sexual partners and fathers of their children. *Journal of Marriage and the Family, 61,* 74–84.

Ennett, S. T., & Bauman, K. E. (1996). Adolescent social networks: School, demographic, and longitudinal considerations. *Journal of Adolescent Research, 11,* 194–215.

Entwisle, D. R., & Alexander, K. L. (1993). Entry into school: The beginning school transition and educational stratification in the United States. *Annual Review of Sociology, 19,* 401–423.

Evans, K., & Heinz, W. (1993). Studying forms of transition: Methodological innovation in a cross-national study of youth transition in labour market entry in England and Germany. *Comparative Education, 29,* 145–158.

Farkas, S., & Johnson, J., with Duffett, A., & Bers, A. (1997). *Kids these days: What Americans really think about the next generation.* New York: Public Agenda.

Feldman, S. S., & Elliott, G. R. (Eds.). (1990). *At the threshold: The developing adolescent.* Cambridge, MA: Harvard University Press.

Flacks, R. (1971). *Youth and social change.* Chicago: Markham.

Flanagan, C. A., & Sherrod, L. R. (1998). Youth political development: An introduction. *Journal of Social Issues, 54,* 447–456.

Frønes, I. (1995). *Among peers.* Oslo, Norway: Scandinavian University Press.

Fuligni, A. J., & Stevenson, H. W. (1995). Time use and mathematics achievement among American, Chinese, and Japanese high-school students. *Child Development, 66,* 830–842.

Furstenberg, F. F. (1995). The fading dream: Prospects for marriage in the inner-city. Paper presented at the Family Research Consortium Summer Institute, Ogonquit, ME.

Furstenberg, F. F. (1999). Family change and family diversity: Accounts of the past and scenarios of the future. In N. J. Smelser & J. Alexander (Eds.), *Diversity and its discontents* (pp. 147–165). Princeton, NJ: Princeton University Press.

Furstenberg, F. F., Cook, T. D., Eccles, J., Elder, G. H., Jr., Sameroff, A. (1999). *Managing to make it: Urban families and adolescent success.* Chicago: University of Chicago Press.

Furstenberg, F. F., Modell, J, & Herschberg, T. (1976). Social change and transition to adulthood in historical perspective. *Journal of Family History, 1,* 7–32.

Gauthier, A. H. (1999). *How do young people use their time? A cross-national comparison of time budget surveys.* Unpublished manuscript.

George, L. K. (1993). Sociological perspectives on life transitions. *Annual Review of Sociology, 19,* 353–373.

Gerson, K. (1985). *Hard choices: How women decide about work, career, and motherhood.* Berkeley: University of California Press.

Gerson, K. (1993). *No man's land: Men's changing commitments to family and work.* New York: Basic Books.

Goldscheider, F. (1997). Recent changes in U. S. young adult living arrangements in comparative perspective. *Journal of Family Issues, 18,* 708–724.

Goldscheider, F. K., & Goldscheider, C. (1994). Leaving and returning home in 20th century America. *Population Bulletin, 49,* 1–34.

Goldscheider, F. K., & Waite, L. (1991). *New families, no families: The transformation of the American home.* Berkeley: University of California Press.

Goodman, E. (1999). The role of socioeconomic status gradients in explaining differences in U.S. adolescent's health. *American Journal of Public Health, 89,* 1522–1528.

Graber, J. A., & Brooks-Gunn, J., & Peterson, A. C. (Eds.). (1996). *Transitions through adolescence: Interpersonal domains and context.* Mahwah, NJ: Erlbaum.

Greenberger, E., & Steinberg, L. (1986). *When teenagers work: The psychological and social costs of adolescent employment.* New York: Basic Books.

Grotevant, H. D. (1997). Identity processes: Integrating social psychological and developmental approaches. *Journal of Adolescent Research, 12,* 139–161.

Grotevant, H. D., & Cooper, C. R. (1988). The role of family experience in career exploration: A life-span perspective. *Life-Span Development and Behavior, 8* 231–258.

Grunseit, A., Kippax, S., Aggleton, P., Baldo, M., & Slutkin, G. (1997). Sexuality education and young people's sexual behavior: A review of studies. *Journal of Adolescent Research, 12,* 421–453.

Hagan, J., & Wheaton, B. (1993). The search for adolescent role exits and the transition to adulthood. *Social Forces, 71,* 955–980.

Hall, G. S. (1904). *Adolescence: Its psychology and its relations to physiology, anthropology, sociology, sex, crime, religion and education.* New York: D. Appleton.

Halperin, S. (Ed.). (1998). *The forgotten half revisited: American youth and young families, 1988–2008.* Washington, DC: American Youth Policy Forum.

Hamilton, S. F. (1994). Employment prospects as motivation for school achievement: Links and gaps between school and work in seven countries. In F. K. Silbereisen & E. Todt (Eds.), *Adolescence in context: The interplay of family, school, peers, and work in adjustment.* New York: Springer.

Hamilton, S. F., & Lempert, W. (1996). The impact of apprenticeship on youth: A prospective analysis. *Journal of Research on Adolescence, 6,* 427–455.

Harford, T. C., & Grant, B. F. (1987). Psychosocial factors in adolescent drinking contexts. *Journal of Studies on Alcohol, 48,* 551–557.

Harris, J. R. (1998). *The nurture assumption: Why children turn out the way they do.* New York: Free Press.

Hartup, W. W. (1993). Adolescents and their friends. *Child Development, 60,* 3–22.

Herrnstein, R. J., & Murray, C. (1994). *The bell curve: Intelligence and class structure in American life.* New York: Free Press.

Hoffman, J. P., & Johnson, R. A. (1998). A national portrait of family structure and adolescent drug use. *Journal of Marriage and the Family, 60,* 633–645.

Holland, D. C., & Eisenhart, M. A. (1990). *Educated in romance: Women, achievement, and college culture.* Chicago: University of Chicago Press.

Horowitz, R. (1999). Through my own eyes: Single mothers and the culture of poverty. *Contemporary Sociology, 28,* 299–300.

Hurrelmann, K., & Hamilton, S. F. (Eds.). (1996). *Social problems and social contexts in adolescence.* New York: Aldine de Gruyter.

Hurtado, S., Carter, D. F., & Spuler, A. (1996). Latino student transition to college: Assessing difficulties and factors in successful college adjustment. *Research in Higher Education, 37,* 135–157.

Jacobs, J. A., & Stoner-Eby, S. (1998). Adult enrollment in higher education and cumulative educational attainment, 1970–1990. *The Annals of the American Academy of Political and Social Science, 559,* 91–108.

Jencks, C., & Peterson, P. E. (Eds.). (1991). *The urban underclass.* Washington, DC: Brookings Institute.

Jessor, R. (1993). Successful adolescent development among youth in high-risk settings. *American Psychologist, 48,* 117–126.

Johnson, M. K., Beebe, T., Mortimer, J. T., & Snyder, M. (1998). Volunteerism in adolescence: A process perspective. *Journal of Research on Adolescence, 8,* 309–332.

Johnston, L. D., O'Malley, P. M., & Bachman, J. G. (1999). *National survey results on drug use from The Monitoring the Future Study, 1975–1998* (Vol. I–II). Washington, DC: U.S. Government Printing Office.

Jones, E., Forrest, D., Goldman, N., Henshaw, S., Lincoln, R., Rosoff, J., Westoff, C., & Wulf, D. (1985). Teenage pregnancy in developed countries: Determinants and policy implications. *Family Planning Perspectives, 17,* 53–63.

Kane, T. J., & Rouse, C. E. (1999). The community college: Educating students at the margin between college and work. *Journal of Economic Perspectives, 13,* 63–84.

Kaplan, E. B. (1997). *Not our kind of girl: Unraveling the myths of Black teenage motherhood.* Berkeley: University of California Press.

Katz, M. B. (1975). *People of Hamilton, Canada West: Family and class in a mid-nineteenth-century city.* Cambridge, MA: Harvard University Press.

Kett, J. (1977). *Rites of passage: Adolescence in America, 1790 to the present.* New York: Basic Books.

Kerkhoff, A., & Macrae, J. (1992). Leaving the parental home in Great Britain: A comparative perspective. *Sociological Quarterly, 33,* 281–301.

Knudsen, K., & Waerness, K. (1999). Reactions to global processes of change: Attitudes toward gender roles and marriage in modern nations. *Comparative Social Research, 18,* 161–195.

Lareau, A. (1997). Human capital or cultural capital? Ethnicity and poverty groups in an urban school district. *American Journal of Sociology, 103,* 816–817.

Larson, R. W. (1997). The emergence of solitude as a constructive domain of experience in early adolescence. *Child Development, 68,* 80–93.

Larson, R. W., & Richards, M. H. (1994). *Divergent realities: The emotional lives of mothers, fathers, and adolescents.* New York: Basic Books.

Larson, R. W., Richards, M. H., Moneta, G., Holmbeck, G., & Duckett, E. (1996). Changes in adolescents' daily interactions with their families from ages 10 to 18: Disengagement and transformation. *Developmental Psychology, 32,* 744–754.

Larson, R. W., & Verma, S. (1998). *How children and adolescents spend time across the world: work, play,*

and developmental opportunities. Unpublished manuscript.

Lee, V. E., Burkham, D. T., Zimiles, H., & Ladewski, B. (1994). Family structure and its effect on behavioral and emotional problems in young adolescents. *Journal of Research on Adolescence, 4,* 405–437.

Lerner, R. M. (Ed.). (1993). *Early adolescence: Perspectives on research, policy, and intervention.* Hillsdale, NJ: Erlbaum.

Lerner, R. M., Peterson, A. C., & Brooks-Gunn, J. (Eds.). (1991). *Encyclopedia of adolescence.* New York: Garland.

Lewis, S. K., Ross, C. E., & Mirowsky, J. (1999). Establishing a sense of personal control in the transition to adulthood. *Social Forces, 77,* 1573–1599.

Lichter, D. T., Kephart, G., McLaughlin, D. K., & Landry, D. J. (1992). Race and the retreat from marriage—A shortage of marriageable men. *American Sociological Review, 57,* 781–799.

Luker, K. (1997). *Dubious conceptions.* Cambridge, MA: Harvard University Press.

Lye, D. N., Klepinger, D. H., Hyle, P. D., & Nelson, A. (1995). Childhood living arrangements and adult children's relations with their parents. *Demography, 32,* 261–280.

Maccoby, E. E. (1998). *The two sexes: Growing up apart.* Cambridge, MA: Belknap Press.

Mare, R. D., & Winship, C. (1991). Socioeconomic change and the decline of marriage for Blacks and Whites. In C. Jencks & P. E. Peterson (Eds.), *The urban underclass* (pp. 175–202). Washington, DC: Brookings Institute.

Markel, K. S., & Frone, M. R. (1998). Job characteristics, work-school conflict, and school outcomes among adolescents: Testing a structural model. *Journal of Applied Psychology, 83,* 277–287.

McLoyd, V. C., & Steinberg, L. (1998). *Studying minority adolescents: Conceptual, methodological, and theoretical issues.* Mahwah, NJ: Erlbaum.

Mead, M. (1928). *Coming of age in Samoa.* New York: Blue Ribbon Books.

Medrich, E. A., Roizen, J. A., Rubin, V., & Buckley, S. (1982). *The serious business of growing up: A study of children's lives outside school.* Berkeley: University of California Press.

Mihalic, S. W., & Elliott, D. (1997). Short- and long-term consequences of adolescent work. *Youth & Society, 28,* 464–498.

Millstein, S. G., Petersen, A. C., & Nightingale, E. O. (1993). *Promoting the health of adolescents: New directions for the twenty-first century.* New York: Oxford University Press.

Mirel, J. E. (1991). Twentieth-century America, adolescence in. In R. M. Lerner, A. C. Petersen, & J. Brooks-Gunn (Eds.), *Encyclopedia of adolescence* (Vol. 2, pp. 1153–1167). New York: Garland.

Modell, J. (1989). *Into one's own: From youth to adulthood in the United States, 1920–1975.* Berkeley: University of California Press.

Mortimer, J. T., Pimentel, E. E., Ryu, S., Nash, K., & Lee, C. (1996). Part time work and occupational value formation in adolescence. *Social Forces, 74,* 1405–1418.

Mulder, C. H., & Manting, D. (1994). Strategies of nestleavers—Settling down versus flexibility. *European Sociological Review, 10,* 155–172.

Nathanson, C. A. (1992). *Dangerous passage: The social control of sexuality in women's adolescence.* Philadelphia: Temple University Press.

National Commission on Children. (1991). *Beyond rhetoric: A new American agenda for children and families.* Washington, DC: U.S. Government Printing Office.

National Research Council. (1993). *Losing generations: Adolescents in high-risk settings.* Washington, DC: National Academy Press.

Newman, K. S. (1999a). *Fall from grace: Downward mobility in the age of affluence.* Berkeley: University of California Press.

Newman. K. S. (1999b). *No shame in my game: The working poor in the inner city.* New York: Knopf and Russell Sage Foundation.

Osgood, W., Johnston, L. D., O'Malley, P. M., & Bachman, J. G. (1988). The generality of deviance in late adolescence and early adulthood. *American Sociological Review, 53,* 81–93.

Owens, T. J., Mortimer, J. T., & Finch, M. D. (1996). Self-determination as a source of self-esteem. *Social Forces, 74,* 1377–1404.

Padilla, Y. C. (1997). Determinants of Hispanic poverty in the course of the transition to adulthood. *Hispanic Journal of Behavioral Sciences, 19,* 416–432.

Pascarelli, E. T., Edison, M., Nora, A., Hagedorn, L. S., & Terenzini, P. T. (1998). Does community college versus four-year college attendance influence students' educational plans? *Journal of College Student Development, 39,* 179–193.

Perkins, D. F., Luster, T., Villarruel, F. A., & Small, S. (1998). An ecological, risk-factor examination of adolescents' sexual activity in three ethnic groups. *Journal of Marriage and the Family, 60,* 660–673.

Petersen, A. C. (1991). History of research on adolescence. In R. M. Lerner, A. C. Petersen, J. Brooks-Gunn (Eds.), *Encyclopedia of adolescence* (Vol. 1, pp. 499–503). New York: Garland.

Phelan, P., Davidson, A. L., & Yu, H. C. (1998). *Adolescents' worlds: Negotiating family, peers, and school.* New York: Teachers College Press.

Phelan, P., Yu, H. C., & Davidson, A. L. (1994). Navigating the psychosocial pressures of adolescence—The voices and experiences of high-school youth. *American Educational Research Journal, 31,* 415–447.

Plomin, R. (1990). The role of inheritance in behavior. *Science, 248,* 4952:183–188.

Popenoe, D. (1996). *Life without father: Compelling new evidence that fatherhood and marriage are indispensable for the good of children and society.* New York: Free Press.

Portes, A. (Ed.). (1996). *The new second generation.* New York: Russell Sage.

Powell, M. A., & Parcel, T. L. (1999). Parental work, family size and social capital effects on early adolescent educational outcomes: The United States and Great Britain compared. *Research in the Sociology of Work, 7,* 1–30.

Resnick, M. D., Bearman, P. S., Blum, R. W., Bauman, K. E., Harris, K. M., Jones, J., Tabor, J., Beuhring, T., Sieving, R., Shew, M., Ireland, M., Behringer, L. H., & Udry, J. R. (1997). Protecting adolescents from harm: Findings from the National Longitudinal Study of Adolescent Health. *Journal of the American Medical Association, 278, 10* :823–832.

Rindfuss, R. R. (1991). The young adult years: Diversity, structural change, and fertility. *Demography, 28,* 493–512.

Rodgers, K. B. (1999). Parenting processes related to sexual risk-taking behaviors of adolescent males and females. *Journal of Marriage and the Family, 61,* 99–109.

Rossi, A., & Rossi, P. (1990). *Of human bonding: Parent-child relations across the life course.* New York: Aldine de Gruyter.

Rowe, D. C., & Rodgers, J. L. (1997). Poverty and behavior: Are environmental measures nature and nurture? *Developmental Review, 17,* 358–393.

Rumbaut, R. G. (1999). Passages to adulthood: The adaptation of children of immigrants in southern California. In D. J. Hernandez (Ed.), *The health and well-being of children of immigrants.* Washington, DC: National Academy Press.

Ryan, B. A., Adams, G. R., Gullotta, T. P., Weissberg, R. P., & Hampton, R. L. (1995). *The family-school connection: Theory, research, and practice.* Thousand Oaks, CA: Sage.

Saetermoe, C. L., Beneli, I., & Busch, R. M. (1999). Perceptions of adulthood among Anglo and Latino parents. *Current Psychology, 18,* 171–184.

Sampson, R. J. (1992). Family management and child development: Insights from social disorganization theory. In J. McCord (Ed.), *Advances in criminological theory* (Vol. 3, pp. 63–93). New Brunswick, ME: Transaction Books.

Saporito, S., & Lareau, A. (1999). School selection as a process: The multiple dimensions of race in framing educational choice. *Social Problems, 46,* 418–439.

Schnaiberg, A., & Goldenberg, S. (1989). From empty nest to crowded nest—The dynamics of incompletely-launched young-adults. *Social Problems, 36,* 251–269.

Settersten, R. A., Jr. (1999). *Lives in time and place: The problems and promises of developmental science.* Amityville, NY: Baywood.

Shavit, Y., & Müller, W. (Eds.). (1998). *From school to work: A comparative study of educational qualifications and occupational destinations.* New York: Oxford University Press.

Sherrod, L. R. (Ed.). (1993). *Late adolescence and the transition to adulthood* [Special issue]. *Journal of Research on Adolescence, 3,* 227–336.

Silverberg, S. B., Vazsonyi, A. T., Schlegel, A. E., & Schmidt, S. (1998). Adolescent apprentices in Germany: Adult attachment, job expectations, and delinquency attitudes. *Journal of Adolescent Research, 13,* 254–271.

Simmons, R., & Blyth, D. A. (1987). *Moving into adolescence: The impact of pubertal change and school context.* New York: Aldine de Gruyter.

Singh, K. (1998). Part-time employment in high school and its effect on academic achievement. *Journal of Educational Research, 91,* 131–139.

Skolnick. A. S. (1991). *Embattled paradise: The American family in an age of uncertainty.* New York: Basic Books.

Small, S. A., & Luster, T. (1994). Adolescent sexual activity: An ecological, risk-factor approach. *Journal of Marriage and the Family, 56,* 181–192.

Smith, H. L., Morgan, S. P., & Koropeckyj-Cox, T. (1996). A decomposition of trends in the nonmarital fertility ratios of Blacks and Whites in the United States, 1960–1992. *Demography, 33,* 141–151.

Stanton-Salazar, R. D. (1997). A social capital framework for understanding the socialization of racial minority children and youths. *Harvard Educational Review, 67,* 1–40.

Steinberg, L., Lamborn, S. D., Darling, N., Mounts, N. S., & Dornbusch, S. M. (1994). Over-time changes in adjustment and competence among adolescents from authoritative, authoritarian, indulgent, and neglectful families. *Child Development, 65,* 754–770.

Steinberg, L., Lamborn, S. D., Dornbusch, S. M., & Darling, N. (1992). Impact of parenting practices on adolescent achievement: Authoritative parenting, school involvement, and encouragement to succeed. *Child Development, 63,* 1266–1281.

Sui-Chu, E. H., & Willms, J. D. (1996). Effects of parental involvement on eighth-grade achievement. *Sociology of Education, 69,* 126–141.

Sullivan, M. L. (1989). *Getting paid: Youth crime and work in the inner city.* Ithaca: Cornell University Press.

Tannenbaum, F. (1938). *Crime and community.* New York: Columbia University Press.

Teachman, J. D., Paasch, K., & Carver, K. (1997). Social capital and the generation of human capital. *Social Forces, 75,* 1343–1359.

Terenzini, P. T., Rendon, L. I., Upcraft, M. L., Millar, S. B., Allison, K. W., Gregg, P. L., & Jalomo, R. (1994). The transition to college-diverse students, diverse stories. *Research in Higher Education, 35,* 57–73.

Thrasher, F. M. (1927). *The gang.* Chicago: University of Chicago Press.

Torney-Purta, J., & Amadeo, J. (1999). *Transitions to adult political identity examined by gender.* Unpublished manuscript.

Udry, J. R. (1994). The nature of gender. *Demography, 31,* 561–573.

U.S. Bureau of the Census. (1976). *The statistical history of the United States: From colonial times to the present.* New York: Basic Books.

U.S. Bureau of the Census. (1996). *Statistical abstract of the United States: 1996* (116th ed.). Washington, DC: U. S. Government Printing Office.

U.S. Department of Health & Human Services. (1999). *Trends in the well-being of America's children and youth.* Washington, DC: U.S. Government Printing Office.

Veevers, J. E., Gee, E. M., & Wister, A. V. (1996). Home-leaving age norms: Conflict or consensus? *International Journal of Aging and Human Development, 43,* 277–295.

Venenziano, R. A., & Rohner, R. P. (1998). Perceived paternal acceptance, paternal involvement, and youths' psychological adjustment in a rural, biracial southern community. *Journal of Marriage and the Family, 60,* 335–343.

Ventura, S. J. (1995). Births to unmarried mothers: United States, 1980–92. *National Center for Health Statistics, Vital Health Statistics, 21,* No. 53.

Wallulis, J. (1998). *The new insecurity: The end of the standard job and family.* Albany: State University of New York Press.

Warner, C. W., Santelli, J. S., Everett, S. A., Kann, L., Collins, J. L., Cassell, C., Morris, L., & Kolbe, L. J. (1998). Sexual behavior among U. S. High School students, 1990–1995. *Family Planning Perspectives, 30,* 170–172, 200.

White, L. (1994). Coresidence and leaving home: Young adults and their parents. *Annual Review of Sociology, 20,* 81–147.

White, L., & Lacy, N. (1997). The effects of age at home leaving and pathways from home on educational attainment. *Journal of Marriage and the Family, 59,* 982–995.

White, L. K., & Rogers, S. J. (1997). Strong support but uneasy relationships: Coresidence and adult children's relationships with their parents. *Journal of Marriage and the Family, 59,* 62–76.

Wigfield, A., Eccles, J. S., & Rodriguez, D. (1998). The development of children's motivation in school contexts. *Review of Research in Education, 23,* 73–118.

Wynn, J. R. (1995). Neighborhood organizations and inner-city youth: Successful programs, currant initiatives. *American Journal of Education, 103,* 218–224.

Zelizer, V. A. (1985). *Pricing the priceless child: The changing social value of children.* New York: Basic Books.

Katherine R. Allen, Rosemary Blieszner, and Karen A. Roberto
Virginia Polytechnic Institute and State University

Families in the Middle and Later Years: A Review and Critique of Research in the 1990s

Research on families in the middle and later years came into its own during the 1990s, documenting the complexity, malleability, and variety of older family connections. We examined 908 articles on family gerontology topics, observing 4 trends: Conceptually, an appreciation for pluralism and resilience as individuals and families age is apparent. Theoretically, life course, feminist, socioemotional selectivity, and family solidarity theories are increasingly applied to intergenerational family relations. Methodologically, new interest in qualitative methods for studying diverse groups has improved the depth with which aging studies can account for variability in old age; new quantitative methodologies have allowed greater sophistication in dealing with longitudinal data. Substantively, there is greater understanding of family caregiving, social support, parent-child relationships, marital transitions, and grandparenting relationships. The field is poised to take even greater risks in fulfilling the promise of studying linked lives over time.

Research on families in the middle and later years came into its own during the 1990s. Earlier decade reviews of the 1960s (Troll, 1971), 1970s (Streib & Beck, 1980), and 1980s (Brubaker, 1990)

Department of Human Development (0416),Virginia Polytechnic Institute and State University Blacksburg, VA 24061 (kallen@vt.edu).

Key Words: aging, decade review, family gerontology, middle years, older adults.

chronicled the emergence of family gerontology as an area of inquiry, charting the structures, functions, roles, and interactions associated with aging individuals in families. In the 1990s, a shift occurred in describing the complexity, malleability, and variety of family connections in the second half of life, generating a more complex view of older families. Our aim in this review of a decade of research is to illuminate innovations and themes in a broad subject matter and to interpret directions in which the field is going.

Our Approach

We examined the titles and abstracts of articles with a relevant family-level focus from 13 social science journals in which family gerontologists routinely publish. Reflecting the multidisciplinary nature of the field, these included journals in family studies (*Journal of Marriage and the Family, Family Relations,* and *Journal of Family Issues*), gerontology (*The Gerontologist, International Journal of Aging and Human Development, Journal of Aging Studies, Journal of Gerontology: Psychological Sciences, Journal of Gerontology: Social Sciences, Journal of Women and Aging, Psychology and Aging,* and *Research on Aging*) and personal relationships (*Journal of Social and Personal Relationships* and *Personal Relationships*). We compiled a list of 908 articles from these publications and identified 30 books on family gerontology topics published over the past 10 years. We also asked six experts on families and aging to nominate works they considered most in-

TABLE 1. RANK ORDER OF FAMILY GERONTOLOGY ARTICLES PUBLISHED FROM 1990–1999 ($N = 908$)

Substantive Focus of Article	Percentage (n)
Caregiving	32.6% (296)
Social support and social networks	13.7% (124)
Parent–adult child relations	10.1% (92)
Marital status transitions	9.5% (86)
Grandparenting	7.8% (71)
Family relationships and structures	7.1% (64)
Intergenerational exchanges, processes, and transmission	4.9% (44)
Living arrangements and parent-child coresidence	4.5% (41)
Bereavement, grief, death, and suicide	3.0% (27)
Siblings	2.6% (24)
Health care decision making	1.4% (13)
Theories, methods, reviews, policies	1.3% (12)
Elder abuse and violence	.8% (7)
Oldest old	.4% (4)
Sexual orientation	.3% (3)

fluential in the 1990s. We coded the predominant theme of each publication (see Table 1). Almost half of the journal articles covered aspects of caregiving or social support, and more than four-fifths of the articles were in the top five categories. There is some overlap in subject matter, but our purpose was to highlight the major substantive focus of the articles to demonstrate the scope of family gerontology research in the 1990s.

Several advances characterize the research on midlife and older families in the 1990s. Conceptually, the study of later life families is no longer depicted in monolithic ways. An appreciation for pluralism and resilience as individuals and families age is apparent. The emphasis on difference has expanded from unitary traits to social relations and process, and formerly ignored and stigmatized topics have appeared in the literature. The study of middle aged and older families has been strengthened by the incorporation of life-course and feminist approaches. Theoretical advances created for the specific study of older individuals and families, such as socioemotional selectivity theory and family solidarity theory, have brought greater focus to intergenerational relations over the life span. Methodologically, new interest in qualitative methods for studying diverse groups has improved the depth with which aging studies can account for variability in old age; new quantitative methodologies, such as latent growth curve analysis, have allowed greater sophistication in dealing with longitudinal data. Finally, substantive advances characterizing the 1990s include greater understanding of family caregiving,

social support, parent-child relationships, marital transitions, and grandparenting relationships. Collectively, these contributions have strengthened the research literature on older families, illustrating sensitivity to diversity in age, gender, racial-ethnic background, class, and family circumstances.

CONCEPTUAL ADVANCES

From Aging Individuals to Families in the Middle and Later Years

A family-level perspective has taken hold in the past decade. Much of this work has been carried out by interdisciplinary gerontological, family, and close-relationships scholars. In 1995, Blieszner and Bedford published the first handbook on family gerontology, consolidating much of the interdisciplinary literature on these intersecting fields of study. The handbook provides historical and demographic overviews; analyses of theory and research methods; summaries of research findings on relationships, the contexts of family life, and major turning points in late-life families; and implications for interventions and future research.

Expanding the focus from being exclusively on the individual to including the family context offers the field of gerontology greater depth and the field of family studies greater breadth. Researchers have increasing access to methodologies and theories that allow systemic-level examinations that bring aging individuals into family studies and flesh out the details, ambiguities, and innovations of family life in the later years. Using a family focus forces a complex view of change and adaptation over time. For example, new research on adult sibling relationships, the longest family tie most individuals will experience, has focused attention on older childless adults, immigrants, and those from racial-ethnic groups (Johnson & Barer, 1997). Reviews have documented complexities in sibling relationships by gender, race, class, family structure, and culture (Bedford, 1998; Campbell, Connidis, & Davies, 1999; Cicirelli, 1994). Demographers found that although full sibling relationships are the strongest in adulthood, half- and step-sibling relationships are considered "real" kin, in that they follow similar patterns of visiting and contact to those that occur among biological siblings (White & Reidmann, 1992).

Researchers have begun to shed new light on what was formerly treated as a monolith: families in the middle years (Penning, 1998). Earlier psychological (Erikson, 1950) and sociological (Hill & Rodgers, 1964) theories introduced middle-age to the study of individuals and families but defined the middle-age family as one with children in school and both parents alive. Recent evidence suggests that middle-age has few distinct structural markers. There is no agreed upon chronological or processual definition of middle-age, as evident in ground-breaking work regarding parenting at midlife (see Ryff & Seltzer, 1996). A person can become a parent or a grandparent for the first time at age 40; here, even gender no longer predicts the likelihood of a major life event. A program of research sponsored in part by the MacArthur Foundation Research Network on Successful Midlife Development is now resulting in presentation of newly appreciated complexities of midlife families (Antonucci & Akiyama, 1997), such as assessment of generativity in parent, spouse, and worker roles (MacDermid, Heilbrun, & DeHaan, 1997).

From "The Aging Family" to Aging Families

A focus on diversity, by gender, race, class, and other stratifications, is becoming increasingly common in family gerontology. Research in the 1990s demonstrated that young adults are not the sole innovators in pioneering the changes taking place in family life today. Johnson and Barer (1997) found that the lives of oldest old persons are increasingly characterized by incorporated kin, including fictive kin (e.g., play children, godchildren, foster children) and upgraded kin (e.g., elevating a niece to "like a daughter"). Allen, Blieszner, Roberto, Farnsworth, and Wilcox (1999) demonstrated the pervasiveness of structural diversity and the corresponding processual dynamics in the lives of older adults, their children, and their grandchildren. Based on in-depth interviews, they found that 18 of the 45 participants had experienced a pluralistic pattern themselves, including divorce, cohabitation, and nonmarital childbearing, and that structural diversity was quite apparent in their descendants' lives as well. Only 10 of the 45 elders had adult children whose lives were characterized as conventional in terms of marital and parental careers.

Despite such findings, the focus on diversity presents methodological and theoretical problems for researchers. Given the difficulty, if not impossibility, of even defining "family" with sufficient precision for research purposes, investigators have struggled with how to account for increasing complexity in families. Contrary to established theories of family life as based on obligations among particular members to fulfill unique functions, families are now based more on voluntary ties, choices, and needs than on presumed obligation, particularly as people age (Johnson, 2000a). Too often, a common-sense heuristic that is based on the census definition of a family consisting of two or more people related by blood, marriage, or adoption and residing together has had to suffice, even though conceptually, researchers have recognized that individuals live outside what were once considered normative boundaries as they mature (Cherlin & Furstenberg, 1994). Fully one third of old people live alone, and a large minority do not have physical access to kin (Johnson & Barer, 1997). The lives of older adults, as revealed in qualitative studies in particular, remind us that definitions deduced from the static notion of "the family" are no longer broadly relevant. Bedford and Blieszner (1997) offered a definition that better represents the lived reality of older adults' lives: "A *family* is a set of relationships determined by biology, adoption, marriage, and, in some societies, social designation, and existing even in the absence of contact or affective involvement, and, in some cases, even after the death of certain members" (p. 526). Adopting such a definition and acknowledging the methodological implications requires researchers to ask individuals to indicate who is in their family, rather than making a priori assumptions.

From Gender Differences to Gender Relations

Gender occupied a central role in aging family relationships in the 1990s. A more explicit feminist approach became evident, acknowledging the ambivalence with which most women approach caring relationships, particularly in terms of family household labor (Dressel & Clark, 1991), family caregiving (Abel, 1990; Stoller, 1993), and mother-daughter ties (Walker & Allen, 1991). Building on the salience of mother-daughter ties, researchers examined their relational complexities. For example, Fingerman (1996) introduced the concept of "developmental schism" to account for a key source of interpersonal problems between female intergenerational dyads, which tend to be the strongest and most lasting of filial relationships. Studies of process in men's lives made a stronger appearance in two areas. Researchers began asking husbands and sons more in-depth questions about their caregiving roles and the influence of providing care for their wives and mothers with physical or cognitive impairments on their daily lives (Barnett, Marshall, & Pleck, 1992; Stoller, 1990). For the first time, the lack of connection many divorced men feel with their adult children was also described (Cooney & Uhlenberg, 1990).

Studies of siblings caring for their aging parents provided another window of understanding into the gendered nature of family relationships. Although siblings most often are supportive of their brothers or sisters who take on the family caregiver role (Wolf, Freedman, & Soldo, 1997), they also are sources of stress (Suitor & Pillemer, 1993). Daughters are three times more likely than are sons to give parents assistance with activities of daily living (Dwyer & Coward, 1991). When parents of both sons and daughters select sons as their primary helper, the sons tend to be geographically closer than their daughters, and in reality, it is the daughter-in-law or granddaughter who provides help (Stoller, Forster, & Duniho, 1992). Matthews's (1995) qualitative investigation of siblings in later life found that lone sisters typically take charge of care provision, whereas their brothers' contributions were less acknowledged by either brothers or sisters. In brother-only sibling groups, brothers met their parents' needs by performing "masculine" services. Their wives provided more nurturing types of assistance, but only if they were part of the parental support network (Matthews & Heidorn, 1998).

From Ignored or Stigmatized to Studied Family Relationships

In the 1990s, new light has been shed on areas previously ignored by family gerontologists. One aspect of the caregiving literature receiving greater attention was older parents as caregivers. For example, the increased longevity of persons with mental retardation and other developmental disabilities and the advances in treatments for persons with mental illness brought attention to issues facing lifelong caregivers (Fullmer, Tobin, & Smith, 1997; Pruchno, Patrick, & Burant, 1996; Roberto, 1993; Seltzer, Greenberg, & Krauss, 1995). The contributors to Seltzer and Heller's (1997) special issue of *Family Relations* addressed heterogeneity in the roles and experiences of late-life family caregivers, noting the importance of cultural context, type of disability, background of the family, and relationships with for-

mal services. The HIV/AIDS epidemic imposes new caregiving responsibilities on older parents as children with HIV return home to be cared for by their aging parents (Brabant, 1994).

The lives of the approximately 20% of persons who are childless in later life also received more attention during the 1990s. The focus of most of these investigations was on the availability of instrumental support and care (Wu & Pollard, 1998) and on their psychological well-being (Koropeckyj-Cox, 1998). Overall, older persons who are childless fare no better or worse than do those with children in either domain. Structural variables, such as gender, marital status, and age, appear to have a greater influence on perceived social support and well-being than does parental status (Alexander, Rubinstein, Goodman, & Luborsky, 1992).

New light has been shed on the family relationships of gay and lesbian adults (Allen & Demo, 1995), a topic that was virtually nonexistent in the previous decade. The result has been a more complete understanding of sexual orientation diversity (Quam & Whitford, 1992). Using a case study approach, Shenk and Fullmer (1996) found that older lesbians may be unable to relate to the idea of a public lesbian identity espoused in the current gay community and are unwilling to be open about their private lives to public agencies. Crosbie-Burnett, Foster, Murray, and Bowen (1996) introduced a social-cognitive-behavioral model of family systems as a tool for analyzing the reactions of heterosexual family members when a child or sibling is gay or lesbian.

From a Deficit Approach to a Strengths and Resilience Approach

A strengths and resilience approach is appearing in the literature, in contrast to the previous focus on problems in old age. We have described examples in aging mother–adult daughter relationships and other adaptive caregiving relationships. Recent literature includes evidence of "aging well," a term that signifies effective coping with aging regardless of adversity (Johnson, 1995). For example, older Blacks, although typically having experienced reduced educational opportunities compared with Whites, being in poorer economic circumstances and having fewer offspring to assist them, are more likely than Whites to have created effective helping networks by converting friends into kin (Johnson & Barer, 1997). Rather than merely focus on diminishing kin networks, kin conversion reveals a strengths approach because of the active role that individuals and families play in shoring up their circumstances under harsh conditions, such as the erosion of public assistance for the poor. The reciprocal support that elders give to other family members likewise contributes to their aging well (Adams & Blieszner, 1995), as does their spiritual resiliency (Ramsey & Blieszner, 1999).

THEORETICAL ADVANCES

Resurgence of a Life-Course Perspective

Perhaps the major theoretical advance in the decade of the 1990s has been the elaboration of the life-course perspective. Elder (1998) explained that this theoretical framework, with its focus on historical, social process and on individual time, satisfies two increasingly important considerations in studies of families: how individuals change over time and how their transitions and trajectories are linked across family members. This perspective has been combined with other theories or fields of study, such as family development (Bengtson & Allen, 1993; Dilworth-Anderson & Burton, 1996; White, 1991), human development (Elder), stress (Pearlin & Skaff, 1996), and demography (Uhlenberg, 1996), and it has been applied to topics such as the study of family caregiving and living arrangements (Silverstein & Angelelli, 1998), family interactions and relationships (Henretta, Hill, Li, Soldo, & Wolf, 1997), norms of filial responsibility (Stein et al., 1998), and the linkages of family and work roles (Moen, Robison, & Fields, 1994).

The life-course perspective of the 1990s is not just a demographic approach to longitudinal change. There is a also a renewed linkage to social constructionism, a point of view in which individuals are seen as active agents in creating their own lives. Narrative methods are used to uncover personalized meanings about the ways in which individuals reconstruct their lives as they age, viewing individuals holistically, not as separate facets or domains, but as linked socially to ever-changing historical contexts. The life-course approach improves on earlier efforts by linking macro and micro levels in both theory and research methods, rather than privileging one or the other.

In a comprehensive study of parent-child relationships representing three generations, members of the middle and youngest generations were in the unique position of being able to provide information from the dual perspectives of parent and child (Rossi & Rossi, 1990). These authors confirmed the many ways that current relationships between parents and children are affected by generational position in the family, normative obligations, gender, family size, personality traits, expressions of aid and intimacy, and sociohistorical trends.

Extensions of the life-course perspective are uncovering how race, class, and gender affect life experiences, as Burton (1996) found in her study of three generations of African American women. The emergence of the role of family caregiver in their lives was shaped by culturally and contextually defined family timetables. The influence of age norms, family role transitions, and patterns of intergenerational care on women's caregiving responsibilities differed by class and geographic residence. Urban women described a preference for an on-time entry to parenthood whereas early childbearing was considered a necessity for lower class, rural families to ensure older women the opportunity to experience the parental role. For many of the rural women, the role of parent was not behaviorally experienced until they became a grandmother.

Socioemotional Selectivity Theory

One of the most important theoretical foundations for family gerontology research to emerge in the past decade is socioemotional selectivity theory (Carstensen, 1992). This theory delineates age-related decreases in social interaction and concomitant increases in emotional closeness over the adult years within the close relationship network, showing that as the functions of relationships change over the course of life, individuals strategically adjust their social networks to maximize social and emotional gains.

In studies of various cultural groups, adults displayed increasingly competent emotional regulation across the life span (Gross et al., 1997). Examination of the circle of emotionally close relationships, however, demonstrated that the extent to which both family members and friends are included depends not so much on personality variables as on whether the elder has nuclear family members or not (Lang, Staudinger, & Carstensen, 1998). Family members tend to be the primary focus of emotional energy, if they are available. Being able to accomplish emotionally meaningful goals contributes to well-being, and blocked goals interfere with it. For example, older wives in dissatisfying marriages have more physical and mental health complaints than do older husbands or happily married wives (Carstensen, Gottman, & Levenson, 1995). In contrast to previous ideas about old age relationships, socioemotional selectivity theory addresses social network change in terms of successful adaptation, not merely loss.

Intergenerational Family Solidarity and Beyond

Another major theoretical contribution to family gerontology emerged from the work of Bengtson and colleagues on the University of Southern California Longitudinal Study of Three-Generation Families, begun in 1971. Based upon an ongoing series of interviews with multiple members of the same families, they have constructed and evaluated intergenerational family solidarity theory (Bengtson & Roberts, 1991). Intergenerational solidarity is indicated by six essential components: association or contact, affection or emotional closeness, consensus or agreement, function or instrumental support and resource sharing, familism or normative obligations, and opportunity structures for family interaction. Empirical tests of interrelationships among these elements of solidarity have provided confirmation of the theory and demonstrated its utility for examining the nature and quality of relationships between parents and adult children (Parrott & Bengtson, 1999; Whitbeck, Hoyt, & Huck, 1994), interactions among grandparents and grandchildren (Silverstein & Long, 1998), and the effects of family relationships on the well-being of older adults (e.g., Lawrence, Bennett, & Markides, 1992; Starrels, Ingersoll-Dayton, & Neal, 1995).

Pyke and Bengtson (1996) acknowledged that the Three Generation Families study sample was largely White, and therefore, additional analyses have been needed to understand family solidarity in ethnically diverse contexts. More older adults, primarily because of their children's and grandchildren's life choices, have expanded family boundaries beyond the level of lineal kin (i.e., intergenerational biological ties), and many elders have strong family ties with collateral kin (i.e., siblings, cousins, aunts, uncles, nieces, nephews). These strategies retain social support in the face of vertical family structures with more generations alive concurrently, but with fewer kin in each generation (Bengtson, Rosenthal, & Burton, 1990).

Integrating a Feminist Perspective into Family Gerontology

Calls for integrating feminist and poststructural perspectives into family gerontology have come from various sources (e.g., Baber & Allen, 1992; Calasanti, 1996; Ray, 1996). For example, a socialist feminist perspective attends to the interlocking systems of economic and political oppression stemming from class, gender, and race domination occurring in a given historical context. Socialist feminists question inequalities that arise from capitalism and patriarchy and offer recommendations that benefit women and men alike. Whether applied to retirement (Calasanti, 1993), caregiving (Stoller, 1993), or widowhood (Blieszner, 1993), socialist feminism demonstrates that patriarchal systems of allocating work and economic rewards yields shortcomings for men and women of all backgrounds because constraints put on one part of the family or society have implications for the well-being of others.

METHODOLOGICAL ADVANCES

Researchers entered the 1990s facing several challenges to advancing the scientific study of aging families. For example, critiques of the caregiving literature (Barer & Johnson, 1990; Malonebeach & Zarit, 1991) exposed methodological problems plaguing early studies, including using multiple definitions of "caregiver" and failing to identify the status and needs of care receivers. The focus of caregiving studies came under fire with experts insisting on research grounded in theory, going beyond basic descriptions of caregiving issues, and generating new knowledge about the dynamics of family caregiving (Walker, Pratt, & Eddy, 1995). The call for a more critical examination of family interactions and other limitations of the caregiving literature, such as sample bias, neglect of the total support network, and reliance on cross-sectional designs, also applied to the field of family gerontology in general.

By the end of the decade, researchers had begun to address several of these concerns. Generalizability issues raised because of the use of small convenience samples were addressed with the greater use of larger, random, and often national samples that included older family members. Many of the trends identified in the early family gerontology literature are now validated in studies from national data sets, most notably, the National Survey of Families and Households (NSFH; e.g.,

Aquilino & Supple's 1991 work on parent–adult child coresidence), and the National Long Term Care Study (NLTCS; e.g., Dwyer, Lee, & Jankowski's 1994 work on caregiving). In our review of 908 articles (see Table 1), we observed that a substantial number of the articles published using national databases relied on these two: 55 analyzed data from the NSFH, and 25 analyzed data from the NLTCS. The preference for quantitative research by some premier journals and the major funding agencies (which finance large-scale representative surveys) overshadowed the use of in-depth interviews or ethnographic methods. There were exceptions to this trend, of course, in which excellent studies that used in-depth investigations to get at multiple meanings were funded and published (see Johnson, 2000b, for example). Of the 908 articles we reviewed in which the methodology was evident, we found that 642 articles used a quantitative approach, 93 articles used a qualitative approach, and 65 articles used a combined approach.

Several innovations in qualitative and quantitative studies over the last decade were evident. A new appreciation for using qualitative methodologies has emerged (Gubrium & Sankar, 1994), benefiting family gerontology by charting new territory, as in Gladstone and Westhues's (1998) study of adult adoption reunions, and by offering new ideas about normative assumptions regarding family structure that researchers take as empirical fact. For example, it has long been held that old people are not cut off from family, in that 75% of aged parents have an adult child living within the vicinity (Shanas, 1979). Johnson and Barer (1997) challenged Shanas's view, however, pointing out a class bias. Oldest childless Whites are more likely to be at risk than their Black peers for isolation from kin and thus may have greater need for formal support services. Oldest Blacks, given their history of disadvantage as well as a kinship system in which sibling relationships are highly valued, are able to convert younger kin into surrogate children, thereby replenishing the kin support network as they age. In these ways, qualitative research has been used to deconstruct established arguments and allow new meanings to emerge.

Innovations in quantitative methodologies have allowed researchers to expand their ability to deal with complexity in longitudinal investigations. One of the first studies in family gerontology to use latent growth curve analysis, and thereby model change as nonlinear, was Walker, Acock,

Bowman, and Li's (1996) analysis of four annual interviews with 130 middle-aged daughters caring for their elderly, physically impaired, unmarried mothers. Testing the wear and tear hypothesis, which in its simplest form, assumes a common slope or rate of change in the outcome variable (e.g., caregiving satisfaction), Walker and colleagues confirmed that it is not the passage or length of time that causes stress in caregiving relationships, but rather the giving of increasing amounts of care that raises caregiver burden.

SUBSTANTIVE ADVANCES

Until the 1990s, the focus of research on older families reflected a uniform developmental view. This conceptualization used stages of marriage (intragenerational) and parenthood (intergenerational) as the prototypes for investigating family-level phenomena, often obscuring family networks and processes, as well as nonkin relationships. In the 1990s, however, in keeping with the trends of acknowledging diversity and employing a life course approach, a broader range of family issues was studied. Next, we highlight substantive advances in the top five topics appearing in the literature in the past decade (see Table 1).

Family Caregiving Is Multilayered

When family members' need for instrumental and emotional support is required for their daily well-being, caregiving emerges as a distinct type of social support. We distinguished caregiving from aid given as part of the normal exchange of assistance among family members by focusing on research that primarily addresses relational influences on and outcomes of assistance given on a regular basis for a person with physical or mental impairments.

Family expectations and interactions often change when the need for care occurs. Parents typically adjust their global expectations for care to reflect the specific realities of their adult children's lives (Peek, Coward, Peek, & Lee, 1998), whereas children and grandchildren try to balance the needs of their dependent elders with those of the whole family (Piercy, 1998). Family relationships intensify and interactions may be strained as members take on, or have thrust upon them, caregiving responsibilities (Semple, 1992; Stommel, Given, Given, & Collins, 1995).

Investigating the effects of caregiving on families has broadened as new contexts have been studied. For example, researchers report that the stresses and strains of providing direct elder care negatively influence workplace performance (Scharlach, Sobel, & Roberts, 1991; Starrels, Ingersoll-Dayton, Dowler, & Neal, 1997) and place employed caregivers at risk for adverse personal and job-related consequences (Gottlieb, Kelloway, & Fraboni, 1994). At some point in the cycle of care, often because of undue personal burden (Reinhard & Horwitz, 1995) and stress (Aranda & Knight, 1997), family caregivers connect with the formal helping network. Caregivers frequently struggle with decisions of including formal services to help them with their caregiving responsibilities (Hinrichsen & Ramirez, 1992) and moving their family members to nursing homes (McFall & Miller, 1992; Montgomery & Kosloski, 1994).

Family Support Is Multidimensional

Social support is defined as receiving various forms of informal assistance (e.g., information, tangible help, emotional support, and social integration) from relatives, friends, neighbors, and other community members. Research on social network composition and network characteristics has demonstrated that most older family members have sources of informal support available, including fictive kin, particularly if they are female (e.g., Barker, Morrow, & Mitteness, 1998; Levitt, Weber, & Guacci, 1993; McCrae, 1992). Silverstein and Waite (1993) pointed out that researchers must take into account the intersecting influences of race, gender, and stage of life when examining the availability of social support. Compared with younger adults, older ones expressed satisfaction with the size of their informal network (Lansford, Sherman, & Antonucci, 1998) even though it might be smaller than in the past.

Social support serves key functions in the lives of elderly people and their families. Research in the past decade demonstrates how social support protects elders' health (Roberto, 1992; Samuelsson & Dehlin, 1993) and psychological well-being (Barrett, 1999; McCulloch, 1995; Newsom & Schulz, 1996). Recent research has refined understanding of how social support acts as a buffer against the negative effects of stressful situations. For example, in a study of support and stressors among Black elderly adults, women's (but not men's) level of depression was higher when they had reduced contact with family and friends in the

face of increased instances of life events than when they had sufficient contact (Husaini et al., 1991).

Researchers also gave greater attention to negative aspects of family interaction. Just as positive exchanges are associated with positive affect, negative exchanges are associated with negative affect, particularly when experiencing other stressors (Ingersoll-Dayton, Morgan, & Antonucci, 1997). Krause (1991, 1994, 1995) contributed a series of studies on negative aspects of family support, including the extent to which certain kinds of stressors might promote isolation rather than receipt of support, the relative effects of stressors depending on the salience of the social roles in which they arise, and the effects of the amount of assistance elderly people provide to others on the impact of negative interaction and received support. Rook (1997) pointed out, however, that research on positive versus negative support involves methodological problems such as incomparable measures of support intensity, dissimilar focal time frames, and incomplete sampling of support domains. Relationships include a complex assortment of both positive and negative aspects that research has not yet addressed thoroughly, rendering premature any oversimplified statements about the relative effects of positive and negative support.

An important conceptual framework related to social support, Weiss's (1974) theory of the provisions of social relationships, received empirical confirmation in the 1990s. Weiss posited that various types of relationships typically provide specific kinds of support, which he labeled attachment, social integration, reliable alliance, guidance, reassurance of worth, and opportunity for nurturance. Availability of one type of support does not necessarily compensate for deficit of another. This theory, which had been tested on younger people in previous decades, was evaluated in relation to the support older adults receive from their social networks by Husaini et al. (1991), Mancini and Blieszner (1992), and Reinhardt (1996).

Complexities in Parent–Child Relationships

Parenthood, the most salient adult role, provides a unique source of social integration and mutual reliance across generations (Umberson, 1992). Despite the stresses parents and adult children confront, continuity characterizes most relationships (Mancini & Blieszner, 1989). Typically, however, only normative transitions have been examined in the aging parent–adult child literature (Ryff & Seltzer, 1996), such as becoming a grandparent and assuming caregiving responsibilities for an older relative.

Increasingly, the literature demonstrates that older adults must deal with nonnormative transitions in their adult children's lives, such as interracial marriage (Taylor, Chatters, Tucker, & Lewis, 1990; Tucker & Mitchell-Kernan, 1990) and coresidence with a parent (Aquilino & Supple, 1991; Goldscheider & Lawton, 1998; Lee & Dwyer, 1996; Ward & Spitze, 1996). Nonnormative transitions may threaten parent-child solidarity (Logan & Spitze, 1996; Rossi & Rossi, 1990). How children turn out is important to parental well-being because parents tend to live vicariously through their children's lives (Ryff, Schmutte, & Lee, 1996). Parental well-being may be enhanced if parents perceive their relationships with their offspring as close (Connidis & McMullin, 1993). Parents whose adult children have chronic mental, physical, alcohol, or stress-related problems experience greater depression than other parents (Pillemer & Suitor, 1991). Adult children who have not fulfilled age-related norms for adult status, as in leaving home, marrying, having children, or becoming financially independent, are less likely to be available to care for parents in the later years (Bumpass, 1990).

Researchers in the 1990s gave attention to the influence of earlier interaction patterns on the quality of older parent-child relationships. The evidence suggests that families do build on past relationships, whether positive or negative, as well as considering members' current needs (Hoyert, 1991). Perceptions of past parental unfairness can interfere with adult children's current feelings of affection toward mothers and fathers (Bedford, 1992), which might influence their propensity to provide assistance to parents needing help (Whitbeck et al., 1994). These tendencies are slight, however, and other research showed that a history of overt parent-child conflict does not necessarily prevent adult children from giving aid to their parents (Parrott & Bengtson, 1999).

In the 1990s, researchers explored several new aspects of the parent-child caregiving relationship that provided greater insight into this family event. Ganong, Coleman, McDaniel, and Killian's (1998) investigation of filial responsibilities and obligations for helping older divorced parents and stepparents broadens understanding of the influence of family structural and situational contexts on caregiving. Studies of the experiences of children-in-law reinforced the importance of examining parental care within the context of the family and the quality of previous relationships (Globerman, 1996; Peters-Davis, Moss, & Pruchno, 1999). Although husbands often spend more time with their wives' families than with their families of origin, when there is a need for care, daughters-in-law step into the caregiver role. They provide similar types of care as biological daughters do, but often with less frequency and perceived authority. Even daughters-in-law in both middle- and working-class families who upgrade their relationship with their mothers-in-law to "second mothers" still do not believe they have the same decision-making prerogative as biological children have (Merrill, 1997).

Many researchers focused attention on the influence of caregiving on daughters' relationships with their parents (e.g., Pohl, Boyd, & Given, 1997; Walker, Martin, & Jones, 1992). Typically, when investigators included sons, they focused on gender-related task differences in parental caregiving. An exception to this approach was Harris's (1993) use of in-depth personal interviews to ascertain adult sons' perspectives of providing care for a parent with dementia. Her findings contradict previous research that portray sons as reluctant, intermittent caregivers and suggest greater variability among son caregivers than previously reported. Studies of African American (Fredman, Daly, & Lazur, 1995; Lee, Peek, & Coward, 1998; Young & Kahana, 1992) and Hispanic (Dietz, 1995; Talamantes, Cornell, Espino, Lichtenstein, & Hazuda, 1996) caregivers, although fewer in number, significantly broaden knowledge of parent care, as did cross-cultural comparisons of middle-aged children providing care for their aging parents (Ogawa & Retherford, 1993; Sung, 1994).

Transformations in Marital Relationships

The demography of cohabitation, marriage, divorce, widowhood, and remarriage has significantly altered the nature of intimate relationships in old age. Formerly, the later years were likely to be characterized by widowhood for women and marriage for men. With demographic shifts toward marital dissolution through divorce over the 20th century, one third of adults can now expect to marry, divorce, and remarry during their life time (Cherlin & Furstenberg, 1994). Cohabitation among older adults is also increasing. Chevan (1996) used a trend analysis with Public Use Microdata Samples and found that 2.4% of unmarried individuals aged 60 and over were cohabiting in 1990, compared to virtually 0% in 1960. In addition to gender being a factor in cohabitation, with men having a higher rate than women, class is also a factor. Older adults with higher incomes are more likely to marry, but cohabitation is a response to poverty for others.

Investigators also gave attention to dating (Bulcroft & Bulcroft, 1991), the influence of age on mate selection (Berardo, Appel, & Berardo, 1993), and remarriage among older adults (Burch, 1990). They paid closer heed than in the past to the dynamics of late-life marital relationships, including the impact of self-disclosure on marital satisfaction (Bograd & Spilka, 1996), the nature and effects of power within elderly couples (Kulik, 1997), and perceptions of fairness across husbands and wives at different stages of the family life cycle (Peterson, 1990). These studies are important because they acknowledge the impact that spousal relationships can have on personal well-being (Quirouette & Gold, 1992). Researchers also examined nonnormative types of marital relationships, such as couples in which one partner resided in the community and the other in a nursing home (Kaplan, Ade-Ridder, Hennon, Brubaker, & Brubaker, 1995) and gay and lesbian marital-like relationships (Huyck, 1995).

A decline in a spouse's health almost inevitably places the other member of the marital dyad in the role of primary caregiver. During the 1990s, investigators broadened caregiving research to include studies of couples faced with health conditions other than dementia (Clipp & George, 1993; Owens & Qualls, 1997; Pakenam, 1998; Roberto & Gold, 1997), husbands as caregivers (Kramer, 1997), and the quality of the marital relationship (Suitor & Pillemer, 1994; Townsend & Franks, 1997; Wright, 1991). The experiences of spouses within various illness scenarios suggest some commonalities in their approach to caregiving and similarities in their perceptions of how caregiving influences their emotional well-being. The inclusion of husbands in such studies provided new insight into the meaning and consequences of caregiving for older men.

New Approaches to Grandparenting

Grandparenting research has proliferated in recent years. Initial depictions of grandparenting focused on classifying types or styles of grandparents, as functional assessments of the roles grandparents perform. Kivett (1991, 1993, 1996) furthered the discussion of grandparenting by describing the diverse and complex roles of rural Black and White grandmothers and grandfathers. She noted that geographic distance from grandchildren influenced the frequency of association and exchange of assistance, but not necessarily the quality of the relationships. The contributors to Szinovacz's (1998) handbook on grandparenthood critically addressed demographic and processual variations in grandparenting experiences and thus provide readers with a greater appreciation of the complexities of grandparenting.

For a growing number of elders, grandparenthood takes on a new meaning when they care for their grandchildren. Minkler and Roe (1993) brought this phenomenon to the attention of scholars with their study of urban African-American grandmothers rearing children of the crack cocaine epidemic. The incidence of grandparents rearing grandchildren, however, goes well beyond large urban cities. Across the United States, grandparents representing all class, race, and cultural backgrounds reported that they were providing day-to-day care of their grandchildren (Fuller-Thomson, Minkler, & Driver, 1997). Grandparents take on the parenting role for a variety of reasons, including parental illness or death, divorce, incarceration, and substance abuse. The context of the family situation influences the amount and type of care provided by grandparents, as well as the impact on the lives and well-being of the grandparents (Jendrek, 1994; Roberto, Allen, & Blieszner, 1999; Strawbridge, Wallhagen, Shema, & Kaplan, 1997) and grandchildren (Aquilino, 1996; Solomon & Marx, 1995).

CONCLUSION

Research on families in the middle and later years blossomed in the 1990s. Family scholars and gerontologists described unique processes associated with aging and incorporated complexities linked to race, class, gender, ethnicity, sexual orientation, marital and parental status, and family structural diversity, as well as the intersections among them. New areas of investigation turned the study of aging families from a monolithic conception of "the aging individual within 'The Family' " to greater awareness of the challenges and innovations associated with variability in later family life. New contexts for aging families include multigenerational structural relationships, chosen family bonds and processes, and responsibilities for support and care over the life course, particularly as required by increased longevity.

Four themes highlight the research in the 1990s on families in the middle and later years. Conceptually, family scholars are demonstrating greater appreciation of the diversity and complexity of family relationships and structures over the life course. Theoretically, family scholars have developed qualitative and quantitative ways to take advantage of the insights of a life-course perspective, one that allows complicated linkages across interrelated lives to be addressed conceptually and empirically. Methodologically, the use of several national data sets allows researchers to accumulate findings regarding a number of complex topics, ranging from parent-child coresidence to the impact of health care decisions on marital relationships. A corresponding rise in the number of in-depth qualitative studies was also evident. Finally, as in past decades, caregiving continues to dominate the literature, but greater complexity in caregiving networks and demographics has been elaborated. New areas are also claiming empirical attention, as in elder abuse and violence, oldest old persons, and sexual orientation diversity.

As we look to the next decade, we anticipate even greater interest in families in the middle and later years. Family gerontology as a subfield of aging studies has come of age, and researchers will be free to take greater risks in fulfilling the promise of studying linked lives over time. Given the family transitions that characterize the adult life course, individuals are increasingly likely to live in more than one family, challenging researchers to generate conceptualizations, measures, and methods that can capture such complexity. Creative application of strong theoretical frameworks, more integration of qualitative and quantitative approaches, and sustained attention to the rich diversity of family life trajectories across the adult years will no doubt become a hallmark of the most careful and useful research in the coming decade.

REFERENCES

Abel, E. K. (1990). Family care of the frail elderly. In E. K. Abel & M. K. Nelson (Eds.), *Circles of care* (pp. 65–91). Albany, NY: State University of New York Press.

Adams, R. G., & Blieszner, R. (1995). Aging well with friends and family. *American Behavioral Scientist, 39,* 209–224.

Alexander, B., Rubinstein, R., Goodman, M., & Luborsky, M. (1992). A path not taken: A cultural analysis of regrets and childlessness in the lives of older women. *The Gerontologist, 5,* 618–626.

Allen, K. R., Blieszner, R., Roberto, K. A., Farnsworth, E., & Wilcox, K. L. (1999). Older adults and their children: Family patterns of structural diversity. *Family Relations, 48,* 151–157.

Allen, K. R., & Demo, D. H. (1995). The families of lesbians and gay men: A new frontier in family research. *Journal of Marriage and the Family, 57,* 111–127.

Antonucci, T. C., & Akiyama, H. (1997). Concern with others at midlife: Care, comfort, or compromise? In M. E. Lachman & J. B. James (Eds.), *Multiple paths of midlife development* (pp. 147–169). Chicago: University of Chicago Press.

Aquilino, W. S. (1996). The life course of children born to unmarried mothers: Childhood living arrangements and young adult outcomes. *Journal of Marriage and the Family, 58,* 293–310.

Aquilino, W. S., & Supple, K. R. (1991). Parent-child relations and parent's satisfaction with living arrangements when adult children live at home. *Journal of Marriage and the Family, 53,* 13–27.

Aranda, M. P., & Knight, B. G. (1997). The influence of ethnicity and culture on the caregiver stress and coping process: A sociocultural review and analysis. *The Gerontologist, 37,* 342–354.

Baber, K. M., & Allen, K. R. (1992). *Women and families: Feminist reconstructions.* New York: Guilford Press.

Barer, B. M., & Johnson, C. J. (1990). A critique of the caregiving literature. *The Gerontologist, 30,* 26–29.

Barker, J. C., Morrow, J., & Mitteness, L. S. (1998). Gender, informal social support networks, and elderly urban African Americans. *Journal of Aging Studies, 12,* 199–222.

Barnett, R. C., Marshall, N. L., & Pleck, J. H. (1992). Adult son-parent relationships and their associations with sons' psychological distress. *Journal of Family Issues, 13,* 505–525.

Barrett, A. E. (1999). Social support and life satisfaction among the never married. *Research on Aging, 21,* 46–72.

Bedford, V. H. (1992). Memories of parental favoritism and the quality of parent-child ties in adulthood. *Journal of Gerontology: Social Sciences, 47,* S149–S155.

Bedford, V. H. (1998). Sibling relationship troubles and well-being in middle and old age. *Family Relations, 47,* 369–376.

Bedford, V. H., & Blieszner, R. (1997). Personal relationships in later life families. In S. Duck (Ed.), *Handbook of personal relationships* (2nd ed., pp. 523–539). New York: Wiley.

Bengtson, V. L., & Allen, K. R. (1993). The life course perspective applied to families over time. In P. Boss, W. Doherty, R. LaRossa, W. Schumm, & S. Steinmetz (Eds.), *Sourcebook of family theories and methods: A contextual approach* (pp. 469–499). New York: Plenum Press.

Bengtson, V. L., & Roberts, R. E. L. (1991). Intergenerational solidarity in aging families: An example of formal theory construction. *Journal of Marriage and the Family, 53,* 856–870.

Bengtson, V. L., Rosenthal, C., & Burton, L. M. (1990). Families and aging. In R. Binstock & L. George

(Eds.), *Handbook of aging and the social sciences* (3rd ed., pp. 263–287). San Diego, CA: Academic Press.

Berardo, F. M., Appel, J., & Berardo, D. H. (1993). Age dissimilar marriages: Review and assessment. *Journal of Aging Studies, 7,* 93–106.

Blieszner, R. (1993). A socialist-feminist perspective on widowhood. *Journal of Aging Studies, 7,* 171–182.

Blieszner, R., & Bedford, V. H. (Eds.). (1995). *Handbook of aging and the family.* Westport, CT: Greenwood Press.

Bogard, R., & Spilka, B. (1996). Self-disclosure and marital satisfaction in mid-life and late-life remarriages. *International Journal of Aging and Human Development, 42,* 161–172.

Brabant, S. (1994). An overlooked AIDS affected population: The elderly parent as caregiver. *Journal of Gerontological Social Work, 22,* 131–145.

Brubaker, T. H. (1990). Families in later life: A burgeoning research area. *Journal of Marriage and the Family, 52,* 959–981.

Bulcroft, R. A., & Bulcroft, K. A. (1991). The nature and functions of dating in later life. *Research on Aging, 13,* 244–260.

Bumpass, L. L. (1990). What's happening to the family? Interactions between demographic and institutional change. *Demography, 27,* 483–498.

Burch, T. K., (1990). Remarriage of older Canadians: Description and interpretation. *Research on Aging, 12,* 546–559.

Burton, L. M. (1996). Age norms, the timing of family role transitions, and intergenerational caregiving among aging African American women. *The Gerontologist, 36,* 199–208.

Calasanti, T. M. (1993). Bringing in diversity: Toward an inclusive theory of retirement. *Journal of Aging Studies, 7,* 133–150.

Calasanti, T. M. (1996). Incorporating diversity: Meaning, levels of research, and implications for theory. *The Gerontologist, 36,* 147–156.

Campbell, L. D., Connidis, I. A., & Davies, L. (1999). Sibling ties in later life: A social network analysis. *Journal of Family Issues, 20,* 114–148.

Carstensen, L. L. (1992). Social and emotional patterns in adulthood: Support for socioemotional selectivity theory. *Psychology and Aging, 7,* 331–338.

Carstensen, L. L., Gottman, J. M., & Levenson, R. W. (1995). Emotional behavior in long-term marriage. *Psychology & Aging, 10,* 140–149.

Cherlin, A. J., & Furstenberg, F. F., Jr. (1994). Stepfamilies in the United States: A reconsideration. *Annual Review of Sociology, 20,* 359–381.

Chevan, A. (1996). As cheaply as one: Cohabitation in the older population. *Journal of Marriage and the Family, 58,* 656–667.

Cicirelli, V. G. (1994). Sibling relationships in cross-cultural perspective. *Journal of Marriage and the Family, 56,* 7–20.

Clipp, E. C., & George, L. K. (1993). Dementia and cancer: A comparison of spouse caregivers. *The Gerontologist, 33,* 534–541.

Connidis, I. A., & McMullin, J. A. (1993). To have or have not: Parent status and the subjective well-being of older men and women. *The Gerontologist, 33,* 630–636.

Cooney, T. D., & Uhlenberg, P. (1990). The role of divorce in men's relations with their adult children after mid-life. *Journal of Marriage and the Family, 52,* 677–688.

Crosbie-Burnett, M., Foster, T. L., Murray, C. L., & Bowen, G. L. (1996). Gays' and lesbians' families-of-origin: A social-cognitive-behavioral model of adjustment. *Family Relations, 45,* 397–403.

Dietz, T. L. (1995). Patterns of intergenerational assistance within the Mexican American family: Is the family taking care of the older generation's needs? *Journal of Family Issues, 16,* 344–356.

Dilworth-Anderson, P., & Burton, L. M. (1996). Rethinking family development: Critical conceptual issues in the study of diverse groups. *Journal of Social and Personal Relationships, 13,* 325–334.

Dressel, P. L., & Clark, A. (1991). A critical look at family care. *Journal of Marriage and the Family, 52,* 769–782.

Dwyer, J. W., & Coward, R. T. (1991). A multivariate comparison of the involvement of adult sons versus daughters in the care of impaired parents. *Journal of Gerontology: Social Sciences, 46,* S259–S269.

Dwyer, J. W., Lee, G. R., & Jankowski, T. B. (1994). Reciprocity, elder satisfaction, and caregiver stress and burden: The exchange of aid in the family caregiving relationship. *Journal of Marriage and the Family, 56,* 35–43.

Elder, G. H., Jr. (1998). The life course and human development. In R. M. Lerner (Ed.), *Handbook of child psychology: Vol. 1. Theoretical models of human development* (5th ed., pp. 939–991). New York: Wiley.

Erikson, E. H. (1950). *Childhood and society.* New York: Norton.

Fingerman, K. L. (1996). Sources of tension in the aging mother and adult daughter relationship. *Psychology and Aging, 11,* 591–606.

Fredman, L., Daly, M. P., & Lazur, A. M. (1995). Burden among White and Black caregivers to elderly adults. *Journal of Gerontology: Social Sciences, 50B,* S110–S118.

Fuller-Thomson, E., Minkler, M., & Driver, D. (1997). A profile of grandparents raising grandchildren in the United States. *The Gerontologist, 37,* 406–411.

Fullmer, E. M., Tobin, S. S., & Smith, G. C. (1997). The effects of offspring gender on older mothers caring for their sons and daughters with mental retardation. *The Gerontologist, 37,* 795–803.

Ganong, L., Coleman, M., McDaniel, A. K., & Killian, T. (1998). Attitudes regarding obligations to assist an older parent or stepparent following later-life remarriage. *Journal of Marriage and the Family, 60,* 595–610.

Gladstone, J., & Westhues, A. (1998). Adoption reunions: A new side to intergenerational family relationships. *Family Relations, 47,* 177–184.

Globerman., J. (1996). Daughters- and sons-in-laws caring for relatives with Alzheimer's disease. *Family Relations, 45,* 37–45.

Goldscheider, F. K., & Lawton, L. (1998). Family experiences and the erosion of support for intergenerational coresidence. *Journal of Marriage and the Family, 60,* 623–632.

Gottlieb, B. H., Kelloway, K., & Fraboni, M. (1994). Aspects of eldercare that place employees at risk. *The Gerontologist, 34,* 815–821.

Gross, J. J., Carstensen, L. L., Pasupathi, M., Tsai, J.,

Skorpen, C. G., & Hsu, A. Y. (1997). Emotion and aging: Experience, expression, and control. *Psychology and Aging, 12,* 590–599.

Gubrium, J. F., & Sankar, A. (Eds.). (1994). *Qualitative methods in aging research.* Thousand Oaks, CA: Sage.

Harris, P. B. (1993). The misunderstood caregiver? A qualitative study of the male caregiver of Alzheimer's disease victims. *The Gerontologist, 33,* 551–556.

Henretta, J. C., Hill, M. S., Li, W., Soldo, B. J., & Wolf, D. A. (1997). Selection of children to provide care: The effect of earlier parental transfers. *The Journals of Gerontology Series B, 52B* [Special issue], 110–119.

Hill, R., & Rodgers, R. H. (1964). The developmental approach. In H. T. Christensen (Ed.), *Handbook of marriage and the family* (pp. 171–211). Chicago: Rand McNally.

Hinrichsen, G., & Ramirez, M. (1992). Black and White dementia caregivers: A comparison of their adaptation, adjustment, and service utilization. *The Gerontologist, 32,* 375–381.

Hoyert, D. L. (1991). Financial and household exchanges between generations. *Research on Aging, 113,* 205–225.

Husaini, B. A., Moore, S. T., Castor, R. S., Neser, W., Whitten-Stovall, R., Linn, J. G., & Griffin, D. (1991). Social density, stressors, and depression: Gender differences among the Black elderly. *Journal of Gerontology: Psychological Sciences, 46,* P236–P242.

Huyck, M. H. (1995). Marriage and close relationships of the marital kind. In R. Blieszner & V. H. Bedford (Eds.), *Handbook of aging and the family* (pp. 181–200). Westport, CT: Greenwood Press.

Ingersoll-Dayton, B., Morgan, D., & Antonucci, T. C. (1997). The effects of positive and negative social exchanges on aging adults. *Journal of Gerontology: Social Sciences, 52,* S190–S199.

Jendrek, M. P. (1994). Grandparents who parent their grandchildren: Circumstances and decisions. *The Gerontologist, 34,* 206–216.

Johnson, C. L. (2000a). Kinship and gender. In D. H. Demo, K. R. Allen, & M. A. Fine (Eds.), *Handbook of family diversity* (pp. 128–148). New York: Oxford University Press.

Johnson, C. L. (2000b). Perspectives on American kinship in the late 1990s. *Journal of Marriage and the Family, 62,* 623–639.

Johnson, C. L., & Barer, B. M. (1997). *Life beyond 85 years: The aura of survivorship.* New York: Springer.

Johnson, T. F. (1995). Aging well in contemporary society. *American Behavioral Scientist, 39,* 120–130.

Kaplan, L., Ade-Ridder, L., Hennon, C. B., Brubaker, E., & Brubaker, T. (1995). Preliminary typology of couplehood for community-dwelling wives: "I" versus "we." *International Journal of Aging and Human Development, 40,* 317–337.

Kivett, V. R. (1991). Centrality of the grandfather role among older rural Black and White men. *Journal of Gerontology: Social Sciences, 46,* S250–S258.

Kivett, V. R. (1993). Racial comparisons of the grandmother role: Implications for strengthening the family support system of older Black women. *Family Relations, 42,* 165–172.

Kivett, V. R. (1996). The saliency of the grandmother-granddaughter relationship: Predictors of association. *Journal of Women & Aging, 8* (3/4), 25–39.

Koropeckyj-Cox, T. (1998). Loneliness and depression in middle and old age: Are the childless more vulnerable? *Journal of Gerontology: Social Sciences, 53B,* S303–S312.

Kramer, B. J. (1997). Differential predictors of strain and gain among husbands caring for wives with dementia. *The Gerontologist, 37,* 239–249.

Krause, N. (1991). Stress and isolation from close ties in later life. *Journal of Gerontology: Social Sciences, 46,* S183–S194.

Krause, N. (1994). Stressors in salient social roles and well-being in later life. *Journal of Gerontology: Psychological Sciences, 49,* P137–P148.

Krause, N. (1995). Negative interaction and satisfaction with social support among older adults. *Journal of Gerontology: Psychological Sciences, 50,* P59–P73.

Kulik, L. (1997). Anticipated dependence: A determinant in an integrative model of power relations among elderly couples. *Journal of Aging Studies, 11,* 363–377.

Lang, F. R., Staudinger, U. M., & Carstensen, L. L. (1998). Perspectives on socioemotional selectivity in later life: How personality and social context do (and do not) make a difference. *Journal of Gerontology: Psychological Sciences, 53,* P21–P30.

Lansford, J. E., Sherman, A. M., & Antonucci, T. C. (1998). Satisfaction with social networks: An examination of Socioemotional Selectivity Theory across cohorts. *Psychology and Aging, 13,* 544–552.

Lawrence, R. H., Bennett, J. M., & Markides, K. S. (1992). Perceived intergenerational solidarity and psychological distress among older Mexican Americans. *Journal of Gerontology: Social Sciences, 47,* S55–S65.

Lee, G. R., & Dwyer, J. W. (1996). Aging parent-adult child coresidence: Further evidence on the effects of parental characteristics. *Journal of Family Issues, 17,* 46–59.

Lee, G. R., Peek, C. W., & Coward, R. T. (1998). Race differences in filial responsibility expectations among older parents. *Journal of Marriage and the Family, 60,* 404–412.

Levitt, M. J., Weber, R. A., & Guacci, N. (1993). Convoys of social support: An intergenerational analysis. *Psychology and Aging, 8,* 323–326.

Logan, J. R., & Spitze, G. D. (1996). *Family ties: Enduring relations between parents and their grown children.* Philadelphia: Temple University Press.

MacDermid, S. M., Heilbrun, G., & DeHaan, L. G. (1997). The generativity of employed mothers in multiple roles: 1979 and 1991. In M. E. Lachman & J. B. James (Eds.), *Multiple paths of midlife development* (pp. 207–240). Chicago: University of Chicago Press.

Malonebeach, E., & Zarit, S. (1991). Current research issues in caregiving to the elderly. *International Journal of Aging and Human Development, 32,* 103–114.

Mancini, J. A., & Blieszner, R. (1989). Aging parents and adult children: Research themes in intergenerational relations. *Journal of Marriage and the Family, 51,* 275–290.

Mancini, J. A., & Blieszner, R. (1992). Social provisions in adulthood: Concept and measurement in close relationships. *Journal of Gerontology: Psychological Sciences, 47,* P14–P20.

Matthews, S. H. (1995). Gender and the division of filial responsibility between lone sisters and their brothers. *Journal of Gerontology: Social Sciences, 50B,* S312–S320.

Matthews, S. H., & Heidorn, J. (1998). Meeting filial responsibilities in brothers-only sibling groups. *Journal of Gerontology: Social Sciences, 53B,* S278–S286.

McCrae, H. (1992). Fictive kin as a component of the social networks of older people. *Research on Aging, 14,* 226–247.

McCulloch, B. J. (1995). The relationship of family proximity and social support to the mental health of older rural adults: The Appalachian context. *Journal of Aging Studies, 9,* 65–81.

McFall, S., & Miller, B. H. (1992). Caregiver burden and nursing home admission of frail elderly persons. *Journal of Gerontology: Social Sciences, 47,* S73–S79.

Merrill, G. (1997). *Caring for elderly parents.* Westport, CT: Auburn House.

Minkler, M., & Roe, K. (1993). *Grandmothers as caregivers: Raising children of the crack cocaine epidemic.* Newbury Park, CA: Sage.

Moen, P., Robison, J., & Fields, V. (1994). Women's work and caregiving roles: A life course approach. *Journal of Gerontology: Social Sciences, 49,* S176–S186.

Montgomery, R. J., & Kosloski, K. (1994). A longitudinal analysis of nursing home placement for dependent elders cared for by spouses vs adult children. *Journal of Gerontology: Social Sciences, 49,* S62–S74.

Newsom, J. T., & Schulz, R. (1996). Social support as a mediator in the relationship between functional status and quality of life in older adults. *Psychology and Aging, 11,* 34–44.

Ogawa, N., & Retherford, R. D. (1993). Care of the elderly in Japan: Changing norms and expectations. *Journal of Marriage and the Family, 55,* 585–597.

Owens, S. J., & Qualls, S. H. (1997). Family stress at the time of a geropsychiatric hospitalization. *Family Relations, 46,* 179–185.

Pakenham, K. I. (1998). Couple coping and adjustment to multiple sclerosis in care receiver-carer dyads. *Family Relations, 47,* 269–277.

Parrott, T. M., & Bengtson, V. L. (1999). The effects of earlier intergenerational affection, normative expectations, and family conflict on contemporary exchanges of help and support. *Research on Aging, 21,* 73–105.

Pearlin, L. I., & Skaff, M. M. (1996). Stress and the life course: A paradigmatic alliance. *The Gerontologist, 36,* 239–247.

Peek, M. K., Coward, R. T., Peek, C. W., & Lee, G. R. (1998). Are expectations for care related to the receipt of care? An analysis of parent care among disabled elders. *Journal of Gerontology: Social Sciences, 53B,* S127–S136.

Penning, M. J. (1998). In the middle: Parental caregiving in the context of other roles. *Journal of Gerontology: Social Sciences, 53B,* S188–S197.

Peters-Davis, N. D., Moss, M. S., & Pruchno, R. A. (1999). Children-in-law in caregiving families. *The Gerontologist, 39,* 66–75.

Peterson, C. C. (1990). Husbands' and wives' perceptions of marital fairness across the family life cycle. *International Journal of Aging and Human Development, 31,* 178–188.

Piercy, K. W. (1998). Theorizing about family caregiving: The role of responsibility. *Journal of Marriage and the Family, 60,* 109–118.

Pillemer, K., & Suitor, J. J. (1991). "Will I ever escape my child's problems?" Effects of adult children's problems on elderly parents. *Journal of Marriage and the Family, 53,* 585–594.

Pohl, J. M., Boyd, C., & Given, B. A. (1997). Mother-daughter relationships during the first year of caregiving: A qualitative study. *Journal of Women & Aging, 9* (1&2), 133–149.

Pruchno, R. A., Patrick, J. H., & Burant, C. J. (1996). Aging women and their children with chronic disabilities: Perceptions of sibling involvement and effects on well-being. *Family Relations, 45,* 318–326.

Pyke, K. D., & Bengtson, V. L. (1996). Caring more or less: Individualistic and collectivist systems of family eldercare. *Journal of Marriage and the Family, 58,* 379–392.

Quam, J. K., & Whitford, G. S. (1992). Adaptation and age-related expectations of older gay and lesbian adults. *The Gerontologist, 32,* 367–374.

Quirouette, C., & Gold, D. P. (1992). Spousal characteristics as predictors of well-being in older couples. *International Journal of Aging and Human Development, 34,* 257–269.

Ramsey, J. L., & Blieszner, R. (1999). *Spiritual resiliency in older women.* Thousand Oaks, CA: Sage.

Ray, R. E. (1996). A postmodern perspective on feminist gerontology. *The Gerontologist, 36,* 674–680.

Reinhard, S. C., & Horwitz, A. V. (1995). Caregiver burden: Differentiating the content and consequences of family caregiving. *Journal of Marriage and the Family, 57,* 741–750.

Reinhardt, J. P. (1996). The importance of friendship and family support in adaptation to chronic vision impairment. *Journal of Gerontology: Psychological Sciences, 51,* P268–P278.

Roberto, K. A. (1992). Coping strategies of older women with hip fractures: Resources and outcomes. *Journal of Gerontology: Psychological Sciences, 47,* P21–P26.

Roberto, K. A. (Ed.). (1993). *The elderly caregiver: Caring for adults with developmental disabilities.* Newbury Park, CA: Sage.

Roberto, K. A., Allen, K. R., Blieszner, R. (1999). Older women, their children, and grandchildren: A feminist perspective on family relationships. *Journal of Women & Aging, 11,* 67–84.

Roberto, K., & Gold, D. (1997). Spousal support of older women with osteoporotic pain: Congruity of perceptions. *Journal of Women & Aging, 9,* 17–31.

Rook, K. S. (1997). Positive and negative social exchanges: Weighing their effects in later life. *Journal of Gerontology: Social Sciences, 52B,* S167–S169.

Rossi, A. S., & Rossi, P. H. (1990). *Of human bonding: Parent-child relations across the life course.* New York: Aldine de Gruyter.

Ryff, C. D., Schmutte, P. S., & Lee, Y. H. (1996). How children turn out: Implications for parental self-evaluation. In C. D. Ryff & M. M. Seltzer (Eds.), *The parental experience in midlife* (pp. 383–422). Chicago: University of Chicago Press.

Ryff, C. D., & Seltzer, M. M. (Eds.). (1996). *The parental experience in midlife.* Chicago: University of Chicago Press.

Samuelsson, G., & Dehlin, O. (1993). Family network and mortality: Survival chances through the lifespan of an entire age cohort. *International Journal of Aging and Human Development, 37,* 277–295.

Scharlach, A. E., Sobel, E. L., & Roberts, R. E. (1991). Employment and caregiver strain: An integrative model. *The Gerontologist, 31,* 778–787.

Seltzer, M. M., Greenberg, J. S., & Krauss, M. W. (1995). A comparison of coping strategies of aging mothers of adults with mental illness or mental retardation. *Psychology and Aging, 10,* 64–75.

Seltzer, M. M., & Heller, T. (Eds.). (1997). Family caregiving for persons with disabilities [Special issue]. *Family Relations, 46* (4).

Semple, S. J. (1992). Conflict in Alzheimer's caregiving families: Its dimensions and consequences. *The Gerontologist, 32,* 648–655.

Shanas, E. (1979). Social myth as hypothesis: The case of the family relations of old people. *The Gerontologist, 19,* 3–9.

Shenk, D., & Fullmer, E. (1996). Significant relationships among older women: Cultural and personal constructions of lesbianism. In K. A. Roberto (Ed.), *Relationships between women in later life* (pp. 75–89). New York: Harrington Park Press.

Silverstein, M., & Angelelli, J. (1998). Older parents' expectations of moving closer to their adult children. *Journal of Gerontology: Social Sciences, 53,* S153–S163.

Silverstein, M., & Long, J. D. (1998). Trajectories of grandparents' perceived solidarity with adult grandchildren: A growth curve analysis over 23 years. *Journal of Marriage and the Family, 60,* 912–923.

Silverstein, M., & Waite, L. J. (1993). Are Blacks more likely than Whites to receive and provide social support in middle and old age? Yes, no, and maybe so. *Journals of Gerontology: Social Sciences, 48,* S212–S222.

Solomon, J. C., & Marx, J. (1995). "To grandmother's house we go": Health and school adjustment of children raised solely by grandparents. *The Gerontologist, 35,* 386–394.

Starrels, M. E., Ingersoll-Dayton, B., Dowler, D. W., & Neal, M. B. (1997). The stress of caring for a parent: Effects of the elder's impairment on an employed, adult child. *Journal of Marriage and the Family, 59,* 860–872.

Starrels, M. E., Ingersoll-Dayton, B., & Neal, M. B. (1995). Intergenerational solidarity and the workplace: Employees' caregiving for their parents. *Journal of Marriage and the Family, 57,* 751–762.

Stein, C. H., Wemmerus, V. A., Ward., M., Gaines, M. E., Freeberg, A. L., & Jewell, T. C. (1998). "Because they're my parents": An intergenerational study of felt obligation and parental caregiving. *Journal of Marriage and the Family, 60,* 611–622.

Stoller, E. P. (1990). Males as helpers: The role of sons, relatives, and friends. *The Gerontologist, 30,* 228–235.

Stoller, E. P., Forster, L. E., & Duniho, T. S. (1992).

Systems of parent care within sibling networks. *Research on Aging, 14,* 28–49.

Stoller, E. P. (1993). Gender and the organization of lay health care: A socialist-feminist perspective. *Journal of Aging Studies, 7,* 151–170.

Stommel, M., Given, B. A., Given, C. W., & Collins, C. (1995). The impact of the frequency of care activities on the division of labor between primary caregivers and other care providers. *Research on Aging, 17,* 412–433.

Strawbridge, W. J., Wallhagen, M. I., Shema, S. J., & Kaplan, G. A. (1997). New burdens or more of the same? Comparing grandparent, spouse, and adult-child caregivers. *The Gerontologist, 37,* 505–510.

Streib, G. F., & Beck, R. W. (1980). Older families: A decade review. *Journal of Marriage and the Family, 42,* 937–956.

Suitor, J. J., & Pillemer, K. (1993). Support and interpersonal stress in the social networks of married daughters caring for parents with dementia. *Journal of Gerontology: Social Sciences, 48,* S1–S8.

Suitor, J. J., & Pillemer, K. (1994). Family caregiving and marital satisfaction: Findings from a 1-year panel study of women caring for parents with dementia. *Journal of Marriage and the Family, 56,* 681–690.

Sung, K. T. (1994). A cross-cultural comparison of motivations for parent care: The case of Americans and Koreans. *Journal of Aging Studies, 8,* 195–209.

Szinovacz, M. (Ed.). (1998). *Handbook on grandparenthood.* Westport, CT: Greenwood Press.

Talamantes, M. A., Cornell, J., Espino, D. V., Lichtenstein, M. J., & Hazuda, H. P. (1996). SES and ethnic differences in perceived caregiver availability among young-old Mexican Americans and nonHispanic Whites. *The Gerontologist, 36,* 88–99.

Taylor, R. J., Chatters, L. M., Tucker, M. B., & Lewis, E. (1990). Developments in research on Black families: A decade review. *Journal of Marriage and the Family, 52,* 1–14.

Townsend, A. L., & Franks, M. M (1997). Quality of the relationship between elderly spouses: Influence on spouse caregivers' subjective effectiveness. *Family Relations, 46,* 33–39.

Troll, L. E. (1971). The family of later life: A decade review. *Journal of Marriage and the Family, 33,* 263–290.

Tucker, M. B., & Mitchell-Kernan, C. (1990). New trends in Black American interracial marriage: The social structural context. *Journal of Marriage and the Family, 52,* 209–218.

Uhlenberg, P. (1996). Mutual attraction: Demography and life-course analysis. *The Gerontologist, 36,* 226–229.

Umberson, D. (1992). Relationships between adult children and their parents: Psychological consequences for both generations. *Journal of Marriage and the Family, 54,* 664–674.

Walker, A. J., Acock, A. C., Bowman, S. R., & Li, F. (1996). Amount of care given and caregiving satisfaction: A latent growth curve analysis. *Journal of Gerontology: Psychological Sciences, 51B,* P130–P142.

Walker, A. J., & Allen, K. R. (1991). Relationships between caregiving daughters and their elderly mothers. *The Gerontologist, 31,* 389–396.

Walker, A. J., Martin, S. K., & Jones, L. L. (1992). The

benefits and costs of caregiving and care receiving for daughters and mothers. *Journal of Gerontology: Social Sciences, 47,* S130–S139.

Walker, A. J., Pratt, C. C., & Eddy, L. (1995). Informal caregiving to aging family members: A critical review. *Family Relations, 44,* 402–411.

Ward, R. A., & Spitze, G. (1996). Gender differences in parent-child coresidence experiences. *Journal of Marriage and the Family, 58,* 718–725.

Weiss, R. S. (1974). The provisions of social relationships. In Z. Rubin (Ed.), *Doing unto others* (pp. 17–26). Englewood Cliffs, NJ: Prentice-Hall.

Whitbeck, L. B., Hoyt, D., R., & Huck, S. M. (1994). Early family relationships, intergenerational solidarity, and support provided to parents by their adult children. *Journal of Gerontology: Social Sciences, 49,* S85–S94.

White, J. M. (1991). *Dynamics of family development.* New York: Guilford.

White, L. K., & Reidmann, A. (1992). When the Brady Bunch grows up: Step/half- and full sibling relationships in adulthood. *Journal of Marriage and the Family, 54,* 197–208.

Wolf, D. A., Freedman, V., & Soldo, B. J. (1997). The division of family labor: Care for elderly parents. *The Journals of Gerontology* Series B, *52B* [Special issue], 102–109.

Wright, L. K. (1991). The impact of Alzheimer's disease on the marital relationship. *The Gerontologist, 31,* 224–237.

Wu, Z., & Pollard, M. (1998). Social support among unmarried childless elderly persons. *Journal of Gerontology: Social Sciences, 53B,* S324–S335.

Young, R. F., & Kahana, E. (1995). The context of caregiving and well-being outcomes among African and Caucasian Americans. *The Gerontologist, 35,* 225–232.

JOHN M. GOTTMAN   *University of Washington*

CLIFFORD I. NOTARIUS   *Washington, DC**

Decade Review: Observing Marital Interaction

This article reviews the advances made in the decade of the 1990s in observing marital interaction. Many technological advances in data collection, including synchronization of physiology, behavior, and cognition, and advances in data analysis such as sequential analysis, have yielded new understanding and advances in prediction of marital outcomes. The advances have also included the study of developmental processes, including the transition to parenthood and the study of midlife and older marriages. Central advances have been made in the study of affect and the study of power and in their integration. This advance has included the mathematical modeling of interaction using nonlinear difference equations and the development of typologies. There has been an added focus on health outcomes and the bidirectional effects of marriages on children. There has been an expansion of the study of marital interaction to common comorbid psychopathologies. Most important has been emergent theorizing based on the interaction of behavior, perception, and physiology, as well as their predictive power.

Observational research plays a major role in research on marriage, both for purposes of description and for building theories of the mechanisms underlying central phenomena occurring within

Department of Psychology, University of Washington, Seattle, WA 98115 (johng@u.washington.edu).

*5028 Wisconsin Avenue, NW, Suite 303, Washington, DC 20016

Key Words: comorbidities, interaction, marriage, observation, sequential analysis.

families. It is the main roadway available for the precise study of family process. It has always been obvious to many scientists that observational research can enhance the study of marriages by adding a depth and richness to other, less expensive methods, such as surveys and questionnaires. In the decade of the 1990s, however, it also has become clear that observational methods can add predictive power and theoretical clarity. These important accomplishments stem, in part, from the power of observational data to reveal a replicable portrait of complex social interaction that lies beyond the natural awareness of even the most keenly sensitive spouse or partner, and thus lies beyond assessment with self-report instruments.

Many of these advances also have been enabled by significant technological breakthroughs in observational research that occurred in this past decade. With the arrival of inexpensive computer-assisted coding, live real-time observational coding, or the rapid coding of videotapes synchronized to computer-readable video, time codes became feasible. An observer can now code complex interaction between husbands and wives in real time and later compute onsets, offsets, and durations of speaker/listener events, compute interobserver reliability, and also perform sequential and time-series analyses that require knowledge of exactly when the events occurred. The merging of video and computer technology also has made it possible to time-synchronize the real-time acquisition of physiological and observational data from an interacting couple, and the use of video playback methods made it possible to time-synchronize spouses' perceptions and cognitions of the interaction. Thus, technology has made it possible to study, with time-synchronized data, the dynamic interplay between behavior, cognition, and physiology. Researchers discovered that the isolated study of behavior, cognition, or physiology without careful study of their interdependencies would severely limit mapping findings onto the real interactional world of the couples we were studying. The technical breakthroughs of the 1990's have narrowed the gap between couples' natural experience of their relationship and researchers' precise understanding of study participants.

Advances in understanding marriage stem not only from breakthroughs in technology, but also from innovations in the methodologies used to extract information from the ongoing flow of interaction. Floyd (1989) reviewed research on the choice of coding units of different sizes and complexities. More and more interest was paid to developing global coding systems to capture targeted interactional processes. Basco, Birchler, Kalal, Talbott, and Slater (1991) developed and validated a rapid rating scale called the Clinician Rating of Adult Communication (CRAC). Bèlanger, Sauborin, Laughrea, Dulude, and Wright (1993) compared macroscopic global coding systems (Marital Interaction Coding System-Global and the Global Couple Interaction Coding System) and decided that the convergence was moderate and that it was premature to conclude that these macroscopic coding systems are interchangeable. Julien, Markman, and Lindahl (1989) presented a new global coding system and correlated it to the positive and negative codes of a more microanalytic Couples Interaction Scoring System (CISS). Although negative codes between the two systems showed some convergence, the positive codes did not. Couples high in marital satisfaction reported higher mutuality, whereas couples lower in marital satisfaction reported higher levels of destructive process, coercion, and postconflict distress. Wampler and Halverson (1990) developed a Q-sort observational measure of marital interaction, and they related it to their measures derived from the CISS (Notarius, Markman, & Gottman, 1983).

A more powerful method of creating global categories from more microanalytic categories was a factor analysis reported by Heyman, Eddy, Weiss, and Vivian (1995) using 995 couples' videotaped conflict interactions using the Marital Interaction Coding System (MICS). The factors formed were hostility, constructive problem discussion, humor, and responsibility discussion. It is interesting that these super-categories are quite different from earlier suggestions for a global MICS system made by Weiss and Tolman (1990). An alternative approach to global coding was the work represented by the Gottman and Levenson laboratories in which detailed microanalytic coding with multiple coding systems was undertaken (e.g., Gottman, 1994). This included the coding of facial expressions (the Emotion Facial Action Coding System, Ekman & Friesen, 1978), MICS coding, the development of a more rapid version of the CISS (RCISS, Krokoff, Gottman, & Hass, 1989), and a Specific Affect Coding System (Gottman, McCoy, Coan, & Collier, 1996) that codes macrolevels of emotional expression (e.g., anger, sadness, fear). This work has led to reliable microanalytic real-time observational coding of marital interaction in both conflict and nonconflict contexts. One advantage of coding specific affects is greater precision in studying positive affect. Gottman, Coan, Carrere, and Swanson (1998) found that positive affect was the only predictor of both stability and happiness in a sample of newlyweds. Finally, a more macro look across time at marital interaction was offered in a review by Christensen & Pasch (1993). They broke down marital conflict into seven stages, beginning with the precipitating event and evolving through the fight and then a return to normal.

The decade of the 1990s also saw the more widespread application of sequential analytic methods for the quantitative study of patterns of interaction between two people over time, the use of time-series analyses, and the mathematical modeling of marital interaction. In two landmark papers published in 1993, Griffin (1993a, 1993b) demonstrated an innovative approach for how event history analysis could be applied to the study of insider evaluations of marital interaction. The first paper described the methodology, and the second paper applied it in a study of marital interaction. Couples had two conversations, one about pleasant memories and one about a problem, and then they engaged in a video recall of affect procedure. The self-rating of affect during the video recall were the data for the analyses. The dependent measure was time until there was a transition out of negative affect. Griffin reported that, consistent with the Gottman and Levenson (1986, 1988) hypothesis, wives maintained a negative affect state longer than husbands did, particularly on the problem task.

Griffin and Greene (1994) reported the results of analyzing one case of orofacial bradykinesia exacerbated during marital conflict. They used an interrupted time-series analysis to demonstrate that an increase of the symptoms followed a series of specific negative comments by the spouse in the conversation. Gottman et al. (1998) applied interrupted time-series analyses to their newlywed heart rate data to assess the extent to which a number of marital affective behaviors were either self-soothing or spouse-soothing; in a second step, they then used these data to predict marital outcomes 6 years later. As predicted by Gottman and Levenson (1988), only soothing of the male spouse (primarily self-soothing) predicted positive marital outcomes.

We will focus the remainder of our review on what we see as the two primary advances made in the study of marital interaction in the decade. First, we will examine how researchers have taken the fruits of cross-sectional, hypothesis-generating descriptive research and tested models for predicting the longitudinal course of relationships over time. These prospective studies were a major advance occurring in the decade, and their results demonstrate the maturation of the discipline. Second, we examine the empirical developments in several core content areas: (a) the study of power, (b) the exploration of marital interaction as a proximal determinant of individual well-being and distress, and (b) the study of interrelationships among interactional behavior, perception, and physiology. We will end with a commentary of the decade of research and a discussion of future research for the next decade.

THE STUDY OF COUPLES OVER TIME

Developmental Transitions

The family life cycle has been used to describe the natural history of couples over time. It is intuitively appealing to suppose that the interactional patterns characterizing young couples versus older couples, or young parents versus older parents, for example, are stamped with unique qualities that determine if the couple is adaptively passing through important and challenging family life-cycle transitions or not. Colloquially, couples expect the marriage to be different "once the honeymoon is over," and empirically, we know that parents on the average experience a significant decline in satisfaction after the birth of the first child.

Divorce prediction. Basic descriptive research during the 1980's paved the way in the 1990s for interactional research that can track the longitudinal course of marriages and can predict divorce. For a review of methodological issues, see Bradbury and Karney (1993). Gottman and Krokoff (1989) reported that a different pattern of interaction was related to concurrent marital satisfaction than to the change in marital satisfaction over time; for example, disagreement and anger were related to lower concurrent marital satisfaction, but to improvement in marital satisfaction over time. Buehlman, Gottman, and Katz (1992) reported that, in a sample of families with preschool-aged children, their coding of an Oral History Interview was able to predict divorce or stability over a 3-year period with 94% accuracy using a discriminant function analysis. The oral history variables were also correlated in clear ways with Time 1 marital interaction in both problem solving and affect, the couple's physiological reactivity during marital interaction, as well as Time 1 and Time 2 marital satisfaction. Gottman and Levenson (1992) reported the first prospective longitudinal study of divorce prediction that used observational data. They found that a couple's interaction and spouse's physiological responses observed at Time 1 were associated with a set of variables forming a cascade toward divorce. Couples starting on this cascade toward divorce at Time 1 had interactions that were marked by more negativity than positivity, and they rated their interactions more negatively upon video recall. Wives in these couples also had significantly higher heart rates and smaller finger pulse amplitudes (which could be part of a general alarm response in which blood is drawn into the trunk from the periphery). Subsequent work on the divorce prediction question with another sample of couples (Gottman, 1993, 1994) identified the ratio of positivity to negativity during the conflict discussion, and four specific negative interaction patterns (criticism, defensiveness, contempt, and stonewalling) as highly predictive of divorce (see also Gottman et al., 1998; Matthews, Wickrama, & Conger, 1996).

Transition to marriage. Smith, Vivian, and O'Leary (1990) studied premarital problem-solving discussions and predicted marital satisfaction at 18 months and 30 months after marriage. The negativity of the premarital interaction correlated with concurrent marital unhappiness but was not predictive of postmarital satisfaction. Controlling for premarital relationship satisfaction, affective disengagement during a premarital problem-solving discussion was negatively associated with marital satisfaction at 18 months and 30 months after marriage. Cohan and Bradbury (1997) examined the longitudinal course of marital satisfaction and depressive symptoms in newlywed marriages over an 18-month period. Problem-solving behavior mediated but did not moderate the relationship between life events and adjustment. In particular, angry wives had better adjustment to major and interpersonal events so that their depressive symptoms were reduced and their marital satisfaction increased.

Gottman et al. (1998) reported the results of a multimethod longitudinal study predicting the eventual 6-year marital happiness and stability from newlywed interactions observed in the first months after the wedding. Seven types of process models were explored: (a) anger as a dangerous emotion, (b) active listening, (c) negative affect reciprocity, (d) negative startup by the wife, (e) de-escalation, (f) positive affect models, and (g) physiological soothing of the male spouse. Support was not found for the models of anger as a dangerous emotion, active listening, or negative affect reciprocity in kind, either low or high intensity. Support was found for models of the husband's rejecting his wife's influence, negative startup by the wife, a lack of de-escalation of low-intensity negative wife affect by the husband, or a lack of de-escalation of high-intensity husband negative affect by the wife, and a lack of physiological soothing of the male spouse, all predicting divorce. Support was also found for a contingent positive affect model and for balance models (i.e., ratio models) of positive-to-negative affect predicting satisfaction among stable couples.

Transition to parenthood. In the past decade, four landmark books were published that summarized key longitudinal research projects on the transition to parenthood (Lewis, 1989; Michaels & Goldberg, 1988; Cowan & Cowan, 1992; Belsky & Kelly, 1994). There have been approximately 15 longitudinal studies on the transition to parenthood; many of the others were not prospective, longitudinal studies. The longitudinal findings are remarkably consistent. Most have concluded that for the overwhelming majority of couples this transition can be both extremely stressful and pleasurable. For approximately 40 to 70% of couples, there is a drop in marital quality. In general, marital conflict increases by a factor of 9, people are at risk for depression, there is a precipitous

drop in marital quality within 1 year after the birth of the first child, people revert to stereotypic gender roles, they are overwhelmed by the amount of housework and child care there is to do, fathers withdraw into work, and marital conversation and sex decrease enormously. There is also an increase in joy and pleasure with the baby. The longitudinal studies have all discovered the strong linkages between the prebirth marital system (particularly highlighting the couple's conflict resolution skills, and a sense of "we-ness"), the parent-child system, and the baby's subsequent emotional/social and cognitive development. Belsky and Kelly's study is a rich source of information in understanding the transition. The Cowans' study is the only controlled preventive marital intervention study in the field, and they demonstrated a powerful intervention effect (of 24 hours of group supportive therapy during pregnancy) in reducing the drop in marital satisfaction, preventing divorce, and improving parenting quality. By the time the child reaches age 5, however, there were no differences between the experimental and control groups; it is still a mystery as to what happened to create relapse in the experimental group between years 3½ and 5. Lewis' (1989) landmark work defines very specific prebirth marital "competencies" that provide links to child developmental outcomes through parenting.

Couples at midlife and beyond. Overwhelmingly, the existing observational research on marriage has studied relatively young couples. The data that do exist on older marriages have been limited to self-report data, derived primarily from questionnaires and interviews (Erikson, Erikson, & Kivnick, 1989; Parron, 1982; Sinnett, Carter, & Montgomery, 1972; Guilford & Bengtson, 1979) with some exceptions (Illig, 1977; Zietlow and Sillars; 1988). In the 1990s, this state of affairs began to be remedied. Using an observational system for coding emotional behavior, Carstensen, Gottman, and Levenson (1995) studied the interactions of a representative sample of couples in their 40s or 60s as they attempted to resolve marital conflicts. With respect to negative emotions, the interactions of older couples were clearly less emotional than those of middle-aged couples. Older couples showed less anger, disgust, belligerence, and whining than did middle-aged couples. With respect to the more positive emotions, however, the evidence was mixed. Middle-aged couples expressed more interest and more humor, but older couples expressed more affection. Importantly, these findings of lesser negative emotion and greater affection in older couples when discussing marital problems still held when the authors controlled for differences in the severity of the problems being discussed. The reports of the couples themselves were consistent with their behavioral coding. When they showed spouses the videotapes of their interactions and had them rate how they were feeling from moment to moment during the interaction, older couples indicated feeling more emotionally positive than middle-aged couples (Levenson, Carstensen, & Gottman, 1994).

THE CORE CONTENT AREAS

The Study of Power

It is fortuitous that in 1993 the late Calfred Broderick, originator of the decade review paper series in this journal, published an important book titled *Understanding Family Process*. Broderick organized family process literature, which he called "relational space," into three major areas, the *regulation* of interpersonal distance, the *regulation* of transactions, and the *regulation* of "vertical space," by which he meant power. The idea of "regulation" implied a homeostatic set point theory. In a therapy context, these three areas were respectively discussed as positivity/caring, responsiveness, and status/influence (Gottman, Notarius, Gonso, & Markman, 1976). We will briefly discuss these three areas. Historically, the regulation of interpersonal distance was first explored by examining the clarity of communication. Hypotheses were advanced to explore the role of unclear communication in dysfunctional families and family distress. More specific hypotheses were advanced that unclear communication was responsible for psychopathology (e.g., Bateson, Jackson, Haley, & Weakland, 1956; Watzlawick, Beavin, & Jackson, 1967), and the cybernetic model or the systems approach to family process was born. However, subsequent research over three decades has shown that the regulation of interpersonal distance is all about affect, not about communication clarity (e.g., Gottman, 1993). The regulation of transactions (e.g., signals of switches in speaking turns) has been studied with strangers (e.g., Duncan & Fiske, 1977; Jaffe & Feldstein, 1970) and has yet to be applied to the study of marital interaction.

The regulation of vertical space, that is, the study of power has been much more elusive. It was an area of important activity in the 1990s,

particularly as the study of physically abusive marriages became a major focus of research attention. The empirical fabric of power always appears to disintegrate on closer examination. Broderick (1993) wrote:

> Literally hundreds of studies have been done on family power, who wields it and at whose expense. The matter has turned out to be complicated and elusive. As a result, the scholarly literature on power is voluminous, complex, and often contradictory (see Szinovacz, 1987). The great majority of these studies are based on questionnaires that ask the respondent to report on who wins the most contested decisions in his or her family. (p. 164)

Questionnaires filled out by independent observers do not correlate well, nor are different measures well correlated (see Gray-Little & Burks, 1983); nor have patterns of domination proven stable over time (see Babcock, Waltz, Jacobson, & Gottman 1993). An older paper by Gray-Little (1982) is noteworthy because it combined the observational assessment of talk time during a 6-minute marital conflict discussion and power during a marital game (the SIMFAM game, Straus & Tallman, 1971). Results were complex but included the result that balance in husband-wife power was related to marital quality; however, self-report and observational measures did not show a high level of agreement in classifying couples. The issues of blending the study of affect and power are central to the integration of psychological and sociological approaches to marriage. As we will note, the issue of how to conceptualize and study power may become clarified either through the use of more precise observational measures or the use of more precise data analytic techniques using data from two people that unfolds over time.

Power studied with more precise observations. An example of this approach to clarifying power is a recent study by Gray-Little, Baucom, and Hamby (1996). They assessed power more precisely, using a coding of the couple's influence patterns during a discussion of the Inventory of Marital Conflicts (Olson & Ryder, 1970). They found that egalitarian couples had the highest Time 1 marital satisfaction and fewer negative MICS behaviors (Weiss, Hops, & Patterson, 1973); also, wife-dominant couples improved the most in a 12-week marital therapy study.

Power explored in the context of gender and re-

lational hierarchy. Feminist writers have pointed to the central role that power must play in understanding marriages. Quantitative observational research has now begun to explore these ideas. Women typically start most of the marital conflict discussions in laboratories that use observational methods (Ball, Cowan, & Cowan, 1995; Oggins, Veroff, & Leber, 1993). The degree of negative affect and the amount of criticism with which a conflict discussion starts are also critical in determining its outcome. In one study, for example, the way a marital conflict interaction began determined its subsequent course 96% of the time (Gottman, 1994; Gottman et al., 1998, p. 7). White (1989), in a sequential analysis using the Raush, Barry, Hertl, and Swain (1974) coding system, found evidence for the contention that men display a more coercive style in resolving marital conflict, whereas women display a more affiliative style. Ball et al. reported that couples perceived the wife to be more important than the husband in the mobilization phase of problem talk, which involved raising the issues, planning on how to solve them, being active and taking control by silence and nonresponse. Husbands and wives both viewed this phase as the most stressful aspect of marital problem solving. Men were perceived as more influential in determining the content and emotional depth of later phases of the discussion. Women viewed their power in the early phases as illusory: "their behavior was shaped primarily by the effort to choose strategies that would avoid upsetting their husbands. " (Ball et al., p. 303).

Coan, Gottman, Babcock, and Jacobson (1997) used sequential analysis to investigate the propensity of two types of physically violent men to reject influence from their wives during a marital conflict discussion. The sequence of escalation of the negativity (from complaining to hostility, for example) was used to operationalize the sequence of rejecting influence. As hypothesized, abusive husbands whose heart rates decreased from baseline to the marital conflict discussion (labeled as Type I abusers in the study), rejected any influence from their wives. These men were also generally violent outside the marriage and were more likely to have used a knife or gun to threaten their wives than abusive husbands whose heart rates accelerated from baseline to the conflict discussion (label as Type II abusers in the study). These analyses were repeated for a representative sample of nonviolent newlywed couples in the first few months of marriage, and the escalation sequence of men rejecting influence from their wives pre-

dicted subsequent divorce (Gottman et al., 1998). The sequence of women rejecting influence from their husbands did not predict divorce. This study was the first time that negative affect reciprocity was broken down into responding negatively *in kind* (e.g., anger is met with anger) or *escalation* (e.g., anger is met with contempt). Negative reciprocity in kind was characteristic of all marriages; only the escalation sequence was characteristic of marriages that were later to end in divorce. These findings reconceptualize negative affect reciprocity as the rejection of influence.

Power studied with the mathematical modeling of marital interaction. Power, according to Broderick (1993), "may be most simply defined as the ability to win contested decisions" (p. 164). An alternative definition has emerged in the 1990s, however, using mathematical modeling of marital interaction. This alternative definition defines power quantitatively as the ability of one partner's affect to influence the other's affect. In this modeling (Cook et al., 1995; Gottman, Swanson, & Murray, in press), two influence functions are computed across the affective range of a conversation, one for the husband's influence on the wife, and one for the wife's influence on the husband. This approach to modeling is based on writing down two interlocking nonlinear difference equations for husband and wife, with influence functions computed after controlling for autocorrelation. The method has a venerable history in the marital field. Long ago, Anatol Rapoport (1960, 1972) suggested that two linear differential equations for husband and wife interaction could describe a marital system as escalating out of control or being self-regulated. He never operationalized these variables or applied them to real data; in addition, his equations were linear, and unfortunately, linear equations are usually unstable. Nonetheless, Cook et al., applying the new mathematics of nonlinear dynamic modeling (e.g., Murray, 1989), showed that depending on the shape of the influence functions, couples can have several stable steady states or "attractors," that are self-regulating, homeostatic set points for the marital system. A homeostatic attractor is a point in husband-wife phase space toward which the interaction is repeatedly drawn, and if the system is perturbed, it will move back to the attractor. These influence functions describe the impact of one person's affect on the partner's subsequent affect. This determination is made across the range of affects in the husband-wife dialogue. The influence functions make the study of power more detailed and specific. Power may be specific to particular affects. Asymmetries in influence reflect a power imbalance, and they reported that these asymmetries were predictive of divorce.

Power and marital typologies. An important research monograph was published by Fitzpatrick (1988) in which she presented the results of a series of studies that combined observational data on marital interaction with questionnaire data. She presented a typology of marriage from her analyses of ideology, communication, interdependence, and power dynamics in the marriage. Her work was another example of the integration of the study of power with marital interaction. In a monograph on what marital processes predict divorce, Gottman (1994) also presented a marital typology with three types, looking at interaction and influence, and his types appear to be similar to those of Fitzpatrick. On a conflict task Gottman's types were validating couples, who are high on conflict but wait a while in the discussion and ask questions before engaging in persuasion attempts; volatile couples, who are high in conflict and engage in persuasion attempts immediately; and, Conflict Avoiding couples, who are low in conflict and do not engage in persuasion attempts at all. All three types were equally likely to have stable marriages, but Cook et al. (1995) discovered that mismatches in influence functions between Gottman's types predicted divorce. Noller & Hiscock (1989) replicated most of Fitzpatrick's typology, except for a lack of effect of ideology on traditionalism. Johnson, Huston, Gaines, & Levinger (1992), however, developed a typology (using diary data of work and leisure) and found a very different typology with four major types: symmetrical, parallel, differentiated companionate, and role reversed. The question remains as to what fundamental mismatches in typology are dysfunctional.

Vanlear & Zietlow (1990) related Fitzpatrick's couple typology, marital satisfaction, and relational control. "Relational control" attempts to capture the sequential communication of power or status between spouses (e.g., from assertion to dominance, from collaborative deference to submission). Across couple types, marital satisfaction was associated with interactions confirming equality between partners (i.e., there was an absence of putting self or partner up or down). More important, the study revealed an interaction effect between couple type and relational control on mar-

ital satisfaction. This finding, along with those of Fitzpatrick and Gottman, further encourages researchers to challenge a uniformity assumption holding that all distressed and nondistressed couples are alike in their reactions to specific interactional behaviors.

Marital Interaction as Proximal Determinants of Family and Individual Well-Being

Historically, an important revolution took place in the study of family processes when interactional hypotheses were advanced to explain how specific family interactions were related to and perhaps responsible for an individual family member's psychopathology (e.g., Bateson, Jackson, Haley, & Weakland, 1956; Watzlawick, Beavin, & Jackson, 1968). This marked the beginning of a major conceptual shift away from individual personality as the primary determinant of personal well-being and distress and toward social interaction with significant others as among the most significant determinant of physical and psychological well-being. We will examine the evidence to emerge in the 1990s that represents the next evolution in this 30-year-old revolution.

Health and longevity. An outstanding review by Burman and Margolin (1992) crystallized ongoing work that the psychosocial quality of marriages is linked to mortality and morbidity. In searching for a mechanism for these linkages, they decided that the effect is indirect and nonspecific. Previous research has identified strong links between marital quality and health (e.g., c.f., Burman & Margolin, 1992), and between being married and better health and longevity (e.g., Berkman & Syme, 1979; Berkman & Breslow, 1983). Research now indicates that marital distress is associated with suppressed immune function (e.g., Kiecolt-Glaser et al., 1987; Kiecolt-Glaser, Malarky, Cacioppo, & Glaser, 1994), cardiovascular arousal (e.g., Brown & Smith, 1992; Ewart, Burnett, & Taylor, 1983; Ewart, Taylor, Kraemer, & Agras, 1991; Gottman, 1994; Gottman & Levenson, 1992; Levenson & Gottman, 1983, 1985), and increases in stress-related hormones such as catecholamines and corticosteroids (e.g., Kiecolt-Glaser et al.,1994). There is extensive literature that indicates, that for men, marriage offers health-buffering effects (e.g., Berkman & Syme; Berkman & Breslow; Bernard, 1982; Burman & Margolin, 1992; Shumaker & Hill, 1991) and that women are more likely to experience health-related problems if the marriage is distressed (Kiecolt-Glaser et al.; Gaelick, Bodenhausen, & Wyer, 1985; Ewart et al., 1991; Huston & Ashmore, 1986).

In the 1990s, researchers also broadened the search for associations between marital interaction and specific disorders. Many of these studies are somewhat weak in methodology but nevertheless point the way toward the benefits of more refined study.

Child outcomes. The decade of the 1990s has been rich in discovering linkages across interacting subsystems within the family, and to the child's peer relations as well. The mediating variable in many of these investigations is the concept of emotional regulation of arousal in children, variously defined. Marital conflict, distress, and dissolution are linked to problematic childhood outcomes including depression, withdrawal, poor social competence, deleterious health outcomes, lower academic achievement, and conduct-related incidents (Cowan & Cowan, 1987, 1992; Easterbrooks, 1987; Emery & O'Leary, 1982; Forehand, Brody, Long, Slotkin & Fauber, 1986; Gottman & Katz, 1989; Hetherington, Cox, & Cox, 1978; Katz & Gottman, 1991; Peterson & Zill, 1986; Porter & O'Leary, 1980; Rutter, 1971; Whitehead, 1979). For example, Cummings and colleagues found that children exposed to angry interadult conflict tend to use negative behavior such as physical aggression to cope (Cummings, Zahn-Waxler, & Radke-Yarrow, 1984). El-Sheikh (1994) found that preschool children from highly conflictual marriages displayed behavioral distress and heart rate reactivity when shown tapes of angry adult interactions. Brody, Arias, & Fincham (1996) reported a link between conflict-promoting marital attributions (e.g., seeing one's partner as selfish) and ineffective parent-child communication and to the child's attributions for negative parental behavior. Davies, Myers, and Cummings (1996) showed videotaped segments of adults engaged in brief verbal conflicts, with various endings to two groups of children, 7- to 9-year-olds and 13- to 15-year-olds. They reported that emotionally harmonious endings were crucial in creating a sense of emotional security in both groups of children, regardless of whether the adults' conflicts were about adult or child issues. Explicit verbal resolution was unnecessary. Across both age groups, female children reported more fear whereas male children offered more task-oriented interventions. See also Davies and Cummings

(1994) for an attachment-based theory of emotional regulation.

Margolin, Christensen, and John (1996), in a sequential analysis, reported that distressed couples showed greater continuance of tensions and more spillover, particularly from marital to parent-child interaction. Nonetheless, there may at times be an inverse relationship between marital conflict and parent-child interaction. Mahoney, Boggio and Jouriles (1996) found that mothers were more empathic toward their 4- to 10-year-old, clinic-referred sons after an episode of marital conflict.

Gottman, Katz, and Hooven (1996) reported the results of a longitudinal study in which there were clear linkages between observed marital, parent-child, and child-peer interaction when the child was 4 years old. Furthermore, these linkages were mediated by the child's ability to regulate physiological arousal during parent-child interaction. These linkages predicted a range of longitudinal child outcomes, including child peer relations at age 8. The central concept of this research was "meta-emotion," which refers to the feelings and cognitions that parents had about their own and their children's anger and sadness. Katz and Gottman (1993) found that two distinct and uncorrelated patterns of marital interaction were related to distinct child outcomes. A mutually hostile pattern (which predicted marital dissolution) correlated with child externalizing behavior, whereas a husband angry and withdrawn pattern correlated with child internalizing disorders. Katz and Gottman (1997) reported that variables that index a "coaching" meta-emotion philosophy buffer children from almost all the deleterious consequences associated with marital conflict and dissolution. Coaching parents are aware of their child's emotion, they listen empathetically to the child's feelings, they help the child find words to express the emotion, and then they explore and implement strategies to deal with the emotion. There was a physiological substrate to this buffering effect. Katz and Gottman (1995) found that a central child physiological dimension, called "vagal tone," protected children from marital conflict. Broadly, vagal tone is related to the ability of the parasympathetic branch of the autonomic nervous system to calm the child down. The concept has become central theoretically for many researchers in organizing the bases for the infant's emotional and social development (e.g., Fox, 1994; Garber & Dodge, 1991; Thompson, 1994). For a review on the heritability of vagal tone and other autonomic indices, see Healy (1992).

Rogers and Holmbeck (1997) reported that more frequent and intense interparental aggression was associated with greater adjustment problems for children. They identified cognitive appraisal strategies that were maladaptive for the children and also noted that peer social support could buffer the negative effects of marital conflict.

Once again, after a hiatus of many years, links were again being made in the 1990's between the marital relationship and child sibling relationships. For example, among children aged approximately 4 to 9 years, Erel, Margolin, and John (1998) reported linkages between the wives' negative reports of the marital relationship, the mother-child relationship, and the older siblings' observed negative interaction. The younger siblings' negative interaction was linked with the mother-child and the differential mother-child interaction (across siblings). No such relationship was found for siblings' positive interactions.

Adolescent adjustment was also studied in the context of couples undergoing the transition to remarriage (Hetherington & Clingempeel, 1992). There were three groups of families: stepfamilies with a divorced custodial mother who was in the first months of a remarriage, families with a divorced custodial mother who had not remarried, and nondivorced families. Authoritative parenting was associated with positive adjustment of children in all family groups, but children in nondivorced families were more competent and had fewer behavior problems than children in divorced or remarried families. Nondivorced and remarried couples looked similar on the observational measures. There was remarkable stability in marital interaction over time; however, Deal, Hagan, and Anderson (1992) noted that the new stepfather is in a tenuous position in his new family, and "It may thus be that the primary difference between first marriages and remarriages lies not in the quality of the marital relationship but in the relative importance of the marital relationship within the whole family system" (p. 93).

Common comorbidities. Research in the past decade firmly established that marital interaction is also strongly associated with a broad range of outcomes for family members. Although the direction of cause and effect between marital interaction and spousal or child well-being is often unclear, the strength and importance of these relations documented in the 1990s will surely be pursued in the next decade.

1. Depression. Schmaling, Whisman, Fruzzetti, and Truax (1991) assessed the marital interaction behaviors associated with wives' depression. They found that active summarization by the wife was associated with fewer depressive symptoms and the absence of a diagnosis of major depression. Johnson and Jacob (1997) examined the marital interactions of control couples and couples in which either the wife or the husband was clinically depressed. Depressed couples were more negative than were nondepressed couples, and couples with a depressed wife were more negative than were couples with a depressed husband. McCabe and Gotlib (1993), in a study of depressed and nondepressed couples, reported that depressed wives became increasingly more negative in their verbal behavior over the course of the interaction, and they perceived the interactions as more hostile. After breaking the interaction into thirds, they found that only depressed couples were fairly immediately reactive to their spouse's behavior in the interaction.

Biglan et al. (1985) discovered an interesting set of interactions using sequential analysis, which led to an exciting flurry of theoretically based research. They examined the potential "function" of depressed and aggressive behavior in depression, using sequential analyses. They compared distressed and nondistressed couples, both of which included a depressed wife, with community control subjects. The findings suggested that the marital system might be covertly maintaining depressive symptoms and thereby suggesting the direction of the causal relationship between interaction and individual outcomes.

Biglan et al.'s study was criticized because they had difficulty obtaining nondepressed distressed couples. Schmaling and Jacobson (1990) conducted the full design, crossing high or low marital distress with high or low depression. They did not find interactional patterns that were unique to depression, but that these marital patterns were due to marital distress rather than depression. Similarly, Nelson and Beach (1990) found that the suppression of aggressive behavior was an artifact of the number of months the couples had been discordant. Interestingly, these means were long, 65.0 months for the nondepressed discordant and 94.5 months for the depressed discordant couples. Greater suppression of aggressive behavior was associated with shorter durations of discord within both groups of couples.

2. Violence. This decade saw a huge increase in observational research applied to the study of violent marriages. Burman and Margolin (1993) used sequential analysis to compare the reenactments of physically aggressive, verbally aggressive, withdrawing, and nondistressed low-conflict couples. Physically aggressive couples were characterized by reciprocity of hostile affect and by rigid, highly contingent behavior patterns that were stronger and longer lasting than those of other couples. Nondistressed couples also reciprocated hostility but were able to exit these negative interaction cycles quickly. These sequential results were also obtained by Cordova, Jacobson, Gottman, Rushe, and Cox (1993) for actual marital conflicts in the laboratory rather than reenactments of conflicts at home. These investigators designed elaborate procedures to guarantee the safety of the abused women following actual marital conflicts in the laboratory. The data suggest that violent couples are missing an exit or withdrawal ritual from either reciprocated or escalating hostility.

Gottman, Jacobson, Rushe, and Shortt (1995) reported a typology of batterers based on heart rate reactivity. Two types of batterers were identified: Type 1 men, who lowered their heart rates from baseline to a marital conflict interaction, and Type 2 men, who raised it. Compared with Type 2 men, Type 1 men were more violent outside the marriage (to strangers, coworkers, friends, and bosses), were higher on antisocial and sadistic aggression personality scores, lower on dependency, and were more verbally aggressive toward their wives during marital conflict; wives responded to these men with anger, sadness, and defensiveness. Type 1 men were more likely to threaten their wives using a knife or gun, but both types had inflicted as much actual physical damage (see Jacobson & Gottman, 1998, for more detail). In a subsequent paper on divorce prediction, Jacobson, Gottman, Gortner, Berns, and Shortt (1997) reported among their batterers there was a high divorce/separation rate of 38% and that husband dominance and the wife's reports of his emotional abuse predicted the divorce. During the Time 1 marital interaction, more husband's contempt, less husband humor, less husband neutral affect, more wife defensiveness, and less wife humor predicted divorce. Physiological reactivity variables in both husbands and wives at Time 1 also predicted divorce.

As noted above, the research on violence in marriages has focused attention on the power aspects of marriage. In an unpublished dissertation, Rushe analyzed marital transactions in terms of power and control strategies and concluded that the violent marriage is basically engaged in a power struggle, which is reminiscent of the analyses carried out by Coan et al. (1997) on violent men rejecting influence from women. This notion of violence as a form of power struggle is distinctly different from the emphasis on anger management for batterers in the therapy literature. The power dimension of violence suggests a systematic use of violence to intimidate and control the abused wife, instead of periodic uncontrolled outbursts (see Jacobson & Gottman, 1998). Babcock et al. (1993) reported that violent couples were more likely than nonviolent distressed and happily married couples to engage in the husband demand–wife withdraw pattern. Also, within the domestically violent group, husbands who had less power were more physically abusive toward their wives. Power was measured by communication skill using a structured interview about previous arguments, and marital power outcomes was measured with the Who Does What scale (Cowan, Cowan, Coie, & Coie, 1978).

Positive affect and social support in violent couples have been studied by Holtzworth-Munroe, Stuart, Sandin, Smutzler, and McLaughlin (1997). They found that compared with nonviolent men, violent husbands in the Bradbury social support task (Bradbury & Pasch, 1994) offered less social support than nonviolent husbands. Instead, they were more belligerent/domineering, more contemptuous/disgusted, showed more anger and tension, and were more upset by the wife's problem.

3. Chronic Physical Pain. Romano et al. (1991) developed a methodology for the behavioral observations of chronic pain patients and their spouses. Pain and control groups could be discriminated with ratings of overt verbal and nonverbal pain-related behaviors. Spouses of pain patients showed more solicitous behavior than control spouses. Turk, Kerns, and Rosenberg (1992), however, reviewed evidence that suggested the complexity of the problem: positive attention from spouses to displays of pain were associated with reports of more intense pain, higher observed pain frequency, and greater disability; but, negative spouse responding to pain was associated with increased affective distress.

4. Hostility and Type-A Personality. Harralson, Suarez, and Lawler (1997) studied cardiovascular reactivity in hostile men and women (using the Cook-Medley Hostility scale, Cook & Medley, 1954) and the suppression of anger. Medalie and Goldbourt (1976) in a 5-year prospective study of marital quality and health, found that a wife's love and support was associated with a reduced risk for the development of angina pectoris in husbands. Sanders, Smith, and Alexander (1991) reported a relationship between marital hostile/dominant behavior and Type A or Type B personality pattern in both husbands and wives. Brown and Smith (1992) found a strong relationship between hostility during marital interaction and heart rate reactivity.

5. *Alcohol Abuse.* Jacob and Krahn (1987) used three analytic methods to cluster the marital interactions of 96 couples (with the MICS) in which the husband was either alcoholic, clinically depressed, or a normal control. Cluster analysis revealed that there were three salient dimensions of the behaviors, negative evaluation, problem solving, and positive evaluation. Jacob and Leonard (1992) performed a highly detailed sequential analysis of these marital interactions. They found that couples with a depressed husband were different from the normal controls and couples with an alcoholic husband; couples with an alcoholic husband and normal controls were characterized by similar interaction patterns. Negative reciprocity was lower among the couples with depressed husbands, and husbands were less likely to follow their wives' problem solving with problem solving of their own.

6. *Drug Abuse.* Fals-Stewart and Birchler (1998) used their macro-CRAC coding system to study the marital conflict interactions of couples with drug-abusing husbands and a well-selected control group of non–substance abusing but distressed couples. They thus controlled for distress and varied only the active ingredient of drug abuse. No differences were found between couple types on the self-report inventories, but the couples with the substance-abusing husband interacted significantly differently than the distressed non–drug-abusing couples: they showed higher abusiveness, lower problem-solving skills, and more attribution of blame than the distressed non–drug-abusing couples. In addition, they found that the CRAC total score was negatively related to the husband's percentage of days abstinent during the year before entering substance abuse treatment.

Interrelationships Among Interaction Behavior, Cognition, and Physiology

The 1990s witnessed the blending of multiple measurements with observational measures in one investigation, which makes it possible to ask more sophisticated questions at the interfaces of these three domains. Notarius, Benson, Sloane, Vanzetti, and Hornyak (1989) pioneered a methodology for mapping the interface between perception and behavior in their experimental investigation of Weiss's (1980) concepts of positive or negative sentiment override and Gottman, Notarius, Gonso, and Markman's (1976) concept of editing. The concept of sentiment override implies a discrepancy between a spouse's subjective evaluation of partner's behavior and an outside observer's evaluation of the same precise behavior. The valence of any discrepancy between spouse and unbiased observer in evaluating the partner's behavior would define positive or negative sentiment override. "Editing," on the other hand, implies a precise sequence of interaction in which a spouse responds positively (or even neutrally) immediately after accurately perceiving his or her partner's behavior to be negative (i.e., the perception matches an unbiased observer's assessment of the immediate antecedent.) The important point is that these salient interactional processes can only be studied through an examination of the interface between behavior and perception. Applying log-linear modeling to the observational and subjective data, Notarius et al. (1989) found a surprising similarity among nondistressed wives and distressed and nondistressed husbands. The perception of distressed wives was heavily under the influence of negative sentiment override and these wives were least likely to edit out a negative reply to the their husbands' negative interactions. In contrast, nondistressed wives and distressed and nondistressed husbands were more likely to subjectively evaluate their partner's negative messages as neutral or positive and even when they made a negative evaluation, and they were less likely to respond negatively.

Bradbury and Fincham (1992) reported the results of two studies. In study 1 maladaptive attributions were related to less effective problem solving behaviors (coded globally with rating scales), particularly for wives. In study 2, a more detailed coding system was used combined with lag sequential analysis (Bakeman & Gottman, 1997; Bakeman & Quera, 1996). In this study, maladaptive attributions (controlling for marital satisfaction) were related to the reciprocation of negative partner behavior (hostility or rejection of partner's views). Attributions and behavior were most strongly related for distressed wives. Miller and Bradbury (1995) found that maladaptive attributions were related to hindering problem resolution on two tasks, a problem-solving and a social-support discussion. Attributions and behavior were more strongly related for wives than husbands and for distressed than for nondistressed spouses, again showing that cognitive factors function to impair interaction.

Vanzetti, Notarius, and NeeSmith (1992) studied specific and generalized expectancies that couples had for the outcomes of marital conflict interactions. Distressed couples expected fewer positive and more negative behaviors. Couples high on relational efficacy chose relationship-enhancing attributions more often that low-efficacy couples. Halford and Sanders (1990) used a video recall procedure to assess cognition of each partner during both a problem discussion and a relaxed discussion. Both domains discriminated distressed from nondistressed couples, and negative behavior in the interaction could be predicted better by accounting for both past cognition and behavior than by relying on past behavior alone. Thomas, Fletcher, and Lange (1997), using a thought stream video recall method pioneered by Ickes (e.g., Ickes, Stinson, Bissonnette, & Garcia, 1990), in a study of empathic accuracy, had couples review their own videotapes and describe their own and their partner's "on-line" thoughts and feelings. Partners' assumed similarity was related to marital satisfaction and the positivity of the verbal interaction. Mendolia, Beach, and Tesser (1996) found that the responsiveness to one's partner's self-evaluations was associated with favorable marital interaction during a conflict discussion, whereas responsiveness to one's own self-evaluation was associated with unfavorable marital interaction. These findings may suggest a possible mechanism underlying defensiveness. Fincham, Garnier, Gano-Phillips, and Osborne (1995) developed a new methodology for studying a couple's preinteraction expectations and the "accessibility" of marital satisfaction. To operationalize accessibility, they used two computer tasks and measured response latencies to specific questions about the spouse or the marriage. Response latencies moderated the relationship between satisfaction and expected partner behavior for husbands.

Because there is considerable complexity in studying each separate domain, it is not surprising that work exploring the interrelations that exist between behavior and cognition is not well advanced.

Physiology and Interaction

The use of physiological measures in studies of marital interaction has increased in the decade. Ewart, Taylor, Kraemer, and Agras (1991), in a study of essential hypertension, investigated high blood pressure and marital conflict. They reported that "not being nasty matters more than being nice." This was based on the finding that among women, supportive or neutral messages were unrelated to blood pressure, but hostile interaction and marital dissatisfaction were related. Among men, blood pressure was related only to speech rate. Levenson and Ruef (1992) reported a physiological substrate for empathy. They asked subjects to view a videotaped, 15-minute marital interaction of a couple and to indicate how a particular spouse reported feeling. When the rater's physiological responses matched those of the target spouse being observed, the rater was more accurate predicting the targeted spouse's feelings.

Gottman and Levenson (1992) combined physiological assessment with observational coding of interaction, specific affect, and the subjective evaluation of affect. Using an index based on the aggregate valence of all statements spoken during a speaker turn, two groups of couples were formed. The speaking turns of regulated couples were characterized by a positive slope (i.e., speaker turns were generally characterized by positive affect) over the course of a conversation, whereas the speaking turns of nonregulated couples were characterized by a negative slope (i.e., speaker turns were generally characterized by negative affect) for one or both spouses. Wives in nonregulated interactions showed higher levels of arousal than all other spouses; Gottman and Levenson speculated that this heightened arousal may play in role in the poorer health of wives in distressed marriages. Gottman et al. (1998), using interrupted time-series analysis, found that only husbands' physiological soothing (via self-soothing or through wives' humor) predicted marital stability among newlyweds.

Smith and Brown (1991) related husbands' and wives' MMPI cynical hostility scale scores to two marital interaction conditions, one in which they simply discussed a problem area, and one in which they received rewards for trying to persuade their wives in a win-lose contest. In husbands their cynical hostility scores in the win-lose condition was related to their own increased systolic blood pressure (SBP) and heart rate (HR) reactivity. Husbands' cynical hostility scores also were related to increased systolic blood pressure reactivity in their wives. Wives' cynical hostility scores were unrelated to their own or to their husbands' physiological responses. Brown & Smith (1992) reported that in this win-lose condition, husbands' SBP increases were accompanied by increases in anger and a hostile, coldly assertive style. In wives, this same interactive style occurred, but it was not associated with their own elevated SBP.

PROMISING TRENDS

Extension to Representative and International Samples

There is a need to integrate sociological and psychological methodologies in the future. Psychological studies have relied on samples of convenience that have limited generalizability. A recent exception is Escudero, Rogers, and Gutierrez (1997), who, in a detailed microanalytic investigation also employing sequential analysis, studied marital interaction in Spain. They compared clinic distressed couples with nonclinic nondistressed couples. They used the Rogers relational coding system (Rogers, 1972), which directly codes power transactions, and the CISS for coding affect. They found that clinic couples displayed more domineering, more negative affect, and a stronger association between one-up control and negative affect than was the case for nonclinic couples. Krokoff, Gottman, and Roy (1988) conducted the only random sample study of blue- and white-collar marital interaction known to us. Among their findings, there was more negative affect and negative affect reciprocity for unhappy couples, regardless of occupational status. Zamsky (1997) compared the interactions of distressed and nondistressed, White and African American couples. Replicating interactional findings on more homogeneous groups, Zamsky found large differences between distressed and nondistressed couples, particular for the negative emotionally invalidating behaviors. Surprisingly, communication differences between couples were not attributable to factors of race, socioeconomic status, or any interaction between these variables and marital satisfaction.

Observational study of distressed and nondistressed couples continued in the 1990s to be used in international settings. In studies in Germany, Kaiser, Hahlweg, Fehm-Wolfsdorf, and Groth (1998) showed that a short-term psychoeducational program increased the frequency of self-disclosure, problem solving, acceptance, and nonverbal positive behavior and decreased the frequency of criticism relative to a control group. Hahlweg, Markman, Thurmaier, Engl, and Eckert (1998) showed that many of the changes in communication behaviors following the short-term intervention were maintained through a 3-year follow-up. Gender differences have frequently been observed in studies with U.S. couples (see Baucom, Notarius, Burnett, & Haefner, 1990), particularly concerning wives negativity, and similar differences were observed in the German samples. At the 3-year follow-up, wives in the treatment and control groups were observed to display more nonverbal negative behavior and more self-disclosure compared with their husbands, and wives in the control group displayed more criticism than their husbands.

In a study of distressed and nondistressed Dutch couples, Van Widenfelt (1995) confirmed a pattern of interactional differences that have been replicated in several studies carried out in the United States. She used the Codebook for Marital and Family Interaction (Notarius, Pellegrini, & Martin, 1991) to define interactional behaviors and found nondistressed couples to display significantly more statements to facilitate problem solving, to emotionally validate partner, and to self-disclose thoughts and feelings and distressed couples to display significantly more statements to inhibit problem solving and to emotionally invalidate partner. Van Widenfelt also observed wives in her Dutch sample to display significantly more statements that were emotionally invalidating of their husbands (e.g., criticisms, guilt inductions, character assassinations). Sequential analyses revealed the interaction of nondistressed couples to be characterized by statements that facilitated problem solving, followed by self-disclosure or emotional validation. In contrast, the interaction of distressed couples was characterized by a high frequency of emotional invalidation that was followed by statements that either facilitated or interfered with problem solving, but without any consequent emotional validation.

Observing in Naturalistic Settings

Melby, Ge, Conger, and Warner (1995), in an elegant analysis, compared a marital discussion and a problem-solving task and reported on the importance of task in detecting positive marital interaction. There have been very few studies of marital interaction outside laboratory settings, and this is a direction that needs continuing exploration. An exception is Vuchinich (1985), who studied naturally occurring dinner-time disputes. He found that in 200 examples of conflict, 67% ended in standoffs in which no one yielded and the topic was dropped. In 33% of the conflicts, the most frequent reaction was withdrawal, in which one person refused to continue the discussion. The reaction of submission, in which one person gave in or compromised was rare. Nonetheless, even if not naturalistic, laboratory observation may have validity, particularly if it can be shown to predict important marital outcomes. Older evidence shows that interaction in the lab underestimates differences between distressed and nondistressed couples, compared with tape recordings made in couples' homes (Gottman, 1979). More recently, Hayden et al. (1998) related the mealtime interactions of families to multiple levels of family assessment; the measures were strongly related to both mother and father involvement. The use of a marital interaction diary was pioneered in a study by Halford, Gravestock, Lowe, and Scheldt (1992) in an attempt to discover the behavioral ecology of stressful marital interaction. For example, they found that most stressful interaction occurred in the kitchen during the weekdays and were associated with everyday life stresses; the most stressful interactions resulted from one partner leaving the scene.

Focus on Sequences or Patterns of Interaction

Either through using various tools of sequence analysis, or through the direct observation of sequences, the observational study of marital interaction expanded to the analysis of patterned communication. Probably the most important of these patterns was the investigation of the demand-withdraw pattern. Most commonly, this is observed as wives demanding change (through emotional requests, criticism, and complaints) and husbands withdrawing (through defensiveness and passive inaction). Christensen and his students pioneered the study of this sequence (Christensen & Heavey, 1990; Sagrestano, Christensen, & Heavey, 1998) and showed that this pattern was most likely when discussing a wife issue and could be reversed for a husband issue (Heavey, Layne, & Christensen, 1993). Given that a consistent finding is that women typically raise most of the issues in most marriages, however, this finding may be of only theoretical interest. Heavey, Christensen, and

Malamuth (1995) demonstrated that the withdrawal by men and the female-demand/male-withdraw pattern predicted decline in wives' marital satisfaction 2.5 years later.

Demand-Withdraw Pattern and Power Revisited

The wife-demand/husband-withdraw pattern does not imply that the wife is dominant in this interaction pattern. The husband's withdrawal could be driving the wife's demandingness, for example. In an innovative analysis, Klinetob and Smith (1996) continuously coded demand and withdraw behaviors for both husband and wife. Using bivariate time-series analysis and controlling for autocorrelation, they assessed the direction of influence between demand-withdraw behaviors (and between withdraw-demand) in both husbands and wives. They found that in the wife-demand/husband withdraw pattern, the overwhelming percentage of couples showed a bidirectional influence pattern (especially when it was her issue), with wife dominance as the next most frequent pattern. For the husband-demand/wife-withdraw pattern, once again a bidirectional influence pattern was most common, with husband dominance the next most frequent pattern (particularly when it was his issue). This was an elegant approach to the study of marital power.

The Importance of Positive Affect

Part of the accomplishments in the study of marital interaction over the last 20 years can be traced to the use of common methodologies and data analytic strategies in independent laboratories throughout the United States, in the Netherlands, German, and Australia. One feature of the typical paradigm was a focus on conflict discussions and the negative behaviors that marked the interaction of distressed couples in this context. As we enter the next decade, interactional researchers have begun to look beyond conflict to better understand the contribution that intimacy and other affectional processes makes to relationship satisfaction and stability.

The importance of looking at positive affective reactions is suggested by several studies of marital interaction. Gottman et al. (1998) found that only positive affect during conflict discussions in the early months of marriage predicted both later divorce and the marital happiness of stable couples. Pasch and Bradbury (1998) and Pasch, Bradbury, and Davila (1997) studied social support in marital interaction using a task of only moderate conflict in which spouses discussed personal, nonmarital issues. Longitudinal data showed that wives' "support solicitation and provision behaviors" predicted marital outcomes 2 years later, independent of the negative behaviors exhibited during marital conflict. Beach, Martin, Blum, and Roman (1993) reported that coworkers and marital quality played a significant role in reducing negative affective symptoms (depression and interpersonal stress).

De Koning and Weiss (1997) studied the use of instrumental humor and found that it appears to function differently during the problem-solving conversations of younger couples married an average of 14 years than during the conversations of older couples married an average of 39 years. Among younger couples, instrumental humor was negatively associated with marital satisfaction, but among older couples, instrumental humor was strongly associated with marital happiness. The authors speculated that humor many function as an avoidance maneuver in the younger couples and more genuinely represent positive affect in the older couples. Cordova (1998) is developing a promising behavioral model of intimacy. Intimacy is operationalized as a dyadic event sequence in which one partner's expresses a personal vulnerability and the spouse responds in an accepting, nonpunitive manner. Fruzzetti and Rubio-Kuhnert (1998) found that intimacy, also assessed as a disclosure-validation sequence using Fruzzetti's Intimacy-Distance Process Model Coding System (1995), was significantly associated with relationship satisfaction and individual well-being, both cross-sectionally and longitudinally. Clearly the field is just beginning to explore the interactional basis of marital intimacy.

Immediate Interactional Outcomes

Haefner, Notarius, and Pellegrini (1991) focused on immediate outcomes of a single problem-solving conversation. Satisfaction with an immediately preceding conversation was primarily determined by partners' positive behaviors, especially wives' emotional validation and husbands' problem-solving facilitation. Dimitri-Carlton (1997) also examined proximal interactional determinants of conversational outcomes: Feeling supported versus feeling undermined by one's partner. Interestingly, a set of mild negative behaviors was found to be most predictive of feelings of support and undermining.

Personality Revisited

Karney and Bradbury (1997), in a longitudinal study, examined the relationship between neuroticism, marital interaction, initial levels of marital satisfaction and rates of change in marital satisfaction. They found that neuroticism was associated with initial levels of marital satisfaction but not with rates of change in marital satisfaction. On the other hand, behavior during marital interaction (total positive minus negative codes using the Sillars [1982] coding system) was associated with rates of change in marital satisfaction, but not with initial levels. Kobak and Hazan (1991), using an attachment theory framework with Q-sort methodology, reported that the accuracy of spouse's internal working models as relying on one's partner and the partner being psychologically available were related to observers' positive ratings of communication in problem-solving and confiding tasks. Sayers and Baucom (1991) studied the relationship between femininity and masculinity and marital interaction using the MICS. Femininity was positively related to greater rates of negative behavior among both husbands and wives. A sequential analysis supported the idea that wives' femininity was associated with greater negative reciprocity of the wives. Men's femininity was associated with husbands' tendency to terminate fewer negative sequences of behavior in comparison with their wives. High masculinity of the wives was related to shorter sequences of negative behavior.

Stress Spillover Management

In 1987, Jacobson, Schmaling, and Holtzworth-Munroe conducted a 2-year telephone follow-up study of the couples from their marital therapy study. They studied two groups of couples, those who maintained change and those who relapsed. The only significant difference between the two groups was in the management of stress from nonmarital situations to the marital relationship. Couples who relapsed had more spillover of stress into the marriage than those who maintained change. A Swiss psychologist, Bodenman (1997a) reported that "dyadic coping" with stress predicted longitudinal outcomes (stability and happiness) in a 2-year study of 70 Swiss couples. Bodenman has developed an intervention program focusing of dyadic coping with stress (Bodenman, 1997b). This is an area that needs a great deal of development.

FINAL THOUGHTS

Behavioral observation of marital interaction contributed significantly to our understanding of marriage in the last decade. We would like readers to carefully note that the construct of marital interaction might be assessed using methodologies other than direct observation. For example, a spouse might be asked to report how often his or her partner is critical. This question assesses a personal construction of the marital system; it does not assess actual interaction. Given the cost of observational measures, it is all too tempting to move back to less expensive methodologies. We can see the pull to develop inexpensive questionnaires to assess theoretical constructs that have been derived from careful observational study and validated by cross-sectional and longitudinal study. We believe this would be a mistake. Although it will be necessary to use self-report measures to tap phenomenological constructs of importance, we should not abandon the observational methods that have contributed to the decade's advances in understanding relationships. We must strive to develop reliable measures of phenomenological constructs and anchor these measures to the most reliable and valid data that we have available on couples and families: the observation of interaction. Observational measures will always be most informative data source we will ever get about process, which will be the richest source we will ever have for describing and building theory.

REFERENCES

Babcock, J. C., Waltz, J., Jacobson, N. S., & Gottman, J. M. (1993). Power and violence: The relation between communication patterns, power discrepancies, and domestic violence. *Journal of Consulting and Clinical Psychology, 61,* 40–50.

Bakeman, R., & Gottman, J. M. (1997). *Observing interaction: An introduction to sequential analysis* (2nd ed.). New York: Cambridge University Press.

Bakeman, R., & Quera, V. (1995). *Analyzing interaction: Sequential analysis with SDIS and GSEQ.* New York: Cambridge University Press.

Ball, F. L. J., Cowan, P., & Cowan, C. P. (1995). Who's got the power? Gender differences in partner's perception of influence during marital problem-solving discussions. *Family Process, 34,* 303–321.

Basco, M. R., Birchler, G. R., Kalal, B., Talbott, R., & Slater, M. A. (1991). The clinician rating of adult communication (CRAC): A clinician's guide to the assessment of interpersonal communication skill. *Journal of Clinical Psychology, 47,* 368–380.

Bateson, G., Jackson, D. D., Haley, J., & Weakland, J. (1956). Toward a theory of schizophrenia. *Behavioral Science, 1,* 251–264.

Baucom, D., Notarius, C., Burnett, C., & Haefner, P.

(1990). Gender differences and sex-role identity in marriage. In F. Fincham & T. Bradbury (Eds.), *The psychology of marriage: Basic issues and applications* (pp. 150–171). New York: Guilford Press.

Beach, R. H., Martin, J. K., Blum, T. C., & Roman, P. M. (1993). Effects of marital and co-worker relationships on negative affect: Testing the central role of marriage. *The American Journal of Family Therapy, 21,* 313–323.

Bèlanger, C., Sauborin, S., Laughrea, K., Dulude, D., & Wright, J. (1993). Macroscopic marital interaction coding systems: Are they interchangeable? *Behavior Research and Therapy, 8,* 789–795.

Belsky, J., & Kelly, J. (1994). *The transition to parenthood.* New York: Dell.

Berkman, L. F., & Breslow, L. (1983). *Health and the ways of living: The Alameda County Study.* New York: Oxford University Press.

Berkman, L. F., & Syme, S. L. (1979). Social networks, host resistance, and mortality: A nine-year follow-up study of Alameda County residents. *American Journal of Epidemiology, 109,* 186–204.

Bernard, J. (1982). *The future of marriage.* New Haven, CT: Yale University Press.

Biglan, A., Hops, H., Sherman, L., Friedman, L. S., Arthur, J., & Osteen, V. (1985). Problem solving interactions of depressed women and their spouses. *Behavior Therapy, 16,* 431–451.

Bodenman, G. (1997a). The influence of stress and coping on close relationships: A two-year longitudinal study. *Swiss Journal of Psychology, 56,* 156–164.

Bodenman, G. (1997b). Can divorce be prevented by enhancing the coping skills of couples? *Journal of Divorce and Remarriage, 27,* 177–194.

Bradbury, T. N., & Fincham, F. D. (1992). Attributions and behavior in marital interaction. *Journal of Personality and Social Psychology, 63,* 613–628.

Bradbury, T. N., & Karney, B. R. (1993). Longitudinal study of marital interaction and dysfunction: Review and analysis. *Clinical Psychology Review, 13,* 15–27.

Bradbury, T. N., & Pasch, L. A. (1994). *The Social Support Interaction Coding System (SSICS).* Unpublished coding manual, University of California, Los Angeles.

Broderick, C. B. (1993). *Understanding family process: Basics of family systems theory.* Newbury Park, CA: Sage.

Brody, G. H., Arias, I., & Fincham, F. D. (1996). Linking marital and child attributions to family processes and parent-child relationships. *Journal of Family Psychology, 10,* 408–421.

Brown, P. C., & Smith, T. W. (1992). Social influence, marriage, and the heart: Cardiovascular consequences of interpersonal control in husbands and wives. *Health Psychology, 11,* 88–96.

Buehlman, K. T., Gottman, J. M., & Katz, L. F. (1992). How a couple views their past predicts their future: Predicting divorce from an Oral History Interview. *Journal of Family Psychology, 5,* 295–318.

Burman, B., & Margolin, G. (1992). Analysis of the association between marital relationships and health problems: An interactional perspective. *Psychological Bulletin, 112,* 39–63.

Burman, B., & Margolin, G. (1993). America's angriest home videos: Behavioral contingencies observed in home reenactments of marital conflict. *Journal of Consulting and Clinical Psychology, 61,* 28–39.

Carstensen, L. L., Gottman, J. M., & Levenson, R. W. (1995). Emotional behavior in long-term marriage. *Psychology and Aging, 10,* 140–149.

Christensen, A., & Heavey, C. L. (1990). Gender and social structure in the demand/withdraw pattern of marital conflict. *Journal of Personality and Social Psychology, 59,* 73–81.

Christensen, A., & Pasch, L. (1993). The sequence of marital conflict: An analysis of seven phases of marital conflict in distressed and nondistressed couples. *Clinical Psychology Review, 13,* 3–14.

Coan, J., Gottman, J. M., Babcock, J., & Jacobson, N. S. (1997). Battering and the male rejection of influence from women. *Aggressive Behavior, 23,* 375–388.

Cohan, C. L., & Bradbury, T. N. (1997). Negative life events, marital interaction, and the longitudinal course of newlywed marriages. *Journal of Personality and Social Psychology, 73,* 114–128.

Cook, J., Tyson, R., White, J., Rushe, R., Gottman, J., & Murray, J. (1995). Mathematics of marital conflict: Qualitative dynamic modeling of marital interaction. *Journal of Family Psychology, 9,* 110–130.

Cook, W. W., & Medley, D. M. (1954). Proposed hostility and Pharisaic-virtue scales for the MMPI. *Journal of Applied Psychology, 38,* 414–418.

Cordova, J. (1998). *A behavioral theory for the study of intimacy: Intimate events, suppressive events and the construction of intimate partnerships.* Paper presented at the meeting of the Association for the Advancement of Behavior Therapy, Washington, DC.

Cordova, J. V., Jacobson, N. S., Gottman, J. M., Rushe, R. and Cox, G. (1993). Negative reciprocity and communication in couples with a violent husband. *Journal of Abnormal Psychology, 102,* 559–564.

Cowan, C. P., & Cowan, P. (1992). *When partners become parents: The big life change for couples.* New York: Basic Books.

Cowan, C. P., Cowan, P. A., Coie, L., & Coie, J. D. (1978). Becoming a family: The impact of the first child's birth on the couple's relationship. In W. B. Miller & L. F. Newman (Eds.), *The first child and family formation.* Chapel Hill, NC: Carolina Population Center.

Cowan, P. A., & Cowan, C. P. (1987, April). Couple's relationships, parenting styles and the child's development at three. Paper presented at the Society for Research in Child Development, Baltimore, MD.

Cummings, E. M., Zahn-Waxler, C., & Radke-Yarrow, M. (1984). Developmental changes in children's reactions to anger in the home. *Journal of Child Psychology & Psychiatry & Allied Disciplines, 25,* 63–74.

Davies, P. T., & Cummings, M. E. (1994). Marital conflict and child adjustment: An emotional security hypothesis. *Psychological Bulletin, 116,* 387–411.

Davies, P. T., Myers, R. L., & Cummings, M. E. (1996). Responses of children and adolescents to marital conflict scenarios as a function of the emotionality if conflict endings. *Merrill-Palmer Quarterly, 42,* 1–21.

De Koning, E., & Weiss, R. L. (1997). *A funny thing happened during my marriage.* Paper presented at the meeting of the Association for the Advancement of Behavior Therapy, Miami, FL.

Deal, J. E., Hagan, M. S., & Anderson, E. R. (1992). The marital relationship in remarried families. In E. M. Hetherington & W. G. Clingempeel (Eds.) Coping with marital transitions: A family systems perspective. *Monographs of the Society for Research in Child Development* (Serial No. 227, 57), 73–93. Chicago: The University of Chicago Press.

Dimitri-Carlton, S. (1997). *Feelings of support and undermining in couples' problem-solving conversations.* Unpublished doctoral dissertation, Catholic University, Washington, DC.

Duncan, S. D., & Fiske, D. W. (1977). *Face to face interaction: Research, methods, and theory.* Hillsdale, NJ: Erlbaum.

Easterbrooks, M. A. (1987, April). *Early family development: Longitudinal impact of marital quality.* Paper presented at the Meeting for Research in Child Development, Baltimore, MD.

Ekman, P., & Friesen, W. V. (1978). *Facial action code system.* Palo Alto, CA: Consulting Psychologist Press.

El-Sheikh, M. (1994). Children's emotional and physiological responses to interadult angry behavior: The role of history of interparental hostility. *Journal of Abnormal Child Psychology, 22,* 661–678.

Emery, R. E., & O'Leary, K. D. (1982). Children's perception of marital discord and behavior problems of boys and girls. *Journal of Abnormal Child Psychology, 10,* 11–24.

Erel, O., Margolin, G., & John, R. S. (1998). Observed sibling interaction: Links with the marital and mother-child relationship. *Developmental Psychology, 34,* 288–298.

Erikson, E. H., Erikson, J. M., & Kivnick, H. Q. (1989). *Vital involvement in old age.* New York: Norton.

Escudero, V., Rogers, L., & Gutierrez, E. (1997). Patterns of relational control and nonverbal affect in clinic and nonclinic samples. *Journal of Social and Personal Relationships, 14,* 5–29.

Ewart, C. K., Burnett, K. F., & Taylor, C. B. (1983). Communication behaviors that affect blood pressure: an A-B–A-B analysis of marital interaction. *Behavior Modification, 7,* 331–344.

Ewart, C. K., Taylor, C. B., Kraemer, H. C., & Agras, S. W. (1991). High blood pressure and marital discord: Not being nasty matters more than being nice. *Health Psychology, 10,* 155–163.

Fals-Stewart, W., & Birchler, G. R. (1998). Marital interactions of drug-abusing patients and their partners: Comparisons with distressed couples and relationship to drug-using behavior. *Psychology of Addictive Behaviors, 12,* 28–38.

Fincham, F. D., Garnier, P. C., Gano-Phillips, S., & Osborne, L. N. (1995). Preinteraction expectations, marital satisfaction, and accessibility: A new look at sentiment override. *Journal of Family Psychology, 9,* 3–14.

Fitzpatrick, M. A. (1988). *Between husbands and wives: Communication in marriage.* Beverly Hills, CA: Sage.

Floyd, F. J. (1989). Segmenting interactions: Coding units for assessing marital and family behaviors. *Behavioral Assessment, 11,* 13–29.

Forehand, R., Brody, G., Long, N., Slotkin, J., & Fauber, R. (1986). Divorce/divorce potential and interparental conflict: The relationship to early adolescent social and cognitive functioning. *Journal of Adolescent Research, 1,* 389–397.

Fox, N. A. (Ed.) (1994). The development of emotion regulation: Biological and behavioral considerations. *Monographs of the Society for Research in Child Development, 59* (2–3, Serial. 240). Chicago: The University of Chicago Press.

Fruzzetti, A. (1995). *Intimacy-distance process model coding system.* Unpublished coding manual, University of Nevada, Reno.

Fruzzetti, A., & Rubio-Kuhnert, A. (1998). Observing intimacy: Self-disclosure and validation reciprocity and its impact on relationship and individual well-being. In J. V. Cordova (Chair), *Conceptualizations of intimacy: Theory and research.* Symposium conducted at the meeting of the Association for the Advancement of Behavior Therapy, Washington, DC.

Gaelick, L., Bodenhausen, G. V., & Wyer, R. S. (1985). Emotional communication in close relationships. *Journal of Personality and Social Psychology, 49,* 1246–1265.

Garber, J., & Dodge, K. A. (Eds.). (1991). *The development of emotion regulation and dysregulation.* New York: Cambridge University Press.

Gottman, J. M. (1979). *Marital interaction: Empirical investigations.* New York: Academic Press.

Gottman, J. M. (1993). The roles of conflict engagement, escalation or avoidance in marital interaction: A longitudinal view of five types of couples. *Journal of Consulting and Clinical Psychology, 61,* 6–15.

Gottman, J. M. (1994). *What predicts divorce: The relationship between marital processes and marital outcomes.* Hillsdale, NJ: Erlbaum.

Gottman, J. M., Coan, J., Carrere, S., & Swanson, C. (1998). Predicting marital happiness and stability from newlywed interactions. *Journal of Marriage and the Family, 60,* 5–22.

Gottman, J. M., Jacobson, N. S., Rushe, R. H., Shortt, J. W. (1995). The relationship between heart rate reactivity, emotionally aggressive behavior, and general violence in batterers. *Journal of Family Psychology, 9,* 227–248.

Gottman, J. M., & Katz, L. F. (1989). Effects of marital discord on young children's peer interaction and health. *Developmental Psychology, 25,* 373–381.

Gottman, J. M., Katz, L. F., & Hooven, C. (1996). Parental meta-emotion philosophy and the emotional life of families: Theoretical models and preliminary data. *Journal of Family Psychology, 10,* 243–268.

Gottman, J. M., & Krokoff, L. J. (1989). Marital interaction and satisfaction: A longitudinal view. *Journal of Consulting and Clinical Psychology, 57,* 47–52.

Gottman, J. M., & Levenson, R. W. (1986). Assessing the role of emotion in marriage. *Behavioral Assessment, 8,* 31–48.

Gottman, J. M., & Levenson, R. W. (1988). The social psychophysiology of marriage. In P. Noller & M. A. Fitzpatrick (Eds.), *Perspectives on marital interaction* (pp. 183–200). San Diego, CA: College Hill Press.

Gottman, J. M., & Levenson, R. W. (1992). Marital processes predictive of later dissolution: Behavior, physiology, and health. *Journal of Personality and Social Psychology, 63,* 221–233.

Gottman, J. M., McCoy, K., Coan, J., & Collier, H. (1996). The Specific Affect Coding System (SPAFF) for observing emotional communication in marital and family interaction. In J. M. Gottman (Ed.), *What predicts divorce? The Measures.* Mahwah, NJ: Erlbaum.

Gottman, J. M., Notarius, C., Gonso, J., & Markman, H. (1976). *A couples guide to communication.* Champaign, IL: Research Press.

Gottman, J. M., Swanson, C., & Murray, J. (in press). The mathematics of marital conflict: Dynamic mathematical nonlinear modeling of newlywed marital interaction. *Journal of Family Psychology.*

Gray-Little, B. (1982). Marital quality and power processes among Black couples. *Journal of Marriage and the Family, 44,* 633–646.

Gray-Little, B., Baucom, D. H., & Hamby, S. L. (1996). Marital power, marital adjustment, and therapy outcome. *Journal of Family Psychology, 10,* 292–303.

Gray-Little, B., & Burks, N. (1983). Power and satisfaction in marriage: A review and critique. *Psychological Bulletin, 93,* 513–538.

Griffin, W. A. (1993a). Event history analysis of marital and family interaction: A practical introduction. *Journal of Family Psychology, 6,* 211–229.

Griffin, W. A. (1993b). Transitions from negative affect during marital interaction: Husband and wife differences. *Journal of Family Psychology, 6,* 230–244.

Griffin, W. A., & Greene, S. M. (1994). Social interaction and symptom sequences: A case study of orofacial bradykinesia in Parkinson's disease during negative marital interaction. *Psychiatry: Interpersonal and Biological Processes, 57,* 269–274.

Guilford, R., & Bengtson, V. (1979). Measuring marital satisfaction in three generations: Positive and negative dimensions. *Journal of Marriage and the Family, 39,* 387–398

Haefner, P. T., Notarius, C. I., & Pellegrini, D. S. (1991). Determinants of satisfaction with marital discussions: An exploration of husband-wife differences. *Behavioral Assessment, 13,* 67–82.

Hahlweg, K., Markman, H., Thurmaier, F., Engl, J., & Eckert, V. (1998). Prevention of marital distress: Results of a German Prospective Longitudinal Study. *Journal of Family Psychology, 12,* 543–556.

Halford, W. K., Gravestock, F. M., Lowe, R., & Scheldt, S. (1992). Toward a behavioral ecology of stressful marital interactions. *Behavioral Assessment, 14,* 199–217.

Halford, W. K., & Sanders, M. R. (1990). The relationship between cognition and behavior during marital interaction. *Journal of Social and Clinical Psychology, 9,* 489–510.

Harralson, T. L., Suarez, E. C., & Lawler, K. A. (1997). Cardiovascular reactivity among hostile men and women: The effects of sex and anger suppression. *Women's Health, 3,* 151–164.

Hayden, L. C., Schiller, M., Dickstein, S., Seifer, R., Sameroff, A., J., Miller, I., Keitner, G., & Rasmussen, S. (1998). Levels of family assessment I: Family, marital, and parent-child interaction. *Journal of Family Psychology, 12,* 7–22.

Healy, B. T. (1992). The heritability of autonomic nervous system processes. In: Field, T. M., McCabe, P. M., & Schneiderman, N. (Eds.), *Stress and coping in infancy and childhood* (pp. 69–82). Hillsdale, NJ: Erlbaum.

Heavey, C. L., Christensen, A., & Malamuth, N. M. (1995). The longitudinal impact of demand and withdrawal during marital conflict. *Journal of Consulting and Clinical Psychology, 63,* 797–801.

Heavey, C. L., Layne, C., & Christensen, A. (1993). Gender and conflict structure in marital interaction: A replication and extension. *Journal of Consulting and Clinical Psychology, 61,* 16–27.

Hetherington, E. M., & Clingempeel, W. G. (1992). Coping with marital transitions: A family systems perspective. *Monographs of the Society for Research in Child Development, 57* (Serial No. 227). Chicago: The University of Chicago Press.

Hetherington, E. M., Cox, M., & Cox, R. (1978). The aftermath of divorce. In J. H. Stevens, Jr., & M. Matthews (Eds.), *Mother-child, father-child relations.* Washington DC: National Association for the Education of Young Children.

Heyman, R. E., Eddy, J. M., Weiss, R. L., & Vivian, D. (1995). Factor analysis of the Marital Interaction Coding System (MICS). *Journal of Family Psychology, 9,* 209–215.

Holtzworth-Munroe, A., Stuart, G. L., Sandin, E., Smutzler, N, & McLaughlin, W. (1997). Comparing the social support behaviors of violent and nonviolent husbands during discussions of wife personal problems. *Personal Relationships, 4,* 395–412.

Huston, T. L., & Ashmore, R. D. (1986). Women and men in personal relationships. In R. D. Ashmore & F. D. Boco (Eds.), *The social psychology of female-male relationships.* (pp. 167–210). New York: Academic Press.

Ickes, W., Stinson, L., Bissonnette, V., & Garcia, S. (1990). Naturalistic social cognition: Empathic accuracy in mixed-sex dyads. *Journal of Personality and Social Psychology, 59,* 730–742.

Illig, D. P. (1977). *Distributional structure, sequential structure, multivariate information analysis, and models of communicative patterns of elderly and young married and friendship dyads in problem-solving situations.* Unpublished doctoral dissertation, Pennsylvania State University, University Park.

Jacob, T., & Krahn, G. (1987). The classification of behavioral observation codes in studies of family interaction. *Journal of Marriage and the Family, 49,* 677–687.

Jacob, T., & Leonard, K. (1992). Sequential analysis of marital interactions involving alcoholic, depressed, and nondepressed men. *Journal of Abnormal Psychology, 101,* 647–656.

Jacobson, N. S., & Gottman, J. M. (1998). *When men batter women.* New York: Simon & Schuster.

Jacobson, N. S., Gottman, J. M., Gortner, E., Berns, S., & Shortt, J. W. (1997). The longitudinal course of battering: When do couples split up? When does the abuse decrease? *Violence and Victims, 11,* 371–392.

Jacobson, N. S., Schmaling, K., & Holtzworth-Munroe, A. (1987). Component analysis of behavioral marital therapy: 2-year follow-up and prediction of relapse. *Journal of Marital and Family Therapy, 13,* 187–195.

Jaffe, J., & Feldstein, S. (1970). *Rhythms of dialogue.* New York: Academic Press.

Johnson, M. P., Huston, T. L., Gaines, S. O., & Levinger, G. (1992). Patterns of married life among young couples. *Journal of Social and Personal Relationships, 9,* 343–364.

Johnson, S. L., & Jacob, T. (1997). Marital interactions of depressed men and women. *Journal of Consulting and Clinical Psychology, 65,* 15–23.

Julien, D., Markman, H. J., & Lindahl, K. M. (1989). A comparison of a global and a macroanalytic coding system: Implications for future trends in studying interactions. *Behavioral Assessment, 11,* 81–100.

Kaiser, A., Hahlweg, K., Fehm-Wolfsdorf, G., Groth, T. (1998). The efficacy of a compact psychoeducational group training program for married couples. *Journal of Consulting and Clinical Psychology, 66,* 753–760.

Karney, B. R., & Bradbury, T. N. (1997). Neuroticism, marital interaction, and the trajectory of marital satisfaction. *Journal of Personality and Social Psychology, 72,* 1075–1092.

Katz, L. F., & Gottman, J. M. (1991). Marital discord and child outcomes: A social psychophysiological approach. In J. Garber & K. A. Dodge (Eds.), *The development of emotion regulation and dysregulation.* New York: Cambridge University Press.

Katz, L. F., & Gottman, J. M. (1993). Patterns of marital conflict predict children's internalizing and externalizing behaviors. *Developmental Psychology, 29,* 940–950.

Katz, L. F., & Gottman, J. M. (1995). Vagal tone protects children from marital conflict. *Developmental Psychopathology, 7,* 83–92.

Katz, L. F., & Gottman, J. M. (1997). Buffering children from marital conflict and dissolution. *Journal of Clinical Child Psychology, 26,* 157–171.

Kiecolt-Glaser, J. K., Fisher, L, Ogrocki, P., Stout, J. C., Speicher, C. E., & Glaser, R. (1987). "Marital quality, marital disruption, and immune function." *Psychosomatic Medicine 49* 13–34

Kiecolt-Glaser, J. K., Malarkey, W. B., Cacioppo, J. T., Glaser, R. (1994). Stressful personal relationships: Immune and endocrine function. In R. Glaser & J. K. Kiecolt-Glaser (Eds.), *Human stress and immunity* (pp. 321–339). San Diego, CA: Academic Press.

Klinetob, N. A., & Smith, D. A. (1996). Demand-withdraw communication in marital interaction: Tests of interpersonal contingency and gender role hypotheses. *Journal of Marriage and the Family, 58,* 945–957.

Kobak, R. R., & Hazan, C. (1991). Attachment in marriage: Effects of security and accuracy of working models. *Journal of Personality and Social Psychology, 60,* 861–869.

Krokoff, L. J., Gottman, J. M., & Hass, S. D. (1989). Validation of a global rapid Couples Interaction Scoring System. *Behavioral Assessment, 11,* 65–80.

Krokoff, L. J., Gottman, J. M., & Roy, A. K. (1988). Blue-collar and white-collar marital interaction and communication orientation. *Journal of Social and Personal Relationships, 5,* 201–221.

Levenson, R. W., Carstensen, L. L., & Gottman, J. M. (1994). Influence of age and gender on affect, physiology, and their interrelations: A study of long-term marriages. *Journal of Personality and Social Psychology, 67,* 56–68.

Levenson, R. W., & Gottman, J. M. (1983). Marital interaction: Physiological linkage and affective exchange. *Journal of Personality and Social Psychology, 45,* 587–597.

Levenson, R. W., & Gottman, J. M. (1985). Physiological and affective predictors of change in relationship satisfaction. *Journal of Personality and Social Psychology, 49,* 85–94.

Levenson, R. W., & Ruef, A. M. (1992). Empathy: A physiological substrate. *Journal of Personality and Social Psychology, 63,* 234–246.

Lewis, J. (1989). *The birth of the family: An empirical inquiry.* New York: Brunner/Mazel.

Mahoney, A., Boggio, R. M., & Jouriles, E. N. (1996). Effects of verbal marital conflict on subsequent mother-son interactions in a child clinical sample. *Journal of Child Clinical Psychology, 25,* 262–271.

Margolin, G., Christensen, A., & John, R. S. (1996). The continuance of spillover of everyday tensions in distressed and nondistressed families. *Journal of Family Psychology, 10,* 304–321.

Matthews, L. S., Wickrama, K. A. S., & Conger, R. D. (1996). Predicting marital instability from spouse and observer reports of marital interaction. *Journal of Marriage and the Family, 58,* 641–655.

McCabe, S. B., & Gotlib, I. H. (1993). Interactions of couples with and without a depressed spouse: Self-report and observations of problem-solving situations. *Journal of Personal and Social Relationships, 10,* 589–599.

Medalie, J. H., & Goldbourt, V. (1976). Angina pectoris among 10,000 men: II. Psychosocial and other risk factors as evidenced by a multivariate analysis of a five year incidence study. *American Journal of Medicine, 60,* 910–921.

Melby, J. N., Ge, X., Conger, R. D., & Warner, T. D. (1995). The importance of task in evaluating positive marital interactions. *Journal of Marriage and the Family, 57,* 981–994.

Mendolia, M., Beach, S. R. H., & Tesser, A. (1996). The relationship between marital interaction behaviors and affective reactions to one's own and one's spouse's self-evaluation needs. *Personal Relationships, 3,* 279–292.

Michaels, G. Y., & Goldberg, W. A. (Eds.). (1988). *The transition to parenthood: Current theory and research.* New York: Cambridge University Press.

Miller, G. E., & Bradbury, T. N. (1995). Refining the association between attributions and behavior in marital interaction. *Journal of Family Psychology, 9,* 196–208.

Murray, J. D. (1989). *Mathematical biology.* Berlin, Germany: Springer-Verlag.

Nelson, G. M., & Beach, S. R. H. (1990). Sequential interaction in depression: Effects of depressive behavior on spousal aggression. *Behavior Therapy, 21,* 167–182.

Noller, P., & Hiscock, H. (1989). Fitzpatrick's typology: An Australian replication. *Journal of Social and Personal Relationships, 6,* 87–91.

Notarius, C. I., Benson, P. R., Sloane, D., Vanzetti, N. A., & Hornyak, L. M. (1989). Exploring the interface between perception and behavior: An analysis of marital interaction in distressed and nondistressed couples. *Behavioral Assessment, 11,* 39–64.

Notarius, C. I., Markman, H. J., & Gottman, J. M. (1983). Couples interaction scoring system: Clinical implications. In E. E. Filsinger (Ed.), *Marriage and family assessment* (pp. 117–136). Beverly Hills, CA: Sage.

Notarius, C. I., Pellegrini, D., & Martin, L. (1991). Codebook of Marital and Family Interaction (COM-FI). Unpublished manuscript, Catholic University of America, Washington, DC.

Oggins, J., Veroff, J., & Leber, D. (1993). Perceptions of marital interactions among Black and White newlyweds. *Journal of Personality and Social Psychology, 65,* 494–511.

Olson, D. H., & Ryder, R. G. (1970). Inventory of marital conflicts (IMC): And experimental interaction procedure. *Journal of Marriage and the Family, 32,* 443–448.

Parron, E. M. (1982). Golden wedding couples: Lessons in longevity. *Generations, 7,* 14–16.

Pasch, L. A., & Bradbury, T. N. (1998). Social support, conflict, and the development of marital dysfunction. *Journal of Consulting and Clinical Psychology, 66,* 219–230.

Pasch, L. A., Bradbury, T. N., & Davila, J. (1997). Gender, negative affectivity, and observed social support in marital interaction. *Personal Relationships, 4,* 361–378.

Peterson, J. L., & Zill, N. (1986). Marital disruption, parent-child relationships, and behavior problems in children. *Journal of Marriage and the Family, 48,* 295–307.

Porter, B., & O'Leary, K. D. (1980). Marital discord and childhood behavior problems. *Journal of Abnormal Psychology, 8,* 287–295.

Rapoport, A. (1960). *Fights, games, and debates.* Ann Arbor: University of Michigan Press.

Rapoport, A. (1972). The uses of mathematical isomorphism in general systems theory. In G. J. Klir (Ed.), *Trends in general systems theory* (pp. 42–77). New York: Wiley Interscience.

Raush, H. L., Barry, W. A., Hertl, R. K., & Swain, M. A. (1974). *Communication, conflict and marriage.* San Francisco: Jossey-Bass.

Rogers, L. E. (1972). *Relational communication control coding manual* Unpublished lab manual, Michigan State University, East Lansing.

Rogers, M. J., & Holmbeck, G. N. (1997). Effects of interparental aggression on children's adjustment: The moderating role of cognitive appraisal and coping. *Journal of Family Psychology, 11,* 125–130.

Romano, J., Turner, J. A., Friedman, L. S., Bulcroft, R. A., Jensen, M. P., & Hops, H. (1991). Observational assessment of chronic pain patient-spouse behavioral interactions. *Behavior Therapy, 22,* 549–567.

Rutter, M. (1971). Parent-child separation: Psychological effects on the children. *Journal of Child Psychology and Psychiatry, 12,* 233–260.

Sagrestano, L. M., Christensen, A., & Heavey, C. L. (1998). Social influence techniques during marital conflict. *Personal Relationships, 5,* 75–89.

Sanders, J. D., Smith, T. W., & Alexander, J. F. (1991). Type A behavior and marital interaction: Hostile-Dominant responses during conflict. *Journal of Behavioral Medicine, 14,* 567–580.

Sayers, S. L., & Baucom, D. H. (1991). Role of femininity and masculinity in distressed couples' communication. *Journal of Personality and Social Psychology, 61,* 641–647.

Schmaling, K. B., Whisman, M. A., Fruzzetti, A. E., & Truax, P. (1991). Identifying areas of marital conflict: Interactional behaviors associated with depression. *Journal of Family Psychology, 5,* 145–157.

Schmaling, K. B., & Jacobson, N. S. (1990). Marital

interaction and depression. *Journal of Abnormal Psychology, 99,* 229–236.

Shumaker, S. A., & Hill, D. R. (1991). Gender differences in social support and physical health. *Health Psychology, 10,* 102–111.

Sillars, A. L. (1982). *Verbal tactics coding scheme: Coding manual.* Unpublished manuscript, Ohio State University, Columbus.

Smith, D. A., Vivian, D., & O'Leary, K. D. (1990). Longitudinal prediction of marital discord from premarital expressions of affect. *Journal of Consulting and Clinical Psychology, 58,* 790–798.

Smith, T. W., & Brown, P. C. (1991). Cynical hostility, attempts to exert social control and cardiovascular reactivity in married couples. *Journal of Behavioral Medicine, 14,* 581–592.

Sinnet, N., Carter, L., & Montgomery, J. E. (1972). Older persons' perceptions of their marriages. *Journal of Marriage and the Family, 32,* 428–434.

Straus, M., & Tallman, I. (1971). SIMFAM: A technique for observational measurement and experimental study of families. In J. Aldous, T. Condon, R. Hill, M. Straus, & I. Tallman (Eds.), *Family problem solving* (pp. 379–438). Himsdale, IL: Dryden.

Szinovacz, M. E. (1987). Family power. In M. B. Sussman & S. K. Steinmetz (Eds.), *Handbook of marriage and the family* (pp. 651–694). New York: Plenum Press.

Thomas, G., Fletcher, G. J. O., & Lange, C. (1997). Online empathic accuracy in marital interaction. *Journal of Personality and Social Psychology, 72,* 839–850.

Thompson, R. A. (1994). Emotion regulation: A theme in search of definition. In N. A. Fox (Ed.), The development of emotion regulation: Biological and behavioral considerations. *Monographs of the Society for Research in Child Development, 59* (2–3, Serial. 240). Chicago: The University of Chicago Press.

Turk, D. C., Kerns, R. D., & Rosenberg, R. (1992). Effects of marital interaction on chronic pain and disability: Examining the down side of social support. *Rehabilitation Psychology, 37,* 259–273.

Van Widenfelt, B. M. (1995). *The prediction and prevention of relationship distress and divorce.* The Hague, Netherlands: Cip-Gegevens Koninklijke.

Vanlear, C. A., & Zietlow, P. H. (1990). Toward a contingency approach to marital interaction: An empirical integration of three approaches. *Communication Monographs, 57,* 202–218.

Vanzetti, N. A., Notarius, C. I., & NeeSmith, D. (1992). Specific and generalized expectancies in marital interaction. *Journal of Family Psychology, 6,* 171–183.

Vuchinich, S. (1985). Arguments, family style. *Psychology Today, 19,* 40–46.

Wampler, K. S., & Halverson, C. F., Jr. (1990). The Georgia Marriage Q-Sort: An observational measure of marital functioning. *The American Journal of Family Therapy, 18,* 169–178.

Watzlawick, P., Beavin, J. H., & Jackson, D. D. (1967). *Pragmatics of human communication.* New York: Norton.

Weiss, R. L. (1980). Strategic behavioral marital therapy: Toward a model for assessment and intervention. In J. P. Vincent (Ed.), *Advances in family intervention, assessment and theory* (Vol. 1, pp. 229–271). Greenwich, CT: JAI Press.

Weiss, R. L., Hops, H., & Patterson, G. R. (1973). A framework for conceptualizing marital conflict. In L. A. Hamerlynck, L. C. Handy, & E. J. Marsh (Eds.), *Behavior change: Methodology, concepts, and practice.* (pp. 309–342). Champaign, IL: Research Press.

Weiss, R. L., & Tolman, A. O. (1990). The marital interaction coding system—Global (MICS-G): A global comparison to the MICS. *Behavioral Assessment, 12,* 271–294.

White, B. B. (1989). Gender differences in marital communication patterns. *Family Process, 28,* 89–106.

Whitehead, L. (1979). Sex differences in children's responses to family stress. *Journal of Child Psychology and Psychiatry, 20,* 247–254.

Zamsky, E. (1997). *Racial and socioeconomic status differences in marital interaction.* Unpublished doctoral dissertation, Catholic University of America, Washington, DC.

Zietlow, P. H., & Sillars, A. L. (1988). Life-stage differences in communication during marital conflicts. *Journal of Social & Personal Relationships, 5,* 223–245.

Michael P. Johnson *Pennsylvania State University*

Kathleen J. Ferraro *Arizona State University**

Research on Domestic Violence in the 1990s: Making Distinctions

This review of the family literature on domestic violence suggests that two broad themes of the 1990s provide the most promising directions for the future. The first is the importance of distinctions among types or contexts of violence. Some distinctions are central to the theoretical and practical understanding of the nature of partner violence, others provide important contexts for developing more sensitive and comprehensive theories, and others may simply force us to question our tendency to generalize carelessly from one context to another. Second, issues of control, although most visible in the feminist literature that focuses on men using violence to control "their" women, also arise in other contexts, calling for more general analyses of the interplay of violence, power, and control in relationships. In addition to these two general themes, our review covers literature on coping with violence, the effects on victims and their children, and the social effects of partner violence.

She wandered the streets, looking in shop windows.
Nobody knew her here. Nobody knew what he did when
the door was closed. Nobody knew.

(Brant, 1996, pp. 281)

Department of Sociology, 211 Oswald Tower, University Park, PA 16802 (mpj@psu.edu).

*Women's Studies, Box 873404, Arizona State University, Tempe, AZ 85287-3404.

Key Words: battering, domestic violence, partner violence.

In everyday speech and even in most social science discourse, "domestic violence" is about men beating women. It is estimated that somewhere in the neighborhood of two million women in the United States are terrorized by husbands or other male partners who use violence as one of the tactics by which they control "their woman." Most of the literature on domestic violence is about men controlling women in intimate relationships through the use of violence. This is not, however, the only form of violence between adult or adolescent partners in close relationships, and our review will therefore cover "partner violence" in a broad range of couple relationships, including the marital, cohabiting, and dating relationships of same-gender and opposite-gender couples.

Our reading of the literature on partner violence has led us to the conclusion that two broad themes of the 1990s provide the most promising directions for the future. The first theme is about the importance of making distinctions. Partner violence cannot be understood without acknowledging important distinctions among types of violence, motives of perpetrators, the social locations of both partners, and the cultural contexts in which violence occurs. We will argue that it is difficult to find a question about partner violence for which these distinctions are not relevant and that our ability to draw firm conclusions and to develop effective policies is broadly handicapped by a failure to make distinctions among types of partner violence.

Control, the second promising theme, is most visible in the feminist literature, which has argued that partner violence is primarily a problem of men using violence to maintain control over "their women," a control to which they feel they are entitled and that is supported by a patriarchal culture. We would agree that "domestic violence" or "battering" as it is generally understood by professionals and by the public is primarily a problem of heterosexual male control of women partners. Nonetheless, battering does happen in gay male couples and in lesbian couples, and some heterosexual women do physically assault their male partners and there are forms of partner violence that are quite different from the systematic violence that we call battering.

The Centrality of Distinctions

Types of Violence Against Partners

One of the clearest illustrations of the importance of making distinctions among types of violence arose in the context of the long-standing debate about "battered husbands," and the alleged gender symmetry of partner violence. Johnson (Johnson, 1995, 2000a) argued that at the relationship level, one can distinguish four major patterns of partner violence, which he called "common couple violence" (CCV), "intimate terrorism" (IT), "violent resistance" (VR), and "mutual violent control" (MVC). The distinctions are based not on behavior in a single incident, but on more general patterns of control exercised across the many encounters that comprise a relationship, patterns that are rooted in the motivations of the perpetrator and his or her partner.

Common couple violence. The first type of partner violence identified by Johnson is that which is not connected to a general pattern of control. It arises in the context of a specific argument in which one or both of the partners lash out physically at the other. In a series of empirical papers, Johnson has demonstrated that CCV (compared to IT) has a lower per-couple frequency, is not as likely to escalate over time, is not as likely to involve severe violence, and is more likely to be mutual (Johnson, 1998, 2000a, 2000b). He also has shown that virtually all of the violence in a general sample is CCV, suggesting that research using such samples may be relevant only to this type of partner violence.

Intimate terrorism. The basic pattern in IT is one of violence as merely one tactic in a general pattern of control. The violence is motivated by a wish to exert general control over one's partner. IT involves more per-couple incidents of violence than does CCV, is more likely to escalate over time, is less likely to be mutual, and is more likely to involve serious injury. Nonetheless, IT is not merely "severe violence," as defined in much of the literature. There is considerable variability of severity in both CCV and IT, with some CCV involving homicides and some IT involving a rather low level of violence (Johnson, 2000a). The distinguishing feature of IT is a pattern of violent and nonviolent behaviors that indicates a general motive to control.

The controlling behaviors of IT often involve emotional abuse (Follingstad, Rutledge, Berg, Hause, & Polek, 1990). Kirkwood (1993) provided detailed insights into the processes of emotional abuse that can gradually alter women's views of themselves, their relationships, and their place in the world. Chang's (1996) detailed accounts of psychological abuse also illustrate the processes through which women become demoralized and trapped in abusive relationships. Renzetti's work (1992) on battering in lesbian relationships demonstrates that emotional abuse is not the sole prerogative of men.

Violent resistance. We prefer the term "violent resistance" over "self-defense," because "self-defense" has meanings that are defined (and changing) in the law. Given that the issue of VR has been central to the debate about the gender asymmetry of partner violence and that there is considerable discussion of the "battered woman" self-defense plea in the law, research on the general dynamics of VR is surprisingly meager. One might almost think from the literature that the only women who fight back are the ones who kill their partners (Browne, Williams, & Dutton, 1999; Roberts, 1996). Johnson (2000a) reported that VR is perpetrated almost entirely by women, but he presented no detailed analysis of its characteristics. There is some evidence elsewhere regarding the immediate dangers of VR (Bachman & Carmody, 1994), and Jacobson & Gottman (1998, see pages 160–162) viewed VR as one important indicator that a woman will soon leave her abusive partner. It is time that we give more research attention to the incidence and nature of VR in partner violence.

Mutual violent control. Johnson (1999, 2000a) identified a couple pattern in which both husband and wife are controlling and violent, in a situation that could be viewed as two intimate terrorists battling for control. The pattern seems to be rare and we know little about it, but it raises questions again about the importance of distinctions. Until recently the literature on mutual violence was either framed in terms of "self-defense" or "mutual combat," (Saunders, 1988), but the little we do know about VR, MVC, and mutual violence in CCV suggests a need for much more focused research on what it means when both partners in a relationship are violent.

General implications. We have given these distinctions considerable attention because in our review we found our understanding of the literature to be improved by making distinctions among types of violence. For example, the marital violence literature is rife with studies that claim to show that partner violence is gender symmetric, if not perpetrated more often by women than by men, continuing to leave readers of this literature with the impression that men and women are equally abusive. Almost all of these studies, however, use the sort of general heterosexual sample in which aggregated violence only appears to be gender symmetric because it lumps together IT, which is essentially perpetrated by men; CCV, which is perpetrated slightly more often by men than by women; and VR, which is clearly perpetrated more often by women than by men (Johnson, 2000b). Similarly, Macmillan and Gartner (1999) demonstrated the centrality of such distinctions in causal research. They found three qualitatively distinct forms of spousal violence against women, two of which they identified with CCV and IT. When they used these classes as dependent variables in multivariate analyses, the models for CCV and IT were clearly different.

Types of Perpetrators

We see a major convergence in the many attempts to develop typologies of male batterers, suggesting three types: one involved in CCV and two types of perpetrators of IT.

Holtzworth-Munroe and Stuart (1994) referred to these types as "family-only," "generally-violent-antisocial," and "dysphoric-borderline." It appears to us that the family-only type may involve primarily CCV because they were described by the authors as involved in "the least severe marital violence and . . . the least likely to engage in psychological and sexual abuse" (p. 481). The other types (whom we see as involved in IT) come to their terrorism through two quite different developmental histories and psychological profiles, one type broadly sociopathic and violent, the other deeply emotionally dependent on their relationship with their partner (see also Dutton, 1995).

The types identified by Jacobson and Gottman (1998) in a sample of men that seems to include only intimate terrorists bear a striking similarity to generally-violent-antisocials and dysphoric-borderlines. The sample of couples they studied had identified themselves as involved in violent relationships, and Jacobson and Gottman reported that practically all of the men were emotionally abusive (p. 155) in addition to being violent. The Jacobson and Gottman research is unique in that in addition to being interviewed, observed, and given psychological tests, the couples were monitored physiologically during arguments in the laboratory. One group of men (labeled memorably as "cobras") exhibited a "cold" physiology even in the heat of vicious verbal attacks on their partners, with heart rate and other physiological indicators that suggest a chilling internal calmness. The characteristics of this group and their personal histories resembles those of generally-violent-antisocial batterers. The second group identified by Jacobson and Gottman ("pit bulls") was more physiologically in tune with the emotional displays involved in their verbal attacks on their partner, and in other respects they resembled the dysphoric-borderline type in that they are dependent and needy. Holtzworth-Munroe and Stuart's hypotheses about the development of different types of batterers have received general empirical support in a number of empirical tests (e.g., Hamberger, Lohr, Bonge, & Tolin, 1996; Holtzworth-Munroe, Meehan, Herron, Rehman, & Stuart, in press).

Types of perpetrators within types of violence. We believe that major advances in our understanding of the origins of partner violence will come from bringing together and extending the work on types of violence and types of perpetrators. These distinctions have already demonstrated their usefulness in understanding the causes of battery and in developing treatment programs for batterers (Saunders, 1996), and the Jacobson and Gottman (1998) book is an accessible and compelling demonstration of the importance of such distinctions in matters as far ranging as the childhood precursors of partner violence, the developmental course of violent relationships, the process of escaping such relationships, and matters of public policy and intervention strategies. Most of this perpetrator work is focused on male IT, but we believe it might also be useful to attempt to develop typologies of male and female CCV perpetrators as well (Holtzworth-Munroe & Stuart, 1994; Holtzworth-Munroe et al., in press).

Types of Relationships

The 1990s have also seen an explosion in information about violence in different types of partner relationships. There is now a massive literature on dating and courtship violence and a growing literature on violence in cohabiting relationships. Some of this work has focused on same-gender relationships.

Same-sex relationships. Although a recent issue of the *Journal of Gay and Lesbian Social Services* was devoted to violence within both male and female same-gender relationships (Renzetti & Miley, 1996), we still seem to know more about lesbian battering than we do about violence in gay men's relationships, in part because of the important role of the women's movement in generating research on domestic violence (Dobash & Dobash, 1992) and in part because of Claire Renzetti's (1992) groundbreaking research on lesbian relationships. Her conclusion that psychological abuse was present in all of the violent relationships that she studied, that these abusive partners were extremely threatened by their partner's efforts to establish independent friendships and activities, that jealousy was a major problem, and that power and control were major sources of conflict all suggest to us that her sample tapped into IT. Furthermore, the fact that the majority of women in Renzetti's sample (68%) indicated that their partner's dependency was a source of conflict suggests a similarity to Jacobson and Gottman's "pit bulls" and Holtzworth-Munroe and Stuart's dysphoric-borderline type. Thus, it may be possible that some variation or elaboration of the models developed with heterosexual couples can provide insight into violence in lesbian couples.

Some of the most striking differences between lesbian battery and heterosexual battery have to do with links to the external environment of the relationship. Threats of "outing" women to family members or employers are common forms of psychological abuse and are of course unique to

same-gender couples; battered lesbians are evidently less likely to be supported by friends, who often refuse to believe that a lesbian can be an abuser; and social service workers are often unsupportive as well, assuming that only men batter their partners (Renzetti, 1992).

Although the women's movement has made efforts to educate service providers and the public about lesbian battering (Elliot, 1990), specialized services are rare and research is still quite limited. We still know little about the varieties of partner violence in same-gender relationships (for example, the extent of CCV or IT). The inability to collect information from random samples means that we know almost nothing about incidence. These gaps in our knowledge are troubling not only because they leave policy makers and service providers somewhat on their own, but also because research on partner violence in diverse types of relationships could be an important source of insights into the inadequacies of our "general" theories. Both Merrill and Renzetti (Merrill, 1996; Renzetti, 1992) have pointed out aspects of partner violence in same-gender relationships that seem to fly in the face of theories developed in a heterosexual context. This may be an arena in which much can be gained in terms of the testing and revision of general theory.

Dating and courtship. Research on partner violence in heterosexual dating and courtship relationships began early in the 1980s and has continued throughout the 1990s (Lloyd & Emery, 2000). Although we appear to know a good deal about what was initially a most surprising incidence of partner violence in dating relationships, this literature is as plagued by lack of distinctions as is the marital violence literature. Frequent statements in the literature that there is as much violence in these relationships as there is in marriage imply that there is as much IT, but because the data are drawn from general social surveys, they probably include only CCV.

Rather than review this extensive literature here, we would simply like to point out that it has been a rich source of theoretical insight regarding partner violence. A great many of the multivariate analyses of the correlates of violence have been done in this context (Bookwala, Frieze, Smith, & Ryan, 1992; Foo & Margolin, 1995; Riggs & O'Leary, 1996; Riggs, O'Leary, & Breslin, 1990; Tontodonato & Crew, 1992; Wyatt, 1994). Stets's theoretical work on the centrality of control issues grew from her work on dating violence (Stets &

Pirog-Good, 1990), and Lloyd & Emery's (Lloyd & Emery, 2000) recent book develops a general theoretical framework for understanding physical violence in dating relationships that could be used to address partner violence in all types of relationships.

Cohabitation. Serious discussion of the extent of partner violence in cohabiting relationships can be traced to Stets and Straus's (1990) puzzling finding that cohabiting couples reported more violence than did either married or dating couples, even with controls for age, education, and occupation. Recent studies in New Zealand and Canada also report a higher rate of violence in cohabiting relationships, compared with dating (Magdol, Moffitt, Caspi, & Silva, 1998), and marriage (Johnson, 1996). Although in the United States, the National Violence Against Women Survey appears to present data on cohabitation (Tjaden & Thoennes, 1999, pp. 27–29), the data actually refer to lifetime victimization of respondents who have a history of cohabitation and do not allow for easy interpretation. One possible complication in this cohabitation literature is the confounding of age, length of relationship, and marital status. In Canada, Johnson (1996, pp. 166–168) found that the difference between married and cohabiting unions held only for couples who had been together for 3 years or less.

Stets and Straus (1990) introduced three possible explanations of marital status differences: social isolation, autonomy–control, and investment. Although Stets (1991) claimed to demonstrate that social isolation "explains" the effect, the only measure of social isolation that works in her analysis is "ties to spouse," as measured by the respondents' report of the chances that they will separate. We think it makes more sense to see this as a measure of commitment to the relationship, suggesting only that low commitment is either a consequence or a cause of partner violence in cohabiting relationships. Gaertner and Foshee's (1999) data support this interpretation, showing a negative relationship between commitment and violence in dating relationships. They also reported data relevant to the investment explanation, finding that both duration of relationship and reported investment are *positively* related to violence, the opposite of what Stets and Straus predicted.

Stets and Straus's data actually show that the pattern of more violence occurring in cohabitation than in marriage does not hold for couples in which only the man was violent (p. 240). Perhaps the pattern is relevant only to CCV. Macmillan and Gartner (1999) reported that marriage is negatively related to CCV, but positively to IT. Perhaps marriage, although not a license to hit, is for some people a license to terrorize. Once again, we see an area in which distinctions among types of violence would help to clarify matters.

Demographics, Social Location, and Identity

Gender. The most longstanding and acrimonious debate in the family literature involves the issue of gender symmetry of partner violence (Archer, 2000; Dobash & Dobash, 1992; Dobash, Dobash, Wilson, & Daly, 1992; Johnson, 1995; Kurz, 1989, 1993; Straus, 1990a, 1993). Although papers continue to appear regularly that claim to demonstrate that women are as violent as men in intimate relationships of one kind or another, or in one country or another, a careful assessment of the literature and a look at the few studies that do distinguish among types of violence both indicate that IT is almost entirely a male pattern (97% male in Johnson, 2000a). The evidence seems to indicate that VR is primarily perpetrated by women (Browne, Williams, et al., 1999; Cascardi & Vivian, 1995; Dobash & Dobash, 1992; Johnson, 2000a; Ogle, Maier-Katkin, & Bernard, 1995; Saunders, 1988). CCV appears to be roughly gender symmetric (56% male perpetrators in Johnson, 2000a; see also Milardo, 1998).

Most studies define gender symmetry in terms of the percent of men and women who have perpetrated at least one act of violence in their relationship. To call this gender symmetry, however, is to ignore different male and female frequencies of violence and the different physical consequences of male-to-female and female-to-male violence. As for the former, Johnson (1999) showed that in 31% of the relationships involving "mutual" CCV, the husbands were clearly more frequently violent than were their wives, compared with 8% in which the wives were more frequently violent. With regard to injury, the more serious physical consequences of male-to-female violence are well-established (Brush, 1990; Sorenson, Upchurch, & Shen, 1996; Straus, 1990a, 1999; Tjaden & Thoennes, 1999).

A number of studies have focused on the possibility that the causes of violence are not the same for men and women. Foo and Margolin (1995) reported in a dating context that a set of standard predictor variables explains 41% of the variance in male-to-female violence, but only 16%

for female-to-male violence (see also Anderson, 1997).

Although work on the gender symmetry issue is of interest in itself, it has also provided an important site for both methodological developments and theoretical insights into the nature of partner violence. Methodologically, the debate has prompted a number of developments, including a new version of the CTS (Straus, Hamby, Boney-McCoy, & Sugarman, 1996), a major reconsideration of the interview context of assessments of violence (Straus, 1999; Tjaden & Thoennes, 1999), and discussions of couple-data issues (Szinovacz & Egley, 1995). The debate has also generated attention to the sampling issues involved in various research designs (Johnson, 2000b; Straus, 1990a).

With regard to theory, the debate has prompted Straus to consider some of the social roots of women's violence toward their male partners (Straus, 1999). He discussed factors such as women's assumption that their violence is harmless (Fiebert & Gonzalez, 1997) and that under some conditions slapping a man is an appropriately "feminine" behavior. Johnson (1995) also provided a rudimentary list of gendered causal factors in partner violence, and he argued that some combinations of them might produce CCV, whereas others produce IT. Other theoretical work of the decade that has arisen from a focus on gender includes theory focused on the broader social context (Dobash & Dobash, 1992, 1998; Straus, 1999), social construction of gender models (Anderson, 1997; Dobash & Dobash, 1998), and evolutionary models (Buss & Shackelford, 1997; Wilson & Daly, 1996, 1998). Of course, gender also is centrally implicated in the literature on gay and lesbian relationships in ways that may prompt further theoretical development as we are forced to ask ourselves which aspects of the gendering of partner violence are a function of male-female differences and which are more related to the specifically gendered nature of heterosexual relationships (Renzetti & Miley, 1996; West, 1998).

Race and ethnicity in North America. Most of the earliest race and ethnicity scholarship did not give serious attention to ethnic differences in experiences of abuse or responses to it, focusing instead primarily on Black-White differences in incidence (Crenshaw, 1994). That literature has continued into the 1990s with survey research regularly indicating higher levels of partner violence among Blacks than among Whites (Anderson, 1997; Ca-

zenave & Straus, 1990; Greenfield & Rand, 1998; Sorenson, 1996; Tjaden & Thoennes, 1999). Recent work has broadened ethnic comparisons to cover other groups, however. For example, only 13% of Asian and Pacific Islander women in the 1995–1996 National Violence Against Women Survey (Tjaden & Thoennes, pp. 22–26) reported having been physically assaulted by an intimate partner. For White women, the figure is 21%, for African Americans 26%, for American Indian and Alaska Natives 31%, and for Mixed Race 27%.

There are two important questions we have to ask about these differences. First, what kind of violence are we talking about? These surveys do not make distinctions among the various types of violence discussed above. We do not know if higher incidence of violence reported in these surveys necessarily means more IT. It is more likely to be CCV. We cannot develop good theories about race differences until we make such distinctions. Second, we have to ask about the extent to which "race" differences have less to do with race and ethnicity than they do with socioeconomic status, as has been shown in National Family Violence Survey data (Cazenave & Straus, 1990). Lockheart's (1991) more recent survey of 307 African American and European American women, drawn equally from high-, middle-, and low-income brackets, found no significant racial differences in rates of violence.

Beyond questions of incidence, there is now a growing literature that focuses on more institutional and cultural matters. Are the dominant social institutions addressing domestic violence effectively in various cultural and ethnic contexts? Are the services women need available in their communities? Are kin, friends, and community willing to face issues of domestic violence and to work to eliminate it? Are the psychological and social consequences the same in different groups? For example, Eng (1995) noted that acknowledgment of battering is highly shameful for many immigrant Asian women who are socialized to believe that marital failure is always the fault of a wife (see also Song, 1996). Gondolf, Fisher, & McFerron (1991) examined 5,708 Texas shelter residents and found no significant differences in the amounts of violence experienced by White, African American, and Hispanic women but did find that Hispanic women were relatively disadvantaged economically and tended to endure battering for a longer time than White and African American women. Crenshaw (1994) was one of the first scholars to identify gaps in domestic violence services for women of color and insensitivity to issues of race and ethnicity in developing policy agendas such as mandatory arrest. Such issues are beginning to be addressed for a number of major ethnic and racial groups in North America, including American Indian people (Bachman, 1992; Fairchild, Fairchild, & Stoner, 1998; McEachern, Winkle, & Steiner, 1998; Norton & Manson, 1995; Tom-Orme, 1995; Waller, Risley-Curtis, Murphy, Medill, & Moore, 1998), Asian and Pacific Island people (Abraham, 1995; Ho, 1990; Song, 1996; Yick & Agbayani-Siewert, 1997), Latino groups (Perilla, Bakerman, & Norris, 1994), and African Americans (Dennis, Key, Kirk, & Smith, 1995; Marsh, 1993; Richie, 1996).

As this literature grows, it will be important to attend to two general questions. First, can we identify social forces that shape experiences similarly across subsets of "minority" groups, such as similarities produced by common experiences of exclusion and domination, or the experience of recent immigration (Cervantes & Cervantes, 1993; Root, 1996; Sorenson, 1996)? Second, what are the unique ways in which each particular racial and ethnic context shapes domestic violence, its consequences, and community responses to it? Even within "standard" racial and ethnic categories, there are important distinctions that cannot be ignored. In one illustration of the importance of making such distinctions, Sorenson and Telles (1991, pp. 3) reported no difference between non-Hispanic Whites and Mexican Americans in their sample until immigration status was taken into account: "Mexican Americans born in the US reported rates 2.4 times higher than those born in Mexico." This finding can serve to remind us not only of the importance of differences among specific groups in North America, but also of matters of cultural roots and immigrant status that have global implications (Kane, 1999).

Global complexities. We can only begin to address the global complexity of partner violence in this review, involving as it does issues of cultural differences, economic and social structure, effects of conflict and warfare, and the position of immigrant and refugee populations. To begin, we can simply draw attention to a number of overviews of the international scope of partner violence (Heise, 1996; Heise, Raikes, Watts, & Zwi, 1994; Human Rights Watch, 1995; Klein, 1998; Levinson, 1989; Sewall, Vasan, & Schuler, 1996; United Nations, 1989). In addition, scholarly work in English on domestic violence in specific other countries is beginning to become available (Alexander, 1993; Dawud-Noursi, Lamb, & Sternberg, 1998; Fawcett, Heise, Isita-Espejel, & Pick, 1999; Glantz, Halperin, & Hunt, 1998; Gondolf & Shestakou, 1997; Grandin & Lupri, 1997; Haj-Yahia, 1998; Handwerker, 1998; Kalu, 1993; Ofei-Aboagye, 1994; Schuler, Hashemi, Riley, & Akhter, 1996; Stewart, 1996; Tang, 1994). Finally, we would like to address briefly a few specific international issues.

First, in a global context domestic violence has now been defined as a human rights issue (Richters, 1994). Second, there appears to be considerable variability in the incidence of partner violence in various countries (Heise, 1994). Of course, we do not know what type of violence these statistics reference. Furthermore, as we consider these clues to the social and cultural roots of partner violence, it will be important to monitor our interpretations for ethnocentrism. For example, Bhattacharjee (1997) questions the assumption of Western White feminism that Southeast Asian women are more subservient to husbands.

Third, a literature is developing that explores the effects of war, internal conflict, and terrorism on matters related to partner violence. McWilliams (1998) framed the issue as one of "societies under stress," using the case of Northern Ireland as her major example. Community resources are diverted to the conflict, a higher priority is placed on keeping families together, public agencies may be controlled by the "enemy," calls for ingroup solidarity militate against making internal conflicts such as domestic violence public, and "warrior" images reinforce patriarchal ideology. As we read McWilliams' chapter, we were intrigued by the possibility that many of these same processes might be relevant to racial and ethnic minorities in the United States who are under siege, albeit a "siege" that generally falls short of the open intergroup violence that applies in the cases McWilliams discusses.

In countries recovering from war, pronatalist policies may limit access to contraceptive devices or reduce women's ability to procure employment that might allow them to escape an abusive situation. Additionally, people suffering from the continuing effects of occupation, such as the majority of indigenous groups worldwide, have high rates of interpersonal and domestic violence related to the destruction of culture and oppressive economic and social conditions (McWilliams, 1998, p. 123–124). Scholarship on the effects of colonization, decolonization, war, and development on rates and forms of partner violence is in its infancy. Filling this gap is an important task for the next decade of research.

Finally, immigrant and refugee status (sometimes a result of flight from the kind of societal stress discussed above) creates special difficulties for women trying to escape abusive relationships. Immigrant women experiencing violence in their homes often are restricted by language barriers, fear of deportation, lack of transportation, fear of loss of child custody, and cultural taboos (Hogeland & Rosen, 1990).

Summary

Some distinctions are central to the theoretical and practical understanding of the nature of partner violence (e.g., types of violence and perpetrators), others provide important contexts for developing more sensitive and comprehensive theories (e.g., types of relationships or gender differences), and others may simply force us to question our tendency to generalize carelessly from one context to another. Such distinctions were a major theme of the domestic violence literature of the 1990s, and they must continue to be so into the next decade.

CONTROL

A second major theme of the 1990s has been control. Whatever the immediate precipitator of violence may be, it generally gives the perpetrator some measure of control, but once again we see distinctions among types of violence as central. The control may be specific, focused narrowly on winning a particular argument or having one's way in some narrowly defined matter (CCV). In other cases the control may be broad, involving the establishment or maintenance of general control over one's partner (IT, MVC). Sometimes the control issue is one of wresting some modicum of control from a generally abusive partner (VR). We believe that the most progress will be made in our understanding of domestic violence by assuming that the origins and dynamics of the different kinds of control motives are not the same.

In our review of this literature, we want to make a somewhat arbitrary distinction. Some writers have come to their focus on control issues through an analysis of the patriarchal roots of wife beating (Dobash & Dobash, 1992; Johnson, 1995; Pence & Paymar, 1993). Although this is our own primary orientation, we believe that a full understanding of partner violence must go beyond this

feminist analysis to ask questions about the role of control in the generation of violence that may have little to do either with patriarchal traditions and structures or with individual patriarchal motives.

The Gender Context

Johnson's (1995) discussion of IT as violence embedded in a general pattern of control tactics draws heavily on the work of the Duluth shelter activists Pence and Paymar (1993). The "power and control wheel" that is the heart of the Duluth educational model for intervention with batterers is drawn directly from the accounts of women who have come to shelters for help. Kirkwood's (1993) study of women who left abusive relationships also relied heavily on an analysis of the dynamics of control. Dobash and Dobash's (1992); analysis of the dynamics of wife beating was likewise formed by the perspectives of battered women, in this case women whom they interviewed in their early research in Scotland, but they also drew heavily on a more sociological and historical analysis of the patriarchal form of the family and other institutions. They now are beginning to explore control issues from the perspective of the violent men themselves (Dobash & Dobash, 1998). Their arguments regarding the importance of context refer not only to the relationship context in which a particular man may feel he has the right to control "his woman," but also the more general context in which relations between men and women are formed and in which other institutions react to men's violence against their female partners.

Whereas Dobash and Dobash, as well as other feminists, tend to move the analysis up from the relationship to the broader societal context of wife beating, Jacobson and Gottman (1998) moved down to the individual level, asking questions about the childhood roots of the personalities of the two types of perpetrators whom they identified among their sample of men who batter their partners. Similarly, other psychologists who focus on wife beating but do not rely heavily on a feminist analysis search for the developmental roots of men's violent behavior toward their female partners (Dutton, 1995; Dutton & Starzomski, 1993; Holtzworth-Munroe et al., in press; Holtzworth-Munroe, Stuart, & Hutchinson, 1997).

Prospects for a More General Analysis of Control

The problem with the analyses of control discussed above is that they are so focused on male

IT that they probably provide little insight into CCV or VR, and they seem to have little relevance for any type of partner violence in same-gender relationships. We need a more general approach to issues of violence and control that can encompass IT in heterosexual relationships but also go beyond it.

Beginning with a study that focused on the connection between relationship control and violence, Jan Stets and her colleagues have developed two lines of analysis of the role of control in intimate relationships (Stets & Pirog-Good, 1990). One line of work focuses on a "compensatory model" in which it is assumed that individuals act to maintain a reasonable level of control in their lives, becoming more controlling of their partner when their level of control is threatened either within the relationship itself (Stets, 1993, 1995b) or in other areas of their life (Stets, 1995a). In a slightly different approach, paying more attention to individual differences, the concepts of "control identity" and "mastery identity" were explored in terms of their relationships to gender, gender identity, and controlling behavior in intimate relationships (Stets, 1995c; Stets & Burke, 1994, 1996).

If this literature could be brought back to its initial connection with violence, and perhaps informed more by feminist analyses of the gendering of control issues in relationships, it might provide a context for major theory development. We expect that the most fruitful approaches will bring together a variety of levels of analysis from the societal through the interpersonal to the individual (for example, see Lloyd & Emery, 2000).

SOME OTHER CONTINUING THEMES

Coping With Partner Violence

Most of the literature on coping with violence is focused on IT. In the 1990s, the dominant view shifted from seeing women in abusive relationships as victims to defining them as "survivors," focusing on the decisions women make to escape, to end the violence, or to cope with it in some other manner (Ferraro, 1997). Campbell and her colleagues (Campbell, Miller, Cardwell, & Belknap, 1994; Campbell, Rose, Kub, & Nedd, 1998) argued that the women they studied over a 2½-year period showed great resourcefulness in their resistance to the pattern of violent control in which they were enmeshed. Strategies included (a) active problem solving, (b) responding to identifiable pivotal events, and (c) negotiating first with oneself and then directly or indirectly with the male partner. By the end of the 2½ years, three fourths of the battered women were no longer in a violent relationship, 43% having left and 32% having successfully negotiated an end to the violence. This is yet another area in which distinctions among types of violence and types of relationship are likely to be useful. Strategies of negotiation and barriers to leaving are likely to differ rather dramatically for IT and CCV and across dating, cohabiting, same-gender and cross-gender relationships.

Leaving. The coping strategy that has received the most attention is "leaving," all-too-often addressed from a misguided sense of puzzlement that women do not leave abusive relationships. We still see papers and sections of literature reviews and textbooks headed "Why do they stay?" Well, the truth is, they don't stay (Campbell et al., 1994; Holtzworth-Munroe, Smutzler, & Sandin, 1997, pp. 194–95). We need to watch our language; there is no good reason why a study in which two thirds of the women have left the violent relationship is subtitled, "How and why women stay" instead of "How and why women leave" (Herbert, Silver, & Ellard, 1991).

One theoretical approach that seems promising draws upon commitment theory. Rusbult and Martz (1995) make use of Rusbult's investment model to investigate the effects of commitment, rewards, costs, alternatives, and investments on whether women in abusive relationships stay or leave within the time frame of the study. We believe, however, that the best work on staying and leaving will have to treat leaving as a process. Choice & Lamke (1997) did that to some extent, identifying two stages of leaving in which women ask themselves first "Will I be better off?" and second "Can I do it?" But there is other work that focuses in more detail on the process of leaving.

Kirkwood's (1993) marvelous book takes us into both the process by which abusive men entrap their partners and the process by which those women engineer their escape. Her two metaphors of a "web" of entrapment and of a "spiral" of escape capture the details of the process simply and vividly. These men use a wide range of tactics of control not only to control the intact relationship, but also to ensure as best they can that their partner will never be able to leave them. Johnson's (1998) analysis of the shelter movement addressed this process in terms of the abuser's manipulation of personal, moral, and structural commitments to the relationship in order to entrap his partner. He argued that the major strategies of the battered women's movement (temporary safe housing, support groups, empowerment counseling, networking with social support services, legal advocacy, coordinated community response) empower women to neutralize those commitments. Kirkwood also acknowledged the role of shelter advocates in helping the women she studied as they went through a process of leaving and returning, each time gaining more psychological and social resources, each time coming closer to escaping for good, metaphorically spiraling outward until they escaped from the web.

Psychological and Behavioral Consequences of Partner Violence

As we approach the end of this article, we come upon a huge research literature dealing with the psychological consequences of partner violence for the adults involved and for their children. Once again, however, we have to note the difficulties created by not taking care to distinguish among types of violence. Although some of the studies in this literature make use of samples in which the violence is clearly IT, others analyze survey data in which the measurement of violence does not attend to differences that may have critical implications in terms of consequences. A slap in the face sometime in the last 12 months is likely to have little impact on self-esteem and may not even be witnessed by the children. A systematic pattern of assault and psychological abuse is another story.

The victims. Nevertheless, the literature confirms that IT and perhaps other forms of partner violence *against women* have negative effects in terms of injuries and longer-term physical and psychological health (Giles-Sims, 1998; Holtzworth-Munroe et al., 1997, pp. 184–189; Johnson & Leone, 2000). The psychological effects include posttraumatic stress disorder, depression, and lowered self-esteem.

There is another interesting line of research that focuses not on psychological health, but on women's attributions regarding the causes of the violence they are experiencing. Holtzworth-Munroe and her colleagues (Holtzworth-Munroe, Jacobson, Fehrenbach, & Fruzzetti, 1992) argue, on the basis of a literature review, that the evidence

shows women do not generally blame themselves for their partner's violence (see also Cantos, Neidig, & O'Leary, 1993). Nonetheless, the fact that issues of victim self-blame are raised often in the more qualitative literature suggests that research on attributions as moderating variables, affecting the consequences of violence, might be useful (Andrews & Brewin, 1990; Fincham, Bradbury, Arias, Byrne, & Karney, 1997).

Studies that have compared physical and psychological consequences for men and women find more serious consequences for women (Browne, Williams, et al., 1999; Brush, 1990; Dobash et al., 1992; Grandin, Lupri, & Brinkerhoff, 1998; Sorenson et al., 1996; Straus, 1999; Vivian & Langhinrichson-Rohling, 1994). Of course, the danger in these comparisons is that they may be comparing apples and oranges because most of them deal with survey data in which no distinctions among types of violence are made. It is unlikely that many of the men in such surveys are experiencing IT, whereas a significant number of the female victims of violence are (Johnson, 2000a). Qualitative and anecdotal evidence suggest that the consequences of terroristic violence may be as severe for men as they are for women (Cook, 1997; Island & Letellier, 1991; Letellier, 1996).

The children. There is also a substantial literature regarding the effects of partner violence on children who witness it (Kolbo, Blakely, & Engleman, 1996; Wolak & Finkelhor, 1998). Behavioral effects include aggression and delinquency, among others. Psychological effects include anxiety, depression, and low self-esteem. There is even evidence of long-term effects, with college-age women who remember violence between their parents having lower self-esteem, greater depression, and lower levels of social competence (Henning, Leitenberg, Coffey, Bennett, & Jankowski, 1997; Silvern, Karyl, Waelde, Hodges, & Starek, 1995). Again, however, we have to point out that although some of these studies deal with populations in which the nature of the parental violence is relatively clear, in most cases the measures do not allow the necessary distinctions. The reported effects are generally small, but we do not know if exposure to IT might in fact have powerful effects that are muted by their aggregation with the effects of CCV.

Intergenerational nontransmission of violence. One particular type of long-term effect on children has been studied enough to merit its own section.

Although it is not unusual for scholars to take the position that "violence in the family of origin is probably the mostly widely accepted risk marker for the occurrence of partner violence (Kantor & Jasinski, 1998, p.16), we are struck by the weakness of the relationship in the studies we reviewed. In this as in other areas of socialization research, the widespread use of the metaphor of "transmission" introduces a gross distortion of the reality of family-of-origin effects on the adult lives of children. Nevertheless, scholars have moved on to assessment of the mechanisms by which "transmission" takes place, in many cases with data that effectively show no "transmission" to begin with. For example, Simons, Lin, & Gordon (1998) presented structural equation models of the process by which parental behavior affects dating violence of their children, failing to draw our attention to the fact that the largest zero-order correlation they find is .12, representing roughly 1% of the variance in dating violence. Then there is a study of marriage and marriagelike relationships (Lackey & Williams, 1995) that takes intergenerational transmission for granted and restricts its major analyses to investigating the conditions under which men whose parents were violent do not become violent themselves. Buried in their appendix is the correlation that represents the intergenerational effect in their data ($r = .10$), once again an explained variance of 1%. Foshee, Bauman, and Linder (1999) similarly tested models of intervening variables for effects the largest of which represent 2% of the variance in dating violence.

The important point here is not just that the effects are small. Social scientists indeed often do make much of such small effects in other areas as well. Our concern is that the metaphor of transmission, and the use of terms such as "cycle of violence," imply that partner violence is inexorably passed on from generation to generation. We want to drive home our concern here with widely cited data that may represent the strongest intergenerational effect ever reported in this literature. Analyzing data from the first National Family Violence Survey, Straus, Gelles, and Steinmetz (1988, p.101) reported that "the sons of the most violent parents have a rate of wife-beating 1,000 percent greater than that of the sons of nonviolent parents . . . ." What we deleted with our ellipses is the actual rate of 20%, meaning that even among this group of men whose parents were two standard deviations above average in level of partner violence, 80% of the adult sons had not even

once in the last 12 months committed any acts of severe violence toward their partners as defined by the CTS. What about the 20% who *were* violent? We must return to our old refrain that we have no way of knowing which type of violence these men (or their parents) perpetrated.

Social Consequences of Partner Violence

During the 1990s, scholarship began to focus on the interconnections of partner violence, poverty, welfare, and homelessness. This work became particularly relevant with the passage of so-called welfare reform in 1996, which included the possibility for states to exempt battered women from some of its most restrictive mandates (Kurz, 1998). Research focusing specifically on low-income women has uncovered an extraordinarily high level of interpersonal violence, which interferes with social and economic success. Zorza (1991) found that at least half of homeless women were forced from residences because of violence from their intimate partners. Browne and Bassuk (1997) interviewed 220 homeless and 216 housed low-income women in Massachusetts about childhood abuse and adult intimate violence. Nearly one third of respondents reported that their current or most recent partner had perpetrated severe physical violence against them. Browne and her colleagues (Browne, Salomon, & Bassuk, 1999) also reported that "Controlling for a variety of factors, women who experienced physical aggression/violence by male partners during a 12-month period had only one third the odds of maintaining employment for at least 30 hrs per week for 6 months or more during the subsequent year as did women without these experiences." Other examinations of the effects of battering on women's employment (Brandwein, 1998; Lloyd, 1999) have reported that abusive men deliberately undermine women's employment by depriving them of transportation, harassing them at work, turning off alarm clocks, beating them before job interviews, and disappearing when they promised to provide child care. Some abusers simply prohibit their partners from working. Battering also indirectly undermines employment by (a) causing repeated absences; (b) impairing women's physical health, mental agility and concentration; and (3) lowering self-esteem and aspirations. Thus, although surveys and crime statistics indicate higher levels of partner violence among low-income couples and in lower income neighborhoods (Anderson, 1997; Lupri, Grandin, & Brinkerhoff, 1994;

Miles-Doan, 1998; Straus, 1990b), for many women violence may be the *precipitating* factor for poverty, and it is surely a barrier to raising income and employment status.

CONCLUSION

The 1990s were a time of tremendous growth in the literature on partner violence, including considerable growth in attention to the need to make distinctions among various types of violence. Unfortunately, our major conclusion from this review of the decade is that in spite of increasing evidence of the importance of distinctions, almost all of our general theoretical and empirical work is severely handicapped by the failure to attend to these distinctions. The modeling of the causes and consequences of partner violence will never be powerful as long as we aggregate behaviors as disparate as a "feminine" slap in the face, a terrorizing pattern of beatings accompanied by humiliating psychological abuse, an argument that escalates into a mutual shoving match, or a homicide committed by a person who feels there is no other way to save her own life.

Even more troubling, however, is the possibility that the aggregation of such disparate phenomena can produce serious errors, as it did in the gender symmetry debate. Everything from lists of risk factors, to inferences about causal processes from multivariate analyses, to statements about differences in incidence across groups or across time—all of it—is called into question. Going back through this review, one can hardly find a section in which we did not feel the need to question generalization across types of violence. We need to return to our research, make distinctions among types of violence, and find out which of our pronouncements apply to which forms of violence.

We hope that the beginning of this century will see work on partner violence that is more careful to make important distinctions among types of violence and to develop theories that take into account the different causes, dynamics, and consequences of the different forms of violence. Equally important is the presentation of our knowledge to each other and to the general public in terms that clearly reflect those differences, so that public opinion and policy development can make *appropriate* use of what we learn.

REFERENCES

Abraham, M. (1995). Ethnicity, gender, and marital violence: South Asian women's organizations in the United States. *Gender and Society, 9,* 450–468.

Alexander, R. (1993). Wife battering—An Australian perspective. *Journal of Family Violence, 8,* 229–251.

Anderson, K. L. (1997). Gender, status and domestic violence: An integration of feminist and family violence approaches. *Journal of Marriage and the Family, 59,* 655–669.

Andrews, B., & Brewin, C. R. (1990). Attributions of blame for marital violence: A study of antecedents and consequences. *Journal of Marriage and the Family, 52,* 757–767.

Archer, J. (in press). Sex differences in aggression between heterosexual partners: A meta-analytic review. *Psychological Bulletin.*

Bachman, R. (1992). *Death and violence on the reservation: Homicide, family violence, and suicide in American Indian populations.* Westport, CT: Autumn House.

Bachman, R., & Carmody, D. (1994). Fighting fire with fire: The effects of victim resistance in intimate versus stranger perpetrated assaults against females. *Journal of Family Violence, 9,* 317–331.

Bhattacharjee, A. (1997). The public/private mirage: Mapping homes and undomesticating violence work in the South Asian immigrant community. In M. J. Alexander & C. T. Mohanty (Eds.), *Feminist genealogies, colonial legacies, democratic futures* (pp. 308–329). New York: Routledge.

Bookwala, J., Frieze, I. H., Smith, C., & Ryan, K. (1992). Predictors of dating violence: A multivariate analysis. *Violence and Victims, 7,* 297–311.

Brandwein, R. A. (1998). *Battered women, children, and welfare reform: The ties that bind.* Thousand Oaks, CA: Sage.

Brant, B. (1996). Wild Turkeys. In S. Koppelman (Ed.), *Women in the trees: U.S. women's short stories about battering & resistance, 1839-1994* (pp. 199–230). Thousand Oaks, CA: Sage.

Browne, A., & Bassuk, S. S. (1997). Intimate violence in the lives of homeless and poor housed women: Prevalence and patterns in an ethnically diverse sample. *American Journal of Orthopsychiatry, 67,* 261–278.

Browne, A., Salomon, A., & Bassuk, S. S. (1999). The impact of recent partner violence on poor women's capacity to maintain work. *Violence Against Women, 5,* 393–426.

Browne, A., Williams, K. R., & Dutton, D. G. (1999). Homicide between intimate partners: A 20-year review. In M. D. Smith & M. A. Zahn (Eds.), *Homicide: A sourcebook of social research* (pp. 149–164). Thousand Oaks, CA: Sage.

Brush, L. D. (1990). Violent acts and injurious outcomes in married couples: Methodological issues in the National Survey of Families and Households. *Gender & Society, 4,* 56–67.

Buss, D. M., & Shackelford, T. K. (1997). From vigilance to violence: Mate retention tactics in married couples. *Journal of Personality and Social Psychology, 72,* 346–361.

Campbell, J. C., Miller, P., Cardwell, M. M., & Belknap,

R. A. (1994). Relationship status of battered women over time. *Journal of Family Violence, 9,* 99–111.

Campbell, J. C., Rose, L., Kub, J., & Nedd, D. (1998). Voices of strength and resistance: A contextual and longitudinal analysis of women's responses to battering. *Journal of Interpersonal Violence, 13,* 743–762.

Cantos, A. L., Neidig, P. H., & O'Leary, K. D. (1993). Men and women's attributions of blame for domestic violence. *Journal of Family Violence, 8,* 289–302.

Cascardi, M., & Vivian, D. (1995). Context for specific episodes of marital violence: Gender and severity of violence differences. *Journal of Family Violence, 10,* 265–293.

Cazenave, N. A., & Straus, M. A. (1990). Race, class, network embeddedness, and family violence: A search for potent support systems. In M. A. Straus & R. J. Gelles (Eds.), *Physical violence in American families* (pp. 321–339). Brunswick, NJ: Transaction.

Cervantes, N. N., & Cervantes, J. M. (1993). A multicultural perspective in the treatment of domestic violence. In M. Harway & M. Hansen (Eds.), *Battering and family therapy: A feminist perspective* (pp. 156–174). Newbury Park, CA: Sage.

Chang, V. N. (1996). *I Just lost myself: Psychological abuse of women in marriage.* Westport, CT: Praeger.

Choice, P., & Lamke, L. K. (1997). A conceptual approach to understanding abused women's stay/leave decisions. *Journal of Family Issues, 18,* 290–314.

Cook, P. W. (1997). *Abused men: the hidden side of domestic violence.* Westport, CT: Praeger/Greenwood.

Crenshaw, K. (1994). Mapping the margins: Intersectionality, identity politics, and violence against women of color. In M. A. Fineman & R. Mykitiuk (Eds.), *The public nature of private violence: The discovery of domestic abuse* (pp. 93–118). New York: Routledge.

Dawud-Noursi, S., Lamb, M. E., & Sternberg, K. J. (1998). The relations among domestic violence, peer relationships, and academic performance. In C. Feiring (Ed.), *Families, risk, and competence* (pp. 207–226). Mahwah, NJ: Erlbaum.

Dennis, R. E., Key, L. J., Kirk, A. L., & Smith, A. (1995). Addressing domestic violence in the African American community. *Journal of Health Care for the Poor and Underserved, 6,* 284–293.

Dobash, R. E., & Dobash, R. P. (1992). *Women, violence and social change.* New York: Routledge.

Dobash, R. E., & Dobash, R. P. (1998). Violent men and violent contexts. In R. E. Dobash & R. P. Dobash (Eds.), *Rethinking violence against women* (pp. 141–168). Thousand Oaks, CA: Sage.

Dobash, R. P., Dobash, R. E., Wilson, M., & Daly, M. (1992). The myth of sexual symmetry in marital violence. *Social Problems, 39,* 71–91.

Dutton, D. G. (1995). *The batterer: A psychological profile* (with Susan K. Golant). New York: Basic Books.

Dutton, D. G., & Starzomski, A. J. (1993). Borderline personality in perpetrators of psychological and physical abuse. *Violence and Victims, 8,* 327–338.

Elliot, P. (Ed.). (1990). *Confronting lesbian battering: A manual for the battered women's movement.* St. Paul, MN: Minnesota Coalition for Battered Women.

Eng, P. (1995). Domestic violence in Asian/Pacific Island communities. In D. L. Adams (Ed.), *Health is-sues for women of color* (pp. 78–88). Thousand Oaks, CA: Sage.

Fairchild, D. G., Fairchild, M. W., & Stoner, S. (1998). Prevalence of adult domestic violence among women seeking routine care in a Native American health care facility. *American Journal of Public Health, 88,* 1515–1517.

Fawcett, G., Heise, L. L., Isita-Espejel, L., & Pick, S. (1999). Changing community responses to wife abuse: A research and demonstration project in Iztacalco, Mexico. *American Psychologist, 54,* 41–49.

Ferraro, K. J. (1997). Battered women: Strategies for survival. In A. Carderelli (Ed.), *Violence among intimate partners: Patterns, causes and effects* (pp. 124–140). New York: Macmillan.

Fiebert, M. S., & Gonzalez, D. M. (1997). College women who initiate assaults on their male partners and the reasons offered for such behavior. *Psychological Reports, 80,* 583–590.

Fincham, F. D., Bradbury, T. N., Arias, I., Byrne, C. A., & Karney, B. R. (1997). Marital violence, marital distress, and attributions. *Journal of Family Psychology, 11,* 367–372.

Follingstad, D. R., Rutledge, L. L., Berg, B. J., Hause, E. S., & Polek, D. S. (1990). The role of emotional abuse in physically abusive relationships. *Journal of Family Violence, 5,* 107–120.

Foo, L., & Margolin, G. (1995). A multivariate investigation of dating aggression. *Journal of Family Violence, 10,* 351–377.

Foshee, V. A., Bauman, K. E., & Linder, G. F. (1999). Family violence and the perpetration of adolescent dating violence: Examining social learning and social control processes. *Journal of Marriage and the Family, 61,* 331–342.

Gaertner, L., & Foshee, V. (1999). Commitment and the perpetration of domestic violence. *Personal Relationships, 6,* 227–239.

Giles-Sims, J. (1998). The aftermath of partner violence. In J. L. Jasinski & L. M. Williams (Eds.), *Partner violence: A comprehensive review of 20 years of research* (pp. 44–72). Thousand Oaks, CA: Sage.

Glantz, N. M., Halperin, D. C., & Hunt, L. M. (1998). Studying domestic violence in Chiapas, Mexico. *Qualitative Health Research, 8,* 377–392.

Gondolf, E. W., Fisher, E., & McFerron, J. R. (1991). Racial differences among shelter residents: A comparison of Anglo, Black and Hispanic battered women. In R. L. Hampton (Ed.), *Black family violence.* Lexington, MA: Lexington Books.

Gondolf, E. W., & Shestakou, D. (1997). Spousal homicide in Russia versus United States: Preliminary findings and implications. *Journal of Family Violence, 12,* 63–74.

Grandin, E., & Lupri, E. (1997). Intimate violence in Canada and United States: A cross-national comparison. *Journal of Family Violence, 12,* 417–443.

Grandin, E., Lupri, E., & Brinkerhoff, M. B. (1998). Couple violence and psychological distress. *Canadian Journal of Public Health, 89,* 43–47.

Greenfield, L. A., & Rand, M. R. (1998). *Violence by Intimates* (NCJ-167237). Washington, DC: U.S. Department of Justice.

Haj-Yahia, M. M. (1998). A patriarchal perspective of beliefs about wife beating among Palestinian men from the West Bank and the Gaza Strip. *Journal of Family Issues, 19,* 595–621.

Hamberger, L. K., Lohr, J. M., Bonge, D., & Tolin, D. F. (1996). A large sample empirical typology of male spouse abusers and its relationship to dimensions of abuse. *Violence & Victims, 11,* 277–292.

Handwerker, W. P. (1998). Why violence? A test of hypotheses representing three discourses on the roots of domestic violence. *Human Organization, 57,* 200–208.

Heise, L. L. (1994). *Violence against women: The hidden health burden.* Washington, DC: World Bank.

Heise, L. L. (1996). Violence against women: Global organizing for change. In J. L. Edleson & Z. C. Eisikovits (Eds.), *Future interventions with battered women and their families* (pp. 7–33). Thousand Oaks, CA: Sage.

Heise, L. L., Raikes, A., Watts, C. H., & Zwi, A. B. (1994). Violence against women: A neglected public health issue in less developed countries. *Social Science and Medicine, 39,* 1165–1179.

Henning, K., Leitenberg, H., Coffey, P., Bennett, T., & Jankowski, M. K. (1997). Long-term psychological adjustment to witnessing interparental physical conflict during childhood. *Child Abuse and Neglect, 21,* 501–515.

Herbert, T. B., Silver, R. C., & Ellard, J. H. (1991). Coping with an abusive relationship: I. How and why do women stay? *Journal of Marriage and the Family, 53,* 311–325.

Ho, C. K. (1990). An analysis of domestic violence in Asian American communities: A multicultural approach to counseling. *Women and Therapy, 9,* 129–150.

Hogeland, C., & Rosen, K. (1990). *Dreams lost, dreams found: Undocumented women in the land of opportunity.* San Francisco: Coalition for Immigrant and Refugee Rights and Services.

Holtzworth-Munroe, A., Jacobson, N. S., Fehrenbach, P. A., & Fruzzetti, A. (1992). Violent married couples' attributions for violent and nonviolent self and partner behaviors. *Behavioral Assessment, 14,* 53–64.

Holtzworth-Munroe, A., Meehan, J. C., Herron, K., Rehman, U., & Stuart, G. L. (in press). Testing the Holtzworth-Munroe and Stuart batterer typology. *Journal of Consulting and Clinical Psychology.*

Holtzworth-Munroe, A., Smutzler, N., & Sandin, E. (1997). A brief review of the research on husband violence: Part II: The psychological effects of husband violence on battered women and their children. *Aggression and Violent Behavior, 2,* 179–213.

Holtzworth-Munroe, A., & Stuart, G. L. (1994). Typologies of male batterers: Three subtypes and the differences among them. *Psychological Bulletin, 116,* 476–497.

Holtzworth-Munroe, A., Stuart, G. L., & Hutchinson, G. (1997). Violent versus nonviolent husbands: Differences in attachment patterns, dependency, and jealousy. *Journal of Family Psychology, 11,* 314–331.

Human Rights Watch (Ed.). (1995). Domestic violence. In *The Human Rights Watch Global Report on Women's Human Rights* (pp. 341–409). New York: Author.

Island, D., & Letellier, P. (1991). *Men who beat the men who love them: Battered gay men and domestic violence.* New York: Haworth Press.

Jacobson, N., & Gottman, J. (1998). *When men batter women: New insights into ending abusive relationships.* New York: Simon & Schuster.

Johnson, H. (1996). *Dangerous domains: Violence against women in Canada.* Toronto: Nelson Canada.

Johnson, M. P. (1995). Patriarchal terrorism and common couple violence: Two forms of violence against women. *Journal of Marriage and the Family, 57,* 283–294.

Johnson, M. P. (1998, June). *Commitment and entrapment.* Paper presented at the Ninth International Conference on Personal Relationships, Saratoga Springs, NY.

Johnson, M. P. (1999, November). *Two types of violence against women in the American family: Identifying patriarchal terrorism and common couple violence.* Paper presented at the National Council on Family Relations annual meetings, Irvine, CA.

Johnson, M. P. (2000a). Conflict and control: Images of symmetry and asymmetry in domestic violence. In A. Booth, A. C. Crouter, & M. Clements (Eds.), *Couples in conflict.* Hillsdale, NJ: Erlbaum.

Johnson, M. P. (2000b). Domestic violence is not a unitary phenomenon: A major flaw in the domestic violence literature. Unpublished manuscript.

Johnson, M. P., & Leone, J. (2000, July). *The differential effects of patriarchal terrorism and common couple violence: Findings from the National Violence Against Women Survey.* Paper presented at the International Conference on Personal Relationships, Brisbane, Australia.

Kalu, W. J. (1993). Battered spouse as a social concern in work with families in two semi-rural communities of Nigeria. *Journal of Family Violence, 8,* 361–373.

Kane, E. W. (1999, August). *Race, ethnicity, and beliefs about gender inequality.* Paper presented at the Society for the Study of Social Problems, Chicago.

Kantor, G. K., & Jasinski, J. L. (1998). Dynamics and risk factors in partner violence. In J. L. Jasinski & L. M. Williams (Eds.), *Partner violence: A comprehensive review of 20 years of research* (pp. 1–43). Thousand Oaks, CA: Sage.

Kirkwood, C. (1993). *Leaving abusive partners: From the scars of survival to the wisdom for change.* Newbury Park, CA: Sage.

Klein, R. C. A. (Ed.). (1998). *Multidisciplinary perspectives on family violence.* New York: Routledge.

Kolbo, J. R., Blakely, E. H., & Engleman, D. (1996). Children who witness domestic violence: A review of empirical literature. *Journal of Interpersonal Violence, 11,* 281–293.

Kurz, D. (1989). Social science perspectives on wife abuse: Current debates and future directions. *Gender and Society, 3,* 489–505.

Kurz, D. (1993). Physical assaults by husbands: A major social problem. In R. J. Gelles & D. R. Loseke (Eds.), *Current controversies on family violence* (pp. 88–103). Newbury Park, CA: Sage.

Kurz, D. (1998). Women, welfare, and domestic violence. *Social Justice, 25,* 105–122.

Lackey, C., & Williams, K. R. (1995). Social bonding and the cessation of partner violence across generations. *Journal of Marriage and the Family, 57,* 295–305.

Letellier, P. (1996). Twin epidemics: Domestic violence

and HIV infection among gay and bisexual men. In C. M. Renzetti & C. H. Miley (Eds.), *Violence in gay and lesbian domestic partnerships* (pp. 69–81). New York: Harrington Park Press.

Levinson, D. (Ed.). (1989). *Family violence in a cross-cultural perspective.* Newbury Park, CA: Sage.

Lloyd, S. (1999). The effects of male violence on female employment. *Violence Against Women, 5,* 370–392.

Lloyd, S. A., & Emery, B. C. (2000). *The dark side of courtship: Physical and sexual aggression.* Thousand Oaks, CA: Sage.

Lockheart, L. L. (1991). Spousal violence: A cross-racial perspective. In R. L. Hampton (Ed.), *Black family violence* (pp. 85–101). Lexington, MA: Lexington Books.

Lupri, E., Grandin, E., & Brinkerhoff, M. B. (1994). Socioeconomic status and male violence in the Canadian home: A reexamination. *Canadian Journal of Sociology, 19,* 47–73.

Macmillan, R., & Gartner, R. (1999). When she brings home the bacon: Labour-force participation and the risk of spousal violence against women. *Journal of Marriage and the Family, 61,* 947–958.

Magdol, L., Moffitt, T. E., Caspi, A., & Silva, P. A. (1998). Hitting without a license: Testing explanations for differences in partner abuse between young adult daters and cohabitors. *Journal of Marriage and the Family, 60,* 41–55.

Marsh, C. E. (1993). Sexual assault and domestic violence in the African American community. *Western Journal of Black Studies, 17,* 149–155.

McEachern, D., Winkle, M. V., & Steiner, S. (1998). Domestic violence among the Navajo: A legacy of colonization. In E. A. Segal & K. M. Kilty (Eds.), *Pressing issues of inequality and American Indian communities* (pp. 31–46). New York: Haworth Press.

McWilliams, M. (1998). Violence against women in societies under stress. In R. E. Dobash & R. P. Dobash (Eds.), *Rethinking violence against women* (pp. 11–140). Thousand Oaks, CA: Sage.

Merrill, G. S. (1996). Ruling the exceptions: Same-sex battering and domestic violence theory. In C. M. Renzetti & C. H. Miley (Eds.), *Violence in gay and lesbian domestic partnerships* (pp. 9–21). New York: Haworth Press.

Milardo, R. M. (1998). Gender asymmetry in common couple violence. *Personal Relationships, 5,* 423–438.

Miles-Doan, R. (1998). Violence between spouses and intimates: Does neighborhood context matter? *Social Forces, 77,* 623–645.

Norton, I. M., & Manson, S. M. (1995). A silent minority: Battered American Indian women. *Journal of Family Violence, 10,* 307–318.

Ofei-Aboagye, R. O. (1994). Altering the strands of fabric: A preliminary look at domestic violence in Ghana. *Signs, 19,* 924–938.

Ogle, R. S., Maier-Katkin, D., & Bernard, T. J. (1995). A theory of homicidal behavior among women. *Criminology, 33,* 173–193.

Pence, E., & Paymar, M. (1993). *Education groups for men who batter: The Duluth model.* New York: Springer.

Perilla, J. L., Bakerman, R., & Norris, F. H. (1994). Culture and domestic violence: The ecology of abused Latinas. *Violence & Victims, 9,* 325–339.

Renzetti, C. M. (1992). *Violent betrayal: Partner abuse in lesbian relationships.* Thousand Oaks, CA: Sage.

Renzetti, C. M., & Miley, C. H. (1996). *Violence in gay and lesbian domestic partnerships.* New York: Haworth Press.

Richie, B. (1996). *Compelled to Crime: The gender entrapment of battered Black women.* New York: Routledge.

Richters, A. (1994). *Women, culture and violence: a development, health and human rights issue.* Leiden, The Netherlands: Women and Autonomy Centre.

Riggs, D. S., & O'Leary, K. D. (1996). Aggression between heterosexual dating partners: An examination of a causal model of courtship aggression. *Journal of Interpersonal Violence, 11,* 519–540.

Riggs, D. S., O'Leary, K. D., & Breslin, F. C. (1990). Multiple correlates of physical aggression in dating couples. *Journal of Interpersonal Violence, 5,* 61–73.

Roberts, A. R. (1996). Battered women who kill: A comparative study of incarcerated participants with a community sample of battered women. *Journal of Family Violence, 11,* 291–304.

Root, M. P. (1996). Women of color and traumatic stress in "domestic captivity": Gender and race as disempowering statuses. In A. J. Marsella & M. J. Friedman (Eds.), *Ethnocultural aspects of posttraumatic stress disorder: Issues, Research, and Clinical Applications* (pp. 363–387). Washington, DC: American Psychological Association.

Rusbult, C. E., & Martz, J. M. (1995). Remaining in an abusive relationship: An investment model analysis of nonvoluntary dependence. *Personality and Social Psychology Bulletin, 21,* 558–571.

Saunders, D. G. (1988). Wife abuse, husband abuse, or mutual combat? A feminist perspective on the empirical findings. In K. Yllo & M. Bograd (Eds.), *Feminist perspectives on wife abuse* (pp. 90–113). Newbury Park, CA: Sage.

Saunders, D. G. (1996). Feminist-cognitive-behavioral and process-psychodynamic treatments for men who batter: Interactions of abuser traits and treatment model. *Violence and Victims, 4,* 393–414.

Schuler, S. R., Hashemi, S. M., Riley, A. P., & Akhter, S. (1996). Credit programs, patriarchy and men's violence against women in rural Bangladesh. *Social Science and Medicine, 43,* 1729–1742.

Sewall, R. P., Vasan, A., & Schuler, M. A. (Eds.). (1996). *State responses to domestic violence: current status and needed improvements.* Washington, DC: Institute for Women, Law & Development.

Silvern, L., Karyl, J., Waelde, L., Hodges, W., & Starek, J. (1995). Retrospective reports of parental partner abuse: Relationships to depression, trauma symptoms and self-esteem among college students. *Journal of Family Violence, 10,* 177–202.

Simons, R. L., Lin, K.-H., & Gordon, L. C. (1998). Socialization in the family of origin and male dating violence: A prospective study. *Journal of Marriage and the Family, 60,* 467–478.

Song, Y. (1996). *Battered women in Korean immigrant families: The silent scream.* New York: Garland.

Sorenson, S. B. (1996). Violence against women: Examining ethnic differences and commonalities. *Evaluation Review, 20,* 123–145.

Sorenson, S. B., & Telles, C. A. (1991). Self-reports of spousal violence in a Mexican American and a non-

Hispanic White population. *Violence and Victims, 6,* 3–16.

Sorenson, S. B., Upchurch, D. M., & Shen, H. (1996). Violence and injury in marital arguments: Risk patterns and gender differences. *American Journal of Public Health, 86,* 35–40.

Stets, J. E. (1991). Cohabiting and marital aggression: The role of social isolation. *Journal of Marriage and the Family, 53,* 669–680.

Stets, J. E. (1993). Control in dating relationships. *Journal of Marriage and the Family, 55,* 673–685.

Stets, J. E. (1995a). Job autonomy and control over one's spouse: A compensatory process. *Journal of Health and Social Behavior, 36,* 244–258.

Stets, J. E. (1995b). Modeling control in relationships. *Journal of Marriage and the Family, 57,* 489–501.

Stets, J. E. (1995c). Role identities and person identities: Gender identity, mastery identity, and controlling one's partner. *Sociological Perspectives, 38,* 129–150.

Stets, J. E., & Burke, P. J. (1994). Inconsistent self-views in the control identity model. *Social Science Research, 23,* 236–262.

Stets, J. E., & Burke, P. J. (1996). Gender, control, and interaction. *Social Psychology Quarterly, 59,* 193–220.

Stets, J. E., & Pirog-Good, M. A. (1990). Interpersonal control and courtship aggression. *Journal of Social and Personal Relationships, 7,* 371–394.

Stets, J. E., & Straus, M. A. (1990). The marriage license as hitting license: A comparison of assaults in dating, cohabiting, and married couples. In M. A. Straus & R. J. Gelles (Eds.), *Physical violence in American families: risk factors and adaptations to violence in 8,145 families* (pp. 227–244). New Brunswick, NJ: Transaction.

Stewart, S. (1996). Changing attitudes toward violence against women: The Musasa Project. In S. Zeidenstein & K. Moore (Eds.), *Learning about sexuality: A practical beginning* (pp. 343–362). New York: International Women's Health Coalition, Population Council.

Straus, M. A. (1990a). Injury and frequency of assault and the 'representative sample fallacy' in measuring wife beating and child abuse. In R. J. Gelles & M. A. Straus (Eds.), *Physical violence in American families: Risk factors and adaptations to violence in 8,145 families* (pp. 75–91). New Brunswick, NJ: Transaction.

Straus, M. A. (1990b). Social stress and marital violence in a national sample of American families. In M. A. Straus & R. J. Gelles (Eds.), *Physical violence in American families: Risk factors and adaptations to violence in 8,145 families* (pp. 181–201). New Brunswick, NJ: Transaction.

Straus, M. A. (1993). Physical assaults by wives: A major social problem. In R. J. Gelles & D. R. Loseke (Eds.), *Current controversies on family violence.* Newbury Park, CA: Sage.

Straus, M. A. (1999). The controversy over domestic violence by women: A methodological, theoretical, and sociology of science analysis. In X. B. Arriaga & S. Oskamp (Eds.), *Violence in intimate relationships* (pp. 17–44). Thousand Oaks, CA: Sage.

Straus, M. A., Gelles, R. J., & Steinmetz, S. K. (1988).

Behind closed doors: Violence in the American family. Newbury Park, CA: Sage. (Original work published 1980)

Straus, M. A., Hamby, S. L., Boney-McCoy, S., & Sugarman, D. B. (1996). The revised Conflict Tactics Scales (CTS2): Development and preliminary psychometric data. *Journal of Family Issues, 17,* 283–316.

Szinovacz, M. E., & Egley, L. C. (1995). Comparing one-partner and couple data on sensitive marital behaviors: The case of marital violence. *Journal of Marriage and the Family, 57,* 995–1010.

Tang, C. S.-K. (1994). Prevalence of spouse aggression in Hong Kong. *Journal of Family Violence, 9,* 347–356.

Tjaden, P., & Thoennes, N. (1999). *Extent, nature, and consequences of intimate partner violence: Findings from the national violence against women survey.* Washington, DC: National Institute of Justice/Centers for Disease Control and Prevention.

Tom-Orme, L. (1995). Native American women's health concerns. In D. L. Adams (Ed.), *Health issues for women of color* (pp. 27–41). Thousand Oaks, CA: Sage.

Tontodonato, P., & Crew, B. K. (1992). Dating violence, social learning theory, and gender: A multivariate analysis. *Violence and Victims, 7,* 3–14.

United Nations. (1989). *Violence against women in the family.* New York: United Nations.

Vivian, D., & Langhinrichson-Rohling, J. (1994). Are bi-directionally violent couples mutually victimized? A gender-sensitive comparison. *Violence and Victims, 9,* 107–124.

Waller, M. A., Risley-Curtis, C., Murphy, S., Medill, A., & Moore, G. (1998). Harnessing the positive power of language: American Indian women, a case example. In E. A. Segal & K. M. Kilty (Eds.), *Pressing issues of inequality and American Indian communities* (pp. 63–81). New York: Haworth.

West, C. M. (1998). Leaving a second closet: Outing partner violence in same-sex couples. In J. L. Jasinksi & L. M. Williams (Eds.), *Partner violence: A comprehensive review of 20 years of research* (pp. 163–183). Thousand Oaks, CA: Sage.

Wilson, M. I., & Daly, M. (1996). Male sexual proprietariness and violence against wives. *Current Directions in Psychological Science, 5,* 2–7.

Wilson, M., & Daly, M. (1998). Lethal and nonlethal violence against wives and the evolutionary psychology of male sexual proprietariness. In R. E. Dobash & R. P. Dobash (Eds.), *Rethinking violence against women* (pp. 199–230). Thousand Oaks, CA: Sage.

Wolak, J., & Finkelhor, D. (1998). Children exposed to partner violence. In J. L. Jasinski & L. M. Williams (Eds.), *Partner violence: A comprehensive review of 20 years of research* (pp. 73–112). Thousand Oaks, CA: Sage.

Wyatt, G. E. (1994). Sociocultural and epidemiological issues in the assessment of domestic violence. *Journal of Social Distress and the Homeless, 3,* 1,7–21.

Yick, A. G., & Agbayani-Siewert, P. (1997). Perceptions of domestic violence in a Chinese-American community. *Journal of Interpersonal Violence, 12,* 832–846.

Zorza, J. (1991). Woman battering: A major cause of homelessness. *Clearinghouse Review, 25,* 421.

Thomas N. Bradbury   *University of California—Los Angeles*

Frank D. Fincham   *State University of New York—Buffalo*

Steven R. H. Beach   *University of Georgia*

Research on the Nature and Determinants of Marital Satisfaction: A Decade in Review

Scientific study of marital satisfaction attracted widespread attention in the 1990s from scholars representing diverse orientations and goals. This article highlights key conceptual and empirical advances that have emerged in the past decade, with particular emphasis on (a) interpersonal processes that operate within marriage, including cognition, affect, physiology, behavioral patterning, social support, and violence; (b) the milieus within which marriages operate, including microcontexts (e.g., the presence of children, life stressors and transitions) and macrocontexts (e.g., economic factors, perceived mate availability); and (c) the conceptualization and measurement of marital satisfaction, including 2-dimensional, trajectory-based, and social-cognitive approaches. Notwithstanding the continued need for theoretical progress in understanding the nature and determinants of marital satisfaction, we conclude by calling for more large-scale longitudinal research that links marital processes with sociocultural contexts, for more disconfirmatory than confirmatory research, and for research that directly guides preventive, clinical, and policy-level interventions.

Department of Psychology, UCLA, Los Angeles, CA 90095–1563 (bradbury@psych.ucla.edu).

Key Words: communication, divorce, intervention, longitudinal study, marital satisfaction.

Even when compared with the high level of scholarly output in previous decades, the 1990s witnessed a vast number of papers published on a wide array of topics pertaining to marital satisfaction. The sheer magnitude of this work attests to the continued importance placed on understanding the quality of marriage, as an end in itself and as a means to understanding its effect on numerous other processes inside and outside the family. The rationale for studying marital satisfaction stems from its centrality in individual and family well-being (e.g., Stack & Eshleman, 1998), from the benefits that accrue to society when strong marriages are formed and maintained (e.g., desistance from crime; Laub, Nagin, & Sampson, 1998), and from the need to develop empirically defensible interventions for couples that prevent (e.g., Hahlweg, Markman, Thurmaier, Engl, & Eckert, 1998) or alleviate (e.g., Baucom, Shoham, Mueser, Daiuto, & Stickle, 1998) marital distress and divorce.

The present analysis comes at a time when the American divorce rate has declined for the eighth straight year, owing, perhaps, to the sharp increase in the age at first marriage over this same period (U.S. Bureau of the Census, 1998). Nonetheless, about half of all first marriages are projected to end in permanent separation or divorce, the level of satisfaction in intact first marriages has declined since at least the mid-1970s (National Marriage Project, 1999; Rogers & Amato, 1997), and there is growing recognition that marital strife prior to divorce accounts, in part, for the widely publicized differences in functioning between children who do and do not come from households marked by divorce (see Amato, this volume; Amato & Booth, 1997). Further tempering any optimism elicited by the slowing divorce rate is recent evidence that, on average, marital satisfaction probably does not follow a U-shaped function over the marital career, as was once believed (e.g., Rollins & Feldman, 1970), but instead drops markedly over the first 10 years of marriage on average and then drops more gradually in the ensuing decades (Glenn, 1998; Vaillant & Vaillant, 1993). Systematic study of marital satisfaction therefore remains vital, and the social significance of studying how and why marriages vary in their quality is matched only by the complex range of factors that must be considered when doing so.

The impressive breadth and scope of work on marital satisfaction in the 1990s shows that research on this topic is not a literature unto itself but is dispersed over several overlapping, yet generally distinct, literatures. These focus, for example, on psychological factors, sociodemographic variables and trends, parenting, physical health, and psychopathology, or some combination of these, all in relation to some aspect of marital quality. It is not possible to capture the subtleties and nuances of each of these literatures in a single review and, arguably, little would be gained from a large-scale integration of specific findings.

In view of these constraints, the task we have set for ourselves in this article is to identify and explore a series of key ideas and emerging trends that may be germane to scholars who approach the study of marital satisfaction with diverse goals and agendas. The article is organized around two themes that we believe represent the sine qua non of a thorough understanding of variability in marital satisfaction, namely, the interpersonal processes that operate within marriages and the sociocultural ecologies and contexts within which marriages operate. We adopt this distinction because we believe it serves well in organizing research conducted on marital satisfaction in the 1990s and because doing so draws attention to the constraints to understanding that arise from analyses of interpersonal processes bereft of their environmental milieus and from ecological or contextual analyses that fail to consider what transpires between spouses. A third and final theme emphasized in the article is the conceptualization and measurement of marital satisfaction,

a topic that continues to attract attention from marital and family scholars and that has evolved in important ways in the past 10 years. In addressing these three themes, we acknowledge and emphasize at the outset that we are psychologists by training with strong interests in refining theory, collecting data, and developing interventions with the applied goal of bringing about stronger marriages and families. This probably leads us to focus more on marital processes and differences between couples in marital processes than is typical of prior reviews of marital satisfaction appearing in this forum, and it yields an analysis that complements rather than updates explicitly the most recent decade review written by Glenn (1990).

INTERPERSONAL PROCESSES IN MARRIAGE

Detailed analysis of the behaviors exchanged by spouses was instigated more than 25 years ago, in part by Harold Raush and colleagues' assertion that "Studying what people say about themselves is no substitute for studying how they behave . . . . Questionnaires and scales of marital satisfaction and dissatisfaction have yielded very little. We need to look at what people do with one another" (Raush, Barry, Hertel, & Swain, 1974, p. 5) and in part by research-oriented clinicians who sought to study how maritally discordant spouses shaped each others' coercive behaviors and thereby caused or perpetuated their discord (e.g., Stuart, 1969). Interest in understanding interpersonal processes in marriage remains strong, yet research reported in the 1990s indicated that, despite some advances, these processes are not easily studied, and a comprehensive understanding of them is not yet at hand.

In keeping with its applied clinical origins, recent research on interpersonal processes in marriage retains a strong focus on behaviors exchanged during marital conflict and marital problem-solving discussions. To understand this focus and the findings that accumulated in the 1990s, it is necessary to consider research trends from earlier decades. The need to capture interdependencies between husband and wife behavior, as distinct from the raw number or proportion of behaviors displayed by the husband and the wife, became evident early in this line of work. The resulting methodological sophistication yielded compelling findings about the sequential patterns of behavior that differentiated maritally distressed and nondistressed couples. For example, Margolin and Wampold (1981) showed that, compared with those of happy couples, the interactions of distressed couples were characterized by higher levels of negative reciprocity (i.e., increased likelihood of negative behavior following negative behavior by the partner) and by higher levels of negative reactivity (i.e., suppression of positive behaviors below base rates following negative behavior by the partner). In the 1980s and 1990s, researchers extended this work by focusing on less immediately observable aspects of marital interaction, (including interpretations of interactional behaviors, emotions experienced and displayed during interaction, physiological responses to interaction) and on global patterns of interaction, neglected prosocial dimensions of marital behavior, and marital violence. We highlight key findings in each of these areas below.

Cognition

The strong focus on marital cognition in the 1980s, which was supported by longitudinal studies of spouses' maladaptive attributions or interpretations for negative partner behaviors (e.g., Fincham & Bradbury, 1987a) and their autonomic physiology before interaction (presumed to be an indicator of the meaning spouses assign to their interactions; e.g., Levenson & Gottman, 1985), has carried through into the 1990s. Major developments in the literature on spouses' attributions include cross-cultural evidence for the association between maladaptive explanations for marital events and marital satisfaction (Sabourin, Lussier, & Wright, 1991), continued elaboration of the internal structure and organization of attributions and other cognitive factors (e.g., Sayers & Baucom, 1995), and further longitudinal data linking attributions to marital deterioration (e.g., Karney & Bradbury, 2000). There also is now evidence that maladaptive attributions covary with elevated rates of negative behaviors during marital problem-solving discussions (e.g., Bradbury, Beach, Fincham, & Nelson, 1996), and a series of studies shows that key associations in this literature are not an artifact of such potential confounds as neurotic personality, self-esteem, physical aggression, depression, or measurement procedures (see Fincham, in press). As a result, attributions now figure prominently in models of marital disruption (e.g., Gottman, 1993a) and in programs designed to prevent adverse marital outcomes (e.g., Markman, Stanley, & Blumberg, 1994).

Although research in the 1990s has satisfied much of the speculation in the 1980s about the importance of attributions in marital functioning, a host of new and important questions now present themselves. These include questions about attributions themselves, such as whether specific patterns of attributions correspond with distinct emotional expressions (e.g., anger versus sadness) and whether the manipulation of attributions can yield enduring changes in marital functioning. Other questions pertain more broadly to cognitive variables in marriage, such as how spouses' understanding of their specific negative marital interactions affects future interactions and how broader cognitive schemas (e.g., lay theories about relationships, stories that couples form about their marriage) organize and guide marital functioning.

Affect

Occurring largely in parallel with this work on cognition is a dramatic surge in research on the affective dimension of marital interaction (e.g., Johnson & Greenberg, 1994; Matthews, Wickrama, & Conger, 1996; Newton, Kiecolt-Glaser, Glaser, & Malarkey, 1995; Thomas, Fletcher, & Lange, 1997). As a result of this work, there is now reasonably clear evidence that this is an essential dimension to consider in accounting for variability in the quality of marriage. Nevertheless, the details of this association remain to be clarified because some studies show, for example, that negative affect is detrimental for marriage, whereas others show that it promotes marital quality or is unrelated to it (for discussions, see Fincham & Beach, 1999a; Gottman & Notarius, this volume). The lack of replication across laboratories and even within laboratories underscores the need for further theoretical development and the low yield that is likely from further atheoretical descriptive work. More specifically, definitive statements about the role of affect in eroding or supporting marital satisfaction await refinements in the conceptual underpinnings of affect-related constructs and in the methods used to observe emotional expressions and to discern their effects on marriage over time.

Physiology

Developing in conjunction with the increased emphasis on affect in marriage is a rapidly growing literature on physiological concomitants of interaction. For example, recent research addresses questions about marital influence attempts and blood pressure changes (Brown, Smith, & Benjamin, 1998), heart rate and skin conductance changes displayed by spouses while listening to their partner talk about chronic low back pain (Stampler, Wall, Cassisi, & Davis, 1997), and gender differences in endocrine and immune functioning during marital problem solving (Kiecolt-Glaser et al., 1996). Some of these findings are intriguing; Thomsen and Gilbert (1998), for example, found greater synchrony or correspondence in physiological systems among maritally satisfied couples than among maritally dissatisfied couples. Malarkey, Kiecolt-Glaser, Pearl, and Glaser (1994) found increases in pituitary and adrenal hormones as a function of increased levels of hostility in newlyweds' marital conflict (see Booth, this volume, for an expanded discussion). This line of work is significant because it provides an expanded, multisystems view of events arising within marital interaction, and it promises to delineate the specific mechanisms by which physiological processes mediate the widely acknowledged link between marital functioning and physical well-being (see Burman & Margolin, 1992; Uchino, Cacioppo, & Kiecolt-Glaser, 1996). At the same time, this literature shows that it can be difficult to obtain reliable physiological data during spontaneous social interaction (e.g., Sanders, Halford, & Behrens, 1999) and that, perhaps as a consequence, promising hypotheses involving physiological data (e.g., that arousal before and during marital interaction would foreshadow marital deterioration; Levenson & Gottman, 1985) have not been supported upon further analysis (Gottman & Levenson, 1992). In any case, the integration of overt behavioral data and accompanying physiology as antecedents of change in physical and marital well-being remains an important task for the future.

Patterns

In contrast to the microanalytic studies of sequential patterns in behavior that typified the 1980s, the 1990s witnessed a movement away from these patterns and toward higher order features of interaction. Foremost among these is the demand/withdraw pattern, whereby one spouse, typically the wife, criticizes and nags the partner for change, while the partner, typically the husband, avoids the discussion and disengages from confrontation. According to this view, increased demands lead to increased avoidance, which in turn leads to increased demands for engagement, with the end result being a decline in marital satisfac-

tion (e.g., Christensen, 1987; Watzlawick, Beavin, & Jackson, 1967). Many important aspects of this model have been supported, using observational data (e.g., Klinetob & Smith, 1996), longitudinal designs (e.g., Heavey, Christensen, & Malamuth, 1995), and cross-cultural samples (e.g., Bodenmann, Kaiser, Hahlweg, & Fehm-Wolfsdorf, 1998). At present, it appears that demand/withdrawal tendencies are at least partially responsive to conflict structure (i.e., who wants to change; see Heavey, Layne, & Christensen, 1993) and that the usual gender differences may be reversed in couples characterized by violence (Babcock, Waltz, Jacobson, & Gottman, 1993). A similar shift toward macroanalytic approaches is evident in Gottman's (1993b) typology, which identifies, using interaction data, three groups of couples who were in stable marriages over a 4-year period (e.g., validators, avoiders) and two groups of unstable couples (i.e., hostile and hostile-detached). Although reports using sequential analysis have appeared in recent years, these tend to focus on descriptive studies of populations that have not been examined extensively using behavioral data (e.g., couples with a depressed wife, Nelson & Beach, 1990; couples with a violent spouse, Burman, Margolin, & John, 1993).

This new focus, which might be characterized as yielding relatively encompassing behavioral patterns derived at least partially from clinical or quasi-clinical observation (i.e., a top-down approach), would seem to be a natural progression from the bottom-up approach to behavioral data that predominated in the past. As this line of work continues, it will be important to establish a reasonably exhaustive set of key macrolevel patterns, to demonstrate that these patterns have predictive validity beyond the specific codes that comprise them, to establish that sampling methods do not misrepresent systematically couples having a particular pattern (e.g., disengaged patterns), and to clarify the extent to which these patterns change over key periods in the life of a marriage.

Social Support

Research on interpersonal processes in marriage focuses heavily on conflict and problem solving. Nonetheless, there is some ambiguity in the association between problem-solving behavior and marital outcomes (as noted above), data suggest that the longitudinal association between negative behavior and marital outcomes is moderated by spouses' expressions of affection (Huston & Chorost, 1994), the actual frequency of overt conflict in a typical marriage is proving to be surprisingly low (McGonagle, Kessler, & Schilling, 1992), and there is growing recognition that the continued increase in dual-career couples places a premium on the manner in which spouses help each other handle problems that arise largely outside the marriage. Although support processes in marriage have long been a topic of interest (e.g., Barker & Lemle, 1984; Coyne & DeLongis, 1986), for the reasons noted here the topic is now being addressed with increased vigor (e.g., Acitelli & Antonucci, 1994; Bodenmann, 1997; Coyne & Smith, 1994; Katz, Beach, Smith, & Myers, 1997). Support processes have been reliably linked in these studies with marital functioning and with important health outcomes in families (Collins, Dunkel-Schetter, Lobel, & Scrimshaw 1993).

An important feature in recent studies of marital support is the use of methods that permit more detailed investigation of potentially supportive transactions. Observational methods for assessing the provision and receipt of supportive behaviors have been developed (e.g., Cutrona, 1996). The resulting behaviors have been linked to marital quality and changes in marital quality, even after controlling for behaviors observed in standard problem-solving discussions (Pasch & Bradbury, 1998; also see Carels & Baucom, 1999; Saitzyk, Floyd, & Kroll, 1997). Daily diary methods have also proven to be powerful in clarifying the operation of support in marriage; for example, in a study of couples in which one spouse was preparing to take the bar exam, Bolger, Zuckerman, & Kessler (1998) showed that the examinees' distress did not rise as the exam drew near to the extent that the partner provided increasing levels of support. This emerging line of work stands in sharp contrast to studies of conflict in marriage, and it promises to enrich our understanding of both conflict (e.g., it may be less consequential in marriages characterized by higher levels of support) and the determinants of marital quality. It is also likely to influence the large literature on the effects of marital interaction on child adjustment, which has focused almost exclusively on the effects of conflict on child well-being (e.g., Cummings & Davies, 1994; Fincham, Grych, & Osborne, 1994; Jouriles, Norwood, McDonald, Vincent, & Mahoney, 1996). These effects might be weaker in families where compassionate, supportive behavior is displayed routinely by the parents and stronger in those families where it is not

(Fincham, 1998). As the work on support continues to develop, it will be important to recognize that interpersonal processes within a marriage might be affected by the nature of support obtained by spouses outside the marriage (Bryant & Conger, 1999). In an observational study of wives talking with their confidants, for example, Julien, Markman, Leveille, Chartrand, & Begin, (1994) demonstrated that wives reported relatively more emotional distress and more perceived distance from their husband following the discussion to the extent the confidant made more comments that interfered with or undermined the wife's marriage.

Violence

The final aspect of interpersonal process in marriage that we consider is physical violence (also see Johnson & Ferraro, this volume). Important strides in estimating the prevalence of marital violence made in the 1980s (e.g., Straus & Gelles, 1986) have resulted in a large amount of research on marital and family violence in the 1990s (cf. Berardo, 1980). Although direct observation of actual physical aggression in marriage typically is not possible (cf. Capaldi & Crosby, 1997), a series of observational studies has been conducted on the interactional styles in violent and nonviolent marriages. Even when compared with distressed couples who are not violent, for example, the interactions of distressed violent couples are marked by higher levels of negative reciprocation, anger, and contempt (e.g., Cordova, Jacobson, Gottman, & Rushe, 1993; Holtzworth-Munroe, Smutzler, & Stuart, 1998). These findings help to clarify how disagreements can escalate in violent marriages, and they also confirm that behavioral differences between distressed and nondistressed couples can exist in the absence of physical aggression. Other noteworthy advances in this area include enhanced measurement of aggression (e.g., Straus, Hamby, Boney-McCoy, & Sugarman, 1996), analysis of the contributing role of alcohol use to violent marital incidents (e.g., Quigley & Leonard, 1999), and recognition that some form of physical aggression is present at high levels in newlywed marriage (e.g., 57% in O'Leary et al., 1989). Growing interest in domestic violence among European researchers has the potential to help identify cross-cultural commonalities as well as unique cultural factors that influence the manifestation of aggression in marriage (see Klein, 1998). Likewise, investigations of ethnic differences in level of physical aggression within the United States suggest that such differences are attributable to differences in family income (Cazenave & Strauss, 1990). Nonetheless, other factors, such as level of acculturation, must play a role in any comprehensive explanation (Sorenson & Telles, 1991). Finally, the link between physical aggression and diminished marital quality typically is assumed rather than demonstrated, and the low rate with which aggression is reported as a problem in couples seeking therapy, even when present, indicates that some couples may tolerate aggression in their relationship (cf. Ehrensaft & Vivian, 1996). This raises questions about whether and how aggression comes to erode marriages (e.g., Leonard & Roberts, 1998; Rogge & Bradbury, 1999) and the factors controlling desistance in aggression (Jacobson, Gottman, Cortner, Berns, & Shortt, 1996; Quigley & Leonard, 1996). In short, although important questions remain, research conducted in the 1990s demonstrates plainly that marriage cannot be studied or treated effectively without giving due consideration to the possibility that spouses are or have been physically aggressive.

MARITAL PROCESSES IN CONTEXT

Although there is widespread endorsement of the view that "the stuff and substance of an interpersonal relationship is the behavioral interaction between the partners" (Berscheid, 1995, p. 531), many scholars adhere to the position that the meaning and implications of behavioral interaction cannot be fully understood without considering the broader context in which those interactions occur. The ways in which couples manage conflict may be important for the long-term quality of their relationship, for example, but is a certain pattern of negative behavior more consequential for blue-collar versus white-collar workers? Does our understanding of social support in relation to marital satisfaction change when we consider how much stress couples experience? Does one's family background influence the meaning of different kinds of interpersonal behaviors in marriage? Is marital instability less prevalent in settings where there are few versus many available mates? Answering questions such as these can sharpen our understanding of marital satisfaction, and indeed questions of this sort received considerable attention in the 1990s.

In addition to its obvious scientific merit, there are important applied benefits to be gained from addressing the ways in which contextual factors—

those that are unique to particular couples as well as those that are common to many couples—contribute to interpersonal processes and moderate links between those processes and marital outcomes. Here it must be recognized that causes of marital dysfunction and the solutions pursued in the hopes of alleviating it can diverge considerably and that the causes of the problem can be linked to viable solutions for a problem in tenuous ways (see Christensen, 1998). To reason by analogy, variability in skin cancer across individuals is presumably due to environmental factors to which people are exposed or to environment by organism (e.g., pigmentation) interactions, but they can be counteracted by individual-level interventions (e.g., applying sunscreen, wearing a hat). Thus, effective solutions that alleviate marital dysfunction may overlap only partially with the actual causes of marital dysfunction.

Research on contextual or ecological factors in relationship functioning has expanded dramatically in recent years, suggesting that a more balanced view of interpersonal and environmental causes—and solutions—will emerge in the decade ahead. Marriages exist in highly complex, multifaceted environments, of course, and a full understanding of how these environments interact and impinge upon marriage is just beginning to develop. In the sections below, we highlight a few key environments and contexts, and we outline associated research as a way of illustrating recent progress. Where possible, we draw attention to studies that link contextual variables with specific interpersonal processes rather than more global indicators of marital functioning. We focus first on three *microcontexts,* which we define as settings and circumstances that are likely to be salient to couples and that will have relatively direct links to interpersonal functioning in marriage, and then we move on to consider some *macrocontexts,* or broader social conditions and institutions likely to be less salient to couples and perhaps more indirect or subtle in their effects.

Microcontexts

Children. Children figure prominently in how marriage is experienced for many couples. Research suggests that children have the paradoxical effect of increasing the stability of marriage, at least when children are relatively young, while decreasing its quality (e.g., Belsky, 1990; Waite & Lillard, 1991). Researchers for some time have turned to examine how couples negotiate the transition to parenthood and the ensuing years as a means of understanding the putative effects of children on marital satisfaction, and numerous studies on this topic were published in the 1990s (e.g., Cowan & Cowan, 1992; Johnson & Huston, 1998; Levy-Shiff, Goldshmidt, & Har-Even, 1991). Perhaps the most important advance in this literature has been the recognition of enormous variability across couples in how they change from, typically, the last trimester of pregnancy through several months or a few years postpartum. Belsky and Rovine (1990) called attention to this point, noted that many couples do not change much on important variables over the transition to parenthood, and demonstrated how differing pathways through this transition could be predicted from demographic and personality data and, in some instances, from indices of infant temperament. A subsequent study of marital change patterns from the time firstborn sons were 10 to 60 months old indicated that spouses' personality traits covaried with marital functioning at any one point in time, whereas marital dynamics—particularly uncooperative coparenting behavior observed in the home—predicted deterioration in marital functioning over the study period (Belsky & Hsieh, 1998). Using a continuous rather than categorical measure of marital change through 2 years postpartum, with multiwave trajectories derived for observational and self-report data, Cox, Paley, Burchinal, and Payne (1999) showed that declines in marital quality and increases in negative interaction were predicted by symptoms of depression, child gender, and whether the pregnancy was planned.

This is an exciting line of research because it is beginning to specify the individual, child, and marital characteristics that render a family vulnerable to a difficult transition to parenthood. Identification of marital trajectories over this important transition is likely to lead to additional questions about how the transition to parenthood and parenting are embedded in a more encompassing developmental view of marriage and marital quality. How does marital satisfaction figure in to couples' decisions to have a child? Do children born at different times in marriage have different effects on marital satisfaction? How do marital processes predict later parenting (cf. Katz & Gottman, 1993)? How do parenting stress and satisfaction with parenting relate to marital satisfaction (cf. Kurdek, 1996; Rogers & White, 1998)? As questions such as these are addressed, there will be a greater understanding of how the transition to par-

enthood figures in the more general developmental course of marriage, and a stronger basis for intervention with at-risk couples will be established (cf. Cowan & Cowan, 1995).

Spouses' backgrounds and characteristics. Evidence that marital processes are associated with marital satisfaction and change in marital satisfaction leads naturally to questions about antecedents of those processes. Numerous studies on this topic appeared in the past decade, and they were complemented by a continuing interest in the intergenerational consequences of marital and family functioning for offspring as they themselves move into long-term committed relationships. Research on intergenerational transmission effects reported in the 1980s (e.g., McLanahan & Bumpass, 1988) are now being examined with increased precision, both with regard to those aspects of the family of origin that appear to be consequential and to the subsequent effects that they produce in families of procreation (e.g., Webster, Orbuch, & House, 1995). There is now evidence, for example, that parental divorce is associated with poorer communication observed among their offspring around the time of marriage (Sanders et al., 1999) and that the association between parental divorce and offspring divorce is mediated by problematic behaviors, such as hostility and jealousy, reported by the younger generation (Amato, 1996). Marital satisfaction in the parents' marriage may prove to be more important than their divorce in these associations (Booth & Edwards, 1989). Along similar lines, Marks, Wieck, Checkly, and Kumar (1996) have shown that marital processes moderate the effects of a history of affective disorder on relapse following the birth of a child; Gotlib, Lewinsohn, and Seeley (1998) have shown that individuals with a history of depression during adolescence are more likely to marry earlier and to experience higher rates of marital dissatisfaction than are individuals with other diagnoses or no diagnosis. Data of this kind demonstrate that a history of psychopathology is proving to be an important antecedent of marital functioning and, together with concurrent symptomatology, cannot be overlooked in models of marital functioning (cf. Beach, in press).

Perhaps the most dramatic upsurge in research on spousal characteristics and relationship functioning occurred in the literature on attachment, which aims to address questions about how the experience of relationships early in life are manifest in individuals' working models of relationships and subsequent interpersonal functioning in adulthood (Bowlby, 1969; see Simpson & Rholes, 1998). Although data on early parent-child functioning are typically not examined directly in this literature, self-reports of attachment style in adulthood or retrospective interview-based assessments of attachment to parents have been used to show that marital quality is greater to the extent that an individual, and that individual's partner, report secure versus avoidant or anxious ambivalent attachment styles (e.g., Feeney, Noller, & Callan, 1994; Hazan & Shaver, 1987). Longitudinal links between attachment styles and subsequent relationship quality are beginning to be established (e.g., Klohnen & Bera, 1998), and the specific interpersonal behaviors that mediate this association—particularly behaviors reflecting the regulation of emotion—are being pursued. Kobak and Hazan (1991), for example, showed that wives displayed more rejection during a problem-solving discussion to the extent that they described themselves as less reliant on their husband and that they described their husband as less psychologically available to them (also see Rholes, Simpson, & Orina, 1999). Although the richness of theorizing about the role of attachment in adult relationships can sometimes exceed the data used to test key hypotheses and although there is greater interest in attachment among dating partners than spouses, data in this area have improved rapidly in a short period of time. They provide strong, conceptually guided evidence for how an overarching framework can integrate individual-level variables and interpersonal processes to clarify determinants of marital satisfaction.

Life stressors and transitions. The social learning approach, which has been influential in the study of marriage, focuses heavily on the interior of marital relationships as the generative mechanism in marital functioning, leaving relatively little room for the ecological niches in which marriages are situated or for the intersection between interior processes and external factors that impinge upon them. This is reflected, for example, in the assertion that "distress, in this model, is assumed to be a function of couples' interaction patterns. Inevitably, couples have wants and needs that conflict. Distress results from couples' aversive and ineffectual responses to conflict" (Koerner & Jacobson, 1994, p. 208). This focus can be understood in part from the clinical orientation of this model, as there is a clear need to emphasize potentially changeable determinants of marital quality. None-

theless, building on a series of studies that link marital environments, stressors, and transitions to marital outcomes, a large body of research now indicates that the social learning perspective may be viewed more appropriately as one component, albeit a key component, in a more inclusive model of marital functioning.

At the risk of oversimplifying a large and complex literature, research on marital environments tends to address either discrete, often traumatic events; economic and work-related stressors; or the total set of stressors and events to which couples might be exposed. In the interest of space, we will focus on the first two lines of research here; examples of the third line of research can be found in Tesser and Beach (1998) and Whiffen and Gotlib (1989). The traumatic events that have been studied in relation to marital functioning are numerous and range, for example, from a hurricane (Moore & Moore, 1996), World War II (Pavalko & Elder, 1990), child illness or death (e.g., Hoekstra-Weebers, Jaspers, Kamps, & Klip, 1998), and testicular cancer (Gritz, Wellisch, Siau, & Wang, 1990). Many of these studies document not only the diverse ways that couples adapt to these extreme difficulties, but also the remarkable resilience that they display when doing so. For example, Gritz and colleagues, in their study of testicular cancer and marriage, commented on how this illness strengthens marital ties for many couples, Schwab (1998) dispelled the myth that the death of a child necessarily increases risk of divorce, and Ward and Spitze (1998) commented on how couples taking care of growing children and aging parents are able to sustain a strong marriage (perhaps due to selection effects; see Loomis & Booth, 1995). These studies are important because they often identify specific marital processes that are affected by or that buffer the effects of traumatic events (e.g., Quittner et al., 1998; Umberson, 1995) and because they help to bring balance to a portrayal of marriage that often is characterized by fragility and impermanence.

Economic and work-related stressors comprise the largest body of research on environmental influences on marriage. Adding to a long line of self-report studies outlining links between job characteristics and marital quality (e.g., Hughes, Galinsky, & Morris, 1992), several of these studies use observational or diary methods to specify the interactional processes that are affected by financial and work stress (see Menaghan, 1991). Repetti (1989), for example, used a diary procedure with air traffic controllers and their wives to show that wives' social support can increase husbands' social withdrawal and decrease anger in the home following workdays marked by high levels of air traffic volume and poor visibility. Using observational methods, Krokoff, Gottman, and Roy (1988) demonstrated that displays of negative affect, but not reciprocation of negative affect, were linked to occupational status in a sample of white- and blue-collar workers. And in perhaps the most comprehensive analysis of economic stress and marital functioning to date, Conger, Rueter, and Elder (1999), found support for a model whereby economic pressure in a sample of predominantly rural families at Time 1 predicted individual distress and observed marital conflict at Time 2, which in turn predicted marital distress at Time 3; the effect of economic pressure on emotional distress was greater in marriages poor in observed social support.

In short, recent research on life events and transitions enriches our understanding of the association between interpersonal processes in marriage and marital functioning. Several researchers testify to the remarkable resilience of couples and families under stress, and the ways in which marital processes moderate the influence of the environment on spouses' evaluations of marriage are becoming apparent. There is now a growing need to map out the life events that are and are not influential for different couples and for different stages of marriage, to clarify how individuals and marriages may inadvertently generate stressful events, and to examine how spouses take life events into account when making evaluations of their relationship (see Tesser & Beach, 1998). Also warranted are experimental studies designed to strengthen relationships by effecting change either in the events that couples confront (e.g., job loss; see Howe, Caplan, Foster, Lockshin, & McGrath, 1995) or in their responses to these specific events.

Macrocontexts

The final set of contextual factors we consider involves the broader social conditions and institutions that can affect individual mates and their marriages. In addition to the contextual factors already noted—children, spouses' backgrounds and characteristics, life stressors and transitions—it is necessary to recognize that there are more encompassing, relatively slow-changing factors that can influence, to varying degrees, entire cohorts of couples. Although links between these macrocon-

textual factors and specific marital processes are not typically addressed, in part because survey methods are often used to examine them, recent work indicates that marital functioning can covary with aspects of these broader contexts.

The following studies help to illustrate the type of findings obtained recently using this level of analysis. South and Crowder (1999), for example, showed that higher levels of neighborhood socioeconomic disadvantage are associated with higher rates of premarital childbearing and earlier timing of first marriage. Other studies have shown that mate availability, perceptions of mate availability, and local employment rates can have far-reaching effects on the development and course of marriage, most notably in African American communities (see Massey & Sibuya, 1995; Tucker & Mitchell-Kernan, 1995). Recognizing that many spouses consider extramarital relationships before divorce, South and Lloyd (1995) combined data from the National Survey of Families and Households and census data to demonstrate that risk for marital dissolution is greater in those regions characterized by high geographic mobility, high levels of unmarried women in the labor force, and high numbers of potential mates. And, finally, there is not only continued interest in the links between various aspects of religiosity and marital functioning (e.g., Booth, Johnson, Branaman, & Sica, 1995; Call & Heaton, 1997), but also in studying how couples' involvement in religious institutions and practices are related to specific dyadic aspects of marriage. Mahoney and colleagues (1999), for example, presented data showing that various aspects of marital functioning, including marital satisfaction, conflict frequency, and use of verbal aggression, are predicted by joint religious activities (e.g., praying together) and by perceptions of the sacred qualities of one's marriage, even after controlling for individual religiousness and religious homogamy.

Although their potential effects on marriage may not be as immediately apparent as some interpersonal processes (e.g., overt conflict or physical aggression), a host of environmental and contextual variables may well influence whether and how couples form their relationship, the obstacles they may confront along the way, and the resources they can use to maintain their relationship. For example, the impact of racism and acculturation processes on marital satisfaction would seem to be especially important to understand. How people understand these factors and the degree to which they engage the relevant institutions may be at least as important as mere exposure to them (e.g., perceptions of mate availability versus actual mate availability; spiritual activity versus religious identity) and that as a result, there are likely to be important differences in how different individuals and couples respond to otherwise identical milieu or the related experiences they have had. Although there appears to be a more accepting attitude of divorce now compared with 20 years ago, for example, such an acceptance might be greater among individuals whose parents divorced (see Amato, 1996). In any event, this line of work underscores the value of studying the external circumstances to which marriages are exposed, and it highlights the possibility that these circumstances can be modified to enhance marital functioning.

Conceptualizing and Measuring Marital Satisfaction

Up to this point, we have provided little direct analysis of the concept that is the central focus of this article, marital satisfaction itself. Nevertheless, there have been important developments in the conceptualization and measurement of marital satisfaction in recent years, and we review the highlights of these developments (also see Berscheid & Reis, 1998; Kluwer, 2000; Sternberg & Hojjat, 1997).

As a result of analyses in the 1980s by Fincham and Bradbury (1987b), Huston, McHale, and Crouter (1986), Norton (1983), and others, there is now widespread recognition that standard measures of marital satisfaction—such as Locke and Wallace's (1959) Marital Adjustment Test (MAT) and Spanier's (1976) Dyadic Adjustment Scale (DAS)—consist of different types of items, including evaluative judgments about marital quality, as well as reports of specific behaviors and general interaction patterns. As a result, the use of these scales can inflate associations between marital quality and self-report measures of interpersonal processes in marriage. This development had clear benefits for the interpretation of extant findings and for the execution of much subsequent research, but it has had at least two unfortunate side effects. First, some researchers are now more inclined to develop and employ nonstandard global measures of marital satisfaction, which limits the degree to which otherwise similar studies can be integrated. We recommend against the further development and proliferation of nonstandard measures of marital satisfaction and, in

the absence of data to the contrary, we encourage researchers to administer global measures that are used routinely in the field (e.g., the Quality Marriage Index, Norton, 1983). Second, the notion that measures such as the MAT and DAS are not appropriate for some applications has been overextended to the point where they are believed to be inappropriate for all applications. Most notably, in longitudinal analyses of the association between a behavioral variable and later marital satisfaction, where earlier levels of marital satisfaction are controlled statistically, it would appear that the problem does not emerge. This is because of the statistical controlling of the variability due to the behavioral items in the satisfaction measure. In any case, the original arguments about the overlapping item content between the MAT or DAS and other measures were made with reference to cross-sectional data, and there is some evidence that measures such as the MAT and DAS perform similarly to global measures of satisfaction in longitudinal designs (Karney & Bradbury, 1997).

Four other important developments in the conceptualization and measurement of satisfaction are on the horizon. First, there is growing appreciation for the view that a satisfying marriage is not merely a relationship characterized by the absence of dissatisfaction, as is implied by the routine use of the term *nondistressed* to describe couples who are maritally satisfied. Factors that lead to marital distress may not be the simple inverse of the factors that lead to a satisfying relationship. Recent discussion of the defining features of a healthy marriage (Halford, Kelly, & Markman, 1997), continuing interest in the attributes of long-term satisfying relationships (e.g., Kaslow & Robison, 1996), and a growing emphasis on social support and other positive behaviors in marriage (e.g., Cutrona, 1996), all point to a developing conception of marriage and marital quality in which the unique dimensions of dissatisfying and satisfying relationships are recognized.

Second, prior efforts that conceptualize marital satisfaction as a global evaluation of the marriage have operationally defined this concept as a single dimension: Marital dissatisfaction reflects an evaluation of the marriage in which negative features are salient and positive features are relatively absent, and marital satisfaction reflects an evaluation in which positive features are salient and negative features are relatively absent. Fincham and colleagues have challenged this view, with the argument that positive and negative evaluations in marriage can be conceptualized and measured as separate, although related, dimensions (Fincham, Beach, & Kemp-Fincham, 1997). Data obtained with a simple measure used to capture this two-dimensional conception of marital quality indicate that the dimensions have different correlates and account for unique variance in reported marital behaviors and attributions. Moreover, two groups of wives who were indistinguishable in their MAT scores—those who were high in positivity and high in negativity versus those who were low in positivity and low in negativity—differed reliably in their behavior and attribution scores (Fincham & Linfield, 1997). This line of work is noteworthy because it draws attention to the important but largely overlooked distinction between positive and negative dimensions of marriage made in prior research that incorporated reports of behavior in assessments of marital quality (cf. Braiker & Kelley, 1979; Johnson, White, Edwards, & Booth, 1986; Orden & Bradburn, 1968). Additionally, the measure derived from this view will enable more detailed descriptions of change in marital satisfaction and the factors that account for these changes.

A third important development in the conceptualization and measurement of marital satisfaction is the notion that satisfaction is appropriately conceptualized not simply as a judgment made by spouses at one point in time but as a trajectory that reflects fluctuations in marital evaluations over time. Such a trajectory is computed for individual spouses using multiple waves of data, and parameters of this trajectory—especially its slope, or rate of change over time—can be examined in relation to other variables of theoretical interest. According to this view, a marital satisfaction score assessed at one point in time cannot be fully understood without reference to earlier or later data points; a score of 95 on the MAT, for example, has a different meaning depending on whether the individual scored 110 or 80 six months before it was obtained. The advantages of this perspective are that it encourages multiwave longitudinal research on marriage (where two-wave longitudinal designs have predominated; see Karney & Bradbury, 1995), it allows researchers to have direct access to the variable reflecting longitudinal change in satisfaction (where two-wave longitudinal designs provide indirect access to this variable, typically by way of residualized change scores), and it encourages researchers to specify a model of marital change (where two-wave longitudinal designs assume a simple linear model). Use of a trajectory-based view of marital satisfaction is increasing (e.g., Cox et al., 1999; Karney

& Bradbury, 1997; Kurdek, 1991; Raudenbush, Brennan, & Barnett, 1995; Wickrama, Lorenz, Conger, & Elder, 1997) and holds considerable promise for testing refined models of marital change.

A fourth important development has been the application of a social-cognitive perspective to the conceptualization of marital satisfaction. One example of this approach is the reconceptualization of marital satisfaction as an *attitude* toward the partner or relationship. Analyzing marital satisfaction with reference to the literature on attitudes highlights the idea that satisfaction can vary not only in degree but also in the strength of the association between the evaluation (i.e., self-reported satisfaction) and the object of the evaluation (i.e., the partner). This association, or level of *attitude accessibility,* may be assessed independent of the valence of the evaluation (Fazio, 1995) and thus may increase prediction of response to partner behavior (e.g., Fincham & Beach, 1999b). Such findings suggest that the correlation of marital satisfaction with marital behavior and interpretations of marital behavior may be different for those with highly accessible attitudes compared with those who have less accessible attitudes (Fincham, Garnier, Gano-Phillips, & Osborne, 1995). They also imply that spouses whose marital satisfaction is highly accessible should report more stable satisfaction over time (they engage in top-down processing) relative to spouses whose satisfaction is less accessible (they engage in bottom-up processing); data collected over 18 months of marriage are also consistent with this implication (Fincham et al., 1997). In short, it may be necessary to revisit many of the correlates of marital satisfaction to determine whether they hold to a greater degree for persons with more accessible marital attitudes.

Researchers in the social-cognitive tradition have also examined the way partners engage in effortful cognitive transformations to change potentially damaging responses to negative partner behavior into responses that are more benign (e.g., Yovetich & Rusbult, 1994). Because these transformations are effortful, introducing a cognitive load can result in more negative reactions than would have otherwise occurred. As a result, this perspective suggests that certain stressful contexts may exert a negative effect on relationship satisfaction by interfering with effortful cognitive transformations and so disrupting patterns of prosocial interaction. In addition, social-cognitive models of assimilation and contrast effects lead to the prediction that evaluation of the quality of family relationships should be affected adversely by a stressful life context, but only up to a point. After a certain point, an increase in stress should result in a contrast or sharp increase in reported satisfaction (e.g., Tesser & Beach, 1998). Accordingly, although not yet full articulated for the family, this perspective has considerable promise for providing new insights regarding the correlates of satisfaction, reactions to partner behavior, and the impact of various life contexts on satisfaction.

CONCLUSION

Scientific work published in the 1990s on marital satisfaction evokes both optimism and pessimism about what can be expected in the decade ahead. The optimism derives in part from the fact that this topic is addressed with surprising vigor by scholars from diverse disciplinary backgrounds. More important, it derives from the progress that has been made in understanding (a) marital processes that covary with and may foreshadow changes in satisfaction, (b) the complex environments to which spouses and couples adapt, and (c) how best to conceptualize and assess the quality of marriage. A central goal of this article has been to illustrate and evaluate this progress, both in terms of the individual research themes we have highlighted and the broader notion that a complete portrayal of variability in marital quality requires analysis of interpersonal exchanges within marriage, the milieus in which marriages are embedded, and the interplay between these interior and exterior forces. Our analysis cannot be considered comprehensive, of course, because research on marital satisfaction extends well beyond what we have presented here. Research on satisfaction in relationships other than marriage (e.g., siblings, Brody, 1998; gay and lesbian couples, Kurdek, 1998; cohabiting couples, Stack & Eshleman, 1998), which is important by itself and as a complement to research on marriage, would extend the scope of this analysis even further.

Pessimism about future work in this area stems from our perception that progress in the field is characterized more by the adding of ideas within a given research area than by building upon, and where appropriate, discarding existing ideas. This is perhaps inevitable—the more we look, the more we see—yet the tendency to supplement rather than supplant or even integrate our hypotheses and ideas hinders cumulative growth in the field. We must be careful to not exaggerate this concern

and thereby overlook the numerous contributions that have been made, and we must be careful to mark progress by the degree of sophistication in the questions that are asked and not solely by the systematic accumulation of empirical findings. Nevertheless, the apparent increase in breadth without a corresponding increase in depth may be part of the price that is paid for conducting research on a complex topic where research designs usually preclude strong inferences of causation. The increased use of longitudinal designs advocated in earlier reviews (e.g., Berardo, 1990) is an important step in the right direction, but the inferential power in these studies tends to be lower than desired, particularly because attrition tends to be high and nonrandom, more than two waves of data are rarely collected or analyzed simultaneously, and data are often collected from only one spouse (see Glenn, 1990; Karney & Bradbury, 1995).

The research published in the 1990s and in prior decades contains a wealth of ideas and information about marital satisfaction. A first step toward generating better work on this topic in the next decade may be to delve deeply into the theories and findings in this work—in those areas close to our research interests as well as those on the periphery. Theoretical and methodological analysis of existing research is needed, and this can serve as a foundation for studies that clarify and complement what is already known about marital satisfaction. We believe that these studies will be of greatest consequence to the extent they meet the following three criteria. First, there is a continuing need for large, well-funded intensive longitudinal studies of couples, particularly those that sample marital functioning at several points in time. Basic research on how marriages develop and deteriorate is deficient in several key respects, and data are badly needed that will illuminate the factors that account for changes in satisfaction over key periods of marital development. Second, because most of the research that we can anticipate in the decade ahead will be nonexperimental in nature, studies that rule out plausible counterhypotheses will be particularly valuable. Most studies on marital quality tend to be confirmatory in their focus and emphasize convergent validity, but studies that provide discriminant information and compare competing models against each other (rather than solely against the null hypothesis) will yield the most progress. Finally, it will be important to conduct research that directly informs and guides specific preventive, clinical, and policy-level interventions involving couples and families, not simply because of the inherent value in applied work and the experimental designs that are permissible there, but also because an applied orientation—an orientation toward solving specific problems pertinent to marriages and families—will greatly focus and sharpen our basic research efforts.

REFERENCES

Acitelli, L. K., & Antonucci, T. C. (1994). Gender differences in the link between marital support and satisfaction in older couples. *Journal of Personality and Social Psychology, 67,* 688–698.

Amato, P. R. (1996). Explaining the intergenerational transmission of divorce. *Journal of Marriage and the Family, 58,* 628–640.

Amato, P. R., & Booth, A. (1997). *A generation at risk: Growing up in an era of family upheaval.* Cambridge, MA: Harvard University Press.

Babcock, J. C., Waltz, J., Jacobson, N. S., & Gottman, J. M. (1993). Power and violence: The relation between communication patterns, power discrepancies, and domestic violence. *Journal of Consulting and Clinical Psychology, 61,* 16–27.

Barker, C., & Lemle, R. (1984). The helping process in couples. *American Journal of Community Psychology, 12,* 321–336.

Baucom, D. H., Shoham, D. H., Mueser, K. T., Daiuto, A. D., & Stickle, T. R. (1998). Empirically supported couple and family interventions for marital distress and adult mental health problems. *Journal of Consulting and Clinical Psychology, 66,* 53–88.

Beach, S. R. H. (in press). *Marital and family processes in depression: A scientific foundation for clinical practice.* Washington, DC: APA Press.

Belsky, J. (1990). Children and marriage. In F. D. Fincham & T. N. Bradbury (Eds.), *The psychology of marriage* (pp. 172–200). New York: Guilford Press.

Belsky, J., & Hsieh, K.-H. (1998). Patterns of marital change during the early childhood years: Parent personality, coparenting, and division-of-labor correlates. *Journal of Family Psychology, 12,* 511–528.

Belsky, J., & Rovine, M. (1990). Patterns of marital change across the transition to parenthood: Pregnancy to three years post-partum. *Journal of Marriage and the Family, 55,* 5–20.

Berardo, F. M. (1980). Decade preview: Some trends and directions for family research and theory in the 1980s. *Journal of Marriage and the Family, 42,* 723–728.

Berardo, F. M. (1990). Trends and directions in family research in the 1980s. *Journal of Marriage and the Family, 52,* 809–817.

Berscheid, E. (1995). Help wanted: A grand theorist of interpersonal relationships, sociologist or anthropologist preferred. *Journal of Social and Personal Relationships, 12,* 529–533.

Berscheid, E., & Reis, H. T. (1998). Attraction and close relationships. In D. T. Gilbert, S. T. Fiske, & G. Lindzey (Eds.), *The handbook of social psychology* (4th ed., pp. 193–281). Boston: McGraw-Hill.

Bodenmann, G. (1997). Dyadic coping: A systemic-transactional view of stress and coping among couples: Theory and empirical findings. *European Review of Applied Psychology, 47,* 137–141.

Bodenmann, G., Kaiser, A., Hahlweg, K., & Fehm-Wolfsdorf, G. (1998). Communication patterns during marital conflict: A cross-cultural replication. *Personal Relationships, 5,* 343–356.

Bolger, N., Zuckerman, A., & Kessler, R. (1998). *Visible support, invisible support, and adjustment to stress.* Manuscript submitted for publication.

Booth, A., & Edwards, J. N. (1989). Transmission of marital and family quality over the generations: The effect of parental divorce and unhappiness. *Journal of Divorce, 13,* 41–58.

Booth, A., Johnson, D. R., Branaman, A., & Sica, A. (1995). Belief and behavior: Does religion matter in today's marriage? *Journal of Marriage and the Family, 57,* 661–671.

Bowlby, J. (1969). *Attachment and loss: Volume 1. Attachment.* New York: Basic.

Bradbury, T. N., Beach, S. R. H., Fincham, F. D., & Nelson, G. (1996). Attributions and behavior in functional and dysfunctional marriages. *Journal of Consulting and Clinical Psychology, 64,* 569–576.

Braiker, H. B., & Kelley, H. H. (1979). Conflict in the development of close relationships. In R. L. Burgess & T. L. Huston (Eds.), *Social exchange in developing relationships* (pp. 135–168). New York: Academic Press.

Brody, G. H. (1998). Sibling relationship quality: Its causes and consequences. *Annual Review of Psychology, 49,* 1–24.

Brown, P. C., Smith, T. W., & Benjamin, L. S. (1998). Perceptions of spouse dominance predict blood pressure reactivity during marital interactions. *Annals of Behavioral Medicine, 20,* 286–293.

Bryant, C. M., & Conger, R. D. (1999). Marital success and domains of social support in long-term relationships: Does the influence of network members ever end? *Journal of Marriage and the Family, 61,* 437–450.

Burman, B., & Margolin, G. (1992). Analysis of the association between marital relationships and health problems: An interactional perspective. *Psychological Bulletin, 112,* 39–63.

Burman, B., Margolin, G., & John, R. S. (1993). America's angriest home videos: Behavioral contingencies observed in home reenactments of marital conflict. *Journal of Consulting and Clinical Psychology, 61,* 28–39.

Call, V. R. A., & Heaton, T. B. (1997). Religious influence on marital stability. *Journal for the Scientific Study of Religion, 36,* 382–392.

Capaldi, D. M., & Crosby, L. (1997). Observed and reported psychological and physical aggression in young, at-risk couples. *Social Development, 6,* 184–206.

Carels, R. A., & Baucom, D. H. (1999). Support in marriage: Factors associated with on-line perceptions of support helpfulness. *Journal of Family Psychology, 13,* 131–144.

Cazenave, N. A., & Straus, M. A. (1990). Race, class, network embeddedness, and family violence. In M. A. Straus & R. J. Gelles (Eds.), *Physical violence in American families* (pp. 321–339). Brunswick, NJ: Transaction.

Christensen, A. (1987). Detection of conflict patterns in couples. In K. Hahlweg & M. J. Goldstein (Eds.), *Understanding major mental disorders: The contribution of family interaction research* (pp. 250–265). New York: Family Process Press.

Christensen, A. (1998). On intervention and relationship events: A marital therapist looks at longitudinal research on marriage. In T. N. Bradbury (Ed.), *The developmental course of marital dysfunction* (pp. 377–392). New York: Cambridge University Press.

Collins, N. L., Dunkel-Schetter, C., Lobel, M., & Scrimshaw, S. C. (1993). Social support in pregnancy: Psychosocial correlates of birth outcomes and postpartum depression. *Journal of Personality and Social Psychology, 65,* 1243–1258.

Conger, R. D., Rueter, M. A., & Elder, G. H. Jr. (1999). Couple resilience to economic pressure. *Journal of Personality and Social Psychology, 76,* 54–71.

Cordova, J., Jacobson, N. S., Gottman, J. M., & Rushe, R. (1993). Negative reciprocity and communication in couples with a violent husband. *Journal of Abnormal Psychology, 102,* 559–564.

Cowan, C. P., & Cowan, P. A. (1992). *When partners become parents: The big life change for couples.* New York: Basic Books.

Cowan, C. P., & Cowan, P. A. (1995). Interventions to ease the transition to parenthood: Why they are needed and what they can do. *Family Relations, 44,* 412–423.

Cox, M. J., Paley, B., Burchinal, M., & Payne, C. C. (1999). Marital perceptions and interactions across the transition to parenthood. *Journal of Marriage and the Family, 61,* 611–625.

Coyne, J. C., & DeLongis, A. (1986). Going beyond social support: The role of social relationships in adaptation. *Journal of Consulting and Clinical Psychology, 54,* 454–460.

Coyne, J. C., & Smith, D. A. F. (1994). Couples coping with a myocardial infarction: Contextual perspective on patient self-efficacy. *Journal of Family Psychology, 8,* 43–54.

Cummings, E. M., & Davies, P. (1994). *Children and marital conflict: The impact of family dispute and resolution.* New York: Guilford Press.

Cutrona, C. (1996). *Social support in couples.* Thousand Oaks, CA: Sage.

Ehrensaft, M. K., & Vivian, D. (1996). Spouses' reasons for not reporting existing marital aggression as a marital problem. *Journal of Family Psychology, 10,* 443–453.

Fazio, R. H. (1995). Attitudes as object-evaluation associations: Determinants, consequences, and correlates of attitude accessibility. In R. E. Petty & J. A. Krosnick (Eds.), *Attitude strength: Antecedents and consequences* (pp. 247–282). Mahwah, NJ: Erlbaum.

Feeney, J. A., Noller, P., & Callan, V. J. (1994). Attachment style, communication, and satisfaction in the early years of marriage. In K. Bartholomew & D. Perlman (Eds.), *Attachment processes in adulthood* (pp. 269–308). London: Jessica Kingsley.

Fincham, F. D. (1998). Child development and marital relations. *Child Development, 69,* 543–574.

Fincham, F. D. (in press). Attributions in close relationships: From balkanization to integration. In G. J. O Fletcher & M. S. Clark (Eds.), *Blackwell handbook of social psychology, Volume 2: Interpersonal processes.* Oxford, U.K.: Blackwell.

Fincham, F. D., & Beach, S. R. H. (1999a). Conflict in marriage: Implications for working with couples. *Annual Review of Psychology, 50,* 47–77.

Fincham, F. D., & Beach, S. R. H. (1999b). Marriage in the new millennium: Is there a place for social cognition in marital research? *Journal of Social and Personal Relationships, 16,* 685–704.

Fincham, F. D., Beach, S. R. H., & Kemp-Fincham, S. (1997). Marital quality: A new theoretical perspective. In R. J. Sternberg & M. Hojjat (Eds.), *Satisfaction in close relationships* (pp. 275–304). New York: Guilford Press.

Fincham, F. D., & Bradbury, T. N. (1987a). The impact of attributions in marriage: A longitudinal analysis. *Journal of Personality and Social Psychology, 53,* 510–517.

Fincham, F. D., & Bradbury, T. N. (1987b). The assessment of marital quality: A reevaluation. *Journal of Marriage and the Family, 49,* 797–809.

Fincham, F. D., Garnier, P. C., Gano-Phillips, S., Osborne, L. N. (1995). Pre-interaction expectations, marital satisfaction, and accessibility: A new look at sentiment override. *Journal of Family Psychology, 9,* 3–14.

Fincham, F. D., Grych, J. H., & Osborne, L. N. (1994). Does marital conflict cause child maladjustment? Directions and challenges for longitudinal research. *Journal of Family Psychology, 8,* 128–140.

Fincham, F. D., & Linfield, K. J. (1997). A new look at marital quality: Can spouses feel positive and negative about their marriage? *Journal of Family Psychology, 11,* 489–502.

Glenn, N. D. (1990). Quantitative research on marital quality in the 1980s: A critical review. *Journal of Marriage and the Family, 52,* 818–831.

Glenn, N. D. (1998). The course of marital success and failure in five American 10-year marriage cohorts. *Journal of Marriage and the Family, 60,* 569–576.

Gotlib, I. H., Lewinsohn, P. M., & Seeley, J. R. (1998). Consequences of depression during adolescence: Marital status and marital functioning in early adulthood. *Journal of Abnormal Psychology, 107,* 686–690.

Gottman, J. M. (1993a). A theory of marital dissolution and stability. *Journal of Family Psychology, 7,* 57–75.

Gottman, J. M. (1993b). The roles of conflict engagement, escalation, and avoidance in marital interaction: A longitudinal view of 5 types of couples. *Journal of Consulting and Clinical Psychology, 61,* 6–15.

Gottman, J. M., & Levenson, R. W. (1992). Marital processes predictive of later dissolution: Behavior, physiology, and health. *Journal of Personality and Social Psychology, 63,* 221–233.

Gritz, E. R., Wellisch, D. K., Siau, J., & Wang, H. (1990). Long-term effects of testicular cancer on marital relationships. *Psychosomatics, 31,* 301–312.

Hahlweg, K., Markman, H. J., Thurmaier, F., Engl, J., & Eckert, V. (1998). Prevention of marital distress: Results of a German prospective longitudinal study. *Journal of Family Psychology, 12,* 543–556.

Halford, W. K., Kelly, A., & Markman, H. J. (1997). The concept of a healthy marriage. In W. K. Halford & H. J. Markman (Eds.), *Clinical handbook of mar-*

riage and couples interventions (pp. 3–12). New York: Wiley.

Hazan, C., & Shaver, P. (1987). Romantic love conceptualized as an attachment process. *Journal of Personality and Social Psychology, 52,* 511–524.

Heavey, C. L., Christensen, A., & Malamuth, N. M. (1995). The longitudinal impact of demand and withdrawal during marital conflict. *Journal of Consulting and Clinical Psychology, 63,* 797–801.

Heavey, C. L., Layne, C., & Christensen, A. (1993). Gender and conflict structure in marital interaction: A replication and extension. *Journal of Consulting and Clinical Psychology, 61,* 16–27.

Hoekstra-Weebers, J. E. H., Jaspers, J. P. C., Kamps, W. A., & Klip, E. C. (1998). Marital dissatisfaction, psychological distress, and the coping of parents of pediatric cancer patients. *Journal of Marriage and the Family, 60,* 1012–1021.

Holtzworth-Munroe, A., Smutzler, N., & Stuart, G. L. (1998). Demand and withdraw communication among couples experiencing husband violence. *Journal of Consulting and Clinical Psychology, 66,* 731–743.

Howe, G. W., Caplan, R. D., Foster, D., Lockshin, M., & McGrath, C. (1995). When couples cope with job loss: A strategy for developing and testing preventive interventions. In L. R. Murphy & J. J. Hurrell Jr. (Eds.), *Job stress interventions* (pp. 139–157). Washington, DC: APA Press.

Hughes, D., Galinsky, E., & Morris, A. (1992). The effects of job characteristics on marital quality: Specifying linking mechanisms. *Journal of Marriage and the Family, 54,* 31–42.

Huston, T. L., & Chorost, A. F. (1994). Behavioral buffers on the effect of negativity on marital satisfaction: A longitudinal study. *Personal Relationships, 1,* 223–239.

Huston, T. L., McHale, S., & Crouter, A. (1986). When the honeymoon's over: Changes in the marriage relationship over the first year. In R. Gilmour & S. Duck (Eds.), *The emerging field of personal relationships* (pp. 109–132). Hillsdale, NJ: Erlbaum.

Jacobson, N. S., Gottman, J. M., Gortner, E., Berns, S., & Shortt, J. W. (1996). Psychological factors in the longitudinal course of battering: When do couples split up? When does the abuse decrease? *Violence and Victims, 11,* 371–392.

Johnson, D. R., White, L. K., Edwards, J. N., & Booth, A. (1986). Dimensions of marital quality: Toward methodological and conceptual refinement. *Journal of Family Issues, 7,* 31–49.

Johnson, E., & Huston, T. L. (1998). The perils of love, or why wives adapt to husbands during the transition to parenthood. *Journal of Marriage and the Family, 60,* 195–204.

Johnson, S. M., & Greenberg, L. S. (Eds.). (1994). *The heart of the matter: Perspectives on emotion in marital therapy.* New York: Brunner/Mazel.

Jouriles, E. N., Norwood, W. D., McDonald, R., Vincent, J. P., & Mahoney, A. (1996). Physical violence and other forms of marital aggression: Links with children's behavior problems. *Journal of Family Psychology, 10,* 223–234.

Julien, D., Markman, H. J., Leveille, S., Chartrand, E., & Begin, J. (1994). Networks' support and interference with regard to marriage: Disclosures of marital problems to confidants. *Journal of Family Psychology, 8,* 16–31.

Karney, B. R., & Bradbury, T. N. (1995). The longitudinal course of marital quality and stability: A review of theory, method, and research. *Psychological Bulletin, 118,* 3–34.

Karney, B. R., & Bradbury, T. N. (1997). Neuroticism, marital interaction, and the trajectory of marital satisfaction. *Journal of Personality and Social Psychology, 72,* 1075–1092.

Karney, B. R., & Bradbury, T. N. (2000). Attributions in marriage: State or trait? A growth curve analysis. *Journal of Personality and Social Psychology, 78,* 295–309.

Kaslow, F., & Robison, J. A. (1996). Long-term satisfying marriages: Perceptions of contributing factors. *American Journal of Family Therapy, 24,* 153–170.

Katz, J., Beach, S. R. H., Smith, D. A., & Myers, L. B. (1997). Personality and the marital context: The case for interactive conceptualizations of needs for spousal support. In G. R. Pierce & B. Lakey (Eds.), *Sourcebook of social support and personality* (pp. 257–278). New York: Plenum.

Katz, L. F., & Gottman, J. M. (1993). Patterns of marital conflict predict children's internalizing and externalizing behaviors. *Developmental Psychology, 29,* 940–950.

Kiecolt-Glaser, J. K., Newton, T., Cacioppo, J. T., MacCallum, R. C., Glaser, R., & Malarkey, W. B. (1996). Marital conflict and endocrine function: Are men really more physiologically affected than women? *Journal of Consulting and Clinical Psychology, 64,* 324–332.

Klein, R. C. A. (Ed.). (1998). *Multidisciplinary perspectives on family violence.* London: Routledge.

Klinetob, N. A., & Smith, D. A. (1996). Demand-withdraw communication in marital interaction: Tests of interpersonal contingency and gender role hypotheses. *Journal of Marriage and the Family, 58,* 945–957.

Klohnen, E. C., & Bera, S. (1998). Behavioral and experiential patterns of avoidantly and securely attached women across adulthood: A 31-year longitudinal perspective. *Journal of Personality and Social Psychology, 74,* 211–223.

Kluwer, E. (2000). Marital quality. In R. M. Milardo & S. W. Duck (Eds.), *Families as relationships* (pp. 59–78). London: Wiley.

Kobak, R. R., & Hazan, C. (1991). Attachment in marriage: Effects of security and accuracy in working models. *Journal of Personality and Social Psychology, 60,* 861–869.

Koerner, K., & Jacobson, N. S. (1994). Emotion and behavioral couple therapy. In S. M. Johnson & L. S. Greenberg (Eds.), *The heart of the matter: Perspectives on emotion in marital therapy* (pp. 207–226). New York: Brunner/Mazel.

Krokoff, L. J., Gottman, J. M., & Roy, A. K. (1988). Blue-collar and white-collar marital interaction and communication orientation. *Journal of Social and Personal Relationships, 5,* 201–221.

Kurdek, L. A. (1991). Predictors of increases in marital distress in newlywed couples: A 3-year prospective longitudinal study. *Developmental Psychology, 27,* 627–636.

Kurdek, L. A. (1996). Parenting satisfaction and marital

satisfaction in mothers and fathers with young children. *Journal of Family Psychology, 10,* 331–342.

Kurdek, L. A. (1998). Relationship outcomes and their predictors: Longitudinal evidence from heterosexual married, gay cohabiting, and lesbian cohabiting couples. *Journal of Marriage and the Family, 60,* 553–568.

Laub, J. H., Nagin, D. S., & Sampson, R. J. (1998). Trajectories of change in criminal offending: Good marriages and the desistance process. *American Sociological Review, 63,* 225–238.

Leonard, K., & Roberts, L. (1998). Marital aggression, quality, and stability: Findings from the Buffalo Newlywed Study. In T. N. Bradbury (Ed.), *The developmental course of marital dysfunction* (pp. 44–73). New York: Cambridge University Press.

Levenson, R. W., & Gottman, J. M. (1985). Physiological and affective predictors of change in relationship satisfaction. *Journal of Personality and Social Psychology, 49,* 85–94.

Levy-Shiff, R., Goldschmidt, I., & Har-Even, D. (1991). Transition to parenthood in adoptive families. *Developmental Psychology, 27,* 131–140.

Locke, H. J., & Wallace, K. M. (1959). Short marital adjustment prediction tests: Their reliability and validity. *Marriage and Family Living, 21,* 251–255.

Loomis, L. S., & Booth, A. (1995). Multigenerational caregiving and well-being: The myth of the beleaguered sandwich generation. *Journal of Family Issues, 16,* 131–148.

Mahoney, A., Pargament, K. I., Jewell, T., Swank, A. B., Scott, E., Emery, E., & Rye, M. (1999). Marriage and the spiritual realm: The role of proximal and distal religious constructs in marital functioning. *Journal of Family Psychology, 13,* 321–338.

Malarkey, W. B., Kiecolt-Glaser, J. K., Pearl, D., & Glaser, R. (1994). Hostile behavior during marital conflict alters pituitary and adrenal hormones. *Psychosomatic Medicine, 56,* 41–51.

Margolin, G., & Wampold, B. E. (1981). Sequential analysis of conflict and accord in distressed and nondistressed marital partners. *Journal of Consulting and Clinical Psychology, 49,* 554–567.

Markman, H. J., Stanley, S., & Blumberg, S. L. (1994). *Fighting for your marriage.* New York: Jossey-Bass.

Marks, M., Wieck, A., Checkly, S., & Kumar, C. (1996). How does marriage protect women with histories of affective disorder from post-partum relapse? *British Journal of Medical Psychology, 69,* 329–342.

Massey, D. S., & Sibuya, K. (1995). Unraveling the tangle of pathology: The effect of spatially concentrated joblessness on the well-being of African-Americans. *Social Science Research, 24,* 352–366.

Matthews, L. S., Wickrama, K. A. S., & Conger, R. D. (1996). Predicting marital instability from spouse and observer reports of marital interaction. *Journal of Marriage and the Family, 58,* 641–655.

McGonagle, K. A., Kessler, R. C., & Schilling, E. A. (1992). The frequency and determinants of marital disagreements in a community sample. *Journal of Social and Personal Relationships, 9,* 507–524.

McLanahan, S., & Bumpass, L. (1988). Intergenerational consequences of family disruption. *American Journal of Sociology, 94,* 130–152.

Menaghan, E. G. (1991). Work experiences and family interaction processes: The long reach of the job? *Annual Review of Psychology, 17,* 419–444.

Moore, D. P., & Moore, J. W. (1996). Posthurricane burnout: An island township's experience. *Environment and Behavior, 28,* 134–155.

National Marriage Project (1999). *The social health of marriage in America.* Rutgers University, New Brunswick, NJ.

Nelson, G. M., & Beach, S. R. H. (1990). Sequential interaction in depression: Effects of depressive behavior on spousal aggression. *Behavior Therapy, 21,* 167–182.

Newton, T. L., Kiecolt-Glaser, J. K., Glaser, R., & Malarkey, W. B. (1995). Conflict and withdrawal during marital interaction: The roles of hostility and defensiveness. *Personality and Social Psychology Bulletin, 21,* 512–524.

Norton, R. (1983). Measuring marital quality: A critical look at the dependent variable. *Journal of Marriage and the Family, 45,* 141–151.

O'Leary, K. D., Barling, J., Arias, I., Rosenbaum, A., Malone, J., & Tyree, A. (1989). Prevalence and stability of physical aggression between spouses: A longitudinal analysis. *Journal of Consulting and Clinical Psychology, 57,* 263–268.

Orden, S. R., & Bradburn, N. M. (1968). Dimensions of marriage happiness. *American Journal of Sociology, 73,* 715–731.

Pasch, L. A., & Bradbury, T. N. (1998). Social support, conflict, and the development of marital dysfunction. *Journal of Consulting and Clinical Psychology, 66,* 219–230.

Pavalko, E. K., & Elder, G. H. (1990). World War II and divorce: A life-course perspective. *American Journal of Sociology, 95,* 1213–1234.

Quigley, B. M., & Leonard, K. E. (1996). Desistance of husband aggression in the early years of marriage. *Violence and Victims, 11,* 355–370.

Quigley, B. M., & Leonard, K. E. (1999). Husband alcohol expectancies, drinking, and marital conflict styles as predictors of severe marital violence among newlywed couples. *Psychology of Addictive Behaviors, 13,* 49–59.

Quittner, A. L., Espelage, D. L., Opipari, L. C., Carter, B., Eid, N., & Eigen, H. (1998). Role strain in couples with and without a child with a chronic illness: Associations with marital satisfaction, intimacy, and daily mood. *Health Psychology, 17,* 112–124.

Raudenbush, S. W., Brennan, R. T., & Barnett, R. C. (1995). A multivariate hierarchical model for studying psychological change within married couples. *Journal of Family Psychology, 9,* 161–174.

Raush, H. L., Barry, W. A., Hertel, R. K., & Swain, M. A. (1974). *Communication, conflict and marriage.* San Francisco: Jossey-Bass.

Repetti, R. (1989). Effects of daily workload on subsequent behavior during marital interaction: The roles of social withdrawal and spouse support. *Journal of Personality and Social Psychology, 57,* 651–659.

Rholes, W. S., Simpson, J. A., & Orina, M. M. (1999). Attachment and anger in an anxiety-provoking situation. *Journal of Personality and Social Psychology, 76,* 940–957.

Rogers, S. J., & Amato, P. R. (1997). Is marital quality declining? The evidence from two generations. *Social Forces, 75,* 1089–1100.

Rogers, S. J., & White, L. K. (1998). Satisfaction with parenting: The role of marital happiness, family structure, and parents' gender. *Journal of Marriage and the Family, 60,* 293–308.

Rogge, R. D., & Bradbury, T. N. (1999). Till violence does us part: The differing roles of communication and aggression in predicting adverse marital outcomes. *Journal of Consulting and Clinical Psychology, 67,* 340–351.

Rollins, B. C., & Feldman, H. (1970). Marital satisfaction over the family life cycle. *Journal of Marriage and the Family, 32,* 20–28.

Sabourin, S., Lussier, Y., & Wright, J. (1991). The effects of measurement strategy on attributions for marital problems and behaviors. *Journal of Applied Social Psychology, 21,* 734–746.

Saitzyk, A. R., Floyd, F. J., & Kroll, A. B. (1997). Sequential analysis of autonomy-interdependence and affiliation-disaffiliation in couples' social support interactions. *Personal Relationships, 4,* 341–360.

Sanders, M. R., Halford, W. K., & Behrens, B. C. (1999). Parental divorce and premarital couple communication. *Journal of Family Psychology, 13,* 60–74.

Sayers, S. L., & Baucom, D. H. (1995). Multidimensional scaling of spouses' attributions for marital conflicts. *Cognitive Therapy and Research, 19,* 667–693.

Schwab, R. (1998). A child's death and divorce: Dispelling the myth. *Death Studies, 22,* 445–468.

Simpson, J. A., & Rholes, W. S. (Eds.). (1998). *Attachment theory and close relationships.* New York: Guilford Press.

Sorenson, S. B., & Telles, C. A. (1991). Self-reports of spousal violence in a Mexican-American and non-Hispanic White population. *Violence and Victims, 6,* 3–15.

South, S. J., & Crowder, K. D. (1999). Neighborhood effects on family formation: Concentrated poverty and beyond. *American Sociological Review, 64,* 113–132.

South, S. J., & Lloyd, K. M. (1995). Spousal alternatives and marital dissolution. *American Sociological Review, 60,* 21–35.

Spanier, G. (1976). Measuring dyadic adjustment: New scales for assessing the quality of marriage and similar dyads. *Journal of Marriage and the Family, 38,* 15–28.

Stack, S., & Eshleman, J. R. (1998). Marital status and happiness: A 17-nation study. *Journal of Marriage and the Family, 60,* 527–536.

Stampler, D. B., Wall, J. R., Cassisi, J. E., & Davis, H. (1997). Marital satisfaction and psychophysiological responsiveness in spouses of patients with chronic pain. *International Journal of Rehabilitation and Health, 3,* 159–170.

Sternberg, R. J., & Hojjat, M. (1997). *Satisfaction in close relationships.* New York: Guilford Press.

Straus, M. A., & Gelles, R. J. (1986). Societal change and change in family violence from 1975 to 1985 as revealed by two national surveys. *Journal of Marriage and the Family, 48,* 465–479.

Straus, M. A., Hamby, S. L., Boney-McCoy, S., & Sugarman, D. B. (1996). The revised Conflict Tactics Scales (CTS2): Development and preliminary psychometric data. *Journal of Family Issues, 17,* 283–316.

Stuart, R. B. (1969). Operant-interpersonal treatment for marital discord. *Journal of Consulting and Clinical Psychology, 33,* 675–682.

Tesser, A., & Beach, S. R. H. (1998). Life events, relationship quality, and depression: An investigation of judgment discontinuity in vivo. *Journal of Personality and Social Psychology, 74,* 36–52.

Thomas, G., Fletcher, G. J. O., & Lange, C. (1997). Online empathic accuracy in marital interaction. *Journal of Personality and Social Psychology, 72,* 839–850.

Thomsen, D. G., & Gilbert, D. G. (1998). Factors characterizing marital conflict states and traits: Physiological, affective, behavioral, and neurotic variable contributions to marital conflict and satisfaction. *Personality and Individual Differences, 25,* 833–855.

Tucker, M. B., & Mitchell-Kernan, C. (Eds.). (1995). *The decline in marriage among African Americans.* New York: Russell Sage Foundation.

Uchino, B. N., Cacioppo, J. T., & Kiecolt-Glaser, J. K. (1996). The relationship between social support and physiological processes: A review with emphasis on underlying mechanisms and implications for health. *Psychological Bulletin, 119,* 488–531.

Umberson, D. (1995). Marriage as support or strain: Marital quality following the death of a parent. *Journal of Marriage and the Family, 57,* 709–723.

U.S. Bureau of the Census. (1998, March). Marital status and living arrangements (update). *Current Population Reports,* (Series P20–514).

Vaillant, C. O., & Vaillant, G. E. (1993). Is the U-curve of marital satisfaction an illusion? A 40-year study of marriage. *Journal of Marriage and the Family, 55,* 230–239.

Waite, L. J., & Lillard, L. A. (1991). Children and marital disruption. *American Journal of Sociology, 96,* 930–953.

Ward, R. A., & Spitze, G. (1998). Sandwiched marriages: The implications of child and parent relations for marital quality in midlife. *Social Forces, 77,* 647–666.

Watzlawick, P., Beavin, J. H., & Jackson, D. D. (1967). *Pragmatics of human communication: A study of interactional patterns, pathologies, and paradoxes.* New York: Norton.

Webster, P. S., Orbuch, T. L., & House, J. S. (1995). Effects of childhood family background on adult marital quality and perceived stability. *American Journal of Sociology, 101,* 404–432.

Whiffen, V. E., & Gotlib, I. H. (1989). Stress and coping in maritally distressed and nondistressed couples. *Journal of Social and Personal Relationships, 6,* 327–344.

Wickrama, K. A. S., Lorenz, F. O., Conger, R. D., & Elder, G. H. Jr. (1997). Marital quality and physical illness: A latent growth curve analysis. *Journal of Marriage and the Family, 59,* 143–155.

Yovetich, N. A., & Rusbult, C. E. (1994). Accommodative behavior in close relationships: Exploring transformation of motivation. *Journal of Experimental Social Psychology, 30,* 138–164.

Maureen Perry-Jenkins   *University of Massachusetts—Amherst*

Rena L. Repetti   *University of California—Los Angeles**

Ann C. Crouter   *Pennsylvania State University***

Work and Family in the 1990s

This review highlights four themes emerging from the work and family literature of the 1990s. The first theme evolves from the historical legacy of the maternal employment literature with its focus on children's well-being. The second theme, work socialization, is based on the premise that occupational conditions, such as autonomy and complexity, shape the values of workers who in turn generalize these lessons off the job. Research on work stress, the third theme, explores how experiences of short- and long-term stress at work make their mark on workers' behavior and well-being off the job. Finally, the multiple roles literature focuses on how individuals balance roles, such as parent, spouse, and worker, and the consequences for health and family relationships. In addition to these four major themes, advances in work and family policy initiatives over the past decade are discussed. Suggestions for future research focus on addressing issues of causality, attending to the complexity of social contexts, linking research to policy, and developing interdisciplinary theories and research designs.

The domain of "work and family" emerged as a distinct area of research in the 1960s and 1970s. By the 1980s, what had begun as a narrow research area, focused on dual-career families and "working mothers," had evolved into a sprawling domain of study involving researchers from several disciplines and theoretical perspectives. Menaghan and Parcel (1990) helped define the field in their decade review of research from the 1980s. Ten years later, researchers continue to be intrigued by the interplay between work and family, with particular emphasis on short- and long-term consequences of work for the quality of family life and the development of family members.

The 1990s stand out as a time of technological and economic change, broad trends that made their mark on the work-family interface in ways that are as yet poorly understood. The growing use of computers, pagers, and cell phones, for example, meant that, for some employees, work could be performed almost anywhere: at home, on the highway, or in an airplane. The American economy boomed throughout much of this decade, but the boom affected people quite differently depending on their place in the social structure: The income and opportunity gap widened between rich and poor and the skilled and unskilled (Mishel, Bernstein, & Schmitt, 1999; White & Rogers, 2000).

The 1990s witnessed continuing rate gains of

Department of Psychology, University of Massachusetts, Amherst, MA 01002 (mpj@psych.umass.edu).

*Department of Psychology, University of California—Los Angeles, CA 90095-1563.

**College of Health and Human Development, 105 White Henderson Building, Penn State University, University Park, PA 16802.

Key Words: job stress, parental employment, work and family, work-family policy.

labor force participation for women, particularly mothers. Following a temporary interruption in the growth of women's labor force participation in the early part of the decade, women's employment slowly increased over the 1990s but at a slower rate than in the 1970s and 1980s. In 1997, the overall employment rate of women was 59.5%, with 63.9% of women with children under age 6 and 78.3% of women with children ages 6 to 17 employed (Hayghe, 1997). Latino and American Indian mothers were less likely to be employed than their European, African, and Asian American counterparts.

Although more Americans were employed in the 1990s than ever before, many experienced an increase in work hours and job instability, and, for low wage earners, a decline in real earned income (Mishel et al., 1999). The number of contingent workers, those holding jobs without long-term contracts, grew (Polivka, 1996; Rogers, 2000). A major study of the U.S. labor market suggests that growth in the labor force in the next 20 years will not keep pace with a continuing expansion in the number of jobs that are available, particularly for individuals proficient in math, science, and the English language. The projected shortage of workers is expected to lead to increases in benefits that attract and retain skilled workers. At the same time, Americans with low levels of education and technological expertise will face declining real wages (Judy & D'Amico, 1997).

We organize our review around four broad themes: maternal employment, work socialization, work stress, and multiple roles. The maternal employment literature is the legacy of more than six decades of developmental research on the potentially problematic effects of maternal work on children. In the 1990s, research in this tradition has expanded its focus to include the timing of work, as well as child care and parenting processes that may mediate or moderate the effects of both mothers' and fathers' work involvement on children. Grounded in the sociology of work and occupations, the work socialization literature stems from the premise that occupational conditions, such as autonomy and substantive complexity, shape the beliefs and values of workers who in turn generalize these lessons to other parts of their lives, including childrearing. Research on work stress, with roots in both occupational health and clinical psychology, explores how short- and long-term stress at work make their mark on workers' behavior and well-being off the job. The multiple roles literature, a product of both social

psychological and sociological theorizing about social roles, focuses on how individuals manage the roles of parent, spouse, and worker and the consequences of this balance for health and family relationships. We highlight the rare cases where researchers have directly explored the family-to-work relationship and, in so doing, address the thorny issue of causality in the work-family literature. Finally, reflecting the fact that work and family polices became part of the national policy scene in the 1990s, we close with a look at how public policy, for better and for worse, has addressed the lives of working families.

Given the enormity of the work-family literature, several topics will not be addressed in this review. The effects of paid employment on families depend in part on how men and women divide unpaid family work, such as household chores and child care. Although we address the interrelationship between paid and unpaid work when relevant, paid work is our primary focus (see Coltrane, current issue, for a review of research on the division of household labor). Research on unemployment and economic distress, child and adolescent employment, and aging and retirement issues, are also beyond the purview of this review. The issue of elder care has become a pressing concern for many employed adults; we refer readers to the review by Allen, Blieszner, and Roberto (current issue) on families in later life that addresses this topic.

THE MATERNAL EMPLOYMENT TRADITION: OLD THEMES AND NEW DIRECTIONS

Impact of Maternal Employment on Children

The effect of maternal employment on children is an old theme in the work and family literature, but researchers gave it some new twists in the 1990s. Early in this decade, a number of studies explored the effects of early maternal employment on child outcomes, with inconsistent results. Using large, nationally representative data sets such as the National Longitudinal Survey of Youth (NLSY), some studies reported significant relationships between maternal employment in the child's first year of life and negative cognitive and social outcomes (Baydar & Brooks-Gunn, 1991; Belsky & Eggebeen, 1991), whereas others found enhanced cognitive outcomes for children as a function of early maternal employment (Vandell & Ramanan, 1992) or no overall net effect (Blau & Grossberg, 1990).

Using the latest NLSY data, Harvey (1999) reviewed the diverse methodological approaches to sample construction, measurement of outcomes, and the construction of early maternal employment variables in the early studies that may have led to such discrepant findings. In her reanalysis, neither early maternal nor paternal employment status, nor the timing and continuity of maternal employment, were consistently related to child outcomes. The few significant findings revealed that, for mothers, working more hours in the first 3 years was associated with slightly lower vocabulary scores up through age 9. Maternal employment during the 1st year of the child's life appeared to be slightly more beneficial for the children of single mothers, and early employment of mothers and fathers was related to more positive child outcomes for low-income families. Neither job satisfaction nor race moderated these effects. Although these results suggest parental employment status has few negative effects on young children, other research in the 1990s illuminated some of the conditions under which parental work makes its mark on family relations.

How Much and When Parents Work

The issue of how much adults—especially parents—work was a hot one in the 1990s, stimulated in part by the publication of Juliet Schor's (1991) *The Overworked American,* which argued that men's and women's work hours had increased the equivalent of "an extra month per year" from 1969 to 1987. The image of "overworked" mothers and fathers caught the attention of journalists and researchers alike. Using qualitative interview and observational data from one Fortune 500 "family-friendly" company, Hochschild (1997) argued that, for many workers, work had become home and home had become work with the result that workers were putting in increasingly long hours in the workplace as a way to avoid family time.

Other researchers questioned the notion of "overwork." Using time-use data, Robinson and Godbey (1997) argued that Americans had not increased the amount of time they devoted to work, but that the pace of their lives had quickened, with the result that many felt overworked. Jacobs and Gerson (in press) performed a more fine-grained analysis of work hours, focusing not only on actual hours worked but on employees' work hour preferences. They found evidence of "overwork" for professional, managerial, and technical workers who worked long hours but preferred to work less, and evidence of underemployment for the least educated segment of the workforce, a group that was more likely to work part-time but preferred to work (and earn) more. Parental overwork and underemployment matter for children. Parcel and Menaghan (1994) found, for example, that when fathers worked less than full-time during their children's early years, children had elevated behavior problems, whereas overtime paternal hours were linked to decreased verbal facility.

Studies focused on parents' work hours have tended to ignore the temporal patterning of those hours, with most of the work-family literature assuming that workers hold jobs with fixed, daytime schedules (Presser, 1994). Presser's research suggests, however, that the overlap in spouses' employment schedules has important implications for family life. The less husbands' and wives' schedules overlap, the more husbands are involved in family work (Presser), including child care (Brayfield, 1995). White and Keith (1990) found, however, that non-daytime hours of employment are associated with higher levels of divorce. The "risk" of working nonstandard hours or days is not randomly distributed across the labor force; indeed, this work circumstance appears to exacerbate inequalities in family life. Less educated mothers are much more likely to work nonstandard hours and days than are better educated mothers (Presser & Cox, 1997), as are never-married mothers, a group that is disproportionately overrepresented in low-level, service-sector jobs (Cox & Presser, in press).

Temporal variations in work across the seasons of the year, days of the week and the hours of the day received some attention in this decade (Crouter & Larson, 1998). Crouter and McHale (1993) examined variations in family processes as a function of season of the year, finding "temporal rhythms" in patterns of parent-child involvement in joint activities and parental monitoring across the year, especially for parents whose involvement in paid work decreased sharply from winter to summer. The day can also be parsed into qualitatively different periods that vary in terms of their meaning. Larson and Richards (1994), who collected time use and mood data from family members by "beeping" them at random times of day, found that emotional affect during the early evening hours differed dramatically for husbands and wives in dual-earner families. For husbands, it was a time to relax, recover from the stresses of the workday, and begin leisure activities; for wives, it was a time to gear up after the relatively enjoyable workday and to focus on housework and child care.

Developmental researchers have been slow to recognize the dynamic nature of parents' work. An exception was a study by Moorehouse (1991), which focused on mechanisms that may buffer children from potentially negative effects of changes in mothers' levels of involvement in paid employment. She found that when mothers frequently engaged in shared activities with their children, such as reading books and telling stories, the potentially disruptive effects of changes in employment status on children's social and cognitive competence were mitigated.

Child-Care Quality as a Link Between Parental Work and Child Functioning

One of the most important moderators of the relationship between parental employment and child functioning is the nature and quality of alternative care that children experience. In the largest study of its kind, the National Institute of Child Health and Development's (NICHD) Early Child Care Research Network set out to ascertain whether nonmaternal care in the 1st year of life had detrimental effects on children's development. The 10-site study found no evidence in support of this controversial hypothesis (NICHD, 1997a, 1997b). Findings clearly indicated that child care by itself was unrelated to the quality of mother-infant attachment. Results, however, did point to less secure attachment relationships when the combined effects of poor-quality care, unstable care, and more than minimal amounts of care were coupled with insensitive mothering (NICHD, 1997b).

Care and supervision issues continue to be important throughout childhood and adolescence. Crouter, MacDermid, McHale, and Perry-Jenkins (1990) identified parental monitoring—parents' day-to-day knowledge about their school-aged children's companions, activities, and whereabouts—as a moderator of the effects of maternal work hours on academic and conduct outcomes. In one of the few studies that examined after-school care during middle childhood, Marshall et al. (1997) found that, for lower income (but not middle-income) children, unsupervised after-school time was associated with more externalizing behaviors, whereas attending an after-school program was associated with fewer internalizing problems. Studies that examined the relationship between maternal employment and adolescent functioning consistently revealed no direct relationships between maternal work hours and adolescents' adjustment (Armistead, Wierson, & Forehand, 1990), parent-adolescent relations (Paulson, Koman, & Hill, 1990), or academic achievement (Muller, 1995). Muller, however, emphasized the importance of the time spent without adult supervision as an important moderator. Adolescents performed better on math achievement tests when mothers were employed part-time or not at all; this finding was entirely explained by unsupervised time after school, however. Muller concluded that full-time employment of mothers may negatively affect adolescents' academic achievement when mothers lack time, resources, or both to secure supervised activities for their children outside of school hours.

New Directions for Future Research

A strength of research in the maternal employment tradition is its attention to children and its multifaceted approach to assessing child functioning. Its weakness lies in the fairly unidimensional assessments of work and the lack of attention to the role of fathers and extended kin in the work-family relationship. Ironically, the maternal employment and day-care literatures are virtually separate fields of study, despite the fact that they are so intimately intertwined in the real world. A next step for child development scholars is to add school or day care to the study of work and family. In addition, some researchers are beginning to ask children directly what they think about their parents' work and family roles. Galinsky (1999), for example, suggested that children may perceive a more positive picture of work-family linkages than their parents do. We urge the next generation of scholars to include a wider range of child "outcomes," including children's own perceptions of their mothers' and fathers' work.

THE WORKPLACE AS A CONTEXT FOR ADULT SOCIALIZATION

Work Complexity, Home Environments, and Child Functioning

Among the most significant contributions to the work-family literature this decade has been greater scrutiny of the work environment. The groundbreaking work of Kohn and Schooler (Kohn & Schooler,1982; Kohn, 1995) laid the foundation for much of the research in the 1990s that explored how occupational self-direction (that is, the extent to which work offers opportunities for employees to exercise autonomy and to focus on substantively complex tasks with minimal supervision), socializes the worker in ways that are generalized to life off the job. As Kohn originally formulated these ideas, workers' value orientations, particularly the extent to which they value self-direction (vs. conformity) for themselves and their children, were a pivotal link between occupational conditions and workers' behavior off the job. Contemporary research, however, has tended to infer, rather than measure, workers' value orientations; thus, the full process by which work shapes the developing cognitions of employed adults, who in turn operationalize those ideas in their daily family lives, awaits future research.

Important research by Menaghan and Parcel throughout the 1990s revealed that the occupational complexity of mothers' work is related to the extent to which they create a positive home environment for their children, meaning a family context that provides cognitive stimulation, emotional support, and safety (Menaghan & Parcel, 1991; Parcel & Menaghan, 1994a, 1994b). In addition to attending to the variability in the work context, these researchers explored family conditions and maternal resources as they influence child outcomes, attempting to tease apart the direct and combinative effects of work conditions and family conditions on child functioning. A particular strength of their research is the careful effort to account for variables that might indicate selection effects into more complex jobs, such as educational, intellectual, and psychological resources.

Parcel and Menaghan (1993) hypothesized that workers subjected to greater autonomy and self-supervision on the job will place less emphasis on direct parental control over their children and instead promote children's ability to internalize parental norms, which in turn lowers the probability of behavior problems. Testing this hypothesis with a sample of married couples with at least one child, they found that higher levels of occupational complexity for fathers served as a protective factor against later child behavior problems. For mothers, substantively complex work was not directly related to children's behavior problems; however, having a more substantively complex job was subsequently more protective for children of divorced or separated mothers. Cooksey, Menaghan, and Jekielek (1997) elaborated on this line of research with a larger subsample of the NLSY

that included single- and two-parent families. These researchers found that when controlling for family structure, maternal employment characterized by more autonomy, working with people, and problem solving predicted decreases in child behavior problems.

Turning to similar analyses that examined children's cognitive functioning, increases in mothers' job complexity was related to enhanced reading scores for children (Parcel & Menaghan, 1994a). Moreover, mothers' intellectual ability interacted with job complexity such that the benefits of mothers' higher levels of intellectual skills were greater when mothers' cognitive skills were continually reinforced in a highly complex work environment (Parcel & Menaghan). The most interesting findings document how combinations of changing work and family circumstances influence changes in the quality of children's home environments. Mothers who began employment in jobs characterized by low to average complexity showed decrements over time in the quality of the home environment they provided their children. Mothers who experienced the greatest gains from highly complex work settings were continuously employed single mothers (Menaghan & Parcel, 1995). Two important themes emerge from this line of research. The first is the importance of considering the multiplicative effects of social contexts, and the second is the significance of lagged effects whereby work and family conditions have greater effects over time than concurrently. Parcel and Menaghan's findings support the notion that holding a job low in complexity, or entering such a job, may drain parental energy, discourage mothers' intellectual growth, and discourage childrearing values and practices that teach children to internalize norms (Parcel & Menaghan, 1994b).

Parcel and Menaghan's studies laid important groundwork for understanding how experiences on the job shape the lives of workers and their children. As noted in these studies, however, because of constraints of the NLSY sample, the authors were unable to examine an important intervening variable in the socialization hypothesis, namely, parenting behavior. Related studies, however, provide additional support for the socialization hypothesis. Grimm-Thomas and Perry-Jenkins (1994) found that fathers with greater complexity and autonomy at work reported higher self-esteem which, in turn, was linked to less authoritarian parenting. Greenberger, O'Neil, & Nagel (1994) reported that parents whose jobs were more complex responded with greater warmth to their children and offered verbal explanations to them that were of higher quality than was the case for parents with less complex work. Similarly, in a sample of White, rural, dual-earner couples with adolescent children, Whitbeck et al. (1997) found that fathers, but not mothers, with more job autonomy had more flexible parenting styles that were, in turn, linked to a sense of mastery and control in their adolescent children.

New Directions for Research on Work Socialization

Parcel and Menaghan have paved the way toward a more complete understanding of the work-family interface by revealing specific cases where the interaction and timing of work and family circumstances either enhance or undermine positive child functioning. Despite efforts to examine how factors such as race and family structure may moderate processes linking work complexity to child outcomes, few significant results emerged (Menaghan & Parcel, 1991). Before concluding that social context does not play a role in these relationships, however, it may be important to construct and examine multidimensional ecological niches that include layers of contexts such as social class, family structure, and race. Processes linking work complexity to home environment may differ markedly for a low-income, White, single mother, for example, than for a middle-income, Latino, married mother (Perry-Jenkins & Gillman, in press).

Findings from the work socialization tradition hold important implications for workplace innovations and policy. A complete approach to family-supportive policy would go beyond enabling employees to take time away from work (e.g., leave time, flextime) or to increase their time at work (e.g., on-site child care) to focus on changing the conditions of work that are related to individual and family functioning (Lambert, 1993, 1999; MacDermid & Targ, 1995). As Menaghan and Parcel (1995) have suggested, welfare reform policies that push parents into jobs with low wages, low complexity, and long hours may hold negative consequences for the children of the working poor.

THE IMPACT OF OCCUPATIONAL STRESS ON FAMILIES

Work stress has probably received more attention from work-family researchers than any other job condition. This literature is based on the idea that any effect that stress has on an individual's psychological, and even physiological, functioning will ultimately influence his or her behavior at home and, in so doing, have an impact on the family and all of its members. We distinguish in our review between job *stressors,* objective conditions at work that tax an individual's emotional, physical, and cognitive stores, and *stress,* the individual's internal response to those conditions. We also distinguish between two different research paradigms: investigations of the possible long-term impact of chronic job stress and a growing literature on the effects of short-term fluctuations in job stressors.

The Transfer of Chronic Job Stress Into Families

There is now a substantial body of research suggesting that chronic job stressors influence families when they cause feelings of overload or conflict between the roles of worker and family member. Hughes, Galinsky, & Morris (1992) found that the association between chronic stressors at work and marital tension was mediated by the worker's perception that work and family life interfered with each other. Crouter, Bumpus, Maguire, & McHale (1999) found that mothers and fathers who described more pressure at work also reported greater role overload and a feeling of being overwhelmed by multiple commitments. Higher levels of role overload were, in turn, associated with increased conflict with adolescent offspring. A structural equation model supported a path from work pressure to role overload to parent-adolescent conflict to adolescent well-being. MacDermid and Williams (1997) reported similar findings in a study of female bank workers. Those who reported poor supervision at work also described greater difficulty managing work and family demands, which was linked to mothers' reports of increased child behavior problems via its association with less nurturing parenting.

In the model that underlies most chronic-stress transfer research, the predictor of family outcomes tends not to be an objective job characteristic (e.g., a job stressor), but rather internal distress in response to experiences in work and family roles. For example, feelings of job stress have been related to self-reports of distress, such as depression, which have in turn been linked to poorer marital relations (Barling & MacEwen, 1992; Sears & Galambos, 1992). People who report more conflict and overload due to the combination of work and family roles tend to also describe more emotional distress (Gerstel & Gallagher, 1993; Guelzow, Bird, & Koball, 1991; Paden & Buehler, 1995), and these experiences are linked to problematic parent-child relations and negative child outcomes (Bird & Kemerait, 1990; Bowen, 1998; Galambos, Sears, Almeida, & Kolaric, 1995; MacEwen & Barling, 1991). One of the shortcomings in this approach is the assumption of causal priority. Little effort has been devoted to the testing of recursive models whereby emotional distress and family functioning affect perceptions of job stress and role strain.

One of the interesting features of the chronic stress transfer studies published in the 1990s is that they tended to report either no direct correlation or very little correlation between an individual's scores on global measures of stress at work and assessments of individual or family functioning. The link to a marital or parent-child relationship outcome was only observed through an individual well-being mediator, such as role strain or emotional distress (Barling & MacEwen, 1992; Crouter et al., 1999; Galambos & Maggs, 1990; Greenberger et al., 1994; Sears & Galambos, 1992). In addition, some of the modest, although statistically significant, cross-sectional correlations between self-reported job stress and unsatisfying or dysfunctional family relationships are subject to respondent-bias explanations (Stewart & Barling, 1996; Wortman, Biernat, & Lang, 1991).

Studies that assessed specific job stressors in homogenous samples were more likely to find associations between job stressors and family outcomes (e.g., Hughes et al., 1992). Repetti (1994), studying fathers in a single occupation (air traffic control), found a propensity for members of work teams with a negative social climate at work (e.g., little or no "group spirit," interpersonal conflicts, etc.) to describe daily after-work interactions with their children as having a more negative emotional tone. This association was observed even when measure of the team social climate was based solely on descriptions provided by the air traffic controllers' coworkers.

To the extent that chronic work stress influences general patterns of family interaction, one might also expect to observe an impact on individual family members. Tests of a direct association between an individual's experience of stressors at work and the well-being of other family members, sometimes referred to as a "cross-over

effect," have been inconclusive. In some studies, a spouse's feelings of depression or overload have been greater when a husband (Crouter et al., 1999) or a wife (Wortman et al., 1991) reported more pressure or overloads at work. Other studies, however, have failed to detect cross-over effects from wives' job pressures and overloads to their husbands' well-being, (Crouter et al., 1999) or marital adjustment (Sears & Galambos, 1992). At least one study found that mothers' reports of more demands at work were directly associated with their reports of more behavior problems in their children (MacDermid & Williams, 1997). No evidence for cross-over has been found when parents' reports of job stressors were related to information about children from independent sources, such as teachers' descriptions of child behavior problems (Stewart & Barling, 1996) or adolescents' self-reports of their psychological adjustment (Crouter et al., 1999; Galambos & Maggs, 1990).

Why are uniform, across-the-board chronic-stress transfer effects often not observed in studies that use heterogeneous samples and global measures of stress? Why are even the significant findings generally not strong? We believe that individual, family, and social context differences exert important influences on the transfer of stress from work to family. Research in the next decade should focus much more heavily on these moderators by asking under *what conditions* are *which job stressors* transferred to *which families*; *how* is stress transmitted, and what *different types of outcomes* are observed? Research in the 1990s has already provided some important clues.

Job stressors have an impact on families when they cause some experience of stress within the individual, such as emotional distress, fatigue, a sense of conflict between work and family roles, or role overload. In the absence of one or more of these intervening links, stress transfer cannot occur. That may explain why many well-designed studies have not found direct associations between job stressors and family outcomes. Many men and women report no work-family strains at all (Marshall & Barnett, 1993). Responses to any stressor, including job stressors, are shaped by personality, coping style, and social support. Recent research points to characteristics of work and family that shape the transfer of stress process.

Vulnerability to role strain seems to vary according to structural characteristics of both job and family, such as the number and flexibility of work hours, family size, and ages of children

(Guelzow et al., 1991; Marshall & Barnett, 1991; O'Neil & Greenberger, 1994). Role commitment and involvement, occupational prestige, and spouse support are other factors that may influence one's experience of role strain (Frone, Russell, & Cooper, 1992; O'Neil & Greenberger, 1994). Marital quality appears to act as a particularly important moderator. On one hand, stress may transfer more readily between people in close, stable relationships. If greater emotional involvement carries with it a "burden of care" (Rook, Dooley, & Catalano, 1991), individuals who are committed and happy in their family roles may find work-family conflicts more distressing (Wortman et al., 1991). On the other hand, an unhappy marriage can exacerbate the effects of job stressors. In one study, a father's highly demanding job interfered with the parents' monitoring of their sons' daily activities, but only if the parents also described their marriage as (relatively) low in love and commitment (Bumpus, Crouter, & McHale, 1999). There is also evidence to suggest that the nature of work-family conflicts, and their impact on families, varies by race, occupation, and social class (Frone, Russell, & Cooper; Marshall & Barnett).

Throughout the 1990s, there have been important methodological improvements. Although many of the studies relied on cross-sectional, self-report questionnaire data, there were at least two prospective longitudinal studies (Galambos & Maggs, 1990; Rook, Dooley, & Catalano, 1991). Many studies avoided the problem of respondent biases inflating correlations between self-report measures by obtaining independent assessments of key variables. To answer questions about the conditions under which particular job stressors are transferred to particular families, research efforts in the next decade should shift from attempts to identify uniform stress transfer effects to investigations of individual and social context variables that moderates these connections.

The Study of Daily Stress Transfer Processes

The stress transfer research cited above focused on the possible long-term impact of chronic job stress. These studies suggest that changes over time in the employed individual's emotional and psychological functioning, particularly feelings of distress, role overload, and work-family conflict, result in interactions with family members that are less sensitive and responsive, and more negative and conflictual. Some researchers have attempted to observe "up close" the process of stress affecting behavior at home using short-term, repeated measures designs.

Repetti (1994; Repetti & Wood, 1997a), for example, has found that employed spouses and parents tend to withdraw from family interaction following high stress days at work. Social withdrawal, which may help adults to cope in the short run with certain types of stressors, involves a pervasive reduction both in the amount of social interaction and in emotional responsiveness (Repetti, 1992). In one study, both maternal self-reports and independent observers indicated that mothers were more withdrawn from their preschoolers on days when the mothers had experienced greater workloads or interpersonal stress at work (Repetti & Wood, 1997a). Repetti (1994) also found evidence of social withdrawal in an analysis of daily data from air traffic controllers. Other analyses showed withdrawal from daily marital interactions following high workload shifts at the airport (Repetti, 1989). The potential short-term benefits of social withdrawal for the family are suggested by findings indicating that solitary time buffers the transmission of negative emotions from mothers to their children (Larson & Gillman, 1999).

In contrast to a social withdrawal response, negative emotion spillover occurs when feelings of frustration, anger, or disappointment at work lead to the expression of greater irritability and impatience or more power assertion at home. The air traffic controllers who were fathers appeared to respond to an increase in social stressors at work with both social withdrawal and negative emotional spillover (Repetti, 1994).

Evidence that an increase in stressful conditions at work is often followed by changes in behavior at home is supplemented by daily studies that point to the possible psychological and emotional mediators of these behavioral responses. Barling and his colleagues have used daily data to show that feelings of role overload and role conflict are associated with distressed emotional states and that these states are, in turn, linked to anger and withdrawal during marital interactions (Barling & Macintyre, 1993; MacEwen & Barling, 1994; MacEwen, Barling, & Kelloway, 1992). Other studies using intensive, repeated measures designs found that increases in job stressors, both distressing social interactions and work overload, are associated with a short-term deterioration in mood and physical well-being and increases in physiological arousal (Jamner, Shapiro, Goldstein, & Hug, 1991; Repetti, 1993). An exciting new literature on *emotional transmission* in families fills in a critical link by showing that events or emotions in one family member's experience predict subsequent emotions or behaviors in another family member (Larson & Almeida, 1999).

When put together, the findings from studies using intensive, repeated measures designs trace daily increases in certain stressful experiences at work to changes in individual psychological and physiological states, to social behaviors and interactions at home, to the feelings and well-being of other family members, all within several days. These studies have also investigated factors that moderate stress transfer processes. The evidence suggests that both stable individual and group differences, as well as circumstances that may change over time, help to shape how an increase in work stress might be subsequently transferred to the family. For example, both emotional reactivity to stressors and the process of negative emotional transmission within a family were strengthened when problems occurred earlier in the day (Almeida, Wethington, & Chandler, 1999; Marco & Suls, 1993) and were accompanied by other life stressors (Larson & Gillman, 1999).

Individual differences in personality and emotional functioning also shape short-term stress-transfer processes. Studies have found exaggerated emotional responses to work stressors, as well as other daily stressors, among individuals with higher levels of negative affectivity or neuroticism (Bolger & Schilling, 1991; Marco & Suls, 1993). Similarly, Repetti & Wood (1997a) found that daily job stressors had a much stronger impact on the parenting behavior of mothers with higher scores on type A behaviors, depression, and anxiety. The transmission of negative emotions within families also seems to be enhanced when there are marital or child conduct problems (Margolin, Christensen, & John, 1996) and when parenting is overcontrolling (Larson & Gillman, 1999).

Depending on the circumstances, immediate responses to what is usually considered to be a job stressor can range from no detectable impact on the family, to increased irritability and anger, to social withdrawal. Our review suggests that individual, family, occupational, and other social context factors shape how an individual will respond to a day at work that taxes his or her emotional, physical, and cognitive stores.

New Directions for Occupational Stress Research

Two distinct approaches to the study of occupational stress have emerged: one that examines long-term chronic job stress and another that focuses on short-term fluctuations of job stress across multiple days. The next step is to integrate what we have learned about short-term and long-term stress transmission processes. For example, although social withdrawal may be an adaptive, short-term coping response for both the individual and the family, over time, repeated instances of withdrawal may corrode feelings of closeness and lead to feelings of resentment and negative interactions (Repetti & Wood, 1997b). Our review also suggests a need to clearly distinguish between objective job characteristics and the individual's subjective experience of those characteristics. Although the two are obviously related, global self-reports of "stress" or feelings of role overload and role conflict should not be confused with specific job characteristics that are presumed to be stressful, such as poor supervision, a negative social climate, or overloads at work. Other research suggests that a high level of control offers workers an opportunity to cope with occupational stressors such as work overload, with benefits for the individual's health (Karasek & Theorell, 1990; Repetti, 1993; Schnall, Schwartz, Landsbergis, Warren, & Pickering, 1998). The simultaneous study of both job demands and job control may allow the theoretical models and empirical findings from work socialization studies, which often assess the effects of autonomy at work, to be integrated into research on the effects of job pressures and demands. Finally, we need to identify key moderating variables that shape the process by which stress is transmitted.

MULTIPLE ROLES PERSPECTIVES IN WORK-FAMILY RESEARCH

An ongoing theme in the work-family research has been the implications of managing the multiple roles of worker, spouse, and parent for individuals' mental health and the quality of their family relationships. White and Rogers (current issue) point out that, in light of men's declining wages, women's increased employment often has allowed families to maintain their standard of living. These changes, however, call into question the gendered ideology of family life that so often ascribes breadwinning to men (Coltrane, 1996; Deutsch, 1999). Some research has revealed that the demands of multiple roles have the potential to increase stress levels and undermine well-being (O'Neil & Greenberger, 1994), as well as to compromise physical health (Repetti, 1993). Most of the recent literature on multiple roles, however, has emphasized the "expansion hypothesis" (Barnett & Baruch, 1985), a view that holds that multiple roles bring rewards—such as "monetary income, heightened self esteem, the power to delegate onerous role obligations, opportunities for social relationships, and challenge" (Barnett, 1999, p. 152)—that have an energizing effect on people. From this perspective, role quality (Barnett, 1994) and the combination of certain roles (Barnett, Marshall, & Pleck, 1992) enhance well-being. The multiple roles literature also has addressed the interactive nature of roles whereby a supportive marital relationship may buffer the negative effects of job stressors (Repetti, 1998). Voydanoff and Donnelly (1999a) found, however, that satisfaction with one's parental role does not serve as a buffer between the stress of managing multiple roles and psychological distress.

Marks and MacDermid (1996) contended that the multiple roles literature has lost sight of the theoretical underpinnings of role theory, which hold that one must examine a total role system rather than treat individual roles as distinct entities separable from the whole. An assumption of some role theorists is that role systems are inherently hierarchical, and thus the problem of juggling roles requires favoring one role over another (Thoits, 1992). In contrast, Marks and MacDermid proposed that although this is how roles may be organized for some, "role balance," where roles are given relatively equal attention and weight, may be optimal for many. This theoretical debate awaits more research to disentangle the ways in which individuals organize their life roles and the implications for individuals and family relationships.

A serious limitation of studies that address multiple roles, whether it be from a balance or strain perspective, is a lack of attention to the connection between role enactment (e.g., the behaviors linked to a role) and role responsibility (e.g., taking on psychological responsibility for a role). A gender perspective challenges researchers to examine how individuals construct and give meaning to their roles, for ultimately it is the meaning attached to role behavior that holds consequences for individual and family functioning (Ferree, 1990). Research on the meaning of the provider role for women and men has consistently found that employment status alone reveals little about the meaning and value of that role for the individual (Hood, 1983; Perry-Jenkins & Crouter,

1990; Perry-Jenkins, Seery, & Crouter, 1992; Potuchek, 1992).

The question of how race may moderate work-family role relationships has been addressed by a few scholars (Broman, 1991; McLoyd, 1993). In a study that explored work and family roles in black families, Broman found that involvement in multiple roles had differential effects on Black women and men. Specifically, married, employed women reported the lowest levels of family life satisfaction, whereas married, employed men reported the highest family satisfaction. In addition, different organization of work and family role responsibilities were related to assessments of family life satisfaction, but not to psychological well-being outcomes. Broman suggested that the usefulness of social role theory may be domain-specific for Blacks, useful in understanding family life satisfaction but not mental health. He and McLoyd argued further that the different historical experiences of Blacks and Whites in the United States have implications not only for differential work and family role configurations as a function of race, but for different associations between role patterns and family and individual outcomes for Blacks and Whites. Greater attention to race and ethnicity as they shape work and family experiences remains an important direction for the field.

New Directions for Research on Multiple Roles

Future research should examine the meaning men and women assign to their roles as parents, workers, and marital partners. One study of the transition to parenthood for working-class, dual-earner couples has shown that in families where both mother and father rank "parent" as their most important role, there is great variation in their definitions of what a parent actually does (Perry-Jenkins, Pierce, Haley, & Goldberg, 1999). More than half of the men reported that providing income was their primary responsibility as a parent, whereas others listed characteristics such as being a role model, nurturing, and spending time with their children. Simon (1997) not only found gendered differences in the meaning that men and women gave to the costs and benefits of certain roles, but also that these different meanings were related to differing degrees of distress.

Research in the multiple roles tradition often views work and family roles as static, despite research that points to the fluid and dynamic nature of many roles. Future work on roles would benefit from a life-course perspective, an approach that guides researchers to examine differing work and family trajectories that take shape over time, with attention to the precursors and outcomes of these different paths. New methodological strategies that focus on the dyad as the unit of analysis will make it possible to understand how spouses shape each others' attitudes and behaviors over time, as well as the consequences of those interactions for the marriage and individual psychological functioning (Raudenbush, Brennan, & Barnett, 1995).

THE IMPACT OF FAMILIES ON THE WORKPLACE

Despite the continued recognition that work-family relationships are bidirectional, few studies emerged in the past decade that explored how families shape behavior in the workplace. The question of the direction of effects has proven to be a thorny issue in work-family research. Although trained not to use causal language, social scientists tend to think causally and to develop causal theories, even when their data and research designs preclude the possibility of making causal conclusions. One reason why it is particularly challenging to think about causal relationships in research on work and family has to do with selection effects at several levels. First, people tend to select their work on the basis of goals, interests, skills, training, and experience. Evidence for the nonrandom nature of these processes comes from Cooksey, Menaghan, and Jekielek (1997), who found that mothers with low self-esteem and those with early histories of delinquent behavior were subsequently less likely to attain jobs that were high in complexity. Second, individuals have to negotiate some work issues (such as schedules, work hours, and overtime) with their marital partner, creating another layer of selection effects. In a large, qualitative study, Deutsch (1999) described how parents often made conscious (and probably unconscious) decisions about jobs that were unsuitable because of time demands, inadequate income, and inflexibility. In fact, job decisions were often gendered decisions, in large part based on who was seen as responsible for supporting the family, as opposed to the nature of the job. Finally, the workplace also plays a role in selection, hiring some employees and firing others, providing opportunities for some workers and discriminating against others. Researchers can control for some of these preexisting qualities and decisions, but it is impossible to fully anticipate or measure all relevant phenomena. Indeed, one reason why the findings on the impact of short-

term work stress on family relations are so powerful is that those research designs bypass the selection effects problem by utilizing each individual respondent as his or her own "control."

What questions did researchers in the 1990s ask about family-to-work effects? A handful of scholars developed or incorporated (or both developed and incorporated) self-report family-to-work conflict scales that require respondents to assess the ways that their family demands have affected their work-related activities (Gutek, Searle, & Klepa, 1991; Netemeyer, Boles, & McMurrian, 1996). Family-to-work conflict was found to be negatively related to work performance (Frone, Yardley, & Markel, 1997) and positively related to work withdrawal (MacEwen & Barling, 1994).

Some support emerged for the hypothesis that distressing or disruptive family relationships negatively impact workplace productivity and absenteeism. Using cross-sectional data from the National Comorbidity Survey, Forthofer, Markman, Cox, Stanley, & Kessler (1996) found that marital distress was positively, albeit modestly, related to work loss, operationalized as the number of days the employee was unable to work and carry out normal activities. The findings were most robust for men in their first 10 years of marriage.

In one of the only longitudinal studies to examine the effects of family conditions on work, Rogers (1999) found that, as marital discord increased, so too did wives' income because increases in marital discord increased the likelihood that nonemployed wives would enter the labor force. Rogers' findings may portray some of the early precursors of marital dissolution, or, more optimistically, reveal a process whereby unhappy wives acquire new bargaining power. In a similar vein, Attewell (1999) concluded that, with regard to the relationship between divorce and unemployment, "causation appears to run in both directions" (p. 81); controlling for demographic and occupational characteristics, unemployment increased the likelihood of subsequent divorce and being divorced increased the likelihood of subsequent unemployment.

New Directions for Research on Family-to-Work Effects

More work is needed that examines how family conditions shape work life in terms of both long-term decisions and short-term daily interactions. As a first step, it would be instructive for researchers to test work-to-family and family-to-work hypotheses in the same data set using recursive models. This approach still begs the question of causality. Some of the most exciting possibilities for studying cause and effect lie in intervention programs. In the context of welfare reform, for example, we may be able to piggyback work and family questions on to studies that randomly assign people to jobs or build questions about work into family interventions. Forthofer et al. (1996) noted that interventions designed to decrease marital conflict may have the side benefit of lowering employers' costs due to work loss and absenteeism. This hypothesis is worth pursuing in marital intervention studies with random assignment to experimental and control conditions.

INSIGHTS ON WORK AND FAMILY FROM POLICY-ORIENTED RESEARCH

In the early 1990s, a great deal of attention focused on federal and workplace policies as sources of support for working families in the United States. Ferber, O'Farrell, and Allen (1991) reviewed the state of policies and programs for working families and outlined the agenda and challenges for the upcoming decade. In 1993, landmark legislation was passed in the form of the Family and Medical Leave Act (FMLA), which allows for 12 weeks of unpaid leave with job protection for employees having or adopting children or for the care of an ill child, spouse, or parent. Although an important milestone in the area of family policy, the FMLA excludes 95% of employers and 50% of employees (because it applies only to workplaces with 50 or more employees), is of little assistance to part-time, seasonal, or temporary workers, and is unavailable to same-gender couples. Moreover, because this leave time is unpaid, low-income families often cannot take advantage of it (Gerstel & McGonagle, 1999), leading some to argue that the act represents "an emerging class cleavage in workplace family policy" (Estes & Glass, 1996, p. 429). Even in companies with a "family-friendly" image, informal barriers often exist that make it difficult for employees either to take a leave or to take as long a leave as they would like. Fried (1998) discussed the inherent contradiction workers interested in parental leave face in a corporate environment that equates dedication with long work hours. Even in Sweden, a country with a much more generous parental leave policy than that of the United States, informal workplace culture often has made it difficult for men to take advantage of parental leave (Haas, 1992).

Only a handful of studies have addressed the implications of work-family policies for parental or child well-being. Hyde, Klein, Essex, and Clark (1995) found that short maternity leaves were a risk factor in predicting maternal depression when coupled with another risk factor such as marital concerns. Clark, Hyde, Essex, and Klein (1997) found that mothers with shorter maternity leaves who were either more depressed or who had babies with more difficult temperaments exhibited less positive interactions with their infants compared with mothers with longer leaves.

The question of why the United States continues to have such a half-hearted response to the needs of working families is compelling. In an excellent historical overview of "the limited and uneven policy response" to maternal employment over the past three decades, Pleck (1992) suggested that one explanation centers on many Americans' continued ambivalence about maternal employment. Given the consistency with which social scientists have documented the absence of effects of maternal employment on children, however, our scientific attention must focus on those conditions of employment that hold implications for families, and our policies, in turn, should enhance those conditions that support families and minimize those circumstances that pose risks.

An historical perspective on family policy can provide insights into the forces that shape social change. Burstein and Bricher (1997), in reviewing the development of public policy around issues of work, family, and gender from 1945 through the 1990s, pointed to the importance of understanding how policy actually emerges. Major changes in policy require the conjunction of three processes: (a) defining the problem, (b) developing new solutions, and (c) pressure on Congress (Burstein & Wierzbicki, in press). Rayman and Bookman (1999) highlighted three examples of policy initiatives in the work-family area: (a) The White House Conference on Families during the late 1970s; (b) The Infant Care Leave Project, organized by the Bush Center in Child Development and Social Policy at Yale University in the mid-1980s; and (c) the Carnegie Corporation of New York's effort to underscore the importance of the first 3 years of life. In each case, the initiatives produced increased public awareness but little in terms of dramatic changes in public policy, perhaps reflecting "a lack of national consensus about what is the proper role of government in supporting working families" (Rayman & Bookman, p. 206). If policy changes regarding work and family issues are to occur in the future, family scholars and advocates could benefit from the lessons of history that recommend focus, creativity, and diligence in our efforts. Disseminating research in forms that are accessible and interesting to the public is an essential part of this process.

On another policy front, changes in the American welfare system that took place in the last decade hold important implications for the lives of poor families. The 1996 Personal Responsibility and Work Opportunity Reconciliation Act shifted authority for welfare reform from the federal government to state governments. The new legislation, Temporary Assistance for Needy Families (TANF), requires that able-bodied welfare recipients work after 2 years. This new legislation provides block grants to states and gives them the power to use this money as they deem appropriate, with an important feature being that states are allowed to *keep every dollar they save from their reform package.* Thus, incentives to cut costs are high. Studies have already begun to document the price that many families pay as a result of this new legislation. Edin and Lein's (1997) work with single mothers highlights the reality that public assistance and low-wage jobs do not provide enough income to cover basic needs. They conclude that the primary problem with the current welfare system is that the kind of jobs these women can attain are low paying, offer little security, and provide few long term opportunities. To make ends meet, many mothers were involved in "off-the-books" work to sustain their families, an aspect of the work-family interface that we know little about. Iverson and Farber (in press) highlight the importance of intergenerational transmission of values regarding work and self-sufficiency in their sample of Black teen mothers and nonparent peers. Their research points to the importance of familial role models, tangible support, direct verbal messages, job training and consultation for poor, young women striving to become financially independent. A number of researchers have raised concerns regarding maternal and child well-being in situations where mothers are in poorly paid, stressful jobs and have not voluntarily chosen to work (Lambert, 1999; Moore & Driscoll, 1997; Parcel & Menaghan, 1997). As this social experiment extends into the next decade, researchers must focus on the short- and long-term outcomes of different types of welfare-to-work initiatives.

CHARTING NEW TERRAIN FOR THE NEXT DECADE

We have woven critiques and recommendations throughout this review. Rather than summarizing those points, we close by highlighting several broad themes that cut across these areas and point the direction for future research. First and foremost, issues of definition and meaning regarding the weighty terms of "work" and "family" must be addressed. Although feminist scholars have challenged the use of these terms in compelling ways (Ferree, 1990; Ishii-Kuntz, 1994; Thorne, unpublished data), most research in the 1990s was rooted in notions of the nuclear family and images of routine, full-year, 9-to-5, paid jobs. We will benefit from efforts that question and explore the social constructions of work and family. As Thorne suggested, "fruitful topics illuminate social processes that don't necessarily stop at the prespecified boundaries of 'work' and 'family.'" For example, how might kin offer instrumental and emotional support that allows for trade-offs and reciprocity across all domains of life, especially during times of economic and social upheavals? In addition, efforts to reconceptualize "work and family" would benefit greatly from more cross-cultural and comparative studies (Ishii-Kuntz).

Second, we need a more nuanced approach to work and family research, attainable by consistently asking to whom our models apply. Answering this question requires samples that vary in terms of gender, race, ethnicity, class, occupation, and family structure. When we succeed in identifying such diverse samples, a first approach should be to explore whether our models are universal or apply in certain delimited contexts. We need to rethink the common tendency to control statistically for race, class, and other indicators of location in the social structure. Rather, we should think through which combinations of social circumstances are most likely to produce the patterns in which we are interested. In attending to social circumstances, we also should take into account how social and historical time shapes the meaning we give to work and family issues.

Sometimes a strategic first step to understanding the complexity of work and family dynamics is to focus on an exemplar occupation, as in Repetti's study of air traffic controllers, who work in a high-stress occupation likely to produce daily fluctuations in challenges and demands. After identifying the processes of interest in a specific, theoretically relevant occupation, we then need to broaden our occupational sampling to specify the conditions under which the linkages of interest are evident.

A third, related direction emphasizes embracing complexity. Some of the most interesting research in the 1990s examined interaction effects, how, for example, occupational complexity in combination with family circumstances shapes the quality of the home environment parents provide for their children. We need to press forward in this direction by building better measures of family processes, family relationships, and employed adults' interpretations and constructions of their work and family roles into studies of occupational conditions.

We have already stressed the ubiquitous problem of selection effects in work and family research. To date, however, most research in the area has focused on working parents themselves. We need to know far more about child effects and their contributions to work and family research. To what extent do parents make work decisions on the basis of what their children are like or what they think their children need? Do child effects operate in the same ways for mothers versus fathers?

Finally, the field would benefit greatly from experimental research designs. Given the attention to workplace policies and conditions in the past decade, the next decade may bring actual change and innovation on the work front. We must be prepared to study these social experiments as they unfold, for it is these types of experimental manipulations that will allow us to pinpoint critical aspects of work that can enhance family life while giving us a handle on the selection effects so pervasive in work and family research.

It is our hope that we will see in the next decade inventive, interdisciplinary research that illuminates the complex processes linking these social settings. The research themes highlighted in this review come from rich disciplinary traditions, each with unique strengths and weaknesses. Future research that integrates the strengths of both a work socialization perspective, with its careful attention to work conditions, and a developmental perspective, with its wealth of knowledge regarding adult and child development and family relationships, would greatly enhance our knowledge base. Moreover, methodological and conceptual advances in the work stress and multiple roles literatures provide insights into the objective and subjective mediators that bridge the relationship between work and family. Finally, heeding Thorne's

(unpublished data) cautions, we must be careful to avoid reifying static, bounded concepts of "work" and "family" in research. Research will better reflect life when our images of work and family issues shift from the confines of black boxes linked by arrows, to more complex, colorful imagery that blurs boundaries and is shaded by multiple layers of social context. In the next decade, researchers in the work and family field, building on its strong multidisciplinary foundation, should forge integrative theories and research designs that mirror the realities and complexities of our work and family lives.

NOTE

The authors wish to express their appreciation to Francine Deutsch, Naomi Gerstel, and Susan McHale for their constructive comments on earlier drafts of this paper. Preparation of this manuscript was supported by a grant from the National Institute of Mental Health (NIMH, R29-MH56777) to the first author, a grant from NIMH (R29–48593) to the second author, and grants from the National Institute for Child Health and Human Development (R01-HD29409 and R01-HD32336) to the third author.

REFERENCES

Allen, K. R., Blieszner, R., & Roberto, K. A. (2000). Families in the middle and later years: A review and critique of research in the 1990s. *Journal of Marriage and the Family, 62,* 911–926.

Almeida, D. M., Wethington, E., & Chandler, A. L. (1999). Daily transmission of tensions between marital dyads and parent-child dyads. *Journal of Marriage and the Family, 61,* 49–61.

Armistead, L., Wierson, M., & Forehand, R. (1990). Adolescents and maternal employment: Is it harmful to have an employed mother? *Journal of Early Adolescence, 10,* 260–278.

Attewell, P. (1999). The impact of family on job displacement and recovery. *The Annals of the American Academy of Political and Social Science, 562,* 66–82.

Barling, J., & MacEwen, K. E. (1992). Linking work experiences to facets of marital functioning. *Journal of Organizational Behavior, 13,* 573–583.

Barling, J., & Macintyre, A. T. (1993). Daily work role stressors, mood and emotional exhaustion. *Work and Stress, 7,* 315–325.

Barnett, R. C. (1994). Home to work spillover revisited: A study of full-time employed women in dual-earner couples. *Journal of Marriage and the Family, 56,* 647–656.

Barnett, R. C. (1999). A new work-life model for the twenty-first century. *The Annals of the American Academy of Political and Social Science, 562,* 143–158.

Barnett, R. C., & Baruch, G. K. (1985). Women's involvement in multiple roles and psychological distress. *Journal of Personality and Social Psychology, 49,* 135–145.

Barnett, R. C., Marshall, N. L., & Pleck, J. H. (1992).

Men's multiple roles and their relationship to men's psychological distress. *Journal of Marriage and the Family, 54,* 358–367.

Baydar, N., & Brooks-Gunn, J. (1991). Effects of maternal employment and child-care arrangements on preschoolers' cognitive and behavioral outcomes: Evidence from the children of the National Longitudinal Survey of Youth. *Developmental Psychology, 27,* 932–945.

Belsky, J., & Eggebeen, D. (1991). Early and extensive maternal employment and young children's socioemotional development: Children of the National Longitudinal Survey of Youth. *Journal of Marriage and the Family, 53,* 1083–1110.

Bird, G. W., & Kemerait, L. N. (1990). Stress among early adolescents in two-earner families. *Journal of Early Adolescence, 10,* 344–365.

Blau, F. D., & Grossberg, A. J. (1990). *Maternal labor supply and children's cognitive development* (NBER Working Paper no. 3536). Cambridge, MA: National Bureau of Economic Research.

Bolger, N., & Schilling, E. A. (1991). Personality and the problems of everyday life: The role of neuroticism in exposure and reactivity to daily stressors. *Journal of Personality, 59,* 355–386.

Bowen, G. (1998). Effects of leader support in the work unit on the relationship between work spillover and family adaptation. *Journal of Family and Economic Issues, 19,* 25–52.

Brayfield, A. (1995). Juggling jobs and kids: The impact of employment schedules on fathers' caring for children. *Journal of Marriage and the Family, 57,* 321–332.

Broman, C. L. (1991). Gender, work-family roles, and psychological well-being of Blacks. *Journal of Marriage of Family, 53,* 509–520.

Bumpus, M. F., Crouter, A. C., & McHale, S. M. (1999). Work demands of dual-earner couples: Implications for parents' knowledge about children's daily lives in middle childhood. *Journal of Marriage and the Family, 61,* 465–475.

Burstein, P., & Bricher, M. (1997). Problem definition and public policy: Congressional committees confront work, family and gender, 1945–1990. *Social Forces, 76,* 135–168.

Burstein, P., & Wierzbicki, S. (in press). Public opinion and congressional action on work, family, and gender, 1945–1990. In T. L. Parcel & D. B. Cornfield (Eds.), *Work and family: Research informing policy* (pp. 97–130).

Clark, R., Hyde, J. S., Essex, M. J., & Klein, M. H. (1997). Length of maternity leave and quality of mother-infant interaction. *Child Development, 68,* 364–383.

Coltrane, S. (1996). *Family man: Fatherhood, housework, and gender equity.* New York: Oxford University Press.

Coltrane, S. (2000). Research on household labor: Modeling and measuring the social embeddedness of routine family work. *Journal of Marriage and the Family, 62,* 1208–1233.

Cooksey, E. C., Menaghan, E. G., & Jekielek, S. M. (1997). Life course effects of work and family circumstances on children. *Social Forces, 76,* 637–667.

Cox, A. G., & Presser, H. (in press). Nonstandard employment schedules among American mothers: The relevance of marital status. In T. L. Parcel & D. B. Cornfield (Eds.), *Work and family: Research informing policy* (pp. 97–130).

Crouter, A. C., Bumpus, M. F., Maguire, M. C., & McHale, S. M. (1999). Linking parents' work pressure and adolescents' well-being: Insights into dynamics in dual-earner families. *Developmental Psychology, 35,* 1453–1461.

Crouter, A. C., & Larson, R. (Eds.). (1998). Temporal rhythms in adolescence: Clocks, calendars, and the coordination of daily life. *New Directions in Child and Adolescent Development, Number 82.* San Francisco: Jossey-Bass.

Crouter, A. C., MacDermid, S. M., McHale, S. M., & Perry-Jenkins, M. (1990). Parental monitoring and perceptions of children's school performance and conduct in dual-earner and single-earner families. *Developmental Psychology, 26,* 649–657.

Crouter, A. C., & McHale, S. M. (1993). Temporal rhythms in family life: Seasonal variation in the relation between parental work and family processes. *Developmental Psychology, 29,* 198–205.

Deutsch, F. (1999). *Halving it all: How couples create equally-shared parenthood.* Boston: Harvard University Press.

Edin, K., & Lein, L., (1997). *Making ends meet: How single mothers survive welfare and low-wage work.* New York: Sage.

Estes, S. B., & Glass, J. L. (1996). Job changes following childbirth: Are women trading compensation for family-responsive work conditions? *Work and Occupations, 23,* 405–436.

Ferber, M. A., O'Farrell, B., & Allen, L. (1991). *Work and family: Policies for a changing work force.* Washington, DC: National Academy Press.

Ferree, M. M. (1990). Beyond separate spheres: Feminism and family studies. *Journal of Marriage and the Family, 52,* 866–884.

Forthofer, M. S., Markman, H. J., Cox, M., Stanley, S., & Kessler, R. C. (1996). Associations between marital distress and work loss in a national sample. *Journal of Marriage and the Family, 58,* 597–605.

Fried, M. (1998). *Taking time: Parental leave policy and corporate culture.* Philadelphia: Temple University Press.

Frone, M. R., Russell, M., & Cooper, M. L. (1992). Antecedents and outcomes of work-family conflict: Testing a model of the work-family interface. *Journal of Applied Psychology, 77,* 65–78.

Frone, M. R., Yardley, J. K., & Markel, K. S. (1997). Developing and testing an integrative model of the work-family interface. *Journal of Vocational Behavior, 50,* 145–167.

Galambos, N., & Maggs, J. L. (1990). Putting mothers' work-related stress in perspective: Mothers and adolescents in dual-earner families. *Journal of Early Adolescence, 10,* 313–328.

Galambos, N. L., Sears, H. A., Almeida, D. M., & Kolaric, G. C. (1995). Parents' work overload and problem behavior in young adolescents. *Journal of Research on Adolescence, 5,* 201–223.

Galinsky, E. (1999). *Ask the children: What America's children really think about working parents.* New York: Morrow.

Gerstel, N., & Gallagher, S. K. (1993). Kinkeeping and distress: Gender, recipients of care, and work-family conflict. *Journal of Marriage and the Family, 55,* 598–608.

Gerstel, N., & McGonagle, K. (1999). Job leaves and the limits of the Family and Medical Leave Act: The effects of gender, race, and family. *Work and Occupations, 26,* 1208–1233.

Greenberger, E., O'Neil, R., & Nagel, S. K. (1994). Linking workplace and homeplace: Relations between the nature of adults' work and their parenting behaviors. *Developmental Psychology, 30,* 990–1002.

Grimm-Thomas, K., & Perry-Jenkins, M. (1994). All in a day's work: Job experiences, self-esteem, and fathering in working-class families. *Family Relations, 43,* 174–181.

Guelzow, M. G., Bird, G. W., & Koball, E. H. (1991). An exploratory path analysis of the stress process for dual-career men and women. *Journal of Marriage and the Family, 53,* 151–164.

Gutek, B. A., Searle, S., & Klepa, L. (1991). Rational versus gender role explanations for work-family conflict. *Journal of Applied Psychology, 4,* 560–568.

Haas, L. (1992). *Equal parenthood and social policy: A study of parental leave in Sweden.* Albany: State University of New York Press.

Harvey, E. (1999). Short-term and long-term effects of parental employment on children of the National Longitudinal Survey of Youth. *Developmental Psychology, 35,* 445–459.

Hayghe, H. V. (1997, September). Developments in women's labor force participation. *Monthly Labor Review,* 41–46.

Hochschild, A. R. (1997). *The time bind: When work becomes home and home becomes work.* New York: Holt.

Hood, J. (1983). *Becoming a two-job family.* New York: Praeger.

Hughes, D., Galinsky, E., & Morris, A. (1992). The effects of job characteristics on marital quality: Specifying linking mechanisms. *Journal of Marriage and the Family, 54,* 31–42.

Hyde, J. S., Klein, M. H., Essex, M., & Clark, R. (1995). Maternity leave and women's mental health. *Psychology of Women Quarterly, 19,* 257–285.

Ishii-Kuntz, M. (1994). Work and family life: Findings from international research and suggestions for future study. *Journal of Family Issues, 15,* 490–506.

Iverson, R. R., & Farber, N. B. (in press). Transmission of family values, work, and welfare among poor urban Black women. In T. L. Parcel & D. B. Cornfield (Eds.), *Work and family: Research informing policy* (pp. 97–130).

Jacobs, J. A., & Gerson, K. (in press). Do Americans feel overworked? Comparing ideal and actual working time. In T. L. Parcel & D..B. Cornfield (Eds.), *Work and family: Research informing policy* (pp. 71–95).

Jamner, L. D., Shapiro, D., Goldstein, I. B., & Hug, R. (1991). Ambulatory blood pressure and heart rate in paramedics: Effects of cynical hostility and defensiveness. *Psychosomatic Medicine, 53,* 393–406.

Judy, R. W., & D'Amico, C. (1997). *Workforce 2020: Work and workers in the 21st century.* Indianapolis, IN: Hudson Institute.

Karasek, R., & Theorell, T. (1990). *Healthy work: Stress, productivity and the reconstruction of working life.* New York: Basic Books.

Kohn, M. L. (1995). Social structure and personality through time and space. In P. Moen, G. H. Elder, Jr., & Luscher (Eds.), *Examining lives in context: Perspectives on the ecology of human development* (pp. 141–168). Washington, DC: American Psychological Association.

Kohn, M. L., & Schooler, C. (1982). Job conditions and personality: A longitudinal assessment of their reciprocal effects. *American Journal of Sociology, 87,* 1257–1286.

Lambert, S. J. (1993, June). Workplace policies as social policy. *Social Service Review,* 237–260.

Lambert, S. J. (1999). Lower-wage workers and the new realities of work and family. *The Annals of the American Academy of Political and Social Science, 562,* 174–190.

Larson, R., & Richards, M. H. (1994). *Divergent realities: The emotional lives of mothers, fathers and adolescents.* New York: Basic Books.

Larson, R. W., & Almeida, D. M. (1999). Emotional transmission in the daily lives of families: A new paradigm for studying family process. *Journal of Marriage and the Family, 61,* 5–20.

Larson, R. W., & Gillman, S. (1999). Transmission of emotions in the daily interactions of single-mother families. *Journal of Marriage and the Family, 61,* 21–37.

MacDermid, S. M., & Targ, D. B. (1995). A call for greater attention to the role of employers in developing, transforming, and implementing family policies. *Journal of Family and Economic Issues, 16,* 145–167.

MacDermid, S. M., & Williams, M. L. (1997). A within-industry comparison of employed mothers' experiences in small and large workplaces. *Journal of Family Issues, 18,* 545–566.

MacEwen, K. E., & Barling, J. (1991). Effects of maternal employment experiences on children's behavior via mood, cognitive difficulties and parenting behavior. *Journal of Marriage and the Family, 53,* 635–644.

MacEwen, K. E., & Barling, J. (1994). Daily consequences of work interference with family and family interference with work. *Work and Stress, 8,* 244–254.

MacEwen, K. E., Barling, J., & Kelloway, E. K. (1992). Effects of short-term role overload on marital interactions. *Work and Stress, 6,* 117–126.

Marco, C. A., & Suls, J. (1993). Daily stress and the trajectory of mood: Spillover, response assimilation, contrast, and chronic negative affectivity. *Journal of Personality and Social Psychology, 64,* 1053–1063.

Margolin, G., Christensen, A., & John, R. S. (1996). The continuance and spillover of everyday tensions in distressed and nondistressed families. *Journal of Family Psychology, 10,* 304–321.

Marks, S. R., & MacDermid, S. M. (1996). Multiple roles and the self: A theory of role balance. *Journal of Marriage and the Family, 58,* 417–432.

Marshall, N. L., & Barnett, R. C. (1991). Race, class, and multiple role strains and gains among women employed in the service sector. *Women and Health, 17,* 1–16.

Marshall, N. L., & Barnett, R. C. (1993). Work-family strains and gains among two-earner couples. *Journal of Community Psychology, 21,* 64–77.

Marshall, N. L., Coll, C. G., Marx, F., McCartney, K.,

Keefe, N., & Ruh, J. (1997). After-school time and children's behavioral adjustment. *Merrill-Palmer Quarterly, 43,* 497–514.

McLoyd, V. C. (1993). Employment among African-American mothers in dual-earner families: Antecedents and consequences for family life and child development. In J. Frankel (Ed.), *The employed mother in the family context.* New York: Springer.

Menaghan, E. G., & Parcel, T. L. (1990). Parental employment and family life: Research in the 1980s *Journal of Marriage and the Family, 52,* 1079–1098.

Menaghan, E. G., & Parcel, T. L. (1991). Determining children's home environments: The impact of maternal characteristics and current occupational and family conditions. *Journal of Marriage and the Family, 53,* 417–431.

Menaghan, E. G., & Parcel, T. L. (1995). Social sources of change in children's home environment: The effects of parental occupational experiences and family conditions. *Journal of Marriage and the Family, 57,* 69–84.

Mishel, L., Bernstein, J., & Schmitt, J. (1999). *The state of working America.* Ithaca, NY: Cornell University Press.

Moore, K. A., & Driscoll, A. K. (1997, Spring). Low-wage maternal employment and outcomes for children: A study. *The future of children, 7,* 122–128.

Moorehouse, M. J. (1991). Linking maternal employment patterns to mother-child activities and children's school competence. *Developmental Psychology, 27,* 295–303.

Muller, C. (1995). Maternal employment, parent involvement, and mathematics achievement among adolescents. *Journal of Marriage and the Family, 57,* 85–100

Netemeyer, R. G., Boles, J. S., & McMurrian, R. (1996). Development and validation of work-family conflict and family-work conflict scales. *Journal of Applied Psychology, 81,* 400–410.

NICHD Early Child Care Research Network (1997a). Familial factors associated with the characteristics of nonmaternal care for infants. *Journal of Marriage and the Family, 59,* 389–408.

NICHD Early Child Care Research Network (1997b). The effects of infant child care on infant-mother attachment security: Results of the NICHD Study of Early Child Care. *Child Development, 68,* 860–879.

O'Neil, R., & Greenberger, E. (1994). Patterns of commitment to work and parenting: Implications for role strain. *Journal of Marriage and the Family, 56,* 101–118.

Paden, S. L., & Buehler, C. (1995). Coping with the dual-income lifestyle. *Journal of Marriage and the Family, 57,* 101–110.

Parcel, T. L., & Menaghan, E. G. (1993). Family social capital and children's behavior problems. *Social Psychology Quarterly, 56,* 120–135.

Parcel, T. L., & Menaghan, E. G. (1994a). Early parental work, family social capital, and early childhood outcomes. *American Journal of Sociology, 99,* 972–1009.

Parcel, T. L., & Menaghan, E. G. (1994b). *Parents' jobs and children's lives.* New York: Aldine de Gruyter.

Parcel, T. L., & Menaghan, E. G. (1997, Spring). Effects of low wage employment on family well-being. *The Future of Children, 7,* 116–121.

Paulson, S. E., Koman, J. J., III, & Hill, J. P. (1990). Maternal employment and parent-child relations in families of seventh graders. *Journal of Early Adolescence, 10,* 279–295.

Perry-Jenkins, M., & Crouter, A. C. (1990). Men's provider-role attitudes: Implications for housework and marital satisfaction. *Journal of Family Issues, 11,* 136–156.

Perry-Jenkins, M., & Gillman, S. (in press). Parental job experiences and children's well-being: The case of working-class, two-parent and single-mother families. *Journal of Family and Economic Issues.*

Perry-Jenkins, M., Pierce, C., Haley, H., & Goldberg, A. (1999, November). *Creating role salience and balance across the transition to parenthood: The meaning of multiple roles.* Paper presented at the meeting of the National Council on Family Relations, Irvine, CA.

Perry-Jenkins, M., Seery, B., & Crouter, A. C. (1992). Linkages between women's provider-role attitudes, psychological well-being, and family relationships. *Psychology of Women Quarterly, 16,* 311–329.

Pleck, J. H. (1992). Work-family policies in the United States. In H. Kahne & J. Z. Giele (Eds.), *Women's work and women's live: The continuing struggle worldwide.* San Francisco: Westview Press.

Polivka, A. E. (1996, October). Contingent and alternative work arrangements, defined. *Monthly Labor Review,* 3–9.

Potuchek, J. L. (1992). Employed wives' orientations to breadwinning: A gender theory analysis. *Journal of Marriage and the Family, 54,* 548–558.

Presser, H. B. (1994). Employment schedules among dual-earner spouses and the division of household labor by gender. *American Sociological Review, 59,* 348–364.

Presser, H. B. (1999). Toward a 24-hour economy. *Science, 284,* 1778–1779.

Presser, H. B., & Cox, A. G. (1997, April). The work schedules of low-educated American women and welfare reform. *Monthly Labor Review,* 25–34.

Raudenbush, S. W., Brennan, R. T., & Barnett, R. C. (1995). A multivariate hierarchical model for studying psychological change within married couples. *Journal of Family Psychology, 9,* 161–174.

Rayman, P. M., & Bookman, A. (1999). Creating a research and public policy agenda for work, family and community. *The Annals of the American Academy of Political and Social Science, 562,* 191–211.

Repetti, R.L. (1989). Effects of daily workload on subsequent behavior during marital interaction: The roles of social withdrawal and spouse support. *Journal of Personality and Social Psychology, 57,* 651–659.

Repetti, R. L. (1992). Social withdrawal as a short term coping response to daily stressors. In Friedman, Howard S. (Ed.), *Hostility, Coping, and Health,* 151–165.

Repetti, R. L. (1993). Short-term effects of occupational stressors on daily mood and health complaints. *Health Psychology, 12,* 126–131.

Repetti, R. L. (1994). Short-term and long-term processes linking job stressors to father-child interaction. *Social Development, 3,* 1–15.

Repetti, R. L. (1998). The promise of a multiple roles paradigm for women's health research. *Women's Health: Research on Gender, Behavior, and Policy, 4,* 273–280.

Repetti, R. L., & Wood, J. (1997a). Effects of daily stress at work on mothers' interactions with preschoolers. *Journal of Family Psychology, 11,* 90–108,

Repetti, R. L., & Wood, J. (1997b). Families accommodating to chronic stress: Unintended and unnoticed processes. In B. H. Gottlieb et al. (Eds.), *Coping with chronic stress. The plenum series on stress and coping* (pp. 191–220). New York: Plenum Press.

Robinson, J. P., & Godbey, G. (1997). *Time for life: The surprising ways Americans use their time.* University Park, PA: Penn State University Press.

Rogers, J. (2000). *Temps.* Ithaca, NY: Cornell University Press.

Rogers, S. J. (1999). Wives' income and marital quality: Are there reciprocal effects? *Journal of Marriage and the Family, 61,* 123–132.

Rook, K., Dooley, D., & Catalano, R. (1991). Stress transmission: The effects of husbands' job stressors on the emotional health of their wives. *Journal of Marriage and the Family, 53,* 165–177.

Schnall, P. L., Schwartz, J. E., Landsbergis, P. A., Warren, K., Pickering, T. G., (1998). A longitudinal study of job strain and ambulatory blood pressure. Results from a three-year follow-up. *Psychosomatic Medicine, 60,* 697–706.

Schor, J. (1991). *The overworked American.* New York: Basic Books.

Sears, H. A., & Galambos, N. L. (1992). Women's work conditions and marital adjustment in two earner couples: A structural model. *Journal of Marriage and the Family, 54,* 789–797.

Simon, R. W. (1997). The meanings individuals attach to role identities and their implications for mental health. *Journal of Health and Social Behavior, 38,* 256–274.

Stewart, W., & Barling, J. (1996). Fathers' work experiences effect children's behaviors via job-related affect and parenting behaviors. *Journal of Organizational Behavior, 17,* 221–232.

Thoits, P. A. (1992). Identity structures and psychological well-being: Gender and marital status comparisons. *Social Psychology Quarterly, 54,* 101–112.

Vandell, D. L., & Ramanan, J. (1992). Effects of early and recent maternal employment on children from low-income families. *Child Development, 63,* 938–949.

Voydanoff, P., & Donnelly, B. W. (1999a). Multiple roles and psychological distress: The intersection of the paid worker, spouse, and parent role with the role of the adult child. *Journal of Marriage and the Family, 61,* 725–735.

Voydanoff, P., & Donnelly, B. W. (1999b). The intersection of time in activities and perceived unfairness in relation to psychological distress and marital quality. *Journal of Marriage and the Family, 61,* 739–753.

Whitbeck, L. B., Simons, R. L., Conger, R. D., Wickrama, K. A. S., Ackley, K. A., & Elder G. H., Jr. (1997). The effects of parents' working conditions and family ecomomic hardship on parenting behaviors and children's self-efficacy. *Social Psychology Quarterly, 60,* 291–303.

White, L., & Keith, B. (1990). The effect of shift work on the quality and stability of marital relations. *Journal of Marriage and the Family, 52,* 453–462.

White, L., & Rogers, S. (2000). Economic circumstances and family eocomes. *Journal of Marriage and the Family, 64,* 1035–1051

Wortman, C., Biernat, M., & Lang, E. (1991). Coping with role overload. In Frankenhauser, et al. (Eds.), *Women, Work, and Health: Stress and Opportunities,* 85–110.

F. Scott Christopher *Arizona State University*

Susan Sprecher *Illinois State University**

Sexuality in Marriage, Dating, and Other Relationships: A Decade Review

In this article, we review the major research advances made during the 1990s in the study of sexuality in marriage and other close relationships. More specifically, we provide a critical review of the empirical findings from the last decade on such sexual phenomena as sexual behavior, sexual satisfaction, and sexual attitudes within the context of marriage, dating, and other committed relationships. After highlighting the major theoretical and methodological advances of the 1990s, we focus on the research literatures of: (1) frequency and correlates of sexual activity in marriage; (2) sexual satisfaction, including its association with general relationship satisfaction; (3) sexuality in gay and lesbian committed relationships; (4) trends in sexual behavior and attitudes in dating relationships; and (5) the role of sexuality in dating relationships. We also incorporate brief reviews of the past decade's research on sexual assault and coercion in marriage and dating and on extramarital sex. We end our decade review with recommendations for the study of sexuality into the next decade.

Department of Family Resources & Human Development, Arizona State University, Tempe, AZ 85287-2502 (Scott.Christopher@asu.edu).

*Department of Sociology & Anthropology, Illinois State University, Normal, IL 61790-4660.

Key Words: close relationships, marital sexuality, premarital sexuality, review of sexuality, sexuality, sexuality in dating.

Sexuality is woven into the fabric of many close relationships. It is sanctioned in marriage; it is often explored in dating; and it is an intricate part of other committed romantic relationships. The past decade saw a marked increase in scholarly interest in sexuality within a relational context. This increased interest posed a challenge for us as we developed the foci of this review. In deciding what areas of research to review, we considered the interests of family scientists balanced with the sexual phenomena explored by scholars from a variety of disciplines, including but not limited to family studies, sociology, psychology, communication, public health, and women's studies. More specifically, the purpose of our review was to identify, summarize, and critique theoretical, methodological, and empirical breakthroughs in sexuality research from the 1990s as they relate to marriage and other relationships that occur prior to or outside of marriage.

We open by identifying major theoretical and methodological advancements in sexuality research of the 1990s that have relevance to marriage, dating, and committed relationships. In the second section, we review the empirical literature from the 1990s on sexuality in marriage and other committed relationships. In the third section, we review the past decade's literature on sexuality in dating (premarital) relationships. Although most of our review concentrates on sexuality's positive aspects, sexuality also has a "dark side" involving sexual coercion and assault. Hence, our review of the literatures on marital and dating sexuality includes findings on this aspect of sexuality. We end the review with recommendations for research on sexuality for the coming decade.

Because of page limits, we could not review all topics relevant to sexuality. For example, we did not include a review of adolescent sexuality, contraceptive use, or teenage pregnancy (for reviews see Gullotta, Adams, & Montemayor, 1993; Moore, Miller, Glei, & Morrison, 1995). Furthermore, although the 1990s saw an increase in research on risk behaviors and individual and family outcomes related to AIDS, these topics are also beyond the scope of this review (see Kelly, 1995, for a review). Moreover, the topics we were able to cover were limited primarily to research conducted in North America, although advances were also made in sexuality research in other countries and cross-culturally.

ADVANCEMENTS IN THE 1990S

We wish to identify several advancements in sexuality research in the 1990s that have relevance to family science. These can be aggregated broadly into two areas: (1) advancements in conceptualization and theory involving sexuality-related phenomena and (2) advancements in methodology.

The 1990s witnessed an increased focus on sexuality within a relational context, which broadened the concepts, topics, and theories linked to sexuality (e.g., McKinney & Sprecher, 1991). The science of interpersonal relationships is one of the most rapidly growing areas in behavioral sciences (Berscheid & Reis, 1998), and it is now chronicled in two multidisciplinary journals (*Journal of Social and Personal Relationships* and *Personal Relationships*) that have published several articles on sexuality. Scholars from the close relationships field have examined how sexuality is related to such relationship phenomena as attraction, satisfaction, intimacy, equity, love, communication, and stability. Reflecting the general lack of government funding for research on intimate relationships, most of these investigations are based on smaller convenience samples (Gierveld, 1995). However, because the issues examined by relationship scholars have not, in general, also been examined in the larger, national studies, we highlight some of their findings in this review because of their insights and heuristic promise.

Overall, theoretical advancements in sexuality research were somewhat limited during this past decade. However, there was an increase in the number of scholars who employed an evolutionary perspective, either as an explanation for their findings or to test a priori hypotheses derived from this perspective. Evolutionary approaches focus on distal causes of sexual behavior and argue that current patterns of sexual behavior, including gender differences in these behaviors, exist because they have been associated with reproductive success in our ancestral past. According to this perspective, current gender differences in a variety of sexual behaviors can be traced to the smaller investment that men, relative to women, need to make in order to create offspring, balanced against women's more limited access to resources needed to ensure their offsprings' survival. In particular, evolutionary perspectives were used to explain gender differences in extramarital behavior, jealousy reactions to extradyadic affairs, sexual conflict in marriage, and choice of sexual influence tactics in dating. Despite the increase in evolutionary-based research, more of the research on sexuality in the 1990s was atheoretical than theoretical (see discussion by Weis, 1998). There is little reason for this to continue. Near the end of the decade, *The Journal of Sex Research* devoted a special issue to theory, which included reviews and critiques of social constructionism (DeLamater & Hyde, 1998), sexual strategy theory (Buss, 1998), social exchange (Sprecher, 1998), symbolic interactionism (Longmore, 1998), social learning theory (Hogben & Byrne, 1998), and systems theory (Jurich & Myers-Bowman, 1998) as they apply to sexuality. This collected work provides a solid reference for informing sexual research in the coming decade.

A number of methodological advances were worthy of recognition. First, there was an increased availability of large-scale national studies that included sexuality data. Knowledge of patterns of sexual behavior was increased significantly with the publication of data from the National Health and Social Life Survey (NHSLS; Laumann, Gagnon, Michael, & Michaels, 1994; Michael, Gagnon, Laumann, & Kolata, 1994). For this study, a probability sample of 3,432 Americans, aged 18 to 59, was interviewed, and respondents completed a brief questionnaire with more sensitive questions about sexuality. Approximately 54% of the sample were married, and another 7% were in cohabiting relationships. Several other ongoing and first-time large-scale probability studies provided data about adult or adolescent sexuality in the 1990s (e.g., General Social Survey—GSS, The National Survey of Men—NSM,

The National Study of Adolescent Health—Add Health). In general, it became more legitimate to ask about sexual behaviors and attitudes in national studies because information on sexual patterns was relevant to the AIDS crisis. More government and private funding was placed into this type of research.

Another methodological advancement was the maturation of several longitudinal studies conducted with married or committed couples. Researchers who began longitudinal studies in the 1980s continued to follow the couples over several years and multiple waves, which allowed them to examine, when sexuality data were available, how sexual phenomena change over time and how the sexual health of the relationship at one time might be related to a future outcome of the relationship. Two longitudinal studies in particular have included measures of sexuality over time: The Early Years of Marriage Project, based on a sample of Black and White married couples in the Detroit area (e.g., Oggins, Leber, & Veroff, 1993); and the Marital Instability over the Lifecourse Project, which was based on a national sample of married individuals obtained through random digit dialing (e.g., Edwards & Booth, 1994).

A final methodological advancement we want to note is an increase in the sophistication and accessibility of information on particular methods and measurement. For example, a recent issue of *The Journal of Sex Research* was devoted to methodological advances (Catania, 1999a). Several of the works will likely prove valuable to family scientists into the next decade. Gribble, Miller, Rogers, and Turner (1999) reviewed the advantages of incorporating new technologies into survey work, including computer-assisted personal and telephone interviewing; these are technologies that, when compared to traditional survey and interview methods, appear to increase respondents' reports of engaging in sensitive sexual practices. Morrison, Leigh, and Gillmore (1999) provided a useful comparison of three different methods of daily data collection: individual-initiated phone calls, investigator-initiated phone calls, and self-administered questionnaires. Two papers focused on reporting bias. Wiederman (1999) identified volunteer biases among college students who typically participate in sexuality research. Catania (1999b) provided a thoughtful analysis of the origins of reporting biases in interviews. Finally, Binik, Mah, and Kiesler (1999) examined ethical issues connected with conducting research

using the Internet, a practice that will likely increase in the coming decade. In addition to the special journal issue, several methodological issues were discussed in an edited volume sponsored by the Kinsey Institute (Bancroft, 1997). Furthermore, Davis, Yarber, Bauserman, Schreer, and Davis (1998) published a handbook of over 200 sexuality measures, including information on their reliability and validity. The advances in methodology, coupled with an increased accessibility of measures of sexuality-related variables, will likely increase the volume of research conducted on sexuality in the next decade.

In addition to advances in conceptualizations, theory, and methods, scholars' empirical investigations revealed new insights into the sexuality of adults in relationships. We begin our review of these findings by examining sexuality in marriage and other committed romantic relationships.

SEX IN (AND OUTSIDE OF) MARRIAGE AND OTHER COMMITTED RELATIONSHIPS

The most socially approved context for sexual activity is the marital relationship. Because sex and marriage are legally and morally linked, marital sex is generally not viewed as a social problem or as a phenomenon likely to lead to negative outcomes. As a result, marital sex has not been the central focus of much research in the past decade. This scarcity of research on marital sex has also been noted in previous decades (Greenblat, 1983). Nonetheless, several studies were conducted in the 1990s that included data on sexuality in marriage or other committed relationships, as described below.

Descriptive Information about Sexual Activity

One issue that received research attention, before and during the 1990s, is the frequency of couples' sexual activity. Scientific interest in frequency of marital sex is based in part on its association with both fertility and quality of marriage. Although data collected on this topic prior to 1990 were based on nonprobability samples (e.g., Blumstein & Schwartz, 1983; Hunt, 1974; Kinsey, Pomeroy, & Martin, 1948; Kinsey, Pomeroy, Martin, & Gebhard, 1953), this past decade yielded data on sexual frequency from national probability samples.

Because the national samples included respondents from across the life-span, how sexual frequency is associated with marital duration or age, two passage-of-time variables that are highly confounded, was examined. The National Survey of Families and Households (NSFH), based on interviews conducted in 1987–88 (Wave 1) with a randomly selected sample of over 13,000 Americans, included a question on frequency of sexual intercourse in the self-administered questionnaire completed by the respondents. Call, Sprecher, and Schwartz (1995) reported that the NSFH Wave 1 married respondents had an overall mean frequency of sex of 6.3 times per month. Couples under the age of 24 had a mean frequency of 11.7, but the frequency declined with each subsequent age group. For example, in the 75 and older age group, the mean frequency was slightly less than once per month. Call, Sprecher, and Schwartz (1996) reported a similar negative association of sexual frequency with age at Wave 2 (1992–1994) of the NSFH. With slightly different foci and subsamples from the NSFH Wave 1 data, Rao and DeMaris (1995), Marsiglio and Donnelly (1991), and Donnelly (1993) published similar findings about marital sexual frequency. The decline in sexual frequency seems to be due to both psychological and biological factors associated with the aging process. Any decreases due to habituation resulting from being with the same partner seem to occur early in the marriage (Call et al., 1995). A habituation perspective can also explain the finding from NSFH (Call et al.) that a remarriage was associated with an increase in marital sex, controlling for other factors including age.

Measures of sexual frequency were included in the National Health and Social Life Survey (NHSLS) (Laumann et al., 1994; Michael et al., 1994), the large-scale national study referred to earlier. The researchers provided data on the sample members' frequency of sexual activity in various ways, but, for our interests, reported a mean frequency of sexual activity per month of 6.9 for married men and 6.5 for married women. The cohabitors had a higher level of sexual activity (which was also found in the NSFH data; e.g., Call et al., 1995; Rao & DeMaris, 1995), whereas the single individuals had the lowest level of sexual activity. Laumann and colleagues (1994) also reported the ubiquitous decrease in sexual frequency with age, although the data were presented for the entire sample, married and unmarried.

The General Social Survey (GSS), an interview study on a variety of attitudes and experiences conducted biennially by the National Opinion Research Center with probability samples of Americans, also contains data on sexual frequen-

cy. As reported in Smith (1994b, based on 1993 GSS data), married respondents engaged in sexual intercourse an average of 67 times per year, or slightly over once a week. The frequency rates were highest among the young and those married less than 3 years.

Only a few longitudinal studies were conducted in the 1990s that included information on sexual frequency, but their findings confirm a decrease in sexual frequency with marital duration. In a longitudinal study of newly married couples selected randomly from central Pennsylvania, Huston and Vangelisti (1991) found that a decrease in sexual activity and interest began in the first 2 years of marriage. Preliminary analyses based on both waves of the NSFH data (Call et al., 1996) indicated that the younger couples in the original sample experienced a decrease in sexual frequency between Waves 1 and 2. In a four-wave longitudinal study conducted with 570 pregnant women and their husbands or partners, Hyde, DeLamater, Plant, and Byrd (1996) found that the respondents reported having sex 4–5 times per month during pregnancy, had almost no sex in the first month post-partum, said they resumed sexual intercourse approximately 7 weeks postpartum, and had a sexual frequency rate at 4 and 12 months postpartum that was similar to the rate during pregnancy (4–5 times per month). More long-term longitudinal studies are needed to examine the pattern of sexual activity with the passage of time and with other family transitions, including the launching of children and retirement.

The rates of marital sexual activity found in the national probability samples of the 1990s appear to be similar to, and in some cases slightly lower than, those reported in nonprobability samples conducted in previous decades. The major advancement in the 1990s on this topic was the examination of a wide range of possible predictors of sexual frequency through multivariate analyses. Passage of time (i.e., age, duration of marriage) was found to have the strongest (negative) association with frequency of marital sex, although marital satisfaction also had a unique and strong (positive) association with sexual frequency (e.g., Call et al., 1995; Laumann et al., 1994; Smith, 1994b). Social and background characteristics, such as race, social status, and religion, were generally unrelated to marital sexual frequency, with the exception of a few modest associations, such as a Catholic background being associated with a lower frequency (Call et al., 1995). The multivariate results conducted in the 1990s on predictors of sexual frequency indicated only a modest amount of variance in marital sexual frequency explained, despite a notable number of predictor variables (e.g., 20% was explained in Call et al. [1995], using the NSFH data and 18 predictors), suggesting that future research needs to broaden the type of predictors considered.

There was very little discussion in the 1990s of measurement issues associated with sexual frequency. The sexual frequency question varied slightly in format across the studies described above. For example, the question in the NSFH referred to "sexual intercourse" and was open-ended, whereas the NHSLS asked about "sex" and elicited closed-ended responses. Responses might vary in systematic ways as a function of the format of the item, although we suspect not by much. The NSHLS study further explored what couples do when they have sex and found that almost all of the married men and women (95%) had vaginal intercourse in their last sex act. Although a majority of the respondents had engaged in oral sex in their lifetime, less than one-fourth of the married respondents reported having oral sex during their last sex act. Anal sex was even less common—1–2% reported having had it during their last episode, although 9.7% of married men and 7.3% of married women reported engaging in anal sex during the past year. Oral and anal sex were more common among the more highly educated and the White respondents.

A continued focus on documenting frequency of marital sex and its predictors might not be as fruitful as examining other issues about sexual frequency, including how married respondents believe their frequency compares to that of other couples and to what they desire or expect, and the implications of these comparisons. In addition, we suggest that the focus of research move from how often couples have sex overall (e.g., each week on average) to the degree of variation, week to week, both in frequency of sexual activity and in the specific behaviors engaged in and the length of time sex lasts. This intracouple variation (over time) is likely to be linked in complex ways to relationship phenomena, including balance of power, conflict, and communication. We encourage research on this issue, possibly through daily diaries kept by married individuals, a method used infrequently in the 1990s.

Sexual Satisfaction

Married individuals' assessments of the quality of their sexual relationship also received research at-

tention in the 1990s. Consistent with findings from previous decades (e.g., Blumstein & Schwartz, 1983), married couples were generally sexually satisfied. For example, Laumann and colleagues (1994), in the NHSLS, found that 88% of the married individuals in the sample were either extremely or very physically pleased in their relationship. When asked about the specific feelings they experienced after having sex, a majority of the participants reported positive feelings (i.e., felt "loved," "thrilled and excited") and only a small minority reported any negative feelings (e.g., "anxious and worried"). Married respondents, particularly if they were monogamous, reported the highest level of sexual satisfaction; cohabiting and single (i.e., dating) respondents had slightly lower levels of sexual satisfaction. Greeley (1991) also found high sexual satisfaction among his married respondents, obtained from the 1988 and 1989 GSS and from telephone interviews conducted by the Gallup Organization using a national probability sample of married couples. High levels of marital sexual satisfaction were reported in several other studies as well (e.g., Edwards & Booth, 1994; Lawrance & Byers, 1995; Oggins et al., 1993). Couples who become sexually dissatisfied, however, might be less likely to be in these studies because of their greater risk of having divorced early in marriage.

Less consistent information is available on how sexual satisfaction might change with marital duration or age, although the accumulating evidence suggests that it does not decline as rapidly or as dramatically as does frequency of sex. For example, Laumann and colleagues (1994) reported that most of their respondents, regardless of age, were happy with their partnered sex. Although physical pleasure was found to be lower for women over the age of 40 than for women under 40, their analyses were based on all respondents, married and unmarried. Men did not experience the same drop in physical pleasure with age, which, as explained by the authors, might be due to divorced and widowed men's greater likelihood of obtaining new and younger sex partners, relative to their female counterparts. Edwards and Booth (1994), in their national sample of married individuals, found no differences in sexual happiness as a function of age, although wives in their late middle years (48–60) were more likely than younger wives to say that loss of interest in sex was a problem in their relationship (nonetheless, only a small minority had this view). Men and women tended to agree that it was the wife who was more likely to lose interest. Their longitudinal analyses revealed a significant decrease in happiness with sex and a significant increase in loss of interest in sex in the sample over 9 years of marriage. Greeley (1991), in a cross-sectional analysis based on a national sample of married couples, also found a decline in sexual satisfaction with age (and therefore marital duration).

Not surprisingly, sexual satisfaction is associated with sexual frequency. Couples who have the most frequent sex are the most sexually satisfied (Greeley, 1991; Laumann et al., 1994). This past decade, however, did not yield any findings of import about this association. For example, no significant knowledge was gained about how the quantity and quality of sexual activity influence each other over time (is one more likely to lead to the other?), the specific processes that might mediate the association, and the degree to which the strength of the association differs based on other characteristics of the couple such as their ages and relationship duration. That sexual frequency appears to decline more rapidly than sexual satisfaction with age (and marital duration) suggests that the association between the quantity and quality of sex might change with the passage of time. These are issues that need more investigation in the next decade.

In the previous section, we reported that social and demographic characteristics are generally unrelated to frequency of sex. Research conducted in the 1990s indicated that social and demographic variables also are generally unrelated to the degree of sexual satisfaction (e.g., Davidson, Darling, & Norton, 1995; Henderson-King & Veroff, 1994; Laumann et al., 1994; Oggins et al., 1993). An exception is that at Wave 1 of the Early Years of Marriage Project, Black spouses reported more sexual enjoyment than White spouses, controlling for other demographic variables, including income (Henderson-King & Veroff, 1994; Oggins et al., 1993). These researchers also found that higher household income was associated with less sexual satisfaction for women and speculated that higher family income is associated with one or both partners working longer hours or having more work stress, which might be detrimental to women's sexual satisfaction. However, with a national sample, Greeley (1991) reported that after controlling for age there was no association between the wife working and sexual satisfaction in marriage. Another work variable, working different shifts, was found to be associated with sexual problems or sexual dissatisfaction in a national sample of married individuals (White & Keith, 1990).

Investigations designed to identify predictors of sexual satisfaction have been generally atheoretical and focused on personality attributes (as noted by Lawrance & Byers, 1995); these studies are beyond the scope of this review. More relevant to this review, however, are investigations that have focused on how sexual satisfaction might be predicted by behavior and affect in sexual and nonsexual aspects of the relationship. Lawrance and Byers (1995) developed a model of sexual satisfaction that focuses on the interpersonal context and is based on exchange theory. Their Interpersonal Exchange Model of Sexual Satisfaction states that sexual satisfaction is affected by rewards, costs, comparison level, comparison level for alternatives, and equality within the sexual area of the relationship, as well as by relationship satisfaction. Evidence for components of this model was found in a study of married and cohabiting men and women (Lawrance & Byers, 1995), a study of daters (Byers, Demmons, & Lawrance, 1998), and a study of Chinese married men and women (Renaud, Byers, & Pan, 1997). Sexual satisfaction also has been found to be associated with other aspects of the interpersonal environment, including quality of sexual communication (Cupach & Comstock, 1990), sexual self-disclosure as mediated by relationship satisfaction (Byers & Demmons, 1999), and equity (Henderson-King & Veroff, 1994).

Investigations in the 1990s that focused on predictors of sexual satisfaction most often were based on smaller, geographically limited samples, although their strength was the frequent use of either multi-item scales with known reliability and validity, multidimensional measures, or both (e.g., Lawrance & Byers, 1995; Oggins et al., 1993), in contrast to the use of single-item global measures of sexual satisfaction typical of national studies. Ideally, research in the future will combine good sampling techniques with sophisticated measures of sexual satisfaction. In addition, more theoretically driven research is needed to identify how factors associated with the individual, the relationship, and "the environment" might interact to affect sexual satisfaction.

In the next section, we discuss how sexual satisfaction, as well as level of sexual activity, are related to overall relationship satisfaction and other relationship outcome variables.

The Association Between Sexual Dimensions of the Relationship and Relationship Quality

In our discussion, above, of findings from the 1990s on sexual frequency, we noted that sexual frequency was found to be associated positively with general relationship satisfaction in married couples (e.g., Call et al., 1995; Donnelly, 1993; Smith, 1994b). What appears to be a more important predictor of marital satisfaction, however, is sexual satisfaction or other feelings about sex (Greeley, 1991). Several studies conducted in the past decade have demonstrated that sexual satisfaction is associated with higher marital satisfaction (Cupach & Comstock, 1990; Edwards & Booth, 1994; Greeley, 1991; Haavio-Mannila & Kontula, 1997; Henderson-King & Veroff, 1994; Kurdek, 1991; Lawrance & Byers, 1995; Oggins et al., 1993). The quality and quantity of sex also appear to be associated with feelings of love for one's spouse or partner, especially a passionate or erotic type of love (e.g., Aron & Henkemeyer, 1995; Grote & Frieze, 1998; Marston, Hecht, Manke, McDaniel, & Reeder, 1998; Sprecher & Regan, 1998). Sexual intimacy, however, has been found to be a weaker predictor of love or of general relationship quality than have other forms of intimacy, including degree of affection expressed (Huston & Vangelisti, 1991) and supportive communication (Sprecher, Metts, Burleson, Hatfield, & Thompson, 1995).

In the examination of how a sexuality variable (e.g., sexual satisfaction) is associated with a general relationship construct (e.g., relationship satisfaction), caution must be exercised so that the two variables do not overlap in measurement content (e.g., Fincham & Bradbury, 1987). For example, several marital satisfaction scales (e.g., Roach, Frazier, & Bowden, 1981; Spanier, 1976) include an item or two about sexual activity. Measures of other relationship dimensions, including intimacy, love, interdependence, maintenance strategies, and exchange, have also included elements referring to sexuality (for a discussion, see Sprecher & McKinney, 1993). One solution has been to delete from the scale measuring the general relationship construct any items that refer to sexuality (e.g., Kurdek, 1991).

On a broader conceptual level, researchers must determine whether the sexuality variable is the independent or dependent variable. One's theoretical framework guides the determination of the specific causal connections between partners' feelings about the sexual relationship and the overall evaluation of the relationship. In most research, the focus has been on a sexuality variable as the predictor and on a general relationship quality measure as the variable to be explained, often within a multivariate framework (e.g., Edwards & Booth, 1994). However, the reverse causal direction is proposed in some models, such as the Interpersonal Exchange Model of Sexual Satisfaction described earlier (e.g., Lawrance & Byers, 1995). Furthermore, Henderson-King and Veroff (1994), among others, have speculated that marital well-being and sexual feelings are reciprocal and that both causal directions operate over time. More multiple-wave, longitudinal investigations are needed to adequately address the possible reciprocal relation between these variables over time.

Research in the 1990s also examined whether sexual satisfaction predicts marital stability versus dissolution. Oggins et al. (1993), using data from the Early Years of Marriage Project, reported that sexual dissatisfaction at Year 1 predicted marital dissolution by Year 4 of marriage. Based on later analyses, however, Veroff, Douvan, and Hatchett (1995) found that sexual (dis)satisfaction measured in the 3rd year of marriage was not a significant predictor of later relationship dissolution. In their longitudinal study of married individuals, Edwards and Booth (1994) found that a decline in sexual satisfaction over time was associated with the increased likelihood of divorce. Furthermore, in a national study of married individuals (White & Keith, 1990), a measure of sexual problems or dissatisfaction at Time 1 was associated positively with the likelihood of divorce by Time 2, controlling for general marital happiness and other variables. Thus, these limited findings suggest that sexual satisfaction contributes to marital stability. To our knowledge, however, no research has examined the effects of frequency of sexual activity on the likelihood that marriages dissolve over time.

In the next section, we discuss extramarital sex, which has also been found to be associated with negative outcomes for the relationship.

Extramarital Sex

Although sex in marriage is the most socially approved form of sexual outlet, sex by married persons with someone other than their spouse is one of the most stigmatized. The GSS has included an attitudinal question on extramarital sexuality, and, consistently through the years, 70–80% of Americans express complete disapproval of a married person having sex with someone other than his or her spouse, and most others express at least some disapproval (e.g., Smith, 1994a). The NHSLS (Laumann et al., 1994) included a similar attitudinal question and found that 77% of participants said extramarital sex was always wrong. Considerable research has been done to examine predictors of attitudes about extramarital sex, although most of this research was conducted in the decades prior to 1990 (for reviews, see Glass & Wright, 1992; Sponaugle, 1989; Thompson, 1983). Among the variables that have been found to be associated with permissive attitudes toward extramarital sex are: premarital sexual permissiveness, high education, low religiosity, and being male.

Research conducted in the past decade on the incidence of extramarital sex has yielded rates lower than those reported in earlier studies based on nonprobability samples (for a review of the earlier research, see Thompson, 1983). In the NHSLS study (Laumann et al., 1994), approximately 25% of married men and 15% of married women reported having engaged in extramarital sex at least once. Less than 4% of married respondents reported having engaged in sex with someone other than their spouse in the prior year. Similar low rates have been found in other national studies, including the GSS (e.g., Greeley, 1991; Smith, 1994b; Wiederman, 1997), the 1991 National Survey of Men (Billy, Tanfer, Grady, & Klepinger, 1993), the 1991 National Survey of Women (Forste & Tanfer, 1996), and a national sample based on the National AIDS Behavioral Study (Choi, Catania, & Dolcini, 1994). Nonetheless, these percentages translate into a significant number of Americans who have experienced sex with someone other than their spouse at least once. Furthermore, individuals who divorce are less represented in married samples but perhaps more likely to have experienced sex with someone other than their spouse.

Cohabitors have a higher rate of nonmonogamy than do married couples (Forste & Tanfer, 1996; Laumann et al., 1994). In addition, a higher lifetime incidence of extramarital sex is found among men, Blacks, remarried individuals, those in the lowest and highest education categories, those in urban areas, and those low in religiosity (e.g., Laumann et al., 1994; Wiederman, 1997).

Perhaps because of the relatively low incidence of extramarital sex, few studies in the past decade have focused on its association with marital satisfaction. There are two major issues that can be examined, however, about this association: First, does marital dissatisfaction lead to extramarital sex? Second, what are the effects of a partner's infidelity on one's marital satisfaction?

The limited research from the 1990s on the first issue suggests that marital dissatisfaction might play only a small role in married individuals' decision to engage in extramarital sex. For example, Greeley (1991) reported that marital dissatisfaction has only an indirect influence on the likelihood of extramarital sex, mediated by such factors as premarital sexual permissiveness and a lower value placed on fidelity. However, several studies prior to 1990 (reviewed in Bringle & Buunk, 1991, and in Edwards & Booth, 1994) did show an association between extramarital sex and marital dissatisfaction, especially for women. Opportunity and having a reference group that supports nonmonogamy also seem to be important factors leading to the behavior.

Concerning the second issue, research suggests that spouses become upset with a partner's infidelity. Not all spouses find out about a partner's infidelity, but those who do tend to have negative reactions (e.g., Bringle & Buunk, 1991) or say they would if it were to happen (Shackelford & Buss, 1997). Gender differences in negative reactions to partner's real or hypothetical infidelity have been a focus of several studies conducted in the 1990s. This research suggests that men become more upset by the sexual aspect of a partner's infidelity, whereas women become more upset by the emotional aspect. These gender differences are explained most frequently from an evolutionary perspective (e.g., Buss, Larsen, Westen, & Semmelroth, 1992; Buunk, Angleitner, Oubaid, & Buss, 1996). In the aggregate, however, it appears that marital satisfaction is rarely affected by the threat of extramarital sex. For example, in their national study of married individuals, Edwards and Booth (1994) reported that only about 5% of the sample reported that extramarital sex caused a problem in their marriage. However, those who perceived it as a problem were more likely to be dissatisfied in their marriage.

Although laypersons and family scholars alike might not agree on the extent to which extramarital sex is a social problem, most can agree that forced sex in marriage or other committed relationships is indeed a problem and a dark side to human sexuality. We discuss sexual assault and coercion in marriage next.

Husbands' Sexual Assault and Coercion of Wives

In spite of important foundational studies in the 1980s (e.g. Finkelhor & Yllo, 1985; Russel, 1982), husbands' sexual assault and coercion of their wives remains one of the most understudied areas of marriage and sexuality. Perhaps this reflects society's struggle with accepting that sexual assault in marriage actually occurs. The American Law Institute's Model Penal Code recommends exempting spouses from sexual assault laws (Posner & Silbaugh, 1996). Four states follow this recommendation by exempting spouses from sexual assault statutes if a married couple coresides. In addition, many states' statutes allow spouses partial exemptions from their sexual assault laws when a spouse is mentally incapacitated or disabled or, in one state, no penetration occurs.

Knowledge about the exact prevalence of marital sexual assault and coercion remains elusive. Laumann et al. (1994), in their national survey, asked women whether they had been "forced to do something sexual they did not want to" (p. 334). Twenty-two percent of the women had been sexually forced by a man and in 9% of these cases the women referred to a spouse. Extrapolating from these percentages suggests a rate of 2% for married women, although the wording of this item is at best a rough indicator of sexual assault, a problem readily acknowledged by the investigators. The 2% rate is notably lower than the marital rape rates of 10% (Finkelhor & Yllo, 1985) and 14% (Russel, 1982) found in earlier investigations that used area-probability samples and more exact measures.

Knowledge about the marital dynamics associated with sexual coercion and assault in marriage remained equally elusive. Using the first wave of NSFH data, DeMaris (1997) found that the monthly sexual frequency of couples with violent husbands was 2.5 times higher than that for couples with nonviolent husbands, when controlling for other factors. Based on previous findings of an overlap between husbands' physical and sexual abuse of their wives, DeMaris hypothesized that violent husbands sexually coerced their wives into this higher frequency of sexual activity. Unfortunately, the data set contained no direct measures of sexual coercion, although indirect measures provided some support for his hypothesis. Additional work with Swinford (DeMaris & Swinford, 1996) using the National Family Violence Survey also provided partial support for the

hypothesis. DeMaris and Swinford's analyses revealed that husbands' previous attempted or completed rapes of their spouses significantly predicted wives' fear of being hit. Hence, husbands' sexual and physical violence co-occur in some marriages. DeMaris (1997) provides insights into these wives' mental states; couples' coital frequency was positively related to wives' depression if husbands were violent, or, in instances where both spouses were violent, if wives but not husbands suffered physical injuries.

The lack of empirical and theoretical attention to sexual assault and coercion in marriage in the 1990s is striking. Work in the 1980s that combined qualitative and quantitative methods painted compelling and vivid pictures of patriarchal terrorism (see Johnson, 1995, for a definition) and of the long-term effects of these women's experiences (e.g., Finkelhor & Yllo, 1985; Russel, 1982). The role of social, familial, couple, and individual factors in sexual coercion and assault in marriage is unclear at this time. Moreover, investigations have centered primarily on wives and have excluded husbands' reports. We echo the call of others in noting the great need for scholarly attention to this area.

Research also documents that forced sex occurs in other committed relationships, including gay and lesbian relationships (e.g., Waldner-Haugrud & Gratch, 1997). The more positive aspects of sex in gay and lesbian relationships, however, will be discussed next.

Sex in Gay and Lesbian Committed Relationships

Although considerable research was done in the past decade on the sexual behavior of homosexuals, particularly gay men, the focus of most of this research was on risky versus safe-sex behavior (e.g., Barrett, Bolan, & Douglas, 1998). Very little research focused on sexuality in committed, long-term homosexual relationships. Furthermore, the national probability studies conducted on sexuality (e.g., Laumann et al.'s [1994] NHSLS) did not include enough homosexual participants to systematically analyze their results separately. Thus, the Blumstein and Schwartz (1983) study from the 1980s continues to be the most extensive study on the sexuality of gay and lesbian couples to date.

The research that did include gay and lesbian samples and a focus on sex in a relational context (e.g., Deenen, Gijs, & van Naerssen, 1994; Kurdek, 1991; Lever, 1994, 1995) suggests that sexuality in committed lesbian and gay relationships is similar to sexuality in heterosexual married couples. For example, Kurdek (1991) found no differences in sexual satisfaction across four types of couples: gay, lesbian, heterosexual cohabiting, and heterosexual married. He also found that in all four couple types, sexual satisfaction was associated with general relationship satisfaction. Lesbian couples might have sex slightly less often than women in heterosexual marriages (Lever, 1995), and gay couples might have sex slightly more often than other couples, at least early in the relationship. However, sexual frequency declines with relationship duration in lesbian and gay relationships, just as it does among heterosexual married couples. One characteristic that continues to distinguish gay male couples from both heterosexual married couples and lesbian couples is their higher rates and acceptance of nonmonogamy (Kurdek, 1991; Lever, 1994).

The reliance on volunteer samples, including magazine surveys (e.g., Lever, 1994, 1995), for data on sexuality in committed gay and lesbian couples is problematic because sexuality in couples open about their sexual orientation might differ from those who are less public. National probability samples have oversampled for other groups in society with small populations (e.g., Blacks, Hispanics, certain religious groups) and then allowed for a weight adjustment based on probability of selection when the data are analyzed in the aggregate; future national studies could also oversample homosexual couples. In addition, studies of married couples should not automatically exclude committed gay and lesbian couples simply because they do not have a legal tie. Realistically, however, it can be expected that most of the research on sex in gay and lesbian relationships will continue to rely on nonprobability samples. We encourage such research because it is through the accumulation of such findings that we can build a knowledge base about the role of sexuality in committed gay and lesbian relationships.

SEXUALITY IN DATING RELATIONSHIPS

General Trends in Sexual Behavior and Attitudes in Dating

Then-current and representative studies in the 1990s attested to a striking shift in coital incidence of adolescents during this decade. Four cross-sectional, national probability samples of high school students from the Youth Risk Behavior Survey, collected between 1991 and 1997, showed an 11% increase in the incidence of virgin adolescents (*Centers for Disease Control and Prevention,* 1998). Change was not uniform; male but not female youths, and White and Black but not Hispanic youths contributed to this increase. This represents a significant reversal from the higher incidence of nonvirginity among adolescents during the 1970s and 1980s.

Such decreases in coital experiences were not evident for the single adult population. Analysis of the National Survey of Men ages 20–39 indicated that 88% of never-married men were coitally experienced (Billy et al., 1993). When investigators asked about the previous 1.5 years, most of these men had a single coital partner, but 18.3% had four or more partners. Laumann and colleagues (1994) reported similar findings. When they queried never-married men ages 18–29 about the previous 12 months, they found that 40.7% had one partner, 30.5% had two to four partners, and 14.2% had five or more.

Comparable findings were reported for women. Tanfer and Cubbins' (1992) use of the National Survey of Unwed Women (NSUW) ages 20–29 showed that 80.75% were nonvirgins. Seidman, Mosher, and Aral's (1992) examination of the 1988–1996 GSS data indicated that 7.9% of never-married women ages 15–44 had two or more partners over a 3-month period. Using a 12-month period, Laumann and colleagues (1994) reported that 56.6% of never-married women ages 18–29 had one partner, 24.2% had two to four partners, and 6.2% had five or more. Taken together, these findings from multiple sources suggest that young, single, adult men and women continue to be sexually active. Possibly this is an outgrowth of the delay in marriage that characterizes this age cohort (U.S. Bureau of the Census, 1988), combined with the overall acceptance of engaging in sex before marriage (Smith, 1994a).

In light of this coital activity, some scholars have investigated predictors of having multiple intercourse partners. Bogaert and Fisher's (1995) smaller scale study suggests age, hypermasculinity, sensation seeking, and testosterone levels are associated positively with men's experiences of high numbers of coital partners. Youthful coital experiences and low levels of religiosity predicted number of partners for Black and White women, and living in a major city was an additional and positive predictor for Whites (Seidman et al., 1992).

Other scholars have examined predictors of co-ital frequency among unmarried young adults. Analysis of the 1983 NSUW data demonstrated that single Black and White women engaged in coitus more frequently if they experienced early onset of coitus, were in a relationship, and were protected from pregnancy (Tanfer & Cubbins, 1992). Living independently, not being religious, and being in the early stages of dating additionally predicted coital frequency for White women. Comparable analyses were unavailable for single men and represent a well-defined gap in our knowledge.

As in much research from previous decades, a general correspondence continued to be found between the coital activity of singles and societal attitudes about sex before marriage (Roche & Ramsbey, 1993; Smith, 1994b). Using data from the 1972–1991 GSS, Smith notes fewer respondents have rated sexual relations before marriage as *always wrong,* and more have rated them as *not wrong at all,* in recent as compared to earlier years. Smith interpreted these changes as a shift towards being morally neutral about engaging in coitus prior to marriage. Nonetheless, Smith demonstrated that societal approval of premarital sexual relationships has generally remained stable since 1982. Since 1982, roughly 38% of respondents have rated sex before marriage as *not wrong at all,* with an approximate 23% seeing it as *only sometimes wrong.* Smith found that predictors of such sexual permissiveness paralleled pre-1990s findings. Multivariate tests revealed that greater acceptance corresponded most strongly with low religiosity, with not having teens in the household, and with being young, politically liberal, Black, male, single (Smith, 1994b). Roche and Ramsbey's more limited study does show, however, that young adults' sexual permissiveness for dating varies with the commitment level of those involved; higher levels of dating commitment coincide with greater approval for engaging in sexual intercourse. Sprecher and Hatfield (1996) found similar results.

Although these findings collectively demonstrate that most never-married young adults accepted premarital coitus and were sexually active, they concurrently demonstrate that some young adults remain virgins. There are at least four groups of reasons, derived from factor analysis, for this choice (Sprecher & Regan, 1996): (1) not experiencing enough love, (2) feeling fearful (of AIDS, STDs, pregnancy), (3) holding beliefs supportive of virginity, and (4) feeling inadequate or insecure. Women rate the first three of these as more important than men do; the reverse holds for the final group of reasons.

Empirically scrutinizing the general trends in singles' coital behavior and sexual attitudes highlighted in this section continues to be important in light of these variables' association with the increased incidence of STDs such as chlamydia and AIDS among single heterosexuals. Aside from this compelling need, however, this research additionally points to ethnic differences that are not well understood. Researchers typically investigate ethnicity either by making comparisons across ethnic groups or by calculating separate models for each ethnic group. Although these practices increase our knowledge about the similarities among ethnic groups and uniqueness within them, scholars have yet to grapple with the larger question of why ethnic subcultures approach sexuality before marriage uniquely. Measuring ethnicity by using categorical variables fails to capture the richness and complexity that is inherent in ethnicity as a variable. The time is ripe for scholars to take a more comprehensive, possibly qualitative look at the relationship between ethnicity and sexuality, rather than simply to continue documenting commonalties and differences.

Besides ethnic influences, investigations in the last decade revealed that relationship and sexual experiences are often interrelated. We review the findings in this area in the next section.

Sexuality and Dating Relationship Experiences

The 1990s witnessed scholars' increased recognition that sexual and relational experiences covary in myriad ways. This recognition translated into different empirical foci. Issues of sexual influence and consent, including initiating sexual involvement, sexual resistance, and complying with a partner's sexual wishes, constituted one empirical focus. For instance, Greer and Buss (1994) identified sexual initiation tactics that men and women perceived were effective and were commonly used. There was considerable overlap in the tactics men and women used and had used on them, including the tactics of implying commitment, increasing attention, and displaying status cues. Men initiated sexual activity more frequently than women, although no gender difference appeared to exist in how frequently men and women considered initiating sex (O'Sullivan & Byers, 1992). There were more frequent sexual initiations in steady as compared to less committed dating relationships, and these initiations involved both indirect verbal messages and nonverbal behaviors for both men and women.

Some investigations of sexual compliance focused on singles who consent to unwanted sexual acts without sexual coercion or aggression. Women most often comply unwillingly with partners' sexual wishes as a form of relationship maintenance (O'Sullivan & Gaines, 1998; Shotland & Hunter, 1995). In later dating stages, compliant women did not want to disappoint their partners or risk damaging the relationship. Men resist their partners' sexual initiations at times. In fact, examinations of women's attempts to influence reluctant male partners found these to be common experiences, especially in steady dating relationships (O'Sullivan & Byers, 1993). In such instances, men more than women offered the inappropriateness of the relationship as the reason for their reluctance, whereas women more than men identified problems with the time or place.

Scholars have additionally focused on token resistance, as when individuals say "no" but mean "yes" to intercourse. Sprecher, Hatfield, Cortese, Potapova, and Levitskaya (1994) sampled college students in the United States, Russia, and Japan and found that the U.S. samples had the lowest incidence of token resistance among nonvirgins. Gender comparisons that included virgins and nonvirgins revealed that more men than women engaged in token resistance; comparisons within nonvirgins only revealed no gender differences. O'Sullivan and Allgeier (1994) asked singles why they used token resistance, and found that the most frequently offered reasons reflected emotional, relational, and practical concerns. Only a small minority of individuals offered control or game-playing reasons for their actions. Token resistance might also be a sign of ambiguity in coital decision making. Shotland and Hunter (1995) revealed that the use of token resistance was more prevalent among women who had previously engaged in coitus with their partners and might have involved women changing their coital intentions from "no" to "yes" over the course of a date. Such ambivalence about engaging in coitus is often associated with more general concerns about the relationship (O'Sullivan & Gaines, 1998).

This collection of studies demonstrates that issues of influence and sexual consent are complex. Although the use of force by a dyad partner is a clear index of sexual aggression, it is not always clear whether the lack of forceful influence by one dating partner corresponds with the other partner's willing consent to engage in sexual activity. Given that initiations and consent usually involve nonverbal signals, opportunities for miscommunication that can affect the relationship exist. Hence, it is important to continue this line of research into the next decade. Operationalizing variables of influence and consent, however, must be done carefully. For instance, Muehlenhard and Rogers' (1998) recent work demonstrates the need to provide respondents with multiple memory cues, such as asking about incidents with current and past partners, when measuring token resistance. Similarly, O'Sullivan and Allgeier's (1998) careful conceptualization and operationalization of sexual consent demonstrates the importance of differentiating undesired from nonconsensual sexual involvement.

Another research focus during the 1990s centered on motivations, and beliefs about motivations, for sexual expression for singles. Hill and Preston's (1996) examination of motivations for engaging in coitus revealed that feeling nurturing towards one's partner, emotionally valuing one's partner, and experiencing pleasure all predicted individuals' engagement in vaginal, oral, and anal intercourse. Emotionally valuing a partner, however, motivated women more than men to engage in coitus. Women's sexual motivations might be important for predicting sexual involvement for dating couples. Cohen and Shotland (1996) found the concordance between individuals' sexual expectations and actual experiences holds more strongly for women than for men. Thus women's desire to pair emotional and sexual experiences played a more direct role in couples' sexual interactions. Research has consistently shown such a gender difference across pre-1990s studies, so it is not surprising that Oliver and Hyde's (1993) meta-analysis found women less accepting of casual sex than men.

Findings that women link their relationship experiences with their sexual expression resonates with young adults' belief that single women's sexual desire is keyed by professing love and that women's sexuality is strongly related to their relationship experiences (Regan, 1997; Regan & Berscheid, 1995). Women's sexuality, however, might actually be more complicated than this. In a series of studies, Cyranowski and Andersen (1998; Andersen & Cyranowski, 1994) showed that young women's sexual schemas, or self-views, include not only estimations of how romantic and passionate they are—clear indicants of relational experiences—but also self-judgments about how sexually open and direct or how embarrassed and sexually conservative they are.

Additional work points to a range of relationship properties that are related to different facets of couples' sexuality. Regan and Berscheid (1999) combined previous conceptualizations of love with empirical evidence to argue that sexual desire is a component of romantic love and that sexual desire is popularly perceived to be part of the experience of being in love. Long, Cate, Fehsenfeld, and Williams (1996) found sexual conflict related negatively to sexual and relationship satisfaction and positively to dyadic conflict and feelings of obligation to engage in intercourse. Byers and colleagues (1998) found dating individuals' sexual satisfaction strongly related to their relationship satisfaction, as was perceived equality of sexual costs and comparisons of sexual rewards to such costs. Lally and Maddock (1994) proposed that the meaning couples assign to their sexual involvement (i.e., affection, communication, recreation or play) is important. They showed that engaged couples were more apt to develop a joint meaning when those couples cohabited, had attained higher education levels, had the same religious affiliation, and agreed on family planning options.

Although the above investigations focused on relationship experiences that either preceded or were concurrent with sexual involvement, other investigations during this decade explored the effects of sexual involvement on short- and long-term relationship outcomes. For instance, Cate, Long, Angera, and Draper (1993) examined the impact of first coitus in a dating relationship on later relational development. Relationships improved for men and women when relationship quality played a role in coital decision making and when they were sexually satisfied. Being sexually permissive was an additional predictor of improved relationship quality for men. Other investigators looked beyond dating to consider outcomes of sexuality in family and marriage. Using data on women from the 1982 National Survey of Family Growth (NSFG), Miller and Heaton (1991) examined the relationship between age at first coitus and the later timing of marriage and childbirth. They showed that after controlling for other factors, early onset of coitus among adolescents corresponded with earlier age at forming a family and with an increased probability that the family would begin with childbirth as opposed to marriage. Finally, Kahn and London (1991) que-

ried whether engaging in premarital sexual intercourse would put women at risk for divorce. Using White respondents from the 1988 NSFG data, and controlling for other factors, they revealed that women who were virgins at marriage were less likely to be separated or divorced than nonvirgins 10 years into marriage. This difference disappeared when potential differences between virgins and nonvirgins were taken into account (mother's education, strictness of rules, and religiosity at age 14). Kahn and London speculated that women who are virgins at marriage might find divorce less acceptable than would women who are nonvirgins, although this hypothesis could not be directly tested with the data.

These findings extend the previous body of research in this area (see Sprecher & McKinney, 1993, for a review) by illustrating different ways in which sexuality is intertwined with relational experiences for singles and ways in which premarital sexual experiences potentially influence marital and familial experiences. For instance, these studies reveal that singles' relationship satisfaction is associated with a number of sexually related variables. There is a need, however, to develop theory-based models for how sexual cognitions, evaluations, and interactions are intertwined with the relationship dynamics for dating individuals. Byers and colleagues (1998) take important steps in this direction with their use of social-exchange theory, but more comprehensive models are needed.

Sexual Coercion and Aggression in Dating

Scholarly interest in sexual coercion and aggression in dating flourished during the 1990s. The corpus of work developed to the point where a number of general reviews and critiques were written (i.e. Koss & Cleveland, 1997; Marx, Van Wie, & Gross, 1996), and midlevel theoretical models were proposed (Byers, 1996; Craig, 1990; Malamuth, 1998; Porter & Critelli, 1992; Shotland, 1992; Thornhill & Thornhill, 1992). Space limitations prevent us from reviewing all advances in this area. Instead, we highlight new research directions generally not included in previous reviews.

The first of these areas reflects early experiences with and influences on sexual coercion. Evidence continued to accumulate that some adolescents fall victim to sexual coercion (Erickson & Rapkin, 1991; Jordan, Price, Telljohann, & Chesney, 1998). Sexually coerced teens were more sexually active, had poorer peer relationships, and had more same-sex friends who also were sexually active than those who had not suffered coercion (Vicary, Klingaman, & Harkness, 1995). Those who experienced unwanted coitus also were older, experienced less parental monitoring and more parental sexual abuse, and conformed more to peers (Small & Kerns, 1993). A number of investigations pointed to the role that early developmental influences play in later acts of sexual coercion. These include experiences of family violence (Dean & Malamuth, 1997), early history of behavior problems (Lalumiere & Quinsey, 1996), and delinquency (Calhoun, Bernat, Clum, & Frame, 1997; Malamuth, Lintz, Heavey, Barnes, & Acker, 1995).

A second new area of research further illuminated the role that dating experiences play in men's sexual coercion. Sexually coercive men, when compared to noncoercive men, were more apt to endorse a Ludic love style—a style characterized by a noncommittal, manipulative, game-playing approach to love (Kalichman et al., 1993; Sarwer, Kalichman, Johnson, Early, & Ali, 1993). They experienced conflict and ambivalence with their coerced partners; experiences that directly predicted their acts of sexual coercion (Christopher, Madura, & Weaver, 1998; Christopher, Owens, & Stecker, 1993a, 1993b). Such men might also lack skills for communicating well in a relationship. Based on responses to videotapes in which women respond in a variety of ways to a man's sexual advances, Malamuth and Brown (1994) suggest that sexually coercive men use cognitive schemas that discount the truthfulness of women's rejection messages. Hence, sexually coercive men might have a propensity to inaccurately decode women's sexual rejections.

Research evidence also reveals that sexually coercive men are different from noncoercive men in their approach to relationships and sexuality. They date more frequently (Byers & Eno, 1991), begin sexual activity at an early age (Malamuth et al., 1995), and have high numbers of sexual partners (Christopher et al., 1993a, 1993b; Lalumiere, Chalmers, Quinsey, & Seto, 1996), especially in uncommitted dating relationships (Lalumiere & Quinsey, 1996). They also prefer novel and casual sexual encounters (Lalumiere et al., 1996). Koss and Cleveland (1997), in reviewing such findings, speculate that sexually coercive men take a predatory approach to their sexual interactions with women.

Finally, a limited number of investigators in the 1990s focused on female-initiated sexual coercion. Studies comparing single women's and single men's coercion experiences reveal that fewer women are sexually coercive, and when women are coercive, they use less forceful techniques (Christopher et al., 1998). Moreover, when men are victims of coercion, they experience less and shorter term emotional upset as a consequence of their experiences than women (O'Sullivan, Byers, & Finkelman, 1998). These results must be interpreted carefully, because few men in these studies experienced violent sexual aggression. Comparing men who experienced no coercion to those who experienced pressure or violence reveals that men who experienced violent sexual coercion were angrier and more depressed than men in the other two groups (Zweig, Barber, & Eccles, 1997). Examination of the sexual outcomes of coercive acts showed that men's experiences with being coerced most often do not advance beyond kissing or fondling whereas women's experiences most often result in intercourse (Waldner-Haugrud & Magruder, 1995).

Attempts to identify correlates of female-initiated sexual coercion revealed that women who use coercion see themselves as more open, and rate themselves higher in self-esteem and in relationship satisfaction, than female victims of coercion (Busby & Compton, 1997). They also feel hostile towards men, possess a brooding anger, have a history of being sexually coercive, and experience relational conflict with and ambivalence about their coerced partners (Christopher et al., 1993b; Christopher et al., 1998).

Of the new research directions we have highlighted, two are particularly noteworthy. First, the corpus of our knowledge about sexual coercion and aggression in dating relationships is largely limited to what occurs among college students. Sampling from early and middle adolescent populations represents an important first step in breaking out of this limitation. The next decade should see an expansion of investigations into the more general single adult population. Second, research to date has focused primarily on individual-level predictors of sexual aggression. We are encouraged that investigators have tested models that additionally included relational (e.g., conflict) and social (e.g., peer association) variables (Christopher et al., 1998). Such integrated approaches will likely continue to prove useful in advancing our understanding of this phenomenon.

FUTURE DIRECTIONS

Throughout this review, we have suggested possible areas for research in the coming decade. In closing, we want to highlight three directions that hold heuristic promise and represent important next steps in the study of sexuality.

We identified new and noteworthy findings about marital sexuality in this review. More is known about sexuality in marriage at this time than has ever been true in the past. Yet we still have only a limited view of how sexuality is integrated into the normal flow of married life—how it influences and is influenced by other marital phenomena. Thus there exist several viable research questions for the coming decade. Does sexuality play a role in maintaining marital relationships? Does it contribute to couples' commitment or to family cohesion? How is sexuality related to dyadic conflict? How do married couples communicate about their sexuality, and does this communication play a role in relationship functioning? Addressing these and similar questions will provide a better understanding of sexual expression in its most socially approved context.

This review additionally attests that research that includes close relationship and sexuality constructs provides useful insights into sexual phenomena. Sexual interaction takes place in a dyadic context, so it should not be surprising that relational and sexual variables covary. To date, however, this developing literature suffers limitations common to many fields, including small samples that disproportionately represent college students, cross-sectional designs, and a high number of atheoretical investigations. Nonetheless, the findings generated from these empirical efforts are intriguing and should be investigated further, albeit with better designed investigations. We encourage sexuality researchers in the coming decade to include relational constructs in their investigations while simultaneously addressing current shortcomings.

Finally, the 1990s saw theoretical and methodological advances in the study of sexuality. Although the advances in theory were moderate, important foundational and exemplary work now exists (Weis, 1998). Methodological advances were more robust and included insights into survey design and the increased use of national data sets. We end our review with the perennial but necessary comment of other reviewers of social science advances. We encourage sexuality researchers to build from these advances. We encourage the increased use of theory, probability sampling, and longitudinal designs. Incorporating these advances into new research in the coming decade will allow researchers to test causal models that more accurately reflect complex influences on sexual expression and will thereby extend our understanding of sexuality in close relationships.

NOTE

The authors would like to thank Sara Jacobs-Carter for her help with this project and Rod Cate, Lauren Levin, Kathleen McKinney, and Marion C. Willetts for reading earlier drafts or portions of this manuscript. Both authors contributed equally to this project.

REFERENCES

Andersen, B. L., & Cryanowski, J. M. (1994). Women's sexual self-schema. *Journal of Personality and Social Psychology, 67,* 1079–1100.

Aron, A., & Henkemeyer, L. (1995). Marital satisfaction and passionate love. *Journal of Social and Personal Relationships, 12,* 139–146.

Bancroft, J. (Ed.) (1997). *Researching sexual behavior: Methodological issues.* Bloomington, IN: Indiana University Press.

Barrett, D. C., Bolan, G., & Douglas, J. M., Jr., (1998). Redefining gay male anal intercourse behaviors: Implications for HIV prevention and research. *The Journal of Sex Research, 35,* 381–389.

Berscheid, E., & Reiss, H. T. (1998). Attraction and close relationships. In D. R. Gilbert, S. T. Fisk, & G. Lindzey (Eds.), *The handbook of social psychology* (Vol. 2, 4th ed., pp. 196–281). New York: McGraw-Hill.

Billy, J. O. G., Tanfer, K., Grady, W. R., & Klepinger, D. H. (1993). The sexual behavior of men in the United States. *Family Planning Perspectives, 25,* 52–60.

Binik, Y. M., Mah, K., & Kiesler, S. (1999). Ethical issues in conducting sex research on the internet. *The Journal of Sex Research, 26,* 82–90.

Blumstein, P., & Schwartz, P. (1983). *American couples.* New York: William Morrow.

Bogaert, A. F., & Fisher, W. A. (1995). Predictors of university men's number of sexual partners. *The Journal of Sex Research, 32,* 119–130.

Bringle, R. G., & Buunk, B. P. (1991). extradyadic relationships and sexual jealousy. In K. McKinney & S. Sprecher (Eds.), *Sexuality in close relationships* (pp. 135–153). Hillsdale, NJ: Erlbaum.

Busby, D. M., & Compton, S. V. (1997). Patterns of sexual coercion in adult heterosexual relationships: An exploration of male victimization. *Family Process, 36,* 81–94.

Buss, D. M. (1998). Sexual strategies theory: Historical origins and current status. *The Journal of Sex Research, 35,* 19–31.

Buss, D. M., Larsen, R., Westen, D., & Semmelroth, J. (1992). Sex differences in jealousy: Evolution, physiology, and psychology. *Psychological Science, 3,* 251–255.

Buunk, B., Angleitner, A., Oubaid, V., & Buss, D. (1996). Sex differences in jealousy in evolutionary and cultural perspectives: Tests from the Netherlands, Germany, and the United States. *Psychological Science, 7,* 359–363.

Byers, E. S. (1996). How well does the traditional sexual script explain sexual coercion? Review of a program of research. Journal of Psychology & Human Sexuality, 8, 7–25.

Byers, E. S., & Demmons, S. (1999). Sexual satisfaction and sexual self-disclosure within dating relationships. *The Journal of Sex Research, 36,* 180–189.

Byers, E. S., Demmons, S., & Lawrance, K. (1998). Sexual satisfaction within dating relationships: A test of the interpersonal exchange model of sexual satisfaction. *Journal of Social and Personal Relationships, 15,* 257–267.

Byers, E. S., & Eno, R. J. (1991). Predicting men's sexual coercion and aggression from attitudes, dating history, and sexual response. *Journal of Psychology and Human Sexuality, 4,* 55 70.

Calhoun, K. S., Bernat, J. A., Clum, G. A., & Frame, C. L. (1997). Sexual coercion and attraction to sexual aggression in a community sample of young men. *Journal of Interpersonal Violence, 12,* 392–406.

Call, V., Sprecher, S., & Schwartz, P. (1995). The incidence and frequency of marital sex in a national sample. *Journal of Marriage and the Family, 57,* 639–650.

Call, V., Sprecher, S., & Schwartz, P. (1996, November). *Changes over time in the incidence and frequency of marital sex: Longitudinal data from a U.S. National Sample.* Paper presented at the National Council on Family Relations. Portland, OR.

Catania, J. A. (1999a). A comment on advancing the frontiers of sexological methods. *The Journal of Sex Research, 36,* 1–2.

Catania, J. A. (1999b). A framework for conceptualizing reporting bias and its antecendents in interviews assessing human sexuality. *The Journal of Sex Research, 36,* 25–38.

Cate, R. M., Long, E., Angera, J. J., & Draper, K. K. (1993). Sexual intercourse and relationship development. *Family Relations, 42,* 158–164.

Centers for Disease Control and Prevention. (1998, September 18). Trends in sexual risk behaviors among high school students—United States, 1991–1997. *Morbidity and Mortality Weekly Report* [Online] *47,* 749–751. Available: http://www.cdc.gov/epo/mmwr/preview/mmwrhtml/00054814.htm

Choi, K., Catania, J. A., & Dolcini, M. M. (1994). Extramarital sex and HIV risk behavior among US adults: Results from the national AIDS behavioral survey. *American Journal of Public Health, 84,* 2003–2007.

Christopher, F. S., Madura, M., & Weaver, L. (1998). Premarital sexual aggressors: A multivariate analysis of social, relational, and individual variables. *Journal of Marriage and the Family, 60,* 56–69.

Christopher, F. S., Owens, L. A., & Stecker, H. L. (1993a). Exploring the dark side of courtship: A test model of male premarital sexual aggressiveness. *Journal of Marriage and the Family, 55,* 469–479.

Christopher, F. S., Owens, L. A., & Stecker, H. L. (1993b). An examination of single men and women's sexual aggressiveness in dating relationships. *Journal of Social and Personal Relationships, 10,* 511–527.

Cohen, L. L., & Shotland, R. L. (1996). Timing of first sexual intercourse in a relationship: Expectations, experiences, and perceptions of others. *The Journal of Sex Research, 33,* 291–299.

Craig, M. E. (1990). Coercive sexuality in dating relationships: A situational model. *Clinical Psychology Review, 10,* 395–423.

Cupach, W. R., & Comstock, J. (1990). Satisfaction with sexual communication in marriage. Links to sexual satisfaction and dyadic adjustment. *Journal of Social and Personal Relationships, 7,* 179–186.

Cyranowski, J. M., & Andersen, B. L. (1998). Schemas, sexuality, and romantic attachment. *Journal of Personality and Social Psychology, 74,* 1364–1379.

Davidson, J. K., Sr., Darling, C. A., & Norton, L. (1995). Religiosity and the sexuality of women: Sexual behavior and sexual satisfaction revisited. *The Journal of Sex Research, 32,* 235–243.

Davis, C. M., Yarber, W. L., Bauserman, R., Schreer, G., & Davis, S. L. (1998). *Handbook of sexuality-related measures.* Thousand Oaks, CA: Sage.

Dean, K. E., & Malamuth, N. M. (1997). Characteristics of men who aggress sexually and of men who imagine aggressing: Risk and moderating variables. *Journal of Personality and Social Psychology, 72,* 449–455.

Deenen, A. A., Gijs, L., & van Naerssen, A. X. (1994). Intimacy and sexuality in gay male couples. *Archives of Sexual Behavior, 23,* 421–431.

DeLamater, J. D., & Hyde, J. S. (1998). Essential versus social constructionism in the study of human sexuality. *The Journal of Sex Research, 35,* 10–18.

DeMaris, A. (1997). Elevated sexual activity in violent marriages: Hypersexuality or sexual extortion? *The Journal of Sex Research, 34,* 361–373.

DeMaris, A., & Swinford, S. (1996). Female victims of spousal violence: Factors influencing their level of fearfulness. *Family Relations, 45,* 98–106.

Donnelly, D. A. (1993). Sexually inactive marriages. *The Journal of Sex Research, 30,* 171–179.

Edwards, J. N., & Booth, A. (1994). Sexuality, marriage, and well-being: The middle years. In A. S. Rossi (Ed.), *Sexuality across the life course* (pp. 233–259). Chicago: University of Chicago Press.

Erickson, P. I., & Rapkin, A. (1991). Unwanted sexual experiences among middle and high school youth. *Journal of Adolescent Health, 12,* 319–325.

Fincham, F. D., & Bradbury, T. N. (1987). The assessment of marital quality: A reevaluation. *Journal of Marriage and the Family, 49,* 797–809.

Finkelhor, D., & Yllo, K. (1985). *License to rape: Sexual abuse of wives.* New York: Holt, Rinehard & Winston.

Forste, R., & Tanfer, K. (1996). Sexual exclusivity among dating, cohabiting, and married women. *Journal of Marriage and the Family, 58,* 33–47.

Gierveld, J. J. (1995). Research into relationship designs: Personal relationships under the microscope. *Journal of Social and Personal Relationships, 12,* 583–588.

Glass, S. P., & Wright, T. L. (1992). Justifications for extramarital relationships: The association between attitudes, behaviors, and gender. *The Journal of Sex Research, 29,* 361–387.

Greeley, A. M. (1991). *Faithful attraction: Discovering intimacy, love, and fidelity in American marriage.* New York: Doherty.

Greenblat, C. S. (1983). The salience of sexuality in the early years of marriage. *Journal of Marriage and the Family, 45,* 289–299.

Greer, A. E., & Buss, D. M. (1994). Tactics for promoting sexual encounters. *The Journal of Sex Research, 31,* 185–201.

Gribble, J. N., Miller, H. G., Rogers, S. M., & Turner, C. F. (1999). Interview mode and measurement of sexual behaviors: Methodological issues. *The Journal of Sex Research, 36,* 16–24.

Grote, N. K., & Frieze, I. H. (1998). Remembrance of things past: Perceptions of marital love from its beginnings to the present. *Journal of Social and Personal Relationships, 15,* 91–109.

Gullotta, T. P., Adams, G. R., & Montemayor, R. (Eds.) (1993). *Adolescent sexuality.* Newbury Park, CA: Sage.

Haavio-Mannila, E., & Kontula, O. (1997). Correlates of increased sexual satisfaction. *Archives of Sexual Behavior, 26,* 399–419.

Henderson-King, D. H., & Veroff, J. (1994). Sexual satisfaction and marital well-being in the first years of marriages. *Journal of Social and Personal Relationships, 11,* 509–534.

Hill, C. A., & Preston, L. K. (1996). Individual differences in the experience of sexual motivation: Theory and measurement of dispositional sexual motives. *The Journal of Sex Research, 33,* 27–45.

Hogben, M., & Byrne, D. (1998). Using social learning theory to explain individual differences in human sexuality. *The Journal of Sex Research, 35,* 58–71.

Hunt, M. (1974). *Sexual behavior in the 1970's.* Chicago: Playboy Press.

Huston, T. L., & Vangelisti, A. L. (1991). Socioemotional behavior and satisfaction in marital relationships: A longitudinal study. *Journal of Personality and Social Psychology, 61,* 721–733.

Hyde, J. S., DeLamater, J. D., Plant, E. A., & Byrd, J. M. (1996). Sexuality during pregnancy and the year postpartum. *The Journal of Sex Research, 33,* 143–151.

Johnson, M. P. (1995). Patriarchal terrorism and common couple violence: Two forms of violence against women. *Journal of Marriage and the Family, 57,* 283–294.

Jordan, T. R., Price, J. H., Telljohann, S. K., & Chesney, B. K. (1998). Junior high school students' perceptions regarding nonconsensual sexual behavior. *Journal of School Health, 68,* 289–300.

Jurich, J. A., & Myers-Bowman, K. S. (1998). Systems theory and its application to research on human sexuality. *The Journal of Sex Research, 35,* 72–87.

Kahn, J. R., & London, K. A. (1991). Premarital sex and the risk of divorce. *Journal of Marriage and the Family, 53,* 845–855.

Kalichman, S. C., Sarwer, D. B., Johnson, J. R., Ali, S. A., Early, J., & Tuten, J. T. (1993). Sexually coercive behavior and love styles: A replication and extension. *Journal of Psychology & Human Sexuality, 6,* 93–106.

Kelly, J. A. (1995). Advances in HIV/AIDS education and prevention. *Family Relations, 44,* 345–353.

Kinsey, A. C., Pomeroy, W. B., & Martin, C. E. (1948). *Sexual behavior in the human male.* Philadelphia: Saunders.

Kinsey, A. C., Pomeroy, W. B., Martin, C. E., & Geb-hard, P. H. (1953). *Sexual behavior in the human female.* Philadelphia: Saunders.

Koss, M. P., & Cleveland, H. H. (1997). Stepping on toes: Social roots of date rape lead to intractability and politicization. In M. D. Schwartz (Ed.), *Researching sexual violence against women: Methodological and personal perspectives* (pp.4–21). Thousand Oaks, CA: Sage.

Kurdek, L. A. (1991). Sexuality in homosexual and heterosexual couples. In K. McKinney & S. Sprecher (Eds.), *Sexuality in close relationships* (pp. 177–191). Hillsdale, NJ: Erlbaum.

Lally, C. F., & Maddock, J. W. (1994). Sexual meaning systems of engaged couples. *Family Relations, 43,* 53–60.

Lalumiere, M. L., Chalmers, L. J., Quinsey, V. L., & Seto, M. C. (1996). A test of the mate deprivation hypothesis of sexual coercion. *Ethology and Sociobiology, 17,* 299–318.

Lalumiere, M. L., & Quinsey, V. L. (1996). Sexual deviance, antisociality, mating effort, and the use of sexually coercive behaviors. *Personality and Individual Differences, 21,* 34–48.

Laumann, E. O., Gagnon, J. H., Michael, R. T., & Michaels, S. (1994). *The social organization of sexuality: Sexual practices in the United States.* Chicago: University of Chicago Press.

Lawrance, K., & Byers, E. S. (1995). Sexual satisfaction in long-term heterosexual relationships: The interpersonal exchange model of sexual satisfaction. *Personal Relationships, 2,* 267–285.

Lever, J. (1994, August 23). Sexual revelations. *The Advocate,* 17–24.

Lever, J. (1995, August 22). Lesbian sex survey. *The Advocate,* 21–30.

Long, E. C. J., Cate, R. M., Fehsenfeld, D. A., & Williams, K. M. (1996). A longitudinal assessment of a measure of premarital sexual conflict. *Family Relations, 45,* 302–308.

Longmore, M. A. (1998). Symbolic interactionism and the study of sexuality. *The Journal of Sex Research, 35,* 44–57.

Malamuth, N. M. (1998). The confluence model as an organizing framework for research on sexually aggressive men: Risk moderators, imagined aggression, and pornography consumption. In R. G. Geen & E. Donnerstein (Eds.), *Human aggression: Theories, research, and implications for social policy* (pp. 227–245). San Diego, CA: Academic Press.

Malamuth, N. M., & Brown, L. M. (1994). Sexually aggressive men's perceptions of women's communications: Testing three explanations. *Journal of Personality and Social Psychology, 67,* 699–712.

Malamuth, N. M., Lintz, D., Heavey, C. L., Barnes, G., & Acker, M. (1995). Using the confluence model of sexual aggression to predict men's conflict with women: A 10-year follow-up study. *Journal of Personality and Social Psychology, 69,* 353–369.

Marsiglio, W., & Donnelly, D. (1991). Sexual intercourse in later life: A national study of married persons. *Journal of Gerontology, 46,* 338–344.

Marston, P. J., Hecht, M. L., Manke, M. L., McDaniel, S., & Reeder, H. (1998). The subjective experience of intimacy, passion, and commitment in heterosexual loving relationships. *Personal Relationships, 5,* 15–30.

Marx, B. P., Van Wie, V., & Gross, A. M. (1996). Date rape risk factors: A review and methodological critique of the literature. *Aggression and Violent Behavior, 1,* 27–45.

McKinney, K., & Sprecher, S. (Eds.). (1991). *Sexuality in close relationships.* Hillsdale, NJ: Erlbaum.

Michael, R. T., Gagnon, J. H., Laumann, E. O., & Kolata, G. (1994). *Sex in America: A definitive survey.* Boston: Little, Brown.

Miller, B. C., & Heaton, T. B. (1991). Age at first sexual intercourse and the timing of marriage and childbirth. *Journal of Marriage and the Family, 53,* 719–732.

Moore, K. A., Miller, B. C., Glei, D., & Morrison, D. R. (1995). *Adolescent sex, contraception, and childbearing: A review of recent research.* Washington, DC: Child Trends.

Morrison, D. M., Leigh, B. C., & Gillmore, M. R. (1999). Daily data collection: A comparison of three methods. *The Journal of Sex Research, 36,* 76–81.

Muehlenhard, C. L., & Rodgers, C. S. (1998). Token resistance to sex. *Psychology of Women Quarterly, 22,* 443–463.

Oggins, J., Leber, D., & Veroff, J. (1993). Race and gender differences in black and white newlyweds' perceptions of sexual and marital relationships. *The Journal of Sex Research, 30,* 152–160.

Oliver, M. B., & Hyde, J. S. (1993). Gender differences in sexuality: A meta-analysis. *Psychological Bulletin, 114,* 29–51.

O'Sullivan, L. F., & Allgeier, E. R. (1994). Disassembling a stereotype: Gender differences in the use of token resistance. *Journal of Applied Social Psychology, 24,* 1035–1055.

O'Sullivan, L. F., & Allgeier, E. R. (1998). Feigning sexual desire: Consenting to unwanted sexual activity in heterosexual dating relationships. *The Journal of Sex Research, 35,* 234–243.

O'Sullivan, L. F., & Byers, E. S. (1992). College students' incorporation of initiator and restrictor roles in sexual dating interactions. *The Journal of Sex Research, 29,* 435–446.

O'Sullivan, L. F., & Byers, E. S. (1993). Eroding stereotypes: College women's attempts to influence reluctant male sexual partners. *The Journal of Sex Research, 30,* 270–282.

O'Sullivan, L. F., Byers, E. S., & Finkelman, L. (1998). A comparison of male and female college students' experiences of sexual coercion. *Psychology of Women Quarterly, 22,* 177–195.

O'Sullivan L. F., & Gaines, M. E. (1998). Decision-making in college students' heterosexual dating relationships: Ambivalence about engaging in sexual activity. *Journal of Social and Personal Relationships, 15,* 347–363.

Porter, J. F., & Critelli, J. W. (1992). Measurement of sexual aggression in college men: A methodological analysis. *Archives of Sexual Behavior, 21,* 525–542.

Posner, R. A., & Silbaugh, K. B. (1996). *A guide to America's sex laws.* Chicago: University of Chicago Press.

Rao, K. V., & DeMaris, A. (1995). Coital frequency among married and cohabiting couples in the U.S. *Journal of Biosocial Science, 27,* 135–150.

Regan, P. C. (1997). The impact of male sexual request style on perceptions of sexual interactions: The mediational role of beliefs about female sexual desire. *Basic and Applied Social Psychology, 19,* 519–532.

Regan, P. C., & Berscheid, E. (1995). Gender differences in beliefs about the causes of male and female sexual desire. *Personal Relationships, 2,* 345–358.

Regan, P. C., & Berscheid, E. (1999). *Lust: What we know about human sexual desire.* Thousand Oaks, CA: Sage

Renaud, C., Byers, E. S., & Pan, S. (1997). Sexual and relationship satisfaction in mainland China. *The Journal of Sex Research, 34,* 1–12.

Roach, A. J., Frazier, L. P., & Bowden, S. R. (1981). The marital satisfaction scale. *Journal of Marriage and the Family, 40,* 537–546.

Roche, J. P., & Ramsbey, T. W. (1993). Premarital sexuality: A five-year follow-up study of attitudes and behavior by dating stage. *Adolescence, 28,* 67–80.

Russel, D. E. H. (1982). *Rape in marriage.* Bloomington, IN: Indiana University Press.

Sarwer, D. B., Kalichman, S. C., Johnson, J. R., Early, J., & Ali, S. A. (1993). Sexual aggression and love styles: An exploratory study. *Archives of Sexual Behavior, 22,* 265–275.

Seidman, S. N., Mosher, W. D., & Aral, S. O. (1992). Women with multiple sexual partners: United States, 1988. *American Journal of Public Health, 82,* 1388–1394.

Shackelford, T. K., & Buss, D. M. (1997). Anticipation of marital dissolution as a consequence of spousal infidelity. *Journal of Social and Personal Relationships, 14,* 793–808.

Shotland, R. L. (1992). A theory of the causes of courtship rape: Part 2. *Journal of Social Issues, 48,* 127–143.

Shotland, R. L., & Hunter, B. A. (1995). Women's "token resistant" and compliant sexual behaviors are related to uncertain sexual intentions and rape. *Personality and Social Psychology Bulletin, 21,* 226–236.

Small, S. A., & Kerns, D. (1993). Unwanted sexual activity among peers during early and middle adolescence: Incidence and risk factors. *Journal of Marriage and the Family, 55,* 941–952.

Smith, T. W. (1994a). Attitudes toward sexual permissiveness: Trends, correlates, and behavioral connections. In Rossi, A. S. (Ed.), *Sexuality across the life course* (pp. 63–97). Chicago: University of Chicago Press.

Smith, T. W. (1994b). *The demography of sexual behavior.* Menlo Park, CA: Kaiser Family Foundation.

Spanier, G. B. (1976). Measuring dyadic adjustment. *Journal of Marriage and the Family, 38,* 15–28.

Sponaugle, G. C. (1989). Attitudes toward extramarital relations. In K. McKinney & S. Sprecher (Eds.), *Human sexuality: The societal and interpersonal context* (pp. 187–209). Norwood, NJ: Ablex.

Sprecher, S. (1998). Social exchange theories and sexuality. *The Journal of Sex Research, 35,* 32–43.

Sprecher, S., & Hatfield, E. (1996). Premarital sexual standards among U.S. college students: Comparison with Russian and Japanese students. *Archives of Sexual Behavior, 25,* 261–288.

Sprecher, S., Hatfield, E., Cortese, A., Potapova, E., & Levitskaya, A. (1994). Token resistance to sexual intercourse and consent to unwanted sexual intercourse: College students' dating experiences in three countries. *The Journal of Sex Research, 31,* 125–132.

Sprecher, S., & McKinney, K. (1993). *Sexuality*. Newbury Park, CA: Sage.

Sprecher, S., Metts, S., Burleson, B., Hatfield, E., & Thompson, A. (1995). Domains of expressive interaction in intimate relationships: Associations with satisfaction and commitment. *Family Relations, 44,* 203–210.

Sprecher, S., & Regan, P. C. (1996). College virgins: How men and women perceive their sexual status. *The Journal of Sex Research, 33,* 3–15.

Sprecher, S., & Regan, P. C. (1998). Passionate and companionate love in courting and young married couples. *Sociological Inquiry, 68,* 163–185.

Tanfer, K., & Cubbins, L. A. (1992). Coital frequency among single women: Normative constraints and situational opportunities. *The Journal of Sex Research, 29,* 221–250.

Thompson, A. (1983). Extramarital sex: A review of the research literature. *The Journal of Sex Research, 19,* 1–22.

Thornhill, R., & Thornhill, N. W. (1992). The evolutionary psychology of men's coercive sexuality. *Behavioral and Brain Sciences, 15,* 363–421.

U.S. Bureau of the Census. (1988). *Households, families, marital status, and living arrangements: March, 1988* [Advance Report] (Current Population Reports, Series P-20, No. 432). Washington, DC: Govenment Printing Office.

Veroff, J., Douvan, E., & Hatchett, S. J. (1995). *Marital instability: A social and behavioral study of the early years.* Westport, CT: Praeger.

Vicary, J. R., Klingaman, L. R., & Harkness, W. L. (1995). Risk factors associated with date rape and sexual assault of adolescent girls. *Journal of Adolescence, 18,* 289–306.

Waldner-Haugrud, L. K., & Gratch, L. V. (1997). Sexual coercion in gay/lesbian relationships: Descriptives and gender differences. *Violence and Victims, 12,* 87–98.

Waldner-Haugrud, L. K., & Magruder, B. (1995). Male and female sexual victimization in dating relationships: Gender differences in coercion techniques and outcomes. *Violence and Victims, 10,* 203–215.

Weis, D. L. (1998). The use of theory in sexuality research. *The Journal of Sex Research, 35,* 1–9.

White, L., & Keith, B. (1990). The effect of shift work on the quality and stability of marital relations. *Journal of Marriage and the Family, 52,* 453–462.

Wiederman, M. W. (1997). Extramarital sex: Prevalence and correlates in a national survey. *The Journal of Sex Research, 34,* 167–174.

Wiederman, M. W. (1999). Volunteer bias in sexuality research using college student participants. *The Journal of Sex Research, 36,* 59–66.

Zweig, J. M., Barber, B. L., & Eccles, J. S. (1997). Sexual coercion and well-being in young adulthood. *Journal of Interpersonal Violence, 12,* 291–308.

ALAN BOOTH, KAREN CARVER, AND DOUGLAS A. GRANGER*
Pennsylvania State University

Biosocial Perspectives on the Family

New theoretical models conceptualize families as systems affected by, and effecting change in, reciprocal influences among social, behavioral, and biological processes. Technological breakthroughs make noninvasive assessment of many biological processes available to family researchers. These theoretical and measurement advances have resulted in significant increases in research on family processes and relationships that integrate knowledge from the fields of behavioral endocrinology, behavior genetics, and, to a lesser degree, evolutionary psychology. This review covers a broad spectrum, including the topics of parenthood, early child development, adolescent and middle child development, parent-child relations, courtship and mate selection, and the quality and stability of marital and intimate relations. Our intention is to introduce, by example, the relevance of the biosocial approach, encourage family researchers to consider the application of these ideas to their interests, and increase the participation of family researchers in the next generation of studies.

This is the first appearance of a decade-in-review article devoted to biosocial perspectives on the family. There are several decades of research ex-

Department of Sociology, 211 Oswald Tower, Pennsylvania State University, University Park, PA 16802 (axb24@psu.edu).

*Biobehavioral Health Department, Pennsylvania State University, University Park, PA 16802.

Key Words: *child development, evolution, family relations, genetics, hormones.*

amining the links between biology and individual development (e.g., perception, memory, maturation), but it is only recently that research has focused on families. Although the information is still fragmented, we now have enough to devote an article to biosocial research as it pertains to families. By biosocial we mean concepts linking psychosocial factors to physiology, genetics, and evolution. This article is a prelude to an explosion of biosocial research related to families anticipated over the next decade. We offer a hint of things to come and hope to perhaps encourage readers to start their own biosocial research project.

Early social scientists, such as William James (1842–1910), assumed that physiological processes were critical components of the behavioral and social phenomena they were studying. Until recently, however, the influence of those assumptions on scientific thinking was limited by significant gaps in knowledge. The nature of many physiological processes was largely unknown, and the technology necessary to operationalize physiological variables was in its infancy. Given these limitations, it is not surprising that research on human development and the family largely focused on the interface between the social environment and individual behavior. Many of those who did study physiological processes looked for simplistic models in which reductionist principles could be applied to reveal "the biological determinants" of behavior. The application of this focus led to clearly drawn boundaries between the social and biological sciences, the exceptions being studies of individual prenatal, infant, and adolescent development.

In the last 2 decades, significant effort has been

focused on reversing this trend. Technical and conceptual advances have begun to break down disciplinary walls. Specifically, advances that enable noninvasive and inexpensive measurement of many physiological processes have given behavioral and social researchers new opportunities to integrate biological measures into their programs (Granger, Schwartz, Booth, & Arentz, 1999). In parallel, a series of paradigm shifts have occurred in scientific thinking about the relative contributions of both nature and nurture to behavioral phenomena (McClearn, 1993) and individual development (Gottlieb, 1992).

Dynamic models have replaced the simple reductionist ones of the past. They can best be described as systems models positing that individuals and families are best understood as the product of reciprocal influences among environmental (primarily social), behavioral, and biological processes (e.g., Cairns, Gariepy, & Hood, 1990; Gottlieb, 1991, 1992). In these models, biological functions set the stage for behavioral adaptation to environmental challenge. At the same time, environmental challenges may induce behavioral change that in turn affects fast-acting (e.g., hormone secretion) and slower-responding (gene expression) biological processes. Biological activities that facilitate a particular behavioral response, and behavioral activities that set the stage for changes in biological processes, may be stimulated or attenuated by environmental challenges (immediately or at some earlier stage in the individual's life). Evidence suggests that these interacting factors are capable of affecting differences in developmental trajectories, even for individuals with the same genetic constitution (e.g., identical twins).

Hereafter we focus on topics addressed by family scholars for which methodologically sound biosocial research has advanced knowledge on the topic and for which further research has the potential to yield new information. We focus primarily on behavioral endocrinology and behavioral genetics but briefly cover studies from evolutionary psychology and behavioral pharmacology. Following a primer on each biological topic, this article is organized around the family themes of parenthood, early child development and parent-child relations, adolescents and parent-child relations, courtship and mate selection, and marital and intimate relations. We conclude with notes on next steps in biosocial research and on how family scholars can become involved.

Primer on Biological Connections

Behavioral Endocrinology

The endocrine system produces several hundred hormones and releases them in response to signals from the brain, either nerve signals or other blood-borne chemical messengers. Hormones are chemical messengers that regulate, integrate, and control bodily functions by turning gene expression (influences) on or off. Hormones mediate both short-term processes, such as immediate responses to stress (e.g., fight or flight), and longer-term processes, such as growth, development, and reproduction. Researchers are interested in basal as well as reactive levels of hormones. Behavioral endocrinology is in the forefront of the integration of biological measures into studies of children and families because recent research has shown that hormones may play an integral role in furthering our understanding of individual differences in developmental trajectories, family relationships, and factors that mediate these processes. One of the reasons behavioral endocrinology is at the forefront is that technical advances have made possible the assessment of many important hormones in saliva (Kirschbaum, Read, & Hellhammer, 1992). For introductory reading on the operation of the endocrine system and its role in regulating many aspects of human biology and behavior, we recommend Nelson (1999). The following hormones are discussed in this review.

Testosterone is one of several androgens produced by the endocrine system. Men produce levels several times higher than do women. In women, the primary sources are the ovaries and the adrenal glands, whereas in men the sources are the testes and the adrenal glands. The hormone is implicated in the development of secondary sexual characteristics, reproduction, dominant behavior (which is sometimes antisocial and aggressive), and interest in activities that are traditionally masculine. It also plays an important role in men's competitive activities that involve gaining, maintaining, and losing social status (Mazur & Booth, 1998).

Dehydroepiandrosterone (DHEA) is a hormone produced by the adrenal glands that has a wide range of effects and is a precursor of other hormones. Preliminary studies indicate a possible association with health risk behavior (i.e., alcohol use and smoking), cognitive abilities, and emotionality. There are dramatic developmental differences in DHEA; levels are very low until about age 6 (adrenarche), and then it increases through age 15. In prepubertal children and in females, peripheral conversion of DHEA is the major pathway for testosterone production and may be an early marker for physiological development (McClintock & Herdt, 1996).

Oxytocin affects a variety of cognitive, grooming, affiliative, sexual, maternal, and reproductive behaviors. It is known to be important in parturition and lactation and may be implicated in maternal-infant interactions (Turner, Altemus, Enos, Cooper, & McGuinness, 1999).

Estradiol is the primary female reproductive hormone. It is implicated in the onset of puberty, menstruation, sexual and reproductive capacity, pregnancy, and menopause. It is associated with maternal behavior and may be important to general social affiliative behavior as well (Fleming, Rube, Krieger, & Wong, 1997).

Cortisol is an endocrine product that enables individuals to adapt to the vicissitudes of life and to environmental changes. Men and women produce the same amount of cortisol. Cortisol regulates metabolism, the fight-flight response, immune activity, sensory acuity, and aspects of learning and memory. Cortisol is particularly interesting because its levels are affected by a variety of environmental processes (the amount of social, physical, and immune stimuli; Stansbury & Gunnar, 1994).

Behavioral Genetics

Behavioral genetics is the study of the relative contribution of genes and the environment to individual differences in behavior. The amount of genetic influence may be derived from the correlation of a behavioral measurement within pairs of siblings with known differences in genetic relatedness. For example, the correlation of antisocial behavior within pairs of identical (monozygotic) twins, who share 100% of their genes, is compared with the correlation within pairs of fraternal (dizygotic) twins, who share 50% of their genes. In one study (Reiss, 1995), the correlation for identical twins was .81, whereas for fraternal twins it was .62. To estimate the genetic influence, the difference between the two correlations is multiplied by 2 (2 × .19 = .38). In this example, 38% of the variance in antisocial behavior may be

attributed to genetic influences. Studies typically employ multiple sibling pairs (full siblings, half siblings, adopted siblings, siblings from blended families), multiple measures of the same phenomena (child estimates, parent estimates, teacher estimates), and structural equation modeling to determine the fit between genetic relatedness and measures of behavior (Neale & Cardon, 1992; Plomin, 1994).

Environmental contributions are parceled out to those shared by siblings (e.g., home, parents, family wealth, parents' education) and those not shared and which make siblings from the same family different from one another (e.g., parental treatment, sibling gender and age, peers, teachers). The distinction between shared and nonshared environment is important because the influence of the latter is stronger and increases throughout the life course. The portion of variance that is shared can be obtained by subtracting the heritability estimate from the identical twin correlation. In the above example, 43% of the variation would be from shared factors (.81–.38). The remaining variance (19%) would be the effect of the influence of the nonshared environment. A powerful method of estimating genetic influence involves estimating differences in behavior among identical twins who have been reared together versus those who have been reared apart. With a few exceptions, results across methods are similar (Rowe, 1994).

Knowledge about the ways genes influence behavior is limited. Complex sets of genes are instrumental in influencing such things as intelligence and antisocial behavior. Nonetheless, it is unlikely that genes are specifically coded for IQ or criminal behavior. Rather, genes affect such things as memory or speed of processing in the case of intelligence, and impulse control and sensation seeking in the case of antisocial behavior. Some genetic influence is passive, derived from the fact that parents and children share genes. Smart kids live in parent-designed, intellectually challenging environments. Some genetic influence is reactive, stemming from the way parents and others respond to genetically influenced behavior. Antisocial behavior may cause parents to be less affectionate. Finally, some genetic influence is active, that is, genetically influenced behaviors cause children to seek and create environments that in turn affect their behavior. The risk-taking child may seek like-minded individuals as friends.

Two lines of research are of interest to family researchers: one focuses on genetic contributions to measures of family environments (stemming from reactive and active processes); and the other focuses on the way in which environmental factors moderate the expression of genetically influenced behavior. In the former, variance in such independent variables as the home environment, parenting styles, offspring's television viewing, and characteristics of peer groups are subject to genetic influences—especially as the child matures and exercises more control over his or her environment (Scarr & McCartney, 1983). Research on the factors that moderate by amplifying and reducing genetic influences include historical and cohort variables, as well as parenting practices. For example, authoritative parenting may reduce genetic influences, whereas laissez faire practices may increase them.

There are two reasons for introducing genetics into family studies. The first is to correctly identify the source of change in variables such as cognitive development and antisocial behavior to avoid attributing genetic influences to environmental ones and vice versa. The clinical and programmatic significance of this knowledge is that intervention strategies can be targeted to those aspects of the environment that can be altered. The second reason to consider genetic variables is to develop better fitting models to explain dependent variables. Those interested in expanding their understanding of behavioral genetics should read articles by Reiss (1995) and Plomin (1995).

Evolutionary Psychology

Evolutionary psychology focuses on (a) behavior that has enhanced genetic replication in past generations and (b) the way in which contemporary behavior effects reproductive success. In humans, women tend to invest more in offspring than do men and tend to be more selective in their choice of mates—mostly on the basis of men's willingness and ability to make a parental contribution. Men tend to invest less in parenting and may increase their chances of passing on their genetic material by being more promiscuous and concerned about the fidelity of their mates. One example of such behavior is the finding that when compared with biological offspring, stepchildren elect to leave or are "pushed out" of their home earlier (White & Booth, 1985). This may be attributable to the stepparent's lack of desire to invest in children who do not have his or her genetic material.

Theory and research on evolutionary psychol-

ogy interests family scholars because there is evidence that it affects virtually every aspect of family life. Mate selection and offspring-parent relations, as well as topics such as the quality and stability of stepfamilies, family violence, incest, and the impact of the support capability of the environment, are all considered under the rubric of evolutionary psychology. For introductory reading, we suggest Buss and Schmitt (1993), Daly and Wilson (1983), and Davis and Daly (1997).

Behavioral Psychopharmacology and the Family

Progress made in describing the biological processes involved in regulating behavior has led to breakthroughs in the design and availability of drugs that stimulate or attenuate those processes. Examples include hormone-replacement therapies (i.e., testosterone, estradiol) to resolve midlife changes in negative moods, attitudes, and behavior; Viagra to address impotence and sexual dysfunction; Prozac for affective disorder; and Ritalin for disruptive behavior disorders of childhood. With the exception of Ritalin (Barkley, 1989), little is known about the effect of these agents on family relationships. Although space limitations prevent us from dealing with this topic, family researchers should be on alert for novel opportunities to test and develop theoretical models by studying the impact of the behavioral, cognitive, and attitudinal changes induced by these medications within the broader social ecology of the family.

One of the challenges facing biosocial research is that investigators in each of the fields involved (behavioral endocrinology, behavioral genetics, evolutionary psychology, behavioral psychopharmacology) tend not to be concerned about the other. Their practitioners rarely cite one another. Moreover, they seldom draw on the other fields to help explain the imponderables in their own work. The biosocial sciences can benefit from heeding Wilson's (1998) call for greater unification of the social and biological sciences.

PARENTHOOD

Biosocial research has focused on numerous aspects of becoming a parent. Evolutionary psychology is implicated in establishing a mating relationship. Hormones are examined with respect to the decision to have children, as well as decisions about the timing of sexual intercourse and parenting behavior following birth.

Establishing a Stable Sexual Relationship

To ensure survival, a period of several years of intense parental care is required. By the time they are age 3 or 4 children stand a good chance of reaching adulthood, and the need for intense care wanes. Humans ensure the needed care by establishing monogamous relationships, whereas most other primates do so through other forms of social organization. Compared with men, women are much more discriminating because future investment in offspring will be higher. Women select mates partly based on the resources they control and partly on the resources they can bring to bear on the support of the mother and her offspring (Daly & Wilson, 1983).

Cashdan (1995) added another dimension to reproductive strategies by taking into account women's dominance, status, and access to resources, some of which are associated with the hormone testosterone. Cashdan's research indicated that women with higher testosterone-associated dominance are less in need of a partner and are less selective in the sense they have more sexual partners and are less likely to agree with the statement, "I would not want to have sex with a man unless I am convinced that he is serious about a long-term commitment." On the other hand, women with low testosterone levels who expect or need partner involvement will be more selective and engage in behavior that is more likely to attract a man, such as minimizing assertiveness and sexual activity to assure the man that her offspring are his.

The Decision to Have Children

The decision to have a child is not well understood socially or biologically. Testosterone may be implicated. In a study explaining a wide range of gendered behavior in 250 women aged 27–30, Udry, Morris, and Kovenock (1995) found high testosterone related to a wide range of nontraditional behaviors related to the family, including not marrying, assigning a lower priority to marrying, having fewer children, and enjoying childcare activities less. It would appear that women's decisions to have a child may be related, in part, to basal levels of testosterone.

Not yet examined is whether female engagement in more competitive, aggressive, independent, or solitary activities, or activities with unrelated men, further increases testosterone. If so, it suggests a feedback mechanism that may help explain participation in parenting. Furthermore, the role of estradiol and other hormones related to reproduction remain to be explored as factors influencing decisions to have children. Whether testosterone or some other hormone influences men's decisions to have children is unknown.

Research supports a moderate heritable component for fertility expectations and desires. Rodgers and Doughty (in press) used the National Longitudinal Study of Youth to investigate ideal, desired, and expected family size. Findings suggest that both fertility expectations and completed fertility have a heritable component, although expectations have a higher level of genetic influence than do outcomes.

Timing of Sexual Intercourse

The role of biological processes in the timing of sexual intercourse is central to parenting. Females of all nonhuman mammals exhibit hormonally related signs of receptivity (visual, pheromonal, behavioral, and combinations of these) at the time of ovulation. The research on humans has been less consistent, mostly because of the difficulty in collecting enough data throughout the menstrual cycle. The only study showing that all the links are present (Van Goozen, Weigant, Endert, Helmond, & Van de Poll, 1997) focused on sexually active, normally, and regularly menstruating women who were not on the pill. Blood samples were obtained every other day, as were measures of sexual activity and mood. Testosterone and estradiol were highest at the ovulatory phase, as were female-initiated sexual activity and interest in sexual activity. It appears that hormones and sexual activity are greatest when women were most likely to conceive. Still, much has to be learned about signals linking the hormones and sexual behavior. Potentially contributing to the functioning of this intricate pattern of linkages between hormones and behavior is interest in having children, early experience with infants or young children, or harsh environments that threaten infant viability. These topics warrant research.

Parenting Behavior Following Birth

Parenting behavior shortly after birth is linked to biological factors. During pregnancy, many hormones are elevated to levels much higher than at any other time in life. Within weeks of birth mothers' hormone levels decline to normal levels. In cases where postpartum decline in estradiol is gradual, mothers report a greater feeling of attachment to their infants (Fleming, Ruble, Krieger, & Wong, 1997). This may be because estradiol triggers the production of oxytocin (Uvnas-Moberg, 1997), which appears to be implicated in mother's preoccupation with their infant children (Lechman & Mayes, 1998) and in their calm feelings while breast-feeding (Altemus, Deuster, Galliven, Carter, & Gold, 1995). Apparently, breast-feeding itself is a factor in the amount and quality of mother-child interaction. A comparison study indicated that mothers exposed to sucking during skin-to-skin contact shortly after birth talked to their babies more and spent more time with them than did mothers just experiencing skin-to-skin contact (Widstrom et al., 1990). Thus, the links among oxytocin, breast-feeding, and maternal care appear to be important in parent-child relations. Another study implicates the hormone prolactin, as well as oxytocin. Comparisons of women 4 days postpartum and a control group indicated these hormones were associated with lower levels of muscular tension, anxiety, and aggression (Uvnas-Moberg, Widstrom, Nissen, & Bjorvell, 1990). In men, a drop in basal testosterone immediately following the birth of a child has been noted (Storey, Walsh, Quinton, & Wynne-Edwards, in press). This may increase feelings of nurturing on the part of the father. Whether these biological factors continue to play a role as the child develops is not known.

Progress has been made in identifying important biosocial relationships in many phases of becoming a parent. Evolutionary factors that contribute to producing viable offspring have been identified in mate selection. Genetic influences have a role in fertility preferences. Hormones may be important in establishing unions that increase the chances of offspring survival, creating interest in having children, setting the timing of sexual intercourse, and shaping the quality of infant care. The research to date is largely descriptive, however, and little is known about direction of effects or pathways of influence.

EARLY CHILD DEVELOPMENT AND PARENT-CHILD RELATIONS

Hormonal and genetic factors are implicated in the development of gendered behavior and other aspects of cogitative development. They also are linked to the development of the parent-infant bond.

Gendered Behavior

Prenatal testosterone production (and perhaps other androgens) during the second trimester of pregnancy affects gendered behavior in adult female offspring in their late 20s (Udry et al., 1995). Gendered behavior refers to one in which males and females differ. More than 20 different measures were used to examine gendered behavior, including such things as marriage, number of births, domestic division of labor, feminine appearance, vocational interests, employment in male-dominated occupations, and personality measures. In this bipolar concept of gender, the higher the score, the more feminine the individual. Using this same data, Udry (1999) found that the greater the mother's testosterone, the smaller the effect of daughter's testosterone on adult-gendered behavior. Moreover, the greater the prenatal (mother's) testosterone, the less sensitive the female child was (during the teen years) to the mother's socialization efforts with respect to feminine behavior. This is probably because the early androgen exposure permanently organizes the brain. Female adolescents with low exposure to prenatal androgen were much more responsive to parental socialization efforts.

The development of gender differences in young children is clear and predictable, with boys preferring aggressive rough and tumble play and traditionally masculine toys and girls preferring more sedentary activities and gender-specific toys. Androgens appear to be implicated in defining the behavior. Most of the research linking hormones and play comes from studies of children with hormone-related disorders (e.g., females with congenital adrenal hyperplasia are exposed to very high levels of androgens from their adrenal glands, and males with idiopathic hypogonadotropic hypogonadalism generate very low levels of androgens). These studies are valuable because they represent essentially natural experiments that randomly assign an affected child and a control sibling to experimental and control conditions. Nonetheless, they may not represent how these processes occur in the population at large (see Collaer and Hines, 1995, for detailed review of the research).

Cognitive Development

A study of genetic influences on the home environment and on its relationship with cognitive development in 1- and 2-year-old children reveals substantial influences (Braungart, Fulker, & Plomin, 1992). The study compares adopted sibling pairs with a matched sample of sibling pairs living with biological parents. The home environment was measured by the Home Observation for Measure of Environment (HOME) scale, which estimates the intellectual resources (e.g., books and other stimulating resources along with material responsiveness and stimulation) available in the home. Cognitive development was measured by the Mental Development Index (MDI). More than one third of the variance in the HOME scores was accounted for by genetic influences, and approximately half the HOME-MDI relationship was mediated by genetic influences. Thus, offspring genetics plays an important role in the family intellectual environment, even in infancy.

Parent-Child Attachment

Research suggests that infant and early childhood experiences alter short- and long-term patterns of cortisol production. Maternal separation, for example, affects the threshold for cortisol production as well as the size of the cortisol increase (Gunnar, Mangelsdorf, Larsen, & Herstgaard, 1998). Young children with histories of child abuse tend to have atypical cortisol profiles throughout the day (Hart, Gunnar, & Cicchetti, 1995). Even cultural differences in care-giving and child-rearing practices (such as maternal emphasis on emotional expression, consistency in daily schedules, and degree of stimulation) are linked to cortisol profiles in infants (Super, Harkness, & Granger, preliminary data). Studies of institutionalized Romanian orphans indicate that severe social and tactile deprivation in early childhood may result in disruption of the circadian pattern of cortisol production (Carlson & Earls, 1997).

In middle childhood, traumatic events within the family are significant sources of cortisol activation for children. Children from families with high levels of conflict, punishment, serious quarreling, and fighting tend to have the highest cortisol levels (Flynn & England, 1995). Cortisol production increases in response to changes in family composition, such as men migrating in and out of the household for seasonal work opportunities, as well as for children living with a stepfather or distant relatives (Flynn & England, 1995).

The patterns of cortisol production noted above (e.g., basal level, response threshold, size of increase, and daily pattern) have the potential for affecting numerous aspects of child development.

Children's cortisol increase resulting from parent-child conflict is associated with high levels of offspring social difficulties, withdrawal, anxiety, and a low sense of control related-beliefs (Granger, Weisz, & Kauneckis, 1994). In addition, cortisol increases are associated with internalizing behavior problems, symptoms of anxiety disorders, and negative patterns of control-related beliefs (Granger, Weisz, McCracken, Ikeda, & Douglas, 1996). Children's low basal cortisol also is associated with maternal dysfunction and psychopathology and parenting stress, and interrelationships between mother and child cortisol levels (Granger et al., 1998). Taken together, these studies suggest that the individual differences in children's cortisol response to features of the family environment contribute to children's behavioral adjustment and development.

No doubt part of the relationship between cortisol response and family relationships has genetic origins. For example, genetic influences have been observed for several measures of parenting behavior that would affect mother-child attachment. They include parental warmth (Braungart, 1994), affection, punitive parenting (Plomin, Reiss, Hetherington, & Howe, 1994), expressiveness (Plomin, McClearn, Pedersen, Nesselroade, & Bergeman, 1988), and inconsistency (Braungart, 1994). Most of these findings are from twin studies.

Evolutionary psychology also suggests how parental interest in reproductive success influences parent-child attachment in infants. There is evidence that parents are reluctant to invest in newborns if the offspring is of poor quality and unlikely to survive or there is little food or few other resources such that infant care would threaten the reproducing pair or older children. Fathers are reluctant to support newborns if they have doubts about the paternity of the child. Stepparents who have no genetic investment in the child are more inclined to abuse their children than are biological parents (Daly & Wilson, 1988).

Both hormones and genetic influences on measures of the family environment are implicated in the cognitive development of infants. Cortisol has a major role responding to and defining the parent-child bond, as well as offspring internalizing and externalizing behavior. An intergenerational component appears to be in evidence. Behavioral genetic research indicates that offspring genes influence numerous aspects of the family environment. Evolutionary psychology helps us understand aspects of the dark side of parent-child bonds. Given the range of biological influences, integrated studies are needed to understand how early development is linked to the three biological models.

LATER CHILD DEVELOPMENT AND PARENT-CHILD RELATIONS

Adolescent dominance, aggression, and sexual behavior, along with antisocial behavior and depression, appear to have biological links. Special attention is given to gender differences in the link between testosterone and behavior. In addition to children's genetic effects on the environment, we also consider the way environment moderates genetic influences.

Sexual Development

Although puberty is evident around age 12 for girls and age 14 for boys—a time when gonadal development is clearly apparent—the organization of the process is established prenatally. Recent research suggests the early stages of puberty begin at age 6, when the adrenal cortex begins to mature and secrete low levels of the hormone DHEA. The metabolism of DHEA leads to the production of both testosterone and estradiol (McClintock & Herdt, 1996). By age 10, DHEA production is significant and corresponds with children's first sexual attraction, sexual fantasy, and sexual activity. DHEA is a much-overlooked marker with a wide range of behavioral, cognitive, and neural effects. As a precursor to potent hormones such as estradiol and testosterone, its effects may be much larger than current research suggests.

Dominance and Aggression

The period of adolescence is marked by physiological changes, in addition to a withdrawal (sometimes estrangement) from the family of origin, increased involvement with peers, and an increase in dominance and aggression for both boys and girls. Much of the testosterone and estradiol production goes toward organizing physiological development but some is manifested in behavior. One study of boys in childhood and early adolescence (ages 6 to 13) suggests that taking body mass as well as testosterone into account differentially predicts dominance and aggression (Tremblay et al., 1998). Increasing testosterone and body mass predict dominance, but only body mass predicts physical aggression. Thus, the relation between testosterone and physical aggression in

this age group (and perhaps others) may be moderated by body mass. Boys with greater body mass may elicit aggression or find it easier to deal with individuals by being aggressive. Further research is needed to determine whether the relationship holds true for girls.

There remains the question of whether it is hormones or some other variable that produces changes in dominance (and possibly aggression). Evidence that hormones produce the change may be found in a randomized, double-blind, placebo-controlled crossover study of 35 boys and 14 girls who were in treatment for pubertal delay. Administrations of hormones to males and females were followed by an increase in physically aggressive behaviors and impulses but not verbal aggression (Finkelstein et al., 1997). It is noteworthy, however, that there is substantially less information regarding the link between testosterone and dominance in female subjects.

Sexual Behavior

Testosterone change in boys is also associated with changes in sexual behavior. A longitudinal study of 82 boys 12–13 years of age assessed over three years linked normal changes in testosterone with changes in sexual behavior. Monthly changes in saliva testosterone and weekly reports of sexual activity revealed that increases in testosterone were associated with coital initiation, frequency of coitus, and the rising incidence of other sexual behavior (Halpern, Udry, & Suchindran, 1998). Noteworthy is another study of this same sample that found serum testosterone collected semiannually and cumulative reports of sexual behavior over a 3-year period were unrelated. The more frequent collection of testosterone in saliva (which represents an estimate of the biologically active hormone in blood that is available to affect behavior) and improved measure of sexual activity detected changes not revealed in the earlier study. This suggests that longitudinal studies of behavior should make frequent assessments and measure free testosterone so that specific changes can be linked to alterations in behavior close to the time at which they occur.

A behavioral genetics study indicated a moderating effect of environmental factors on the heritability of the age of onset of sexual intercourse. Dunne et al. (1997) showed that genetic factors explained more of the variance in age at first sexual intercourse for a younger cohort (born 1952–1965) of twins than for an older cohort (born

1922–1952). Effects were interpreted to mean that parents of younger twins exercised less social control over offspring behavior.

Sex Differences

It is clear that there are marked gender differences in the link between testosterone and risky or nonconforming behavior. Although androgens result in increased interest in such behavior, Udry (1988) demonstrated that social controls (father presence and participation in sports) reduced the relationship between testosterone and sexual activity among adolescent girls, whereas these same controls had little impact on the testosterone–sexual-behavior link among boys. The differential impact of social controls on boys and girls suggests that although there are similarities in the hormone-behavior link (e.g., interest in sex and masculine behavior), there are important differences that require exploration.

Nowhere is this more evident than in studies of competition among male subjects. Testosterone is shown to rise in anticipation of competition. Following competition, testosterone remains high or climbs further in winners but drops in losers (Booth, Johnson, & Granger, 1989), a finding that has been replicated numerous times. Nonetheless, testosterone does not have the same role in female competitors. There is no anticipatory rise in female competitors, nor does winning and losing affect testosterone production (Mazur, Susman, & Edelbrock, 1997). In a pilot study (Booth & Dabbs, 1996), it appears that cortisol was implicated in the preparation for and outcome of competitive events. Although untested, DHEA also may have a role in female competition because it is a precursor of testosterone.

The relevance of competition studies to families is that family members confer and take away status from one another. For example, the preferential treatment of one child over another is a way of giving status to one and taking it away from another. Children who receive more favorable treatment may experience an increase in testosterone, which is then expressed in more dominating behavior toward the less favored sibling. Giving and withholding support from spouse in family problem solving is another way status is gained and lost that, in turn, could affect hormone production and may then affect the quality of subsequent family interaction. Given the paucity of research on competing women, it is uncertain how and which hormones may be involved in the conferring and taking away of status from female family members.

Parental Relations, Adolescent Depression, and Antisocial Behavior

Genetically influenced characteristics of children also affect aspects of adolescent family environment. Significant genetic influences were found for children's and parents' ratings of positive factors (such as warmth, support, empathy, and mutual involvement in enjoyable activities), as well as for negative factors (such as frequency and intensity of disputes and feelings of anger). No influence was observed for control as assessed by monitoring offspring activities (Plomin et al., 1994; Rowe, 1981, 1983). Significant nonshared influences also were noted.

In an analysis of the impact of parents' negativity (anger, coercion, and conflict) on adolescent depression (as assessed by three scales) and antisocial behavior (measured from the Behavioral Problems Index antisocial scale), significant nonshared environment, as well as genetic contributions, were observed for the independent variable and the dependent variables (Pike, McGuire, Hetherington, Reiss, & Plomin, 1996). The nonshared environment contribution was modest in comparison with the genetic influence, accounting for nearly two thirds of the contribution. Moreover, the genetic influence accounts for most of the relation between parents' negativity and adolescent adjustment.

Genetic studies also reveal that environmental factors moderate the genetic influence on adolescent depression and antisocial behavior. Among adopted twins without a biological risk of antisocial behavior (as measured by having a biological parent without an antisocial personality disorder), the correlation between the family environment and becoming antisocial was trivial among those growing up in an adverse family environment. In contrast, among twins with a biological risk, there was a strong correlation between an adverse family environment and antisocial behavior (Cadoret, Yates, Troughtoh, Woodworth, & Stewart, 1995). In other words, children without genetic risk for antisocial behavior do not manifest such behavior, even in adverse environments, whereas children with a genetic predisposition are much more likely to display antisocial behavior in adverse environments than in more positive environments. A similar finding was observed among twins with and without a biological risk of depression. In this case, the interaction was between being at risk for depression and experiencing stressful life events (Kendler et al., 1995).

Transition to Adulthood

Studies have illustrated the implications of hormone production in youth for problems in adulthood. Numerous adolescents engage in antisocial or deviant behavior. For a few, it extends into adulthood; for others, it is limited to adolescence (Moffitt, 1993). One study revealed that adolescent boys who had been expelled or suspended from school, ran away from home, fought, stole, or were arrested were far more likely to commit a crime as an adult if they had high levels of testosterone than if their testosterone production was average or below (Booth & Osgood, 1993). Social factors such as marriage and full-time employment tended to dampen the impact of testosterone on adult male antisocial behavior. Another study using the same sample of men demonstrated that high testosterone is related to low occupational status and periods of unemployment (Dabbs, 1992). Testosterone-related low occupational success was attributable in part to testosterone-related antisocial behavior during adolescence that got the young men into trouble at school.

Still another study suggests that father's testosterone may be linked to parent-child relationships. Julian, McKenry, and McKelvey (1990) found that fathers with low testosterone had a better quality relationship with offspring 12–18 years of age than did high-testosterone men. Thus, part of the research agenda facing us is to address the issue of why testosterone is related to antisocial behavior in some individuals but not in others. What personal experiences and environmental factors explain the differential impact of the hormone?

One of the few areas of study that combines behavioral endocrinology, genetics, and evolutionary psychology stems from an investigation by Belsky, Steinberg, and Draper (1991), which proposes that early family relationships that are harsh, rejecting, and opportunistic (versus sensitive, supportive, and rewarding) result in an earlier onset of puberty that leads to a precocious and promiscuous reproductive strategy. Although early studies produced mixed results, recent longitudinal studies have clarified the causal paths. There is a genetic influence in that mother's early marriage and childbearing accounts for part of the

early onset of daughter's puberty (Ellis & Garber, in press). This study reveals that the mother's low-quality romantic relationship with the biological father, stepfather, or boyfriend has an independent effect on the early onset of puberty, as does the presence of a stepfather or boyfriend. The authors suggest that the effect of the presence of an unrelated man may be similar to that observed in studies of other mammals in which pheromones produced by the unrelated adult male accelerate female pubertal maturation (Sanders & Reinisch, 1990). A second longitudinal study suggests that positive care giving from the biological father plays a unique and pivotal role in delaying pubertal development (Ellis, Dodge, Pettit, & Bates, in press). Mother's care giving was found to be redundant of paternal involvement. Further research is needed to clarify the mechanisms involved and to more precisely estimate genetic influences on pubertal maturation.

Hormones have a particularly strong influence on adolescent development. They are related to social dominance and reproductive behavior but seem to have different effects on boys and girls. Testosterone appears to influence behavior that is eventually expressed in adult antisocial behavior and poor socioeconomic achievement. Environmental factors are found to be important moderators of genetic influences on adjustment. Studies combining biosocial models add to our understanding of the onset of female puberty and subsequent promiscuous behavior.

COURTSHIP AND MATE SELECTION

Among the most fascinating—but also puzzling—recent findings are those that suggest an association between a basic feature of the immune system and the process of selecting a mate. Immunologists long ago identified basic features of our cells that enable the immune system to recognize self versus other and subsequently eliminate potentially damaging molecules it determines as other. The basic feature of this part of the immune system is proteins found on cell surfaces called human leukocyte antigens (HLA) or the major histocompatibility complex (MHC). Put simply, the MHC defines for each person a unique "immunological fingerprint." Recent findings suggest that interpersonal cues signal information about individual differences in MHC. Humans can detect individual differences in odors (sweat) associated with MHC, which influence decisions regarding mate selection and perceived attractiveness (Wedekind,

Seebeck, Bettens, & Paepke, 1995). In other words, mate selection might be influenced by olfactory or other cues that signal immunological differences. The greater the immunological differences, the greater the chances of producing a viable infant. Inbreeding avoidance may be the most important function of MHC-associated mating preferences (Potts, Manning, & Wakeland, 1994). Studies of mice suggest that MHC preferences come about through imprinting (Yamazaki et al., 1988). Infants learn how their own MHC type smells, and evolutionary forces have evolved a preference for dissimilar types.

It is of interest that scores of studies find behavioral and social similarity important to understanding mate selection. Winch, Ktsanes, and Ktsanes's (1954) theory of complementary needs never received much support (e.g., Udry, 1964). The MHC studies draw family scholars back to exploring complementarity, albeit in a different form, as an explanatory variable.

This preference for immunological differences would certainly help to explain mate selection studies of Kibbutz marriages and Chinese arranged marriages. Shepher (1971) studied mate selection in Israel Kibbutz where from the time of birth, children were raised in child-care facilities. Parents saw them a few hours a day, but most of the time they were with the care providers and other children. Shepher observed that, upon reaching adulthood, individuals never married someone from the same facility. Wolf (1995) studied arranged marriages in China that took place in the early part of this century. Marriages were often arranged when children were very young. In some communities, the female child would go to live in the male's home where she was treated as one of the children. In other communities, the female remained with the birth parents until mature, whereupon she moved to the male's family. Compared with those who did not reside together until maturity, the couples who lived together as children had unsuccessful marriages. Many were never consummated, and few had children. Men were consistently unfaithful and had children with mistresses. For MHC preferences to be the explanatory mechanism in these studies, we would need evidence of imprinting (akin to the mouse studies) to explain the rejection of kibbutz-mates and sons of foster families.

Family researchers should find this work of interest not only because of its relation to mate preferences and incest avoidance, but also because of its relation to birth outcomes. For example, HLA similarity has been associated with repeated spontaneous abortions (Thomas, Harger, Wagener, Rabin, & Gill, 1985), and lower birth weight (Ober et al., 1987).

Students of contraceptive use also will find the HLA studies of interest. Estradiol reduces women's ability to discriminate immunological differences among potential mates. High estradiol may be found among pregnant women and women on "the pill." A modern contraceptive method may be resulting in poor mate selection from the standpoint of producing children who are less likely to survive. The inability of these women to detect appropriate mates may affect the stability of courtship relationships. Cohabiting pill users have significantly higher rates of union dissolution (controlling for a wide assortment of suspected covariates) than other nonhormonal-based contraceptors (Carver, 1998).

Developments in another line of research bear watching because of their relevance to mate selection. Faces judged to have above average symmetry are regarded as more attractive. Facial symmetry may be associated with greater immunological competence and increased gene variation, which means that mating with such individuals would increase the chances of infant survival (Gangestad & Buss, 1993; Gangestad & Thornhill, 1998; Grammar & Thornhill, 1994; Mitton, 1993; Thornhill & Gangestad, 1993). Preference for masculine facial features has been observed to vary during the phase of the menstrual cycle. When conception is most likely, women prefer less masculine faces than during the rest of the menstrual cycle (Penton-Voak et al., 1999). The masculine faces may signal immunological competence, whereas the less masculine faces may indicate paternal interest and investment in offspring. Gangestad and Simpson (in press) integrate these findings into a theory that suggests women vary their reproductive strategy according to the harshness of the environment. When the environment is difficult, women place more weight on indications of genetic fitness than they do when the environment is less demanding. How these findings, if borne out by subsequent studies, would play out in mate selection or extra-pair sexual relationships is deserving of study.

The integration of measures of basic features of the immune system into mate selection and courtship research serves to increase understanding of incest avoidance, contraceptive use, and unstable courtship relations as they relate to the evolutionary need to produce viable offspring.

Testosterone's links to marrying and divorcing are considered first, followed by reports of research on the relationship between marital quality and testosterone. Genetic influences on divorce are considered, as is the association between marital conflict and immunity.

Marital Status

In the preceding section, several biological mechanisms were suggested that may define marital relationship quality and stability. Insight is obtained from evidence that testosterone levels in men drop after they marry. In a 10-year longitudinal study of Air Force officers who underwent four physical exams over that period of time, Mazur and Michalek (1998) were able to compare changes in testosterone with changes in marital status. Unmarried men's testosterone levels were high, but following marriage, they decreased. One scenario is that single men are mostly in the company of other men, and everyday competition (some of which may be over women) keeps testosterone levels elevated (e.g., Booth, Shelly, Mazur, Tharp, & Kittok, 1989). Once married, exposure to other men declined, and the need to compete for women disappeared. Another scenario is that the marriage itself lowered testosterone—similar to what was observed after the birth of an infant. Wives expect men to behave in supportive and nurturing ways, and lowering testosterone may be crucial to successfully enacting the caring spousal and parent roles. Alternatively, biological messages (e.g., pheromones) having to do with sex or reproduction may cause testosterone to decrease.

Relationship Quality

Even though marriage is accompanied by a drop in testosterone, hormones may still be related to marital quality. An analysis of men from a representative sample of 4,462 former military servicemen between the ages of 33 and 42 showed that men with higher testosterone production were less likely to marry in the first place; once married, they were more likely to divorce (Booth & Dabbs, 1993). The likelihood of never marrying was 50% higher for men whose testosterone levels were one standard deviation above the mean compared with those whose testosterone levels were one standard deviation below the mean. Similarly, men at the higher level were 43% more likely to

divorce than were those at the lower level. Once married, men with higher testosterone levels were 31% more likely to leave home because of a troubled relationship with their wife, 38% more likely to have extra-marital sex, and 13% more likely to report hitting or throwing things at their spouse. In addition, high-testosterone men were more likely to report low-quality marital interaction, a finding supported by Julian and McKenry (1989). These findings were net of other social variables such as low socioeconomic status or deviant behavior in other arenas. It is important to note, however, that substantial numbers of men with high testosterone had excellent marriages. The mechanism that explains this differential marital success is unknown. There is also the caveat that cross-sectional studies do not clarify whether conflictual marriages raise testosterone.

On the other hand, marriage does play a protective role with respect to the link between testosterone and antisocial behavior and depression. Men with high testosterone levels are at risk of committing a crime and being depressed. Marriage, along with steady employment, reduces the likelihood of both (Booth, Johnson, & Granger, 1999; Booth & Osgood, 1993). Because these studies are based on cross-sectional data, it is not possible to estimate the causal ordering of the variables. The work of Mazur and Michalek (1998) and Gubernick, Worthman, and Stallings (1991) has suggested that marriage may reduce the likelihood that high-testosterone men commit crimes and get depressed. The nature of the mechanism is unclear, however.

We know little about hormones and women's marriages. Having low levels of testosterone may be important to relationship quality, or quality may be associated with hormones associated with reproduction, such as estradiol or oxytocin. Equally important is dyadic research on marital partners to see how hormone-behavior links in one individual are related to hormone-behavior links in the spouse.

Genetics and Divorce

Given that divorce rates are so consistent from society to society (Goode, 1993), it is not surprising that a number of studies have shown genes to influence divorce. Estimates of the heritability of divorce have ranged from .26 (Turkheimer, Lovett, Robinette, & Gottesman, 1992) to .53 (Jockin, McGue, & Lykken, 1996; McGue & Lykken, 1992). Jockin et al. (1996) hypothesized that personality traits play a key role. They demonstrated that between 30% and 42% of the heritability of divorce risk comes from genetic factors affecting personality. This finding is supported by a study of the association between parent and offspring divorce indicating that behavior problems mediate a significant share of the link (Amato, 1996). Analysis is needed that combines methods used by family researchers (survival analysis) with behavior genetics methods to explain the genetic mediation of divorce (e.g., Meyer, Eaves, Heath, & Martin, 1991).

The consequences of divorce for children may also have genetic origins. In a large-scale study of divorce, Block, Block, and Gjerde (1986) and Cherlin and colleagues (1991) both demonstrated that boys' elevated risk for behavior problems observed after divorce disappeared when behavior problems many years before divorce were controlled. Although Cherlin, Chase-Lansdale, and McRae (1998) demonstrated in a later study that the gap between children from divorced and nondivorced families widened as children moved into young adulthood, there remains a significant amount of unexplained variance. It is possible that the behavior problems of the boys before and after divorce are related because of underlying enduring personality characteristics and not because a high-conflict marital relationship generates the problems. This is an example of a finding that could be greatly informed by including a genetic component in the study.

Marital Conflict, Immunity, and Health

Data from large epidemiological studies suggest that poor personal relationships are a major risk factor for morbidity and mortality (House, Landis, & Umberson, 1988). The search for mechanisms has revealed substantial evidence regarding the role of immune function. Kiecolt-Glaser, Glaser, Cacioppo, and Malarkey (1998) demonstrated that abrasive marital interactions have important endocrine and immunological correlates. In general, marital separation or divorce, higher marital conflict, and lower marital satisfaction are associated with lower immune function. Such stress-related immunological changes may be a pathway through which close personal relationships influence health (e.g., infectious diseases, cancer, wound healing).

Testosterone is related to poor union quality and stability, as are genetic influences. In contrast, evidence that environmental factors influence hormone levels involves the finding that testosterone declines when men marry. Marital conflict and instability may compromise the immune system, which in turn affects health.

FUTURE DIRECTIONS

Recent Research Advances

The biosocial research community is now poised to construct and test multivariate and latent models of the interacting effects of genetic, endocrine, environmental, historical, and behavioral factors that will increase our understanding of family relationships and processes, as well as developmental outcomes (Susman, 1998). Researchers have cleared several major hurdles that now make such advances possible. First, we have reliable and valid noninvasive methods to obtain measurements of biological systems with direct relevance to biosocial research. Second, gene mapping is progressing at a rapid rate, which will advance our ability to disentangle genetic and environmental influences. Third, large public use data sets are now, or soon will be, available that contain biological markers, as well as representative samples of household pairs (twins, siblings, and unrelated adolescents residing in the same household) needed to more accurately estimate genetic variance. The National Longitudinal Study of Adolescent Health (Bearman, Jones & Udry, 1997), rich in biological, behavior, social, and contextual data, is the premiere study in this category.

Increased Involvement in Biosocial Research by Social and Behavioral Scientists

Contemporary social and behavioral scientists have expressed renewed interest in how the factors they study influence and are influenced by physiological and genetic processes. A content analysis of articles in three journals that publish family research revealed a substantial growth in the number of articles per issue involving biological variables. Issues from 1990 to mid-1998 were compared to issues from 1980 to 1989. For *Journal of Marriage and the Family,* the number per issue increased by 47% (.76 to 1.12), for *Social Forces,* 121% (.28 to .62), and for *Journal of Personality and Social Psychology,* 18% (1.10 to 1.30).

Development of Infrastructure Support

The National Institutes of Health have established new priorities that designate "studies on the interactions between biological and behavioral processes" as being of "high program relevance." The National Science Foundation's Division of Social, Behavioral, and Economic Research has as one of its goals to advance fundamental knowledge about "biological factors related to human behavior." In short, there is now a national agenda to facilitate the integration of biosocial perspectives into research on child and adult well-being and development within the context of the family.

How to Get Involved

This does not mean that family scholars must become biologists to take an active role in this line of research. Rather, we envision family researchers and trainees learning enough biology to become part of an interdisciplinary scientific team. This team approach contrasts with the notion of training one investigator who "knows all" about several fields of knowledge. The latter scenario seems problematic because ultimately depth of knowledge in any one field may be sacrificed to breadth of knowledge. We expect future family researchers to have specialized skills in traditional disciplines but also to have the practical and theoretical biological training needed to speak the common language and facilitate collaboration between investigators who represent different disciplinary perspectives. Family researchers may obtain that knowledge by reading references cited here, attending the meetings of scholarly groups such as the International Society for Psychoneuroendocrinology, Society for Behavioral Medicine, Behavior Genetics Association, and International Workshop on Methodology of Twin and Family Studies.

NOTE

We are indebted to Paul Amato, Jay Belsky, Ann C. Crouter, Daniel Lichter, J. Richard Udry, Susan Welch, and Lynn White for very helpful comments on earlier versions of this manuscript. This research is supported in part by the Pennsylvania State University Population Research Institute, with core support from the National Institute of Child Health and Human Development, grant 1-HD28263.

REFERENCES

Altemus, M., Deuster, P., Galliven, E., Carter, C., & Gold, P. (1995). Suppression of hypothalamic-pituitary-adrenal axis responses to stress in lactating women. *Journal of Clinical Endocrinology Metabolism, 80,* 2954–2959.

Amato, P. (1996). Explaining the intergenerational transmission of divorce. *Journal of Marriage and the Family, 58,* 628–640.

Baker, L. A., & Daniels, D. (1990). Nonshared environmental influences and personality differences in adult twins. *Journal of Personality and Social Psychology, 58,* 103–110.

Barkley, R. (1989). Hyperactive girls and boys: Stimulant drug effects on mother-child interactions. *Journal of Child Psychology and Psychiatry, 30,* 336–341.

Bearman, P. S., Jones, J., & Udry, J. R. (1997). *The National Longitudinal Study of Adolescent Health: Research design.* Available at: http://www.cpc.unc.edu/projects/addhealth/design.html.

Belsky, J., Steinberg, L., & Draper, P. (1991). Childhood experience, interpersonal development, and reproductive strategy: An evolutiionary theory of socialization. *Child Development, 62,* 642–670.

Block, J., Block, J., & Gjerde, P. (1986). The personality of children prior to divorce: A prospective study. *Child Development, 57,* 827–840.

Booth, A., & Dabbs, J. (1993). Testosterone and men's marriages. *Social Forces, 72,* 463–477.

Booth, A., & Dabbs, J. (1996). *Cortisol, testosterone, and competition among women.* Unpublished manuscript.

Booth, A., Johnson, D., & Granger, D. (1999). Testosterone and men's depression: The role of social behavior. *Journal of Health and Social Behavior, 40,* 130–140.

Booth, A., & Osgood, D. (1993). The influence of testosterone on deviance in adulthood. *Criminology, 31,* 93–117.

Booth, A., Shelley, G., Mazur, A., Tharp, G., & Kittok, R. (1989) Testosterone, and winning and losing in human competition. *Hormones and Behavior, 23,* 556–571.

Braungart, J., Fulker, D., & Plomin, R. (1992). Genetic mediation of the home environment during infancy: A sibling adoption study of the HOME. *Developmental Psychology, 28,* 1048–1055.

Braungart, J. M. (1994). Genetic influences on "environmental" measures. In J. C. DeFries, R. Plomin, & D. W. Fulker (Eds.), *Nature and nurture during middle childhood* (pp. 233–248). Oxford, U.K.: Blackwell.

Buss, D. M., & Schmitt, D. P. (1993). Sexual strategies theory: An evolutionary perspective on human mating. *Psychological Review, 100,* 204–232.

Cadoret, R., Yates, W., Troughtoh, E., Woodworth, G., & Stewart, M. (1995). Genetic-environmental interaction in the genesis of aggressive and conduct disorders. *Archives of General Psychiatry, 52,* 916–924.

Cairns, R., Gariepy, J., & Hood, K. (1990). Development, microevolution, and social behavior. *Psychological Review, 97,* 49–65.

Carlson, M., & Earls, F. (1997). Psychological and neuroendocrinological sequelae of early social deprivation in institutionalized children in Romania. In C. Carter, I. Lederhendler, & B. Kirkpatrick (Eds.), *The integrative neurobiology of affiliation* (pp. 419–428). New York: New York Academy of Sciences.

Carver, K. (1998). *The effect of hormonal contraceptive*

use on the risk of union dissolution in the United States. Unpublished manuscript.

Cashdan, E. (1995). Hormones, sex, and status in women. *Hormones and Behavior, 29,* 354–366.

Cherlin, A., Chase-Lansdale, P., & McRae, C. (1998). Effects of parental divorce on mental health throughout the life course. *American Sociological Review, 63,* 239–249.

Cherlin, A., Furstenberg, F. F., Chase-Lansdale, P. L., Kiernan, K., Morrison, D. R., & Teitler, J. (1991). Longitudinal studies of effects of divorce on children in Great Britain and the United States. *Science, 252,* 1386–1389.

Collaer, M., & Hines, M. (1995). Human behavioral sex differences: A role for gonadal hormones during early development? *Psychological Bulletin, 118,* 55–107.

Dabbs, J. (1992). Testosterone and occupational achievement. *Social Forces, 70,* 813–824.

Daly, M., & Wilson, M. (1983). *Sex, evolution, and behavior.* Boston: Willard Grant Press.

Daly, M., & Wilson, M. (1988). Evolutionary social psychology and family homicide. *Science, 242,* 519–524.

Davis, J., & Daly, M. (1997). Evolutionary theory and the human family. *The Quarterly Review of Biology, 72,* 407–435.

Dunne, M. P., Martin, N. G., Statham, D. J., Slutske, W. S., Dinwiddie, S. H., Bucholz, K. K., Madden, P. A., & Heath, A. C. (1997). Genetic and environmental contributions to variance in age at first sexual intercourse. *Psychological Science, 8,* 211–216.

Ellis, B., Dodge, K., Pettit, G., & Bates, J. (in press). Quality of early family relationships and individual differences in the timing of pubertal maturation in girls: A longitudinal test of an evolutionary model. *Journal of Personality and Social Psychology.*

Ellis, B., & Garber, J. (in press). Psychosocial antecedents of variation in girls' pubertal timing: Marital depression, stepfather presence, and marital and family stress. *Child Development.*

Finkelstein, J., Susman, E., Chinchilli, V., Kunselman, S., D'arcangelo, R., Schwab, J., Demers, L., Liben, L., Lookingbill, G., & Kulin, H. (1997). Estrogen or testosterone increases self-reported aggressive behaviors in hypogonadal adolescents. *Journal of Clinical Endocrinology and Metabolism, 82,* 2433–2438.

Fleming, A., Ruble, D., Krieger, H., & Wong, P. (1997). Hormonal and experiential correlates of maternal responsiveness during pregnancy and the puerperium in human mothers. *Hormones and Behavior, 31,* 145–158.

Flynn, M., & England, B. (1995). Childhood stress and family environment. *Current Anthropology, 36,* 854–866.

Gangestad, W. W., & Buss, D. M. (1993). Pathogen prevalence and human mate preferences. *Ethology and Sociobiology, 14,* 89–96.

Gangestad, W. W., & Simpson, J. A. (in press). The evolution of human mating: Trade offs and strategic pluralism. *Behavioral and Brain Sciences.*

Gangestad, W. W., & Thornhill, R. (1998). Menstrual cycle variation in women's preferences for the scent of symmetrical men. *Proceedings of the Royal Society of London, B, 265,* 927–933.

Goode, W. J. (1993). *World changes in divorce patterns.* New Haven, CT: Yale University Press.

Gottlieb, G. (1991). Experiential canalization of behavioral development: Theory. *Developmental Psychology 27,* 4–13.

Gottlieb, G. (1992). *Individual development and evolution: The genesis of novel behavior.* New York: Oxford University Press.

Grammar, K., & Thornhill, R. (1994). Human (*Homo sapiens*) facial attractiveness and sexual selection: The role of symmetry and averageness. *Journal of Comparative Psychology, 108,* 233–242.

Granger, D. A., Schwartz, E. B., Booth, A., & Arentz, M. (1999). Salivary testosterone determination in studies of child health and development. *Hormones and Behavior, 36,* 18–27.

Granger, D. A., Serbin, L. A., Schwartzman, A. E, Lehoux, P., Cooperman, J., & Ikeda, S. (1998). Children's salivary cortisol, internalizing behavior problems, and family environment: Results from the Concordia Longitudinal Risk Project. *International Journal of Behavioral Development, 22,* 707–728.

Granger, D. A., Weisz, J. R., & Kauneckis, D. (1996). Neuroendocrine reactivity, internalizing behavior problems, and control-related cognitions in clinic-referred children and adolescents. *Journal of Abnormal Psychology, 103,* 267–276.

Granger, D. A., Weisz, J. R., McCracken, J. T., Ikeda, S., & Douglas, P. (1996). Reciprocal influences among adrenocortical activation, psychosocial processes, and clinic-referred children's short-term behavioral adjustment. *Child Development, 67,* 3250–3262.

Gubernick, D., Worthman, C., & Stallings, J. (1991). *Hormonal correlates of fatherhood in man.* Unpublished manuscript.

Gunner, M., Mangelsdorf, S., Larsen, M., & Herstgaard, L. (1998). Attachment, temperament, and adrenocortical activity in infancy: A study of psychoendocrine regulation. *Developmental Psychology, 25,* 355–363.

Halpern, C., Udry, J., & Suchindran, C. (1998). Monthly measures of salivary testosterone predict sexual activity in adolescent males. *Archives of Sexual Behavior, 27,* 445–465.

Hart, J., Gunnar, M., & Cicchetti, D. (1995). Salivary cortisol in maltreated children: Evidence of relations between neuroendocrine activity and social competence. *Development and Psychopathology, 7,* 11–26.

House, J. S., Landis, K. R., & Umberson, D. (1988). Social relationships and health. *Science, 241,* 540–545.

Jockin, V., McGue, M., & Lykken, D. T. (1996). Personality and divorce: A genetic analysis. *Journal of Personality and Social Psychology, 71,* 288–299.

Julian, T., & McKenry, P. (1989). Relationship of testosterone to men's family functioning at mid-life: A research note. *Aggressive Behavior, 15,* 281–289.

Julian, T., McKenry, P., & McKelvey, M. (1990). Mediators of relationships stress between middle-aged fathers and their adolescent children. *Journal of Genetic Psychology, 152,* 381–386.

Kendler, K., Kessler, R., Walters, E., Maclean, C., Neale, M., Heath, A., & Eaves, L. (1995). Stressful life events, genetic liability, and onset of an episode of major depression in women. *American Journal of Psychiatry, 154,* 1398–1404

Kiecolt-Glaser, J. K., Glaser, R., Cacioppo, J. T., & Malarkey, W. B. (1998). Marital stress: Immunological, neuroendocrine, and autonomic correlates. *Annals of the New York Academy of Sciences, 840,* 656–663.

Kirschbaum, C., Read, G. F., & Hellhammer, D. H. (1992). *Assessment of hormones and drugs in saliva in biobehavioral research.* Kirkland, WA: Hogrefe & Huber.

Lechman, J., & Mayes, L. (1998). Maladies of love—An evolutionary perspective on some forms of obsessive-compulsive disorder. In D. Hann, L. Huffman, I. Lederhendler, & D. Meinecke (Eds.), *Advancing research on developmental plasticity: Integrating the Behavioral Science and Neuroscience of Mental Health* (publication 98, pp. 134–152). Washington, DC: National Institute of Mental Health.

Mazur, A., & Booth, A. (1998). Testosterone and dominance in men. *Behavioral and Brain Sciences, 21,* 353–363.

Mazur, A., & Michalek, J. (1998). Marriage, divorce, and male testosterone. *Social Forces, 77,* 315–330.

Mazur, A., Susman, E., & Edelbrock, S. (1997). Sex differences in testosterone response to a video game contest. *Evolution and Human Behavior, 18,* 317–326.

McClearn, G. (1993). Behavior genetics: The last century and the next. In R. Plomin & G. McClearn (Eds.), *Nature, nuture and psychology.* (pp. 27–51) Washington, DC: American Psychological Association.

McClintock, M., & Herdt, G. (1996). Rethinking puberty: The development of sexual attraction. *Current Directions in Psychological Science, 5,* 178–183.

McGue, M., & Lykken, D. T. (1992). Genetic influence on risk of divorce. *Psychological Science, 3,* 368–373.

Meyer, J. M., Eaves, L. J., Heath, A. C., & Martin, N. G. (1991). Estimating genetic influences on the age-at-menarche: A survival analysis approach. *American Journal of Medical Genetics, 39,* 148–154.

Mitton, J. B. (1993). Enzyme heterozygosity, metabolism, and developmental stability. *Genetica, 89,* 47–66.

Moffitt, T. (1993). Adolescence-limited and life-course-persistent antisocial behavior: A developmental taxonomy. *Psychological Review, 100,* 674–701.

Neale, M. C., & Cardon, L. R. (1992). *Methodology for genetic studies of twins and families.* The Netherlands: Kluwer Academic.

Nelson, R. J. (1999). *An introduction to behavioral endocrinology.* New York: Sinauer.

Ober, C., Simpson, J. L., Ward, M., Radvany, R. M., Andersen, R., Elias, S., Sabbagha, R., & The DIEP Study Group. (1987). Prenatal effects of maternal-retal HLA compatibility. *American Journal of Reproductive Immunology and Microbiology, 15,* 141–149.

Penton-Voak, I. S., Perrett, D. I., Castles, D. L., Kobayashi, T., Burt, D. M., Murray, L. K., & Minamisawa, R. (1999). Menstrual cycle alters face preference. *Nature, 399,* 741–742.

Pike, A., McGuire, S., Hetherington, E., Reiss, D., & Plomin, R. (1996). Family environment and adolescent depressive symptoms and antisocial behavior: A multivariate genetic analysis. *Developmental Psychology, 32,* 590–603.

Plomin, R. (1994). *Genetics and experience: The interplay between nature and nuture.* Thousand Oaks, CA: Sage.

Plomin, R. (1995). Genetics and children's experiences in the family. *Journal of Child Psychology and Psychiatry, 36,* 33–68.

Plomin, R., McClearn, G., Pedersen, G., Nesselroade, J., & Bergeman, C. (1988). Genetic influence on adults' ratings of their current family environment. *Journal of Marriage and the Family, 51,* 791–803.

Plomin, R., Reiss, D., Hetherington, E., & Howe, G. (1994). Nature and nurture: Genetic influence on measures of family environment. *Developmental Psychology, 30,* 32–43.

Potts, W. K., Manning, C. J., & Wakeland, E. K. (1994). The role of infectious disease, inbreeding and mating preferences in maintaining MHC genetic diversity: An experimental test. *Philosophical Transactions of the Royal Society of London, Series B: Biological Sciences, B, 346,* 369–378.

Reiss, D. (1995). Genetic influence on family systems: Implications for development. *Journal of Marriage and the Family, 57,* 543–560.

Rodgers, J. L. and D. Doughty. (in press). Genetic and environmental influences on fertility expectations and outcomes using NLSY kinship data. In J. L. Rodgers, D.C. Rowe, & W. B. Miller (Eds.), *Genetic influences on fertility and sexuality.* Boston: Kluwer Academic.

Rowe, D. C. (1981). Environmental and genetic influences on dimensions of perceived parenting: A twin study. *Developmental Psychology, 17,* 203–208.

Rowe, D. C. (1983). A biometrical analysis of perceptions of family environment: A study of twin and singleton sibling kinships. *Child Development, 54,* 416–423.

Rowe, D. C. (1994). *The limits of family influence: Genes, experience, and behavior.* New York: Guilford Press.

Sanders, S., & Reinisch, J. (1990). Biological and social influences on the endocrinology of puberty: Some additional considerations. In J. Bancroft & J. Reinisch (Eds.), *Adolescence and puberty* (pp. 50–62). New York: Oxford University Press.

Scarr, S., & McCartney, K. (1983). How people make their own environments: A theory of genotype→environment effects. *Child Development, 54,* 424–435.

Shepher, J. (1971). Mate selection among second generation Kibbutz adolescents and adults: Incest avoidance and negative imprinting. *Archives of Sexual Behavior, 1,* 293–307.

Stansbury. K., & Gunnar, R. (1994). Adrenocortical activity and emotion regulation. In N. Fox (Ed.), The development of emotion regulation: Biological and behavioral considerations. *Monographs of the Society for Research in Child Development, 59,* 108–134.

Storey, A. E., Walsh, C. J., Quinton, R. L., & Wynne-Edwards, K. E. (in press). Hormonal correlates of paternal responsiveness in new and expectant fathers. *Evolution and Human Behavior.*

Susman, E. (1998). Biobehavioral development: An integrative perspective. *International Journal of Behavioral Development, 22,* 671–679.

Thomas, M. L., Harger, J. H., Wagener, D. K., Rabin, B. S., & Gill, T. J. (1985). HLA sharing and spontaneous abortion in humans. *American Journal of Obstetrics and Gynecology, 151,* 1053–1058.

Thornhill, R., & Gangestad, S. W. (1993). Human facial

beauty: Averageness, symmetry and parasite resistance. *Human Nature, 4,* 237–269.

Tremblay, R., Schaal, B., Boulerice, B., Arseneault, L., Soussignan, R., Paquette, D., & Lauret, D. (1998). Testosterone, physical aggression, dominance and physical development in early adolescence. *International Journal of Behavioral Development, 22,* 753–777.

Turkheimer, E., Lovett, G., Robinette, C. D., & Gottesman, I. I. (1992). The heritability of divorce: New data and theoretical implications [abstract]. *Behavior Genetics, 22,* 757.

Turner, R. A., Altemus, M., Enos, T., Cooper, B., & McGuinness, T. (1999). Preliminary research on plasma oxytocin in normal cycling women: Investigating emotion and interpersonal distress. *Psychiatry: Interpersonal & Biological Processes, 62,* 97–113.

Udry, J. R. (1964). Complementarity in mate selection: A perceptual approach. *Marriage and Family Living, 25,* 281–289.

Udry, J. R. (1988). Biological predispositions and social control in adolescent sexual behavior. *American Sociological Review, 53,* 709–722.

Udry, J. R. (in press). Biological limits of gender construction. *American Sociological Review.*

Udry, J. R., Morris, N., & Kovenock, J. (1995). Androgen effects on women's gendered behavior. *Journal of Biosocial Science, 27,* 359–369.

Uvnas-Moberg, K. (1997). Physiological and endocrine effects of social contact. In C. Carter, I. Lederhendler, & B. Kirkpatrick (Eds.), *The integrative neurobiology of affiliation* (pp. 146–163). New York: New York Academy of Sciences.

Uvnas-Moberg, K., Widstrom, A., Nissen, E., & Bjorvell, H. (1990). Personality traits in women 4 days postpartum and their correlation with plasma levels of oxytocin and prolactin. *Journal of Psychosomatic Obstetrics and Gynaecology, 11,* 261–273.

Van Goozen, S., Weigant, V., Endert, E., Helmond, F., & Van de Poll, N. (1997). Psychoendocrinological assessment of the menstrual cycle: The relationship between hormones, sexuality, and mood. *Archives of Sexual Behavior, 26,* 359–382.

Wedekind, C., Seebeck, T., Bettens, F., & Paepke, A. J. (1995). MHC-dependent mate preferences in humans. *Proceedings of the Royal Society of London, B, 260,* 245–249.

White, L., & Booth, A. (1985). The quality and stability of remarriages: The role of stepchildren. *American Sociological Review, 50,* 689–698.

Widstrom, A., Wahlbert, V., Matthiesen, A., Eneroth, P., Unvas-Moberg, K., Werner, S., & Winberg, J. (1990). Short-term effects of early sucking on maternal behavior and breast-feeding performance. *Early Human Development, 21,* 153–163.

Wilson, E. O. (1998). *Consilience: The unity of knowledge.* New York: Knopf.

Winch, R. F., Ktsanes, T., & Ktsanes, V. (1954). The theory of complementary needs in mate-selection. *American Sociological Review, 19,* 241–249.

Wolf, A. (1995). *Sexual attraction and childhood association.* Stanford, CA: Stanford University Press.

Yamazaki, K., Beauchamp, G. K., Kupniewski, D., Bard, J., Thomas, L., & Boyse, E. A. (1988). Familial imprinting determines H-2 selective mating preferences. *Science, 240,* 1331–1332.

Lynn White   *University of Nebraska—Lincoln*

Stacy J. Rogers   *Pennsylvania State University**

Economic Circumstances and Family Outcomes:
A Review of the 1990s

This review documents the economic context within which American families lived in the 1990s. Despite nearly full employment and growing income and wealth for many Americans, problem areas included persistent racial gaps in economic well-being, growing inequality, and declining wages for young men. Women showed stronger income growth than men in the decade, and 2-earner households became increasingly associated with advantage. We review the consequences of these trends and of economic well-being generally on 4 dimensions of family outcomes: family formation, divorce, marital quality, and child well-being. Despite hypotheses suggesting that women's earnings might have different effects on family outcomes than men's earnings, generally the review supports the expectation that both men's and women's economic advantage is associated with more marriage, less divorce, more marital happiness, and greater child well-being. Important issues regarding measurement, reciprocal relations between family structure and economic well-being, and race and gender effects remain unresolved.

Department of Sociology, University of Nebraska-Lincoln, Lincoln, NE 68588-0324 (lwhite3@unl.edu).

*Department of Sociology, Pennsylvania State University, University Park, PA 16802.

Key Words: economic status, marriage market.

In *The Sociological Imagination,* C. Wright Mills (1959) argued for the importance of seeing the intimate realities of our own lives within the larger social and historical context of our times. In this review of family research in the 1990s, we consider the economic context of family experience. We begin by summarizing the economic climate of the 1990s, followed by a review of research that has examined the consequences of income, employment, and economic hardship on family life. We limit this review by focusing on the United States and on a limited set of family outcomes—family formation, marital quality, divorce, and child well-being. The review is necessarily in broad strokes, and important variations in economic circumstances in rural, regional, and other subpopulations are omitted. We conclude with a discussion of needed research and unanswered questions.

THE ECONOMIC CLIMATE OF THE 1990S

Two contradictory conditions characterized the economic climate of the 1990s. On one hand, the United States economy was robust. Economic growth averaged 3% per year during the decade, and median per capita income increased, as did the wealth of that segment of the population with significant holdings in the stock market. At the end of the decade, inflation was low, and the unemployment rate was the lowest it had been in 25 years (Auerbach & Belous, 1998). These gains were most obvious for women, for two-earner families, and for the college educated.

Below this surface of affluence and security were several problem areas, some of which are illustrated in Table 1. First, African Americans and Hispanics continued to experience rates of unemployment 2 to 3 times higher than those for non-Hispanic Whites (U.S. Bureau of Labor Statistics, 1998a, 1998b). Second, poverty, especially among children, was immune to general economic growth, and 19% of children under the age of 18 remained in poverty at the end of the decade. For children in mother-headed families, regardless of race, nearly 60% of children under age 6 were in poverty (Dalaker & Naifeh, 1998). Third, many workers, including those with lower levels of education and young men, experienced stagnation or decline in earnings during most of the 1990s. Median earnings (in constant dollars) for young adult men decreased from 1980 to 1995, whereas the median earnings of young women increased over the same period. Fourth, a growing number of families faced financial uncertainty due to economic restructuring, contingent work, and the changing locations of jobs (Wilson, 1996). Finally, Table 1 also indicates that there was growing inequality in income from 1980 to the late 1990s as those at the upper ends of the income distribution experienced gains, whereas those in the lower quintiles experienced loss.

Most analysts agree that economic conditions in the 1990s extended long-term trends. To summarize briefly, from World War II to approximately 1973, rapid growth in manufacturing, construction, and shipping industries contributed to steady growth in individual income and good jobs for workers at all education levels. The economic boom, according to Farley (1996), created the American middle class. Beginning around the time of the 1973 oil crisis, economic growth changed course. An increased reliance on consumer spending on services and the internationalization of markets and production contributed to an eventual shift away from manufacturing, as well as an increased use of technology in manufacturing. This restricted opportunities for "good jobs" in manufacturing for those with less education. In addition, growth in service and technology-based sectors of the economy increased the opportunities for technologically skilled workers (Farley; Wilson, 1996). These changes, in conjunction with changes in family structure and in women's economic roles, affected the relation between the family and the economy during the 1990s. Below we review some of the ways this has occurred.

Labor Force Participation and Unemployment

Table 1 indicates that from 1980 to the late 1990s, labor force participation increased for women but generally decreased slightly for men, continuing the long-term convergence of men's and women's work experience. In 1990, 74% of women aged 25 to 54 years were in the labor force, compared with 94% of men. By 1998, rates had increased to 77% for women and decreased to 92% for men (U.S. Bureau of Labor Statistics, 1998b). Although women's labor force participation rates remain lower than men's, their growing commitment to paid work is demonstrated in overall increases and in growing convergence among women, as factors such as marital status, age, race, and motherhood became less influential in determining women's labor force participation (Spain & Bianchi, 1996).

Table 1 indicates that the total unemployment rate among those aged 16 years and over declined from 7% in the mid-1980s to 4.5% by 1998 (U.S. Bureau of Labor Statistics, 1998b). All groups experienced declines in unemployment during the decade, but race and education continued to differentiate work opportunity. When White unemployment reached a low of 4% in 1998, African American rates were 9%, and Hispanic rates were 7% (U.S. Bureau of Labor Statistics). Even during this period of very low unemployment, nearly 20% of African American men ages 20 to 24 seeking employment were unable to find it (U.S. Bureau of the Census). Inequality in employment opportunity was further exacerbated by educational differentials. Unemployment rates in 1998 were 7% for those with less than a high school education compared with 2% for individuals with a college degree (U.S. Bureau of Labor Statistics). Perhaps because those who remain unemployed in periods of high employment demand represent a multiple-problem population, the average length of unemployment spells increased during this decade (U.S. Bureau of the Census).

Individual Earnings

Finding work has been easier than finding work that offers good pay and job security. Job growth during the 1990s was most pronounced in services and in information and technology industries (Hout, Arum, & Voss, 1996), contributing to the

TABLE 1. CHANGES IN SELECTED ECONOMIC AND FAMILY-RELATED INDICATORS, 1980 TO THE LATE 1990s

Indicator	1980	1985	1990	1995	1998
Employment					
Percent of men of prime working age in					
labor force (age 25–54 years)	94.2	93.9	93.5	91.6	91.8
White	95.0	94.8	94.4	92.7	92.9
African American	88.4	87.8	87.4	84.1	84.4
Hispanic	93.0	92.2	92.3	91.0	91.6
Asian/Pacific Islanders	89.5	89.1	88.3	88.7	90.1
Percentage of women of prime working age					
in labor force (ages 25–54 years)	64.0	69.6	74.1	75.6	76.5
White	63.4	69.4	74.4	76.3	76.6
African American	67.6	71.7	73.7	74.4	78.3
Hispanic	54.5	57.3	62.3	62.9	65.8
Asian/Pacific Islanders	64.8	66.9	67.8	67.6	71.4
Percentage of married women in labor force					
(1997) (ages 16 and over, all races)	50.1	54.2	58.2	61.1	62.1
With children under 6 years	45.1	53.4	58.9	63.5	63.6
With children 6 to 17 years only	61.7	67.8	73.6	76.2	77.6
Unemployment					
Total unemployment rate (ages 16 and over)	7.1	7.2	5.6	5.6	4.5
White	6.3	6.2	4.8	4.9	3.9
African American	14.3	15.1	11.4	10.4	8.9
Hispanic	10.1	10.5	8.2	9.3	7.2
Asian/Pacific Islander			Not available		
Income and earnings					
Median earnings for young adults (ages 25					
to 34) (1998 dollars, in thousands, all races)					
Women	13.81	14.97	15.70	16.64	18.26
Men	30.86	28.27	26.68	25.25	28.12
Median family income (1998 dollars, in					
thousands, all races)					
All Families	41.64	42.02	44.09	43.44	46.74
Married Couples	45.83	47.11	49.75	50.33	54.18
Married couple, wife employed	53.24	55.19	58.34	59.71	63.37
Married couple, wife not employed	37.58	37.20	37.74	34.62	35.67
Father-headed families	34.70	34.27	36.22	32.47	35.68
Mother-headed families	20.61	20.69	21.11	21.06	22.16
Percentage of aggregate income received					
by each fifth and by the top 5% of families					
(all races)					
Top 5%	14.6	16.1	17.4	20.7	20.7
Highest quintile	41.1	43.1	44.3	47.2	47.2
Fourth quintile	24.4	24.3	23.8	23.0	23.0
Third quintile	17.6	16.9	16.6	15.7	15.7
Second quintile	11.6	11.0	10.8	9.9	9.9
Lowest quintile	5.3	4.8	4.6	4.2	4.2
Percentage of children living in poverty					
(under age 18)					
All races	18.3	20.7	20.6	20.8	18.9
White	11.8	12.8	12.3	11.2	10.6
African American	42.3	43.6	44.8	41.9	36.7
Hispanic	33.2	40.3	38.4	40.0	34.4
Asian/Pacific Islander	n/a	n/a	17.6	19.5	18.0

Note: Information compiled from the following sources:

U.S. Bureau of the Census (1998). *Statistical Abstract of the United States* (118th ed.). Washington, DC: U.S. Government Printing Office. Tables 84, 654.

U.S. Bureau of the Census. Historical income tables—people, (Table) P-7, age of people by median income and gender: 1947–1997. Retrieved July 21, 2000 from the World Wide Web: http://www.census.gov/hhes/income/histinc/p07.html

U.S. Bureau of the Census. Historical income tables—families. (Table) F-7, type of family (all races) by median income and mean income: 1947–1997. Retrieved July 21, 2000 from the World Wide Web: http://www.census.gov/hhes/income/histinc/f07.html

U.S. Bureau of the Census. Historical poverty tables—people, (Table) 3, poverty status of people, by age, race, and Hispanic origin: 1959–1997. Retrieved July 21, 2000 from the World Wide Web: http://www.census.gov/hhes/poverty/histpov/hstpov3.html

U.S. Bureau of the Census (1997).

U.S. Bureau of Labor Statistics. Accessed March 10, 1999 at ftp://ftp.bls.gov/pub/special.requests/ep/labor.force/clra8096.dta

U.S. Bureau of Labor Statistics. (1998a).

U.S. Bureau of Labor Statistics (1998b).

growth of jobs at both ends of the spectrum. Farley (1996) noted the simultaneous growth in the 1980s and early 1990s of "bad" jobs, which required less education and paid minimum wage, and of "good" jobs that required more education and skill and paid more than $25 dollars per hour. At the same time, job growth in the middle of the earning and education distributions declined, and manufacturing jobs that once provided security and good wages for workers with less education became more scarce (Hout et al.).

Consistent with this bifurcation in job opportunities, individual earnings growth varied by education. Between 1963 and 1997, the median income for men with a bachelor's degree or higher increased 22% from $38,496 to $47,126 (in 1997 constant dollars). For all other education levels, men's incomes have actually fallen during this period. For example, among men with a high school diploma, median income declined 12% from $28,914 in 1963 to $25,453 in 1997. Men without a high school diploma experienced an even more dramatic decline in income of 32%. In contrast, women's incomes have increased at all levels of education over the period from 1963 to 1997 (U.S. Bureau of the Census, 1998a). The largest increases, however, were for women with a bachelor's degree, whose median incomes rose 53%, from $19,443 in 1963 to $29,781 in 1997 (in constant dollars).

As a result of these trends, the earnings gap between women and men continued to close during the 1990s. In 1998, the female-to-male median weekly earnings ratio was 76% for full-time workers. This ratio was 85% among African Americans and 86% for Latinos (U.S. Bureau of Labor Statistics, 1999). Among workers with a high school education or less, women's relative gains were primarily the result of declines in men's wages and increases in women's annual weeks of work. Among workers with a college degree, some of the closing gender gap reflected growing opportunities for college-educated women in the expanding service sector of the economy in which women are concentrated. In addition, cohort replacement affected women's earnings as older women left the labor force and were replaced by a larger group of younger, more educated women who were more likely to work full-time (Danziger & Gottschalk, 1995; Spain & Bianchi, 1996).

To the extent that men's lower earnings delay family formation or significantly inhibit men's ability to support their children, the stagnation of young men's wages is particularly important (Cherlin, 1992; Wilson, 1996). Until recently, each generation of men has fared better, in terms of median income, than their father's generation fared at comparable ages. In the last 2 decades, however, young men's fortunes stagnated and declined and, even after a substantial recovery between 1995 and 1998, young men's median earnings in 1998 remain below those of 20 years ago. In contrast, young women have experienced continuing economic improvement in earnings relative to their mothers' generation (Spain & Bianchi, 1996). In sum, the 1990s was a decade of declining economic resources for young men and those with less than a college degree. At the same time, advances in women's earnings helped offset these declines for many two-earner families.

Family Income

The link between family structure and family income grew during the 1990s. Table 1 indicates that the median income of married couple families continued to be higher than that for families with one parent, regardless of the gender of the parent. Until relatively recently, the economic advantage of married-couple families stemmed from their having access to male earnings, which were much higher than female earnings. During the 1980s and continuing through the 1990s, however, their advantage was increasingly due to the presence of two earners (Cattan, 1998; Levy, 1995; McNeil, 1998). Having two earners was normative among married couples of all races during the 1990s. In 1994, for those couples in which the husband was employed, wives were also employed in 61% of Hispanic, 79% of African American, and 75% of White couples in 1994 (Cattan). Furthermore, wives' earnings made significant contributions to family resources. Table 1 indicates that the median income for married couple families without an employed wife actually declined from 1980 to 1998, from $37,580 in 1980 to $35,670 in 1998 (in 1998 constant dollars). When wives were employed, the median family income in married couple families rose over this period from $53,240 in 1980 to $63,370 in 1998 (in 1998 constant dollars). Paralleling general trends in income by gender, single-mother families experienced slight income gain during the period ($20,610 in 1980 to $22,160 in 1998), whereas single-father families experienced actual income declines in the early 1980s and early 1990s.

These data provide important evidence for the

essential nature of women's economic contributions to their families. All of the increases in median income for married couples during this period were due to the growing economic contributions of wives (McNeil, 1998). Hispanic, African American, and White couples with two earners were one fourth as likely to be poor as similar couples with only a male earner (Cattan, 1998).

Income Inequality

Changes in family income during the 1990s were strongly influenced by position within the income distribution. Families in the upper quintiles of the income distribution benefited disproportionately from economic growth. Virtually all of the gains during the 1990s went to the top 20% of the income distribution. As Table 1 indicates, the top 5% enjoyed the most improvement whereas the incomes of the lower two quintiles fell (Freeman, 1998; Levy, 1995; Yellen, 1998). This is true for African Americans and Hispanics as well as for Whites (U.S. Bureau of the Census, 1997). Put another way, although the percentage of Americans whose incomes were below the poverty line has remained close to constant at 13%, the proportion of American families earning more than 7 times the poverty rate nearly doubled from 6 to 12% (Danziger, 1996).

The effect of these increases in income inequality could be moderated if social class mobility increased. In a study of family income mobility patterns from 1967 to 1991, however, Gittleman and Joyce (1999) indicated that mobility has changed little during this period and that the likelihood of upward mobility is especially low for those in families headed by young adults or by individuals with less than a college degree.

Three explanations are offered for growing inequality. First, it reflects the divergent economic prospects of the well educated and the poorly educated discussed above (Yellen, 1998). Second, most observers have argued that increases in employment among wives with higher earning husbands increased the advantage to families already at the upper end of the income distribution. This was in contrast to previous decades, when most employed wives were married to low-earning husbands, and their contributions helped enlarge the incomes in the middle of the income distribution (Farley, 1996; Levy, 1995). A recent paper by Cancian and Reed (1999), however, suggests that increases in wives' income over the last 25 years

have actually countered the trend toward rising inequality in family income. Finally, scholars argue that increases in mother-headed households have contributed to growth in the lower portion of the income distribution (Eggebeen & Lichter, 1991). These households have lower incomes because they lack a second wage earner, because women tend to earn less, on average, than men, and because some of these women are not employed (Yellen).

Job Security

Throughout the 1990s, downsizing, rightsizing, and overseas job flight were staples of headline news, yet the unemployment rate declined rather than increased. In addition to being reflected in the replacement of good jobs by poor jobs, industrial restructuring was reflected in the growth of contingent jobs and the reduction in job tenure. Reflective of the times, the Bureau of Labor Statistics conducted the first assessment of contingent workers in 1995. Approximately 5% of the employed population qualified as contingent workers in 1995: They held jobs designed to be of short duration without a contract (Hipple, 1998). Contingent workers tended to be disadvantaged in work hours, earnings, and employer-provided benefits relative to their noncontingent counterparts, and many expressed a preference for noncontingent employment (Hipple).

A recent summary of employee tenure by the Bureau of Labor Statistics (U.S. Bureau of Labor Statistics, 1998c) indicated that between 1983 and 1998, median employee tenure declined modestly for men in all age groups (from approximately 4.1 years to 3.8 years) and grew modestly for women (from 3.1 to 3.4 years). Declining tenure may reflect either layoffs or positive job changes, as workers take advantage of opportunities in a tight labor market. Whether movement is voluntary or involuntary, it may negatively affect pay, benefits, and the seniority of individual workers, and lower job tenure may be associated with increasing feelings of economic insecurity.

Summary

The economic climate of the 1990s has been a continuation of several long-term trends that have resulted in strong overall economic growth and lower unemployment, but which have failed to eliminate and have even exacerbated long-term economic inequalities. Men who are young or who have less than a college degree have experienced considerable erosion in their incomes, both in absolute terms and relative to previous cohorts of young men and, perhaps as important, relative to women in their own cohort. Although important segments of the male population have experienced worsening income and worsening income trajectories, women's earnings have increased steadily. These increases have often allowed families to maintain their standard of living and avoid poverty despite men's declining resources, but they challenge the breadwinner model that lingers in the normative fabric of family life and may signal more fundamental changes in how men and women live together. Long-term demographic trends in household composition have also played a role in affecting families' economic well-being, increasing the number of dual-earner, high-income households, as well as the number of mother-headed households facing economic hardship. The question the rest of this review addresses is whether these economic conditions have been demonstrated to have important effects on family life.

THE EFFECTS OF ECONOMIC CIRCUMSTANCE ON FAMILY OUTCOMES

Marriage and Family Formation

Galvanized by sharply declining marriage rates, the growth in nonmarital cohabitation and childbearing, a growing racial gap in marriage behavior, and by provocative hypotheses that attribute these trends to men's or women's economic behavior, many excellent studies have addressed the link between earnings, employment, and family formation behavior. The work is divided into two camps, depending on whether men's or women's economic behavior is thought to have the strongest effect. We review the theoretical and empirical work on each hypothesis and then summarize their specific implications for the three basic family formation options in the 1990s—marriage, cohabitation, and nonmarital childbearing.

The male-based hypothesis has several theoretical roots, but its empirical prediction is straightforward: Men with higher earnings, better and more secure jobs, and stronger economic prospects are more likely to marry. This prediction is based on the notion that such men enjoy greater attractiveness in the marriage market because of their greater ability to set up an independent household and to perform the conventional

breadwinning role (Becker, 1981). Because real wages for young men have declined in the last decade, this hypothesis has seemed a likely candidate to explain declining marriage rates. In particular, Wilson's (1987) concept of the male marriageable pool index provided a persuasive argument that declining opportunities for young African American men might explain the growing racial gap in marital behavior.

The female-based hypothesis is more complex. On the one hand, scholars such as Oppenheimer (1997b) have argued that, in a fashion parallel to men, better earning, employed women make more attractive partners and are more likely to marry. On the other hand, it has been argued that women who are able to support themselves through their own work (or through welfare benefits) will feel less pressure to marry for economic need and may choose not to marry or to form families through cohabitations or nonmarital childbearing (Cherlin, 1992). That this "independence effect" is hypothesized for women but not men rests on a trading model that has been criticized as a "narrow (if not impoverished) notion of what marriage is about" (Oppenheimer, 1995) and implies that a gender-based division of labor is more important to the marital decision than are economies of scale, risk reduction, or maximization of economic resources.

Empirical Tests of the Male Hypothesis. Men's earnings and employment consistently have been demonstrated to increase the likelihood of marriage (Lloyd & South, 1996; Oppenheimer, Kalmijn, & Lim, 1997) and, specifically, of moving from cohabitation to marriage (Bumpass, Sweet, & Cherlin, 1991; Manning & Smock, 1995; Smock & Manning, 1997). It might have been expected that male earning capacity would matter less as women's earnings and labor force attachment increased; however, women—and especially mothers—still find it reasonable to assess breadwinning potential in deciding whether to marry (Huinink & Mayer, 1995; Sorensen, 1995). Ethnographic work on young unmarried mothers (Farber, 1990) confirms that neither young women nor their parents see any reason to marry a man who is not working.

These statistically strong effects do not account for a substantial share of the percentage of young men who are married at any given time (Oppenheimer, 1997b), for more than a small share of the decline in proportion married (Koball, 1998; Mare & Winship, 1991; Testa & Krogh, 1995), or for more than 20% of the racial gap in marriage (Lichter, LeClere, & McLaughlin, 1991; Lichter, McLaughlin, Kephart, & Landry, 1992; Lloyd & South, 1996; Raley, 1996).

The plausibility of the male earnings hypothesis and the consistent support for the effect of income and prospects on marriage rates across time and race have lead to efforts to salvage the hypothesis that declining economic prospects for young men play a role in trends and in racial differentials. One possibility is that better measurement, including multidimensional assessment of prospects, earnings, and stability, as well as employment, might explain more of the period and race effects (Danziger, 1995). Another possibility is an interaction effect. As Wilson (1996) said, "The weaker the norms against premarital sex, out-of-wedlock pregnancy, and nonmarital parenthood, the more that economic considerations affect decisions to marry" (p. 97). He pointed out, for example, that in 1960, the man's unemployment or low income would not have been a good enough reason not to legitimate a premarital conception but that it is reason enough today (e.g., Farber, 1990). Because the stigma of nonmarital sex and parenthood is weaker now than it used to be (Thornton, 1989) and weaker among African Americans than Whites (Trent & South, 1992), this hypothesis seems plausible.

In support of the hypothesis of period interactions, Testa and Krogh (1995) demonstrated a strong interaction between cohort and employment in their analysis of Black men's odds of marrying the mother of their first child. Using a small sample of inner-city Black men interviewed as part of the Urban Poverty and Family Structure study, they show that employed men were 1.4 times more likely to marry the mother of their first child than the unemployed in the cohort born in the 1940s, but that this effect had grown to 7.4 times in the 1960s cohort. Koball (1998), however, found no cohort interactions in the effect of men's employment on marriage timing.

The race-interaction hypothesis receives support from a consistent set of findings that male employment, earnings, and prospects matter more in African American than White women's decisions to marry (Bulcroft & Bulcroft, 1993; South 1991). No studies have examined whether this is truly a race effect, however, or whether it appears to be so because effects are stronger at lower income levels.

Empirical Results for the Female Hypothesis

A growing body of evidence suggests that women who are employed, who have higher earnings, and who have higher earning potential are more likely to marry compared with less economically advantaged women. Not only are they generally more likely to marry (McLaughlin & Lichter, 1997; Oppenheimer & Lewin, 1999), they are more likely to marry before a birth if they become premaritally pregnant (Manning & Landale, 1996) and to remarry after divorce (Smock, 1990). Further, attitudinal evidence shows that men would prefer to marry women with good earnings (South, 1991).

Evidence for the independence effect—that women's earnings, education, or employment reduce their marriage rates—is weak. One need only compare the median incomes of single and married women (Table 1) to demonstrate that women's own earnings have not reduced the economic gains to marriage (Sorensen, 1995). Manning and Smock (1995) found that women's economic prospects are weighted less strongly than are men's prospects in the decision to move from cohabitation to marriage, and two ecological studies show evidence that marriage rates are higher when women's labor market opportunities are worse (Cready, Fossett, & Kiecolt, 1997; Lichter et al., 1991). The best that can be said in the support of the independence effect is that longer school enrollment does postpone marriage (Oppenheimer, 1997b) and that the positive effects of women's earnings are not as large or consistent as for men's earnings (Sassler & Schoen, 1999; Smock & Manning, 1997).

Because the effect of women's education, earnings, and labor force attachment on marriage are generally positive, women's growing earnings and labor force attachment logically cannot explain declining marriage behavior, nor is it very plausible that Black women's labor force attachment explains their low marriage rates. In fact, paralleling results for men, women's income is more important in predicting African American than White marriage (Bulcroft & Bulcroft, 1993; Oppenheimer & Lewin, 1999; South 1991).

Effect on Nonmarital Family Formation

To the extent that positive earnings of both men and women encourage marriage, it seems logical that the same factors would be associated with lower likelihood of using nonmarital routes to family formation, namely cohabitation and nonmarital fertility.

In the case of nonmarital fertility, the evidence is largely consistent with this expectation. Adolescents and young women with higher social class backgrounds, higher school attainment, and stable family economic histories have lower levels of nonmarital births (Kahn & Anderson, 1992; Upchurch & McCarthy, 1990; Wu, 1996). A study by Manning and Landale (1996) went further to demonstrate that not only are women with higher educations less likely to become pregnant while unmarried, they are more likely to marry before birth in the event that they do become pregnant. The only study to address the issue of racial differences demonstrated that education has a much stronger effect in dampening African American than White women's nonmarital fertility rates (South & Lloyd, 1992). None of these studies has directly assessed the effect of the male partner's economic prospects on the likelihood of premarital pregnancy or nonmarital birth. One might hypothesize that the effect of male earnings on postconception marriage would depend on women's alternative resources, including welfare.

The possibility that welfare specifically encourages nonmarital childbearing and discourages marriage has been the focus of scholarly and policy debate. Studies have documented a positive association between the size of welfare payments and various measures of nonmarital childrearing (e.g., Lichter, McLaughlin, & Ribar, 1997) and also demonstrated that unmarried mothers receiving welfare are less likely to marry than are unmarried mothers who are not on welfare (Bennett, Bloom, & Miller, 1995). Nevertheless, Moffitt (1998) concluded in a thorough review that the generally negative effect of welfare on marriage cannot explain long-term declines in marriage rates or racial differentials in nonmarriage.

How cohabitation is related to economic circumstances is directly addressed in a study by Clarkberg (1999), who assessed the comparative effects of men's and women's economic resources on the likelihood of cohabiting rather than marrying. When contrasted to the alternative of singlehood, cohabitation is positively related to men's and women's earnings but also positively related to job instability. Because women's income is a stronger predictor of cohabitation than of marriage, Clarkberg speculated that "higher earning women may prefer cohabitation as a way to enjoy the benefits of couplehood without having to sacrifice their careers during the vulnerable

period of adulthood" (p. 964). Against this hypothesis, however, must be matched her findings that income relative to earnings is a strong and comparable predictor of men's and women's likelihood of marriage and has much smaller effects on cohabitation.

Summary

Overall, the evidence suggests that, although men's earnings continue to be somewhat more important than women's in family formation, the role of economic factors in women's and men's family formation decisions is remarkably similar. Both men and women with better educations, job prospects, and earnings are more likely to marry because both are attractive commodities in a marriage market that seems to rely less on notions of role complementarity and more on economies of scale, reduction of economic risk, and income maximization. Although improvements in women's earnings and economic independence might be expected to increase the likelihood that women who are better off will attempt to enjoy family life through cohabitation or nonmarital fertility rather than by tying themselves to traditional gender roles still symbolized by marriage, studies in the 1990s do not support this argument. It seems more likely that women's economic independence and, even more importantly, their growing commitment to education and career building in early adulthood may delay marriage and thus increase the likelihood of cohabitation (Sassler & Schoen, 1999). A full understanding of these trade-offs would require direct specification of alternatives, including both partners' incomes and the ability of women to translate economic resources into marital equity.

MARITAL STABILITY

Theoretical arguments surrounding the effects of economic circumstances on divorce generally parallel those used to explain marriage rates. The gender-neutral hypothesis is that lower income, job insecurity and instability, and unemployment of either partner raise the risk of divorce by causing the other to reevaluate their marriage market bargain and by raising strain and tension. The gendered hypothesis is similar to that adduced for marriage: Men's employment, earnings, and prospects reduce divorce, whereas women's employment, earnings, and prospects increase divorce (an independence effect).

Consistent evidence demonstrates a positive effect of men's earnings on marital stability (Hoffman & Duncan, 1995; South & Lloyd, 1995), especially when wives have no earnings (Ono, 1998). Men's unemployment doubles the risk of divorce in the first 5 years of marriage, whereas wife's unemployment has no effect as long as her husband is employed (Bumpass, Castro Martin, & Sweet, 1991). Recent trends in divorce rates, however, cannot be explained by changing economic circumstances. For example, Hoffman and Duncan noted that whereas men's rising real incomes between 1963 and 1971 should have led to a fall in divorce, the divorce rate rose. The effects of more recent changes in men's economic prospects have not been assessed yet in studies of divorce; nevertheless, both the gendered and the gender-neutral hypotheses lead to the prediction of a growing class split in divorce as better prospects should reduce divorce among college-educated men and increase divorce among the less advantaged.

Wives' greater labor force attachment and the growing share of family income that wives contribute are two of the strongest economic trends of this decade. Evidence regarding the effects of these trends on marital dissolution is mixed. Some evidence suggests that women's higher earnings stabilize marriages (Hoffman & Duncan, 1995), although this positive effect can be counteracted by traditional gender-role ideology (Greenstein, 1995; Sayer & Bianchi, 1998). Other evidence shows that women's wages and employment are associated with a greater hazard of divorce (Heidermann, Suhomlinova, & O'Rand, 1998), especially when husband's earnings or total family income are low (Heckert, Nowak, & Snyder, 1998; Ono, 1998). A study by Rogers (1999) lent support to the possibility of two-way causality by using panel data to demonstrate that the path from marital discord to earnings (through increased labor force attachment) was stronger than the path from earnings to marital discord. Other studies show no effect of wife's earnings on divorce (South & Lloyd, 1995; Tzeng & Mare, 1995). Perhaps the safest conclusion is that there is no consistent evidence that wives' success as coproviders reduces marital stability, although there are hints here and in the family violence literature (e.g., McCloskey, 1996) that problems arise when wives' employment and earnings are substantially greater than their husbands' earnings.

The effect of income change on divorce has been addressed in three studies. Tzeng and Mare (1995) showed no effect of year-to-year changes in husband's or wife's income or weeks worked, but Weiss and Willis (1997) showed that increases in either spouse's income reduce the divorce hazard, and Yeung and Hofferth (1998) showed that income loss and especially loss of work hours increase the divorce hazard.

Two other measures of social class are consistently related to hazards of divorce. Both husbands' and wives' educations reduce odds of divorce (Bumpass et al., 1991; Teachman & Polonko, 1990; Tzeng & Mare, 1995) and home ownership deters divorce (Heiderman et al., 1998; Ono, 1998; Weiss & Willis, 1997) These findings suggest that a broad conception of social class that includes wealth, education, earnings, security, and debt would be a useful extension of current research.

Consistent findings that earnings and unemployment, particularly men's, are related to divorce raise the question whether differential economic opportunity explains the racial gap in divorce. Ruggles (1997) claimed that increases in female labor force participation and decreases in male economic prospects fully account for racial differences in divorce rates between 1880 and 1990 and in any given census year, concluding that "it is possible ... that the declining market-labor participation of black men since 1970 is the single most important source of rising marital instability for blacks" (p. 465). His results have been challenged on the basis of measurement, model specification, and murky causal order (Oppenheimer, 1997a; Preston, 1997), however, and it seems appropriate to consider this an open question. In an analysis of odds of divorce among the NLSY sample, for example, Tzeng and Mare (1995) concluded that little of the race difference in divorce could be explained by the very complete set of economic variables they investigated (including level of, changes in, and differences between husbands and wives in income, education, and labor force attachment).

The consistent finding that economic factors are more central to African American than White marriage decisions raises the question about whether earnings and employment stability also play a stronger role in marital instability within African American families. Partial support for this expectation is provided by Yeung and Hofferth (1998), who showed that the effect of job loss on the hazard of divorce is 2 to 3 times stronger in African American couples than in White couples.

MARITAL QUALITY

Although scholars in earlier decades were concerned about the effect of low income and unemployment on marital quality and family process (e.g., Komarovsky, 1940), direct examinations of income, employment, and wealth effects have been relatively scarce in the last decade compared with examinations using subjective measures of economic pressure. Subjective assessments of financial worry have been shown consistently to correlate negatively with marital happiness in general American samples (Conger et al., 1990; Fox & Chancey, 1998), as well as in African American samples (Broman & Forman, 1997; Clark-Nicolas & Gray-Little, 1991). This relationship is elaborated most thoroughly in panel studies from the Iowa State project fielded by Conger and associates (e.g., Conger & Elder, 1994; Conger et al., 1990), which show that economic pressure increases husband's hostility and wife's depression and, through these paths, reduces both husband's and wife's marital happiness.

The few studies that have addressed income directly report mixed results. Rogers and Amato (1997) demonstrated that lower income from young husbands is a significant factor in explaining why a current cohort of early marriages reports more marital problems than did an early cohort, but direct examinations of the link between income and measures of marital quality show no effect (Amato & Rogers, 1997). A positive effect of income is reported by Brody and associates (1994), who found that higher per capita incomes were associated with higher marital happiness and lower marital conflict in their small sample of rural African Americans. This is counterbalanced by two other studies of African American marriages, however, that report weak or no effect of family income on measures of marital quality or problems (Broman & Forman, 1997; Clark-Nicolas & Gray-Little, 1991). Taken together, this is not a strong case for income as an important determinant of marital happiness.

Only a few studies have examined economic indicators other than family income. In their small Tennessee study, Fox and Chancey (1998) showed that husband's job insecurity has a significant positive effect on wives' reports of marital conflict and thoughts of divorce, controlling for income and subjective economic well-being. Interestingly, wives' job insecurity and job instability also have positive effects on husbands' reports of marital conflict. The Iowa State project includes an ad-mirable array of economic measures, including asset-to-debt ratios, job security, and unemployment, as well as family income-to-needs ratios. Although they would seem to have the best opportunity to assess the total effect of economic circumstances on marital quality, they have modeled the effects of all objective economic indicators as indirect through a measure of economic hardship, and none of their reports assesses total effects.

Where reports offer coefficients for both objective and subjective economic indicators, subjective indicators are more strongly correlated with marital outcomes than are objective measures of income or employment (e.g., Clark-Nicolas & Gray-Little, 1991; Fox & Chancey, 1998). This stronger effect arises in part because of common method bias (Lorenz, Conger, Simons, Whitbeck, & Elder, 1991), but also because subjective hardship is more proximate than structural measures.

Given evidence that income and employment are related to divorce and that perceived economic hardship predicts marital quality, it is difficult to accept weak and null effects of income on marital quality at face value. Qualitative research certainly supports a strong association between economic insecurity and marital trouble (Rubin, 1994). It is possible that negative effects are concentrated at lower income levels (threshold effects) or that income interacts with other stressors, such as unemployment. Certainly, consistent findings show that spousal violence is associated with low income and unemployment (Strauss, 1990). Further, unemployment ranks as one of the most stressful life events (Catalano, 1991), and we would expect it to have negative effects on marital quality through depression, stress, and hostility. If the Iowa State project were to unpack their broad range of economic measures and examine their total as well as indirect effects, we would expect to see stronger effects of objective economic conditions on marital quality than have been previously demonstrated.

A second issue is raised by the disjuncture between studies showing no effect of income on marital quality in African American families and findings showing that low income and unemployment have stronger effects on the divorce hazard among African American than White couples. Broman and Forman (1997) revived the idea that "protective resources within African American communities . . . . such as cohesive extended families, spiritual beliefs, and ethnic coping orientations" (p. 243) provide some protection, but this argument is challenged both by the divorce data and by direct examinations of social support mechanisms (e.g., Roschelle, 1997). An alternative hypothesis is that economic issues carry relatively more weight than relationship quality issues in African American divorce decisions, a hypothesis that can only be tested in studies that combine sociodemographic variables with measures of marital happiness in large mixed samples.

Child Outcomes

Much of the research on child outcomes and parents' economic circumstances focuses on poverty and is reviewed in Seccombe (this issue). Because these studies bear on the larger issue of how economic circumstances affect families, however, we review this work briefly.

A variety of studies using different data sets document positive effects of family income on a broad array of child outcome measures, including child health (Dawson, 1991), internalizing and externalizing problems (Hanson, McLanahan, & Thomson, 1997), and school attainment and achievement (Duncan, Yeung, Brooks-Gunn, & Smith, 1998). To a significant extent, these findings regarding income (or income-to-needs) have been replicated using other measures of social class. For example, occupational status and complexity (Menaghan & Parcel, 1991), assets (Axinn, Duncan, & Thornton, 1997), education (Day, 1992), debt (Hanson et al.), and unemployment (McLoyd, Epstein Jayaratne, Ceballo, & Borquez, 1994) have been shown to be related to child outcomes for both single-parent and two-parent families (Hanson et al.; McLoyd et al.).

Some of the strongest arguments for the effect of income on children's outcomes are indirect. McLanahan and Sandefur (1994) argued that income accounts for nearly half of the substantial deficits on outcomes such as school performance, high school graduation, teen pregnancy, and young-adult idleness that they document for children raised by single mothers. Other studies using the same analytic strategy, however, show weaker effects of income (e.g., Sandefur, McLanahan, & Wojtkiewicz, 1992).

In addition, a substantial set of research, largely from the Iowa State project (but also see McLoyd et al., 1994; Takeuchi, Williams, & Adair, 1991), has demonstrated the ways in which subjective economic pressure affects the quality of parenting, children's psychological well-being, and finally children's outcomes, such as internalizing and externalizing problems and school attainment (Simons, Whitbeck, Melby, & Wu, 1994). Summarizing how economic pressure reverberates through the family system, Simons and associates (pp. 219–220) noted that

> parents who are under high economic strain are liable to be preoccupied and minimally involved in the parenting role until serious or flagrant child misbehavior jars them into action. Such transgressions are likely to demand a harsh response, so that the pattern of parenting displayed is inconsistent and explosive.

Simons and associates concluded that economic pressure jeopardizes the child's psychological and behavioral outcomes.

The most comprehensive examination of economic effects on child outcomes is the project organized by Duncan and Brooks-Gunn (1997), who commissioned a dozen research groups (including most of those cited in the two preceding paragraphs) to test the effects of family income on a broad array of child outcome measures using separate data sets but a common model. The consensus from this comparative project is that income itself has surprisingly narrow effects on child outcomes. They concluded that family income has important and consistent effects on ability and achievement but that income effects on behavior, mental health, and physical health are narrower and less consistent. Income effects are smaller in the studies that focus on adolescence than those that focus on early childhood. As one might expect, however, premarital births and college attendance are more sensitive to family income in adolescence than in early childhood (Duncan et al., 1998). They interpreted the results as showing that increments in income at and around the poverty level matter more than income differences higher in the continuum for most child outcomes and that "In no case did the evidence here suggest that income transfers alone would produce a dramatic improvement in physical health, mental health, or in behavioral development of children" (Duncan & Brooks-Gunn, p. 608).

The conclusion that "income transfers alone" would not make a dramatic difference in children's health, behavior, or well-being and the provocative book by Mayer (1997), *What Money Can't Buy,* raise important questions about measurement and conceptualization. Neither Marxist theories of class nor mainstream theories of social class suggest that income alone, much less income controlling for education and other measures of socioeconomic status, is the critical variable measuring social inequality. Policy-related studies such as Mayer's and those in the Duncan and Brooks-Gunn volume are designed to assess the effect of a single variable that is relatively easily manipulated by available public policy instruments (i.e., family income), rather than to assess the costs of disadvantage. If the latter were the focus, then broader and more process-oriented measures, such as education and labor markets, would need to be assessed. As the authors of one of the contributions to the Duncan and Brooks-Gunn volume concluded, "overly economistic thinking may have diverted researchers from other major sources, dimensions, and consequences of social inequality" (Hauser & Sweeney, 1997). Nevertheless, the finding that income alone has such small effects outside of status attainment is an important contribution. Rather than undercutting arguments for various government programs, however, it may be a testament to the effectiveness with which "government policies . . . ensure that poor children get basic necessities most of the time" (Mayer, p. 143).

DISCUSSION

Analysis of economic trends in the 1990s documents general prosperity and growing median earnings, particularly of women and the college educated. At the same time, we have documented remarkably persistent poverty and stagnating or declining wages for young men and the poorly educated. Both of these economic circumstances have been implicated in marriage rates and children's educational attainment and, to a lesser extent, in divorce rates, marital quality, and general child well-being. Several important issues remain unresolved.

Measuring Economic Well-Being and Hardship

Objective Indicators. Theoretical treatments of economic inequality usually refer to a multidimensional set of indicators including education, occupational prestige, employment, employment security, wealth, and income. For the most part, however, family research has tended to rely on a narrow subset of these indicators, often using only education and family income and sometimes only income (Smith & Graham, 1995). This may lead to underestimates of the true effect of class inequality on family outcomes, such as that discussed in regard to child outcomes. Our focus on

income may well be driven by the narrowness of policy options feasible in today's political climate, but it is possible that a broader set of scholarly work would provide the impetus for broadening our policy scope beyond minor income redistributions to consider factors such as job quality and security and public education, among others (Danziger, 1996; Hout et al., 1996).

Level of Analysis. Although family studies in the 1990s for the most part focused on individual economic circumstances, an important tradition emphasized larger social ecologies, including the importance of the opportunity structure and economic well-being of the communities in which families live. In particular, the high levels of joblessness in the central cities, especially among minorities and the less well educated, and the growing segregation of rich and poor have been suggested to exacerbate both individual advantage and disadvantage (Farley, 1996). The economic well-being of the community has been addressed in studies of the marriage market (e.g., Cready et al., 1997; Lichter et al, 1991) and family violence (Miles-Doan, 1998), and the effects of social capital of communities on children's outcomes has been addressed in several studies (e.g., Furstenberg & Hughes, 1995), but research on the main and interactive effects of community economies on family outcomes remains undeveloped. The review of families and local ecologies by Burton and Jarrett found in this issue addresses some of these issues.

Subjective measures. The Iowa State project provides the most detailed rationale for using subjective measures of economic hardship. The conceptual framework that underlies their work is that objective economic measures—such as debt-to-asset ratios, income, and unemployment—have indirect effects on family members' psychological states and on family processes and outcomes through the intervening variable of economic pressure (Conger & Elder, 1994). In the Iowa State model, economic pressure is a latent variable reflected in three domains of content: assessment of whether income is sufficient for regular expenses, the extent to which the family members have enough money to buy the kinds of consumer goods they would like to have, and a checklist of economic adjustments (such as borrowing or going into debt) that families might have had to make because of financial need. The focus on feelings of economic pressure instead of on objective economic circumstances is both a strength and a weakness. It provides indirect evidence about other dimensions of class analysis such as consumer class and class identification by tapping issues of relative deprivation and insecurity. It provides a partial window through which to view how American families feel about their prospects for the future and the growing inequality documented in Table 1. As an individual social psychological variable, it is used most often to explain other individual social psychological attributes, such as happiness, depression, and hostility. The disadvantage of this focus is that it contributes to a psychologizing of class issues in place of more structural analyses of how class affects life chances.

For those concerned with the effects of economic transformation and social class on the family, it would be useful to present alternative models in which both the total and the indirect effects of income, wealth, and employment insecurity were assessed. It would also be helpful to examine interaction effects between objective and subjective indicators. Many more families are in economic distress than are in poverty (Fox & Chancey, 1998; Takeuchi et al., 1991), and it would be useful to understand the degree to which the negative effects of economic stress are limited to those who face objective hardship or are experienced equally by those with incomes of $60,000 a year but who have aspirations suitable for $90,000.

Developing a Life-Course Understanding of Economic Effects

Family income and economic status are surprisingly volatile (Duncan, 1984; Duncan et al., 1998), but only a handful of studies examine broad patterns of economic change and their effects on family outcomes. A partial exception is Yeung and Hofferth (1998), who used the Panel Study of Income Dynamics to assess families' experiences with job loss and income loss over 15 years following the birth of a child. Defining significant income loss as a 50% decline in income-to-needs ratio and significant work reduction as a 20% decrease in husband's annual work hours plus an unemployment episode, they reported that one half of all children's families experienced a major economic setback before the children reached age 15. Although economic setbacks were most common among those in the poorest quartile (more than 75% of poor families experienced at

least one of these setbacks), no group was immune: Approximately one third of White families, as well as African American families in the highest quartile, experienced either significant income or work loss. Income loss was associated with greater residential mobility and increased probability of divorce or separation.

We have a growing number of national studies with multiple waves, such as the Panel Study of Income Dynamics, the National Survey of Families and Households, the National Longitudinal Studies, and the Marital Instability Over the Life Course project, that would allow us to track more directly the economic fortunes of families and their consequences. It is possible that broad-based measurement of economic trajectories would help explain racial differentials—not only in marriage and divorce behavior, but also in child outcomes—better than has been possible with one-time measures or year-to-year changes.

Which Comes First? Economic Condition or Family Structure?

Much has been made of the poverty of single-mother households (e.g., McLanahan & Sandefur, 1994). One outcome is that policy discussions and the media often "blame the victim" by suggesting that the poverty of single-mother households could be solved simply by marriage. Nevertheless, we know that nonmarital births are more likely among those whose parents have lower educations (Kahn & Anderson, 1992) and low and declining incomes (Duncan et al., 1998; Wu, 1996) and among young women with few attractive alternative prospects (Upchurch & McCarthy, 1990). Poverty among African American, single-mother families is especially likely to be "reshuffled poverty" (McLanahan & Sandefur). Two-thirds of Black women who were poor after divorce were also poor when married (Bane, 1986)—and probably many were poor before marriage. This research focusing on the extent to which class and social class affect who ends up in which family structures has been overshadowed by the research on the consequences of family structures, and the result is a biased public discussion. We would enhance the quality of policy discourse if our research gave greater emphasis to the determinants of family structure.

Understanding the Interaction of Race and Disadvantage on Family Outcomes

Large racial differences in income and unemployment are a persistent feature of the American class picture. Aside from Ruggles' (1997) claim that these differences explain the racial difference in divorce, the evidence we have assessed does not provide a strong case for attributing observed differences in family outcomes to different structures of opportunity. This raises the old issue of whether ameliorating processes of social support in African American families somehow counterbalance greater economic risk (Broman & Forman, 1997). Alternatively, if economic effects are nonlinear, simple main effects models may underestimate the extent to which earnings and employment explain racial differences. Another possibility is that using a wider variety of economic measures (e.g., job security and stability, career versus dead-end jobs) or more dynamic measures might show stronger effects (Danziger, 1995). Because race is arguably the defining and most persistent inequality in America and because of the strong linkage among race, marriage, and economic well-being, this issue deserves more analysis.

Integrating Women's Role as Providers Into Family Models

Research in the last decade suggested that role complementarity models of marriage are less effective than coprovider models in predicting marriage, divorce, and marital quality. Women and men are increasingly similar in their economic roles, and class is replacing gender as a major determinant of women's economic condition (Huinink & Mayer, 1995). Growing equalities in earnings and labor force attachment raise questions about the extent to which they are paralleled by growing equalities in the domestic division of labor, the internal division of resources within the family, the use of power and coercion in the family, and the socialization of boys and girls.

CONCLUSION

One of the major economic trends of the 1990s, women's growing contribution to family income, appears to have had largely positive effects on family outcomes. Rather than seeing a decreased importance of men's earnings on family outcomes, however, we see significant positive effects of both women's and men's earnings and employment on marriage, marital stability, marital quality, and child outcomes. Many questions remain unresolved, however, including the effects on families of persistent racial inequalities in economic opportunity and a growing disparity be-

tween rich and poor. For the past 2 decades, American families in the middle of the income distribution masked men's stagnating wages by reducing the number of children and increasing wives' labor force participation (Levy, 1995). With these strategies already implemented, economic inequality may seem more visible and problematic in the future. Will Americans, like the Japanese and many Europeans, cut fertility even further, to an average of little over one child? Has marriage, like a Lexus, become an obvious marker of social class? Or is marriage a form of capital that the well off have used to increase their advantage? Questions such as these suggest fruitful fields for further research and a continued vital intersection between the family and social inequality.

NOTE

We appreciate the comments of Alan Booth, Paul Amato, and Bob Schoen on earlier drafts of this manuscript.

REFERENCES

Amato, P. R., & Rogers, S. J. (1997). A longitudinal study of marital problems and subsequent divorce. *Journal of Marriage and the Family, 59,* 612–624.

Auerbach, J. A., & Belous, R. S. (1998). *The inequality paradox: Growth of income disparity.* Washington, DC: National Policy Association.

Axinn, W., Duncan, G. J., & Thornton, A. (1997). The effects of parents' income, wealth and attitudes on children's completed schooling and self-esteem. In G. Duncan & J. Brooks-Gunn (Eds.), *Consequences of growing up poor* (pp. 518–540). New York: Russell Sage Foundation.

Bane, M. J. (1986). Household composition and poverty. In. S. Danziger & D. Weinberg (Eds.), *Fighting poverty: What works and what doesn't?* (pp. 209–231), Cambridge, MA: Harvard University Press.

Becker, G. S. (1981). *A treatise on the family.* Cambridge, MA: Harvard University Press.

Bennett, N. G., Bloom, D. E., & Miller, C. K. (1995). The influence of nonmarital childbearing on the formation of first marriages. *Demography, 32,* 47–62.

Brody, G. H., Stoneman, Z., Flor, D., McCrary, D., Hastings, L., & Conyers, O. (1994). Financial resources, parent psychological functioning, parent co-caregiving, and early adolescent competences in rural two-parent African-American families. *Child Development, 65,* 590–605.

Broman, P. J., & Forman, T. A. (1997). Instrumental and expressive family roles among African American fathers. In R. J. Taylor, J. S. Jackson, & L. M. Chatters (Eds.), *Family life in Black America* (pp. 216–249). Newbury Park, CA: Sage.

Bulcroft, R. A., & Bulcroft, K. A. (1993). Race differences in attitudinal and motivational factors in the decision to marry. *Journal of Marriage and the Family, 55,* 338–355.

Bumpass, L. L., Castro Martin, T., & Sweet, J. A.

(1991). The impact of family background and early marital factors on marital disruption. *Journal of Family Issues, 12,* 22–42.

Bumpass, L. L., Sweet, J. A., & Cherlin, A. (1991). The role of cohabitation in declining rates of marriage. *Journal of Marriage and the Family, 53,* 913–927.

Cancian, M., & Reed, D. (1999). The impact of wives' earnings on income inequality: Issues and estimates. *Demography, 36,* 173–184.

Catalano, R. (1991). The health effects of economic insecurity. *The American Journal of Public Health, 81,* 1148–1153.

Cattan, P. (1998, March). The effect of working wives on the incidence of poverty. *Monthly Labor Review Online.* Retrieved June 25, 2000, from the World Wide Web: http://www.bls.gov/opub/mlr/1998/03/contents.htm

Cherlin, A. (1992). *Marriage, divorce, remarriage* (2nd ed.). Cambridge, MA: Harvard University Press.

Clark-Nicolas, P., & Gray-Little, B. (1991). Effect of economic resources on marital quality in Black married couples. *Journal of Marriage and the Family, 53,* 645–655.

Clarkberg, M. (1999). The price of partnering: The role of economic well-being in young adults' first union experiences. *Social Forces, 66,* 945–968.

Conger, R. D., & Elder, G. H. (1994). *Families in troubled times: Adapting to change in rural America.* New York: Aldine de Gruyter.

Conger, R. D., Elder, G. H., Lorenz, F. O., Conger, K. J., Simons, R. L., Whitbeck, L. B., Huck, S., & Melby, J. N. (1990). Linking economic hardship to marital quality and instability. *Journal of Marriage and the Family, 52,* 643–656.

Cready, C. M., Fossett, M. A., & Kiecolt, K. J. (1997). Mate availability and African American family structure in the U.S. nonmetropolitan South, 1960–1990. *Journal of Marriage and the Family, 59,* 192–203.

Dalaker, J., & Naifeh, M. (1998). U.S. Bureau of the Census, *Current Population Reports* (Series P60-201, Poverty in the United States: 1997). Washington, DC: U.S. government printing office.

Danziger, S. (1995). Commentary. In M. B. Tucker & C. Mitchell-Kerman (Eds.), *The decline in marriage among African Americans* (pp. 59–95). New York: Russell Sage Foundation.

Danziger, S. (1996). Comment on "The age of extremes: Concentrated affluence and poverty in the twenty-first century." *Demography, 33,* 413–416.

Danziger, S., & Gottschalk, P. (1995). *America unequal.* Cambridge, MA: Harvard University Press.

Dawson, D. A. (1991). Family structure and children's health and well-being: Data from the 1988 health interview survey on child health. *Journal of Marriage and the Family, 53,* 573–584.

Day, R. D. (1992). The transition to first intercourse among racially and culturally diverse youth. *Journal of Marriage and the Family, 54,* 749–762.

Duncan, G. J. (1984). *Years of poverty, years of plenty.* Ann Arbor: Institute for Social Research, University of Michigan.

Duncan, G. J., & Brooks-Gunn, J. (1997). Income effects across the life span: Integration and interpretation. In G. J. Duncan & J. Brooks-Gunn (Eds.), *The consequences of growing up poor* (pp. 596–610). New York: Russell Sage Foundation.

Duncan, G. J., Yeung, W. J., Brooks-Gunn, J., & Smith, J. R. (1998). How much does childhood poverty affect the life chances of children? *American Sociological Review, 63,* 406–423.

Eggebeen, D. J., & Lichter, D. T. (1991). Race, family structure, and changing poverty among American Children. *American Sociological Review, 56,* 801–817.

Farber, N. (1990). The significance of race and class in marital decisions among unmarried adolescent mothers. *Social Problems, 37,* 51–63.

Farley, R. (1996). *The new American reality.* New York: Russell Sage Foundation.

Fox, G. L., & Chancey, D. (1998). Sources of economic distress: Individual and family outcomes. *Journal of Family Issues, 19,* 725–749.

Freeman, R. B. (1998). Is the new income inequality the Achilles' heel of the American economy? In J. Auerbach & R. S. Belous (Eds.), *The inequality paradox: Growth of income disparity.* (pp. 219–229). Washington, DC: National Policy Association.

Furstenberg, F. F., Jr., & Hughes, M. E. (1995). Social capital and successful development among at-risk youth. *Journal of Marriage and the Family, 57,* 580–592.

Gittleman, M., & Joyce, M. (1999). Have family income mobility patterns changed? *Demography, 36,* 295–314.

Greenstein, T. N. (1995). Gender ideology, marital disruption, and the employment of married women. *Journal of Marriage and the Family, 57,* 31–42.

Hanson, T. L., McLanahan, S., & Thomson, E. (1997). Economic resources, parental practices, and children's well-being. In G. Duncan & J. Brooks-Gunn (Eds.), *The consequences of growing up poor* (pp. 180–238). New York: Russell Sage Foundation.

Hauser, R. M., & Sweeney, M. M. (1997). Does poverty in adolescence affect the life chances of high school graduates? In G. Duncan & J. Brooks-Gunn (Eds.), *The consequences of growing up poor* (pp. 541–595). New York: Russell Sage Foundation.

Heckert, D. A., Nowak, T. C., & Snyder, K. A. (1998). The impact of husbands' and wives' relative earnings on marital disruption. *Journal of Marriage and the Family, 60,* 690–703.

Heidermann, B., Suhomlinova, O., & O'Rand, A. M. (1998). Economic independence, economic status, and empty nest in midlife marital disruption. *Journal of Marriage and the Family, 60,* 690–703.

Hipple, S. (1998). Contingent work: Results from the second survey. *Monthly Labor Review, 124,* no. 11.

Hoffman, S. D., & Duncan, G. J. (1995). The effect of incomes, wages, and AFDC benefits on marital disruption. *Journal of Human Resources, 30,* 19–42.

Hout, M., Arum, R., & Voss, K. (1996). The political economy of inequality in the "age of extremes." *Demography, 33,* 421–425.

Huinink, J., & Mayer, K. U. (1995). Gender, social inequality, and family formation in West Germany. In K. O. Mason & A-M. Jensen (Eds.), *Gender and family change in industrialized countries* (pp. 168–199). Oxford, U.K.: Clarendon.

Kahn, J. R., & Anderson, K. E. (1992). Intergenerational patterns of teenage fertility. *Demography, 29,* 39–57.

Koball, H. (1998). Have African American men become

less committed to marriage? Explaining the twentieth century racial cross-over in men's marriage timing. *Demography, 35,* 251–258.

Komarovsky, M. (1940). *The unemployed man and his family.* New York: Dryden Press.

Levy, F. (1995). Incomes and income inequality. In R. Farley (Ed.), *State of the nation: Volume 1. Economic trends.* (pp. 1–57). New York: Russell Sage Foundation.

Lichter, D. T., LeClere, F. B., & McLaughlin, D. K. (1991). Local marriage markets and the marital behavior of Black and White women. *American Journal of Sociology, 96,* 843–867.

Lichter, D. T., McLaughlin, D. K., Kephart, G., & Landry, D. J. (1992). Race and the retreat from marriage: A shortage of marriageable men? *American Sociological Review, 57,* 781–799.

Lichter, D. T., McLaughlin, D. K., & Ribar, D. C. (1997). Welfare and the rise in female-headed families. *American Journal of Sociology, 103,* 112–143.

Lloyd, K. M., & South, S. J. (1996). Contextual influences on young men's transitions to first marriages. *Social Forces, 74,* 1097–1119.

Lorenz, F. O., Conger, R. D., Simons, R. L., Whitbeck, L. B., & Elder, G. H., Jr. (1991). Economic pressure and marital quality: An illustration of the method variance problem in the causal modeling of family processes. *Journal of Marriage and the Family, 53,* 375–388.

Manning, W. D., & Landale, N. S. (1996). Racial and ethnic differences in the role of cohabitation in premarital childbearing. *Journal of Marriage and the Family, 58,* 63–77.

Manning, W. D., & Smock, P. J. (1995). Why marry? Race and the transition to marriage among cohabitors. *Demography, 32,* 509–520.

Mare, R. D., & Winship, C. (1991). Socioeconomic change and the decline of marriage for Blacks and Whites. In C. Jencks & P. E. Peterson (Eds.), *The urban underclass* (pp. 175–202). Washington, DC: Brookings Institute.

Mayer, S. E. (1997). *What money can't buy: Family income and children's life chances.* Cambridge, MA: Harvard University Press.

McCloskey, L. A. (1996). Socioeconomic and coercive power within the family. *Gender and Society, 10,* 449–463.

McLanahan, S., & Sandefur, G (1994). *Growing up with a single parent.* Cambridge, MA: Harvard University Press.

McLaughlin, D. K., & Lichter, D. T. (1997). Poverty and the marital behavior of young women. *Journal of Marriage and the Family, 59,* 582–594.

McLoyd, V. C., Epstein Jayaratne, T., Ceballo, R., & Borquez, J. (1994). Unemployment and work interruption among African American single mothers: Effects on parenting and adolescent socioemotional functioning. *Child Development, 65,* 562–589.

McNeil, J. (1998). *Changes in median household income: 1969 to 1996* (U.S. Bureau of the Census, Current Population Reports. Special Studies, P23-196). Washington, DC: U.S. Government Printing Office.

Menaghan, E. G., & Parcel, T. L. (1991). Determining children's home environments: The impact of maternal characteristics and occupational and family con-

ditions. *Journal of Marriage and the Family, 53,* 417–431.

Miles-Doan, R. (1998). Violence between spouses and intimates. Does neighborhood context matter? *Social Forces, 77,* 623–645.

Mills, C. W. (1959). *The sociological imagination.* New York: Oxford University Press.

Moffitt, R. A. (1998). The effect of welfare on marriage and fertility. In R. A. Moffitt (Ed.), *Welfare, the family, and reproductive behavior: Research perspectives* (pp. 50–97). Washington, DC: National Academy Press.

Ono, H. (1998). Husbands' and wives' resources and marital dissolution. *Journal of Marriage and the Family, 60,* 674–689.

Oppenheimer, V. K. (1995). The role of women's economic independence in marriage formation: A skeptic's response to Annemette Sorensen's remarks. In H.-P. Blossfeld (Ed.), *The new role of women: Family formation in modern societies* (pp. 236–243). Boulder, CO: Westview Press.

Oppenheimer, V. K. (1997a). Comment on "The rise of divorce and separation in the United States, 1880–1990." *Demography, 34,* 467–472.

Oppenheimer, V. K. (1997b). Women's employment and the gain to marriage: The specialization and trading model. *Annual Review of Sociology, 23,* 431–453.

Oppenheimer, V. K., Kalmijn, M., & Lim, N. (1997). Men's career development and marriage timing during a period of rising inequality. *Demography, 34,* 311–330.

Oppenheimer, V. K., & Lewin, A. (1999). Career development and marriage formation in a period of rising inequality: Who is at risk? What are their prospects? In A. Booth, A. C. Crouter, & M. J. Shanahan (Eds.), *Transition to adulthood in a changing economy* (pp. 189–225). New York: Praeger.

Preston, S. H. (1997). Comment on Steven Ruggles's "The rise of divorce and separation in the United States, 1880–1990." *Demography, 34,* 473–474.

Raley, R. K. (1996). A shortage of marriageable men? A note on the role of cohabitation in Black-White differences in marriage rates. *American Sociological Review, 61,* 973–983.

Rogers, S. J. (1999). Wives' income and marital quality: Are there reciprocal effects? *Journal of Marriage and the Family, 61,* 123–132.

Rogers, S. J., & Amato, P. R. (1997). Is marital quality declining? The evidence from two generations. *Social Forces, 75,* 1089–1100.

Roschelle, A. R. (1997). *No more kin.* Thousand Oaks, CA: Sage.

Rubin, L. B. (1994). *Families on the fault line.* New York: HarperCollins.

Ruggles, S. (1997). The rise of divorce and separation in the United States, 1880–1990. *Demography, 34,* 455–466.

Sandefur, G. D., McLanahan, S., & Wojtkiewicz, R. A. (1992). The effects of parental marital status during adolescence on high school graduation. *Social Forces, 71,* 103–122.

Sassler, S., & Schoen, R. (1999). The effect of attitudes and economic activity on marriage. *Journal of Marriage and the Family, 61,* 147–159.

Sayer, L., & Bianchi, S. M. (1998, August). Independence or interdependence? Re-examining women's economic independence and the probability of divorce. Paper presented at the 1998 meetings of the American Sociological Association, San Francisco, CA.

Simons, R. L., Whitbeck, L. B., Melby, J. N., & Wu, C-I. (1994). Economic pressure and harsh parenting. In R. D. Conger & G. H. Elder, Jr. (Eds.), *Families in troubled times: Adapting to change in rural America* (pp. 207–222). New York: Aldine de Gruyter.

Smith, T. E., & Graham, P. G. (1995). Socioeconomic stratification family research. *Journal of Marriage and the Family, 57,* 930–940.

Smock, P. J. (1990). Remarriage patterns of Black and White women: Reassessing the role of educational attainment. *Demography, 27,* 467–474.

Smock, P. J., & Manning, W. D. (1997). Cohabiting partners' economic circumstances and marriage. *Demography, 34,* 331–341.

Sorensen, A. (1995). In H.-P. Bossfeld (Ed.), *The new role of women: Family formation in modern societies* (pp. 229–235). Boulder, CO: Westview Press.

South, S. J. (1991). Sociodemographic differentials in mate selection preferences. *Journal of Marriage and the Family, 53,* 928–940.

South, S. J., & Lloyd, K. M. (1992). Marriage markets and nonmarital fertility in the United States. *Demography, 29,* 247–264.

South, S. J., & Lloyd, K. M. (1995). Spousal alternatives and marital dissolution. *American Sociological Review, 60,* 21–35.

Spain, D., & Bianchi, S. M. (1996). *Balancing act: Motherhood, marriage, and employment among American women.* New York: Russell Sage Foundation.

Straus, M. A. (1990). Social stress and marital violence in a national sample of American families. In M. A. Straus & R. J. Gelles (Eds.), *Physical violence in American families* (pp. 181–202). New Brunswick, NJ: Transaction.

Takeuchi, D. T., Williams, D. R., & Adair, R. K. (1991). Economic stress in the family and children's emotional and behavioral problems. *Journal of Marriage and the Family, 53,* 1031–1041.

Teachman, J. D., & Polonko, K. A. (1990). Cohabitation and marital stability in the United States. *Social Forces, 69,* 207–220.

Testa, M., & Krogh, M. (1995). The effect of employment on marriage among Black males in inner-city Chicago. In M. B. Tucker & C. Mitchell-Kernan (Eds.), *The decline in marriage among African Americans* (pp. 59–95). New York: Russell Sage Foundation.

Thornton, A. (1989). Changing attitudes toward family issues in the United States. *Journal of Marriage and the Family, 51,* 873–893.

Trent, K., & South, S. J. (1992). Sociodemographic status, parental background, childhood family structure, and attitudes toward family formation. *Journal of Marriage and the Family, 54,* 427–439.

Tzeng, J. M., & Mare, R. D. (1995). Labor market and socioeconomic effects on marital stability. *Social Science Research, 24,* 329–351.

Upchurch, D., & McCarthy, J. (1990). The timing of a first birth and high school completion. *American Sociological Review, 55,* 224–234.

U.S. Bureau of the Census. (1997). Historical Income Table-Families, (TableF-2): Share of aggregate income received by each fifth and top 5 percent of families (all races): 1947–1997. *Historical Income Table–Families,* Retrieved July 21, 2000, from the World Wide Web: http://www.census.gov/hhes/income/histinc/f02.html

U.S. Bureau of the Census. (1998a). Current Population Reports, P60-203, Measuring 50 years of economic change using the March Current Population Survey. Washington, DC: U.S. Government Printing Office.

U.S. Bureau of the Census. (1998b). Labor force statistics from the Current Population Survey (Table A-3): Employment status of the civilian population 25 years and over by educational attainment. Retrieved July 21, 2000 from the World Wide Web: http://www.bls.gov/webapps/legacy/cpsatab3.htm

U.S. Bureau of Labor Statistics. (1998a). Labor force statistics from the Current Population Survey (Table A-1): Employment status of the civilian population by age and sex. Retrieved July 21, 2000 from the World Wide Web: http://www.bls.gov/webapps/legacy/cpsatab1.html

U.S. Bureau of Labor Statistics (1998b). Labor force statistics from the Current Population Survey (Table A-2): Employment status of the civilian population by race, sex, age, and Hispanic origin. Retrieved July 21, 2000 from the World Wide Web: http://www.bls.gov/webapps/legacy/cpsatab2.htm

U.S. Bureau of Labor Statistics. (1998c). Employee tenure in 1998. Published September 23, 1998. Retrieved July 21, 2000, from the World Wide Web: http://www.bls.gov/bls_news/archives/all_nr.htm #TENURE

U.S. Bureau of Labor Statistics. (1999). Another real raise in 1998. Monthly Labor Review Online. The editor's desk July 21, 2000. Retrieved from the World Wide Web: http://www.bls.gov/opub/mlr/1999/01/lmir/htm

Weiss, Y., & Willis, R. J. (1997). Match quality, new information, and marital dissolution. *Journal of Labor Economics, 15,* S293–330.

Wilson, W. J. (1987). *The truly disadvantaged.* Chicago: University of Chicago Press.

Wilson, W. J. (1996). *When work disappears: The world of the new urban poor.* New York: Vintage Books.

Wu, L. (1996). Effects of family instability, income, and income instability on the risk of a premarital birth. *American Sociological Review, 61,* 386–406.

Yellen, J. L. (1998). Trends in income inequality. In J. Auerbach & R. S. Belous (Eds.), *The inequality paradox: Growth of income disparity.* (pp.7–17). Washington, DC: National Policy Association.

Yeung, W. J., & Hofferth, S. (1998). Family adaptations to income and job loss in the United States. *Journal of Family and Economic Issues, 19,* 255–283.

CHARLOTTE J. PATTERSON   *University of Virginia*

Family Relationships of Lesbians and Gay Men

The family lives of lesbian and gay people have been a source of controversy during the past decade. Despite prejudice and discrimination, lesbians and gay men have often succeeded in creating and sustaining family relationships. Research on same-gender couple relationships, parent-child relationships, and other family relationships is reviewed here. In general, the picture of lesbian and gay relationships emerging from this body of work is one of positive adjustment, even in the face of stressful conditions. Research is also beginning to address questions about individual differences among the family relationships of lesbians and gay men. Future work in this area has the potential to affect lesbian and gay lives, influence developmental and family theory, and inform public policies in the decade ahead.

The family lives of lesbian and gay people have been a subject of controversy during the past decade. Because of the stigma attached to nonheterosexual identities, those who declare lesbian or gay identities often do so at the risk of relationships in families of origin. In the United States, as in most other nations, the law does not recognize marriages between same-gender partners, nor—in many jurisdictions—does it protect relationships between lesbian or gay parents and their children. Despite such obstacles, however, lesbian and gay people have often succeeded in creating and sustaining meaningful family relationships.

Department of Psychology, Gilmer Hall, P.O. Box 400400, University of Virginia, Charlottesville, VA 22904 (cjp@virginia.edu).

Key Words: families, gay men, lesbians, parenting, relationships.

How this has been accomplished, at what cost, and with what results, is the subject of this essay.

A preliminary issue concerns the assessment of sexual orientation itself, a notoriously challenging topic (McWhirter, Sanders, & Reinisch, 1990; Michaels, 1996). Common understandings of terms such as "lesbian," "gay," and "bisexual" generally rest on the belief that sexual attractions, sexual behaviors, and sexual identities coincide. For instance, a man who is sexually attracted to other men is generally expected to have sexual relations mainly or exclusively with men and to identify as gay. Such expectations are not always correct, however (Diamond, 1998; Golden, 1987; Savin-Williams, 1998b). Felt attractions, actual sexual behavior, and sexual identities may match one another for some individuals, but for others the situation may be quite different. Furthermore, although it is generally assumed that sexual orientation is a stable part of a person's identity over the entire life course, and although this may often be the case, mounting evidence suggests that, particularly for women, sexual identities may shift over time (e.g., Kitzinger & Wilkinson, 1995). When such considerations are combined with controversies over the extent to which categorical or dimensional systems are best in the assessment of sexual orientation (McWhirter et al., 1990), it becomes clear that simple two- or three-category schemes often may fail to capture the complexity of many lives.

This article presents an overview of recent research on the family lives of lesbians and gay men (see also Laird & Green, 1996; Patterson & D'Augelli, 1998). Research on lesbian and gay couples is described first, followed by studies of lesbian and gay parents and their children, and then by research on other family relationships. The review of research is followed by a discussion of some limitations of existing work and suggestions about directions for future research.

Research on lesbian and gay couples has addressed a variety of interrelated issues. In this section, I give an overview of findings on love and commitment, power and the division of labor, sexual behavior, problems and conflict in relationships, and the ending of couple relationships. For other recent reviews of research and theory on lesbian and gay couples, see James and Murphy (1998), Klinger (1996), Kurdek (1995), McWhirter and Mattison (1996), Murphy (1994), Peplau (1991), and Peplau, Veniegas, and Campbell (1996).

Love and Commitment

Many if not most lesbians and gay men express the desire for an enduring love relationship with a partner of the same gender. Indeed, research findings suggest that many are successful in creating such relationships. Survey data suggest that 40 to 60% of gay men and 45 to 80% of lesbians are currently involved in steady romantic relationships (see Peplau & Cochran, 1990; Peplau et al., 1996). Because most surveys involve many young adults who may not yet have found romantic partners, these figures may underestimate the actual numbers.

When asked about their current relationship, lesbians and gay men report as much satisfaction with their relationships as do heterosexual couples; the great majority describe themselves as happy (Cardell, Finn, & Maracek, 1981; Kurdek & Schmidt, 1986a, 1986b; Peplau, Padesky, & Hamilton, 1982). For example, Peplau and Cochran (1990) described a study of 50 lesbians, 50 gay men, 50 heterosexual women, and 50 heterosexual men who were currently involved in romantic relationships. Both lesbians and gay men reported very positive feelings about their partners and rated their relationships as very satisfying. There were no differences as a function of sexual orientation on any of the measures of relationship quality (Peplau & Cochran, 1990).

Research also has focused on factors related to differences in relationship satisfaction between couples. The correlates of relationship quality for lesbian and gay couples include feelings of having equal power, perceiving many attractions and few alternatives to the relationship, endorsing few dysfunctional beliefs about the relationship, placing a high value on the relationship, and engaging in shared decision making (Blumstein & Schwartz, 1983; Kurdek, 1994, 1995).

Power and Division of Labor

The great majority of lesbian and gay couples believe that an equal balance of power is desirable (Peplau & Cochran, 1990), but not all report that they achieve equality. In Peplau and Cochran's study, only 59% of lesbians, 38% of gay men, 48% of heterosexual women, and 40% of heterosexual men reported that the balance of power in their current relationship was exactly equal. Others have found that majorities of gay as well as lesbian couples report equal power (see Peplau et al., 1996).

When power is unequal in a relationship, which partner has more power in an intimate relationship and why? Social exchange theory predicts that the partner with greater personal resources (e.g., income, education) should have greater power (Peplau, 1991), and results of a number of studies have supported this view. For example, Harry found that older, wealthier men tended to have more power in their intimate relationships (Harry, 1984; Harry & DeVall, 1978). Caldwell and Peplau, in a study of young lesbians (1984), reported that wealthier, better educated women tended to have more power than their partners. In an early study, Blumstein and Schwartz (1983) reported that the partner with greater financial resources had more power in money management issues in gay, married heterosexual, and unmarried (but cohabiting) heterosexual couples, but not in lesbian couples. The extent to which financial resources affect balance of power in lesbian couples remains an open question (see Peplau et al., 1996).

Other predictions from exchange theory have also received empirical support (Kurdek, 1995; Peplau, 1991; Peplau et al., 1996). In social exchange theory, the "principle of least interest" states that when one person is more dependent or involved than the other, the more dependent partner is expected to have less power (Peplau, 1991). Consistent with this view, Caldwell and Peplau (1984) found associations between unequal involvement and unequal power among lesbian couples. As predicted by social exchange theory, the woman who was less involved in the relationship had more power.

Although some expect that, in same-gender couples, one partner plays a traditionally "male" and one a traditionally "female" role, research has consistently found that this is rarely the case (Kurdek, 1995; Peplau et al., 1996). For example, Bell and Weinberg reported in 1978 that most lesbians and gay men in their sample reported sharing domestic tasks equally. More recently, Kurdek (1993) reported egalitarian divisions of labor among lesbian and gay couples without children. Others have described similar findings among lesbian and gay couples who are raising children together (Chan, Brooks, Raboy, & Patterson, 1998; Dunne, 1998; Gartrell et al., 1999; McPherson, 1993; Patterson, 1995c; Sullivan, 1996; Tasker & Golombok, 1998).

Sexual Behavior

Sexual behavior among lesbian and gay couples has been found to vary considerably as a function of gender. First, the frequency of genital sexual behavior has been reported to decline with the duration of a relationship, and this is true of reports given by lesbian, gay, heterosexual married, and unmarried (but cohabiting) heterosexual couples (Kurdek, 1995). These declines are less pronounced among gay and more pronounced among lesbian couples than among heterosexual couples, whether married or not. The frequency of genital sexual relations, as reported in surveys, thus appears to increase with the number of men in a couple. It is also possible that lesbian couples have different conceptions of sexuality and of sexual behavior than do gay men or heterosexual couples (Blumstein & Schwartz, 1983).

Another area in which strong gender differences emerge is in that of the degree of a couple's desire for and accomplishment of sexual exclusivity. Lesbians and heterosexual couples have generally been found to be more supportive than gay men of monogamy in their relationships, and their reported behavior corresponds to these views. In their classic study, Blumstein and Schwartz (1983) reported that among couples who had been together between 2 and 10 years, most lesbian and heterosexual couples preferred and experienced monogamous sexual relationships, whereas most gay couples did not. These data were collected before the HIV/AIDS epidemic had attracted public attention. Nonetheless, data collected during 1988–1989, after HIV infection had become wide-

spread in the United States, revealed the same pattern of results (Bryant & Demian, 1994).

Despite differences in preferences and in actual behavior, however, lesbian, gay, heterosexual married, and unmarried (but cohabiting) heterosexual couples all report similar satisfaction with their sexual relationships (Bryant & Demian, 1994). Thus, although gender differences in sexual attitudes and sexual behavior would appear to be substantial, reported sexual satisfaction within couple relationships has not varied as a function of sexual orientation or gender of partners (Kurdek, 1995; Peplau, 1991).

Problems and Conflict in Couples

When lesbian and gay couples experience problems in their relationships, some of these stem from the same roots from which difficulties in heterosexual relationships also arise. As in heterosexual relationships, problems can arise because of different religious, racial, ethnic, or socioeconomic backgrounds and because of the different values that these backgrounds may have inculcated. Relationship difficulties can also arise as a result of problems at either partner's job, financial pressures on the couple, friction with members of extended family networks, and so forth, just as they do in heterosexual relationships. Kurdek (1994, 1995) reported that the top five areas of conflict for lesbian and gay couples were finances, driving style, affection/sex, being overly critical, and division of household tasks.

There are some conflicts that are probably unique to lesbian and gay couples and prominent among these are issues created by negative social attitudes toward homosexuality (Kurdek & Schmidt, 1987). When a couple disagrees about the extent to which they should disclose the lesbian or gay nature of their relationship, problems in their relationship can ensue (James & Murphy, 1998). Resolution of such conflicts may be central to the success of the couple relationship over time (Peplau et al., 1996).

The longevity of lesbian and gay relationships has also been a topic of some research. Blumstein and Schwartz (1983) found that for couples who had been together 10 years, breakup rates over the 18 months of their study were low; only 6% of lesbian couples, 4% of gay couples, and 4% of married couples separated during this period. For couples who had been together less than 2 years, 22% of lesbian couples, 16% of gay couples, 17% of cohabiting (but unmarried) heterosexual couples, and only 4% of heterosexual married couples had separated; thus, being married was associated with low break-up rates, but otherwise there were no differences. A more recent study (see Kurdek, 1995) also found low rates of separation and no differences in break-up rates between lesbian and gay couples.

Kurdek and Schmidt (1986a) compared the attractions that a relationship held for the partners and also the barriers to exiting a relationship for lesbian, gay, unmarried (but cohabiting) heterosexual, and married heterosexual couples. They found no differences among these four types of couples in the strength of attractions toward their relationships but did find significant differences in barriers to leaving the relationships. Specifically, married heterosexual spouses reported more obstacles to exiting the relationship than did members of the other three types of couples.

In addition to all the usual ways in which couple relationships can end, gay relationships in particular have been subject to unusual stresses because of the HIV/AIDS epidemic (Mattison & McWhirter, 1994; Paul, Hays & Coates, 1995). In the early 1990's, a survey of a large group of gay men in New York City found that nearly one third had suffered the loss of a close friend or lover to AIDS (Martin & Dean, 1993). Such men may not only have cared for a dying partner through a long illness, but also experienced bereavement without many of the supports available to surviving members of heterosexual couples (D'Augelli & Garnets, 1995; Paul et al., 1995).

LESBIAN AND GAY PARENTS AND THEIR CHILDREN

When considering lesbian and gay parents and their children, it is helpful to recognize the diversity of family constellations (Arnup, 1995; Benkov, 1994). One important distinction (Patterson, 1992) is between families in which children were born or adopted in the context of heterosexual marriages that later dissolved when one or both parents came out as gay or lesbian on the one hand, and those in which children were born or adopted after parents had affirmed lesbian or gay identities on the other. Families of the first type have undergone the tensions and reorganizations characteristic of parental divorce and separation, whereas families of the second type have not necessarily experienced these transitions. Children's histories are likely to be different in these two types of families.

Within each of these two types of families, there are of course many additional forms of diversity (Lewin, 1993). Apart from the ethnic, religious, economic, and other forms of diversity that characterize other families, there are also a number of forms of diversity that are more specific to lesbian and gay family formation (Martin, 1993; Patterson, 1994b; Weston, 1991). For instance, a lesbian couple and a gay couple may agree to conceive children together and raise them jointly. Variants on this kind of arrangement might involve a gay couple and a single lesbian, or a lesbian couple and a single gay man.

One important impetus for research in the area of lesbian and gay parents has come from extrinsic sources, such as judicial concerns about the psychological health and well-being of divorced lesbian mothers and their children compared with that of divorced heterosexual mothers and their children. Other work has emerged from concerns that are more intrinsic to the families themselves, such as the role of biological linkages in the formation of family relationships. In some areas, existing research addresses only those concerns arising from extrinsic sources, but wherever possible, I address both types of issues. Other recent reviews of this literature can be found in Brewaeys and Van Hall (1997), Falk (1994), Flaks (1994), Kirkpatrick (1996), Parks (1998), Patterson (1992, 1995a, 1997), Patterson and Chan (1997), Tasker and Golombok (1991, 1997), and Victor and Fish (1995).

Divorced Lesbian Mothers

Research comparing lesbian and gay parents and their children with heterosexual parents and their children often has been designed to address negative assumptions that have been expressed in judicial opinions, legislative initiatives or public policies relevant to lesbian and gay parents and their children (Patterson & Redding, 1996). Thus, many studies have been conducted to evaluate the accuracy of negative expectations about lesbian and gay parents or about their children.

Because it often has been raised as an issue by judges presiding over custody disputes (Falk, 1989), a number of studies have assessed the overall mental health of lesbian compared with heterosexual mothers. Consistent with data on the mental health of lesbians in general (Gonsiorek, 1991), research in this area has revealed that divorced lesbian mothers score at least as high as divorced heterosexual mothers on assessments of psychological health. For instance, studies have found no differences between lesbian and heterosexual mothers on self-concept, happiness, overall adjustment, or psychiatric status (Falk, 1989, 1994; Patterson, 1992, 1997).

Another area of judicial concern has focused on maternal gender role behavior and its potential impact on children (Patterson, 1995a, 1995b). Stereotypes cited by the courts suggest that lesbians might be unusually masculine and that they might interact inappropriately with their children. In contrast to expectations based on the stereotypes, however, neither lesbian mothers' reports about their gender role behavior nor their self-described interest in childrearing have been found to differ from those of heterosexual mothers. Reports about responses to child behavior and ratings of warmth toward children have been found not to differ significantly between lesbian and heterosexual mothers.

Differences between lesbian and heterosexual mothers also have been reported. Among the most straightforward of these are the early reports by Lyons (1983) and Pagelow (1980) that divorced lesbian mothers in their samples had more fears about loss of child custody than did divorced heterosexual mothers. Similarly, Green, Mandel, Hotvedt, Gray, and Smith (1986) reported that lesbian mothers were more likely than heterosexual mothers to be active in feminist organizations.

A few other scattered differences seem more difficult to interpret. For instance, Miller, Jacobsen, and Bigner (1981) reported that lesbian mothers they studied were more child-centered than were heterosexual mothers in their discipline techniques. In a sample of African American lesbian and heterosexual mothers, Hill (1987) found that lesbian mothers reported being more flexible about rules, more relaxed about sex play and modesty, and more likely to have nontraditional expectations for their daughters.

Several studies have also examined the social circumstances and relationships of lesbian mothers. Divorced lesbian mothers have consistently been reported to be more likely than divorced heterosexual mothers to be living with a romantic partner (Harris & Turner, 1985/1986; Kirkpatrick, Smith, & Roy, 1981; Pagelow, 1980). Whether this represents a difference between lesbian and heterosexual mother-headed families or it reflects a sampling bias of the research cannot be determined on the basis of information in the published reports. Information is sparse about the impact of such relationships in lesbian-mother families, but

that which has been published suggests that, like heterosexual stepparents, coresident lesbian partners of divorced lesbian mothers can be important sources of conflict as well as support in the family.

Relationships with the fathers of children in lesbian-mother homes have also been a topic of study. Few differences in the likelihood of paternal financial support have been reported for lesbian and heterosexual families with children; Kirkpatrick and her colleagues (1981) reported, for example, that only about one half of heterosexual and about one half of lesbian mothers in their sample received financial support from the fathers of their children. Findings about frequency of contact with the fathers are mixed, with some (e.g., Kirkpatrick et al., 1981) reporting no differences as a function of maternal sexual orientation and others (e.g., Golombok, Spencer, & Rutter, 1983) reporting more contact among lesbian than among heterosexual mothers.

Although most research to date has involved assessment of possible differences between lesbian and heterosexual mothers, a few studies have reported other types of comparisons. For instance, in a study of divorced lesbian mothers and divorced gay fathers, Harris and Turner (1985/1986) found that gay fathers were likely to report higher incomes and that they encouraged more gender-typed toy play among their children whereas lesbian mothers were more likely to see benefits for their children (e.g., increased empathy and tolerance for differences) as a result of having lesbian or gay parents. In comparisons of relationship satisfaction among lesbian couples who did or did not have children, Koepke, Hare, and Moran (1992) reported that couples with children scored higher on overall measures of relationship satisfaction and of the quality of their sexual relationship.

Another important set of questions, as yet little studied, concerns the conditions under which lesbian mothers experience enhanced feelings of well-being, support, and ability to care for their children. Rand, Graham, and Rawlings (1982) reported that psychological health of lesbian mothers was associated with the mothers' openness about her sexual orientation with her employer, ex-husband, children, and friends, and with her degree of feminist activism. Kirkpatrick (1987) found that lesbian mothers living with partners and children had greater economic and emotional resources than those living alone with their children.

Many other issues that have arisen in the context of divorced, lesbian-mother families are also in need of study. For instance, when a mother is in the process of coming out as a lesbian to herself and to others, at what point in that process should she address the topic with her child, and in what ways should she do so—if at all? And what influence ought the child's age and circumstances have in such a decision? Reports from research and clinical practice suggest that early adolescence may be a particularly difficult time for parents to initiate discussions of this topic and that disclosure may be less stressful at earlier or later points in a child's development (Patterson, 1992; 1995a). Similarly, many issues remain to be addressed regarding step-family and blended family relationships that may emerge as a lesbian mother's household seeks new equilibrium following her separation or divorce from the child's father.

Divorced Gay Fathers

Although considerable research has focused on the overall psychological adjustment of lesbian mothers compared with that of heterosexual mothers, no published studies of gay fathers make such comparisons with heterosexual fathers. This may be attributable to the greater role of judicial decision making as an impetus for research on lesbian mothers (Patterson & Redding, 1996). In jurisdictions where the law provides for biases in custody proceedings, these are likely to favor female and heterosexual parents. Perhaps because, other things being equal, gay fathers are unlikely to win custody battles over their children after divorce, fewer such cases seem to have reached the courts. Consistent with this view, only a minority of divorced gay fathers have been described as living in the same households as their children (Bigner & Bozett, 1990; Bozett, 1980, 1989).

Research on the parenting attitudes of gay versus heterosexual divorced fathers has been reported, however. Bigner and Jacobsen (1989a, 1989b) compared gay and heterosexual fathers, each of whom had at least two children. Their results revealed that, with one exception, there were no significant differences between gay and heterosexual fathers in their motives for parenthood. The single exception concerned the greater likelihood of gay than heterosexual fathers to cite the higher status accorded to parents as compared with non-parents as a motivation for parenthood (Bigner & Jacobsen, 1989a).

Bigner and Jacobsen (1989b) also asked gay and heterosexual fathers in their sample to report on their behavior when interacting with their children. Although no differences emerged in the fathers' reports of involvement or intimacy, gay fathers reported that their behavior was characterized by greater responsiveness, more reasoning, and more limit setting than was that of heterosexual fathers. These reports by gay fathers of greater warmth and responsiveness on the one hand and of greater control and limit setting on the other are strongly reminiscent of findings from research with heterosexual families and would seem to raise the possibility that gay fathers are more likely than their heterosexual counterparts to exhibit authoritative patterns of parenting behavior such as those described by Baumrind (Baumrind & Black, 1967).

In addition to research comparing gay and heterosexual fathers, a handful of studies have made other comparisons. For instance, Robinson and Skeen (1982) compared gender-role orientations of gay fathers with those of gay men who were not fathers and found no differences. Similarly, Skeen and Robinson (1985) found no evidence to suggest that gay men's retrospective reports about relationships with their own parents varied as a function of whether they were parents themselves. As noted above, Harris and Turner (1985/1986) compared gay fathers and lesbian mothers and reported that although gay fathers had higher incomes and were more likely to report encouraging their children to play with gender-typed toys, lesbian mothers were more likely to believe that their children received positive benefits such as increased tolerance for diversity from having lesbian or gay parents. Findings such as these suggest a number of issues for research on gender, sexual orientation, and parenting behavior.

Much research in this area has also arisen from concerns about the gay father identity and its transformations over time. Thus, work by Miller (1978, 1979) and Bozett (1980, 1981a, 1981b, 1987) sought to provide a conceptualization of the processes by which a man who considers himself to be a heterosexual father may come to identify himself, both in public and in private, as a gay father. Based on extensive interviews with gay fathers in the United States and Canada, these authors emphasized the pivotal nature of identity disclosure itself and of the reactions to disclosure by significant people in a man's life. Miller (1978) suggested that although a number of factors such as the extent of occupational autonomy and amount of access to gay communities may affect how rapidly a gay man discloses his identity to others, the most important of these is likely to be the experience of falling in love with another man. It is this experience, more than any other, Miller argued, that leads a man to integrate the otherwise compartmentalized parts of his identity as a gay father.

Lesbians and Gay Men Choosing to Become Parents

Although for many years lesbian mothers and gay fathers were generally assumed to have become parents in the context of previous heterosexual relationships, both men and women are believed increasingly to be undertaking parenthood in the context of preexisting lesbian and gay identities (Beers, 1996; Crawford, 1987; Gartrell et al., 1996, 1999; Patterson, 1994a, 1994b). Although a substantial body of research addresses the transition to parenthood among heterosexuals (e.g., Cowan & Cowan, 1992), little research has explored this transition among gay men or lesbians.

The first question concerns whether to pursue parenthood at all (Beers, 1996; Sbordone, 1993). In one study of gay men who were not parents, Beers found that about half of the participants reported that they would like to become parents. Interestingly, those who expressed the desire to become parents were also assessed at higher levels of psychosocial development (assessed within an Eriksonian framework) and at higher levels of identity formation with regard to their gay identities, but there were no differences in retrospective reports of experiences with their own parents. Sbordone studied gay men who had become parents through adoption or surrogacy arrangements after coming out and compared them with gay men who were not fathers. There were no differences between fathers and nonfathers on reports about relationships with the men's own parents. Gay fathers did, however, report higher self-esteem and fewer negative attitudes about homosexuality than did gay men who were not fathers.

An interesting result of the Sbordone (1993) study was that more than half of the gay men who were not fathers indicated that they would like to rear a child. Those who said that they wanted children were younger than those who said they did not, but the two groups did not differ otherwise (e.g., on income, race, education, or attitudes about homosexuality). Given that fathers had higher self-esteem and fewer negative attitudes about homosexuality than either group of nonfathers, Sbordone suggested that gay fathers' higher

self-esteem might be a result rather than a cause of parenthood. No comparable results have been reported as yet in the literature on transition to parenthood among lesbian women.

Having made the decision to pursue parenthood, a number of interrelated issues are often faced by lesbians and gay men (Crawford, 1987; Patterson, 1994b; Pies, 1985). One of the first needs is for accurate, up-to-date information on how lesbians and gay men can become parents, how their children are likely to develop, and what supports are available. Lesbians and gay men who are seeking biological parenthood are also likely to encounter various health concerns, ranging from medical screening of prospective birthparents to assistance with donor insemination techniques, prenatal care, and preparation for birth. As matters progress, legal concerns about the rights and responsibilities of all parties may also emerge. Associated with all of these will generally be financial issues; in addition to the support of a child, auxiliary costs of medical and legal assistance may be considerable. Finally, social and emotional concerns of many different kinds are also likely to surface (Martin, 1998; Pies, 1985, 1990; Patterson; Rohrbaugh, 1988).

As this brief overview of issues suggests, numerous questions are posed by the emergence of prospective lesbian and gay parents. What are the factors that influence lesbians' and gay men's inclinations to make parenthood a part of their lives, and through what processes do they exert an influence? What effects does parenting have on lesbians or gay men who undertake it, and how do these effects compare with those experienced by heterosexuals? How effectively do special services such as support groups serve the needs of lesbian and gay parents and prospective parents for whom they were designed? What are the elements of a social climate that is supportive for gay and lesbian parents and their children? As yet, little research has addressed such questions.

RESEARCH ON CHILDREN OF LESBIAN AND GAY PARENTS

In this section, research on children born in the context of heterosexual relationships is presented first, followed by a description of work with children born to or adopted by lesbian and gay parents. Most samples studied to date have been composed mainly of White, middle-class, largely professional families. Whenever samples differ from this description, that fact is specifically noted in the discussion.

Research on Children Born in the Context of Heterosexual Relationships

As with research on lesbian mothers, much of the impetus for research in this area has come from judicial concerns about the welfare of children residing with gay or lesbian parents (Patterson & Redding, 1996). Research in each of three main areas of judicial concern—namely, children's sexual identity, other aspects of children's personal development, and children's social relationships—is summarized here. For other recent reviews of this material, see Gibbs (1988), Green and Bozett (1991), Patterson (1992, 1995c, 1997, 1998), Perrin (1998), and Tasker and Golombok (1991, 1997).

Reflecting issues relevant in the largest number of custody disputes, most of the research compares development of children with custodial lesbian mothers to that of children with custodial heterosexual mothers. Because many children living in lesbian mother-headed households have undergone parental divorce and separation, it has been widely believed that children living in families headed by divorced but heterosexual mothers provide the best comparison group.

Sexual identity. Research on the development of sexual identity has explored the development of gender identity, gender-role behavior, and sexual orientation. Gender identity concerns a person's self-identification as male or female. Gender-role behavior involves the extent to which a person's activities and occupations are regarded by the culture as masculine, feminine, or both. Sexual orientation refers to a person's choice of sexual partners (e.g., heterosexual, homosexual, or bisexual). To examine the possibility that children in the custody of lesbian mothers experience disruptions of sexual identity, research has addressed each of these three major facets of sexual identity.

Research on gender identity has failed to reveal any differences in the development of children as a function of their parents' sexual orientation. In an early study, Kirkpatrick et al. (1981) compared development among children of lesbian mothers with that among same-aged children of heterosexual mothers. In projective testing, most children in both groups drew a same-gender figure first, a finding that fell within expected norms. Of those who drew an opposite-gender figure first, only

three (one with a lesbian mother, and two with heterosexual mothers) showed concern about gender issues in clinical interviews. Similar findings have been reported in projective testing by other investigators (e.g., Green et al., 1986), and studies using more direct methods of assessment (e.g., Golombok et al., 1983) have yielded similar results.

Research on gender-role behavior has also failed to reveal difficulties in the development of children with lesbian mothers. For instance, Green (1978) reported that a large majority of children of lesbian mothers in his sample named a favorite toy consistent with conventional gender-typed toy preferences and that all reported vocational choices fell within typical limits for conventional gender roles. In interviews with 56 children of lesbians and 48 children of heterosexual mothers, Green and his colleagues (1986) found no differences with respect to favorite television programs, television characters, games, or toys. These investigators reported that daughters of lesbian mothers were more likely to be described as taking part in rough and tumble play or as playing with "masculine" toys such as trucks or guns, but found no comparable differences for sons.

A number of investigators have also studied sexual orientation, the third component of sexual identity. For instance, Huggins (1989) interviewed a group of teenagers, half of whom were the offspring of lesbian mothers and half of heterosexual mothers. No child of a lesbian mother identified as lesbian or gay, but one child of a heterosexual mother did. Similar results have been reported by other investigators (e.g., Golombok & Tasker, 1996; Gottman, 1990). Studies of the offspring of gay fathers have yielded similar results (Bozett, 1987).

Two studies conducted from a behavior genetic perspective have recently added to this literature. Pattatucci and Hamer (1995) studied a large sample of women, some of whom identified as lesbian or bisexual. Of the 19 such women in their sample with daughters old enough to report sexual orientation, six daughters were identified as lesbian or bisexual using relatively loose criteria for this assessment. When more restrictive criteria were used, however, only one of seven adult daughters were identified as lesbian or bisexual. No significant results emerged for sons of nonheterosexual mothers in this sample. Bailey, Bobrow, Wolfe, and Mikach (1995) interviewed gay fathers and inquired as to the sexual orientation of their adult sons. They reported that 7 of 75 (9%) of the sons in their sample were identified as gay or bisexual. No information about the daughters of gay fathers was collected in this study. Definitive interpretation of these numbers depends on the population base rates for nonheterosexual identities, and as noted earlier, these are not known. Thus, the clearest conclusion from these and the earlier studies is that the great majority of children with lesbian or gay parents grow up to identify themselves as heterosexual (Bailey & Dawood, 1998).

As clear as these results are, it should be recognized that research on the development of sexual identity among the offspring of lesbian and gay parents has been criticized from a number of perspectives. For instance, many lesbian women do not self-identify as lesbians until adulthood (see Brown, 1995); for this reason, studies of sexual orientation among adolescents may count as heterosexual some individuals who will identify as lesbian later in life. Concern has also been voiced that in many studies that compare children of divorced heterosexual mothers with children of divorced lesbian mothers, the lesbian mothers were more likely to be living with a romantic partner; in these cases, maternal sexual orientation and relationship status have been confounded. Although these and other methodological issues await resolution, it remains true that no significant problems in the development of sexual identity among children of lesbian mothers have yet been identified.

Other aspects of personal development. Studies of other aspects of personal development among children of gay and lesbian parents have assessed a broad array of characteristics (Patterson, 1995a; Tasker & Golombok, 1995). Among these have been psychiatric evaluations and assessments of behavior problems, personality, self-concept, locus of control, moral judgment, and intelligence. Concerns about possible difficulties in personal development among children of lesbian and gay parents have not been sustained by the results of research (Patterson, 1992, 1995a, 1997). As was true for sexual identity, studies of other aspects of personal development have revealed no significant differences between children of lesbian or gay parents and children of heterosexual parents. Thus, fears that children of gay and lesbian parents suffer deficits in personal development are without empirical foundation.

Social relationships. Studies assessing potential differences between children of gay and lesbian

versus heterosexual parents have sometimes included assessments of children's social relationships. Because of concerns voiced in legal settings that children of lesbian and gay parents might encounter difficulties among their peers, the most common focus of attention has been on peer relations. Research has consistently found that children of lesbian mothers report normal peer relations and that adult observers agree with this judgment (Patterson, 1992). Anecdotal accounts sometimes describe children's worries about being stigmatized as a result of their parents' sexual orientation (e.g., Pollack & Vaughn, 1987), but research findings to date provide no evidence to suggest that children of lesbian mothers have difficulties in peer relations (Tasker & Golombok, 1995).

Research has also been directed toward description of children's relationships with adults, especially fathers. For instance, Golombok and her colleagues in the United Kingdom (1983) found that children of lesbian mothers were more likely than children of heterosexual mothers to have contact with their fathers. Most children of lesbian mothers had some contact with their fathers during the year preceding the study, but most children of heterosexual mothers had not; indeed, almost one third of the children of lesbian mothers reported at least weekly contact with their fathers, whereas only 1 in 20 of the children of heterosexual mothers reported this. Kirkpatrick and her colleagues (1981) also reported that lesbian mothers in their sample were more concerned than heterosexual mothers that their children have opportunities for good relationships with adult men, including fathers. Lesbian mothers' social networks have been found to include both men and women, and their offspring as a result have contact with adults of both genders. Overall, results of research to date suggest that children of lesbian parents have satisfactory relationships with adults of both genders.

Concerns that children of lesbian or gay parents are more likely than children of heterosexual parents to be sexually abused have also been voiced by judges in the context of child custody disputes (Patterson, 1992). Results of research in this area show that the great majority of adults who perpetrate sexual abuse are men; sexual abuse of children by adult women is extremely rare. Lesbian mothers are thus extremely unlikely to abuse their children. Existing research findings suggest that gay men are no more likely than heterosexual men to perpetrate child sexual abuse

(Jenny, Roesler, & Poyer, 1994). Fears that children in custody of gay or lesbian parents might be at heightened risk for sexual abuse are without empirical foundation (Patterson, 1992, 1995a, 1997).

Diversity Among Children With Divorced Lesbian or Gay Parents

Despite the great diversity evident within gay and lesbian communities, research on differences among children of lesbian and gay parents is as yet relatively sparse.

One important dimension of difference among gay and lesbian families concerns whether the custodial parent is involved in a romantic relationship, and if so what implications this may have for children. Pagelow (1980), Kirkpatrick et al. (1981), and Golombok et al. (1983) reported that in their samples, divorced lesbian mothers were more likely than divorced heterosexual mothers to be living with a romantic partner. Huggins (1989) reported that self-esteem among daughters of lesbian mothers whose lesbian partners lived with them was higher than that among daughters of lesbian mothers who did not live with a partner. This finding might be interpreted to mean that mothers who are high in self-esteem are more likely to be involved in romantic relationships and to have daughters who are also high in self-esteem, but many other interpretations are also possible. In view of the small sample size and absence of conventional statistical tests, Huggins' finding should be interpreted with great caution. Particularly in view of the judicial attention that lesbian mothers' romantic relationships have received during custody proceedings (Falk, 1989), it is surprising that more research has not examined the impact of this variable on children.

Rand et al. (1982) found that lesbian mothers' sense of psychological well-being was related to the extent to which they were open about their lesbian identity with employers, ex-husbands, and children. In their sample, a mother who felt more able to disclose her lesbian identity was also more likely to express a positive sense of well-being. In light of the consistent finding that in heterosexual families, children's adjustment is often related to indexes of maternal mental health (Sameroff & Chandler, 1975), one might expect factors that enhance mental health among lesbian mothers also to benefit the children of these women, but this possibility has not yet been studied.

Another area of great diversity among families with a gay or lesbian parent concerns the degree to which a parent's sexual identity is accepted by other significant people in children's lives. Huggins (1989) found a tendency for children whose fathers were rejecting of maternal lesbianism to report lower self-esteem than those whose fathers were neutral or positive. Because of small sample size and absence of conventional statistical tests, this finding should be seen as suggestive rather than definitive.

Effects of the age at which children learn of parents' gay or lesbian identities have also been a topic of study. Paul (1986) reported that those who were told either in childhood or in late adolescence found it easier to cope with the news than did those who first learned of it during adolescence. Huggins (1989) reported that those who learned of maternal lesbianism in childhood had higher self-esteem than did those who were not informed of it until they were adolescents. Early adolescence may be a particularly difficult time for children to learn of their parents' lesbian or gay identities (Patterson, 1992).

As this discussion reveals, research on diversity among families with gay and lesbian parents is only beginning. Existing data favor early disclosure of identity to children, good maternal mental health, and a supportive milieu, but the available data are still limited. Little information is yet available on differences attributable to race or ethnicity, family economic circumstances, cultural environments, or related variables. Because none of the published work has employed observational measures or longitudinal designs, little is known about the details of actual behavior in these families or about any changes over time.

Research on Children Born to or Adopted by Lesbian Mothers

Many writers have noted recent increases in childbearing among lesbians, but research with these families is as yet relatively new (Kirkpatrick, 1996; Martin, 1993; Patterson, 1992, 1994b). Here, I summarize the research to date on children born to or adopted by lesbian mothers. Although some gay men are also becoming parents after coming out, no research has yet been reported on their children.

In one of the first systematic studies of children born to lesbians, Steckel (1987) compared the progress of separation-individuation among preschool children born via donor insemination to lesbian couples with that among same-aged children of heterosexual couples. She compared independence, ego functions, and object relations among children in the two types of families and reported impressive similarity in development among children in the two groups. Similar findings, based on extensive interviews with a smaller group of lesbian mother families were also reported by McCandlish (1987).

Another early study examining psychosocial development among preschool and school-aged children born to or adopted by lesbian mothers was conducted by Patterson (1994a), who studied 37 four- to nine-year-old children. Using a variety of standardized measures, the study sought to provide an overview of the children's development. Results showed that children scored in the normal range for all measures. For instance, children of lesbian mothers' scores for social competence, internalizing behavior problems, and externalizing behavior problems differed significantly from the scores for a clinical sample but did not differ from the scores for a large normative sample of American children. Likewise, children of lesbian mothers reported gender-role preferences within the expected normal range for children of this age. On most subscales of the self-concept measure, answers given by children of lesbian mothers did not differ from those given by same-aged children of heterosexual mothers studied in a standardization sample.

On two subscales of the self-concept measure, however, Patterson (1994a) found that children of lesbian mothers reported feeling more reactions to stress (e.g., feeling angry, scared, or upset), but a greater sense of well-being (e.g., feeling joyful, content, and comfortable with themselves) than did the same-aged children of heterosexual mothers in the standardization sample. One possible interpretation of this result is that children of lesbian mothers reported greater reactivity to stress because, in fact, they experienced greater stress in their daily lives than did other children. Another possibility is that, regardless of actual stress levels, children of lesbian mothers were better able to acknowledge both positive and negative aspects of their emotional experience.

Contrary to stereotypes of these families as isolated from families of origin, most reported that children had regular (i.e., at least monthly) contact with one or more grandparents, as well as with other adult friends and relatives of both genders (Patterson, Hurt, & Mason, 1998). In families headed by lesbian couples, the parents were likely to maintain egalitarian divisions of labor, but

when differences occurred, biological lesbian mothers were likely to do somewhat more child care and nonbiological lesbian mothers were likely to spend somewhat more time engaged in paid employment (Patterson, 1995c). Even within the relatively small range represented in this sample, families in which child care was divided more evenly were also those in which children exhibited the most favorable adjustment (Patterson, 1995c). These results suggest the importance of family process variables as predictors of child adjustment in lesbian as well as in heterosexual families.

Chan and his colleagues (Chan, Brooks, et al., 1998; Chan, Raboy, & Patterson, 1998) studied a group of 80 families formed by lesbian and heterosexual parents via donor insemination (DI) and reported similar findings. Children's overall adjustment was unrelated to parents' sexual orientation. Regardless of parents' sexual orientation or relationship status, parents who were experiencing higher levels of parenting stress, higher levels of interparental conflict, and lower levels of love for each other had children who exhibited more behavior problems. Among lesbian couples, nonbiological mothers' satisfaction with the division of labor, especially in family decision making, was related to better couple adjustment, which was in turn related to children's positive psychological adjustment (Chan, Raboy, et al., 1998), a result that is consistent with research on heterosexual families (Cowan, Cowan, & Kerig, 1993). Flaks, Ficher, Masterpasqua, & Joseph (1995) also compared children from lesbian mother families with those from heterosexual families and found no differences in the children's level of psychological adjustment as a function of mother's sexual orientation.

In Europe, Brewaeys, Ponjaert, Van Hall, & Golombok (1997) studied adjustment among a group of 4- to 8-year-old children who were conceived via DI by lesbian and heterosexual parents and compared them to a group of children who were conceived by heterosexual parents in the conventional way. When children were asked about their perceptions of parent-child relationships, all children reported positive feelings about their parents, and there were no differences in children's reports as a function family types. Children's behavior and emotional adjustment were also assessed, and results indicated that overall, children who were conceived via DI in heterosexual families exhibited more behavior problems than children who were conceived in the conventional way. Furthermore, girls who were conceived via DI in heterosexual families exhibited more behavioral problems than girls from other family types. Brewaeys concluded that the differences observed in the heterosexual DI families may have been attributable to issues related to secrecy regarding DI; in particular, some fathers wished to conceal information about their own infertility, and this contributed to their wish to maintain secrecy about the use of DI. Such concerns were not relevant to lesbian mother families, whose use of DI did not reflect on their own fertility and who generally disclosed information about their use of DI.

In another European study, Golombok, Tasker, and Murray (1997) reported on the psychological well-being of children raised since birth by lesbian mothers and by heterosexual single mothers. These children were compared with children raised in two-parent heterosexual families. Results indicated that these children did not show unusual emotional or behavior problems (as reported by parents or by teachers), and there were no differences as a function of family type. In terms of children's attachment relationships to their parents, children from mother-only families (lesbian mothers and heterosexual single mothers) scored higher on an attachment-related assessment than did children reared by heterosexual couples, suggesting the possibility that children from mother-only families had more secure attachment relationships with their mothers. With respect to children's perceived competence, children from mother-only families reported lower perceived cognitive and physical competence than those children from father-present families. Thus, key findings in this study seemed to depend on parents' gender rather than parental sexual orientation.

RESEARCH ON OTHER FAMILY RELATIONSHIPS

In addition to parent-child and couple relationships in which they may participate, lesbians and gay men are likely also to maintain contacts with parents, siblings, and other members of their families of origin (Cohen & Savin-Williams, 1996; D'Augelli, Hershberger, & Pilkington, 1998; Herdt & Beeler, 1998; Laird, 1998; Patterson & D'Augelli, 1998; Patterson et al., 1998; Savin-Williams, 1998a). Although, as Herdt and Beeler, Laird, and others have emphasized, many other issues are undoubtedly significant, the largest amount of research to date has focused on the concerns of young lesbians and gay men about

disclosing their sexual identities to members of their families of origin, especially to parents.

Most lesbians and gay men apparently come out first to close friends and only later—if at all—to family members (Herdt & Boxer, 1993; Savin-Williams, 1990). Young people are more likely to come out first to mothers rather than to fathers, perhaps because they expect more positive responses from mothers (Bryant & Demian, 1994; Cohen & Savin-Williams, 1996).

Although it is difficult to predict parental reactions to disclosure of a nonheterosexual orientation by their offspring, the most common initial reactions are negative (Cohen & Savin-Williams, 1996; D'Augelli & Hershberger, 1993; D'Augelli et al., 1998; Strommen, 1989a, 1989b). Negative reactions are likely to be more pronounced among older parents, those with less education, and those whose parent-child relationships were troubled before the disclosure. Although interactions between lesbian and gay young people and their parents often suffer difficulties immediately after disclosure, they most often improve again over time as families assimilate this new information into existing images of the lesbian or gay child. The best predictor of postdisclosure relationships between lesbian and gay young adults and their parents is the quality of their relationships before the disclosure (Cohen & Savin-Williams; Savin-Williams, 1990).

What are the associations between disclosure of lesbian or gay identity to parents and young adults' self-esteem? Because of the significance of parent-adolescent relationships, one might expect parental acceptance to be associated with favorable self-images among lesbian and gay youth. Consistent with this view, Savin-Williams (1990) found that teenaged and young-adult lesbians who reported that their parents were accepting of their sexual identities (or would be accepting if they knew) also reported feeling more comfortable with their sexual orientation. This was true for young men only if they also described their parents as important to their self-image, however (Savin-Williams, 1990). Because the research to date has been correlational in nature, it cannot be determined whether parental acceptance makes lesbian and gay children feel better about themselves, whether youth who already have high self-esteem are more likely to disclose to parents, or whether a cyclical process may be involved.

While some research has focused on young adults' disclosure of lesbian and gay identities to parents, other studies have shown that among samples of older lesbian and gay adults, sizeable proportions have not come out to parents or other family members. When a lesbian or gay identity has not been disclosed, any one of several coping strategies may be employed by the individual and the family (Brown, 1989).

When a family member's nonheterosexual orientation becomes known, Strommen (1989a, 1989b) has described the family's reaction as involving a two-stage process. First, the family members struggle to understand and assimilate this new information about one of its members. The family may then simply reject the lesbian or gay person, or it may reorganize itself over time to accommodate this shift in identity while still including the lesbian or gay person in family activities. Parents in particular often find that the process of reorganization can be difficult, often extending over substantial periods of time. In the end, many discover that the process has brought them unexpected gifts (Bernstein, 1995).

Disclosure of nonheterosexual identity is only one issue of many that are relevant to lesbian and gay family lives. Research has not yet explored at any length the ways in which sexual identities affect other aspects of parent-child or sibling relationships in adulthood (Allen & Demo, 1995). How are experiences of change in romantic relationships, parenting, and occupational lives affected by an individual's assuming either a lesbian or gay identity? How do the sexual identities of family members affect responses to illness, death, and bereavement? How indeed does sexual orientation affect understandings of family membership itself? There is much territory here for research to explore, and there have been some intriguing recent efforts (Badgett, 1998; Herdt & Beeler, 1998; Laird, 1998; Weinstock, 1998); such explorations should lead to a more inclusive understanding of family lives.

DISCUSSION AND DIRECTIONS FOR FUTURE RESEARCH

Research on lesbian and gay couples and on families with children, although relatively new, has nevertheless yielded some important results.

Without denying the consistency of major research findings to date, it is important first to acknowledge that much of the research is subject to various criticisms. For instance, much of the research has involved small samples that are predominantly White, well-educated, middle class, and American; the degree to which results would

hold with other populations is thus difficult to evaluate. It would also be desirable to have data based on observational methods, collected within longitudinal designs. Longitudinal studies are beginning to appear (e.g., Gartrell et al., 1999; Tasker & Golombok, 1997), but observational work is still lacking. Other issues could also be raised (see Patterson, 1995a).

Despite limitations, however, central results of existing research on lesbian and gay couples and families with children are exceptionally clear. Beyond their witness to the sheer existence of lesbian and gay family lives, the results of existing studies, taken together, also yield a picture of families thriving, even in the midst of discrimination and oppression. Certainly, they provide no evidence that psychological adjustment among lesbians, gay men, their children, or other family members is impaired in any significant way. Indeed, the evidence suggests that relationships of lesbian and gay couples are just as supportive and that home environments provided by lesbian and gay parents are just as likely as those provided by heterosexual parents to enable psychosocial growth among family members.

As discussed above, much research on lesbian and gay parenting has focused primarily on comparisons between lesbian and gay families and heterosexual families. This approach presumably reflects the concern of researchers to address prejudices and negative stereotypes that have been influential in judicial decision making and in public policies relevant to lesbian and gay couples, parents, and their children in the United States. Now that results of research have begun to converge so clearly on answers to questions posed in this way, the time has come also to address a broader range of issues in this area.

Many important research questions arise from a focus on the interests of lesbian- and gay-parented families themselves. For instance, many lesbian and gay couples with children are interested in distinctions between the experiences of biological and nonbiological parents (Patterson, 1998). How important, they ask, are the biological linkages in influencing experiences of parenthood? Similarly, both lesbian and gay parented families are concerned about the qualities of children's experiences at school, and some groundbreaking work in this area has been reported by Casper and her colleagues (Casper & Schultz, 1999; Casper, Schultz, & Wickens, 1992). In the future, scholarship likely will increasingly concern itself with the study of sources of strength and resilience in lesbian and gay couples, as well as among lesbian and gay parents and their children.

In the meantime, however, the central results of research to date have important implications. If psychosocial development among children born to lesbian mothers and gay fathers is, as research suggests (Patterson, 1994a), essentially normal, then traditional theoretical emphases on the importance of parental heterosexuality need to be reconsidered. Although many possible approaches to such a task are possible (Patterson, 1992), one promising approach is to focus on the significance of family process rather than structure. Thus, structural variables such as parental sexual orientation may ultimately be seen as less important in mediating children's developmental outcomes than qualities of family interactions, relationships, and processes. By including variables of both types, future research will facilitate comparisons between them.

Results of research with lesbian and gay parents and their children also have implications for what might be termed the "politics of family life." If, as appears to be the case, neither parents nor children in lesbian and gay families run any special risk of maladjustment or other psychosocial problems, then a good rationale for prejudice and discrimination becomes more and more difficult to provide. Without such a rationale, many legal precedents and public policies relevant to lesbian and gay families would require reconsideration. Ultimately, lesbian and gay couples and parents might come to be viewed as couples and parents like others, and policies might be designed to protect their legitimate interests, as well as those of their family members. Although some recent steps in this direction have been taken, much remains to be done.

Considering substantive directions of future research, it is important to note that a number of issues have gone all but unexplored to date in the research literature on lesbian and gay family lives. For instance, little attention has been devoted to assessment of sexual orientation over time (Kitzinger & Wilkenson, 1995). Similarly, the phenomena associated with bisexuality (Paul, 1996) have received relatively little study. Ethnic, racial, and socioeconomic diversity of lesbian and gay family lives have yet to be systematically explored. Little research has been conducted outside of the United States. These gaps all provide important opportunities for future research.

From a methodological perspective, it would be valuable to have more studies that follow couples or parents and their children over time. Longitudinal studies of the relationships between lesbians, gay men, and members of their families of origin over relatively long periods of time could also be helpful in describing predictable sequences of reactions to significant life events (e.g., coming out, having a child) among family members. To avoid the pitfalls associated with retrospective reporting, these studies should utilize prospective designs that follow participants over time.

Another methodological issue in the literature to date is the dearth of observational data. Observational studies of couples, parents, and children, as well as of lesbian and gay adults with members of their families of origin, could provide valuable evidence about similarities and differences between family processes in the family lives of lesbian, gay, and heterosexual adults. Such observational data could be collected from dyads or triads or larger family groups, at home or in the laboratory, in a single visit or in repeated sessions over time; these kinds of data could add tremendously to knowledge about the families of lesbians and gay men.

Overall, the study of lesbian and gay family lives provides a context in which to explore the limits of existing theoretical perspectives and an opportunity to develop new ones. Future research that addresses these challenges has the potential to improve understanding of lesbian and gay family life, increase inclusiveness of theoretical notions about family structure and process, and inform public policies and judicial rulings relevant to lesbian and gay family lives. Rapid change in attitudes, social climates, and even legal rulings relevant to lesbian and gay family lives during the last 25 years in the United States has, in many ways, transformed the daily lives of lesbians and gay men and those of their family members as well. The experiences associated with lesbian and gay family lives will no doubt also be transformed by future events. Another role for research in the years ahead, then, is to document the ways in which secular changes in attitudes, behaviors, and public policies both influence and are influenced by lesbians, by gay men, and by their families.

REFERENCES

Allen, K. R., & Demo, D. H. (1995). The families of lesbians and gay men: A new frontier in family research. *Journal of Marriage and the Family, 57,* 1–17.

Arnup, K. (Ed.). (1995). *Lesbian parenting: Living with*

pride and prejudice. Charlottetown, Canada: Gynergy Press.

Badgett, M. V. L. (1998). The economic well-being of lesbian, gay and bisexual adults' families. In C. J. Patterson & A. R. D'Augelli (Eds.), *Lesbian, gay and bisexual identities in families: Psychological perspectives.* New York: Oxford University Press.

Bailey, J. M., Bobrow, D., Wolfe, M., & Mikach, S. (1995). Sexual orientation of adult sons of gay fathers. *Developmental Psychology, 31,* 124–129.

Bailey, J. M., & Dawood, K. (1998). Behavior genetics, sexual orientation, and the family. In C. J. Patterson & A. R. D'Augelli (Eds.), *Lesbian, gay and bisexual identities in families: psychological perspectives.* New York: Oxford University Press.

Baumrind, D., & Black, A. E. (1967). Socialization practices associated with dimensions of competence in preschool boys and girls. *Child Development, 38,* 291–327.

Beers, J. R. (1996). *The desire to parent in gay men.* Unpublished doctoral dissertation, Columbia University, New York, NY.

Bell, A. P., & Weinberg, M. S. (1978). *Homosexualities: A study of diversity among men and women.* New York: Simon & Schuster.

Benkov, L. (1994). *Reinventing the family: The emerging story of lesbian and gay parents.* New York: Crown.

Bernstein, R. A. (1995). *Straight parents, gay children: Keeping families together.* New York: Thunder's Mouth Press.

Bigner, J. J., & Bozett, F. W. (1990). Parenting by gay fathers. In F. W. Bozett & M. B. Sussman (Eds.), *Homosexuality and family relations* (pp. 155–176). New York: Harrington Park Press.

Bigner, J. J., & Jacobsen, R. B. (1989a). The value of children to gay and heterosexual fathers. In F. W. Bozett (Ed.), *Homosexuality and the family* (pp. 163–172). New York: Harrington Park Press.

Bigner, J. J., & Jacobsen, R. B. (1989b). Parenting behaviors of homosexual and heterosexual fathers. In F. W. Bozett (Ed.), *Homosexuality and the family* (pp. 173–186). New York: Harrington Park Press.

Blumstein, P., & Schwartz, P. (1983). *American couples: Money, work, sex.* New York: William Morrow.

Bozett, F. W. (1980). Gay fathers: How and why they disclose their homosexuality to their children. *Family Relations, 29,* 173–179.

Bozett, F. W. (1981a). Gay fathers: Evolution of the gay-father identity. *American Journal of Orthopsychiatry, 51,* 552–559.

Bozett, F. W. (1981b). Gay fathers: Identity conflict resolution through integrative sanctioning. *Alternative Lifestyles, 4,* 90–107.

Bozett, F. W. (1987). Children of gay fathers. In F. W. Bozett (Ed.), *Gay and lesbian parents* (pp. 39–57). New York: Praeger.

Bozett, F. W. (1989). Gay fathers: A review of the literature. In F. W. Bozett (Ed.), *Homosexuality and the family* (pp. 137–162). New York: Harrington Park Press.

Brewaeys, A., Ponjaert, I., Van Hall, E. V., & Golombok, S. (1997). Donor insemination: Child development and family functioning in lesbian mother families. *Human Reproduction, 12,* 1349–1359.

Brewaeys, A., & Van Hall, E. V. (1997). Lesbian moth-

erhood: The impact on child development and family functioning. *Journal of Psychosomatic Obstetrics and Gynecology, 18,* 1–16.

Brown, L. (1989). Lesbians, gay men, and their families: Common clinical issues. *Journal of Gay and Lesbian Psychotherapy, 1,* 65–77.

Brown, L. (1995). Lesbian identities: Concepts and issues. In A. R. D'Augelli & C. J. Patterson (Eds.), *Lesbian, gay and bisexual identities over the lifespan: Psychological perspectives* (pp. 3–23). New York: Oxford University Press.

Bryant, A. S., & Demian (1994). Relationship characteristics of American gay and lesbian couples: Findings from a national survey. *Journal of Gay and Lesbian Social Services, 1,* 101–117.

Caldwell, M. A., & Peplau, L. A. (1984). The balance of power in lesbian relationships. *Sex Roles, 10,* 587–599.

Cardell, M., Finn, S., & Maracek, J. (1981). Sex-role identity, sex-role behavior, and satisfaction in heterosexual, lesbian, and gay male couples. *Psychology of Women Quarterly, 5,* 488–494.

Casper, V., & Schultz, S. (1999). *Gay parents, straight schools: Building communication and trust.* New York: Teachers College Press.

Casper, V., Schultz, S., & Wickens, E. (1992). Breaking the silences: Lesbian and gay parents and the schools. *Teachers College Record, 94,* 109–137.

Chan, R. W., Brooks, R. C., Raboy, B., & Patterson, C. J. (1998). Division of labor among lesbian and heterosexual parents: Associations with children's adjustment. *Journal of Family Psychology, 12,* 402–419.

Chan, R. W., Raboy, B., & Patterson, C. J. (1998). Psychosocial adjustment among children conceived via donor insemination by lesbian and heterosexual mothers. *Child Development, 69,* 443–457.

Cohen, K. M., & Savin-Williams, R. C. (1996). Developmental perspectives on coming out to self and others. In R. C. Savin-Williams & K. M. Cohen (Eds.), *The lives of lesbians, gays, and bisexuals: Children to adults* (pp. 113–151). New York: Harcourt Brace.

Cowan, C. P., & Cowan, P. A. (1992). *When partners become parents: The big life change for couples.* New York: Basic Books.

Cowan, P. A., Cowan, C. P., & Kerig, P. K. (1993). Mothers, fathers, sons, and daughters: Gender differences in family formation and parenting style. In P. A. Cowan, D. Field, D. Hansen, A. Skolnick, & G. Swanson (Eds.), *Family, self, and society: Toward a new agenda for family research* (pp. 165–195). Hillsdale, NJ: Erlbaum.

Crawford, S. (1987). Lesbian families: Psychosocial stress and the family-building process. In Boston Lesbian Psychologies Collective (Ed.), *Lesbian psychologies: Explorations and challenges* (pp. 195–214). Urbana: University of Illinois Press.

D'Augelli, A. R., & Garnets, L. (1995). Lesbian, gay and bisexual communities. In A. R. D'Augelli and C. J. Patterson (Eds.), *Lesbian, gay and bisexual identities over the lifespan: Psychological perspectives* (pp. 293–320). New York: Oxford University Press.

D'Augelli, A. R., & Hershberger, S. L. (1993). Lesbian, gay and bisexual youth in community settings: Personal challenges and mental health problems. *American Journal of Community Psychology, 21,* 421–448.

D'Augelli, A. R., Hershberger, S. L., & Pilkington, N. W. (1998). Lesbian, gay and bisexual youths and their families: Disclosure of sexual orientation and its consequences. *American Journal of Orthopsychiatry, 68,* 361–371.

Diamond, L. M. (1998). Development of sexual orientation among adolescent and young adult women. *Developmental Psychology, 34,* 1085–1095.

Dunne, G. D. (1998). Add sexuality and stir: Towards a broader understanding of the gender dynamics of work and family life. *Journal of Lesbian Studies, 2,* 1–8.

Falk, P. J. (1989). Lesbian mothers: Psychosocial assumptions in family law. *American Psychologist, 44,* 941–947.

Falk, P. J. (1994). The gap between psychosocial assumptions and empirical research in lesbian-mother child custody cases. In A. E. Gottfried (Ed.), *Redefining families: Implications for children's development.* (pp. 131–156). NewYork: Plenum Press.

Flaks, D. K. (1994). Gay and lesbian families: Judicial assumptions, scientific realities. *William & Mary Bill of Rights Journal, 3,* 345–372.

Flaks, D. K., Ficher, I., Masterpasqua, F., & Joseph, G. (1995). Lesbians choosing motherhood: A comparative study of lesbian and heterosexual parents and their children. *Developmental Psychology, 31*(1), 105–114.

Gartrell, N., Banks, A., Hamilton, J., Reed, N., Bishop, H., & Rodas, C. (1999). The national lesbian family study: II. Interviews with mothers of toddlers. *American Journal of Orthopsychiatry, 69,* 362–369.

Gartrell, N., Hamilton, J., Banks, A., Mosbacher, D., Reed, N., Sparks, C. H., & Bishop, H. (1996). The national lesbian family study: I. Interviews with prospective mothers. *American Journal of Orthopsychiatry, 66,* 272–281.

Gibbs, E. D. (1988). Psychosocial development of children raised by lesbian mothers: A review of research. *Women and Therapy, 8,* 55–75.

Golden, C. (1987). Diversity and variability in women's sexual identities. In Boston Lesbian Psychologies Collective (Ed.), *Lesbian psychologies: Explorations and challenges.* Urbana: University of Illinois Press.

Golombok, S., Spencer, A., & Rutter, M. (1983). Children in lesbian and single-parent households: Psychosexual and psychiatric appraisal. *Journal of Child Psychology and Psychiatry, 24,* 551–572.

Golombok, S., & Tasker, F. (1996). Do parents influence the sexual orientation of their children? Findings from a longitudinal study of lesbian families. *Developmental Psychology, 32,* 3–11.

Golombok, S., Tasker, F. L., & Murray, C. (1997). Children raised in fatherless families from infancy: Family relationships and the socioemotional development of children of lesbian and single heterosexual mothers. *Journal of Child Psychology and Psychiatry. 38,* 783–791.

Gonsiorek, J. C. (1991). The empirical basis for the demise of the illness model of homosexuality. In J. C. Gonsiorek & J. D. Weinrich (Eds.), *Homosexuality: Research implications for public policy.* Beverly Hills, CA: Sage.

Gottman, J. S. (1990). Children of gay and lesbian parents. In F. W. Bozett & M. B. Sussman, (Eds.), *Ho-*

mosexuality and family relations (pp. 177–196). New York: Harrington Park Press.

Green, G. D.& Bozett, F. W. (1991). Lesbian mothers and gay fathers. In J. C. Gonsiorek & J. D. Weinrich, Eds., *Homosexuality: Research implications for public policy.* Beverly Hills, CA: Sage Publications.

Green, R. (1978). Sexual identity of 37 children raised by homosexual or transsexual parents. *American Journal of Psychiatry, 135,* 692–697.

Green, R., Mandel, J. B., Hotvedt, M. E., Gray, J., & Smith, L. (1986). Lesbian mothers and their children: A comparison with solo parent heterosexual mothers and their children. *Archives of Sexual Behavior, 7,* 175–181.

Harris, M. B., & Turner, P. H. (1985/86). Gay and lesbian parents. *Journal of Homosexuality, 12,* 101–113.

Harry, J. (1984). *Gay couples.* New York: Praeger.

Harry, J., & DeVall, W. B. (1978). *The social organization of gay males.* New York: Praeger.

Herdt, G., & Beeler, J. (1998). Older gay men and lesbians in families. In C. J. Patterson & A. R. D'Augelli (Eds.), *Lesbian, gay and bisexual identities in families: Psychological perspectives.* New York: Oxford University Press.

Herdt, G., & Boxer, A. M. (1993). *Children of horizons: How gay and lesbian youth are leading a new way out of the closet.* Boston: Beacon Press.

Hill, M. (1987). Child-rearing attitudes of black lesbian mothers. In the Boston Lesbian Psychologies Collective (Ed.), *Lesbian psychologies: Explorations and challenges* (pp. 215–226). Urbana: University of Illinois Press.

Huggins, S. L. (1989). A comparative study of self-esteem of adolescent children of divorced lesbian mothers and divorced heterosexual mothers. In F. W. Bozett (Ed.), *Homosexuality and the family* (pp. 123–135). New York: Harrington Park Press.

James, S. E., & Murphy, B. C. (1998). Gay and lesbian relationships in a changing social context. In C. J. Patterson & A. R. D'Augelli (Eds.), *Lesbian, gay and bisexual identities in families: Psychological perspectives.* New York: Oxford University Press.

Jenny, C., Roesler, T. A., & Poyer, K. L. (1994). Are children at risk for sexual abuse by homosexuals? *Pediatrics, 94,* 41–44.

Kirkpatrick, M. (1987). Clinical implications of lesbian mother studies. *Journal of Homosexuality, 13,* 201–211.

Kirkpatrick, M. (1996). Lesbians as parents. In R. P. Cabaj & T. S. Stein (Eds.), *Textbook of homosexuality and mental health.* Washington, DC: American Psychiatric Press, Inc.

Kirkpatrick, M., Smith, C., & Roy, R. (1981). Lesbian mothers and their children: A comparative survey. *American Journal of Orthopsychiatry, 51,* 545–551.

Kitzinger, C., & Wilkinson, S. (1995). Transitions from heterosexuality to lesbianism: The discursive production of lesbian identities. *Developmental Psychology, 31,* 95–104.

Klinger, R. L. (1996). Lesbian couples. In R. P. Cabaj & T. S. Stein (Eds.), *Textbook of homosexuality and mental health.* Washington, DC: American Psychiatric Press, Inc.

Koepke, L., Hare, J., & Moran, P. B. (1992). Relationship quality in a sample of lesbian couples with children and child-free lesbian couples. *Family Relations, 41,* 224–229.

Kurdek, L. A. (1993). The allocation of household labor in homosexual and heterosexual cohabiting couples. *Journal of Social Issues, 49,* 127–139.

Kurdek, L. A. (1994). The nature and correlates of relationship quality in gay, lesbian, and heterosexual cohabiting couples: A test of the contextual, investment, and discrepancy models. In B. Greene & G. M. Herek (Eds.), *Lesbian and gay psychology: Theory, research, and clinical applications* (pp. 133–155). Thousand Oaks, CA: Sage.

Kurdek, L. A. (1995). Lesbian and gay couples. In A. R. D'Augelli & C. J. Patterson, (Eds.), *Lesbian, gay and bisexual identities over the lifespan: Psychological perspectives* (pp. 243–261). New York: Oxford University Press.

Kurdek, L. A., & Schmidt, J. P. (1986a). Early development of relationship quality in heterosexual married, heterosexual cohabiting, gay and lesbian couples. *Developmental Psychology, 22,* 305–309.

Kurdek, L. A., & Schmidt, J. P. (1986b). Relationship quality of partners in heterosexual married, heterosexual cohabiting, and gay and lesbian relationships. *Journal of Personality and Social Psychology, 51,* 711–720.

Kurdek, L. A., & Schmidt, J. P. (1987). Perceived support from family and friends in members of homosexual, married, and heterosexual cohabiting couples. *Journal of Homosexuality, 14,* 57–68.

Laird, J. (1998). Invisible ties: Lesbians and their families of origin. In C. J. Patterson & A. R. D'Augelli (Eds.), *Lesbian, gay and bisexual identities in families: Psychological perspectives.* New York: Oxford University Press.

Laird, J., & Green, R. J. (1996). *Lesbians and gays in couples and families.* San Francisco: Jossey-Bass.

Lewin, E. (1993). *Lesbian mothers: Accounts of gender in American culture.* Ithaca, NY: Cornell University Press.

Lyons, T. A. (1983). Lesbian mothers' custody fears. *Women and Therapy, 2,* 231–240.

Martin, A. (1993). *The lesbian and gay parenting handbook.* New York: HarperCollins.

Martin, A. (1998). Clinical issues in psychotherapy with lesbian-, gay-, and bisexual-parented families. In C. J. Patterson & A. R. D'Augelli (Eds.), *Lesbian, gay and bisexual identities in families: Psychological perspectives.* New York: Oxford University Press.

Martin, J., & Dean, L. (1993). Effects of AIDS-related bereavement and HIV-related illness on psychological distress among gay men: A 7-year longitudinal study, 1985–1991. *Journal of Consulting and Clinical Psychology, 61,* 94–103.

Mattison, A. M., & McWhirter, D. P. (1994). Serodiscordant male couples. *Journal of Gay and Lesbian Social Services, 1,* 83–99.

McCandlish, B. (1987). Against all odds: Lesbian mother family dynamics. In F. Bozett, (Ed.), *Gay and lesbian parents* (pp. 23–38). New York: Praeger.

McPherson, D. (1993). *Gay parenting couples: Parenting arrangements, arrangement satisfaction, and relationship satisfaction.* Unpublished doctoral dissertation, Palo Alto, CA: Pacific Graduate School of Psychology.

McWhirter, D. P., & Mattison, A. M. (1996). Male cou-

ples. In R. P. Cabaj & T. S. Stein (Eds.), *Textbook of homosexuality and mental health.* Washington, DC: American Psychiatric Press.

McWhirter, D. P., Sanders, S. A., & Reinisch, J. M. (1990). *Homosexuality/Heterosexuality: Concepts of Sexual Orientation.* New York: Oxford University Press.

Michaels, S. (1996). The prevalence of homosexuality in the United States. In R. P. Cabaj & T. S. Stein (Eds.), *Textbook of homosexuality and mental health.* Washington, DC: American Psychiatric Press, Inc.

Miller, B. (1978). Adult sexual resocialization: Adjustments toward a stigmatized identity. *Alternative Lifestyles, 1,* 207–234.

Miller, B. (1979). Gay fathers and their children. *Family Coordinator, 28,* 544–552.

Miller, J. A., Jacobsen, R. B., & Bigner, J. J. (1981). The child's home environment for lesbian versus heterosexual mothers: A neglected area of research. *Journal of Homosexuality, 7,* 49–56.

Murphy, B. C. (1994). Difference and diversity: Gay and lesbian couples. *Journal of Gay and Lesbian Social Services, 1,* 5–31.

Pagelow, M. D. (1980). Heterosexual and lesbian single mothers: A comparison of problems, coping, and solutions. *Journal of Homosexuality, 5,* 198–204.

Parks, C. A. (1998). Lesbian parenthood: A review of the literature. *American Journal of Orthopsychiatry, 68,* 376–389.

Pattatucci, A. M. L., & Hamer, D. H. (1995). Development and familiality of sexual orientation in females. *Behavior Genetics, 25,* 407–420.

Patterson, C. J. (1992). Children of lesbian and gay parents. *Child Development, 63,* 1025–1042.

Patterson, C. J. (1994a). Children of the lesbian baby boom: Behavioral adjustment, self-concepts, and sex-role identity. In B. Greene & G. Herek (Eds.), *Contemporary perspectives on lesbian and gay psychology: Theory, research, and applications* (pp. 156–175). Beverly Hills: Sage.

Patterson, C. J. (1994b). Lesbian and gay couples considering parenthood: An agenda for research, service, and advocacy. *Journal of Gay and Lesbian Social Services, 1,* 33–55.

Patterson, C. J. (1995a). Lesbian mothers, gay fathers, and their children. In A. R. D'Augelli & C. J. Patterson (Eds.), *Lesbian, gay and bisexual identities over the lifespan* (pp. 262–290). New York: Oxford University Press.

Patterson, C. J. (1995b). Gay and lesbian parenthood. In M. H. Bornstein, (Ed.), *Handbook of parenting* (pp. 255–274). Hillsdale, NJ: Erlbaum.

Patterson, C. J. (1995-c). Families of the lesbian baby boom: Parents' division of labor and children's adjustment. *Developmental Psychology, 31,* 115–123.

Patterson, C. J. (1997). Children of lesbian and gay parents (pp. 235–282). In T. Ollendick & R. Prinz (Eds.), *Advances in Clinical Child Psychology* (Vol. 19). New York: Plenum Press.

Patterson, C. J. (1998). Family lives of children with lesbian mothers. In C. J. Patterson & A. R. D'Augelli (Eds.), *Lesbian, gay and bisexual identities in families: psychological perspectives* (pp. 154–176). New York: Oxford University Press.

Patterson, C. J., & Chan, R. W. (1997). Gay fathers. In M. E. Lamb (Ed.), *The role of the father in child development* (3rd ed., pp. 245–260). New York: Wiley.

Patterson, C. J. & D'Augelli, A. R. (Eds.). (1998). *Lesbian, gay and bisexual identities in families: Psychological perspectives.* New York: Oxford University Press.

Patterson, C. J., Hurt, S., & Mason, C. (1998). Families of the Lesbian Baby Boom: Children's contacts with grandparents and other adults. *American Journal of Orthopsychiatry, 68,* 390–399.

Patterson, C. J., & Redding, R. (1996). Lesbian and gay families with children: Public policy implications of social science research. *Journal of Social Issues, 52,* 29–50.

Paul, J. P. (1986). *Growing up with a gay, lesbian, or bisexual parent: An exploratory study of experiences and perceptions.* Unpublished doctoral dissertation, University of California at Berkeley.

Paul, J. P. (1996). Bisexuality: Exploring/exploding the boundaries. In R. C. Savin-Williams & K. M. Cohen (Eds.), *The lives of lesbians, gays and bisexuals: Children to adults* (pp. 436–461). New York: Harcourt Brace.

Paul, J. P., Hays, R. B., & Coates, T. J. (1995). The impact of the HIV epidemic on U.S. gay male communities. In A. R. D'Augelli & C. J. Patterson (Eds.), *Lesbian, gay and bisexual identities over the lifespan: Psychological perspectives* (pp. 347–397). New York: Oxford University Press.

Peplau, L. A. (1991). Lesbian and gay relationships. In J. C. Gonsiorek & J. D. Weinrich (Eds.), *Homosexuality: Research implications for public policy* (pp. 177–196). Newbury Park, CA: Sage.

Peplau, L. A., & Cochran, S. D. (1990). A relationship perspective on homosexuality. In D. P. McWhirter, S. A. Sanders, & J. M. Reinisch (Eds.), *Homosexuality/heterosexuality: Concepts of sexual orientation* (pp. 321–349). New York: Oxford University Press.

Peplau, L. A., Padesky, C., & Hamilton, M. (1982). Satisfaction in lesbian relationships. *Journal of Homosexuality, 8,* 23–35.

Peplau, L. A., Veniegas, R. C., & Campbell, S. M. (1996). Gay and lesbian relationships. In R. C. Savin-Williams & K. M. Cohen (Eds.), *The lives of lesbians, gays, and bisexuals: Children to adults* (pp. 250–273). New York: Harcourt Brace.

Perrin, E. C. (1998). Children whose parents are lesbian or gay. *Contemporary Pediatrics, 15,* 113–130.

Pies, C. (1985). *Considering parenthood.* San Francisco: Spinsters/Aunt Lute.

Pies, C. (1990). Lesbians and the choice to parent. In F. W. Bozett & M. B. Sussman (Eds.), *Homosexuality and family relations* (pp. 137–154). New York: Harrington Park Press.

Pollack, S., & Vaughn, J. (1987). *Politics of the heart: A lesbian parenting anthology.* Ithaca, NY: Firebrand Books.

Rand, C., Graham, D. L. R., & Rawlings, E. I. (1982). Psychological health and factors the court seeks to control in lesbian mother custody trials. *Journal of Homosexuality, 8,* 27–39.

Robinson, B. E., & Skeen, P. (1982). Sex-role orientation of gay fathers versus gay nonfathers. *Perceptual and Motor Skills, 55,* 1055–1059.

Rohrbaugh, J. B. (1988). Choosing children: Psychological issues in lesbian parenting. *Women and Therapy, 8,* 51–63.

Sameroff, A. J., & Chandler, M. (1975). Reproductive risk and the continuum of caretaking casualty. In F. A. Horowitz, H. Hetherington, S. Scarr-Salapatek, & G. Siegal (Eds.), *Review of Child Development Research* (Vol. 4). Chicago: University of Chicago Press.

Savin-Williams, R. C. (1990). *Gay and lesbian youth: Expressions of identity.* New York: Hemisphere.

Savin-Williams, R. C. (1998-a). Lesbian, gay and bisexual youths' relationships with their parents. In C. J. Patterson & A. R. D'Augelli (Eds.), *Lesbian, gay and bisexual identities in families: Psychological perspectives.* New York: Oxford University Press.

Savin-Williams, R. C. (1998-b). *. . . And then I became gay: Young men's stories.* NY: Routledge Press.

Sbordone, A. J. (1993). *Gay men choosing fatherhood.* Unpublished doctoral dissertation, City University of New York.

Skeen, P., & Robinson, B. (1985). Gay fathers' and gay nonfathers' relationships with their parents. *Journal of Sex Research, 21,* 86–91.

Steckel, A. (1987). Psychosocial development of children of lesbian mothers. In F. W. Bozett (Ed.), *Gay and lesbian parents* (pp. 75–85). New York: Praeger.

Strommen, E. F. (1989a). "You're a what?" Family members' reactions to the disclosure of homosexuality. *Journal of Homosexuality, 18,* 37–58.

Strommen, E. F. (1989b). Hidden branches and growing pains: Homosexuality and the family tree. *Marriage and Family Review, 14,* 9–34.

Sullivan, M. (1996). Rozzie and Harriet? Gender and family patterns of lesbian coparents. *Gender and Society, 10,* 747–767.

Tasker, F., & Golombok, S. (1991). Children raised by lesbian mothers: The empirical evidence. *Family Law, 21,* 184–187.

Tasker, F., & Golombok, S. (1995). Adults raised as children in lesbian families. *American Journal of Orthopsychiatry, 65,* 203–215.

Tasker, F. L., & Golombok, S. (1997). *Growing up in a lesbian family: Effects on child development.* New York: Guilford.

Tasker, F. L., & Golombok, S. (1998). The role of comothers in planned lesbian-led families. In G. A. Dunne (Ed.), *Living difference: lesbian perspectives on work and family life.* New York: Harrington Park Press.

Victor, S. B., & Fish, M. C. (1995). Lesbian mothers and their children: A review for school psychologists. *School Psychology Review, 24,* 456–479.

Weinstock, J. S. (1998). Lesbian, gay, bisexual, and transgender friendships in adulthood. In C. J. Patterson & A. R. D'Augelli (Eds.), *Lesbian, gay and bisexual identities in families: Psychological perspectives.* New York: Oxford University Press.

Weston, K. (1991). *Families we choose: Lesbians, gays, kinship.* New York: Columbia University Press.

Vonnie C. McLoyd   *University of Michigan*

Ana Mari Cauce   *University of Washington**

David Takeuchi   *Indiana University***

Leon Wilson   *Wayne State University****

Marital Processes and Parental Socialization in Families of Color: A Decade Review of Research

Research published during the past decade on African American, Latino, and Asian American families is reviewed. Emphasis is given to selected issues within the broad domains of marriage and parenting. The first section highlights demographic trends in family formation and family structure and factors that contributed to secular changes in family structure among African Americans. In the second section, new conceptualizations of marital relations within Latino families are discussed, along with research documenting the complexities in African American men's conceptions of manhood. Studies examining within-group variation in marital conflict and racial and ethnic differences in division of household labor, marital relations,

and children's adjustment to marital and family conflict also are reviewed. The third section gives attention to research on (a) paternal involvement among fathers of color; (b) the relation of parenting behavior to race and ethnicity, grandmother involvement, neighborhood and peer characteristics, and immigration; and (c) racial and ethnic socialization. The article concludes with an overview of recent advances in the study of families of color and important challenges and issues that represent research opportunities for the new decade.

Center for Human Growth and Development, University of Michigan, 300 North Ingalls, Ann Arbor, MI 48109 (vcmcloyd@umich.edu).

*Department of Psychology, University of Washington, PO Box 351525, Seattle, WA 98195.

**Department of Sociology, Indiana State University, Ballantine Hall 744, 1020 E. Kirkwood Avenue, Bloomington, IN 47405-7103.

***Department of Sociology, Wayne State University, 2237 Faculty/Administration Bldg., 656 W. Kirby, Detroit, MI 48202.

Key Words: families of color, marital processes, parenting.

As a review that closes out a decade and a century, leaving us perched to begin a new millennium, we are bid not only to look backward at what has happened, but also to look forward into the future. A look forward reveals a U.S. demographic profile that will be strikingly different than profiles of prior eras. In the 21st century, our country will no longer be overwhelmingly White; we can no longer describe it as simply "Black and White." It will instead be fully multicultural, equally divided between non-Hispanic European Americans and those of other racial and ethnic groups. Among people of color, Hispanics will become the largest group soon after the turn of the century. Asian American and Pacific Islanders will increase at the most rapid rate, although Hispanics will add more actual numbers to the U.S. population in the next century. By 2050, the U.S. population is expected to be 8% Asian American, 14% African American, 25% Hispanic, and 53% non-Hispanic White. This differential increase in people of color in the United States over the next several decades is due both to increased fertility rates and to the younger average ages of African Americans, Hispanics, and Asian Americans. It is also due to increased immigration among the latter two groups (Lee, 1998; U.S. Bureau of the Census, 1995, 1997a).

Yet, if we look backward at the research that has been published in social science journals over the last 10 years, such changes are scarcely reflected. Instead, notwithstanding some sparing changes in the last decade, our research, especially that in the quantitative domain, continues to largely reflect what Collins (1990) called biracial or dichotomous thinking, where the normative work is conducted using European American families and the "minority" perspective is represented via an examination of African American families. Our review necessarily reflects this fact, with the bulk of the empirical research we examine focusing on African American families. Wherever possible we present research that has been conducted on Hispanic and Asian American families. We also discuss briefly the new conceptual and theoretical frameworks that have been put forth to inform this research. Remarkably little research has been conducted on American Indian families. (For a few examples of recent research focusing on this understudied group, see McCubbin, Thompson, Thompson, & Fromer, 1998.) We present pertinent demographic information on this group wherever possible but make no attempt to summarize a knowledge base so small that generalizations are speculative at best.

We limit our review to selected issues within the broad domains of marriage and parental socialization. The first section reviews demographic changes in family structure, followed by a discussion of research that sought to explain these changes. We then turn to studies of racial and ethnic differences in the division of household labor, the frequency and management of marital conflict, and children's adjustment to marital and family conflict. In addition to highlighting new conceptualizations of gender roles within Latino families, we review research on predictors of marital quality and life-course changes in marital quality and relations among couples of color. The third section

of the article devotes attention to parental socialization processes. Our review reflects relatively little of the recent work published in books and edited volumes, but concentrates on quantitative research that appeared in social science journals during the past decade. More in-depth reviews of recent family research on different racial and ethnic groups in the United States can be found elsewhere (Burton & Jarrett, in press; Gadsden, 1999; Gaines, Buriel, Liu, & Rios, 1997; Leyendecker & Lamb, 1999; McAdoo, 1993; Taylor, 1998).

DEMOGRAPHIC TRENDS IN MARRIAGE, MARITAL TRANSITIONS, AND HOUSEHOLD COMPOSITION

Family Formation and Family Structure

Especially relative to African American families, studies of structural changes of families constituted a major portion of the family-related literature in the last decade. The major trends on which researchers have focused attention are overall declines in the rates of marriages and later age at first marriage, along with concomitant trends such as higher proportions of unwed mothers, higher percentages of single-headed households families, and higher numbers of poor households (Taylor, Tucker, Chatters, & Jayakody, 1997). The research emphasis in the last decade was more on single-parent families than on two-parent families, the latter often being used merely as a basis for comparison. As such, the issues of family configurations and nonmarital patterns are more central to our review than is a direct emphasis on two-parent families.

African Americans. In general, structural changes in African American families continued to be more rapid during the last decade when compared with the general population. Between 1990 and 1998, the percent of individuals aged 15 years and older who were married declined 3.8% among African Americans (42.7% to 38.9%) but declined only 2.3% in the general population (58.8% to 56.5%). Correspondingly, during this same period, the percent of never-married individuals in this age group increased 3.7% among African Americans (40.1% to 43.8%) compared with an increase of 1.6% in the general population (26.4% to 28%). During the past decade, African Americans continued to have higher divorce rates than those in the general population, but the increase in divorce from 1990 to 1998 was slightly smaller among African Americans (9.7% to 10.7%) than in the general population (7.9% to 9.2%; U.S. Bureau of Census, Internet Release 1999a, Table MS-1).

After a 7.3% increase during the 1980s, the percent of single-headed families among African Americans rose only slightly between 1990 and 1998, from 54.6% (51.2% female headed) to 54.8% (51.1% female headed). The increase was somewhat higher for European Americans (3.6%), rising from 19.2% (16.2% female headed) in 1990 to 22.8% (18.2% female headed) in 1998. Female-headed households accounted for 26.2% of all American Indian families at the beginning of the decade, with the figures being slightly higher (29.4%) in urban areas (U.S. Bureau of the Census, 1999a). Sandefur and Liebler (1996) demonstrated that there is considerable variation in female headship across American Indian reservations. Between 1990 and 1998, households headed by single fathers increased .2% among African Americans, 1.6% among European Americans, and 1.5% among Hispanics. Rates of poverty declined substantively over the past decade among African American families (from 29.3% in 1990 to 23.6% in 1997), but not among Hispanic families (from 25% to 24.7% during the same period). The percentage of European American families living in poverty increased slightly, going from 8.1% in 1990 to 8.4% in 1997 (U.S. Bureau of the Census, 1999a, 1999b).

Latinos. Hispanic female-headed families grew to about 31.2% in 1998, an increase of about 1.2% over the 1990 totals. Compared with their White and Asian American counterparts, Latino women in the 1990s, as with African American women, were less likely to be married, more likely to be household heads, and more likely to have younger children at younger ages outside of marriage. Nonetheless, there is considerable variation in rates of female-headed households among Latino subgroups, with rates almost twice as high among Puerto Ricans than among Mexican Americans or Cuban Americans. In addition, Puerto Rican women tend to have their first child before marriage, whereas Mexican American women tend to do so within marriage. Compared with other Latino subgroups, Cuban American women have the lowest fertility rates and are older at the time of their first marriage (U.S. Bureau of the Census, 1995, 1997b). These subgroup differences correspond to differences in poverty rates. In 1996, 35% of Puerto Rican families had incomes below the poverty line, a rate considerably higher than

that of Mexican American families (28%) and almost twice that of Cuban Americans (17%). A noteworthy development during the past decade, though, is the end of the sharp economic decline of Puerto Rican families observed throughout the 1970s and 1980s (Tienda, 1989; U.S. Bureau of the Census, 1997b).

Asian Americans. Discussions of family structure and process within Asian American families cannot be adequately framed in the absence of the concept of the extended family. On average, Asian American households have 3.3 members, a figure that is higher than for European Americans (2.5 members per household) and similar to Hispanic household size averages (3.5). Among Asian Americans, Vietnamese (4.0) and other Southeast Asians such as Cambodians, Hmong, and Laotian (5.1) have the largest average number per household. By contrast, Japanese Americans have the lowest household average (2.5). The greater average household size can largely be attributed to the presence of another relative who is not a child or spouse. Compared with European Americans and African Americans, Asian Americans are more likely to live in households that are comprised exclusively of family members (i.e., family households, as distinguished from households that include individuals who are not related through family ties). Given the relatively high percentage of Asian American families that are extended, researchers who focus exclusively on parents and children as the operational measure of the family unit are prone to lose sight of the social and cultural resources that other relatives bring to Asian American families.

Although differences exist among Asian American subgroups, Asian Americans, on average, wait longer to have children and have fewer children than other ethnic groups (Lee, 1998). Only 6% of all births occur to Asian American women under the age of 20 years. Compare this figure with European Americans (10%), African Americans (23%), and Hispanics (18%) and the differences are quite striking. Asian American mothers have a higher average educational level, are more likely to be foreign-born, and are less likely to give birth out-of-wedlock than are other ethnic categories. Fertility rate data provide evidence of the changing nature of Asian American families. Chinese American (1.4 children per woman) and Japanese American women (1.1 per woman) have a fertility rate that is lower than the replacement level (2.1 children per woman). These rates suggest that these ethnic groups will substantially diminish in size over time. On the other hand, Southeast Asian American women have high fertility rates and tend to have children at earlier ages than Chinese and Japanese Americans (Lee). As fertility factors play a larger role in population increases, the population of Southeast Asians will rise compared with the Japanese and Chinese populations. The next generation of studies on Asian American families will need to redirect its foci to reflect this change.

Recent census estimates, like those of the past, indicate that Asian Americans have lower rates of divorce than U.S. averages. Approximately 4% of Asian American men were divorced, compared with 8% in the general male population. The discrepancy in the proportion who are divorced among Asian American women and the U.S. average is similar—4.7% of Asian American females were divorced compared with 10.3% of the U.S. female population (U.S. Census Bureau, 1999a). In a cogent series of analysis, Barringer, Gardner, and Levin (1993) demonstrated that nativity is associated with divorce. In general, Asian Americans who are born in the United States are much more likely to be divorced than are their counterparts who immigrated to the United States. Among Asian American men, the never-married segment is high at 35%, a percentage higher than that for European American men but lower than that for African American men. The reasons for this relatively high never-married rate may be attributed to the high male immigration pattern in the early part of this century (Barringer et al.; Gardner, Robey, & Smith, 1985).

Explanations of Changes in Family Structure

Little research has focused on contributors to increases in female-headed households among Latinos and Asian Americans over the past few decades. Nor has there been serious examination of the factors that account for marked differences among Latino and Asian American subgroups in rates of female-headed households. The past decade brought refinements of the explanations for changing family patterns among African Americans, however (McAdoo, 1998).

Economic factors. Economic factors as a reason for the changes in African American family structures assumed some prominence in the later part of the 1980s because of Wilson's (1987) contention that unemployment rates were a major ex-

planatory factor. Wilson's argument suggested a correspondence between rates of male unemployment and rates of marriage, such that the economic potential of a man was directly related to his eligibility as a desirable mate. Studies of this association produced mixed results. Several reported a positive relation between employment and marriage rates (Fossett & Kiecolt, 1993; Lichter, McLaughlin, Kephart, & Landry, 1992), whereas the results of other studies were less conclusive (Mare & Winship, 1991; South & Lloyd, 1992; Testa, 1991). Some studies even suggested that between the 1960s and 1980s, rates of marriage actually declined more among employed than unemployed African American men (Ellwood & Crane, 1990; Jencks, 1992). Later studies, however, seem to support the conclusion that, although stable employment is indeed positively related to marriage rates for Black men, increases in the joblessness rates of Black men do not fully explain the declining rates of marriage among this population (Testa & Krogh, 1995). Employment factors are critical to African American family formation, but they represent only one set of factors (Tucker & Mitchell-Kernan, 1995).

Receipt of welfare benefits as an economic explanation of declining African American marriage rates continued to receive attention in the last decade. Despite the conclusion of Moffitt's (1992) extensive review that most studies find no relation between welfare benefits and African American family formation, some scholars remain committed to this explanation. In fact, some empirical research has found a negative relation between the level of welfare benefits at the aggregate level and the level of welfare benefits at the individual level (Fossett & Kiecolt, 1993; Kiecolt & Fossett, 1997; Lichter, LeClere, & McLaughlin, 1991; South & Lloyd, 1992). The level of welfare benefits may simply be a proxy for unmeasured characteristics of recipients, however (Kiecolt & Fossett). At present, welfare is most consistent as a predictor of young unmarried women's tendency to set up independent households rather than stay with their parents (Moffit, 1994).

Gender ratio imbalance. The second major explanation receiving some attention in the past decade is the imbalance in the gender ratio. Essentially the argument suggests that the imbalanced ratio of Black men to women results in a disincentive for both genders to marry and a reduced commitment of men to stay married (Smith, 1995). Research conducted during the past decade yielded increasing support for these hypotheses (Kiecolt & Fossett, 1995, 1997; Lichter et al., 1992; South & Lloyd, 1992). Nonetheless, individual level data are less predictive of the relation for men than are aggregate-level data (Kiecolt & Fossett, 1995).

Growth in the rate of nonmarital births also is a factor contributing to changes in the structure of African American families. Taylor et al. (1997) refined the analysis of this issue, pointing out that births to adolescents account for only a minority of nonmarital births. Taylor et al. (1997) concluded that nonmarital births significantly affect African American family structure because African American women are now less likely to marry in response to a pregnancy than they were in the 1960s; at the same time, they also are more likely to bear a child before marriage.

Racial and Ethnic Intermarriage

Census data indicate fairly stable overall rates of racial and ethnic intermarriage between 1980 and 1992 (Internet Release 1999b). Racial and ethnic intermarriages accounted for 2% of all marriages in 1980, compared with 2.2% estimated by the Current Population Survey in 1992. Of the projected 1,161,000 interracial and interethnic couples in 1992, 21.2% were of the Black-White combination, with roughly two thirds of these involving a Black husband and a White wife. Of all racial and ethnic intermarriages, the percentages that are Black-White couples increased from 12% in 1980 to 21% in 1992.

Ethnic intermarriage is relatively common among Asian Americans and will play a crucial part in making sense of Asian American family life in the near future. During the past decade, approximately 11% of marriages involving an Asian American partner were interracial or interethnic (Kitano, Fujino, & Sato, 1998). Intermarriages are higher for Asian Americans born in the United States than for those born in another country, and variation exists in the rate of intermarriage within the Asian American category. When Asian Americans intermarry, they are more likely to marry someone within the Asian American category than with African Americans or Hispanics. (Kitano et al.; Lee, 1998). As the sociodemographic characteristics of Asian Americans continue to change (e.g., increase in native-born individuals, higher education and income levels), intermarriage rates are likely to rise. Interracial marriages are more vulnerable to divorce than are marriages among same-race individuals (Clarke,

1995). As the trend toward increased rates of racial and ethnic intermarriage continues, it will become increasingly important to understand what factors promote resilience among such families, given the unique challenges they confront.

MARITAL PROCESSES

Most of the empirical research on marital relations during the past decade focused on African American families, although some important work occurred on the Latino front, especially on a theoretical level. The lack of empirical study on marital relations among Asian Americans stands in marked contrast and provides a challenge for researchers in the coming decade. Indeed, although the importance of family to Asian Americans is cited quite extensively in the literature (Lee, 1998), surprisingly few empirical studies have actually analyzed the nature and impact of marital and family processes among Asian Americans or the role that families play in shaping how and when Asian American children develop particular social and psychological characteristics. When statistical differences are found between Asian Americans and other ethnic groups, social and cultural factors such as family values are invoked to explain the findings without systematic observations of these constructs. This problem plagues much research on people and families of color (Betancourt & Lopez, 1993; Cauce, Coronado, & Watson, 1998).

Gender Role Attitudes and Values

The bulk of the work on Latino marital relations this past decade was conceptual. The earliest research depictions of Latino marital relations emphasized the role of "machismo" and "marianismo," two cultural values ascribed to Latino culture (Ginorio, Gutierrez, Cauce, & Acosta, 1995). "Marianismo," based on the Catholic ideal of the Virgin Mary, emphasizes the woman's role as mother and celebrates the mother's self-sacrifice and suffering for her children. "Machismo," on the other hand, stresses the man's role not as father, but as head of household. Taken together and exaggerated to the point of caricature, these Latino values have been used to paint a portrait of the ideal Latino family type as that of the self-sacrificing mother and the dominant, tyrannical man.

As is not atypical in the rural farming economies that characterized much of Mexico and the

Caribbean through the 1950s, a strongly gendered division of labor, with women's roles largely played out within the domestic sphere, were normative. Despite the rapid changes in the second half of the century, however, stereotypes based on this much earlier period often dominated our views of the Latino family. For example, a review of this decade (Inclan & Herron, 1990) continued to describe the Puerto Rican family as patriarchal and the role of the husband as protector and provider, despite the fact that at the time 44% of Puerto Rican families were headed by women (Ginorio et al., 1995). Feminist re-interpretations focused on correcting such persistent stereotypes, underscoring that these families displayed a much greater diversity of gender role patterns than the emphasis on machismo would have us believe (Ramirez & Arce, 1981; Williams, 1988; Zavella, 1989).

More recent research also focused on how women's increasing participation in the workforce brought with it an increase in women's power both within and outside of the family (Pesquera, 1993; Williams, 1988). Even working class Chicano men who held traditional values about marriage and gender roles counted on their wives' income generated from work outside the home to increase their families' standard of living and upward mobility (Williams). Moreover, Chicana women, like their Anglo counterparts, reported less depression and more satisfaction with their marriages when husbands contributed more to the household upkeep (Saenz, Goudy, & Lorenz, 1989). Although not focusing on marriage specifically, research examining how Latina women exert control over their reproduction, and hence family formation, also suggested that they are adopting values not consonant with stereotypes of passivity or domination by patriarchy, including the patriarchal structure of the Catholic Church (Amaro, 1988; Hurtado, 1995).

Still, the most important contribution of the 1990s may be the feminist critiques of how cultural interpretations of Latino gender roles within families, and Latino family life more generally, serve to mask the role of social-structural factors as shapers of family life and to obscure race and gender as basic organizing principles of society (Baca Zinn, 1994, 1999). Key to this reconceptualization is the premise that social locations rather than cultural differences are the source of ethnic and racial variations in marital relations, family formation, and family lifestyles (Baca Zinn, 1999; Baca Zinn & Eitzen, 1996; Dill, Baca

Zinn, & Patton, 1993). This reconceptualization has the potential to advance our understanding of not only families of color, but of all families, not in group-specific terms, but as part of a socially constructed system.

The decade of the 1990s also was distinguished by efforts to reconceptualize, explain, and document the complexity of gender roles among African American men. As with the discourse on Latinos, this work reflected tensions between structural and cultural interpretations of male gender roles (Duneier, 1992; Hunter & Davis, 1992; Majors & Billson, 1992; Majors & Gordon, 1994). Consistent with a perspective that emerged during the 1980s emphasizing "masculinities" rather than a generic, unidimensional male gender role (Pleck, 1981), Hunter and Davis found that African American men's responses to the question "What do you think it means to be a man?" emphasized four distinct dimensions: self-determinism and accountability, family relations, pride, and spirituality and humanism. In contrast to more stereotyped views of men's conceptions of manhood, attributes associated with masculinity (e.g., physically strong, aggressive, competitive) were rated as only somewhat important, whereas those associated with power were rated as least important. Consonant with the view of social location as a contributor to gender roles (Baca Zinn, 1999), the perceived importance of ownership, manliness, spirituality, and power varied as a function of men's occupational status. Adding yet another level of complexity, Blee and Tickamyer (1995) found that gender role attitudes of both Black and White men change over time in response to marriage and historical period.

Empirical work on race and ethnic differences in gender role attitudes has found that African Americans and Mexican Americans, compared with European Americans, have more positive attitudes toward working wives but ironically are more likely to endorse the traditional role of men as head of household and primary economic provider (Blee & Tickamyer, 1995; Kane, 1992; Taylor, Tucker, & Mitchell-Kernan, 1999). Compared with European American men, African American men report more conservative attitudes about a range of other gender role issues (e.g., responsibility for housework, achievement outside home; Blee & Tickamyer), a pattern consistent with findings reported in the 1970s (McLoyd, 1993). These racial disparities in gender role attitudes may partly account for evidence that in the early years of marriage, race is a salient determinant of whether social context variables such as husband's participation in housework and the presence of children moderate the impact of women's work on the psychological well-being of husbands (Orbuch & Custer, 1995).

An especially noteworthy set of findings from the past decade documents sources of within race and ethnicity variation in gender role schemas. The belief that men are primarily responsible for making economic provisions for the family is stronger among people of color who are older and less educated, as well as among African Americans who are more religious, experience more financial strain, and live in cities with higher percentages of non-Hispanic Black men below the poverty level. Mexican Americans who are not born in the United States and who are less linguistically acculturated espouse this view more strongly than highly acculturated Mexican immigrants and Mexican Americans born in the United States (Taylor et al., 1999). Collectively, the racial, ethnic and economic-related disparities in gender role attitudes and beliefs found in recent research no doubt reflect increased need for wives' income in families of color and heightened sensitivity among men of color to the fact that a combination of inadequate education, high unemployment, underemployment, and racism has limited their ability to be good economic providers (Taylor et al.; Wilson, 1996). Successful performance of the primary provider role is of major psychological significance for men of color. Unmarried African American fathers' evaluations of their performance as primary provider and as fathers are highly correlated, but the former is a much stronger predictor of their psychological well-being (e.g., self-esteem) than is the latter (Bowman & Sanders, 1998).

Division of Household Labor

By the late 1980s, it was well documented that African American husbands, compared with European American husbands, perform a slightly larger share of and spend a little more time on domestic chores (e.g., cooking, cleaning, washing clothes, grocery shopping) and child care. But African American wives, like their European American counterparts, nevertheless assume primary responsibility for household work and child care, irrespective of their employment status (McLoyd, 1993). Studies published during the 1990s based on community and national samples replicated and further differentiated these patterns and ex-

tended the focus to Latino families (Hossain & Roopnarine, 1993; John, Shelton, & Luschen, 1995; Kamo & Cohen, 1998; Oggins, Veroff, & Leber, 1993; Pesquera, 1993; Rubin, 1994; Shelton & John, 1993).

Black husbands or partners are less likely than their White counterparts to view the division of household labor as unfair to their wives or partners (John et al., 1995). It is not surprising that employed husbands who report doing most of the housework have especially low levels of family life satisfaction (Broman, 1991). Although White and Latino husbands and partners do not differ in their total household labor time or attitudes about the fairness of the division of household labor once sociodemographic characteristics are taken into account, contrary to popular stereotypes, some evidence suggests that Hispanic husbands and partners spend more time on typically "female-typed" tasks than do European American husbands, especially if they are employed part time or not at all (Shelton & John, 1993). Qualitative research among dual-earner Chicano families indicates that husbands perform more domestic work if their wives are coproviders (had income roughly equal to their husband's and both husband and wife highly valued the latter's employment) or if husbands had failed to fulfill career aspirations (Coltrane & Valdez, 1993).

Although some have posited that African American husbands' increased involvement in household work is due to reduced hours in paid work, Shelton and John's (1993) work suggests otherwise. These researchers found household labor time varied by race and ethnicity, even after controlling for paid labor time, education, age, presence of children, and husbands' and wives' gender role attitudes. Among both European American and Hispanic husbands, those who were not employed spent more time on household labor than did those who were employed, although this difference was statistically significant only for the former group. In contrast, among African American husbands, the more time they spent in paid labor, the more time they spent on household labor. (Shelton & John). This provocative finding should invite replication studies, especially because husbands' reduced household labor can amplify the negative impact of their unemployment on family life satisfaction, marital quality, and marital stability (Broman, 1988; McLoyd, 1990, 1993).

Not only do employed African American husbands spend more time in household labor if they are employed, they also appear to increase their household labor in response to decreases in their wives' household labor (Kamo & Cohen, 1998). This finding, along with evidence that resource exchange theory (e.g., the notion that the amount of housework a partner performs is inversely related to his or her personal income) is less powerful in explaining African American men's relative share of household work than that of European American men, prompted Kamo and Cohen to advocate for new theoretical models of household division of labor among families of color. These models might incorporate notions of group identity and utility maximization of the family unit as alternatives to models based on assumptions about utility maximization of the individual.

Marital Quality

Frequency and management of conflict. Early work suggested that African American couples and families have more conflictual relations and are more tolerant of open, intense disclosure than their European American counterparts (Aschenbrenner, 1975; Blood & Wolfe, 1969). Such findings may have resulted from a variety of methodological flaws common in these early studies, such as failure to control for social class, income, and family size, biased sampling, and use of measures of unknown or questionable reliability and validity for African American families (Henggeler & Tavormina, 1980). Even with careful controls for factors confounded with race, recent investigations have not resolved this issue. In addition, no consistent patterns of race difference have been found in how couples manage conflict (e.g., confrontation, withdrawal, avoidance) or in the degree of negative affect or hostility expressed by spouses during conflictual encounters (e.g., insults, name calling, bringing up the past, having to have the last word, yelling or shouting; Adelmann, Chadwick, & Baerger, 1996; Mackey & O'Brien, 1998; MacDonald & DeMaris, 1995; Oggins et al., 1993; Sistler & Moore, 1996). Although comparative data are sparse, it appears that Hispanic couples do not differ from European American couples in the frequency of major or overt marital conflict (Lindahl & Malik, 1999; Mackey & O'Brien).

Spousal violence. Although race and ethnicity do not appear to be reliable predictors of the frequency and management of marital conflict, a number of recent studies have found both race and ethnicity to be associated with physical violence among spouses (Anderson, 1997; Hampton & Coner-Edwards, 1993; Sorenson, Upchurch, & Shen, 1996). Even with controls for income, education, urbanicity, age and number of children, and duration of marriage, data from almost 7,000 currently married respondents in the National Survey of Families and Households indicated that Blacks were 1.58 times more likely and Latinos 0.53 times less likely than Whites to report that marital arguments during the past year had escalated into physical violence (i.e., hitting, shoving, throwing things at spouse; Sorenson et al.).

The 1985 National Family Violence Survey found higher rates of husband-to-wife violence and severe violence among both Blacks and Latinos, compared with Whites. Rates of overall wife-to-husband violence and severe violence among Latinos were intermediate between those of Blacks and Whites, with Black women having the highest rates (Hampton & Coner-Edwards, 1993; Hampton & Gelles, 1994; Straus & Smith, 1990). Controlling for income and social class reduces, but does not eliminate, the relation between race and ethnicity and spousal violence (Hampton & Coner-Edwards). Status inequality between partners in terms of earnings and education does not appear to be a central mechanism linking race to domestic violence (Anderson, 1997). Studies of spousal violence that are based on reports by wives (female partners) may actually underestimate race differences in husband-to-wife (male partner-to-female partner) violence. Data from the National Survey of Families and Households indicate that African American women are more likely than European American women to underreport victimization by male partners (i.e., greater percentage of instances among African Americans in which husband (male partner) self-reported his perpetration of violence but wife (female partner) failed to acknowledge victimization; Anderson).

There is some suggestion that Mexican American women, compared with European American women, are more tolerant of physical aggression by their husbands and more conservative in their perception of what constitutes physical abuse (Asbury, 1993; Gondolf, Fisher, & McFerron, 1991). In addition, Mexican American women in shelters report longer duration of abuse, compared with African Americans and European Americans (Gondolf et al.). If indeed these ethnic differences are subsequently replicated in well-designed studies, we need to know the extent to which they are driven by disparities in economic well-being, educational credentials, employability, and availability and appropriateness of services to assist victims of domestic violence.

Our knowledge about sources of spousal violence within families of color also grew during the past decade (Asbury, 1993; Hampton & Coner-Edwards, 1993). Hampton and Gelles (1994), for example, found that lower income, younger age of couple, shorter residence in a community, unemployment of the husband, being hit as an adolescent, and observing parental violence were significant predictors of husband-to-wife violence among African American couples. African American, Hispanic, and Anglo men in positions of lower income status relative to their female partners are more likely to perpetrate domestic assaults, whereas among women, it is those in positions of higher income status who are more likely to perpetrate violence against their male partners. The former finding is consonant with resource theory suggesting that individuals lacking other means of power, such as income or educational status, are more likely to use violence to achieve greater power within the conjugal relationship (Anderson, 1997; Goode, 1971).

Immigration status also has been found to influence rates of spousal violence among Mexican Americans. Being born in the United States increases the risk of wife assault by both Mexican American and Puerto Rican American husbands (Kantor, Jasinski, & Aldarondo, 1994; Sorenson & Telles, 1991). We now need research that identifies the factors that mediate this intriguing country-of-birth effect. Several factors seem worthy of exploration, including perceived acceptability of violence toward spouse, cultural conflicts, sense of relative deprivation, embeddedness within extended family networks, and internalization of mainstream values regarding autonomy and self-reliance.

Predictors of marital quality. To date, there is little evidence to suggest that the major predictors of marital quality and marital conflict differ across racial and ethnic groups. For example, Lindahl and Malik's (1999) recent study found that low levels of family cohesiveness, and hostile marital coalitions (redirecting marital conflicts into attacks on the child) in comparison to balanced family subsystem interactions predicted higher levels of marital conflict, irrespective of family ethnicity (Hispanic, European American, biethnic). In a similar vein, marital interactions (perceived) as-

sociated with marital happiness are generally similar for African American and European American couples (e.g., affective affirmation, unsupportive spouse, frequency of destructive conflict, sexual satisfaction; Oggins et al., 1993).

There is considerable evidence of racial disparity in marital happiness, however. Even when economic resources, education, premarital cohabitation, family constellation, and patterns of marital interaction are taken into account, African American couples report less marital happiness and satisfaction than European American couples (Adelmann et al., 1996; Broman, 1991; Oggins et al., 1993). Furthermore, contrary to popular perception, educational and occupational status inequality between spouses is neither a reliable predictor of marital quality among African American couples nor a significant contributor to race differences in marital happiness and satisfaction (Adelmann et al.; Creighton-Zollar & Williams, 1992). Another popular explanation of racial disparity in marital happiness is African Americans' greater exposure to extrafamilial pressures, such as racial discrimination and negative conditions in the workplace (Oggin et al.). The past decade brought virtually no empirical tests of these hypothesized links, although some work was done on family-work role strain in families of color (Beale, 1997; Rubin, 1994).

Because families of color tend to be less advantaged economically than are European American families, it is not surprising that the impact of economic resources and hardship on marital and interpersonal relations in families of color is an issue that commanded considerable attention during the past decade (Brody, Stoneman, & Flor, 1995; Chadiha, 1992; Clark-Nicolas & Gray-Little, 1991; Gomel, Tinsley, Parke, & Clark, 1998; Gutman & Eccles, 1999; Lawson & Thompson, 1995; McLoyd, Jayaratne, Ceballo, & Borquez, 1994). Perceived economic adequacy is even more potent than income or income loss in its negative impact on the quality of marital relations (Clark-Nicolas & Gray-Little) and family relations among African Americans (Gomel et al.). It also is a crucial pathway by which low family income increases depressive symptoms (McLoyd et al.) and parent-child conflict (Gutman & Eccles) in this population. Some work documented social support as a buffer of the negative effects of economic stress on individual psychological functioning (e.g., McLoyd et al.), whereas other research emphasized individual and dyadic behavior as contributors to resiliency in couples facing economic stress (Chadiha).

Whereas prior studies of the processes through which financial resources influence family relations, parenting, and child functioning were based on samples comprised solely of European Americans or African Americans (Conger, Ge, Elder, Lorenz, & Simons, 1994; Conger, Conger, Elder, Lorenz, Simons, & Whitbeck, 1992; McLoyd et al., 1994; Simons, Lorenz, Conger, & Wu, 1992), by the late 1990s, increasing attention was being given to the question of whether European American families and families of color cope similarly or differently in the face of economic stress (Elder, Eccles, Ardelt, & Lord, 1995; Gomel et al., 1998; Gutman & Eccles, 1999). What gives this question cogency is prior work pointing to racial and ethnic differences in coping resources and the context of economic hardship (Duncan, 1991; Harrison, Wilson, Pine, Chan, & Buriel, 1990).

Life-course changes. The question of how marital quality among couples of color changes over the course of marriage attracted a modest amount of scholarly attention during the past decade. Adelmann and colleagues' (1996) analysis of African Americans and European Americans in their first marriages (with years of marriage ranging from 1 to 65 years), indicated a U-shaped association between years of marriage and marital satisfaction, similar to Glenn's (1989) finding. Nonetheless, years of marriage bore a negative linear relation to negative marital quality, such that marital discord and spousal negative behavior (e.g., ill-treatment, inability to forgive, excessive drinking) decreased with increases in years of marriage. Overall, these trends in marital quality held similarly for African Americans and European Americans, except that negative spouse behaviors decreased more sharply over time among the former than among the latter.

Other researchers focused attention on how management of marital conflict changes during the course of marriage (Crohan, 1996; Mackey & O'Brien, 1998). In Crohan's longitudinal study of newlywed couples, irrespective of race, couples who made the transition to parenthood reported more frequent conflicts, more marital tension, and a greater decline in marital happiness than couples who remained childless. Likewise, conflict behaviors among new parents were linked to marital happiness in similar ways for African American and European American spouses. Destructive conflict (e.g., insulting spouse, calling spouse names)

and active avoidance (leaving the scene of the conflict to cool down) predicted lower marital happiness for both new mothers and fathers, whereas passive avoidance (withdrawal) predicted higher marital happiness. Crohan's investigation did, however, reveal some race differences. Among European American couples, but not African American couples, the tendency to respond to marital conflict by becoming quiet and withdrawn increased after the birth of their child. Although African American couples did not respond to parenthood with an increase in passive avoidance, levels of passive avoidance before the transition to parenthood were actually higher among African American couples than European American couples, whereas the two groups were roughly comparable in use of this strategy following parenthood.

Marital and family conflict and child adjustment. A handful of studies, most conducted within the past decade, suggest that marital and family conflict is linked to psychological distress, externalizing behavior, reduced life satisfaction, lower academic competence, and reduced self-regulation among children of color (Brody et al., 1995; Buehler et al., 1998; Dumka, Roosa, & Jackson, 1997; DuRant, Getts, Cadenhead, Emans, & Woods, 1995; Spencer, Cole, DuPree, Glymph, & Pierre, 1993). During the past decade, some scholars speculated that children of color may be less vulnerable than are European American children to the adverse effects of parental discord, separation, and divorce (Amato & Keith, 1991). Proponents of this hypothesis pointed out, first, that marital discord and dissolution as experienced by children of color often occurs in the context of an overabundance of stressful events and ongoing condition, potentially diminishing unique psychosocial effects. Second, the increased embeddedness of children of color in extended family networks, compared with their European American counterparts (Bahr, 1994; Dalla & Gamble, 1998; Fuller, Holloway, & Liang, 1996; Hunter, 1997; Ramos-McKay, Comas-Diaz, & Rivera, 1988; Vega, 1995; Wilson, 1986; Wilson & Tolson, 1990), is thought to ease the psychosocial burden that marital conflict places on the child by increasing economic resources, increasing the number of nurturant and supportive adults in the child's environment, and reducing children's exposure to marital conflict following separation (Amato & Keith; Smith, 1997).

Although the attenuation hypothesis lacks

strong, direct empirical support, the convergence of three strands of evidence published during the past decade bolsters its plausibility. First, Amato and Keith's (1991) meta-analysis comparing effect sizes across studies of parental divorce and adult well-being indicated that the impact of parental divorce on separation, divorce, nonmarital childbearing, and educational attainment were significantly greater for European American adults than for African American adults. Some, but not all, of the findings from two recent prospective studies of child externalizing behavior preceding and following marital transitions follow this general pattern (Mason et al., 1994; Shaw, Winslow, & Flanagan, 1999).

A second strand of evidence lending support to the attenuation hypothesis are studies that assess marital conflict directly and report racial and ethnic differences in children's response to it. Buehler et al. (1998) found that the association between overt hostile conflict styles among parents (e.g., calling each other names, threatening each other) and externalizing problems in fifth to eighth graders was much weaker among Mexican Americans than among European Americans; the slope for the latter group (which included some ethnically mixed youth) was twice that of the slope for Mexican American youth. Likewise, Smith (1997) reported that the impact of parental separation on the school grades of seventh and ninth graders was weaker among African Americans than European Americans. In Lindahl and Malik's (1999) recent study, however, marital discord was found to affect externalizing behavior similarly in Latino and White boys.

A third strand of research evidence that provides indirect support for the attenuation hypothesis comes from Gohm and colleagues' (Gohm, Oishi, Darlington, & Diener, 1998) large international survey study of college students from 39 countries on six continents. The negative association of parental marital status and conflict to life satisfaction and affect balance (negative affect minus positive affect) was much weaker in students from collectivist countries (e.g., Ghana, Zimbabwe, China, Columbia) than students from individualistic countries (e.g., United States, Germany, Japan, Italy). Collectivism lessened both the impact of divorce following a high-conflict marriage and the impact of marital conflict when a parent remarried. The authors attributed this effect to higher levels of child-directed social support from extended family members in countries that are more collectivistic than individualistic. Collective-

ly, these findings about families of color, juxtaposed with those reported by Gohm et al., lend considerable plausibility to the notions that even within the American context, embeddedness in extended family networks protects children against the negative psychosocial effects of interparental conflict and that variation in extended family embeddedness may mediate racial and ethnic differences in children's response to marital conflict. Given their tenability and popularity, direct tests of these hypotheses clearly are warranted.

PARENTAL SOCIALIZATION PROCESSES

Although research on parenting and parent-child relations in families of color remains sparse compared with work on European American families, the 1990s saw a modest increase in both conceptual and empirical work focusing on African American, Latino, and Asian American groups. One important trend in conceptual work on the parenting of children of color was the increasing focus on identifying the positive influence on children of color of socialization practices based on cultures of origin (Garcia Coll & Magnuson, 1997; McAdoo, 1993). The shift from deficit models of parenting and child development to more sophisticated, ecological models that place parents and children of color at the center is well illustrated by the work of Garcia Coll et al. (1996). Their integrative model situates parenting within a larger framework that includes social position variables, racism, adaptive culture, and the wider social environment of schools and neighborhoods, among others. Such frameworks remind us that family relations—whether marital, parent-child, or kinship ties—do not occur within a vacuum, a resonant theme in the best work of the last decade.

Paternal Involvement

Earlier studies and writings, preoccupied as they were with the effect of poor fathers' absence on children, tended to portray fathers as uninvolved and distant from their children and largely ignored Latino fathers. Recent research in this area departs from earlier work by giving attention to both resident and nonresident African American and Latino fathers from economically diverse backgrounds. The empirical literature on the role of Asian American fathers continues to be extremely limited.

Quantity and quality of involvement. Roopnarine and colleagues (Ahmeduzzaman & Roopnarine, 1992; Hossain & Roopnarine, 1993, 1994) found that levels of involvement in primary caregiving (e.g., feeding, bathing) by African American fathers in middle-income and lower middle-income, dual-earner families with infant and preschool children tended to be as high, if not higher, than those reported for fathers from other ethnic groups. Increases in the number of hours the wife worked predicts increases in the amount of time African American fathers spend playing, reading, and directly interacting with their preschool children (Fagan, 1998) but appears to have no influence on how much time they spend in primary caregiving activities with infants (Hossain & Roopnarine, 1993). Not unlike their European American counterparts, African American husbands are more likely to spend time playing with the infant than in primary caregiving but, importantly, neither they nor their wives show differential time investment in caring for boys and girls (Hossain & Roopnarine, 1993, 1994). Low-income African American and Hispanic fathers (and mothers) do not differ in their level of parental involvement (Fagan; Hossain, Field, Pickens, Malphurs, & Del Valle, 1997), although African American parents, compared with their Hispanic counterparts, report receiving more assistance from extended family members in caring for their children (Hossain et al.). African American fathers and Hispanic fathers are more likely than are European American fathers to report monitoring and supervising their children's activities. In addition, survey data indicate that Latino fathers spend more time with their children in shared activities than do European American fathers, a finding consonant with the notion of familism (strong value for family closeness and cohesion) as a distinguishing feature of Hispanic cultures (Toth & Xu, 1999).

Research points to a range of individual and social factors as antecedents of paternal involvement and responsiveness. Regardless of racial and ethnic background (Hispanic, African American, and European American), fathers who are more involved with their children overall tend to be ones who hold nontraditional gender role and egalitarian family role ideologies, are highly committed to fatherhood and the family, and value obedience and compliance with family rules (Ahmeduzzaman & Roopnarine, 1992; Toth & Xu, 1999; Hossain & Roopnarine, 1994). In general, levels of various dimensions of paternal involve-

ment and nurturance (e.g., socialization, child care, availability) increase in African American and Puerto Rican two-parent families as income rises, and among African American families with increases in education, duration of marriage, fathers' family communication skills, fathers' self-esteem, and extrafamilial assistance to fathers in their parental role (Ahmeduzzaman & Roopnarine, 1992; Fagan, 1996, 1998; Hossain & Roopnarine). Among Ojibwa Indian fathers, paternal nurturance is greater among those who perceived that their own fathers were more nurturant during their upbringing, whereas the quantity of paternal involvement is higher among fathers who report higher community leadership expectations for their children (Williams, Radin, & Coggins, 1996).

Contributions to child functioning. A critical question in the literature is whether father involvement exerts unique effects on children's development beyond maternal characteristics and provision of economic support. Black, Dubowitz, and Starr (1999) found that nurturance displayed by fathers and father figures during play predicted advanced receptive language skills among low-income African American preschoolers, even after controlling for fathers' financial contributions and maternal age, education, and parenting satisfaction. Nonetheless, paternal nurturance was unrelated to children's IQ scores and problem behavior. In other research, father presence (continuous father coresidence; early vs. late onset of coresidence) predicted more advanced receptive language skills among Latino and African American children, but these effects disappeared once controls were introduced for economic resources and maternal IQ and education (Crockett, Eggebeen, & Hawkins, 1993).

Other studies report that greater paternal involvement is associated with higher cognitive and academic functioning in children of color, but the absence of controls for maternal and economic factors makes it impossible to claim that these relations represent unique effects of fathering (Hrabowski, Maton, & Greif, 1998; Williams et al., 1996; Zambrana-Ortiz & Lidz, 1995).

In sum, unique effects of fathering on the development of children of color have not yet been well documented. By countering the stereotype of fathers of color as a homogeneous group largely uninvolved and distant from their children, however, research conducted during the past decade laid the groundwork for more methodologically rigorous and sophisticated study of relations be-tween fathers of color and their children.

Discipline and Parenting Styles

Race and ethnic influences. The work of Dorn-busch, Steinberg and colleagues (Dornbusch, Rit-ter, Leiderman, Roberts, & Fraleigh, 1987; Stein-berg, Mounts, Lamborn, & Dornbusch, 1991) suggests that the more authoritarian parenting style of African American and Latino parents is not conducive to school performance. These same studies, however, indicate that the authoritarian style of Asian American parents does not lead to lower school performance in this subgroup. Stein-berg, Dornbusch, and Brown (1992) explained this contradictory pattern in terms of the role of peers, arguing that the high premium on school achievement reinforced within Asian American peer culture mitigates the more authoritarian par-enting style of their parents. The basic classifica-tory system undergirding this work, which de-scribes parents as either authoritarian or authoritative, came under scrutiny this past de-cade. Scholars of color, especially, questioned its generalizability outside a European American middle-class context and took issue with the ap-parently contradictory nature of the findings (Cau-ce & Gonzales, 1993; Chao, 1994). A recent study suggested that the "stricter" parenting styles of African Americans may be more in the eye of the (European American) beholder than in African American parenting. When both African Ameri-can (ingroup) and non–African American (out-group) observers watched and coded mother-daughter interactions, outgroup observers rated the mothers' parenting styles as more restrictive in their use of control. They also noted more con-flict in the interactions than did ingroup observers (Gonzales, Cauce, & Mason, 1996).

Another important development in this area of research is Lindahl and Malik's (1999) distinction between "hierarchical" parenting and authoritar-ian parenting, somewhat akin to the distinction that scholars make between strictness and puni-tiveness (Baldwin, Baldwin, & Cole, 1990; Baum-rind, 1972). Definitions of both parenting styles encompass parental decision making and the level of behavioral control parents use. However, whereas typical definitions of authoritarian par-enting incorporate a cold and unresponsive emo-tional style, Lindahl and Malik explicitly excluded emotional components from their definition of hi-erarchical parenting. They posited and found ev-

idence that hierarchical parenting is more adaptive in Latino families than in European American families, presumably because of the former group's strong value of respecting parents, other authority figures, and intrafamilial boundaries. For both European American and biethnic families, but not for Latino families, hierarchical parenting predicted higher levels of externalizing behavior in grade-school boys than did democratic parent-ing. For all three ethnic groups, though, lax and inconsistent parenting predicted more problem be-havior than did democratic parenting.

The past decade also witnessed challenges to conventional wisdom about parenting among Asian Americans. In her inventive study of par-enting attitudes, Chao (1994) asked Chinese American and European American parents to rate both prototypical items endorsing authoritarian parenting and Chinese child-rearing items related to the concept of *chiao shun* or training. Chinese American parents were much more likely than were European American parents to score higher on the concept of training, even after accounting for parental control and authoritarian parenting. Chao concluded that characterizing such parents as controlling and authoritarian is inappropriate and ethnocentric. Chinese Americans see their parenting styles as neither controlling nor author-itarian but aligned more with the notion of pro-viding clear and concrete guidelines for behavior.

During the past decade, scholars engaged in an intense conversation about the contribution of cul-ture versus other factors to race differences in par-ents' use of physical discipline and its impact on children's development (e.g., Baumrind, 1997; Huesmann, 1997; Lytton, 1997), stimulated prin-cipally by research and theorizing by Dodge and his colleagues (Deater-Deckard & Dodge, 1997a, 1997b; Deater-Deckard, Dodge, Bates, & Pettit, 1996). Deater-Deckard and colleagues' (1996) longitudinal study indicated that parents' use of physical discipline predicted higher levels of ex-ternalizing behavior among European American children, but not among African American chil-dren. In explaining these findings, these research-ers asserted that within African American culture compared with European American culture, phys-ical discipline short of abuse is more acceptable and more likely to be viewed as an appropriate display of positive parenting (Deater-Deckard & Dodge, 1997a). Consonant with this view is evi-dence that African American parents are more likely than European American parents to use physical punishment as a discipline strategy, even taking account of socioeconomic status (Deater-Deckard et al.; Day, Peterson, & McCracken, 1998; Gils-Sims, Straus, & Sugarman, 1995; Hill & Sprague, 1999). Deater-Deckard and Dodge (1997a) posited normativeness of physical coercion and punishment during slavery, combined with existing racial oppression and threat of societal punishment, as factors underlying African Americans' increased preference for physical discipline. Tests of the replicability of the moderating effects of race found by Deater-Deckard et al. and rigorous data-based evaluations of whether variation in the acceptability, meaning, and parental attributes associated with spanking underlie race differences in the effects of physical discipline would be highly valuable contributions to the field.

One problem in comparing research on parenting in families of color and parenting in White families is the different methodologies used. The gold standard for studies of parent-child interactions requires an observational and interactional component to supplement questionnaires or surveys, which are completed by both parents and children. This provides a broad-based understanding of family dynamics from the perspective of parent, child, and outside observer. This methodology is extremely rare in studies of families of color, despite advances in normative research systematizing observational assessment and micro- and macro-level coding procedures (Okazaki & Sue, 1995). There are no published studies of Asian American family interactions that include an observational component, and there are only a few that focus on Latino or African American families (e.g., Fagan, 1996, 1998; Florsheim, Tolan, & Gorman-Smith, 1996; Lindahl & Malik, 1999).

In sum, although there is some evidence that the childrearing practices of African American, Latino, and Asian American parents may not always reflect European American middle-class norms, there is no clear consensus on just how they differ. This is, in part, because research directly addressing this issue is sparse and generally not up to the rigorous methodological standards now commonplace among the best studies examining parenting among European Americans. Nonetheless, the lack of clear-cut differentiations in parenting across ethnic groups may also reflect the wide diversity in parenting within these groups. To rival the conceptual advances of this decade, empirical research of the next decade will need to find ways to retain a focus on culture and

ethnicity while treating it as one of a number of factors that interact to affect family and child functioning.

Grandmother involvement. Keen interest in the impact on parenting of Latino and African American grandmothers' involvement in family processes began during the 1980s and was sustained throughout the 1990s. In most cases, the work focused on adolescent mothers, who are viewed as particularly vulnerable and whose children are considered at high risk for a host of negative outcomes. Some of this work paints a very positive portrait of grandmother involvement and support. African American and Latino adolescent mothers who report higher levels of grandmother support experience less psychological distress (Leadbeater & Linares, 1992), more positive interactions with their babies (Chase-Lansdale, Brooks-Gunn, & Zamsky, 1994), and higher levels of educational attainment (Furstenberg, Brooks-Gunn, & Morgan, 1987). Based in part on the belief that it is better for both the adolescent mother and her child(ren) to live with her mother, some welfare policies require adolescents to reside with a parent to receive benefits (Leven-Epstein, 1996).

Upon closer inspection, however, the impact of grandmother involvement, especially when mother and grandmother are coresiding, coparenting, or both, is decidedly mixed. For example, Latina adolescent mothers who report very high levels of support from their mothers have been found to display less maternal sensitivity (Contreras, Mangelsdorf, Rhodes, Diener, & Brunson, in press). Studies of Black and White urban or high-risk families have also suggested that coresidence and high levels of grandmother involvement can predict lower quality parenting by adolescent mothers (Black & Nitz, 1996; Oyserman, Radin, & Saltz, 1994; Unger & Cooley, 1992). These discordant findings beckon us to seek a better understanding of what types of support from grandmothers are helpful, what types are inert or detrimental, and under what circumstances these outcomes vary. Some work along these lines has been done (Chase-Lansdale et al., 1994; Contreras, Lopez, Rivera-Mosquera, Raymond-Smith, & Rothstein, 1999), but more is needed.

Neighborhood and peer influences. The well-designed and richly textured study conducted by Furstenberg and colleagues (Furstenberg, Cook, Eccles, Elder, & Sameroff, 1999) of African American and European American families living in Philadelphia produced evidence that neighborhood characteristics have modest effects on two types of family management strategies: promotive strategies intended to foster children's talents and opportunities and preventive strategies that aim to reduce children's exposure to various types of dangerous circumstances. In terms of promotive strategies, parents in high-resource neighborhoods were more likely than parents in low-resource neighborhoods to enroll their adolescents in and take them to organized programs, whereas parents in low-resource neighborhoods were more likely to use verbal strategies, such as pointing out what might happen if the child did not develop his or her talents. Parents in low-resource communities used more preventive strategies than parents in high-resource communities and, in particular, were more likely to keep children home as much as possible, talk to them about dangers, and get them involved in prosocial activities outside their neighborhood. Parents in high-resource communities were more likely than those in low-resource communities to get their child involved in activities within their neighborhood as a preventive measure.

Other research affirmed the salutary effects of parental responsiveness to neighborhood conditions and peers (Baldwin et al., 1990; Jarrett, 1995). For example, Mason, Cauce, Gonzales, and Hiraga (1996) found that among adolescents who reported that their peers engaged in relatively low levels of problem behavior, the optimal level of behavioral control by mothers was low, whereas for those reporting that their peers were involved in higher levels of problem behavior, the optimal level of control was higher. Deviations from the optimal level of control had greater negative consequences on problem behavior among the latter group than the former group.

Immigration influences. Immigration accounted for a net increase in the United States from 1970 to 1990 of approximately 10 million people—a rare growth spurt that matches the rise in the immigrant population at the onset of the 20th century. The estimated number of undocumented migrants increases the figure by another two million (Muller, 1993). A major difference between the rise in immigrants coming to the United States in the early 1900s and the current increase is the source of immigration. At the turn of the century, most immigrants came from Europe and Canada, whereas the recent immigration has come primarily from Asia and Latin America (Portes & Rumbaut, 1990).

It is not surprising, then, that much of the sparse research on Latino and Asian American families focused on issues related to acculturation. Most of this work suggests that as Latino and Asian American parents become acculturated, their childrearing practices (e.g., teaching and play interactions, use of reasoning) and attitudes become more similar to those of parents born in the United States (Kelley & Tseng, 1992; Perez-Febles, 1992). Although most theories and studies of acculturation and assimilation place individuals and families on a linear path from immigration to assimilation to acculturation, the recent work of Zhou and Bankston (1998) provides a more complex picture of how families choose different paths toward adaptation and mobility. Because Vietnamese families typically live in low-income neighborhoods that may be divorced from the mainstream, they can choose from at least two paths. They can become marginal to their own ethnic community, abandon their ethnic identity, and adapt an identity common to inner cities that has few options for upward mobility. Or they can choose to adhere to Vietnamese community values and follow Vietnamese authority figures, which may eventually lead to more opportunities for upward mobility. Other research illustrates how acculturation may erode some primary cultural differences, even when others are maintained. For example, in an empirical study of cultural values, parents from four immigrant groups (Cambodians, Filipinos, Mexicans, and Vietnamese) were contrasted with Anglo American and Mexican American parents (Okagaki & Divecha, 1993). Immigrant parents placed more importance on promoting behaviors that conform to external standards, whereas the two American groups placed more value on promotion of autonomous functioning. Nonetheless, only European Americans rated cognitive factors as more important than noncognitive factors as determinants of whether a first grader was "intelligent."

Adding to the complexity of the acculturation process is the finding that the speed of this process may vary by generation. Children adjust to new environments and adapt to new values more quickly than do their parents. Hence, another area of research focuses on how acculturation affects intergenerational conflict between children and their parents. This line of research has been best elaborated over the past two decades by Szapocznik and his colleagues (Santiesteban et al.,

1996; Szapocznik & Kurtines, 1989, 1993; Szapocznik, Kurtines, Santiesteban, & Rio, 1990; Szapocznik, Rio, Hervis, Mitrani, Kurtines, & Faraci, 1991). These scholars have illuminated how acculturative stresses can lead to family conflict that, when handled poorly, can engender increased problem behaviors among Cuban American and, more recently, non-Cuban Latino youth in South Florida. They illustrate how culturally sensitive, conceptually grounded, and empirically driven family treatment and intervention can ameliorate these difficulties and improve Latino family and youth functioning. This work is among the only to examine programmatically and empirically the utility of a family therapy strategy developed specifically for families of color at various stages of acculturation.

Fuligni and colleagues' investigation of the attitudes toward autonomy, family cohesion, and family obligations of adolescents with Filipino, Chinese, Mexican, Central and South American, and European backgrounds, many of them immigrant, reveals that immigrant and first-generation youth display influences of both their culture-of-origin and American culture. For example, Asian American and Latino youth, whose cultures have been considered more collectivistic, possessed stronger values and greater expectations regarding their obligation to assist and support their families than did European American youth (Fuligni, Tseng, & Lam, 1999). Both Mexican and Filipino youth were less willing than White American youth to disagree with their fathers. Yet developmental trends toward increasing autonomy over time, including greater willingness to disagree with parents, were the same across all groups (Fuligni, 1998). Fuligni concluded that immigrant youth may have difficulty maintaining some traditional values (e.g., lower levels of autonomy) when they move to a new society that does not support those values, but other values (e.g., accepting and fulfilling familial obligations) remain strong.

Racial and Ethnic Socialization

Building on extensive conceptual and psychometric work and a handful of empirical studies published between 1980 and 1990, scholarly attention to the contents and correlates of racial and ethnic socialization intensified during the past decade. Although the bulk of this research continued to focus on African Americans, the past decade brought increasing attention to these issues in other groups of color. It is also noteworthy that many of these studies included both mothers and fathers (DeBerry, Scarr, & Weinberg, 1996; Hughes & Chen, 1997; Phinney & Chavira, 1995; Thomas & Speight, 1999).

Nature and content of messages. Parents of color and White parents alike talk to their children about race, but they do so with very different goals. Whereas White parents discuss race with their children to promote attitudes of tolerance and equality, African American parents' discussions of race with their children tend to focus on preparing their children for prejudice (Kofkin, Katz, & Downey, 1995). Within-group analysis indicates that parents of color convey messages about children's cultural heritage and the importance of racial pride more frequently than they convey messages about racial bias and discrimination and how to prepare for these circumstances (Hughes & Chen, 1997; Marshall, 1995; Phinney & Chavira, 1995; Thomas & Speight, 1999). In addition, especially when they are first-generation, Asian American and Latino families typically teach their children the traditions and values of their cultures-of-origin (Buriel & DeMent, 1997; Garcia Coll & Magnuson, 1997; Kibria, 1997). Messages intended to promote racial mistrust are a comparatively minor, if not rare, element of racial socialization, at least among African American parents (Hughes & Chen; Thomas & Speight). Nonetheless, these general patterns inexplicably are not found when offspring, rather than parents, are informants about parental racial socialization (Sanders-Thompson, 1994).

Racial and ethnic differences. African American parents vary considerably in the importance they attach to preparing their children to deal with racial stereotyping and discrimination and in the frequency with which they reportedly engage in racial socialization (Hughes & Chen, 1997; Marshall, 1995; Thornton, Chatters, Taylor, & Allen, 1990). Nonetheless, they generally provide more extensive racial and ethnic socialization than other parents of color studied thus far, a finding in keeping with the especially virulent and egregious discrimination that African Americans have historically faced and continue to experience (Feagin, 1991; Jaynes & Williams, 1989). Phinney and Chavira's (1995) study of a triethnic sample indicated that African American parents were more likely to report talking with their adolescent children about racial and ethnic prejudice as a problem and how to handle it than were Mexican American parents, who in turn were more likely to talk about these issues than were Japanese American parents. The themes that parents emphasize during the course of ethnic socialization are also related to race and ethnicity. Whereas Japanese American parents are more disposed than African American and Mexican American parents to underscore the importance of achievement, without mention of prejudice, African American parents report a greater tendency than the other two groups to discuss both achievement and themes dealing with prejudice.

Sources of within-group variation in racial and ethnic socialization. Among African American parents, factors that predict greater parental racial and ethnic socialization include higher levels of exposure to parental racial socialization during the parent's own childhood, heightened perception of racial bias in the parent's workplace (Hughes & Chen, 1997), and having a race-linked self-concept wherein racial identity is internalized with one's self-concept (Thomas & Speight, 1999). Among Mexican American mothers, those who engage in greater ethnic socialization tend to have a higher level of comfort with Mexican culture (e.g., speaking Spanish, enjoyment of Mexican foods and activities) and conversely a lower level of comfort with American culture. They also are more likely to have husbands whose families have been in the United States for fewer generations (Knight, Bernal, Garza, Cota, & Ocampo, 1993). Research is mixed regarding whether socioeconomic factors are related to racial and ethnic socialization (Hughes & Chen; Phinney & Chavira, 1995).

Racial socialization reportedly is more frequent among parents of adolescents than parents of children in middle childhood, who in turn report more frequent racial socialization than parents of children in preschool and the early years of grade school (Hughes & Chen, 1997). No consistent relation has been found between child gender and the frequency and content of parental racial socialization (Phinney & Chavira, 1995; Thomas & Speight, 1999; Sanders-Thompson, 1994).

Relations between racial and ethnic socialization and children's development. Studies of African American children report weak, scattered associations or no relation of racial and ethnic socialization to children's racial identity, school achievement, or beliefs about the best way of dealing with racial and ethnic stereotyping and discrimination (DeBerry et al., 1996; Marshall, 1995; Phinney & Chavira, 1995). Studies of Mexican Americans also have failed to find robust relations between parental ethnic socialization and children's psychological functioning. Knight and colleagues' (1993) investigation indicated that children whose mothers taught more about Mexican culture and lived in homes with more Mexican objects possessed a greater number of correct ethnic self-labels, engaged in more ethnic-linked behaviors (e.g., piñatas at birthday parties; speaking Spanish at home) and had more ingroup ethnic preferences. Nonetheless, no overall relation was found between ethnic socialization and children's ethnic identity. Quintana, Castaneda-English, and Ybarra (1999) found that parental ethnic socialization predicted higher levels of ethnic identity achievement among Mexican American adolescents but was unrelated to adolescents' level of understanding or construction of ethnicity (e.g., focus on physical features vs. internal psychological features). This weak pattern of relation between racial and ethnic socialization and children's development may be due to the small samples characteristic of most studies or may indicate that relations are domain-specific.

CONCLUSIONS AND FUTURE DIRECTIONS

Research on families of color made some noteworthy strides in the last decade. For African Americans, the research literature evolved from documenting demographic changes in family structure and formation to investigating the underlying causes of such changes and from a unidimensional perspective on gender roles among African American men to one suggestive of the complexities of this issue. For Latinos, studies began to explode the myth that the macho man and submissive woman are the norm. Our knowledge is much greater than heretofore about the nature and determinants of the division of household labor and marital processes in both African American and Latino families. We also have at least begun to examine Asian American families. In addition to the flourishing of research on racial and ethnic socialization, we witnessed a burgeoning of interest in the role of African American and Latino fathers, the emergence of more culturally valid constructs of parenting for all three racial and ethnic groups, and a remarkable growth in our understanding of how parenting in families of color is shaped by neighborhood context, grandmother involvement, children's peers, immigration, and acculturation. Although not a theory as such, the growing emphasis on an ecological framework allowed for an examination of a variety of issues within a larger contextual framework. Also discernible, however faintly, is a broadening of the generic perspective on familial socialization from one framed almost exclusively in terms of the parent-child dyad to one concerned with the family system and marital processes as contributors to children's functioning.

Recent increases in the number of studies that focused specifically and exclusively on families of color from a specific ethnic group have important implications for the development of theory. These studies advance a more diverse portrait of people of color, including an appreciation of the role that social class plays within each group. In addition, although rarely acknowledged, many of these studies were conducted by people of color. As such, interpretations are often made from an insider's perspective, in contrast to the outsider's view more common in the 1980s.

Notwithstanding these achievements, social science research on marital processes and familial socialization has considerable distance to go before it adequately reflects the ethnic and racial diversity of the United States. If people from a distant country or planet had to deduce the current racial and ethnic composition of the United States based on reading our family studies and child development journals, they probably would conclude that it is 85 to 90% White and about 10% Black, with a miniscule percentage of Latinos and Asian Americans. It would be easy to miss that there are any American Indian or multiracial families at all. This disconnection between the demographic reality of the United States and our data base is unfortunate and must change if our work is to remain relevant to policy makers or professionals who work directly with families and children. The dearth of family research is a special area of concern because the demographic revolution is already present in the classrooms, schools, and lives of our children. For real progress to occur, we not only need more studies, but higher quality ones (McLoyd & Steinberg, 1998). Studies characterized by poor measurement, inappropriate constructs, or both do not yield useful information. One of the most important advances in the last decade was the new conceptual frameworks that urge us to place families in context and to take into account that ethnicity and race do not exist in isolation from class and gender hierar-

chies. A major challenge for the new century is translation of these sophisticated and nuanced models into sound empirical research. An examination of the interactive and joint effects of culture and context offers to greatly enrich research in the coming decade.

Another important challenge is applying to studies of families of color the methodological sophistication characteristic of the best research on European American families. State-of-the-art work on European American families is typically longitudinal and includes careful observation, yet there are few studies of families of color that encompass these methodologies. Most of our knowledge base on the latter families still depends on cross-sectional studies or short-term longitudinal ones. It is still relatively rare for normative studies of families of color to include both the perspective of parents and children, and still fewer include an observational component. Prevention and intervention studies, review of which was beyond the scope of this paper, are the most common types of longitudinal research conducted with families and children of color. But when our core knowledge on family processes among European Americans is based on normative studies, whereas that on people of color is based on follow-ups of high-risk families, there is grave danger that our work will reinforce common stereotypes and prejudices. Advances in theory and methods throughout the 1990s provide a clear road map for the type of research needed in the future. The road is not an easy one, and we will undoubtedly encounter many unanticipated bumps and detours along the way, but there is no good alternative to continuing the journey. Given projected demographic changes, to do otherwise means short-changing half the American population.

NOTE

The authors express sincere appreciation to Charlea Tracey McNeal and Autumn Kelly for their diligent bibliographic assistance and Sheba Shakir for her superb secretarial and editorial assistance.

REFERENCES

Adelmann, P. K., Chadwick, K., & Baerger, D. R. (1996). Marital quality of Black and White adults over the life course. *Journal of Social and Personal Relationships, 13,* 361–384.

Ahmeduzzaman, M., & Roopnarine, J. L. (1992). Sociodemographic factors, functioning style, social support, and fathers' involvement with preschoolers in African-American families. *Journal of Marriage and the Family, 54,* 699–707.

Amaro, H. (1988). Women in the Mexican-American community: Religion, culture, and reproductive attitudes. *Journal of Community Psychology, 16,* 6–20.

Amato, P. R. & Keith, B. (1991). Parental divorce and adult well-being: A meta-analysis. *Journal of Marriage and the Family, 53,* 43–58.

Anderson, K. L. (1997). Gender, status, and domestic violence: An integration of feminist and family violence approaches. *Journal of Marriage and the Family, 59,* 655–669.

Asbury, J. (1993). Violence in the families of color in the United States. In R. Hampton, T. Gullotta, G. Adams, E. Potter, & R. Weissberg (Eds.), *Family violence: Prevention and treatment* (pp. 159–178). Newbury Park, CA: Sage.

Aschenbrenner, J. (1975). *Lifelines: Black families in Chicago.* New York: Holt, Rinehart & Winston.

Baca Zinn, M. (1994). Feminist rethinking from racial-ethnic families. In M. Baca Zinn & B. T. Dill (Eds.), *Women of color in U.S. society.* Philadelphia: Temple University Press.

Baca Zinn, M. (1999). Social science theorizing for Latino families. In S. Coontz, M. Parson, & F. Raley (Eds.), *American families: A multicultural reader.* New York: Routledge Press.

Baca Zinn, M., & Eitzen, D. S. (1996). *Diversity in families* (4th ed). New York: Harper Collins.

Bahr, K. S. (1994). The strengths of Apache grandmothers: Observations on commitment, culture and caretaking. *Journal of Comparative Family Studies, 25,* 233–248.

Baldwin, A. L., Baldwin, C., & Cole, R. (1990). Stress resistant families and stress resistant children. In J. Rolf, A. S. Masten, D. Cicchetti, K. Nuechterlein, & S. Weintraub (Eds.), *Risk and protective factors in the development of psychopathology,* (pp. 257–280). Cambridge, England: Cambridge University Press.

Barringer, H., Gardner, R. W., & Levin, M. J. (1993). *Asians and Pacific Islanders in the United States.* New York: Russell Sage.

Baumrind, D. (1972). An exploratory study of socialization effects on black children: Some black-white comparisons. *Child Development, 43,* 261–267.

Baumrind, D. (1997). Necessary distinction. *Psychological Inquiry, 8,* 176–182.

Beale, R. L. (1997). Multiple familial-worker role strain and psychological well-being: Moderating effects of coping resources among Black American parents. In R. J. Taylor, J. Jackson, & L. M. Chatters (Eds.), *Family life in Black America* (pp. 132–145). Thousand Oaks, CA: Sage.

Betancourt, H., & Lopez, S. R. (1993). The study of culture, ethnicity, and race in American psychology. *American Psychologist, 48,* 629–637.

Black, M. M., Dubowitz, H., & Starr, R. H. (1999). African American fathers in low income, urban families: Development, behavior, and home environment of their three-year-old children. *Child Development, 70,* 967–978.

Black, M. M., & Nitz, K. (1996). Grandmother co-residence, parenting, and child development among low-income urban teen mothers. *Journal of Adolescent Health, 18,* 218–226.

Blee, K., & Tickamyer, A. (1995). Racial differences in men's attitudes about women's gender roles. *Journal of Marriage and the Family, 57,* 21–30.

Blood, R., & Wolfe, E. (1969). Negro-white differences in blue-collar marriages in a northern metropolis. *Social Forces, 48,* 59–64.

Bowman, P. J., & Sanders, R. (1998). Unmarried African American fathers: A comparative life span analysis. *Journal of Comparative Family Studies, 29,* 39–56.

Brody, G., Stoneman, Z., & Flor, D. (1995). Linking family processes and academic competence among rural African American youths. *Journal of Marriage and the Family, 57,* 567–579.

Broman, C. L. (1988). Household work and family life satisfaction. *Journal of Marriage and the Family, 50,* 743–748.

Broman, C. L. (1991). Gender, work-family roles, and psychological well-being of blacks. *Journal of Marriage and the Family, 53,* 509–520.

Buehler, C., Krishnakumar, A., Stone, G., Anthony, C., Pemberton, S., Gerard, J., & Barber, B. (1998). Interparental conflict styles and youth problem behavior: A two-sample replication study. *Journal of Marriage and the Family, 60,* 119–132.

Buriel, R., & DeMent, T. (1997). Immigration and sociocultural changes in Mexican, Chinese, and Vietnamese American families. In A. Booth, A. C. Crouter, & N. Landale (Eds.), *Immigration and the family: Research and policy on U.S. immigrants.* Mahwah, NJ: Erlbaum.

Burton, L., & Jarrett, R. (2000). In the mix, yet on the margins: The place of families in urban neighborhood and child development research. *Journal of Marriage and the Family, 64,* 1114–1135.

Cauce, A. M., Coronado, N., & Watson, J. (1998). Conceptual, methodological, and statistical issues in culturally competent research. In M. Hernandez & M. R. Isaacs (Eds.), *Promoting cultural competence in children's mental health services. Systems of care for children's mental health* (pp. 305–329). Baltimore: Paul H. Brookes.

Cauce, A. M., & Gonzales, N. (1993). Slouching towards culturally competent research: Adolescents and families of color in context. *Focus: Psychological Study of Ethnic Minority Issues, 7*(2), 8–9.

Chadiha, L. A. (1992). Black husbands' economic problems and resiliency during the transition to marriage. *Families in Society: The Journal of Contemporary Human Services, 73,* 542–552.

Chao, R. (1994). Beyond parental control and authoritarian parenting style: Understanding Chinese parenting through the cultural notion of training. *Child Development, 65,* 1111–1119.

Chase-Lansdale, P. L., Brooks-Gunn, J., & Zamsky, E. (1994). Young African American multigenerational families in poverty: Quality of mothers and grandmothering. *Child Development, 65,* 373–393.

Clark-Nicolas, P., & Gray-Little, B. (1991). Effect of economic resources on marital quality in Black married couples. *Journal of Marriage and the Family, 53,* 645–655.

Clarke, S. C. (1995). Advance report of final divorce statistics, 1989 and 1990. *Monthly Vital Statistics Report, 42,* 8.

Collins, P. H. (1990). *Black feminist thought: Knowledge, consciousness, and the politics of empowerment. Perspectives on gender,* (Vol. 2). Boston: Unwin Human.

Coltrane, S., & Valdez, E. O. (1993). Reluctant compliance. In J. Hood (Ed.), *Men, work, and family* (pp. 151–175). Newbury Park, CA: Sage.

Conger, R. D., Conger, K. J., Elder, G. H., Lorenz, F., Simons, R. L., & Whitbeck, L. B. (1992). A family process model of economic hardship and adjustment of early adolescent boys. *Child Development, 63,* 526–541.

Conger, R. D., Ge, X., Elder, G., Lorenz, F., & Simons, R. (1994). Economic stress, coercive family process, and developmental problems of adolescents. *Child Development, 65,* 541–561.

Contreras, J. M., Lopez, I. R., Rivera-Mosquera, E. T., Raymond-Smith, L., & Rothstein, K. (1999). Social support and adjustment among Puerto Rican adolescent mothers: The moderating effect of acculturation. *Journal of Family Psychology, 13,* 228–243.

Contreras, J., Mangelsdorf, S., Rhodes, J., Diener, M., & Brunson, L. (1999). Parent-child interaction among Latina adolescent mothers: The role of family and social support. *Journal of Research in Adolescence, 9,* 417–439.

Creighton-Zollar, A., & Williams, S. J. (1992). The relative educational attainment and occupational prestige of Black spouses and life satisfaction. *Western Journal of Black Studies, 16,* 57–63.

Crockett, L. J., Eggebeen, D. J., & Hawkins, A. J. (1993). Fathers' presence and young children's behavioral and cognitive adjustment. *Journal of Family Issues, 14,* 355–377.

Crohan, S. E. (1996). Marital quality and conflict across the transition to parenthood in African American and White couples. *Journal of Marriage and the Family, 58,* 933–944.

Dalla, R. L., & Gamble, W. C. (1998). Social networks and systems of support among American Indian Navajo American youth. In H. I. McCubbin, E. A. Thompson, A. I. Thompson, & J. E. Fromer (Eds.), *Resiliency in Native American and immigrant families* (pp. 183–198). Thousand Oaks, CA: Sage.

Day, R. D., Peterson, G. W., & McCracken, C. (1998). Predicting spanking of younger and older children by mothers and fathers. *Journal of Marriage and the Family, 60,* 79–94.

Deater-Deckard, K., & Dodge, K. (1997a). Externalizing behavior problems and discipline revisited: Nonlinear effects and variation by culture, context, and gender. *Psychological Inquiry, 8,* 161–175.

Deater-Deckard, K., & Dodge, K. A. (1997b). Spare the rod, spoil the authors: Emerging themes in research on parenting and child development. *Psychological Inquiry, 8,* 230–235.

Deater-Deckard, K., Dodge, K. A., Bates, J. E., & Pettit, G. S. (1996). Physical discipline among African American and European American mothers: Links to children's externalizing behaviors. *Developmental Psychology, 32,* 1065–1072.

DeBerry, K. M., Scarr, S., & Weinberg, R. (1996). Family racial socialization and ecological competence: Longitudinal assessments of African-American transracial adoptees. *Child Development, 67,* 2375–2399.

Dill, B. T., Baca Zinn, M., & Patton, S. (1993). Feminism, race, and the politics of family values. *Report from the Institute for Philosophy and Public Policy, 13,* 13–18.

Dornbusch, S. M., Ritter, P. L., Leiderman, P. H., Roberts, D., & Fraleigh, M. (1987). The relation of parenting style to adolescent school performance. *Child Development, 58,* 1244–1257.

Dumka, L. E., Roosa, M. W., & Jackson, K. M. (1997). Risk, conflict, mothers' parenting, and children's adjustment in low-income, Mexican immigrant, and Mexican American families. *Journal of Marriage and the Family, 59,* 309–323.

Duncan, G. (1991). The economic environment of childhood. In A. Huston (Ed.), *Children in poverty: Child development and public policy* (pp. 23–50). New York: Cambridge University Press.

Duneier, M. (1992). *Slim's table: Race, respectability, and masculinity.* Chicago: University of Chicago Press.

DuRant, R., Getts, A., Cadenhead, C., Emans, S., & Woods, E. (1995). Exposure to violence and victimization and depression, hopelessness, and purpose in life among adolescents living in and around public housing. *Developmental and Behavioral Pediatrics, 16,* 233–237.

Elder, G., Eccles, J. S., Ardelt, M., & Lord, S. (1995). Inner-city parents under economic pressure: Perspectives on the strategies of parenting. *Journal of Marriage and the Family, 57,* 771–784.

Ellwood, D., & Crane, J. (1990). Family change among black Americans: What do we know? *Journal of Economic Perspectives, 4,* 65–84.

Fagan, J. (1996). A preliminary study of low-income African American fathers' play interactions with their preschool-age children. *Journal of Black Psychology, 22,* 7–19.

Fagan, J. (1998). Correlates of low-income African American and Puerto Rican fathers' involvement with their children. *Journal of Black Psychology, 24,* 351–367.

Feagin, J. R. (1991). The continuing significance of race: Antiblack discrimination in public places. *American Sociological Review, 56,* 101–116.

Florsheim, P., Tolan, P. H. & Gorman-Smith, D. (1996). Family processes and risk for externalizing behavior problems among African American and Hispanic boys. *Journal of Consulting and Clinical Psychology, 64,* 1222–1230.

Fossett, M. A. & Kiecolt, K. J. (1993). Mate availability and family structure among African Americans in U.S. metropolitan areas. *Journal of Marriage and the Family, 55,* 288–302.

Fuligni, A. J. (1998). Authority, autonomy, parent-adolescent conflict and cohesion: A study of adolescents from Mexican, Chinese, Filipino, and European backgrounds. *Developmental Psychology, 34,* 782–792.

Fuligni, A. J., Tseng, W., & Lam, M. (1999). Attitudes toward family obligations among American adolescents with Asian, Latin American, and European backgrounds. *Child Development, 70,* 1030–1044.

Fuller, B., Holloway, S., & Liang, X. (1996). Family selection of child-care centers: The influence of household support, ethnicity, and parental practices. *Child Development, 67,* 3320–3337.

Furstenberg, F., Brooks-Gunn, J., & Morgan, S. (1987). Adolescent mothers in later life. New York: Cambridge University Press.

Furstenberg, F., Cook, T. D., Eccles, J., Elder, G. H., & Sameroff, A. J. (1999). *Managing to make it: Urban families and adolescent success.* Chicago: University of Chicago Press.

Gadsden, V. (1999). Black families in intergenerational and cultural perspective. In M. Lamb (Ed.), *Parenting and child development in "nontraditional" families* (pp. 221–246). Mahwah, NJ: Erlbaum.

Gaines, S., Buriel, R., Liu, J., & Rios, D. (1997). *Culture, ethnicity, and personal relationship processes.* New York: Routledge.

Garcia Coll, C. T., Lamberty, G., Jenkins, R., McAdoo, H. P., Crnic, K., Wasik, B. H., & Vazquez Garcia, H. (1996). An integrative model for the study of developmental competencies in minority children. *Child Development, 67,* 1891–1914.

Garcia Coll, C. T., & Magnuson, K. (1997). The psychological experience of immigration: A developmental perspective. In A. Booth, A. C. Crouter, & N. Landale (Eds.), *Immigration and the family: Research and policy on U.S. immigrants.* Mahwah, NJ: Erlbaum.

Gardner, R. W., Robey, B., & Smith, P. C. (1985). Asian Americans: Growth, change, and diversity. *Population Bulletin, 40*(4). Washington, DC: U.S. Census Bureau.

Gils-Sims, J., Straus, M., & Sugarman, D. (1995). Child, maternal, and family characteristics associated with spanking. *Family Relations, 44,* 170–176.

Ginorio, A., Gutierrez, L., Cauce, A. M., & Acosta, M. (1995). The psychology of Latinas. In C. Travis (Ed.), *Feminist perspectives on the psychology of women* (pp. 331–342). Washington, DC: American Psychological Association.

Glenn, N. D. (1989). Duration of marriage, family composition, and marital happiness. *National Journal of Sociology, 3,* 3–24.

Gohm, C. L., Oishi, S., Darlington, J., & Diener, E. (1998). Culture, parental conflict, parental marital status, and the subjective well-being of young adults. *Journal of Marriage and the Family, 60,* 319–334.

Gomel, J. N., Tinsley, B. J., Parke, R., & Clark, K. M. (1998). The effects of economic hardship on family relationships among African American, Latino, and Euro-American families. *Journal of Family Issues, 19,* 436–467.

Gondolf, E., Fisher, E., & McFerron, R. (1991). Racial differences among shelter residents: A comparison of Anglo, Black, and Hispanic battered women. In R. Hampton (Ed.), *Black family violence: Current research and theory* (pp. 103–113). Lexington, MA: Heath.

Gonzales, N. A., Cauce, A. M., & Mason, C. A. (1996). Interobserver agreement in the assessment of parental behavior and parent-adolescent conflict: African American mothers, daughters, and independent observers. *Child-Development, 67,* 1483–1498.

Goode, W. (1971). Force and violence in the family. *Journal of Marriage and the Family, 33,* 624–636.

Gutman, L. M., & Eccles, J. S. (1999). Financial strain, parenting behaviors, and adolescents' achievement: Testing model equivalence between African American and European American single- and two-parent families. *Child Development, 70,* 1464–1476.

Hampton, R. L., & Coner-Edwards, A. (1993). Physical and sexual violence in marriage. In R. Hampton, T. Gullotta, G. Adams, E. Potter, & R. Weissberg (Eds.), *Family violence: Prevention and treatment* (pp. 113–141). Newbury Park, CA: Sage.

Hampton, R. L., & Gelles, R. (1994). Violence toward Black women in a nationally representative sample of Black families. *Journal of Comparative Family Studies, 25,* 105–119.

Harrison, A. O., Wilson, M. N., Pine, C. J., Chan, S. Q., & Buriel, R. (1990). Family ecologies of ethnic minority children. *Child Development, 61,* 347–362.

Henggeler, S., & Tavormina, J. (1980). Social class and race differences in family interaction: Pathological, normative, or confounding methodological factors. *Journal of Genetic Psychology, 137,* 211–222.

Hill, S., & Sprague, J. (1999). Parenting in black and white families: The interaction of gender with race and class. *Gender and Society, 13,* 480–502.

Hossain, Z., Field, T., Pickens, J., Malphurs, J., & Del Valle, C. (1997). Fathers' caregiving in low-income African-American and Hispanic-American families. *Early Development and Parenting, 6,* 73–82.

Hossain, Z., & Roopnarine, J. L. (1993). Division of household labor and child care in dual-earner African-American families with infants. *Sex Roles, 29,* 571–583.

Hossain, Z., & Roopnarine, J. L. (1994). African-American fathers' involvement with infants: Relationships to their functioning style, support, education, and income. *Infant Behavioral and Development, 17,* 175–184.

Hrabowski, F. A., III, Maton, K. I., & Greif, G. I. (Eds.). (1998). *Beating the odds: Raising academically successful African American males.* New York: Oxford University Press.

Huesmann, L. R. (1997). No simple relation. *Psychological Inquiry, 8,* 200–204.

Hughes, D., & Chen, L. (1997). When and what parents tell children about race: An examination of race-related socialization among African American families. *Applied Developmental Science, 1,* 200–214.

Hunter, A., & Davis, J. (1992). Constructing gender: An exploration of Afro-American men's conceptualization of manhood. *Gender and Society, 6,* 464–479.

Hunter, A. G. (1997). Counting on grandmothers: Black mothers' and fathers' reliance on grandmothers for parenting support. *Journal of Family Issues, 18,* 251–269.

Hurtado, A. (1995). Variations, combinations, and evolutions: Latino families in the United States. In R. E. Zambrana (Ed.), *Understanding Latino families: Scholarship, policy, and practice* (pp. 40–61). Thousand Oaks, CA: Sage.

Inclan, J. E., & Herron, D. G. (1990). Puerto Rican adolescents. In J. T. Gibbs & L. N. Huang (Eds.), *Children of color* (pp. 251–279). San Francisco: Jossey-Bass.

Isaacs, M. B., & Leon, G. (1987). Race, marital dissolution and visitation: An examination of adaptive family strategies. *Journal of Divorce, 11,* 17–31.

Jarrett, R. (1995). Growing up poor: The family experiences of socially mobile youth in low-income African American neighborhoods. *Journal of Adolescent Research, 10,* 111–135.

Jaynes, G., & Williams, R. (Eds.). (1989). *A common destiny: Blacks and American society.* Washington, DC: National Academy Press.

Jencks, C. (1992). *Rethinking social policy: Race, pov-*

erty and the underclass. Cambridge, MA: Harvard University Press.

John, D., Shelton, B. A., & Luschen, K. (1995). Race, ethnicity, gender and perceptions of fairness. *Journal of Family Issues, 16,* 357–379.

Kamo, Y., & Cohen, E. L. (1998). Division of household work between partners: A comparison of Black and White couples. *Journal of Comparative Family Studies, 29,* 131–145.

Kane, E. (1992). Race, gender, and attitudes toward gender stratification. *Social Psychology Quarterly, 55,* 311–320.

Kantor, G. K., Jasinski, J. L., & Aldarondo, E. (1994). Sociocultural status and incidence of marital violence in Hispanic families. *Violence and Victims, 9,* 207–222.

Kelley, M., & Tseng, H. (1992). Cultural differences in child rearing: A comparison of immigrant Chinese and Caucasian American mothers. *Journal of Cross-Cultural Psychology, 23,* 444–455.

Kibria, N. (1997). The concept of "bicultural families" and its implications for research on immigrant and ethnic families. In A. Booth, A. C. Crouter, & N. Landale (Eds.), *Immigration and the family: Research and policy on U.S. immigrants* (pp. 243–260). Mahwah, NJ: Erlbaum.

Kiecolt, K. J., & Fossett, M. A. (1995). Mate availability and marriage among African Americans: Aggregate and individual level analyses. In M. B. Tucker & C. Mitchell-Kernan (Eds.), *The decline in marriage among African Americans: Causes, consequences and policy implications* (pp. 121–135). New York: Russell Sage.

Kiecolt, K. J., & Fosset, M. A. (1997). The effects of mate availability on marriage among black Americans: A contextual analysis. In R. J. Taylor, J. S. Jackson, & L. M. Chatters (Eds.), *Family life in black America* (pp. 63–78). Thousands Oaks, CA: Sage.

Kitano, H., & Fujino, D., & Sato, J. (1998). Interracial marriages: Where are the Asian Americans and where are they going? In L. C. Lee & N. W. S. Zane (Eds.), *Handbook of Asian American psychology* (pp. 233–260). Thousand Oaks, CA: Sage.

Knight, G. P., Bernal, M. E., Garza, C. A., Cota, M. K., & Ocampo, K. A. (1993). Family socialization and the ethnic identity of Mexican-American children. *Journal of Cross-Cultural Psychology, 24,* 99–114.

Kofkin, J. A., Katz, P. A., & Downey, E. P. (1995, March). *Family discourse about race and the development of children's racial attitudes.* Paper presented at the meeting of the Society for Research on Child Development, Indianapolis, IN.

Lawson, E. J., & Thompson, A. (1995). Black men make sense of marital distress and divorce: An exploratory study. *Family relations, 44,* 211–218.

Leadbeater, B., & Linares, I. (1992). Depressive symptoms in Black and Puerto Rican adolescent mothers in the first three years post-partum. *Development and Psychopathology, 4,* 451–468.

Lee, S. (1998). Asian Americans: diverse and growing. *Population Bulletin, 53.* Washington, DC: Population Reference Bureau.

Leven-Epstein, J. (1996). *Teen parent provisions in the new law.* Washington, DC: Center for Law and Social Policy.

Leyendecker, B., & Lamb, M. (1999). Latino families. In M. Lamb (Ed.), *Parenting and child development in "nontraditional" families* (pp. 247–262). Mahwah. NJ: Erlbaum.

Lichter, D. T., LeClere, F. B., & McLaughlin, D. K. (1991). Local marriage markets and the marital behavior of black and white women. *American Journal of Sociology, 96,* 843–867.

Lichter, D. T., McLaughlin, D. K., Kephart, G., & Landry, D. J. (1992). Race and retreat from marriage: A shortage of marriageable men? *American Sociological Review, 57,* 781–799.

Lindahl, K. M., & Malik, N. M. (1999). Marital conflict, family processes, and boys' externalizing behavior in Hispanic American and European American families. *Journal of Clinical Child Psychology, 28,* 12–24.

Lytton, H. (1997). Physical punishment is a problem, whether conduct disorder is endogenous or not. *Psychological Inquiry, 8,* 211–214.

MacDonald, W., & DeMaris, A. (1995). Remarriage, stepchildren, and marital conflict: Challenges to the incomplete institutionalization hypothesis. *Journal of Marriage and the Family, 57,* 387–398.

Mackey, R. A., & O'Brien, B. A. (1998). Marital conflict management: Gender and ethnic differences. *Social Work, 43,* 128–141.

Majors, R., & Billson, J. (1992). *Cool pose: Dilemmas of Black manhood in America.* New York: Lexington Books.

Majors, R., & Gordon, J. (Eds.). (1994). *The American black male: His present status and his future.* Chicago: Nelson-Hall.

Mare, R. D., & Winship, C. (1991). Socioeconomic change and the decline of marriage for blacks and whites. In C. Jencks & P. Peterson (Eds.), *The Urban underclass* (pp. 175–202). Washington, DC: Brookings Institute.

Marshall, S. (1995). Ethnic socialization of African American children: Implications for parenting, identity development, and academic achievement. *Journal of Youth and Adolescence, 24,* 377–397.

Mason, C. A., Cauce, A. M., Gonzales, N., & Hiraga, Y. (1996). Neither too sweet nor too sour: Problem peers, maternal control, and problem behavior in African American adolescents. *Child Development, 67,* 2115–2130.

Mason, C. A., Cauce, A. M., Gonzales, N., & Hiraga, Y., & Grove, K. (1994). An ecological model of externalizing behaviors in African American adolescents: No family is an island. *Journal of Research on Adolescence, 4,* 639–655.

McAdoo, H. P. (1993). The social cultural contexts of ecological developmental family models. In P. G. Boxx, W. J. Doherty, R. LaRossa, W. Shumm, & S. Steinmetz (Eds.), *Sourcebook of family theories and methods: A contextual approach* (pp. 298–301). New York: Plenum.

McAdoo, H. P. (1998). African American families. In C. H. Mindel, R. W. Habenstein, & R. Wright (Eds.), *Ethnic families in America,* (pp. 361–381). Upper Saddle River, NJ: Prentice Hall.

McCubbin, H., Thompson, E., Thompson, A., & Fromer, J. (Eds.) (1998). *Resiliency in Native American and immigrant families.* Thousand Oaks, CA: Sage.

McLoyd, V. C. (1990). The impact of economic hardship on Black families and children: Psychological distress, parenting, and socioemotional development. *Child Development, 61,* 311–346.

McLoyd, V. C. (1993). Employment among African American mothers in dual earner families: Antecedents and consequences for family life and child development. In J. Frankel (Ed.), *The employed mother and the family context* (pp. 180–226). New York: Springer.

McLoyd, V. C., Jayaratne, T., Ceballo, R., & Borquez, J. (1994). Unemployment and work interruption among African American single mothers: Effects on parenting and adolescent socioemotional functioning. *Child Development, 65,* 562–589.

McLoyd, V. C., & Steinberg, L. (Eds.) (1998). *Studying minority adolescents: Conceptual, methodological, and theoretical issues.* Mahwah, NJ: Erlbaum.

Moffit, R. (1992, March). Incentive effects of the U.S. welfare system: A review. *Journal of Economic Literature, 30,* 1–61.

Moffit, R. (1994). Welfare effects on female headship with area effects. *Journal of Human Resources, 29,* 621–629.

Muller, T. (1993). *Immigrants and the American city.* New York: New York University.

Oggins, J., Veroff, J., & Leber, D. (1993). Perceptions of marital interaction among Black and White newlyweds. *Journal of Personality and Social Psychology, 65,* 494–511.

Okagaki, L., & Divecha, D. J. (1993). Development of parental beliefs. In T. Luster & L. Okagaki (Eds.), *Parenting: An ecological perspective* (pp. 35–68). Hillsdale, NJ: Erlbaum.

Okazaki, S., & Sue, S. (1995). Methodological issues in assessment research with ethnic minorities. *Psychological Assessment, 7,* 367–375.

Orbuch, T., & Custer, L. (1995). The social context of married women's work and its impact on black husbands and white husbands. *Journal of Marriage and the Family, 57,* 333–345.

Oyserman, D., Radin, N., & Saltz, E. (1994). Predictors of nurturant parenting in teen mothers living in three generational families. *Child Psychiatry and Human Development, 24,* 215–239.

Perez-Febles, A. M. (1992). Acculturation and international styles of Latina mothers and their infants. Unpublished honors thesis, Brown University, Providence, RI. [Cited in Garcia Coll, C. T., Meyer, E. C., & Brillon, L. (1995). Ethnic minority parenting. In M. Bornstein (Ed.), *Handbook of parenting: Vol. 2. Biology and ecology of parenting* (pp. 189–209). Hillsdale, NJ: Erlbaum.]

Pesquera, B. M. (1993). In the beginning he couldn't even lift a spoon: The division of household labor. In A. de la Torre & B. M. Pesquera (Eds.), *Building with our hands: New directions in Chicana Studies.* Berkeley: University of California Press.

Phinney, J. S., & Chavira, V. (1995). Parental ethnic socialization and adolescent coping with problems related to ethnicity. *Journal of Research on Adolescence, 5,* 31–54.

Pleck, J. (1981). *The myth of masculinity.* Cambridge, MA: MIT Press.

Portes, A., & Rumbaut, G. R. (1990). *Immigrant America: A portrait.* Berkeley: University of California Press.

Quintana, S. M., Castaneda-English, P., & Ybarra, V. C. (1999). Role of perspective-taking abilities and ethnic socialization in development of adolescent ethnic identity. *Journal of Research on Adolescence, 9,* 161–184.

Ramirez, O., & Arce, C. H. (1981). The contemporary Chicano family: An empirically based review. In A. Baron, Jr. (Ed.), *Explorations in Chicano psychology.* New York: Prager.

Ramos-McKay, J. M., Comas-Diaz, L., & Rivera, L. (1988). Puerto Ricans. In L. Comas-Diaz & E. H. Griffith (Eds.), *Clinical guidelines in cross-cultural mental health* (pp. 204–232). New York: Wiley.

Rubin, L. (1994). *Families on the fault line: America's working class speaks about the family, the economy, race, and ethnicity.* New York: HarperCollins.

Saenz, R., Goudy, W., & Lorenz, F. O. (1989). The effects of employment and marital relations on depression among Mexican American women. *Journal of Marriage and the Family, 58,* 239–251.

Sandefur, G. D., & Liebler, C. A. (1996). The demography of American Indian families. In G. Sandefur, R. R. Rindfuss, & B. Cohen (Eds.), *Changing numbers, changing needs: American Indian demography and public health* (pp. 196–217). Washington, DC: National Academy Press.

Sanders-Thompson, V. L. (1994). Socialization to race and its relationship to racial identification among African Americans. *Journal of Black Psychology, 20,* 175–188.

Santiesteban, D. A., Szapocznik, J., Perez-Vidal, A., Murray, E. J., Kurtines, W. M., & LaPerriere, A. (1996). Efficacy of intervention for engaging youth and families into treatment and some variables that may contribute to differential effectiveness. *Journal of Family Psychology, 10,* 35–44.

Shaw, D. S., Winslow, E. B., & Flanagan, C. (1999). A prospective study in the effects of marital status and family relations on young children's adjustment among African American and European American families. *Child Development, 70,* 742–755.

Shelton, B. A., & John, D. (1993). Ethnicity, race, and difference: A comparison of White, Black, and Hispanic men's household labor time. In J. Hood (Ed.), *Men, work, and family* (pp. 131–149). Newbury Park, CA: Sage.

Simons, R. L., Lorenz, F. O., Conger, R. D., & Wu, C. (1992). Support from spouse as a mediator and moderator of the disruptive influence of economic strain on parenting. *Child Development, 63,* 1282–1301.

Sistler, A. B., & Moore, G. M. (1996). Cultural diversity in coping with marital stress. *Journal of Clinical Geropsychology, 2,* 77–82.

Smith, T. E. (1997). Differences between Black and White students in the effect of parental separation on school grades. *Journal of Divorce and Remarriage, 27,* 25–42.

Smith, W. (1995). Mate availability and marriage: Commentary. In M. B. Tucker & C. Mitchell-Kernan (Eds.), *The decline in marriage among African Americans: Causes, consequences and policy implications* (pp. 136–141). New York: Russell Sage.

Sorenson, S. B., & Telles, C. A. (1991). Self-reports of spousal violence in a Mexican American and non-Hispanic White population. *Violence and Victims, 6,* 3–16.

Sorenson, S. B., Upchurch, D. M., & Shen, H. (1996).

Violence and injury in marital arguments: Risk patterns and gender differences. *American Journal of Public Health, 86,* 34–40.

South, S. J., & Lloyd, K. M. (1992). Marriage opportunities and family formation: Further implications of imbalanced sex ratios. *Journal of Marriage and the Family, 54,* 440–451.

Spencer, M. B., Cole, S., DuPree, D., Glymph, A., & Pierre, P. (1993). Self-efficacy among urban African American adolescents: Exploring issues of risk, vulnerability, and resilience. *Development and Psychopathology, 5,* 719–739.

Steinberg, L., Dornbusch, S. M., & Brown, B. B. (1992). Ethnic differences in adolescent achievement: An ecological perspective. *American-Psychologist, 6,* 723–729.

Steinberg, L., Mounts, N. S., Lamborn, S. D., & Dornbusch, S. M. (1991). Authoritative parenting and adolescent adjustment across varied ecological niches. *Journal of Research on Adolescence, 1,* 19–36.

Straus, M., & Smith, C. (1990). Violence in Hispanic families in the United States: Incidence rates and structural interpretations. In M. A. Straus & R. Gelles (Eds.), *Physical violence in American families: Risk factors and adaptations in 8,145 families* (pp. 341–368). New Brunswick, NJ: Transaction.

Szapocznik, J., & Kurtines, W. (1989). *Breakthroughs in family therapy with drug abusing problem youth.* New York: Springer.

Szapocznik, J., & Kurtines, W. (1993). Family psychology and cultural diversity: Opportunities for theory, research, and application. *American Psychologist, 48,* 400–407.

Szapocznik, J., Kurtines, W. M., Santiesteban, D. A., & Rio, A. T. (1990). The interplay of advances among theory, research, and applications in treatment interventions aimed at behavior problem children and adolescents. *Journal of Consulting and Clinical Psychology, 58,* 696–703.

Szapocznik, J., Rio, A. T., Hervis, O. E., Mitrani, V. B., Kurtines, W., & Faraci, A. M. (1991). Assessing change in family functioning as a result of treatment: The structural family systems rating scale (SFSR). *Journal of Marriage and Family Therapy, 17,* 295–310.

Taylor, P. L., Tucker, M. B., & Mitchell-Kernan, C. (1999). Ethnic variations in perceptions of men's provider role. *Psychology of Women Quarterly, 23,* 741–761.

Taylor, R. (Ed.). (1998). Minority families in the United States: A multicultural perspective. Upper Saddle River, NJ: Prentice Hall.

Taylor, R. J., Tucker, M. B., Chatters, L. M., & Jayakody, R. (1997). Recent demographic trends in African American family structure. In R. J. Taylor, J. S. Jackson, & L. M. Chatters (Eds.), *Family life in Black America* (pp. 14–62). Thousands Oaks, CA: Sage.

Testa, M. (1991). *Male joblessness, nonmarital parenthood and marriage.* Paper presented at the Chicago Urban Poverty and Family Life Conference, Chicago IL.

Testa, M., & Krogh, M. (1995). The effects of employment on marriage among Black males in inner city Chicago. In M. B. Tucker & C. Mitchell-Kernan (Eds.), *The decline in marriage among African Americans: Causes, consequences and policy implications* (pp. 59–105). New York: Russell Sage.

Thomas, A. J., & Speight, S. L. (1999). Racial identity and racial socialization attitudes of African American parents. *Journal of Black Psychology, 25,* 152–170.

Thornton, M. C., Chatters, L., Taylor, R., & Allen, W. (1990). Sociodemographic and environmental correlates of racial socialization by black parents. *Child Development, 61,* 401–409.

Tienda, M. (1989). Puerto Ricans and the underclass debate. *Annals of the American Academy of Political and Social Science, 501,* 105–119.

Toth, J. F., & Xu, X. (1999). Ethnic and cultural diversity in fathers' involvement: A racial/ethnic comparison of African American, Hispanic, and White fathers. *Youth and Society, 31,* 76–99.

Tucker, M. B., & Mitchell-Kernan, C. (Eds.). (1995). *The decline in marriage among African Americans: Causes, consequences and policy implications.* New York: Russell Sage.

Unger, D., & Cooley, M. (1992). Partner and grandmother contact in Black and White teen parent families. *Journal of Adolescent Health, 13,* 546–552.

U.S. Bureau of the Census. (1995, September). The Nation's Hispanic population—1994. *Statistical Brief, 95/25.*

U.S. Bureau of the Census. (1997a, September 11). Facts for Hispanic Heritage Month. Press Release, 97–110. Washington, DC: Author.

U.S. Bureau of the Census. (1997b). Hispanic population for the March 1994 Current Population Survey. Washington, DC: U.S. Government Printing Office.

U.S. Bureau of the Census. (1999a, July). Selected social characteristics of the population, by region and race. Washington, DC: Author.

U.S. Bureau of the Census. (1999b). *Statistical abstract of the United States: 1999.* Washington, DC: Author.

Vega, W. A. (1995). The study of Latino families: A point of departure. In R. E. Zambrana (Ed.), *Understanding Latino families: Scholarship, policy, and practice* (pp. 3–17). Thousand Oaks, CA: Sage.

Williams, E., Radin, N., & Coggins, K. (1996). Parental involvement in childrearing and the school performance of Ojibwa children: An exploratory study. *Merrill-Palmer Quarterly, 42,* 578–595.

Wilson, M. N. (1986). The black extended family: An analytic consideration. *Developmental Psychology, 22,* 246–258.

Wilson, M. N., & Tolson, T. (1990). Familial support in the Black community. *Journal of Clinical Child Psychology, 19,* 347–355.

Williams, N. (1988). Role making among married Mexican American women: Issues of class and ethnicity. *Journal of Applied Behavioral Sciences, 24,* 203–217.

Wilson, W. J. (1987). *The truly disadvantaged: The inner city, the underclass, and public policy.* Chicago: University of Chicago Press.

Wilson, W. J. (1996). *When work disappears: The world of the new urban poor.* New York: Knopf.

Zambrana-Ortiz, N. Z., & Lidz, C. S. (1995). The relationship between Puerto Rican mothers' and fathers' mediated learning experiences and the competence of their preschool children. *Journal of Cognitive Education, 4,* 17–31.

Zavella, P. (1989). The problematic relationship of feminism and Chicana studies. *Womens Studies: An Interdisciplinary Journal, 17,* 25–36.

Zhou, M., & Bankston, C. L., III. (1998). *Growing up American: How Vietnamese children adapt to life in the United States.* New York: Russell Sage.

KAREN SECCOMBE   *Portland State University*

Families in Poverty in the 1990s: Trends, Causes, Consequences, and Lessons Learned

During the 1990s, poverty rates in the United States remained relatively stable despite a robust economy in which unemployment and inflation were at their lowest points in many years. Approximately 13% of individuals, 11% of families, and 19% of children lived below the poverty line in 1998, a decline of only 1% or less for each of these categories since 1990. These high rates of poverty result in many severe consequences. This essay reviews the research and theoretical and conceptual developments during the past decade, including: (a) a background on how the poverty line was developed; (b) general research themes in the 1990s; (c) the causes of the virtually unchanged poverty rate; (d) the consequences of poverty, particularly for children; and (e) the lessons we have learned from research over the past decade, with some directions for the future.

When President John Kennedy was elected to office in 1960, more than 22% of the U.S. population lived below the poverty level. Perhaps even more alarming, nearly 27% of children under the age of 18 lived in poverty (U.S. Bureau of the Census, 1999, tables 2, 3). The dire circumstances of the poor were brought to light in Michael Harrington's book, *The Other America* (1963), which described the vicelike impoverishment that was common in specific geographic regions of the country. President Kennedy considered this cause

Department of Sociology, Portland State University, Portland, OR 97207-0751 (seccombek@pdx.edu).

Key Words: inequality, poverty, welfare, working poor.

for great concern and began a series of programs and policies designed to combat poverty in the United States. President Johnson continued and expanded these after Kennedy's assassination in 1963. Collectively known as *The War on Poverty,* these programs and policies, such as Medicaid, Medicare, Head Start, Job Corps, and Food Stamps (along with a strong economy), helped reduce the overall poverty rate to 12.6%, and the child poverty rate to 14.9% by 1970 (U.S. Bureau of the Census, 1999, tables 2, 3).

Since this period, however, there has been an increase in the percentage of people who live in poverty, particularly among children, as shown in Table 1. By 1990, 13.5% of the general population, 12.0% of families, and 19.9% of children in the United States, or nearly one child in five, lived in impoverished households (U.S. Bureau of the Census, 1999, tables B1, B2). That figure has remained remarkably consistent throughout this decade, rising slightly in the early 1990s, leveling off by the middle of the decade, then dipping slightly. The most recent data available as this essay goes to press indicates that in 1998, 12.7% of the overall population, 11.2% of families, and 18.9% of children under the age of 18 lived below the poverty line (U.S. Bureau of the Census, 1999, tables B1, B2). Thus, we end the 1990s with poverty rates that are only slightly less than those in which we began. This is ironic, given the unusually robust economy during the decade. Unemployment and inflation were at their lowest rates in decades (Auerbach & Belous, 1998; U.S. Bureau of the Census, 1998, tables 679, 772).

TABLE 1. HISTORICAL RATES OF POVERTY: PERSONS, FAMILIES AND CHILDREN, BY ETHNICITY

Year	Total	White/Not Hispanic	Black	Hispanic	Asian
Percentage of persons below the poverty level					
1970	12.6	N/A[a]	33.5	N/A	N/A
1980	13.0	9.1	32.5	25.7	N/A
1990	13.5	8.8	31.9	28.1	12.2
1995	13.8	8.5	29.3	30.3	14.6
1998	12.7	8.2	26.1	25.6	12.5
Percentage of families below the poverty level					
1970	10.9	N/A	32.2	N/A	N/A
1980	11.5	7.4	31.1	25.1	N/A
1990	12.0	7.0	31.0	26.9	11.3
1995	12.3	6.6	28.5	29.2	13.0
1998	11.2	6.3	24.7	24.3	11.4
Percentage of children below poverty level					
1970	14.9	N/A	41.5	N/A	N/A
1980	17.9	11.8	42.3	33.2	N/A
1990	19.9	12.3	44.8	38.4	17.6
1995	20.2	11.2	41.9	40.0	19.5
1998	18.9	10.6	36.7	34.4	18.0

Note: Data are from the U.S. Bureau of the Census. (1999, September) *Poverty in the United States, 1998.* pp. 60–207, tables B1–B2. Retrieved from World Wide Web: http://www.census.gov/pub/hhes/www/poverty.html.

[a] Early census reports did not distinguish between Whites and White Hispanic groups as did later reports. Here I keep them separated so that we can see the effects of ethnicity on poverty rates.

These data contrast sharply with other industrialized nations, many of which have poverty rates of one half or even one quarter of those found in the United States (Bergmann, 1996; Casper, McLanahan, & Garfinkel, 1994; Rainwater, 1995; Rainwater & Smeeding, 1995).

Moreover, the full impact of welfare reforms implemented in the late 1990s has not yet been fully assessed (see the General Accounting Office, 1999, for a list of recent tracking efforts). Welfare caseloads declined dramatically between March 1994 and March 1999, from 5 million to 2.6 million (U.S. Department of Health and Human Services, 1999). But early evaluations of welfare reforms (General Accounting Office, 1999; Loprest, 1999) and the anecdotal evidence of a dramatic increase in the use of food banks and homeless shelters (Associated Press, 1999; Bernstein, 1997) suggest that many people are worse off than they were before welfare reform. Journalist Jason DeParle summed up research findings on welfare reform in an article in the *New York Times* on December 30, 1999 as the decade was coming to a close:

> Less welfare and more work—it sounds like an impressive achievement, . . . Yet for most families the work has failed to translate into economic progress. Among those who went to work in 1998, average annual earnings were just $7,700,

> $400 less than they would have received by staying on welfare. . . . After leaving welfare for work, poor families were 50% more likely to say they did not have enough money for groceries, a finding that rings true after many conversations with former welfare families who spontaneously talked about their struggles for food. (pp. A1, A12)

Poverty is not randomly distributed; race, gender, family structure, and parental education all have a significant effect on the likelihood of experience poverty. For example, as shown in Table 1, in 1998, 10.6% of White, non-Hispanic children under the age of 18 were poor, in contrast to 36.7% of African American, 34.4% of Hispanic, and 18.0% of Asian and Pacific Islander children, respectively (U.S Bureau of the Census, 1999, table 3). Minority groups are also significantly more likely to live in "deep poverty," defined as families with cash incomes less than 50% of the poverty line (Wertheimer, 1999). As shown in Table 1, however, African Americans have also experienced the largest declines in poverty during the decade, declining by nearly 20%. Yet the problems remain severe. Rank and Hirschl (1999), using data from the Panel Study of Income Dynamics, found 34% of children overall will have spent at least 1 year in poverty; however, that increases to 69% of Black children, 81% of children in single parent households, and 63% of children whose head of household had not completed 12 years of school. The effects of combining these characteristics are glaring. Ninety-nine percent of children who are Black, who live in a single parent household, and who live with a head of household who has less than 12 years of education have experienced poverty, compared with only 15% of children who are White, who live in two-parent households, and who live with a head of household who has completed at least 12 years of education.

Poverty is usually depicted statistically. Statistical data are important because they allow us to compare the vulnerability of different groups within the population and to assess the ways in which poverty expands or contracts, or which groups are becoming relatively more or less vulnerable. Nonetheless, numbers alone may present a sterile picture of economic, social, and material hardship. Consequently, during the 1990s, we witnessed an explosion of ethnographic studies designed to allow the outsider "in"—and show what the experience of poverty is like for the approximately 36 million U.S. adults and children who experience it (Berrick, 1995; Edin & Lein, 1997; Jarrett, 1994; Kotlowitz, 1991; Kozol, 1992, 1995; Liebow, 1993; Rank, 1994a; Rubin, 1994; Seccombe, 1999; Sidel, 1992, 1996).

Collectively, these studies reveal that being poor involves more than simply having a "low income." It is more than an economic inconvenience easily overcome with increased initiative. Rather, poverty affects one's total existence. It can impede adults' and children's social, emotional, biological, and intellectual growth and development. More than half of poor families experienced at least one of the following deprivations over the course of a year: eviction, utilities disconnected, telephone disconnected, housing with upkeep problems, crowded housing, no refrigerator, no stove, or no telephone (Federman, Garner, Short, Cutter, Kiely, 1996). Ethnographic studies expose the "sting" of these deprivations, the humiliation of being poor and perhaps needing welfare assistance, the coping mechanisms used by both adults and children, and the myriad of ways people try to make sense of their lives and carve out a sense of respectability in a society that places a high premium on wealth and material possessions.

This essay reviews the research and theoretical development on families in poverty that have been published during the 1990s. First, I provide a definition of poverty that is used by the federal government, indicating how this threshold was developed. Then I review the research themes and trends that dominated the literature (in my estimation) during this decade. I examine the research findings on the causes of the relatively stagnant poverty rate among families during a period of otherwise strong economic growth, and I discuss the recent literature delineating the consequences of poverty, particularly for children. In conclusion, I summarize the lessons we have learned over the past decade and offer some directions for future research.

HOW POVERTY IS DEFINED

The official poverty line was established by the Social Security Administration in 1964 (Orshansky, 1965). Survey data in the early 1960s indicated that families spent approximately one third of their income on food. Therefore, the poverty line was calculated from the estimated annual costs of a minimal food budget designed by the U.S. Department of Agriculture (USDA) and then multiplied by three, a method that continues today (U.S. House of Representatives, Committee on Ways and Means, 1996). This food budget parallels the current "Thrifty Food Plan," which forms the basis of Food Stamp benefits and is the least expensive food plan developed by the USDA (Family Economics and Nutrition Review, 1997). It is far below the amount most middle class families spend on food. Families with yearly pretax cash incomes that are below this established threshold are counted as "poor."

The poverty line varies by family size and by whether the individuals are over or under age 65, because food costs are expected to differ. It is revised yearly based on inflationary changes in the Consumer Price Index. The threshold value for the year 1963 for a family of four (two adults and two children) was about $3,100. In 1990, the poverty line for a four-person family under the age of 65 was $13,359 (U.S. House of Representatives, Committee on Ways and Means, 1996). By 1999, the poverty line for a family of four had risen to $16,700 (Federal Register, 1999). It is approximately 25 to 30% higher in Alaska and Hawaii because of higher food costs.

Calculation of the poverty line has been criticized on a number of grounds (Citro & Michael, 1995; Danziger, 1990; Garbarino, 1992; Huston, McLoyd, & Coll, 1994; National Research Council, 1996; Panel on Poverty and Family Assistance, 1999). It is a highly arbitrary measure; that is, because it is an absolute dollar amount, not a percentage of the median income, it is theoretically possible for any specific portion of the population (or everyone) to be above the poverty level. Another concern is whether the basis of three times the costs of a very thrifty food budget is an appropriate basis because there is no empirical evidence that food constitutes a third of a family's expenses. Moreover, the poverty thresholds are uniform across the nation, despite tremendous variation in the cost of living. Also, the official measure does not reflect how far below or above the poverty line people fall. Families with incomes only $1 above the threshold are not counted as poor. Another contention is that the measure is antiquated because it fails to take into account changing family patterns since the poverty line was created, such as the growing need to pay for day care, commuting, or other work-related expenses among dually employed or single-mother families. Instead, the current measure does not distinguish between the needs of families in which the parents are or are not employed. Another concern is whether the measure actually overestimates the number of poor because means-tested noncash transfers, such as Medicaid, food stamps, rent subsidies, and free or reduced school lunches, are not taken into account. Nonetheless, according to federal data, the poverty rate would still have been 10.2% in 1996 if these noncash transfers were taken into account (U.S. Bureau of the Census, 1998, table 766).

Because of the many limitations of the official poverty threshold, the concept of "poverty" is often expanded in research to "economic vulnerability." Instead of the official poverty line, research uses indicators such as parental unemployment, relative poverty, deep poverty, income loss, deprivation, occupational status, low parental education, unmet medical or dental needs, degree of financial strain, or some combination of variables referred to as "socioeconomic status" (Conger, Ge, Elder, Lorenz, & Simons, 1994; Dodge, Pettit, & Bates, 1994; Duncan, Yeung, Brooks-Gunn, & Smith, 1998; Huston et al., 1994; Mills, Grasmick, Morgan, & Wenk, 1992).

RESEARCH THEMES DURING THE 1990S

The study of impoverished families is a burgeoning area of research. A computer search for this review using the words "poverty" and "family" yielded well over a thousand entries focusing on the demographic, psychological, sociological, health, and developmental antecedents and consequences of poverty for families. Using the broader definitions noted above yielded thousands of additional entries. Consequently, this manuscript will synthesize themes rather than provide an exhaustive review of the literature. These themes are derived by examining several hundred abstracts and articles from the computer search, deliberately using those that minimized overlap with other topics included in this special issue. I reviewed all issues of *The Journal of Marriage and the Family* and *Family Relations,* the two journals published by the National Council on Family Relations. I also reviewed issues of *Journal of Family Issues.* Admittedly, because of my background as a sociologist, this review is weighted toward structural dimensions of poverty more than toward psychological dimensions.

This survey of the diverse literature on families in poverty published during the 1990s generally reveals several important themes. These include a focus on the following issues: (a) family diversity, (b) the working poor, (c) poverty's selection and mediating influences, (d) an ecological approach, (e) the contributions of fathers, (f) an integration of macro and micro explanations of poverty, (g) an appreciation of qualitative rich description, and (h) an expanded concern with social policy that was instigated in part by the welfare reform policies of the late 1990s. Each of these are discussed below.

First, there is increasing awareness of the diversity in the poverty experience and that the antecedents and effects of poverty can vary by race, gender, or ethnicity. Instead of using these as simply control variables, an increasing number of studies conducted in the 1990s deliberately explored poverty experiences separately for different subgroups within the population (e.g., Abell, Clawson, Washington, Bost, & Vaughn, 1996; Chase-Lansdale, Brooks-Gunn, & Zamsky, 1994; Franklin, Smith, & McMiller, 1995; Lichter & Landale, 1995; Mulsow & Murry, 1996). Jarrett's research on poor African American mothers, for example, was not designed to generalize the findings to fathers, to Whites, or to other racial or ethnic groups (Jarrett, 1996, 1994). Unapologetically, her research focused solely on the female, poor, African American experience.

When people imagine a "poor family," they are likely to visualize a family on welfare. Yet another important research theme during the 1990s was to highlight the plight of working poor families (e.g., Annie E. Casey Foundation, 1996; Budetti, Duchon, Schoen, & Shikles, 1999; Chilman, 1991; Levitan, Gallo, & Shapiro, 1993; Orthner & Neenan, 1996; Seccombe & Amey, 1995; Wertheimer, 1999). Many families with incomes below or hovering around the poverty line have an adult wage earner in them. Approximately 35 million adults between the ages of 18 and 64 earn less than $20,000 annually (Budetti et al.). More than 5% of persons age 25 and over earned minimum wage of $5.15 an hour in 1997, including 7.4% of employed women over age 25 (U.S. Bureau of the Census, 1998, table 700). A single parent with two children, earning a minimum wage of $5.15 an hour would not earn enough to pull the family above the poverty line. Working poor families face many challenges and obstacles, including reliable transportation, quality day care, safe and affordable housing, affordable health insurance, and other important fringe benefits of a job. Compared with other working families, working poor families are less likely to own a car, to own their own home, to have paid child care for preschoolers, and to have health insurance coverage (Wertheimer). A study conducted by the Commonwealth Fund with a national sample of 5,002 adults aged 18–64, found that more than two thirds (68%) of working-age adults with annual incomes below $20,000 are living on the edge financially: one third (31%) reported that they did not have enough money to meet basic expenses, and another 37% reported that they were just able to meet expenses (Budetti et al.).

Even though most studies report deleterious effects of poverty on both adults' and children's well-being, research during this decade has elaborated on the specific features of poverty that are responsible for these outcomes. For instance, what mechanisms are responsible for the inferior health status of poor adults and children? Life expectancy is significantly lower, infant mortality is higher, and the poor are more likely to suffer a wide variety of acute and chronic conditions. It is possible that these outcomes are due to factors that include limited or no access to medical care (Budetti et al., 1999; Families USA Foundation, 1999; Seccombe, 1996; Weigers, Weinick, & Cohen, 1998); lack of prenatal care (Clarke, Miller, Albrecht, Frentzen, & Cruz, 1999; National Center for Health Statistics, 1996); less healthy lifestyles related to increased smoking, lack of exercise or increased alcohol use (Berlin & Colditz, 1990; Darrow, Russell, Copper, Mudar, & Frone, 1992); or low levels of education or literacy that make it

more difficult to use health services or follow basic educational materials or instructions (Baker, Parker, Williams, Clark, & Nurss, 1997; Meade, McKinney, & Barnas, 1994). What are the effects of these variables on health, independently and simultaneously? And moreover, what are their causes?

There is also a growing awareness of the importance of factors outside the family, which have critical impacts on the well-being of children. This ecological approach (Bronfenbrenner, 1979) went beyond simply studying family influences and examined the importance of environmental systems such as neighborhoods, schools, day-care centers, and peer groups. Research in the 1990s has examined the effects of poverty within this broader social context (e.g., Bowen & Chapman, 1996; Brooks-Gunn, Duncan, Klebanov, & Sealand, 1993; Brooks-Gunn, Duncan, & Aber, 1997; Coulton & Pandey, 1992; Crane, 1991; Franklin, Smith, & McMiller, 1995; Mayer, 1991; South & Crowder, 1999; Tienda, 1991).

The literature published during the 1990s also included an increased focus on the contributions that fathers make within families. These included not only financial contributions but also fathers' role in child development and in promoting the social and emotional well-being of children (e.g., Amato & Rivera, 1999; Coltrane, 1996; Harris & Marmer, 1996; McLanahan & Sandefur, 1994). Although Harris and Marmer found that mothers' appear to play a more critical role in protecting poor children from adverse outcomes than do fathers, they noted that fathers, too, play an important role and buffer the effects of poverty by reducing delinquency.

Research conducted during the 1990s made further attempts to integrate macro and micro explanations of poverty. Why are people poor? What are the consequences of poverty? Numerous factors influence the likelihood of being poor, including cognitive attainment, family background, drug and alcohol abuse, and domestic violence. Research during the decade moved away from mere individual explanations (e.g., motivation, personality, cognitive attainment, levels of human capital) and instead situated poverty within a broader social milieu (e.g., capitalism, racism, sexism). Yet individualistic explanations continue to be highly popular within the general population. People often assume that the poor are simply lazy, unmotivated, or unwilling to defer their immediate gratification by pursuing long-term goals to improve their job prospects, such as education or training programs (see, for example, Gilens, 1999; Hunt, 1996; Smith & Stone, 1989). Indeed, poor persons themselves often hold such views of others that are impoverished (Seccombe, James, & Battle Walters, 1998). Nonetheless, research during the 1990s made headway in improving our understanding of the causes of and selection into poverty by examining the utility of both micro and macro explanations. It notes the ways in which individual behavior is shaped by the larger structural forces within society, such how the movement of jobs from the inner city to the suburbs may shape the marriage and fertility behavior of poor, urban African Americans, which in turn shapes poverty and its consequences (Wilson, 1987, 1996).

A review of the literature also reveals that, as our conceptions of poverty become more complex, rich descriptions of the poverty experience have become increasingly valued. Qualitative studies provide an inside look at the lived experience of poor families. These add in-depth and highly personalized accounts that are important supplements to the quantitative data that are available from a number of sources (see, for example, Berrick, 1995; Edin & Lein, 1997; Jarrett, 1994; Rank, 1994a; Rubin, 1994; Seccombe, 1999; Sidel, 1992, 1996; Wilson, 1996). Rank, for example, used three separate sources of data throughout his book on welfare, *Living on the Edge*: (a) quantitative analysis with a longitudinal sample drawn from caseloads in Wisconsin, (b) in-depth interviews with 50 families from the larger sample, and (c) fieldwork that included visits to welfare offices and job training programs (1994a).

Finally, poverty research during the 1990s, particularly during the latter part of the decade, became increasingly concerned with social policy. For example, there has been a growing interest in family health and health policy, fueled by rising health care costs, and interest in the effects of welfare reform on poor families (e.g., Chafel, 1993; Chavkin, 1999; Families USA Foundation, 1999; Greenberg, 1998; Heymann & Earle, 1999; Loprest, 1999). Special issues or special sections of issues devoted to family policies have appeared in a multitude of journals.

WHY HAS POVERTY REMAINED VIRTUALLY UNCHANGED DURING THE 1990S?

Despite a strong economy, a low rate of unemployment and relatively low inflation, the percentage of individuals, families, and children in poverty at the end of the decade has been reduced by only 1% (or less) since 1990. This can be traced to several reasons, including: (a) changing labor market conditions, (b) erosion of a safety net for poor families, and (c) the increase in the number of single-parent families.

Changing Labor Market Conditions

Several significant changes in our labor market occurred during the 1990s, which have influenced the poverty rate in the United States. The structure of lower skilled work is changing and becoming more tenuous, often throwing people into poverty who otherwise would be in the ranks of the "lower middle class." In the past, many people with low levels of education were able to secure manufacturing jobs that could reasonably support a family (Devine & Wright, 1993). The economic recession during the 1980s hit lower income families hard, with factories closing throughout the nation, and these families have not recovered. Consequently, the distribution of income and wealth has become increasingly polarized, with the rich getting richer and the poor getting poorer (Auerbach & Belous, 1998; Danziger & Gottschalk, 1995; Phillips, 1990; U.S. Bureau of the Census, 1997, table 725). There is a paucity of well-paying jobs for persons with little education. For example, whereas the unemployment rate for Whites overall was less than 5% in 1996, the rate was nearly 20% for African American women aged 15 to 25 who had only a high school diploma (Bernstein, 1997; U.S. Bureau of the Census, 1997, Table 621). The U.S. Department of Labor estimated that more than half of available jobs by the year 2000 would require advanced education or technical training (Sansone, 1998).

One concern is that the job growth tends to be concentrated in the service sector, particularly in entry level or "secondary sector" jobs, such as cashier, waitress, or sales clerk. These jobs typically pay near minimum wage and generally do not offer benefits such as health insurance, paid sick leave, or vacations. Lichter and Eggebeen suggested, "the problem is not finding a job, but rather a job that pays well enough to lift the family (and its children) out of poverty" (1994, p. 633). They also found that the higher rates of poverty among African American children are not simply the result of a low labor-market attachment among their parents but reflect differences in the kinds of jobs available to parents.

Second, the minimum wage in the United

States, at $5.15 an hour in 1999, comes nowhere near lifting even a small family out of poverty. Employment at minimum wage, working full-time for 52 weeks a year, yields less than $11,000 a year, which is well below the poverty line of $16,700 for a family of four. Yet almost two thirds of workers making minimum wage are adults aged 20 or older, and 40% of them provide the sole income for their families (*U.S. News Online,* 1996). Adjusted for inflation, the value of the federal minimum wage has dropped by more than a dollar since the early 1970s (U.S. Bureau of Labor Statistics, n.d.).

A third concern is the movement of jobs from the inner city to the outlying suburban regions (Wilson, 1987, 1996). The loss of well-paying manufacturing jobs from urban areas has had a disastrous effect on those persons living in inner cities. Male unemployment and subsequent poverty increased dramatically, thereby reducing the pool of men eligible for marriage and increasing the number of children born out of wedlock. Moreover, the middle class migrated out of urban areas, leading to the further development of ghettos.

A fourth concern is the growing number of part-time, contingency, subcontracted, or temporary jobs, often with irregular work schedules and high layoff and turnover rates (Castro, 1993; Hipple, 1998; Presser & Cox, 1997). Manpower, an agency specializing in temporary employment, was the largest private employer during the early 1990s (Castro). Hipple reported that 5% of all workers were contingent workers in 1995, and contingent workers were generally disadvantaged with respect to pay, benefits, and job security. Part-time temporary workers made up approximately one quarter of the labor force in 1988 but are estimated to constitute nearly one half of the labor force by the year 2000 (Castro; Morrow, 1993).

Fifth is the erosion of union coverage (U.S. Bureau of the Census, 1998). The protections offered by unions are well established; for example, union workers averaged more than $14,000 more in wages than their nonunionized counterparts in 1992 (Feagin & Feagin, 1994). More than one third of workers were members of unions in the 1950s, whereas the figure has declined significantly in recent years (Goldfield, 1987). By 1990, 16.1% of wage and salary workers in the United States were union members, declining to 14.1% by 1997 (U.S. Bureau of the Census, 1998, table 712).

Finally, fringe benefits for low-income persons, such as health insurance, have eroded during the past decade. Approximately 41 million Americans today, or nearly 18% of the population, are uninsured (Kaiser Commission on Medicaid and the Uninsured, 1998) This has caused more families to fall into poverty and suffer adverse health consequences (Children's Defense Fund, 1998; O'Brien & Feder, 1998; Weigers, Weinick, & Cohen, 1998). For example, the percentage of families with a wage level of less than $7 an hour who had health insurance from any source, including an employer or the government, declined by 12% between 1987 and 1996, down from 54% to 42%. Likewise, health insurance coverage among families with wages between $7 and $10 an hour eroded 7% during this period. Access to employer-sponsored coverage declined as well during the 1990s; fewer employers were offering health benefits to their workers, particularly their low-wage workers. Despite the passage of federal programs to help finance children's health insurance (e.g., CHIP), it remained that approximately 15% of children under age 18 were uninsured. Moreover, most of these children (61%) lived in a household in which at least one parent was employed full time, according to the March 1998 Current Population Survey (Office of Health Policy, 1998).

The Erosion of a Safety Net

Another reason that poverty increased during the 1990s was that government benefits declined. The real purchasing power of cash welfare programs decreased substantially over the past two decades. When inflation is taken into account, the average grant from Aid to Families with Dependent Children declined from $676 in 1970 to $373 in 1993 (Congressional Digest, 1995). In 1979, 41% of poor children were lifted out of poverty as a result of cash and noncash transfers, compared with only 32% of poor children in 1991. Thus, the safety net designed to help the most vulnerable has eroded in recent decades (Ozawa, 1995).

With the advent of welfare reform, with work requirements and time limits, many poor families will be pushed off welfare programs altogether. The number of persons receiving Aid to Families with Dependent Children or Temporary Assistance to Needy Families declined nearly 50% between March 1994 and March 1999, from 5 million to 2.6 million families (U.S. Department of Health and Human Services, 1999). Medicaid enrollment has fallen as well, from 36.3 million to 35.1 million between 1995 and 1996. The decline is particularly apparent among children; the number of children under 15 years covered by Medicaid decreased from 15.5 million in 1995 to 15.1 million in 1996 (Greenberg, 1998). Employer-sponsored insurance does not fill in the gaps when Medicaid coverage is eliminated among poor families (Kaiser Commission on Medicaid and the Uninsured, 1998; Moffitt & Slade, 1997). Among children from families with incomes less than 100% of poverty, 25% are uninsured, compared with only 6% of children whose families earn more than 500% of poverty (Office of Health Policy, 1998).

An Increase in Single-Parent Families

Poverty has also increased during the past decade because of the rise in the numbers of single-parent families, particularly those with single mothers (see Arendell in this issue; Eggebeen & Lichter, 1991; U.S. Bureau of the Census, 1998; Zimmerman, 1992;). In 1980, approximately 20% of children under the age of 18 lived in single-parent families, rising to 25% by 1990 and 28% by 1997 (U.S. Bureau of the Census, 1998, table 84). If we examine the income of families by quintile—that is, dividing the population up into five equally sized segments—we see that single-parent families, particularly single-mother families are significantly more likely to have incomes that put them in the lowest quintile. Obviously, because there is only one wage earner, single-parent households are particularly vulnerable to being impoverished. But gender also influences poverty status. Nearly half (48.8%) of all female-headed households have incomes in the lowest quintile, compared with 28.5% of single male-headed households and only 12.7% of married-couple families (U.S. Bureau of the Census, 1997, table 725). More than one third of female-headed households (35.8%) are poor (U.S. Bureau of the Census, 1998, table 762).

The risk of poverty in single-mother families is especially high for many reasons. One explanation is the lower wages paid to women generally, particularly minority women (U.S. Bureau of the Census, 1998, table 696). Women aged 25 and over working full time in 1997 earned $462 a week, compared to $615 for men of the same age. Welfare recipients also earn low wages when they leave welfare for work, averaging between $6 and $7 an hour (General Account Office, 1999; Lo-

prest, 1999). Referring to their research focusing on poverty among Latino children, Lichter and Landale suggested:

> Although policies aimed at strengthening the family or promoting maternal employment may enhance children's economic well-being, they are unlikely to eliminate racial and ethnic differences in child poverty . . . they suffer from limited human capital (e.g., low education and language proficiency), racial discrimination in job opportunities and pay, and continuing gender wage inequality, which diminishes the ability of single mothers to support their children. (1995, p. 353)

The correlation between single parent households and poverty is also due to the limited receipt of child support (Peterson & Nord, 1990; Smock & Manning, 1997; Teachman, 1991) and decreased levels of social capital (Furstenberg & Hughes, 1995; McLanahan & Sandefur, 1994), particularly among never-married mothers. Using data from nonresidential parents (mostly fathers) the Panel Study of Income Dynamics, Smock and Manningfound that only 52% reported paying child support. This figure corresponds with data from the U.S. Bureau of the Census (1998, table 609). It also corresponds with the percentage of residential parents (mostly mothers) who claim to receive child support—roughly 55%.

When looking at single mothers as a whole, the proportion who receive child support is virtually unchanged since the mid-1970s (Urban Institute, 1999). Nonetheless, this fact is somewhat misleading. Although the likelihood of receiving child support among divorced and separated women has increased only slightly during this period, up from 36% to 42%, there has actually been a fourfold increase in child support receipt between 1976 and 1997 among mothers who have never married, up from 4% to 18%. But because the number of never-married mothers is large and growing rapidly (increasing in size from 17 to 46% of all single mothers), it depresses any improvement we might see in overall statistics.

Would further enforcing child support orders eliminate or reduce poverty? Male partners of welfare recipients tend to earn little at the time their child was born, but their incomes typically increase over time. A study in Wisconsin found that child support payments of these fathers would average between $200 and $460 a month if child support laws were perfectly enforced, which could improve the lives of impoverished children considerably, if not lift them from poverty altogether (Brien & Willis, 1997). Sorensen (1997) found that if all nonresidential fathers paid the same percentage of their income as payers do, they would pay, on average, between 12 and 15% of their income on child support. This would average between $2,837 and $3,321 a year, enough to lift at least some families out of poverty, albeit marginally.

Another factor is the large number of young mothers who are unmarried (Corcoran & Kunz, 1997; Harris, 1997; Trent & Crowder, 1997; U.S. Bureau of the Census, 1998, table 101). According to Ambert (1998), teen mothers are overwhelmingly poor, have less education than their peers, are less likely to receive prenatal care than other pregnant women, and often do not have a diet that is conducive to healthy fetal development. A baby born to an adolescent parent may be an at-risk infant. These children are more likely to start their lives with fewer material and social advantages than are children born to married, older parents.

McLaughlin and Lichter (1997) reported that young women who are poor are less likely to marry than are women who are not poor and that poor women who have jobs are more likely to marry than are those who do not have jobs. They find no differences in the likelihood of marriage between poor African American and poor White women, after controlling for differences in economic independence, mate availability, family culture, and living arrangements.

CONSEQUENCES OF POVERTY ON CHILDREN

The increased rate of child poverty during the 1990s, the rise in the proportion of children in "deep poverty," (i.e. below 50% of the poverty line), and the negative consequences of poverty for children have been well documented in the literature (see Chafel, 1993; Duncan et al., 1994, 1998; Lichter, 1997, for example). Children reared in poverty have poorer physical and mental health, do worse in school, experience more punitive discipline styles and abuse, live in poorer neighborhoods, and are more likely to engage in deviant or delinquent acts. These deleterious effects on children are intensified for older children or the longer a child lives in poverty (Duncan et al., 1994; Lichter, 1997; McLeod & Shanahan, 1993). Indeed, children who are exposed to poverty or welfare in their family of origin are more likely to be poor or use welfare themselves (Gottschalk, 1990, 1992; Rank & Cheng, 1995); however,

Rank and Cheng's research reminds us that most welfare recipients did not grow up on the system.

The literature over the past decade has attempted to further document (a) the specific negative outcomes caused by poverty, such as in physical health, mental health, and academic achievement; and (b) the mediators between family income and negative childhood outcomes, such as family stress and neighborhood effects. These are discussed below.

Physical Health

Research is unequivocal on the relationship between poverty and health (see Feinstein, 1993, and Williams, 1990, for reviews of research). Poverty puts the health of children at risk first by increasing the frequency of low-birth-weight babies and undernutrition, which in turn increase their likelihood of serious chronic and acute illness (Bradley et al., 1994; Children's Defense Fund, 1994, 1998; Halfon & Newacheck, 1993; Montgomery & Carter, 1993; Miller & Korenman, 1994; Rosenbaum, 1992; Weigers, Weinick, & Cohen, 1998). Children living in poverty have a higher risk for infant mortality because of biological factors such as low birth weight or birth defects and environmental hazards during the fragile first year of life. Mothers also often receive inadequate prenatal care. Gerstan (1992) asserted that there are several risk factors that are common to poor women during pregnancy, including inadequate medical care, serious maternal illnesses such as hypertension and diabetes, maternal nutritional deficiencies in vitamin A and iron, maternal intravenous drug abuse (which also increases the risk of being positive for the AIDS virus).

Poor children continue to suffer from a variety of ailments at higher rates than do more affluent children. For example, they are more than three times more likely to be iron deficient; one-and-a-half times more likely to have frequent diarrhea or colitis; two times more likely to suffer from severe asthma; and one-and-a-half times more likely to suffer partial or complete blindness or deafness (Children's Defense Fund, 1994). Moreover, poor preschoolers are three times more likely than their more affluent counterparts to have lead levels in their bloodstream of at least 10 micrograms of lead per deciliter of blood, a level at which harmful effects to the brain and nervous system have been noted. An estimated three million poor children may be at risk of impaired physical and mental development related to ingesting lead-based paint flaking off the walls in older homes (Needleman, Schell, Bellinger, Leviton, & Allred, 1990).

Finally, as many as 12 million children each year go without food at some point every month (Jackson, 1993), suffering the immediate pain of hunger and the more long-term consequences of malnutrition. Without proper nutrition, children are in a weakened state. They run the risk of more frequent colds, ear infections and other infectious diseases, impaired brain function, and stunted growth; they are also more vulnerable to lead and other environmental toxins. Data from the Continuing Survey of Food Intake by Individuals reported that the percentage of households claiming that they sometimes or often did not have enough to eat increased from less than 8% to approximately 11% among low-income families between 1989 and 1991. The age group most likely to be affected were youths aged 12 to 19 (reported in Lewit & Kerrebrock, 1997).

Children (and adults) living in poor families are not only at higher risk for serious medical problems, but often these problems go untreated. According to the Commonwealth Study, nearly one in four adults (24%)—an estimated 40 million people—reported that they had failed to visit a doctor when sick, had not followed up on recommended treatment or testing, or had not filled a prescription in the past year because of the cost (Budetti et al., 1999). Some poor children have Medicaid insurance, particularly if their mothers receive the cash assistance program formerly known as Aid to Families with Dependent Children, now known as Temporary Assistance to Needy Families. However children (and adults) on Medicaid are less likely to have a regular physician providing them with continuous care, and they are more likely to use the emergency rooms rather than doctors' clinics (St. Peter, Newacheck, & Halfon, 1992; U.S. Congress, Office of Technology, 1992). But many poor children do not receive Medicaid (U.S. House of Representatives, Committee on Ways and Means, 1996). In fact, 14% of children under the age of 11 had no health insurance at all from any source in 1998, including Medicaid, and one third of these children live below the poverty line (Office of Health Policy, 1998).

Rosenbaum (1992) suggested a number of health improvements that would improve the lives of poor children, as well as reduce the total number of children living in poverty. These programs include prenatal care, nutrition, immunization, preventative pediatric care, family planning, expanded Medicaid coverage, and federal and state attempts to improve the supply of providers in medically underserved communities.

Children's Mental Health, Adjustment, and Well-Being

Children living in poverty have more socioemotional and behavioral problems than do more affluent children. They are more likely to suffer from depression and social withdrawal, to have peer relationship difficulties, to have low self-esteem, to have behavioral and conduct disorders, and to do poorly in school (Conger, Conger, & Elder, 1997; Conger et al., 1992, 1993; Cooksey, Dumka, Roosa, & Jackson, 1997; Downey, 1994; Duncan et al., 1994; Farrington, 1991; Gerard & Buehler, 1999; Leadbeater & Bishop, 1994; Mayer, 1997; McLeod & Edwards, 1995; McLeod & Shanahan, 1993; McLoyd, 1990; Takeuchi, Williams & Adair, 1991; Whitbeck et al., 1991). For example, Takeuchi et al. found that children on welfare or in families that experience financial stress are more likely to exhibit impulsive, antisocial, and depressive behaviors. They also noted, however, that children from families experiencing stress at two different points in time, separated by 5 years, did not differ from children whose families were under financial stress at only one point in time. Gerhard and Buehler explained how poverty influences preadolescent and early adolescent problem behaviors:

> The association between poverty and youth problem behaviors may be explained by possible links among educational quality of home environments, academic difficulties, and increased problem behaviors. Poor families have fewer resources to commit to educationally relative tools such as computers, books, and calculators. This type of impoverishment is associated with academic failure (Downey, 1994), which, in turn, may prompt or sustain misbehavior or emotional distress in school. (1999, p. 356)

McLeod and Edwards (1995), using data from the Children of the National Longitudinal Survey of Youth, found that the effects of poverty on children's mental health has different effects across race and ethnicity, with stronger effects for Hispanics and American Indians than for Blacks and Whites. Weinger (1998) conducted a qualitative survey to hear directly from children themselves how they are affected emotionally by poverty. She found that poor children have a difficult time holding on to positive self-images. They view poverty as a deprivation and perceive messages in society highly critical of the poor. She found that they internalize many of these negative messages.

McLeod and Shanahan (1993, 1996) examined children's mental health and found that "the mental health disadvantages that poor children face increase with the length of time that their families are poor" (1996, p. 207). For example, children who suffered long-term poverty had higher rates of depression than did children whose poverty was of shorter duration. Research by Dubow and Ippolito (1994) also confirms the association between length of poverty spell and negative outcomes. Their results suggest that the actual number of years in poverty predicted marked increases in antisocial behavior in children. Likewise, Coll, Buckner, Brooks, Weinreb, and Bassuk (1998) examined homeless youth and children living in low-income housing and concluded that the negative effects of poverty on children increase the longer children are impoverished.

Academic and School Achievement

Research conducted during the 1990s indicates that children living below the poverty level are more likely to suffer academically than are children who are not poor, although there is little consensus over the size of the effects. Overall, poor children receive lower grades, receive lower scores on standardized tests, are less likely to finish high school, and are less likely to attend or graduate from college than are nonpoor youth (Downy, 1994; Dubow & Ippolito, 1994; Duncan et al., 1998; Entwisle & Alexander, 1995; McLanahan & Sandefur, 1994; Pong, 1997; Smith, Brooks-Gunn, & Klebanov, 1997; Teachman, Paasch, Day, & Carver, 1997). Nonetheless, Entwisle and Alexander, in their attempt to distinguish economic standing from family structure, found that neither two-parent homes nor families' economic resources affected test scores during the school year, but in the summer period, when schools were closed, family income was an important source of variance in achievement.

Specifically, Smith et al. (1997), using data from the National Longitudinal Survey of Youth and the Infant Health and Development Program, found that children in families with incomes less than one half of the poverty line scored between 6 and 13 points lower on various standardized tests than did children in families with incomes between 1.5 and 2.0 times the poverty line. In all cases, the differences were statistically significant. Children living in families whose incomes were higher but still below the poverty line also did significantly worse on the majority of tests compared with the higher reference group. Duncan et al. (1998), using the Panel Study of Income Dynamics, reported that economic conditions in early childhood have the biggest impact on levels of achievement. Lipman and Offord (1997) agreed and summarized, "poverty appears to be most detrimental to academic performance when it occurs early in a child's life" (p. 281). Dubow and Ippolito (1994) found that persistent poverty predicted decreases in math and reading scores.

Smith et al. (1997) examined the consequences of poverty on young children's cognitive and verbal ability and on their early school achievement. They used three types of assessment: IQ, verbal ability, and achievement tests. They found that the duration of poverty had a significantly negative effect on all three assessment tests. They noted that the degree of poverty also affected children's scores: Children's cognitive abilities dramatically increased as family income increased from very poor to near poor. Duncan et al. (1998) speculated that income in a child's early years affects school achievement throughout the life course. They suggested the following:

> poverty has a strong association with a low level of preschool ability, which is associated with low test scores later in childhood as well as grade failure, school disengagement, and dropping out of school, even when controls for family characteristics such as maternal schooling, household structure, and welfare receipt are included. (p. 420)

Poor Black and Hispanic children experience more frequent and more severe poverty than do Whites, with fewer prospects for improvement in their economic circumstances. This increases their risk for dropping out of school or being involved in a teen pregnancy (Crane, 1991; Mayer, 1991).

Mediating Effects Within the Family: Stresses, Parenting Styles, Discipline, and Abuse

It is well documented that poverty affects how parents interact with their children. The Home

Observation of the Measurement of the Environment (HOME) is a widely used interview and observation measure of parent-child interaction. Its measures include maternal warmth and learning experiences provided to the child, and it is associated with a variety of child outcomes. Miller and Davis (1997) reported that poverty had a statistically significant effect on the quality of the home environment after controlling for the effects of other model variables. Improvements in family income had the strongest effects on improving the quality of the home environment for children who were born to a poor family. Miller and Davis found, using data from the National Longitudinal Survey of Youth, that differences among income groups were larger for the cognitive stimulation component than for the emotional component of the HOME score. Mayer also reported that children in poor families have, on average, less educationally stimulating home environments (1997).

Conger et al. (1992, 1993), Dodge et al. (1994), Hashima and Amato (1994), McLeod and Shanahan (1993), and McLoyd (1990) found that parents are less nurturing, more authoritarian, and use more inconsistent and harsh physical discipline as a family's economic situation worsens. Moreover, research conducted during the 1990s suggests that poor children have a higher probability of being abused and neglected and to be injured more severely by the abuse than do their more affluent peers (Children's Defense Fund, 1994; DiLeonardi, 1993; Gelles, 1992; Kruttschnitt, McLeod, & Dornfeld, 1994; U.S. Advisory Board on Child Abuse and Neglect, 1990; Wolfner & Gelles, 1993). As Gelles reported:

> Abusive violence is more likely to occur in poor homes. Specific social and demographic characteristics increase the likelihood that poverty will lead to abuse. Poor young parents who are raising young children have an elevated risk of using the most abusive forms of violence toward their children, as do poor single mothers. (p. 271)

What is it about an impoverished family environment that increases the likelihood of negative outcomes for children? One likely culprit is that parents who are living in poor conditions have a high level of stress related to their situation (Brooks-Gunn, Duncan, & Maritato, 1997; Coulton, Korbin, Su, & Chow, 1995; Edin & Lein, 1997; Elder, Eccles, Ardelt, & Lord, 1995; Ensminger, 1995; Gillham, Tanner, Cheyne, Free-man, Rooney, & Lambie, 1998; McLoyd, 1990; Quint, Bos, & Polit, 1997; Seccombe, 1999). Elder et al. reported that parents with low and unstable incomes experience more emotional distress and see themselves as less effective parents than do parents with higher incomes.

Increased social support from family and friends has been shown to reduce the amount of stress poor families experience, to reduce the degree of violence or harsh discipline poor children may experience, and to foster improved self-esteem and the ability on the part of the child in overcoming adversity (Bowen & Chapman, 1996; Jennings, Stagg, & Conners, 1991; Hashima & Amato, 1994). Some of the most vulnerable poor families, such as those who are homeless, tend to have little social support (Letiecq, Anderson, & Koblinsky, 1998). Nonetheless, the importance of social support and other coping strategies has been shown to vary across different ethnic groups (Gomel, Tinsley, Parke & Clarke, 1998). Using data collected from focus groups in conjunction with survey data, Gomel et al. found that social supports and individual self-help coping strategies were more important to improving Latino family relationships than they were for White or African American families.

Other possible mediating effects include the lack of social capital or antisocial qualities of the parent or parents (Bank, Forgatch, Patterson, & Fetrow, 1993; McLanahan & Sandefur, 1994; Simons, Beaman, Conger, & Chao, 1993). Some researchers have also identified that high levels of male unemployment are significantly correlated with child abuse and deprivation (Gillham et al., 1998). Thomson, Hanson, and McLanahan (1994) and McLanahan and Sandefur, drawing on a variety of national data sources, found that growing up in a single-mother household is associated with poorer academic performance, teen births, delinquency, and a variety of other negative outcomes that undermine their chances of future success. But they also exercise caution:

> But are single mother and father absence therefore the root cause of child poverty, school failure, and juvenile delinquency? Our findings lead us to say no. While living with just one parent increases the risk of each of these negative outcomes, it is not the only, or even the major cause of them. Growing up with a single parent is just one among many factors that put children at risk of failure, just as lack of exercise is only one among many factors that put people at risk for heart disease. (p. 2)

Extrafamilial Mediating Effects: The Neighborhood

A developing area of research during the past decade examines the macrolevel structural influences that may have an effect on the negative outcomes for children living in poverty. For example, some researchers have explored the effects of the neighborhoods in which children live to determine their independent and mediating effects on child well-being (Bowen & Chapman, 1996; Brooks-Gunn et al., 1997; Coulton & Pandey, 1992; Crane, 1991; Drake & Pandey, 1995; Mayer, 1991; South & Crowder, 1999; Vartanian, 1999). Poor children are increasingly spatially isolated from the nonpoor in their neighborhoods and communities (Lichter, 1993; Massey & Denton, 1993; O'Hare, 1995). Some findings suggest that those neighborhoods characterized by "poverty, excessive numbers of children per adult resident, population turnover, and the concentration of female-headed families are at highest risk for maltreatment" (Coulton et al., 1995, p. 1262). Neighborhood conditions are generally found to be significant predictors of children's development. Poor children often live in inner cities where violence, crime, truancy, loitering, and a sense of despair predominate. Drake and Pandey found a positive relationship between neighborhood poverty and three types of maltreatment: neglect, physical abuse, and sexual abuse, with the strongest relationship appearing between neglect and neighborhood poverty.

There are at least three ways in which neighborhoods may affect poverty and the use of welfare among children. As Vartanian summarized:

> The social isolation theory hypothesizes that the more economically depressed the neighborhood during childhood, the more likely a child is to use welfare during adulthood. The epidemic theory hypothesizes that only when children live in the most economically depressed neighborhoods will their likelihood of welfare use during adulthood increase. The relative deprivation theory hypothesizes that, when poor children live in wealthier neighborhoods, they will be more likely to use welfare as an adult. (1999, p. 228)

South and Crowder (1999), using data from the Panel Study of Income Dynamics, found that growing up in poor neighborhoods had different effects for African Americans and Whites. Likewise, Vartanian (1999) reported that family characteristics (e.g., parents' economic conditions, whether the parent received welfare, adult education levels, and number of children in the household) are more important for reproducing poverty and welfare use among African American girls, whereas neighborhood characteristics (e.g., neighborhood poverty rate, percentage of adults without a high school degree, male employment rate, and percentage receiving public assistance) were more significant for White girls.

LESSONS LEARNED FROM RESEARCH

As is often the case, good research often raises at least as many questions as it answers. Poverty remains a critical issue for families as we head into the 21st century. Millions of families continue to face the "sting" of poverty daily, whereas millions more face the threat of impoverishment from situations over which they have little control: job layoffs, the ending of relationships, racial or gender discrimination, or the erosion of regular hours or fringe benefits at work. From the research conducted during the 1990s, we have learned a number of important lessons about the causes and consequences of poverty and about the policies that could reduce, if not eliminate the suffering that poor families routinely experience.

We have discovered that many seemingly straightforward mechanisms for reducing poverty are considerably more complex and multifaceted than they appear at first glance. One notable example is that of child support. Despite the initial enthusiasm behind the Child Support Act passed in the late 1980s, the majority of single mothers do not receive child support. Parents without custody—usually fathers—fail to pay child support regularly or they fail to pay the full amount owed in approximately half of all cases. Many families will likely remain impoverished until more rigid enforcement is enacted so children get the money that they are due. At the same time, we should not assume that the collection of child support alone would eliminate poverty substantially. Why? Because absentee fathers who fail to pay child support are more likely to be school dropouts and low earners themselves than are resident fathers (Garfinkel, McLanahan, Meyer, & Seltzer, 1998), and their resources are limited. Moreover, there is another side to the child support debate that is rarely aired. Through the collection of articles in the book *Fathers Under Fire*, Garfinkel et al., suggested that enforcing child support has both positive and unintended negative effects that should be considered. One possible negative effect is that vigorous child-support enforcement may contribute to a decline in rates of remarriage, which ironically could do more to keep mothers impoverished than inadequate child support collection (Bloom, Conrad, & Miller, 1998). Another possibility is that increases in child support payments may lead to more serious parental conflict (Seltzer, McLanahan, & Hanson, 1998). Thus, Garfinkel et al., suggested that even something as seemingly straightforward as child-support enforcement is a complex phenomenon. Although the authors did not intend to minimize the importance of collecting money that is clearly owed, they reminded readers that these issues are multifaceted.

A second lesson that we have learned from research is that significant changes must occur within our social structure for poverty to be significantly reduced. The large number of families in poverty represent a social problem, not merely an individual problem. Many people are poor or live with the threat of impoverishment because of structural impediments such as gender or racial discrimination, working in the lower rungs of a dual labor market, child-care costs, the costs associated with the U.S. fee-for-service health care system, or transportation policies favoring private auto ownership rather than public transportation. For example, a full-time job is not necessarily a ticket out of poverty. Minimum wage is currently woefully inadequate to support a family. Because of inflation, the real value of minimum wage has eroded significantly since the 1980s. Using 1996 dollars to hold inflation constant, minimum wage was equal to $7.20 an hour at its peak during the 1980s. It would take increases of approximately $2 an hour to regain these losses (U.S. Bureau of Labor Statistics, n.d.). Other research suggests that the minimum wage should be raised even further, by several dollars an hour, so that working families will be above the poverty line (Edin & Lein, 1997; Seccombe, 1999). Edin and Lein's interviews with 214 women on welfare revealed that it would take a job paying $8 or $9 an hour, working full time, or roughly $16,000 a year, for welfare families to be self-sufficient (in the mid 1990s). Economists are not in agreement as to the consequences such large increases would have on the economy. Although some suggest that raising the minimum wage would have a critical inflationary effect and would reduce the number of jobs, others suggest that the income gains from a minimum wage hike would outweigh the job losses and price increases.

Third, access to quality health care is increasingly being demonstrated as an important dimension of social stratification in the United States. Research demonstrates that families without health insurance use the health care system less frequently, are in poorer health, suffer more adverse effects from their illnesses because of forgoing treatment, and are less likely to have a regular source of health care than are their insured counterparts. Low-income families may slip into poverty as they try to pay their health care costs. One of the lessons we have learned through the 1990s is that health, access to health care, social inequality, and family well-being are invariably linked. One way to reduce the numbers of people who are impoverished, as well as to improve the standard of living for those who are poor, is to allow them to have access to high-quality health care at an affordable cost.

And finally, the ideas and recommendations of the poor themselves are increasingly being sought in our research. Programs and policies may be more successful if they are created to reflect the needs that the poor themselves articulate. The growing number of in-depth qualitative studies, when used in conjunction with statistical data from large representative samples, infuse new ideas in the discussion and answer old questions in new and creative ways. For example, in-depth interviews with welfare recipients have revealed generally positive feelings towards a restructuring of the welfare system with an eye toward employment, especially if reforms are applied with compassion (Quint et al., 1999; Rank, 1994b; Seccombe et al., 1999). This view conflicts dramatically with popular folklore suggesting that welfare recipients enjoy the "free ride" they receive at the expense of the taxpayer (Gilens, 1999). Listening to poor families by way of the research process will go a long way to further our understanding of the causes and consequences of poverty, as well as to create the policies needed to ameliorate this widespread and demeaning social problem.

Despite our progress during the 1990s, the research agenda for the next decade remains substantial. Both basic and applied research are sorely needed to further specify the intricate causes and multifaceted consequences of poverty and to continue to develop adequate solutions. Poverty is not stagnant; poverty rates rise and fall, individuals weave in and out of impoverishment, and public policies come and go. But this assessment is not meant to be discouraging. An aggressive and committed research agenda can indeed be the critical first step in understanding and ameliorating the impoverishment that grips millions of families.

NOTE

I extend my sincere thanks to Amy Arnett for her significant contributions to the section on the consequences of poverty on children and to Richard T. Meenan for his insightful comments and suggestions on the manuscript.

REFERENCES

Abell, E., Clawson, M., Washington, W. N., Bost, K. K., & Vaughn, B. E. (1996). Parenting values, attitudes, behaviors, and goals of African American mothers from a low-income population in relation to social and societal contexts. *Journal of Family Issues, 17,* 593–613.

Amato, P., & Rivera, F. (1999). Paternal involvement and children's behavior problems. *Journal of Marriage and the Family, 61,* 375–384.

Ambert, A. M. (1998). *The web of poverty: Psychosocial perspectives.* New York: Hawthorne Press.

Annie E. Casey Foundation. (1996). *Kids count data book.* Baltimore, MD: Annie E. Casey Foundation.

Associated Press. (1999, January 19). People leave welfare for jobs, find they can't afford essentials. *The Oregonian.* p. D8.

Auerbach, J. A., & Belous, R. S. (1998). *The inequality paradox: Growth of income disparity.* Washington, DC: National Policy Association.

Baker, D. W., Parker, R. M., Williams, M. V., Clark, W. S., & Nurss, J. (1997). The relationship of patient reading ability to self-reported health and use of health services. *American Journal of Public Health, 87,* 1027–1030.

Bank, L., Forgatch, M. S., Patterson, G. R., & Fetrow, R. A. (1993). Parenting practices of single mothers: Mediators of negative contextual factors. *Journal of Marriage and the Family, 55,* 371–384.

Bergmann, B. R. (1996). *Saving our children from poverty: What the United States can learn from France.* New York: Russell Sage Foundation.

Berlin, J. A., & Colditz, G. A. (1990). A meta-analysis of physical activity in the prevention of coronary heart disease. *American Journal of Epidemiology, 132,* 612–628.

Bernstein, A. (1997, December 22). Off welfare—and worse off. Business Week, p. 38.

Berrick, J. D. (1995). *Faces of poverty.* New York: Oxford University Press.

Bloom, D. E., Conrad, C., & Miller, C. (1998). Child support and fathers' remarriage and fertility. In I. Garfinkel, S. S. McLanahan, D. R. Meyer, & J. A. Seltzer (Eds.), *Fathers under fire* (pp. 94–127). New York: Russell Sage Foundation.

Bowen, G. L., & Chapman, M. V. (1996). Poverty, neighborhood danger, social support, and the individual adaptation among at-risk youth. *Journal of Family Issues, 17,* 641–666.

Bradley, R. H., Whiteside, L., Munford, D. J., Casey, P. H., Kelleher, K. J., & Pope, S. K. (1994). Early indications of resilience and their relation to experiences in the home environments of lowbirth weight, premature children living in poverty. *Child Development, 65,* 346–360.

Brien, M. J., & Willis, R. J. (1997). The partners of welfare mothers: Potential earnings and child support. *The Future of Children, 7,* 65–73.

Bronfenbrenner, U. (1979). *The ecology of human development: Experiments by nature and design.* Cambridge, MA: Harvard University Press.

Brooks-Gunn, J., Duncan, G. J., & Aber, J. L. (Eds.). (1997). *Neighborhood poverty* (Vols. 1–2). New York: Russell Sage Foundation.

Brooks-Gunn, J., Duncan, G. J., Klebanov, P. K., & Sealand, N. (1993). Do neighborhoods influence child and adolescent development? *American Journal of Sociology, 99,* 353–395.

Brooks-Gunn, J., Duncan, G. J., & Maritato, N. (1997). Poor families, poor outcomes: The well-being of children and youth. In G. J. Duncan & J. Brooks-Gunn (Eds.), *Consequences of growing up poor* (pp. 1–17). New York: Russell Sage Foundation.

Budetti, J., Duchon, L., Schoen, C., & Shikles, J. (1999, September). *Can't afford to get sick: A reality for millions of working Americans.* New York: Commonwealth Fund.

Casper, L. M., McLanahan, S. S., & Garfinkel, I. (1994). The gender-poverty gap: What can we learn from other countries. *American Sociological Review, 59,* 594–605.

Castro, J. (1993, March 29). Disposable workers. *Time,* 43–47.

Chafel, J. A. (1993). *Child poverty and public policy.* Washington, DC: Urban Institute.

Chase-Lansdale, P. L., Brooks-Gunn, J., & Zamsky, E. S. (1994). Young African-American multigenerational families in poverty: Quality of mothering and grandmothering. *Child Development, 65,* 373–393.

Chavkin, W. (1999). What's a mother to do? Welfare, work, and family. *American Journal of Public Health, 89,* 477–478.

Children's Defense Fund. (1994). *Wasting America's future: The children's defense fund report on the cost of child poverty.* Washington, DC: Author.

Children's Defense Fund. (1998). *The state of America's children yearbook.* Washington, DC: Author.

Chilman, C. S. (1991). Working poor families: Trends, causes, effects, and suggested policies. *Family Relations, 40,* 191–198.

Citro, C. F., & Michael, R. T. (1995). *Measuring poverty: A new approach.* Washington, DC: National Academy Press.

Clarke, L. L., Miller, M. K., Albrecht, S. L., Frentzen, B., & Cruz, A. (1999). The role of medical problems and behavioral risks in explaining patterns of prenatal care use among high-risk women. *Health Services Research, 34,* 145–170.

Coll, C. G., Buckner, J. C., Brooks, M. G., Weinreb, L. F., & Bassuk, E. L. (1998). The developmental status and adaptive behavior of homeless and low-income housed infants and toddlers. *American Journal of Public Health, 88,* 1371–1374.

Coltrane, S. (1996). *Family man.* New York: Oxford University Press.

Conger, R., Conger K., & Elder, G. (1997). Family economic hardship and adolescent adjustment: Mediating and moderating processes. In G. J. Duncan & J. Brooks-Gunn (Eds.), *Consequences of growing up poor* (pp. 288–310). New York: Russell Sage Foundation.

Conger, R. D., Conger, K. J., Elder G. H., Jr., Lorenz, R. O., Simons, R. L., & Whitbeck, L. B. (1992). A family process model of economic hardship and adjustment of early adolescent boys. *Child Development, 63,* 526–541.

Conger, R. D., Conger, K. J., Elder, G. H., Lorenz, R. O., Simons, R. L., & Whitbeck, L. B. (1993). Family economic stress and adjustment of early adolescent girls. *Developmental Psychology, 29,* 206–219.

Conger, R. D, Ge, X., Elder G. H., Jr., Lorenz, F. O., & Simons, R. L. (1994). Economic stress, coercive family process, and developmental problems of adolescents. *Child Development, 65,* 541–561.

Congressional Digest. (1995, June–July). *Welfare overview* (pp. 163–165). Washington, DC: U.S. Government Printing Office.

Cooksey, E. C., Dumka, L. E., Roosa, M. W., & Jackson, K. M. (1997). Risk, conflict, mothers' parenting, and children's adjustment in low-income, Mexican immigrant and Mexican American families. *Journal of Marriage and the Family, 59,* 309–323.

Corcoran, M. E., & Kunz, J. P. (1997). Do unmarried births among African American teens lead to adult poverty? *Social Service Review, 71,* 274–287.

Coulton, C. J., Korbin, J. E., Su, M., & Chow, J. (1995). Community level factors and child maltreatment rates. *Child Development, 66,* 1262–1276.

Coulton, C. J., & Pandey, S. (1992). Geographic concentration of poverty and risk to children in urban neighborhoods. *American Behavioral Scientist, 35,* 238–257.

Crane, J. (1991). Effects of neighborhoods on dropping out of school and teenage childbearing. In C. Jencks & P. E. Peterson (Eds.), *The urban underclass* (pp. 299–320). Washington, DC: Brookings Institute.

Danziger, S. (1990). Antipoverty policies and child poverty. *Social Work Research and Abstracts, 26,* 171–24.

Danziger, S., & Gottschalk, P. (1995). *American unequal.* Cambridge, MA: Harvard University Press.

Darrow, S. L., Russell, M., Copper, M. L., Mudar, P., & Frone, M. R. (1992). Sociodemographic correlates of alcohol consumption among African-American and White women. *Women And Health, 18,* 35–51.

DeParle, J. (1999, December 30). Bold effort leaves much unchanged for the poor. *New York Times,* pp. A1, A12.

Devine, J. A., & Wright, J. D. (1993). *The greatest of all evils.* New York: Aldine De Gruyter.

DiLeonardi, J. W. (1993). Families in poverty and chronic neglect of children. *Families in Society: The Journal of Contemporary Human Services, 79,* 557–562.

Dodge, K. A., Pettit, G. S., & Bates, J. E. (1994). Socialization mediators of the relation between socioeconomic status and child conduct problems. *Child Development, 65,* 649–665.

Downey, D. B. (1994). The school performance of children from single-mother and single-father families: Economics or interpersonal deprivation? *Journal of Family Issues, 15,* 129–147.

Drake, B., & Pandey, S. (1995). Understanding the relationship between neighborhood poverty and specific types of child maltreatment. *Child Abuse and Neglect, 20,* 1003–1018.

Dubow, E. F., & Ippolito, M. F. (1994). Effects of poverty and quality of the home environment on changes in the academic and behavioral adjustments of elementary school age children. *Journal of Clinical Child Psychology, 23,* 401–412.

Duncan, G. J., Brooks-Gunn, J., & Klebanov, P. K. (1994). Economic deprivation and early childhood development. *Child Development, 65,* 296–318.

Duncan, G. J., Yeung, W-J. J., Brooks-Gunn, J., & Smith, J. R. (1998). How much does childhood poverty affect the life chances of children? *American Sociological Review, 63,* 406–423.

Edin, K., & Lein, L. (1997). *Making ends meet.* New York: Russell Sage Foundation.

Eggebeen, D. J., & Lichter, D. T. (1991). Race, family structure, and changing poverty among American children. *American Sociological Review, 56,* 801–817.

Elder, G. H., Jr., Eccles, J. S., Ardelt, M., & Lord, S. (1995). Inner-city parents under economic pressure: Perspectives on the strategies of parenting. *Journal of Marriage and the Family, 57,* 771–784.

Ensminger, M. E. (1995). Welfare and psychological distress: A longitudinal study of African American urban mothers. *Journal of Health and Social Behavior, 36,* 346–359.

Entwisle, D. R., & Alexander K. L. (1995). A parent's economic shadow: Family structure versus family resources as influences on early school achievement. *Journal of Marriage and the Family, 57,* 399–409.

Families USA Foundation. (1999, May). *Losing health insurance: The unintended consequences of welfare reform.* Washington, DC: Author.

Family Economics and Nutrition Review. (1997). Cost of food at home. *Family Economics and Nutrition Review, 10,* 56.

Farrington, D. P. (1991). Childhood aggression and adult violence: Early precursors and later-life outcomes. In D. J. Pepler & K. H. Rubin (Eds.), *The development and treatment of child aggression* (pp. 5–29). Hillsdale, NJ: Erlbaum.

Feagin, J., & Feagin, C. B. (1994). *Social problems: A critical power-conflict perspective* (4th ed.). New York: Prentice Hall.

Federal Register (1999, March 18). Vol. 64, No. 52, pp. 13428–13430.

Federman, M., Garner, T. I., Short, K., Cutter, W. B., IV, & Kiely, J. (1996, May). What does it mean to be poor in America? *Monthly Labor Review,* pp. 3–17.

Feinstein, J. (1993). The relationship between socioeconomic status and health: A review of the literature. *Milbank Quarterly, 71,* 279–322.

Franklin, D. L., Smith, S. E., & McMiller, W. E. (1995). Correlates of marital status among African American mothers in Chicago neighborhoods of concentrated poverty. *Journal of Marriage and the Family, 57,* 141–152.

Furstenberg, F. F., Jr., & Hughes, M. E. (1995). Social capital and successful development among at-risk youth. *Journal of Marriage and the Family, 57,* 593–609.

Garbarino, J. (1992). The meaning of poverty in the world of children. *American Behavioral Scientist, 35,* 220–237.

Garfinkel, I., McLanahan, S. S., Meyer, D. R., & Seltzer, J. A. (1998). *Fathers under fire.* New York: Russell Sage Foundation.

Gelles, R. J. (1992). Poverty and violence toward children. *American Behavioral Scientist, 35,* 258–274.

General Accounting Office. (1999, April). *Welfare reform: Information on former recipients' status* (GOA/ HEHS-99–48).

Gerard, J. M., & Buehler, C. (1999). Multiple risk factors in the family environment and youth problem behaviors. *Journal of Marriage and the Family, 61,* 343–361.

Gerstan, J. C., (1992). Families in poverty. In M. E. Procidano & C. B. Fisher (Eds.), *Contemporary families: A handbook for school professionals* (pp. 137–158). New York: Teachers College Press.

Gilens, M. (1999). *Why Americans hate welfare.* Chicago: University of Chicago Press.

Gillham, B., Tanner, G., Cheyne, B., Freeman, I., Rooney, M., & Lambie, A. (1998). Unemployment rates, single parent density, and indices of child poverty: Their relationship to different categories of child abuse and neglect. *Child Abuse and Neglect, 22,* 79–90.

Goldfield, M. (1987). *The decline of organized labor in the United States.* Chicago: University of Chicago Press.

Gomel, J. N., Tinsley, B. J., Parke, R. D., & Clarke, K. M. (1998). The effects of economic hardship on family relationships among African Americans, Latino, and European American families. *Journal of Family Issues, 19,* 436–467.

Gottschalk, P. (1990). AFDC participation across generations. *American Economic Review, 80,* 367–371.

Gottschalk, P. (1992). The intergeneration transmission of welfare participants: Facts and possible causes. *Journal of Policy Analysis and Management, 11,* 254–272.

Greenberg, M. (1998). *Participation in welfare and Medicaid enrollment* [Issue paper]. Washington, DC: Kaiser Commission on Medicaid and the Uninsured.

Halfon, N., & Newacheck, P. (1993). Childhood asthma and poverty: Differential impacts and utilization of health services. *Pediatrics, 91,* 56–61.

Harrington, M. (1963). *The other America: Poverty in the United States.* New York: Penguin Books.

Harris, K. M. (1997). *Teen mothers and the revolving welfare door.* Philadelphia: Temple University Press.

Harris, K. M., & Marmer, J. K. (1996). Poverty, paternal involvement, and adolescent well-being. *Journal of Family Issues, 17,* 614–640.

Hashima, P. Y., & Amato, P. R. (1994). Poverty, social support, and parental behavior. *Child Development, 65,* 394–403.

Heymann, S. J., & Earle, A. (1999). The impact of welfare reform on parents' ability to care for their children's health. *American Journal of Public Health, 89,* 502–505.

Hipple, S. (1998). Contingent work: Results from the second survey. *Monthly Labor Review, 124,* no. 11.

Hunt, M. O. (1996). The individual, society, or both? A comparison of Black, Latino, and White beliefs about the causes of poverty. *Social Forces, 75,* 293–322.

Huston, A. C., McLoyd, V. C., & Coll, C. G. (1994). Children in poverty: Issues in contemporary research. *Child Development, 65,* 275–282.

Jackson, S. A. (1993). Opportunity to learn: The health connection. *The Journal of Negro Education, 62,* 377–393.

Jarrett, R. (1994). Living poor: Family life among single-parent African American women. *Social Problems, 41,* 30–49.

Jarrett, R. (1996). Welfare stigma among low-income African American single mothers. *Family Relations, 45,* 368–374.

Jennings, K. D., Stagg, V., & Conners, R. E. (1991). Social networks and mothers' interactions with their preschool children. *Child Development, 62,* 966–978.

Kaiser Commission on Medicaid and the Uninsured. (1998). *The uninsured and their access to health care.* September. Washington, DC: Henry J. Kaiser Family Foundation.

Kotlowitz, A. (1991). *There are no children here: The story of two boys growing up in the other America.* New York: Doubleday.

Kozol, J. (1992). *Savage inequalities: Children in America's schools.* New York: Harper Collins.

Kozol, J. (1995). *Amazing grace: The lives of children and the conscience of a nation.* New York: Crown.

Kruttschnitt, C., McLeod, J. D., & Dornfield, N., (1994). The economic environment of child abuse. *Social Problems, 41,* 299–315.

Leadbeater, B. J., & Bishop, S. J. (1994). Predictors of behavior problems in preschool children of inner-city Afro-American and Puerto Rican adolescent mothers. *Child Development, 65,* 638–648.

Letiecq, B. L., Anderson, E. A., & Koblinsky, S. A. (1998). Social support of homeless and housed mothers: A comparison of temporary and permanent housing arrangements. *Family Relations, 47,* 415–421.

Levitan, S. A., Gallo, F., & Shapiro, I. (1993). *Working but poor: America's contradiction* (rev. ed.). Baltimore: Johns Hopkins University Press.

Lewit, E. M., & Kerrebrock, N. (1997). Childhood hunger. *The Future of Children, 7,* 128–137.

Lichter, D. T. (1993). Migration, population redistribution, and the new spatial inequality. In D. L. Brown, D. Field, &. J. Suites (Eds.), *Demography of rural life* (pp. 19–46). University Park, PA: NE Reg. Center Rural Development.

Lichter, D. T. (1997). Poverty and inequality among children. *Annual Review of Sociology, 23,* 121–145.

Lichter, D. T., & Landale, N. S. (1995). Parental work, family structure, and poverty among Latino children. *Journal of Marriage and the Family, 57,* 346–354.

Lichter, D. T., & Eggebeen, D. J. (1994). The effect of parental employment on child poverty. *Journal of Marriage and the Family, 56,* 633–645.

Liebow, E. (1993). *Tell them who I am: The lives of homeless women.* New York: Penguin.

Lipman, E. L., & Offord, D. R. (1997). Psychosocial morbidity among poor children in Ontario. In G. J. Duncan & J. Brooks-Gunn (Eds.), *Consequences of growing up poor* (pp. 239–287). New York: Russell Sage Foundation).

Loprest, P. (1999, July). *Families who left welfare: Who are they and how are they doing?* (pp. 99–102). Washington, DC: Urban Institute.

Massey, D. S., & Denton, N. A. (1993). *American apartheid: Segregation and the making of the underclass.* Cambridge, MA: Harvard University Press.

Mayer, S. (1991). How much does a high school's racial

and socioeconomic mix affect graduation and teenage fertility rates? In C. Jencks & P. E. Peterson (Eds.), *The urban underclass* (pp. 321–341). Washington, DC: Brookings Institute.

Mayer, S. (1997). *What money can't buy.* Cambridge, MA: Harvard University Press.

McLanahan, S., & Sandefur, G. D. (1994). *Growing up with a single parent: What hurts, what helps.* Cambridge MA: Harvard University Press.

McLaughlin, D. K., & Lichter, D. T. (1997). Poverty and the marital behavior of young women. *Journal of Marriage and the Family, 59,* 582–594.

McLeod, J. D., & Edwards, K. (1995). Contextual determinants of children's responses to poverty. *Social Forces, 73,* 1487–1516.

McLeod, J. D., & Shanahan, M. J. (1993). Poverty, parenting, and children's mental health. *American Sociological Review, 58,* 351–366.

McLeod, J. D., & Shanahan, M. J. (1996). Trajectories of poverty and children's mental health. *Journal of Health and Social Behavior, 37,* 207–220.

McLoyd, V. C. (1990). The impact of economic hardship on Black families and children: Psychological distress, parenting, and socioemotional development. *Child Development, 61,* 311–346.

Meade, C. D., McKinney, W. P., & Barnas, G. P. (1994). Educating patients with limited literacy skills: The effectiveness of printed and videotaped materials about colon cancer. *American Journal of Public Health, 84,* 119–121.

Miller, J. A., & Davis, D. (1997). Poverty history, marital history, and quality of children's home environments. *Journal of Marriage and the Family, 59,* 996–1007.

Miller, J. E., & Korenman, S. (1994). Poverty and children's nutritional status in the United States. *American Journal of Epidemiology, 140,* 233–243.

Mills, R. J., Grasmick, H. G., Morgan, C. S., & Wenk, D. (1992). The effects of gender, family satisfaction, and economic strain on psychological well-being. *Family Relations, 41,* 440–445.

Moffit, R. A., & Slade, E. P. (1997). Health care coverage for children who are on and off welfare. *The Future of Children, 7,* 87–98.

Montgomery, L., & Carter, P. (1993). Health status by social class and/or minority status:Implications for environmental equity research. *Toxicology and Industrial Health, 9,* 41–50.

Morrow, L. (1993, March 29). The temping of America. *Time,* pp. 40–41.

Mulsow, M. H., & Murry, V. M. (1996). Parenting on edge: Economically stressed, single, African American adolescent mothers. *Journal of Family Issues, 17,* 704–721.

National Center for Health Statistics. (1996). Prenatal care in the United States, 1980–94. *Vital and Health Statistics* (Vol. 21). Hyattsville, MD: Public Health Service.

National Research Council. (1996). *Measuring poverty: A new approach.* Washington, DC: National Academy Press.

Needleman, H. L., Schell, A., Bellinger, D., Leviton, A., & Allred, E. L. (1990). The long-term effects of exposure to low doses of lead in childhood. *New England Journal of Medicine, 322,* 83–88.

O'Brien, E., & Feder, J. (1998). How well does the employment-based health insurance system work for low-income families? *Kaiser Commission on Medicaid and the Uninsured.* Washington, DC: Henry J. Kaiser Family Foundation.

O'Hare, W. P. (1995). 3.9 million U.S. children in distressed neighborhoods. *Population Today, 22,* 4–5.

Office of Health Policy. (1998). *Chartbook on children's insurance status.* Washington, DC: Assistant Secretary for Planning and Evaluation. Retrieved August 8, 1999, from the World Wide Web: http://www.aspe.os.dhhs.gov/health/98Chartbk/98-chtbk.htm

Orshansky, M. (1965). Counting the poor: Another look at poverty. *Social Security Bulletin, 28,* 3–29.

Orthner, D., & Neenan, P. A. (1996). Children's impact on stress and employability of mothers in poverty. *Journal of Family Issues, 17,* 667–687.

Ozawa, M. N. (1995). Antipoverty effects of public income transfers on children. *Child Youth Service Review, 17* :43–59.

Panel on Poverty and Family Assistance. (1999). *Concepts, information needs, and measuring methods.* Retrieved February 12, 1999, from the World Wide Web: http://www.nap.edu/readingroom/books/poverty/

Peterson, J. L., & Nord, C. W. (1990). The regular receipt of child support: A multistep process. *Journal of Marriage and the Family, 52,* 539–551.

Phillips, K. (1990). *The politics of the rich and the poor.* New York: Random House.

Pong, S.-L. (1997). Family structure, school context, and eighth-grade math and reading achievement. *Journal of Marriage and the Family, 59,* 734–746.

Presser, H. B., & Cox, A. G. (1997, April). The work schedules of low-educated American women and welfare reform. *Monthly Labor Review,* 25–33.

Quint, J., Bos, H., & Polit, H. (1997). *New chance: Final report on a comprehensive program for young mothers in poverty and their children.* New York: Manpower Demonstration Research.

Quint, J., Edin, K., Buck, M. L., Fink, B., Padilla, Y. C., Simmons-Hewitt, O., & Valmont, M. E. (1999, April). *Big cities and welfare reform: Early implementation and ethnographic findings from the project on devolution and urban change.* New York: Manpower Demonstration Research Corporation. Retrieved August 3, 1999, from the World Wide Web: http://www.mdrc.org/Reports99/UrbanChange/UC-ExecSum.html

Rainwater, L. (1995). Poverty and the income packaging of working parents: The United States in comparative perspective. *Child Youth Service Review, 17,* 11–41.

Rainwater, L., & Smeeding, T. (1995). *Doing poorly: The real income of American children in a comparative perspective* [Working paper no. 127] Syracuse, NY: Maxwell School, Syracuse University.

Rank, M. R. (1994a). *Living on the edge.* New York: Columbia University Press.

Rank, M. R. (1994b). A view from the inside out: Recipients' perceptions of welfare. *Journal of Sociology and Social Welfare, 21,* 27–47.

Rank, M. R., & Cheng, L. (1995). Welfare use across generations: How important are the ties that bind? *Journal of Marriage and the Family, 57,* 673–684.

Rank, M. R., & Hirschl, T. A. (1999). The economic risk of childhood poverty in America: Estimating the probability of poverty across the formative years. *Journal of Marriage and the Family, 61,* 1058–1067.

Rosenbaum, S. (1992). Child health and poor children. *American Behavioral Scientist, 35,* 275–389.

Rubin, L. (1994). *Families on the fault line.* New York: Harper Perennial.

Sansone, F. (1998). Social support's contribution to reduced welfare dependency: Program outcomes of long term welfare recipients. *Journal of Sociology and Social Welfare, 25,* 105–126.

Seccombe, K. (1996). Health insurance coverage and the working poor: Changes from 1977–1987. *Research in the Sociology of Health Care, 13,* 199–227.

Seccombe, K. (1999). *So you think I drive a Cadillac? Welfare recipients' perspectives on the system and its reform.* Needham Heights, MA: Allyn & Bacon.

Seccombe, K., & Amey, C. (1995). Playing by the rules and losing: Health insurance and the working poor. *Journal of Health and Social Behavior, 36,* 168–181.

Seccombe, K., Battle Walters, K., & James, D. (1999). Welfare mothers welcome reform, urge compassion. *Family Relations, 48,* 197–206.

Seccombe, K., James, D., & Battle Walters, K. (1998). "They think you ain't much of nothing": The social construction of the "welfare mother." *Journal of Marriage and the Family, 60,* 849–865.

Seltzer, J. A., McLanahan, S. S., & Hanson, T. L. (1998). Will child support enforcement increase father-child contact and parental conflict after separation? In I. Garfinkel, S. S. McLanahan, D. R. Meyer, & J. A. Seltzer (Eds.), *Fathers under fire* (pp. 128–156). New York: Russell Sage Foundation.

Sidel, R. (1992). *Women and children last: The plight of poor women in affluent America.* New York: Penguin.

Sidel, R. (1996). *Keeping women and children last: America's war on the poor.* New York: Penguin.

Simons, R. L., Beaman, J., Conger, R. D., & Chao, W. (1993). Stress, support, and antisocial behavior trait as determinants of emotional well-being and parenting practices among single mothers. *Journal of Marriage and the Family, 55,* 385–398.

Smith, J., Brooks-Gunn, J., & Klebanov, P. (1997). Consequences of growing up poor for young children. In G. J. Duncan, & J. Brooks-Gunn (Eds.) *Consequences of growing up poor.* New York: Russell Sage Foundation.

Smith, K. B., & Stone, L. H. (1989). Rags, riches, and bootstraps: Beliefs about the causes of wealth and poverty. *The Sociological Quarterly, 30,* 93–107.

Smock, P. J., & Manning, W. D. (1997). Nonresident parents' characteristics and child support. *Journal of Marriage and the Family, 59,* 798–808.

Sorensen, E. (1997). A national profile of nonresident fathers and their ability to pay child support. *Journal of Marriage and the Family, 59,* 785–797.

South, S. J., & Crowder, K. D. (1999). Neighborhood effects on family formation: Concentrated poverty and beyond. *American Sociological Review, 64,* 113–132.

St. Peter, R. F., Newacheck, P. W., & Halfon, N. (1992). Access to care for poor children. Separate and unequal? *Journal of the American Medical Association, 267,* 2760–2764.

Takeuchi, D. T., Williams, D. R., & Adair, R. K. (1991). Economic stress in the family and children's emotional and behavior problems. *Journal of Marriage and the Family, 53,* 1031–1041.

Teachman, J. D. (1991). Who pays? Receipt of child support in the United States. *Journal of Marriage and the Family, 53,* 759–772.

Teachman, J. D., Paasch, K. M., Day, R. D., & Carver, K.P. (1997). Poverty during adolescence and subsequent educational attainment. In J. Duncan & J. Brooks-Gunn (Eds.), *Consequences of growing up poor* (pp. 382–418). New York: Russell Sage Foundation.

Tienda, M. (1991). Poor people, poor places: Deciphering neighborhood effects on poverty outcomes. In J. Huber (Ed.), *Macro-micro linkages in sociology* (pp. 244–262). Newbury Park, CA: Sage.

Trent, K., & Crowder, K. (1997). Adolescent birth intentions, social disadvantage, and behavioral outcomes. *Journal of Marriage and the Family, 59,* 523–535.

Thomson, E., Hanson, T. L., & McLanahan, S. (1994). Family economic structure and child well-being: Economic resources vs. parental behavior. *Social Forces, 73,* 221–242.

Urban Institute (1999). Child Support Enforcement. In *New federalism: policy research and resources* (p. 1). Washington, DC: Urban Institute.

U.S. Advisory Board on Child Abuse and Neglect. (1990). *Child abuse and neglect: Critical first steps in response to a national emergency.* Washington, DC: U.S. Government Printing Office.

U.S. Bureau of the Census. (1997). *Statistical abstract of the United States: 1997* (117th ed.). Washington, DC: U.S. Government Printing Office.

U.S. Bureau of the Census. (1998). *Statistical abstract of the United States: 1998* (11th ed.). Washington, DC: U.S. Government Printing Office.

U.S. Bureau of the Census. (1999, September). *Poverty in the United States, 1998* (Current Population Survey; pp. 60–207; Tables B-1, B-2).

U.S. Bureau of Labor Statistics. (n.d.). *The value of the federal minimum wage, 1954–1996.* Retrieved February 1999, from the World Wide Web: http://www.dol.gov./dol/esa/public/minwage/chart2.htm

U.S. Congress, Office of Technology Assessment. (1992). *Does health insurance make a difference?* [Background paper] (OTA-BP-H-99). Washington, DC: U.S. Government Printing Office.

U.S. Department of Health and Human Services. (1999, August). Changes in TANF caseloads. Administration for Children and Families.

U.S. House of Representatives, Committee on Ways and Means. (1996). *1996 green book.* Washington, DC: U.S. Government Printing Office.

U.S. News Online. (1996, April 29). *Raise the minimum wage?* Retrieved from the World Wide Web: http://www.usnews.com/usnews/ISSUE/WAGE.HTM

Vartanian, T. P. (1999). Childhood conditions and adult welfare use: Examining neighborhood and family factors. *Journal of Marriage and the Family, 61,* 225–237.

Weigers, M. W., Weinick, R. M., & Cohen, J. W. (1998). Children's health insurance, access to care, and health status: New findings. *Health Affairs, 17,* 127–136.

Weinger, S. (1998). Poor children "know their place": Perceptions of poverty, class, and public messages. *Journal of Sociology and Social Welfare, 25,* 100–118.

Wertheimer, R. (1999). Trends in the well-being of America's children and youth: 1999. Washington, DC: Child Trends.

Whitbeck, L. B., Simons, R. L., Conger, R. D, Lorenz, F. O., Huck, S., & Elder G. H., Jr. (1991). Family economic hardship, parental support, and adolescent self-esteem. *Social Psychology Quarterly, 54,* 353–363.

Williams, D. R. (1990). Socioeconomic differences in health: A review and redirection. *Social Psychology Quarterly, 53,* 81–99.

Wilson, W. J. (1987). *The truly disadvantaged: The inner city, the underclass, and public policy.* Chicago: University of Chicago Press.

Wilson, W. J. (1996). *When work disappears: The world of the new urban poor.* New York: Knopf.

Wolfner, G. D., & Gelles, R. J. (1993). A profile of violence toward children: A national study. *Child Abuse and Neglect, 17,* 197–212.

Zimmerman, S. L. (1992). Family trends: What implications for family policy? *Family Relations, 41,* 423–429.

Linda M. Burton *The Pennsylvania State University*

Robin L. Jarrett *University of Illinois—Urbana-Champaign**

In the Mix, Yet on the Margins:

The Place of Families in Urban Neighborhood

and Child Development Research

In the 1990s, the most popular theoretical and empirical research issue concerning the local ecologies of families focused on the impact of family structures (e.g., household composition) and processes (e.g., child management strategies) on the relationship between urban neighborhoods and child and adolescent development. In this article, we synthesize and critically examine the decade's prevailing literature on the topic, organizing this review into three areas: (a) the research designs of quantitative and ethnographic studies of urban neighborhoods, families, and child outcomes; (b) the conceptual approaches used in these studies; and (c) the role of structural and behavioral features of family and parenting as factors that influence the relationship between urban neighborhoods and child development in ethnically and racially diverse populations. Results suggest that although family has been center stage in the neighborhood effects research question of the decade, it has remained on the margins in terms of theoretical and methodological specificity. Recommendations for future research are also offered.

In this decade review, we synthesize and critique the current scientific literature linking urban neighborhoods, families, and child and adolescent outcomes. Our focus emerged from the dominant conceptual and empirical question posed by researchers about this topic in the 1990s: What impact do structural (e.g., household composition) and process (e.g., child management strategies) features of families have on the relationship between urban neighborhoods and child and adolescent development?

Widespread scholarly and public interest in this question was driven by several coalescent forces, including the following: (a) a precipitous rise in concentrated poverty in urban, primarily ethnic and racial minority neighborhoods (Fine & Weis, 1998; Jargowsky, 1997; Kasarda, 1993; Moore & Pinderhughes, 1993; Wilson, Quane, & Rankin, 1998); (b) the dramatic influx of immigrants to the United States, accompanied by notable growth in the number and density of ethnic enclaves in urban and suburban settings (Alba, Logan, Stults, Maran, & Zhang, 1999; Freidenberg, 1995; Margolis, 1998; Portes & Rumbaut, 1996; Zhou,

Department of Human Development and Family Studies, 106 Henderson Building, Penn State University, University Park, PA 16802 (burton@pop.psu.edu).

*Department of Human and Community Development, University of Illinois at Urbana-Champaign, M-C 180, 269 Bevier Hall, 905 South Goodwin Avenue, Urbana, IL 61801.

Key Words: child development, families, urban neighborhoods.

333

1992); (c) vivid journalistic and media accounts of social pathologies in inner cities that heightened public concern about the safety of children growing up in economically disadvantaged, high-risk environments and catalyzed an intervention movement for youth and community development initiatives (Aber, Jones, Brown, Chaudry, & Samples, 1998; Armstead & Wexler, 1997; Colley-Quille, Turner, & Beidel, 1995; Gambone, 1999; Jessor, 1993; Kotlowitz, 1991; Melton, 1992; Schwab-Stone, Ayers, & Kasprow, 1995; Simon & Burns, 1997); and (d) a groundswell of efforts by individual social and applied scientists and interdisciplinary teams of researchers to develop new, and reframe existing, theories of urban neighborhoods and human development (Brooks-Gunn, Duncan, & Aber, 1997; Moen, Elder, & Luscher, 1995; Sampson, 1999) and test innovative methodological and statistical procedures for examining the lives of families and children in multiple ecological contexts (Earls, McGuire, & Shay 1993; Robertson & Weir, 1998; Raudenbush & Sampson, 1999).

The decade's academic and applied research activities with regard to urban neighborhoods, families, and children led to a number of comprehensive literature reviews. Several focused on quantitative studies of urban neighborhoods and child outcomes and, to a limited degree, the impact of family structure and parental monitoring on this relationship (Gephart, 1997; Jencks & Mayer, 1990; Leventhal & Brooks-Gunn, 2000). Others concentrated specifically on qualitative and ethnographic studies of family processes, low-income neighborhoods, and child development (Burton, Obeidallah, & Allison, 1996; Jarrett, 1998b). To date, no review has provided an integrated discussion of quantitative and qualitative studies, as well as conceptual and methodological issues, concerning the role of family structure and process in neighborhood effects and child development research. This article presents a synthesis and critique of relevant literature on the topic, devoting special attention to the conceptual, methodological, and empirical "place" of family in the prevailing discourse.

Paradoxically, our review of the literature indicates that although family has been a major focus of the contextual question of the decade, the conceptual and methodological treatment of family variables range from unspecified and vaguely implied to modestly defined and measured in most studies. We argue that, in part, this circumstance prevails because family scientists did not "weigh

in heavily" in neighborhood effects research efforts in the 1990s. Thus, we couch our review in the metaphor, "in the mix," connoting the designated centrality of family in the decade's prominent research question, "yet on the margins" in terms of both the modest theoretical and methodological specificity received by family variables in this line of research and family scientists' peripheral involvement in prevailing research efforts.

We begin our review with a brief description of the research designs used in recent quantitative and ethnographic studies on the topic. Next, we highlight the conceptual approaches and definitions of urban neighborhoods, family structure and process, and child development outcomes used in these studies. We then look intently at "the place" of family in this body of research. Specifically, we explore the role of structural and behavioral features of family and parenting as factors that impact the relationship between urban neighborhoods and child outcomes. We conclude our review and critique of the literature with recommendations for future research.

QUANTITATIVE AND ETHNOGRAPHIC STUDIES IN THE 1990s: A PROFILE OF RESEARCH DESIGNS

In tandem with Leventhal and Brooks-Gunn's (2000, p. 11) recent comprehensive review of survey and quasi-experimental research on neighborhoods and child development, the quantitative studies we evaluate represent a range of designs, including surveys that comprise national probability samples (Brewster, 1994; Chase-Lansdale, Gordon, Brooks-Gunn, & Klebanov, 1997); multi-city studies of individuals and families (Brooks-Gunn et al., 1997; Elliott et al., 1996); city or regional studies on neighborhood effects (Ensminger, Lamkin, & Jacobson, 1996; Loeber & Wikstrom, 1993; Paschall & Hubbard, 1998; Spencer, Cole, Jones, & Swanson, 1997); neighborhood-based studies such as the Project on Human Development in Chicago Neighborhoods (Sampson, Raudenbush, & Earls, 1997); and experimental and quasi-experimental design studies in which families were randomly assigned to live in particular types of neighborhoods (Briggs, 1998; Ludwig, Duncan, & Hirschfield, 1998).

Most of the quantitative studies we examined test models in which family variables either mediate or moderate the influence of neighborhood effects on child outcomes (Cook, Shagle, & Degirmencioglu, 1997). Many of the data sets used for these analyses have a limited repertoire of neighborhood and family variables and were not designed, a priori, to test such models.

Similar to quantitative studies, several of the qualitative and ethnographic studies we reviewed were not explicitly designed to explore the relationship among urban neighborhoods, family structure and process, and child outcomes, although the issue was addressed implicitly to some degree. These studies were primarily descriptive, representing a broad range of substantive foci, including family and kinship organization, parenting and childrearing practices, peer relationships, and schooling.

The studies included in this review are diverse in the ethnic and racial groups they involve, primarily featuring African Americans and including, to varying degrees, Mexican Americans, Puerto Ricans, non-Hispanic Whites, and Asian immigrants. In the quantitative studies, Mexican Americans and Puerto Ricans were often grouped indistinguishably under the ethnic categories of "Hispanic" or "Latino." Comparable ethnic grouping strategies were noted for Asian Americans and recent immigrants. Native American families were visibly absent in existing studies (Mitchell & Beals, 1997). Snipp (1996) indicated that the absence of Native Americans in urban neighborhoods is in part due to the reality that Native American families are more likely to live in rural, nonmetropolitan areas, and the few who do reside in large urban communities still consider the reservation their neighborhood or "homeplace" (John, 1998; Miller & Moore, 1979).

We also noted a significant limitation in the ethnographic studies relative to ethnic and racial comparisons and neighborhood quality. Many of the studies we reviewed did not focus equally on a range of urban neighborhood types (e.g., working class, suburban, "ghetto"). With the exception of Patillo-McCoy's (1998, 1999) recent ethnography of the neighborhood-based social life of middle-class African Americans and several ethnographies on middle-class Asian immigrants (Bacon, 1996; Min, 1998; Wong, 1998), most studies of ethnic and minority families were conducted in economically disadvantaged, unstable urban communities, whereas those involving non-Hispanic White families were conducted in stable, working-class neighborhoods (Freeman, 1995; Furstenberg, Cook, Eccles, Elder, & Sameroff, 1999; MacLeod, 1995; Moore, 1991; Perez-Granados & Callanan, 1997). Comparable neighborhood selectivity biases and sample endogeneity were noted in the quantitative studies we reviewed (Korbin, in press; Tienda, 1991).

CONCEPTUAL PERSPECTIVES: NEIGHBORHOODS, CHILD AND YOUTH OUTCOMES, AND FAMILIES

Conventional wisdom implies, and a number of studies suggest, that families play a major role in determining how urban environments impact the lives of their children. Nonetheless, conclusively identifying the precise paths through which families influence the relationship between urban neighborhoods and child outcomes was a significant challenge for researchers in the 1990s despite theoretical advances made in that decade. This challenge is particularly obvious in studies involving ethnically and racially diverse populations and comprising families with an array of culture- and situation-based family structures and processes. Burton (in press) and Duncan and Raudenbush (in press) have suggested that the challenge is mired in unmeasured neighborhood and family effects—the result, in part, of the multiple ways in which neighborhoods, families, and child and youth development have been conceptualized in existing empirical studies (Randolph, 1996).

Neighborhoods

During the 1990s several conceptual and methodological approaches were generated for studying neighborhood contexts and children. Jencks and Mayer (1990), in a now classic review, identified five theoretical frameworks for linking child outcomes with neighborhood effects: (a) neighborhood resources, which suggest that child outcomes are related to the level of resources (e.g., community centers, parks, day care) available in neighborhoods; (b) collective socialization, which proposes a relationship between child outcomes and the prevalence of neighborhood adults who can serve as role models and monitors of the behavior of neighborhood children; (c) the contagion or epidemic model, which posits that the negative behaviors of neighborhood peers strongly influences the spread of behavior problems among children in socioeconomic and racially homogeneous communities; (d) competition approaches, which argue that neighborhood effects on children are a function of community residents competing for scarce resources; and (5) relative deprivation models, which focus on how neighborhoods affect children and families via their evaluations of their circumstances relative to their neighbors and peers. These five frameworks tend to focus on problem-based child and adolescent outcomes, differ with respect to the mechanisms through which neighborhoods influence child development, and often omit the active role that some families play in mediating negative neighborhood influences.

In terms of defining and measuring neighborhoods, Burton, Price-Spratlen, and Spencer (1997) described four approaches used in existing work: neighborhood as physical site, perception, network, and culture. Neighborhood as site, the most commonly used conceptualization, is concerned with the sociodemographic milieu (e.g., racial mix, poverty levels, crime rates) and the physical quality (e.g., housing density, street maintenance) of a designated geographic space. Within this approach, designated boundaries of neighborhoods are typically defined by the researcher and usually constitute a census-tract, school or health district, or a zip code area (Bennett, 1993; Chaskin, 1997; Sawicki & Flynn, 1996).

Consistent with the unmeasured effects argument, the site approach has two major weaknesses. First, site analyses are too often driven by the convenience of census or survey data aggregation and do not properly acknowledge the loss of family and individual variability resulting from it. Second, this approach has a limited range of accountability for the diversity of neighborhood influences on any given family or individual. For example, its reliance on the "contextual moment" minimizes the temporal rhythms and life cycles neighborhoods possess. Among other outcomes, this can result in a blindness to dynamic elements critical to the neighborhood-family-child interaction.

Neighborhood as perception involves individuals' personal evaluations of the boundaries, risks, social milieu, and quality of the geographic areas they define as their neighborhood. Social scientists who employ this perspective note that perceptions of a neighborhood, and how that neighborhood is experienced by individuals, vary in meaning and interpretation by gender and race, as well as across generations in families (Aneshensel & Sucoff, 1996; Burton & Price-Spratlen, 1999; Coulton, Korbin, & Su, 1996; Garbarino, Kostelny, & Dubrow, 1991; Lee & Campbell, 1997). Problems in interpreting neighborhood and family effects on children arise most often when parents' perceptions of neighborhoods, rather than the child's own perspective of neighborhood risks and opportunities, are used to predict child outcomes.

The network approach in neighborhood research emphasizes the primacy of interpersonal linkages in context. In doing so, the network model focuses on identifying the types and content of relations with others in the local area. This approach is most commonly employed in studies of neighboring and the structural features of social networks in neighborhoods (Yen & Kaplan, in press). To date, few studies have used this approach to explore the relationship among urban neighborhoods, families, and child and adolescent outcomes (Logan & Spitze, 1994).

Neighborhood as culture is concerned with symbolic meanings, including actions, beliefs, language, gossip, and rituals of daily life in a geographic space. This framework is primarily used in the ethnographic studies we reviewed (Anderson, 1990; Fordham, 1996; Fernandez-Kelly, 1994; Newman, 1992; Williams & Kornblum, 1994). This perspective's principal weakness involves the definition of neighborhood boundaries relative to the loci of local culture. Because culture can be fluid across geographic spaces, identifying its epicenter or assigning concrete street boundaries to its perimeter is difficult. Thus, determining the impact of neighborhood culture on child outcomes is complicated by the spatial diffuseness of culture.

Developmental Outcomes of Children and Adolescents

Most of the quantitative studies on urban neighborhoods, families, and children published in the 1990s are embedded in traditional linear theories of normative development. Developmental outcomes of interest included, but were not limited to, birth weight and physical health (O'Campo, Xue, Wang, & Caughy, 1997; Roberts, 1997); school readiness (Attar, Guerra, & Tolan, 1994; Chase-Lansdale et al., 1997; Duncan, Brooks-Gunn, & Klebanov, 1994); educational attainment (Buchel & Duncan, 1998; Clark, 1992; Dornbush, Ritter, & Steinberg, 1991; Entwisle, Alexander, & Olson, 1994; Gonzales, Cauce, Freiedman, & Mason, 1996); depression (Dubrow, Edwards, & Ippolito, 1997; Simmons, Johnson, Beaman, Conger, & Whitbeck, 1996); childhood aggression (Kuperschmidt, Griesler, DeRosier, Patterson, & Davis, 1995); juvenile delinquency (Gottfredson, McNeill, & Gottfredson, 1991; Loeber & Wikstrom, 1993); antisocial behavior (Seidman et al., 1998); substance abuse (Allison et al., 1999); child abuse (Coulton, Korbin, & Su, 1999; Korbin, Coulton, Chard, Platt-Houston, & Su, 1998); and teenage pregnancy (Billy, Brewster, & Grady, 1994; Brewster, 1994; Burton, 1995; Crane, 1991; Ku, Sonenstein, & Pleck, 1993).

Although normative domains of development are clearly important, a number of social scientists have questioned whether traditional theories of development are appropriate for studying the lives of minority children and adolescents growing up in high-risk urban neighborhoods (Randolph, 1996; Spencer, in press). In these environments, children and teens may attach different meanings to their roles and behaviors than do their mainstream counterparts, thus calling into question the relevance of outcome variables derived from traditional developmental approaches and applied to these populations (Ogbu, 1991; Seidman, 1991). This issue is particularly salient given that most research on urban neighborhoods, families, and child outcomes focuses on ethnic and racial minorities, specifically low-income African Americans.

Many of the ethnographic studies integrate contextually relevant as well as traditional normative approaches to development. For example, Burton, Obeidallah, and Allison (1996, p. 4), in a review of the ethnographic literature on development among inner-city African American teens, identified contextually relevant adolescent outcomes, such as the "revised American dream," commitment to religious and spiritual activities, and kin-care abilities, and established the relative importance of these outcomes for understanding families' expectations concerning their children's behavior in high-risk urban environments. Spencer (in press) and Sullivan (in press) discussed the survival function of hypermasculinity as a developmental outcome for male African Americans growing up in hyperghettos; they also underscored the challenges created by this attribute for men who manifest it in normative contexts such as schools. Jarrett (1998a, p. 4), in a synthesis of the qualitative literature on neighborhood effects and African American children, described "street" and "nonstreet" developmental pathways and their implication for parental monitoring strategies and the social mobility of youth.

What is most relevant about highlighting the range of traditional and contextually relevant developmental outcomes present in the literature is that a number studies on urban neighborhoods, although testing important normative outcomes, do not explore alternative outcomes that are consistent with the realities of the children's and ado-

lescents' environment. Moreover, when only traditional outcomes are considered, particularly when deficit-models undergird the research, youth may be erroneously assigned aberrant attributions when in fact their behaviors represent a cadre of actions that fit contextual demands (South, in press; Spencer, in press). This issue has conspicuous implications for assessing the "place" of family in neighborhood effects research. The questions this issue generates are comparable to the "getting the context right" dilemma posed by Duncan and Raudenbush (in press): Do existing studies focus on the "right" child and adolescent outcomes? Is the "fit" between these outcomes and the family structure and process variables tested in neighborhood effects research a contextually relevant one?

Families: Structures and Processes

Family characteristics assessed in existing studies fall into three general categories: collectivist perspectives, family structure and socioeconomic indicators, and familial and parenting processes.

Collectivist perspectives adopt a broad community view of family akin to the African proverb, "It takes a village to raise a child" (Booth & Crouter, in press; Schorr, 1997; Stevenson, 1998). The construct most endemic to this perspective is *collective efficacy* (Sampson, Morenoff, & Earls, 1999). Collective efficacy is the extent to which social ties among community residents facilitate the collective monitoring of children relative to shared neighborhood norms and practices.

During the 1990s, collective efficacy, defined as neighborhoods that operate as "families" on children's behalf, experienced conceptual and empirical rebirth and prominence, most notably in the Project on Human Development in Chicago Neighborhoods (Sampson, Raudenbush, & Earls, 1997). In addition, it has become a guiding principle in neighborhood-based youth development programs (McLaughlin, Irby, & Langman, 1994; Tarlov & Pittman, 1994). Darling and Steinberg (1997), however, suggested that the relative importance of collective efficacy in the lives of children requires further empirical investigation, given that current research does not indicate the conditions under which integration into a "community family" operates in the child's best interest. Moreover, to date, researchers have not empirically assessed whether this collectivist construct is linked to family- and parenting-level variables.

The second category of family variables, structural and socioeconomic indicators, were principally used in large survey studies. The most common conceptualization of family structure used in these studies was a dichotomized construct that contrasts the effects of intact (e.g., both biological parents are present in the household) and nonintact (e.g., single-parent households) families relative to a specific child or adolescent outcome. Socioeconomic indicators included family income and poverty level (Bowen, 1996; Brooks-Gunn, Duncan, Klebanov, & Sealand, 1993; Chase-Lansdale & Gordon, 1996; Corcoran & Adams, 1995; Crane, 1991; Klebanov, Brooks-Gunn, McCarton, McCormick, 1998; Vartanian, 1999) and parents' education and occupational status (Buchel & Duncan, 1998; Dubrow, 1997; Duncan, 1994).

A number of social scientists have argued that although family structure and socioeconomic indicators provide broad insights on the role of family in neighborhood effects research, these indicators are, in effect, omnibus variables comprising multiple unmeasured features of relevant family conditions (Burton, in press; Elder, Eccles, Adelt, & Lord, 1995). These unmeasured features most likely represent the mechanisms that produce true family effects relative to urban neighborhoods and child outcomes.

What might these unmeasured features of family be? To address this question, we relied on the existing handful of survey and experimental studies that explored family- and parental-level process variables relative to neighborhood effects, but most notably, we looked to the qualitative and ethnographic literature for possible answers.

THE "PLACE" OF FAMILY IN URBAN NEIGHBORHOOD AND CHILD DEVELOPMENT RESEARCH

In discussing the "place" of family in neighborhood effects and child outcomes research, it is important to note that few researchers explicitly defined, conceptually or operationally, the family processes they explored. Many of these domains were implicit in their work and thus "on the margins" with respect to conceptual and methodological specificity.

Neighborhood Effects on Child Development: The Domains and Paths of Family Influence

Leventhal and Brooks-Gunn (2000, p. 325) reported four main findings from quantitative studies of neighborhood effects on child and adolescent development: (a) there is a positive relationship between the socioeconomic status of neighborhoods (comprising indicators such as household incomes, high school drop out rates, levels of female headship and female employment, number of managerial and professional workers) and the school readiness, academic achievement, mental health, externalizing and internalizing behavior problems, and coital and fertility outcomes of children and adolescents; (b) "the most consistent neighborhood effects are reported in studies involving national samples as compared with city- and regional-based studies"; (c) "many studies report small to modest neighborhood effects and account for five upwards of ten percent of the variance in child and adolescent outcomes"; and (d) "family-level variables tend to be more strongly associated with child and outcomes than neighborhood-level variables."

With respect to the "place" of family in this body of research, debate continues concerning the precise domains and paths of family influences on the relationship between urban neighborhoods and child outcomes. Most social scientists agree that the child's age and gender indirectly affect, via family structures and processes, neighborhood influences on child development. Cook et al. (1997) and Duncan and Raudenbush (in press, p. 16) have suggested that family variables play two substantial roles in neighborhood studies: "as mediators that account for the "reduced form" effects of neighborhood conditions on youth outcomes" and "as moderators in which families and neighborhoods jointly influence youth outcomes." Spencer (in press) and South (in press, p. 4) have suggested a reciprocal relationship between neighborhoods and family with this question: "Are parenting strategies a direct reaction to neighborhood conditions, or are they a reaction to children's behavior which, in turn, is partly a function of neighborhood attributes?"

Whatever the analytic approach adopted by researchers, most studies suggest that family is "in the mix" relative to neighborhood effects and child development and the influence occurs at the family (e.g., households and extended kin networks) and parent (e.g., mother, father, primary care provider) levels. The following overview of these influences highlights ethnic and racial similarities and differences to the extent allowed by the literature.

Family-Level Variables

The family-level variables that emerged in our review of the decade's quantitative and ethnographic studies of neighborhood effects include family structure and socioeconomic indicators, residential movements, extended kin networks, family role flexibility, family routines, family protection strategies, family orientation, and ideology of distinctiveness (see Table 1).

Family structure and socioeconomic indicators. As Table 1 illustrates, family structure and socioeconomic indicators have been the most commonly used family variables in neighborhood effects research, particularly studies involving African American and non-Hispanic White populations. Taken as a whole, these studies suggest that the effects of neighborhoods on child outcomes via family structural and socioeconomic characteristic are not uniform, and the number of replications of any one study has not been sufficient to conclusively support a particular relationship.

In effect, most of the studies that explore the impact of family structure and socioeconomic characteristics relative to neighborhood effects and child outcomes examine whether neighborhoods *or* families are more powerful predictors of child outcomes. Brooks-Gunn, Duncan, and Aber (1997), summarizing findings of five quantitative studies, noted that although neighborhood conditions were often significant predictors of children's development (depending on factors, including race, age, and gender of the child, and the outcome of interest), "the *size* of the estimated effects of neighborhood conditions were usually much smaller than the estimated effects of family structure and socioeconomic indicators were. For example, when available in the data, family income and mother's education were almost always fairly powerful predictors of children's cognitive development; these measures and family structure were usually significant predictors of behavioral development as well" (p. 281).

Researchers who use family structure and socioeconomic indicators acknowledge the "proxy" status of these variables and suggest that to unpack the influence of these indicators on neighborhood effects and child outcomes, more dynamic features of family should be tested in these models. Examples of more dynamic features include the fluidity of family structure, which comprises the frequency and pace of changes in family composition as a function of marriage, childbearing, conjugal dissolutions, death, economic hardship, familial excommunication, or personal choice (Burton & Jayakody, in press; Jarrett & Burton, 1999) and the timing and persistence of a family's economic and social resources relative to neighborhood risks and opportunities (Duncan, 1994; Entwisle et al., 1994).

The Residential Moves of Families. Poverty, race, social mobility, and place are innate themes in neighborhood effects studies. Not surprisingly, they also are cornerstone constructs in residential mobility research. Recent state-of-the-art discussions of neighborhood effects have encouraged a marriage between the two (Brooks-Gunn, Duncan, & Aber, 1997). Furstenberg and Hughes (1997), for example, suggested that residential mobility data, particularly length of time in the neighborhood, reasons for moving, and characteristics of the previous neighborhood, are aspects of family life that are critical to assessing the effects of neighborhoods on children.

To date, only a few studies have explored the impact of families' residential moves relative to neighborhood effects on child outcomes (Crane, 1991; Ensminger et al., 1996; Wood, Halfon, Scarlata, Newacheck, & Nessim, 1993). A guiding assumption of this research is that parents often move to better neighborhoods to reduce their children's involvement in "noxious neighborhood activities" (Long, 1992, p. 865). Several studies indicate, however, that although families change their children's residence by moving, they do not necessarily change the types of neighborhoods in which their children spend most of their time. For example, Solon, Page, and Duncan (1997) suggested that residential moves, particularly for economically disadvantaged families, occur between similar neighborhoods. Burton and Graham (1998), reporting findings from an ethnographic study of neighborhoods, families, and teenage pregnancy among African Americans, noted that when families moved to better neighborhoods, their teens frequently visited and retained strong ties with troubled peers in the previous neighborhood or other high-risk communities.

Brooks-Gunn, Duncan, and Aber (1997) noted that the most likely source of information for advancing knowledge on the impact of neighborhoods, families' residential moves, and child outcomes is housing demonstration data from the Gautreaux Assisted Housing Program (Kaufman & Rosenbaum, 1992; Rosenbaum, 1991) and the Moving to Opportunity Program (Briggs, 1998;

TABLE 1. FAMILY LEVEL FEATURES AND RELEVANT STUDIES BY RACIAL COMPOSITION OF THE STUDY SAMPLES

Feature	African American	Non-Hispanic Whites	Mexican American	Puerto Rican	Asian American
Structure and socioeconomic indicators	Aber et al., 1998; Aneshensal & Sucoff, 1996; Bowen, 1996; Brewster, 1994; Brooks-Gunn et al., 1993, 1996, 1998; Chase-Lansdale et al., 1996; Corcoran et al., 1995; Coulton et al., 1995, 1996, 1997; Crane, 1991; Dubow et al., 1997; Duncan, 1994; Earls et al., 1994; Ensminger et al., 1996; Entwisle et al., 1994; Gonzales 1996; Gordon et al., 1997; Gottfredson et al., 1991; Klebanov et al., 1994, 1997, in press; Korbin et al., 1996, 1998; Kuperschmidt et al., 1995; Lamborn et al., 1996; Lewis-Epstein, 1986; Ludwig et al., 1998; Paschall et al., 1998; Peeples & Loeber, 1994; Quane & Rankin, 1998; Sampson et al., 1997; Seidman et al., 1998; Stern & Smith, 1995; Sucoff, 1998; Vartanian, 1999	Aber et al., 1998; Aneshensal & Sucoff, 1996; Bowen, 1996; Brewster, 1994; Brooks-Gunn et al., 1993, 1996, 1998; Chase-Lansdale et al., 1996; Corcoran et al., 1995; Coulton et al., 1995, 1996, 1997; Crane, 1991; Dubow et al., 1997; Duncan, 1994; Earls et al., 1994; Entwisle et al., 1994; Klebanov et al., 1994, 1997, in press; Korbin et al., 1996, 1998; Kuperschmidt et al., 1995; Lamborn et al., 1996; Lewis-Epstein, 1986; Ludwig et al., 1998; Sampson et al., 1997; Seidman et al., 1998; Stern & Smith, 1995; Vartanian, 1999	Aber et al., 1998; Aneshensal & Sucoff, 1996; Brooks-Gunn et al., 1998, 1993; Crane, 1991; Dubow et al., 1997; Gottfredson et al., 1991; Klebanov et al., 1994; Lamborn et al., 1996; Sampson et al., 1997; Seidman et al., 1998; Stern & Smith, 1995	Aber et al., 1998; Aneshensal & Sucoff, 1996; Brooks-Gunn et al., 1993, 1998; Dubow et al., 1997; Earls et al., 1994; Klebanov et al., 1994; Lamborn et al., 1996; Seidman et al., 1998	Aber et al., 1998; Aneshensal & Sucoff, 1996; Dubow et al., 1997; Lamborn et al., 1996; Seidman et al., 1998
Residential mobility	Briggs, 1998; Burton & Graham, 1998; Ensminger et al., 1996; Stack, 1996				
Extended kin network	Anderson, 1990; Burton & Jayakody, in press; Davidson, 1996; Furstenberg, 1993; Gordon et al., 1997; Jarrett, 1998b; Jarrett & Burton, 1999; Stack, 1996; Stevenson, 1998	Furstenberg, 1993	Gandara, 1995; Moore & Pinderhughes, 1993; Romo & Falbo, 1996; Suarez-Orozco & Suarez-Orozco, 1995	Alicea, 1997; Hidalgo, 1992; Sullivan, 1993; Toro-Morn, 1995; Volk, 1994, 1997	Kibria, 1993
Family role flexibility	Anderson, 1990; Burton, Obeidallah, & Allison, 1996; Jarrett, 1998; Stack & Burton, 1993		Romo & Falbo, 1996		

TABLE 1. CONTINUED

Feature	African American	Non-Hispanic Whites	Mexican American	Puerto Rican	Asian American
Family routines Family protection strategies	Burton, 1991; Jarrett, 1992; Anderson, 1990; Brodsky, 1996; Burton, 1991; Burton & Graham, 1998; Cole & Hoffman, 1996; Cook & Fine, 1995; Dubow et al., 1997; Edin & Lein, 1997; Fordham, 1993, 1996; Furstenberg, 1993; Puntenney, 1997	Dubow et al., 1997	Gandara, 1995; Vigil, 1997 Dubow et al., 1997; Romo & Falbo, 1996; Vigil 1997	Soto, 1990; Volk, 1997 Bourgois, 1991, 1995; Dubow et al., 1997; Furstenberg, 1993	Dubow et al., 1997
Family orientation	Brodsky, 1996; Jarrett, 1992		Gandara, 1995; Romo & Falbo, 1996; Suarez-Orozco & Suarez-Orozco, 1995; Vigil, 1997	Alicea, 1997; Toro-Morn, 1995; Volk, 1997	
Ideology of distinctiveness	Brodsky, 1996; Fordham, 1993, 1996; Jarrett & Burton, 1999; Newman, 1999; O'Connor, 1997			Bourgois, 1991, 1995; Soto, 1990	

Galster & Killen, 1995; Ludwig et al., 1998). In these programs, low-income families are randomly assigned to reside in particular types of neighborhoods (e.g., suburban areas), providing unique opportunities to use a quasi-experimental design in examining the impact of neighborhood influences as they operate through the families' residential moves, and controlling for the unmeasured characteristics of families that previously allowed them to self-select into certain communities (Tienda, 1991).

Extended kin networks. Ethnographic research suggests that using extended family models rather than dichotomous constructs of family structure provides crucial insights on how the compositional features of family mediate neighborhood effects on children. Extended families can include both blood and nonblood members related by marriage, adoption, and friendship, and sharing domestic and familial caregiving obligations. In many of the ethnographies we reviewed, groups of affiliated relatives were often found in highly functioning families and were able to assist children in circumventing the dangers of high-risk neighborhoods (Patillo-McCoy, 1999; Stevenson, 1998; Sullivan, 1993). Extended kin were frequently geographically dispersed within and across local neighborhoods and, in some cases, other states and countries (Alicea, 1997; Davidson, 1996; Stack, 1996; Toro-Morn, 1995). Center locales in the extended family system served as "outposts" as children and family members moved between households and regions.

Many strong and resilient families were embedded in networks with "better off" kin in these various locales. Extended kin networks, such as those described in Kibria's (1993) work with Vietnamese immigrant families, expanded the resource base of the poorer family members and their children and teens. Kin with higher socioeconomic status provided resources in the form of money, clothing, and housing, as well as access to resource-rich communities with a wider array of institutional, information, and economic assets (Gandara, 1995; Jarrett, 1999b). Extended kin members linked children and adolescents into institutions and social networks that facilitated optimal development.

Relative to other ethnic and racial groups, non-Hispanic White families exhibited the least geographic dispersal of kin networks. The geographic concentration of these kin groups in part reflected earlier patterns of immigration from Europe and the attenuation of kin ties over several generations (Sullivan, 1989).

Family role flexibility. Families' ability to reassign roles as needed emerges in a few of the ethnographic studies as an important family domain relative to the study of neighborhood effects and child outcomes. This flexibility allows some families in high-risk environments to function with little external institutional support without compromising parents' ability to work and children's needs for contextual monitoring. Moreover, interdependence and team work are critical to the dual management of responsibilities and neighborhood dangers.

Jarrett's (1992) case study of a multigeneration family detailed how the youngest adult daughter in an extended family system took responsibility for the daily management of the household, caring for her sister's children (and her own), and nursing her ailing father. This woman's assumption of key family roles facilitated her mother's and sister's employment and the close monitoring of children and adults by kin. Anderson's (1990) observational study of an impoverished neighborhood blighted by drugs chronicled the important role of grandmothers. These women assumed a maternal role, taking full responsibility for the children of addicted parents. Burton (1991), in studies of drug-infested urban neighborhoods, found that uncles and great-grandfathers, as well as grandmothers, assume parenting roles for children, helping them to navigate the negative pulls of high-risk environments.

Family routines. According to a number of studies, families who avoid many of the stresses associated with residence in impoverished neighborhoods have a reoccurring and orderly schedule for executing domestic and household tasks (Clark, 1983). Soto's (1990) observational study of Puerto Rican American families with young children noted that a "feeling of organization" permeated these homes. Family routines resulted in "well-kept" households and meals prepared ahead of time. Findings from Volk's (1994) study of Puerto Rican American families were complementary. She observes that kindergarten-age children contributed to family routines—dusting and putting away groceries, among other activities.

Leventhal and Brooks-Gunn (2000) noted that in the past, the link between neighborhood effects and child outcomes vis-a-vis routines has not been empirically examined in quantitative studies, although it is central to models of community socialization as proposed by Wilson (1987). There are several emerging and on-going national studies of welfare reform and families that are explicitly designed to test this issue, however (Winston et al., 1999).

Family protection strategies. Several studies underscore the point that families institute unit-based actions to safeguard members from the physical and moral dangers of impoverished neighborhoods (Duncan, 1996; Elder et al, 1995; Furstenberg et al., 1999; Peeples & Loeber, 1994; Richters & Martinez, 1993). Family members avoid dangerous sections of the neighborhood (Brodsky, 1996; Cook & Fine, 1995); identify "safe" neighborhood "niches" (Furstenberg, 1993); carry out domestic chores during "safe" times (Burton, 1991; Burton & Graham, 1998); require older brothers, sisters, cousins, or family friends to accompany children on their daily rounds in and out of the neighborhood (Clark, 1983; Jarrett, 1998b); facilitate children staying in contact with their care givers via telephone contact or beepers (Edin & Lein, 1997); evade unconventional neighbors (Anderson, 1990); restrict neighboring relations to "desirable" neighbors (Puntenney, 1997); and generate ruses to avoid home burglary and personal victimization (Jarrett, 1992). In addition, consistent with notions of collective efficacy, many families work with neighbors to institute group-based strategies to defend and survey neighborhoods, as well as to keep them socioeconomically segregated (DeSena, 1990).

Family orientation. In a handful of ethnographic studies, families who reject street values and emphasize a commitment to family relations are able to mediate the impact of high-risk neighborhoods on their children. Women in Brodsky's (1996) case studies of "resilient" single mothers stressed the importance of their homes as havens for themselves and their children. They also viewed themselves as "homebodies." Vigil's (1997) study of Mexican-descent youth exemplified family orientation in action. Family members shared "ethnic" meals, watched television, and participated in recreational and festive activities such as birthday parties, coming-of-age ceremonies, and father's day observances.

Ideology of distinctiveness. One of the strategies employed by families to survive and thrive in high-risk environments is to believe and act as though they are distinct from their neighbors (Patillo-McCoy, 1999). This "ideology of distinctiveness" symbolically isolates families from disreputable neighbors and insulates them from the stigma associated with individual and neighborhood impoverishment. In the East Harlem Puerto Rican American neighborhood studied by Bourgois (1995) and the Harlem neighborhoods studied by Newman (1999), respectable families "shunned" the lifestyles of local drug dealers and unemployed residents who dominated the streets. Families in Fordham's (1996) case studies of high-achieving African American teens denigrated the lifestyles of nonmobile residents, viewing themselves as more ambitious and disciplined.

Parental-Level Processes

The parental-level factors we identified in the literature comprise the following: parental role commitment, generational role boundaries, parenting styles, resource-seeking behaviors, advocacy efforts, child-monitoring strategies, in-home learning strategies, and normative value orientations concerning education, social mobility and humanistic values (see Table 2).

Parental role commitment. Studies view the quality of and commitment to the parental role as a central variable in assessing the impact of family on the relationship between neighborhood effects and child outcomes. Jarrett (1997) noted that the sheltered development of promising children and youth relied on the dedication and commitment of at least one parent, usually a mother. Multiple accounts document the sacrifices made by mothers rearing children and teens in impoverished neighborhoods. Mothers in Fordham's (1996) study quit critically needed jobs to supervise and protect their adolescents "from the streets." Studies on the role of extended kin in the lives of families residing in economically disadvantaged contexts indicate that grandparents similarly left jobs to care for their grandchildren or to facilitate their adult child's employment or academic plans (Burton, 1995). Brodsky's (1996) work further identified mothers who sacrificed their own companionship needs to nurture the development of their daughters.

Generational role boundaries. A small number of studies specifically examine the impact of the generational age distance between parents and their children and the parents' ability to effectively help

their child or adolescent negotiate their environment (Burton, 1996). The more positive outcomes for children are noted when parents, in part as a function of a reasonable age distance (e.g., 21 years) between generations compared with a truncated one (e.g., 14 years), encourage superior-subordinate role distinctions between themselves and their adolescents.

Qualitative studies by Fordham (1996) and Romo and Falbo (1996) revealed that parents demand "respect" or make rules that are not to be questioned. These parents assert superiority by virtue of their status as parents. As a means to insure firm authority and compliance, mothers did not "run around" with their teens. Such behaviors enhanced mothers' abilities to enforce neighborhood regulations on their children. Mothers in Jarrett and Burton's (1999) research reinforced generational boundaries and, relatedly, respect, by differentiating their behavior from that of their children. Kibria's (1993) and Freeman's (1995) studies revealed that the focus on generational boundaries is particularly strong among Vietnamese immigrant families.

Parenting styles. Parenting styles are second only to structural and socioeconomic indicators and parental monitoring as important factors to consider in neighborhood effects and child development research (Alicea, 1997; Garbarino & Kostelny, 1993; Gonzales et al., 1996; Lamborn, Dornbusch, & Steinberg, 1996; Stern & Smith, 1995). Qualitative accounts of well-functioning families in urban neighborhoods document two key parenting styles: individualistic and communal (Jarrett, 1998b). Furstenberg's (1993) comparative neighborhood study of African American and Latino families with adolescents detailed the nature of the individualistic pattern. Some parents rear teens alone, receiving little or no assistance from other adults. They assert that neighbors cannot be trusted and assume full responsibility for their teen's development. For some of these families kin also are unavailable because of geographic distance (e.g., Puerto Rico) or lifestyle differences (involvement in drug dealing).

Jarrett's (1995) interviews with mothers of Head Start children detailed the communal pattern. Mothers in this study reared children with assistance from kin. Childcare responsibilities were dispersed among grandmothers, great-grandmothers, and aunts and sometimes took place in different households. Effective communal parent-

TABLE 2. PARENTAL LEVEL FEATURES AND RELEVANT STUDIES BY RACIAL COMPOSITION OF THE SAMPLE

Feature	African Americans	Non-Hispanic Whites	Mexican Americans	Puerto Rican	Asian Americans
Parental role commitment	Brodsky, 1996; Cook & Fine, 1995; Edin & Lein, 1997; Jarrett, 1998	Edin & Lein, 1997	Gandara, 1995; Vigil 1997	Furstenberg, 1993	
Generational role boundaries	Brodsky, 1996; Burton, 1996; Fordham, 1993, 1996; Jarrett & Burton, 1999		Romo & Falbo, 1996		Freeman, 1995; Kibria, 1993
Parenting styles	Anderson, 1990; Brodsky, 1996; Cook & Fine, 1995; Elder et al., 1995; Fordham, 1993, 1996; Furstenberg, 1993, Furstenberg et al., 1999; Jarrett, 1992, 1994, 1998; Spencer, 1999	Elder et al., 1995; Fursten-berg, 1993; Furstenberg et al., 1999	Romo & Falbo, 1996; Vigil, 1997	Alicea, 1997; Furstenberg, 1993	
Parental resource seeking behaviors	Brodsky, 1996; Cook & Fine, 1995; Furstenberg, 1993; Newman, 1999; Polakow, 1993; Puntenny, 1997; Williams & Kornblum, 1994	Furstenberg, 1993	Romo & Falbo, 1996	Furstenberg, 1993	
Parental advocacy efforts	Brodsky, 1996; Coley & Hoffman, 1996; Cook & Fine, 1995; Fordham, 1993, 1996; Furstenberg, 1993; Furstenberg et al., 1999; MacLeod, 1995; O'Connor, 1997	Coley & Hoffman, 1996; Furstenberg, 1993; Fursten-berg et al., 1999	Gandara, 1995; Okagaki & Frensch, 1995; Romo & Falbo, 1996	Furstenberg, 1993; Soto, 1990; Volk, 1994	
Parental monitoring strategies	Anderson, 1990; Brodsky, 1996; Burton, 1991; Coley & Hoffman, 1996 Cook & Fine, 1995; Darling & Steinberg, 1997; Davidson, 1996; Edin & Lein, 1997; Fordham, 1993, 1996; Furstenberg et al., 1999; Jarrett, 1992; Korbin & Coulton, 1997; Patillo-McCoy, 1999; Puntenny, 1997; Quane & Rankin, 1998	Coley & Hoffman, 1996; Darling & Steinberg, 1997; Edin & Lein, 1997; Furstenberg, 1993; Furstenberg et al., 1999 Korbin & Coulton, 1997	Darling & Steinberg, 1997; Reese, et al., 1995; Romo & Falbo, 1996; Vigil, 1997	Furstenberg, 1993; Soto, 1990; Volk, 1994	Darling & Steinberg, 1997

TABLE 2. CONTINUED

Feature	African Americans	Non-Hispanic Whites	Mexican Americans	Puerto Rican	Asian Americans
In-home learning strategies	Cook & Fine, 1995; Fordham, 1996; MacLeod, 1995; Rosier & Corsaro, 1993		Gandara, 1995; Okagaki & French, 1995; Pease-Alvarez & Vasquez, 1994; Perez-Granados & Callanan, 1997; Vigil, 1997	Soto, 1990; Volk, 1994, 1997	Freeman, 1995; Kibria, 1993
Stress on education and social mobility	Brodsky, 1996; Fordham, 1996; Jarrett, 1995; MacLeod, 1995; Newman, 1999; Williams & Kornblum, 1994		Gandara, 1995; Lucas, Henze & Donato, 1997; Reese et al., 1995; Romo & Falbo, 1996; Suarez-Orozco & Suarez-Orozco, 1995; Vigil, 1997	Soto, 1990; Volk, 1997; Williams & Kornblum, 1994	
Stress on humanistic values	Cook & Fine, 1995; MacLeod, 1995; Williams & Kornblum, 1994			Soto, 1990	

ing depended on accessible and trustworthy kin who shared similar lifestyles and values.

Other aspects of parenting styles deemed important in this area of research include the indicators of parental warmth, harshness, and control (Elder et al., 1995; Gonzales et al., 1996; Klebanov, Brooks-Gunn, & Duncan, 1994); parents' potential for violence and child abuse (Coulton, Korbin, & Su, 1999; Deccio, Horner, & Wilson, 1994; Earls et al., 1994; Korbin et al., 1998; Paschall & Hubbard, 1998) and the different socialization styles employed by parents for their male and female children and their young compared with their adolescent offspring (Delgado-Gaitan, 1994; MacLeod, 1995; Rosier & Corsaro, 1993).

Parental resource-seeking behaviors. Parents' ability to locate opportunities for their children and teens is highlighted as critical in impoverished neighborhoods with relatively few resources. Rosier and Corsaro (1993) and Polakow (1993), detailed how African American mothers of preschool children used Head Start programs to enhance their children's development. Romo and Falbo's (1996) study of Mexican-descent teens, Williams and Kornblum's (1994) study of African American and Latino teens, and MacLeod's (1995) study of African American youth described the significant investment of time by parents in identifying institutional resources for their teens, such as after-school programs, youth social service agencies, tutoring programs, job training programs, and recreational and sports centers. Parents believe their investments will increase the likelihood of their offsprings' success.

Parental advocacy efforts. As part of their resource-seeking activities, parents not only identify supportive institutions and programs, but also ensure that their children and teens receive benefits from them. Two studies of parents of young children identified a collaborative form of advocacy. Okagaki and Frensch (1995) detailed how parents formed a partnership with school staff to enhance their children's prospects. These parents were in frequent contact with teachers and staff, discussing their children's progress. Similarly, Volk (1994) found that mothers of young children advocated on behalf of their children by volunteering in the classroom. As volunteers, parents could ensure that their children received their share of teachers' attention and time.

Other research has revealed more defensive patterns of parental advocacy. Parents in

O'Connor's (1997) study of African American high achievers actively challenged teachers who were unresponsive or withheld learning opportunities from their teens. Similarly, African American mothers interviewed by Cook and Fine (1995) scheduled meetings with "uppity" school staff when they believed that their children's educational needs were not being met.

Parental monitoring strategies. Perhaps more than any other parenting process, monitoring strategies have been the most extensively documented in the ethnographic literature. Korbin (in press) raised a major question here: Are parenting strategies a direct reaction to neighborhood conditions or to children's behavior, which, in turn, is partly a function of neighborhood attributes? In other words, are certain parenting strategies more effective in some neighborhoods than in others?

Parents use a variety of supervisory strategies to control the time, space, and friendships of their offspring and to protect them from neighborhood dangers (Coley & Hoffman, 1996; Sampson, 1992). Jarrett (1998b) indicated that parents use verbal accounts in the form of stories, homilies, discussion, chastisements, and conversations to caution children against undesirable peers (Brodsky, 1996; Mark, 1993; Romo & Falbo, 1996); encourage relationships with conventionally oriented peers (Korbin & Coulton, 1997); chaperone children and teens on their daily rounds in the neighborhood (Cook & Fine, 1995; Puntenney, 1997; Soto, 1990; Volk, 1994); confine young children to the household (Burton 1991; Reese, Goldenberg, Loucky, & Gallimore, 1995); institute curfews (Ensminger et al., 1996; Fordham, 1996; Romo & Falbo, 1996); restrict teens' out-of-home activities (Clark, 1983; Furstenberg et al., 1999); prohibit children from wearing specific clothing or playing with toys that may put them in a threatening situation in the neighborhood (Jarrett, 1995); and in extreme cases, send teens to live in safer neighborhoods (Davidson, 1996).

Significantly, the most capable parents institute monitoring strategies while their children are young and continue them through adolescence. Although parents are sometimes less restrictive with adolescents, they nevertheless are well informed of their teens' friendships, activities, and whereabouts at all times.

In-home learning strategies. To supplement poorly functioning neighborhood schools, several studies have suggested that capable parents institute in-home activities that enhance the intellectual development of their children and teens. These studies reveal that parents of young children are most directly involved with their children's academic development (Gandara, 1995; Goldenberg, Reese, & Gallimore, 1992; Pease-Alvarez & Vasquez, 1994; Perez-Granados & Callanan, 1997; Reese et al., 1995; Rosier & Corsaro, 1993; Soto, 1990; Volk, 1994, 1997). Parents assist with school assignments, use everyday activities to impart academic skills, supervise trips to the library, teach children simple educational tasks (such as learning their numbers, writing their names, and reciting the alphabet), and facilitate language proficiency when English is the second language. Using Infant Health and Development Program data, Brooks-Gunn et al. (1993) indicated that part of the effect of neighborhood on preschool children's IQ at age 3 is mediated by the provision of learning experiences in the home and that the addition of the home variables to the model increases the variance as well.

Parents of teens, especially those with limited literacy skills, use comparable means to facilitate their offsprings' academic performance. They institute and supervise homework routines, endorse teacher directives and authority, provide school supplies, emphasize their teens' intelligence, and acknowledge satisfactory school progress (Clark, 1983; Fordham, 1996; MacLeod, 1995).

Stress on humanistic values. Successful parents actively monitor the moral life of their children and youth. Studies of children and teens highlight the values stressed by some inner-city parents who taught their offspring "super morals" that focus on self-respect, personal dignity, a concern for others, and hope for the future. Humanistic values are sometimes tied to religion and serve several functions. They bolster positive self-esteem, discourage adoption of the predatory and competitive street ethos that pervade social relations in impoverished neighborhoods, counter the stigma and denigration associated with neighborhood impoverishment, and give meaning to deprivation and struggle (Cook & Fine, 1995; MacLeod, 1995; Williams & Kornblum, 1994).

Stress on education and social mobility. As a means to escape impoverished neighborhood, parents emphasize the importance of education and hard work to their children and teens. Parents in the Suarez-Orozco and Suarez-Orozco (1995) study firmly believed that education was the key to social and economic mobility. As Lucas, Duncan, and Hirschfield (1997) discovered, parents sometimes used their own lack of education and the hardship it entailed to encourage striving. Romo and Falbo (1996) found that siblings who had not completed school or who had become involved in street life were similarly used to encourage social mobility. The research of Reese et al. (1995) summarized a widely shared belief held by parents: "[Education] is the best inheritance that a parent can give a child" (p. 210).

More generally, Jarrett (1995) identified the "community bridging" pattern of socialization as a strategy to promote the social mobility prospects of children and teens. This pattern entails a parental focus on mainstream values of success and "getting ahead" and characterizes families from diverse ethnic and racial groups. Parental emphasis on conventional means of striving for their offspring challenges unconventional behaviors and values that truncates developmental trajectories.

DISCUSSION AND CONCLUSION

The purpose of this decade review was to discuss the "place" of family in the link between characteristics of neighborhoods and developmental outcomes for children. We provided an overview of research designs and conceptual approaches used in existing studies of urban neighborhoods, family, and child development outcomes. We then looked at the place of family in this body of research. Specifically, we explored the role of structural (e.g., household composition) and behavioral (e.g., daily routines) features of family and parenting in ethnically and racially diverse families as factors which impact the relationship between urban neighborhoods and child outcomes.

What did research in the 1990s tell us about family influences on the relationship between urban neighborhoods and child and adolescent outcomes? Our review supported the notion that family domains are "in the mix" with respect to neighborhood effects studies but clearly "on the margins" in terms of the modest theoretical and methodological specificity they often receive in this literature. In light of this circumstance, a major challenge facing researchers is how to resolve the dilemma of unmeasured family effects.

Unmeasured family effects emerge from a number of sources. In part, the unmeasured effects dilemma reflects inconsistencies across studies in the ways in which family, neighborhood, and child development domains are theoretically and

operationally defined in existing research. A second source concerns the lack of attention given to cultural and contextual perspectives of family processes, most notably in the quantitative studies we reviewed. Most of the quantitative and several of the qualitative studies were not explicitly designed, a priori, to explore the relationship among family, neighborhoods, and child outcomes and thus had a limited repertoire of relevant variables. This issue posed a measurement specificity and relevance conundrum, given that most of the neighborhood effects studies, to date, focus on low-income urban African American populations.

Working within the limitations of available variables, family structure and socioeconomic indicators frequently were used as family process proxies in the quantitative studies we reviewed. Although these indicators provided some insights to the place of family in this research, they left us wanting in terms of understanding how dynamic family processes impact the relationship between neighborhoods and child outcomes. Looking to qualitative and ethnographic data, we were able to identify family- and parental-level domains that may be important to consider in future research, particularly studies that involve ethnically and socioeconomically diverse populations. These domains should be viewed as suggestive, however, and require further theoretical discussion and testing to determine the role they play in neighborhood effects research.

To be sure, in the 1990s, academic and public concern about urban neighborhoods and children propagated an important context-family question, and the field is moving toward providing the answer(s) to it. To furnish the answer(s), however, future research will need to address several issues. First, developing new and reframing existing (e.g, collective socialization) conceptual frameworks to incorporate distinct, contextually and culturally relevant, and dynamic process features of family is imperative. These frameworks need not be restricted to testing mediating and moderating models of family effects. Rather, a series of alternative models should be explored.

Drawing on the insights gleaned from the ethnographic literature, a plausible line of research might involve examining the impact of parenting strategies on neighborhood environments. A related research question is: How do individualistic parenting strategies in a neighborhood impact larger neighborhood stability or decline? Other approaches include testing reciprocal models of influence and given that neighborhoods, families, and children all have their own unique developmental courses, exploring the "goodness" of fit between these stages, for example, posing the question: How do older neighborhoods, with midlife parents, and very young children influence each other's development?

Second, future studies need to move beyond the current focus on concentrated disadvantage and explore the relationship between neighborhood, family, and child development in understudied contexts and populations. Information on neighborhood effects relative to economically advantaged populations (DeFrances, 1996; Patillo-McCoy, 1999) is sorely needed, as is data on rural families (Davidson, 1995; Dill, 1999; Duncan, 1999; Elder & Conger, 2000; Fitchen, 1991; Snipp, 1996; Stack, 1996), young children (Brooks-Gunn, Duncan, & Aber, 1997), the elderly (Cummings, 1998), and Mexican American, Puerto Rican, Asian American, and recent immigrant populations (Friedenberg, 1995).

Third, the study of neighborhood effects is an enterprise that requires interdisciplinary thinking and the integration of survey, quasi-experimental, and ethnographic methods. Several recently initiated studies involving ethnically and socioeconomically diverse populations in urban neighborhoods have adopted this perspective (Duncan & Raudenbush, in press; Winston et al., 1999). The initial promise of these studies is that they will wrestle with the unmeasured effects dilemma and, perhaps, move the field forward with respect to clearly defining the place of family in neighborhood effects research.

Our review of the literature suggests that there are many avenues to explore and much work to be done in discerning the place of family in neighborhood effects studies. Research conducted in the 1990s has primed the field to meet the challenge. We hope this review encourages more family scientists to participate actively in this discourse. Moving family from the margins in neighborhood effects research to theoretically and methodologically precise places in the mix is an assuredly worthy pursuit.

NOTE

Writing and research for this article were supported by grants to Linda M. Burton from the National Institute of Mental Health and the National Institute of Child Health and Human Development (R29 MH46057–01, RO1 MH49694–07, and RO1 HD36093–02); by support services provided by the Population Research Institute, The Pennsylvania State University, which has core support from National Institute of Child Health and Human Development Grant 1-HD 28263; by a National Science Foundation Award for the Study of Race, Urban Poverty, and Social Policy at Northwestern University, a Hatch Award, a University of Illinois Research Board Award, and a Visiting Scholar Award from the Russell Sage Foundation to Robin L. Jarrett; and by a Faculty Scholars Award from the William T. Grant Foundation and grants from the Social Science Research Council's Program on the Urban Underclass to Linda M. Burton and Robin L. Jarrett. We extend thanks to Frank Avenilla, Davon Carter, Tera Hurt, Stephanie Jefferson, Marla Kibler, Monica McManus, Zena Mello, Romney Norwood, Aureen Roach, and Rachel Ryterske for their assistance in the preparation of the bibliographic materials for this article. We also wish to thank Sonya Salmon, Dawn Obeidallah, and members of the Social Science Research Council's Working Group on Communities, Neighborhoods, Families, and Individuals and the Family Research Consortium on Diversity, Family Process, and Child/Adolescent Mental Health for their insightful comments on earlier versions of this article.

REFERENCES

Aber, J. L., Jones, S. M., Brown, J. L., Chaudry, N., & Samples, F. (1998). Resolving conflict creatively: Evaluating the developmental effects of a school-based violence prevention program in neighborhood and classroom context. *Development and Psychopathology, 10,* 187–213.

Alba, R. D., Logan, J. R., Stults, B. J., Maran, G., & Zhang, W. (1999). Immigrant groups in the suburbs: A reexamination of suburbanization and spatial assimilation. *American Sociological Review, 64,* 446–460.

Alicea, M. (1997). A chambered nautilus: The contradictory nature of Puerto Rican women's role in the social construction of a transnational community. *Gender and Society, 11,* 597–626.

Allison, K. W., Burton, L., Marshall, S., Perez-Febles, A., Yarrington, J., Kirsh, L. B., & Merriwether-de-Vries, C. (1999). Life experiences among urban adolescents: Examining the role of context. *Child Development, 70,* 1017–1029.

Anderson, E. (1990). *Streetwise: Race, class, and change in an urban community.* Chicago: University of Chicago Press.

Aneshensel, C. S., & Sucoff, C. A. (1996). The neighborhood context of adolescent mental health. *Journal of Health and Social Behavior, 37,* 293–310.

Armstead, P. J., & Wexler, M. B. (1997). *Community development and youth development.* Washington, DC: National Academy Press.

Attar, B. K., Guerra, N. G., & Tolan, P. H. (1994). Neighborhood disadvantage, stressful life events, and adjustment in urban elementary school children. *Journal of Clinical Child Psychology, 23,* 391–400.

Bacon, J. (1996). *Lifelines: Community, family, and assimilation among Asian Indian immigrants.* New York: Oxford University Press.

Bennett, L. (1993). Rethinking neighborhoods, neighborhood research, and neighborhood policy: Lessons from uptown. *Journal of Urban Affairs, 15,* 245–257.

Billy, O. J., Brewster, K. L., & Grady, W. R. (1994). Contextual effects on the sexual behavior of adolescent women. *Journal of Marriage and the Family,* 56, 387–404.

Booth, A., & Crouter, A. C. (Eds.). (in press). *Does it take a village? Community effects on children, adolescents, and families.* Mahwah, NJ: Erlbaum.

Bourgois, P. (1995). *In search of respect: Selling crack in El Barrio.* New York: Cambridge University Press.

Bowen, G. L. (1996). Poverty, neighborhood danger, social support, and the individual adaptation among at-risk youth in urban areas. *Journal of Family Issues,* 17, 641–666.

Bradley, R. H. (1995). Environment and parenting. In M. Bornstein (Ed.), *Handbook of parenting* (pp. 235–261). Hillsdale, NJ: Erlbaum.

Brewster, K. L. (1994). Race differences in sexual activity among adolescent women: The role of neighborhood characteristics. *American Sociological Review,* 59, 408–424.

Briggs, X. (1998). Brown kids in White suburbs: Housing mobility and the many faces of social capital. *Housing Policy Debate,* 9, 177–212.

Brodsky, A. E. (1996). Resilient single mothers in risky neighborhoods: Negative psychological sense of community. *Journal of Community Psychology,* 24, 347–363.

Brooks-Gunn, J., Duncan, G. J., & Aber, J. L. (Eds.). (1997). *Neighborhood poverty* (Vols. I & II). New York: Russell Sage Foundation.

Brooks-Gunn, J., Duncan, G. J., Klebanov, P. K., & Sealand, N. (1993). Do neighborhoods influence child and adolescent development? *American Journal of Sociology,* 99, 353–395.

Brooks-Gunn, J., Klebanov, P. K., & Duncan, G. J. (1996). Ethnic differences in children's intelligence test scores: Role of economic deprivation, home environment, and maternal characteristics. *Child Development,* 67, 396–408.

Brooks-Gunn, J., McCormick, M. C., Klebanov, P. K., & McCarton, C. (1998). Health care use of 3-year-old low birth weight premature children: Effects of family and neighborhood poverty. *Journal of Pediatrics,* 132, 971–975.

Buchel, F., & Duncan, G. J. (1998). Do parents' social activities promote children's school attainments? Evidence from the German socioeconomic panel. *Journal of Marriage and Family,* 60, 77–90.

Burton, L. M. (1991). Caring for children: Drug shifts and impact on families. *American Enterprise,* 2, 34–37.

Burton, L. M. (1995). Family structure and nonmarital fertility: Perspectives from ethnographic research. *Report to congress on out-of-wedlock childbearing* (Pub. No. (PHS) 95-1257; pp. 147–165). Washington, DC: Department of Health and Human Services.

Burton, L. M. (1996). Age norms, the timing of family role transitions, and intergenerational caregiving among aging African American women. *Gerontologist,* 36, 199–208.

Burton, L. M. (in press). One step forward and two steps back: Neighborhoods and adolescent development. In A. Booth & A. C. Crouter (Eds.), *Does it take a village? Community effects on children, adolescents, and families.* Mahwah, NJ: Erlbaum.

Burton, L. M., & Graham, J. (1998). Neighborhood rhythms and the social activities of adolescent mothers. In R. Larson & A. C. Crouter (Eds.), *Temporal rhythms in adolescence: Clocks, calendars, and the coordination of daily life* (pp. 7–22). San Francisco: Jossey-Bass.

Burton, L. M., & Jayakody, R. (in press). Rethinking family structure and single parenthood: Implications for future studies of African-American families and children. In A. Thorton (Ed.), *Family and child well-being: Research and data needs.* Ann Arbor: University of Michigan Press.

Burton, L. M., Obeidallah, D. A., & Allison, K. (1996). Ethnographic insights on social context and adolescent development among inner-city African-American teens. In R. Jessor, A. Colby, & R. Shweder (Eds.), *Ethnography and human development: Context and meaning in social inquiry* (pp. 395–418). Chicago: University of Chicago Press.

Burton, L. M., & Price-Spratlen, T. (1999). Through the eyes of children: An ethnographic perspective on neighborhoods and child development. In A. Masten (Ed.), *Minnesota symposium on child psychology: Cultural processes in child development* (Vol. 29, pp. 77–96). Hillsdale, NJ: Erlbaum.

Burton, L. M., Price-Spratlen, T., & Spencer, M. (1997). On ways of thinking about and measuring neighborhoods: Implications for studying context and developmental outcomes for children. In G. Duncan, J. Brooks-Gunn, & L. Aber (Eds.), *Neighborhood poverty: Context and consequences for children* (Vol. II, pp. 132–144). New York: Russell Sage Foundation.

Chase-Lansdale, P. L., & Gordon, R. A. (1996). Economic hardship and the development of five- and six-year-olds: Neighborhood and regional perspectives. *Child Development,* 67, 3338–3367.

Chase-Lansdale, P. L., Gordon, R. A., Brooks-Gunn, J., & Klebanov, P. (1997). Neighborhood and family influences on the intellectual and behavioral competence of preschool and early school-age children. In J. Brooks-Gunn, G. J. Duncan, & J. L. Aber (Eds.), *Neighborhood poverty: Context and consequences for children* (Vol. I, pp. 79–118). New York: Russell Sage Foundation.

Chaskin, R. J. (1997, December). Perspectives on neighborhood and community: A review of the literature. *Social Service Review,* 521–547.

Clark, R. (1983). *Family life and school achievement: Why poor black children succeed or fail.* Chicago: University of Chicago Press.

Clark, R. (1992). *Neighborhood effects on dropping out of school among teenage boys.* Washington, DC: Urban Institute.

Coley, R. L., & Hoffman, L. W. (1996). Relations of parental supervision and monitoring to children's functioning in various contexts: Moderating effects of families and neighborhoods. *Journal of Applied Developmental Psychology,* 17, 51–68.

Colley-Quille, M. R., Turner, S. M., & Beidel, D. C. (1995). Emotional impact of children's exposure to community violence: Preliminary study. *Journal of the American Academy of Child and Adolescent Psychiatry,* 34, 1362–1368.

Cook, D. A., & Fine, M. (1995). Motherwit: Childbearing lessons from African-American mothers of low-income. In B. B. Wadener & S. Lubeck (Eds.), *Children and families "at promise"* (pp. 118–142). Albany: State University of New York Press.

Cook, T. D., Shagle, S. C., & Degirmencioglu, S. M.

(1997). Capturing social process for testing mediational models of neighborhood effects. In J. Brooks-Gunn, G. Duncan, & J. L. Aber (Eds.), *Neighborhood poverty: Policy implications in studying neighborhoods* (Vol. II, pp. 94–119). New York: Russell Sage Foundation.

Corcoran, M., & Adams, T. (1995). Family and neighborhood welfare dependency and sons' labor supply. *Journal of Family and Economic Issues, 16,* 239–264.

Coulton, C. J., Korbin, J. E., & Su, M. (1996). Measuring neighborhood context for young children in an urban area. *American Journal of Community Psychology, 24,* 5–32.

Coulton, C. J., Korbin, J. E., & Su, M. (1999). Neighborhoods and child maltreatment: A multi-level study. *Child Abuse and Neglect, 23,* 1019–1040.

Coulton, C. J., Korbin, J. E., Su, M., & Chow, J. (1995). Community level factors and child maltreatment rates. *Child Development, 66,* 1262–1276.

Crane, J. (1991). The epidemic theory of ghettos and neighborhood effects on dropping out and teenage childbearing. *American Journal of Sociology, 96,* 1226–1259.

Cummings, S. (1998). *Left behind in Rosedale: Race relations and the collapse of community institutions.* Boulder, CO: Westview Press.

Cutright, P. (1995). Neighborhood social structures and lives of Black and White children. *Sociological Focus, 27,* 243–255.

Darling, N., & Steinberg, L. (1997). Assessing neighborhood effects using individual-level data. In J. Brooks-Gunn, G. J. Duncan, & J. L. Aber (Eds.), *Neighborhood poverty* (Vol. I, pp. 120–131). New York: Russell Sage Foundation.

Davidson, A. L. (1996). *Making and molding identity in schools: Student narratives on race, gender, and academic engagement.* Albany: State University of New York Press.

Davidson, O. G. (1995). *Broken heartland: The rise of America's rural ghetto.* Iowa City: University of Iowa Press.

Deccio, G., Horner, W. C., & Wilson, D. (1994). High-risk neighborhoods and high-risk families: Replication research related to the human ecology of child maltreatment. *Journal of Social Science Research, 18,* 123–137.

DeFrances, C. J. (1996). The effects of racial ecological segregation on quality of life: A comparison of middle-class Blacks and middle class Whites. *Urban Affairs Review, 31,* 799–809.

Delgado-Gaitan, C. (1994). Parenting in two generations of Mexican American families. *International Journal of Behavioral Development, 16,* 409–427.

DeSena, J. N. (1990). *Protecting one's turf: Social strategies for maintaining urban neighborhoods.* New York: University Press of America.

Dill, B. (1999). *Poverty in the rural U.S.: Implications for children, families, and communities.* Literature review prepared for the Annie E. Casey Foundation, Baltimore, MD.

Dornbush, S. M., Ritter, L. P., & Steinberg, L. (1991). Community influences on the relation of family status to adolescent school performance: Differences between African Americans and non-Hispanic Whites. *American Journal of Education, 38,* 543–567.

Dubrow, E. F., Edwards, S., & Ippolito, M. F. (1997). Life stressors, neighborhood disadvantage, and resources: A focus on inner-city children's adjustment. *Journal of Clinical Child Psychology, 26,* 130–144.

Duncan, C. M. (1999). *Worlds apart: Why poverty persists in rural America.* New Haven, CT: Yale University Press.

Duncan, D. F. (1996). Growing up under the gun: Children and adolescents coping with violent neighborhoods. *Journal of Primary Prevention, 16,* 343–356.

Duncan, G. J. (1994). Families and neighbors as sources of disadvantage in the schooling decisions of White and Black adolescents. *American Journal of Education, 103,* 20–53.

Duncan, G. J., Brooks-Gunn, J., & Klebanov, P. K. (1994). Economic deprivation and early childhood development. *Child Development, 65* (2), 296–318.

Duncan, G. J., & Raudenbush, S. (in press). Neighborhoods and adolescent development: How can we determine the links? In A. Booth & A. C. Crouter (Eds.), *Does it take a village? Community effects on children, adolescents, and families.* Mahwah, NJ: Erlbaum.

Earls, F., McGuire, J., & Shay, S. (1993). Evaluating a community intervention to reduce the risk of child abuse: Methodological strategies in conducting neighborhood surveys. *Child Abuse and Neglect, 18,* 473–485.

Edin, K., & Lein, L. (1997). *Making ends meet: How single mothers survive welfare and low-wage work.* New York: Russell Sage Foundation.

Elder, G. H., Jr., & Conger, R. (2000). *Children of the land: Adversity and success in rural America.* Chicago: University of Chicago Press.

Elder, G. H., Jr., Eccles, J. S., Ardelt, M., & Lord, S. (1995). Inner-city parents under economic pressure: Perspectives on the strategies of parenting. *Journal of Marriage and the Family, 57,* 771–784.

Elliott, D. S., Wilson, W. J., Huizinga, D., Sampson, R. J., Elliot, A., & Rankin, B. (1996). The effects of neighborhood disadvantage on adolescent development. *Journal of Research in Crime and Delinquency, 33,* 389–426.

Ensminger, M. E., Lamkin, R. P., & Jacobson, N. (1996). School leaving: A longitudinal perspective including neighborhood effects. *Child Development, 67,* 2400–2416.

Entwisle, D. R., Alexander, K. L., & Olson, L. S. (1994). The gender gap in math: Its possible origins in neighborhood effects. *American Sociological Review, 59,* 822–838.

Fernandez-Kelly, P. (1994). Towanda's triumph: Social and cultural capital in the transition to adulthood in the urban ghetto. *International Journal of Urban and Regional Research, 18,* 88–111.

Fine, M., & Weis, L. (1998). *The unknown city: The lives of poor and working class young adults.* Boston: Beacon Press.

Fitchen, J. M. (1991). *Endangered spaces, enduring places: Change, identity, and survival in rural America.* Boulder, CO: Westview Press.

Fordham, S. (1996). *Blacked out: Dilemmas of race, identity and success at Capital High.* Chicago: University of Chicago Press.

Freeman, J. M. (1995). *Changing identities: Vietnamese Americans 1975–1995.* Boston: Allyn and Bacon.

Freidenberg, J. (Ed.). (1995). *The anthropology of lower income urban enclaves: The case of East Harlem.* New York: New York Academy of Sciences.

Furstenberg, F. F. (1993). How families manage risk and opportunity in dangerous neighborhoods. In W. J. Wilson (Ed.), *Sociology and the public agenda* (pp. 231–258). Newbury Park, CA: Sage.

Furstenberg, F. F., Cook, T., Eccles, J., Elder, G. H., Jr., & Sameroff, A. (1999). *Managing to make it: Urban families in high-risk neighborhoods.* Chicago: University of Chicago Press.

Furstenberg, F. F., & Hughes, M. E. (1997). The influence of neighborhoods on children's development: A theoretical perspective and a research agenda. In J. Brooks-Gunn, G. Duncan, & J. L. Aber (Eds.), *Neighborhood poverty: Context and consequences for children* (pp. 23–47). New York: Russell Sage Foundation.

Galster, G. C., & Killen, S. P. (1995). The geography of metropolitan opportunity: A reconnaissance and conceptual framework. *Housing Policy Debate, 6,* 10–47.

Gambone, M. A. (1999). *Community action and youth development.* Queensland, Maryland: Aspen Institute Roundtable for Comprehensive Community Initiatives.

Gandara, P. (1995). *Over the ivy walls: The educational mobility of low-income Chicanos.* Albany: State University of New York Press.

Garbarino, J., & Kostelny, K. (1993). Neighborhood and community influences on parenting. In T. Luster & L. Okagaki (Eds.), *Parenting: An ecological perspective* (pp. 203–226). Hillsdale, NJ: Erlbaum.

Garbarino, J., Kostelny, K., & Dubrow, N. (1991). What children can tell us about living in danger. *American Psychologist, 46,* 376–383.

Gephart, M. (1997). Neighborhoods and communities as contexts for development. In J. Brooks-Gunn, G. Duncan, & L. Aber (Eds.), *Neighborhood poverty: Context and consequences for children* (pp. 1–43). New York: Russell Sage Foundation.

Goldenberg, C., Reese, L., & Gallimore, R. (1992). Effects of literacy materials from school on Latino children's home experiences and early reading achievement. *American Journal of Education, 100,* 497–536.

Gonzales, N. A., Cauce, A., Freiedman, R. J., & Mason, C. A. (1996). Family, peer and neighborhood influences on academic achievement among African-American adolescents: One-year prospective effects. *American Journal of Community Psychology, 24,* 365–387.

Gordon, R. A., Chase-Lansdale, P. L., Matjasko, J. L., & Brooks-Gunn, J. (1997). Young mothers living with grandmothers and living apart: How neighborhood and household contexts relate to multigenerational coresidence in African American families. *Applied Developmental Science, 1,* 89–106.

Gottfredson, D. C., McNeill, R. J. M., III., & Gottfredson, G. D. (1991). Social area influences on delinquency: A multilevel analysis. *Journal of Research on Crime and Delinquency, 28,* 197–226.

Harvey, D. L. (1993). *Potter addition: Poverty, family, and kinship in a heartland community.* New York: Aldine De Gruyter.

Jargowsky, P. A. (1997). *Poverty and place: Ghettos, barrios, and the American city.* New York: Russell Sage Foundation.

Jarrett, R. L. (1992). A family case study: An examination of the underclass debate. In J. Gilgun, G. Handel, & K. Daley (Eds.), *Qualitative methods in family research* (pp. 172–197). Newbury Park, CA: Sage.

Jarrett, R. L. (1995). Growing up poor: The family experiences of socially mobile youth in low-income African American neighborhoods. *Journal of Adolescent Research, 10,* 111–135.

Jarrett, R. L. (1997). African American family and parenting strategies in impoverished neighborhoods. *Qualitative Sociology, 20,* 275–288.

Jarrett, R. L. (1998a). African American children, families, and neighborhoods: Qualitative contributions to understanding developmental pathways. *Applied Developmental Science, 2,* 2–16.

Jarrett, R. L. (1998b). *Indicators of family strengths and resilience that influence positive child-youth outcomes in urban neighborhoods: A review of quantitative and ethnographic studies.* Background paper prepared for the Neighborhood Transformation and Family Development Initiative of the Annie E. Casey Foundation, Baltimore, MD.

Jarrett, R. L., & Burton, L. M. (1999). Dynamic dimensions of family structure in low-income African American families: Emergent themes in qualitative research. *Journal of Comparative Family Studies, 30,* 177–188.

Jencks, C., & Mayer, S. E. (1990). The social consequences of growing up in a poor neighborhood. In L. E. Lynn, Jr., & M. G. H. McGeary (Eds.), *Inner-city poverty in America* (pp. 111–186). Washington, DC: National Academy Press.

Jessor, R. (1993). Successful adolescent development among youth in high-risk settings. *American Psychologist, 48,* 117–126.

John, R. (1998). Native American families. In C. H. Mindel, R. W. Habenstein, & R. Wright, Jr. (Eds.), *Ethnic families in America: Patterns and variations* (4th ed., pp. 382–421). New York: Prentice-Hall.

Kasarda, J. D. (1993). Inner city concentrated poverty and neighborhood distress. *Housing Policy Debate, 4,* 253–302.

Kaufman, J., & Rosenbaum, J. (1992). The education and employment of low-income Black youth in White suburbs., *Educational Evaluation and Policy Analysis, 14,* 229–240.

Kibria, N. (1993). *Family tightrope: The changing lives of Vietnamese Americans.* Princeton, NJ: Princeton University Press.

Klebanov, P. K., Brooks-Gunn, J., & Duncan, G. J. (1994). Does neighborhood and family poverty affect mothers' parenting, mental health, and social support? *Journal of Marriage and the Family, 56,* 441–455.

Klebanov, P. K., Brooks-Gunn, J., McCarton, C., & McCormick, M. C. (1998). The contribution of neighborhood and family income upon developmental test scores over the first three years of life. *Child Development, 69,* 1420–1436.

Korbin, J. (in press). Context and meaning in neighborhood studies of children and families. In A. Booth & A. C. Crouter (Eds.), *Does it take a village: Community effects on children, adolescents, and families.* Mahwah, NJ: Erlbaum.

Korbin, J. E., & Coulton, C. J. (1997). Understanding the neighborhood context for children and families: Combining epidemiological and ethnographic approaches. In J. Brooks-Gunn, G. Duncan, & J. L. Aber (Eds.), *Neighborhood poverty: Context and consequences for children* (Vol. II, 65–79). New York: Russell Sage Foundation.

Korbin, J. E., Coulton, C. J., Chard, S., Platt-Houston, C., & Su, M. (1998). Impoverishment and child maltreatment in African American and European American neighborhoods. *Development and Psychopathology, 10,* 215–233.

Kotlowitz, A. (1991). *There are no children here.* New York: Anchor.

Ku, L., Sonenstein, F. L., & Pleck, J. H. (1993). Neighborhood, family, and work: Influences on the premarital behaviors of adolescent males. *Social Forces, 72,* 479–503

Kuperschmidt, J. B., Griesler, P. C., DeRosier, M. E., Patterson, C. J., & Davis, P. W. (1995). Childhood aggression and peer relations in the context of family and neighborhood factors. *Child Development, 66,* 360–375.

Lamborn, S. D., Dornbusch, S. M., & Steinberg, L. (1996). Ethnicity and community context as moderators of the relations between family decision making and adolescent adjustment. *Child Development, 67,* 283–301.

Lee, B. A., & Campbell, K. E. (1997). Common ground? Urban neighborhoods as survey respondents see them. *Social Science Quarterly, 78,* 922–936.

Leventhal, T. L., & Brooks-Gunn, J. (2000). The neighborhoods they live in: The effects of neighborhood residence upon child and adolescent outcomes. *Psychological Bulletin, 126,* 309–337.

Loeber, R., & Wikstrom, P. H. (1993). Individual pathways to crime in different types of neighborhoods. In D. P. Farrington, R. J. Sampson, & P. H. Wikstrom (Eds.), *Integrating individual and ecological aspects of crime* (pp. 1169–1204). Stockholm, Sweden: National Council for Crime Prevention.

Logan, J. R., & Spitze, G. D. (1994). Family neighbors. *American Journal of Sociology, 100,* 453–476.

Long, L. (1992). International perspectives on the residential mobility of America's children. *Journal of Marriage and the Family, 54,* 861–869.

Lucas, T., Henze, R., & Donato, R. (1997). Promoting the success of Latino language-minority students: An exploratory study of six high schools. In A. Darder, R. D. Torres, & H. Gutierrez (Eds.), *Latinos and education: A critical reader.* New York: Routledge.

Ludwig, J., Duncan, G. J., & Hirschfield, P. (1998). *Urban poverty and juvenile crime: Evidence from a randomized housing-mobility experiment.* Unpublished manuscript, Georgetown University, Washington, DC.

MacLeod, J. (1995). *Ain't no makin' it: Leveled aspirations in a low-income community.* Boulder, CO: Westview Press.

Margolis, M. L. (1998). *An invisible minority: Brazilians in New York city.* Boston: Allyn and Bacon.

Mark, D. L. (1993). *High-achieving African American children in low-income families: The home learning environment.* Unpublished doctoral dissertation, University of New York, Buffalo.

McLaughlin, M. W., Irby, I. A., & Langman, J. (1994). *Urban sanctuaries: Neighborhood organizations in the lives and futures of inner-city youth.* San Francisco: Jossey-Bass.

Melton, G. B. (1992). It's time for neighborhood research and action. *Child Abuse and Neglect, 16,* 909–913.

Miller, D. L., & Moore, C. D. (1979). The Native American family: The urban way. In National Institute on Mental Health (Ed.), *Families and the outside world* (pp. 441–484). Washington, DC: U.S. Government Printing Office.

Min, P. G. (1998). *Changes and conflicts: Korean immigrant families in New York.* Boston: Allyn and Bacon.

Mitchell, C. M., & Beals, J. (1997). The structure of problem and positive behavior among American Indian adolescents: Gender and community differences. *American Journal of Community Psychology, 25,* 257–274.

Moen, P., Elder, G. H., & Luscher, K. (Eds.). (1995). *Examining lives in context: Perspectives on the ecology of human development.* Washington, DC: American Psychological Association.

Moore, J. W. (1991). *Going down to the barrio: Homeboys and homegirls in change.* Philadelphia: Temple University Press.

Moore, J. W., & Pinderhughes, R. (1993). *In the barrios: Latinos and the underclass debate.* New York: Russell Sage Foundation.

Newman, K. S. (1992). *The view from the corner: Neighborhood influences on children and adolescents.* New York: Social Science Research Council.

Newman, K. S. (1999). *No shame in my game: The working poor in the inner city.* New York: Knopf and Russell Sage Foundation.

O'Campo, P., Xue, X., Wang, M. C., & Caughy, M. O. (1997). Neighborhood risk factors and low birth weight in Baltimore: A multilevel analysis. *American Journal of Public Health, 87,* 1113–1118.

O'Connor, C. (1997). Dispositions toward (collective) struggle and educational resilience in the inner city: A case analysis of six African-American high school students. *American Educational Research Journal, 34,* 593–629.

Ogbu, J. (1991). Minority coping responses and school experience. *Journal of Psychohistory, 18,* 433–356.

Okagaki, L., & Frensch, P. A. (1995). Parental support for Mexican-American children's school achievement. In H. I. McCubbin, E. A. Thompson, A. I. Thompson, & J. E. Fromer (Eds.), *Resiliency in ethnic minority families: Native and immigrant American families* (Vol. 1, pp. 325–342). Madison: University of Wisconsin Press.

Paschall, M. J., & Hubbard, J. (1998). Effects of neighborhood and family stressors on African American male adolescents' self worth and propensity for violent behavior. *Journal of Consulting & Clinical Psychology, 66,* 825–831.

Patillo-McCoy M. (1998). Sweet mothers and gangbangers: Managing crime in a Black middle-class neighborhood. *Social Forces, 76,* 747–774.

Patillo-McCoy, M. (1999). *Black picket fences.* Chicago: University of Chicago Press.

Pease-Alvarez, C. & Vasquez, O. (1994). Language socialization in ethnic minority communities. In F. Genese (Ed.), *Educating second language children: The whole child, the whole curriculum, the whole community* (pp. 82–102). New York: Cambridge University Press.

Peeples, F., & Loeber, R. (1994). Do individual factors and neighborhood context explain ethnic differences in juvenile delinquency? *Journal of Quantitative Criminology, 10,* 141–157.

Perez-Granados, D. R., & Callahan, M. (1997). Parents and siblings as early resources for young children's learning in Mexican-descent families. *Hispanic Journal of Behavioral Sciences, 19,* 3–33.

Polakow, V. (1993). *Lives on the edge; Single mothers and their children in the other America.* Chicago: University of Chicago Press.

Portes, A., & Rumbaut, R. G. (1996). *Immigrant America: A portrait (2nd ed.).* Berkeley: University of California Press.

Puntenney, D. L. (1997). The impact of gang violence on the decisions of everyday life: Disjunctions between policy assumptions and community conditions. *Journal of Urban Affairs, 19,* 143–161.

Quane, J. M., & Rankin, B. H. (1998). Neighborhood poverty, family characteristics, and commitment to mainstream goals. *Journal of Family Issues, 19,* 769–794.

Randolph, S. M. (1996). Studying the role of family and school in the development of African American preschoolers in violent neighborhoods. *Journal of Negro Education, 6,* 282–294.

Raudenbush, S. W., & Sampson, R. J. (1999). Econometrics: Toward a science of assessing ecological settings, with application to the systematic social observation of neighborhoods. *Sociological Methodology, 29,* 1–41.

Reese, L., Goldenberg, C., Loucky, J., & Gallimore, R. (1995). Ecocultural context, cultural activity, and emergent literacy: Sources of variation in home literacy experiences of Spanish-speaking children. In S. W. Rothstein (Ed.), *Class, culture, and race in American schools: A handbook* (pp. 199–224). Westport, CT: Greenwood Press.

Richters, J. E., & Martinez, P. E. (1993). Violent communities, family choices, and children's chances. *Development and Psychopathology, 5,* 609–627.

Roberts, E. M. (1997). Neighborhood social environment and the distribution of low birthweight in Chicago. *American Journal of Public Health, 87,* 597–603.

Robertson, J. G., & Weir, K. R. (1998). Using geographic information systems to enhance community-based child welfare services. *Child Maltreatment, 3,* 224–234.

Romo, H. D. & Falbo, T. (1996). *Latino high school graduation: Defying the odds.* Austin: University of Texas Press.

Rosenbaum, J. (1991). Black pioneers—do their moves to the suburbs increase economic opportunities for mothers and children? *Housing Policy Debate, 2,* 1179–1213.

Rosier, K. B., & Corsaro, W. A. (1993). Competent parents, complex lives: Managing parenthood in poverty. *Journal of Contemporary Ethnography, 22,* 171–204.

Sampson, R. J. (1992). Family management and child development: Insights from social disorganization theory. In J. McCord (Ed.), *Facts, frameworks, and forecasts: Advances in criminological theory* (Vol. 3, pp. 63–93). New Brunswick, NJ: Transition Press.

Sampson, R. J. (1999). What "community" supplies. In R. Ferguson & W. T. Dickens (Eds.), *Urban problems and community development.* Washington, DC: Brookings Institution.

Sampson, R. J., Morenoff, J. D., & Earls, F. (1999). Beyond social capital: Spatial dynamics of collective efficacy for children. *American Sociological Review, 64,* 633–660.

Sampson, R. J., Raudenbush, S. W., & Earls, F. (1997). Neighborhoods and violent crime: A multilevel study of collective efficacy. *Science, 277,* 918–924.

Sawicki, D. A., & Flynn, P. (1996). Neighborhood indicators: A review of the literature and assessment of conceptual and methodological issues. *Journal of American Planning, 62,* 165–183.

Schorr, L. (1997). *Common purpose: Strengthening families and neighborhoods to rebuild America.* New York: Doubleday.

Schwab-Stone, M., Ayers, T. S., & Kasprow, W. (1995). No safe haven: A study of violence exposure in an urban community. *Journal of the American Academy of Child and Adolescent Psychiatry, 34,* 1343–1352.

Seidman, E. (1991). Growing up the hard way: Pathways of urban adolescents. *American Journal of Community Psychology, 19,* 173–205.

Seidman, E., Yoshikawa, H., Roberts, A., Chesir-Teran, D., Allen, L., Friedman, J. L., & Aber, J. L. (1998). Structural and experiential neighborhood contexts, developmental stage, and antisocial behavior among urban adolescents in poverty. *Development and Psychopathology, 10,* 259–281.

Simmons, R. I., Johnson, C., Beaman, J. J., Conger, R. D., & Whitbeck, L. B. (1996). Parents and peer group as mediators of the effect of community structure on adolescent behavior. *American Journal of Community Psychology, 24,* 145–171.

Simon, D., & Burns, E. (1997). *The corner: A year in the life of an inner-city neighborhood.* New York: Broadway Books.

Snipp, C. M. (1996). Understanding race and ethnicity in rural America. *Rural Sociology, 61,* 125–142.

Solon, G., Page, M. E., & Duncan, G. J. (1997). *Correlations between neighboring children in their subsequent educational attainment* (Mimeo). University of Michigan, Ann Arbor.

Soto, L. D. (1990). *Families as learning environments: Reflections on critical factors affecting differential achievement.* Technical Report, Pennsylvania State University, University Park.

South, S. J. (in press). Issues in the analysis of neighborhoods, families, and children. In A. Booth & A. C. Crouter (Eds.), *Does it take a village? Community effects on children, adolescents, and families.* Mahwah, NJ: Erlbaum.

Spencer, M. B. (in press). Resiliency and fragility factors associated with the contextual experiences of low resource urban African American male youth and families. In A. Booth & A. C. Crouter (Eds.), *Does it take a village? Community effects on children, adolescents, and families.* Mahwah, NJ: Erlbaum.

Spencer, M. B., Cole, S. P., Jones, S. M., & Swanson, D. P. (1997). Neighborhood and family influences on young urban adolescents' behavior problems: A multisample, multisite analysis. In J. Brooks-Gunn, G. J.

Duncan, & J. L. Aber (Eds.), *Neighborhood poverty* (Vol. I, pp. 200–218). New York: Russell Sage Foundation.

Stack, C. B. (1996). *Call to home.* New York: Basic Books.

Stern, S. B., & Smith, C. A. (1995). Family processes and delinquency in an ecological context. *Social Service Review, 69,* 703–731.

Stevenson, H. C. (1998). Raising safe villages: Cultural-ecological factors that influence the emotional adjustment of adolescents. *Journal of Black Psychology, 24,* 44–59.

Suarez-Orozco, C., & Suarez-Orozco, M. (1995). *Transformations: Immigration, family life, and achievement motivation among Latino adolescents.* Stanford, CA: Stanford University Press.

Sucoff, C. A. (1998). Neighborhood context and the risk of childbearing among metropolitan-area black adolescents. *American Sociological Review, 63,* 571–585.

Sullivan, M. L. (1989). *Getting paid: Youth crime and work in the inner city.* Ithaca, NY: Cornell University Press.

Sullivan, M. L. (1993). Puerto Ricans in Sunset Park, Brooklyn: Poverty amidst ethnic and economic diversity. In J. Moore & R. Pinderhughes (Eds.), *Poor Latino communities in the United States: Beyond the underclass debate* (pp. 1–26). New York: Russell Sage Foundation.

Sullivan, M. L. (in press). Hyperghettos and hypermasculinity: The phenomenology of exclusion. In A. Booth & A. C. Crouter (Eds.), *Does it take a village: Community effects on children, adolescents, and families.* Mahwah, NJ: Erlbaum.

Tarlov, S. M., & Pittman, K. (1994). *Integrating youth participation and neighborhood development: Expressions from the field.* Washington, DC: Center for Youth Development and Policy Research, Academy for Educational Development.

Tienda, M. (1991). Poor people in poor places: Deciphering neighborhood effects on poverty outcomes. In J. Huber (Ed.), *Macro-micro linkages in sociology* (pp. 244–262). Newbury Park, CA: Sage.

Toro-Morn, M. (1995). Gender, class, family, and migration: Puerto Rican women in Chicago. *Gender and Society, 9,* 706–720.

Valdes, G. (1996). *Con respto: Bridging the distances between culturally diverse families and schools.* New York: Columbia University, Teachers College Press.

Vartanian, T. P. (1999). Childhood conditions and adult welfare use: Examining neighborhood and family factors. *Journal of Marriage and the Family, 61,* 225–237.

Vigil, J. D. (1997). *Personas Mexicanas: Chicano high schoolers in a changing Los Angeles.* Fort Worth, TX: Harcourt Brace College.

Volk, D. (1994). A case study of parent involvement in the homes of three Puerto Rican kindergartners. *Journal of Educational Issues of Language Minority Students, 14,* 89–113.

Volk, D. (1997). Questions in lessons: Activity settings in the homes and school of two Puerto Rican kindergartners. *Anthropology and Education Quarterly, 28,* 22–49.

Williams, T., & Kornblum, W. (1994). *The uptown kids: Struggle and hope in the projects.* New York: G. P. Putnam.

Wilson, W. H. (1998). *Hamilton Park: A planned Black community in Dallas.* Baltimore, MD: Johns Hopkins University Press.

Wilson, W. J. (1987). *The truly disadvantaged: The inner city, the underclass, and public policy.* Chicago: University of Chicago Press.

Wilson, W. J., Quane, J. M., & Rankin, B. H. (1998). The new urban poverty: Consequences of the economic and social decline of inner-city neighborhoods. In F. R. Harris & L. A. Curtis (Eds.), *Locked in the poorhouse: Cities, race, and poverty in the United States.* New York: Rowman & Littlefield.

Winston, P., Angel, R., Burton, L., Chase-Lansdale, P. L., Cherlin, A., Moffitt, R., & Wilson, W. J. (1999). *Welfare, children, and families: A three city study. Overview and design.* Baltimore: Johns Hopkins University Press.

Wong, B. P. (1998). *Ethnicity and entrepreneurship: The new Chinese immigrants in the San Francisco Bay Area.* Boston: Allyn and Bacon.

Wood, D., Halfon, N., Scarlata, D., Newacheck, D., & Nessim, S. (1993). Impact of family relocation on children's growth, development, school function, and behavior. *Journal of the American Medical Association, 270,* 1334–1338.

Yen, I., & Kaplan, G. (in press). Neighborhood social environment and risk of death: Multilevel evidence from the Alameda County Study. *American Journal of Epidemiology.*

Zhou, M. (1992). *Chinatown: The socioeconomic potential of an urban enclave.* Philadelphia: Temple University Press.

KAREN BOGENSCHNEIDER   *University of Wisconsin—Madison*

Has Family Policy Come of Age? A Decade Review of the State of U.S. Family Policy in the 1990s

Family policy has come of age in the 1990s, yet it has not achieved a status commensurate with that of economic or environmental policy. Because family policy has been difficult to define, this review proposes an explicit definition of the term family policy *and a companion implicit term,* a family perspective in policy making. *It updates the rationale for family policy, arguing that family commitment at its core is particularly consequential in an individualistic market economy with a small social safety net. It chronicles recent developments including philanthropic commitments, state and federal policy initiatives, and the use of research to inform family policy making. Selected family policy issues including family and work conflict, long-term care, family poverty, and marriage, are overviewed. The paper concludes with developments during the decade in theory, methods, and dissemination that hold the potential for capitalizing on the current popularity of families as a theme in policy making.*

The field of family policy was conceived in the 1970s and has come of age in the 1990s. A watershed event in the field's formative years, the 1980 White House Conference on Families, was instrumental in putting families on the political agenda, but it proved so politically contentious

University of Wisconsin—Madison, 201a Child & Family Studies, 1430 Linden Drive, Madison, WI 53706 (kpbogens@facstaff.wisc.edu).

Key Words: family perspective in policy making, family policy.

that it stymied any federal development for almost a decade. With its reemergence in the 1990s, family policy is much like an adolescent on the cusp of adulthood, its future hanging in the balance. Was family policy in the 1990s a futile endeavor with a short life expectancy, as prophesied by doomsayers in the early 1980s (Steiner, 1981), or did it mature into "a full-fledged adult in the policy world" (Jacobs & Davies, 1994, p. 290)?

At the dawn of the decade, family policy was a concept without a consistent definition, a perspective lacking a solid rationale, a field in need of legitimization, and a rhetoric in search of grounding and guidance from theory and practice. This article reviews progress on each of these fronts by addressing six fundamental questions: First, has the field reached consensus on definitions of family policy to guide research and action? Second, what evidence has emerged in the decade in support of the rationale that policy making should aim to strengthen families? Third, given that families have historically been considered primarily a private matter, have family issues been a legitimate focus of policy making during the decade? Fourth, what family policy issues of the 1990s are likely to be debated in the new millennium? Fifth, has research been used to inform the design and implementation of family policies? Finally, what developments during the decade in theory, methods, and dissemination hold potential for advancing the field?

Reviewing 10 years of research in a field that spans as many disciplines as family policy does is clearly an impossible task, so this review is nec-

355

essarily selective. Specifically, I focused on child, adolescent, communitarian, family, psychology, and sociology journals and paid less attention to ethics, family law, family history, or political science journals. Moreover, foundations, government agencies, public interest groups, and think tanks issue a huge number of policy reports, and I have drawn from some of these, but clearly not all.

HAS THE FIELD REACHED CONSENSUS ON DEFINITIONS?

Defining family policy has proven so difficult that it has been likened to "swimming in molasses or nailing Jell-O to a tree" (Blankenhorn, 1990, p. 5). This issue, raised in the 1990 decade review (Aldous & Dumon, 1990), is still not resolved. Scholars have been unable to agree on definitions but have agreed that an essential first task in moving the field forward, in terms of research or action, is to reach some consensus on what family policy means (e.g., see Moen & Jull, 1995; Wisensale, in press). Definitions are important because progress depends on identifying what the parameters are—what family policy is, what it is not, and what it can achieve (Schattschneider, 1960). Imprecise language invites imposters who borrow the politically popular, nonpartisan family label (Skocpol, 1997) as a "Trojan horse" for narrow individualistic agendas (Blankenhorn, 1988b, p. 6; Ooms, 1990).

Definitions of the term family policy have been marked by differences in scope, content, target, and source. Kamerman and Kahn (1978) defined the scope of family policy as "everything that government does to and for the family" (p. 3). Critics have contended that defining family policy broadly enough to include defense policy or economic edicts results in a concept so elastic that it encompasses almost everything and consequently loses any integrity. Conversely, Moen and Schorr (1987, p. 795) defined family policy as "a widely agreed-on set of objectives for families, toward the realization of which the state (and other major social institutions) deliberately shapes programs and policies." Critics have contended that definitions requiring "deliberate" and "widely agreed upon" actions are so limiting that the definition becomes virtually meaningless. Some definitions restrict family policy to the economic functions of families (Seaberg, 1990), to families with children (Rosenberg & Limber, 1996), or to actions by governmental bodies (Aldous & Dumon, 1990), thereby disregarding the large number of family

policies that emanate from employers and non-profit organizations.

Family Policy and a Family Perspective in Policy Making

Perhaps this confusion can be clarified by returning to the roots of the field in the early writing of Kamerman and Kahn (1978), who made a clear distinction between explicit policies designed to achieve specific goals regarding families and implicit policies not specifically or primarily intended to affect families but having indirect consequences on them. Paralleling this distinction, explicit and implicit terms are proposed, both of which build on a broad definition of policy as the development, enactment, and implementation of a law, rule, code, or judicial decision in the public or private sector. The explicit term, *family policy,* is a subfield of social policy, which focuses on "family business" (Blankenhorn, 1990, p. 18), specifically four family functions: (a) family creation, (b) economic support, (c) childrearing, and (d) family caregiving (Consortium of Family Organizations, 1990; Ooms, 1990). Obviously, families also provide members with love and emotional support, but such aspects matter to social policy only when they interfere with these four major functions (Ooms).

A companion implicit term, *a family perspective in policy making,* acknowledges the important role that family considerations can play on a broad range of policy issues (Kamerman & Kahn, 1978; Ooms, 1990). A family perspective in policy making analyzes the consequences of any policy or program, regardless of whether it is explicitly aimed at families, for its impact on family well-being (e.g., family stability, family relationships, and the family's ability to carry out its responsibilities).

To clarify these terms, Ooms (1990) offered several examples. Family policy would include issues encompassed under the four family functions, such as child care, child support, divorce, family violence, juvenile crime, long-term care, and teenage pregnancy. Tax provisions that create a child care tax credit or decrease the marriage penalty would be classified as family policy. However, a tax reform law that lowers taxes for individuals, many of whom live in families, would not be considered family policy. Other issues such as health care, housing, poverty, substance abuse, and unemployment would not be considered family policies because they are not aimed specifically at families. Nevertheless, these issues would certainly benefit from a family perspective that examines in what ways families contribute to problems, how families are affected by problems, and whether they need to be involved in solutions (Ooms).

At the heart of both terms is the critical family element, which moves beyond one individual to a relationship between two or more individuals, a distinction that is often overlooked in policy circles. For example, children's policy or women's policy is often incorrectly equated with family policy even though an individual, not a family relationship, is targeted. Family, when mentioned in policy debate, is sometimes misused to represent some, but not all, relationships in families. For example, *family* can be a code word for mother and child, with scant, if any, attention to father (Blum, 1993). The commonly used term *single-parent family* masks the role of noncustodial parents in the lives of their children (Walsh, 1995). Or *family* is used as a shorthand term to represent the relationship of parent and child, often ignoring the relationship of the adults in the family through marriage or other partnerships.

What Evidence Has Emerged That Policy Making Should Aim to Strengthen Families?

A rationale for why and how policies can strengthen families has emerged from several sources in the previous decade, three of which are discussed here: broad-based popular support for family-focused policy making, research on the value of families in American society, and evaluation studies documenting the effectiveness of family-focused policies and programs.

Broad-Based Support for Family-Focused Policy Making

Political interest in children and families has rebounded from the lows of the 1980s, which has led to claims that families as a theme in policy making is at its highest peak in the last 20 years among policy makers, professionals, and the public (Hutchins, 1998; Ooms, 1995; Whitehead, 1992). In studies of policy makers, state legislative leaders have called child and family issues a "surefire vote winner" (State Legislative Leaders Foundation, 1995, introduction). Importantly, this concern for families is not Republican or Democratic, conservative or liberal (Jacobs & Davies, 1994). For example, in the 1994 Republican Con-

tract with America, 4 of the 10 proposals dealt specifically with families; less than 2 years later, the Democrats rallied around "Families First" as their campaign slogan (Wisensale, 1999). In the 1996 bid for the presidency, both candidates battled to be the bearer of the family banner (Rosenberg & Limber, 1996).

Professionals have called for family-focused policy making in several reports issued by national commissions, nonprofit organizations, and professionals who serve families (Finance Project, 1996; Institute for Educational Leadership, 1997; Kumpfer, 1993; National Commission on America's Urban Families, 1993; National Commission on Child Welfare and Family Preservation, 1990; National Commission on Children, 1991a; State Legislative Leaders Foundation, 1995; U.S. Department of Education Office of Educational Research and Improvement, 1991). Of these organizations, perhaps the most influential is the bipartisan National Commission on Children, which met for 2½ years, reviewed the current state of knowledge on children and families, conducted a national opinion survey, and held hearings and focus groups in 11 communities across the country. Liberal and conservative members of the commission endorsed an agenda for children and families that contained 11 principles, three of which dealt with the primary role of families in rearing children and the obligation of society to help families fulfill this responsibility.

In a recent public opinion poll (Bennett, Petts, & Blumenthal, 1999), a resounding 99% of Americans reported that loving family relationships are extremely (91%) or somewhat (9%) important to them, beliefs that a 1982 survey indicated are almost identical among Blacks and Whites (Wilson, 1999). Nine of ten married people find their greatest joy in the family, but so do more than half of single Americans and almost three fourths of those who are currently divorced (Mellman, Lazarus, & Rivlin, 1990). Yet, in recent polls of families with children, four out of five reported that it is harder to be a parent today than it used to be (Hewlett & West, 1998; National Commission on Children, 1991b), owing in part to conditions outside the family that could potentially be shaped by policy—economic pressures, social isolation, and unsafe streets and neighborhoods (National Commission on Children). Most Americans would probably agree that childrearing is primarily the responsibility of families, yet they believe that government has a responsibility to create the conditions under which parents can do their best. In

1998, only 6% of parents said government was doing a great deal to help them with their concerns, yet 47% said government could be doing a great deal to help them, and 37% said government could do something to help them (Hewlett & West).

Research on the Value of Families in American Society

Families teach the powerful moral lesson of the value of commitment (Bayme, 1991; Doherty, 1995) and perhaps have always done so (Kane & Penrod, 1995). This commitment is universal in all human societies because the prospects that the young will survive depend on close association with older members of the species (e.g., Bronfenbrenner & Weiss, 1983; Eastman, 1996). Yet commitment may be particularly consequential in the United States to counter the self-interest of an individualistic culture, the materialistic pressures of a market economy, and the meager assistance of a small social safety net.

Family commitment in an individualistic culture. In his classic writing on democracy in the United States in the 1830s, Tocqueville (1945) worried that freedom was threatened by individualism, the tendency of Americans to isolate themselves from their responsibilities to the larger society by focusing exclusively on themselves and their families. If unchecked, individualism could isolate people from their ancestors, their contemporaries, and even their descendants as they come to believe they control their own destinies with nothing expected from or owed to others. Tocqueville observed that American individualism was tempered by religious and democratic political participation and the large number of voluntary associations he observed, but particularly by associations in the family, the first institution to teach "habits of the heart" that can counter isolationism with a larger view of public responsibility.

The individualism Tocqueville observed in the last century remains pervasive in American culture today (Bellah, Madsen, Sullivan, Swidler, & Tipton, 1996). Early in the decade, the Responsive Communitarian Platform (1992) issued a call for a better balance between our rights as individuals and our responsibilities as members of families and communities. Like our Founding Fathers, communitarians believe that democracy cannot be sustained without a citizenry willing to respect the rights of others and to assume responsibilities for

the collective good, even when such actions exact a personal cost (Glendon, 1992). Like Tocqueville, communitarians believe that cultivating the moral foundations for balancing obligations to self and others begins in the family. As exemplified in recent cross-cultural research, American mothers typically perceive their babies as being born dependent and parent them in ways that build independence and self-reliance, whereas Japanese mothers view babies as being born independent, so their parenting is aimed at building dependence and reliance on the group (Barratt, 1993).

The consequences of individualism have become even more apparent in the past decade (Bellah et al., 1996; Blankenhorn, 1990; Bumpass, 1990). Two contemporary examples of the individualistic tendency to pursue private interests and ignore obligations to the rest of society are the highest rates of income inequality between the rich and the poor in recent U.S. history and declines in the Tocquevillian life of civic engagement (Bellah et al.).

In an analysis of American civic engagement in the 1990s, Putnam (1995) noted that voter turnout has dropped by nearly 25% since 1960, attendance at public meetings has fallen by more than a third since 1970, union membership has plummeted by about half since the mid-1950s, participation in parent-teacher organizations has dropped by 40% since the 1960s, and church membership has stagnated or declined since the 1970s. Many major civic organizations also have experienced a sudden substantial decline in membership. Overall, Putnam concluded that associational memberships have fallen by about one fourth in the last quarter century among all educational and social sectors. Given that such associations build tolerance and social trust (Boyte & Etzioni, 1993; Wilson, 1999), declining civic engagement may account, in part, for drops in Americans' belief that most people can be trusted, down from 58% in 1960 to 37% in 1993 (Putnam). Putnam's analysis has been criticized because he assessed only the quantity, not the quality, of social ties and because he omitted some relevant associations such as work-related groups that Americans may join. Yet even his critics acknowledge that the richness of social ties has declined and selfishness in America has increased (Wolfe, 1998).

Family commitment in a strong market economy. The family ethos of commitment may assume greater importance in capitalistic countries to temper the self-interest that often drives market economies (Schor, 1991) and that can undermine our connections to others (Bellah, 1990). For example, between 1969 and 1987, the average employed American worked an additional 163 hours annually, or an extra month each year. Some of these extra hours are obviously worked out of necessity, but not all of them are; work hours have increased irrespective of income or family structure. The extra income apparently buys more material goods, as Americans own and consume twice as much as their 1948 counterparts (Schor). Bellah warned that the greatest threat to strong families and a good society is an economy that becomes too coercive, creating a culture of consumerism so potent that it transforms "today's luxuries" into "tomorrow's necessities" (Schor, p. 122).

Consumerism also has invaded families in other ways. For example, Americans complain that spending more time at work steals time away from their families, yet only one third report that they would refuse a job that offered more money or prestige even though it would mean less time for their family (Mellman et al., 1990). Perhaps most disturbing is a recent study primarily of a Fortune 500 company that indicates a cultural reversal of the meaning of work and home (Hochschild, 1997). A surprising 85% of employees reported that home often feels like work, and 58% reported that work often feels like home. When asked about their performance in each setting, 86% said their performance was good or unusually good on the job, but only 59% give these same ratings to their performance in the family.

Family commitment in a society with a weak social safety net. The family often serves as the failsafe in the United States with its small social safety net (i.e., government antipoverty programs). Compared with the education system in societies with extensive government support, American schools rely more on parents for children's academic readiness. With privatized health care, hospitals send patients home before they have recuperated, assuming that families will take up the slack. With a declining union presence, employers have come to expect that families will contribute to employee productivity by tolerating longer work hours and relieving the employee of routine family obligations as well as caregiving responsibilities during special events such as the birth, adoption, or illness of a family member (Giele, 1996). When safety nets are smaller and less certain, families serve more prominent roles as health

care providers, educators, social workers, and personnel managers for their members.

Evaluation Studies Documenting the Effectiveness of Family Approaches

Perhaps the most crucial issue in establishing a rationale for family policy is whether policies and programs would be more effective if approached from a family perspective rather than an individual perspective. The best evidence of the value of family-focused policies has emerged from experimental studies that train parents to improve their child management practices and then track the behavior of their children over time. Two streams of research are especially illustrative, one that focuses on a social problem, juvenile crime, and a second that focuses on a method of family support, home visiting.

Juvenile crime. Researchers have learned that 30 to 40% of the antisocial behavior of early offenders—who are those most likely to become chronic and violent offenders later—is tied to harsh, inconsistent parenting during the preschool years (e.g., Patterson, 1986). Yet most programs to prevent juvenile crime have focused on individuals and few have shown lasting success (Zigler, Taussig, & Black, 1992). Programs that focus on parenting have proven more promising. For example, in the Oregon Social Learning Center's parent education program, parents receive, on average, 20 hours of training on specific child management practices. Children from participating families displayed less antisocial behavior, with improvements large enough to bring the target child (and sibling) into the range of normal functioning (e.g., Patterson) and with effects lasting up to 4½ years (Baum & Forehand, 1981).

A more direct test of the value of a family-focused approach emerged from an experimental study of the Oregon Social Learning Center's Adolescent Transition Program, which compared a randomly assigned control group with interventions for parents only, youth only, both parents and youth, and self-directed materials (Dishion, Andrews, Kavanagh, & Soberman, 1996). In the long-term analysis, the teen-only group actually reported more smoking and worse school behavior than did the control group. Apparently, bringing high-risk youth together, no matter how skillfully, glamorized inappropriate behavior so that participants more eagerly adopted it. Compared with the combined control and self-directed groups, the parent-only training proved most effective in improving youth behavior at school and also in reducing tobacco and marijuana use 1 year later. Contrary to expectations, no benefits occurred for the combined parent-teen intervention. Thus, interventions retain their cost-effectiveness if training parents is emphasized and aggregating young adolescents is avoided (Dishion, McCord, & Poulin, 1999).

Home visiting. Home visiting has attracted considerable attention from policy makers despite inconclusive evaluations (Gomby, Culross, & Behrman, 1999). Promising results have emerged, however, from the methodologically sound longitudinal studies of nurse home visiting. Nurses visited low-income mothers, many of whom were unmarried teenagers, prenatally and during the first 2 years of the children's lives. Compared with families that received only transportation and developmental screening, nurse home visiting resulted in benefits to children's behavior and the mothers' life course 15 years later. The 15-year-olds born to low-income, nurse-visited mothers had 46% fewer verified reports of child abuse and neglect and also 56% fewer arrests. The nurse-visited mothers had an average of 69% fewer arrests, 37 fewer months on food stamps, 30 fewer months on Aid to Families With Dependent Children (AFDC), 23 fewer months on Medicaid, one fifth fewer subsequent births, and a spacing of 28 months more between first and second children (Olds et al., 1997, 1998). This successful intervention targeted parents at a key family transition point—the birth of a first child.

Taken together, these studies provide compelling examples of the potential of family-focused approaches. Not all family approaches have been this encouraging, however, particularly evaluations of teenage pregnancy prevention programs (Kirby, 1997) and two-generation welfare programs (St. Pierre, Layzer, & Barnes, 1996). Exaggerating the effectiveness of family programs to policy makers can be counterproductive, yet ignoring this demonstrated potential seems shortsighted.

HAVE FAMILY ISSUES BEEN A LEGITIMATE FOCUS OF POLICY MAKING DURING THE DECADE?

The legitimacy of family policy is contingent on whether families are perceived primarily as a personal matter or as a proper target for policy mak-

ing. This section chronicles family policy developments of the 1990s, including private philanthropic commitments and public policy initiatives enacted by federal and state governments. Developments at the federal and state levels are profiled because the 1990s have been characterized as a "Dr. Jekyll and Mr. Hyde decade," referring to the devolution of authority for policies from the federal to the state level and a simultaneous countertrend toward centralization and federal preemption of state authority (Tubbesing, 1998, p. 14). Special attention is devoted to efforts to collect family-related data because its absence has stymied progress in the field (Ooms, 1995). Obviously, the courts have played an active role in family issues during the decade, although a review of these cases is beyond the scope of this paper (see the annual review of federal and state legislative and judicial developments in the winter issue of *Family Law Quarterly*).

Philanthropic Commitments

During the 1990s, several foundations launched major initiatives that shaped the family field, influencing what issues might be legitimate topics for government actions and evaluating whether the actions taken by government legitimately reached their objectives for families. For example, the Edna McConnell Clark Foundation has a historical commitment to the doctrine of family preservation (i.e., cautioning the too-easy removal of children from families in which abuse or neglect is suspected or substantiated) that was later picked up by state and federal governments (Ooms, personal communication, October 16, 1999). The fatherhood movement was launched, in part, by the Funders Collaborative on Fathers and Families, which included the Casey, Danforth, Ford, and Mott Foundations (Carter, 1995). The Carnegie Council's Task Force on Meeting the Needs of Young Children and their Council on Adolescent Development led to several federal initiatives on children and adolescence (Ooms; Zigler, 1998). In the wake of welfare reform, 16 foundations have funded Assessing the New Federalism, an Urban Institute multiyear project to track the effects of the devolution of social welfare programs from the federal government to the states. In 1999, the inaugural issue of "Snapshots of American Families" was released, which provides a comprehensive overview of family well-being including employment, income, child support, program participation, and family life based on data from

44,461 randomly selected households and 900 low-income families with children in 13 states (see www.urban.org).

Federal Initiatives

During this decade, as in the past, the question faced by policy makers in the debate of family issues was not whether families needed support, but whether support should be provided by government, particularly the federal government (Trzcinski, 1995). During the decade, policies were enacted to address issues such as adoption, child abuse and neglect, child care, children's health insurance, child support, domestic violence, education, family leave, family preservation, family poverty, same-sex marriage, telecommunications, and welfare reform (see Table 1). In a recent analysis of public expenditures during the first half of the decade, Kamerman and Kahn (in press) reported a tripling of expenditures on child care, a doubling of direct cash benefits to families, and a 50% increase in family services. Federal and state expenditures have also increased during the second half of the decade, but firm data are not yet available. In 1997, President Clinton signed an executive order requiring family impact statements on policies affecting families, which, ironically, superseded a broader executive order issued by President Reagan in 1987 requiring agencies to review any proposed new policies for their potential impact on families (Elrod & Spector, 1998). During the decade, the National Governors' Association has been focusing gubernatorial attention on children and families, with special attention to welfare reform, child care, early childhood development, before and after school child care programs, and fatherhood (see www.nga.org). The National Conference of State Legislatures focused on child welfare and responsible fatherhood during the decade and expanded its efforts on child care and early education (see www.ncsl.org).

A new source of family data emerged, in part, from a national workshop calling for accessible, high-quality data on families to maximize connections to policy (see Hendershot & LeClere, 1993, for the proceedings published by the National Council on Family Relations). A 1997 executive order established the Interagency Forum on Child and Family Statistics, which requires the Office of Management and Budget to publish an annual report on the condition of America's children and families based on data from 18 federal agencies (see www.childstats.gov). Also, a guide to national surveys and other sources of family data was published by Westat and Child Trends (Zill & Daly, 1993).

State Initiatives

Family matters such as marriage, divorce, property distribution, and child welfare have traditionally fallen into the purview of state governments. Landmark devolution legislation in the 1990s transferred federal responsibility to states on a range of other issues including children's health insurance, family preservation, and welfare reform (Tubbesing, 1998). Devolution began early in the decade as states increasingly sought federal waivers but gained momentum in 1995 with the passing of the Unfunded Mandate Reform Act, which limited the ability of the federal government to mandate programs for which state and local governments must foot the bill. Devolution has provided state legislatures and governors with more responsibility and flexibility because categorical funding has been replaced with block grants (Tubbesing). The hallmarks of devolution are typically greater specificity by the federal government in elaborating the ends to be achieved through block grants, more discretion for states in the means of reaching those ends, and a growing shift of services from public to private sector providers such as Medicare health maintenance organizations and for-profit vendors for child care, prisons, and welfare programs (Pratt, 1998). The trend toward devolution has been counterbalanced, however, by proposed federal child care standards, national regulations on managed care practices (e.g., length of maternity stays), and tobacco settlements that preempt such state laws as sales to minors and vending machine sales.

State involvement in family policy during the decade has been extensive, and selected examples are cited here. State commissions, councils, or subcabinets were created in 30 states, primarily in the 1990s to assign greater priority to child and family issues, to facilitate better coordination among existing services, and to promote child and family collaboratives (see Hutchins, 1998). In 1994, the Finance Project was formed to develop strategies for public financing and administration of community-based family collaboratives to overcome rigidly categorical funding streams and entrenched bureaucratic structures. This nonprofit organization conducted policy research, provided policy maker forums and public education, and

TABLE 1. SELECTED FEDERAL FAMILY POLICIES ENACTED DURING THE 1990s

Year	Law	Provisions
1990	Child Care and Development Block Grant	Provided $22.5 billion to help states improve child care; provided child care tax credits; developed a new health insurance credit for broadening Head Start eligibility; initiated full-year Head Start Programming; expanded the earned income tax credit (EITC); and provided an additional EITC credit for infants (Wisensale, in press).
1992	Child Support Recovery Act	Made it a federal crime to willfully fail to pay child support awarded in another state; created a Commission on Child and Family Welfare with responsibilities for such issues as child custody, visitation, and domestic violence (Walker & Elrod, 1993).
1993	Family and Medical Leave Act	Provided 12 weeks of unpaid leave for a serious illness or to care for an ailing family member; ensured job security and health coverage during the leave (Wisensale, 1997).
1993	Family Preservation and Support Act	Provided almost $1 billion over 5 years (Jacobs & Davies, 1994) for community-based family services, including prevention and intervention programs to avoid unnecessary out-of-home placements (Early & Hawkins, 1994; Ooms, 1998).
1993	International Parental Kidnapping Crime Act	Established international parental abduction as a felony (Elrod, 1995).
1993	Omnibus Budget Reconciliation Act	Expanded the EITC by providing an additional $21 billion over 5 years (Jacobs & Davies, 1994); addressed court reforms in foster care and adoption cases; and mandated states to establish quick paternity procedures (Elrod, 1995).
1993	National Child Protection Act	Encouraged states' criminal background checks on child care providers (Elrod, 1995).
1994	Educate America Act	Promoted parental involvement in their children's schooling (Zimmerman, 1998).
1994	Full Faith and Credit for Child Support Orders Act	Required states to enforce child support orders established in other states; required employers to comply with child support orders that require noncustodial children to be included in health coverage (Elrod, 1995).
1994	Federal Budget	Allocated $550 million to Head Start with full funding by 1999 (Jacobs & Davies, 1994); initiated Early Head Start (McMurrer & Sawhill, 1998).
1994	Violence Against Women Act	As part of the Omnibus Crime Act, increased funding for battered women and established a national domestic violence hotline (Elrod, 1995).
1996	Debt Collection and Improvement Act	Denied federal loans and authorized interception of federal payments to parents owing child support (Elrod & Spector, 1997).
1996	Defense of Marriage Act	Defined marriage as a union between one man and one woman, which denied Social Security benefits to same-sex couples; stipulated that no state is required to recognize a same-sex marriage performed in another state (Elrod & Spector, 1997).
1996	Personal Responsibility and Work Opportunity Reconciliation Act (PRWORA)	Eliminated public assistance as an entitlement that ensured benefits if eligibility criteria were met. For families, the major federal provisions (some of which can be modified by states) are a 60-month time limit on welfare receipt using Temporary Assistance for Needy Families (TANF) funds, work requirements after 24 months of welfare receipt, the option to institute family caps that deny additional benefits to children born to parents receiving assistance, requirements that teen parents live with parents or other adults, stronger child support enforcement programs, mandates that states establish paternity for 90% of all births to unmarried women, restrictions on education and training to meet PRWORA requirements, the scaling back of food stamp benefits, a narrowing of supplemental security income eligibility standards, an elimination of federally funded public assistance for newly arriving immigrants, limitations on assistance to legal residents who are not citizens, and financial incentives for states to provide abstinence education (Wisensale, in press; Zaslow, Tout, Smith, & Moore, 1998).
1996	Telecommunications Reform Law	Mandated that new televisions include a V-chip to allow parents to screen out programs they judge inappropriate for their children (Galston, 1996).
1997	Adoption and Safe Family Act	Provided $875 million for a 3-year reauthorization of the Family Preservation and Support Act; promoted adoption and moving children quickly into safe, permanent placements.
1997	Balanced Budget Act	Provided a $500 child tax credit; authorized $24 billion for state health insurance for uninsured children; restored welfare benefits for disabled legal immigrants; and initiated Hope Scholarship tax credits of up to $1,500 per year (Wisensale, in press).
1998	Deadbeat Parents Act	Made it a felony for anyone who crosses a state line to evade a child support obligation (Elrod, Spector, & Atkinson, 1999).

drafted sample legislation for changes in state stat-utes (Finance Project, 1996).

Several developments transpired in the collec-tion of state-level family data in the 1990s. For example, because of budget cuts in 1995, the Na-tional Center on Health Statistics no longer com-piles national data from state reports on marriage and divorce, which limits the ability to describe trends within and across states (Ooms, 1998). In 1990, the Annie Casey Foundation began publish-ing *Kids Count,* an annual report card comparing states on key measures of child well-being which, by 1995, was also being published in every state. In 1995, *Map and Track* was launched by the Na-tional Center for Children in Poverty to track changes over time in state-initiated programs and policies for young children and their families (Knitzer & Page, 1996, 1998). In 1997, *Map and Track* also began tracking state initiatives to en-courage responsible fatherhood in cooperation with the Council of Governors' Policy Advisors and the National Center on Fathers and Families (Bernard & Knitzer, 1999; Knitzer, Bernard, Bren-ner, & Gadsden, 1997).

In the 1998 *Map and Track* report, more than two thirds of the states (34) were funding state-wide programs for preschoolers, about half (24) were funding statewide programs for infants and toddlers, and half (25) were funding statewide programs on parenting (Knitzer & Page, 1998). Despite this progress, the report concluded that state leadership was not strong enough and state investments not extensive enough. For example, only 10 states explicitly linked welfare strategies to comprehensive child and family initiatives oth-er than child care. In 1996 and 1998, only eight states met the criteria of *Map and Track* for com-prehensive initiatives, and seven states reported no state-initiated statewide programs for young chil-dren and families. In regard to fathering, state ef-forts have focused predominantly on financial in-volvement, particularly child support (Ooms, 1998). *Map and Track* reported that only four states demonstrated exemplary efforts in promot-ing both the financial and emotional involvement of fathers with their children. To date, state efforts focus primarily on teen fathers and low-income noncustodial fathers, with little attention to father-friendly workplace policies or fathers in two-par-ent families (Bernard & Knitzer, 1999).

Across the decade, so many family policy ini-tiatives were undertaken and so many family pol-icies enacted that the legitimacy question appears to be answered—families are a legitimate focus of government at all levels, although debate over how and when government should intervene will undoubtedly continue.

WHAT FAMILY POLICY ISSUES OF THE 1990s ARE LIKELY TO BE DEBATED IN THE NEW MILLENNIUM?

During the decade, several family policies have achieved prominence—albeit sometimes fleeting (see Table 1). For illustrative purposes, this sec-tion focuses on four issues that are likely to be front-burner family policies beyond the 1990s: family and work conflict, long-term care, family poverty, and marriage. The role of family diver-sity in developing and sustaining family policies is also examined.

Family and Work Conflict

The concern voiced most often by parents, conflict between work and family, transcends class, race, ethnicity, and family structure (Moen & Jull, 1995). Family and work conflict has been coined the "double squeeze" (Skocpol, 1997, p. 119)— a squeeze on economic resources and a simulta-neous squeeze on the time and energy needed for family and community commitments (Hewlett & West, 1998). Schor (1991) explained that between 1969 and 1987, the average employed Ameri-can—irrespective of income, marital status, or oc-cupation—worked an additional 163 hours annu-ally on the job. Because time spent on domestic labor, including housework and child care, re-mained almost the same, this statistic means that Americans worked, on average, 1 extra month each year. The time that family members spent in the labor force continued to increase between 1989 and 1995 (Center on Budget and Policy Pri-orities, 1998), with families raising children log-ging in the longest hours (Moen & Yu, 1999).

Some Americans prefer to work longer hours (Hochschild, 1997), but many do not. In a nation-ally representative sample of 4,554 married cou-ples, 44% of men and 34% of women reported working substantially more hours than they pre-ferred (Clarkberg & Moen, 1999). Only 15% re-ported a preference for full-time employment even though 48% worked full-time, and half of these worked more than 40 hours in a typical week. This preference for less than full-time employ-ment held for all ages and education levels in this nationally representative sample (Families and Work Institute, 1995). Those who work more hours than they prefer experience more work-life conflict, more stress, more overload, and an impaired sense of coping and mastery (Moen & Yu, 1999).

In studies of how parental work affects child outcomes, no uniform effects of parental employment have emerged. Instead, the effects appear to depend on several mediating, moderating, and developmental influences, such as the complexity of the job, the time and material resources of the parent, and demands on parental resources such as the partner's job, the number of siblings, and the recent birth of an additional child (Parcel & Menaghan, 1994). Increases in family income appear to benefit the child (see Perry-Jenkins, Repetti, & Crouter, this volume), but small negative effects are reported if both mother and father worked overtime (Parcel & Menaghan) and if the mother worked more hours during the early years (Baydar & Brooks-Gunn, 1991; Belsky & Eggebeen, 1991; Bogenschneider & Steinberg, 1994; Harvey, 1999).

Three theoretical approaches have been proposed to guide policy responses when family and work conflict (Parasuraman & Greenhaus, 1997). First, the situation can be modified by restructuring or role negotiation through such policies as providing more flexible time schedules, improving child care, and making family leave a legal right. In a recent national survey, 90% of mothers and fathers wanted access to compressed work weeks, flextime, job sharing, and part-time work with benefits (Hewlett & West, 1998). Yet policies need to move beyond enabling employees to increase their time at work or take more time away from work, to changing the conditions of work that harm family life (see Perry-Jenkins et al., this volume). Others have advocated for a fundamental restructuring that moves beyond a "family-friendly corporation" to a "family-friendly society" (Goggins, 1997, p. 230) in which family life is more broadly supported by friends, schools, service agencies, and civic organizations.

A second theoretical perspective proposes that employees could learn specific techniques for better managing work-induced strain. For example, recent studies have identified specific strategies that married couples use to scale back, such as placing limits on job demands, choosing a one-job/one-career marital pattern, and trading off these strategies (Becker & Moen, 1999). Finally, a third theoretical orientation suggests modifying the meaning of the situation through personal role reorientation. Some working families are in a time

bind because they *want* to work more hours to earn more money (Schor, 1991) or to avoid family conflicts and responsibilities (Hochschild, 1997); these findings imply the need for policies that promote personal commitments to family life and foster a cultural climate that supports these commitments.

Long-Term Care

Long-term care includes a broad range of services given over a sustained period to the disabled or the frail elderly whose disability results in long-term difficulties in functioning (Kane, Kane, & Ladd, 1998). Long-term care is a family issue because four of five disabled elderly living in the community rely on assistance from family and others, with three of five relying exclusively on unpaid help, usually from wives and daughters (Stone, 1999). Families make care arrangements, respond in emergencies, and offer assistance with such daily living activities as shopping, cleaning, and meal preparation. Long-term care needs are increasing because of the aging of the baby boomers and advances in medical technology, which keep people alive longer. The over-65 population is expected to double by 2040, and the ratio of available caregivers to those needing care is expected to decline by almost two thirds by the year 2050 (Stone).

For caregivers, a prominent law in the decade is the 1993 Family and Medical Leave Act, which requires employers with more than 50 workers to provide up to 12 weeks of unpaid leave to care for an ailing family member. Although federal oversight and dollars exist, long-term care is largely controlled by the states (Kane et al., 1998). In an analysis of long-term care policies in 13 states, three general strategies have emerged: (a) offsetting state spending by encouraging the purchase of private long-term care insurance, maximizing Medicaid financing of long-term care, and reducing Medicaid estate planning whereby individuals manage assets to appear poor enough to qualify for Medicaid-financed care; (b) reorganizing health care delivery to make it more efficient through expanding home- and community-based options and extending managed care to include long-term care; and (c) using traditional cost-saving measures such as controlling the supply of providers and lowering reimbursement rates. Nursing homes have been the predominant long-term care providers, but younger people with disabilities recently advocated for more home- and community-based options (Wiener & Sullivan, 1995). Given the amount of need and the number of affected parties—nursing homes and other providers, health professionals, advocates for the disabled and the elderly—long-term care promises to continue as a contentious family policy issue (Kane et al.).

Family Poverty

Poverty rates have been lower recently than in the past, yet these trends are offset by growing income disparity between the rich and the poor. In their 1998 and 1999 State of the Union messages, President Clinton and his Republican critics made no mention of income disparity, an issue that has received considerable scholarly attention, but less scrutiny outside academia (e.g., Center on Budget and Policy Priorities, 1998; Hewlett & West, 1998; McMurrer & Sawhill, 1998; Wilson, 1997). This economic trend seems an anomaly in an otherwise strong economy—low unemployment rates, rising consumer confidence, and a record high percentage of adults who are employed (Larin, 1998). Yet, contrary to what happened in the 3 decades after World War II, this strong economic growth has not been shared equally among all families. For example, between 1979 and 1995, family incomes rose by 26% in the top fifth of families and fell by 9% in the bottom fifth. This widening gap between the rich and the poor has been consistent across Black and White households (Center on Budget and Policy Priorities; Wilson) and also across states. From 1994 to 1996, the top fifth of families with children had, on average, almost 13 times the income of the bottom fifth, with differentials among states ranging from a low of 7 to a high of almost 20. In the 1970s, no state had an income differential greater than 10, whereas in the mid-1990s, 30 states did (Larin).

These economic trends have repercussions for families and particularly the well-being of children (see White & Rogers, this volume). Family income is a potent predictor of children's development across income groups, with one third to one half of its impact accounted for by parenting practices, the home learning environment, and family structure (McMurrer & Sawhill, 1998). Of a number of policies that address family poverty, four are discussed here. First, the 1996 Personal Responsibility and Work Opportunity Reconciliation Act (PRWORA), with its provisions that address marriage, teenage parenting, fathering, child

support, and family caps, was one of the decade's most significant family policies (see provisions in Table 1). Through its Temporary Assistance for Needy Families (TANF) program, PRWORA accelerated trends that transformed the culture of welfare from a focus on income support to work and self-sufficiency. By January 1999, every state had in place a new welfare system based on work (Tweedie, 1999). Some believe that TANF, with its work requirements, sanctions, and marginal tax rates, is simply another name for welfare. Yet the Welfare Peer Assistance Network, a group of senior welfare administrators from the Midwest, believes that further shifts may be occurring toward community and family concerns, particularly the well-being of children (Corbett, 2000). Former welfare agencies are dealing with child welfare, domestic violence, teenage pregnancy, education, and juvenile crime. Work remains a major goal, but increasingly as a way of stabilizing families, improving parents' ability to function as caregivers, and encouraging fuller participation in society (Corbett).

With TANF reauthorization approaching, several major evaluation studies are underway to measure the success of welfare reform (see the Web site of the Research Forum on Children, Families, and the New Federalism at www. researchforum.org). Success may be measured by reductions in caseloads, which currently have dropped by at least 50%. Because of media and policymaker attention to these plummeting caseloads (Pratt, 1998), the welfare reform debate has been primarily one-generational, focusing on enhancing parents' self-sufficiency or breadwinning capacity. As an alternative, scholars have proposed two-generation approaches that simultaneously focus on parents' caregiving capacity (e.g., Smith, Blank, & Collins, 1992), arguing that if children are neglected and unable to become self-sufficient adults, the investment in their parents' employment may well be squandered (Blum, 1992). Family scholars caution that welfare reform should not be declared a success without an examination of family outcomes such as child maltreatment rates, child poverty rates, the quality of parenting and the home environment, homelessness, and the accessibility, affordability, and quality of child care (e.g., Pratt).

A second policy that is credited with lifting 4.3 million Americans out of poverty in 1997 is the Earned Income Tax Credit (EITC) program. The EITC targets working families with children and was expanded under Democratic and Republican administrations during the decade (Hotz & Scholz, 2000). In an attempt to reward working families and reduce reliance on welfare, a cash subsidy is provided to earnings up to a specific income level, but no money is granted to those without earnings. The EITC is an appealing policy to assist low-income working families because of its work incentive, its relatively low administrative costs, and its targeting. About two thirds of all EITC payments go to taxpayers with wages in the bottom quartile of all workers with children (Hotz & Scholz). At least 12 states have adopted state EITCs and others are considering it.

A third policy response has been to fund a broad array of investments in children, including early childhood programs, quality child care, home visiting, and Head Start. The interest of federal and state policy makers in early intervention may be due, in part, to the heightened need for child care as welfare recipients entered employment, to media attention to early brain development, and to scientific evidence on the importance of the early years. Of particular relevance to policy was longitudinal research linking home visits conducted prenatally and during the first 2 years of a baby's life to the mother's reduced reliance on AFDC, food stamps, and Medicaid 15 years later (Olds et al., 1997, 1998). Also, longitudinal studies of the Abecedarian Project demonstrated high-quality, multifaceted interventions beginning early in infancy can alter the course of intellectual development. At age 21, the benefits included delayed parenthood, higher IQs, higher reading and math scores, and more years of formal education especially for teenage mothers (Ramey et al., 1999; Ramey & Ramey, 1999).

Finally, an obvious policy question that arises from growing income inequality is whether people, particularly the disadvantaged, can move out of poverty by climbing up the rungs of the economic ladder. Mobility rates have remained substantial, but virtually unchanged, over the last 25 years. In the 1980s, a college education became and has remained the ticket to mobility. The family is a powerful influence on school success and increasingly so (McMurrer & Sawhill, 1998). For example, a family's socioeconomic status (i.e., education, income, and occupation) is a powerful predictor of whether children attend college and, when enrolled, whether they complete a degree (McMurrer & Sawhill). Yet educational reform has focused primarily on school organization, course curriculum, instructional methods, and

teacher training. Steinberg (1996) concluded that 15 years of such reforms have accomplished little because academic achievement is shaped more by the conditions of students' lives outside school. Despite evidence of a substantial family component to school success and economic mobility, family scholars have traditionally ignored educational issues (Seeley, 1985), and family advocates typically exclude education from their policy agenda (for an exception, see Lewis & Henderson, 1997).

Marriage

Three major demographic trends were on the family policy radar screen in the 1990s: Almost one third of all births were outside marriage; nearly 40% of children did not live with their biological father; and more than half of all first marriages in the United States are estimated to end in divorce (see Teachman, Tedrow, & Crowder, 2000). A phenomenon underlying these trends has received little public attention—the pervasive decline in marriage across all sectors of society (Ooms, 1998).

Ooms (1998) argued that marriage should be on the public agenda for four reasons. First, married men and women are healthier, live longer, and have fewer emotional problems (Eastman, 1996). A recent study confirmed the relationship between marriage and personal happiness in 16 of 17 industrialized countries, with marriage contributing to happiness substantially more than cohabitation (Stack & Eshleman, 1998). Second, married fathers are more apt to be involved with their children because fathers' relationship to their offspring, more than mothers', is tied to the quality of the relationship between parents (Doherty, Kouneski, & Erickson, 1998). Third, although debate continues about the effect of single parenthood or stepfamilies on child well-being, there is little question that children do well economically, socially, and psychologically if their biological parents have a strong, conflict-free marriage (Glenn, 1996; McLanahan & Sandefur, 1994). Finally, marriage has economic impacts in that married people work harder, earn and save more, and accumulate greater wealth (Forthofer, Markman, Cox, Stanley, & Kessler, 1996).

With 90% of Americans wanting to marry and expecting to stay married (Thornton, 1996), marriage would seem to be a nonpartisan issue. Yet policy efforts so far have been sporadic, uncoordinated, and unsupported by think tanks, foundations, or government commissions, amid concerns that marriage is a code word for an ideological agenda to de-liberate women, stigmatize single parents, or force women to remain in abusive patriarchal relationships. Acknowledging these concerns, Ooms (1998) proposed an agenda that would strengthen marriage "to make it better to be in rather than more difficult to get out of" (p. 5).

The first federal laws to explicitly address marriage emerged this decade with the passage of the 1996 welfare law, which promoted two-parent families, and the 1996 Defense of Marriage Act, which limited marriage to heterosexual couples. Family resource centers have sprung up around the country, but they focus almost exclusively on improving parent-child relationships, and little or no attention is paid to the couple relationship despite its contribution to the quality of parenting. Oklahoma, with the second highest divorce rate in the nation, has recently launched a statewide initiative to strengthen marriage using $10 million of unused TANF funds. Florida passed a Marriage Preparation and Preservation Act in 1998, Louisiana passed a Covenant Marriage Act in 1997, and Arizona passed a similar bill in 1998 (Ooms, 1998). For updates, see the Couples and Marriage Policy Resource Center Web site: www.marriagepolicy.org.

Family Diversity Issues

Progress has been made in the decade on addressing inequities of gender, race, and ethnicity, but class divisions have deepened (Bellah et al., 1996; McMurrer & Sawhill, 1998; Wilson, 1997). For example, to predict the life chances of a child born in the United States in 1998, it is more important to know the parents' socioeconomic status than the child's race or gender. High school completion rates of Blacks and Whites are now similar, and the earnings of Blacks have almost caught up to those of Whites with similar educational backgrounds (McMurrer & Sawhill). Nonetheless, disparities in racial wealth (i.e., the net value of assets such as stocks, savings, real estate, and business ownership) may limit parents' ability to pass along advantage to their children (Oliver & Shapiro, 1997). The disproportionate concentration of poverty among racial and ethnic minorities suggests the need for ongoing discussions of disadvantage as a function of race and ethnicity, discussions that might draw on developmental contextualism as a theoretical framework for

conceptualizing family diversity (Lerner, Sparks, & McCubbin, 2000).

For research purposes, studying diversity is important to disentangle the influence of class, race, ethnicity, and gender on family outcomes. For policy purposes, however, identifying similarities across diverse families is equally important. Understanding how families are different is essential to designing effective policies, but understanding how families are similar enhances the prospects that policies will muster widespread, sustainable political support (see Bogenschneider, 1999; Skocpol, 1997; Wilson, 1997, 1999). The fate of a family agenda hinges on the prospects of pulling together coalitions that transcend class and race (Skocpol & Greenberg, 1997) to promote "common solutions to shared problems" (Wilson, 1997, p. 77). A common experience across the usual divides of class, race, ethnicity, and gender is the family, and recent studies indicate enormous unity on family issues (Hewlett & West, 1998). Issues such as child care, child support, family leave, or income disparity could well become rallying points for parent-teacher associations, unions, churches, businesses, and other community groups across the political spectrum (Skocpol).

HAS RESEARCH BEEN USED TO INFORM THE DESIGN AND IMPLEMENTATION OF FAMILY POLICIES?

Policy analysis has been touted as one of the growth industries in late-20th-century America (Dunn, 1994), which raises an important question: Has the growth in scientific knowledge of policy analysis and family development culminated in the development of better family policies? Scholars disagree. Some claim little influence of research on family policy, and others claim considerable impact.

One prominent view is that research had little influence on family policy in the decade. With a couple notable exceptions, researchers lament that the history of the utilization of social science knowledge in the past 50 years has yielded few examples of research being used to inform policy making (DeLeon, 1996). Because of the nature of the political process and because of recent changes in the political landscape, anecdote can triumph over scientific data, passion over reason, and the media's 30-second sound bite over substantive debate (Kirp, 1992; Shonkoff, 2000).

As one of the only countries in the world without a mention of family in its constitution, American government was built on individualistic principles that have pervaded policy making in ways the founding fathers might not have intended. For example, at the federal level, 15 congressional committees and five executive branch departments have some jurisdiction over the family (Sawhill, 1992), but no single federal agency oversees family issues and devotes its attention exclusively to families (Eshleman, 1991). At the state level, slightly more than half of state legislatures have a specific committee or commission that deals with family issues, but many do not (State Legislative Leaders Foundation, 1995). The United States has no explicit national family policy, so policy makers pass piecemeal legislation that responds to specific individual needs but does not provide a comprehensive vision for families (Elrod, 1999). Four examples will be cited here.

First, in a 1998 United Nations study of 152 countries, the United States is one of only six countries that does not have paid family leave (International Labor Organization, 1997). Second, some tax policies have a built-in marriage penalty, with the strongest disincentives for those on the economic margins of society, such as low-income working couples participating in the EITC program. If they marry, two individuals with one child who both work full-time at minimum wage may suffer financial losses as substantial as $8,000 per year in higher taxes and lost benefits (Ooms, 1998). Third, if tax breaks for families had kept pace with inflation, the exemption for dependents would have been $7,800 in 1990 rather than $2,050 (Sawhill, 1992). Finally, the 1997 Child Health Insurance Program increased federal reimbursement rates to states for health care coverage of children but not for their parents.

In contrast to this view, some policy observers counter that research has influenced family policy more extensively than is commonly believed. Politicians such as Senator John D. Rockefeller, IV, credit the base of knowledge developed and synthesized by the National Commission on Children with providing the momentum for policies such as the 1993 expansion of the EITC program, the 1996 strengthening of child support enforcement, and the 1997 partially fundable child tax credit (Rockefeller, 1998). Also, research was cited in the debate of family issues such as family leave (Trzcinski, 1995), regulation of television and Internet violence (Wilcox & Kunkel, 1996), and violence prevention (Zuckerman, 1999).

These contradictory conclusions on whether research has benefited family policy making may be attributable, in part, to the outcome that is assessed and the time span that is considered. Scholars' assessment of the value of research will be meager if it is narrowly measured by counting only blockbuster effects, that is, whether policy makers implement an alternative suggested by research. Instead, research may serve an enlightenment function by influencing policy incrementally in more subtle ways, such as projecting ideas into political discourse, framing the terms of policy debate, shaping citizen preferences (Weiss, 1986), and generating popular support for the democratic process by retroactively verifying the wisdom of decisions made by policy makers (Shulock, 1999).

The best indicator of whether research benefits family policy is typically derived not from a single study but from the replication of findings that gradually become so well accepted that they are considered common sense. For example, the development of Head Start was spurred by years of research documenting that intelligence is not fixed but can be shaped by the environment. More recently, the 1994 Early Head Start program for children aged 1 to 3 was launched, in part, by the accumulation of decades of research on the importance of the early years (Zigler, 1998). Thus, it may be too early to identify the greatest impact of family research in the 1990s, which could well be the gradual development of a body of knowledge documenting the contributions that stable, well-functioning families make to society and the potential of social policy to promote the stability and functioning of families. Granted, the evidence is not all in, but it appears that some progress has been made in using research to improve family policy making, but the links are still not as direct or consistent as their importance warrants.

What Development in Theory, Methods, and Dissemination Holds Potential for Advancing the Field

Several barriers threaten to impede progress of the field. Family policy has proven so controversial that value conflicts and ideological clashes often undercut the consensus needed for political action. Few methods have been articulated for overcoming the narrow, individualistic agendas of many special interest groups, think tanks, and political action committees. Policy makers voice support for families but still are uncertain how to translate this rhetoric into specific policies. This section reviews selected advances in theory, methods, and dissemination during the decade that have the potential to overcome these barriers.

Advances in Theory During the Decade

In controversial arenas, some politicians polarize issues by casting them in simplistic either-or terms or as liberal or conservative political ploys that make rousing campaign speeches and catchy 30-second sound bites. Yet these political characterizations are oftentimes inaccurate and frequently generate "more heat than light, more politics than policies, more slogans than solutions" (Bayme, 1991, p. 14). In an attempt to overcome this polarization and break the policy making impasse, the following theoretical perspective frames issues in a way that identifies common ground by recognizing the validity and utility of seemingly antithetical viewpoints.

This theory builds on Rappaport's (1981) compelling concept of true paradox—two ideas or principles that seem, on first blush, irreconcilable with each other but prove, on closer scrutiny, simultaneously valid (see Bogenschneider, 1997; 2000). Rappaport illustrated this notion with the contradiction between two widely held but opposite values in American politics—freedom and equality. Allowing total freedom might result in the powerful dominating the weak, thereby obliterating equality. Conversely, promoting total equality would impose more limits on some people than others, thereby constraining freedom. Thus, freedom and equality exemplify a true paradox because they are valid yet opposing schools of thought that are nevertheless intimately intertwined. Maximizing one of these poles necessarily limits the other. Because both poles need attention, people become one-sided when they focus on only one pole and ignore its equally compelling counterpart. An important role of scientists is to first discover true paradox and, if imbalance occurs, to push in the ignored direction (Rappaport). To demonstrate the potential of the theory, it will be applied to the substance of family policy (e.g., welfare reform), a frame of reference (e.g., the family perspective), and the locus of policy response (e.g., individual versus structural solutions).

Applying the theory of paradox to the substance of family policy. According to Corbett (1993), welfare reformers face the dilemma of balancing two important yet contradictory goals—reducing family dependency on welfare and reducing child poverty. Reaching either goal alone would be relatively simple, but attempting to reach both goals simultaneously has proven extraordinarily difficult. For example, Corbett claimed that dependency could easily be ended by eliminating welfare benefits, thereby providing the poor with no program on which to depend. Ending welfare programs, however, would increase the number of children living in poverty, thereby jeopardizing children's well-being. Alternatively, child poverty could be ended by increasing welfare benefits. Yet, making welfare more attractive would run the risk of increasing the number of welfare recipients and increasing the prospects that they might become dependent on government assistance. Thus, the crux of welfare reform is to reduce welfare dependency by encouraging parental self-sufficiency but doing so in a way that does not increase child poverty and harm child well-being—a policy dilemma that, in Rappaport's (1981) terms, is a true paradox.

True paradox can precipitate paralysis in policy making. A true paradox is not always self-evident and can escape notice if advocates become enticed by the persuasiveness of their political rhetoric and entrenched in the belief that their position alone represents what is true, right, and good. When faced with a true paradox, Rappaport (1981) encouraged social scientists to examine whether one pole of the dialectic is being emphasized at the expense of the other. Social scientists have done just that, in the example of welfare reform, by calling for evaluations that focus not only on the current preoccupation with reduced caseloads but also on child outcomes such as the safety net's ability to lift children out of poverty. One insight that the theory of paradox brings to policy making is that two virtually opposite yet valid policy goals can be developed by reasonable, well-meaning people and can be pursued simultaneously. Social scientists should welcome and embrace these contradictory solutions, because more solutions typically mean better, not worse, policies (Rappaport).

Applying the theory to a frame of reference in policy making. As argued earlier in this paper, a family perspective in policy making is valid and defensible. The theory of paradox, however, would raise the question of whether this familism is only one pole of a dialectic that has an equally compelling opposite pole. The obvious counterpoint is individualism. Focusing exclusively on familism can interfere with hard-fought individual rights, such as women's career opportunities, equal wages, and reproductive rights (Ooms, 1998). Yet unfettered individualism, as evidenced by excessive striving for occupational advancement, social status, material gains, or pleasure seeking, can interfere with the time and self-sacrifice that solid marriages, effective parenting, and strong civil societies require (Hewlett & West, 1998). I argue that individualism is so pervasive in America that its one-sidedness justifies pushing in the ignored direction toward familism. Yet this approach does not rule out the reverse possibility that, at some future time, familism might become so rampant that a push toward individualism would be warranted. Thus, the familism-individualism dichotomy is a true paradox that raises the ominous specter of pushing too far in either direction.

According to the theory of paradox, the optimum response may derive from pushing in the ignored direction, or it may be an elegant integration that takes both perspectives into account by falling somewhere in between. Moving toward the middle ground is not mealy-mouthed politics that leads to mediocre policy, but often the only way that policy gets done in the real world (Elshtain, 1995).

Applying the theory to the locus of policy response. A decision that often polarizes policy debate, albeit needlessly, is the source of policy responses, whether it be government, civil society, the market (Wolfe, 1989) or a cultural shift such as occurred with women's equality, civil rights, and environmentalism. One obvious fault line has been liberals' preference for structural solutions that provide the conditions for change and conservatives' preference for individual solutions that provide the motivation for change.

In policy circles, the extreme positions have tempered recently because both poles have gravitated toward the middle. For example, those typically classified as conservative have nevertheless recognized the need for more "extensive governmental programs offering monetary support and social services for families" (Popenoe, 1990, p. 47), specifically "parental leaves for childbirth, job sharing, flexible work hours and benefits, and on-site or nearby child care" (Blankenhorn, 1988a, p. 6). These structural supports respond to new family realities, but at the core is the conservative principle of allowing parents more time with their children (Blankenhorn). Those typically allied with the liberal perspective have noted that

culture, although not an exclusive explanation, should not be dismissed as a contributor to problems of the poor (e.g., Cherlin, 1997). Liberals such as Jesse Jackson continue to advocate for structural solutions but suggest they be accompanied by a moral revolution.

This blurring of the traditional fault lines between liberals and conservatives is epitomized in a recent proposal by Skocpol (1997) that family support for working parents would be the best focus for the Democratic party even though it is "'conservative' in the best sense of the word" (p. 120). Her vision is liberal because she advocates for policies that create the social conditions that parents need, such as decent wages and benefits, job training, and family leave. Nonetheless, this progressive vision depends on some policies that are typically considered conservative—taxes and benefits that encourage married parenthood and tough crime laws to make neighborhoods safe. The irony, however, is that liberal policies often flourish amid the family-friendly environment that conservative policies typically foster. For example, workplace supports are more apt to materialize in a cultural climate that values childrearing; conversely, when the cultural climate supports childrearing, parents will be more likely to take advantage of available supports (Skocpol).

Is the theory of paradox a Pollyannaish portrayal, or is it politically feasible? Disagreements have been greatly exaggerated, according to political observers, and a broad middle ground exists that could push family policies forward (Ooms, 1995; Skocpol, 1997). The American public tends not to gravitate toward one extreme or the other and instead longs for less political posturing and more consensus building to create a bipartisan family agenda (Bayme, 1991). According to Blankenhorn (1988a), a national family agenda is "neither liberal nor conservative . . . the core issues facing the American family . . . will fit the strategic need of either party. Thus, it is twice blessed: good policy and good politics" (p. 2).

Advances in Methods During the Decade

Two recent historical analyses of the family field posit two methods for moving the family policy field forward. Paralleling the dual definitions proposed earlier, Skocpol (1995) proposed a specific, broad-based family policy program that would promote family security, whereas Ooms (1995) proposed a series of efforts aimed at promoting a family perspective in policy making across a broad range of policies. In keeping with the spirit of the theory of paradox, these two alternative methods of promoting a family agenda should not be viewed as contradictory, but should be embraced as complementary approaches that can be pursued simultaneously to reach the shared goal of strengthening families.

Promoting a specific family policy. Skocpol (1995, p. 312) claims that "the only progressive vision that has any chance of social effectiveness and political viability in the foreseeable future" is an effort aimed at family security that would support work and responsible parenting in single- and two-parent families. Skocpol believes this family security proposal is politically feasible, not only because it embodies conservative and liberal elements as described earlier, but also because of the success of other broad-based U.S. social programs. In her historical analysis, Skocpol dispelled the stereotype of the United States as a social policy laggard by pointing to several examples of U.S. social policies that have successfully provided security and support to a broad range of citizens. For example, the United States provided the world's first system of universal public education, which was considered the most inclusive in the industrialized world. Following the Civil War, the United States became a "defacto world leader" in providing veterans with generous disability and old-age pensions. In the early 20th century, legislation such as the Shephard-Towner Act provided a number of benefits to mothers and children, and 44 states passed mothers' pensions so widows could care for their children at home. The 1935 Social Security Act and its Medicare expansion in 1965 provided the framework for the country's most effective antipoverty program. The 1944 GI Bill and its successor provided millions of veterans with free medical care; generous disability pensions; access to education or training loans; and grants or loans for homes, businesses, and farms.

Skocpol (1995, 1996, 1997) identified four common characteristics of these successful programs that can be used as touchstones to assess the feasibility of implementing other broad-based family policies. First, for a family policy agenda to be successful, it would need to articulate the valuable services that families provide to society, such as raising children and caring for the elderly. In an aging society, the value of children and caregivers may increase as the number of workers for each retiree drops from 3.7 in 1970 to an esti-

mated 2 in 2030 (Moen, 1996). Second, family policies would have the greatest chances for success if built on the principle that Skocpol called "targeting within universalism"—the practice of making room for the less privileged in universal programs that benefit all. The most widespread and long-term programs have provided benefits to the advantaged and the disadvantaged through the same policy rubric. Third, family policies are more apt to flourish if promoted through a voluntary association, preferably one with a local, state, and national presence. Obvious candidates are the Parent Teacher Association, which has a membership of about 7 million (Putnam, 1995); the General Federation of Women's Clubs, with a U.S. membership of 220,000; or the new National Parenting Association (Hewlett & West, 1998), with a membership of 7,000. Finally, Skocpol (1995) predicted that to ensure the secure resources that underlie successful social policies, Americans will pay more taxes for programs addressing widely felt needs that benefit not only the disadvantaged, but also their own families and friends.

Promoting a family perspective in policy making. In contrast to a broad-based social program, Ooms (1995) proposed that what is needed is a focused effort to promote a family perspective in policy making on a broad range of policy issues. Policy makers' interest in families is at an all-time high, yet what remains elusive is how policy makers can best act on this interest. What is needed is better packaged information and tools to help policy makers design, analyze, and implement policies that strengthen families. For example, the Family Impact Seminar developed a checklist for assessing the family impact of policies, published family impact analyses of proposed legislation, collaborated with community organizations to conduct family impact assessments of local programs and policies, coordinated Family Impact Seminars for federal policy makers, conducted roundtable meetings for federal officials to help them implement family-centered legislation, and prepared a checklist for self-assessing a program's family supportiveness.

Ooms (1995) believes that family impact statements, originally proposed to parallel environmental impact statements, is too limited a concept. What is needed is a cadre of family professionals committed to a broader vision of a family perspective in policy making that would include monitoring family trends and their implications for policy, assessing the impact of actual and proposed policies on families, gathering evidence on the effectiveness of family-focused policies and programs, promoting the development and enactment of policies that are attuned to family well-being, developing innovative methods of connecting family research and policy making, fostering effective implementation of family-focused policies, and collaborating with like-minded organizations to reach these goals. The leadership for these functions could be provided by a cabinet-level Council of Family Advisors similar to the Council of Economic Advisors, a recommendation from the Consortium of Family Organizations that seems as relevant today as in 1988 when it was first proposed.

Advances in Dissemination During the Decade

During the decade, theoretical approaches have emerged that articulate roles for professionals in building family policy (Bogenschneider, 1995; Pratt, 1995). Also, several dissemination strategies for building family policies and promoting a family perspective in policy making have emerged. Selected examples are listed here, with the reader referred to Bogenschneider (2000) for a complete description.

The Family Impact Seminar, established in 1976 to promote a family perspective in policy making, closed its doors in 1999 and transferred its mission to the newly established Policy Institute for Family Impact Seminars directed by Bogenschneider at the University of Wisconsin at Madison. Because the institute aims to connect research and policy making, one of its first initiatives is to build a network of states that will conduct Family Impact Seminars—a series of seminars, briefing reports, and follow-up activities for state policy makers (see Bogenschneider, 1995; Bogenschneider, Olson, Linney, & Mills, 2000; Mayer & Hutchins, 1998; McClintock, 1999).

The Packard Foundation took the unprecedented step of producing and widely disseminating a journal, *The Future of Children,* which has the explicit purpose of synthesizing research in a format that is accessible to policy makers, practitioners, legislators, and professionals in the public and private sectors. In an era of devolution, strategies are being developed for working with state policy makers on child and family issues (Bogenschneider et al., 2000; Kaufman, 1993; Monroe, 1991; Pratt, 1998; State Legislative Leaders Foundation, 1995). For example, the Wel-

fare Peer Assistance Network brings together state-level welfare officials in the Midwest on a regular basis to facilitate cross-state peer assistance (Corbett et al., 1998). Because program responsibilities have devolved from federal to state and local governments, providing a mechanism for similarly situated professionals or practitioners to pool insights, expertise, and intellectual resources is a concept with obvious implications beyond welfare reform.

Some innovations were initiated but not sustained. A family magazine was launched in 1997, with sponsorship by the Institute for Families at the University of South Carolina and several other collaborators, to provide practice-oriented summaries of research in an accessible format (Melton, 1997). The Society for Research on Adolescence, the Society for Research on Child Development, and the International Conference of Infant Studies developed a series of five research briefs for policy makers, which summarized the current state of knowledge on issues such as child care and teenage parenthood (Brooks-Gunn, 1995).

Other efforts launched before the 1990s continue. The National Issues Forum Institute (1996), which provides opportunities for citizens to gather in communities to debate controversial public issues, featured the family in 1995. The Harvard Family Research Project (1992a, 1992b) continues to publish informative publications on designing and evaluating innovative family support and education programs. Several universities promote policy development at the local, state, and federal levels in a variety of venues that benefit children, youth, and families (for examples, see Lerner & Simon, 1998).

For family policy researchers, guidelines were published on providing data of more direct relevance to policy makers using qualitative (Rist, 1994) and epidemiological methodologies (Scott, Mason, & Chapman, 1999). For teachers of family policy, several publications appeared (Anderson & Skinner, 1995; Bogenschneider, 2000; Quoss, 1992; Skinner & Anderson, 1993; Zimmerman, 1992, 1995), and for practitioners, a family policy Web site (http://sohe.wisc.edu/familyimpact) was developed by the National Network for Family Resiliency (Bogenschneider, 2000; Mills & Bogenschneider, 1998). For advocates, the Society for Research on Child Development published a guide to providing expert testimony (McCartney & Phillips, 1993), and the National Council on Family Relations published a compendium that described 27 nonprofit national family organizations—their history, major publications, and activities including social advocacy (Chilman, 1997).

CONCLUSION

Family policy came of age in the 1990s, dispelling doomsayers who predicted a short life expectancy, yet it has not matured into a full-fledged adult with a stature commensurate to that of economic or environmental policy. The core of U.S. family policy is fostering family commitment, which this review argues is particularly consequential in an individualistic, market-based economy with a small social safety net. The dilemma for family policy scholars is that the very conditions that make family commitments so important also constitute some of the most entrenched barriers to progress.

This review of the state of U.S. family policy in the 1990s reveals several advances. As a concept, family policy has been more clearly defined. As a perspective, its rationale has been strengthened with a growing body of scholarship on the important functions families perform for society and the important role policy plays in fostering stable, well-functioning families. As a field, it has gained legitimacy through numerous philanthropic commitments and through state and federal policy initiatives that are chronicled in this review. Several advances in theory, methods, and dissemination during the decade have the potential to capitalize on the popularity that families currently command as a theme in policy making among policy makers, professionals, and the public.

Curiously, family policy is still not a term that is widely used in policy circles. Family research has been used to strengthen policy making, but the examples are not as frequent, varied, or comprehensive as their importance warrants, and the debate of family policy issues continues to generate deep-seated passion and controversy among policy makers and scholars alike.

This review raises several challenges for family professionals, four of which are detailed here. First, scholars need to reach consensus on definitions of family policy as a basis for research and action. Second, basic research on families and family policy is critical to solidifying the rationale for the field, yet basic researchers could ask more policy-sensitive and family-relevant questions, could utilize measures and methods for assessing dyadic or family relationships (see Maguire, 1999), and could employ epidemiological methods that provide data more pertinent to policy makers, such as the prevalence of a problem, its risk to the population, and the potential cost-savings of policy responses (see Scott et al., 1999). Third, because family scholars' ability to generate high-quality research has outpaced their ability to disseminate this research into policy making, innovative technologies for connecting research and policy making are needed, as are equally innovative methods of evaluating the effectiveness of dissemination efforts that are not expected to have large, immediate, or singular impacts. Finally, the field needs not more activity, but more strategic efforts that build on the advances of the decade. The efforts of professionals to inform family policy making are particularly important now amid observations that American policy making is "more polarized, short-sighted, fragmented—and often less intelligent—than it should be" (Smith, 1991, p. xxi). Those of us who work for families can be heartened to stay the course in the new millennium by the advice of an anonymous state legislator (State Legislative Leaders Foundation, 1995, p. 29): "Persist with well-researched and accredited information and keep at it. Politics belongs to the persistent."

NOTE

I am deeply grateful to several colleagues who provided thoughtful comments on all or parts of this manuscript: Inge Bretherton, Thomas Corbett, Ann Crouter, Thomas Kaplan, Theodora Ooms, Julian Rappaport, David Riley, and Steven Wisensale. Special acknowledgment is extended to Theodora Ooms, whose work has profoundly influenced my thinking. I also extend appreciation to Meg Wall-Wild and Karen Dorman for preparing and editing the manuscript.

REFERENCES

Aldous, J., & Dumon, W. (1990). Family policy in the 1980's: Controversy and consensus. *Journal of Marriage and the Family, 52,* 1136–1151.

Anderson, E. A., & Skinner, D. A. (1995). The components of family policy education. *Journal of Family and Economic Issues, 16,* 65–76.

Barratt, M. S. (1993). Early childrearing in Japan: Cross-cultural and intracultural perspectives. *Early Development and Parenting, 2,* 3–6.

Baum, C. G., & Forehand, R. (1981). Long term follow-up assessment of parent training by use of multiple outcome measures. *Behavior Therapy, 12,* 643–652.

Baydar, N., & Brooks-Gunn, J. (1991). Effects of maternal employment and childcare arrangements on preschooler's cognitive and behavioral outcomes: Evidence from the Children of the National Longitudinal Survey of Youth. *Developmental Psychology, 27,* 932–945.

Bayme, S. (1991). A new synthesis on family policy? *Family Affairs, 4,* 14.

Becker, P. E., & Moen, P. (1999). Scaling back: Dual-earner couples' work-family strategies. *Journal of Marriage and the Family, 61,* 995–1007.

Bellah, R. N. (1990). The invasion of the money world. In D. Blankenhorn, S. Bayme, & J. B. Elshtain (Eds.), *Rebuilding the nest: A new commitment to the American family* (pp. 227–236). Milwaukee, WI: Family Service America.

Bellah, R. N., Madsen, R., Sullivan, W. M., Swidler, A., & Tipton, S. M. (1996). *Habits of the heart: Individualism and commitment in American life.* Berkeley: University of California Press.

Belsky, J., & Eggebeen, D. (1991). Early and extensive maternal employment and young children's socioeconomic development: Children of the National Longitudinal Survey of Youth. *Journal of Marriage and the Family, 53,* 1083–1110.

Bennett, Petts, & Blumenthal. (1999). *Adult attitudes towards sexual problems: National survey of American adults aged 25 and older.* Conducted during March 25–31, 1999, for the Gender and Human Sexuality: A Continuing Medical Education Conference held April 30, 1999, Washington, DC.

Bernard, S. N., & Knitzer, J. (1999). *Map and track: State initiatives to encourage responsible fatherhood, 1999 edition.* New York: National Center for Children in Poverty, Columbia University School of Public Health.

Blankenhorn, D. (1988a). Cosby for president? *Family Affairs, 1,* 1–6.

Blankenhorn, D. (1988b). What are "family values" anyway? *Family Affairs, 1,* 6.

Blankenhorn, D. (1990). American family dilemmas. In D. Blankenhorn, S. Bayme, & J. Elshtain (Eds.), *Rebuilding the nest: A new commitment to the American family* (pp. 3–25). Milwaukee, WI: Family Service America.

Blum, R. (1992). Preface. In S. Smith, S. Blank, & R. Collins (Eds.), *Pathways to self-sufficiency for two generations: Designing welfare-to-work programs that benefit children and strengthen families.* New York: Foundation for Child Development.

Blum, R. (1993). Critical issues for the family research agenda and their use in policy formulation. In G. E. Hendershot & F. B. LeClere (Eds.), *Family health: From data to policy* (pp. 110–112). Minneapolis, MN: National Council on Family Relations.

Bogenschneider, K. (1995). Roles for professionals in building family policy: A case study of state family impact seminars. *Family Relations, 44,* 5–12.

Bogenschneider, K. (1997). Parental involvement in adolescent schooling: A proximal process with transcontextual validity. *Journal of Marriage and the Family, 59,* 718–733.

Bogenschneider, K. (1999). Foreword. In R. M. Lerner, E. E. Sparks, & L. D. McCubbin (Eds.), *Family diversity and family policy: Strengthening families for America's children.* Norwell, MA: Kluwer.

Bogenschneider, K. (2000). *Putting families on the political agenda: The family litmus test.* Manuscript in preparation, University of Wisconsin—Madison.

Bogenschneider, K., Olson, J. R., Linney, K. D., & Mills, J. (2000). Connecting research and policymaking: Implications for theory and practice from the Family Impact Seminars. *Family Relations, 49,* 327–339

Bogenschneider, K., & Steinberg, L. (1994). Maternal employment and adolescents' academic achievement: A developmental analysis. *Sociology of Education, 67,* 60–77.

Boyte, H. C., & Etzioni, A. (1993). Redefining politics, Part II. *The Responsive Community: Rights and Responsibilities, 3,* 83–88.

Bronfenbrenner, U., & Weiss, H. B. (1983). Beyond policies without people: An ecological perspective on child and family policy. In E. F. Zigler, S. L. Kagan, & E. Klugman (Eds.), *Children, families, and government: Perspectives on American social policy* (pp. 393–414). Cambridge, U.K.: Cambridge University Press.

Brooks-Gunn, J. (1995, Spring). Research briefs to inform policy. *SRA Newsletter, 1–2,* 4.

Bumpass, L. L. (1990). What's happening to the family? Interactions between demographic and institutional change. *Demography, 27,* 483–498.

Carter, N. (1995). *See how we grow: A report on the status of parenting education in the U.S.* Philadelphia: Pew Memorial Trust.

Center on Budget and Policy Priorities. (1998). *Poverty rates fall, but remain high for a period with such low unemployment.* Washington, DC: Author. Retrieved June 23, 2000, from the World Wide Web: http://www.cbpp.org/9-24-98pov.htm

Cherlin, A. J. (1997). What's most important in a family textbook? *Family Relations, 46,* 209–211.

Chilman, C. S. (1997, October). *Principles, policies, and programs of selected national family organizations: An analytic survey by the public policy committee of NCFR.* Minneapolis, MN: National Council on Family Relations.

Clarkberg, M., & Moen, P. (1999, January). *The time-squeeze: The mismatch between work-hours patterns and preferences* (BLCC Working Paper #99-04). Ithaca, NY: Cornell University, Bronfenbrenner Life Course Center.

Consortium of Family Organizations (1990). *Family Policy Report, 1.*

Corbett, T. (1993). Child poverty and welfare reform: Progress or paralysis? *Focus, 15,* 1–46. Madison: University of Wisconsin Institute for Research on Poverty.

Corbett, T. (2000). From income support to child and family support: Some rather surprising consequences of national welfare reform. In K. Bogenschneider & J. Mills (Eds.), *Helping poor kids succeed: Welfare, tax, and early intervention policies* (Wisconsin Family Impact Seminar Briefing Report No. 14, pp. 1–12). Madison, WI: University of Wisconsin Center for Excellence in Family Studies.

Corbett, T., Burkett-Simms, C., Crandall, L., Howard, D., Le, N., Powers, P., Rabb, J., Rogers, J. J., Sells, S., Semmons, A., Snell, T., Titus-Cunningham, S., & Wulf, K. (1998). *The Midwest welfare peer assistance network: Leading the nation beyond welfare reform* (Rev ed.). Madison: University of Wisconsin Institute for Research on Poverty.

DeLeon, P. H. (1996). Public policy and public service: Our professional duty. In R. P. Lorion, I. Iscoe, P. H. DeLeon, & G. R. VandenBos (Eds.), *Psychology and public policy: Balancing public service and profes-*

sional need. Washington, DC: American Psychological Association.

Dishion, T. J., Andrews, D. W., Kavanagh, K., & Soberman, L. H. (1996). Preventive interventions for high-risk youth: The adolescent transitions program. In R. D. Peters & R. J. McMahon (Eds.), *Preventing childhood disorders, substance abuse, and delinquency* (pp. 184–214). Thousand Oaks, CA: Sage.

Dishion, T. J., McCord, J., & Poulin, F. (1999). When interventions harm: Peer groups and problem behavior. *American Psychologist, 54,* 755–764.

Doherty, W. J. (1995). *Soul searching: Why psychotherapy must promote moral responsibility.* New York: Basic Books.

Doherty, W. J., Kouneski, E. F., & Erickson, M. F. (1998). Responsible father: An overview and conceptual framework. *Journal of Marriage and the Family, 60,* 277–292.

Dunn, W. N. (1994). *Public policy analysis: An introduction* (2nd ed.). Englewood Cliffs, NJ: Prentice-Hall.

Early, B. P., & Hawkins, M. J. (1994). Opportunity and risks in emerging family policy: An analysis of family preservation legislation. *Children and Youth Services Review, 16,* 309–318.

Eastman, M. (1996). Myths of marriage and family. In D. Popenoe, J. B. Elshtain, & D. Blankenhorn (Eds.), *Promises to keep: Decline and renewal of marriage in America* (pp. 35–68). Lanham, MD: Rowman & Littlefield.

Elrod, L. D. (1995). A review of the year in family law. *Family Law Quarterly, 28,* 541–571.

Elrod, L. D. (1999). Epilogue: Of families, federalism, and a quest for policy. *Family Law Quarterly, 33,* 843–863.

Elrod, L. D., & Spector, R. G. (1997). A review of the year in family law: Of welfare reform, child support, and relocation. *Family Law Quarterly, 30,* 765–809.

Elrod, L. D., & Spector, R. G. (1998). A review of the year in family law: A search for definitions and policy. *Family Law Quarterly, 31,* 613–665.

Elrod, L. D., Spector, R. G., & Atkinson, J. (1999). A review of the year in family law: Children's issues dominate. *Family Law Quarterly, 32,* 661–717.

Elshtain, J. B. (1995). *Democracy on trial.* New York: Basic Books.

Eshleman, R. (1991). *The family: An introduction.* Boston: Bacon.

Families and Work Institute. (1995, May). *Women: The new providers. Whirlpool Foundation Study, Part One.* (Available from the Families and Work Institute, 330 Seventh Avenue, 14th Floor, New York, NY 10001)

Finance Project (1996, December). *Building strong communities: Crafting a legislative foundation.* Washington, DC: Author.

Forthofer, M. S., Markman, H. J., Cox, M., Stanley, S., & Kessler, R. C. (1996). Associations between marital distress and work loss in a national sample. *Journal of Marriage and the Family, 58,* 597–605.

Giele, J. Z. (1996). Decline of the family: Conservative, liberal, and feminist views. In D. Popenoe, J. B. Elshtain, & D. Blankenhorn (Eds.), *Promises to keep: Decline and renewal of marriage in America* (pp. 271–290). Lanham, MD: Rowman & Littlefield.

Glendon, M. A. (1992). The second national commu-nitarian teach-in. *The Responsive Community, 2,* 54–58.

Glenn, N. D. (1996). Values, attitudes, and the state of American marriage. In D. Popenoe, J. B. Elshtain, & D. Blankenhorn (Eds.), *Promises to keep: Decline and renewal of marriage in America* (pp. 15–33). Lanham, MD: Rowman & Littlefield.

Goggins, B. K. (1997). Shared responsibility for managing work and family relationships: A community perspective. In S. J. Parasuraman & J. H. Greenhaus (Eds.), *Integrating work and family: Challenges and choices for a changing world* (pp. 220–231). Westport, CT: Quorum Books.

Gomby, D. S., Culross, C. L., & Behrman, R. E. (1999, Spring/Summer). Home visiting: Recent program evaluations—Analysis and recommendations. *The Future of Children Report, 9,* 4–26.

Harvard Family Research Project. (1992a). *Innovative states: Emerging family support and educational programs (Arkansas, Iowa, Oregon, Vermont, and Washington)* (2nd ed.). Cambridge, MA: Author.

Harvard Family Research Project. (1992b). *Pioneering states: Innovative family support and education programs (Arkansas, Iowa, Oregon, Vermont, and Washington)* (2nd ed.). Cambridge, MA: Author.

Harvey, E. (1999). Short-term and long-term effects of early parental employment on children of the National Longitudinal Survey of Youth. *Developmental Psychology, 35,* 445–459.

Hendershot, G. E., & LeClere, F. B. (1993). *Family health: From data to policy.* Minneapolis, MN: National Council on Family Relations.

Hewlett, S. A., & West, C. (1998). *The war against parents: What we can do for America's beleaguered moms and dads.* New York: Houghton Mifflin.

Hochschild, A. R. (1997). *The time bind: When work becomes home and home becomes work.* New York: Metropolitan Books.

Hotz, V. J., & Scholz, J. K. (2000). Not perfect, but still pretty good: The EITC and other policies to support the U.S. low-wage labor market. *OECD Economic Studies, 2000, 31* 26–42.

Hutchins, J. (1998). *Coming together for children and families: How cabinet-level collaboration is changing state policymaking.* Washington, DC: Family Impact Seminar.

Institute for Educational Leadership. (1997). *Partnerships for stronger families: Building intergovernmental partnerships to improve results for children and families* (Special Report #9). Washington, DC: Author.

International Labor Organization. (1997). *Maternity protection at work. Report of the Maternity Protection Convention (Revised), 1952 (No. 103) and Recommendation, 1952 (No. 95).* Geneva, Switzerland: Author.

Jacobs, F. H., & Davies, M. W. (1994). On the eve of a new millennium. In F. H. Jacobs & M. W. Davies (Eds.), *More than kissing babies? Current child and family policy in the United States.* Westport, CT: Auburn House.

Kamerman, S. B., & Kahn, A. J. (1978). Families and the idea of family policy. In S. B. Kamerman & A. J. Kahn (Eds.), *Family policy: Government and families in fourteen countries* (pp. 1–16). New York: Columbia University Press.

Kamerman, S. B., & Kahn, A. J. (in press). Child and family policies in an era of social policy retrenchment and restructuring. In T. Smeeding & K. Vlemincks (Eds.), *Child well-being and poverty: Policy in modern nations.*

Kane, R. A., Kane, R. L., & Ladd, R. C. (1998). *The heart of long-term care.* New York: Oxford University Press.

Kane, R. A., & Penrod, J. D. (1995). In search of family caregiving policy: General considerations. In R. A. Kane & J. D. Penrod (Eds.), *Family caregiver applications series: Vol. 5. Family caregiving in an aging society: Policy perspectives* (pp. 1–14). Thousand Oaks, CA: Sage.

Kaufman, I. (1993). Family research in state and local policy making. In G. E. Hendershot & F. B. LeClere (Eds.), *Family health: From data to policy* (pp. 113–115). Minneapolis, MN: National Council on Family Relations.

Kirby, D. (1997, March). *No easy answers: Research findings on programs to reduce teen pregnancy (Summary).* Washington, DC: The National Campaign to Prevent Teen Pregnancy.

Kirp, D. L. (1992). The end of policy analysis: With apologies to Daniel (The End of Ideology) Bell and Francis (The End of History) Fukiyama. *Journal of Policy Analysis and Management, 2,* 693–696.

Knitzer, J., Bernard, S., Brenner, E., & Gadsden, V. (1997). *Map and track: State initiatives to encourage responsible fatherhood.* New York: Columbia University School of Public Health, National Center for Children in Poverty.

Knitzer, J., & Page, S. (1996). *Map and track: State initiatives for young children and families.* New York: Columbia University School of Public Health, National Center for Children in Poverty.

Knitzer, J., & Page, S. (1998). *Map and track: State initiatives for young children and families, 1998 edition.* New York: Columbia University School of Public Health, National Center for Children in Poverty.

Kumpfer, K. L. (1993, September). *Strengthening America's families: Promising parenting strategies for delinquency prevention—User's guide* (U.S. Department of Justice Publication No. NCJ140781). Washington, DC: Office of Juvenile Justice and Delinquency Prevention.

Larin, K. (1998, November). *Income inequities among families in the U.S. and internationally: Problems and policies.* Paper presented at the annual meeting of the National Council on Family Relations, Milwaukee, WI.

Lerner, R. M., & Simon, L. K. (1998). *University-community collaborations for the twenty-first century: Outreach scholarship for youth and families.* New York: Garland.

Lerner, R. M., Sparks, E. E., & McCubbin, L. D. (2000). Family diversity and family policy: Strengthening families for America's children. Boston: Kluwer.

Lewis, A., & Henderson, A. (1997). *Urgent message: Families crucial to school reform.* Washington, DC: Center for Law and Education.

Maguire, M. C. (1999). Treating the dyad as the unit of analysis: A primer on three analytic approaches. *Journal of Marriage and the Family, 61,* 213–223.

Mayer, R., & Hutchins, V. L. (1998). District of Columbia family policy seminar: A tool for devolution. *Maternal and Child Health Journal, 2,* 59–62.

McCartney, K., & Phillips, D. (1993). *An insider's guide to providing expert testimony before Congress.* Ann Arbor, MI: Society for Research in Child Development.

McClintock, C. (1999). Policy seminars for state and community leaders. In T. R. Chibucos & R. M. Lerner (Eds.), *Serving children and families through community: University partnerships success stories* (pp. 269–274). Norwell, MA: Kluwer.

McLanahan, S., & Sandefur, G. (1994). *Growing up with a single parent: What hurts, what helps.* Cambridge, MA: Harvard University Press.

McMurrer, D. P., & Sawhill, I. V. (1998). *Getting ahead: Economic and social mobility in America.* Washington, DC: Urban Institute Press.

Mellman, M., Lazarus, E., & Rivlin, A. (1990). Family time, family values. In D. Blankenhorn, S. Bayme, & J. B. Elshtain (Eds.), *Rebuilding the nest: A new commitment to the American family* (pp. 73–92). Milwaukee, WI: Family Service America.

Melton, G. B. (1997). Going where the kids are. *Family Futures, 1,* 4–5.

Mills, J., & Bogenschneider, K. (1998, November). *Informing family policy: Resources on the Internet.* Paper presented at the annual meeting of the National Council on Family Relations, Milwaukee, WI.

Moen, P. (1996). Change age trends: The pyramid upside down? In U. Bronfenbrenner, P. McClelland, E. Wethington, P. Moen, & S. J. Ceci (Eds.), *The state of Americans: This generation and the next* (pp. 208–258). New York: Free Press.

Moen, P., & Jull, P. M. M. (1995). Informing family policies: The uses of social research. *Journal of Family and Economic Issues, 16,* 79–107.

Moen, P., & Schorr, A. L. (1987). Families and social policy. In M. B. Sussman & S. K. Steinmetz (Eds.), *Handbook of marriage and the family* (pp. 795–813). New York: Plenum.

Moen, P., & Yu, Y. (1999, January). *Effective work/life strategies: Working couples, gender, and life quality* (BLCC Working Paper #99-06). Ithaca, NY: Cornell University, Bronfenbrenner Life Course Center.

Monroe, P. A. (1991). Participation in state legislative activities: A practical guide for family scientists. *Family Relations, 40,* 324–331.

National Commission on America's Urban Families. (1993). *Families first.* Washington, DC: Author.

National Commission on Child Welfare and Family Preservation. (1990). *A commitment to change.* Washington, DC: American Public Welfare Association.

National Commission on Children. (1991a). *Beyond rhetoric: A new American agenda for children and families.* Washington, DC: Author.

National Commission on Children. (1991b). *Speaking of kids: A national survey of children and parents.* Washington, DC: Author.

National Issues Forum Institute. (1996). *The troubled American family: Which way out of the storm?* Washington, DC: Author.

Olds, D., Eckenrode, J., Henderson, C. R., Jr., Kitzman, H., Powers, J., Cole, R., Sidora, K., Morris, P., Pettitt, L., & Luckey, D. (1997). Long-term effects of home visitation on maternal life course and child abuse and neglect: 15-year follow-up of a randomized trial.

Journal of the American Medical Association, 278, 637–643.

Olds, D., Henderson, C. R., Jr., Cole, R., Eckenrode, J., Kitzman, H., Luckey, D., Pettitt, L., Sidora, K., Morris, P., & Powers, J. (1998). Long-term effects of nurse home visitation on children's criminal and antisocial behavior: 15-year follow-up of a randomized controlled trial. *Journal of the American Medical Association, 280,* 1238–1244.

Oliver, M. L., & Shapiro, T. M. (1997). *Black wealth/ white wealth: A new perspective on racial inequality.* New York: Routledge.

Ooms, T. (1990). Families and government: Implementing a family perspective in public policy. *Social Thought, 16,* 61–78.

Ooms, T. (1995, October). *Taking families seriously: Family impact analysis as an essential policy tool.* Paper presented at Expert Meeting in Leuven, Belgium.

Ooms, T. (1998). *Towards more perfect unions: Putting marriage on the public agenda.* Washington, DC: Family Impact Seminar.

Parasuraman, S., & Greenhaus, J. H. (1997). *Integrating work and family: Challenges and choices for a changing world.* Westport, CT: Quorum Books.

Parcel, T. L., & Menaghan, E. G. (1994). *Parents' jobs and children's lives.* New York: Aldine de Gruyter.

Patterson, G. R. (1986). Performance model for antisocial boys. *American Psychologist, 41,* 432–444.

Popenoe, D. (1990). Family decline in America. In D. Blankenhorn, S. Bayme, & J. B. Elshtain (Eds.), *Rebuilding the nest: A new commitment to the American family.* Milwaukee, WI: Family Service America.

Pratt, C. C. (1995). Family professionals and family policy: Strategies for influence. *Family Relations, 44,* 56–62.

Pratt, C. C. (1998, September). *Family policy in an era of devolution.* Paper presented at the annual meeting of the National Public Policy Education Conference, Portland, OR.

Putnam, R. D. (1995). Bowling alone: America's declining social capital. *Journal of Democracy, 6,* 65–78.

Quoss, B. (1992). Teaching family policy through advocacy and empowerment. *Family Relations, 41,* 39–43.

Ramey, C. T., Campbell, F. A., Burchinal, M., Skinner, M. L., Gardner, D. M., & Ramey, S. L. (1999). Persistent effects of early intervention on high-risk children and their mothers. *Applied Developmental Science, 4,* 2–14.

Ramey, S. L., & Ramey, C. T. (1999). Early experience and early intervention for children at risk for developmental delay and mental retardation. In S. L. Ramey, C. T. Ramey, & M. J. Friedlander (Eds.), *Mental retardation and developmental disabilities research reviews* (Vol. 5, pp. 1–10). NY: Wiley.

Rappaport, J. (1981). In praise of paradox: A social policy of empowerment over prevention. *American Journal of Community Psychology, 9,* 1–25.

Responsive Communitarian Platform. (1992). *The Responsive Community: Rights and Responsibilities, 2* (2), 4–20.

Rist, R. C. (1994). Qualitative program evaluation: Practice and promise. In N. Denzin & Y. Lincoln (Eds.), *Handbook of qualitative research* (pp. 545–558). Thousand Oaks, CA: Sage.

Rockefeller, J. D., IV. (1998, October 2). *Measuring our success at the turn of the century: A report card on kids and family issues.* Invited address presented to the Georgetown Public Policy Institute, Georgetown University, Washington, DC.

Rosenberg, A., & Limber, S. P. (1996). Contributions of social science research to issues of family policy. *Journal of Social Issues, 52,* 1–9.

St. Pierre, R. G., Layzer, J. I., Barnes, H. B. (1996). *Regenerating two-generation programs.* Cambridge, MA: Abt Associates.

Sawhill, I. V. (1992). Young children and families. In H. J. Aaron & C. L. Schultze (Eds.), *Setting domestic policy: What can government do?* (pp. 147–184). Washington, DC: Brookings Institute.

Schattschneider, E. E. (1960). The semisovereign people: A realist's view of democracy in America. New York: Holt, Rinehart, & Winston.

Schor, J. B. (1991). *The overworked American: The unexpected decline of leisure.* New York: Basic Books.

Scott, K. G., Mason, C. A., & Chapman, D. A. (1999). The use of epidemiological methodology as a means of influencing public policy. *Child Development, 70,* 1263–1272.

Seaberg, J. R. (1990). Family policy revisited: Are we there yet? *Social Work, 35,* 548–554.

Seeley, D. (1985). *Education through partnership.* Washington, DC: American Enterprise Institute on Public Policy Research.

Shonkoff, J. P. (2000). Science, policy, and practice: Three cultures in search of a shared mission. *Child Development, 71,* 181–187.

Shulock, N. (1999). The paradox of policy analysis: If it is not used, why do we produce so much of it? *Journal of Policy Analysis and Management, 18,* 226–244.

Skinner, D. A., & Anderson, E. (1993). *Teaching family policy: A handbook of course syllabi, teaching strategies, and resources.* Minneapolis, MN: National Council on Family Relations.

Skocpol, T. (1995). *Social policy in the United States: Future possibilities in historical perspective.* Princeton, NJ: Princeton University Press.

Skocpol, T. (1996, November). *The missing middle: Working parents in U.S. democracy and social policy.* Paper presented at the annual meeting of the National Council on Family Relations, Kansas City, MO.

Skocpol, T. (1997). A partnership with American families. In S. B. Greenberg & T. Skocpol (Eds.), *The new majority: Toward a popular progressive politics* (pp. 104–129). New Haven, CT: Yale University Press.

Skocpol, T., & Greenberg, S. B. (1997). A politics for our times. In S. B. Greenberg & T. Skocpol (Eds.), *The new majority: Toward a popular progressive politics* (pp. 104–129). New Haven, CT: Yale University Press.

Smith, J. A. (1991). *The idea brokers: Think tanks and the rise of the new policy elite.* New York: Free Press.

Smith, S., Blank, S., & Collins, R. (1992). *Pathways to self-sufficiency for two generations: Designing welfare-to-work programs that benefit children and strengthen families.* New York: Foundation for Child Development.

Stack, S., & Eshleman, J. R. (1998). Marital status and happiness: A 17-nation study. *Journal of Marriage and the Family, 60,* 527–536.

State Legislative Leaders Foundation. (1995). *State legislative leaders: Keys to effective legislation for children and families.* Centerville, MA: Author.

Steinberg, L. (1996). *Beyond the classroom: Why school reform has failed and what parents need to do.* New York: Simon & Schuster.

Steiner, G. Y. (1981). *The futility of family policy.* Washington, DC: Brookings Institute.

Stone, R. I. (1999). Long term care: Coming of age in the 21st century. In R. Butler, L. Grossman, & M. Oberlink (Eds.), *Life in an older America.* New York: Twentieth Century Fund.

Teachman, J. D., Tedrow, L. M., & Crowder, K. D. (2000). The changing demography of America's families. *Journal of Marriage and the Family, 62,* 1234–1246.

Thornton, A. (1996). Comparative and historical perspectives on marriage, divorce, and family life. In D. Popenoe, J. B. Elshtain, & D. Blankenhorn (Eds.), *Promises to keep: Decline and renewal of marriage in America* (pp. 69–87). Lanham, MD: Rowman & Littlefield.

Tocqueville, A. (1945). *Democracy in America* (Vol. 2). New York: Vintage Books.

Trzcinski, E. (1995). The use and abuse of neoclassical theory in the political arena: The example of family and medical leave in the United States. In E. Kuiper & J. Sap (Eds.), *Out of the margin: Feminist perspectives on economics* (pp. 231–248). London: Routledge.

Tubbesing, C. (1998). The dual personality of federalism. *State Legislatures, 24,* 14–19.

Tweedie, J. (1999). Eight questions to ask about welfare reforms. *State Legislatures, 25,* 32–35.

U.S. Department of Education Office of Educational Research and Improvement. (1991). *Policy perspectives: Parental involvement in education* (Publication No. PIP 91-983) Washington, DC: U.S. Government Printing Office.

Walker, T. B., & Elrod, L. D. (1993). Family law in the fifty states: An overview. *Family Law Quarterly, 16,* 319–421.

Walsh, F. (1995). From family damage to family challenge. In R. H. Miskell, S. H. Lusterman, & S. H. McDaniel (Eds.), *Integrating family therapy: Handbook of family psychology and system theory* (pp. 587–606). Washington, DC: American Psychological Association.

Weiss, C. H. (1986). Research and policy making: A limited partnership. In F. Heller (Ed.), *The use and abuse of social science* (pp. 214–235). Newbury Park, CA: Sage.

Whitehead, B. D. (1992). A new familism? *Family Affairs, 5,* 1–5.

Wiener, J. M., & Sullivan, C. M. (1995). Long-term care for the younger population: A policy synthesis. In J.

M. Weiner, S. B. Clauser, & D. L. Kennell (Eds.), *Persons with disabilities: Issues in health care financing and service delivery* (pp. 291–324). Washington, DC: Brookings Institute.

Wilcox, B. L., & Kunkel, D. (1996). Taking television seriously: Children and television policy. In E. Zigler & N. W. Hall (Eds.), *Children, families, and government: Preparing for the 21st century* (pp. 333–352). New York: Cambridge University Press.

Wilson, W. J. (1997). The new social inequity and affirmative opportunity. In S. B. Greenberg & T. Skocpol (Eds.), *The new majority: Toward a popular progressive politics* (pp. 57–77). New Haven, CT: Yale University Press.

Wilson, W. J. (1999). *The bridge over the racial divide: Rising inequality and coalition politics.* Berkeley: University of California Press.

Wisensale, S. K. (1997). The White House and Congress on child care and family leave policy: From Carter to Clinton. *Policy Studies Journal, 25,* 75–86.

Wisensale, S. K. (1999). Family values and presidential elections: The use and abuse of the Family and Medical Leave Act in the 1992 and 1996 campaigns. *New England Journal of Public Policy, 15,* 35–50.

Wisensale, S. K. (in press). Twenty years of family policy: From Carter to Clinton. In S. Garasky & J. Mercier (Eds.), *Redefining family policy implications for the 21st century.*

Wolfe, A. (1989). *Whose keeper?* Berkeley: University of California Press.

Wolfe, A. (1998). Developing civil society: Can the workplace replace bowling? *The Responsive Community: Rights and Responsibilities, 8,* 41–47.

Zaslow, M., Tout, K., Smith, S., & Moore, K. (1998). Implications of the 1996 welfare legislation for children: A research perspective. *Social Policy Report, 12,* 1–35.

Zigler, E. (1998). A place of value for applied and policy studies. *Child Development, 69,* 532–542.

Zigler, E., Taussig, C., & Black, K. (1992). Early childhood intervention: A promising preventative for juvenile delinquency. *American Psychologist, 47,* 997–1006.

Zill, N., & Daly, M. (1993). *Researching the family: A guide to survey and statistical data on U.S. families.* Washington, DC: U.S. Department of Health and Human Services.

Zimmerman, S. L. (1988/1995). *Understanding family policy: Theoretical approaches* (pp. 86–100). Newbury Park, CA: Sage.

Zimmerman, S. L. (1992). *Family policies and family well-being: The role of political culture.* Newbury Park, CA: Sage.

Zimmerman, S. L. (1998). Educational policy and the role of advocacy. In M. L. Fuller & G. Olson (Eds.), *Home-school relations: Working successfully with parents and families* (pp. 332–352). Needham, MA: Allyn & Bacon.

Zuckerman, D. (1999). Research watch. *Youth Today, 8,* 16–17.

GREER LITTON FOX *University of Tennessee, Knoxville*

VELMA McBRIDE MURRY *University of Georgia**

Gender and Families: Feminist Perspectives and Family Research

This review provides a selective overview of scholarship on gender and families over the past decade. First, we discuss four characteristics of feminist perspectives to theoretical and methodological issues in social science. Then we describe briefly how feminist sensibility has been reflected in family scholarship over the past decade. We conclude with brief observations on the disjuncture between academic work on gender and the feminist backlash apparent in the contemporary culture.

In family studies, as in many other scholarly disciplines, feminist perspectives have reshaped traditional approaches to theorizing about and conducting and interpreting research. In this review, we describe several characteristics of feminist approaches to scholarship and then suggest how feminist sensibilities are reflected in contemporary research with families.

Many labels have been used to depict the orientation to social thought that we refer to as "feminism," including *feminism, feminist perspective, gender lens,* and *gender perspective.* In this re-

view, we use the labels *feminism, gender perspective, feminist perspective,* or *feminist approach* interchangeably to refer in the most general terms to an intellectual orientation to scholarship that makes certain assumptions about the importance of men and women to social life, the connectedness of structures and processes found in macro and micro settings, and the interdependence of one's personal orientation and professional concerns. Specifically, feminism assumes that women and men are of equal importance in social action, that structures and processes at work in the larger social arena have impact on relations in intimate environments and vice versa, and that one's personal experiences and sensibilities are not separable from the conduct of one's professional life. Across varied disciplinary fields, feminism as an intellectual orientation has taken a critical eye to received traditions of scholarship and epistemology (Reinharz, 1992). Wood (1995) further defines feminist approaches as follows:

> Encompassing diverse, sometimes conflicting intellectual traditions, feminist enquiry is unified by the belief that females and males, femininity and masculinity are equally valuable. Feminist scholars seek to identify, critique and alter structures and practices that actively or passively hinder equality. Participating in a broadly based critique of received notions of knowledge and cultural life, feminist enquiry typically supplants grand theory with tentative, situated and interpretive analyses. . . . The axis of feminist enquiry is gender, which consists of deeply ensconced social meanings and their derivative, power. Not

Department of Child and Family Studies, University of Tennessee, 1215 W. Cumberland Avenue, #115, Knoxville, TN 37996–1900 (glfox@utk.edu).

*Department of Family and Human Development, University of Georgia, Athens, GA 30602

Key Words: feminist perspectives, feminist research, gender and families.

a code word for women, gender is a cultural construction that profoundly affects women, men, and relationships between them. (p. 104)

Characteristics of Feminist Approaches to Scholarship

Despite the variety of feminist traditions (for example, Marxist feminism, radical lesbian feminism, neotraditionalist feminism, Black feminism), it is possible to isolate several elements that are commonly characteristic of feminist approaches to scholarship. We discuss four of these: reflexivity, the centrality of practice, a focus on social processes, and a critical stance toward traditional paradigms and theories.

Reflexivity in Scholarship

Reflexivity refers to a self-conscious reflection about the part one plays in the generation of knowledge (Gouldner, 1970; Mills, 1959). One of the hallmarks of reflexivity is recognition by the scholar that he or she is an actor intimately involved in the generation of knowledge, rather than simply a recorder and reporter of what is seen outside oneself. Such a self-aware stance on the part of a researcher fosters a critical approach to epistemology. For example, reflexivity calls into question the notion that objectivity is the only orientation a scholar may legitimately take to his or her study. Thus, it opens the door to the recognition that subjectivity not only is a valid and valuable orientation to research but may also be a necessary stance for good research. An example of the impact of a researcher's awareness of self on the research process and product comes from Stacey's (1990) ethnography of two Silicon Valley families in which she describes her struggles with her own biases about evangelical Christian groups as an impediment to her ability to hear, see, interpret, and reflect—in other words, conduct accurate research with—her primary respondents.

Another hallmark of reflexivity as a research orientation is the willingness to engage in continuous self-criticism, that is, a conscious second guessing of one's expertness, a questioning of the traditional posture of the researcher as the "knower," apart from and unrelated to those whom he or she is studying. This kind of self-critical orientation opens the doors to recognition of the ways in which scholars and the products of their research (as well as the institutional structures that support research) can foster and perpetuate a knowledge-based hierarchy in which the voices and views of some participants (the researchers) are valued more highly than those of the researched or in which the researched may be valued only as objects of study.

Reflexivity is notable as well in the self consciousness of feminist researchers in relation to their research participants. Feminists take issue with the concept of the researcher as somehow standing beyond the perimeter of the research arena, apart from the research frame. Instead of conceptualizing research as something done to (or for) research subjects by an objective observer outside the research setting, feminists acknowledge that their orientations, actions, interpretations, biases, and interests will become integral to the research process and its outcomes, and they seek to understand how it happens as it is happening during the process of their research.

We make no claim that feminist scholarship is the only place one finds self-critical sensitivity in the conduct of scholarship. Indeed, it has been the searing critiques of the scholarship of White, middle-class feminists by women of color that has fostered an awareness of what has been labeled "academic colonialism" (Collins, 1986). Academic colonialism is a reference to the potential for the academic research enterprise to exploit rather than to empower those who are the subject of study (Baca Zinn & Dill, 1994). In response to such critiques, feminist scholars have attempted to be more deliberately conscious of how scholarly practices affect those whose lives are studied and to attend to patterns of inclusion and exclusion. One of the implications for family research has been to broaden the base of research with families of color, as will be described in a later section. This has also renewed attention to one of the central characteristics of feminist approaches, and that is an emphasis on praxis.

The Centrality of Practice

Wood (1995) describes a "vibrant dialectic" in feminist scholarship between theorizing and practice, a dialectical tension that arises from the recognition that scholarship about the structures and processes that give rise to inequality is inherently political. The knowledge gained from feminist research must be applied not solely in the reshaping of theory but also in arenas of social change so as to reshape existing social conditions toward greater equality for men and women. Some feminists argue that the feminist scholar has a compelling involvement in implementation of his or her research and suggest a seamlessness between research and practice, including advocacy for change (Allen & Baber, 1992a; Reinharz, 1992).

Research for what? The concern with practice, that is, with the application and implementation of research findings beyond the academic environment, promotes a conscious attention to the relative importance of research questions and topics. Feminist scholars value the lives of women, and this concern is reflected in their choices of topics, settings, and approaches for study. Feminist scholarship has illuminated the dynamics of inequality and power through studies that have focused on the mundane aspects of women's everyday routines, including housework, caregiving, serving and allocating food, and balancing work and home (Hertz, 1997; Marks, 1998; Ribbens, 1994). Research that focuses on the physical, economic, and legal vulnerabilities of women has also been characteristic of choices of feminist scholars (Jarrett, 1994; Johnson, 1995; Konradi, 1996; Margolin, 1992; McCloskey, 1996).

Teaching. During the early years of this decade, attention turned to the incorporation of feminist perspectives and sensibilities into conventional materials on "the traditional family" and into conventional classroom teaching styles. One finds concern not only with what to teach (Allen & Baber, 1992b; Dilworth-Anderson, Burton, & Turner, 1993; Walker, 1993) but how (Lewis, 1995). Both content and practice concerns are reflected in articles that discuss the need for sensitivity to diverse student experiences and the value in building connections among and empowering students (MacDermid, Jurich, Myers-Walls, & Pelo, 1992), the planned use of reflexivity (Allen & Farnsworth, 1993), empathy (Thompson & Walker, 1995), self-disclosure (Allen, 1995), and restraint (Marks, 1995). Others focused beyond the content and pedagogy in family studies courses to address feminist pedagogy in family therapy training programs (Leslie & Clossick, 1992).

As the decade has progressed, attention continues to be given to sexist practices in the classroom and their effects on both women and men students and faculty (Maher & Tetrault, 1994; Myers & Dugan, 1996). In addition, new concerns have surfaced about student hostility toward women teachers and faculty in both secondary and higher education classrooms and with the combined effects of racism and sexism on classroom environments (Jarrett et al., 1999). The attention given by feminist scholars to the practice of the profession, with the correlative placement of the self in both research and teaching activities, legitimates this area of the professional literature. It also illustrates a central component of feminist thought on the artificiality of role segregation into professional and personal spheres.

A Central Focus on Process

A third characteristic of feminist research is its concern with process, as reflected both in the focus and conduct of research. Feminist research interest lies not solely in describing and analyzing current empirical realities in the lives of women and men and the associated inequalities, constraints, and privileges that accompany their different statuses. A feminist approach takes as centrally problematic the social processes through which the described patterns are generated, sustained over time, and come to reproduce themselves. A focus on the centrality of studying process is exemplified by Chafetz's (1991) work on the persistence of gender stratification. The choice to focus on understanding process is a strategic one. Knowledge of processes of gender differentiation and stratification can be used for intervention in and change of those processes and the inequalities they produce.

The focus on process also grows out of a sense that life, more particularly the lives of men and women, may be more adequately captured with a sense of time that is ongoing and seamless rather than divided into intervals or stages or marked by discrete events, roles, and achievements. There is interest in the unfolding of the processes themselves as objects of study. Thus, feminist approaches to parenting, for example, have focused on the myriad processes involved in caregiving (Cowan & Cowan, 1990), the unfolding nature of a parent's sense of himself or herself as part of and distinct from parenting activities (Cohen, 1987), and the processes through which a parent incorporates others into a scaffold of care for the child (Ribbens, 1994).

A third way in which process is central to feminist research is in the conduct of the research itself, regardless of the particular methodological approach taken by the researcher. Emphasis on the process of research is consistent with and part of a broader questioning of the nature and conduct of research, fueled by postmodernist and antipositivist trends in social philosophy (Lemert, 1999). Along with reflexivity, characteristics of feminist research practices include the conscious articulation of values, awareness of and attendance to the sensibilities of research participants, attention to the ethics of research, especially the linkages between the purpose of the basic research and its application to human need and the grounding of research questions and insights in human experience (Reinharz, 1992; Thompson, 1992; Thompson & Walker, 1995).

Small (1995) considers feminist research as action research and compares feminist methods with three other forms of action-oriented research. He notes particularly the concern of feminist research with advocacy on behalf of women (see Allen & Baber, 1992b). By contrast, in an extensive review of feminist methods in social research, Reinharz (1992) notes that although feminist research is concerned ultimately with change in inequitable structures, not all feminist researchers are activists or advocates. Moreover, the earlier debates about whether qualitative or quantitative approaches were able not only to capture more faithfully the voices of research participants but also to reflect the values and orientations of feminist scholars have been largely superseded by the publication of Reinharz's encyclopedic assessment of the diversity of research techniques employed by feminist scholars across the social sciences. Reinharz observes that feminist scholars work simultaneously from two vantage points—their disciplinary methodology plus the insights of feminism.

Rethinking Received Paradigms

A fourth characteristic of feminist scholarship is the questioning of received disciplinary wisdom, including prevailing epistemologies (Ferree, 1990; Thompson & Walker, 1995). It is of concern to feminist scholars that the accepted canon has largely been produced in an academy heretofore dominated by men and by masculinist ideologies about what is of importance. Scholarship that has been conducted outside a feminist perspective becomes suspect, given the understanding that knowledge is a product of the producer and that values about what to study and how have been determined by those in positions of power, that is, predominantly by men (Lemert, 1999; Wood, 1995). Moreover, the realization that the works of women and of men of color have largely been ignored and omitted from the accepted bodies of classic knowledge in the social science disciplines

underlines the concern that the canon is partial and that understandings of the nature of the phenomena we study are incomplete and therefore need careful reassessment (Allen, 2000; Baca Zinn & Dill, 1994; Lemert).

Fostering the critical stance toward the social science canon is the articulation of standpoint theory. Standpoint theory is succinctly expressed by Gubrium and Holstein (1990) in their aphorism, "truth = fact + perspective." That is, what is seen or experienced as authentic and real depends upon one's standpoint, one's perspective (Haraway, 1999). Acknowledgment of the centrality of gender to perspective and incorporation into research designs of the idea that gender shapes one's reality are two of the signal contributions of feminist scholarship to family research over the past decade.

Gender Roles and "Doing Gender"

Two formulations of the nature of gender are dominant, the gender roles perspective and the social constructionist approach. Stemming from role theory and with linkages to structure-functionalism, the first approach treats gender as a social role, characterized by a distinct and well integrated set of attitudes and behaviors. Viewed as a social role, gender is enacted or played out according to scripts that are carefully taught and repeatedly rehearsed until behavior governed by one's gender role script becomes so natural as to be seen as an integral part of oneself—second nature, as it were.

This taken-for-granted quality, the imperceptible slide from gender as role into gender as the essence of the self, has given rise to critiques of the role approach to gender. The role perspective encourages the social analyst to ignore the difference between the sex of the person playing a role and the gendered nature of the role, a critical omission if the goal is to understand how gender can shape perspective, structure social action, and express cultural values.

When gender is conceptualized as a role, women and men are seen as enacting roles that are separable, often complementary, and necessary elements to the integrity of the social settings or structures in which the roles are embedded. The role perspective on gender, with an emphasis on the content of roles and the processes by which they are learned and expressed, continues to characterize much contemporary work on gender in families, perhaps finding its fullest expression in textbooks on marriage and family relations (Glenn, 1997).

The second approach views gender as a social construct embodying cultural meanings of masculinity and femininity. Here, gender is defined as a constituent element of social structures, intricately interwoven with other elements of social structures such as class and race. Gender not only expresses cultural values but—as do class and race—also organizes the social distribution of societal resources. Gender, then, is centrally tied to distributions of merit, privilege, power, autonomy, and the resources they command. Ferree's (1990) description of the social constructionist perspective on gender appeared early in this decade and continues to stand as an excellent account of this approach.

This perspective specifically directs attention to the covert and overt processes that differentiate and then assign value and privilege on the basis of sex. This perspective reveals the systematic privileging of men relative to women, or less often, of women relative to men. Differential gender privilege, in turn, reinforces the establishment and maintenance of a culturally constructed, shared understanding of the differentness of men from women. This perspective on gender thus attends to processes in ongoing social interactions, as well as the resulting microstructures of power and privilege that result from those social interactions.

The social constructionist perspective on gender suggests that despite gender role socialization and because gender is not synonymous with the self, men and women not only vary in their degree of masculinity and femininity but have to be constantly persuaded or reminded to be masculine and feminine. That is, men and women have to "do" gender rather than "be" a gender. West and Zimmerman (1987) provided one of the first uses of this perspective in their analysis of the ways that individuals construct gender continuously in their ongoing social interactions. More recent work that follows in this tradition would include Martin's study (1998) of the creation of gendered children. Through careful ethnographic work in preschool settings, the author shows how child care personnel create children's identities as gendered boys and girls through typical preschool practices. Examples included teachers' disciplining girls' voices differently than boys' voices. The boys were allowed to be louder, and teachers' instructions were given to boys in groups rather than individually directed, as they were toward girls. Children's bodies were also disciplined such that more freedom of action and expression was allowed to boys than to girls. These practices were then incorporated by the children to provide a gendered structure to their subsequent interactions. Heimer and Staffen (1995) describe how nursing practices in newborn intensive care units result in gendered parenting. Specifically, young unwed fathers become left out of the newborn baby's circle of care by both intentional and unintentional acts of hospital staff. McGuffey and Rich (1999) used ethnographic procedures to analyze the strategies used by boys and girls in middle childhood to mark and maintain gender boundaries in both social and physical playground space. Their work is especially notable for the incorporation of social class and race into their analyses of children's coalitions and behaviors.

Thompson and Walker (1995) concluded that researchers and practitioners in the family field have yet to appreciate fully the power of this approach to gender. Relative to the more common role perspective, social constructionism remains on the margins of mainstream work on families and is used more often as a sensitizing framework rather than as a guide for research on families and family processes. Nonetheless, the impact of both this and the role perspective on gender can be traced in family research over the decade.

REFLECTIONS OF FEMINIST SENSITIVITIES IN FAMILY RESEARCH

Distinction between Sex and Gender

One of the most important reflections of feminist sensitivities in family research is the distinction between sex and gender. When gender is understood as the product of social processes and as embodying cultural meanings of masculinity and femininity, then it becomes possible to distinguish a person's gender from his or her sex. The former can be understood as sociocultural, the latter as biological; and while the two are correlated, they are not synonymous or isomorphic. This distinction offers clarity on often-confusing matters of measurement and interpretation of data by sex and gender.

Relative to measurement, one implication is to question the unexamined, often unstated, assumption that the meanings of attitudinal and behavioral measurement items (such as Likert-type questions) are the same for all male and female respondents. In other words, gender neutrality and within-gender homogeneity are assumed in much family studies research. With few exceptions, little attention has been given to the validity of the same measures for women and men. Notable exceptions are efforts to explore the differential meanings attached to fertility intentions (Thomson & Brandreth, 1995), money (Zelizer, 1989) and breadwinning (Potuchek, 1997). Far more common is research that employs measures without regard to the potential for differential meaning to men and women. For example, Sabatelli and Waldron (1995) provide an otherwise excellent discussion of issues in the measurement of parenting, but they do not discuss the problem of gender validity. Likewise, the conflict tactics scale (Straus, Hamby, Boney-McCoy, & Sugarman, 1996), widely used in studies of domestic violence, assumes that such terms as *conflict, argue,* and *hit* are interpreted in similar ways by men and women. To assume cross-gender validity and within-gender homogeneity ignores the impact of social position on social perception, which the feminist perspective would hold to be an inadequate representation of social reality.

The conventions of social survey research require that researchers measure attitudes, beliefs, values, or behaviors by exposing all respondents to the same stimuli, that is, by asking them all the same questions. When both partners in a couple dyad are included, it is possible to compare their responses and determine the degree of couple consistency in response patterns as well as patterns of under- and overreporting (Melby, Ge, Conger, & Warner, 1995; Svinovacz & Egley, 1995). But it is not possible to assert that the meanings attached to the items (that is, the subjective context out of which the respondents responded to the same items) were invariant across gender. Indeed, the recognition of gender bias in measures deserves the kind of attention that race and class bias has received (McGuire & Earls, 1993). To the extent that the empirical base in family studies increasingly comes to rest on analyses of large-scale, national-sample, survey data sets, which presume gender, class, and race neutrality in their measures, then to that extent, our knowledge base is problematic.

A second implication of distinguishing between sex and gender can be seen in the interpretation of data that demonstrate attitudinal or behavioral differences between men and women. How one interprets such empirical differences depends to some extent on one's perspective toward gender. For example, Mason's (1999) narrative analysis of men and women convicted of white-collar felonies showed that women described themselves as motivated by family need. They minimized their criminality by references to the small sums of money involved and its use for family necessities, such as groceries. Men, by contrast, described themselves as motivated by high achievement goals and felt their desire for a faster track to success justified embezzling large sums of money. There are sharp differences between men and women in the narrative accounts of their crimes, despite conspicuous similarities in their actual family situations and class backgrounds. One might interpret the empirical differences in their stories as reflective of an essential difference between men and women, or, alternatively, as a reflection of the different (gendered) cultural materials available to men and women from which they constructed their accounts. Similarly, one might interpret the difference in the economic value of their crimes as reflective of some kind of essential sex difference in criminal expression, such as a greater capacity of men for risk taking, or, alternatively, as an artifact of the gendered structure of corporate hierarchies that give more men than women unscrutinized access to large sums of money. The choice among these interpretations is less important than that they illustrate the interpretive richness that becomes available by viewing empirical differences between men and women not solely as evidence of biological or "essential" differences between the sexes but also as reflective of sociocultural and political processes of gender.

Recognition of Gendered Standpoints

The sensitivity of feminist scholarship to gendered standpoints is also reflected in family research. Safilios-Rothschild (1969), in the now-classic article entitled "Family sociology or wives' family sociology?", three decades ago called attention of family researchers to the importance of standpoint. Subsequent scholarship has continued to emphasize the influence of the researcher's standpoint on research. Wood (1995, pp. 111–112) suggests, "Scholars who rely on any single standpoint risk (mis)interpreting data in ways that overlook and therefore, distort some participants' motives and meanings. . . ." Wood continues, "Because Western culture defines men and masculine perspectives as normative, an androcentric point of view is often assumed and imposed, yet not acknowledged in either social life or research practice" (p. 112).

Interpretations of research findings. We highlight three examples in which scholars used multiple standpoints to advantage in interpreting their research on one of the most persistent work-family issues over the decade, the management of dependent care. Recent family research recognizes that the way in which family members provide care for one another is a political issue within the family. Hertz's (1997) analysis of the management of child care in dual-earner families is exemplary. Approaches used by couples in her study to construct their family lives included mothering, which maximized the working mother's time spent in parenting; parenting, in which the couple restructured their jobs to maximize both parents' involvement with parenting; and a market approach, in which couples allocated economic resources to replace the mother-as-parent by professional caregivers and left intact the father's limited role in family work. By viewing both employment and parenting as functions that could vary in the degree to which the couples gendered the roles, Hertz was able to discover a complex array of outcomes resulting from couple negotiations.

That negotiations within the family about how to provide care are centrally affected by larger societal trends and conditions has received some attention. Within the context of culture conflicts that impinge upon the availability of options for child care, Ross and Van Willigen (1996) track the impact of such societal inconsistencies in their analysis of gender, parenthood, and anger. In this study, the higher levels of anger among mothers than fathers and nonparents were accounted for by a combination of economic strain, status as the primary care provider, and the difficulties of finding, arranging, and paying for child care outside the home. In other words, the heightened levels of anger among mothers were not seen as characterological flaws or as personal weakness but as an outgrowth of situational demands and structural constraints that themselves were differentially distributed by gender.

Marks (1998) compared the impact of dependent-care providing, including the provision of care at home for a disabled child, spouse, or parent and care for neighbors or friends, on indicators of emotional well-being of middle-aged men and women. In general, more men than women reported reaping large benefits from providing care. The one exception was that men who provided care for a spouse reported experiencing significantly more hostility than women who provided spousal care, even after controlling for spillover stress from work and family. Androcentric ideologies of caregiving suggest that providing dependent care is a family domain in which women dominate because of their greater capacities for nurturance and self-sacrifice and the lower market value of their time relative to that of other adult family members. Among the outcomes of Marks' study is evidence that men are more involved in caregiving than such ideologies might suggest and that men are neither ill-equipped emotionally to care nor unable to gain satisfaction from caring for others.

Omission in problem definition. The use of gendered standpoints can cause researchers to overlook certain issues as research problems. Such was the case with family violence, which was not systematically studied until the 1970s (Gelles, 1980). We would argue that family security is also an issue that has been overlooked in part because of gendered standpoints. Ensuring the safety of family members from external threats is only occasionally studied and primarily only among families living in extreme environments. Research attention to family safety over the past two decades has given priority to recognition of the threat that family members themselves pose to one another. Thus, studies of intrafamilial violence, especially the serious violence of men against women, have appropriately dominated the focus of studies of family security, and gender and gender stratification are centrally involved in these patterns of intrafamilial violence. However, given the high levels of concern with crime, family, and personal safety voiced in national opinion surveys, the relative lack of attention to ensuring family safety from external threats is surprising.

Family security is stereotypically gendered work, and the male as family protector has been described as an enduring gender myth. Indeed, there is evidence to suggest that both men and women take seriously and support the assignment of family security to men. The male protector myth is mythical only in that it obscures the work that women do to secure the safety of their homes and children and in that it fails to suggest that the work that most men do to secure their families often endangers rather than protects them.

The work women do to protect their children from harm takes on heroic proportions in certain circumstances (Fox, Von Bargen, & Jester, 1996; Garbarino, Dubrow, Kostelney, & Pardo, 1992). More commonly, family security is a byproduct of women's common, daily community activities

(Hunter, Pearson, Ialongo, & Kellam, 1998). Ribbens (1994) describes in detail how mothers carefully construct a web of social relationships in their neighborhoods, primarily to provide a base of friendships for their children and in part to scaffold their children's security. Furstenberg et al. (1993) describe how the social relationships in which women envelop their children vary from one community to another, so that depending upon the characteristics of the community, those social relationships can complement, compensate for, or detract from the resources—including safety—that mothers on their own provide. Others, too, have found stark social class differences in the safety strategies women teach to their children and in the extent to which women can draw on neighborhood resources to help secure their children's safety (Brodsky, 1996; Fox, 2000; Hunter et al.; Jarrett, 1994).

In contrast to security strategies embedded in community-based social relationships, which have been uncovered in studies of mothers, there is much less evidence that fathers are involved in family safety work beyond the confines of the privatized household. In their own homes, men are more likely than women to purchase guns and to justify gun ownership in terms of family security needs and self-defense (Reiss & Roth, 1993). That such weapons-based family security strategies are often counterproductive is suggested by studies that show that both homicide and suicide are more likely in homes with guns than in comparable gun-free homes (Kellerman et al., 1992, 1993). The National Crime Victimization surveys suggest that victims rarely defend themselves with guns. In fewer than 5% of residential burglaries did homeowners defend themselves with firearms, and self-defense rates were even lower for other categories of personal crime (Reiss & Roth). In addition to posing inadvertent threats to their families, there is plentiful evidence that men are more likely to use firearms to kill family members intentionally than to be similarly victimized by family members (Daly & Wilson, 1988; Reiss & Roth). Finally, there is evidence that unrelated men in the household, such as boyfriends and stepfathers, may expose women and children to special risk (Margolin, 1992); and that fathers, when asked, give voice to concerns about the potential risk that other men pose to their children (Fox & Bruce, 1999). In sum, we suggest that family safety, as a topic of study, merits more explicit attention from family scholars, particularly as it relates to the well-researched and theorized area of family violence. Further, taking a gender perspective to the study of family security would help make explicit how women and men can be differentially steered into the use of strategies that play out gendered stereotypical behaviors and, similarly, are steered away from strategies that could prove to be more effective approaches to ensuring family safety.

Model misspecification. The use of gendered, androcentric standpoints can also foster model misspecification. The increasingly widespread use of the concept of social capital in family studies provides an example. Social capital as articulated by Coleman (1988) refers to the ways that social relationships are cumulated, stored, and utilized in the service of one's ends or goals, much as human capital, financial capital, and physical capital. Social capital inheres in social relationships characterized by ties of obligation, expectation, and trustworthiness and that serve as information channels. Coleman suggested that social norms that carry effective sanctions within a community are also a form of social capital. Interestingly, Coleman drew on family examples for both his abstract and empirical illustrations of the concept, showing how parents can build social capital and expend it in the service of their children's human capital accumulation.

Social capital conceptualizes the work that members of families do in building and using ties of mutual obligation, expectation, and trust with one another and with others in their neighborhoods and communities. It also conceptualizes how social relations in communities and neighborhoods can facilitate or hamper family work (Furstenberg & Hughes, 1995; Hunter et al., 1998; Murry & Brody, 1999; Sampson, Morenoff, & Earls, 1999). Thus, the concept stands as a useful addition to the theoretical work on the family-community interface because it makes visible the work that men and women do to build social supports around their families in order to accomplish or secure certain ends. By conceptualizing such family work within a broader set of microeconomic theories that have credence with those in the disciplinary mainstreams, it links the analysis of this kind of family work with central theoretical concerns of the field.

At the same time, the concept of social capital has been used without regard to its gender implications. A gender perspective raises several questions that need to be addressed by those who would use the concept of social capital. First, the implicit presumption of symmetry in the ties of mutual obligation and expectation (the social relations in which social capital inheres) may be inappropriate and misleading. Blumberg and Coleman's (1989) concept of *net economic value,* which takes into account a variety of discount factors that enhance or diminish the value of women's contributions, is relevant here. As with women's financial and human capital, it is likely that women's activities in the generation of social capital are subject to discounting or devaluation (for example, women's informational channels are disparaged as "mere gossip"). It is likely that women must expend or cash in relatively more social capital than men in transactions to accomplish similar ends. It is likely that men will tend to underinvest in social relations with women, both in the family and the community, because of the devaluation or underestimation of the capital value of such social relations. Finally, women may be as likely as men to devalue their social relations with other women and to discount or underestimate the power and effectiveness of their neighborly ties with women to secure valued social ends (Komter, 1989).

Contextualizing Family Relationships

Sensitizing family scholars to the importance of placing their studies of families within a broader social context has been one of the most important influences of feminist perspectives in family research. This has been reflected in family scholarship over the decade in several ways. First, there is greater sensitivity to the inclusion of people of color in study samples. The increased use of large-scale national sample surveys relevant to family-related phenomena, such as the National Survey of Families and Households, that include sufficient numbers of families of color to allow for both within-group and cross-group analyses has facilitated attention to families of color. Likewise, smaller surveys and ethnographies focused on specific ethnic family groups have increased understanding of contextual influences on families (Murry & Brody, 1999). Moreover, the increased emphasis on ethnic diversity across the academic curriculum, including the emergence of courses and texts focused on family diversity, has also fostered, indeed necessitated, new research on underrepresented ethnic groups (McAdoo, 1993; Mindel, Habenstein, & Wright, 1999; Pedraza & Rumbaut, 1996).

Second, there is recognition of the importance

of the challenge posed by Collins' (1986) articulation of the matrix of domination as the context out of which family life is constructed. That is, race, class, and gender are relational categories of domination. To understand how family life is structured, each must be studied in relation to the others, not alone. Studies have emerged that seek the source of differences in family patterns within the structural matrix formed by these three axes of hierarchy (Baca Zinn, 1994; Dill, 1994; Glenn, 1992; Segura, 1994).

Finally, family scholars have contextualized their research on family relationships by recognition of the myriad ways in which intimate family interactions are shaped by broader social currents, prevailing power relations, and dominant ideologies (Komter, 1989; Mullings, 1994). Examples include studies of men's decisions about time allocation between work and parent roles (Berry & Rao, 1997; Daly, 1996), decisions about marriage timing and family formation (Adler, 1997; Albrecht, Fossett, Cready, & Kiecolt, 1997; Koball, 1998), husband-to-wife violence (Macmillan & Gartner, 1999), the use of money (Treas, 1991), and household division of labor (Gallagher & Smith, 1999; Hossain & Roopnarine, 1993; Orbuch & Eyster, 1997).

Attending to Power Processes

Attending to the importance of process is one of the sensitizing influences of feminist scholarship in family research. Power processes, both overt and covert, have been an important focus of study. Kudson-Martin and Mahoney (1998) sought to identify marital processes that foster equal marriages, which they defined as those in which each partner held equal status, in which accommodation in the relationship was mutual, in which attention to the other in the relationship was mutual, and in which there was mutual well-being of partners. In equal marriages, each spouse has roughly the same capacity to get the other to cooperate in attaining goals and attending to his or her needs, desires, and wants. Couples were selected for study who viewed themselves as having a marriage they characterized as equal and who described their roles as non–gender specific. They found, however, that despite the couples' self-descriptions as egalitarian, gender inequality was perpetuated by subtle power processes that were both visible and latent. Wives were more likely than husbands to accommodate their partners' needs or desires and to speak of fitting their lives around their partner's schedule. In addition, wives were more likely than husbands to describe attending to their partners' needs, worrying about upsetting or offending their partners, and doing what their partner wanted or needed. Other researchers have reported similar gender inequalities in marriages in terms of the subtle power processes involved in determining the direction of conversations and problems that get discussed in marriages (Ball, Cowan, & Cowan, 1995; Zvonkovic, Schmiege, & Hall, 1994). Viewing one's marriage as equal and family roles as egalitarian, despite experiencing marital inequality, serves several functions in preserving marriages (Gallagher & Smith, 1999; Rosenbluth, Steil, & Whitcomb, 1998). It conceals the existence of male domination and female submission in modern couple relationships and keeps partners from recognizing the existence of covert power, which if acknowledged could create marital conflict (Hare-Mustin, 1991; Komter, 1989).

CONCLUSION

In this review, we have outlined four characteristics of feminist scholarship and have suggested how each is reflected in contemporary research in family studies. Throughout the review, we have tried to suggest areas of continuity with earlier work on gender—specifically, in the work that focuses on division of labor, work-family issues, and providing care for family members. We have also suggested areas that merit continued exploration through the perspective of gender, such as validity assessments of measures, the conceptualization of social capital, and family safety.

We choose to close with our vague sense of discomfort with the seeming disjuncture between the body of work on family and gender as represented in some areas of academic study of the family and evidence of a strong antifeminism, antiwoman backlash that has surfaced in many parts of the contemporary U.S. culture. Both overt and covert expressions that in the quest for gender equality, women have stepped beyond their proper place can be found among religious activist groups, privately funded think tanks, and even in academia and academic and professional organizations. Anecdotal reports of suspected censorship of feminist scholarship by journal reviewers, editors, and funding agencies circulate in the informal information channels of academia (e.g., listservs, newsletters, e-mails). The concerns are reminiscent of a similar concern about the selectivity of research on race reported more than a decade ago (Baptiste, 1986). Gamson (1999) has spoken of the social knowledge process of "facticity;" that is, the validation of certain information as "factual." Information that is consistent with hegemonic story-lines is privileged, and alternative information is ignored, suppressed, unseen, and unheard.

Family scholars need to exercise oversight and caution about the knowledge processes in our field, and we would suggest that a study of the typical career of feminist scholarship in family studies might be timely. For example, rates of funding of research, presentation and publication of family scholarship utilizing feminist perspectives might be tracked over time. Beyond academia, we suggest that the growing antifeminist sensibility in the culture at large deserves study in its own right, especially as the organizations that give voice to it claim to speak in the best interests of families. It also merits attention because it will be part of the sociocultural context out of which new social theories of families and gender will be born.

REFERENCES

Adler, M. A. (1997). Social change and declines in marriage and fertility in Eastern Germany. *Journal of Marriage and the Family, 59,* 37–49.

Albrecht, C. M., Fossett, M. A., Cready, C. M., & Kiecolt, K. J. (1997). Mate availability, women's marriage prevalence, and husbands' education. *Journal of Family Issues, 18,* 429–452.

Allen, K. R. (1995). Opening the classroom closet: Sexual orientation and self-disclosure. *Family Relations, 44,* 136–131.

Allen, K. R. (2000). A conscious and inclusive family study. *Journal of Marriage and the Family, 62,* 4–17.

Allen, K. R., & Baber, K. M. (1992a). Ethical and epistemological tension in applying a postmodern perspective to feminist research. *Psychology of Women Quarterly, 16,* 1–15.

Allen, K. R., & Baber, K. M. (1992b). Starting a revolution in family life education: A feminist vision. *Family Relations, 41,* 378–384.

Allen, K. R., & Farnsworth, E. B. (1993). Reflexivity in teaching about families. *Family Relations, 42,* 351–356.

Baca Zinn, M. (1994). Feminist rethinking from racial-ethnic families. In M. Baca Zinn & B. T. Dill (Eds.), *Women of color in U.S. society* (pp. 303–314). Philadelphia: Temple University Press.

Baca Zinn, M., & Dill, B. T. (1994). Difference and domination. In M. Baca Zinn & B. T. Dill (Eds.), *Women of color in U.S. society* (pp. 3–12). Philadelphia: Temple University Press.

Ball, J., Cowan, P., & Cowan, P. (1995). Who's got the power? Gender differences in partners' perceptions of influence during marital problems-solving discussions. *Family Process, 34,* 303–321.

Baptiste, D. A., (1986). The image of the black family portrayed by television: A critical comment. *Marriage and Family Review, 10,* 41–65.

Berry, J. O., & Rao, J. M. (1997). Balancing employment and fatherhood: A systems perspective. *Journal of Family Issues, 18,* 386–402.

Blumberg, R. L., & Coleman, M. T. (1989). A theoretical look at the gender balance of power in the American couple. *Journal of Family Issues, 10,* 225–250.

Brodsky, A. E. (1996). Resilient single mothers in risky neighborhoods: Negative psychological sense of community. *Journal of Community Psychology, 24,* 347–363.

Chafetz, J. C. (1991). The gender division of labor and the reproduction of female disadvantage: Toward an integrated theory. In R. L. Blumberg (Ed.) *Gender, family, and economy: The triple overlap* (pp. 74–94). Newbury Park, CA: Sage.

Cohen, T. F. (1987). Remaking men: Men's experiences becoming and being husbands and fathers and their implications for reconceptualizing men's lives. *Journal of Family Issues, 8,* 55–77.

Coleman, J. S. (1988). Social capital in the creation of human capital. *American Journal of Sociology, 94,* S95–S120.

Collins, P. H. (1986). Learning from the outsider within: The sociological significance of black feminist thought. *Social Forces, 33,* 514–532.

Cowan, P. A., & Cowan, C. P. (1990). Becoming a family: Research and intervention. In I. E. Sigel and G. H. Brody (Eds.), *Methods of family research: Biographies of research projects. Vol. 1: Normal families* (pp. 1–52). Hillsdale, NJ: Erlbaum.

Daly, K. J. (1996). Spending time with the kids: Meaning of family time for fathers. *Family Relations, 45,* 466–476.

Daly, M., & Wilson, M. (1988). *Homicide.* New York: Aldine de Gruyter.

Dill, B. T. (1994). Fictive kin, paper sons, and compadrazgo: Women of color and the struggle for family survival. In M. Baca Zinn & B. T. Dill (Eds.), *Women of color in U.S. society* (pp. 149–170). Philadelphia: Temple University Press.

Dilworth-Anderson, P., Burton, L. M., & Turner, W. L. (1993). The importance of values in the study of culturally diverse families. *Family Relations, 42,* 238–242.

Ferree, M. M. (1990). Beyond separate spheres: Feminism and family research. *Journal of Marriage and the Family, 52,* 866–884.

Fox, G. L. (2000). No time for innocence, no place for innocents: Children's exposure to extreme violence. In G. L. Fox & M. L. Benson (Eds.), *Families, crime, and criminal justice* (pp. 163–181). London: JAI/Elsevier.

Fox, G. L., & Bruce, C. (1999). The anticipation of single parenthood: A profile of men's concerns. *Journal of Family Issues, 20,* 485–506.

Fox, G. L., Von Bargen, J., & Jester, M. (1996). Managing murder: Parents as mediators of children's experience. *Journal of Family Issues, 17,* 732–757.

Furstenberg, F. F., Jr., Belzer, A., Davis, C., Levine, J. A., Morrow, K., & Washington, M. (1993). How families manage risk and opportunity in dangerous neighborhoods. In W. J. Wilson (Ed.), *Sociology and the public agenda* (pp. 231–258). Newbury Park, CA: Sage.

Furstenberg, F. F., Jr., & Hughes, M. (1995). Social capital and successful development among at-risk youth. *Journal of Marriage and the Family, 57,* 580–592.

Gallagher, S. K., & Smith, C. (1999). Symbolic traditionalism and pragmatic egalitarianism: Contemporary evangelicals, families, and gender. *Gender and Society, 13,* 211–233.

Gamson, W. (1999). Half-truths with real consequences: Journalism, research, and public policy. *Contemporary Sociology, 28,* 23–26.

Garbarino, J., Dubrow, N., Kostelney, K., & Pardo, C. (1992). *Children in danger.* San Francisco: Jossey-Bass.

Gelles, R. (1980). Violence in the family: A review of research in the seventies. *Journal of Marriage and the Family, 42,* 873–886.

Glenn, E. N. (1992). From servitude to service work: Historical continuities in the racial division of paid reproductive labor. *Signs: Journal of Women in Culture and Society, 18,* 1–43.

Glenn, N. D. (1997). A critique of twenty family and marriage and the family textbooks. *Family Relations, 46,* 197–208.

Gouldner, A. W. (1970). *The coming crisis of western sociology.* New York: Basic Books.

Gubrium, J. F., & Holstein, J. A. (1990). *What is family?* Mountain View, CA: Mayfield.

Haraway, D. (1999). The cyborg manifesto and fractured identities. In C. Lemert (Ed.), *Social theory* (pp. 539–543). Boulder, CO: Westview Press.

Hare-Mustin, R. (1991). Sex, lies, and headaches: The problem is power. In T. J. Goodrich (Ed.), *Women and power: Perspectives for family therapy* (pp. 63–85). New York: Norton.

Heimer, C. A., & Staffen, L. R. (1995). Interdependence and reintegrative social control: Labeling and reforming "inappropriate" parents in neonatal intensive care units. *American Sociological Review, 60,* 635–654.

Hertz, R. (1997). A typology of approaches to child care: The centerpiece of organizing family life for dual-earner couples. *Journal of Family Issues, 18,* 355–385.

Hossain, Z., & Roopnarine, F. L. (1993). Division of household labor and child care in dual earner African-American families with infants. *Sex Roles, 29,* 571–583.

Hunter, A. G., Pearson, J. L., Ialongo, N. S., & Kellam, S. G. (1998). Parenting alone to multiple caregivers: Child care and parenting arrangements in black and white urban families. *Family Relations, 47,* 343–353.

Jarrett, R. L. (1994). Living poor: Family life among single parent, African American women. *Social Problems, 41,* 30–45.

Jarrett, R., Lamanna, M., Baker, P., Higginbotham, E., Rakowski, C., & Sprague, J. (1999, August). *Evaluating Teaching: Does Gender Matter?* Panel presentation at the American Sociological Association meetings, Chicago.

Johnson, M. P. (1995). Patriarchal terrorism and common couple violence: Two forms of violence against women. *Journal of Marriage and the Family, 57,* 283–294.

Kellerman, A. L., Rivara, F. P., Rushforth, N. B., Banton, J. G., Reay, D. T., Francisco, J. T., Locci, A. B.,

Prodzinski, J., Hackman, B. B., & Somes, G. (1993). Gun ownership as risk factor for homicide in the home. *New England Journal of Medicine, 329,* 1084–1091.

Kellerman, A. L., Rivara, F. P., Somes, G., Reay, D. T., Francisco, J. T., Banton, J. G., Prodzinski, J., Fligner, C., & Hackman, B. B. (1992). Suicide in the home in relation to gun ownership. *New England Journal of Medicine, 327,* 467–472.

Koball, H. (1998). Have African American men become less committed to marriage? Explaining the twentieth century racial cross-over in men's marriage timing. *Demography, 35,* 251–258.

Komter, A. (1989). Hidden power in marriage. *Gender and Society, 3,* 187–216.

Konradi, A. (1996). Preparing to testify: Rape survivors negotiating the criminal justice system. *Gender and Society, 10,* 404–432.

Kudson-Martin, C., & Mahoney, A. R. (1998). Language processes in the construction of equality in marriages. *Family Relations, 47,* 81–91.

Lemert, C. (1999). After modernity. In C. Lemert (Ed.), *Social theory* (pp. 451–463). Boulder, CO: Westview Press.

Leslie, L. A., & Clossick, M. L. (1992). Changing set: Teaching family therapy from a feminist perspective. *Family Relations, 41,* 256–263.

Lewis, E. A. (1995). Toward a tapestry of impassioned voices: Incorporating praxis into teaching about families. *Family Relations, 44,* 149–152.

MacDermid, S. M., Jurich, J. A., Myers-Walls, J. A., & Pelo, A. (1992). Feminist teaching: Effective education. *Family Relations, 41,* 31–38.

Macmillan, R., & Gartner, R. (1999). When she brings home the bacon: Labor-force participation and the risk of spousal violence against women. *Journal of Marriage and the Family, 61,* 947–958.

Maher, F. A., & Tetrault, M. K. T. (1994). *The feminist classroom: An inside look at how professors and students are transforming higher education for a diverse society.* New York: Basic Books.

Margolin, L. (1992). Mothers' boyfriends and child abuse: Why the overrepresentation? *Child Abuse and Neglect, 16,* 541–551.

Marks, N. F. (1998). Does it hurt to care? Caregiving, work-family conflict, and midlife well-being. *Journal of Marriage and the Family, 60,* 951–966.

Marks, S. R. (1995). The art of professing and holding back in a course on gender. *Family Relations, 44,* 142–148.

Martin, K. A. (1998). Becoming a gendered body: Practices of preschools. *American Sociological Review, 63,* 494–511.

Mason, K. (1999). *Middle class, white collar criminals: Needy women, greedy men?* Unpublished doctoral dissertation. University of Tennessee, Knoxville.

McAdoo, H. P. (Ed.) (1993). *Family ethnicity: Strength in diversity.* Newbury Park, CA: Sage.

McCloskey, L. A. (1996). Socioeconomic and coercive power within the family. *Gender and Society, 10,* 449–463.

McGuffey, C. S., & Rich, B. L. (1999). Playing in the gender transgression zone: Race, class, and hegemonic masculinity in middle childhood. *Gender and Society, 13,* 608–627.

McGuire, J., & Earls, F. (1993). Exploring the reliability of measures of family relations, parental attitudes, and parent-child relations in a disadvantaged minority population. *Journal of Marriage and the Family, 55,* 1042–1046.

Melby, J. N., Ge, X., Conger, R. D., Warner, T. D. (1995). The importance of task in evaluating positive marital interactions. *Journal of Marriage and the Family, 57,* 981–994.

Mills, C. W. (1959). *The sociological imagination.* New York: Oxford University Press.

Mindel, C. H., Habenstein, R. W., & Wright, R., Jr. (Eds.). (1999). *Ethnic families in America: Patterns and variations.* Upper Saddle River, NJ: Prentice-Hall.

Mullings, L. (1994). Images, ideology, and women of color. In M. Baca Zinn & B. T. Dill (Eds.), *Women of color in U.S. society* (pp. 265–89). Philadelphia: Temple University Press.

Murry, V. M., & Brody, G. H. (1999). Self-regulation and self-worth of Black children reared in economically stressed, rural, single-mother headed families. *Journal of Family Issues, 20,* 456–482.

Myers, D. J., & Dugan, K. B. (1996). Sexism in graduate school classrooms: Consequences for students and faculty. *Gender and Society, 10,* 330–350.

Orbuch, T. L., & Eyster, S. L. (1997). Division of household labor among black couples and white couples. *Social Forces, 76,* 301–333.

Pedraza, S., & Rumbaut, R. G. (1996). *Origins and destinies: Immigration, race, and ethnicity in America.* Belmont, CA: Wadsworth.

Potuchek, J. L. (1997). *Who supports the family? Gender and breadwinning in dual-earner marriages.* Stanford, CA: Stanford University Press.

Reinharz, S. (1992). *Feminist methods in social research.* New York: Oxford University Press.

Reiss, A. J., Jr., & Roth, J. A., Eds. (1993). *Understanding and preventing violence.* Washington, DC: National Academy Press.

Ribbens, J. (1994). *Mothers and their children: A feminist sociology of childrearing.* London: Sage.

Rosenbluth, S. C., Steil, J. M., & Whitcomb, J. H. (1998). Marital equality: What does it mean? *Journal of Family Issues, 19,* 227–244.

Ross, C. E., & Van Willigen, M. (1996). Gender, parenthood, and anger. *Journal of Marriage and the Family, 58,* 572–584.

Sabatelli, R. M., & Waldron, R. J. (1995). Measurement issues in the assessment of the experiences of parenthood. *Journal of Marriage and the Family, 57,* 969–980.

Safilios-Rothschild, C. (1969). Family sociology or wives' family sociology? A cross-cultural examination of decision-making. *Journal of Marriage and the Family, 31,* 290–301.

Sampson, R. S., Morenoff, J. D., & Earls, F. (1999). Beyond social capital: Spatial dynamics of collective efficacy for children. *American Sociological Review, 64,* 633–660.

Segura, D. A. (1994). Inside the work worlds of Chicana and Mexican immigrant women. In M. Baca Zinn & B. T. Dill (Eds.), *Women of color in U.S. society* (pp. 95–111). Philadelphia: Temple University Press.

Small, S. A. (1995). Action-oriented research: Models and methods. *Journal of Marriage and the Family, 57,* 941–955.

Stacey, J. (1990). *Brave new families: Stories of domestic upheaval in late twentieth century America.* New York: Basic Books.

Straus, M. A., Hamby, S. L., Boney-McCoy, S., & Sugarman, D. B. (1996). The revised conflict tactics scale (CTS2): Development and preliminary psychometric data. *Journal of Family Issues, 17,* 283–316.

Szinovacz, M. E., & Egley, L. C. (1995). Comparing one-partner and couple data on sensitive marital behaviors: The case of marital violence. *Journal of Marriage and the Family, 57,* 995–1010.

Thomson, E., & Brandreth, Y. (1995). Measuring fertility demand. *Demography, 32,* 81–96.

Thompson, L. (1992). Feminist methodology for family studies. *Journal of Marriage and the Family, 54,* 3–18.

Thompson, L., & Walker, A. (1995). The place of feminism in family studies. *Journal of Marriage and the Family, 57,* 847–865.

Treas, J. (1991). The common pot or separate purses? A transaction cost interpretation. In R. L. Blumberg (Ed.), *Gender, family, and economy: The triple overlap* (pp. 211–224). Newbury Park, CA: Sage.

Walker, A. J. (1993). Teaching about race, gender, and class diversity in United States families. *Family Relations, 42,* 342–350.

West, C., & Zimmerman, D. (1987). Doing gender. *Gender and Society, 1* 125–151.

Wood, J. T. (1995). Feminist scholarship and the study of relationships. *Journal of Social and Personal Relationships, 12,* 103–120.

Zelizer, V. A. (1989). The social meaning of money: "Special monies." *American Journal of Sociology, 95,* 342–377.

Zvonkovic, A. M., Schmiege, C. J., & Hall, L. D. (1994). Influence strategies used when couples make work-family decisions and their importance for marital satisfaction. *Family Relations, 43,* 182–188.

WILLIAM MARSIGLIO   *University of Florida*

PAUL AMATO   *The Pennsylvania State University**

RANDAL D. DAY   *Brigham Young University***

MICHAEL E. LAMB   *National Institute of Child Health and Human Development****

Scholarship on Fatherhood in the 1990s and Beyond

Throughout the 1990s, scholars interested in fatherhood have generated a voluminous, rich, and diverse body of work. We selectively review this literature with an eye toward prominent theoretical, methodological, and substantive issues. This burgeoning literature, complemented by social policy makers' heightened interest in fathers and families, focuses on fatherhood in at least 4 key ways. First, theorists have studied fatherhood as a cultural representation that is expressed through different sociocultural processes and embedded in a larger ecological context. Second, researchers have conceptualized and examined the diverse forms of fatherhood and father involvement. Third, attempts have been made to identify the linkages between dimensions of the father-child relationship and developmental outcomes among children and fathers. Fourth, scholars have explored the father identity as part of a reciprocal process negotiated by men, children, mothers, and other interested parties. Our review highlights research that examines the relationships between dimensions of the father-child relationship and children's well-being and development. We conclude by discussing promising avenues of scholarship for the next generation of research on fatherhood.

Department of Sociology, University of Florida, Gainesville, FL 32611 (marsig@soc.ufl.edu).

*Department of Sociology, The Pennsylvania State University, University Park, PA 16803.

**Department of Marriage, Family, and Human Development, Brigham Young University, Provo, UT 84604.

***National Institute of Child Health and Human Development, Bethesda, MD 20892.

Key Words: father-child relationship, fatherhood, father identity, fathering, father involvement.

THE CONTEXT FOR SCHOLARSHIP ON FATHERHOOD

Building on the scholarly interest in fatherhood that emerged in the 1970s and 80s (Lamb, 2000), the 1990s produced a more extensive and eclectic social science literature on numerous aspects of fatherhood. Throughout the decade, interest in fatherhood grew, the number and diversity of fatherhood researchers expanded, and efforts to promote the study of fatherhood intensified. These developments, punctuated by expanding social policies targeting fathers, present us with a timely opportunity to survey the recent literature on fatherhood and suggest promising avenues for future scholarship.

The multilayered fatherhood terrain is represented by a wide range of issues, including cultural representations of and discourses about fatherhood, conceptual and empirical analyses of the diverse forms of fatherhood and father involvement, linkages between dimensions of the father-child relationship and children's and fathers' well-being and development, and the social psychology of paternal identity and fathering. Given the breadth of work on these topics, our review incorporates various disciplinary perspectives on the different aspects of fatherhood and focuses largely on the fathering of children and adolescents (for discussions of fathering with adult children, see Rossi & Rossi, 1990; Snarey, 1993).

Our summary and assessment of the scholarly record on fatherhood during the past decade is informed by our recognition of the larger sociopolitical context and its role in shaping research agendas. A variety of specialized conferences and roundtables during the 1990s raised the visibility of research on fathers while accentuating its social policy implications (Marsiglio, 1998; National Center on Fathers and Families [NCOFF], 1997). Most notable among these conferences were the series of national meetings sponsored by the Federal Interagency Forum on Child and Family Statistics in 1996–1997. Organized in response to President Clinton's 1995 executive order directing federal agencies to support fathers' positive involvement in their families while ensuring that federally funded research on children and families incorporated fathers, these multidisciplinary meetings culminated in 1998 in the publication of *Nurturing Fatherhood: Improving Data and Research on Male Fertility, Family Formation, and Fatherhood.* This document, drawing on the efforts of over 100 researchers, policy analysts, and public officials, reviewed and analyzed the state of data collection, research, and theory on a range of issues related to fatherhood. The larger federal initiative has provided an intellectual foundation and incentive for launching a new wave of research on fatherhood while sensitizing policy makers and funding agencies to its relevance.

During the past decade, scholarship on fatherhood was also encouraged when several journals, including *Families in Societies* (1993), *Journal of Family Issues* (1993 & 1994; 1999), *Demography* (1998), *Journal of Men's Studies* (1998), *Journal of Family History* (2000), and *Marriage and Family Review* (2000), devoted special issues to this topic. A number of edited volumes (Booth & Crouter,1998; Bozett & Hanson, 1991; Daniels, 1998; Garfinkel, McLanahan, Meyer, & Seltzer, 1998; Hawkins & Dollahite, 1997; Hood, 1993; Lamb, 1997; Marsiglio, 1995a; Shapiro, Diamond, & Greenberg, 1995) provided additional outlets for the growing body of research on fa-

therhood. The impressive activity in this area is further illustrated by the emergence, continuing efforts, or both of organizations across the country to promote research, social policy analyses, community programs, or the dissemination of information and value-based messages about fatherhood (National Center for Fathers and Families; Center on Fathers, Families, and Public Policy; National Center for Fathering; National Fatherhood Initiative; and the Fatherhood Project). In addition, the directors of major national surveys (e.g., Panel Study of Income Dynamics, National Survey of Labor Market Experience—Youth, National Survey of Adolescent Males, National Survey of Families and Households [NSFH], and National Survey of Family Growth) have recently responded to the surge of interest in fatherhood by adding questions about fathering to recent or forthcoming waves of data collection (see Federal Interagency Forum on Child and Family Statistics, 1998). Research initiatives such as these are novel and significant because they ask the fathers themselves about their family roles.

These noteworthy activities have occurred against a backdrop of fundamental shifts in family life, gender relations, men's declining wages, and increases in both women's participation in the paid labor force and men's involvement as primary nonmaternal care providers (Gerson, 1993). At the same time, heated public debates have emerged over numerous issues relevant to fatherhood, including divorce and single parenthood, "deadbeat dads" and "androgynous" fathers, welfare reform, teenage pregnancy and nonmarital childbearing, fathers' rights and responsibilities, the definition of "family," and fathers' potentially unique contributions to child development. Discussions of these issues often make reference to serious social problems assumed to arise from the diverse conditions of *fatherlessness* and *father absence* (Blankenhorn, 1995; Popenoe, 1996). Despite scholarly disagreement over the meaning of these concepts and the extent and consequences of father absence, these debates influence how the public, policy makers, and the research community frame various questions concerning fathers and families (Daniels, 1998; Griswold, 1993). Fears about the growing numbers of fathers who are disconnected from their children have inspired stakeholders to develop organized responses to particular features of fatherhood. Male-only social movements and events such as the Promise Keepers, the Million Man March on Washington, the Mythopoetic movement, and fathers' rights groups have each wrestled with fathers' voluntary or involuntary lack of involvement with their children and, in the process, served to heighten public awareness about the meaning and relevance of fathers in children's lives (Marsiglio & Cohan, 2000; Messner, 1997; Stacey, 1998).

PERSPECTIVES ON FATHERHOOD

An impressive body of literature appearing during the 1990s advanced the way we conceptualize and theorize aspects of fatherhood. These multidisciplinary efforts illustrate the complexity of the issues involved and, at times, the competing ways in which core questions have been framed and addressed. Without claiming to be exhaustive, we discuss briefly some of the leading perspectives that have guided the literatures that take fatherhood or fathering as their subject and emphasize where appropriate the significance of fathers' diverse life course and family circumstances.

Historical Perspectives

Our understanding of late-20th-century fatherhood has been enriched by efforts to clarify how it can be viewed as an historically varying social construction (Griswold, 1993; Jaret, 1991; LaRossa, 1997; LaRossa, Gordon, Wilson, Bairan, & Mintz, 1998; Pleck & Pleck, 1997; Stearns, 1991; see also Kimmel, 1996; Rotundo, 1993). These insightful critiques of fatherhood in the United States since the colonial era have painted a more complex image of fathering than was available earlier. Scholars have shown that within every historical epoch, a great deal of variability has always existed, with the dominant motif in any period coexisting alongside concerns about other important conceptions of fatherhood. Breadwinning has always been a concern, for example, even though moral leadership may have been emphasized in the colonial period and gender role modeling in the mid-20th century. Recent analyses have alerted us to the historical flexibility of fatherhood, the fundamental linkages between cultural images of mothering and fathering, the futility of searching for prototypical "traditional" families and fathers, and the diversity of men's family roles in previous eras (Cherlin, 1998; Lamb, 1998). At the same time, we are also reminded that our historical understanding of fatherhood is quite limited because materials are typically drawn from White middle-class sources and are seldom representative of their contempo-

raries from different ethnic, racial, cultural, and economic backgrounds. Although those interested in the history of fatherhood have been encouraged to study the unique historical events relevant to men from different ethnic or racial backgrounds and to focus on the unique combinations of these experiences across race and ethnicity, Burton and Snyder (1998) point out that little has been accomplished in this regard (see Griswold (1993); and Parke & Buriel (1998) for possible exceptions).

Conceptual and Theoretical Perspectives

One of the more noteworthy recent developments involves attempts to refine and expand conceptualizations of father involvement to capture the range of activities that fathers can do that influence their children's lives. Lamb, Pleck, Charnov, and Levine's (1987) conceptualization identifying engagement, accessibility, and responsibility as forms of paternal involvement continued to influence fatherhood scholars in the 1990s. Building on this conceptualization, Palkovitz (1997) explicitly identified 15 general categories of paternal involvement (e.g., doing errands, planning, providing, sharing activities, teaching, thinking about children). In the process, Palkovitz extended Lamb and colleagues' notion of responsibility by calling for a more systematic and fuller treatment of the cognitive manifestations of father involvement (see also Walzer, 1998). Moreover, he delineated and discussed some of the useful continua (e.g., time invested, degree of involvement, observability, salience, directness) that researchers should take into account when examining the nature and consequences of different types of father involvement. These and other related discussions (Hawkins & Palkovitz, 1999) highlight the complex nature of father involvement and warrant further consideration.

From a social constructionist perspective, it is clear that the growing diversity of life course and residency patterns for men and children today, as well as stakeholders' vested interests in emphasizing particular images of fatherhood and paternal involvement, need to be recognized when conceptualizations of paternal involvement are broadened (Marsiglio, Day, & Lamb, 2000). In a related vein, a focus on family processes such as distance regulation (parents' tolerance for individuality and emotional connection), parental support, and flexibility provides opportunities to examine the ways men develop, negotiate, and sustain their rights, privileges, and obligations as fathers in different types of family structures. This type of approach is consistent with an appreciation for the increasingly complex set of social, cultural, and legal forces associated with the multiple pathways to paternity, social fatherhood, and responsible fathering (Daniels, 1998; Marsiglio, 1998).

Other theorists have examined fatherhood using the concept of social capital (e.g., family and community relations that benefit children's cognitive and social development). The quality of the relationships between fathers and children (as reflected in behaviors such as paternal warmth and helping) represents one obvious example of social capital. Fathers who cooperate with and share parenting styles and values with their children's mother provide another example. Fathers also contribute to their children's development through their connections with other individuals and organizations in the community. For example, fathers build social capital when they know their children's friends and the parents of their children's friends. Social capital also is created when fathers are involved with institutions in the community, such as schools, churches, sports teams, and neighborhood organizations in which their children participate. Fathers who maintain contact with their children's teachers, coaches, employers, ministers, and neighbors help to bring about closure (or structural integration) in children's social networks. Closure makes it easier for care providers to share information about children, supervise and guide children, treat children in a consistent manner, and help children internalize a coherent set of social norms. Finally, fathers can build social capital by connecting their children to their own social networks. A father working in a factory may introduce his child to his supervisor, who may eventually hire the child. This father can also share knowledge that will help his child succeed at his tasks and fit in with his coworkers (Amato, 1998; Coleman, 1988, 1990; Furstenberg, 1998; Furstenberg & Hughes, 1995; Hagan, MacMillan, & Wheaton, 1996; Seltzer, 1998a). Additional research is indirectly relevant to our understanding of how fathers' opportunities for contributing social capital are affected by co-parents' perspectives on shared parenting (Dienhart, 1998; Dienhart & Daly, 1997) and mothers' gatekeeping roles when fathers co-reside with (Allen & Hawkins, 1999) or live apart from their children (Braver & O'Connell, 1998). The notion of social capital is useful because it provides a conceptual linkage between the actions of fathers, children's

developmental trajectories, and the larger network of social relations within which fathers and children are embedded.

Use of the social capital concept to enrich the analysis of father involvement is consistent with a family systems or ecological perspective. Although not referring to social capital explicitly, Doherty, Kouneski, and Erickson (1998) outlined a systemic ecological approach for conceptualizing the linkages between individual, interpersonal, and social factors that affect the context for so-called responsible fathering for either resident or nonresident biological fathers. This model, which focuses on several aspects of the father-child connection (including the establishment of paternity), underscores how fathering, compared with mothering, is "uniquely sensitive to contextual influences" (p. 289). In some ways, this approach parallels the multilevel scripting perspective that has been used to conceptualize fatherhood and men's involvement in the procreative realm (Marsiglio, 1995a, 1998).

Scholars' interest in responsible fathering is consistent with a recent willingness among social scientists to incorporate value-sensitive positions into their social analysis (Doherty et al., 1998), including conceptualizations of fatherhood (Blankenhorn, 1995; Hawkins & Dollahite, 1997; Levine & Pitt, 1995; Pleck, 1997). Although these perspectives on fathering take many forms and often make contradictory assumptions about fathering, they each highlight moral positions toward fathering using value-based language.

One of the more cohesive value-directed approaches, the *generativity perspective,* emerged in response to what has been perceived as a deficit paradigm and a role-inadequacy perspective. These latter terms have been used to characterize and assail an approach that views fathering as a "*social role* that men generally perform inadequately" (Hawkins & Dollahite, 1997, p. 3). Snarey (1993) borrowed the term *generativity* from the work of Erik Erikson (1982) and applied that particular psychosocial label to activities or work involving fathers. As Snarey (1993) says,

> [His book]. . . is about good fathers. By good, I mean "generative" fathers: men who contribute to and renew the ongoing cycle of the generations through the care that they provide as birth fathers (biological generativity), childrearing fathers (parental generativity), and cultural fathers (societal generativity). (p. 1)

The generative-fathering framework emphasizes the kind of activities and work fathers do in response to the needs of their children rather than in response to the role obligations superimposed upon men by sociocultural prescriptions (Dollahite & Hawkins, 1998; Hawkins & Dollahite, 1997). Generativity theorists suggest that the generative work of fathers involves a sense of responsible caring, a desire to facilitate the needs of the next generation, and attention to fostering a fit between men's activities and children's needs. Recent work based on this perspective has increasingly focused attention on how religious beliefs shape fathers' generative work (Dollahite, 1998).

Developmentalists' conceptions of father-child relationships and paternal influence patterns have also matured in the 1990s. Although these scholars had previously dealt with audiences implicitly or explicitly skeptical about the possible significance of father-child relationships, substantial consensus now exists within developmental psychology that father-child relationships can be remarkably influential (compare Lamb, 1981, with Lamb, 1997). More than ever before, developmentalists are willing to recognize the extent to which father-child relationships must be viewed in the context of a network of mutually interdependent relationships within the family, with fathers influencing these children (and vice versa) both directly, by way of these direct interactions with one another, and indirectly, by way of their impact on other significant members of their social ecologies shared by children and their fathers (e.g., Parke & Buriel, 1998). Although indirect patterns of influence (i.e., patterns of influence mediated via the behavior of third parties, such as mothers) were described by some scholars decades ago (e.g., Lewis, Feiring, & Weinraub, 1981; Lewis & Weinraub, 1976; Parke, Power, & Gottman, 1979), their significance was not universally recognized and studied until the 1990s.

Appreciation of the broader social context within which father-child relationships must be viewed is evidenced by the increasingly sophisticated observational research on the extent to which children are influenced by the quality of the interactions between their parents (Cummings & O'Reilly, 1997; Parke & Buriel, 1998). Similarly, Parke and his colleagues, among others, have described how the pattern of relationships children experience within their families affect children's behavior outside the family (e.g., their peer relationships) as well (Carson & Parke, 1996; Henggeler, Edwards, Cohen, & Summerville, 1992; Isley, O'Neil, & Parke, 1996).

Of course, the emergent concern with intrafamily dynamics and complex multidirectional patterns of influence has achieved center stage at a time when growing numbers of families deviate from the modal family type that developmentalists have typically studied (Lamb, 1999a). In recent years, developmentalists have been more willing to acknowledge the dramatic rise in the number of children being exposed to their parents' separation, being raised for part or all of their childhoods in single-parent households, or both. Likewise, they have become more aware that there are cultural and subcultural variations in the ways in which parents perceive their family roles and responsibilities and that these variations undoubtedly shape parental behavior as well as its influence on children. This diversity has not only fostered interest in parent- (including father-) child relationships in other cultures (e.g., Hewlett, 1992; Parke & Buriel, 1998) and diverse ethnic groups (Gadsden, 1999) but has also dissuaded developmentalists from offering sweeping recommendations that ignore the variability of family structures and circumstances.

Whereas developmentalists have decades of experience studying fathers, scholars who explore the subjective experiences of men as fathers using a symbolic interactionist perspective, and in some cases identity theory, are relatively new to the study of fatherhood (Armato & Marsiglio, 1998; Daly, 1995; Fox & Bruce, 1999; Futris & Pasley, 1997; Ihinger-Tallman, Pasley, & Buehler, 1995; Marsiglio, 1995b, 1998; Marsiglio & Cohan, 2000; Minton & Pasley, 1996). Although they have focused on different theoretical and substantive questions, these theorists have been committed to understanding how men perceive and construct their identities as fathers in diverse situations. Theorists have grown more sensitive to the co-constructed nature of men's identities and their actual fathering activities. Moreover, these theorists recognize that it is critical to understand the nature, bases, and consequences of father's commitment to their children. The recent popularity of the symbolic interactionist perspective not coincidentally comes at a time when more and more men are experiencing complex family-based life course transitions and, in the process, are struggling to make sense of poorly defined fathering roles and competing images of ideal fathering.

Informed by poststructuralist and phenomenological perspectives, other scholars have argued that fatherhood should be viewed as a continually changing ontological state, a site of competing discourses and desires that can never be fully and neatly shaped into a single "identity" and that involves oscillation back and forth between various modes of subject positions even within the context of a single day. (Lupton & Barclay, 1997, p. 16)

These authors challenge mainstream thinking on fatherhood in several ways. Most important, they invite scholars to view the meanings and experiences associated with fatherhood as existing through specific sociocultural processes rather than as a stable identity. Although they appear too eager to discount the stable, continuous, and orderly patterns of many fathers' experiences when they evaluate identity theory, their plea for scholars to pay more attention to the emotional and subjective aspects of fathering resonates with growing numbers of scholars (Garbarino, 1996). Likewise, their call for a discourse analysis that assesses the competing sociocultural forces contributing to the construction of fatherhood is particularly timely given the recent surge in government-sponsored fatherhood initiatives and the public's keen interest in fatherhood issues.

Though brief and selective, the preceding discussion illustrates the number and breadth of theoretical lenses that have been used to view the fatherhood terrain and its many dimensions. These diverse perspectives have captured fatherhood as a cultural representation that is expressed through different sociocultural processes and embedded in a larger ecological context, as a reflection of the interpersonal processes that lead to developmental outcomes among children and fathers, and as an identity that is part of a reciprocal process negotiated by men, children, mothers, and other interested parties. An important legacy of this literature will be its role in encouraging scholars to expand their vision of fatherhood and paternal involvement while reinforcing the need to examine fathering within a systemic and ecological context.

METHODOLOGICAL ISSUES

Scholars' attempts to view fathering more broadly, coupled with the changing composition of families, have complicated efforts to study fathers in recent years. Researchers in the 1990s became more attentive to methodological issues associated with the quality of data on fathers, as evidenced by the Methodology Working Group's report for the Federal Interagency Forum on Child and Family Statistics (1998). This report systematically as-

sessed the key methodological issues involving population identification, data collection procedures, and study designs in this area. The authors speculated that standard household surveys were most problematic because of the outdated assumption that an individual respondent from each household can provide accurate information about the entire family unit. In fact, standard household surveys clearly provide incomplete information about nonresident fathers: They underestimate the number of nonresident fathers because many men underreport children who are not living with them, and they inadequately account for men's sexual, reproductive, and union histories in many instances. The most basic of the report's many recommendations was a suggestion that resident and nonresident fathers be included in future research designs. Researchers were also encouraged to deal with undercounting and undercoverage problems by exploring strategies for augmenting current household rosters and using administrative records. These efforts may be vital for securing the participation of nonmarried fathers, particularly those with low incomes, who tend to be more loosely attached to households compared with their married, more affluent counterparts. Special sampling strategies to include fathers in jail, prison, and the military were deemed important to ensure more representative samples, especially of African American men.

Researchers also need to develop and assess survey measures that better represent fathers' diverse experiences, including the cognitive work they do as fathers, by considering new opportunities to incorporate time-diary methods into studies of fathers and children (Juster & Stafford, 1985). Likewise, A-CASI (audio, computer-assisted self-interview) technology should be considered for studies that address sensitive aspects of fathers' experiences (e.g., child support payments, physical discipline, father-child closeness). This computer-based technique enhances privacy because respondents listen to questions through a headset and then enter their responses directly into a computer. It was recently and successfully used in the 1995 National Survey of Adolescent Males, and there are plans to experiment with it in the 2001 National Survey of Family Growth interviews with men (W. Mosher, personal communication, July 8, 1998). Methodological studies based on these and other initiatives with men are especially warranted because it appears more difficult to obtain valid and complete responses about fertility and parenting from men than from women, partly because some men may misrepresent their affiliations to avoid legal action, custody requirements, and paternity connections. Some men may also fail to provide accurate reports because they anchor their time lines differently than do women, and fertility and union sequences in questionnaires have typically been designed for women respondents.

Finally, fathers' pre- and postnatal experiences should be studied using a range of observational, ethnographic, and in-depth qualitative interview approaches (Marsiglio & Cohan, 2000). These types of methodologies, especially when used in longitudinal studies, may play a crucial role in developing a rich understanding of the cultural context and interpersonal processes associated with how fathers construct and negotiate their self-images as fathers and are directly and indirectly involved in their children's lives. These approaches may also prove useful for survey researchers who wish to improve the substantive content and interviewing procedures associated with their closed-ended survey items.

National Surveys and Fathering Measures

Large national data sets that contain measures of parent-child interaction continue to be a valuable resource as researchers attempt to measure father involvement, predict patterns of father-child relations, and assess the impact of father involvement on children's well-being. The data sets used most frequently to study fatherhood are the National Longitudinal Survey of Youth (NLS-Y), Michigan Panel Study of Income Dynamics (PSID), NSFH, and National Longitudinal Survey of Adolescent Health (Add Health). (See Federal Interagency Forum on Child and Family Statistics, 1998, for a more complete description of the relevant items in these data sets).

Two kinds of measures are generally found in these data sets: (a) a gross measure of father absence or presence at the time of the interview or in previous years and (b) some inquiry regarding broad categories of father involvement, such as communication, teaching, monitoring, feelings, planning, providing, and negative involvement (PSID—Child Development Supplement) or communication, monitoring, time-in-contact, providing for the child, affection, and negative involvement (NSFH).

The most recent large national survey to gather information about father involvement is the Add Health survey. In the first wave of this planned longitudinal survey, data were collected about several important dimensions of adolescent-father relationships, including measures of presence and absence, communication, co-activities, teaching, and conflict.

Although large, nationally representative data sets provide us with excellent opportunities to understand fathers' family roles, these data sets have limitations. Even those data sets that specifically target family interactional variables (e.g., NSFH, Add Health, and PSID) provide few measures of the diverse theoretical constructs that have been developed in recent years. Another shortcoming is that fathers, especially nonresident ones, are underrepresented in household surveys. The PSID is one of the few data collection efforts where securing the participation of nonresident fathers was a primary objective. Finally, national surveys can develop more effective ways of asking sensitive questions about the most intimate aspects of father involvement (e.g., emotional displays, prayer).

Measurement Issues

The technical issues dealing with shared-method variance, discrepancies among respondents' reports, and the reliability of observational data deserve special comment here. Shared-method variance is present whenever researchers use the same source (fathers, mothers, children, teachers, or observers) for data on independent and dependent variables. This occurs, for example, when children report on (a) the amount of time spent with their fathers and (b) their self-esteem. Under these circumstances, shared-method variance tends to increase the correlation between variables, resulting in an overestimate of the true association. In our review of 72 studies dealing with paternal involvement and child outcomes in two-parent families conducted in the 1990s, 39 studies (54%) were based entirely on data from a single source, making it impossible to know whether the observed correlations have an objective basis or exist entirely within the minds of the informants. For this reason, studies using multiple informants are preferable to those based on a single source. However, some research questions make individuals' perceptions important in their own right, not simply as vehicles for defining some objective reality. For example, children's perceptions of their fathers may directly influence their own feelings and behavior, regardless of how other family members (including the fathers themselves) see their fathers.

Relatedly, researchers have shown that when asked to describe family processes (such as the amount of contact, affection, and conflict between fathers and children), different informants' accounts appear to be only modestly correlated. For example, Tein, Roosa, and Michaels (1994) found that correlations reflecting father-child agreement regarding paternal acceptance, rejection, and discipline ranged from .19 to .31. Similarly, Paulson, Hill, and Holmbeck (1991) found that correlations between reports of parent-child closeness by different informants ranged from .33 (between fathers and adolescent sons) to .58 (between mothers and adolescent daughters). Correlations between the reports of objective observers and family members tend to fall in the same range. Simons, Whitbeck, Melby, and Wu (1995) found that observers' ratings of parental harsh discipline correlated at .30 with children's reports and .31 with fathers' reports. Meanwhile, other studies have shown that married fathers report doing more child care than their wives acknowledge (Coltrane, 1996), whereas divorced fathers report paying more child support than their ex-wives concede (Braver, Fitzpatrick, & Bay, 1991; Braver & O'Connell, 1998; see also Seltzer & Brandreth, 1995). Finally, although there was modest but statistically significant agreement between mothers and preadolescents in violent families regarding the children's behavior problems in one study, fathers' reports were not significantly related to those of either mothers or children (Sternberg et al., 1993, 1994). On the other hand, another study found that fathers and adolescents were more likely than mothers and adolescents to agree with one another regarding the levels and types of family violence (Sternberg, Lamb, & Dawud-Noursi, 1998).

It is tempting to conclude that the lack of agreement between independent observers exists because people's views are entirely idiosyncratic and that researchers should abandon the search for descriptions of paternal behavior that are verified by different persons. But care must be taken when interpreting these seemingly modest correlations. First, these modest correlations partly reflect problems with measurement error, which attenuates the magnitude of associations. Second, it is important to recognize that a correlation of .3 between fathers' and children's ratings means that the correlation between their respective ratings and the latent, unobserved variable (e.g., father involvement) is actually .55. This is the case because the correlation of .3 is the product of the path between

the latent variable and the fathers' rating and the path between the latent variable and the child's rating (i.e., .55 × .55). In this light, one gains a new respect for interrater correlations as low as .3.

Nevertheless, a pattern of positive but modest correlations between observers also suggests that measures of paternal involvement (and other dimensions of paternal behavior) have a subjective as well as an objective component. Researchers should distinguish between those phenomena that have a clear objective basis and those that are completely subjective, for instance, how children and fathers feel about each other. The meaning of associations between multiple-source reports may be quite different depending upon whether behaviors or feelings are being studied. In either case, a subjective element is present, and the subjectivity associated with perceptions of behavior is linked to individuals' emotional reactions to these behaviors. Consequently, the nonshared variance in multiple respondents' ratings often reflects more than mere measurement error.

Although understanding fathers and family life is enhanced by obtaining different family members' perspectives, this strategy raises the question of how one analyzes multiple-source data. This topic is too complex to address here; nevertheless, new statistical methods for analyzing multiple-source data (such as hierarchical linear modeling) allow researchers to model both the agreement and the discrepancies between observers (Maquire, 1999). The innovative work of Smith and Morgan (1994) represents another approach. Consequently, advancing research on father involvement will require researchers to obtain data from more than one family member.

Another methodological issue relates to growing concerns about the reliability of developmentalists' observational studies of fathers. Just as the reliability of measurement obtained using self-report questionnaires increases with the number of observations (questionnaire items), the same is true of observational (behavioral) data (Epstein, 1979, 1980). Using data obtained in extended observations of independent samples of upper-middle-class White Americans, Central American immigrants to the United States, and middle-class Costa Ricans, Leyendecker and her colleagues reported that reliable measures of individual behavior and the more theoretically important interaction patterns were not obtained unless each of the families was observed for several hours (Leyendecker, Lamb, & Schölmerich, 1997; Leyendecker, Lamb, Schölmerich, & Fricke, 1997) and that measures continued to become more reliable as the length of observation increased. Of course, the actual amount of time needed to obtain reliable measures would undoubtedly change as a function of the specific coding system involved (Leyendecker et al. used a rather gross 20-second observe, 10-second record time-sampling system), the extent to which the observers focused on carefully specified functional contexts, and the age of those being observed. The data of Leyendecker et al. nevertheless demonstrate that the typical study, sampling 10 to 30 minutes of interaction, is unlikely to provide reliable measures of individuals. These findings should encourage researchers to check and report the reliability of their observational data and underscore the need for careful replication. Moreover, because fathers typically spend shorter periods of time with their children, naturalistic observations of children will necessarily need to embrace even longer periods of time to ensure adequate sampling and thus reliable assessments of father-child relationships.

FATHERHOOD: DEMOGRAPHIC AND CULTURAL DIVERSITY

Although interest in fatherhood diversity predates the 1990s, researchers have recently accelerated their efforts to study the shifting demography of fatherhood and cultural aspects of fathering. The literatures in these areas have accentuated fathers' diverse experiences resulting from their varied living arrangements, responsibility for early off-time births, racial or ethnic background, and experiences as gay parents. Much of this research has profiled and studied divorced fathers (Arendell, 1995; Shapiro & Lambert, 1999), nonresident or "absent" fathers (Braver & O'Connell, 1998; Braver, Wolchik, Sandler, Gogas, & Zvetina, 1991; Clarke, Cooksey, & Verropoulou, 1998; Furstenberg & Harris, 1992; Hetherington & Stanley-Hagan, 1999; Mott, 1990, 1994; Nord & Zill, 1996a, 1996b; Rettig, Leichtentritt, & Stanton, 1999; Seltzer, 1991, 1998b; Seltzer & Brandreth, 1995; Stewart, 1999; Thompson & Laible, 1999) resident single-father families (Bianchi, 1995; Brown, 1996; Downey, Ainsworth-Darnell, & Dufur, 1998; Eggebeen, Synder, & Manning, 1996; Garasky & Meyer, 1996; Grief, 1990; Grief & DeMaris, 1995; Heath & Orthner, 1999; Meyer & Garasky, 1993; see also Fox & Bruce, 1999), stepfathers (Bray & Berger, 1993; Fine, Ganong, & Coleman, 1997; Hawkins & Eggebeen, 1991;

Hetherington, 1993; Hetherington & Henderson, 1997; Larson, 1992; MacDonald & DeMaris, 1996; Marsiglio, 1995b), young fathers of children born to teenage mothers (Kiselica, 1995; Landry & Forrest, 1995; Lerman & Ooms, 1993; Lindberg, Sonenstein, Ku, & Martinez, 1997; Marsiglio & Cohan, 1997), and fathers in violent and neglectful families (Dubowitz, 1999; Sternberg & Lamb, 1999). Relatedly, some researchers have considered the socioeconomic and family life consequences associated with premarital, adolescent, or both those types of fatherhood (Heath & McKenry, 1993; Nock, 1998).

This literature is too expansive for us to provide a detailed review of the substantive issues here, but several findings warrant brief comment. Scholars in the 1990s have increasingly recognized the need to move beyond simplistic analyses of fathers' presence or absence in the household, family, or both, noting the complexity, fluidity, and cultural variations associated with fathers' multifaceted connections to particular households, families, or individual household members. Similarly, researchers have recently highlighted how our understanding of the changing demography of single-father families requires us to account for the significant roles cohabiting partners play in the lives of many single fathers. A number of researchers have also focused on the critical gatekeeping role many women play in nonresident fathers' and stepfathers' relationships with their children, whereas others have attempted to clarify the factors that account for nonresident fathers' declining level of involvement in their children's lives after their romantic relationships with the children's mothers have ended. There is also mounting evidence that stepfathers frequently exhibit a disengaged parenting style, which needs to be considered in the context of the circumstances that influence the quality of stepfather-stepchild relationships and the factors associated with the adjustment to life with a stepfather.

Researchers interested in the cultural diversity of fathering have focused primarily on variations in racial or ethnic background or on status as gay fathers. Although some studies conducted during the 1990s improved our understanding of how the social ecology of race affects men's lives as fathers, research in the U.S.A. has focused disproportionately on men from lower socioeconomic backgrounds and has been largely limited to African Americans (Allen & Doherty, 1996; Furstenberg, 1995; Gadsden, 1999; Hammer, 1997; McAdoo, 1993; Roy, 1999). Some cross-national comparative research has produced valuable insights related to familial perceptions and paternal involvement within American, Japanese, and German families (Ishii-Kuntz, 1992, 1995), and Hewlett (1991) has explored the remarkably intimate relations between Aka Pygmy fathers and infants. Meanwhile, other researchers have extended our understanding of culture and fatherhood by exploring gay fathers' unique experiences resulting from societal misgivings about gay parenting compounded by factors associated with nonresident or single fatherhood (Crosbie-Burnett & Helmbrecht, 1993; Patterson & Chan, 1997).

FATHER INVOLVEMENT AND CHILD OUTCOMES

Many studies conducted in the 1990s explored the patterns as well as the possible causes and consequences of varied forms of father involvement (see Pleck, 1997 for an extensive review; Parke, 1996; Russell, 1999). Most researchers focused on behaviors such as financial support and visitation patterns (especially among nonresident fathers), on one-on-one engagement activities (e.g., sharing a leisure activity, helping with homework, instructional talks), or on more general indicators of the absence or presence of the father in the home. Recent research focusing on nonfinancial forms of father involvement continued to document a slow increase in the level of father involvement in two-parent households since the 1970s, both in proportionate and absolute terms, although levels of fathers' engagement and accessibility remained significantly lower than those for mothers (Pleck, 1997).

Fathers' Economic Support

One way in which fathers contribute to their children's well-being is through the provision of economic support. Many researchers have documented the harmful toll that economic hardship takes on children, including a greater risk of poor nutrition, health problems, low school grades, dropping out of school, emotional distress, and behavioral difficulties (Brooks-Gunn, Britto, & Brady, 1999; Duncan & Brooks-Gunn, 1997; Klerman, 1991; Mayer, 1997; McLoyd & Wilson, 1991). Because women earn less money than men and are less likely to be employed full-time, children's economic status is largely determined by their fathers. In other words, most children are poor either because their fathers earn little money or be-

cause their fathers are absent and pay little or no child support.

Surprisingly few studies of two-parent families have estimated the independent influence of paternal and maternal income. However, two studies have shown that fathers' earnings are positively associated with the educational attainment (Kaplan, Lancaster, & Anderson, 1998) and psychological well-being of young adult offspring (Amato, 1998), even when mothers' earnings are controlled. Other studies yield less clear results (Blau & Grossberg, 1992). Overall, however, the evidence suggests that fathers' earnings are positively and independently associated with offspring outcomes in two-parent families.

With respect to nonresident fathers, it is not the total income earned but the amount that is transferred to children that is central. Consequently, the most relevant studies focus on fathers' payment of child support. We located 12 studies published since 1990, including journal articles and book chapters, that examined associations between fathers' payment of child support and child outcomes. Most studies were based on different data sets. A couple of studies used the same data set (the Add Health data) but relied on different subsamples or child outcomes. Of the 12 studies, 9 reported positive and significant associations between the amount of child support paid by nonresident fathers and aspects of children's well-being, including school grades and behavior problems at school (McLanahan, Seltzer, Hanson, & Thomson, 1994), reading and math scores (King, 1994), and years of educational attainment (Graham, Beller, and Hernandez, 1994; Knox and Bane, 1994). In general, these associations do not appear to vary with the sex or race of the children. Of course, not all findings are consistent (e.g., Simons, Whitbeck, Beaman, & Conger, 1994), but a recent meta-analysis of this literature confirmed that nonresident fathers' child support payments are positively associated with children's educational success and negatively associated with children's externalizing problems (Amato & Gilbreth, 1999).

The Father-Child Relationship

Fathers in two-parent families. A large number of studies in the 1990s have dealt with the links between child outcomes and various dimensions of paternal behavior, such as spending time with children, providing emotional support, giving everyday assistance, monitoring children's behavior, and noncoercive disciplining. Most of these behaviors can be subsumed under the general category of *authoritative parenting*. Developmentalists have consistently indicated that authoritative parenting is the parenting style that best predicts more desirable outcomes among children (Baumrind, 1968, 1991; Parke & Buriel, 1998). Relevant child outcomes include academic success (test scores, grades, years of education), lower levels of externalizing behavior problems (conduct problems, delinquency) or internalizing problems (depression, self-esteem, life satisfaction), and positive social behavior (social competence, popularity, size of support networks).

We found 72 studies in journal articles or book chapters published in the 1990s of fathers and children with continuously married parents. Of these studies, 55 dealt with young children or adolescents (aged 0–19), and 17 dealt with young adult offspring (aged 20 or older). These studies used different data sets, with the exception of three studies based on the NSFH, three studies based on the National Survey of Children, and five studies based on Conger and Elder's (1994) sample of families in Iowa. These latter 11 studies, however, all reported data on different subsamples or dependent variables.

For studies of young children and adolescents, the mean zero-order correlation between paternal authoritative parenting and children's behavior problems was −.23. The corresponding mean correlation for children's internalizing problems was −.27. These results indicate that the associations between paternal behavior and offspring outcomes were, on average, moderate rather than large. The percentage of studies reporting significant results did not vary with the ages of children sampled. Furthermore, similar associations were apparent for racial minorities as well as Whites. For example, in a sample of African American urban adolescent boys, Zimmerman, Salem, and Maton (1995) found that the amount of time spent with fathers and the amount of emotional support obtained from fathers were associated with less depression, higher self-esteem, higher life satisfaction, and less delinquency. In addition, Amato and Rivera (1999) found that the estimated positive influence of paternal involvement on children's behavior was similar for White, African American, and Latino fathers. Overall, these results are consistent with the belief that positive father involvement is generally beneficial to children.

However, three qualifications to this conclusion are necessary. First, as noted earlier, the majority of studies relied on a single source of data; consequently, shared-method variance may have inflated the magnitude of the observed correlations and increased the risk of type I errors. Second, many researchers did not control for the quality of the mother-child relationship when estimating the impact of the father-child relationship. In fact, maternal and paternal behaviors are highly correlated in many studies. For example, Clark-Lempers, Lempers, and Netusil (1990) found a correlation of .82 between children's reports of support from mothers and fathers. Meanwhile, Wright, Peterson, and Barnes (1990) reported a correlation of .63 between children's reports of positive communication with mothers and fathers. Perhaps these high correlations reflect the fact that effective mothers tend to encourage fathers to be highly involved with their children, but whatever the reason, significant zero-order associations between paternal behavior and child outcomes drop to nonsignificant levels in some studies after controls for the quality of the mother-child relationship (which are usually significant) are introduced (e.g., Barnett, Kibria, Baruch, & Pleck, 1991; Brody, Stoneman, Flor, McCrary, Hastings, & Conyers, 1994; Wright et al., 1990). Other studies, however, continue to show significant associations between paternal behavior and child outcomes, even with maternal behavior controlled.

Of the 72 studies identified, only eight used data from independent sources and controlled for the quality of the mother-child relationship. Of these, five revealed significant associations between positive father involvement and child outcomes. For example, Browne and Rife (1991) found that teachers' reports that children had few problems at school (such as failing a grade or poor attendance) were associated significantly with children's reports of supportive paternal behavior, even after controlling for variations in the level of supportive maternal behavior. Overall, the majority of studies that use multiple sources and control for maternal characteristics support the notion that positive father involvement is linked with desirable outcomes among children, although the number of methodologically sound studies is disappointingly small.

A third qualification deals with the time ordering of variables. The great majority of studies are correlational and consequently provide little evidence of causal relationships between paternal behavior and offspring outcomes. The conclusion that fathers influence their children is stronger when paternal behavior is measured prior to assessments of the children's status. The few extant longitudinal studies tend to support the hypothesis that fathers affect their children (e.g., Amato & Booth, 1997; Franz, McClelland, & Weinberger, 1991; Koestner, Franz, & Weinberger, 1990; Snarey, 1993). For example, Amato and Booth (1997) found that parents' reports of paternal involvement in 1980 were associated with adult offspring's reports of greater social integration in 1992. Similarly, Franz et al. (1991) reported that fathers' warmth (as reported by children's mothers when children were age 5) predicted offspring well-being (marital success and supportive social networks) at age 41. Nevertheless, more longitudinal research on this topic is necessary, including studies that model possible reciprocal relationships between offspring and fathers.

Nonresident fathers. Divorce is often followed by a decline in the quality and quantity of contact between fathers and children. Never-married fathers are even less likely than divorced fathers to keep in contact with their children. Nevertheless, some nonresident fathers manage to see their children frequently and maintain positive relationships. If the father-child relationship is an important resource for children, then a close relationship with nonresident fathers should predict positive outcomes for children (Lamb, 1999b; Thompson & Laible, 1999).

In 38 studies published since 1990, researchers examined linkages between children's well-being and their relationships with nonresident fathers. In general, these studies do not provide strong support for the belief that visitation with nonresident fathers benefits children. Of the 24 studies that included data on the frequency of contact, only 10 (42%) found that contact significantly predicted some aspect of children's well-being. Other studies focused not on contact but on how close children feel to their fathers. Of these 10 studies, only 3 found significant associations in the predicted direction. Taken together, these studies suggest that the frequency of visitation and children's feelings about their fathers are not good predictors of children's development or adjustment.

An additional nine studies focused on the extent to which nonresident fathers exhibit aspects of authoritative parenting. Consistent with studies of two-parent families, eight of these nine studies found significant associations in the predicted direction between paternal behavior and children's well-being. For example, Barber (1994) found that adolescents who frequently obtained advice from

nonresident fathers (about educational plans, employment goals, and personal problems) were less likely than other adolescents to experience symptoms of depression. Similarly, Simons et al. (1994) found that the quality of nonresident fathers' parenting (as reflected in emotional support, giving reasons for decisions, providing consistent discipline, and praising children's accomplishment) was negatively related to externalizing problems among adolescent sons and daughters. The assumption that the authoritative parenting of nonresident fathers is associated with positive child outcomes was confirmed in a recent meta-analysis by Amato and Gilbreth (1999).

In general, these studies suggest that it is not the amount of time that nonresident fathers spend with their children but how they interact with their children that is important. The same principle applies to two-parent families. For example, Young, Miller, Norton, and Hill (1995) found that when married fathers engaged in authoritative parenting (such as providing encouragement and talking over problems), children tended to have high levels of life satisfaction. But merely spending time with fathers (by going out to dinner or seeing movies together) was not related to children's life satisfaction. Unfortunately, contact between nonresident fathers and children tends to be recreational rather than instrumental. Compared with fathers in two-parent households, nonresident fathers provide less help with homework, are less likely to set and enforce rules, and provide less monitoring and supervision of their children (Furstenberg & Cherlin, 1991). If nonresident fathers rarely engage in authoritative parenting, then mere contact, or even sharing good times together, may not contribute in a positive way to children's development.

Frequent contact also provides opportunities for parents to quarrel. Because conflict is harmful to children, conflict between parents may cancel, or even reverse, any benefits associated with frequent visitation. Thus, for example, Amato and Rezac (1994) reported that contact with nonresident fathers following divorce appeared to lower sons' behavior problems when conflict between the parents was low but increased behavior problems when conflict between the parents was high. A similar result was reported by Healy, Malley, and Stewart (1990).

In conclusion, recent research suggests that nonresident fathers play an important role in their children's lives to the extent that they provide authoritative parenting—especially if this occurs within the context of cooperative relationships between the parents. Unfortunately, nonauthoritative fathering within the context of minimal interparental cooperation is the pattern observed in most families. For this reason, nonresident fathers may have a difficult time making positive contributions to their children's development.

FUTURE DIRECTIONS

We now selectively highlight several of the compelling issues that are likely to guide the next generation of research on fatherhood, relying heavily on recommendations proposed by the interdisciplinary working groups for the Federal Interagency Forum on Child and Family Statistics (1998). Our general comments emphasize the four areas we identified earlier: cultural representations of and discourses about fatherhood, conceptual and empirical analyses of the diverse forms of fatherhood and paternal involvement, linkages between dimensions of the father-child relationship and children's well-being and development, and the interpretive practices surrounding paternal identity and fathering. Where appropriate, we comment on the intersections among demographic trends, research agendas, and social policy concerns involving fathers.

Because the culture of fatherhood has grown more fragmented and politicized, scholars will be challenged to understand the familial, social, and legal processes through which men in diverse settings appropriate and negotiate their status as father, with its accompanying rights, obligations, and privileges. These efforts must be complemented by initiatives to develop a richer portrait of how men, women, and children from different cultural and social backgrounds view aspects of fatherhood. What types of distinctive cultural (e.g., social class, race, community) and organizational (e.g., work place, Promise Keepers' movement, fathers' rights groups) contexts contribute to the definition and evaluation of good or responsible fathering? In what ways and to what extent are men's visions of fathering and their actual paternal behaviors affected by their exposure to these cultural forces? How are various forms of father involvement fostered or impeded by external factors? Efforts to address these and related questions must be informed by recent attempts to broaden the way father involvement and paternal influence are conceptualized.

Developing a broader conceptualization of fathering, one that more fully acknowledges the cognitive and indirect dimensions (e.g., via emotional support of the mother) of father involvement, will shape the substantive questions researchers ask concerning the ways and extent to which fathers affect their children's well-being and development, especially during the childhood and adolescent years. Researchers appear poised to study more seriously how father involvement patterns and consequences are affected by the larger ecological context within which they occur. Recent efforts to examine the contributions of fathers' social capital to their children's lives through their familial and community relations are consistent with this development. Likewise, researchers need to turn their attention to the ways fathers affect their children through their participation in various family processes (e.g., distance regulation, social support, and monitoring). These analyses require researchers to make good on their commitment to secure data from multiple family members' perspectives. A high priority should be to study how fathering is often a co-constructed accomplishment, tied as it is to familial processes involving various participants, most notably the children's mothers. Relatedly, researchers must examine more closely how children's behaviors, personalities, and perceived needs influence men's identities and behaviors as fathers as well as how fathering affects men's individual development. A significant, complex, and politicized theme that inevitably will continue to shape some research agendas focuses on whether men have gendered practices as fathers that uniquely contribute to their children's development. Finally, research is needed that explores the wide range of formal and informal ways fathers actively contribute to their children's moral, religious, and spiritual development.

Meanwhile, more conventional, policy-oriented lines of research that examine the relationship between certain aspects of father involvement (e.g., financial child support, visitation, varied parenting styles) and child outcomes (e.g., school performance, psychosocial health, juvenile delinquency) are likely to remain in vogue given the political and cultural climate surrounding welfare reform and crime prevention. Researchers studying child support/visitation patterns and child outcomes are hopeful that recent and proposed data collection efforts (e.g., Add Health, NLSY, PSID) that include more information directly obtained from fathers, enhanced efforts to enroll hard-to-reach fathers, and new approaches for analyzing data will enable them to answer various questions more convincingly. Data from the large national surveys we reviewed are a critical source of information about how fathers are involved in the lives of children and how differing levels and types of care affect children's well-being. We therefore urge funding agencies to continue to recognize the value of these costly data collection efforts as researchers struggle to understand important family processes.

The growing diversity and transitional nature of men's experiences as fathers in recent years also invites researchers to explore how structural, interpersonal, and individual level factors influence the types and intensity of men's commitments to their biological and step children. Research agendas built on these concerns are closely tied to a variety of specific social policy initiatives related to paternity establishment, divorce, blended families, child support, and visitation. Researchers are likely to become increasingly attentive to the significance of studying how pregnancy resolution dynamics and union formation and dissolution patterns, coupled with shifts in residency arrangements, affect paternal involvement in both low income and more advantaged familial environments. Understanding how fathering roles are defined, negotiated, and expressed in diverse contexts and transitional periods will become increasingly important. As alluded to earlier, the scope and utility of these types of analyses will depend on methodological innovations designed to help researchers identify, enroll, and interview diverse and hard-to-reach samples of men as well as make sense of data from multiple respondents. Finally, researchers ideally should strive to develop research designs that allow them to explore the connections and transitions between men's fatherhood experiences prior to conception, during pregnancy, and after birth.

Although research agendas have been and will continue to be defined in large part by pressing social policy concerns, researchers should continue to study fathers' involvement with and influence on their children in healthy, stable families. Fortunately, given the burgeoning number and diversity of scholars interested in studying fathers during the 1990s, the immediate prospects are promising that a wide range of interdisciplinary perspectives are likely to characterize future advances.

REFERENCES

Allen, S. M., & Hawkins, A. J. (1999). Maternal gatekeeping: Mothers' beliefs and behaviors that inhibit greater father involvement in family work. *Journal of Marriage and the Family, 61,* 199–212.

Allen, W. D., & Doherty, W. J. (1996). The responsibilities of fatherhood as perceived by African American teenage fathers. *Families in Society: The Journal of Contemporary Human Services, 77,* 142–155.

Amato, P. (1998). More than money?: Men's contributions to their children's lives. In A. Booth & N. Crouter (Eds.), *Men in families: When do they get involved? What difference does it make?* (pp. 241–278). Mahwah, NJ: Erlbaum.

Amato, P. A., & Gilbreth, J. G. (1999). Nonresident fathers and children's well-being: A meta-analysis. *Journal of Marriage and the Family, 61,* 557–573.

Amato, P. R., & Booth, A. (1997). *A generation at risk: Growing up in an era of family upheaval.* Cambridge, MA: Harvard University Press.

Amato, P. R., & Rezac, S. (1994). Contact with nonresidential parents, interparental conflict, and children's behavior. *Journal of Family Issues, 15,* 191–207.

Amato, P. R., & Rivera, F. (1999). Paternal involvement and children's behavior. *Journal of Marriage and the Family 61,* 375–384.

Arendell, T. (1995). *Fathers & divorce.* Thousand Oaks, CA: Sage.

Armato, M., & Marsiglio, W. (1998, August). *Godly men at home: Promise Keepers' father identity.* Paper presented at the Society for the Study of Social Problems Conference, San Francisco.

Barber, B. L. (1994). Support and advice from married and divorced fathers: Linkages to adolescent adjustment. *Family Relations, 43,* 433–438.

Barnett, R. C., Kibria, N., Baruch, G. K., & Pleck, J. H. (1991). Adult daughter-parent relationships and their associations with daughters' subjective well-being and psychological distress. *Journal of Marriage and the Family, 53,* 29–42.

Baumrind, D. (1968). Authoritarian versus authoritative parental control. *Adolescence, 3,* 255–272.

Baumrind, D. (1991). The influence of parenting style on adolescent competence and substance use. *Journal of Early Adolescence, 11,* 56–95.

Bianchi, S. M. (1995). The changing demographic and socioeconomic characteristics of single parent families. In S. M. H. Hanson, M. L. Heims, D. J. Julian, & M. B. Sussman (Eds.), *Single parent families: Diversity, myths, and realities* (pp. 71–97). New York: Haworth Press.

Blankenhorn, D. (1995). *Fatherless America: Confronting our most urgent social problem.* New York: Basic Books.

Blau, F. D., & Grossberg, A. J. (1992). Maternal labor supply and children's cognitive development. *Review of Economics and Statistics, 74,* 474–481.

Booth, A., & Crouter, A. C. (1998). *Men in families: When do they get involved? What difference does it make?* Mahwah, NJ: Erlbaum.

Bozett, F. W., & Hanson, S. M. H. (1991). *Fatherhood and families in cultural context.* New York: Springer.

Braver, S. H., Wolchik, S. A., Sandler, I. N., Gogas, B. S., & Zvetina, D. (1991). Frequency of visitation of divorced fathers: Differences in reports by fathers and mothers. *American Journal of Orthopsychiatry, 61,* 448–454.

Braver, S. L., Fitzpatrick, P. J., & Bay, R. C. (1991).

Noncustodial parent's report of child support payments. *Family Relations, 40,* 180–186.

Braver, S. L., & O'Connell, D. (1998). *Divorced dads: Shattering the myths.* New York: Tarcher/Putnam.

Bray, J. H., & Berger, S. H. (1993). Developmental issues in Stepfamilies Research Project: Family relationships and parent-child interactions. *Journal of Family Psychology, 7,* 1–17.

Brody, G., Stoneman, Z., Flor, D., McCrary, C., Hastings, L., & Conyers, O. (1994). Financial resources, parental psychological functioning, parent co-caregiving, and early adolescent competence in rural two-parent African-American families. *Child Development, 65,* 590–605.

Brooks-Gunn, J., Britto, P. R., & Brady, C. (1999). Struggling to make ends meet: Poverty and child development. In M. E. Lamb (Ed.), *Parenting and child development in "nontraditional" families* (pp. 279–304). Mahwah, NJ: Erlbaum.

Brown, B. V. (1996, October). *The single father family: Recent trends in demographic, economic, and public transfer use characteristics.* Paper presented at the Conference of Fathers' Involvement, National Institute of Child Health and Human Development, Bethesda, MD.

Browne, C. S., & Rife, J. C. 1991. Social, personality, and gender differences in at-risk and not-at-risk sixth grade students. *Journal of Early Adolescence, 11,* 482–495.

Burton, L. M., & Snyder, T. R. (1998). The invisible man revisited: Historical perspectives on men's roles in African American Families. In A. Booth & N. Crouter (Eds.), *Men in families: When do they get involved? What difference does it make?* (pp. 31–39). Mahwah, NJ: Erlbaum.

Carson, J., & Parke, R.D. (1996). Reciprocal negative affect in parent-child interactions and children's peer competency. *Child Development, 67,* 2217–2226.

Cherlin, A. J. (1998). On the flexibility of fatherhood. In A. Booth & A. C. Crouter (Eds.), *Men in families: When do they get involved? What difference does it make?* (pp. 41–46). Mahwah, NJ: Erlbaum.

Clark-Lempers, D. S., Lempers, J. D., & Netusil, A. J. (1990). Family financial stress, parental support, and young adolescents' academic achievement and depressive symptoms. *Journal of Early Adolescence, 10,* 21–36.

Clarke, L., Cooksey, E. C., & Verropoulou, G. (1998). Fathers and absent fathers: Sociodemographic similarities in Britain and the United States. *Demography, 35,* 217–228.

Coleman, J. (1988). Social capital in the creation of human capital. *American Journal of Sociology, 94,* 95–120.

Coleman, J. (1990). *Foundations of social theory.* Cambridge, MA: Harvard University.

Coltrane, S. (1996). *Family man: Fatherhood, housework, and gender equity.* New York: Oxford University Press.

Conger, R. D., & Elder, G. H. (1994). *Families in troubled times.* Hawthorne, NY: Aldine de Gruyter.

Crosbie-Burnett, M., & Helmbrecht, L. (1993). A descriptive empirical study of gay male stepfamilies. *Family Relations, 42,* 256–262.

Cummings, E. M., & O'Reilly, A. W. (1997). Fathers in family context: Effects of marital quality on child adjustment. In M. E. Lamb (Ed.), *The role of the father in child development* (pp. 49–65, 318–375). New York: Wiley.

Daly, K. J. (1995). Reshaping fatherhood: Finding the models. In Marsiglio, W. (Ed.), *Fatherhood: Contemporary theory, research, and social policy* (pp. 21–40) Thousand Oaks, CA: Sage.

Daniels, C. R. (1998). *Lost fathers: The politics of fatherlessness in America.* New York: St. Martin's Press.

Dienhart, A. (1998). *Reshaping fatherhood: The social construction of shared parenting.* Thousand Oaks, CA: Sage.

Dienhart, A., & Daly, K. J. (1997). Men and women cocreating father involvement in a nongenerative culture. In A. J. Hawkins & D. C. Dollahite (Eds.), *Generative fathering: Beyond deficit perspectives* (pp. 147–164). Thousand Oaks, CA: Sage.

Doherty, W. J., Kouneski, E. F., & Erikson, M. F. (1998). Responsible fathering: An overview and conceptual framework. *Journal of Marriage and the Family, 60,* 277–292.

Dollahite, D. C. (1998). Fathering, faith, and spirituality. *Journal of Men's Studies, 7,* 3–15.

Dollahite, D. C., & Hawkins, A. J. (1998). A conceptual ethnic of generative fathering. *Journal of Men's Studies, 7,* 109–132.

Downey, D. B., Ainsworth-Darnell, J. W., & Dufur, M. J. (1998). Sex of parent and children's well-being in single-parent households. *Journal of Marriage and the Family, 60,* 878–902.

Dubowitz, H. (1999). The families of neglectful children. In M. E. Lamb (Ed.), *Parenting and child development in "nontraditional" families* (pp. 327–345). Mahwah, NJ: Erlbaum.

Duncan, G. J., & Brooks-Gunn, J. (1997). Consequences of growing up poor. New York: Russell Sage Foundation Press.

Eggebeen, D. J., Snyder, A. R., & Manning, W. D. (1996). Children in single-father families in demographic perspective. *Journal of Family Issues, 17,* 441–465.

Epstein, S. (1979). The stability of behavior I: On predicting most of the people much of the time. *Journal of Personality and Social Psychology, 37,* 1079–1126.

Epstein, S. (1980). The stability of behavior II: Implications for psychological research. *American Psychologist, 35,* 790–806.

Erikson, E. H. (1982). *The life cycle completed.* New York: Norton.

Federal Interagency Forum on Child and Family Statistics. (1998). *Nurturing fatherhood: Improving data and research on male fertility, family formation, and fatherhood.* Washington, DC: Author.

Fine, M. A., Ganong, L. H., & Coleman, M. (1997). The relation between role constructions and adjustment among stepfathers. *Journal of Family Issues, 18,* 503–525.

Fox, G. L., & Bruce, C. (1999, November). *Conditional fatherhood: Identity theory and parental investment theory as competing explanations of fathering.* Paper presented at the Symposium on Social Psychological Perspectives on Fatherhood. National Council on Family Relations. Irvine, CA.

Fox, G. L., & Bruce, C. (1999). The anticipation of

single parenthood: A profile of men's concerns. *Journal of Family Issues, 20,* 458–506.

Franz, C. E., McClelland, D., & Weinberger, J. (1991). Childhood antecedents of conventional social accomplishment in midlife adults: A 36-year prospective study. *Journal of Personality and Social Psychology, 60,* 586–595.

Furstenberg, F. F., Jr. (1995). Fathering in the inner city: Paternal participation and public policy. In W. Marsiglio (Ed.), *Fatherhood: Contemporary theory, research, and social policy* (pp. 119–147). Thousand Oaks, CA: Sage.

Furstenberg, F. F., Jr. (1998). Social capital and the role of fathers in the family. In A. Booth & N. Crouter (Eds.), *Men in families: When do they get involved? What difference does it make?* (pp. 295–301). Mahwah, NJ: Erlbaum.

Furstenberg, F. F., Jr., & Cherlin, A. J. (1991). *Divided families.* Cambridge, MA: Harvard University Press.

Furstenberg, F. F., Jr., & Harris, K. (1992). The disappearing American father? Divorce and the waning significance of biological parenthood. In S. S. South & S. E. Tolnay (Eds.), *The changing American family: Sociological and demographic perspectives* (pp. 197–223). Boulder, CO: Westview.

Furstenberg, F. F., Jr., & Hughes, M. E. (1995). Social capital and successful development among at-risk youth. *Journal of Marriage and the Family, 57,* 580–592.

Futris, T. G., & Pasley, K. (1997, November). *The father role identity: Conceptualizing and assessing within-role variability.* Paper presented at the Theory Construction and Research Methodology Workshop, National Council on Family Relations, Washington, DC.

Gadsden, V. (1999). Black families in intergenerational and cultural perspective. In M. E. Lamb (Ed.), *Parenting and child development in "nontraditional" families* (pp. 221–246). Mahwah, NJ: Erlbaum.

Garasky, S., & Meyer, D. R. (1996). Reconsidering the increase in father-only families. *Demography, 33,* 385–393.

Garbarino, J. (1996, October). *The soul of fatherhood.* Paper presented at Conference on Father Involvement, National Institute of Health, Bethesda, MD.

Garfinkel, I., McLanahan, S., Meyer, D., & Seltzer, J. (1998). *Fathers under fire: The revolution of child support enforcement.* New York: Russell Sage Foundation Press.

Gerson, K. (1993). *No man's land: Men's changing commitments to family and work.* New York: Basic Books.

Graham, J. W., Beller, A. H., & Hernandez, P. M. (1994). The effects of child support on educational attainment. In I. Garfinkel, S. S. McLanahan, & P. K. Robins (Eds.), *Child support and child well-being* (pp. 317–354). Washington, DC: Urban Institute.

Grief G. L. (1990). *The daddy track and the single father.* New York: Macmillan/Lexington.

Grief, G. L., & DeMaris, A. (1995). Single fathers with custody: Do they change over time? In W. Marsiglio (Ed.), *Fatherhood: Contemporary theory, research, and social policy* (pp. 193–210). Thousand Oaks, CA: Sage.

Griswold, R. L. (1993). *Fatherhood in America: A history.* New York: Basic Books.

Hagan, J., MacMillan, R., & Wheaton, B. (1996). New kid in town: Social capital and the life course effects of family migration on children. *American Sociological Review, 61,* 368–385.

Hammer, J. F. (1997). The fathers of "fatherless" black children. *Families in Society: The Journal of Contemporary Human Services, 78,* 564–578.

Hawkins, A. J., & Dollahite, D. C. (1997). *Generative fathering: Beyond deficit perspectives.* Thousand Oaks, CA: Sage.

Hawkins, A. J., & Eggebeen, D. J. (1991). Are fathers fungible? Patterns of coresident adult men in maritally disrupted families with young children's well-being. *Journal of Marriage and the Family, 53,* 958–972.

Hawkins, A. J., & Palkovitz, R. (1999). Beyond ticks and clicks: The need for more diverse and broader conceptualizations and measures of father involvement. *Journal of Men's Studies 8,* 11–32.

Healy, J. M., Malley, J. E., & Stewart, A. J. (1990). Children and their fathers after parental separation. *American Journal of Orthopsychiatry, 60,* 531–543.

Heath, D. T., & McKenry, P. C. (1993). Adult family life of men who fathered as adolescents. *Families in Society: The Journal of Contemporary Human Services, 74,* 36–45.

Heath, D. T., & Orthner, D. K. (1999). Stress and adaptation among male and female single parents. *Journal of Family Issues, 20,* 557–587.

Henggeler, S.W., Edwards, J.J. Cohen, R., & Summerville, M.B. (1992). Predicting changes in children's popularity: The role of family relations. *Journal of Applied Developmental Psychology, 12,* 205–218.

Hetherington, E. M. (1993). An overview of the Virginia Longitudinal Study of Divorce and Remarriage with a focus on early adolescence. *Journal of Family Psychology, 7,* 39–56.

Hetherington, E. M., & Henderson, S. H. (1997). Fathers in stepfamilies. In M. E. Lamb (Ed.), *The role of the father in child development* (3rd ed., pp. 212–226, 369–373). New York: Wiley.

Hetherington, E. M., & Stanley-Hagan, M. M. (1999). Stepfamilies. In M. E. Lamb (Ed.), *Parenting and child development in "nontraditional" families* (pp. 137–159). Mahwah, NJ: Erlbaum.

Hewlett, B. S. (1991). *Intimate fathers.* Ann Arbor, MI: University of Michigan Press.

Hewlett, B.S. (1992). *Father-child relations: Cultural and biosocial contexts.* New York: Aldine de Gruyter.

Hood, J. (1993). *Men, work, and family.* Thousand Oaks, CA: Sage.

Ihinger-Tallman, M., Pasley, K., & Buehler, C. L. (1995). Developing a middle-range theory of father involvement postdivorce. In W. Marsiglio (Ed.), *Fatherhood: Contemporary theory, research, and social policy* (pp. 57–77). Thousand Oaks, CA: Sage.

Ishii-Kuntz, M. (1992). Are Japanese families "fatherless"? *Sociology and Social Research, 76,* 105–109.

Ishii-Kuntz, M. (1995). Paternal involvement and perception toward fathers' roles: A comparison between Japan and the United States. In W. Marsiglio (Ed.), *Fatherhood: Contemporary theory, research, and social policy* (pp. 102–118). Thousand Oaks, CA: Sage.

Isley, S., O'Neil, R., & Parke, R.D. (1996). The relation of parental affect and control behavior to children's classroom acceptance: A concurrent and predictive analysis. *Early Education and Development, 7,* 7–23.

Juster, F. T., & Stafford, F. P. (1985). *Time, goods, and well-being.* Ann Arbor, MI: Survey Research Center, University of Michigan.

Kaplan, H. S., Lancaster, J. B., & Anderson, K. G. (1998). Human parental investment and fertility: The life histories of men in Albuquerque. In A. Booth and A. C. Crouter (Eds.), *Men in Families* (pp. 55–109). Mahwah, NJ: Erlbaum.

Kimmel, M. (1996). *Manhood in America: A cultural history.* New York: Free Press.

King, V. (1994). Nonresident father involvement and child well-being: Can Dads make a difference? *Journal of Family Issues, 15,* 78–96.

Kiselica, M. S. (1995). *Multicultural counseling with teenage fathers: A practical guide.* Thousand Oaks, CA: Sage.

Klerman, L. V. (1991). The health status of poor children: Problems and programs. In A. C. Huston (Ed.), *Children in Poverty: Child Development and Public Policy* (pp. 136–157). Cambridge, MA: Cambridge University Press.

Knox, V. W., & Bane, M. J. (1994). Child support and schooling. In I. Garfinkel, S. S. McLanahan, & P. K. Robins (Eds.), *Child support and child well-being* (pp. 285–316). Washington, DC: Urban Institute.

Koestner, R., Franz, C. E., & Weinberger, J. (1990). The family origins of empathic concern: A 26-year longitudinal study. *Journal of Personality and Social Psychology, 58,* 709–717.

Lamb, M.E. (1981). *The role of the father in child development* (2nd ed.). New York: Wiley.

Lamb, M.E. (1997). *The role of the father in child development* (3rd ed.). New York: Wiley.

Lamb, M.E. (1998). Fatherhood then and now. In A. Booth & A. C. Crouter (Eds.), *Men in families: When do they get involved? What difference does it make?* (pp. 47–52). Mahwah, NJ: Erlbaum.

Lamb, M.E. (in press). Research on father involvement: An historical overview. *Marriage and Family Review.*

Lamb, M. E. (1999a). *Parenting and child development in "nontraditional" families.* Mahwah, NJ: Erlbaum.

Lamb, M. E. (1999b). Noncustodial fathers and their impact on the children of divorce. In R. A. Thompson & P. Amato (Eds.), *The postdivorce family: Research and policy issues* (pp. 105–125) Thousand Oaks, CA: Sage.

Lamb, M. E., Pleck, J. H., Charnov, E. L., & Levine, J. A. (1987). A biosocial perspective on paternal behavior and involvement. In J. B. Lancaster, J. Altmann, A. S. Rossi, & L. R. Sherrod (Eds.), *Parenting across the lifespan: Biosocial dimensions* (pp. 111–142). New York: Aldine de Gruyter.

Landry, D. J., & Forrest, J. D. (1995). How old are U. S. fathers? *Family planning perspectives, 27,* 159–161, 165.

LaRossa, R. (1997). *The modernization of fatherhood: A social and political history.* Chicago: University of Chicago Press.

LaRossa, R., Gordon, B. A., Wilson, R. J., Bairan, A., & Jaret, C. (1991). The fluctuating image of the 20th century American father. *Journal of Marriage and the Family, 53,* 987–997.

Larson, J. (1992, July). Understanding stepfamilies. *American Demographics,* 36–40.

Lerman, R. I., & Ooms, T. J. (1993). *Young unwed fathers: Changing roles and emerging policies.* Philadelphia: Temple University Press.

Levine, J. A., & Pitt, E. W. (1995). *New expectations: Community strategies for responsible fatherhood.* New York: Families and Work Institute.

Lewis, M., Feiring, C., & Weinraub, M. (1981). The father as a member of the child's social network. In M.E. Lamb (Ed.), *The role of the father in child development* (2nd ed., pp. 259–294). New York: Wiley.

Lewis, M., & Weinraub, M. (1976). The father's role in the child's social network. In M.E. Lamb (Ed.), *The role of the father in child development* (pp. 157–184). New York: Wiley.

Leyendecker, B., Lamb, M.E., & Schölmerich, A. (1997). Studying mother-infant interaction: The effects of context and length of observation in two subcultural groups. *Infant Behavior and Development, 20,* 325–337.

Leyendecker, B., Lamb, M.E., Schölmerich, A., & Fricke, D.M. (1997). Contexts as moderators of observed interactions: A study of Costa Rican mothers and infants from differing socioeconomic backgrounds. *International Journal of Behavioral Development, 21,* 15–34.

Lindberg, L. D., Sonenstein, F. L., Ku, L., & Martinez, G. (1997). Age differences between minors who give birth and their adult partners. *Family Planning Perspectives, 29,* 61–66.

Lupton, D., & Barclay, L. (1997). *Constructing fatherhood: Discourses and experiences.* Thousand Oaks, CA: Sage.

MacDonald, W. L., & DeMaris, A. (1996). Parenting stepchildren and biological children: The effects of stepparent's gender and new biological children. *Journal of Family Issues, 17,* 5–25.

Maquire, M. C. (1999). Treating the dyad as the unit of analysis: A primer on three analytic approaches. *Journal of Marriage and the Family, 61,* 213–224.

Marsiglio, W. (1995a). *Fatherhood: Contemporary theory, research, and social policy.* Thousand Oaks, CA: Sage.

Marsiglio, W. (1995b). Stepfathers with minor children living at home: Parenting perceptions and relationship quality. In W. Marsiglio (Ed.), *Fatherhood: Contemporary theory, research, and social policy* (pp. 211–229) Thousand Oaks, CA: Sage.

Marsiglio, W. (1998). *Procreative man.* New York: New York University Press.

Marsiglio, W., & Cohan, M. (1997). Young fathers and child development. In M E. Lamb (Ed.), *The role of the father in child development* (3rd ed., pp. 227–244, 373–376). New York: Wiley.

Marsiglio, W., & Cohan, M. (in press). Contextualizing father involvement and paternal influence: Sociological and qualitative themes. *Marriage & Family Review.*

Marsiglio, W., Day, R., & Lamb, M. E. (in press). Exploring fatherhood diversity: Implications for conceptualizing father involvement. *Marriage and Family Review.*

Mayer, S. E. (1997). *What money can't buy: Family income and children's life chances.* Cambridge, MA: Harvard University Press.

McAdoo, J. L. (1993). The roles of African American fathers: An ecological perspective. *Families in Soci-*

ety: The Journal of Contemporary Human Service, 74, 28–35.

McLanahan, S. S., Seltzer, J. A., Hanson, T. L., & Thomson, E. (1994). Child support enforcement and child well-being: Greater security or greater conflict? In I. Garfinkel, S. S. McLanahan, & P. K. Robins (Eds.), *Child support and child well-being* (pp. 285–316). Washington, DC: Urban Institute.

McLoyd, V. C., & Wilson, L. (1991). The strain of living poor: Parenting, social support, and child mental health. In A. C. Huston (Ed.), *Children in poverty: Child development and public policy* (pp. 105–135). Cambridge, MA: Cambridge University Press.

Messner, M. (1997). *Politics of masculinities: Men in movements.* Thousand Oaks, CA: Sage.

Meyer, D. R., & Garasky, S. (1993). Custodial fathers: Myths, realities, and child support policy. *Journal of Marriage and the Family, 55,* 73–89.

Minton, C., & Pasley, K. (1996). Fathers' parenting role identity and father involvement: A comparison of nondivorced and divorced, nonresident fathers. *Journal of Family Issues, 17,* 26–45.

Mintz, S. (1998). From patriarchy to androgyny and other myths: Placing men's family roles in historical perspective. In A. Booth & N. Crouter (Eds.), *Men in families: When do they get involved? What difference does it make?* (pp. 3–30). Mahwah, NJ: Erlbaum.

Mott, F. L. (1990). When is a father really gone? Paternal-child conduct in father-absent homes. *Demography, 27,* 499–517.

Mott, F. L. (1994). Sons, daughters and fathers' absence: Differentials in father-leaving probabilities and in home environments. *Journal of Family Issues, 5,* 97–128.

National Center on Fathers and Families. (1997). *Fathers and families roundtables: Discussions on the seven sore learnings, 1995–1997. National Center on Fathers and Families.* Philadelphia: University of Pennsylvania.

Nock, S. (1998). The consequences of premarital fatherhood. *American Sociological Review, 63,* 250–263.

Nord, C. W., & Zill, N. (1996a). *Non-custodial parents' participation in their children's lives: Evidence from the Survey of Income and Program Participation: Volume I, Summary of SIPP Analysis* (Report to the Office of Human Services Policy). Washington, DC: U.S. Department of Health and Human Services.

Nord, C. W., & Zill, N. (1996b). *Non-custodial parents' participation in their children's lives: Evidence from the Survey of Income and Program Participation: Volume II, synthesis of the literature* (Report to the Office of Human Services Policy). Washington, DC: U.S. Department of Health and Human Services.

Palkovitz, R. (1997). Reconstructing "involvement": Expanding conceptualizations of men's caring in contemporary families. In A. J. Hawkins & D. C. Dollahite (Eds.), *Generative fathering: Beyond deficit perspectives* (pp. 200–216). Thousand Oaks, CA: Sage.

Parke, R.D. (1996). *Fatherhood.* Cambridge, MA: Harvard University Press.

Parke, R.D., & Buriel, R. (1998). Socialization in the family: Ethnic and ecological perspectives. In W. Damon & N. Eisenberg (Eds.), *Handbook of child psy-*

chology. Vol. 3. Social, emotional, and personality development (5th ed., (pp. 463–552). New York: Wiley.

Parke, R.D., Power, T.G., & Gottman, J.M. (1979). Conceptualization and quantifying influence patterns in the family triad. In M.E. Lamb, S.J. Suomi, & G.R. Stephenson (Eds.), *Social interaction analysis: Methodological issues* (pp. 231–253). Madison, WI: University of Wisconsin Press.

Patterson, C. J., & Chan, R. W. (1997). Gay fathers. In M. E. Lamb (Ed.), *The role of the father in child development* (pp. 245–260, 376–380). New York: Wiley.

Paulson, S. E., Hill, J. P., & Holmbeck, G. N. (1991). Distinguishing between perceived closeness and parental warmth in families with seventh-grade boys and girls. *Journal of Early Adolescence, 11,* 276–293.

Pleck, E. H., & Pleck, J. H. (1997). Fatherhood ideals in the United States: Historical dimensions. In M. E. Lamb (Ed.), *The role of the father in child development* (3rd ed., pp. 33–48, 413–318). New York: Wiley.

Pleck, J. H. (1997). Paternal involvement: Levels, sources, and consequences. In M. E. Lamb (Ed.), *The role of the father in child development* (3rd ed., pp. 66–103, 325–332). New York: John Wiley & Sons.

Popenoe, D. (1996). *Life without father.* New York: Free Press.

Rettig, K. D., Leichtentritt, R. D., & Stanton, L. M. (1999). Understanding noncustodial fathers' family and life satisfaction from resource theory perspective. *Journal of Family Issues, 20,* 507–538.

Rossi, A., & Rossi, P. (1990). *Of human bonding: Parent-child relations across the life course.* New York: Aldine De Gruyter.

Rotundo, E. A. (1993). *American manhood: Transformations in masculinity from the Revolution to the modern era.* New York: Basic Books.

Roy, K. (1999). Low-income single fathers in an African American community and the requirements of welfare reform. *Journal of Family Issues, 20,* 432–457.

Russell, G. (1999). Primary caregiving fathers. In M. E. Lamb (Ed.), *Parenting and child development in "nontraditional" families* (pp. 57–81). Mahwah, NJ: Erlbaum.

Seltzer, J. A. (1991). Relationships between fathers and children who live apart: The father's role after separation. *Journal of Marriage and the Family, 53,* 79–101.

Seltzer, J. A. (1998a). Men's contributions to children and social policy. In A. Booth & N. Crouter (Eds.), *Men in families: When do they get involved? What difference does it make?* (pp. 303–314). Mahwah, NJ: Erlbaum.

Seltzer, J. A. (1998b). Father by law: Effects of joint legal custody on nonresident fathers' involvement with children. *Demography, 35,* 135–146.

Seltzer, J. A., & Brandeth, Y. (1995). What fathers say about involvement with children after separation. In W. Marsiglio (Ed.), *Fatherhood: Contemporary theory, research, and social policy* (pp. 166–192) Thousand Oaks, CA: CA: Sage.

Shapiro, A., & Lambert, J. D. (1999). Longitudinal effects of divorce on the quality of the father-child relationship and on father's psychological well-being. *Journal of Marriage and the Family, 61,* 397–408.

Shapiro, J. L., Diamond, M. J., & Greenberg, M. (1995). *Becoming a father.* New York: Springer.

Simons, R. L., Whitbeck, L. B., Beaman, J., & Conger, R. D. (1994). The impact of mothers' parenting, involvement by nonresidential fathers, and parental conflict on the adjustment of adolescent children. *Journal of Marriage and the Family, 56,* 356–374.

Simons, R. L., Whitbeck, L. B., Melby, J. N., & Wu, C.-I. (1995). Economic pressure and harsh parenting. In R. D. Conger and G. H. Elder, Jr. (Eds.), *Families in troubled times: Adapting to change in rural America.* New York: Aldine De Gruyter.

Smith, H. L., & Morgan, S. P. (1994). Children's closeness to father as reported by mothers, sons and daughters: Evaluating subjetive assessments with the Rasch model. *Journal of Family Issues, 15,* 3–29.

Snarey, J. (1993). *How fathers care for the next generation.* Cambridge, MA: Harvard University Press.

Stacey, J. (1998). Dada-ism in the 1990s: Getting past baby talk about fatherlessness. In C. R. Daniels (Ed.), *Lost fathers: The politics of fatherlessness in America* (pp. 51–83). New York: St. Martin's Press.

Stearns, P. N. (1991). Fatherhood in historical perspective. The role of social change. In F. Bozett & S. Hanson (Eds.), *Fatherhood and families in cultural context* (pp. 28–52). New York: Springer.

Sternberg, K. J., & Lamb, M. E. (1999). Violent families. In M. E. Lamb (Ed.), *Parenting and child development in "nontraditional" families* (pp. 305–325). Mahwah, NJ: Erlbaum.

Sternberg, K. J., Lamb, M. E., & Dawud-Noursi, S. (1998). Using multiple informants to understand domestic violence and its effects. In G. W. Holden, R. Geffner, & E. N. Jouriles (Eds.), *Children exposed to marital violence: Theory, research, and applied issues* (pp. 121–156). Washington, DC: American Psychological Association.

Sternberg, K. J., Lamb, M. E., Greenbaum, C., Cicchetti, D., Dawud, S., Cortes, R. M., Krispin, O., & Lorey, F. (1993). Effects of domestic violence on children's behavior problems and depression. *Developmental Psychology, 29,* 44–52.

Sternberg, K. J., Lamb, M. E., Greenbaum, C., Dawud, S., Cortes, R. M., & Lorey, F. (1994). The effects of domestic violence on children's perceptions of their perpetrating and nonperpetrating parents. *International Journal of Behavioral Development, 17,* 779–795.

Stewart, S. D. (1999). Disneyland dads, Disneyland moms? How nonresident parents spend time with absent children. *Journal of Family Issues, 20,* 539–556.

Tein, J., Roosa, M., & Michaels, M. (1994). Agreement between parent and child reports on parental behavior. *Journal of Marriage and the Family, 56,* 341–355.

Thompson, R. A., & Laible, D. J. (1999). Noncustodial parents. In M. E. Lamb (Ed.), *Parenting and child development in "nontraditional" families* (pp. 103–123). Mahwah, NJ: Erlbaum.

Walzer, S. (1998). *Thinking about the baby: Gender and transitions into parenthood.* Philadelphia: Temple University Press.

Wright, D. W., Peterson, L. R., & Barnes, H. L. (1990). The relation of parental employment and contextual variables with sexual permissiveness and gender role attitudes of rural early adolescents. *Journal of Early Adolescence, 10,* 382–398.

Young, M. H., Miller, B. C., Norton, M. C., & Hill, E. J. (1995). The effect of parental supportive behaviors on life satisfaction of adolescent offspring. *Journal of Marriage and the Family, 57,* 813–822.

Zimmerman, M. A., Salem, D. A., & Maton, K. I. (1995). Family structure and psychosocial correlates among urban African-American adolescent males. *Child Development, 66,* 1598–1613.

TERRY ARENDELL   *Colby College*

Conceiving and Investigating Motherhood:
The Decade's Scholarship

Mothering and motherhood are the subjects of a rapidly expanding body of literature. Considered in this decade review are two predominant streams in this work. One is the theorizing of mothering and motherhood and the other is the empirical study of the mothering experience. Conceptual developments have been propelled particularly by feminist scholarship, including the increasing attention to race and ethnic diversity and practices. The conceptualizations of the ideology of intensive mothering and of maternal practice are among the significant contributions. Study of mothering has focused attention on a wide array of specific topics and relationships among variables, including issues of maternal well-being, maternal satisfaction and distress, and employment.

Today's scholarship on mothering and motherhood considers mothers' activities, understandings, and experiences. This represents a broadening of much of the earlier work focused on the quality of mothering and its supposed effects on a child. The study of mothering both expanded dramatically over the course of the past decade and became more multidisciplinary.

Scholarly work on mothering focuses on the person who does the relational and logistical work of child rearing. Definitions of mothering share a theme: the social practices of nurturing and caring for dependent children. Mothering, thus, involves dynamic activity and always-evolving relationships. Scholars Glenn, Brown, and Forcey (Forcey, 1994, p. 357), for example, define mothering as "a socially constructed set of activities and relationships involved in nurturing and caring for people." Mothering is particularly significant because it is "the main vehicle through which people first form their identities and learn their place in society." Multifaceted and complex, mothering is symbolically laden, representing what often is characterized as the ultimate in relational devotion (e.g., Phoenix, Woollett, and Lloyd, 1991).

Mothering is associated with women because universally, it is women who do the work of mothering. Motherhood is entwined with notions of femininity (Chodorow, 1989, 1990; Glenn, 1994), and women's gender identity is reinforced by mothering (McMahon, 1995). Especially since the 19th century, mothering has been presumed to be a primary identity for most adult women. That is, womanhood and motherhood are treated as synonymous identities and categories of experience. Yet not all women mother, and mothering as nurturing and caring work is not inevitably the exclusive domain of women (Forcey, 1994; Rothman, 1994; Ruddick, 1994; Schwartz, 1994).

Many of the most pressing political and social debates of recent years—such as abortion, women's employment, welfare reform, and reproductive technologies—have had definitions of mothers and mothering at their center (Glenn, 1994, p. 3; Luker, 1996). The debates involve disputed ex-

Department of Sociology, Colby College, Waterville, Maine 04901 (tjarende@colby.edu).

Key Words: families, family ideology, gender, motherhood, motherhood ideology, mothering.

411

pectations of women and womanhood and, as well, of men and manhood, family, and adulthood, and challenges to the gender-based division of labor (e.g., Barnard & Martell, 1995; Blaisure & Allen, 1995; Stacey, 1996; see Thompson & Walker, 1995). These controversies about mothers and mothering are about children—the evolving conceptualizations of childhood and arguments about what children's needs are and whether or not they are being met.

What follows is a review of some of the pivotal scholarly work of the past decade on mothering and motherhood. I limit the discussion to North American scholarship and to women's experiences and practices, and, consistent with the literature and general practice, I focus on mothering as women's activity. First, I address developments in the theorizing of mothering and motherhood. I survey the dominant American ideology of motherhood, challenges posed to the ideology, and discourses of maternal deviancy, including in this latter section a brief overview of demographic and employment trends. Second, I consider the phenomenology of mothering—experiences and understandings of mothering. I present findings on mothers' well-being, including issues of emotional work, maternal satisfaction, distress, and social support. I turn to mothers' employment and, briefly, to the economic hardship experienced by high numbers of mothers and related policy issues. I conclude with some thoughts regarding gaps in our knowledge and prospects for future study.

I move in this essay from an overview of recent conceptual developments to specific empirical findings. This reflects the parallel existence of two general approaches—conceptual and empirical—in the increasingly voluminous scholarship on mothering. Drawing on and posing somewhat unique intellectual histories and theoretical, epistemological, methodological, and discursive approaches, the contributions of the two traditions are somewhat distinctive. Lacking in the literature overall is an integration of the two approaches.

On the one hand is work on mothering that can be characterized as interpretive, critical, hermeneutic, qualitative, and feminist. These perspectives, although they vary some from each other, share a focus on both the construction of shared meanings and the historical, cultural, and situational contexts out of which people act. Meanings are seen to be multiple and shifting. Terms such as *mothering, motherhood, family,* and *childhood* are problematicized, and variations are foregrounded and explored. Moreover, dominant ideologies are deconstructed; language, as well as action, is subjected to careful analysis.

On the other hand is the scholarly tradition, which adheres, more or less, to the classical conventions of positivist social science. In this approach, statistical methodologies underpin the scholarship; variable relationships are explored and causation patterns determined. Survey research is common, and findings are intended to be verifiable, reliable, and generalizable. Coming especially out of psychology, human development, and child and family studies, this body of work is extensive and generally considered to be mainstream in the study of mothering.

One of the most pressing challenges in the coming decade for scholars engaged in the endeavor to more fully describe, analyze, and explain motherhood is to bridge the schism between these two bodies of work—the interpretive and the positivistic. Integrating the respective contributions—for purposes of both attaining a more complete understanding of mothering and for establishing a starting place for future theory development and empirical research—is the larger task.

CONCEPTUALIZING MOTHERING

Feminist constructionism dominates U.S. contemporary theory development on mothering in the social sciences and humanities. That is, mothering and motherhood are viewed as dynamic social interactions and relationships, located in a societal context organized by gender and in accord with the prevailing gender belief system. Definitions and practices of mothering are understood to be historically variable (see Apple & Golden, 1997), rather than being seen as "natural, universal, and unchanging" (Glenn, 1994, p. 4), the product of biological reproduction. What is vital to explore is not that women, as females, have the capacity to conceive, gestate, give birth, and lactate, but that some women engage in the ongoing, demanding activities of child rearing and nurture. How these biological activities are culturally organized and given meaning are the provocative questions.

Feminist scholarship has opened up fresh conceptualizations of mothering practices and of women's lives and family, more generally, and pushed for study of varied activities in relation and in contrast to the dominant ideologies of motherhood (Adams, 1995; Ross, 1995). Related, and also energizing and expanding the study of motherhood, has been the inclusion of minority and working- and lower-income class definitions, representations, and practices (Collins, 1994; Glenn, Chang, & Forcey, 1994). All of these discussions continue a trend propelled by both the women's movement and writings, personal and conceptual, by well-known writers and theorists, such as Carol Stack (1974), Dorothy Dinnerstein (1976), Adrienne Rich (1977), Nancy Chodorow (1978, 1989), Sara Ruddick (1980), Alice Walker (1983), Audre Lorde (1984), and Jessica Benjamin (1988).

Continued feminist revisiting and reformulation of psychoanalytic theory illumine the meanings and complexities of mothering (Benjamin, 1990, 1994; Chodorow, 1989, 1990; Vegetti-Finzi, 1996). Everyone was mothered, and many are mothers, and these experiences can impede study and understanding (e.g., Bassin, Honey, & Kaplan, 1994, p. 2; Schwartz, 1994). Feminist attention to care and caring has also animated the scholarship on mothering (see Sevenhuijsen, 1998; Tronto, 1996; Waerness, 1996). Mothers and children form relationships of care (Gordon et al., 1996), and "caring as experienced in the family has come to act as the metaphor and standard for all forms of caring" (Tarlow, 1996, p. 56). Caring occurs in many social spheres and relationships, however, not just in the mother-child dyad (Tronto).

Within feminist constructionist efforts to portray the broad landscape of mothering is an investigation of motherhood ideology. The prevailing ideology in North America is that of *intensive mothering*. This motherhood mandate declares that mothering is exclusive, wholly child centered, emotionally involving, and time-consuming (Hays, 1996). The mother portrayed in this ideology is devoted to the care of others; she is self-sacrificing and "not a subject with her own needs and interests" (Bassin et al., 1994, p. 2). She is the good mother (Ribbens, 1994; Thurer, 1993).

Motherhood ideology is entwined with idealized notions of the family, presuming the institution and image of the idealized White, middle-class heterosexual couple with its children in a self-contained family unit (see Thorne, 1993). Family law and social policies presume and support the heterosexual nuclear family and center the spousal, not mother and child, relationship (Abramovitz, 1996; Fineman, 1995). Literary, film, and other cultural representations portray and reinforce the conventional notions of mothering and motherhood (Gillis, 1997; Kaplan, 1992). Inten-

sive mothering ideology both assumes and reinforces the traditional gender-based division of labor (Fineman).

Maternal Practice—A Universalist Approach

Central in the conceptual work on mothering and motherhood is work aimed at delineating what it is that mothers do. Mothers share, by definition and condition, a set of activities even though they vary as individuals and across cultures (Ruddick, 1994; see Phoenix et al., 1991). They engage in "maternal practice"—the nurturing, protecting, and training of their children (see also Ladd-Taylor, 1994; Leonard, 1996). Certain kinds of responses are evoked by children's (supposed) common core of basic needs (Bailey, 1994), and the daily activities of mothering foster a "practicalist" form of reasoning—an intellectual style, way of thinking, and "thoughtful project" (Ruddick). As theorist Ruddick observed, "Mothers are identified not by what they feel but by what they try to do" (p. 34). Maternal practice involves intimate relationships as well as skill. Through dynamic interaction with their children, mothers foster and shape a profound affectional relationship, a deeply meaningful connection (Oberman & Josselson, 1996). In this relationship of care, the child has physical, emotional, and moral claims on the mother (see Leonard, 1996). Influencing women's particular mothering actions are their beliefs about family, individuality, the nature of childhood, and the nature of their child (Ribbens, 1994). Mothers actively interpret both cultural messages about childhood and their experiences with children, shaping their parental role in accordance with their evolving beliefs (Lightfoot & Valsiner, 1992). "Mothering is learned in the process of interaction with the individual mothered" (Barnard & Martell, 1995, p. 22).

Motherwork—A Particularistic Approach

Some theorists call into question a unitary model of mothering, insisting that women's various standpoints must be taken into account (Dill, 1994a, 1994b; Glenn, 1992). Mothering, these scholars argue, is not universally a relationship between a woman and her children, a private, singular, or even primary activity understood to be separate and distinct from economic provision (see Collins, 1991, 1994; Coontz, 1997). Cultural and economic contexts variously shape mothers' activities and understandings. Mothering takes place within "specific historical contexts framed by interlocking structures of race, class, and gender" (Collins, 1994, p. 56, 1991; see Baca Zinn, 1990, 1994; Stack & Burton, 1993). Women's social locations—the intersections of regional and local political economy with class, ethnicity, culture, and sexual preference—"condition the strategies and meanings that working mothers fashion through their agency," for example (Lamphere, Zavella, & Gonzales, 1993, p. 4).

Mothers' responses to children vary; mothers do not nurture, protect, or socialize their children in identical ways or circumstances, nor do they necessarily provide such care at all (see Scheper-Hughes, 1992). Having limited or no access to class and racial privilege constricts the range of options and resources available to minority mothers (Baca Zinn, 1990, p. 468, 1994). Three issues, according to sociologist Collins (1991, 1994), form the "bedrock" of the "motherwork" of women of color: survival, power, and identity (see Altschuler, 1997; Bailey, 1994; Kaplan, 1997). And motherwork is conducted not only on behalf of individual children but also on behalf of the larger social group in which they are situated (see Stack & Burton, 1993). Further, the view that mothers are the "source of children's current and later personal stability" is not universal (Ambert, 1994, p. 531), despite the implications of universalist models.

Deviancy Discourses

Intensive mothering ideology remains, despite cultural contradictions and diverse arrangements and practices, the normative standard, culturally and politically, by which mothering practices and arrangements are evaluated. A variety of deviancy discourses derive from this ideological construct of mothering—the mother absorbed in nurturing activities and situated in the biological nuclear family. The discourses are targeted, albeit differentially, at mothers who do not conform to the script of full-time motherhood in the context of marriage. Single mothers, welfare mothers, minority mothers, immigrant mothers, and lesbian mothers—often overlapping but not mutually exclusive categories—are subjects of deviancy discourses of mothering (see Fineman, 1995; Kurz, 1995; Sidel, 1996). Especially spotlighted by the discourses are mothers of color who are unmarried and not engaged in paid work but dependent on public assistance to support their children. Indeed, in contradiction to intensive mothering ideology,

low-income racial and ethnic and immigrant mothers are expected to prioritize employment, if not marriage to a good provider, as has been the case across the century (Boris, 1994; Chang, 1994; Segura, 1994; U.S. Bureau of the Census for the Bureau of Labor Statistics, 1999).

Demographic trends. Adding fuel to the discursive rhetoric both on motherhood and the deviancy discourses, more specifically, are several trends, demographic and employment. Childbearing, overall, is delayed compared with the case in earlier decades (Ventura, Martin, Curtis, & Mathews, 1996). Although declining across all racial and ethnic groups, fertility rates remain highest among women of color, and there has been less convergence in the fertility rates of minority women and White women than previously predicted (Casterline, Lee, & Foote, 1996). Immigration patterns contribute to the diversity in fertility rates among groups of women.

Of particular importance, and fueling the ideological debates about mothers' roles, and women's roles more generally, is the increase in single motherhood and the growing separation of marriage and maternity (Manning, 1995; Spain & Bianchi, 1996). Two phenomena account for these trends. One is the continued high rate of divorce, in which over half of young mothers are or are likely to become divorced (Spain & Bianchi, p. 50). Moreover, mothers' remarriage rates are declining and lower than fathers' (National Center for Health Statistics, 1998). The other major component of the rise in single mothers is the increasing proportion of births to unwed women. Unmarried women account for one-third of births in the United States. This constitutes a significant change in recent decades: the proportion of births to unwed women was roughly one in five in 1980 and one in ten in 1970 (Ventura et al., 1996). Given present patterns, the proportion of births to unwed women is likely to increase, as is the case in numerous European countries (Welles-Nystrom, 1997, p. 280).

Significant racial and ethnic differences in unwed motherhood persist. Roughly one quarter of births to White, Latina, and Asian American women and more than two thirds of births to Black women are to unmarried women. Further, poorly educated women are overrepresented in the ranks of never-married mothers (Mathews & Ventura, 1997; Ventura et al., 1996), although teenagers no longer comprise the majority of unwed mothers. And although the vast majority of unwed mothers are heterosexual, growing numbers of women raising children are lesbians—between 1.5 and 5 million (Allen, 1997; see Allen & Demo, 1995; Lewin, 1993; Patterson, 1995). Conservative social commentators view these trends with alarm, seeing them as threats not only to the American family unit but to the larger society more generally (e.g., Blankenhorn, 1995; Blankenhorn, Bayme, & Elshtain, 1992; Whitehead, 1993).

Mothers' employment. White married mothers who are employed, especially if they are middle class, are also subjects of deviancy discourses by virtue of their employment (see Coontz, 1997; Presser, 1995; Stacey, 1996). The activities of mothering and working for pay are undertaken simultaneously by a large majority of mothers rather than, as in the past, sequentially. Tripling over the past 30 years, maternal employment increased steadily for all racial and ethnic groups (Spain & Bianchi, 1996). Seventy-five percent of all mothers with dependent children under age 18 and 60% of mothers with children under age 6 are in the paid labor force. Well over half of all mothers of infants are employed, and married mothers' employment falls just short of that of unmarried mothers' (Bachu, 1997; Ventura et al., 1996). Further, surveys show that maternal employment generally would be even higher if child care costs were more reasonable (Scarr, 1998).

Assisted reproductive technologies. An emerging subject of motherhood deviancy discourses are women who resist the underlying assumptions and approaches related to assisted reproductive technologies. These technologies are rapidly expanding but in a societal context that has yet to address conflicts of values and objectives (Donchin, 1996; Ginsburg & Rapp, 1995; Rae, 1994; Rothman, 1994). These technologies extend the medicalization of maternity in dramatic and often unexamined ways (see Rapp, 1996) and stress the primacy of male genetic ties to offspring (Callahan, 1995). Definitions of mothers and mothering are co-opted by scientific and medical experts and determined by legal contracts (Fineman, 1995; Schwartz, 1994), and birth giving and motherhood are commodified. Rather than affording reproductive freedoms, technologies may countermand them by dictating women's choices and behaviors, for instance (see Baber & Allen, 1992; Rothman). Women who break contractual agreements or who assert their autonomy in the process of utilizing

assisted reproductive technologies are potential subjects for an expanded deviancy discourse. But for that matter, women who use such technologies are potentially subjects of deviancy discourses, seen to be interfering with the natural processes of reproduction.

THE PHENOMENOLOGY OF MOTHERING

Disjunctures prevail between the ideologies of mothering and motherhood and the experiences of real women. The mothering experience is replete with dialectical tensions; for example, "mothering can confer both maternal power and an immense burden of responsibility" (Oberman & Josselson, 1996, p. 344). Mothering is a font of personal fulfillment, growth, and joy, on the one hand, and one of distress, depression, and anxiety, on the other (e.g., Ross, 1995). Child raising may bring personal development but also increased work and economic stress; it brings feelings of liberation and transformation but also of oppression and subordination (Marshall, Barnett, & Sayer, 1998; Roxburgh, 1997). Mothering is neither a unitary experience for individual women nor experienced similarly by all women. It carries multiple and often shifting meanings (Josselson, 1996; McMahon, 1995).

With respect to identity, mothering is more powerful than either marital status or occupation (Rogers & White, 1998). Mothering may hold even greater salience for women of color, given racial and ethnic communities' extended family ties and loyalties (see Dill, 1994b; McAdoo, 1993; Polatnick, 1996; Segura & Pierce, 1993). Women with children report experiencing greater meaning in their lives than do women without children (Ross & Van Willigen, 1996, p. 583).

Emotional Work

Modern mothering entails extensive, ongoing emotional work (Benjamin, 1990, 1994; Chodorow, 1989; Thurer, 1993). Feelings shift. There is no single emotion—love—that children inspire in mothers, and feelings must be managed and directed. A mother's emotions can vary within the course of a day and certainly over time, depending upon the behavior of her children, the space, time, and services available to her, and myriad other desires and frustrations (Ruddick, 1994, p. 34; see Josselson, 1996). Mothering is a site of warm and tender caretaking and nurture and also, inevitably, of interpersonal conflicts, as is the case with family life more generally (Presser, 1995; Thorne, 1993). Maternal ambivalence is grounded in the paradoxical character of the mothering experience. The uncertainty of children's long-term outcomes intensifies maternal ambivalence.

Mothers' negative feelings are understudied. Some research, however, suggests that married mothers experience significantly higher levels of anger than do fathers. Economic hardships and child care are the primary strains. Women report that their anger is targeted primarily at husbands, who do little to ease wives' burdens, and directed secondarily at children (Ross & Van Willigen, 1996, p. 582).

Married mothers in dual-income households generally experience more positive affect at work and more negative at home. In contrast, their husbands experience the reverse: experiencing more negative emotion at work and more positive at home. What seems to account for these differences is that these men do less housework and cooking, engage less with their children, and enjoy more relaxation and leisure when at home than do their wives. Employed single mothers are more similar to married fathers than to married mothers. They view their home situations as being more flexible than do married mothers, even though they carry sole responsibility for their children and homes (Larsen, 1998; Larson & Richards, 1994). Single and married mothers spend roughly the same amount of time in total family and child care responsibilities (Bianchi & Robinson, 1997; Duxbury, Higgins, & Lee, 1994).

Maternal Satisfaction

Mothering one's biological offspring rather than stepchildren brings greater maternal satisfaction. Not related to maternal satisfaction are the number and ages of children, social class, or employment patterns (Rogers & White, 1998, p. 305). Also related to maternal satisfaction is parenting approach. Mothers who utilize an authoritative style of parenting—that is, are democratic; are controlling and demanding; and are also warm, receptive, and rational in their relations with their children—are more satisfied with parenting than are those who use an authoritarian approach (see Rogers & White, 1998). Warmth, acceptance, and respect for their children influence the parental functioning of divorced mothers also (Stewart, Copeland, Chester, Malley, & Barenbaum, 1997). Well-educated mothers are more likely to use authoritative parenting approaches and are emotionally closer to

their children than poorly educated mothers (Amato & Booth, 1997, p. 50).

Mothers are more satisfied with parenting than fathers. Also, however, not surprisingly, given their more intensive involvement in parenting work, mothers experience more parental strain over the course of child rearing than do fathers. But strain is not necessarily a negative phenomenon: it "may indicate greater emotional intimacy and, as such, is a positive sign of a close relationship" (Scott & Alwin, 1989, p. 500). Indeed, both mothers and children in general report that children feel more closely attached to their mothers than to their fathers (Larson & Richards, 1994). Mothers generally are more positive and supportive than fathers of their children (Kerig, Cowan, & Cowan, 1993, p. 931; Starrels, 1994). Marital dissatisfaction negatively influences mothers' parenting approaches (Kerig et al.).

Distress

Notwithstanding the affirmative meanings women find in its activities and relationships, mothering is often negatively associated with psychological well-being. Distress, defined as "symptoms of depression, anxiety, physiological malaise, and lack of happiness" (Goldsteen & Ross, 1989, p. 505), is a common maternal experience. The most stressed of all mothers are those who are married, employed, have young children, and encounter difficulty in locating and affording child care and handle child rearing mostly alone (Benin & Keith, 1995; Hughes & Galinsky, 1994; Marshall, Barnett, et al., 1998; Neal, Chapman, Ingersol-Dayton, & Emlen, 1993; Sears & Galambos, 1993). Such mothers' depression levels are twice those of mothers having sufficient resources (Goldsteen & Ross, 1989, pp. 507–508). Mothers having preschool-aged or multiple children and living in crowded conditions feel more overburdened than other mothers. Young mothers experience greater distress and have fewer psychological resources than do older mothers (Brooks-Gunn & Chase-Lansdale, 1995). Each additional child increases younger mothers' feelings of being overburdened (Goldsteen & Ross). When economic conditions are constant, single and married women experience similar levels of maternal distress (Ross & Van Willigen, 1996).

Employed mothers experience lower levels of distress than do full-time mothers (Marshall, Barnett, et al., 1998). Mothers able both to locate and afford high-quality child care; who are supported by their partners; and who can avail themselves of flexible workplace options and, thus, have a sense of control over their work lives are benefited the most by paid work (see Duxbury et al., 1994; Hughes & Galinsky, 1994; Roxburgh, 1997).

Social Support

Mothers often receive precious little assistance with the work of parenting. Despite much attention in recent years to the so-called "new, nurturing father" and some change on men's part, women still do most child rearing (and homemaking) (Coltrane, 1996; Coltrane & Adams, 1998). Divorced and unwed fathers, especially, do little in the way of parenting (Arendell, 1995). In point of fact, "although people are moving toward the idea that fathers should be more involved with children, demographic and social changes have resulted in fathers being less involved with children than perhaps at any time in U.S. history" (Amato & Booth, 1997, p. 228). Other family members, in general, also provide little in the way of practical support to mothers. Poor mothers are no more likely than affluent ones to receive family assistance. Single mothers, generally, get no more help than married mothers from family members (Benin & Keith, 1995).

Differences exist along racial and ethnic lines in mothers' reliance on family and friends for childrearing assistance, with minority women receiving more aid than White women. Nonetheless, the variations between the two groups are less pronounced now than in earlier decades, and "a significant proportion of African American women are not receiving assistance from family or friends or neighbors" (Benin and Keith, 1995, p. 294; see Jayakody, Chatters, & Taylor, 1993; Kaplan, 1997; Polatnick, 1996). In comparison, African American mothers rely more on extended family for assistance with child care, and White mothers rely more on neighbors and friends. Employed single mothers in both groups are more likely than married mothers to turn to family for help when a child is ill but are no more likely to turn to friends and neighbors (Benin & Keith; see Jayakody et al.; Logan & Spitze, 1994). Hispanic mothers rely mostly on other household residents—their partner and other adults or children—and less than either Black or White mothers on extended family or nonrelatives, even when taking residential proximity into account (Lamphere et al., 1993; Marshall, Marx, McCartney, & Garcia Coll, 1998).

Maternal Employment

Maternal employment adds layers of complexity to the general portrait of mothers' well-being and parental satisfaction. Overall, employment is conducive to mothers' mental health and parenting gratification. But employment is not an unmitigated blessing: paid work and mothering are structured and defined as distinctive spheres in U.S. society (Moen, 1992). Many mothers (and fathers) experience a time bind (Daly, 1996; Hochschild, 1997; Robinson & Godbey, 1997) and pay a high personal price trying to balance work and family demands. Loss of sleep, curtailed leisure time, and feeling overloaded and stressed are the currencies extorted from mothers involved both in paid work and child raising (e.g., Presser, 1995).

Employed and full-time mothers generally engage in the same array of child care activities, with the exception that full-time mothers watch more television with their children (Bryant & Zick, 1996; DeMeis & Perkins, 1996). Mothers holding employment do not spend less time with their children than full-time homemaker mothers (see Bianchi & Robinson, 1997). Further, many employed mothers "compensate for their absence from the home during work hours by increasing the amount of time they spend in intense interaction with children during nonwork hours [Mischel and Fuhr, 1988]" (Amato & Booth, 1997, p. 60). Educational attainment is a factor in employed mothers' time involvement with their children: those with higher levels of education spend more time with their children than women with lower levels (Bianchi & Robinson; Bryant & Zick, 1996).

Mothers typically experience greater work-family strains than fathers (see Barnett, Brennan, & Marshall, 1994; Duxbury et al., 1994; Marshall, Barnett, et al., 1998). Given their primary responsibility for child care (England, 1996), mothers have fewer options for easing their overall situations (Jacobs & Gerson, 1997). Mothers are more commonly interrupted at work both by children seeking contact or child care or school personnel reporting children's illnesses or injuries (see England; Rosenbloom, 1993). The mothering identity and responsibilities are carried into the workplace: "Even when at work, one is still a parent and time is spent thinking, worrying, planning for children (*this was particularly true for female respondents* [italics added])" (Thorpe & Daly, 1999, p. 15; see Neal et al., 1993). Further, mothers typically "perceive a conflict between responsibility for child care arrangements and opportunity for workplace advancement," unlike fathers (Peterson & Gerson, 1992, p. 533). In the longer term, adjustments made to accommodate family needs when children are young adversely affect mothers' economic well-being (Presser, 1995; Waldfogel, 1997).

African American mothers generally may experience greater psychological satisfaction and less stress in combining parenting and paid work than do Anglo women, although they, like all mothers, must contend with role conflicts between child raising and working for pay. African American mothers' employment rates have been higher for a longer period of time and are recognized within the community as being essential to family survival (Collins, 1991, 1994; Glenn, 1992; Polatnick, 1996; Segura, 1994).

Although most mothers are employed, social attitudes remain critical of women's work-related absence from their children. The roots of the debates about working mothers run deep and long in American culture (Gordon, 1993, 1994; Ladd-Taylor, 1994; Ross, 1995), in tandem with a rhetoric of mother-blame (Garey & Arendell, 1998; Presser, 1995; Thurer, 1993; Turkel, 1994). Thus, mothers who violate the ideology of intensive mothering by being engaged in paid work must contend with others' judgments and their own feelings of ambivalence and guilt about leaving their children (Arendell, 1999; Hertz & Ferguson, 1996; Walzer, 1997). "Idealized, stay-at-home motherhood eludes most American women with children. As an ideology, however, it tells them what should be, rendering them failures as women when they enter the labor market" (Segura, 1994). These cultural contradictions—condemnation of working mothers even as most mothers work for pay—complicate women's experiences and assessments of mothering.

Strategizing Employment

Mothers actively and continuously strategize the handling of family life and employment (England, 1996; Pridham, Denney, Pascoe, Chiu, & Creasey, 1995). Most mothers must rely on their own resources and innovations in managing paid work and child raising. Their personal and individualistic solutions are due, in large measure, to the dearth of formal programs and supports to which to turn for assistance (Martin, 1997; Mitchell, 1997). Mothers alter their strategies for coordinating work and family in accord with their perceptions of children's developmental trajectories

and well-being (Arendell, 1999). They cope with the stresses of the two roles by emphasizing efficiency and organization, planning ahead, and cognitively restructuring their attitudes and assessments (Paden & Buehler, 1995). Mothers reframe their views about their performances without reducing their roles; that is, they seek to emphasize the positive and downplay the negative aspects of being a working mother (DeMeis & Perkins, 1996). Some married mothers work shifts different from their husbands, and other mothers, both single and married, work evening or night shifts in order to be at home during their children's waking hours (Garey, 1999). Dual-earner couples often use the strategy of shared parenting to enhance parental time involvement (Barnett et al., 1994; Hertz, 1997; Hertz & Ferguson, 1996). Immigrant mothers sometimes resort to transnational caring strategies, using a pattern of circular migration and leaving their children in the home country in the care of extended family members for a period of time, then bringing them to the United States (see Hondagneu-Sotel & Avila, 1997; Orellana, Thorne, Lam, & Chee, 1998).

Relationships and interactions between mothers and their paid child caretakers are a focus of recent study. Mothers and their child care providers actively negotiate and redefine mothering, devising ways not only to secure care for children, but also to create and maintain certain meanings pertaining to motherhood. The strategies constructed vary, influenced by beliefs about mothering as well as about children, for example (Hertz, 1997; Macdonald, 1998; Nelson, 1994; Uttal, 1996; Wrigley, 1995). Studies to date have granted more attention to the effects of class differences than to cultural differences between mothers and child care workers, with only few exceptions (e.g., Uttal, 1998).

Economic Distress

Access to economic resources and its influences on mothers' experiences, objectives, and strategies is a significant but understudied dimension of mothering. Income inadequacies and insecurities adversely impact mothers, adding multiple stressors and obstacles to effective child rearing (Flores, Douglas, & Ellwood, 1998; Zill, Moore, Smith, Steif, & Coiro, 1995). Several factors contribute to mothers'—and their children's—poverty: the increase in mother-only families, the underpayment of child support, the insufficiency of the minimum wage, changes in public assistance programs, and the persistence of gender stratification and occupational segregation in the workplace (Children's Defense Fund, 1998; McLanahan & Kelly, 1998).

Social and economic trends and the persistently high rates of poverty for mothers and children constitute the racialization and feminization of poverty (Dickerson, 1995; Edin & Lein, 1997; Kaplan, 1997; McLanahan & Kelly, 1998; Sidel, 1996). Martial status is crucial to mothers' economic well-being. The income gap among mothers is increasing rapidly, with those raising children alone being at great risk of economic hardship. Female-headed households with children present have a poverty rate of 31.6 percent, in contrast to a poverty rate among married couple families with children of 5.2%. White mother–headed families have a poverty rate of 27.7%, Black, 39.8%, and Hispanic, 47.6%. Poverty rates among married-couple families vary by racial and ethnic groups as well: White families have a poverty rate of 4.8%, Black families 8%, and Hispanic families, 17.4%. The poverty rate for all families with children is 19.2%. Twenty-six percent of the total population, children are 40% of the poor (U.S. Bureau of the Census, 1998). Children's poverty is tied to mothers', just as mothers' is tied to their children's.

A joint report issued by the Children's Defense Fund and the National Coalition for the Homeless shows that many families have lost ground with the move from welfare to work. This involves the abolition of the Aid for Dependent Children program and implementation of the Personal Responsibility and Work Opportunity Reconciliation Act of 1996, with its Temporary Assistance for Needy Families program. Many families caught in this transition lack food, medical care, and stable housing, and extreme poverty among children is on the rise. Nearly all mothers who have found employment receive wages that leave them far below the poverty line. Further, as families expend their time-restricted benefits over the course of the next several years, the numbers of mothers and children falling into desperate economic conditions are expected to increase significantly (Children's Defense Fund, 1998; Flores et al., 1998; Sherman, Ameyu, Duffeld, Ebb, & Weinstein, 1998). Mothers with children under age 7 are especially prone to extreme poverty and are the fastest growing group of the homeless (Lee et al., 1992; see Martin, 1997; Sidel, 1996; Welles-Nystrom, 1997).

Social Policy

The United States, a welfare state laggard, has extraordinarily high rates of maternal and child poverty in comparison to the other advanced industrial societies, even those having much higher rates of female-headed families (see Martin, 1997; McLanahan & Kelly, 1998). Mothers' poverty is not a new phenomenon (Abramovitz, 1996; Skocpol, 1992): Throughout American history, mothers, particularly unmarried mothers, have been at a disproportionate risk of economic hardship (Boris, 1994; Gordon, 1993, 1994; Ladd-Taylor, 1994). Poor women have been long the object of policy regulation. Social policies have been used to enforce the idealized version of women's roles; to maintain a double standard of womanhood; to reward and punish women based on their race, class, and marital status; to reconcile the competing demands for women's low-paid market and unpaid domestic work; and to accommodate other labor market needs (Abramovitz, 1996, p. xii–xiii; see Boris, 1994; Brush, 1996; Gordon, 1994; Koven & Michel, 1993; Skocpol, 1992).

Social policy, thus, has reinforced the dominant ideologies of the good mother, promoting, in the process, a particular view of appropriate women's roles. Overall, married and widowed mothers have fared significantly better under American social policies, especially White women, than divorced, separated, deserted, or never-married mothers (Martin, 1997).

Specifically, mothers are systematically disadvantaged in the employment sector by the lack or limited scope of programs aimed at accommodating their child raising (Waldfogel, 1997). The 1993 Family and Medical Leave Act (FMLA) excludes a majority of working mothers; only full-time employees working for organizations that employ more than 50 people qualify to use the leave policy, and then the individual must be able to afford to take unpaid leave. Relatively few women who do qualify actually utilize the leave offered under FMLA, mostly because of concerns about their future employment standing and assessment of opportunity costs given the present structure of the system (Fried, 1998). The FMLA offers a step forward, however, because it conceives "of the worker as both an individual and as a family member and...allows room for recognizing the special needs of new mothers" (Martin, 1997, pp. 303, 319).

Political questions face policy advocates in their pursuits. How, for example, do we press for greater social valuing of mothering and provide social supports for those doing this necessary activity without reducing women's lives to motherhood? How do we acknowledge the socially necessary work of mothers and "support women's claims to integrity, autonomy, dignity, security, and political voice" (Brush, 1996, p. 430; Ladd-Taylor, 1994) without resorting to a rhetoric of maternalism? How do we recognize and press to ease the burdens without becoming blinded to the pleasures of mothering? Such dilemmas point to the interrelatedness of cultural ideologies and social policy objectives and assumptions and highlight questions of difference—among women, those who mother and those who do not, and between women and men.

CONCLUSION AND RECOMMENDATIONS

Mothering and motherhood are the subjects of rapidly expanding bodies of literature. Study of mothering spans efforts to develop general conceptual models to careful examinations of selected social and psychological variables. For all of the contributions to our understanding of mothering and mothers' lives, however, we are left with major gaps.

Areas calling for our attention in the study of mothering can be described as falling into four broad, overlapping domains: identities and meanings of mothering; relationships, with both children and others; experiences and activities of mothering; and the social locations and structural contexts from within which women mother. At the heart of each of these thematic domains must be attention to and respect for the enormous multiplicity of mothering circumstances. Class, race, ethnicity, gender, sexual orientation, national origin, and immigrant experience must be at the forefront of our considerations. Not only is American society increasingly diverse, but the experiences and perceptions of minority women—as legitimate and valuable in their own right and not as measures by which White, heterosexual, middle-class mothering is reified—have been given too little attention. At the same time, this respect for diversity and pluralism, in their many forms, need not divert us from also considering what mothers hold in common. Here I borrow from feminist theorist Susan Bordo (1990, p. 140): "Certainly, we often err on the side of exclusion and thus submerge large areas of human history and experience. But attending too vigilantly to difference can just as problematically construct an Other who

is an exotic alien, a breed apart." Women do, after all, actively participate in a shared larger social context: there is experiential continuity and structural common ground among women (see Marks, 1996, p. 568).

I raise several questions in each of the four areas I've delineated as one way to think about continued study of mothering. These broad categories offer literally dozens of more narrowly defined subjects for study.

Meanings and Identities

How do various women feel about being mothers; what meanings do they ascribe to mothering? How do identities, and subjectivities, differ between full-time mothers, those who combine employment and child raising, and others? How does mothering complement or conflict with other identities? How are women's sexual lives, desires, and experiences affected by mothering activities and the status of motherhood? How do mothers attend to, balance, and negotiate their immediate needs with longer-term ones—relational, economic, health, and emotional? What is the mothering project, as mothers see it? Feminist Ann Snitow's (1992, p. 49) question posed almost a decade ago remains salient: "To what extent is motherhood a powerful identity?... To what extent is it a patriarchal construction that inevitably places mothers outside of the realm of the social, the changing, the active?"

Relationships

What is the character of the relationships between particular mothers and their children? How and why do mothering relationships diverge across mother-child units and also across time for individuals? What are the relationships between mothers' perceptions of their own needs and desires and children's well-being and needs? Where and how do intimate adult relationships fit into the relationships between mothers and children? How is maternal power perceived and exercised, and to what purpose? How are gender and family politics bargained, more generally?

Experiences and Activities

What, exactly, do mothers do? What is the character of mothers' daily lives? How do mothers negotiate the activities of child rearing? How do these negotiations shift with children's growth into new developmental stages and across mothers' own life courses? How are women affected by mothering, and how does this change as children grow and develop, and as women mature and change? What is the full sweep of mothers' emotions and attitudes? How is ambivalence experienced and handled? How do women's experiences of mothering vary by sexual orientation or preference? Where does biology fit into mothering and mothers' experiences?

Social Locations and Structural Context

How do women actively resist the dominant ideologies of mothering and family? Where does mothering fit into the shifting landscape of gender politics? How is mothering affected by the increasing tide of global capitalism and by more-local production and service economies, many of which are receding? How does region influence mothers' activities? For instance, what does it mean to raise children in rural areas, urban areas, or as immigrants? How do women mediate between their children and others, between the family unit and other institutions? How do women collaborate with others in mothering activities? How do they make room for men who wish to mother? What is the political economy of motherhood and mothering?

In conclusion, we need more attention to the lives of particular mothers—to mothers' own voices—and to the lives and voices of diverse groups of mothers. By focusing our investigations on mothers' identities, experiences, and activities, and their understandings of each, we can secure far more realistic and less normative portrayals of mothers' lives than those afforded by sweeping images. At the same time, we need to study the influences on mothers' activities and experiences of various political, economic, and other social arrangements and developments. We need work that connects mothers' personal beliefs and choices with their social situations. We will benefit from greater conceptual clarity, empirical depth, and better integration of theory and data. We especially need theory building grounded in mothers' experiences. Through such work, drawing on a variety of methods, we will attain not only a fuller, richer, and deeper understanding of mothering but, also, more generally, of practices of caring and ethics of care (see Tronto, 1996).

Social constructionism offers an exceptionally strong framework for considering mothering and motherhood. The paradigm affords a means for looking at, and taking seriously, interaction, interpretative processes (including those of the researchers and writers), social context, and, importantly, relationships. Specifically, feminist conceptual models, which have driven much of the recent scholarship on mothering, allow us to acknowledge the gendered character of mothering, as well as of most caregiving. Constructionist and feminist constructionist perspectives focus attention on the interrelated systems of gender, race, ethnicity, and class stratification.

Finally, the past decade's advances in the study of mothering and motherhood are significant, as is the fact that mothering is being studied from diverse perspectives and disciplines, treated as a worthy subject in its own right. The recent scholarship marks what is often a dense landscape for future research and writing. Assuredly, the near future will yield exciting developments in the study of mothers and motherhood.

NOTE

The work on this essay was generously supported by the Alfred P. Sloan Foundation's Center for Working Families, University of California—Berkeley. I thank numerous friends and colleagues for their comments on earlier drafts and, especially, Andrea Altschuler, Pam Blake, Louise Lamphere, and Barrie Thorne for their insightful reviews. Mary Larios and Lisa Stampnitsky performed heroic library research and bibliographic work.

References

Abramovitz, M. (1996). *Regulating the lives of women: Social welfare policy from colonial times to the present* (2nd ed.). Boston: South End Press.

Adams, A. (1995). Maternal bonds: Recent literature on mothering. *Signs: Journal of Women in Culture and Society, 20,* 414–427.

Allen, K. (1997). Lesbian and gay families. In T. Arendell (Ed.), *Contemporary parenting: Challenges and issues* (pp. 196–218). Newbury Park, CA: Sage.

Allen, K., & Demo, D. H. (1995). The families of lesbians and gay men: A new frontier in family research. *Journal of Marriage and the Family, 57,* 111–127.

Altschuler, A. (1997). *Contexts of care: Mothers and their young children's health.* Unpublished doctoral dissertation, University of California, Berkeley.

Amato, P. R., & Booth, A. (1997). *A generation at risk: Growing up in an era of family upheaval.* Cambridge, MA: Harvard University Press.

Ambert, A. M. (1994). An international perspective on parenting: Social change and social constructs. *Journal of Marriage and the Family, 56,* 529–543.

Apple, R. D., & Golden, J. (1997). Introduction: Mothers, motherhood, and historians. In *Mothers and motherhood: Readings in American history* (pp. x–xvii). Columbus, OH: Ohio State University Press.

Arendell, T. (1995). *Fathers and divorce.* Newbury Park, CA: Sage.

Arendell, T. (1999, April). *Hegemonic motherhood: Deviancy discourses and employed mother's accounts of out-of-school time issues* (Center for Working Families Working Paper No. 9). Berkeley: University of Caifornia.

Baber, K. M., & Allen, K. R. (1992). *Women and families: Feminist reconstructions.* New York: Guilford Press.

Baca Zinn, M. (1990). Family, feminism, and race. *Gender & Society, 4,* 68–82.

Baca Zinn, M. (1994). Adaptation and continuity in Mexican-origin families. In R. Taylor (Ed.), *Minority families in the United States: A multicultural perspective* (pp. 64–81). Englewood Cliffs, NJ: Prentice Hall.

Bachu, A. (1997). *Fertility of American women: June 1995 (update)* (Current Population Reports). U.S. Department of the Census. Washington, DC: U.S. Government Printing Office.

Bailey, A. (1994). Review essay: Mothering, diversity, and peace politics. *Hypatia, 9,* 188–192.

Barnard, K. E., & Martell, L. K. (1995). Mothering. In M. H. Bornstein (Ed.), *Handbook of parenting. Status and social conditions of parenting* (Vol. 3, pp. 3–26). Mahwah, NJ: Erlbaum.

Barnett, R. C., Brennan, R. T., & Marshall, N. L. (1994). Gender and the relationship between parent role quality and psychological distress. *Journal of Family Issues, 15,* 229–252.

Bassin, D., Honey, M., & Kaplan, M. M. (1994). Introduction. In D. Bassin, M. Honey, & M. M. Kaplan (Eds.), *Representations of motherhood* (pp. 1–25). New Haven, CT: Yale University Press.

Benin, M., & Keith, V. M. (1995). The social support of employed African American and Anglo mothers. *Journal of Family Issues, 16,* 275–297.

Benjamin, J. (1988). *The bonds of love: Psychoanalysis, feminism, and the problem of domination.* New York: Pantheon Books.

Benjamin, J. (1990). An outline of intersubjectivity. *Psychoanalytic Psychology, 7,* 33–46.

Benjamin, J. (1994). The omnipotent mother: A psychoanalytic study of fantasy and reality. In D. Bassin, M. Honey, & M. M. Kaplan (Eds.), *Representations of motherhood* (pp. 129–146). New Haven, CT: Yale University Press.

Bianchi, S., & Robinson, J. (1997). What did you do today? Children's use of time, family composition, and the acquisition of social capital. *Journal of Marriage and the Family, 59,* 332–344.

Blaisure, K. R., & Allen, K. R. (1995). Feminists and the ideology and practice of marital equity. *Journal of Marriage and the Family, 57* (1), 5–19.

Blankenhorn, D. (1995). *Fatherless America: Confronting our most urgent social problem.* New York: Basic Books.

Blankenhorn, D., Bayme, S., & Elshtain, J. B. (1992). *Rebuilding the nest: A new commitment to the American family.* Milwaukee, WI: Family Service America, Inc.

Bordo, S. (1990). Feminism, postmodernism, and gender-skepticism. In L. J. Nicholson (Ed.), *Feminism/postmodernism* (pp. 133–156). New York: Routledge.

Boris, E. (1994). *Home to work: Motherhood and the politics of industrial homework in the United States.* New York: Cambridge University Press.

Brooks-Gunn, J., & Chase-Lansdale, P. L. (1995). Adolescent parenthood. In M. H. Bornstein (Ed.), *Handbook of parenting: Status and social conditions of parenting* (Vol. 3, pp. 113–149). Mahwah, NJ: Erlbaum.

Brush, L. D. (1996). Love, toil, and trouble: Motherhood and feminist politics. *Signs: A Journal of Women in Culture and Society, 21,* 429–454.

Bryant, W. K., & Zick, C. D. (1996). An examination of parent-child shared time. *Journal of Marriage and the Family, 58,* 227–237.

Callahan, J. (1995). Editor's introduction. In J. Callahan (Ed.), *Reproduction, ethics, and the law: Feminist perspectives* (pp. 1–15). Bloomington: Indiana University Press.

Casterline, J., Lee, R., & Foote, K. (Eds.). (1996). *Fertility in the United States: New patterns, new theories 1996.* Washington, DC: U.S. Government Printing Office.

Chang, G. (1994). Undocumented Latinas: The new "employable" mothers. In E. N. Glenn, G. Chang, & L. R. Forcey (Eds.), *Mothering: Ideology, experience, and agency* (pp. 259–285). New York: Routledge.

Children's Defense Fund. (1998). *The state of America's children yearbook 1998.* Washington, DC: Author.

Chodorow, N. (1978). *The reproduction of mothering: Psychoanalysis and the sociology of gender.* Berkeley: University of California Press.

Chodorow, N. (1989). *Feminism and psychoanalytic theory.* New Haven, CT: Yale University Press.

Chodorow, N. (1990). Gender, relation, and difference in psychoanalytic perspective. In C. Zanardi (Ed.), *Essential papers on the psychology of women* (pp. 420–436). New York: New York University Press.

Collins, P. H. (1991). *Black feminist thought: Knowledge, consciousness, and the politics of empowerment.* Boston: Unwin Hyman.

Collins, P. H. (1994). Shifting the center: Race, class, and feminist theorizing about motherhood. In D. Bassin, M. Honey, & M. M. Kaplan (Eds.), *Representations of motherhood* (pp. 56–74). New Haven, CT: Yale University Press.

Coltrane, S. (1996). *Family man: Fatherhood, housework, and gender equity.* New York: Oxford University Press.

Coltrane, S. L., & Adams, M. A. (1998, November). *Experiencing gendered divisions of labor in American households: Resources, entitlement, and perceptions of fairness.* Paper presented at the Work and Family: Today's Realities and Tomorrow's Visions Conference, Boston.

Coontz, S. (1997). *The way we really are: Coming to terms with America's changing families.* New York: Basic Books.

Daly, K. (1996). *Families & time: Keeping pace in a hurried culture.* Newbury Park, CA: Sage.

DeMeis, D. K., & Perkins, H. W. (1996). "Supermoms" of the nineties: Homemaker and employed mothers' performance and perceptions of the motherhood role. *Journal of Family Issues, 17,* 777–792.

Dickerson, B. J. (Ed.). (1995). *African American single mothers: Understanding their lives and families.* Newbury Park, CA: Sage.

Dill, B. T. (1994a). *Across the boundaries of race and*

class: An exploration of work and family among Black female domestic servants. New York: Garland.

Dill, B. T. (1994b). Fictive kin, paper sons, and compadrazago: Women of color and the struggle for family survival. In M. B. Zinn & B. Dill (Eds.), *Women of color in U.S. society* (pp. 149–169). Philadelphia: Temple University Press.

Dinnerstein, D. (1976). *The mermaid and the minotaur: Sexual arrangements and the human malaise.* New York: Harper & Row.

Donchin, A. (1996). Feminist critiques of new fertility technologies: Implications for social policy. *The Journal of Medicine and Philosophy, 21,* 475–498.

Duxbury, L., Higgins, C., & Lee, C. (1994). Work-family conflict: A comparison by gender, family type, and perceived control. *Journal of Family Issues, 15,* 449–466.

Edin, K., & Lein, L. (1997). *Making ends meet: How single mothers survive welfare and low-wage work.* New York: Russell Sage Foundation.

England, K. (1996). Mothers, wives, workers: The everyday lives of working mothers. In K. England (Ed.), *Who will mind the baby: Geographies of child care and working mothers* (pp. 109–122). New York: Routledge.

Fineman, M. A. (1995). *The neutered mother, the sexual family and other twentieth century tragedies.* New York: Routledge.

Flores, K., Douglas, T., & Ellwood, D. A. (1998). *The children's budget report: A detailed analysis of spending on low-income children's programs in 13 states* (Occasional Paper Number 14). Washington, DC: Urban Institute.

Forcey, L. R. (1994). Feminist perspectives on mothering and peace. In E. N. Glenn, G. Chang, & L. R. Forcey (Eds.), *Mothering: Ideology, experience, and agency* (pp. 355–375). New York: Routledge.

Fried, M. (1998). *Taking time: Parental leave policy and corporate culture.* Philadelphia: Temple University Press.

Garey, A. I. (1999). *Weaving work and motherhood.* Philadelphia: Temple University.

Garey, A., & Arendell, T. (1998, November). *Children, work and family: Some thoughts on "mother-blame."* (Center for Working Families Working Paper No. 4). Berkeley, CA: University of California.

Gillis, J. R. (1997). *A world of their own making: Myth, ritual, and the quest for family values.* Cambridge, MA: Harvard University Press.

Ginsburg, F. D., & Rapp, R. (Eds.). (1995). *Conceiving the new world order: The politics of reproduction.* Berkeley: University of California Press.

Glenn, E. N. (1992). From servitude to service work: Historical continuities in the racial division of paid reproductive labor. *Signs: Journal of Women in Culture and Society, 18,* 1–43.

Glenn, E. N. (1994). Social constructions of mothering: A thematic overview. In E. N. Glenn, G. Chang, & L. R. Forcey (Eds.), *Mothering: Ideology, experience, and agency* (pp. 1–29). New York: Routledge.

Glenn, E. N., Chang, G., & Forcey, L. R. (Eds.). (1994). *Mothering: Ideology, experience, and agency.* New York: Routledge.

Goldsteen, K., & Ross, C. E. (1989). The perceived burden of children. *Journal of Family Issues, 10,* 504–526.

Gordon, L. (1993). Family violence, feminism, and social control. In B. Thorne & M. Yalom (Eds.), *Rethinking the family: Some feminist questions* (2nd ed., pp. 262–286). Boston: Northeastern University Press.

Gordon, L. (1994). *Pitied but not entitled: Single mothers and the history of welfare, 1890–1935.* New York: Maxwell Mamillan International.

Gordon, S., Benner, P., & Noddings, N. (Eds.). (1996). *Caregiving: Readings in knowledge, practice, ethics, and politics.* Philadelphia: University of Pennsylvania Press.

Hays, S. (1996). *The cultural contradictions of motherhood.* New Haven, CT: Yale University Press.

Hertz, R. (1997). A typology of approaches to child care: The centerpiece of organizing family life for dual-earner couples. *Journal of Family Issues, 18,* 355–385.

Hertz, R., & Ferguson, F. (1996). Childcare choices and constraints in the United States: Social class, race, and the influence of family views. *Journal of Comparative Family Studies, 27,* 249–280.

Hochschild, A. (1997). *The time bind: When work becomes home and home becomes work.* New York: Metropolitan Books.

Hondagneu-Sotel, P., & Avila, E. (1997). "I'm here, but I'm there": The meanings of Latina transnational motherhood. *Gender & Society, 11,* 548–571.

Hughes, D., & Galinsky, E. (1994). Work experiences and marital interactions: Elaborating the complexity of work. *Journal of Organizational Behavior, 15,* 423–438.

Jacobs, J., & Gerson, K. (1997). *The endless day or the flexible office? Working hours, work-family conflict, and gender equity in the modern workplace.* Philadelphia: Alfred P. Sloan Foundation.

Jayakody, R., Chatters, L. M., & Taylor, R. J. (1993). Family support to single and married African American mothers: The provision of financial, emotional, and child care assistance. *Journal of Marriage and the Family, 55,* 261–275.

Josselson, R. (1996). *Revising herself: The story of women's identity from college to midlife.* New York: Oxford University Press.

Kaplan, E. A. (1992). *Motherhood and representation: The mother in popular culture and melodrama.* New York: Routledge.

Kaplan, E. B. (1997). *Not our kind of girl: Unraveling the myths of Black teenage motherhood.* Berkeley, CA: University of California Press.

Kerig, P. K., Cowan, P. A., & Cowan, C. P. (1993). Marital quality and gender differences in parent-child interaction. *Developmental Psychology, 29,* 931–939.

Koven, S., & Michel, S. (Eds.). (1993). *Mothers of a new world: Maternalist politics and the origins of the welfare state.* New York: Routledge.

Kurz, D. (1995). *For better or for worse: Mothers confront divorce.* New York: Routledge.

Ladd-Taylor, M. (1994). *Mother-work: Women, child welfare, and the state, 1890–1930.* Chicago: University of Illinois Press.

Lamphere, L., Zavella, P., & Gonzales, F., with Peter B. Evans. (1993). *Sunbelt working mothers: Reconciling family and factory.* Ithaca, NY: Cornell University Press.

Larsen, R. (1998, November). *Changes in the lives of women and men.* Paper presented at the Work and

Family: Today's Realities and Tomorrow's Visions Conference, Boston.

Larson, R., & Richards, M. H. (1994). *Divergent realities: The emotional lives of mothers, fathers, and adolescents.* New York: Basic Books.

Lee, M. A., Haught, K., Redlener, I., Fant, A., Fox, E., & Somers, S. A. (1992). Health care for children in homeless families. In P. Brickner, L. Scharer, B. Conanan, M. Savarese, & B. Scanlan (Eds.), *Under the safety net: The health and social welfare of the homeless in the United States* (pp. 119–138). New York: Norton.

Leonard, V. W. (1996). Mothering as a practice. In S. Gordon, P. Benner, & N. Noddings (Eds.), *Caregiving: Readings in knowledge, practice, ethics, and politics* (pp. 124–140). Philadelphia: University of Pennsylvania Press.

Lewin, E. (1993). *Lesbian mothers: Accounts of gender in American culture.* Ithaca, NY: Cornell University Press.

Lightfoot, C., & Valsiner, J. (1992). Parental belief systems under the influence: Social guidance of the construction of personal cultures. In I. E. Sigel, A. V. McGillicuddy-DeLisi, & J. J. Goodnow (Eds.), *Parental belief systems: The psychological consequences for children* (2nd ed., pp. 393–414). Hillsdale, NJ: Erlbaum.

Logan, J. R., & Spitze, G. D. (1994). Family neighbors. *American Journal of Sociology, 100,* 453–476.

Lorde, A. (1984). *Sister outsider: Essays and speeches.* Trumansburg, NY: Crossing Press.

Luker, K. (1996). *Dubious conceptions: The politics of teenage pregnancy.* Cambridge: Harvard University Press.

Macdonald, C. L. (1998). Manufacturing motherhood: The shadow work of nannies and au pairs. *Qualitative Sociology, 21,* 25–48.

Manning, W. D. (1995). Cohabitation, marriage, and entry into motherhood. *Journal of Marriage and the Family, 57,* 191–200.

Marks, S. (1996). The problem and politics of wholeness in family studies. *Journal of Marriage and the Family, 58* (3), 565–571.

Marshall, N. L., Barnett, R. C., & Sayer, A. (1998). The changing workforce, job stress, and psychological distress. In N. L. Marshall (Ed.), *Work and family today: Recent research at the Center for Research on Women* (pp. 1–15). Wellesley, MA: Center for Research on Women.

Marshall, N. L., Marx, F., McCartney, K., & Garcia Coll, C. (1998). It takes a village to raise a child: Parenting networks of urban families. In N. L. Marshall (Ed.), *Work and family today: Recent research at the Center for Research on Women* (pp. 194–107). Wellesley, MA: Center for Research on Women.

Martin, G. T., Jr. (1997). An agenda for family policy in the United States. In T. Arendell (Ed.), *Contemporary parenting: Issues and challenges.* Newbury Park, CA: Sage.

Mathews, T. J., & Ventura, S. J. (1997). *Mother's educational level influences birth rate and fertility rates by educational attainment: United States, 1994.* Washington, DC: U.S. Government Printing Office.

McAdoo, H. P. (1993). Ethnic families: Strengths that are found in diversity. In H. McAdoo (Ed.), *Family

ethnicity: Strength in diversity* (pp. 3–14). Newbury Park, CA: Sage.

McLanahan, S. S., & Kelly, E. L. (1998). *The feminization of poverty: Past and future.* Princeton, NJ: Office of Population Research.

McMahon, M. (1995). *Engendering motherhood: Identity and self-transformation in women's lives.* New York: Guilford Press.

Mischel, H., & Fuhr, R. (1988). Maternal employment: Its psychological effects on children and their families. In S. M. Dornbusch & M. Strober (Eds.), *Feminism, children, and the new families* (pp. 191–211). New York: Guilford Press.

Mitchell, O. S. (1997). Work and family benefits. In F. D. Blau & R. G. Ehrenberg (Eds.), *Gender & family issues in the workplace* (pp. 269–276). New York: Russell Sage.

Moen, P. (1992). *Women's two roles: A contemporary dilemma.* New York: Auburn House.

National Center for Health Statistics. (1998). *Vital statistics for the United States.* Hyattsville, MD: U.S. Public Health Service.

Neal, M. B., Chapman, N. J., Ingersol-Dayton, B., & Emlen, A. C. (Eds.). (1993). *Balancing work and caregiving for children, adults, and elders* (Vol. 3). Newbury Park, CA: Sage.

Nelson, M. K. (1994). Family day care providers: Dilemmas of daily practice. In E. N. Glenn, G. Chang, & L. R. Forcey (Eds.), *Mothering: Ideology, experience, and agency* (pp. 181–209). New York: Routledge.

Oberman, Y., & Josselson, R. (1996). Matrix of tensions: A model of mothering. *Psychology of Women Quarterly, 20,* 341–359.

Orellana, M. F., Thorne, B., Lam, W. S. E., & Chee, A. (1998, July). *Transnational childhoods: The participation of children in processes of family migration.* Paper presented at the 14th World Congress of Sociology, Montreal, Canada.

Paden, S. L., & Buehler, C. (1995). Coping with the dual-income lifestyle. *Journal of Marriage and the Family, 57:* 101, 110.

Patterson, C. J. (1995). Lesbian mothers, gay fathers, and their children. In A. R. D'Augelli & C. J. Patterson (Eds.), *Lesbian, gay, and bisexual identities across the lifespan* (pp. 262–290). New York: Oxford University Press.

Peterson, R. R., & Gerson, K. (1992). Determinants of responsibility for child care arrangements among dual-earner couples. *Journal of Marriage and the Family, 54,* 527–536.

Phoenix, A., Woollett, A., & Lloyd, E. (1991). *Motherhood: Meanings, practices, and ideologies.* Newbury Park, CA: Sage.

Polatnick, M. R. (1996). Diversity in women's liberation ideology: How a Black and a White group of the 1960s viewed motherhood. *Signs: Journal of Women in Culture and Society, 21,* 679–706.

Presser, H. B. (1995). Are the interests of women inherently at odds with the interests of children or the family? A viewpoint. In K. O. Mason & A.-M. Jensen (Eds.), *Gender and family change in industrialized countries* (pp. 297–319). New York: Clarendon Press.

Pridham, K., Denney, N., Pascoe, J., Chiu, Y., & Creasey, D. (1995). Mothers' solutions to childrearing problems: Conditions and processes. *Journal of Marriage and the Family, 57,* 785–799.

Rae, S. B. (1994). *The ethics of commercial surrogate motherhood: Brave new families?* Westport, CT: Praeger.

Rapp, R. (1996). Constructing amniocentesis: Maternal and medical discourses. In F. Ginsburg & A. L. Tsing (Eds.), *Uncertain terms* (pp. 28–42). Boston: Beacon Press.

Ribbens, J. (1994). *Mothers and their children: A feminist sociology of childrearing.* London: Sage.

Rich, A. (1977). *Of woman born: Motherhood as experience and institution.* New York: Bantam Books.

Robinson, J. P., & Godbey, G. (1997). *Time for life: The surprising ways Americans use their time.* University Park, PA: Pennsylvania State University Press.

Rogers, S. J., & White, L. K. (1998). Satisfaction with parenting: The role of marital happiness, family structure, and parents' gender. *Journal of Marriage and the Family, 60,* 293–308.

Rosenbloom, S. (1993). Women's travel patterns at various stages of their lives. In C. Katz & J. Monk (Eds.), *Full circles: Geographies of women over the life course* (pp. 208–242). New York: Routledge.

Ross, E. (1995). New thoughts on "the oldest vocation:" Mothers and motherhood in recent feminist scholarship. *Signs: Journal of Women in Culture and Society, 20,* 397–413.

Ross, C. E., & Van Willigen, M. (1996). Gender, parenthood, and anger. *Journal of Marriage and the Family, 58,* 572–584.

Rothman, B. K. (1994). Beyond mothers and fathers: Ideology in a patriarchal society. In E. N. Glenn, G. Chang, & L. R. Forcey (Eds.), *Mothering: Ideology, experience, and agency* (pp. 139–157). New York: Routledge.

Roxburgh, S. (1997). The effect of children on the mental health of women in the paid labor force. *Journal of Family Issues, 18,* 270–289.

Ruddick, S. (1980). Maternal thinking. *Feminist Studies, 6,* 343–367.

Ruddick, S. (1994). Thinking mothers/conceiving birth. In D. Bassin, M. Honey, & M. M. Kaplan (Eds.), *Representations of motherhood* (pp. 29–46). New Haven, CT: Yale University Press.

Scarr, S. (1998). American child care today. *American Psychologist, 53,* 95–108.

Scheper-Hughes, N. (1992). *Death without weeping: The violence of everyday life in Brazil.* Berkeley, CA: University of California Press.

Schwartz, A. (1994). Taking the nature out of mother. In D. Bassin, M. Honey, & M. M. Kaplan (Eds.), *Representations of motherhood* (pp. 240–255). New Haven, CT: Yale University Press.

Scott, J., & Alwin, D. F. (1989). Gender differences in parental strain: Parental role or gender role? *Journal of Family Issues, 10,* 482–503.

Sears, H. A., & Galambos, N. L. (1993). The employed mother's well-being. In J. Frankel (Ed.), *The employed mother and the family context* (pp. 7–30). New York: Springer.

Segura, D. A. (1994). Working at motherhood: Chicana and Mexican immigrant mothers and employment. In E. N. Glenn, G. Chang, & L. R. Forcey (Eds.), *Mothering: Ideology, experience, and agency* (pp. 211–233). New York: Routledge.

Segura, D. A., & Pierce, J. L. (1993). Chicana/o family structure and gender personality: Chodorow, feminism, and psychoanalytic sociology revisited. *Signs: Journal of Women in Culture and Society, 19,* 62–91.

Sevenhuijsen, S. (1998). Citizenship and the ethics of care: Feminist considerations on justice, morality and politics (Savage, L., Trans.). New York: Routledge.

Sherman, A., Ameyu, C., Duffeld, B., Ebb, N., & Weinstein, D. (1998). *Welfare to what? Early findings on family hardship and well-being.* Washington, DC/New York: Children's Defense Fund/National Coalition for the Homeless.

Sidel, R. (1996). *Keeping women and children last.* New York: Penguin Books.

Skocpol, T. (1992). *Protecting soldiers and mothers: The political origins of social policy in the United States.* Cambridge, MA: Harvard University Press.

Snitow, A. (1992). Feminism and motherhood: An American reading. *Feminist Review, 40,* 32–49.

Spain, D., & Bianchi, S. M. (1996). *Balancing act: Motherhood, marriage, and employment among American women.* New York: Russell Sage.

Stacey, J. (1996). In the name of the family: Rethinking family values in a postmodern age. Boston: Beacon Press.

Stack, C. (1974). *All our kin: Strategies for survival in a Black community.* New York: Harper & Row.

Stack, C., & Burton, L. (1993). Kinscripts. *Journal of Comparative Family Studies, 24,* 157–170.

Starrels, M. E. (1994). Gender differences in parent-child relations. *Journal of Family Issues, 15,* 148–165.

Stewart, A. J., Copeland, A. P., Chester, N. L., Malley, J. E., & Barenbaum, N. B. (1997). *Separating together: How divorce transforms families.* New York: Guilford Press.

Tarlow, B. (1996). Caring: A negotiated process that varies. In S. Gordon, P. Benner, & N. Noddings (Eds.), *Caregiving: Readings in knowledge, practice, ethics, and politics* (pp. 56–82). Philadelphia: University of Pennsylvania Press.

Thompson, L., & Walker, A. J. (1995). The place of feminism in family studies. *Journal of Marriage and the Family, 57* (4),847–865.

Thorne, B. (1993). Feminism and the family: Two decades of thought. In B. Thorne & M. Yalom (Eds.), *Rethinking the family: Some feminist questions* (2nd ed., pp. 3–30). New York: Longman.

Thorpe, K., & Daly, K. (1999). Children, parents, and time: The dialectics of control. In C. Sheehan (Ed.), *Through the eyes of the child: Revisioning children as active agents of family life* (Vol. 1, pp. 1–31). Greenwich, CT: JAI Press.

Thurer, S. (1993). Changing conceptions of the good mother in psychoanalysis. *Psychoanalytic Review, 80,* 519–540.

Tronto, J. (1996). Care as a political concept. In N. J. Hirschmann & C. D. Stefano (Eds.), *Revisioning the political: Feminist reconstructions of traditional concepts in western political theory* (pp. 139–156). Boulder, CO: Westview Press.

Turkel, A. R. (1994). Hiding behind motherhood. *Journal of the American Academy of Psychoanalysis, 24,* 163–177.

U.S. Bureau of the Census. (1998). *People and families in poverty by selected characteristics: 1989, 1996, and 1997* (Current Population Survey). Washington, DC: U.S. Government Printing Office.

U. S. Bureau of the Census for the Bureau of Labor Statistics. (1999). *Civilian employment population, 1998* (Current Population Survey). Washington, DC: U.S. Government Printing Office.

Uttal, L. (1996). Custodial care, surrogate care, and co-ordinated care: Employed mothers and the meaning of child care. *Gender & Society, 10,* 291–311.

Uttal, L. (1998). Racial safety and cultural maintenance: The child care concerns of employed mothers of color. In K. Hansen & A. Garey (Eds.), *Families in the U.S.: Kinship and domestic politics* (pp. 597–606). Philadelphia: Temple University Press.

Vegetti-Finzi, S. (1996). *Mothering: Toward a new psychoanalytic construction* (K. Jason, Trans.). New York: Guilford Press.

Ventura, S., Martin, J., Curtin, S., & Mathews, T. J. (1996). *Report of final natality statistics, 1996.* Washington DC: U.S. Government Printing Office.

Waerness, K. (1996). The rationality of caring. In S. Gordon, P. Benner, & N. Noddings (Eds.), *Caregiving: Readings in knowledge, practice, ethics, and politics* (pp. 231–255). Philadelphia: University of Pennsylvania Press.

Waldfogel, J. (1997). Working mothers then and now: Cross-cohort analysis of the effects of maternity leave on women's pay. In F. D. Blau & R. G. Ehrenberg (Eds.), *Gender & family issues in the workplace* (pp. 92–126). New York: Russell Sage.

Walker, A. (1983). *In search of our mothers' gardens: Womanist prose.* San Diego, CA: Harcourt Brace Jovanovich.

Walzer, S. (1997). Contextualizing the employment decisions of new mothers. *Qualitative Sociology, 20,* 211–227.

Welles-Nystrom, B. (1997). The meaning of postponed motherhood for women in the United States and Sweden: Aspects of feminism and radical timing strategies. *Health Care for Women International, 18,* 279–299.

Whitehead, B. D. (1993). Dan Quayle was right. The *Atlantic Monthly, 271,* 47–84.

Wrigley, J. (1995). *Other people's children: An intimate account of the dilemmas facing middle-class parents and the women they hire to raise their children.* New York: Basic Books.

Zill, N., Moore, K. A., Smith, E. W., Steif, T., & Coiro, M. J. (1995). The life circumstances and development of children in welfare families: A profile based on national survey data. In P. Chase-Lansdale & J. Brooks-Gunn (Eds.), *Escape from poverty: What makes a difference for children?* (pp. 38–59). New York: Cambridge University Press.

SCOTT COLTRANE   *University of California—Riverside*

Research on Household Labor: Modeling and Measuring the Social Embeddedness of Routine Family Work

This article reviews more than 200 scholarly articles and books on household labor published between 1989 and 1999. As a maturing area of study, this body of research has been concerned with understanding and documenting how housework is embedded in complex and shifting social processes relating to the well-being of families, the construction of gender, and the reproduction of society. Major theoretical, methodological, and empirical contributions to the study of household labor are summarized, and suggestions for further research are offered. In summary, women have reduced and men have increased slightly their hourly contributions to housework. Although men's relative contributions have increased, women still do at least twice as much routine housework as men. Consistent predictors of sharing include both women's and men's employment, earnings, gender ideology, and life-course issues. More balanced divisions of housework are associated with women perceiving fairness, experiencing less depression, and enjoying higher marital satisfaction.

American families are facing complex and contradictory challenges as we embark on the 21st century. Although beliefs about the appropriate roles of men and women in the workplace have undergone substantial shifts in the past several decades,

Sociology Department, University of California, Riverside, CA 92521–0419 (coltrane@ucr.edu).

Key Words: division of labor, domestic labor, fairness, family, gender, housework.

assumptions about who should perform unpaid family work have changed more slowly. And changes in domestic behavior have been slower still. Although the vast majority of both men and women now agree that family labor should be shared, few men assume equal responsibility for household tasks. On average, women perform two or three times as much housework as men, and the vast majority of men, as well as most women, rate these arrangements as fair. In part, this is because most husbands are employed more hours and earn more income than do their wives. Compared with past decades, women are doing less housework and men are doing slightly more, but the redistribution of household labor has been slower and less profound than anticipated. In this review, I suggest that these patterns can only be understood by attending to the symbolic significance of household labor in the social construction of gender and by analyzing the social, cultural, economic, and political contexts in which men and women form families, raise children, and sustain households.

As a topic worthy of serious academic study, housework came of age in the 1990s. Not only did the number of books and articles on the subject expand dramatically during that decade, but scholars from a wide range of academic disciplines turned their attention to isolating the causes and consequences of divisions of household labor for men, women, children, families, and society. Many of these studies attempted to operationalize concepts and test hypotheses emerging from the time-use research tradition (Berk & Berk, 1979;

Robinson, 1977), or from past interview and observational studies (Hochschild, 1989; Hood, 1983). The more than 200 works cited in this review do not exhaust research on the topic, but they do represent a cross-section of influential social science works in the field. Because the foundation for this research was laid in past decades, readers interested in the history and development of the field are encouraged to consult classic housework and marriage studies (Bernard, 1972; Blood & Wolfe, 1960; Oakley, 1974; Vanek, 1974), and earlier reviews (England & Farkas, 1986; Ferree, 1990; Miller & Garrison, 1982; Osmond & Thorne, 1993; Shelton & John, 1996; Szinovacz, 1987; Thompson & Walker, 1989).

The most important theme to emerge from household labor studies in the past decade is that housework is embedded in complex and shifting patterns of social relations. Although most studies focus on only a few aspects of this embeddedness, taken together, they reveal how housework cannot be understood without realizing how it is related to gender, household structure, family interaction, and the operation of both formal and informal market economies. Recent research documents how household labor both reflects and perpetuates cultural understandings of family love and personal fulfillment, as well as helping to structure race, class, and gender relations. In particular, studies from the 1990s investigate how the allocation of household labor is linked to life-course issues, marital quality, kin relations, interpersonal power, symbolic exchange, social comparison, fairness evaluation, gender ideology and display, provider role identification, and the scheduling and performance of paid labor. This review summarizes how researchers have attempted to specify and evaluate these linkages using various measurement and modeling techniques. I first discuss some reasons for studying household labor, define important terms, and suggest how gender and housework are related. Major theoretical approaches are then presented, followed by a brief discussion of methodological issues and a review of empirical findings organized into sections on major predictors, fairness evaluations, and outcome assessments.

WHY STUDY HOUSEHOLD LABOR?

Human existence depends on the routine activities that feed, clothe, shelter, and care for both children and adults. In theoretical terms, this family work—or social reproductive labor—is just as important to the maintenance of society as the productive work that occurs in the formal market economy. Recent estimates suggest that the total amount of time spent in unpaid family work is about equal to the time spent in paid labor (Robinson & Godbey, 1997). Nevertheless, family work—and especially housework—tends to be trivialized in the popular imagination, in part because it is considered "women's work." Recent research confirms that family work is sharply divided by gender, with women spending much more time on these tasks than do men and typically taking responsibility for monitoring and supervising the work even when they pay for domestic services or delegate tasks to others. Research also shows that women perform more of the housework when they are married and when they become parents, whereas men tend to perform less housework when they marry and assume a smaller share of the household work after their wives have children. Because new mothers tend to reduce their employment hours, and new fathers often increase theirs, findings about housework are best understood within larger economic, social, and family contexts. When time spent on both paid and unpaid work is combined, most studies find that the total number of hours contributed by husbands and wives is much more equal. Nevertheless, when women shoulder a disproportionate share of responsibility for housework, their perceptions of fairness and marital satisfaction decline, and depending on gender ideology and other mediating factors, marital conflict and women's depression increase. For men, in contrast, divisions of household labor and perceptions of fairness are typically unrelated to personal well-being or marital satisfaction.

Because gender is a major organizing feature of household labor, research has explored how men's and women's task performance differs and how their experience and evaluation of housework tend to diverge. In general, women have felt obligated to perform housework, and men have assumed that domestic work is primarily the responsibility of mothers, wives, daughters, and low-paid female housekeepers. In contrast, men's participation in housework has appeared optional, with most couples—even those sharing substantial amounts of family work—characterizing men's contributions as "helping" their wives or partners (Coltrane 1996). Much recent research also attempts to isolate the conditions under which men and women might come to share more of the housework. Most studies show that women who are employed longer hours, earn more money, have more education, and endorse gender equity do less housework, whereas men who are employed fewer hours, have more education, and endorse gender equity do more of the housework. A preponderance of research also shows that when husbands do more, wives are likely to evaluate the division of labor as fair, which, in turn, is associated with various measures of positive marital quality.

Because of the potential benefits of sharing family work, the rapid increase in women's labor force participation, and increasing popular endorsement of equity ideals in marriage, many observers predicted that the division of household labor would become more gender-neutral. Nevertheless, studies published in the 1970s and 1980s seemed to offer little support for this notion (Miller & Garrison, 1982; Thompson & Walker, 1989). This left researchers with a major unanswered question: "Why don't men do more?" Before analyzing what 1990s research tells us about this and other questions, I define some important terms.

WHAT IS HOUSEHOLD LABOR?

In most studies, the concept of housework or household labor is rarely defined explicitly, except for explaining how variables are measured and providing some indication of whether child care is included in its definition. As Shelton and John (1996, p. 300) note, however, a fairly consistent conceptualization has emerged in the literature: "Housework most often refers to unpaid work done to maintain family members and/or a home." Although this concept can include child minding, household management, and various kinds of emotional labor, most household labor studies have excluded these less visible or overlapping types of "work" from study (Ferree, 1990; Thompson & Walker, 1989). As discussed below, studies in the 1990s both continued and problematized this conceptualization of housework, but the lack of attention to child care and emotional labor continued to be a major shortcoming of research on housework. In addition, whereas previous studies tended to predict absolute hours of total household labor performed by women or men, many studies in the 1990s used proportional measures for married couples and considered the gender-segregation of tasks. As noted below, some studies also began to look at the contributions of children, kin, and paid help, as well

as considering nonmarried households (e.g., single parents, cohabitors, gay or lesbian couples, single persons), and refining various techniques for collecting household labor data.

According to several large-sample national surveys conducted in the United States, the five most time-consuming major household tasks include (a) meal preparation or cooking, (b) housecleaning, (c) shopping for groceries and household goods, (d) washing dishes or cleaning up after meals, and (e) laundry, including washing, ironing, and mending clothes (Blair & Lichter, 1991; Robinson & Godbey, 1997). As discussed below, these household tasks are not only the most time-consuming, but also are less optional and less able to be postponed than other household tasks such as gardening or house repairs. These seemingly never-ending tasks have been labeled "nondiscretionary," "mundane," "repetitive," "onerous," "unrelenting," and "boring" (Blair & Lichter, 1991; Starrels, 1994; Thompson & Walker, 1989). In this article, I label these activities "routine housework," or simply "housework" (see also Coltrane, 1996; DeMaris & Longmore, 1996). Although some people find pleasure in doing this work, especially the cooking, most men and women report that they do not like housework (DeVault, 1991; Robinson & Milkie, 1997, 1998). I label residual tasks such as household repairs, yard care, driving other people, or paying bills as "occasional" or "other" household labor. In general, these other tasks have been found to be more time flexible, more discretionary, and more enjoyable than everyday routine housework tasks (Coltrane, 1998; Larson, Richards, & Perry-Jenkins, 1994).

GENDER AND HOUSEHOLD LABOR

National surveys and time-diary studies show that American household members spend 2 or 3 hours on routine housework for every hour they spend on other household labor. According to the National Survey of Families and Households (NSFH), in 1992–1993 the average married woman did about three times as much routine housework as the average married man (32 vs. 10 hours per week), and the average married man did a little less than twice as much occasional household labor as the average married woman (10 vs. 6 hours per week). This division of labor is so influenced by gender that the average man would have to reallocate more than 60% of his family work to other chores before gender equality would be achieved in the distribution of labor time across all domestic tasks (Blair & Lichter, 1991, p. 99).

Some research still combines all forms of household labor into one summary measure of hours worked, failing to distinguish between routine tasks and occasional tasks (Lye & Biblarz, 1993; Sanchez & Thomson, 1997; Shelton & John, 1993a, 1993b). In general, this approach explains only a small portion of the variance in household labor as a dependent variable and is less successful than alternate approaches in specifying how and why household labor might influence fairness evaluations or marital satisfaction. Similarly, a focus on men's absolute hours of housework has had limited success. Reviewing previous studies, Blair and Lichter (1991) concluded "the singular focus on husbands' hours worked may be inappropriate or even misleading" (p. 100).

A majority of household labor studies now recognize and measure differences between task types and construct proportional measures to compare husbands' and wives' contributions. In acknowledging the gender typing of household labor, many researchers refer to the routine housework chores of cooking, cleaning, and shopping as "female" (Presser, 1994); "female-dominated" (Blair & Lichter, 1991); "female-stereotypic" (Sanchez & Kane, 1996); "female gender-typed" (Starrels, 1994); "traditionally feminine" (Orbuch & Eyster, 1997), or just "feminine" (Antill, Goodnow, Russell, & Cotton, 1996). Conversely, less frequent tasks such as household repairs, mowing the lawn, and taking care of cars are often labeled "male," "male-dominated," "male-typed,"or "masculine" (Blair & Lichter; Shelton, 1992). A few researchers also use a third category of "gender-neutral" when neither men nor women are found to perform a preponderance of the hours for a particular task (e.g., bill paying, driving).

Often researchers signal that the tasks to which they assign gendered terms are neither inherently nor absolutely gendered by, for example, putting the term in quotes: "masculine tasks" (Blair & Lichter, 1991), "'feminine' tasks" (Hall, Walker, & Acock, 1995), "traditionally 'female'" (Lennon & Rosenfeld, 1994). In applying gendered labels to these activities, researchers explicitly acknowledge that gender influences household labor allocation, although such labeling also carries a danger of perpetuating popular cultural understandings about housework as "women's work." Recent research suggests that specific

tasks can carry different meanings about gender, that these meanings are subject to change, and that there may be several gendered thresholds that men must cross to become high participators (Twiggs, McQuillan, & Ferree, 1999). In addition, some researchers use nomenclature that focuses on the content, timing, or character of the tasks themselves. For example, Baxter (1997) captured the distinction between cooking and cleaning on the one hand and yard work and auto maintenance on the other by labeling them "inside" versus "outside" domestic tasks. Starrels (1994) used the term "daily" to measure cooking and meal cleanup but noted that other "female gender-typed tasks" such as shopping for groceries and cleaning house are more likely to occur on a weekly or nondaily basis. Barnett and Shen (1997) developed a promising distinction between "high-schedule-control" and "low-schedule-control" household tasks (see also Bird & Ross, 1993; Ross & Mirowsky, 1992). In employing the terms "routine housework" and "other household labor" in this review, I call attention to the character of the tasks themselves, rather than to cultural beliefs about the suitability of one gender to perform them.

WHO DOES WHAT?

Recent studies using random samples and precise measurement techniques demonstrate that women—especially employed women—are doing less housework than they used to and that men are doing somewhat more. Based on national time-diary studies, Robinson and Godbey (1997) reported that American women's time spent on housework declined from 24 hours per week in 1965 to 16 hours in 1985, a decline of one third. During that period, employed women cut back on the time they devoted to housework and shifted many chores to the weekends, so that they were doing about one third less family work than nonemployed women. At the same time, men's contributions to routine housework increased from about 2 hours per week to about 4 hours per week (Robinson & Godbey, 1997). As a consequence, men's proportionate contribution to housework doubled between 1965 and 1985, from about 15% to 33% of the total. Using a different methodology, the NSFH shows that women's housework contributions declined slightly from 1987–1988 to 1992–1993, as men's continued to increase slowly. Broadly similar results have been reported using other national data such as the National Survey of Children, the National Longitudinal Surveys of Young Women, and the Panel Study of Income Dynamics. The rate of increase in men's absolute hours of routine housework actually exceeded the rate of decrease in women's hours, but because men were starting from such a low level, their contributions have not approached those of women. Because the average woman still does about three times the amount of routine housework as the average man does, researchers have focused on the importance of gender in the allocation of domestic work. In the last decade review, for example, Thompson and Walker (1989) dismissed virtually all other commonly advanced predictors for household labor sharing: "women's employment, time availability, resources, conscious ideology, and power do not account for why wives still do the bulk of family work" (p. 857). Similarly, Calasanti and Bailey (1991) argued that "focusing on the *persistence* of the gender difference in the division of domestic labor rather than on factors accounting for the small amount of change may be more fruitful for understanding and eradicating inequality" (p. 49).

Whether the household labor "glass" appears half empty or half full depends on how much change one expects. Recent research shows we are far from reaching gender parity in the sharing of household work, yet most Americans judge their divisions of labor to be "fair." As a result, significant attention has been turned toward understanding the role of fairness evaluations in the allocation of household labor. As noted below, women continue to feel responsible for family members' well-being and are more likely than are men to adjust their work and home schedules to accommodate others (Sanchez & Thomson, 1997; Shelton, 1992; Spain & Bianchi, 1996). Married women are still expected to manage home and family (Coltrane, 1996; Ferree, 1991; Hays, 1996; Mederer, 1993), and wives spend two or three times as many hours on housework as their husbands (Demo & Acock, 1993; Hersch & Stratton, 1997; Presser, 1994). Not surprisingly, employed wives enjoy less leisure and experience more stress than their husbands do (Barnett & Shen, 1997; Hochschild, 1989; Milkie & Petola, 1999; Robinson & Godbey, 1997; Schor, 1991).

Despite continuing gender segregation in household tasks, many American households are renegotiating norms and behaviors. Among married women, 40% indicate that they want their husbands to do more housework, and men are more likely than ever to report that they enjoy

cooking and cleaning, especially if they are under 30 years of age (Robinson & Godbey, 1997). In light of such findings, and in contrast to previous pessimism about men's assumption of housework (e.g., Miller & Garrison, 1982; Thompson & Walker, 1989), researchers in the 1990s tended to voice guarded optimism about a narrowing of the gender gap in housework. Many projected that as women's opportunities in the labor market improve and as public support for gender equity increases, there will be more sharing of housework (Barnett & Shen, 1997; Brayfield, 1992; Hersch & Stratton, 1994; Pittman, Solheim, & Blanchard, 1996; Presser, 1994; Waite & Goldscheider, 1992). Because findings of greater proportionate sharing among married couples are driven more by women's time adjustments than men's, other scholars focus on how domestic labor allocation continues to perpetuate women's oppression (Hartmann, 1993; Sanchez, 1996).

Finally, household labor research in the 1990s became much more sophisticated in its theories, methods, and research questions. As noted below, recent studies show that a wide range of social, economic, and interpersonal factors combine to influence household labor and that housework performance has complex effects on marital and family relationships. Following some path-breaking studies in previous decades (e.g., Goodnow, 1988), more attention has been paid to the household tasks of children, with results generally suggesting that teenage housework is at least as gendered as that of adults. In addition, researchers have moved beyond married couples to analyze the causes and consequences of household labor performance for cohabitors, gay and lesbian couples, single parent households, single persons, retirees, kin networks, and paid domestic laborers. Researchers also have begun documenting similarities and differences in housework among race/ethnic groups and some studies have compared patterns of housework in various countries. Taken as a whole, these studies of household labor provide us with a better understanding of the embeddedness of housework in various social institutions and interpersonal processes and offer promise for predicting future trends.

THEORETICAL DEVELOPMENTS IN THE STUDY OF HOUSEHOLD LABOR

The typical introductory section of an empirical household labor journal article refers to three "theories" of labor allocation as (a) relative resources, (b) socialization-gender role attitudes, and (c) time availability-constraints. The first "theory" suggests that a person with more income will do less housework, the second suggests that people socialized to believe in gender-segregated work will conform to those beliefs, and the third suggests that when people spend more time in paid work they will spend less time in housework. Control variables are typically added and these three discrete hypotheses are tested in an effort to specify how and why couples divide housework. In the 1990s, an increasing number of scholars published articles and books presenting more elaborate reasons for accepting, challenging, and understanding the allocation of family work. Some explored in greater detail the multifaceted underpinnings to the three common housework predictors and argued for a more complex theoretical understanding of the many psychological, interpersonal, institutional, cultural, and economic forces involved. In the following brief review, I discuss conceptual developments in household labor studies under seven general headings. The fuzzy boundaries between categories suggest that theories in this area are neither exhaustive nor mutually exclusive, and deserve greater elaboration in the coming decade.

Gender Construction

Given the failure of neo-classical economic theories and the three common housework predictors to explain domestic divisions of labor in past decades, researchers in the 1990s increasingly turned to theories that incorporate gender in its symbolic and performance dimensions. Perhaps the most popular approach to emerge in the last decade, gender construction theories suggest that women and men perform different tasks because such practices affirm and reproduce gendered selves, thus reproducing a gendered interaction order. Drawing on symbolic interactionist, phenomenological, ethnomethodological, and feminist understandings of everyday life, the gender construction approach posits active subjects limited by situational exigencies, social structural constraints, and submerged power imbalances (Ferree, 1991; Hochschild, 1989; Hood, 1983; Komter, 1989; Pestello & Voydanoff, 1991; West & Fenstermaker, 1993). These theories are most similar to the hypothesis of socialization-gender role attitudes noted above, but they reject the assumption that people are automatically socialized into rigid gender roles or that they develop relatively fixed attitudes or deeply gendered personalities. Gender construction theories are variously labeled "gender theory" (Ferree, 1990, 1991; Potuchek, 1992), "doing gender" (Coltrane, 1989; West & Fenstermaker, 1993), "gender perspective" (Osmond & Thorne, 1993; Thompson, 1993); "interactionist" (Pestello & Voydanoff, 1991), "relational" (Thompson & Walker, 1989), "symbolic exchange" (Brines, 1993; Hochschild, 1989), or gender "display" (Brines 1994; Fenstermaker, 1996). Doing specific household tasks provides opportunities to demonstrate to oneself and to others that one is a competent member of a sex category with the capacity and desire to perform appropriately gendered behaviors (Berk, 1985; West & Fenstermaker, 1993). Hartmann (1993) called such theories "gender-plus" because they begin to specify how the performance of tasks is about something else besides or in addition to the housework, thus questioning assumptions of human capital or rational choice models (see below). A large number of authors during the 1990s drew on a version of gender construction theory to help explain household labor results (Blain, 1994; DeVault, 1990, 1991; Erickson, 1993; Greenstein, 1996a; Hall et al., 1995; Mederer, 1993; Perkins & DeMeis, 1997; Perry-Jenkins & Crouter, 1990; Perry-Jenkins, Seery, & Crouter, 1992; Piña,& Bengtson, 1993, 1995; Risman & Johnson-Sumerford, 1998; Sanchez & Kane, 1996; Thompson, 1991; Van Every, 1997; Zvonkovic, Greaves, Schmiege, & Hall, 1996).

Economic and Exchange Perspectives

Brines (1993, p. 303) suggested that three overlapping economic models of household labor allocation have "come to dominate the research agenda." The neoclassical economic theory of human capital investment and its "new household economics" variants suggest that men and women allocate time to household or paid work based on maximizing overall utility or efficiency (Becker, 1981). Human capital is typically measured by education, previous labor market experience, and the wages or jobs available to an employee (Bergen, 1991). The resource-bargaining perspective focuses on family power. It views the division of household labor as an outcome of negotiation between people who use valued resources to strike the best deal based on self-interest (Brines, 1993). The economic dependency model (which others might place in the institutional or socialist-feminist categories discussed below) focuses on marital exchanges in the context of gender and class inequalities. In this variant, women are assumed to enter into a "contract" wherein they exchange household labor in return for economic support from a main breadwinner (Brines, 1993, 1994).

In most household labor studies, these three economic-exchange approaches are lumped into a single relative resource hypothesis, though Becker's human capital theory, with its assumptions about the efficiency of labor specialization by gender, is sometimes operationalized using time availability. As others have noted (Bergen, 1991; Ferree, 1991; Peterson & Gerson, 1993), these theories are putatively gender neutral, emphasize choice, and assume that housework allocation is governed by the rules and principles of exchange relations. All three theories share an emphasis on how partners' earnings enter into the allocation of housework between husbands and wives. Beller (1993) noted that Becker's division-of-labor model does not account for individuals deriving utility directly from spending time in certain activities, rather than just from what is produced; in other words the model ignores that couples might get enjoyment out of cooking a meal together or value equity as a goal along with marginal utility. Even if they accept some of the utility maximization assumptions of neoclassical models of labor allocation, most sociologists insist that social and cultural factors be included in theoretical models along with macroeconomic opportunity structures, the family economy, and human capital characteristics (e.g., Bergen 1991; Bielby, 1993; Blumberg & Colemen, 1989). Refuting related assumptions of neoclassical choice models, Glass and Camarigg (1992) showed that occupational gender segregation does not result from women choosing jobs that afford them more opportunities to perform domestic tasks.

Although rarely citing the literature noted above, some economists in the 1990s also began to challenge simplifying assumptions of human capital and household production theories, including the ideas that tastes or preferences for housework are fixed, exogenous, or irrelevant and that social and interpersonal influences on market and nonmarket labor allocation are epiphenomenal (Barmby, 1994). For example, Juster and Stafford (1991, p. 506) noted that the human capital literature on opportunity costs of different workers ignores the preferences of household members for different activities, even though there is well-documented evidence that those preferences differ. Recent econometric studies also have called into question the assumption that labor supply and household labor demand are separate (Nicol & Nakamura, 1994) and have suggested that when women do more housework, their wage rates are depressed (Heath, Ciscel, & Sharp, 1998; Hersch & Stratton, 1994, 1997). A small but increasing number of economists recommend that theoretical models should attempt to incorporate more sociological factors related to gender or work preferences (Kooreman & Kapteyn, 1990; Van der Lippe & Siegers, 1994).

Institutional Influences

Related to the economic and exchange theories described above are conceptual approaches that focus on the constraints imposed by the formal economy, informal markets, state services, and other institutions. Recent studies focus on job scheduling, showing that shift work and flex-time promote housework sharing, as do non-overlapping employment schedules for spouses (Manke, Crouter, & McHale, 1994; Presser, 1994). Promising new research and theorizing in this area also focus on the purchase of domestic services, including meals, child care, and house cleaning (Bergen, 1991; Cohen, 1998; Oropesa, 1993; Presser, 1994), and on working-class and immigrant women who provide these services (Baca Zinn, 1990; Glenn, 1992; Graham, 1991). Other research looks at the organization of domestic and child-care work through kinship networks and neighborhood support (e.g., Abel & Nelson, 1990; Gallagher, 1994; Gerstel & Gallagher, 1994; Padgett, 1997). Some cross-cultural research in this tradition has looked at how global economies and immigration influence divisions of labor; other studies have examined the role of the state in promoting child care and enforcing tax policies that influence the allocation of housework (Baxter, 1997; Hondagneu-Sotelo, 1992; Miraftab, 1994; Sanchez, 1994b). Other theories in the general institutional category have provided a more comprehensive explanation for gender stratification by relying on various levels of analysis and postulating an interplay among technological, market, political, cultural, interactional, and personal factors in the distribution of labor. Such theories posit reciprocal links between the gender organization of reproduction and the gender organization of production. They also consider sexual politics, political economy, resource mobilization, social conflicts, and social movements as they relate to the changing life options of men and women (Chafetz, 1990; Collins, Chafetz, Blumberg, Coltrane, & Turner, 1993; Curtis & MacCorquodale, 1990). Such integrated theories lend themselves to cross-national studies (Baxter, 1997; Chafetz & Hagan, 1996; Sanchez 1993, 1994b), but can also explain individual behavior (Blumberg & Coleman, 1989; Gerson, 1993).

Socialist-Feminist Theories

Socialist-Feminist theories were some of the first to stress the systemic importance of the sexual division of labor (e.g., Hartmann, 1981). A distinctive feature of this approach is its continued emphases on the dual systems of capitalism and patriarchy (Agger & Shelton, 1993; Wright, Shire, Hwang, Dolan, & Baxter, 1992). Other distinctive features include its political activism and its attention to historical dynamics leading to the present oppressive situation for working-class women (Baxter 1993; Calasanti & Bailey, 1991; Jackson, 1992; Kynaston, 1996). Socialist-feminism assumes that asking about "sex-role" attitudes will not reveal how the sexual division of labor serves the interests of both men and capital. This approach shares some assumptions with economic theories but denies the free-market and individual choice premises of those theories. Socialist-feminist research on housework also contains analyses of institutions, with primary emphasis on how race, class, and gender constitute overlapping but relatively autonomous hierarchies in the world system (Baca Zinn, 1990; Glenn, 1992; VanEvery, 1997).

Morality Theories

Morality theories are simultaneously the oldest and newest to be applied to housework. They can be considered foundational because they come from ancient teachings in religion and philosophy and because family social science was founded by social reformers and moral crusaders. Morality theories of housework also seem new, however, because few family scholars from the 1950s through the 1970s felt compelled to invoke moral arguments when discussing who should perform household tasks. The general category of morality theories could be subsumed under gender construction or institutional approaches but is highlighted here because of its increasing prominence in public debates. Moral arguments have became more common in the scholarly literature as academics (along with politicians and religious lead-

ers) have staked out positions on family values, divorce, same-sex marriage, domestic partner laws, abortion rights, welfare, covenant marriage, responsible fatherhood, custody, and other issues (e.g., Glenn, 1997; Popenoe, 1996; Stacey, 1996). The general debates about culture and morality are too broad to address here, but more narrow debates about family work tend to revolve around issues of whether women are uniquely qualified to perform family service and whether housework reflects caring love, oppression, or both. Conservative and religious versions suggest that most academic models of housework focus too much on individualism, conflict, and inequality and not enough on spirituality and the positive aspects of moral obligation and service to family members (Ahlander & Bahr, 1995; Bahr & Ahlander, 1996). Liberal and feminist versions suggest that power, inequality, and love are uniquely intertwined within the household economy, religion, and the general culture (Hays, 1996; Sanchez, 1996; Thompson, 1993). Recent scholarship in the philosophy of morals has begun to reconceptualize social justice as it relates to gender, citizenship, and the care of others inside and outside of families, but this work has rarely been recognized or appreciated by family science scholars (Cancian & Oliker, 1999; Okin, 1989; Tronto, 1993).

Life-Course Factors

The 1990s saw a proliferation of middle-level hypotheses about the impact on housework of age, work experiences, living arrangements, family structure, life transitions, marriage, remarriage, childbearing, teenagers, and other life-course issues. This category reflects a loose conglomeration of hypotheses rather than a unified body of research or theory. The conceptual apparatus for these various hypotheses often is left implicit, but role theory, family ecology, and various developmental and socialization theories provide a backdrop for interpreting empirical results. For many of the reasons noted above and because of normative pressures, transitions into marriage and childbearing are expected to increase women's household labor more than men's (Blair & Lichter, 1991; Cowan & Cowan, 1992; South & Spitze, 1994). Because they are assumed to be less subject to marriage norms and because they are thought to embrace egalitarian ideals, comparison groups of cohabitors and same-sex couples are expected to share more household labor than do married couples (Kurdek, 1993; VanEvery, 1993;

but see Giddings, 1998). Because of the independence and multiple role identities available to those who wait longer to marry or have children, delayed transitions to marriage and parenthood are also expected to contribute to more equal contributions from husbands and wives (Coltrane, 1990; Pittman & Blanchard, 1996). Remarriage and a more extensive work history are also theorized to decrease women's share of housework because of the socializing impacts of prior experience and weaker norms governing behavior (Demo & Acock, 1993; Ishii-Kuntz & Coltrane, 1992b; Sullivan, 1997). Childless couples and single, divorced, or widowed people are also expected to do less housework because of reduced workload, although predictions for retirees are more mixed (South & Spitze, 1994; Szinovacz, 1992; Szinovacz & Harpster, 1994). Whereas having more and younger children is expected to increase the demand for housework, having fewer and older children is expected to contribute to its performance, especially if they are daughters (Waite & Goldscheider, 1992). Not only might children add to demand for and performance of housework, but parents' desires to instill family obligation in children or to teach them gender-typed skills are expected to influence family work patterns (Goodnow, Bowes, Warton, Dawes, & Taylor, 1991). Although often neglected, housing variables (tenure, dwelling size, length of residence) are also related to life stages and are expected to influence household labor demand, performance capability, normative obligations, and labor allocation. Research in the coming decade ought to include more of these demographic and life-course variables and strive to articulate theoretical relationships among overlapping hypotheses.

Psychological and Socialization Theories

Psychological or socialization theories suggest that men and women with "traditional" attitudes will share less housework, whereas men and women with "nontraditional" attitudes will share more housework. These theories assume that from childhood on, men and women are socialized to conform to predetermined "sex roles" and thereby develop gendered personalities and preferences. Some research in the 1990s continued tests of whether "androgynous" individuals (those high on "femininity" and "masculinity") shared more housework (Gunter & Gunter, 1990). More common in recent studies, however, are "gender traditionalism" scales, including questions about the rights of women, the appropriate work and family roles of men and women, and whether children will be harmed if they spend time away from their mothers. One of the NSFH items that best predicts sharing of housework among couples simply asks "Do you believe that men and women should share housework when both are employed?" As proponents of gender construction approaches argue, theoretical interpretation of attitude findings is difficult, and scholars do not agree on the depth or stability of gender attitudes and gendered personalities. Simple "tests" of socialization versus social structural explanations for housework allocation have become less common recently because researchers have begun to focus on various mediators and consequences. Often invoking theoretical constructs such as role overload, role strain, or role conflict, more studies are investigating causal factors and mediating conditions in respondents' depression and individual well-being, as well as in couples' conflict and marital satisfaction. A final use of psychological theories about household labor comes from clinical, counseling, and social work fields. Most theories postulate that women in general, and employed women in particular, will function better and be less depressed if they can shed total responsibility for housework and child care. Therapists and researchers propose various nonthreatening ways to encourage men to pay more attention to housework and specify some of the potential beneficial impacts on marriages and on men's emotional development (Hawkins & Roberts, 1992; Mintz & Mahalik, 1996; Rasmussen, Hawkins, & Schwab, 1996). Others suggest how existing counseling models ignore issues of power and fail to hold men fully accountable for housework and family management (Braverman, 1991).

Important concepts within each of the approaches noted above offer researchers theoretical tools to explore questions about how and why housework is divided and how divisions of household labor influence individuals and families. Theories within each category are sometimes overlapping and sometimes competing, and there is significant interplay among the categories. Although it is inappropriate to assume that one can test fully the utility of one theory versus another, with the introduction of comprehensive data sets (e.g., NSFH) and new data analysis techniques, researchers are beginning to specify the conditions under which one theory better predicts measurable outcomes. As noted below, given fairly narrow research questions, precise measurement techniques, and comparable levels of analysis, several robust predictors have begun to emerge. The task for the next decade is to specify conceptual links among common predictors and to develop more comprehensive theoretical models of household production, labor segmentation, gender differentiation, family functioning, and personal well-being.

METHODOLOGICAL ISSUES

Information about household labor in the 1990s was collected using time diaries and survey questions, but studies also used other methods such as qualitative depth interviews, direct observations, discourse analysis, historical-comparative methods, and longitudinal study designs.

Time Diaries

In time diary studies, individuals are asked to complete logs accounting for time spent on various activities, usually for a 24-hour period, with results collected via phone, mail, or in person (Harvey, 1993; Marini & Shelton, 1993; Robinson & Godbey, 1997). Important temporal variables within the time diary method include length of recording period and whether respondents are asked to report activities at the end of the day or retrospectively on the next day. Daily activity collected on the next day differs little from that collected on the same day, and weekend information often is collected up to a week later with little distortion (Robinson & Godbey, 1997). Time diaries generally are considered to generate the most accurate (and lower) estimates of time spent on specific activities, although simultaneous activities are sometimes ignored or underestimated, and if the day selected is not representative, other biases may enter (Niemi, 1993; Robinson & Godbey, 1997). Most researchers report that variations in question format produce only minor changes in results (Harvey, 1993; Shelton & John, 1996), although differences in diary layout can slightly change estimates of activity patterns over the day (Geurts & DeRee, 1993). The diary-like Experience Sampling Method, in which participants carry pagers and are signaled at random times and asked to fill out activity and subjective state reports, has also been used to verify time diary estimates (Juster & Stafford, 1991) and to study how household labor is associated with emotional well-being or distress (Larson et al., 1994; Larson & Almeida, 1999).

Survey Questions

Direct questions about time spent on household labor have been asked in many national and some regional phone, mail, and in-person interview surveys. Respondents typically are asked how much time they "usually" spend per week on specific household activities or how much time they spent "yesterday" on selected activities. Comparisons with time diary studies show that results are highly correlated but that direct-question surveys produce estimates of time spent that are often 25%–50% higher, especially for frequently performed activities (Juster & Safford, 1991; Marini & Shelton, 1993; Press & Townsley, 1998). For less frequently performed activities, survey questions may produce lower estimates, especially if the period of recall is long (Marini & Shelton, 1993; Shelton & John, 1996). Both men and women tend to overestimate their own contributions in direct-question surveys and to double-count time spent in simultaneous activities; some studies suggest that men may inflate their estimates more than women because of cognitive biases relating to salience effects and ego-enhancement (Coltrane, 1996; Kiger & Riley, 1996; Marini & Shelton, 1993; Press & Townsley, 1998). In addition, missing responses may predominate among couples in which husbands contribute little to housework, leading to overestimates of husbands' contributions in data sets such as the NSFH (Szinovacz & Harpster, 1994), and more research is needed on how and why couples who do not answer detailed questions on housework might differ from others. Proportional estimates of a spouse's time spent in household labor are approximately equal whether diaries or surveys are used (Sullivan, 1997), but while they may be both reliable and valid, proportional measures are difficult to interpret because they cannot be used for all households, do not measure how much time is spent on housework, and do not reflect whether shifts result from wives doing less or husbands doing more (Marini & Shelton, 1993).

Variation in question wording for survey items include asking how much time respondents spend in a typical week on "housework" (Brines, 1994); asking who does each of a list of tasks (Baxter, 1997; Ferree, 1991), sometimes followed by questions about how often (Robinson & Spitze, 1992); asking what percentage of each task was done by each spouse (Wright et al., 1992); and asking whether women had sole responsibility or shared responsibility for a list of tasks (Waite & Goldscheider, 1992). In general, researchers have moved away from asking simple proportionate questions (who does more tasks) and toward collecting hourly estimates of performance because more narrowly defined tasks produce more accurate estimates (Shelton & John, 1996). As noted above, many researchers convert hourly estimates into proportionate measures of routine housework to capture task segregation (Blair & Lichter, 1991; Coltrane & Ishii-Kuntz, 1992; Demo & Acock, 1993; Glass & Fujimoto, 1994; Perry-Jenkins & Folk, 1994). Using hourly estimates alone can mask issues of equity, but using proportional measures alone can mask substantial differences in performance, so some researchers advocate using both (Barnett & Shen, 1997). Whereas past studies often collected information about various household members' task performance from wives only, many studies in the 1990s used estimates of self and spouse contributions to each task from both husbands and wives (typically averaged to minimize reporting biases; see Coltrane, 1996). Some recent studies also collect housework information from and about children (Antill et al., 1996; Goodnow, Bowes, Warton, Dawes, & Taylor, 1991; Manke et al., 1994; McHale, Bartko, Crouter, & Perry-Jenkins, 1990). Finally, although most housework studies have not included measures of child care, using both in the same models can help explicate their interrelations (Almeida, Maggs, & Galambos, 1993; Ishii-Kuntz & Coltrane, 1992a).

Several innovations in survey design and content also emerged in the 1990s, including the use of card-sorting techniques to measure relative task performance (Coltrane, 1996; Risman & Johnson-Sumerford, 1998). Researchers devised new questionnaire instruments to measure fairness (Hawkins, Marshall, & Allen, 1998), task management (Mederer, 1993), maternal gatekeeping (Allen & Hawkins, 1999), control over housework scheduling (Barnett & Shen, 1997), personal obligation to perform tasks (Perkins & DeMeis, 1996), family social class (Wright et al., 1992), and provider role identity (Perry-Jenkins et al., 1992). Others employed survey variables not often used in household labor studies, such as non-overlapping work hours (Presser, 1994), work-place authority (Brayfield, 1992), occupational autonomy for both spouses (Perry-Jenkins & Folk, 1994), paid domestic labor (Oropesa, 1993), home ownership (South & Spitze, 1994), age at first birth (Coltrane & Ishii-Kuntz, 1992), and previous cohabitation (Sullivan 1997). The availability of large national data sets such as the NSFH, with substantial information on both household labor and family functioning, allowed for the testing of various hypotheses about the entire U.S. population and specific subgroups, although problems associated with frequent reanalysis of the same data also emerged in the 1990s. Relatively recent and more sophisticated data-analytic and modeling techniques were also introduced to household labor studies during the decade: log linear modeling (Dancer & Gilbert, 1993), multinominal logistic regression (Waite & Goldscheider, 1992), hierarchal structural equation modeling—LISREL (Coltrane & Ishii-Kuntz, 1992; Piña & Bengtson, 1995), hierarchical regression (Perry-Jenkins & Folk, 1994), maximum likelihood estimation—TOBIT (Brines, 1994), and multiple classification analysis (Robinson & Milkie, 1998).

Other Methods

Although most household labor studies in the decade collected and analyzed quantitative data, many studies used observational and less structured interview techniques to generate qualitative data, describe social processes, and construct ideal types. Perhaps best known of the studies in this category are Hochschild's *The Second Shift* (1989) and *The Time Bind* (1997) and DeVault's *Feeding the Family* (1991), both of which generated new insights and hypotheses. Other case studies and interview-based research projects illuminated how family life, gender, and household labor are intertwined and mutually produced (e.g., Coltrane, 1996; Doucet, 1995; Gager, 1998; Gerson, 1993; Hays, 1996; Potuchek, 1992; Ribbens & Edwards, 1995; Risman & Johnson-Sumerford, 1998; Wharton, 1994; Zvonkovic et al., 1996). A few studies explicitly adopted discourse analysis to understand how housework, gender, and family are constructed through narratives (Blain, 1994; DeVault, 1990; West & Fenstermaker, 1993).

A new development in household labor studies was signaled by the large number of comparative and cross-national studies that appeared during the decade. Although results were often limited, using the nation-state as a unit of analysis showed promise for developing a sociological understanding of links between household labor and other cultural, institutional, and structural factors. In general, men in virtually all countries studied increased their contributions to household labor slightly from previous decades (Juster & Stafford, 1991). Canadian studies show results broadly similar to similar studies conducted in the United States, with Canadian men perhaps doing a little more than U.S. men (Baxter, 1997; Blain, 1994; Brayfield, 1992; Haddad, 1994; Harrell, 1995; Nakhaie, 1995; Wright et al., 1992). Studies in Australia yielded similar results to those from Canada (Antill et al., 1996; Baxter, 1997; Wright et al., 1992), and studies in England, mostly qualitative, report extremely wide diversity in results (Bonney & Reinbach, 1993; Doucet, 1995; Hakim, 1996; Sullivan, 1997; VanEvery, 1997). With some variation, studies show that Swedish men do slightly more housework than U.S. men and Norwegian men (Baxter, 1997; Calasanti & Bailey, 1991; Juster & Stafford, 1991; Kalleberg & Rosenfeld, 1990; Wright et al., 1992). Conversely, studies show that Japanese men do less than U.S. men (Juster & Stafford, 1991; Kamo, 1994; Strober & Chan, 1998). Few comparisons have been made to less developed countries, although Sanchez (1993, 1994b) found that three of five Asian countries have greater rates of sharing than is exhibited in the United States. Other researchers investigate household labor in Turkey (Bolak, 1997), the former Yugoslavia, (Massey, Hahn, & Sekulic, 1995), and Mexico (Miraftab, 1994). Although these transnational and comparative studies often set out to isolate the potential impact of state policy or taxation on domestic labor sharing, methodological problems are great, and finding significant differences in predicted directions is rare (Kalleberg & Rosenfeld, 1990).

One of the most important methodological developments of the decade was a move toward longitudinal studies. Because correlations from cross-sectional analyses can reflect spurious associations, many researchers called for more detailed longitudinal studies (Jacobs, 1993; Sanchez & Thomson, 1997). The availability of housework questions in national longitudinal data sets such as the NSFH, the National Longitudinal Surveys of Young Women, and the Panel Study of Income Dynamics made testing of causal pathways more possible during the 1990s. Led by developmental paradigms, both quantitative and qualitative studies looked at changes in parenting and housework over time (Almeida et al., 1993; Cowan & Cowan, 1992; Deutsch, Lussier, & Servis, 1993; Johnson & Huston, 1998; MacDermid, Huston, & McHale, 1990; Pittman et al., 1996; Sullivan, 1997; Zvonovic et al., 1996). Part method and part subject matter, the ultimate longitudinal approach—historical studies—continued to inform our understanding of household labor during the 1990s.

With the proliferation of historical studies of everyday life, historians of housework have a wealth of new material from which to draw. Historical studies of housework can inform economic models and refine estimates of productive output (Folbre & Wagman, 1993), but cultural histories carry the most potential for understanding housework in its social context. Analyses of the emergence of separate spheres and an ideology of intensive mothering are particularly enlightening (Hays, 1996; Jackson, 1992; Siegel, 1998), as are studies of how immigrants and women of color have performed domestic labor (Glenn, 1992; Palmer, 1989; Romero, 1992). Historical studies suggest that future household labor research should incorporate measures of paid domestic labor, substitution of services, and housework standards into their allocation models.

EMPIRICAL FINDINGS

Predictors of Household Labor

In contrast to research conducted in earlier decades, 1990s studies find that men's share of housework has several consistent predictors, including women's employment patterns, ideology, and earnings, followed by men's employment hours and ideology. Other predictors of men's relative share of housework, including age, life-course issues, marital status, and children, are also found to influence the relative share of housework performed by men. The few studies that measure initiation or management of family work find that women almost invariably assume a manager role, with men occasionally serving as their helpers (Blain, 1994; Coltrane, 1996; Gunter & Gunter, 1990; Hawkins, Roberts, Christiansen, & Marshall, 1994; Mederer, 1993; West & Fenstermaker, 1993). The gender division of household labor is typically attributed to men's reluctance to assume responsibility, but some studies also discuss women's reluctance to relinquish control over family work (Allen & Hawkins, 1999; Ferree, 1991; Haas, 1992; Hawkins & Roberts, 1992; Hays, 1996). Studies using measures of men's absolute time spent on all types of household labor identify fewer significant predictors and explain less variance than studies using women's hours or proportional measures of routine housework. In addition, the same predictors do not necessarily apply to all people or even to the same person at different times or under different circumstances (Gerson, 1993), leading some to promote looking at breadwinner-homemaker families separately from dual-earner families or dividing samples according to family structure or life stage (Bonney & Reinbach, 1993; Doucet, 1995; Hakim, 1996; Perry-Jenkins et al., 1992; Sullivan, 1997).

Women's Employment. Of the time availability variables, women's employment hours have the strongest and most consistent effects on women's absolute levels of housework and men's share of housework. Robinson and Godbey (1997) report that employed women do one third less family work than nonemployed women. With few exceptions, dual-earner couples are found to share more family work than male-only breadwinner couples (DeMeis & Perkins, 1996; Fish, New, & Van Cleave, 1992; Presser, 1994; Starrells, 1994; Sullivan, 1997; but see Hossain & Roopnarine, 1993). Studies now find that women routinely spend less time on housework when they are employed longer hours, and men living with them do a greater share of the domestic work (Almeida et al., 1993; Baxter, 1993; Blair & Lichter, 1991; Brayfield, 1992; Calasanti & Bailey, 1991; Coltrane & Ishii-Kuntz, 1992; Demo & Acock, 1993; Goldscheider & Waite, 1991; Greenstein, 1996a; Heath & Bourne, 1995; Kalleberg & Rosenfeld, 1990; Peterson & Gerson, 1993; Shelton, 1990; Shelton & John, 1993a; Wright et al., 1992). When women spend more time on the job, they also spend less time providing help and support to extended kin (Gerstel & Gallagher, 1994). The relationship between women's employment hours and men's housework is more varied. Some studies find that women's employment hours are related both to men's absolute hours and proportional contributions to housework (Almeida et al., 1993; Blair & Lichter, 1991), whereas others find that women's employment hours are significantly related only to men's proportionate contributions (Larson et al., 1994). When women are involved in shift-work or flex-time employment, men contribute more to housework (Silver & Goldscheider, 1994), especially if there is non-overlap between spouses' employment hours (Presser, 1994). Other aspects of women's employment also may influence household labor allocation. Some small sample studies suggest that women in professional jobs do more housework because they compensate for gender-atypical breadwinning patterns (Biernat & Wortman, 1991; Deutsch et al., 1993; Hochschild, 1989), but other studies using representative samples find that women with higher occupational prestige, or more workplace authority tend to share more of the housework with their husbands (Brayfield, 1992; Perry-Jenkins & Folk, 1994; Presser, 1994; but see Brines, 1993).

Men's Employment. As for women, less paid work generally means more family work for men, but low levels of housework and greater variation among men produces some mixed results. Men's commitment to employment is a weaker and less consistent predictor of household labor than it is for women, especially when a large number of predictors are entered into multivariate models. Using national samples, researchers typically find that men who are employed fewer hours do a greater share of housework, child care, or both (Baxter, 1993; Brines, 1993; Ishii-Kuntz & Coltrane, 1992a; Greenstein, 1996a; Haddad, 1994; Hersch & Stratton, 1994; Waite & Goldscheider, 1992), as do men whose employment hours do not overlap with their wives' (Presser, 1994). In contrast, some studies find no relationship between men's employment hours and their housework (Almeida et al, 1993; John & Shelton, 1997; Sullivan, 1997). Results concerning men's unemployment are also mixed, with some finding that Black and White unemployed men do more housework (Orbuch & Eyster, 1997) and others finding that unemployed Black men do less housework (Shelton & John, 1993b). Small sample studies from the 1990s continue to show that most men identify themselves as primary breadwinners and that both men and women are reluctant to accept wives as equal providers (Bergen, 1991; Biernat & Wortman, 1991; Larson et al., 1994; Perry-Jenkins & Crouter, 1992; Rubin, 1994). In some studies, accepting wives as coproviders is identified as the key factor in reallocating family work (Coltrane & Valdez, 1993; Hood, 1993; Potuchek, 1992).

Earnings. In general, wives who make more money enjoy more equal divisions of labor. Results were mixed in past studies, whereas research in the 1990s suggested that when relative earnings between husbands and wives are more equal, the relative distribution of household tasks is more balanced. Some find that when women's absolute levels of earnings go up, their absolute levels of time spent on housework go down (Beller, 1993; Brines, 1993; Hersch & Stratton, 1997; Silver & Goldscheider, 1994). Smaller absolute income differences between husbands and wives are associated with more housework sharing (Baxter, 1993), and wives' proportionate share of earnings is consistently associated with more equal divisions of housework (Blair & Lichter, 1991; Brayfield, 1992; Calasanti & Bailey, 1991; Coltrane, 1996; Deutsch et al., 1993; Greenstein, 1996a; Harrell, 1995; Heath & Bourne, 1995; Hersch & Stratton, 1994; Sanchez & Thomson, 1997; Starrels, 1994; Steil & Weltman, 1991; Sullivan, 1997; Van der Lippe & Siegers, 1994).

A simple economic or power interpretation of these results does not hold across the full range of incomes. As noted above, when men are unemployed, they sometimes do less housework. For example, Brines (1994) found that dependent husbands do less housework the more they depend on their wives for income, noting that this dynamic is particularly evident among (although not limited to) married men in low-income households. At the opposite end of the income pyramid, different patterns emerge. Wealthier men do little housework, but the amount their wives do varies significantly. Women's higher occupational status and income (but not men's) is strongly associated with the purchase of domestic services (Cohen, 1998; Oropesa, 1993). Results from sample surveys using quantitative data and results from historical and ethnographic studies using qualitative data thus converge on a general finding: women's economic resources allow them to reduce their own housework contributions and "buy out" of gendered domestic obligations. Upwardly mobile and well-educated women are the most likely to purchase domestic services, whether performed in their own homes or embedded in the food and products they purchase for the family from outside the home (Oropesa, 1993). It is predominantly White, middle-class women who consume these services and products, and it is immigrant, ethnic minority, and working-class women who produce and provide them (Glenn, 1992). How women near the bottom of the earnings pyramid manage to care for their own homes and families is a topic that more survey and quantitative studies of household labor should address in the coming decade.

Education. Education often is used as a control variable in multivariate models predicting household divisions of labor. Interpretation of findings is complicated by conceptual confusion about whether years of education should be considered a measure of human capital accumulation, a relative resource, a component of social class, an indicator of ideology or attitudes, or a life-course transition experience. In general, studies suggest that women with more education do less house-

work (Bergen, 1991; Hersch & Stratton, 1994; Pittman & Blanchard, 1996; Presser, 1994; Orbuch & Eyster, 1997; Sanchez & Thomson, 1997; South & Spitze, 1994), purchase more domestic services (Cohen, 1998), and have children who do less housework (Waite & Goldscheider, 1992). In contrast, men with more education generally do more housework (Bergen, 1991; Haddad, 1994; Orbuch & Eyster, 1997; Pittman & Blanchard, 1996; Presser, 1994; South & Spitze, 1994; Waite & Goldscheider, 1992).

Ideology. Studies from the 1990s show that women's egalitarian gender ideology is a consistent predictor of household labor sharing. When wives feel more strongly that both paid work and family work should be shared and when they agree more fully with statements about equality between women and men, they are more likely to share housework with husbands. Some studies also show that more egalitarian men share more housework or child care (Almeida et al., 1993; Blair & Johnson, 1992; Baxter, 1993; Calasanti & Bailey, 1991; Greenstein, 1996a, 1996b; Harrell, 1995; Ishii-Kuntz & Coltrane, 1992a; Mederer & Weinstein, 1992; Orbuch & Eyster, 1997; Perry-Jenkins & Crouter, 1990; Pittman & Blanchard, 1996; Presser, 1994; Starrels, 1994; Waite & Goldscheider, 1992; Wright et al., 1992; but see Sanchez & Thomson, 1997). The fit between spouses' attitudes is also important: Spouses with similar views are likely to put those ideals in practice (i.e., more congruent egalitarians share more housework, more congruent traditionals share less) (Greenstein, 1996a; MacDermid et al., 1990). Baxter (1993) suggested that one's own attitudes impinge more directly on one's own tasks than do the attitudes of one's spouse. Starrels (1994) found that an earnings gender attitudes interaction term is the best predictor of housework sharing in multivariate models.

Age and Life-Course Issues. Because the meaning of housework varies between generations, some studies focus on cohort effects in its distribution (Barnett & Shen, 1997). In general, younger women do less housework and share more of it than do older women (Hersch & Stratton, 1994; Shelton & John, 1993a; Van der Lippe & Siegers, 1994), prompting some to call for studies of young just-marrieds (South & Spitze, 1994; Perkins & DeMeis, 1996). Others find that when ideology and other variables are entered into multivariate models, cohort effects become nonsignificant (Presser, 1994). Another finding related to age is that the larger the age gap between spouses, the less the couple shares housework (Presser, 1994). Some studies find that men increase their contributions to household labor after retirement, although they do so for affiliative reasons and remain in a helper role (Piña & Bengtson, 1995; Szinovacz, 1992). Some suggest that retirement does not change the gender division of labor significantly, although some women expect it (Robinson & Spitze, 1992; Ward, 1993), and others specify how past employment, retirement, and gender interact to influence task allocation (Szinovacz & Harpster, 1994).

Marital Status. Being married means more housework for women and less for men (Gupta, 1999; Nock, 1998; Shelton, 1992). Single and cohabiting women perform less housework than do married women, but single and cohabiting men perform more housework than do married men (Nock, 1998; Perkins & DeMeis, 1996; Shelton & John, 1993a). Because single mothers perform about as much housework as do married mothers (Demo & Acock, 1993), married fathers may do about as much household work as they create (Hartmann, 1981). When single-mother and single-father households are compared, women do more housework than do men, suggesting that even without a spouse, housework is still gendered (Fassinger, 1993; Hall et al., 1995). Nevertheless, single fathers do more housework than do married fathers, and therefore the difference between men's and women's housework in single parent families is less than it is in two-parent families. The first marriage may be the most likely to produce gendered divisions of labor because remarried households share more than first married ones (Demo & Acock, 1993; Ishii-Kuntz & Coltrane, 1992b; Pyke & Coltrane, 1996; Sullivan, 1997; but see Presser, 1994).

Presence of Children. Studies show that the transition to parenthood is associated with movement toward less sharing of family work between men and women (Cowan & Cowan, 1992; Johnson & Huston, 1998; MacDermid et al., 1990; Shelton, 1992). Women tend to feel more obligation to perform household labor when they have children, just as they do when they get married (Perkins & DeMeis, 1996; Wharton, 1994). When couples have children, men tend to work more hours at paid jobs but do not necessarily put in more hours of housework. Women, in contrast, tend to work

fewer hours on the job and begin to put in significantly more hours of domestic work (Sanchez & Thomson, 1997; Shelton, 1992). Other studies show that more preschool children are associated with more hours of household labor for both men and women (Baxter, 1994; Bergen, 1991; Presser, 1994; Van der Lippe & Seigers, 1994). Nevertheless, because women increase their hours more than men do, they end up doing a larger share of family work as the number of children increases (Greenstein, 1996a; Hersch & Stratton, 1994; Shelton & John, 1993a; Perkins & DeMeis, 1996; Presser, 1994; Shelton & John, 1993a, 1996; Van der Lippe & Seigers, 1994; but see Kamo, 1991 on the nonlinearity of effects). A few studies suggest that later transitions to parenthood produce more equal divisions of child care and housework (Coltrane, 1990; Coltrane & Ishii-Kuntz, 1992; Pittman & Blanchard, 1996). As men do more child care, they may also do more housework, especially if the firstborn child is a boy (Fish et al., 1996; Ishii-Kuntz & Coltrane, 1992a; Presser, 1994).

Race and Ethnicity. Household labor studies in the 1990s began to take race seriously. Most studies find that Black men do more housework than do White men, net of other predictors, but that Black women still do almost twice as much housework as do Black men (Bergen, 1991; Broman, 1991; Heath & Bourne, 1995; Hossain & Roopnarine, 1993; John & Shelton, 1997; Orbuch & Eyster, 1997; Padgett, 1997; Sanchez & Thomson, 1997). Some find that common predictor variables work somewhat differently for Blacks, in part because of more egalitarian attitudes and greater employment and earnings equality between spouses (Orbuch & Eyster, 1997). For example, employed Black women do fewer hours of housework than do other women (Silver & Goldscheider, 1994) but Black men do more hours of housework if they are employed (Shelton & John, 1993b). Some find that Black men are less likely to perceive the division of household labor as unfair to their wives as are White men (DeMaris & Longmore, 1996; John, Shelton, & Luschen, 1995). Others find unique patterns of labor allocation in Black families when extended kin are included, with Black adult children living at home contributing more than Whites (Spitze & Ward, 1995) and Black men doing more (Padgett, 1997) or less (Wilson, Tolson, Hinton, & Kiernan, 1990) when grandmothers and other kin contribute. Preliminary findings also suggest that nonresident Black fathers contribute more than do nonresident White fathers (Wilson et al., 1990).

Findings are contradictory concerning the sharing of family work in Latino families, with some suggesting there is slightly more sharing than among White families (Mirande, 1997; Shelton & John, 1993b) and some suggesting there is less (Golding, 1990). Most studies show similar patterns of association between variables whether the couples are Latino or Anglo (Coltrane & Valdez, 1993; Golding, 1990; Herrera & del Campo, 1995; John et al., 1995), although DeMaris and Longmore (1996) found Latino men and women to be less likely to view household labor as unfair to the wife than did Anglo men and women. In a unique contribution, Hondagneu-Sotelo (1992) documented the independent effects of immigration on labor sharing in Mexican American families. Work on other ethnic minorities in North America is still rare, although Johnson (1998) found some cultural norms promoting sharing among Vietnamese and Laotians in the United States, and Brayfield (1992) found that French Canadians share more housework than do English Canadians.

Fairness Evaluations

Although women perform two thirds of the total household labor, only about one third of them rate their division of labor as unfair, prompting researchers in the 1990s to investigate what fairness evaluations mean. According to Lennon and Rosenfeld (1994), couples do not use 50% as an "equity point"—men find the division of labor to be fair when they contribute 36% of the time devoted to household tasks, whereas women find the division of labor to be fair when they contribute 66% of the total. Such findings suggest that unequal divisions of labor are accepted as normal and help explain why past studies have found little relation between actual divisions of labor and perceptions of fairness. Nevertheless, research in the 1990s begins to isolate conditions associated with labeling divisions of household labor as "fair" or "unfair." Some also call attention to measurement problems in the area of fairness evaluations, especially with an NSFH item that lacks unidimensionality and is difficult to interpret (Smith, Gager, & Morgan, 1998).

Resource theories and their derivatives predict how people make fairness evaluations about housework. Classical exchange theory suggests that women will see as fair those situations in which they are doing the least amount of housework and unfair those in which they are doing the most (Suitor, 1991). Equity theory posits that partners will feel uncomfortable with situations in which they are either over- or under-benefitted, suggesting that both men and women will see as most fair those situations in which they share the household labor about equally (Piña & Bengtson, 1993). Challenges to these theories come from studies showing that even employed women tend to label unbalanced divisions of labor as fair and from research showing that men who do little persist in seeing the allocation of household tasks as fair (Ward, 1993). Suitor (1991) replicated the oft-cited U-shaped curve of marital satisfaction by finding that wives' satisfaction with the division of household labor is highest in the preparental and postparental stages and lowest when children are present (i.e., when women do the most domestic work). In contrast, husbands' fairness ratings and satisfaction with housework show little variation across the life course.

Thompson (1991) refined Major's (1987) distributive justice framework to show how outcome values, comparison referents, and justifications shape gendered differences in entitlement that lead wives to evaluate unbalanced divisions of labor as fair (see also Ferree, 1990; Gager, 1998; Hochschild, 1989; Major, 1993; Pyke & Coltrane, 1996). In brief, wives should better grasp the injustice of the existing division of housework if they lack valued outcomes, compare their husband's contributions to their own, and reject justifications for unequal performance (Major, 1993; Thompson, 1991). Contrary to earlier findings showing little variation in fairness evaluations, many 1990s studies showed that wives' participation in household labor (measured in absolute hours, as a proportion of couple time in housework, or as responsibility for household management) is associated with variation in women's, and sometimes men's, sense of fairness (Greenstein, 1996b; Hawkins, Marshall, & Meiners, 1995; Mederer, 1993; Sanchez, 1994a; Sanchez & Kane, 1996). Although most people rate their own contributions as fair, men's lower levels of participation in household labor generally are associated with both men and women seeing more unfairness in the division of family work (Blair & Johnson, 1992; Dancer & Gilbert, 1993; Greenstein, 1996b; Sanchez 1994a), especially when men contribute little to the routine tasks of cooking, cleaning, and washing (DeMaris & Longmore, 1996; John et al., 1995; Lennon & Rosenfield, 1994; Perry-Jenkins

& Folk, 1994; Robinson & Spitze, 1992; but see Wilkie, Ferree, & Ratcliff, 1998). Findings differ on how much men and women pay attention to their own contributions, but most studies find that when one spouse does less and the other does more, the chances of perceiving unfairness increase (Dancer and Gilbert, 1993; John et al., 1995; Robinson & Spitze, 1992). In contrast, as men do more of the occasional tasks (such as washing the car), both spouses are more likely to judge the division of household labor as fair to wives (DeMaris & Longmore, 1996).

Fairness evaluations also are influenced by employment, education, and ideology, but 1990s results were mixed. Several studies find a negative relationship between women's paid work hours and fairness evaluations (Greenstein, 1996b; Sanchez, 1994a; Sanchez & Kane, 1996; but see Blair & Johnson, 1992). Some find that men's greater employment hours are related to their own evaluations of fairness in the division of household labor (Ward, 1993), whereas others find that men's greater employment hours are related to their evaluations of unfairness (Robinson & Spitze, 1992). DeMaris & Longmore (1996) found that husbands' greater employment hours, relative to wives', encourage wives (but not husbands) to see the division of housework as fair to her. Women with less education than their husbands and those who perceive the costs of leaving the marriage to be high perceive more fairness (Lennon & Rosenfield, 1994; Wilkie et al., 1998), and higher levels of education for both spouses are associated with seeing less fairness in the division of labor (DeMaris & Longmore, 1996; John et al., 1995; Robinson & Spitze, 1992). Some studies show that women, and sometimes men, with more egalitarian gender attitudes see more unfairness to the wife in household labor allocation (Blair & Johnson, 1992; DeMaris & Longmore, 1996; John et al., 1995; Sanchez & Kane, 1996), and some find that women's fairness evaluations are disproportionately influenced by men's conventional gender attitudes (Sanchez, 1994a). Greenstein (1996b) noted a significant interaction between gender ideology and housework, with the actual division of labor having less effect on fairness evaluations the more conventional the wife's views on gender.

We can better understand fairness evaluations if we acknowledge the insight from gender construction theories that women (and sometimes men) perceive both their own and their spouse's housework to carry emotional messages, frequently representing love, caring, or appreciation

(Blain, 1994; Blair & Johnson, 1992; Coltrane, 1996; DeVault, 1991; Erickson, 1993; Gager, 1998; Hawkins et al., 1995; Johnson & Huston, 1998; Kane & Sanchez, 1994; Piña & Bengtson, 1993; Stohs, 1994; Thompson, 1993). Although this symbolic equation of housework and care can lead to demands for more task performance, it can also encourage women to consider men's expressions of affection or positive intent as sufficient, thereby lowering their expectations and judging current unbalanced labor arrangements as fair (Hochschild, 1989). In addition, men's contributions to housework tend to be noticed and negotiated, whereas women's are taken for granted (Robinson & Spitze, 1992). As predicted, the selection and use of cross-gender referents seems to lead women to judge divisions of labor as less fair (Hawkins et al., 1995), whereas the selection of same-gender referents is associated with evaluations of greater fairness (Coltrane, 1990; Gager, 1998). In a related finding, invoking high housekeeping standards tends to provide justification for husbands' nonperformance of household tasks (Allen & Hawkins, 1998; Coltrane, 1996; Ferree, 1990; Hawkins et al., 1995).

Other studies consider fairness as a mediating, or intervening, variable between the division of household labor and personal or marital well-being (Dancer & Gilbert, 1993; Kluwer, Heesink, & Van de Vliert, 1996; Lennon & Rosenfield, 1994; Perry-Jenkins & Folk, 1994; Piña & Bengtson, 1993; Robinson & Spitze, 1992; Suitor, 1991; Ward, 1993; Wilkie et al., 1998). Wives are less satisfied with the division of labor when the actual time they spend on housework is higher than what they would prefer to spend (Kluwer et al., 1996). Fairness evaluations also affect personal well-being. When the distribution of household tasks appears to be fair, wives display few symptoms of depression, but when it is perceived as unfair, women's depression is higher (Glass & Fujimoto, 1994; Lennon & Rosenfield, 1994). Satisfaction with spousal help is positively associated with positive marital interaction, marital closeness, affirmation, and positive affect; it is negatively related to marital conflict, thoughts of divorce, negative affect, and depression (Piña & Bengtson, 1993). Similarly, although perceived unfairness predicts both unhappiness and distress for women, it predicts neither for men (Robinson & Spitze, 1992). Perceived fairness also contributes to marital satisfaction or marital quality, especially for women (Blair, 1993; Dancer & Gilbert, 1993; Suitor, 1991; Ward, 1993; Wilkie et al., 1998).

Spouses who hold more comparable perceptions of fairness also report higher marital satisfaction (Dancer & Gilbert, 1993). Wives' perceptions of unfairness also are related to marital conflict (Kluwer et al., 1996; Perry-Jenkins & Folk, 1994; Stohs, 1995), with those couples having more conventional gender ideology more likely to avoid conflict and experience negative consequences (Kluwer, Heesink, & Van de Vliert, 1997). Finally, dissatisfaction with the household division of labor may be a more important catalyst for change than perceptions of its unfairness. Men are almost universally satisfied with the division of housework, whereas women are often less satisfied, especially if they hold egalitarian attitudes and like their paid work (Baxter & Western, 1998). Although findings about fairness evaluations vary considerably, the majority of studies in the 1990s concluded that the single most important predictor of a wife's fairness evaluation is what portion of the routine housework her husband contributes.

Outcome Assessments

Divisions of household labor are directly and indirectly linked to depression. Although detailed outcome studies are still rare, research indicates that performing larger amounts of routine, repetitive housework is associated with more depression in women and sometimes in men (Barnett & Shen, 1997; Glass & Fujimoto, 1994; Golding, 1990; Larson et al., 1994). Previous studies finding no such relationship for men typically did not differentiate between types of household labor nor control for the frequency and schedule flexibility of the tasks (see Barnett & Shen, 1997). Some researchers have found that women's "homemaker-role quality" moderates the relationship between job stress and psychological well-being (Barnett, 1994; Kibria, Barnett, Baruch, Marshall, & Pleck, 1990). It appears that it is primarily men's participation in the routine repetitive chores of cooking, cleaning, and washing that relieves women's burden, contributes to their sense of fairness, and hence lowers their chances of being depressed. For their part, men often report some difficulty assuming more responsibility for family work, although initial frustration is typically short lived (Coltrane, 1996; Cowan & Cowan, 1992; Hawkins et al., 1994).

Several studies also have found that marital satisfaction increases in relation to the amount of routine housework that is shared by spouses (Biernat & Wortman, 1991; Erickson, 1993; Orbuch &

Eyster, 1997; Piña & Bengtson, 1993). Most studies find that the fit between husband's and wive's ideology is extremely important to marital satisfaction, as is the congruence between spouses' attitudes and actions. In general, if spouses align their attitudes and divisions of household labor, then their marital happiness is higher (McHale & Crouter, 1992; Perry-Jenkins & Crouter, 1990). Because men continue to do substantially less housework than do women, however, a gender-bifurcated pattern emerges: Women who believe in sharing housework tend to have lower marital satisfaction than others and men who believe in sharing tend to have higher marital satisfaction than others (Lye & Biblarz, 1993). Similarly, when men are more egalitarian than wives, marital disagreements are fewer, but when wives are more egalitarian than husbands (the more typical case), then marital disagreements are more common (Lye & Biblarz, 1993). Because housework is typically perceived as optional for men and required of women, it is generally up to women to bring about change. Only when women perceive the division of labor to be unfair, does the level of marital conflict go up (Blair, 1993; Perry-Jenkins & Folk, 1994; Wilkie et al., 1998). Marital conflict, in turn is related to lower marital satisfaction and higher rates of depression. Women are thus faced with a double bind: They can push for change, threatening the relationship, or they can accept an unbalanced division of labor, labeling it "fair" (Hochschild, 1989).

Children's Housework

Household labor studies of the 1990s were also more likely to include children. Questions were asked about how much and under what conditions sons and daughters perform housework and what impact such performance has for the children and families. Using NSFH data, Blair (1992a) reported that in families with school-aged children, 5.9 hours of routine housework are performed by (all) children each week, representing about 13% of the routine housework hours for the household (almost as much as contributed by fathers). Children do the work because parents are attempting to socialize them or because the parents (and children) are responding to household labor demand (Blair, 1992a; Gill, 1998; Goodnow et al., 1991). According to Goodnow et al. (1991), children's housework is analyzed according to gender, age of child, and purpose of the tasks—primarily in terms of self versus family care. Younger children's housework is less typed by gender than that of adults or teenagers (Hilton & Haldeman, 1991; McHale et al., 1990). As children approach the teenage years, however, they take on more tasks, which become more segregated by gender (Antill et al., 1996; Benin & Edwards, 1990; Goldscheider & Waite, 1991; Goodnow et al., 1991). Studies find that young teenage girls do about twice the amount of household labor as young teenage boys do (Juster & Stafford, 1991), with girls concentrating their efforts on routine inside chores of cooking and cleaning and boys concentrating their efforts on occasional outside chores such as yard care (Antill et al., 1996; Blair, 1992b; Goldscheider & Waite, 1991; McHale et al., 1990). Some researchers have found that children in two-parent, dual-earner families and children of highly educated parents do less housework than do children in other family types (Benin & Edwards, 1990; Demo & Acock, 1993; Manke et al., 1994; Waite & Goldscheider, 1992). Whereas girls in single-parent families often do all types of tasks and tend to put in more household work hours than girls in other family types, boys in single-parent families have been found to do less routine housework than boys in two-parent families (Hilton & Haldeman, 1991; McHale et al., 1990). If the mother's hours of employment are longer, children (especially girls) perform more of the housework, suggesting that daughters are substituting for the mother's hours (Bergen, 1991; Blair, 1992a; Goldscheider & Waite, 1991). Some studies also have suggested that daughters' housework time substitutes for fathers' housework time (Manke et al., 1994; Waite & Goldscheider, 1992; but see Padgett, 1997), although girls' participation in household tasks seems to be dwindling to boys' levels in many households (Goldscheider & Waite, 1991). Stepparents, parents with egalitarian gender ideology, and those who give their children more encouragement are more likely to have sons who share more of the routine housework (Antill et al., 1996; Blair, 1992b; Demo & Acock, 1993; Weisner & Garnier, 1994). Conversely, first-married biological parents and those with more conventional gender ideology are more likely to assign gender-typed tasks to their children and to require that daughters do more (Benin & Edwards, 1990; Blair, 1992b). Following a similar pattern, boys from dual-earner families who do more housework are more satisfied, less stressed, and have better relations with their parents, whereas boys from single-earner families who do more housework report being less satisfied, more stressed, and have worse relations with their parents (Crouter, McHale, & Bartko, 1993). Finally, adult sons living with their parents create more housework than they perform, whereas adult daughters perform more housework than they create (South & Spitze, 1994). In addition, Glenn (1992) discussed how privileged White children learn a subtle form of racism watching women of color perform the dirtiest domestic work.

CONCLUSION

In conclusion, most men still do much less housework than women do, with married men creating about as much demand for household labor as they perform. In the past decade, researchers have documented how women's contributions to housework have declined and shown how men's contributions have increased at a slower pace. Although we can better predict variation in women's performance of housework, we are just beginning to understand why men do so little and to specify the conditions associated with men doing more. We also have begun to isolate causes and consequences of various divisions of paid and unpaid labor for individuals, families, and society.

Women still perform most routine cooking and cleaning tasks, and although fewer men confine their efforts to the occasional outside chore, husbands rarely take full responsibility for a wide range of household tasks. We now know that when men perform more of the routine housework, employed women feel that the division of labor is fairer, are less depressed, and enjoy higher levels of marital satisfaction. Using refined measures and more representative samples, we also know that the employment hours of both men and women, their relative earnings, their beliefs about gender and family, and their living arrangements all influence the allocation of household tasks. Family size, age, life stage, ethnicity, presence and contribution of children, and a host of other factors also enter into the household labor allocation process. Although we cannot yet adjudicate between most competing theories, we are better able to understand that household labor embodies a set of complex material and symbolic practices that constitute and reproduce daily life. Because most housework continues to be performed by women, wives, and daughters, and because most women buy out of onerous domestic tasks when they can afford to, we ought not lose sight of the fact that domestic labor allocation is embedded in social arrangements that perpetuate class, race, and gender inequities. The task before us is thus to specify in more detail how the performance of housework in different families is implicated in various cultural, economic, and gender-reproductive processes. In particular, we need to do a better job of assessing contributions to routine chores in a wider range of households, use both absolute and proportional measures, and focus on how relative resources, gender ideology, interpersonal relations, and economic factors influence fairness evaluations and individual well-being. Only by refining our measurement and data analysis techniques, specifying linkages among different levels of analysis, and continuing to evaluate competing theoretical approaches will we be able to assess how and why household labor is associated with gender and how it might change in the future.

NOTE

I thank Michele Adams for expert research assistance.

REFERENCES

Abel, E. K., & Nelson, M. K. (1990). *Circles of care: Work and identity in women's lives.* Albany, NY: State University of New York Press.

Agger, B., & Shelton, B. A. (1993). Shotgun wedding, unhappy marriage, no-fault divorce? Rethinking the feminism-Marxism relationship. In P. England (Ed.), *Theory on gender/feminism on Theory* (pp. 25–41). New York: Aldine de Gruyter.

Ahlander, N. R., & Bahr, K. S. (1995). Beyond drudgery, power, and equity: Toward an expanded discourse on the moral dimensions of housework in families. *Journal of Marriage and the Family, 57,* 54–68.

Allen, S. M., & Hawkins, A. J. (1999). Maternal gatekeeping: Mothers beliefs and behaviors that inhibit greater father involvement in family work. *Journal of Marriage and the Family, 61,* 199–212.

Almeida, D. M., Maggs, J. L., & Galambos, N. L. (1993). Wives' employment hours and spousal participation in family work. *Journal of Family Psychology, 7,* 233–244.

Antill, J. K., Goodnow, J. J., Russell, G., & Cotton, S. (1996). The influence of parents and family context on children's involvement in household tasks. *Sex Roles: A Journal of Research, 34,* 215–236.

Baca Zinn, M. (1990). Family, feminism, and race. *Gender & Society, 4,* 68–82.

Bahr, K. S., & Ahlander, N. R. (1996). Morality, feminism, and family work—Reply. *Journal of Marriage and the Family, 58,* 520–525.

Barmby, T. (1994). Household labor supply: Some notes on estimating a model with Pareto optimal outcomes. *The Journal of Human Resources, 29,* 932–940.

Barnett, R. C. (1994). Home-to-work spillover revisited—a study of full-time employed women in dual-earner couples. *Journal of Marriage and the Family, 56,* 647–656.

Barnett, R. C., & Shen, Y.-C. (1997). Gender, high- and low-schedule-control housework tasks, and psychological distress: A study of dual-earner couples. *Journal of Family Issues, 18,* 403–428.

Baxter, J. (1993). *Work at home: The domestic division of labour.* Queensland, Australia: University of Queensland Press.

Baxter, J. (1997). Gender equality and participation in housework: A cross-national perspective. *Journal of Comparative Family Studies, 28,* 220–247.

Baxter, J., & Western, M. (1998). Satisfaction with housework: Examining the paradox. *Sociology, 32,* 101–120.

Becker, G. A. (1981). *A treatise on the family.* Cambridge, MA: Harvard University Press.

Beller, A. H. (1993). The division of labor by gender. *Rationality and Society, 5,* 398–407.

Benin, M. H., & Edwards, D. A. (1990). Adolescents&abos; chores: The difference between dual- and single-earner families. *Journal of Marriage and the Family, 52,* 361–373.

Bergen, E. (1991). The economic context of labor allocation: Implications for gender stratification. *Journal of Family Issues, 12,* 140–157.

Berk, R. A., & Berk, S. F. (1979). *Labor and leisure at home: The content and organization of the household day.* Beverly Hills, CA: Sage.

Berk, S. F. (1985). *The gender factory: The apportionment of work in American households.* New York: Plenum Press.

Bernard, J. (1972). *The future of marriage.* New York: World.

Bielby, D. D. (1993). Explaining gender stratification and inequality in the workplace. *Rationality and Society, 5,* 367–374.

Biernat, M., & Wortman, C. B. (1991). Sharing of home responsibilities between professionally employed women and their husbands. *Journal of Personality and Social Psychology, 60,* 844–860.

Bird, C. E., & Ross, C. E. (1993). Houseworkers and paid workers: Qualities of the work and effects on personal control. *Journal of Marriage and the Family, 55,* 913–925.

Blain, J. (1994). Discourses of agency and domestic labor: Family discourse and gendered practice in dual-earner families. *Journal of Family Issues, 15,* 515–549.

Blair, S. L. (1992a). Children's participation in household labor: Child socialization versus the need for household labor. *Journal of Youth and Adolescence, 21,* 241–258.

Blair, S. L. (1992b). The sex-typing of childrens' household labor: Parental influence on daughters' and sons' housework. *Youth and Society, 24,* 178–203.

Blair, S. L., (1993). Employment, family, and perceptions of marital quality among husbands and wives. *Journal of Family Issues, 14,* 189–212.

Blair, S. L., & Johnson, M. P. (1992). Wives' perceptions of the fairness of the division of household labor: The intersection of housework and ideology. *Journal of Marriage and the Family, 54,* 570–581.

Blair, S. L., & Lichter, D. T. (1991). Measuring the division of household labor: Gender segregation of housework among American couples. *Journal of Family Issues, 12,* 91–113.

Blood, R. O., & Wolfe, D. M. (1960). *Husbands and wives.* New York: Free Press.

Blumberg, R. L., & Coleman, M. T. (1989). A theoretical look at the balance of power in the American couple. *Journal of Family Issues, 10,* 225–250.

Bolak, H. C. (1997). When wives are major providers: Culture, gender, and family work. *Gender & Society, 11,* 409–433.

Bonney, N., & Reinach, E. (1993). Housework reconsidered: The Oakley thesis 20 years later. *Work, Employment, and Society, 7,* 615–627.

Braverman, L. (1991). The dilemma of housework: A feminist response to Gottman, Napier, and Pittman. *Journal of Marital and Family Therapy, 17,* 25–28.

Brayfield, A. A. (1992). Employment resources and housework in Canada. *Journal of Marriage and the Family, 54,* 19–30.

Brines, J. (1993). The exchange value of housework. *Rationality and Society, 5,* 302–340.

Brines, J. (1994). Economic dependency, gender, and the division of labor at home. *American Journal of Sociology, 100,* 652–688.

Broman, L. L. (1991). Gender, work, family roles, and psychological well-being of Blacks. *Journal of Marriage and the Family, 53,* 509–520.

Calasanti, T. M., & Bailey, C. A. (1991). Gender inequality and the division of household labor in the United States and Sweden: A socialist-feminist approach. *Social Problems, 38,* 34–53.

Cancian, F., & Oliker, S. (1999). *Gender and care.* Newbury Park, CA: Sage.

Chafetz, J. S. (1990). *Gender equity: An integrated theory of stability and change.* Newbury Park, CA: Sage.

Chafetz, J. S., & Hagan, J. H. (1996). The gender division of labor and family change in industrial societies: A theoretical accounting. *Journal of Comparative Family Studies, 27,* 187–216.

Cohen, P. N. (1998). Replacing housework in the service economy: Gender, class, and race-ethnicity in service spending. *Gender & Society, 12,* 219–231.

Collins, R., Chafetz, J. S., Blumberg, R. L., Coltrane, S., & Turner, J. (1993). Toward an integrated theory of gender stratification. *Sociological Perspectives, 36,* 185–216.

Coltrane, S. (1989). Household labor and the routine production of gender. *Social Problems, 36,* 473–490.

Coltrane, S. (1990). Birth timing and the division of labor in dual-earner families: Exploratory findings and suggestions for future research. *Journal of Family Issues, 11,* 157–181.

Coltrane, S. (1996). *Family man: Fatherhood, housework, and gender equity.* New York: Oxford University Press.

Coltrane, S. (1998). *Gender & Families.* Newbury Park, CA: Pine Forge Press.

Coltrane, S., & Ishii-Kuntz, M. (1992). Men's housework: A life-course perspective. *Journal of Marriage and the Family, 54,* 43–57.

Coltrane, S. & Valdez, E. (1993). Reluctant compliance: Work/family role allocation in dual-earner Chicano families. In J. C. Hood (Ed.), *Men, work and family* (pp. 151–175). Newbury Park, CA: Sage.

Cowan, C. P., & Cowan, P. A. (1992). *When partners become parents: The big life change for couples.* New York: Basic Books.

Crouter, A. C., McHale, S. M., & Bartko, W. T. (1993). Gender as an organizing feature in parent-child relationships. *Journal of Social Issues,* 161–174.

Curtis, R. F., & MacCorquodale, P. (1990). Stability and change in gender relations. *Sociological Theory, 8,* 136–152.

Dancer, L. S., & Gilbert, L. A. (1993). Spouses' family work participation and its relation to wives' occupational level. *Sex Roles: A Journal of Research, 28,* 127–145.

DeMaris, A., & Longmore, M. A. (1996). Ideology, power, and equity: Testing competing explanations for the perception of fairness in household labor. *Social Forces, 74,* 1043–1071.

DeMeis, D. K., & Perkins, H. W. (1996). "Supermoms" of the nineties: Homemaker and employed mothers' performance and perceptions of the motherhood role. *Journal of Family Issues, 17,* 776–792.

Demo, D. H., & Acock, A. C. (1993). Family diversity and the division of domestic labor: How much have things really changed? *Family Relations, 42,* 323–331.

Deutsch, F. M., Lussier, J. B., & Servis, L. J. (1993). Husbands at home: Predictors of paternal participation in childcare and housework. *Journal of Personality and Social Psychology, 65,* 1154–1166.

DeVault, M. (1990). Conflict over housework: A problem that (still) has no name. In L. Kriesberg (Ed.), *Research in social movements, conflict, and change.* Greenwich, CT: JAI Press.

DeVault, M. (1991). *Feeding the family: The social organization of caring and gendered work.* Chicago: University of Chicago Press.

Doucet, A. (1995). Gender equality and gender differences in household work and parenting. *Women's Studies International Forum, 18,* 271–284.

England, P., & Farkas, G. (1986). Households, employment, and gender: A social, economic, and demographic view. New York: Aldine.

Erickson, R. J. (1993). Reconceptualizing family work: The effect of emotion work on perceptions of marital quality. *Journal of Marriage and the Family, 55,* 888–900.

Fassinger, P. A. (1993). Meanings of housework for single fathers and mothers. In J. Hood (Ed), *Men, Work, and Family* (pp. 195–216). Newbury Park, CA: Sage.

Fenstermaker, S. (1996). The dynamics of time use. *Journal of Family and Economic Issues, 17,* 231–243.

Ferree, M. M. (1990). Beyond separate spheres: Feminism and family research. *Journal of Marriage and the Family, 52,* 866–884.

Ferree, M. M. (1991). The gender division of labor in two-earner marriages: Dimensions of variability and change. *Journal of Family Issues, 12,* 158–180.

Fish, L. S., New, R. S., & Van Cleave, N. J. (1992). Shared parenting in dual-income families. *American Orthopsychiatric Association, Inc. 62,* 83–92.

Folbre, N., & Wagman, B. (1993). Counting housework: New estimates of real product in the United States, 1800–1860. *Journal of Economic History, 53,* 275–288.

Gager, C. T. (1998). The role of valued outcomes, justifications, and comparison referents in perceptions of fairness among dual-earner couples. *Journal of Family Issues, 19,* 622–649.

Gallagher, S. K. (1994). Doing their share—comparing patterns of help given by older and younger adults. *Journal of Marriage and the Family, 56,* 567–578.

Gerson, K. (1993). *No man's land: Men's changing commitment to family and work.* New York: Basic Books.

Gerstel, N., & Gallagher, S. (1994). Caring for kith and kin: Gender, employment, and the privatization of care. *Social Problems, 41,* 519–539.

Geurts, J., & De Ree, J. (1993). Influence of research design on time use estimates. *Social Indicators Research, 30,* 245–284.

Giddings, L. A. (1998). Political economy and the construction of gender: The example of housework within same-sex households. *Feminist Economics, 4,* 97–106.

Gill, G. K. (1998). The strategic involvement of children in housework: An Australian case of two-income families. *International Journal of Comparative Sociology, 39,* 301–314.

Glass, J., & Camarigg, V. (1992). Gender, parenthood, and job-family compatibility. *American Journal of Sociology, 98,* 131–151.

Glass, J., & Fujimoto, T. (1994). Housework, paid work, and depression among husbands and wives. *Journal of Health and Social Behavior, 35,* 179–191.

Glenn, E. N. (1992). From servitude to service work: Historical continuities in the racial division of paid reproductive labor. *Signs: Journal of Women in Culture and Society, 18,* 1–43.

Glenn, N. (1997). *Closed hearts, closed minds: The textbook story of marriage.* New York: Institute for American Values.

Golding, J. M. (1990). Division of household labor, strain, and depressive symptoms among Mexican Americans and Non-Hispanic Whites. *Psychology of Women Quarterly, 14,* 103–117.

Goldscheider, F. K., & Waite, L. J. (1991). *New families, no families?* Berkeley, CA: University of California Press.

Goodnow, J. J. (1988). Children's housework: Its nature and functions. *Psychological Bulletin, 163,* 5–26.

Goodnow, J. J., Bowes, J. M., Warton, P. M., Dawes, L. J., & Taylor, A. J. (1991). Would you ask someone else to do this task? Parents' and children's ideas about household work requests. *Developmental Psychology, 27,* 817–828.

Graham, H. (1991). The concept of caring in feminist research: The case of domestic service. *Sociology, 25,* 61–79.

Greenstein, T. N. (1996a). Husbands' participation in domestic labor: Interactive effects of wives' and husbands' gender ideologies. *Journal of Marriage and the Family, 58,* 585–595.

Greenstein, T. N. (1996b). Gender ideology and perceptions of the fairness of the division of household labor: Effects on marital quality. *Social Forces, 74,* 1029–1042.

Gunter, N. C., & Gunter, B. G. (1990). Domestic division of labor among working couples: Does androgyny make a difference. *Psychology of Women Quarterly, 14,* 355–370.

Gupta, S. (1999). The effects of marital status transitions on men's housework performance. *Journal of Marriage and the Family, 61,* 700–711.

Haas, L. (1992). *Equal parenthood and social policy.* Albany, NY: SUNY Press.

Haddad, T. (1994). Men's contribution to family work:

A re-examination of "time-availability." *International Journal of Sociology of the Family, 24,* 87–111.

Hakim, C. (1996). The sexual division of labour and women's heterogeneity. *British Journal of Sociology, 47,* 178–188.

Hall, L. D., Walker, A. J., & Acock, A. C. (1995). Gender and family work in one-parent households. *Journal of Marriage and the Family, 57,* 685–692.

Harrell, W. A. (1995). Husband's involvement in housework: Effects of relative earning power and masculine orientation. *Psychological Reports, 77,* 1331–1337.

Hartmann, H. (1981). The family as the locus of gender, class, and political struggle: The example of housework. *Signs: Journal of Women in Culture and Society, 6,* 366–394.

Hartmann, H. (1993). Comment on the exchange value of housework and theories of gender stratification. *Rationality and Society, 5,* 375–385.

Harvey, A. S. (1993). Guidelines for time use data collection. *Social Indicators Research, 30,* 197–228.

Hawkins, A. J., Marshall, C. M., & Allen, S. M. (1998). The orientation toward domestic labor questionnaire: Exploring dual-earner wives' sense of fairness about family work. *Journal of Family Psychology, 12,* 244–258.

Hawkins, A. J., Marshall, C. M., & Meiners, K. M. (1995). Exploring wives' sense of fairness about family work: An initial test of the distributive-justice framework. *Journal of Family Issues, 16,* 693–721.

Hawkins, A. J., & Roberts, T.-A. (1992). Designing a primary intervention to help dual-earner couples share housework and child care. *Family Relations, 41,* 169–177.

Hawkins, A. J., Roberts, T.-A., Christiansen, S. L., & Marshall, C. M. (1994). An evaluation of a program to help dual-earner couples share the second shift. *Family Relations, 43,* 213–220.

Hays, S. (1996). *The cultural contradictions of motherhood.* New Haven, CT: Yale University Press.

Heath, J. A. (1990). Non-employed women, marriage and the Sisyphus Syndrome. *Journal of Economic Issues, 24,* 103–114.

Heath, J. A., & Bourne, W. D. (1995). Husbands and housework: Parity or parody. *Social Science Quarterly, 76,* 195–202.

Heath, J. A., Ciscel, D. H., & Sharp, D. C. (1998). Too many hours–too little pay: The impact of market and household hours on women's work lives. *Journal of Economic Issues, 32,* 587–594.

Herrera, R. S., & del Campo, R. L. (1995). Beyond the superwoman syndrome: Work satisfaction and family functioning among working-class, Mexican American women. *Hispanic Journal of Behavioral Sciences, 17,* 49–60.

Hersch, J., & Stratton, L. S. (1997). Housework, fixed effects, and wages of married workers. *Journal of Human Resources, 32,* 285–307.

Hersch, J., & Stratton, L. S. (1994). Housework, wages, and the division of housework time for employed spouses. *American Economic Review, 84,* 120–125.

Hilton, J. M., & Haldeman, V. A. (1991). Gender differences in the performance of household tasks by adults and children in single-parent and two-parent, two-earner families. *Journal of Family Issues, 12,* 114–130.

Hochschild, A. R. (1997). *The time bind.* New York: Holt.

Hochschild, A. R., with Machung, A. (1989). *The second shift.* New York: Avon.

Hondagneu-Sotelo, P. (1992). Overcoming patriarchal constraints: The reconstruction of gender relations among Mexican immigrant women and men. *Gender & Society, 6,* 393–415.

Hood, J. C. (1983). *Becoming a two-job family.* New York: Praeger.

Hood, J. C. (1993). *Men, work, and family.* Newbury Park, CA: Sage.

Hossain, Z., & Roopnarine, J. L. (1993). Division of household labor and child care in dual-earner African-American families with infants. *Sex Roles, 29,* 571–583.

Ishii-Kuntz, M., & Coltrane, S. (1992a). Predicting the sharing of household labor: Are parenting and housework distinct? *Sociological Perspectives, 35,* 629–647.

Ishii-Kuntz, M., & Coltrane, S. (1992b). Remarriage, stepparenting, and household labor. *Journal of Family Issues, 13,* 215–233.

Jackson, S. (1992). Towards a historical sociology of housework: A materialist feminist analysis. *Women's Studies International Forum, 15,* 153–172.

Jacobs, J. (1993). Economic and sociological explanations of gender inequality. *Rationality and Society, 5,* 386–397.

John, D., & Shelton, B. A. (1997). The production of gender among Black and White women and men: The case of household labor. *Sex Roles: A Journal of Research, 36,* 171–193.

John, D., Shelton, B. A., & Luschen, K. (1995). Race, ethnicity, gender and perceptions of fairness. *Journal of Family Issues, 16,* 357–379.

Johnson, E. M., & Huston, T. L. (1998). The perils of love, or why wives adapt to husbands during the transition to parenthood. *Journal of Marriage and the Family, 60,* 195–204.

Johnson, P. J. (1998). Performance of household tasks by Vietnamese and Laotian refugees: Tradition and change. *Journal of Family Issues, 19,* 245–273.

Juster, F. T., & Stafford, F. P. (1991). The allocation of time: Empirical findings, behavioral models, and problems of measurement. *Journal of Economic Literature, 29,* 471–522.

Kalleberg, A. L., & Rosenfeld, R. A. (1990). Work in the family and in the labor market: A cross-national, reciprocal analysis. *Journal of Marriage and the Family, 52,* 331–346.

Kamo, Y. (1991). A non-linear effect of the number of children on the division of household labor. *Sociological Perspectives, 34,* 205–218.

Kamo, Y. (1994). Division of household work in the United States and Japan. *Journal of Family Issues, 15,* 348–378.

Kane, E. W., & Sanchez, L. (1994). Family status and criticism of gender inequality at home and work. *Social Forces, 72,* 1079–1102.

Kibria, N., Barnett, R. C., Baruch, G. K., Marshall, N. L., & Pleck, J. H. (1990). Homemaking-role quality and the psychological well-being and distress of employed women. *Sex Roles: A Journal of Research, 22,* 327–347.

Kiger, G., & Riley, P. J. (1996). Gender differences in perceptions of household labor. *The Journal of Psychology, 130,* 357–370.

Kluwer, E. S., Heesink, J. A. M., & Van de Vliert, E. (1996). Marital conflict about the division of household labor and paid work. *Journal of Marriage and the Family, 58,* 958–969.

Kluwer, E. S., Heesink, J. A. M., & Van de Vliert, E. (1997). The marital dynamics of conflict over the division of labor. *Journal of Marriage and the Family, 59,* 635–653.

Komter, A. (1989). Hidden power in marriage. *Gender & Society, 3,* 187–216.

Kooreman, P., & Kapteyn, A. (1990). On the empirical implementation of some game theoretic models of household labor supply. *The Journal of Human Resources, 25,* 584–598.

Kurdek, L. A. (1993). The allocation of household labor in gay, lesbian, and heterosexual married couples. *Journal of Social Issues, 49,* 127–139.

Kynaston, C. (1996). The everyday exploitation of women: Housework and the patriarchal mode of production. *Women's Studies International Forum, 19,* 221–237.

Larson, R. W., & Almeida, D. M. (1999). Emotional transmission in the daily lives of families: A new paradigm for studying family process. *Journal of Marriage and the Family 61,* 5–20.

Larson, R. W., Richards, M. H., & Perry-Jenkins, M. (1994). Divergent worlds: The daily emotional experience of mothers and fathers in the domestic and public spheres. *Journal of Personality and Social Psychology, 67,* 1034–1046.

Lennon, M. C., & Rosenfield, S. (1994). Relative fairness and the division of housework: The importance of options. *American Journal of Sociology, 100,* 506–531.

Lye, D. N., & Biblarz, T. J. (1993). The effects of attitudes toward family life and gender roles on marital satisfaction. *Journal of Family Issues, 14,* 157–188.

MacDermid, S. M., Huston, T. L., & McHale, S. M. (1990). Changes in marriage associated with the transition to parenthood: Individual differences as a function of sex-role attitudes and changes in the division of household labor. *Journal of Marriage and the Family, 52,* 475–486.

Major, B. (1987). Gender, justice, and the psychology of entitlement. P. Shaver & C. Hendricks (Eds.), *Review of personality and social psychology (pp. 124–140).* Newbury Park, CA: Sage.

Major, B. (1993). Gender, entitlement, and the distribution of family labor. *Journal of Social Issues, 49,* 141–159.

Manke, B. S. B. L., Crouter, A. C., & McHale, S. M. (1994). The three corners of domestic labor: Mother's, father's, and children's weekday and weekend housework. *Journal of Marriage and the Family, 56,* 657–668.

Marini, M. M., & Shelton, B. A. (1993). Measuring household work: Recent experience in the United States. *Social Science Research, 22,* 361–382.

Massey, G., Hahn, K., & Sekulic Dusko. (1995). Women, men and the "second shift" in socialist Yugoslavia. *Gender & Society, 9,* 359–379.

McHale, S. M., Bartko, W. T., Crouter, A. C., & Perry-Jenkins, M. (1990). Children's housework and psychosocial functioning: The mediating effects of parents' sex-role behaviors and attitudes. *Child Development, 61,* 1413–1426.

McHale, S. M., & Crouter, A. C. (1992). You can't always get what you want—incongruence between sex-role attitudes and family work roles and its implications for marriage. *Journal of Marriage and the Family, 54,* 537–547.

Mederer, H. J. (1993). Division of labor in two-earner homes: Task accomplishment versus household maintenance as critical variables in perceptions about family work. *Journal of Marriage and the Family, 55,* 133–145.

Mederer, H. J., & Weinstein, L. (1992). Choices and constraints in a two-person career: Ideology, division of labor, and well-being among submarine officers' wives. *Journal of Family Issues, 13,* 334–350.

Milkie, M., & Peltola, P. (1999). Playing all the roles: Gender and the work-family balancing act. *Journal of Marriage and the Family, 61,* 476–490.

Miller, J., & Garrison, H. H. (1982). Sex roles: The division of labor at home and in the workplace. *Annual Review of Sociology, 8,* 237–262.

Mintz, R. D., & Mahalik, J. R. (1996). Gender role orientation and conflict as predictors of family roles for men. *Sex Roles: A Journal of Research, 34,* 805–821.

Miraftab, F. (1994). (Re)production at home: Reconceptualizing home and family. *Journal of Family Issues, 15,* 467–489.

Mirande, A. (1997). Hombres et Machos: Masculinity and Latino Culture. Boulder, CO: Westview.

Nakhaie, M. R. (1995). Housework in Canada: The national picture. *Journal of Comparative Family Studies, 26,* 409–429.

Nicol, C. J., & Nakamura, A. (1994). Labor supply and child status effects on household demands. *The Journal of Human Resources, 29,* 588–599.

Niemi, I. (1993). Systematic error in behavioral measurement: Comparing results from interview and time budget studies. *Social IndicatorsResearch, 30,* 229–244.

Nock, S. (1998). *Marriage in men's lives.* New York: Oxford University Press.

Oakley, A. (1974). *The sociology of housework.* New York: Pantheon.

Okin, S. M. (1989). *Justice, gender, and the family.* New York: Basic Books.

Orbuch, T. L., & Eyster, S. L. (1997). Division of household labor among Black couples and White couples. *Social Forces, 76,* 301–332.

Oropesa, R. S. (1993). Using the service economy to relieve the double burden: Female labor force participation and service purchases. *Journal of Family Issues, 14,* 438–473.

Osmond, M. W., & Thorne, B. (1993). Feminist theories: The social construction of gender in families and society. In P. G. Boss, W. J. Doherty, R. LaRossa, W. R. Shumm, & S. K. Steinmetz (Eds.), *Sourcebook of family theories and methods* (pp. 591–623). New York: Plenum.

Padgett, D. L. (1997). The contribution of support networks to household labor in African American families. *Journal of Family Issues, 18,* 227–250.

Palmer, P. (1989). *Domesticity and dirt: Housewives and domestic servants in the United States, 1920–1945.* Philadelphia: Temple University Press.

Perkins, H. W., & DeMeis, D. K. (1996). Gender and family effects on the second-shift domestic activity of college-educated young adult. *Gender & Society, 10,* 78–93.

Perry-Jenkins, M., & Crouter, A. C. (1990). Men's provider-role attitudes: Implications for household work and marital satisfaction. *Journal of Family Issues, 11,* 136–156.

Perry-Jenkins, M., & Folk, K. (1994). Class, couples, and conflict: Effects of the division of labor on assessments of marriage in dual-earner families. *Journal of Marriage and the Family, 56,* 165–180.

Perry-Jenkins, M., Seery, B., & Crouter, A. C. (1992). Linkages between women's provider-role attitudes, psychological well-being, and family relationships. *Psychology of Women Quarterly, 16,* 311–329.

Pestello, F. G., & Voydanoff, P. (1991). In search of mesostructure in the family: An interactionist approach to division of labor. *Symbolic Interaction, 14,* 105–128.

Peterson, R. R., & Gerson, K. (1993). A social-structural explanation of mens' and womens' domestic responsibility. *Journal of Marriage and the Family, 55,* 508–510.

Piña, D. L., & Bengtson, V. L. (1993). The division of household labor and wive's happiness—Ideology, employment, and perceptions of support. *Journal of Marriage and the Family, 55,* 901–912.

Piña, D. L., & Bengtson, V. L. (1995). Division of household labor and the well-being of retirement-aged wives. *The Gerontologist, 35,* 308–317.

Pittman, J. F., & Blanchard, D. (1996). The effects of work history and timing of marriage on the division of household labor: A life-course perspective. *Journal of Marriage and the Family, 58,* 78–90.

Pittman, J. F., Solheim, C. A., & Blanchard, D. (1996). Stress as a driver of the allocation of housework. *Journal of Marriage and the Family, 58,* 456–468.

Popenoe, D. (1996). Life without father: Compelling new evidence that fatherhood and marriage are indispensable for the good of children and society. New York: Martin Kessler/Free Press.

Potuchek, J. L. (1992). Employed wives' orientations to breadwinning: A gender theory analysis. *Journal of Marriage and the Family, 54,* 548–558.

Press, J. E., & Townsley, E. (1998). Wives' and husbands' housework reporting: Gender, class, and social desirability. *Gender & Society, 12,* 188–218.

Presscr, H. B. (1994). Employment schedules among dual-earner spouses and the division of household labor by gender. *American Sociological Review, 59,* 348–364.

Pyke, K., & Coltrane, S. (1996). Entitlement, obligation, and gratitude in family work. *Journal of Family Issues, 17,* 60–82.

Rasmussen, K. S., Hawkins, A. J., & Schwab, K. P. (1996). Increasing husband's involvement in domestic labor: Issues for therapists. *Contemporary Family Therapy, 18,* 209–223.

Ribbens, J., & Edwards, R. (1995). Introducing qualitative research on women in families and households. *Women's Studies International Forum, 18,* 247–258.

Risman, B. J., & Johnson-Sumerford, D. (1998). Doing it fairly: A study of postgender marriages. *Journal of Marriage and the Family, 60,* 23–40.

Robinson, J. (1977). *How Americans use time.* New York: Praeger.

Robinson, J., & Spitze, G. (1992). Whistle while you work? The effect of household task performance on women's and men's well-being. *Social Science Quarterly, 73,* 844–861.

Robinson, J., & Godbey, G. (1997). *Time for life.* University Park, PA: Pennsylvania State University Press.

Robinson, J. P., & Milkie, M. (1997). Dances with dust bunnies: Housecleaning in America. *American Demographics, 59,* 37–40.

Robinson, J. P., & Milkie, M. A. (1998). Back to the basics: Trends in and role determinants of women's attitudes toward housework. *Journal of Marriage and the Family, 60,* 205–218.

Romero, M. (1992). *Maid in the U.S.A.* New York: Routledge.

Ross, C. E., & Mirowsky, J. (1992). Households, employment, and the sense of control. *Social Psychology Quarterly, 55,* 217–235.

Rubin, L. (1994). *Families on the fault line.* New York: Harper.

Sanchez, L. (1993). Women's power and the gendered division of domestic labor in the third-world. *Gender & Society, 7,* 434–459.

Sanchez, L. (1994a). Gender, labor allocations, and the psychology of entitlement within the home. *Social Forces, 73,* 533–553.

Sanchez, L. (1994b). Material resources, family structure resources, and husband's housework participation: A cross-national comparison. *Journal of Family Issues, 15,* 379–402.

Sanchez, L. (1996). Feminism, family work, and moral discourse—Beyond drudgery, power, and equity—Comment. *Journal of Marriage and the Family, 58,* 514–520.

Sanchez, L., & Kane, E. W. (1996). Women's and men's constructions of perceptions of housework fairness. *Journal of Family Issues, 17,* 358–387.

Sanchez, L., & Thomson, E. (1997). Becoming mothers and fathers: Parenthood, gender, and the division of labor. *Gender & Society, 11,* 747–772.

Schor, J. (1991). *The overworked American.* New York: BasicBooks.

Shelton, B. A. (1990). The distribution of household tasks: Does wife's employment status make a difference? *Journal of Family Issues, 11,* 115–135.

Shelton, B. A. (1992). *Women, men and time: Gender differences in paid work, housework and leisure* (Contributions in Women's Studies 127). New York: Greenwood Press.

Shelton, B. A., & John, D. (1993a). Does marital status make a difference? Housework among married and cohabiting men and women. *Journal of Family Issues, 14,* 401–420.

Shelton, B. A., & John, D. (1993b). Ethnicity, race, and difference: A comparison of White, Black, and Hispanic men's household labor time. In J. C. Hood (Ed.), *Men, work, and family* (pp. 131–150). Newbury Park, CA: Sage.

Shelton, B. A., & John, D. (1996). The division of household labor. *Annual Review of Sociology, 22,* 299–322.

Siegel, R. B. (1998). Valuing housework: Nineteenth-century anxieties about the commodification of domestic labor. *American Behavioral Scientist, 41,* 1437–1451.

Silver, H., & Goldscheider, F. (1994). Flexible work and housework: Work and family constraints on women's domestic labor. *Social Forces, 72,* 1103–1119.

Smith, H. L., Gager, C. T., & Morgan, S. P. (1998). Identifying underlying dimensions in spouses' evaluations of fairness in the division of household labor. *Social Science Research, 27,* 305–327.

South, S. J., & Spitze, G. (1994). Housework in marital and nonmarital households. *American Sociological Review, 59,* 327–347.

Spain, D., & Bianchi, S. (1996). *Balancing act: Motherhood, marriage and employment among American women.* New York: Russell Sage Foundation.

Spitze, G., & Ward, R. (1995). Household labor in intergenerational households. *Journal of Marriage and the Family, 57,* 355–361.

Stacey, J. (1996). *In the name of the family: Rethinking family values in the postmodern age.* Boston: Beacon Press.

Starrels, M. E. (1994). Husbands' involvement in female gender-typed household chores. *Sex Roles: A Journal of Research, 31,* 473–491.

Steil, J. M., & Weltman, K. (1991). Marital inequality: The importance of resources, personal attributes, and social norms on career valuing and the allocation of domestic responsibilitie. *Sex Roles: A Journal of Research, 24,* 161–179.

Stohs, J. H. (1994). Alternative ethics in employed women's household labor. *Journal of Family Issues, 15,* 550–561.

Stohs, J. H. (1995). Predictors of conflict over the household division of labor among women employed full-time. *Sex Roles: A Journal of Research, 33,* 257–275.

Strober, M. H., & Chan, A. M. K. (1998). Husbands, wives, and housework: Graduates of Stanford and Tokyo universities. *Feminist Economics, 4,* 97–127.

Suitor, J. J. (1991). Marital quality and satisfaction with the division of household labor across the family life cycle. *Journal of Marriage and the Family, 53,* 221–230.

Sullivan, O. (1997). The division of housework among "remarried" couples. *Journal of Family Issues, 18,* 205–223.

Szinovacz, M. (1987). Family power. In M. Sussman & S. Steinmetz (Eds.), *Handbook of Marriage and the Family.* New York: Plenum.

Szinovacz, M. (1992). Is housework good for retirees? *Family Relations, 41,* 230–238.

Szinovacz, M., & Harpster, P. (1994). Couples' employment/retirement status and the division of household tasks. *Journals of Gerontology, 49,* S125–S137.

Thompson, L. (1991). Family work: Women's sense of fairness. *Journal of Family Issues, 12,* 181–196.

Thompson, L. (1993). Conceptualizing gender in marriage: The case of marital care. *Journal of Marriage and the Family, 55,* 557–569.

Thompson, L., & Walker, A. J. (1989). Gender in families: Women and men in marriage, work, and parenthood. *Journal of Marriage and the Family, 51,* 845–871.

Tronto, J. C. (1993). *Moral boundaries: A political argument for an ethic of care.* New York: Routledge.

Twiggs, J. E., McQuillan, J., & Ferree, M. M. (1999). Meaning and measurement: Reconceptualizing measures of the division of household labor. *Journal of Marriage and the Family, 61,* 712–724.

Vanek, J. (1974). Time spent in housework. *Scientific American, 231,* 116–120.

Van der Lippe, T., & Siegers, J. J. (1994). Division of household and paid labour between partners: Effects of relative wage rates and social norms. *KYKLOS, 47,* 109–136.

VanEvery, J. (1997). Understanding gendered inequality: Reconceptualizing housework. *Women's Studies International Forum, 20,* 411–420.

Waite, L., & Goldscheider, F. K. (1992). Work in the home: The productive context of family relationships. S. J. South, & S. E. Tolnay (Eds.), *The changing American family* (pp. 267–299). Boulder, CO: Westview.

Ward, R. A. (1993). Marital happiness and household equity in later life. *Journal of Marriage and the Family, 55,* 427–438.

Weisner, T. S., & Garnier, H. (1994). Domestic tasks, gender egalitarian values and children's gender typing in conventional and nonconventional families. *Sex Roles: A Journal of Research, 30,* 23–54.

West, C., & Fenstermaker, S. (1993). Power and the accomplishment of gender. In P. England (Ed.), *Theory on gender/feminism on theory* (pp. 151–174). New York: Aldine de Gruyter.

Wharton, C. S. (1994). Finding time for the "Second Shift": The impact of flexible work schedules on women's double days. *Gender & Society, 8,* 189–205.

Wilkie, J. R., Ferree, M. M., & Ratcliff, K. S. (1998). Gender and fairness: Marital satisfaction in two-earner couples. *Journal of Marriage and the Family, 60,* 577–594.

Wilson, M. N., Tolson, T. F. J., Hinton, I. D., & Kiernan, M. (1990). Flexibility and sharing of childcare duties in Black families. *Sex Roles: A Journal of Research, 22,* 409–425.

Wright, E. O., Shire, K., Hwang, S.-L., Dolan, M., & Baxter, J. (1992). The non-effects of class on the gender division of labor in the home: A comparative study of Sweden and the United States. *Gender & Society, 6,* 252–282.

Zvonkovic, A. M., Greaves, K. M., Schmiege, C. J., & Hall, L. D. (1996). The marital construction of gender through work and family decisions: A qualitative analysis. *Journal of Marriage and the Family, 58,* 91–100.

JAY D. TEACHMAN, LUCKY M. TEDROW, AND KYLE D. CROWDER
Western Washington University

The Changing Demography of America's Families

We use data from a variety of sources to describe recent dramatic changes in the composition, economic stability, and diversity of American families. The declining prevalence of early marriage, increasing level of marital dissolution, and growing tendency to never marry, especially among some racial and ethnic groups, reflect changes in the relative economic prospects of men and women and support the conclusion that marriage is becoming less valued as a source of economic stability. These developments also imply that relatively more children are born outside of marriage, spend at least part of their childhood in a single-parent household, and endure multiple changes in family composition. Paralleling these trends have been sharp changes in the economic stability of families, characterized most notably by a growing importance of women's income and increasing economic inequality among American families.

The American family has never been static. On the 50th anniversary of *Journal of Marriage and the Family,* Glick (1988) outlined a series of studies that detailed long-term changes in marriage, divorce, remarriage, childbearing, cohabitation, and household structure, using the family life cycle as an organizing principle for understanding these changes. Glick has been joined by others in detailing the fluidity of family-related events as individuals and families respond to the opportu-

Demographic Research Laboratory, Department of Sociology, Western Washington University, Bellingham, WA 98225-9081 (teachman@cc.wwu.edu).

Key Words: demography of families, family change, family economic status, family trends.

nities and constraints presented by the fortunes of war, the economy, and underlying shifts in values.

Continued change in patterns of fertility, nuptiality, and divorce has prompted some scholars to speculate about the future of the American family. Citing the loss of functions to other institutions, some researchers have argued that the family is in decline (Popenoe, 1988, 1993; Skolnick, 1991) and have warned that its demise holds negative consequences for all Americans. Other authors are more sanguine and have simply noted that change is inevitable and may even be for the best, especially for women (Stacey, 1990, 1993). In this article, we provide more fuel for this heated debate by outlining continued change in the family over the past 3 decades with attention to variations by race and ethnicity.

DEFINING THE FAMILY

America is made up of a multiplicity of family types including two-parent families, one-parent families, cohabiting couples, gay and lesbian families, and extended-family households. Unfortunately, comparable, national-level data are not available to track variation in each of these family types across time and important social characteristics such as race and social class. We are forced by our need for comparable, high-quality data to make use of official statistics that all assume a legal definition of marriage and the family. The census defines a family as "a group of two persons or more (one of whom is a householder) related by birth, marriage or adoption and residing together" (U.S. Bureau of the Census, 1998c). A married couple is defined as a "husband and wife

FIGURE 1. Rates of Marriage and Divorce in the United States: 1940-1996. Source: U.S. Bureau of the Census (1999).

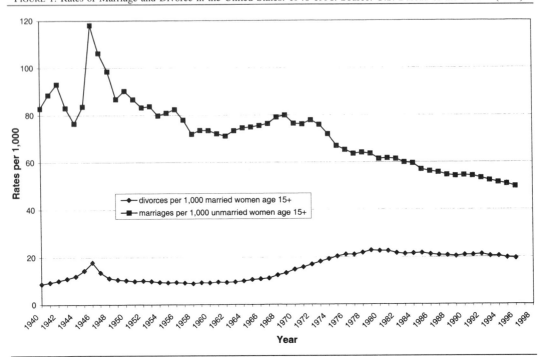

enumerated as members of the same household." An unmarried couple is defined as "two unrelated adults of the opposite sex (one of whom is the householder) who share a housing unit with or without the presence of children under 15 years old." Among the limitations of this definition is the fact that equating families with households inevitably ignores increasingly common family relationships that extend across households. Similarly, the definition precludes the examination of increasingly common unmarried but cohabiting couples.

Even within the official definition of what constitutes a family, we are further limited by the fact that information is often not available for some subgroups of the population. For example, it is difficult to obtain information about Native American or Asian American families (particularly data that allow a perspective across time) simply because the requisite questions have not been asked. The information we do have about finely grained subgroups of the American population is too often based on anecdote and small, nonrepresentative samples. These data limitations are unfortunate because available research indicates that family change takes different forms and proceeds at different rates across race and ethnic groups (Bennett, Bloom, & Craig, 1992; Cherlin, 1992; Tucker & Mitchell-Kernan, 1995).

Changes in Marriage, Divorce, and Remarriage

Long-term shifts in rates of marriage and divorce from 1940 to 1998 are shown in Figure 1. There has been a reasonably consistent decline in the rate of first marriage since the end of World War II. By the middle of the 1990s, the rate of marriage was as low or lower than observed during the Great Depression. The rate of divorce has evidenced a slow, but steady increase over the period covered. The increase in the divorce rate was particularly great over the 1970s but has slowed considerably since then.

The trends shown in Figure 1 indicate a general decline over time in the early formation of marriages and an increase over time in the dissolution of marriages. In patterns mirroring those occurring in most Western, industrialized nations (Kammerman, 1995), rates of marriage in the United States have decreased since the late 1940s, whereas rates of divorce have increased (with a flattening of the rate of divorce in recent years).

FIGURE 2. Percent of Women 20–24 Ever Married: 1975–1998. Source: U.S. Bureau of the Census (1996a, 1998c).

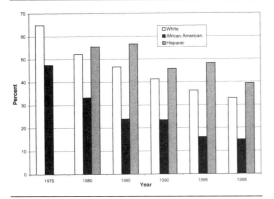

Marriage

Figure 2 provides a more detailed description of the changes in marriage that have occurred during the last 25 years. Because Figures 2 represent trends within a specific age group, it is unaffected by shifts in the age structure of the American population. This is not true of Figure 1. Thus, at least part of the shifts in rates shown in Figure 1 can be attributed to changes in age structure (changes in race and ethnicity and educational composition could also play a role in these shifts). For example, some of the upswing in divorce during the 1970s can be attributed to the substantial increase in marriages of short duration (where the risk of divorce is high) associated with the first marriages of members of the baby boom cohort.

Figure 2 shows the trend in the percent of women aged 20 to 24 by race or ethnic status who are ever married. The changes illustrated are dramatic. Among Whites, the percent of women aged 20 to 24 ever married declined by about 32 percentage points between 1975 and 1998. By 1998, only one third of White women this age had married. Among African Americans, the decline between 1975 and 1998 was also about 32 percentage points. The end result of this decline was much more dramatic than it was for Whites, however, simply because the prevalence of marriage among young African American women was already substantially lower at the beginning of this time period. Thus, by the late 1990s only 15% of African American women aged 20 to 24 had ever married.

The observed change in the prevalence of marriage among Hispanic women has been much more moderate. The percentage of Hispanic wom-

en aged 20 to 24 ever married changed little between 1980 and 1985 (data on Hispanics are not available before 1980). Between 1985 and 1990, however, Hispanics witnessed a decline of about 11 percentage points in the share of women in this age group who had ever married. Between 1990 and 1995, the percentage ever married rose slightly before experiencing another 9-percentage-point drop between 1995 and 1998. Still, Hispanic women in the 1990s are more likely than either Whites or African Americans to have formed a marriage by age 20 to 24.

Recent decades have also been characterized by group-specific changes in the percentage of women remaining single into their mid-30s. Historically, only a small fraction of women not married by age 35 to 39 subsequently marry (Rodgers & Thornton, 1985; Schoen, 1987), so changes in the percentage not ever married by this age imply changes in permanent singlehood. Of course, this basic conclusion does not take into consideration the percent of women who form nonmarital unions. As discussed later, part of the decline in marriage has been matched by an increase in the rate at which nonmarital unions are formed.

For Whites, there has been relatively little change in the likelihood of permanent singlehood over the past 20 years. Between 1975 and 1998, the percentage ever married among White women aged 35 to 39 declined by only about 7 percentage points. Similar modest declines among Hispanic women are also evident. For African Americans, however, there has been a much more substantial change in the likelihood of permanent singlehood. The percent of women ever married by age 35 to 39 has declined from nearly 90% in 1975 to just over 65% in 1998. This result implies that nearly one in three African American women may never marry.

The available evidence is consistent in showing a retreat from early marriage and a decline in marriage overall for African American women. What factors might explain these trends? First, some authors have suggested that the rise of the welfare state has negated the economic role of marriage, particularly for low-income women (Murray, 1984). Although this argument would seem to be consistent with the decline in early marriage, especially for low-income women, and the overall retreat from marriage for African American women, supporting evidence is weak. Few researchers have found consistent evidence that welfare benefits reduce the likelihood of marriage (Moffitt, 1990, 1992; Schultz, 1994). Those researchers who have found an effect have not found it to be substantively important (Lichter, LeClere, & McLaughlin, 1991; McLanahan & Casper, 1995). Moreover, rates of marriage have continued to decline at the same time the value of Aid to Families with Dependent Children (AFDC) benefits have fallen dramatically (Schultz). The most consistent evidence for a welfare effect is that it appears to encourage young unmarried women who become pregnant to set up their own households rather than remain at home with their parents (Moffitt, 1994).

Second, it has been proposed that an increasing value placed on individualism by Americans has decreased the perceived benefits of marriage (Bellah, Madsen, Swidler, Sullivan, & Tipton, 1985; South, 1992). Cherlin (1992) provided a compelling discussion of the role that African American culture plays in mediating the effects of larger structural constraints and opportunities on rates of African American marriage. Although attractive in its power and simplicity, this argument is nonetheless difficult to test empirically.

Third, growth in the economic independence of women and decline in the economic power of men have been emphasized in two interrelated arguments concerning changes in marriage patterns. Both arguments assume that one of the major functions of marriage is to provide economic security, particularly for the bearing and raising of children. Becker (1981) has argued that the exchange between home and market production has become increasingly threatened by the growing ability of women to support themselves outside marriage. At the same time, Wilson (1987, 1996) has argued that the decline in job opportunities for young African American men, particularly in inner cities, has sharply diminished their ability to form and support a family. In concert with Wilson's argument, other researchers have documented the declining economic prospects of young men, both African American and White, who came of age in the 1970s and 1980s (Duncan, Boisjoly, & Smeeding, 1996; Levy & Murnane, 1992).

The changing economic fortunes of men and women appear to offer a testable explanation of changes in the likelihood of marriage across time, as well as observed marital differences between Whites and African Americans. McLanahan and Casper (1995) found that among Whites, marriage is more common when men are employed and have more education and higher incomes. Conversely, marriage is less common among Whites

when women are employed and have more education and higher incomes. The result is that increases in female earning power explain about 70% of the recent decline in marriage for White women with another 8% of the decline explained by the stagnant earning power of White men.

Among African Americans, however, neither the increased earning power of women, nor the decreased earning power of men explains much of the decline in marriage (McLanahan & Casper, 1995). Just as important as the differential impacts of these variables by race is McLanahan and Casper's finding that race-specific economic characteristics explain little of the overall African American–White difference in the propensity to marry. Other recent research on the economic position of men and women supports the same conclusion— that the race differential in marriage cannot be explained by race differences in the relative economic position of men and women (Ellwood & Crane, 1990; Levy & Michael, 1991).

Given these findings, one is tempted to return to arguments such as differences in the value of marriage to explain persistent race differentials in marital formation. Before doing so, however, additional structural factors affecting marriage need to be considered. In particular, the availability of suitable spouses in a local marriage market has been presented as an important determinant of marital behavior (Lichter et al., 1991; Lichter, McLaughlin, Kephart, & Landry, 1992; South & Lloyd, 1992). According to this argument, marriage depends not only on one's personal characteristics but also on the availability of suitable spouses and on the characteristics of others competing for those potential spouses.

A number of studies have shown that after accounting for individual characteristics, the availability of economically attractive men (men with steady employment) is positively linked to rates of marriage for women (Lichter et al., 1991, 1992; South & Lloyd, 1992). It is possible, therefore, that the source of the African American–White differential in marriage may lie in the character of the marriage markets in which they are located, if not their individual characteristics. For instance, African American women tend to live in areas (often measured at the level of a metropolitan community) in which the deficit of economically attractive potential mates is much more pronounced than it is in areas occupied by White women (Fossett & Kiecolt, 1991; Lichter et al., 1992). Indeed, the true heart of Wilson's (1987, 1996) argument was that it is the decline in the pool of "marriageable" men in local marriage markets that has led to the retreat from marriage among African Americans.

Lichter et al. (1992) showed that differences in local marriage markets do more to explain race differences in marriage than do individual characteristics. About one fifth of the existing race differential in rates of marriage can be explained by the more restrictive marriage market conditions faced by African American women in comparison to those faced by Whites. Similar results have been provided by other researchers (Mare & Winship, 1991; South & Lloyd, 1992; Testa, Astone, Krogh, & Neckerman, 1991).

Two additional issues complicate efforts to pinpoint race differences in marriage. First, nonmarital cohabitation has increased substantially in recent years, and African Americans are more likely to cohabit nonmaritally than are Whites (Schoen & Owens, 1992). Indeed, considering nonmarital cohabitation along with marital unions, race differences in union formation are substantially reduced (Bumpass, Sweet, & Cherlin, 1991; Qian & Preston, 1993; Raley, 1996).

Nonmarital unions are much less stable than marital unions, however, and African Americans are less likely than Whites to convert a nonmarital union into marriage (Manning & Smock, 1995; Schoen & Owens, 1992). Thus, the fact that racial differences in union formation are less pronounced when nonmarital unions are considered does not necessarily imply that African Americans and Whites have similar experiences in terms of either the number or the duration of their unions. Nor is it clear that nonmarital unions fulfill the same functions as marital unions (Brown & Booth, 1996; Nock, 1995; Rindfuss & Vanden-Heuvel, 1990).

A second issue confounding the interpretation of race differences in marriage is that there is some evidence that more recent cohorts of women have responded differently to their economic independence than earlier cohorts of women. That is, although early evidence suggested that a woman's participation in the labor market and her higher wages tended to reduce the likelihood that she married (Espenshade, 1985; Farley & Bianchi, 1987; Lichter et al., 1991; Teachman, Polonko, & Leigh, 1987), evidence for more recent cohorts of women suggests that these factors now have the reverse effect (Lichter et al., 1992).

These findings imply that marriage is contextualized not only by local marriage markets, but also by historical period. Among more recent co-

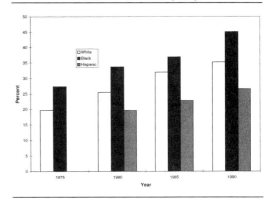

FIGURE 3. Percent of Ever-Married Women 40–44 Divorced: 1975, 1980, 1985, and 1990. Source: U.S. Bureau of the Census (1992).

horts of women, financial resources may facilitate the transition to marriage by making women more attractive as potential mates or providing the resources to support a marriage. In part, this finding likely stems from the stagnant or declining economic prospects of young men (Duncan et al., 1996).

Divorce

We now shift attention to a consideration of marital stability. We begin with a simple yet useful assumption. If one assumes that marriage is becoming less valued and less important as a source of economic stability and exchange, it makes sense to expect an increase in marital dissolution in addition to a retreat from early marriage. Figure 3 clearly indicates that such a decline in marital stability has taken place in recent decades. The proportion of ever-married women divorced from their first marriage by age 40 to 44 rose sharply between 1975 and 1990 for all three race and ethnic groups for which we have data. (Although the use of this measure misses women who end their first marriage at older ages, Figure 3 accurately portrays general trends in divorce).

For Whites, the increase was particularly large from 1975 to 1985 (from 20% to 32%) with some slowing in the 1985–1990 period (32% to 35%). For African Americans, the increase in the percent divorced has been more steady, rising from slightly less than 30% in 1975 to 45% in 1990. Hispanic women have also experienced an increase in the percent of women aged 40 to 44 divorced from their first marriage (from just less than 20% in 1980 to around 27% in 1990).

Remarriage

The growing prevalence of divorce after first marriage has been matched by a pronounced decline in the percent of women remarrying after their divorce. For Whites, the percent of women who were remarried by age 40 to 44 declined from 71.9% in 1975 to 67.5% in 1985 before rebounding slightly to 69.5% by 1990. The trends for African American women follow a similar pattern but with a much sharper decline in remarriage between 1975 and 1985 (from 57% to 45%). In comparison to Whites, both African American and Hispanic women experienced a more pronounced increase in the level of remarriage between 1985 and 1990 (from 45% to 50% for African Americans and from 51% to 54% for Hispanic women).

Most of the arguments concerning changes in these demographic behaviors mirror those put forward with respect to the formation of marriages (Becker, 1981; Becker, Landes, & Michael, 1977; Espenshade, 1985; Grossbard-Shiechtman, 1993; South & Spitze, 1986). Indeed, one of the most active areas of research concerning marital stability is a consideration of the influence of husbands' and wives' economic resources (Greenstein, 1990, 1995; Heckert, Nowak, & Snyder, 1998; Hoffman & Duncan, 1995; Ono, 1998). This research suggests that wives' earnings have a nonlinear, U-shaped relationship with marital dissolution that varies according to the level of husbands' earnings and each spouses' gender ideology.

This is not to say that all factors related to marital dissolution and remarriage are identical to those for marital formation. Clearly, aspects of marital interaction and experience that affect the likelihood of marital dissolution have little influence on union formation (Glenn, 1990, 1998; Orbuch, House, Mero, & Webster, 1996). There appear to be elements of common influence, however, especially with respect to the opportunities and constraints imposed by changing social and economic conditions. There is even evidence that characteristics of local marriage markets also affect the likelihood of divorce through variations in the availability of economically attractive marriage partners (South & Lloyd, 1995).

Changes in the Context of Childbearing and Childrearing

As American women spend a smaller fraction of their childbearing years in marriage, the opportunity for nonmarital childbearing increases. Thus, recent changes in marital behavior alone should lead to concomitant increases in the proportion of children born outside of marriage. Indeed, the data indicate that the relative number of births occurring to unmarried mothers has increased in recent decades, and racial differences in nonmarital childbearing mirror race differentials in marital behavior. In 1995, about 25% of White births occurred outside of marriage, compared with 41% of Hispanic births and 70% of African American births. Just 15 years earlier, these figures were 14.5% for Whites, 29.5% for Hispanics, and 60% for African Americans (U.S. Bureau of the Census, 1998a).

The proportion of births that are nonmarital is determined by the rates of both marital fertility and nonmarital fertility. For example, a drop in marital fertility will lead to a greater proportion of births occurring outside of marriage even if the rate of nonmarital fertility remains constant (Smith & Cutright, 1988; Smith, Morgan, & Koropeckyj-Cox, 1996). For African Americans, the increase in the proportion of births that are nonmarital has resulted from the fact that rates of marital fertility have declined more rapidly than rates of nonmarital fertility (National Center for Health Statistics, 1995a). For Whites, the rate of nonmarital childbearing has increased consistently across time. While marital fertility has declined for Whites as well, the increase in the rate of nonmarital fertility has played a stronger role in determining the increasing proportion of nonmarital births over time (National Center for Health Statistics, 1995a).

What does the increasing proportion of nonmarital births, combined with the retreat from early and stable marriage, imply for the living arrangements of children? Figure 4 indicates that the proportion of children living with a single parent at any given point in time has increased markedly over time. In 1970, nearly 90% of White children lived with two parents (biological, adopted, or stepparents). This figure dropped to just 74% by 1998. A similar trend has occurred for Hispanic children, with a decline from just under 78% to about 64% between 1970 and 1998. The percent for African American children fell from under 60 in 1970 to about 36 in 1998.

The statistics in Figure 4 reflect the impact of out-of-wedlock childbearing and the formation and dissolution of marriages by parents on the living arrangements of their children at a given point in time. This series of snapshots, however, does not reflect the fact that over time children move

FIGURE 4. Percent of Children Under 18 Living With Two Parents: 1970–1980. Source: U.S. Bureau of the Census (1996b, 1998c).

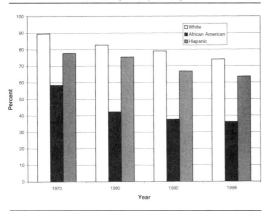

FIGURE 5. Childhood Living Arrangements of Women: 1950–1954, 1960–1964, and 1970–1974 Birth Cohorts by Race. Source: Author Tabulations from the 1995 National Survey of Family Growth.

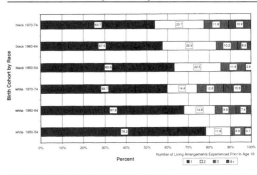

into and out of several different family types as a function of these events. Taking these life-course changes into account, nearly 50% of White children and two thirds of African American children are likely to spend at least part of their childhood in a single-parent family (Bumpass & Sweet, 1989; Martin & Bumpass, 1989), often with detrimental consequences (McLanahan & Sandefur, 1994).

A growing body of literature indicates that change in childhood living arrangements, beyond any effect associated with experiencing a single-parent family, is also detrimental to the well-being of children (An, Haveman, & Wolfe, 1993; Cherlin et al., 1991; Seltzer, 1994; Wu, 1996). The changes we have outlined in marriage, divorce, and remarriage imply that an increasing percentage of children are experiencing change in their childhood living arrangements. We illustrate this point in Figure 5 using data from the 1995 National Survey of Family Growth (National Center for Health Statistics, 1998). These data provide information on a wide range of different living arrangements experienced by women when they were children, including living with two biological parents, a parent and stepparent, a single parent of either gender, a parent who cohabited, grandparents, other relatives, and group living quarters.

For women born in the period from 1950 to 1954, about 22% of White women and 37% of African American women experienced more than one living arrangement during their childhood before age 19. For women born between 1960 and 1964, these figures were 32% and 43%, respec-

tively. For women born between 1970 and 1974, 40% of White women and 46% African American women had experienced more than one living arrangement while growing up. For the youngest cohort of women, roughly 25% of both Whites and African Americans experienced three or more childhood living arrangements.

The combined impact of the retreat from marriage and the shifting context of childbearing and childrearing on changes in the composition of American households is shown in Figure 6. (Although part of the change in household structure shown in Figure 6 may be attributed to change in the age structure of the American population, this effect is likely to be small; Santi, 1988). In 1970, about 40% of all households consisted of a married couple with at least one child living in the household. This share declined to just under 26% by 1998. There were substantial increases in the percent of households made up of persons living alone and other families with children (mainly households headed by a single woman). Other,

FIGURE 6. Household Composition: 1970–1998. Source: U.S. Bureau of the Census (1995, 1998c).

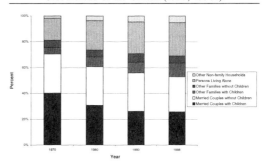

FIGURE 7. Median Income of Families: 1970–1997.
Source: U.S. Bureau of the Census (1998b).

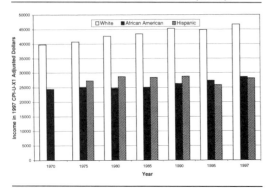

FIGURE 8. Median Family Income by Family Type:
1970–1997. Source: U.S. Bureau of the Census (1998a,
1998b).

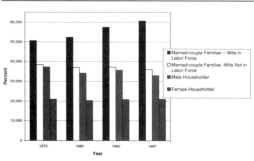

nonfamily households (nonrelated individuals living together) also witnessed a gain during recent decades.

Married couples have declined as a fraction of all households, from over 70% in 1970 to just 53% in 1998. The percent of nonfamily households has increased along with the relative number of families that do not include a married couple. In sum, the changes in marriage, divorce, remarriage, and childbearing discussed earlier have resulted in increased diversity in the types of households to be found in America. Consideration of the growing number of stepparent families, which is not reflected separately in Figure 6, adds to this diversity.

The Changing Economic Fortune of America's Families

We begin the discussion of the economic well-being of America's families by presenting information on their median income from 1970 to 1997 in Figure 7. For White families, there has been a modest upward shift in median income, from just under $40,000 in 1970 (in constant 1997 dollars) to just under $47,000 in 1997. This represents a gain of about 17.5% over a 27-year period, or about .65% per year.

For African American families, median income also increased slightly from about $24,400 in 1970 to $28,600 in 1997. This change represents an increase of about 17.2% over the 27-year period, or .64% annually. The increase in median income for Hispanic families was even more modest, going from just over $27,000 in 1975 to just over $28,000 in 1997 for an annual increase of only .14%. Thus, whereas Hispanic families

earned slightly more than African American families in 1975, this ordering had reversed by 1997.

Most of the gain in median family income during recent decades has been constrained to families where either the husband or wife has a college education. For example, the 1997 median family income of families in which the highest level of education was a high school degree was $40,040. For families in which at least one member had a college degree, the 1997 median income was $73,578, 84% higher than in 1970.

Income by family type over the period 1970 to 1997 in constant 1997 dollars is presented in Figure 8. Married-couple families in which the wife was in the labor force increased their income from just under $51,000 to nearly $61,000, or about 20%. In contrast, married couples without the wife in the labor force not only had consistently lower levels of income in comparison to two-earner families, but actually experienced a slight decline in their median income between 1970 and 1997 (from $38,441 to $36,027 or about −6.3%). These data suggest that the increase in median family income shown in Figure 7 was driven in large part by increases in the income of married-couple families in which the wife was employed.

One of the most striking features of Figure 8 is the very poor and remarkably constant economic position of families headed by women. In 1970, these families earned slightly more than $21,000 (in constant 1997 dollars), a figure that was virtually unchanged by 1997. Although the income of single male-headed families (male householder families) remains higher than for single female-headed families (female householder families), this group also lost ground over the past 27 years (from about $37,234 to $32,960, or about −11.5%).

FIGURE 9. Labor Force Participation Rates of Men and Women Aged 16–64: 1960–1997. Source: U.S. Bureau of the Census (1998a, 1998b).

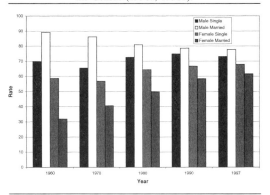

FIGURE 10. Median Income of Men and Women With Earnings: 1970–1997 by Race. Source: U.S. Bureau of the Census (1998a, 1998b).

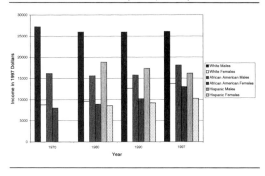

The increasing importance of women's income to the family can be traced to differences in the labor-market fortunes of men and women. We consider two dimensions of labor-market experience, changes in the rate of labor force participation and changes in income among those in the labor force. Figure 9 outlines the changes in labor force participation for men and women aged 16 to 64. The figure indicates a steady decline in the participation of married men in the labor force, from just under 90% in 1960 to about 78% in 1997, reflecting in part the increased coverage of American men by pension plans and social security (Wise, 1997). In contrast, there has been a rush of married women into the labor force. In 1960, about three out of 10 married women worked for pay. In 1997, this figure had grown to more than 6 out of 10 married women. Compared with married women, married men were 2.8 times more likely to be in the labor force in 1960, but only 1.3 times more likely to be in the labor force in 1997. Figure 9 is interesting because it indicates a decline in the ability to predict labor force participation based on gender and marital status.

Figure 10 sketches changes in the income of men and women by race and ethnicity over the period 1970 to 1997 (in constant 1997 dollars). In 1970, the median income of White men was about $27,200. In 1997, this figure had declined to just over $26,100. A decline in income also occurred for Hispanic men, from about $18,800 in 1980 to about $16,200 in 1997. The median income for African American men remained virtually constant between 1970 and 1990, fluctuating slightly around $16,000. By 1997, however, the median

income for African American men with earnings had increased to just over $18,000.

Among women, there has been a steady increase in median earnings for Whites, African Americans, and Hispanics. The increased labor force participation and income for women is especially interesting in light of the declines over the past 3 decades in the level of labor force participation of men and their relatively stagnant or declining incomes. The combination of these trends points to the growing importance of wives' income to the economic survival of families.

These changes in the distribution of family income illustrated in Figures 7–10 have corresponded with a more general trend toward greater wage inequality in America (Danziger & Gottschalk, 1993, 1995; Fischer et al., 1996; McFate, Lawson, & Wilson, 1995). In 1980, the poorest fifth of families earned 5.3% of all income. In 1996, this value had fallen to 4.2% (U.S. Bureau of the Census, 1998b). In contrast, in 1980, the richest fifth of families earned 41.1% of all income, a value that grew to 46.8% in 1996. The richest 5% of American families increased their share of all income from 14.6% to 20.3% over the same period.

Not only is the distribution of family income becoming more unequal, but also the richest families are getting richer, and the poorest families are getting poorer. That is, the growth in inequality is not simply the result of rich families gaining income more rapidly than poor families. In 1980, the upper income limit for the poorest fifth of families was $19,827 in constant 1996 dollars (U.S. Bureau of the Census, 1998b). By 1996, the upper limit for the poorest families had fallen to $19,680. In contrast, the lower income limit for the richest fifth of families increased from $66,344 in 1980 to $75,316 in 1996.

Karoly and Burtless (1995) reported that family income at the lowest levels has fallen for two reasons. First, there has been an increase in single-parent families headed by persons with low skills and low incomes. That is, the number of families at the lowest end of the income scale is growing more rapidly than the number of higher-income families. Second, there has been an increase in income inequality among men, such that men at the lower end of the distribution have seen their wages fall (see Figure 10). Thus, families at the lower end of the income distribution either do not have access to male earnings or have seen these earnings decrease over time.

At higher income levels, family income has grown because of two factors. First, the income of men at the upper end of the distribution has grown substantially. Second, employed women tend to be concentrated in higher income families. This latter fact is consistent with increases in the educational homogamy (i.e., positive assortative mating) of marriages over time (Mare, 1991), and means that valued labor market skills are increasingly concentrated in two-earner families. Karoly (1993) also reported that income inequality increased more among African American and Hispanic families than among White families across the 1970s and 1980s.

The economic health of American families is also reflected in the percent of families with incomes below the poverty line. Trends in this level of family poverty point to several striking facts. First, there was a substantial reduction in poverty for both African Americans and Whites over the decade of the 1960s, reflecting the increases in income among the poorest Americans under Lyndon Johnson's Great Society programs. In just 10 years, the percent of African American Americans with incomes below the poverty line fell nearly 20 percentage points, going from 54.9% in 1960 to 32.2% in 1970. For White Americans, the poverty rate was halved, from 16.2% in 1960 to 8.1% in 1970.

The second interesting fact is the overwhelming stability of rates of poverty for most groups since 1970. For both Whites and Hispanics, the percentage of families below the poverty line has changed very little for a period of almost 30 years. Among Hispanic families, the rate has fluctuated around 25% at least since 1980, whereas the rate for White families is much lower but has remained constant at about 8 to 9% since 1970.

In a similar fashion, the poverty rate among Black families remained virtually unchanged between 1970 and 1990. In contrast to the stable poverty rates for White and Hispanic families, however, the percent of Black families living in poverty dropped sharply during the 1990s. After hovering at close to 31% for the previous 20 years, the Black poverty rate fell to just under 24% between 1990 and 1997. These most recent statistics indicate that the level of Black poverty is now actually below that of Hispanics (24.7%), although still almost 3 times the level among White families (8.4%).

This recent decline in the rate of family poverty among Blacks provides an interesting contrast to evidence indicating a decline in the economic standing of the lowest fifth of the income distribution and a corresponding increase in the level of income inequality. This contrast appears to indicate that, although the nation's recent economic expansion has allowed a larger number of Black families to rise above the poverty threshold, it has apparently done little to improve the economic conditions of the most destitute. Understanding the intricacies of changing levels of poverty and the expanding economic inequality among American families continues to be considered an important goal for future research.

DISCUSSION

Clearly, the past quarter century has seen increased diversity in the demographic structure of American families. There has been a retreat from universal early marriage, and among some groups, particularly African Americans, there has been a retreat from marriage altogether. In addition, fewer households are composed of families, and of family households, an increasing proportion are not composed of two parents living with their children. It is no longer the case that a child born today can expect to live his or her childhood with both biological parents.

How can we make sense of the changes that have occurred to America's families? Part of the answer appears to lie in a rapid shift in the economic environment facing families. Economic stagnation and growing uncertainty about the economic future has plagued young men, whereas economic opportunities have increased for young women. These changes have made it extremely difficult for young men and women to achieve the type of family modeled by their parents or grandparents. These economic changes reflect a continuation of long-term shifts in production and family roles associated with the industrial revolution (Goode, 1963).

Men and women have had to renegotiate taken-for-granted assumptions about the division of economic and household labor, as well as their notions about acceptable economic security. The period of renegotiation has been difficult, as witnessed by the substantial delay in marriage, the rise in the divorce rate, and declining stability in the living arrangements of children. Nonetheless, there are small signs that new types of families may be emerging. For example, female employment now seems to be encouraging marriage rather than discouraging it (Lichter et al., 1992). Younger men also appear to be more willing to accept an egalitarian division of labor, reducing the terrible work burden often facing wives in dual-earner families (Goldscheider & Waite, 1991).

At the same time as there is evidence of new families forming, substantial challenges to marriage remain among the most economically deprived Americans. At the extreme, poverty and lack of economic opportunity remain barriers to a productive and fulfilling family (Massey, 1996; Wilson, 1987). The retreat of public support for education and the dubious impact of ongoing welfare reform make the future even more uncertain for individuals at the lowest ranks of the income distribution. It is among these individuals that the threat of family decline remains most salient.

NOTE

This article is based on a chapter by Teachman, J. (2000): The social and economic context of increasing demographic diversity of families. In D. Demo, K. Allen, & M. Fine (Eds.), *Handbook of family diversity* (pp. 32–58). New York: Oxford University Press.

REFERENCES

An, C., Haveman, R., & Wolfe, B. (1993). Teen out-of-wedlock births and welfare receipt: The role of childhood events and economic circumstances. *Review of Economics and Statistics, 75,* 195–208.

Becker, G. (1981). *A treatise on the family.* Cambridge, MA: Harvard University Press.

Becker, G., Landes, E., & Michael, R. (1977). An economic analysis of marital instability. *Journal of Political Economy, 85,* 1141–1187.

Bellah, R., Madsen, R., Swidler, A., Sullivan, W., & Tipton, S. (1985). *Habits of the heart: Individualism and commitment in American life.* Berkeley: University of California Press.

Bennett, N., Bloom, D., & Craig, P. (1992). American marriage patterns in transition. In S. South & S. Tolnay (Eds.), *The changing American family* (pp. 89–108). Boulder, CO: Westview Press.

Brown, S. L., & Booth, A. (1996). Cohabitation versus marriage: A comparison of relationship quality. *Journal of Marriage and the Family, 58,* 668–78.

Bumpass, L., & Sweet, J. (1989). Children's experience in single-parent families: Implications of cohabitation and marital transitions. *Family Planning Perspectives, 21,* 256–260.

Bumpass, L, Sweet, J., & Cherlin, A. (1991). The role of cohabitation in declining rates of marriage. *Journal of Marriage and the Family, 53,* 913–927.

Cherlin, A. (1992). *Marriage, divorce, remarriage* (rev. ed.). Cambridge, MA: Harvard University Press.

Cherlin, A., Furstenberg, F., Lindsay Chase-Lansdale, P., Kiernan, K., Robins, P., Morrison, D., & Teitler, J. (1991). Longitudinal studies of effects of divorce on children in Great Britain and the United States. *Science, 252,* 1386–1389.

Danziger, S., & Gottschalk, P. (1993). *Uneven tides: Rising Inequality in America.* New York: Russell Sage Foundation.

Danziger, S., & Gottschalk, P. (1995). *American unequal.* Cambridge, MA: Harvard University Press.

Duncan, G., Boisjoly, J., & Smeeding, T. (1996). Economic mobility of young workers in the 1970s and 1980s. *Demography, 33,* 497–509.

Ellwood, D., & Crane, J. (1990). Family change among African American Americans: What do we know? *Journal of Economic Perspectives, 4,* 65–84.

Espenshade, T. (1985). Marriage trends in America: Estimates, implications and underlying causes. *Population and Development Review, 11,* 193–245.

Farley, R., & Bianchi, S. (1987). The growing racial difference in marriage and family patterns (Research report No. 87–107). Ann Arbor: Population Studies Center, University of Michigan.

Fischer, C., Hout, M., Jankowski, M., Lucas, S., Swidler, A., & Voss, K. (1996). *Inequality by design: Cracking the bell curve myth.* Princeton, NJ: Princeton University Press.

Fossett, M., & Kiecolt, J. (1991). A methodological review of the sex ratio: Alternatives for comparative research. *Journal of Marriage and the Family, 53,* 941–957.

Glenn, N. (1990). Quantitative research on marital quality in the 1980s: A critical review. *Journal of Marriage and the Family, 52,* 818–831.

Glenn, N. (1998). The course of marital success and failure in five American 10-year marriage cohorts. *Journal of Marriage and the Family, 60,* 569–576.

Glick, P. (1988). Fifty years of family demography: A record of social change. *Journal of Marriage and the Family, 50,* 861–874.

Goldscheider, L., & Waite, L. (1991). *New families, no families? The transformation of the American home.* Berkeley: University of California Press.

Goode, W. (1963). *World revolution and family patterns.* New York: Free Press.

Greenstein, T. (1990). Marital disruption and the employment of married women. *Journal of Marriage and the Family, 52,* 657–676.

Greenstein, T. (1995). Gender ideology, marital disruption, and the employment of married women. *Journal of Marriage and the Family, 57,* 31–42.

Grossbard-Shiechtman, S. (1993). *On the economics of marriage: A theory of marriage, labor and divorce.* Boulder, CO: Westview Press.

Heckert, A., Nowak, T., & Snyder, K. (1998). The impact of husbands' and wives' relative earnings on marital disruption. *Journal of Marriage and the Family, 60,* 690–703.

Hoffman, S., & Duncan, G. (1995). The effect of wages and AFDC benefits on marital disruption. *Journal of Human Resources, 30,* 19–41.

Kammerman, S. (1995). Gender role and family structure changes in the advanced industrialized west: Implications for social policy. In K. McFate, R. Lawson, & W. Wilson (Eds.), *Poverty, inequality and the future of social policy: Western states in the new world order* (pp. 231–256). New York: Russell Sage Foundation.

Karoly, L. (1993). The trend in inequality among families, individuals, and workers in the United States: A twenty-five year perspective. In S. Danziger & P. Gottschalk (Eds.), *Uneven tides: Rising inequality in America* (pp. 19–97). New York: Russell Sage Foundation.

Karoly, L., & Burtless, G. (1995). Demographic change, rising earnings inequality, and the distribution of personal well-being, 1959–1989. *Demography, 32,* 379–405.

Levy, F., & Michael, R. (1991). *The economic future of American families: Income and wealth trends.* Washington, DC: Urban Institute.

Levy, F., & Murnane, R. (1992). U. S. earnings levels and earnings inequality: A review of recent trends and proposed explanations. *Journal of Economic Literature, 30,* 1333–1381.

Lichter, D., LeClere, F., & McLaughlin. (1991). Local marriage markets and the marital behavior of African American and White women. *American Journal of Sociology, 96,* 843–867.

Lichter, D., McLaughlin, D., Kephart, G., & Landry, D. (1992). Race and the retreat from marriage: A shortage of marriageable men? *American Sociological Review, 57,* 781–799.

Manning, W., & Smock, P. (1995). Why marry? Race and the transition to marriage among cohabitors. *Demography, 32,* 509–520.

Mare, R. (1991). Five decades of educational assortative mating. *American Sociological Review, 56,* 15–32.

Mare, R., & Winship, C. (1991). Socioeconomic change and the decline of marriage for Blacks and Whites. In C. Jencks & P. Peterson (Eds.), *The urban underclass* (Pp. 175–202). Washington, DC: Urban Institute Press.

Martin, T., & Bumpass, L. (1989). Recent trends in marital disruption. *Demography, 26,* 37–51.

Massey, D. (1996). The age of extremes: Concentrated affluence and poverty in the twenty-first century. *Demography, 33,* 395–412.

McFate, K., Lawson, R., & Wilson, W. (1995). *Poverty, inequality and the future of social policy: Western states in the new world order.* New York: Russell Sage Foundation.

McLanahan, S., & Casper, L. (1995). Growing diversity and inequality in the American family. In R. Farley (Ed.), *State of the union: America in the 1990s. Volume 2: Social Trends* (pp. 1–45). New York: Russell Sage Foundation.

McLanahan, S., & Sandefur, G. (1994). *Growing up with a single parent.* Cambridge, MA: Harvard University Press.

Moffitt, R. (1990). The effect of the U.S. welfare system on marital status. *Journal of Public Economics, 41,* 101–124.

Moffitt, R. (1992). Incentive effects of the U.S. welfare system: A review. *Journal of Economic Literature, 30,* 1–61.

Moffitt, R. (1994). Welfare effects on female headship with area effects. *Journal of Human Resources, 29,* 621–636.

Murray, C. (1984). *Losing ground.* New York: Basic Books.

National Center for Health Statistics. (1995a). Births to unmarried mothers: United States, 1980–1992. *Vital and Health Statistics* (Series 21-53). Washington, DC: U.S. Government Printing Office.

National Center for Health Statistics. (1995b). Advance report of final divorce statistics, 1989 and 1990. *Monthly Vital Statistics Report 43(Suppl.),* 8 Hyattsville, MD: U. S. Government Printing Office.

National Center for Health Statistics. (1995c). Advance report of final marriage statistics, 1989 and 1990. *Monthly Vital Statistics Report, 43*(Suppl.), 12, Hyattsville, MD: U. S. Government Printing Office.

National Center for Health Statistics. (1998). Sample design, sampling weights, and variance estimation in the 1995 *National Survey of Family Growth.* Washington, D. C.: U. S. Government Printing Office.

Nock, S. (1995). A comparison of marriages and cohabiting relationships. *Journal of Family Issues, 16,* 53–76.

Ono, H. (1998). Husbands' and wives' resources and marital dissolution. *Journal of Marriage and the Family, 60,* 674–689.

Orbuch, T., House, J., Mero, R., & Webster, P. (1996). Marital quality over the life course. *Social Psychology Quarterly, 59,* 162–171.

Popenoe, D. (1988). *Disturbing the nest: Family change and decline in modern society.* New York: Aldine de Gruyter.

Popenoe, D. (1993). American family decline, 1960–1990: A review and appraisal. *Journal of Marriage and the Family, 55,* 527–542.

Qian, Z., & Preston, S. (1993). Changes in American marriage, 1972 to 1987: Availability and forces of attraction by age and education. *American Sociological Review, 58,* 482–495.

Raley, R. (1996). A shortage of marriageable men? A note on the role of cohabitation in Black-White differences in marriage rates. *American Sociological Review, 61,* 973–983.

Rindfuss, R., & VandenHeuvel, A. (1990). Cohabitation: A precursor to marriage or an alternative to being single? *Population and Development Review, 16,* 703–726.

Rodgers, W., & Thornton, A. (1985). Changing patterns of first marriage in the United States. *Demography, 22,* 265–279.

Santi, L. (1988). The demographic context of recent change in the structure of American households. *Demography, 25,* 509–519.

Schoen, R. (1987). The continuing retreat from marriage: figures from 1983 marital status life tables. *Social Science Research, 71,* 108–109.

Schoen, R., & Owens, D. (1992). A further look at first marriages and first unions. In S. South & S. Tolnay

(Eds.), *The changing American family* (pp. 109–114). Boulder, CO: Westview Press.

Schultz, T. (1994). Marital status and fertility in the United States: Welfare and labor market effects. *Journal of Human Resources, 29,* 637–669.

Seltzer, J. (1994). Consequences of Marital Dissolution for Children. *Annual Review of Sociology, 20,* 235–266.

Skolnick, A. (1991). *Embattled paradise: The American family in an age of uncertainty.* New York: Basic Books.

Smith, H., & Cutright, P. (1988). Thinking about change in illegitimacy ratios: United States, 1963–1983. *Demography, 25,* 235–248.

Smith, H., Morgan, S., & Koropeckyj-Cox, T. (1996). A decomposition of trends in the nonmarital fertility ratios of Blacks and Whites in the United States, 1960–1992. *Demography, 33,* 141–151.

South, S. (1992). For love or money? Sociodemographic determinants of the expected benefits of marriage. In S. South & S. Tolnay (Eds.), *The changing American family* (pp. 171–194) Boulder, CO: Westview Press.

South, S., & Lloyd, K. (1992). Marriage opportunities and family formation: Further implications of imbalanced sex ratios. *Journal of Marriage and the Family, 54,* 440–451.

South, S., & Lloyd, K. (1995). Spousal alternatives and marital dissolution. *American Sociological Review, 60,* 21–35.

South, S., & Spitze, G. (1986). Determinants of divorce over the marital life course. *American Sociological Review, 51,* 583–590.

Stacey, J. (1990). *Brave new families: Stories of domestic upheaval in late 20th century America.* New York: Basic Books.

Stacey, J. (1993). Good riddance to "the family": A response to David Popenoe. *Journal of Marriage and the Family, 55,* 545–547.

Teachman, J., Polonko, K., & Leigh, G. (1987). Marital timing: Race and sex comparisons. *Social Forces, 66,* 239–268.

Testa, M., Astone, N., Krogh, M., & Neckerman, K. (1991). Employment and marriage among inner-city fathers. *The Annals of the American Academy of Political and Social Science, 51,* 79–91.

Tucker, M. B., & Mitchell-Kernan, C. (1995). Trends in African American family formation: A theoretical and statistical overview. In M. B. Tucker & C. Mitchell-Kernan (Eds.), *The decline of marriage among African Americans* (pp. 3–26). New York: Russell Sage Foundation.

U.S. Bureau of the Census. (1992). Marriage, divorce and remarriage in the 1990's. *Current Population Reports* (Series P23-180). Washington, DC: U.S. Government Printing Office.

U.S. Bureau of the Census. (1996a). Marital status and living arrangements: March, 1995 Update. *Current Population Reports* (Series P20-491). Washington, DC: U.S. Government Printing Office.

U.S. Bureau of the Census. (1996b). Marital status and living arrangements: March, 1994. *Current Population Reports* (Series P20-484). Washington, DC: U.S. Government Printing Office.

U.S. Bureau of the Census. (1995). Household and family characteristics: March, 1994. *Current Population Reports* (Series P20-483). Washington, DC: U.S. Government Printing Office.

U.S. Bureau of the Census. (1998a). *Statistical abstract of the United States, 1998.* (118th ed.) Washington, DC: U.S. Government Printing Office.

U.S. Bureau of the Census. (1998b). Money income in the United States: 1997. (With separate data on valuation of noncash benefits. *Current Population Reports* (Series P60-200). Washington, DC: U.S. Government Printing Office.

U.S. Bureau of the Census. (1998c). Marital status and living arrangements: March, 1998. *Current Population Reports* (Series P20-514). Washington, DC: U.S. Government Printing Office.

U.S. Bureau of the Census. (1999). *Statistical abstract of the United States, 1999* (119th ed.) Washington, DC: U.S. Government Printing Office.

Wilson, W. (1987). *The truly disadvantaged.* Chicago: University of Chicago Press.

Wilson, W. (1996). *When work disappears: The world of the new urban poor.* New York: Vintage Books.

Wise, D. (1997). Retirement against the demographic trend: More older people living longer, working less, and saving less. *Demography, 34,* 83–95.

Wu, L. (1996). Effects of family instability and income instability on the risk of a premarital birth. *American Sociological Review 61,* 386–406.

Judith A. Seltzer   *University of California—Los Angeles*

Families Formed Outside of Marriage

Cohabitation and childbearing outside of marriage are increasingly common family arrangements in the United States. Cohabitation is becoming more like formal marriage in that both are childrearing institutions. Attempts to study the meaning of families formed outside of marriage face the challenge of studying a moving target because the rapid rise in nonmarital families contributes to new meanings and institutional supports. Among these institutions are state policies that formalize ties between members of nonmarital families. This review summarizes the changing demography of cohabitation and nonmarital childbearing, considers the causes and effects of these changes, and describes some recent policies that formalize the relationship between members of families formed outside of marriage. These policies may affect family members' behavior.

Marriage and childbearing within marriage are the centerpiece of family studies. Researchers investigate the formation and dissolution of relationships, the quality of marital and parental relationships, and the effects of marriage and changes in marital status on individuals. Marriage forms alliances between kin groups and allows the exchange of property and other resources. Children are the most important of the resources created in marriage. Individual and family-level processes, such as who marries, who has children and how the children are raised affect reproduction. State

Department of Sociology, 2201 Hershey Hall, Box 951551, University of California—Los Angeles, Los Angeles, CA 90095-1551 (seltzerj@ucla.edu).

Key Words: childbearing, childrearing, cohabitation, couples, nonmarital childbearing, nonmarital families.

policies and community-level processes also affect reproduction, for instance, through social practices, norms, and laws about marriage and about parents' rights and responsibilities for children.

Scholars have provided new insights into family relationships by broadening their studies to include greater emphasis on nonmarital relationships. Although studies of nonmarital relationships are not new phenomena, recent data facilitate a broader conceptualization of families formed outside of marriage than was possible before this decade. In particular, social scientists have collected improved data on cohabiting unions and childbearing outside of marriage. Investing resources in better data on nonmarital families acknowledges that cohabitation and childbearing outside of marriage are important aspects of U.S. family life. Because the number and social significance of families formed outside of marriage have grown over recent decades, the place of these relationships in contemporary kinship has changed. Studies of nonmarital families focus on a moving target.

This review considers two ways in which families are formed outside of marriage: by coresidence, as when a couple lives together without being married, and by having children outside of marriage. The review considers intimate relationships between adults or "conjugal" relationships and relationships between parents and minor children. I treat coresidence and childbearing behaviors as defining characteristics of families. This behavioral definition differs from definitions of families formed by marriage because marriage is defined, in part, by laws. Couples who marry obtain marriage licenses, in contrast to couples who live together without marrying and who require no formal license. The phrases "out-of-wedlock" and "illegitimate" childbearing also highlight the legal distinction between families formed outside of marriage and families formed in marriage. I follow convention by using the phrase "nonmarital cohabitation" and "cohabitation" synonymously to describe heterosexual couples who live together as intimate partners but are not married to each other. My review complements other recent reviews by Casper and Bianchi (in press), Patterson's review of gay and lesbian families (2000); Prinz (1995); Smock (2000); Thomson, Bachrach, Kaye, and Ventura (1998); the Department of Health and Human Services 1995 *Report to Congress on Out-of-Wedlock Childbearing* (Thornton, 1995); Thornton, Amaudo, Marsiglio, Sugland, and Waite (1998); and the 1998 National Institute of Child Health and Human Services (NICHD) *Ties That Bind* conference (Waite, Bachrach, Hindin, Thomson, & Thornton, 2000). The large number of new publications on this topic is consistent with the growing importance of these family arrangements in the U.S. kinship system.

As families formed outside of marriage grow in number, policy makers and individuals try to formalize aspects of nonmarital family relationships, such as when the father of a child born outside of marriage is formally identified as that child's father through the establishment of legal paternity. I consider research on the trend toward formalizing the rights and responsibilities of families formed outside of marriage at the end of this review.

Marriage licenses parenthood (Malinowski, 1964). I start from this assumption and ask whether cohabitation is also an institution for childrearing. This necessarily emphasizes young families over older families in which members are beyond reproductive age, although nonmarital family relationships among older persons may be increasingly important in the United States and other Western societies with aging populations (Chevan, 1996; Gonnot, Keilman, & Prinz, 1995; see also Allen, Blieszner, & Roberto, 2000). My focus on young adults excludes grandparent-grandchild households, from which the middle generation is absent, and other aspects of grandparents' involvement in childrearing, although these family ties are certainly important. Emphasis on younger adults takes into account that this is a time when many make important decisions about forming families and, as a result, they may provide unique

insight into new meanings of cohabitation and nonmarital childbearing. (See Thornton and Fricke, 1989, for a similar strategy in a comparative analysis of changing kinship.) Finally, I focus on nonmarital families in the United States, but draw on evidence from other countries.

The review is organized as follows. The next section discusses the effects of social context on the meaning of families formed outside of marriage. It also considers how individuals' expectations about the stability of cohabiting relationships or relationships that produce children may change as a result of things that happen to the couple once they start living together or after their child is born. The next several sections review research on cohabitation. First, I chart the increase in cohabitation and consider group differences in rates of cohabitation. I then review the debate about whether cohabitation is a stage in the courtship process leading up to marriage or whether cohabitation is an end in itself. The sections after that consider the stability of cohabiting unions, how cohabitors organize their daily lives, and the associations among cohabitation, childbearing, and childrearing. Then I turn my attention to nonmarital childbearing more generally. This is followed by a discussion of conceptual and methodological issues that affect the interpretation of past research and should be considered in new work on nonmarital families. I then examine the increasing efforts to formalize relationships between members of families formed outside of marriage. The review ends with a short discussion of cohabitation as a kinship institution.

TRIAL ARRANGEMENTS AND CHANGING EXPECTATIONS

It is a sociological truism that the meaning of cohabitation outside of marriage and other family relationships depends on the social context in which they occur. For example, many Latin American countries have long histories of socially accepted consensual unions, which may substitute for formal unions in some groups (De Vos, 1999; Parrado & Tienda 1997). Laws about taxes and housing and child allowances treat unmarried and married couples the same in Sweden, where premarital cohabitation is nearly universal (Hoem, 1995). In contrast, in the United States, where cohabitation was uncommon until recently, family law gives cohabitors few of the rights of married couples (Gordon, 1998/1999). Similarly, U.S. children born outside of marriage lack some advantages that accrue to children born in marriage, unless the former have legally identified fathers.

As cohabitation and nonmarital childbearing become more common, individuals are less likely to think of them as deviant behaviors. Individuals also have fewer incentives to marry before having a child when children born outside of marriage are eligible for the same benefits and accorded the same social recognition as children born in marriage. In the United States, individuals are marrying and forming nonmarital families in a changing social context. Marriage, as an institution, is increasingly defined as a short-term relationship. Divorce is more acceptable now than in the past (Thornton, 1989). Laws no longer assume that marriage is forever (Weitzman, 1985), and celebrations of marriage are less likely to emphasize its permanence (Furstenberg, 1997). The meaning of cohabitation is shifting, in part because the meaning of marriage has shifted. Marriage offers fewer benefits relative to cohabitation now than in the past. Most young people expect to marry and believe that it is important to have a good marriage and family life, but most do not believe that they must marry to live a good life (Thornton, 1995).

The meaning of cohabitation and nonmarital relationships also depends on the expectations of those who form the union and on individuals' own experiences within the relationship. Individuals' attitudes on the appropriate conditions for marriage and childbearing, on whether relationships involve lifetime commitments, and on the different rights and responsibilities of women and men in cohabiting and marital relationships affect how they understand their personal relationships. Marriage is an economic arrangement, notwithstanding the expressions of love that accompany the formalization of such unions. Economic uncertainty and scarcity of economic resources increase the likelihood of cohabitation compared with marriage, but rates of cohabitation have risen among those with both low and high levels of education, an indicator of likely economic success. Individuals who decide to live together instead of marrying may do so as a way to evaluate whether their partner will end up as a good economic match (Oppenheimer, 1988) or an egalitarian partner (Cherlin, 2000). Once couples begin living together, they also develop new ties that bring them closer together (Berger & Kellner, 1974). Having children together connects cohabiting partners in addition to the symbolic connections adults create. For some couples, these symbolic and child-based

sources of solidarity may reinforce their plans to marry. For other couples, these bonds may make the idea of formalizing their union through marriage less important than when they began living together. The secular rise in the public's acceptance of cohabitation and of childbearing outside of marriage contributes to a decline in cohabiting partners' expectations about whether marriage is the "next step" in their own relationship.

THE RISE IN COHABITATION AND GROUP DIFFERENCES IN COHABITATION

It was clear by the start of this decade that cohabitation was an important aspect of couple relationships in the United States. Between the mid-1970s and 1980s, young adults became more accepting of nonmarital cohabitation, with increasing percentages agreeing that cohabitation was a "worthwhile experiment" and that it was a good idea to live together before marrying (Thornton, 1989). Approval of cohabitation is likely to continue to increase in the future through the process of cohort replacement because young adults are more likely than older adults to believe that it is all right for an unmarried couple to live together even if they have no plans to marry (Bumpass & Sweet, 1995; Oropesa, 1996). British data also show that compared with older persons, young adults are much more likely to say that they would advise a young person to live with a partner before they marry the partner (Kiernan & Estaugh, 1993; see Thornton, 1995, for a review of attitudes about cohabitation and changing family patterns). Trends in behavior follow a similar pattern, with each recent birth cohort more likely to cohabit than previous cohorts (Bumpass & Sweet, 1989; Chevan, 1996). Rates of cohabitation have increased even among older adults, however (Waite, 1995). By 1997, there were approximately 4.1 million cohabiting couples of all ages, up from 2.9 million in 1990, an increase of 46% (Casper & Cohen, 2000).

The rise in cohabitation is best understood in the context of delayed marriage for recent cohorts compared with cohorts born between the post–World War II period and the mid-1960s. About two thirds of the decline between 1970 and 1985 in the proportion of young adults married by age 25 can be attributed to the rise in nonmarital cohabitation (Bumpass, Sweet, & Cherlin, 1991, Table 1). Although much discussion of cohabitation among young adults considers it a stage in the transition to first marriage, Bumpass and his colleagues showed that cohabiting unions also occur after a marriage dissolves and that rising rates of postmarital cohabitation compensated for the decline in remarriage among couples separated in the early 1980s.

These trends have continued for U.S. women in the 1990s. Nearly 40% of women aged 19 to 24 years in 1995 had ever cohabited, compared with just under 30% of women that age in the late 1980s (Bumpass & Lu, 2000, Table 1). More than half of first unions in the early 1990s began with cohabitation (Bumpass & Lu, Table 3). The increase in nonmarital cohabitation occurred for all education groups and for Whites, Blacks, and Hispanics, although the increases were greater for those with a high school degree or less and for non-Hispanic Whites than for other groups (Bumpass & Lu, Table 2). Cohabitation continues to offset the decline in marriage for young women (Bumpass & Lu).

Cohabitation remains more common among those with less education and for whom economic resources are more constrained (Bumpass & Lu, 2000; Clarkberg, 1999; Willis & Michael, 1994), perhaps because cohabiting unions require less initial commitment to fulfill long-term economic responsibilities (Clarkberg, Stolzenberg, & Waite, 1995; Smock & Manning, 1997). Because the institution of marriage includes expectations about economic roles, couples may think that they should reach specific financial goals, such as steady employment or housing of a certain quality, before it is appropriate to marry. Those with low incomes may also think that marriage, with its legal rules about marital property and inheritance, is irrelevant for them given their few material assets (Cherlin, 1992). Consistent with higher rates of cohabitation among the economically disadvantaged, cohabitors with more financial resources are more likely to expect to marry their partners (Bumpass et al., 1991). They are also more likely to realize their expectations about marriage than cohabiting couples who are economically disadvantaged (Smock & Manning).

Cohabitation rates have increased at the same time as marriage rates have declined for both Blacks and Whites. By 1998, about two thirds of White women aged 20 to 24 were never married, nearly doubling the percentage never married in 1970. Marriage is even less common for Black women age 20–24, among whom 85% were never married in 1998 (Cherlin, 1992; Teachman, Tedrow, & Crowder, 2000; U.S. Bureau of the Census, 1998).

Rates of marriage or nonmarriage exaggerate Black-White differences in union formation. When one considers both informal unions (cohabitation) and formal unions (marriages), the race difference in the percentage of young women who have entered a union is reduced by about one half (Raley, 1996). Puerto Ricans also enter informal unions at high rates. Compared with non-Hispanic Whites, Puerto Ricans are less likely to marry their cohabiting partners (Landale & Forste, 1991). Explanations for race and ethnic differences in cohabitation patterns draw on both cultural and economic factors. Landale and Fennelly (1992), for example, argued that the long history of social recognition of consensual unions in many Latin American countries explains in part why Puerto Rican women, compared to non-Hispanic White women, are less likely to formalize their unions, even when children are involved.

When men's economic circumstances are precarious, young adults delay marriage (Oppenheimer, Kalmijn, & Lim, 1997). Those who are economically insecure, including those still enrolled in school, may choose cohabitation over marriage (Thornton, Axinn, & Teachman, 1995; Willis & Michael, 1994). Among cohabiting couples, those in which the male partner is more economically secure are more likely to marry than those in which the male partner is economically insecure (Smock & Manning, 1997). Economic factors alone, however, do not explain race differences in union formation (Raley, 1996), pointing again to the need for explanations that take account of both cultural and economic factors. That men's declining labor market prospects explain some, but not all, of the delay in marriage between 1960 and 1980 for Black and White men reinforces the need to consider both economic and noneconomic factors to account for temporal and cross-sectional differences in union formation (Mare & Winship, 1991).

COHABITATION AS A STAGE BEFORE MARRIAGE OR AS AN END IN ITSELF

That family scholars in the 1980s regarded cohabitation in the United States as a transitional stage between being single and marrying is evident from the organization of the 1990 *Journal of Marriage and the Family* decade reviews. Ten years ago, cohabitation was examined in the review of research on mate selection and premarital relationships (Surra, 1990). Cohabitors themselves also saw their unions as a way to assess marital compatibility (Bumpass et al., 1991, Table 7). Most either had definite plans to marry their cohabiting partner or thought they would marry their partner (Bumpass et al., Table 9). Among young adults, never-married cohabitors are usually intermediate between those who are single and those who are in first marriages on attitudes and socioeconomic characteristics. On most of these dimensions, cohabitors are more similar to single, noncohabiting adults than to those who are married (Rindfuss & VandenHeuvel, 1990). Because cohabitation may occur either before a first marriage or with a new partner after a divorce, it is instructive to compare the characteristics of single and cohabiting persons, taking account of whether they have ever been married. Casper and Bianchi (in press, Table 3) show that, among 25- to 34-year-old adults, never-married singles and cohabitors are more similar to each other than they are to ever-married singles and cohabitors on education, per capita income, and use of food stamps. Ever-married singles and cohabitors resemble each other on these characteristics and are generally more disadvantaged than the never-marrieds, regardless of cohabitation status. Comparisons on other characteristics show more variation in which groups bear the greatest resemblance.

Not surprisingly, cohabiting women are more similar to married women than to single women in their sexual and contraceptive behavior due to their greater exposure to risk (Bachrach, 1987). Although adults in cohabiting relationships report that they have sex more frequently than those who are married, once the younger age of cohabitors is taken into account, the difference diminishes (Laumann, Gagnon, Michael, & Michaels, 1994). Never-married cohabiting couples are less likely to have a child together than are married couples, but they are significantly more likely to have a child compared with single women (Manning & Landale, 1996; Wu, Bumpass, & Musick, 1999). However, race and economic characteristics affect the degree to which cohabiting couples' fertility resembles that of married couples (Loomis & Landale, 1994; Manning & Landale, 1996).

Although cohabitation is often a prelude to marriage, cohabiting unions may be an end in themselves for an increasing percentage of cohabitors. These cohabitors do not necessarily reject marriage. Instead, cohabitors are less likely to see marriage as the defining characteristic of their family lives. Fewer cohabitations end in marriage now than in the past. In the 1970s, about 60% of cohabitors who formed unions at age 25 or older married their partners within 3 years of starting to live together, compared with only about 35% in the early 1990s (Bumpass, 1995, Figure 6; see Bumpass, 1998, for replication using different data). Thus, fewer cohabitations are a stage on the way to marriage, either because the partners never intended to marry in the first place or because other changes in their circumstances altered their intentions or their ability to fulfill their intentions.

Change in the meaning of nonmarital cohabitation also comes from the growing importance of cohabitation as a setting in which couples bear and rear children. The percentage of cohabitors who had biological children together increased from 12% in the early 1980s to 15% in the early 1990s (Bumpass, personal communication, 1999). Although these percentages are still low, the change is a 25% increase over a short time. Having a child in the relationship may change how the couple thinks of their union. For example, among Puerto Rican women interviewed in a survey that allowed them to describe their unions as either informal marriages (i.e., they thought of themselves as married) or cohabitations, women who had borne children outside formal marriage were much more likely to describe their relationship as an informal marriage than women without children (Landale & Fennelly, 1992).

At the same time that cohabitors have become more likely to bear children together, the percentage of all children who are born to unmarried parents in the United States increased from about 18% in 1980 to nearly a third in 1997 (Smith, Morgan, & Koropeckyj-Cox, 1996; Ventura, Martin, Curtin, & Mathews, 1999), a trend I discuss further below. Cohabiting couples are responsible for much of this increase in nonmarital childbearing. In the early 1980s, cohabiting couples had 29% of nonmarital births, compared with 39% a decade later (Bumpass & Lu, 2000). About 20% of nonmarital births occur in cohabiting unions after a first marriage has ended in separation or divorce, among women born since 1945 (Brown, 2000). Children born to cohabiting parents begin life in a household with both biological parents, but researchers and policy makers often assume that these children live in a single-mother household.

Single women who become pregnant are increasingly likely to move in with rather than marry the father of their child. In the past, many of these pregnancies were "premarital" pregnancies that resulted in marital births; a single woman who became pregnant married the father of their child.

(See Parnell, Swicegood, & Stevens, 1994 on declines in "legitimation" in the postwar period.) As recently as the early 1980s, about 20% of single noncohabiting women who had a pregnancy that resulted in a live birth married by the time the child was born. By the early 1990s, only 11% did so. Over this same period, the percentage of pregnant single women who began cohabiting by the time their child was born increased from 6% to 9% (Raley, in press). Thus, women are almost as likely to form nonmarital cohabiting unions as marry when they have a child. Cohabiting couples also care for children brought to the union by only one of the partners. Nearly half of cohabiting couples live with children (Bumpass, personal communication, 1999), and cohabiting couples make up one fourth of all stepfamilies (Bumpass, Raley, & Sweet, 1995).

STABILITY OF COHABITING UNIONS

Cohabiting unions end quickly either because the couple marries or breaks up. Half end in a year or less for one of these reasons (Bumpass & Lu, 2000). Compared with married couples, cohabitors are much more likely to break up. About 29% of cohabitors and only 9% of married couples break up within the first 2 years (Bumpass & Sweet, 1989, Table 4). Over the past decade, cohabiting unions have become even less stable, but this is mainly because of the decline in the percentage of cohabitors who eventually marry their partners (Bumpass & Lu). Within 5 years, more than half of unions begun by cohabitation have ended, regardless of whether the couple formalized the union by marrying (Bumpass & Lu). In Canada, cohabiting unions may also be less stable than in the past (Wu & Balakrishnan, 1995). Informal unions dissolve more quickly than do formal marriages because of differences in the quality of the match between partners who marry and those who do not, the strength of normative consensus favoring marriage, the legal and social institutions that support formal marriage over cohabitation, and differences in the attitudes and resources of cohabitors and those who marry.

Marriages preceded by cohabitation are more likely to end in separation or divorce than marriages in which the couple did not live together previously (Bumpass & Lu, 2000; DeMaris & Rao, 1992; Laumann et al., 1994; Lillard, Brien, & Waite, 1995; Sweet & Bumpass, 1992). For instance, about 16% of marriages preceded by cohabitation broke up within the first 5 years, compared with about 10% of marriages not preceded by cohabitation among women born in the mid-1930s. For women born a decade later who were marrying during the 1960s when divorce rates were rising, the contrast is 31% compared with 16%, respectively (Schoen, 1992, Table 1). However, for women born more recently, there is some evidence of convergence in the rates of marital dissolution between those who cohabited and those who did not (Schoen; but see Bumpass & Lu, 2000, who reported that the higher disruption rates for marriages preceded by cohabitation persist for a more recent period).

In Britain, premarital cohabitation is also associated with higher rates of marital disruption (Berrington & Diamond, 1999). In France, however, Leridon (1990) found that premarital cohabitation does not affect the stability of first marriage. Both cohort and country variation in the association between premarital cohabitation and marital disruption support my earlier claim that the social context affects who cohabits and the meaning and consequences of cohabitation.

In the United States, higher divorce rates for couples who cohabit before marriage may be due to differences in the background, attitudes, and behavior of those who choose premarital cohabitation compared with those who do not. Yet if young adults are correct in their belief that cohabitation is a worthwhile experiment for evaluating the compatibility of a potential spouse, one would expect those who cohabit first to have even more stable marriages than those who marry without cohabiting once preexisting differences between those who cohabit before marriage and those who do not are taken into account. Alternatively, the experience of premarital cohabitation may damage the couple's prospect of having a stable marriage. (See Axinn & Thornton, 1992; and Brüderl, Diekmann, & Engelhardt (1998); Sweet & Bumpass, 1992, who elaborate on these interpretations.)

Evidence for whether cohabitation *causes* an increase in the chance of divorce is mixed. Young men and women with liberal gender-role attitudes are more likely to cohabit than to marry (Clarkberg et al., 1995). Similarly, those who hold more negative attitudes about marriage and are more accepting of divorce have higher rates of cohabitation and generally lower rates of marriage (Axinn & Thornton, 1992). Childhood family characteristics associated with marital disruption also affect whether a person cohabits or marries. Growing up in a single-parent household increases the likelihood of cohabiting in the United States and in

Great Britain (Bumpass & Sweet, 1989; Cherlin, Kiernan, & Chase-Lansdale, 1995; Thornton, 1991). Longitudinal surveys do not measure all of the personality traits and attitudes that distinguish cohabitors from those who marry. Higher rates of marital disruption for those who have previously cohabited disappear when these unobserved differences are taken into account with econometric techniques (Lillard et al., 1995). For German couples, premarital cohabitation actually enhances marital stability after statistical adjustments for unmeasured differences, such as attitudes and the quality of the couple's relationship, between those who cohabit and those who do not (Brüderl et al., 1998). The statistical techniques used in these studies require assumptions that are difficult to meet, but the similarity in findings and their consistency with other longitudinal analyses is reassuring on this point.

Young adults also become more tolerant of divorce as a result of cohabiting, whatever their initial views are (Axinn & Thornton, 1992). Cohabitation may expose partners to a wider range of attitudes about family arrangements than those who marry without first living together. In addition, how cohabitors organize their daily lives may carry over into marriage (see below). Women and men in cohabiting couples divide housework somewhat more equally and bring home more similar earnings than married couples (Brines & Joyner, 1999; Nock, 1995). If these patterns carry over into marriage, they may contribute to higher divorce rates for those who cohabited before marriage because marital solidarity may depend on a specialized division of labor. Couples who cohabited before marriage may find that attempts to pursue a more egalitarian division of labor in marriage, a social institution that promotes a gendered division of labor, creates strain and conflict, which in turn increase the likelihood of divorce (Brines & Joyner). Researchers have done little to address the following questions: How and why do cohabiting couples decide to marry (or not to marry)? And how, if at all, does marriage change their behavior and feelings about the relationship (but see Gupta, 1999, and Singh & Lindsay, 1996, for initial steps in this direction; see Bumpass & Sweet, in press, for a similar point).

On balance, both the "people who cohabit are different" and "cohabitation changes people" interpretations are supported by recent studies. None of the studies cited above provides definitive evidence on which is the better interpretation of higher divorce rates for those who cohabit before

marriage. Much past research focuses on individuals and their attitudes, to the exclusion of partners' attitudes and the characteristics of their union, including how those who cohabit and those who marry organize their lives. Nevertheless, studies using different data and different methods of analysis consistently show that those who live together before marriage come from more "divorce-prone" families and hold more liberal attitudes toward divorce than do those who do not cohabit before marriage. Claims that individuals who cohabit before marriage hurt their chances of a good marriage pay too little attention to this evidence.

Paradoxically, whatever the effect of cohabiting on divorce at the level of the relationship, the instability of individual cohabiting unions stabilizes the rate of divorce. Many relationships that would have been short-term marriages dissolve before couples marry. Living together shows the couple that marriage is not for them, so they break up before formalizing their union. Demographers speculate that this removes some "high-risk" marriages from the pool of marriages that contributes to the formal divorce rate (Bumpass & Lu, 2000; Bumpass & Sweet, 1989). Recently, however, Goldstein's (1999) simulation provides evidence against this interpretation, suggesting that the rise in cohabitation explains little, if any, of the stabilization in the divorce rate.

HOW COHABITORS ORGANIZE THEIR LIVES: WORK, COUPLE, AND KIN TIES

That couples who cohabit differ in their attitudes about gender roles and family institutions suggests that they may organize their daily lives differently from those who choose to marry. Much of what we know about the organization of cohabiting couples' lives and how their lives compare to the lives of married couples builds on the rich information provided by Blumstein and Schwartz (1983) in their study of couple relationships in the United States. Cohabiting couples have greater flexibility in the degree to which they follow the gender-based division of labor and family responsibilities that is characteristic of formal marriage. Because some couples use cohabitation as a testing ground to evaluate a partner's compatibility, women (and men) who want to marry someone who will share most household and childrearing tasks may be particularly likely to live with a partner before marriage to observe and negotiate these arrangements (Cherlin, in press). Whether the greater similarity in women's and men's roles within cohabitation than in marriage is due to the different goals that cohabitors bring to their relationship or to the lack of institutional supports for a gender-based division of labor is still an open question.

Recent data from large, national probability surveys, such as the National Survey of Families and Households (Sweet & Bumpass, 1996), provide similar information on the experiences of heterosexual couples in formal and informal unions. These data show that compared with wives, women in cohabiting couples do fewer hours of housework but more hours of paid work. When differences between married and cohabiting couples in education, paid work, and the presence of children are taken into account, women in cohabiting couples still do about 6 fewer hours of housework than wives do. This is consistent with the finding cited above that compared with those who marry, cohabitors have more liberal gender-role attitudes when they begin their relationship. There are small differences, if any, in housework time for men by whether they are in formal or informal unions (Shelton & John, 1993; South & Spitze, 1994). In both marriage and cohabitation, women do more housework than men do, but the somewhat greater similarity between women's and men's paid and unpaid work in cohabiting unions suggests that the role responsibilities of female cohabiting partners may differ from those of female marriage partners.

Because cohabiting women perceive their relationships as less secure and as more likely to dissolve than formal marriages, they may be less willing to limit their paid labor force participation or to invest extra effort in housework to the detriment of their participation in the paid labor force. Both women and men may be less committed to their relationships when they cohabit than when they marry. Compared with those who are married, women and men in pre- and postmarital cohabiting unions see fewer costs and more benefits to breaking up (Nock, 1995). A recent study in Norway also showed that a majority of cohabitors, regardless of whether they had a child together, are reluctant to marry because marriages are difficult to dissolve (Kravdal, 1999, Table 6). These perceptions of the barriers to breaking up are realistic assessments. Married couples are more likely to pool their financial resources and have other relationship-specific investments, including biological children born to the union, than are cohabiting couples (Blumstein &

Schwartz, 1983; Loomis & Landale, 1994; Singh & Lindsay, 1996). Another indication that spouses are more committed than are cohabitors to their relationships comes from the U.S. National Health and Social Life Survey of adults, which showed that marriages are more likely to be sexually exclusive than cohabitations, even taking account of cohabitors' more permissive values (Treas & Giesen, 2000). We do not know, however, whether partners who invest more in their relationship do so because it is a good relationship or whether the relationship improves and becomes stronger as a result of the partners' investments.

Cohabiting partners may evaluate the success of their union using different criteria than do spouses in formal marriage. For instance, because they hold more egalitarian attitudes, young adult cohabitors may observe how their housework is actually divided to assess whether the relationship is "working." Cohabiting couples in which partners have similar earnings are more stable than those with dissimilar earnings. In contrast, among married couples, a more specialized division of labor, in which wives are not employed but husbands are, increases marital stability, as noted above (Brines & Joyner, 1999).

Cohabiting couples face more disapproval of their relationship and receive less social support than do married couples. The lack of support may contribute to higher rates of disruption for cohabiting unions. Although the general public has grown increasingly tolerant of nonmarital cohabitation, parents may prefer that their children marry rather than cohabit. When mothers think marriage is important, their daughters are less likely to cohabit than when mothers hold less favorable attitudes about marriage (Axinn & Thornton, 1992). Similarly, data from young adults in The Netherlands show that young adults' intentions to cohabit depend on whether they think that their parents and friends would support their decision (Liefbroer & Gierveld, 1993).

Cohabitation may strain relationships between parents and adult children. Members of married couples describe their relationships with parents more positively than do cohabiting couples (Nock, 1995). Parents also report closer relationships with married children than with cohabiting children (Aquilino, 1997). On the other hand, members of cohabiting couples are almost as likely as members of married couples to have been introduced to each other by a family member, which suggests that spouses and cohabiting partners may be part of similar social circles (Laumann et al., 1994,

Table 6.1) Parents whose children cohabit are also more likely than those whose children are single (and not cohabiting) to share with each other leisure activities, meals, and enjoyable times and to have emotionally close relationships (Aquilino).

COHABITATION, CHILDBEARING, AND CHILDREARING

Do Cohabiting Couples Marry Because They Want Children?

If cohabiting unions are experiments that young couples undertake to decide if they should marry, is there an end to the experiment or some precipitating event that prompts couple members to marry? Cohabiting couples who decide that they are ready to have children may decide to marry as a first step toward having a child. Cohabiting couples in which the woman becomes pregnant (and does not have an abortion) are more likely to marry than are couples in which the woman is not pregnant (Manning, 1995), although this effect is greater for White than for Black women (Manning & Smock, 1995). Pregnancy also increases marriage among cohabitors in Sweden, a setting with fewer institutional barriers to childbearing outside of formal marriage than in the United States (Bracher & Santow, 1998). Cohabiting couples in the United States who already have children, whether born to the couple or in previous relationships, are more likely to marry than those without children (Manning & Smock, 1995). This finding is not consistent across settings, however. In Canada, which has also experienced a rise in cohabitation, couples who have a child in their cohabiting union are less likely to marry than those who have not had a child in their union (Wu & Balakrishnan, 1995). Childbearing in cohabitation reduces the chance that a couple will break up, whether or not they formalize their union (Wu & Balakrishnan).

Effects of Cohabitation on Children's Family Experiences

As noted above, much of the recent rise in childbearing outside of marriage can be attributed to childbearing in cohabiting unions. Children in these unions start life in households with both of their biological parents instead of in a single-mother household. For new parents in Oakland, California, and Austin, Texas, about half of unmarried mothers who have just had a child report that they are living with their child's father (McLanahan, Garfinkel, & Padilla, 1999; McLanahan, Garfinkel, & Waller, 1999). Even if these reports overstate the extent of cohabitation at childbirth, perhaps because the interview occurred at a time of great optimism about the strength of the couple's relationship (L. Wu, personal communication, 1999), these children are born into families in which both parents are present, at least for a time.

Inferences about children's living arrangements from parents' marital status provide a misleading picture of recent demographic trends, such as the rise of "single"-father families. For instance, Garasky and Meyer (1996) showed that treating cohabitors as two-parent families reduces estimates of the growth in "single"-father families between 1960 and 1990 from about 240% to about 120%. Cohabitation also reduces the amount of time that children will spend in a single-parent household during childhood. Estimates using marital status to infer whether both parents are present have shown that children in recent cohorts will spend a median of nearly 7 years in a single-parent household from the time they first enter it. When cohabiting parents are taken into account, the median duration drops to 3.7 years (Bumpass & Raley, 1995).

At first glance, taking cohabitation into account suggests that children's lives have become more stable. Yet because cohabiting unions are usually short-term relationships, taking cohabitation into account increases the number of family disruptions children experience. Just over one third of children born in either a marital or cohabiting union will experience the break-up of their parents' relationship before the end of their teenage years, and this fraction increased in the decade between the early 1980s and the 1990s (Bumpass & Lu, 2000, p. 37). Cohabitation also affects children's experience in stepfamilies, many of which are begun informally when a parent brings a new partner into the household, rather than by formal marriage. By the early 1980s, almost two thirds of children who entered a stepfamily did so by cohabitation instead of marriage (Bumpass et al., 1995, Table 2). Once children enter a stepfamily, the rates at which they face the dissolution of their stepfamily are similar whether the stepfamily began by cohabitation or by marriage (Bumpass et al., 1995, Table 4). The similarity in rates of disruption for cohabiting and remarried stepfamilies suggests that there is less selection into cohabiting unions after a first relationship ends than into pre-marital cohabiting unions.

Effects of Cohabitation on Children

Adults who live with children share resources with them. A parent's cohabiting partner is likely to contribute toward the economic costs of raising the child(ren). These contributions may occur because the parent and her partner pool their incomes or because the child shares the household's public goods, such as housing, even if the cohabiting partners do not pool all of their incomes. The National Academy of Sciences report on measuring poverty recognizes that cohabiting partners' resources are important for family members' economic well-being. The report recommends that poverty measures treat cohabitors as part of the same family (Citro & Michael, 1995). Cohabitors are included in the definition of "family" because of their likely pooling of income, economies of scale, and potential for continued resource sharing for several years. Although we know little about the extent to which cohabiting partners pool their incomes, Bauman (1999) finds that compared with spouses, cohabitors pool less of their income. Partners may be more likely to pool their incomes when they have a child together or have lived together a long time (Winkler, 1997).

Income from a parent's cohabiting partner reduces by almost 30% the number of children in cohabiting-couple families who are in poverty (Manning & Lichter, 1996). The rise in cohabitation over the past several decades implies that assessments of trends in poverty may overstate poverty in the more recent period relative to poverty rates a few decades ago. In fact, once cohabiting partners are included as family members and contributors to family income, the increase between 1969 and 1989 in child poverty from 13.1% to 18.7%, as measured by official statistics, would have been about 11% less (Carlson & Danziger, 1999). Children whose parents cohabit are still more likely to be poor than those in married-couple families because of the age, education, and employment differentials between those who cohabit and those who marry.

In addition to the economic implications for children's well-being, married and cohabiting parents may follow different childrearing practices. Compared with stepfathers, male cohabiting partners devote less time to organized youth activities at school, religious, or other community organizations. Otherwise, however, stepfathers and male cohabiting partners pursue similar activities with children (Thomson, McLanahan, & Curtin, 1992). Cohabiting fathers may pursue fewer organized activities because they often are arranged for children's socially recognized parents, and those who are cohabiting may be reluctant to participate unless they are married to the child's mother. We know little about how parents' cohabiting partners affect children's family experience, although studies are beginning to distinguish cohabiting-couple families from married-"intact" families and stepfamilies (Hanson, McLanahan, & Thomson, 1997; Thomson, Hanson, & McLanahan, 1994). Efforts to compare childrearing practices of cohabiting parents to those of married biological parents and married stepparents are limited by small sample sizes, even in studies that include oversamples of cohabiting families (Bumpass & Lu, 2000; Thomson, Mosley, Hansen, & McLanahan, 1998).

DEMOGRAPHIC CONTOURS OF CHILDBEARING OUTSIDE OF MARRIAGE

The high proportions of nonmarital births that occur within cohabiting unions are only part of the story of childbearing outside of marriage in the United States. Increasing numbers of children are also being born to single mothers, women who are neither married nor cohabiting. The demography of childbearing outside of marriage can be summarized with two types of statistics: birth rates for unmarried women (e.g., births per 1,000 unmarried women aged 15–44) and the percentage of children born outside of marriage (births to unmarried women divided by births to all women). Answers to questions about women's or couples' behavior (such as "how does delayed marriage affect childbearing outside of marriage?") should use information about the birth rate for unmarried women. Answers to questions about children and the family resources available to them should use information about the percentage of children born outside of marriage. For instance, children born outside of marriage are somewhat disadvantaged compared with children born to married parents who divorced and more seriously disadvantaged compared with children in two-parent, never-disrupted households (McLanahan & Sandefur, 1994). Plans to meet the next generation's needs depend, in part, on the distribution of children across these family types.

The delay in marriage and rise to high levels of divorce, along with increasing acceptance of sexual intercourse outside of marriage, expose many more U.S. women (couples) to the risk of nonmarital pregnancy. The birth rate for unmarried women increased between 1970 and 1997 from 26.4 to 44.0. There has been a slight downturn since 1994, however, when the rate was 46.9. Nonmarital birth rates were higher for Black women than for White women, 73.4 compared with 37.0, respectively, in 1997. The rate for Hispanic women (of any race) is higher than for either Blacks or Whites (Ventura et al., 1999, Table 18). Women with less education have higher rates of nonmarital childbearing than women with college educations. The education difference accounts for some, but not all, of the racial and ethnic differences in rates of childbearing outside of marriage (Ventura, Bachrach, Hill, Kaye, Hollcombe, & Koff, 1995).

The nonmarital birth ratio also has risen over the past decade. In 1997, 32.4% of children were born outside of marriage, up from 28.0 in 1990 (Ventura et al., 1999, Table 19; Ventura & Martin, 1993, Table 18). Here again there are substantial racial and ethnic differences in levels. Among non-Hispanic Whites in 1997, 21.5% of children were born outside of marriage. For non-Hispanic Blacks, more than two-thirds of children were born to unmarried parents; among Hispanics (of any race) 40.9% were born to unmarried parents (Ventura et al., Table 19).

Not only the level but also the pattern of nonmarital childbearing has changed, primarily because of the rise in the percentage of cohabiting women (Raley, in press). As noted above, higher percentages of nonmarital births occur to cohabiting parents now than in the past. In fact, there was only a slight increase in the percentage of nonunion (nonmarital *and* not to cohabiting parents) births between the early 1980s and early 1990s, from 15% to 17% of births to women under 40 (Bumpass & Lu, 2000, p. 35). Another important change is the degree to which women who have had one nonmarital birth bear all of their children outside of marriage. For women born in the 1930s, about 26% of women who bore a child outside of marriage had all of their children in nonmarital relationships. For women born in the early 1960s, this rose to 70% (Hoffman & Foster, 1997, Table 3). For both early and later cohorts, Black women were more likely to bear all of their children in nonmarital relationships than were White women (Hoffman & Foster, Figure 8).

The increasingly concentrated pattern for women who have one nonmarital birth to have all of their children outside of marriage forces researchers to pay more attention to the conditions of a women's

first birth. Compared with White women, much higher percentages of Black women bore their first child outside of marriage in the early 1990s (34% vs. 81%, respectively; Wu, Bumpass & Musick, 1999, p. 12, Figure 3). The race difference in whether first births were in cohabiting unions is much smaller. Among White women, 12% of first births were in cohabiting unions compared with about 10% of Black first births (Wu et al., pp. 12–13, Figure 4). Compared with Blacks, however, a much higher fraction of White nonmarital first births were to cohabiting parents. The gap between the percentage of Black and White children who begin life in a two-parent household widens somewhat when information on cohabitation is taken into account instead of relying only on information about parents' marital status at the child's birth.

Women of all ages bear children outside of marriage. About 30% of nonmarital births are to women less than 20 years old and about 15.5% to women 30 and older (Ventura, Martin, Curtin, Mathews, & Park, 2000, Table 17). These figures show that the common view of nonmarital childbearing as a teenage phenomenon is false. In fact, births to teenagers are a declining percentage of all nonmarital births. In 1970, births to unmarried teenagers were 50% of all nonmarital births (Ventura et al., 1995, Figure II-2). Rates of teenage childbearing have also declined. During the 1990s, the birthrate for teenagers declined form 16.1 in 1991 to 51.1 in 1998 (Ventura et al., 2000, Table B). The age at which women bear their first child has increased over the past 25 years for both unmarried and married women; however, the increase has been more modest for unmarried women (Wu et al., 1999).

Nonmarital childbearing in the United States has a somewhat different character than it does in some Western European countries. For instance, in Sweden about half of births are to unmarried women, but these are almost all births to cohabiting women, not women living alone (Prinz 1995; Ventura et al., 1995). France is more similar to the United States in the percentages of children born outside of formal marriage (Ventura et al.). Other comparative work to date shows great similarity in patterns, if not levels, of cohabitation and nonmarital childbearing between the United States and Great Britain (Bumpass & Lu, 2000; Ermisch, 1999; Kiernan, 1999). Notwithstanding, the decline in U.S. rates of nonmarital childbearing among teenagers, the United States has higher rates than in other industrialized countries (Ventura et al.).

REASONS FOR THE RISE IN CHILDBEARING OUTSIDE OF MARRIAGE

Just as cohabitation has become more widely accepted, adults in the United States have also become more tolerant toward childbearing outside of marriage. Between 1974 and 1985, the percentage of White women and men who said that it would be acceptable for their daughters to have a child outside of marriage increased from 7.7% to 13.9% for women, and 8.3% to 12.7% for men. Acceptance among Black women was more than twice as likely as acceptance among Whites, 28.5% compared with 13.9%, respectively (Pagnini & Rindfuss, 1993, Tables 1 and 2). Whether the change in attitudes is a cause or consequence of the greater incidence of nonmarital childbearing is unclear, but changes in attitudes and behaviors are probably mutually reinforcing.

Over this same period, delays in marriage have increased the number of years in which young adults face the risk of conceiving and bearing a child outside of marriage. Although contraception is relatively inexpensive and widely available, high percentages of women report unplanned pregnancies. Nearly 90% of pregnancies to never-married women are unintended, compared with about 40% among married women (Brown & Eisenberg, 1995, p. 31). Although about half of unintended pregnancies end in abortion, the percentage of unplanned births seems to be increasing for both married and never-married women (Brown & Eisenberg, Figures 2–2, 2–6, 2–7). Note that estimates of unplanned pregnancies may understate their true occurrence because women are reluctant to report abortions.

Cohabitors differ from both married and single (never-married, not cohabiting) women in the extent to which they have a child at a time when they did not plan a birth. Whereas about 18% of married women report that their first birth did not occur when it was wanted, 44% of cohabiting women and 61% of single women reported that their first birth was mistimed (Manning, 1999, Table 6).

Group differences in whether a woman becomes pregnant, whether the pregnancy was intended and "on-time," use of abortion, and union status at the time of the birth depend on differences in the costs and benefits of various strategies to limit births, as well as the costs and benefits of cohabitation and marriage (Montgomery, 1996; Willis & Haaga, 1996). Because men and women face different role responsibilities and have access to different resources, it is important to develop theories and data that include information from both women and men (Goldscheider & Kaufman, 1996; Montgomery; Willis & Haaga). High rates of marital instability demonstrate to both women and men that marriage may not be a lifetime relationship. Given the greater likelihood that children will live with their mothers after their parents' marriage dissolves or when a child is born outside of marriage, men can anticipate fewer benefits of having children, either in or outside of marriage (Willis & Haaga). Moreover, the financial costs to U.S. men of having a child outside of marriage are considerably less than the child-related costs of divorce, in part because there are fewer formal and informal obligations for men who father children outside of marriage compared with those for divorced fathers. Lower percentages of fathers whose children were born outside of marriage have child support orders, pay child support, or see their children compared with divorced fathers (Beller & Graham, 1993; King, 1994; Seltzer, 1991). Fathers of children born in cohabiting relationships have visiting patterns more similar to those of nonmarital fathers who never lived with their children than to divorced fathers (Seltzer, 2000). For women the costs of childbearing outside of marriage and the relative benefits of childbearing in marriage have also declined as the economic circumstances of potential fathers has deteriorated and women's relative economic circumstances have improved. Individuals who prefer autonomy or intimate partnerships with greater role symmetry than is common in marriage may also see childbearing outside of marriage and cohabitation as relatively more beneficial than formalizing these ties by marriage (Cherlin, 2000; Oppenheimer, 1997). How women and men understand their "options" and the factors that influence their decisions are important components of new theoretical models and data on childbearing outside of marriage (Harris, Boisjoly, & Duncan, 1999; Keane & Wolpin, 1999).

Changes over historical time in how individuals understand and make choices about family relationships are rooted in long-term trends toward greater individual autonomy and the economic arrangements that facilitate individualism (Lesthaeghe, 1995). At a macrolevel, these cultural and broad-based economic changes account for a constellation of family changes in the United States and Western Europe, including rising rates of cohabitation and nonmarital childbearing, but also the related trend toward declining rates of formal marriage and increases in divorce (Lesthaeghe; see also Prinz, 1995, for a review in the context of European trends).

EFFECTS OF NONMARITAL CHILDBEARING ON CHILDREN

Children who spend part of childhood in a single-parent household are disadvantaged on a variety of educational, economic, and social outcomes (McLanahan & Sandefur, 1994). Children born outside of marriage grow up in households with less money than children born to married parents, and this economic difference explains some, but not all, of the association between family structure and children's subsequent well-being. As their mothers move in and out of cohabiting and marital unions, children's lives are disrupted, sometimes in good ways and sometimes in bad ways. Repeated family changes of this type, however, may increase the risk of some negative outcomes (e.g., Wu & Martinson, 1993). Just as mother's marital status is inadequate to determine whether she is cohabiting with the child's father, knowledge of children's living arrangements alone is inadequate to determine whether a child's father is involved in the child's life (Marsiglio, Amato, Day, & Lamb, 2000). Children's relationships with their nonresident biological father also affect their adjustment and well-being (Amato & Gilbreth, 1999; Seltzer, 1994). Research on the effects on children of being born outside of marriage and of changes in parents' cohabitation and marital status must take account of children's developmental stage when the changes occur, as well as changes in parents' economic circumstances, residential mobility, and other aspects of the parents' lives that affect their ability to care for their children. A thorough review of the growing body of research in this area is beyond the scope of my review.

STUDYING COHABITATION AND NONMARITAL CHILDBEARING

The increase in cohabitation in the United States has motivated researchers to develop new ways of studying who cohabits and why. The U.S. Census Bureau changed the way it identifies cohabiting couples first in the Decennial Census and then in the Current Population Survey. The 1990 Decennial Census is the first to include direct information identifying cohabiting couples. That census included the category "unmarried partner" as a response choice identifying a person's relationship to the householder. Before 1990, researchers using decennial census data identified cohabiting couples using indirect methods, which define cohabitors as persons of the opposite sex who live together. Households in which there are multiple adults who meet this criterion make the identification of cohabiting couples ambiguous. The direct indicator of cohabitation also suffers from the problem that it cannot identify cohabiting couples in which one partner is not the householder (i.e., the reference person on the household roster).

Fewer people identified themselves as cohabitors in 1997 than would be treated as cohabiting based on the Census Bureau's indirect method of identifying cohabiting unions, 3,079,000 by self-identification versus 4,125,000 by indirect identification (Casper & Cohen, 2000, Table 2). Estimates of the proportion of the population who are cohabiting vary, depending on the way cohabitors are identified, even among studies such as the National Survey of Families and Households, the National Survey of Youth 1979, and the Panel Study of Income Dynamics, which include more direct measures of cohabiting couples. How the question is asked affects responses, and the degree of variation across surveys differs by respondents' age and other characteristics (Casper & Cohen; Moffitt, Revelle, & Winkler, 1998). The indirect measure used in the past by the Census Bureau undercounts cohabitors who live with children (Casper & Cohen).

As cohabitation and childbearing outside of marriage have become more common, survey respondents may be more willing to identify themselves as cohabiting or as having had a nonmarital birth. This affects both trends and differentials to the extent that subgroups in the population perceive these behaviors as more or less stigmatized. Similarly, trends in nonmarital childbearing based on vital statistics records may overstate the increase since 1970 in nonmarital childbearing, compared with Current Population Survey data, because the vital registration data are more affected by social desirability bias in the early part of the period, which encouraged mothers to report nonmarital births as marital births (Wu et al., 1999). Consistent with this interpretation, discrepancies between the time trends for Whites are significantly larger than those for Blacks, for whom nonmarital childbearing was less stigmatized.

Change in how the Census Bureau estimates cohabitors is only one aspect of the difficulty of defining cohabiting unions. Couple relationships occur along a continuum of greater and lesser intensity, time spent together, and the degree to which the relationship is recognized by the state (marriage vs. nonmarital unions). (Also see Ross, 1995, who treated partnerships on a continuum of social attachment.) In some informal unions, couples spend substantial time together but still maintain separate households. If the maintenance of separate households is a temporary phenomenon as partners make the transition to a single household, it may be difficult for survey respondents— and for researchers—to specify a date that the relationship or even the cohabiting part of the relationship began. Individuals may also be in a long-term, intimate relationship to which they are highly committed but still live apart, sometimes referred to as "Living Apart Together" (Leridon & Villeneuve-Gokalp, 1989; Liefbroer & Gierveld, 1993). How members of a couple think about their relationship and whether they view themselves as "partners," "lovers," or something else may also vary over time. Couples may describe themselves differently to different audiences (parents, friends, co-workers). Members of the same couple also may differ in how they view their relationship, how they describe it, and in whether they consider their children to be planned or unplanned (Thomson et al., 1998; Goldscheider & Kaufman, 1996; Manning, 1999; Montgomery, 1996; Thornton et al., 1998).

This variation poses methodological problems but also raises conceptual questions about what is being studied. We know relatively little about the progress of relationships between "dating" and living together, about how members of a couple think about their relationship, including when each person begins to think of themselves as part of a couple and their expectations for the relationship and how long it will last. Longitudinal data from individuals and those they identify as "dating" or other types of partners would help address these gaps. The design of the National Longitudinal Study of Adolescent Health helps address this need, but the sample members are too young to be used to study adult family relationships. Matched couples, those in which partners agree that they are in a relationship, should be compared with matched couples in which partners disagree about their relationship and to unmatched persons to provide more complete information about why some persons "choose" to be in a relationship and some do not.

One reason that we are able to identify these gaps in the conceptualization and in the data on nonmarital families is the tremendous improvement over the past decade in the quality and extent of data that we do have on cohabiting relationships, on cohabitors, and on childbearing outside of marriage. Many of the results summarized here come from the two waves of the National Survey of Families and Households, the Panel Study of Income Dynamics, and the National Survey of Family Growth (NSFG). The 1979 National Longitudinal Survey of Youth (NLSY79) has become a valuable new data source with the recent release of cohabitation information, including whether male respondents married cohabiting partners, that has been coded from the (mostly) annual household roster information (National Longitudinal Survey of Youth User Services, 2000). Although the rosters will not provide information about cohabitations that began and ended between survey dates, the inclusion of the new data will allow a more careful assessment of union patterns for men than was possible previously with this economic survey (Gryn, Mott, & Burchett-Patel, 2000).

Even without the new information, the NLSY79 provides useful information about children's experience with parents' cohabitation (Graefe & Lichter, 1999). Other data sources, such as The National Longitudinal Survey of the High School Class of 1972 (NLSHS72), provide information about subgroups of interest, such as high school graduates, although in light of the link between economic disadvantage and cohabitation, such studies miss an important subgroup. Longitudinal studies restricted to specific cohorts, such as the NLSHS72 and the 1961 Detroit Area Study, provide invaluable information about the family experiences of individuals as they age. However, rapid change in public opinion and the institutional setting in which individuals make decisions about cohabitation means that we should continue to collect data on new cohorts' experiences to assess change in the meaning of cohabitation and nonmarital childbearing. Otherwise, inferences about the meaning of cohabitation will be based on the meaning for a particular cohort. Willis and Michael (1994), for example, noted that their conclusions about cohabitation as a trial marriage were specific to the cohort who graduated from high school in 1972. The parallel designs of the NLSY79 and the 1997 National Longitudinal Survey of Youth are important steps in the right direction to enable cross-cohort comparisons of cohabiting experiences.

Data from other countries and from different race and ethnic groups within countries open new opportunities to investigate the effects of context on the formation and consequences of families formed outside of marriage. The European Fertility and Family Surveys include data on a common set of questions, including partnership and birth histories, for more than 20 countries. Most of these were conducted in the 1990s and are designed to be comparable to the 1995 NSFG in the United States. These, along with rich data from several British and Canadian surveys and from other U.S. surveys from which much of this review is drawn, suggest that the next *Journal of Marriage and the Family* decade review on families formed outside of marriage will include a summary of more explicitly comparative analyses. These will build on projects like that of Blossfeld (1995) and the contributors to his volume comparing nine countries. A strength of the cross-country comparative design is variation in the social and legal institutions that govern marriage and that affect parents' obligations to children born inside and outside of marriage.

Cohabiting relationships and nonmarital childbearing are best studied with information from or about two partners, in part because members of the same couple see and understand things differently (e.g., whether a union is temporary, whether the couple will live together when a child is born, what rights each person has to common goods, including children). The National Survey of Families and Households design assumes that information from both partners is essential. It includes information from both members of cohabiting couples, married couples, and ex-couples. Unfortunately, low rates of survey participation may bias results from couple samples. Families in which both members of cohabiting couples and both new parents of children born outside of marriage participate in surveys differ in important ways from those in which only one partner or parent participates (McLanahan et al., 1999b; McNally, Sassler, & Schoen, 1997). Men and women may differ in the quality of their reports or their understanding of interviewers' questions. For instance, compared with men, women appear to report both the occurrence and the dates of family events with fewer errors (Auriat, 1993; Rendall, Clarke, Peters, Ranjit, & Verropoulou, 1999) and to interpret the phrase "live with" differently (Tuschen, 1994). In particular, male survey respondents are less likely than female respondents to report about the existence of their children born outside of marriage (Rendall et al.). The hospital-based design of the Fragile Families and Child

Wellbeing Study, which attempts to interview both mothers and fathers at the time their child is born, attempts to address this problem. Survey data on men suffer from both nonparticipation and response bias (Rendall et al.; Schaeffer, Seltzer, & Dykema, 1998).

Finally, most current knowledge about the place of cohabitation and nonmarital childbearing in U.S. kinship comes from studies of young adults and of women in their reproductive years. The focus on the reproductive years provided valuable insight into the experiences of individuals making major decisions about how they will start their adult family lives. But if people are lucky, life is long. Children grow up and form new families. Parents dissolve marriages and form new unions. The process of cohort replacement means that the elderly population of tomorrow will have much more experience with cohabitation, both in their own intimate relationships and in their children's lives. Survey samples of older persons will include more respondents who have ever or are currently cohabiting. We know little about cohabitation in older age. New research on the meaning of cohabitation and other families formed outside of marriage, including "Living Apart Together," should examine age (life stage) differences in couple members' understanding of the obligations of cohabitation and in the way these couples arrange their lives together.

BEHAVIORAL AND LEGAL DEFINITIONS OF FAMILY

Cohabitation and childbearing outside of marriage are central features of growth in families formed outside of marriage. Relationships between cohabiting couples and between many parents of babies born outside of marriage are defined by coresidence and sharing a household. Nonmarital family relationships also cross household boundaries, as when parents and children live apart after divorce. Contact and financial transfers from nonresident parents to minor children help define family ties that may be important for children's welfare (Seltzer, 1991, 1994). Cohabitation, childbearing outside of marriage, and relationships between parents and minor children who live apart are all families that exist largely without formal recognition by the state, although state laws about child support are an important exception to the lack of formal recognition. Individual citizens and policy makers seek to formalize relationships between cohabiting couples and fathers and children who live apart to acquire rights and, from the policy makers' side, establish responsibilities.

Two aspects of cohabiting unions may be formalized: rights and responsibilities within the union, including property and inheritance, and rights and responsibilities with respect to the state and other third parties (e.g., Blumberg, 1981, 1985). Rights within the union can formalized by individual contracts and other legal procedures the couple members can initiate. Establishing these legal contracts may be expensive, which means that they are not universally available because cohabitation is more common among the economically disadvantaged.

Rights with respect to third parties, such as social insurance claims, access to health insurance and other "family" benefits, derive from public action, including the passage of state laws, city ordinances establishing domestic partnership licenses, and policies adopted by employers. Vermont's recent civil union legislation tries to formalize both aspects of nonmarital unions for same-sex couples. The legislation provides same-sex couples who establish a civil union with the rights and obligations of marriage and requires that when a civil union dissolves, it is governed by the laws for marital dissolution. Other domestic partner laws apply to both same-sex and opposite-sex partnerships but may limit the types of heterosexual couples who are allowed to register as domestic partners. For instance, the California Assembly bill (AB 26, 1999–2000) on domestic partners allows same-sex adult partners or seniors to register as partners if they live together and agree to be jointly responsible for each other's living expenses. The bill gives partners the same rights to hospital visitation as members of married families have, as well as rights to health insurance benefits. The substantial variation across states in the availability of domestic partnership registration, the eligibility rules, and the benefits and responsibilities of registration demonstrates public disagreement about the meaning of cohabitation and its place in the U.S. kinship system. The rapidly changing opportunities to acquire domestic partnerships and the diverse record keeping systems make it difficult to study these arrangements. We know little about the prevalence of domestic partnerships, the content of the agreements, who acquires the partnerships, and the consequences of the partnerships for the nature and stability of the relationship, although researchers are beginning to address these questions (e.g., Willetts & Scanzoni 1998).

Evidence about trends and effects of policies formalizing biological fathers' ties to children is somewhat better. Between the mid-1970s and the late 1980s the percentage of divorcing families with joint legal custody increased from about 10% to nearly 30% (author's tabulations). Joint legal custody is the formal right to make decisions about the child's life, as distinct from physical custody or placement, which identifies with whom a child lives. Because most national data sources do not include good measures of joint legal custody, it is not possible to assess whether this trend has continued in the 1990s, although evidence from a small sample suggests that it has (Seltzer, 1998).

Rates of paternity establishment, the mechanism for identifying the biological father of a child born outside of marriage as the child's legal father, have also increased in recent decades, from just under 20% of nonmarital births in 1979 to more than 50% in 1996 (Garfinkel, Meyer, & McLanahan, 1998). Increases in paternity establishment reflect federal emphasis on the need for legal paternity establishment as a first step in assigning child support orders and collecting formal child support on behalf of children born outside of marriage.

Policies advancing joint legal custody and paternity establishment emphasize the rights and responsibilities of biological parents, primarily fathers, because fathers are more likely than mothers to live apart from their children. Advocates of the policies expect that formalizing fathers' ties to children will increase their commitment to childrearing and increase the amount of time and money that the fathers invest in their children. Critics who are skeptical about past work showing a positive association between formal ties and paternal involvement argue that fathers and families who formalize their relationships are already more child-oriented or get along better, and these characteristics explain both the adoption of joint legal custody or legal paternity as well as nonresident fathers' greater involvement with children.

Even after taking account of preexisting differences between families, both joint legal custody and paternity establishment may increase fathers' involvement with children. Joint legal custody increases the frequency of visits between nonresident fathers and children (Seltzer, 1998). Preliminary evidence also suggests that compared with fathers without paternity, those for whom legal paternity has been established are more likely to pay child support and to spend time with their children (Seltzer, 1999). These findings suggest that formalization of a father's rights and responsibilities alters his participation in childrearing and may alter the behavior of the child's mother as well. Whether formalizing relationships between unmarried cohabiting couples also alters their investments in their relationship is an important question for research in the coming decade. Based on research in the 1990s, there is every reason to expect that U.S. families will continue to be formed outside of marriage and, in a sense, outside the law, while at the same time legal institutions will continue to move toward formalizing relationships in these families.

COHABITATION AND NONMARITAL CHILDBEARING: INDIVIDUAL AND SOCIAL MATTERS

Families matter for individuals. What happens in our families affects how we live our lives, whether we are rich or poor, the languages we speak, the work that we do, how healthy we are, and how we feel. Families also matter for the larger social group. Family members take care of each other (some better than others) and bear and rear the next generation. Within a society, the work families do depends on what people believe is the right way to treat parents, siblings, children, grandparents, and other kin. A common understanding about the obligations and rights of family members contributes to the institutionalization of family relationships. General consensus in public opinion about who should be counted as a family member and consistent laws also institutionalize relationships. Cohabitation, like remarriage, is still an incomplete institution in the United States (Cherlin, 1978; Nock 1995). It takes a long time for new behaviors to become institutionalized.

The rapid increase in cohabitation and nonmarital childbearing over the past few decades suggests that these relationships may become more complete institutions in the future, but it is unlikely that they will have the preferred standing of marriage and childbearing in marriage any time soon. Cohabiting couples are very diverse, in part because they are forming their relationships under a rapidly changing set of social rules about marriage, cohabitation, and childbearing outside of marriage. The instability of the environment in which individuals make family choices hampers the enforcement of kin obligations and norms about the acceptability of informal families and makes it even more likely that individuals will experiment in their family lives.

Some cohabitors would prefer formal marriage, but their economic circumstances prevent them from achieving this goal. Others seek a different type of relationship, one with greater gender equality, than they expect to find in marriage or than they found in a previous marriage. Yet another group of cohabitors uses their informal relationship as a trial period during which they negotiate and assess whether to formalize their union through marriage. We do not know the relative size of these groups in the population nor do we know how rapidly each group is growing. The heterogeneity of cohabiting couples poses a challenge to researchers who try to understand what cohabitation means.

Adults have more choices today about whether to cohabit and whether to have a child outside of marriage because the social costs, at least to adults, of forming informal families are much less today than just a few decades ago. Choosing one's family is part of a long-term trend toward greater individual autonomy in West Europe and the United States (Lesthaeghe, 1995). The ability to choose at the individual level, however, does not mean that all choices will or should have the same standing in the public sphere. Nevertheless, the inclusion of a decade review on families formed outside of marriage in the *Journal of Marriage and the Family* demonstrates the greater legitimacy of individual choice in the contemporary United States and suggests even greater variation in informal families in the near future.

NOTE

This work was supported, in part, by a grant from the Council on Research of the UCLA Academic Senate. The paper benefited from discussion with seminar participants at the University of California, Berkeley; University of Washington; University of California, Riverside; RAND; University of Virginia; University of Wisconsin—Madison; and Notre Dame University. I am grateful to Suzanne Bianchi, Larry Bumpass, Lynne Casper, Wendy Manning, Robert Mare, Kelly Musick, R. Kelly Raley, Christine Schwartz, and Pamela Smock for helpful advice, discussion, and comments on previous versions.

REFERENCES

Allen, K. R., Blieszner, R., & Roberto, K. A. (2000). Families in the middle and later years: A review and critique of research in the 1990s. *Journal of Marriage and the Family 62,* 911–926.

Amato, P. R., (2000). The consequences of divorce for

adults and children. *Journal of Marriage and the Family, 62,* 1269–1287.

Amato, P. R., & Gilbreth, J. G. (1999). Nonresident fathers and children's well-being: A meta-analysis. *Journal of Marriage and the Family, 61,* 557–573.

Aquilino, W. S. (1997). From adolescent to young adult: A prospective study of parent-child relations during the transition to adulthood. *Journal of Marriage and the Family, 59,* 670–686.

Auriat, N. (1993). "My wife knows best": A comparison of event dating accuracy between the wife, the husband, the couple, and the Belgium Population Register. *Public Opinion Quarterly, 57,* 165–190.

Axinn, W. G. & Thornton, A. (1992). The relationship between cohabitation and divorce: Selectivity or causal influence? *Demography, 29,* 357–374.

Bachrach, C. A. (1987). Cohabitation and reproductive behavior in the United States. *Demography, 24,* 623–637.

Bauman, K. J. (1999). Shifting family definitions: The effect of cohabitation and other nonfamily household relationships on measures of poverty. *Demography, 36,* 315–325.

Beller, A. H., & Graham, J. W. (1993). *Small change: The economics of child support.* New Haven, CT: Yale University Press.

Berger, P. L., & Kellner, H. (1974). Marriage and the construction of reality. In R. L. Coser (Ed.), *The family: Its structures and functions* (2nd ed., pp. 157–174). New York: St. Martin's Press.

Berrington, A., &. Diamond, I. (1999). Marital dissolution among the 1958 British birth cohort: The role of cohabitation. *Population Studies, 53,* 19–38.

Blossfeld, H.-P. (Ed.). (1995). *The new role of women: Family formation in modern societies.* Boulder, CO: Westview Press.

Blumberg, G. G. (1981). Cohabitation without marriage: A different perspective. *UCLA Law Review, 28,* 1125–1180.

Blumberg, G. G. (1985). New models of marriage and divorce: Significant legal developments in the last decade. In K. Davis with A. Grossbard-Shechtman (Eds.), *Contemporary marriage: Comparative perspectives on a changing institution.* New York: Russell Sage.

Blumstein, P., & Schwartz, P. (1983). *American couples: Money, work and sex.* New York: William Morrow and Co.

Bracher M., & Santow, G. (1998). Economic independence and union formation in Sweden. *Population Studies, 52,* 275–294.

Brines, J., & Joyner, K. (1999). The ties that bind: Principles of cohesion in cohabitation and marriage. *American Sociological Review, 64,* 333–355.

Brown, S. S. (2000). Fertility following marital dissolution: The role of cohabitation. *Journal of Family Issues, 21,* 501–524.

Brown, S. S., & Eisenberg, L. (Eds.). (1995). *The best intentions: Unintended pregnancy and the well-being of children and families.* Washington, DC: National Academy Press.

Brüderl, J., Diekmann, A., & Engelhardt, H. (1997, August). *Premarital cohabitation and marital stability in West Germany.* Paper presented at the annual meeting of the American Sociological Association, Toronto.

Bumpass, L. L. (1995). *The declining significance of marriage: Changing family life in the United States* (National Survey of Families and Households Working Paper no. 66). Center for Demography and Ecology, University of Wisconsin, Madison.

Bumpass, L. L. (1998). The changing significance of marriage in the United States. In K. O. Mason, N. O. Tsuya, & M. K. Choe (Eds.), *The changing family in comparative perspective: Asia and the United States* (pp. 63–79). Honolulu, HI: East-West Center.

Bumpass, L. L., & Lu, H.-H. (2000). Trends in cohabitation and implications for children's family contexts in the United States. *Population Studies, 54,* 29–41.

Bumpass, L. L., & Raley, R. K. (1995). Redefining single-parent families: Cohabitation and changing family reality. *Demography, 32,* 97–109.

Bumpass, L. L., Raley, R. K., & Sweet, J. A. (1995). The changing character of stepfamilies: Implications of cohabitation and nonmarital childbearing. *Demography, 32,* 425–436.

Bumpass, L. L., & Sweet, J. A. (1989). National estimates of cohabitation. *Demography, 26,* 615–625.

Bumpass, L. L., & Sweet, J. A. (1995). *Cohabitation, marriage, and nonmarital childbearing and union stability: Preliminary findings from NSFH2* (National Survey of Families and Households Working Paper no. 65). Center for Demography and Ecology, University of Wisconsin, Madison.

Bumpass, L. L., & Sweet, J. (in press). Marriage, divorce, and intergenerational relationships. In A. Thornton (Ed.), *The Well-Being of Children and Families.* Ann Arbor, MI: University of Michigan Press.

Bumpass, L. L., Sweet. J. A., & Cherlin, A. J. 1991. The role of cohabitation in declining rates of marriage. *Journal of Marriage and the Family, 53,* 913–927.

Carlson, M., & Danziger, S. (1999). Cohabitation and the measurement of child poverty. *Review of Income and Wealth, 2,* 179–191.

Casper, L. M., & Bianchi, S. M. (in press). Cohabitation. In *Trends in the American family.* Thousand Oaks, CA: Sage.

Casper, L. M., & Cohen, P. N. (2000). How does POSSLQ measure up? Historical estimates of cohabitation. *Demography, 37,* 237–245.

Cherlin, A. J. (1978). Remarriage as an incomplete institution. *American Journal of Sociology, 84,* 634–650.

Cherlin, A. J. (1992). *Marriage, divorce, remarriage.* Cambridge, MA: Harvard University Press.

Cherlin, A. J. (2000). Toward a new home socioeconomics of union formation. In L. J. Waite, C. Bachrach, M. Hindin, E. Thomson, & A. Thornton (Eds.), *Ties that bind: perspectives on marriage and cohabitation* (pp. 126–144). Hawthorne, NY: Aldine de Gruyter.

Cherlin, A. J., Kiernan, K. E., & Chase-Lansdale, P. L. (1995). Parental divorce in childhood and demographic outcomes in young adulthood. *Demography, 32,* 299–318.

Chevan, A. (1996). As cheaply as one: Cohabitation in the older population. *Journal of Marriage and the Family, 58,* 656–667.

Citro, C. F., & Michael, R. T. (Eds.). (1995). *Measuring poverty: A new approach.* Washington, DC: National Academy Press.

Clarkberg, J. (1999). The price of partnering: The role of economic well-being in young adults' first union experiences. *Social Forces, 77,* 945–968.

Clarkberg, M., Stolzenberg, R. M., & Waite, L. J. (1995). Attitudes, values, and entrance into cohabitational versus marital unions. *Social Forces, 74,* 609–634.

DeMaris, A., & Rao, K. V. (1992). Premarital cohabitation and subsequent marital stability in the United States: A reassessment. *Journal of Marriage and the Family, 54,* 178–190.

De Vos, S. (1999). Comment of coding marital status in Latin America. *Journal of Comparative Family Studies, 30,* 79–93.

Ermisch, J. (1999, April). *Cohabitation and childbearing outside marriage in Britain.* Paper presented at the Conference on Nonmarital Childbearing, Institute for Research on Poverty, University of Wisconsin, Madison.

Furstenberg, F. F., Jr. (1997, January). *Family change and family diversity: Accounts of the past and scenarios of the future.* Paper prepared for the Conference on Common Values, Social Diversity, and Cultural Conflict, Center for Advanced Study in the Behavioral Sciences, Stanford, CA.

Garasky, S., & Meyer, D. R. (1996). Reconsidering the increase in father-only families. *Demography, 33,* 385–393.

Garfinkel, I., Meyer, D. R., & McLanahan, S. S. (1998). A brief history of child support policies in the United States. In I. Garfinkel, S. S. McLanahan, D. R. Meyer, & J. A. Seltzer (Eds.), *Fathers under fire: The revolution in child support enforcement* (pp. 14–30). New York: Russell Sage.

Goldscheider, F. K., & Kaufman, G. (1996). Fertility and commitment: Bringing men back in. In J. B. Casterline, R. D. Lee, & K. A. Foote (Eds.), *Fertility in the United States: New patterns, new theories* (pp. 87–99). New York: Population Council.

Goldstein, J. R. (1999). The leveling of divorce in the United States. *Demography, 36,* 409–414.

Gonnot, J.-P., Keilman, N., & Prinz, C. (1995). *Social security, household, and family dynamics in aging societies.* Boston: Kluwer Academic.

Gordon, K. C. (1998/1999). The necessity and enforcement of cohabitation agreements: When strings will attach and how to prevent them. A state survey. *University of Louisville Brandeis Law Journal, 37,* 245–257.

Graefe, D. R., & Lichter, D. T. (1999). Life course transitions of American children: Parental cohabitation, marriage, and single motherhood. *Demography, 36,* 205–217.

Gryn, T. A., Mott, F. L., & Burchett-Patel, D. (2000, March). *Relationship trajectories for a contemporary cohort of men in early middle age: Evidence from the NLSY79.* Paper presented at the annual meeting of the Population Association of America, Los Angeles.

Gupta, S. (1999). The effects of transitions in marital status on men's performance of housework. *Journal of Marriage and the Family, 61,* 700–711.

Harris, K. M., Boisjoly, J., & Duncan, G. J. (1999, April). *Great expectations: Consequences of adolescent sexuality, pregnancy, and childbearing on perceptions of adult attainments.* Paper presented at the Conference on Nonmarital Childbearing, Institute for

Research on Poverty, University of Wisconsin, Madison.

Hanson, T. L., McLanahan, S., & Thomson, E. (1997). Economic resources, parental practices, and children's well-being. In G. Duncan & J. Brooks-Gunn (Eds.), *Consequences of growing up poor* (pp. 190–238). New York: Russell Sage.

Hoem, B. (1995). Sweden. In H.-P. Blossfeld (Ed.), *The new role of women: Family formation in modern societies* (pp. 35–55). Boulder, CO: Westview Press.

Hoffman, S. D., & Foster, E. M. (1997). Nonmarital births and single mothers: Cohort trends in the dynamics of nonmarital childbearing. *The History of the Family, 2,* 255–275.

Keane, M. P., & Wolpin, K. I. (1999, April). *Estimating welfare effects consistent with forward-looking behavior.* Paper presented at the Conference on Nonmarital Childbearing, Institute for Research on Poverty, University of Wisconsin, Madison.

Kiernan, K. E. (1999, April). *European perspectives on non-marital childbearing.* Paper presented at the Conference on Nonmarital Childbearing, Institute for Research on Poverty, University of Wisconsin, Madison.

Kiernan, K. E., & Estaugh, V. (1993). *Cohabitation: Extra-marital childbearing and social policy* (Occasional Paper 17). London: Family Policy Studies Centre.

King, V. (1994). Variation in the consequences of nonresident father involvement for children's well-being. *Journal of Marriage and the Family, 56,* 963–972.

Kravdal, O. (1999). Does marriage require a stronger economic underpinning than informal cohabitation? *Population Studies, 53,* 63–80.

Landale, N. S., & Fennelly, K. (1992). Informal unions among mainland Puerto Ricans: Cohabitation or an alternative to legal marriage? *Journal of Marriage and the Family, 54,* 269–280.

Landale, N. S., & Forste, R. (1991). Patterns of entry into cohabitation and marriage among mainland Puerto Rican women. *Demography, 28,* 587–607.

Laumann, E. O., Gagnon, J. H., Michael, R. T., & Michaels, S. (1994). *The social organization of sexuality: Sexual practices in the United States.* Chicago: University of Chicago Press.

Leridon, H. (1990). Cohabitation, marriage, separation: An analysis of life histories of French cohorts from 1968 to 1985. *Population Studies, 44,* 127–144.

Leridon, H., & Villeneuve-Gokalp, C. (1989). The new couples: Number, characteristics, and attitudes. *Population, 44,* 203–235.

Lesthaeghe, R. (1995). The second demographic transition in Western countries: An interpretation. In K. O. Mason & A.-M. Jensen (Eds.), *Gender and family change in industrialized countries* (pp. 17–82). Oxford, UK: Clarendon Press.

Liefbroer, A. C., & Gierveld, J. D. J. (1993). The impact of rational considerations and perceived opinions on young adults' union formation intentions. *Journal of Family Issues 14,* 213–235.

Lillard, L. A., Brien, M. J., & Waite, L. J. (1995). Premarital cohabitation and subsequent marital dissolution: A matter of self-selection. *Demography 32,* 437–457.

Loomis, L. S., & Landale, N. S. (1994). Nonmarital cohabitation and childbearing among Black and

White American women. *Journal of Marriage and the Family 56,* 949–962.

Malinowski, B. (1964). Parenthood, the basis of social structure. In R. L. Coser (Ed.), *The family: Its structure and functions* (pp. 3–19). New York: St. Martin's Press. (Original work published 1930)

Manning, W. D. (1995). Cohabitation, marriage, and entry into motherhood. *Journal of Marriage and the Family, 57,* 191–200.

Manning, W. D. (1999, March). *Childbearing in cohabiting unions: Racial and ethnic differences.* Paper presented at the annual meeting of the Population Association of American, New York.

Manning, W. D., & Landale, N. S. (1996). Racial and ethnic differences in the role of cohabitation in premarital childbearing. *Journal of Marriage and the Family, 58,* 63–77.

Manning, W. D., & Lichter, D. T. (1996). Parental cohabitation and children's economic well-being. *Journal of Marriage and the Family, 58,* 998–1010.

Manning, W. D., & Smock, P. J. (1995). Why marry? Race and the transition to marriage among cohabitors. *Demography, 32,* 509–520.

Mare, R. D., & Winship, C. (1991). Socioeconomic change and the decline of marriage for Blacks and Whites. In C. Jencks & P. E. Peterson (Eds.), *The urban underclass* (pp. 175–202). Washington, DC: Brookings Institute.

Marsiglio, W., Amato, P., Day, R. D., & Lamb, M. E. (current issue). Scholarship on fatherhood in the 1990s and beyond. *Journal of Marriage and the Family, 62,* 1173–1191.

McLanahan, S., Garfinkel, I., & Padilla, Y. (1999a). The Fragile Families and Child Wellbeing Study: Austin, Texas (baseline report). Center for Research on Child Wellbeing, Princeton University, Princeton, NJ.

McLanahan, S., Garfinkel, I., & Waller, M. (1999b). The Fragile Families and Child Wellbeing Study: Oakland, California (baseline report). Center for Research on Child Wellbeing, Princeton University, Princeton, NJ.

McLanahan, S., & Sandefur, G. (1994). *Growing up with a single parent: What hurts, what helps.* Cambridge, MA: Harvard University Press.

McNally, J. W., Sassler, S., & Schoen, R. (1997). *"Misplaced affection": The use of multiple imputation to reconstruct missing cohabiting partner information in the NSFH* (Population Studies and Training Center Working Paper no. 97–09). Brown University, Providence, RI.

Moffitt, R. A., Revelle, R., & Winkler, A. E. (1998). Beyond single mothers: Cohabitation and marriage in the AFDC program. *Demography 35,* 259–278.

Montgomery, M. (1996). Comments on men, women, and unintended pregnancy. In J. B. Casterline, R. D. Lee, & K. A. Foote (Eds.), *Fertility in the United States: New patterns, new theories* (pp. 100–106). New York: Population Council.

National Longitudinal Survey of Youth User Services. (2000). *NLS News* [no. 00–100]. Washington, DC: U.S. Bureau of Labor Statistics. Retrieved July 28, 2000, from the World Wide Web: http://www.bls.gov/pdf/nls100.pdf

Nock, S. L. (1995). A comparison of marriages and cohabiting relationships. *Journal of Family Issues, 16,* 53–76.

Oppenheimer, V. K. (1988). A theory of marriage timing. *American Journal of Sociology, 94,* 563–591.

Oppenheimer, V. K. (1997). Women's employment and the gain to marriage: The specialization and trading model. *Annual Review of Sociology, 23,* 431–453.

Oppenheimer, V. K., Kalmijn, M., & Lim, N. (1997). Men's career development and marriage timing during a period of rising inequality. *Demography, 34,* 311–330.

Oropesa, R. S. (1996). Normative beliefs about marriage and cohabitation: A comparison of non-Latino Whites, Mexican Americans, and Puerto Ricans. *Journal of Marriage and the Family, 58,* 49–62.

Parrado, E. A., & Tienda, M. (1997). Women's roles and family formation in Venezuela: New forms of consensual unions? *Social Biology, 44,* 1–24

Parnell, A. M., Swicegood, G., & Stevens, G. (1994). Nonmarital pregnancies and marriage in the United States. *Social Forces, 73,* 263–287.

Pagnini, D. L., & Rindfuss, R. R. (1993). The divorce of marriage and childbearing: Changing attitudes and behavior in the United States. *Population and Development Review, 19,* 331–347.

Patterson, C. J. (2000). The families of lesbians and gay men. *Journal of Marriage and the Family, 62,* 1052–1069.

Prinz, C. (1995). *Cohabiting, married, or single: Portraying, analyzing, and modeling new living arrangements in the changing societies of Europe.* Brookfield, VT: Avebury.

Raley, R. K. (1996). A Shortage of marriageable men? A note on the role of coinhabitation in Black-White differences in marriage rates. *American Sociological Review, 61,* 973–983.

Raley, R. K. (in press). Increasing Fertility in coinhabiting unions: Evidence for the second demographic transition in the United States? *Demography.*

Rendall, M. S., Clarke, L., Peters, H. E., Ranjit, N., & Verropoulou, G. (1999). Incomplete reporting of men's fertility in the United States and Britain: A research note. *Demography, 36,* 135–144.

Rindfuss, R. R., & VandenHeuvel, A. (1990). Cohabitation: A precursor to marriage or an alternative to being single? *Population and Development Review, 16,* 703–726.

Ross, C. E. (1995). Reconceptualizing marital status as a continuum of social attachment. *Journal of Marriage and the Family, 57,* 129–140.

Schaeffer, N. C., Seltzer, J. A., & Dykema, J. (1998). *Methodological and theoretical issues in studying nonresident fathers: A selective review* (National Center on Fathers and Families Working Paper no. WP98-02). University of Pennsylvania, Philadelphia.

Schoen, R. (1992). First unions and the stability of first marriages. *Journal of Marriage and the Family, 54,* 281–284.

Seltzer, J. A. (1991). Relationships between fathers and children who live apart. *Journal of Marriage and the Family, 53,* 79–101.

Seltzer, J. A. (1994). Consequences of marital dissolution for children. *Annual Review of Sociology, 20,* 235–266.

Seltzer, J. A. (1998). Father by law: Effects of joint legal custody on nonresident fathers' involvement with children. *Demography, 35,* 135–146.

Seltzer, J. A. (1999, April). *Legal fatherhood for chil-*

dren born out of wedlock. Paper presented at the Conference on Nonmarital Childbearing, Institute for Research on Poverty, University of Wisconsin, Madison.

Seltzer, J. A. (2000). Child support and child access: Experiences of divorced and nonmarital families. In J. T. Oldham & M. S. Melli (Eds.), *Child support: The next frontier* (pp. 69–87) Ann Arbor, MI: University of Michigan Press.

Shelton, B. A., & John, D. (1993). Does marital status make a difference? *Journal of Family Issues, 14,* 401–420.

Singh, S., & Lindsay, J. (1996). Money in heterosexual relationships. *The Australian and New Zealand Journal of Sociology, 32,* 57–69.

Smith, H. L., Morgan, S. P., & Koropeckyj-Cox, T. (1996). A decomposition of trends in the nonmarital fertility ratios of Blacks and Whites in the United States, 1960–1992. *Demography, 33,* 141–151.

Smock, P. J. (2000). Cohabitation in the United States: An appraisal of research themes, findings, and implications. *Annual Review of Sociology, 26,* 1–20

Smock, P. J., & Manning, W. D. (1997). Cohabiting partners' economic circumstances and marriage. *Demography, 34,* 331–341.

South, S. J., & Spitze, G. (1994). Housework in marital and nonmarital households. *American Sociological Review, 59,* 327–347.

Surra, C. A. (1990). Research and theory on mate selection and premarital relationships in the 1980s. *Journal of Marriage and the Family, 52,* 844–865.

Sweet, J. A., & Bumpass, L. L. (1992). Disruption of marital and cohabitation relationships: A social demographic perspective. In T. L. Orbuch (Ed.), *Close relationship loss: Theoretical approaches* (pp. 67–89). New York: Springer-Verlag.

Sweet, J. A., & Bumpass, L. L. (1996). *The National Survey of Families and Households—Waves 1 and 2: Data Description and Documentation.* Center for Demography and Ecology, University of Wisconsin, Madison. Retrieved from the World Wide Web: http://www.ssc.wisc.edu/nsfh

Teachman, J. D., Tedrow, L. M., & Crowder, K. D. (2000). The changing demography of America's families. *Journal of Marriage and the Family, 62,* 1234–1246.

Thomson, E., Bachrach, C., Kaye, K., & Ventura, S. (1998). Male fertility in relation to union formation and dissolution. In *Nurturing fatherhood: Improving data and research on male fertility, family formation and fatherhood* (pp. 327–364). Federal Interagency Forum on Child and Family Statistics. Washington, DC. Retrieved July 28, 2000, from the World Wide Web: http://aspe.hhs.gov/fathers/cfsforum/front.htm

Thomson, E., Hanson, T. L., & McLanahan, S. S. (1994). Family structure and child well-being: Economic resources vs. parental behaviors. *Social Forces, 73,* 221–242.

Thomson, E., Mosley, J., Hanson, T. L., & McLanahan, S. S. (1998). *Remarriage, cohabitation and changes in mothering. National Survey of Families and Households* (Working Paper no. 65). Center for Demography and Ecology, University of Wisconsin, Madison.

Thomson, E., McLanahan, S. S., & Curtin, R. B. (1992). Family structure, gender, and parental socialization. *Journal of Marriage and the Family, 54,* 368–378.

Thornton, A. (1989). Changing attitudes toward family issues. *Journal of Marriage and the Family, 51,* 873–893.

Thornton, A. (1991). Influence of the marital history of parents on the marital and cohabitational experiences of children. *American Journal of Sociology, 96,* 868–894.

Thornton, A. (1995). Attitudes, values and norms related to nonmarital fertility. In *Report to Congress on Out-of-Wedlock Childbearing* (pp. 201–215). U.S. Department of Health and Human Services (DHHS Pub. No. [PHS] 95–1257). Hyattsville, MD: U.S. Government Printing Office.

Thornton, A., Arnaudo, D., Marsiglio, B., Sugland, B., & Waite, L. (1998). Data and Research Needs Concerning Union Formation and Dissolution. In *Nurturing Fatherhood: Improving Data and Research on Male Fertility, Family Formation and Fatherhood* (pp. 295–325). Washington, DC: Federal Interagency Forum on Child and Family Statistics. Retrieved July 28, 2000 from the World Wide Web: http://aspe.hhs.gov/fathers/cfsforum/front.htm

Thornton, A., Axinn, W. G., & Teachman, J. D. (1995). The influence of school enrollment and accumulation on cohabitation and marriage in early adulthood. *American Sociological Review, 60,* 762–774.

Thornton, A., & Fricke, T. E. (1989). Social change and the family: Comparative perspectives from the West, China, and South Asia. In J. Mayone Stycos (Ed.), *Demography as an interdiscipline* (pp. 128–161). New Brunswick, NJ: Transaction. (Originally published in *Sociological Forum* 2, Fall 1987)

Treas, J., & Giesen, D. (2000). Sexual infidelity among married and cohabiting Americans. *Journal of Marriage and the Family, 62,* 48–60.

Tuschen, K. L. (1994). When parents "live" with their children. Unpublished honors thesis, Department of Sociology, University of Wisconsin, Madison.

U.S. Bureau of the Census. (1998). *Unpublished tables—Marital status and living arrangements: March 1998 (update).* Retrieved from the World Wide Web: http://www.census.gov/prod/99pubs/p20–514u.pdf

Ventura, S. J., Bachrach, C. A., Hill, L., Kaye, K., Holcomb, P., & Koff, E. (1995). The demography of out-of-wedlock childbearing. In *Report to Congress on Out-of-Wedlock Childbearing* (pp. 1–133). U. S. Department of Health and Human Services (DHHS Pub. No. [PHS] 95-1257). Hyattsville, MD: National Center for Health Statistics.

Ventura, S. J., & Martin, J. A. (1993). Births: Advance report of final natality statistics, 1990. *Monthly Vital Statistics Report, 41* (9; Suppl.). Hyattsville, MD: National Center for Health Statistics.

Ventura, S. J., Martin, J. A., Curtin, S. C., & Mathews, T. J. (1999). Births: Final data for 1997. *National Vital Statistics Reports, 47* (18). Hyattsville, MD: National Center for Health Statistics.

Ventura, S. J., Martin, J. A., Curtin, S. C., Mathews, T. J., & Park, M. M. (2000). Births: Final data for 1998. *National Vital Statistics Reports, 48* (3). Hyattsville, MD: National Center for Health Statistics.

Waite, L. J. (1995). Does marriage matter? *Demography, 32,* 483–507.

Waite, L. J., Bachrach, C., Hindin, M., Thomson, E., & Thornton, A. (Eds.). (2000). *Ties that bind: Perspec-*

tives on marriage and cohabitation. Hawthorne, NY: Aldine de Gruyter.

Weitzman, L. J. (1985). The divorce law revolution and the transformation of legal marriage. In K. Davis with A. Grossbard-Shechtman (Eds.), *Contemporary marriage: Comparative perspectives on a changing institution* (pp. 301–348). New York: Russell Sage.

Willetts, M. C., & Scanzoni, J. (1998, August). *Redefining family: Domestic partnership ordinances.* Paper presented at the annual meeting of the American Sociological Association, San Francisco, CA.

Willis, R. J., & Haaga, J. G. (1996). Economic approaches to understanding nonmarital fertility. In J. B. Casterline, R. D. Lee, & K. A. Foote (Eds.), *Fertility in the United States: New patterns, new theories* (pp. 67–86). New York: Population Council.

Willis, R. J., & Michael, R. T. (1994). Innovation in family formation: Evidence on cohabitation in the United States. In J. Ermisch & N. Ogawa (Eds.), *The family, the market and the state in ageing societies* (pp. 9–45). Oxford, UK: Clarendon Press.

Winkler, A. E. (1997). Economic decision-making by cohabitors: Findings regarding income pooling. *Applied Economics, 29,* 1079–1090.

Wu, L. L., Bumpass, L. L., & Musick, K. (1999, July). *Historical and life course trajectories of nonmarital childbearing.* Revised version of paper presented at the Conference on Nonmarital Fertility, Institute for Research on Poverty, University of Wisconsin, Madison.

Wu, L. L., & Martinson, B. C. (1993). Family structure and the risk of a premarital birth. *American Sociological Review, 58,* 210–232.

Wu, Z., & Balakrishnan, T. R. (1995). Dissolution of premarital cohabitation in Canada. *Demography, 32,* 521–532.

Paul R. Amato *The Pennsylvania State University*

The Consequences of Divorce for Adults and Children

I use a divorce-stress-adjustment perspective to summarize and organize the empirical literature on the consequences of divorce for adults and children. My review draws on research in the 1990s to answer five questions: How do individuals from married and divorced families differ in well-being? Are these differences due to divorce or to selection? Do these differences reflect a temporary crisis to which most people gradually adapt or stable life strains that persist more or less indefinitely? What factors mediate the effects of divorce on individual adjustment? And finally, what are the moderators (protective factors) that account for individual variability in adjustment to divorce? In general, the accumulated research suggests that marital dissolution has the potential to create considerable turmoil in people's lives. But people vary greatly in their reactions. Divorce benefits some individuals, leads others to experience temporary decrements in well-being, and forces others on a downward trajectory from which they might never recover fully. Understanding the contingencies under which divorce leads to these diverse outcomes is a priority for future research.

Of all the changes in family life during the 20th century, perhaps the most dramatic—and the most far-reaching in its implications—was the increase in the rate of divorce. Near the middle of the 19th century, only about 5% of first marriages ended

Department of Sociology, The Pennsylvania State University, University Park, PA 16802-6207 (pxa6@psu.edu).

Key Words: children of divorce, divorce, family-level stressors.

in divorce (Preston & McDonald, 1979). In contrast, demographers estimate that about half of first marriages initiated in recent years will be voluntarily dissolved (Cherlin, 1992). Observers have attributed this change to a number of factors, including the increasing economic independence of women, declining earnings among men without college degrees, rising expectations for personal fulfillment from marriage, and greater social acceptance of divorce (Cherlin, 1992; Furstenberg, 1994; White, 1991).

Remarriage following divorce is common, and nearly one-half of current marriages involve a second (or higher order) marriage for one or both partners (U.S. Bureau of the Census, 1998, Table 157). Second (and higher order) marriages, however, have an even greater likelihood of dissolution than first marriages. As a result, about one out of every six adults endures two or more divorces (Cherlin, 1992). The shift from a dominant pattern of lifelong marriage to one of serial marriage punctuated by periods of being single represents a fundamental change in how adults meet their needs for intimacy over the life course.

The increase in marital dissolution has had major implications for the settings in which children are nurtured and socialized. Slightly more than half of all divorces involve children under the age of 18. More than one million children experience parental divorce every year (U.S. Bureau of the Census, 1998, Table 160), and about 40% of all children will experience parental divorce before reaching adulthood (Bumpass, 1990). The high rate of marital disruption, combined with an increase in births outside marriage, means that about half of all children will reside at least temporarily in single-parent households, usually with their mothers (Castro & Bumpass, 1989). Because of remarriage, about one in seven children currently lives with a parent and a stepparent (Cherlin, 1992), and about one in three children will live with a stepparent for some time prior to reaching age 19 (Glick, 1989). These patterns vary by race. For example, compared with Whites, African Americans are more likely to bear children outside of marriage, more likely to divorce, and more likely to cohabit rather than remarry following divorce (Cherlin, 1992). Nevertheless, regardless of race, the decline in two-parent households, the increase in nonresident parents, and the introduction of parents' new partners (whether married or cohabiting) into the home represent major transformations in the lives of America's children.

The increase in divorce—and the implications of this increase for the lives of adults and children—has generated a high level of interest among social scientists. Indeed, a search of the SOCIOFILE database revealed 9,282 articles published (and dissertations completed) between 1990 and 1999 in which "divorce" appeared in the title or abstract. The authors of these works represent a variety of disciplines, including developmental psychology, clinical psychology, family therapy, sociology, demography, communication studies, family science, history, economics, social work, public health, social policy, and law. The extent and diversity of divorce scholarship pose a sobering challenge to any reviewer attempting to synthesize current knowledge on this topic.

Reviewing the literature on divorce also is challenging because of the ongoing, contentious debate over the consequences of marital disruption for adults and children. Some scholars see the two-parent family as the fundamental institution of society—the setting in which adults achieve a sense of meaning, stability, and security and the setting in which children develop into healthy, competent, and productive citizens. According to this view, the spread of single-parent families contributes to many social problems, including poverty, crime, substance abuse, declining academic standards, and the erosion of neighborhoods and communities (Blankenhorn, 1995; Glenn, 1996; Popenoe, 1996). In contrast, other scholars argue that adults find fulfillment, and children develop successfully, in a variety of family structures. According to this view, divorce, although temporarily stressful, represents a second chance for happiness for adults and an escape from a dysfunctional home environment for children. Poverty, abuse, neglect, poorly funded schools,

and a lack of government services represent more serious threats to the well-being of adults and children than does marital instability (Coontz, 1992; Demo, 1992; Skolnick, 1991; Stacey, 1996).

The polemical nature of divorce scholarship makes it difficult to write on this topic without being identified as either a conservative or a liberal voice. Nevertheless, although complete objectivity is impossible, my goal in this article is to assess the state of knowledge on divorce in a balanced and relatively nonpartisan manner. Indeed, a review of current literature might help to inform the debate between those who see divorce as a major social problem and those who see divorce as a necessary and beneficial alternative to mandatory lifelong marriage.

Because it is impossible to cover the full breadth of divorce scholarship in the 1990s in a single article, my review focuses on the consequences of divorce for the well-being of adults and children. I chose this focus because it encompasses, either directly or indirectly, much of the research in this field and because it is central to debates about the rise in marital instability. I omit (or touch only briefly on) many other aspects of divorce, such as legal issues related to custody determination and child support. I also exclude material on the dissolution of cohabiting relationships (including those with children) because we know relatively little about this topic. Readers should note that my review draws on qualitative as well as quantitative research, although I do not usually identify individual studies on the basis of their methodology.

THEORY

Researchers in the 1990s have employed a variety of theories and conceptual perspectives to explain how divorce affects adults and children; these include feminist theory (Carbonne, 1994), attachment theory (Hazan & Shaver, 1992), attribution theory (Grych & Fincham, 1992), symbolic interactionism (Orbuch, 1992), systems theory (Emery, 1994), the social capital perspective (Teachman, Paasch, & Carver, 1996), and the life-course perspective (Amato & Booth, 1997). The largest number of studies, however, begin with the assumption that marital disruption is a stressful life transition to which adults and children must adjust. Many researchers link their work to established stress perspectives, such as family stress and coping theory (Hill, 1949; McCubbin & Patterson, 1983; Plunkett, Sanchez, Henry, & Rob-

FIGURE 1. THE DIVORCE-STRESS-ADJUSTMENT PERSPECTIVE

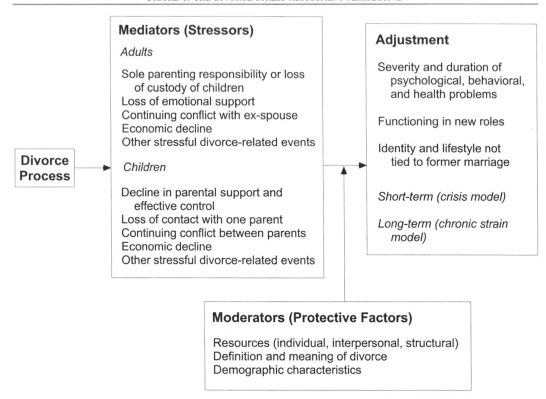

FIGURE 1. THE DIVORCE-STRESS-ADJUSTMENT PERSPECTIVE

inson, 1997), general stress theory (Pearlin, Menaghan, Lieberman, & Mullan, 1981; Thoits, 1995), and the risk and resiliency perspective (Cowan, Cowan, & Schulz, 1996; Hetherington, 1999; Rutter, 1987). Because stress frameworks dominate the literature on divorce, I give them particular attention here. And because these frameworks have much in common, I combine their various elements into a general divorce-stress-adjustment perspective. This conceptual model integrates the assumptions found in many discrete pieces of research, helps to summarize and organize specific research findings from the 1990s, and provides a guide for future research on divorce. This perspective also is useful because it can be applied to children as well as adults.

The Divorce-Stress-Adjustment Perspective

The divorce-stress-adjustment perspective, outlined in the Figure, views marital dissolution not as a discrete event but as a process that begins while the couple lives together and ends long after the legal divorce is concluded. The uncoupling process typically sets into motion numerous events that people experience as stressful. These stressors, in turn, increase the risk of negative emotional, behavioral, and health outcomes for adults and children. The severity and duration of these negative outcomes varies from person to person, depending on the presence of a variety of moderating or protective factors. Successful adjustment occurs to the extent that individuals experience few divorce-related symptoms, are able to function well in new family, work, or school roles, and have developed an identity and lifestyle that is no longer tied to the former marriage (Kitson, 1992; Kitson & Morgan, 1990).

Thinking of divorce as a process leads to several useful insights. Uncoupling begins with feelings of estrangement—feelings that typically emerge after a period of growing dissatisfaction with the relationship (Kayser, 1993). Because virtually all people enter marriage with the expectation (or the hope) that it will be a mutually supportive, rewarding, lifelong relationship, estrangement from one's spouse is typically a painful experience. Estranged spouses might spend considerable time attempting to renegotiate the relationship, seeking advice from others, or simply avoiding (denying) the problem. Consequently, the first negative effects of divorce on adults can occur years prior to final separation and legal dissolution. In addition, overt conflict between parents during this period might lead to behavior problems in children—problems that can be viewed as early effects of marital dissolution (Davies & Cummings, 1994).

Furthermore, it is often the case that one spouse wants the marriage to end more than the other spouse does (Emery, 1994). When this happens, the spouse who is considering divorce might mourn the end of the marriage even though it is still legally and physically intact. Indeed, when the marriage is legally terminated, the initiating spouse often experiences a great deal of relief. The spouse who wanted the marriage to continue, in contrast, might not mourn the end of the marriage until the legal divorce is completed. Spouses, therefore, often experience the greatest degree of emotional distress at different points in the divorce process (Emery, 1994). The same principle applies to children. For example, an older child might experience stress prior to the divorce, during the period when the parents' marriage is unraveling. For this older child, the physical separation of constantly warring parents might come as a relief. For a younger child in the same family, however, the departure of one parent from the household might be a bewildering event that generates considerable anxiety. In other words, members of divorcing families can experience different trajectories of stress and adjustment.

Legal divorce does not necessarily bring an end to the stress associated with an unhappy marriage, even for the partner who initiates the divorce. Instead, during the time in which the marriage is ending, and in the immediate postdivorce period, new events and processes (mediators) emerge that have the potential to affect people's emotions, behavior, and health. For adults, mediators include: having sole responsibility for the care of children (among custodial parents); losing contact with one's children (among noncustodial parents); continuing conflict with the ex-spouse over child support, visitation, or custody; loss of emotional support due to declining contact with in-laws, married friends, and neighbors; downward economic mobility (especially for mothers); and other disruptive life events, such as moving from the family home into less expensive accommodation in a poorer neighborhood. With regard

to children, divorce can result in less effective parenting from the custodial parent, a decrease in involvement with the noncustodial parent, exposure to continuing interparental discord, a decline in economic resources, and other disruptive life events such as moving, changing schools, and additional parental marriages and divorces. These mediating factors represent the mechanisms through which divorce affects people's functioning and well-being. (For discussions of mediators, see Amato, 1993; Kitson, 1992; McLanahan & Booth, 1989; McLanahan & Sandefur, 1994; Rodgers & Pryor, 1998; Simons and Associates, 1996.)

It is important to recognize that mediators can be viewed as outcomes in their own right. For example, a particular study might focus on the impact of divorce on single mothers' standard of living. But a declining standard of living, in turn, can have consequences for single mothers' sense of financial security, children's nutrition, and older adolescents' opportunities to attend college. Mediators, therefore, represent short- or medium-term outcomes of divorce that can have additional long-term consequences for adults' and children's well-being.

Moderators introduce variability into the manner in which divorce and mediating factors are linked to personal outcomes. Protective factors act like shock absorbers and weaken the links between divorce-related events and people's experience of stress, and hence the extent to which divorce is followed by negative emotional, behavioral, or health outcomes (Rutter, 1987). Resources that lessen the negative impact of divorce might reside within the individual (self-efficacy, coping skills, social skills), in interpersonal relationships (social support), and in structural roles and settings (employment, community services, supportive government policies). For example, although divorce often brings about an initial decline in emotional support, people vary in their ability to reconstruct social networks following divorce, including how quickly they are able to form new, supportive intimate relationships. Another moderator refers to the manner in which people regard divorce, with some individuals viewing it as a personal tragedy (typically the partner who is left behind) and others viewing it as an opportunity for personal growth or as an escape from an aversive or dysfunctional marriage (typically the partner who initiates the divorce). Finally, a number of demographic characteristics, such as gender, age, race, ethnicity, and culture can moderate the effects of divorce. As a result of the particular configuration of moderating factors, some individuals are resilient and others are vulnerable following divorce, resulting in a diversity of outcomes. (For discussions of these and other moderators see Bloom, Asher, & White, 1978; Booth & Amato, 1991; Pearlin et al., 1981; Wheaton, 1990).

Imbedded within the divorce-stress-adjustment perspective are two contrary models. The first, a crisis model, assumes that divorce represents a disturbance to which most individuals adjust over time. According to the crisis model, factors such as personal resources and definitions determine the speed with which adjustment occurs. But given a sufficient amount of time, the great majority of individuals return to their predivorce level of functioning. The second model, a chronic strain model, assumes that being divorced involves persistent strains, such as economic hardship, loneliness, and, for single parents, sole parenting responsibilities. Because these problems do not go away, declines in well-being associated with divorce might continue more or less indefinitely. According to the chronic strain model, factors such as personal resources and definitions determine the level of distress that individuals experience, but divorced individuals do not, in general, return to the same level of well-being they experienced early in the marriage.

Some researchers have argued that stress perspectives tend to focus exclusively on the negative aspects of divorce and ignore positive outcomes for adults (Ahrons, 1994; Wheaton, 1990) and children (Barber & Eccles, 1992; Gately & Schwebel, 1991). For example, women (as well as their children) might feel that they are substantially better off when a relationship with an abusive husband ends. The notion that divorce can be beneficial, however, is not inconsistent with the divorce-stress-adjustment perspective. Many stress theorists, such as Thoits (1995) and Wheaton (1990), have argued that potentially stressful events, such as divorce, can have positive long-term consequences when people resolve their problems successfully. Indeed, the divorce-stress-adjustment perspective explicitly focuses on the contingencies that lead to negative, positive, or mixed outcomes for individuals. Nevertheless, the divorce-stress-adjustment perspective assumes that for most people, the ending of a marriage is a stressful experience, even if much of the stress occurs prior to the legal divorce, is temporary, or is accompanied by some positive outcomes.

The Selection Perspective

The main alternative to the divorce-stress-adjustment perspective is based on the notion that poorly adjusted people are selected out of marriage. According to the selection perspective, certain individuals possess problematic personal and social characteristics that not only predispose them to divorce, but also lead them to score low on indicators of well-being after the marriage ends. Consequently, the adjustment problems frequently observed among the divorced might be present early in the marriage or might predate the marriage. Some evidence is consistent with the assumption that people bring traits to marriage that increase the risk of divorce, including antisocial personality traits, depression, and a general history of psychological problems (Capaldi & Patterson, 1991; Davies, Avison, & McAlpine, 1997; Hope, Power, & Rodgers, 1999; Kitson, 1992; Kurdek, 1990). Whereas the divorce-stress-adjustment perspective assumes that marital disruption causes adjustment problems, the selection perspective assumes that adjustment problems cause marital disruption. Selection also can occur if the best adjusted divorced individuals are especially likely to remarry. If this is true, then the mean level of functioning in the divorced (and not remarried) population should decline over time.

The selection perspective, as applied to children, assumes that at least some child problems observed following divorce are present during the marriage—an assumption consistent with several longitudinal studies (Amato & Booth, 1996; Cherlin et al., 1991; Elliot & Richards, 1991; Hetherington, 1999). Many researchers assume that these problems are caused by parents' marital discord or by inept parenting on the part of distressed or antisocial parents. Of course, to the extent that dysfunctional family patterns are reflections of the unraveling of the marriage, then these early effects on children can be viewed as part of the divorce process. But the selection perspective goes one step further and argues that inherent characteristics of parents, such as antisocial personality traits, are direct causes of dysfunctional family patterns and divorce, as well as child problems. The discovery that concordance (similarity between siblings) for divorce among adults is higher among monozygotic than dizygotic twins suggests that genes might predispose some people to behaviors that increase the risk of divorce (McGue & Lykken, 1992; Jockin, McGue, & Lykken, 1996). Consequently, some children from divorced families might exhibit problems because they have inherited genetic traits from their (presumably troubled) parents. According to this perspective, to the extent that parents' personalities and genetically transmitted predispositions are causes of divorce as well as child problems, the apparent effects of divorce on children are spurious.

RESEARCH ON THE CONSEQUENCES OF DIVORCE FOR ADULTS

Comparisons of Divorced and Married Individuals

A large number of studies published during the 1990s found that divorced individuals, compared with married individuals, experience lower levels of psychological well-being, including lower happiness, more symptoms of psychological distress, and poorer self-concepts (Aseltine & Kessler, 1993; Davies et al., 1997; Demo & Acock, 1996b; Kitson, 1992; Lorenz et al., 1997; Marks, 1996; Mastekaasa, 1994a, 1994b, 1995; Robins & Regier, 1991; Ross, 1995; Shapiro, 1996; Simon, 1998; Simon & Marcussen, 1999; Simons & Associates, 1996; Umberson & Williams, 1993; White, 1992). Compared with married individuals, divorced individuals also have more health problems and a greater risk of mortality (Aldous & Ganey, 1999; Hemstrom, 1996; Joung et al., 1997; Lillard & Waite, 1995; Murphy, Glaser, & Grundy, 1997; Rogers, 1996; Zick & Smith, 1991). Although the direction of these differences is consistent, their magnitude varies across studies. For example, Hope, Power, and Rodgers (1999) compared the depression scores of married and divorced mothers in a large, national British sample and found an effect size of .56, which translates into a 188% increase in the odds of depression. Other studies suggest smaller differences, however. Because no one has carried out a systematic evaluation of effect sizes in this literature, it is difficult to make claims about the magnitude of group differences on average.

Research also shows that divorced and married individuals differ on a number of variables that can be viewed not only as outcomes in their own right, but also as mediators of the long-term effects of marital dissolution on well-being. Compared with married individuals, divorced individuals report more social isolation (Joung et al., 1997; Marks, 1996; Mastekaasa, 1997; Peters & Leifbroer, 1997; Ross, 1995; Umberson, Chen,

House, Hopkins, & Slaten, 1996), less satisfying sex lives (Laumann, Gagnon, Michael, & Michaels, 1994), and more negative life events (Kitson, 1992; Lorenz et al., 1997; Simons and Associates, 1996). Divorced individuals also have a lower standard of living, possess less wealth, and experience greater economic hardship than married individuals (Hao, 1996; Marks, 1996; Ross, 1995, Teachman & Paasch, 1994), although this particular difference is considerably greater for women than men. For parents, divorce is associated with more difficulties in raising children (Fisher, Fagor, & Leve, 1998; Hetherington & Clingempeel, 1992), less authoritative parenting (Ellwood & Stolberg, 1993; Simons & Associates, 1996; Thomson, McLanahan, & Curtin, 1992), and greater parental role strain among noncustodial as well as custodial parents (Rogers & White, 1998; Umberson & Williams, 1993). Of course, this literature contains some null findings. But the general conclusion that emerges from studies published in the 1990s—that the divorced are worse off than the married in multiple ways—is consistent with research conducted in the 1980s (Kitson & Morgan, 1990) and in earlier decades (Bloom et al., 1978).

Although the divorce-stress-adjustment perspective assumes that marital dissolution increases the risk of negative outcomes, it allows for the possibility that some individuals experience positive changes. Consistent with this notion, several studies show that divorced individuals report higher levels of autonomy and personal growth than do married individuals (Kitson, 1992; Marks, 1996). Acock and Demo (1994) found that many divorced mothers reported improvements in career opportunities, social lives, and happiness following divorce. Similarly, in a qualitative study, Riessmann (1990) found that women reported more self-confidence and a stronger sense of control following marital dissolution, and men reported more interpersonal skills and a greater willingness to self-disclose. In summary, although the majority of studies document the negative consequences of divorce, a small number of studies indicate that divorce also has positive consequences for many individuals. If more studies explicitly searched for positive outcomes, then the number of studies documenting beneficial effects of divorce would almost certainly be larger.

Causation or Selection?

Studies in the 1990s indicate that divorce is associated with a variety of problematic outcomes.

But does divorce lower people's well-being, or are poorly functioning people especially likely to divorce? Consistent with the divorce-stress-adjustment perspective, and contrary to the selection perspective, longitudinal studies show that people who make the transition from marriage to divorce report an increase in symptoms of depression, an increase in alcohol use, and decreases in happiness, mastery, and self-acceptance (Aseltine & Kessler, 1993; Hope, Rodgers, & Power, 1999; Marks & Lambert, 1998; Power, Rodgers, & Hope, 1999). Given that divorce is a process rather than a discrete event, declines in well-being are likely to begin prior to the legal divorce. In fact, Kitson's (1992) respondents reported (retrospectively) that they had experienced the greatest level of stress prior to making the decision to divorce, the second highest level of distress at the time of the decision, and the least stress following the final separation. Consistent with Kitson's data, longitudinal studies (Booth & Amato, 1991; Johnson & Wu, 1996; Mastekaasa, 1994b, 1997) show that reports of unhappiness and psychological distress begin to rise a few years prior to marital separation. Furthermore, Johnson and Wu (1996) used a fixed-effects model to control for all time-invariant individual variables, thus making it unlikely that selection could account for the increase in distress.

Some longitudinal studies, however, suggest that selection effects operate alongside divorce effects. For example, Mastekaasa (1997) observed personal problems (such as greater alcohol consumption among wives) as early as 4 years prior to divorce. Hope, Rodgers, and Power (1999) found that depression at age 23 predicted becoming a single mother at age 33. Similarly, Davies and colleagues (1997) found that many divorced mothers had a history of depression that predated the marriage. These mothers also reported high levels of adversity in their families of origin, including weak attachment to parents and parental depression. Controlling for these family-of-origin factors decreased the estimated effect of divorce on adult depression (suggesting a selection effect), although the association between divorce and depression remained significant (suggesting divorce causation).

In general, studies support the notion of divorce causation, but a degree of selection also might be operating. This combination can occur in two ways. First, some individuals might be prone to psychological or interpersonal problems prior to divorce but exhibit additional problems following

divorce. That is, long-standing differences between those who divorce and those who remain married might be amplified as divorce becomes imminent. For example, a husband's aggression might contribute to the dissolution of the relationship, but the dissolution of the relationship, in turn, might generate even more serious levels of aggression. Second, some individuals might have long-standing problems that disrupt their marriages, whereas others might be relatively symptom-free until confronted with the stress of marital dissolution. In other words, selection explanations might apply to some groups of people more than others.

Divorce as Crisis or Chronic Strain?

An unresolved issue in the literature of the 1990s is whether divorce represents a temporary crisis to which most individuals adapt or a source of chronic strains that persist indefinitely. Several studies found that unhappiness, distress, depression, alcohol consumption, and health problems had largely subsided 2 or 3 years afterseparation—a result that supports the crisis model (Booth & Amato, 1991; Goldberg, Greenberger, Hamill, & O'Neil, 1992; Kitson, 1992; Lorenz et al., 1997). In contrast, other studies failed to find improvements in people's functioning during the time since divorce, unless they remarried—a result that supports the chronic strain model (Aseltine & Kessler, 1993; DeGarmo & Kitson, 1996; Gray & Silver, 1990; Johnson & Wu, 1996; Mastekaasa, 1995; Neff & Schluter, 1993; Wang & Amato, in press). Furthermore, Umberson and Williams (1993) found that parental strain among divorced fathers increased, rather than decreased, over time. Of course, both the crisis and the chronic strain models might contain some truth. Kitson (1992) found that although half of her respondents improved over time, about one fourth got worse. These results suggest that a crisis model (implying gradual adjustment) might be appropriate for some individuals, and a chronic strain model (implying persistent long-term problems) might be appropriate for others.

Mediators of Divorce Effects

Researchers attempting to identify the mediators of divorce effects have adopted two strategies. Some researchers have examined associations between mediators and measures of well-being using samples composed entirely of divorced individuals. Other researchers have tried to make the mean differences in well-being between divorced and married individuals "disappear" by controlling for presumed mediators. Although within-group studies are useful, between-group studies provide stronger evidence of mediation. Nevertheless, the various types of studies generally yield consistent results.

With regard to parenting, adjustment among custodial mothers is negatively associated with difficulty in finding child care (Goldberg et al., 1992), children's misbehavior (Simons and Associates, 1996), and the number of children in the household (Garvin, Kalter, & Hansell, 1993; Kitson, 1992). Correspondingly, loss of contact with children is associated with increased distress among noncustodial fathers (Lawson & Thompson, 1996; Umberson & Williams, 1993). Other studies have shown that poor adjustment is associated with conflict between ex-spouses (Goodman, 1993; Masheter, 1991), lack of emotional support from others (Marks, 1996; O'Connor, Hawkins, Dunn, Thorpe, & Golding, 1998; Ross, 1995), low income (Booth & Amato, 1991; Garvin et al., 1993; Kitson, 1992; Ross, 1995; Shapiro, 1996; Simons & Associates, 1996; Thabes, 1997), and the number and severity of stressful life changes following divorce (DeGarmo & Kitson, 1996; Kitson, 1992; Lorenz et al., 1997; Miller, Smerglia, Gaudet, & Kitson, 1998; O'Connor et al., 1998; Simons & Associates, 1996). Although some exceptions appear in the literature, research in the 1990s generally demonstrated that difficulties associated with solo parenting, continuing discord with the former spouse, declines in emotional support, economic hardship, and other stressful life events account for much of the gap in well-being between divorced and married adults.

Moderating Factors

What factors make some individuals more vulnerable than others to divorce-induced stress? With regard to resources, several studies show that adjustment among divorced individuals is positively associated with education (Booth & Amato, 1991; Demo & Acock, 1996b; Goldberg et al., 1992), employment (Bisagni & Eckenrode, 1995; Booth & Amato, 1991; Demo & Acock, 1996b; Kitson, 1992; Wang & Amato, in press), and large networks of supportive kin and friends (Aseltine & Kessler, 1993; Cotton, 1999; DeGarmo & Forgatch, 1999; Garvin et al., 1993; Goldberg et al.,

1992; Lawson & Thompson, 1996; Thabes, 1997). Support from a new partner appears to be especially beneficial, because studies consistently show that adjustment is higher among divorced individuals who have formed a new romantic relationship (Funder, Harrison, & Weston, 1993; Garvin et al., 1993; Mastekaasa, 1995; Thabes, 1997; Wang & Amato, in press) or have remarried (Demo & Acock, 1996; Hemstrom, 1996; Marks & Lambert, 1998; Shapiro, 1996; Wang & Amato, in press). Remarriage also improves people's standard of living (Kitson, 1992; Teachman & Paasch, 1994) and accumulation of wealth (Hao, 1996).

One particular resource—having a large network of friends and kin—is not always a blessing, however. Miller and colleagues (1998) found that having someone to confide in decreased distress, but receiving material assistance (such as money or housing) increased distress. Of course, people receiving material assistance might be most in need and therefore most distressed. But support also might come with costs, such as feelings of inadequacy or indebtedness on the part of the receiver. Kitson (1992) found that receiving help with services, finances, or information was associated with lower distress; receiving these forms of assistance in conjunction with advice, however, was associated with higher distress. These findings suggest that aid might be more (rather than less) stressful when it comes with strings attached.

Another protective factor involves the manner in which people cognitively appraise the divorce. Longitudinal studies by Booth and Amato (1991) and by Simon and Marcussen (1999) found that people who strongly believed that marriage is a lifelong commitment reported especially high levels of distress following divorce. Adjustment among these individuals might have been difficult because they were troubled by the moral contradiction involved in seeing their own marriages end. Similarly, DeGarmo and Kitson (1996) found that divorce adjustment was easier for women who were not heavily invested in their marital identity. Other studies show that individuals who initiate divorce, compared with those who do not want the marriage to end, tend to be better adjusted in the postdivorce period (Kitson, 1992; Gray & Silver, 1990; Wang & Amato, in press). Consistent with these findings, individuals who report a large number of problems during the marriage tend to function relatively well in the postdivorce period (Booth & Amato, 1991). Indeed, for individuals who are very distressed during the marriage, divorce appears to decrease symptoms of depression (Aseltine & Kessler, 1993; Wheaton, 1990). As noted earlier, initiators of divorce and their partners are often on different trajectories of divorce adjustment. These results suggest, therefore, that people who initiate divorce might experience distress, but they do this mainly prior to, rather than following, marital dissolution.

Demographic Variables

Are the consequences of divorce more debilitating for women or men? Some studies suggest that the effects of marital disruption on psychological well-being are stronger for women than men (Aseltine & Kessler, 1993; Marks & Lambert, 1998; Simon & Marcussen, 1999; Shapiro, 1996). In contrast, other studies show that marital disruption is more debilitating for the psychological well-being and health of men than women (Funder et al., 1993; Hemstrom, 1996; Masheter, 1991; Mastekaasa, 1994a; Peters & Liefbroer, 1997; Stack & Eshleman, 1998; Zick & Smith, 1991). Yet other studies show no gender differences in psychological well-being (Booth & Amato, 1991; Mastekaasa, 1995; Ross, 1995; White, 1992) or health and mortality (Lillard & Waite, 1995; Murphy et al., 1997). These studies do not provide evidence that one gender is more vulnerable than the other, overall, following divorce.

The main exception to this conclusion involves economic well-being. Research is consistent in showing that the economic consequences of divorce are greater for women than for men (Bianchi, Subaiya, & Kahn, 1999; Hao, 1996; Kitson, 1992; Marks, 1996; Peterson, 1996; Ross, 1995; Smock, 1994). For example, Bianchi and colleagues found—using matched couples—that custodial mothers experienced a 36% decline in standard of living following separation, whereas noncustodial fathers experienced a 28% increase. Overall, mothers' postseparation standard of living was only about one half that of fathers. Similarly, divorced women, compared with married women or divorced men, report more chronic financial difficulties, such as being unable to pay bills or purchase necessary goods (Fisher et al., 1998; Ross, 1995; Shapiro, 1996; Simons & Associates, 1996). These differences exist because women, compared with men, have more interrupted work histories prior to divorce, experience greater work–family conflict (due to their responsibility for children), and are more likely to experience employment and wage discrimination. In general, studies conducted in the 1990s yield re-

sults similar to those of studies conducted in the 1980s in showing that divorced women, especially if they have custody of children, continue to be economically disadvantaged vis-a-vis married women or divorced men.

Relatively little is known about racial and ethnic differences in divorce adjustment. Kitson (1992) reported that Blacks adjusted to divorce more readily than Whites. In contrast, Neff and Schluter (1993) found that the mean differences in depression among divorced, separated, and married individuals were similar for Blacks, Mexican Americans, and Whites. Similar results for happiness for Blacks and Whites were reported by Aldous and Ganey (1999). Wang and Amato (in press) found no evidence that non-Whites adjusted to divorce more easily than Whites. And Lawson and Thompson (1996) found that the problems reported by divorced Black fathers—financial strain, noncustodial parenting, and difficulty meeting child-support payments—were similar to those reported by divorced White fathers (Umberson & Williams, 1993). Available research, therefore, does not suggest strong racial differences in divorce adjustment in the United States.

Turning to cross-national data, Mastekaasa (1994a) found that divorced and separated individuals had lower levels of psychological well-being than married individuals in 19 countries, including cultures as diverse as Japan, Mexico, South Africa, Britain, Germany, France, and Italy. Stack and Eshleman (1998) reported similar findings in a 17-nation study, and Amato (1994a) reported similar findings in India. Overall, available research suggests that divorce has the potential to create stress in the lives of individuals irrespective of culture or nationality.

RESEARCH ON THE CONSEQUENCES OF DIVORCE FOR CHILDREN

Comparisons of Children from Divorced and Two-Parent Families

Early in the decade, Amato and Keith (1991) published a meta-analysis of 92 studies that compared the well-being of children whose parents had divorced with that of children whose parents were married to each other. Their meta-analysis showed that children from divorced families scored significantly lower on a variety of outcomes, including academic achievement, conduct, psychological adjustment, self-concept, and social competence. The differences between groups of children (effect sizes) were small, however, ranging from .08 of a standard deviation for psychological adjustment to .23 of a standard deviation for conduct. For some outcomes, studies conducted in the 1980s yielded smaller effect sizes than earlier studies conducted in the 1960s and 1970s. Amato and Keith (1991) speculated that the gap in well-being between children with divorced and nondivorced parents might have narrowed either because divorce became more socially accepted or because parents were making greater efforts to reduce the potentially disruptive impact of divorce on their children.

During the 1990s, the number of people touched by divorce increased, school-based programs for children of divorce became common, and mediation and education courses for divorcing parents became mandatory in many states (Emery, Kitzmann, & Waldron, 1999). Given these trends, one might expect studies conducted in the 1990s to reveal a continued closing of the gap in well-being between children with divorced parents and children with married parents. An examination of studies conducted in the 1990s, however, does not support this hypothesis.

A large number of studies in the 1990s continued to find that children with divorced parents score lower than children with continuously married parents on measures of academic success (Astone & McLanahan, 1991; Teachman, Paasch, & Carver, 1996), conduct (Doherty & Needle, 1991; Simons and Associates, 1996), psychological adjustment (Forehand, Neighbors, Devine, & Armistead, 1994; Kurdek, Fine, & Sinclair, 1994), self-concept (Wenk, Hardesty, Morgan, & Blair, 1994), social competence (Beaty, 1995; Brodzinsky, Hitt, & Smith, 1993), and long-term health (Tucker et al., 1997). Furthermore, effect sizes in the 1990s appear comparable to those of earlier decades. For example, across 32 studies of children's conduct published in the 1990s, the mean effect size was $-.19$, which is not appreciably different from the mean value of $-.18$ for studies conducted in the 1980s, as reported in Amato and Keith (1991). Similarly, across 29 studies of psychological adjustment published in the 1990s, the mean effect size was $-.17$, which is slightly larger than the mean value of $-.10$ for studies conducted in the 1980s, also as reported in Amato and Keith. In general, the small but consistent gap in well-being between children from divorced and two-parent families observed in earlier decades persisted into the 1990s.

As with studies of adults, a few studies suggest that divorce also has positive consequences for some children. For example, a qualitative study by Arditti (1999) found that many offspring from divorced families, especially daughters, reported developing especially close relationships with their custodial mothers—a finding that is consistent with some quantitative work (Amato & Booth, 1997). In addition, Amato, Loomis, and Booth (1995), Amato and Booth (1997), Hanson (1999), and Jekielek (1998) found that offspring were better off on a variety of outcomes if parents in high-conflict marriages divorced than if they remained married. When conflict between parents is intense, chronic, and overt, divorce represents an escape from an aversive home environment for children. Only a minority of divorces, however, appear to be preceded by a high level of chronic marital conflict (Amato & Booth, 1997). For this reason, divorce probably helps fewer children than it hurts.

CAUSATION OR SELECTION?

The selection perspective holds that differences between children from divorced and nondivorced families are due to factors other than marital disruption, including parents' personality characteristics, inept parenting, predivorce marital discord, or genetic influence. Consistent with a selection perspective, Capaldi and Patterson (1991) found that mothers' antisocial personalities accounted for the association between mothers' marital transitions and boys' adjustment problems. In contrast, other studies found significant estimated effects of divorce even after controlling for aspects of parents' personalities, including depression (Demo & Acock, 1996a) and antisocial personality traits (Simons and Associates, 1996).

Longitudinal studies provide another type of evidence. Cherlin and colleagues (1991) found that children from maritally disrupted families had more postdivorce behavior problems than children from nondisrupted families. These differences, however, were apparent several years prior to divorce, especially for boys. Amato and Booth (1996) found that problems in parent–child relationships (including parents' reports that their children had given them more than the usual number of problems) were present as early as 8 to 12 years before divorce. Aseltine (1996) and Hetherington (1999) obtained comparable results with regard to children's internalizing behavior, externalizing behavior, social competence, and self-esteem, and Doherty and Needle (1991) found comparable results for substance abuse among daughters. These longitudinal studies suggest that some of the negative outcomes observed among children with divorced parents are present years before the marriage ends and hence might be due to parental or family problems other than marital dissolution.

Nevertheless, as noted earlier, marital dissolution is a process that usually begins long before the legal divorce, so the existence of elevated levels of child problems prior to parental separation does not necessarily provide evidence of selection. Furthermore, several longitudinal studies show that many postdivorce child problems cannot be traced to a point in time prior to the divorce (Doherty & Needle, 1991; Forehand, Armistead, & Corinne, 1997; Morrison & Cherlin, 1995). For example, Doherty and Needle found that substance abuse and psychological problems among adolescent boys were elevated after, but not prior to, divorce. Consistent with these findings, Hanson (1999) found that differences in behavior and well-being between children from divorced and nondivorced families continued to be significant even after controlling for children's predivorce levels of behavior problems. And Morrison and Coiro (1999) found that parental divorce was followed by an increase in children's behavior problems above predivorce levels. Similarly, two follow-up studies of the 1991 work by Cherlin and colleagues (Chase-Lansdale, Cherlin, & Kiernan, 1995; Cherlin, Chase-Lansdale, & McRae, 1998) found that the gap in psychological well-being between offspring with divorced and married parents increased between adolescence and young adulthood. A noteworthy aspect of the latter study was the use of a random-effects model, which provides strong evidence for divorce rather than selection as the cause of the gap.

With regard to possible genetic influence, one study found that the association between parental divorce and child problems was similar for adopted and biological children (Brodzinsky, Hitt, & Smith, 1993)—a finding that cannot be explained by genetic transmission. Another study based on a large sample of twins (Kendler, Neale, Kessler, Heath, & Eaves, 1992) found that parental divorce predicted offspring depression in adulthood even with genetic resemblance controlled statistically. These studies suggest that even if predivorce family factors (including genetic factors) predispose children to certain emotional and behavioral problems, divorce itself brings about new conditions that exacerbate these differences.

Divorce as Crisis or Chronic Strain?

The crisis perspective holds that children from divorced families, although distressed at the time of marital disruption, show improvements in functioning in the years following divorce. Consistent with this view, some studies show that children's problems decline with time following divorce (Bussell, 1995; Frost & Pakiz, 1990; Goldberg et al., 1992; Jekielek, 1998). Other studies provide contrary evidence. For example, McLanahan and Sandefur (1994) found that the length of time in a single-parent family was not related to children's graduation from high school or risk of a teenage birth. Similar null results were reported by Hetherington and Clingempeel (1992), Machida and Holloway (1991), and Mauldon (1990) for different child outcomes.

Furthermore, the longitudinal studies of Cherlin and colleagues (Chase-Lansdale et al., 1995; Cherlin et al., 1998) found that the gap in psychological well-being between offspring from divorced and nondivorced families grew larger—not smaller—with the passage of time. Consistent with this finding, a large number of studies have demonstrated that parental divorce is a risk factor for multiple problems in adulthood, including low socioeconomic attainment, poor subjective well-being, increased marital problems, and a greater likelihood of seeing one's own marriages end in divorce (see Amato, 1999, for a review). Why might these problems persist into adulthood? Two mechanisms seem likely. First, economic hardship due to parental divorce might lead some children to abandon plans to attend college, resulting in lower occupational attainment and wages throughout adulthood. Other offspring who were exposed to poor parental models of interpersonal behavior might have difficulty forming stable, satisfying, intimate relationships as young adults. These considerations suggest that even if some children show improvements in functioning a year or two after marital disruption, delayed effects of divorce might appear only when offspring have reached young adulthood.

Mediators of Divorce Effects

A number of studies indicate that divorced custodial parents, compared with married parents, invest less time, are less supportive, have fewer rules, dispense harsher discipline, provide less supervision, and engage in more conflict with their children (Astone & McLanahan, 1991; Hetherington & Clingempeel, 1992; Simons and Associates, 1996; Thompson et al., 1992). Many of these deficits in parenting presumably result from the stress of marital disruption and single parenting. Congruent with this perspective, Larson and Gillman (1999) found that negative emotions were more likely to be transmitted from single mothers to adolescent children than vice versa, especially when mothers were under stress. The quality of parental functioning is one of the best predictors of children's behavior and well-being. Several within-group studies show that either a conflicted relationship with the custodial parent or inept parenting on the part of the custodial parent are linked with a variety of negative child outcomes, including lower academic achievement, internalizing problems, externalizing problems, reduced self-esteem, and poorer social competence (Aseltine, 1996; Buchanan, Maccoby, & Dornbush, 1996; Clark & Clifford, 1996; DeGarmo & Forgatch, 1999; Demo & Acock, 1996; Ellwood & Stolberg, 1993; Hetherington & Clingempeel, 1992; McLanahan & Sandefur, 1994; Simons and Associates, 1996; Tschann, Johnston, Kline, & Wallerstein, 1990). Other studies show that depression among custodial mothers, which is likely to detract from parenting, is related to poor adjustment among offspring (Demo & Acock, 1996a; Mednick, Baker, Reznick, & Hocevar, 1990; Silitsky, 1996; Simons & Associates, 1996).

Although the role of the custodial parent (usually the mother) in promoting children's well-being is clear, the role of the noncustodial parent (usually the father) is ambiguous. A variety of studies conducted in the 1970s and 1980s suggest that contact with noncustodial fathers is not related in a consistent manner with children's behavior or well-being (Amato, 1993). However, in a recent meta-analysis of 63 studies of nonresident fathers and their children, Amato and Gilbreth (1999) found that authoritative parenting on the part of noncustodial fathers consistently predicted children's higher academic achievement and lower internalizing and externalizing problems. Amato and Gilbreth also found that studies of noncustodial fathers in the 1990s (e.g., Simons and Associates, 1996; Barber, 1994) were more likely than studies from earlier decades to report positive effects of father contact. These results tentatively suggest that noncustodial fathers might be enacting the parent role more successfully now than in the past, with beneficial consequences for children.

Interparental hostility and lack of cooperation between parents following divorce is a consistent predictor of poor outcomes among offspring (Bolgar, Zweig-Frank, & Parish, 1995; Buchanan, Maccoby, & Dornbusch, 1996; Clark & Clifford, 1996; Ellwood & Stolberg, 1993; Healy, Malley, & Stewart, 1990; Pearson & Thoennes, 1990; Silitsky, 1996; Simons & Associates, 1996; Tschann et al., 1990; Vandewater & Lansford, 1998). Hetherington (1999) found that direct conflict between divorced parents, but not encapsulated conflict (that is, conflict to which children are not exposed), was related to behavior problems among adolescents. Conflict was especially aversive if it involved physical violence or made children feel as if they were caught in the middle. Interparental conflict is not only a direct stressor for children, but also might interfere with children's attachments to parents, resulting in feelings of emotional insecurity (Davies & Cummings, 1994).

Postdivorce economic hardship also is associated with negative outcomes among children (Aseltine, 1996; Bronstein, Stoll, Clauson, Abrams, & Briones, 1994; Mauldon, 1990; McLanahan & Sandefur, 1994; Morrison & Cherlin, 1995; Pearson & Thoennes, 1990; Simons and Associates, 1996). One study found that income stability, rather than total income, predicts children's well-being (Goldberg et al., 1992). Research showing that fathers' payment of child support is positively related to children's school attainment and behavior provides additional support for the importance of income in facilitating children's postdivorce adjustment (e.g., King, 1994; McLanahan, Seltzer, Hanson, & Thompson, 1994).

Finally, the number of negative life events to which children are exposed is a consistent predictor of children's divorce adjustment (Aseltine, 1996; Buchanon, Maccoby, & Dornbusch, 1996; Ellwood & Stolberg, 1993; Pearson & Thoennes, 1990; Sandler, Wolchik, Braver, & Fogas, 1991; Sheets, Sandler, & West, 1996; Silitsky, 1996). Events such as moving (Amato & Booth, 1997; McLanahan & Sandefur, 1994; Simons & Associates, 1996) and changing schools (Mednick et al., 1990; Teachman, Paasch, & Carver, 1996) appear to be especially disruptive. Unfortunately, moving to poorer neighborhoods is common following divorce as custodial parents are forced to live on smaller household incomes (South, Crowder, & Trent, 1998). Overall, in spite of the fact that some null findings appear in this literature, the majority of studies conducted in the 1990s document the importance of the mediators outlined in the divorce-stress-adjustment model and also are consistent with research trends from the 1970s and 1980s (Amato, 1993).

Moderating Factors

What factors facilitate children's adjustment to divorce? In relation to resources, one study found that children who use active coping skills (such as problem solving and gathering social support) tend to adjust to divorce more quickly than children who rely on avoidance or distraction as coping mechanisms (Sandler, Tein, & West, 1994). Social support appears to be another protective factor. Samera and Stolberg (1993) found that children's social support from peers was positively related to adjustment as rated by children, teachers, and parents. Comparable findings were obtained by Silitsky (1996) and Teja and Stolberg (1993). Access to therapeutic interventions also appears to improve children's postdivorce well-being. For example, school-based support programs for children with divorced parents are widespread, and evidence suggests that these interventions are beneficial (Emery et al., 1999; Kalter, & Schreier, 1993; Lee, Picard, & Blain, 1994). Programs aimed at divorcing parents also are common. Although parents who attend these programs tend to rate them positively, it is not clear whether these programs benefit children (Beuhler, Betz, Ryan, Legg, & Trotter, 1992; Braver, Salem, Pearson, & DeLuse, 1996).

With regard to cognition, children who place some of the blame for the divorce on themselves tend to be more poorly adjusted (Bussell, 1995). Healy, Stewart, and Copeland (1993), in a study of primary school children 6 months after parental separation, found that one third reported some feelings of self-blame; self-blame, in turn, was related to a variety of child problems, including depression, externalizing problems, and lowered feelings of self-competence. In addition to self-blame, Kim, Sandler, and Jenn-Yum (1997) found that children's perceived lack of control over events mediated some of the impact of divorce-related stress on adjustment.

Studies focusing on custody arrangements following divorce tend to show that children fare better under joint physical custody rather than sole mother or father custody (Buchanan, Maccoby, & Dornbush, 1996). This conclusion should be treated cautiously, however, because especially cooperative parents are more likely to choose and maintain joint physical custody than are other parents. Consequently, it is difficult to determine whether it is joint physical custody or some characteristic of parents or their postdivorce relationship that is responsible for children's functioning. Children in sole mother custody and sole father custody show few differences (Downey, Ainsworth-Darnell, & Dufur, 1998; McLanahan & Sandefur, 1994). Although many children in single-mother households are disadvantaged by a lack of economic resources, some children in single-father households are disadvantaged by a lack of interpersonal resources (such as single fathers' relatively low level of involvement in school activities), resulting in roughly equal outcomes (Downey, 1994). Furthermore, it appears to matter little whether children reside with a same-gender or opposite-gender parent (Downey & Powell, 1993). A reasonable conclusion is that no particular custody arrangement is best for all children. Indeed, custody arrangements often require modification as children develop and their relationships with parents change (Buchanan, Maccoby, & Dornbusch, 1996).

Research yields mixed results with regard to parental remarriage. A meta-analytic review of studies (mostly from the 1970s and 1980s) found that children in stepfamilies were no better off, and in some ways worse off, than children living in single-parent households following divorce (Amato, 1994b). In contrast, several recent studies found that offspring with remarried custodial parents were less depressed (Aseltine, 1996) or had fewer interpersonal problems (Bolgar et al., 1995) than children with single custodial parents. McLanahan and Sandefur (1994) found that parental remarriage appeared to benefit African Americans more than Whites. Interestingly, Buchanon, Maccoby, and Dornbusch (1996) found that parental remarriage was associated with fewer child problems, whereas parental cohabitation was associated with more problems, especially among boys. Hetherington and Clingempeel (1992) found few differences, overall, between children in divorced single-parent families and stepfamilies. It might be difficult to reach broad generalizations about the role of parental remarriage in children's adjustment, because these effects vary with children's ages, children's gender, the time since divorce, and other factors (Hetherington & Jodl, 1994). Additional parental divorces, however, appear to be more stressful for offspring than first divorces (Amato & Booth, 1991).

Demographic Variables

In general, evidence for variations in the effects of parental divorce by children's gender and age is inconsistent. Although some studies find stronger estimated effects for one gender than the other (Doherty & Needle, 1991; McLanahan & Sandefur, 1994; Rodgers, 1994), other studies do not (Aseltine, 1996; Simons & Associates, 1996). Similarly, few studies find that age at time of marital disruption matters (e.g., McLanahan & Sandefur, 1994). A few studies of non-White children from divorced families appear in the literature (Bussell, 1995; McLanahan & Sandefur, 1994; Smith, 1997; Teachman, Paasch, & Carver, 1996). The number of studies using samples of non-White families is too small, however, to form any firm generalizations.

CONCLUSIONS

Studies conducted during the 1990s, along with studies conducted in earlier decades, allow us to reach several conclusions about the consequences of divorce for adults and children.

First, we know that adults and children from divorced families, as a group, score lower than their counterparts in married-couple families on a variety of indicators of well-being. Second, although selection can account for some of these differences, the evidence is strong that divorce has an impact on well-being net of selection. Third, we have a good grasp of many of the mechanisms through which divorce affects individuals. These mediators include disruptions in parent–child relationships, continuing discord between former spouses, loss of emotional support, economic hardship, and an increase in the number of other negative life events, such as moving. Fourth, although some adults and children adjust relatively quickly to divorce (supporting a crisis model), others exhibit long-term deficits in functioning (supporting a chronic strain model). Fifth, a number of factors moderate the speed and extent of adjustment. For adults, protective factors include resources such as education and employment, support from a new partner, and being the spouse who initiated the divorce. For children, protective factors include the use of active coping skills, support from family and friends, and having access to therapeutic interventions. For adults as well as children, the end of a highly conflicted marriage is likely to be followed by improvements, rather than declines, in well-being.

Although we know a good deal about divorce, this review suggests several substantive areas that would benefit from additional research. First, more attention should be given to the dissolution of cohabiting relationships. This attention is critical, given that about one fourth of children in single-parent families were born to cohabiting parents (Bumpass, Sweet, & Cherlin, 1991). It seems likely that the ending of a cohabiting relationship has consequences for adults and children that are similar to those of divorce, but we have little evidence to support this conclusion. Second, studies of racial and ethnic minorities are frustratingly rare. New research should consider that some groups, such as African Americans, are more likely than Whites to cohabit (rather than marry) and bear children outside of marriage. Given these racial differences, it would make sense to expand the focus of future research beyond divorce to include the instability of all childbearing unions. Third, researchers have given insufficient attention to interventions for adults and children. An increasing number of states are offering (or mandating) mediation and education courses for divorcing parents, and school-based support programs for children are common. Although some evidence suggests that these interventions are beneficial to adults and children, more evaluation research, especially studies based on randomized trials, is sorely needed.

In conclusion, I return to the contentious debate over divorce that has continued throughout the 1990s. On one side are those who see divorce as an important contributor to many social problems. On the other side are those who see divorce as a largely benign force that provides adults with a second chance for happiness and rescues children from dysfunctional and aversive home environments. Based on the accumulated research of the 1990s—and of earlier decades—it is reasonable to conclude that both of these views represent one-sided accentuations of reality. The increase in marital instability has not brought society to the brink of chaos, but neither has it led to a golden age of freedom and self-actualization. Divorce benefits some individuals, leads others to experience temporary decrements in well-being that improve over time, and forces others on a downward cycle from which they might never fully recover. Continuing research on the contingencies that determine whether divorce has positive, neutral, or negative long-term consequences for adults and children is a high priority. Work on these issues is likely to progress in the next decade. As long as nearly half of all marriages in the United States end in divorce, there will be an enduring need to understand and monitor the implications of marital dissolution for adults, children, and the larger society.

NOTE

I thank Alan Booth, Stacy Rogers, and Lynn White for useful comments on an earlier version of this article.

REFERENCES

Acock, A. C., & Demo, D. H. (1994). *Family diversity and well-being.* Thousand Oaks, CA: Sage.

Ahrons, C. (1994). *The good divorce.* New York: Harper Collins.

Aldous, J., & Ganey, R. F. (1999). Family life and the pursuit of happiness: The influence of gender and race. *Journal of Family Issues, 20,* 155–180.

Amato, P. R. (1993). Children's adjustment to divorce: Theories, hypotheses, and empirical support. *Journal of Marriage and the Family, 55,* 23–38.

Amato, P. R. (1994a). The impact of divorce on men and women in India and the United States. *Journal of Comparative Family Studies, 25,* 207–221.

Amato, P. R. (1994b). The implications of research findings on children in stepfamilies. In A. Booth & J. Dunn (Eds.), *Stepfamilies: Who benefits? Who does not?* (pp. 81–87). Hillsdale, NJ: Erlbaum.

Amato, P. R. (1996). Explaining the intergenerational transmission of divorce. *Journal of Marriage and the Family, 58,* 628–641.

Amato, P. R. (1999). Children of divorced parents as young adults. In E. M. Hetherington (Ed.), *Coping with divorce, single parenting, and remarriage: A risk and resiliency perspective* (pp. 147–164). Mahwah, NJ: Erlbaum.

Amato, P. R., & Booth, A. (1991). Consequences of parental divorce and marital unhappiness for adult well-being. *Social Forces, 69,* 895–914.

Amato, P. R., & Booth, A. (1996). A prospective study of parental divorce and parent–child relationships. *Journal of Marriage and the Family, 58,* 356–365.

Amato, P. R., & Booth, A. (1997). *A generation at risk: Growing up in an era of family upheaval.* Cambridge, MA: Harvard University Press.

Amato, P. R., & Gilbreth, J. (1999). Nonresident fathers and children's well-being: A meta-analysis. *Journal of Marriage and the Family, 61,* 557–573.

Amato, P. R., & Keith, B. (1991). Consequences of parental divorce for children's well-being: A meta-analysis. *Psychological Bulletin, 110,* 26–46.

Amato, P. R., Loomis, L. S., & Booth, A. (1995). Parental divorce, marital conflict, and offspring well-being in early adulthood. *Social Forces, 73,* 895–916.

Arditti, J. A. (1999). Rethinking relationships between divorced mothers and their children: Capitalizing on family strengths. *Family Relations, 48,* 109–119.

Aseltine, R. H. (1996). Pathways linking parental divorce with adolescent depression. *Journal of Health and Social Behavior, 37,* 133–148.

Aseltine, R. H., & Kessler, R. C. (1993). Marital disruption and depression in a community sample. *Journal of Health and Social Behavior, 34,* 237–251.

Astone, N., & McLanahan, S. S. (1991). Family structure, parental practices, and high school completion. *American Sociological Review, 56,* 309–320.

Barber, B. L. (1994). Support and advice from married and divorced fathers: Linkages to adolescent adjustment. *Family Relations, 43,* 433–438.

Barber, B. L., & Eccles, J. S. (1992). Long-term influence of divorce and single parenting on adolescent family- and work-related values, behavior, and aspirations. *Psychological Bulletin, 111,* 108–126.

Beaty, L. A. (1995). Effects of paternal absence on male adolescents' peer relations and self-image. *Adolescence, 30,* 873–880.

Beuhler, C., Betz, P., Ryan, C. M., Legg, B. H., & Trotter, B. B. (1992). Description and evaluation of the orientation for divorcing parents: Implications for postdivorce prevention programs. *Family Relations, 41,* 154–162.

Bianchi, S. M., Subaiya, L., & Kahn, J. R. (1999). The gender gap in the economic well-being of nonresident fathers and custodial mothers. *Demography, 36,* 195–203.

Bisagni, G. M., & Eckenrode, J. (1995). The role of work identity in women's adjustment to work. *American Journal of Orthopsychiatry, 65,* 574–583.

Blankenhorn, D. (1995). *Fatherless America: Confronting our most urgent social problem.* New York: Basic Books.

Block, J. H., Block, J., & Gjerde, P. F. (1986). The personality of children prior to divorce: A prospective study. *Child Development, 57,* 827–840.

Bloom, B. L., Asher, S. J., & White, S. W. (1978). Marital disruption as a stressor: A review and analysis. *Psychological Bulletin, 85,* 867–894.

Bolgar, R., Zweig-Frank, H., & Parish, J. (1995). Childhood antecedents of interpersonal problems in young adult children of divorce. *Journal of the American Academy of Child and Adolescent Psychiatry, 34,* 143–150.

Booth, A., & Amato, P. R. (1991). Divorce and psychological stress. *Journal of Health and Social Behavior, 32,* 396–407.

Braver, S. L., Salem, P., Pearson, J., & DeLuse, S. R. (1996). The content of divorce education programs: Results of a survey. *Family and Conciliation Courts Review, 34,* 41–59.

Brodzinsky, D., Hitt, J. C., & Smith, D. (1993). Impact of parental separation and divorce on adopted and nonadopted children. *American Journal of Orthopsychiatry, 63,* 451–461.

Bronstein, P., Stoll, M. F., Clauson, J., Abrams, C. L., & Briones, M. (1994). Fathering after separation or divorce: Factors predicting children's adjustment. *Family Relations, 43,* 469–479.

Buchanan, C. M., Maccoby, E. E., & Dornbush, S. M. (1996). *Adolescents after divorce.* Cambridge, MA: Harvard University Press.

Bumpass, L. L. (1990). What's happening to the family? Interactions between demographic and institutional change. *Demography, 27,* 483–498.

Bumpass, L. L., Sweet, J. A., & Cherlin, A. (1991). The role of cohabitation in declining rates of marriages. *Journal of Marriage and the Family, 53,* 913–927.

Bussell, D. A. (1995). A pilot study of African American children's cognitive and emotional reactions to parental separation. *Journal of Divorce and Remarriage, 25,* 3–15.

Capaldi, D. M., & Patterson, G. R. (1991). The relation of parental transitions to boys' adjustment problems:

I. A linear hypothesis, and II. Mothers at risk for transitions and unskilled parenting. *Developmental Psychology, 27,* 489–504.

Carbonne, J. R. (1994). A feminist perspective on divorce. *The Future of Children, 4,* 183–209.

Castro, M. T., & Bumpass, L. L. (1989). Recent trends in marital disruption. *Demography, 26,* 37–51.

Chase-Lansdale, P. L., Cherlin, A. J., & Kiernan, K. E. (1995). The long-term effects of parental divorce on the mental health of young adults: A developmental perspective. *Child Development, 66,* 1614–1634.

Cherlin, A. J. (1992). *Marriage, divorce, remarriage.* Cambridge, MA: Harvard University Press.

Cherlin, A. J., Chase-Lansdale, P. L., & McRae, C. (1998). Effects of divorce on mental health throughout the life course. *American Sociological Review, 63,* 239–249.

Cherlin, A. J., Furstenberg, F. F., Jr., Chase-Lansdale, P. L., Kiernan, K. E., Robins, P. K., Morrison, D. R., & Teitler, J. O. (1991). Longitudinal studies of effects of divorce on children in Great Britain and the United States. *Science, 252,* 1386–1389.

Clark, J., & Barber, B. L. (1994). Adolescents in postdivorce and always-married families: Self-esteem and perceptions of father interest. *Journal of Marriage and the Family, 56,* 608–614.

Clark, R., & Clifford, T. (1996). Toward a resources and stressors model: The psychological adjustment of adult children of divorce. *Journal of Divorce and Remarriage, 25,*

Coontz, S. (1992). *The way we never were: American families and the nostalgia trap.* New York: Basic Books.

Cooper, H., & Hedges, L. V. (Eds.). (1994). *Handbook of research synthesis.* New York: Russell Sage Foundation.

Cotton, S. R. (1999). Marital status and mental health revisited: Examining the importance of risk factors and resources. *Family Relations, 48,* 225–233.

Cowan, P. A., Cowan, C. P., & Schulz, M. S. (1996). Thinking about risk and resilience in families. In E. M. Hetherington & E. A. Blechman (Eds.), *Stress, coping, and resiliency in children and families* (pp. 1–38). Mahwah, NJ: Erlbaum.

Davies, L., Avison, W. R., & McAlpine, D. D. (1997). Significant life experiences and depression among single and married mothers. *Journal of Marriage and the Family, 59,* 294–308.

Davies, P. T., & Cummings, E. M. (1994). Marital conflict and child adjustment: An emotional security hypothesis. *Psychological Bulletin, 116,* 387–411.

DeGarmo, D. S., & Forgatch, M. S. (1999). Contexts as predictors of changing maternal parenting practices in diverse family structures. In E. M. Hetherington (Ed.), *Coping with divorce, single parenting, and remarriage: A risk and resiliency perspective* (pp. 227–252). Mahwah, NJ: Erlbaum.

DeGarmo, D. S., & Kitson, G. C. (1996). Identity relevance and disruption as predictors of psychological distress for widowed and divorced women. *Journal of Marriage and the Family, 58,* 983–997.

Demo, D. H. (1992). Parent–child relations: Assessing recent change. *Journal of Marriage and the Family, 54,* 104–114.

Demo, D. H., & Acock, A. C. (1996a). Family structure, family process, and adolescent well-being. *Journal of Research on Adolescence, 6,* 457–488.

Demo, D. H., & Acock, A. C. (1996b). Motherhood, marriage, and remarriage: The effects of family structure and family relationships on mothers' well-being. *Journal of Family Issues, 17,* 388–407.

Doherty, W. J., & Needle, R. H. (1991). Psychological adjustment and substance use among adolescents before and after a parental divorce. *Child Develoment, 62,* 328–337.

Downey, D. B. (1994). The school performance of children from single-mother and single-father families: Economic or interpersonal deprivation? *Journal of Family Issues, 15,* 129–147.

Downey, D. B., Ainsworth-Darnell, J. W., & Dufur, M. J. (1998). Sex of parent and children's well-being in single-parent households. *Journal of Marriage and the Family, 60,* 878–893.

Downey, D. B., & Powell, B. (1993). Do children in single-parent households fare better living with same-sex parents? *Journal of Marriage and the Family, 55,* 55–71.

Elliot, B. J., & Richards, M. P. M. (1991). Children and divorce: Educational performance and behaviour before and after parental separation. *International Journal of Law and the Family, 5,* 258–276.

Ellwood, M. S., & Stolberg, A. L. (1993). The effects of family composition, family health, parenting behavior and environmental stress on children's divorce adjustment. *Journal of Child and Family Studies, 2,* 23–36.

Emery, R. E. (1994). *Renegotiating family relationships: Divorce, child custody, and mediation.* New York: Guilford Press.

Emery, R. E., Kitzmann, K. M., & Waldron, M. (1999). Psychological interventions for separated and divorced families. In E. M. Hetherington (Ed.), *Coping with divorce, single parenting, and remarriage: A risk and resiliency perspective* (pp. 323–344). Mahwah, NJ: Erlbaum.

Fisher, P. A., Fagor, B. I., & Leve, C. S. (1998). Assessment of family stress across low-, medium-, and high-risk samples using the family events checklist. *Family Relations, 47,* 215–219.

Forehand, R., Armistead, L., & Corinne, D. (1997). Is adolescent adjustment following parental divorce a function of predivorce adjustment? *Journal of Abnormal Child Psychology, 25,* 157&–164.

Forehand, R., Neighbors, B., Devine, D., & Armistead, L. (1994). Interparental conflict and parental divorce. *Family Relations, 43,* 387–393.

Frost, A. K., & Pakiz, B. (1990). The effects of marital disruption on adolescents: Time as a dynamic. *American Journal of Orthopsychiatry, 60,* 544–555.

Funder, K., Harrison, M., & Weston, R. (1993). *Settling down: Pathways of parents after divorce.* Melbourne, Australia: Australian Institute of Family Studies.

Furstenberg, F. F., Jr. (1994). History and current status of divorce in the United States. *The Future of Children, 4,* 29–43.

Garvin, V., Kalter, N., & Hansell, J. (1993). Divorced women: Individual differences in stressors, mediating factors, and adjustment outcomes. *American Journal of Orthopsychiatry, 63,* 232–240.

Gately, D. W., & Schwebel, A. I. (1991). The challenge model of children's adjustment to parental divorce:

Exploring favorable postdivorce outcomes in children. *Journal of Family Psychology, 5,* 60–81.

Glenn, N. (1996). Values, attitudes, and the state of American marriage. In D. Popenoe, J. B. Elshtain, & D. Blankenhorn (Eds.), *Promises to keep: Decline and renewal of marriage in America* (pp. 15–34). Lanham, MD: Rowman and Littlefield.

Glick, P. C. (1989). Remarried families, stepfamilies, and stepchildren: A brief demographic profile. *Family Relations, 38,* 24–27.

Goldberg, W. A., Greenberger, E., Hamill, S., & O'Neil, R. (1992). Role demands in the lives of employed single mothers with preschoolers. *Journal of Family Issues, 13,* 312–333.

Goodman, C. C. (1993). Divorce after long-term marriages: Former spouse relations. *Journal of Divorce and Remarriage, 20,* 43–61.

Gray, J. D., & Silver, R. C. (1990). Opposite sides of the same coin: Former spouses' divergent perspectives in coping with their divorce. *Journal of Personality and Social Psychology, 59,* 1180–1191.

Grych, J. H., & Fincham, F. D. (1992). Marital dissolution and family adjustment: An attributional analysis. In T. L. Orbuch (Ed.), *Close relationship loss: Theoretical approaches* (pp. 157–173). New York: Springer-Verlag.

Hanson, T. L. (1999). Does parental conflict explain why divorce is negatively associated with child welfare? *Social Forces, 77,* 1283–1316.

Hao, L. (1996). Family structure, private transfers, and the economic well-being of families with children. *Social Forces, 75,* 269–292.

Hazan, C., & Shaver, P. R. (1992). Broken attachments: Relationship loss from the perspective of attachment theory. In T. L. Orbuch (Ed.), *Close relationship loss: Theoretical approaches* (pp. 90–110). New York: Springer-Verlag.

Healy, J. M., Malley, J. E., & Stewart, A. J. (1990). Children and their fathers after parental separation. *American Journal of Orthopsychiatry, 60,* 531–543.

Healy, J. M., Stewart, A. J., & Copeland, A. P. (1993). The role of self-blame in children's adjustment to parental separation. *Personality and Social Psychology Bulletin, 19,* 279–289.

Hemstrom, O. (1996). Is marriage dissolution linked to differences in mortality risks for men and women? *Journal of Marriage and the Family, 58,* 366–378.

Hetherington, E. M. (1999). Should we stay together for the sake of the children? In E. M. Hetherington (Ed.), *Coping with divorce, single parenting, and remarriage: A risk and resiliency perspective* (pp. 93–116). Mahwah NJ: Erlbaum.

Hetherington, E. M., & Clingempeel, W. G. (1992). Coping with marital transitions. *Monographs of the Society for Research in Child Development, 57,* (2–3). Chicago: University of Chicago Press.

Hetherington, E. M., & Jodl, K. M. (1994). Stepfamilies as settings for child development. In A. Booth & J. Dunn (Eds.), *Stepfamilies: Who benefits? Who does not?* 55–79 Hillsdale, NJ: Erlbaum.

Hill, R. (1949). *Families under stress.* New York: Harper and Row.

Hope, S., Power, C., & Rodgers, B. (1999). Does financial hardship account for elevated psychological distress in lone mothers? *Social Science and Medicine, 29,* 381–389.

Jekielek, S. M. (1998). Parental conflict, marital disruption and children's emotional well-being. *Social Forces, 76,* 905–935.

Jockin, V., McGue, M., & Lykken, D. T. (1996). Personality and divorce: A genetic analysis. *Journal of Personality and Social Psychology, 71,* 288–299.

Johnson, D. R., & Wu, J. (1996). *An empirical test of crisis, social selection and role explanations of the relationship between marital disruption and psychological distress: A pooled time-series analysis of four-wave panel data.* Paper presented at the International Conference on Social Stress Research, Paris, France.

Joung, I. M. A., Stronks, K., van de Mheen, H., van Poppel, F. W. A., van der Meer, J. B. W., & Mackenbach, J. P. (1997). The contribution of intermediary factors to marital status differences in self-reported health. *Journal of Marriage and the Family, 59,* 476–490.

Kalter, N., & Schreier, S. (1993). School-based support groups for children of divorce. *Special Services in the Schools, 8,* 39–66.

Kayser, K. (1993). *When love dies: The process of marital disaffection.* New York: Guilford Press.

Kendler, K. S., Neale, M. C., Kessler, R. C., Heath, A. C., & Eaves, L. J. (1992). Childhood parental loss and adult psychopathology in women. *Archives of General Psychiatry, 49,* 109–116.

Kim, L., Sandler, I. N., & Jenn-Yum, T. (1997). Locus of control as a stress moderator and mediator in children of divorce. *Journal of Abnormal Child Psychology, 25,* 145–155.

King, V. (1994). Nonresident father involvement and child well-being: Can dads make a difference? *Journal of Family Issues, 15,* 78&–96.

Kitson, G. C. (1992). *Portrait of divorce: Adjustment to marital breakdown.* New York: Guilford Press.

Kitson, G. C., & Morgan, L. A. (1990). The multiple consequences of divorce: A decade review. *Journal of Marriage and the Family, 52,* 913–924.

Kurdek, L. A. (1990). Divorce history and self-reported psychological distress in husbands and wives. *Journal of Marriage and the Family, 52,* 701–708.

Kurdek, L. A., Fine, M. A., & Sinclair, R. J. (1994). The relation between parenting transitions and adjustment in young adolescents. *Journal of Early Adolescence, 14,* 412–432.

Larson, R. W., & Gillman, S. (1999). Transmission of emotions in the daily interactions of single-mother families. *Journal of Marriage and the Family, 61,* 21–37.

Laumann, E. O., Gagnon, J. H., Michael, R. T., & Michaels, S. (1994). *The social organization of sexuality.* Chicago: University of Chicago Press.

Lawson, E. J., & Thompson, A. (1996). Black men's perceptions of divorce-related stressors and strategies for coping with divorce. *Journal of Family Issues, 17,* 249–273.

Lee, C. M., Picard, M., & Blain, M. D. (1994). A methodological and substantive review of intervention outcome studies for families undergoing divorce. *Journal of Family Psychology, 8,* 3–15.

Lillard, L. A., & Waite, L. J. (1995). 'Til death do us part: Marital disruption and mortality. *American Journal of Sociology, 100,* 1131–1156.

Lorenz, F. O., Simons, R. L., Conger, R. D., Elder, G.

H., Johnson, C., & Chao, W. (1997). Married and recently divorced mothers' stressful events and distress: Tracing change over time. *Journal of Marriage and the Family, 59,* 219–232.

Machida, S., & Holloway, S. D. (1991). The relationship between divorced mothers' perceived control over child rearing and children's post-divorce adjustment. *Family Relations, 40,* 272–278.

Marks, N. F. (1996). Flying solo at midlife: Gender, marital status, and psychological well-being. *Journal of Marriage and the Family, 58,* 917–932.

Marks, N. F., & Lambert, J. D. (1998). Marital status continuity and change among young and midlife adults. *Journal of Family Issues, 19,* 652–686.

Masheter, C. (1991). Postdivorce relationships between ex-spouses: The roles of attachment and interpersonal conflict. *Journal of Marriage and the Family, 53,* 103–110.

Mastekaasa, A. (1994a). Marital status, distress, and well-being: An international comparison. *Journal of Comparative Family Studies, 25,* 183–206.

Mastekaasa, A. (1994b). Psychological well-being and marital dissolution. *Journal of Family Issues, 15,* 208–228.

Mastekaasa, A. (1995). The subjective well-being of the previously married: The importance of unmarried cohabitation and time since widowhood or divorce. *Social Forces, 73,* 665–692.

Mastekaasa, A. (1997). Marital dissolution as a stressor: Some evidence on psychological, physical, and behavioral changes during the preseparation period. *Journal of Divorce and Remarriage, 26,* 155–183.

Mauldon, J. (1990). The effect of marital disruption on children's health. *Demography, 27,* 431–446.

McCubbin, H. I., & Patterson, J. M. (1983). Stress and the family. In H. I. McCubbin & C. R. Figley (Eds.), *Family stress, coping, and social support* (pp. 5–25). Springfield, IL: Thomas.

McGue, M., & Lykken, D. T. (1992). Genetic influence on risk of divorce. *Psychological Science, 3,* 368–373.

McLanahan S. S., & Booth, K. (1989). Mother-only families: Problems, prospects, and politics. *Journal of Marriage and the Family, 51,* 557–580.

McLanahan, S., & Sandefur, G. (1994). *Growing up with a single parent: What hurts, what helps.* Cambridge, MA: Harvard University Press.

McLanahan, S. S., Seltzer, J. A., Hanson, T. L., & Thompson, E. (1994). Child support enforcement and child well-being: Greater security or greater conflict? In I. Garfinkel, S. S. McLanahan, & P. K. Robins (Eds.), *Child support and child well-being* (pp. 239–256). Washington, DC: Urban Institute Press.

Mednick, B. R., Baker, R. L., Reznick, C., & Hocevar, D. (1990). Long-term effects of divorce on adolescent academic achievement. *Journal of Divorce, 13,* 69–88.

Miller, N. B., Smerglia, V. L., Gaudet, D. S., & Kitson, G. C. (1998). Stressful life events, social support, and the distress of widowed and divorced women. *Journal of Family Issues, 19,* 181–203.

Morrison, D. R., & Cherlin, A. J. (1995). The divorce process and young children's well-being: A prospective analysis. *Journal of Marriage and the Family, 57,* 800–812.

Morrison, D. R., & Coiro, M. J. (1999). Parental conflict and marital disruption: Do children benefit when high-conflict marriages are dissolved? *Journal of Marriage and the Family, 61,* 626–637.

Murphy, M., Glaser, K., & Grundy, E. (1997). Marital status and long-term illness in Great Britain. *Journal of Marriage and the Family, 59,* 156–164.

Neff, J. A., & Schluter, T. D. (1993). Marital status and depressive symptoms: The role of race/ethnicity and sex. *Journal of Divorce and Remarriage, 20,* 137–160.

O'Connor, T. G., Hawkins, N., Dunn, J., Thorpe, K., & Golding, J. (1998). Family type and depression in pregnancy: Factors mediating risk in a community sample. *Journal of Marriage and the Family, 60,* 757–770.

Orbuch, T. L. (1992). A symbolic interactionist approach to the study of relationship loss. In T. L. Orbuch (Ed.), *Close relationship loss: Theoretical approaches* (pp. 90–110). New York: Springer-Verlag.

Pearlin, L. I., Menaghan, E. G., Lieberman, M. A., & Mullan, J. T. (1981). The stress process. *Journal of Health and Social Behavior, 22,* 337–356.

Pearson, J., & Thoennes, N. (1990). Custody after divorce: Demographic and attitudinal patterns. *American Journal of Orthopsychiatry, 60,* 233–249.

Peters, A., & Liefbroer, A. C. (1997). Beyond marital status: Partner history and well-being in old age. *Journal of Marriage and the Family, 59,* 687–699.

Peterson, R. R. (1996). A re-evaluation of the economic consequences of divorce. *American Sociological Review, 61,* 528–536.

Plunkett, S. W., Sanchez, M. G., Henry, C. S., & Robinson, L. C. (1997). The double ABCX model and children's post-divorce adaptation. *Journal of Divorce and Remarriage, 27,* 17–33.

Popenoe, D. (1996). *Life without father.* New York: Free Press.

Power, C., Rodgers, B., & Hope, S. (1999). Heavy alcohol consumption and marital status: Disentangling the relationship in a national study of young adults. *Addictions, 94,* 1477–1497.

Preston, S. H., & McDonald, J. (1979). The incidence of divorce within cohorts of American marriages contracted since the Civil War. *Demography, 16,* 1–26.

Riessmann, C. K. (1990). *Divorce talk: Women and men make sense of personal relationships.* New Brunswick, NJ: Rutgers University Press.

Robins, L. N., & Regier, D. A. (1991). *Psychiatric disorders in America: The epidemiologic catchment area study.* New York: Free Press.

Rodgers, B. (1994). Pathways between parental divorce and adult depression. *Journal of Child Psychology and Psychiatry, 35,* 1289–1308.

Rodgers, B., & Pryor, J. (1998). *Divorce and separation: The outcomes for children.* York, England: Joseph Rowntree Foundation.

Rogers, R. G. (1996). The effects of family composition, health, and social support linkages on mortality. *Journal of Health and Social Behavior, 37,* 326–338.

Rogers, S. J., & White, L. K. (1998). Satisfaction with parenting: The role of marital happiness, family structure, and parents' gender. *Journal of Marriage and the Family, 60,* 293–308.

Ross, C. E. (1995). Reconceptualizing marital status as a continuum of social attachment. *Journal of Marriage and the Family, 57,* 129–140.

Rutter, M. (1987). Psychosocial resilience and protective mechanisms. *American Journal of Orthopsychiatry, 57,* 316–331.

Samera, T., Stolberg, A. L. (1993). Peer support, divorce, and children's adjustment. *Journal of Divorce and Remarriage, 20,* 45–64.

Sandler, I. N., Tein, J. Y., & West, S. G. (1994). Coping, stress, and the psychological symptoms of children of divorce: A cross-sectional and longitudinal study. *Child Development, 65,* 1744–1763.

Sandler, I., Wolchik, S., Braver, S., & Fogas, B. (1991). Stability and quality of life events and psychological symptomatology in children of divorce. *American Journal of Community Psychology, 19,* 501–520.

Shapiro, A. M. (1996). Explaining psychological distress in a sample of remarried and divorced persons. *Journal of Family Issues, 17,* 186–203.

Sheets, V., Sandler, I., & West, S. G. (1996). Appraisals of negative events by preadolescent children of divorce. *Child Development, 67,* 2166–2182.

Silitsky, D. (1996). Correlates of psychosocial adjustment in adolescents from divorced families. *Journal of Divorce and Remarriage, 26,* 151–169.

Simon, R. W. (1998). Assessing sex differences in vulnerability among employed parents: The importance of marital status. *Journal of Health and Social Behavior, 39,* 38–54.

Simon, R. W., & Marcussen, K. (1999). Marital transitions, marital beliefs, and mental health. *Journal of Health and Social Behavior, 40,* 111–125.

Simons, R. L. and Associates. (1996). *Understanding differences between divorced and intact families.* Thousand Oaks, CA: Sage.

Skolnick, A. (1991). *Embattled paradise: The American family in an age of uncertainty.* New York: Basic Books.

Smith, T. E. (1997). Differences between Black and White students in the effects of parental separation on school grades. *Journal of Divorce and Remarriage, 27,* 25–42.

Smock, P. J. (1994). Gender and the short-run economic consequences of marital disruption. *Social Forces, 73,* 243–262.

South, S. J., Crowder, K. D., & Trent, K. (1998). Children's residential mobility and neighborhood environment following parental divorce and remarriage. *Social Forces, 77,* 667–693.

Stacey, J. (1996). *In the name of the family: Rethinking family values in the postmodern age.* Boston: Beacon Press.

Stack, S., & Eshleman, J. R. (1998). Marital status and happiness: A 17-nation study. *Journal of Marriage and the Family, 60,* 527–536.

Sweet, J. A., & Bumpass, L. L. (1987). *American families and households.* New York: Russell Sage Foundation.

Teachman, J. D., & Paasch, K. M. (1994). Financial impact of divorce on children and the family. *Future of Children, 4,* 63–83.

Teachman, J. D., Paasch, K., & Carver, K. (1996). Social capital and dropping out of school early. *Journal of Marriage and the Family, 58,* 773–783.

Teja, S., & Stolberg, A. L. (1993). Peer support, divorce, and children's adjustment. *Journal of Divorce and Remarriage, 20,* 45–64.

Thabes, V. (1997). A survey analysis of women's long-term postdivorce adjustment. *Journal of Divorce and Remarriage, 27,* 163–175.

Thoits, P. A. (1995). Stress, coping, and social support processes: Where are we? What next? *Journal of Health and Social Behavior, 36,* (Ext), 53–79.

Thomson, E., McLanahan, S. S., & Curtin, R. B. (1992). Family structure, gender, and parental socialization. *Journal of Marriage and the Family, 54,* 368–378.

Tschann, J. M., Johnston, J. R., Kline, M., & Wallerstein, J. (1990). Conflict, loss, change and parent-child relationships: Predicting children's adjustment during divorce. *Journal of Divorce and Remarriage, 13,* 1–22.

Tucker, J. S., Friedman, H. S., Schwartz, J. E., Critiqui, M. H., Tomlinson-Keasey C., Wingard, D. L., & Martin, L. R. (1997). Parental divorce: Effects on individual behavior and longevity. *Journal of Personality and Social Psychology, 73,* 381–391.

Umberson, D., Chen, M. D., House, J. S., Hopkins, K., & Slaten, E. (1996). The effect of social relationships on psychological well-being: Are men and women really so different? *American Sociological Review, 61,* 837–857.

Umberson, D., & Williams, C. L. (1993). Divorced fathers: Parental role strain and psychological distress. *Journal of Family Issues, 14,* 378–400.

U.S. Bureau of the Census (1998). *Statistical Abstract of the United States* (118th ed.) Washington, DC: U.S. Government Printing Office.

Vandewater, E. A., & Lansford, J. E. (1998). Influences of family structure and parental conflict on children's well-being. *Family Relations, 47,* 323–330.

Wang, H., & Amato, P. R. (in press). Predictors of divorce adjustment. *Journal of Marriage and the Family.*

Wenk, D., Hardesty, C. L., Morgan, C. S., & Blair, S. L. (1994). The influence of parental involvement on the well-being of sons and daughters. *Journal of Marriage and the Family, 56,* 229–234.

Wheaton, B. (1990). Life transitions, role histories, and mental health. *American Sociological Review, 55,* 209–223.

White, J. M. (1992). Marital status and well-being in Canada. *Journal of Family Issues, 13,* 390–409.

White, L. K. (1991). Determinants of divorce. In A. Booth (Ed.), *Contemporary families* (pp. 141–149). Minneapolis, MN: National Council on Family Relations.

Zick, C. D., & Smith, K. R. (1991). Marital transitions, poverty, and gender differences in mortality. *Journal of Marriage and the Family, 53,* 327–336.

Marilyn Coleman, Lawrence Ganong, and Mark Fine
University of Missouri

Reinvestigating Remarriage: Another Decade of Progress

The body of stepfamily research published this decade exceeded the entire output of the previous 90 years of the century. The complexity and quality of the scholarly work in this decade improved as well—better samples were obtained, methods were more sensitive to stepfamily complexity, longitudinal designs were more frequently employed, and other important methodological gains were made. Unfortunately, many unknowns regarding remarriages and stepfamilies remain. We present an overview of trends regarding topics, research methods, and theories; we critique research methods that have not been productive; and we identify scholarly advances. Finally, new conceptual, methodological, and theoretical directions for future scholarship on remarriages and stepfamilies are proposed.

Remarriages and stepfamilies have always represented a substantial proportion of marriages and families in the United States and other Western countries (Phillips, 1997). However, researchers paid little attention to stepfamilies until the 1970s, when divorce replaced bereavement as the leading precursor to remarriage (Cherlin, 1992). Postdivorce stepfamilies were hard to ignore because unlike postbereavement stepfamilies, remarriage no longer reconstituted the nuclear family, and stepparents often were added "parent figures" rather than substitutes for deceased parents. The

Department of Human Development and Family Studies, 314 Gentry, Columbia, MO 65211-7700 (colemanma@missouri.edu).

Key Words: marital quality, parent-child relationships, remarriage, stepfamily.

complications and new interaction patterns of postdivorce stepfamilies created an explosion of scholarly interest in remarriage, stepparenting, and stepfamilies in the 1980s (Coleman & Ganong, 1990).

Although the 1980s were a productive period for research on remarriage and stepfamilies and although the quality of investigations improved throughout the decade (Coleman & Ganong, 1990), the scholarship left ample room for conceptual and methodological improvement. For example, inadequate attention was given to the structural complexity and diversity of stepfamilies, relationship problems were studied to the near exclusion of positive interactions, and households and stepfamilies were treated as if they were equivalent. The reactivity of measures and methods and the difficulty in obtaining representative samples of remarried families also were problems characteristic of 1980s research. Consequently, in the last decade review article, Coleman and Ganong made a number of recommendations for research on stepfamilies, calling for more complexity in designs and in how researchers thought about remarriages and stepfamilies.

One purpose of this review is to present and summarize research and theory on remarriages and stepfamilies published in the 1990s. This decade was a period of enormous productivity in the study of remarriages and stepfamilies. The body of published work was three times larger than the number of publications on stepfamilies before 1990. We examined more than 850 publications. Given the volume of studies, we decided to emphasize topics that received relatively greater attention by scholars: (a) demographic trends, (b) remarriage relationships, (c) the effects on children of living with a stepparent, (d) stepfamily processes, (e) societal views of stepfamilies, and (f) legal issues. Most (92%) of the decade's research fits into one of these categories. Many excellent reviews of research were written in this decade; interested readers should consult them (e.g., Amato, 1994; Cherlin & Furstenberg, 1994; Ganong & Coleman, 1994b; Hetherington & Henderson, 1997; Ihinger-Tallman & Pasley, 1997; Nielsen, 1999). A second purpose of this review is to identify conceptual and methodological trends in stepfamily research in the past decade. We critique research methods that have not been productive, and we identify scholarly advances. A third purpose of this review is to propose conceptual, methodological, and theoretical directions for future scholarship on remarriages and stepfamilies.

DEMOGRAPHIC TRENDS

Remarriages

Approximately half of the marriages in the United States represent a remarriage for one or both partners (Bumpass, Sweet, & Castro Martin, 1990). Although remarriage rates are lower than in the United States, similar trends were reported in Canada (e.g., Wu, 1994) and Europe (e.g., Kiernan, 1992). Remarriage is a term that encompasses several different types of relationships—both partners may be in a second marriage or a higher-order remarriage (e.g., a third or fourth marriage) or the marriage may be a remarriage for only one of the partners. Historically, remarriages generally have been treated as a uniform group by researchers, although in this decade, researchers began to think about remarriages and stepfamilies in more complex ways (e.g., Bumpass, Raley, & Sweet, 1995). About 75% of divorced people remarry (Furstenberg & Cherlin, 1991), and serial remarriages are increasingly common (National Center for Health Statistics, 1993). Remarriages that end in divorce do so more quickly than first marriages. As people age, however, the divorce rates of first marriages and remarriages converge (Clarke & Wilson, 1994). Remarriages contracted by older adults (i.e., older than 40) may be more stable than first marriages (Wu & Penning, 1997).

Remarriages tend to take place rapidly after prior marriages end; the mean length of time between divorce and remarriage is less than 4 years (Wilson & Clarke, 1992). Thirty percent remarry within a year after the divorce, and the distribution of time between marriages is skewed, peaking for both men and women at 1 month after divorce and 13 months after bereavement. The interval to remarriage lengthens with age for both men and women (Wilson & Clarke).

Men remarry at higher rates than do women (South, 1991), and Blacks and Hispanics remarry at lower rates than Whites (South). For divorced women, the probability of remarriage is lower when they are older (Buckle, Gallup, & Rodd, 1996), have more education, and are employed (Montalto & Gerner, 1998). For men, education increases the likelihood of remarriage (Montalto & Gerner). Divorced men who marry divorced women generally marry someone at least a few years younger than themselves, and it is likely that her children are younger than his (Wilson & Clarke, 1992). Children lower the likelihood of remarriage for both men and women, but the impact of children is greater on women's probability of remarriage (Buckle et al.). High occupational status delays remarriage among women separating at relatively younger ages and hastens it among women separating at relatively older ages. For older women, those least able to support themselves are also least likely to remarry. Thus, among older women, patterns of remarriage tend to increase the concentration of poverty among divorced women.

Fertility in Remarriage

A substantial proportion of all U.S. births occurs in remarriages. For both Blacks and Whites, about half of women in remarriages give birth to at least one child, most within 24 months of remarriage (Wineberg, 1990).

Cohabitation

Remarriage rates have been dropping in the United States except among older adults, but this does not mean that people are recoupling less often. Instead of remarrying after divorce, increasing numbers of divorced individuals are cohabiting, not as a precursor but as an alternative to remarriage (Bumpass et al., 1991, 1995). Moreover, most couples cohabit prior to legally forming a union (Cherlin & Furstenberg, 1994).

Older Adults and New Partners

The marital histories of older Americans are becoming increasingly complex (Cornman & Kingson, 1996). More divorced older adults, increased longevity, and better health throughout life are factors related to increases in remarriage among older adults (Holden & Kuo, 1996). An estimated half million people over the age of 65 in the United States remarry each year (U.S. Census Bureau, 1995). Over 4% of older people do not remarry but cohabit with a new partner (Chevan, 1996).

The numbers of later-life cohabiting relationships, remarriages, and stepfamilies are likely to increase in the next few years as the baby boom generation begins reaching retirement age. About half of the marriages of this cohort will end in divorce, and about 75% of those who have divorced will remarry at least once (Furstenberg & Cherlin, 1991). Among this cohort will be unprecedented numbers of individuals who are stepparents (Cornman & Kingson, 1996).

Stepfamilies

Not all remarriages include children from prior relationships, nor do all stepfamilies incorporate a remarriage. Approximately 25% of the 3.7 million cohabiting couples in the United States are households in which at least one adult brings children from prior relationships, thereby creating cohabiting stepfamily households (Bumpass et al., 1991). In fact, cohabiting couples are more likely (48% versus 37%) to enter a new union with children from previous relationships than are remarried couples (Wineberg & McCarthy, 1998). Some first marriages create stepfamilies and stepparent-stepchild relationships (i.e., when never-married mothers marry a man who is not the child's father).

In 1992, 15% of all children in the United States lived with a mother and a stepfather (U.S. Bureau of the Census, 1995). About one-third of U.S. children will live in a remarried or cohabiting stepfamily household before they reach adulthood (Bumpass et al., 1995; Seltzer, 1994). In fact, children in stepfamilies may have lived in several types of families before they reach adulthood, although fewer than 5% of all remarried couples incorporate three sets of children (i.e., yours, mine, and ours). Complex marital and cohabiting histories over the life course result in complex family histories for children (O'Connor, Pickering, Dunn, Golding, & the ALSAC Study Team, 1999; Wojtkiewicz, 1994) and for adults. For example, about 40% of adult women will likely reside in a remarried or cohabiting stepfamily household as a parent or stepparent at some time

(Bumpass et al.), and 40% of all families include stepgrandparents (Szinovacz, 1998).

The work of demographers in this decade yielded a more complex understanding of stepfamily structures. The importance of knowing about relationship histories in order to more fully comprehend stepfamily dynamics was underscored, and these more elaborated demographic views influenced how other researchers conceptualized stepfamily structure.

REMARRIAGE RELATIONSHIPS

Remarriage research generally focused on marital dynamics, quality, and stability. Samples were often small, and many employed qualitative designs.

Marital Dynamics

Remarriage or cohabitation typically occurs within months after beginning the relationship (Montgomery, Anderson, Hetherington, & Clingempeel, 1992), and we know little about how decisions to cohabit are made or the effects that cohabiting has on the stepfamily system. A common courtship pattern is as follows: (a) male partner spends a few nights per week in the mother's household, followed by (b) a brief period of full-time living together, followed by (c) remarriage (Montgomery et al.).

Studies of the process of building satisfying remarriages were limited, and the effectiveness of strategies used was not determined. Evidence exists that decision making in remarriage is perceived to be equally shared (Crosbie-Burnett & Giles-Sims, 1991; Pyke), primarily because women seek more power in remarriages than in first marriages (Pyke & Coltrane, 1996). Reasons offered for why distribution of power in remarriage is more equitable included the following: (a) personal experiences in prior unions and as divorced single persons cause women to seek more power (Burgoyne & Morison, 1997; Pyke, 1994), (b) the greater resources women often bring to remarriage give them more bargaining power (Crosbie-Burnett & Giles-Sims; Pyke & Coltrane), (c) previously married men and women think differently about marital roles (Burgoyne & Morison; Ishii-Kuntz & Coltrane, 1992), (d) women who are reluctant to remarry gain power (Pyke), and (e) men concede more during marital conflicts than they did in their first marriages (Hobart, 1991).

Women perceived that they have more power regarding financial decisions in their remarriages than in their prior marriages (Burgoyne & Morison, 1997; Pasley, Sandras, & Edmondson, 1994), but it is difficult to determine whether financial decision-making is equitable because finances in remarried families are complex (Burgoyne & Morison; Jacobson, 1993). For example, remarried couples are more likely than first marriages to maintain some economic resources under the individual control of each partner, in part because of financial responsibilities for children from multiple unions, and in part because of individuals' desires to retain financial independence.

Shared decision making does not mean that household tasks are shared equitably, however. Household duties appear to be based on traditional gender roles, and most studies find that remarried women do most of the housework (Demo & Acock, 1993; Pyke & Coltrane, 1996), although remarried husbands do more housework than husbands in first marriages (Deal, Stanley-Hagan, & Anderson, 1992; Ishii-Kuntz & Coltrane, 1992).

Remarriage Quality

Findings are mixed regarding differences in marital quality between individuals in first marriages and in remarriages; some find no differences (Booth & Edwards, 1992; Deal at al., 1992), and others report lower relationship quality for remarried individuals (Brown & Booth, 1996). It has been suggested that different processes may be involved in determining the quality of remarriages and first marriages (Jacobson, 1993; Rogers, 1996b). For example, Kurdek (1991) found that marital satisfaction declined more rapidly over time in stepfather households than in first marriages.

Findings based on behavioral observations and self-reports were that remarried spouses more openly express criticisms, anger, and irritation than do spouses in first marriages (Bray & Kelly, 1998; Hetherington, 1993). Remarried participants also generally report higher levels of tension and disagreement than their counterparts in first marriages (Hobart, 1991). These disagreements generally center on issues related to stepchildren, such as discipline, rules for children, and the distribution of resources to children (Hobart; Pasley, Koch, & Ihinger-Tallman, 1993). Disputes between adults may also result from arguments between stepparents and stepchildren (Clingempeel, Colyar, & Hetherington, 1994). Although the presence of stepchildren is thought to lower marital quality for remarried adults (Brown & Booth,

1996), the effects are not always strong. In fact, Kurdek (1999) found that children born to first marriages lowered marital quality more than stepchildren lowered remarital quality. Nonetheless, marital quality is poorer when both adults have children from prior relationships than when only one adult is a stepparent, presumably because of added complexity and more opportunities for conflict (Hobart).

Remarriage Stability

Remarriages dissolve at higher rates than first marriages (Bumpass et al., 1990), especially for remarried couples with stepchildren (Booth & Edwards, 1992). A number of intrapersonal, interpersonal, and societal-level explanations have been proposed for the greater instability of remarriages. For example, compared with first marriages, remarriages include more people who have personality characteristics (e.g., impulsivity, neuroticism) that predispose them to end relationships more frequently and make them poorer marriage material (Booth & Edwards; Capaldi & Patterson, 1991). Booth and Edwards concluded that remarriages are more fragile because (a) they lack social support and clear norms to follow, (b) a larger proportion of people who remarry than people in first marriages see divorce as a solution to marital problems, and (c) the smaller pool of partners for remarriages results in unions between people with dissimilar interests and values.

Some researchers pointed to greater conflict in remarriages as a reason for higher redivorce rates (Hobart, 1991), but others argued that it is not the amount of conflict that predicts redivorce but the manner in which remarried couples resolve their disagreements (Pasley et al., 1993). Conflict is not inherently negative; some women in the power-sharing couples that Pyke (1994) interviewed reported more conflicts than those in husband-dominant remarriages because the women actively sought power. In such marriages, conflict may represent active problem solving, which may decrease the probability of redivorce.

Effects of Remarriage on Remarried Adults

A few researchers investigated health status, depression, happiness, and psychological distress of remarried adults. The findings were mixed—remarriage was associated with higher levels of depression (e.g., Neff & Schluter, 1993), but other researchers reported less distress for remarried than for divorced individuals (e.g., Shapiro, 1996) and that remarriage was not related to well-being (e.g., Richards, Hardy, & Wadsworth, 1997). Moreover, it is not clear whether men or women benefit more from remarriage (Marks, 1995; Pasley & Ihinger-Tallman, 1990). These mixed findings suggest that factors other than marital status explain adults' well-being. For example, differential selection into remarriage may potentially explain differences between remarried and divorced adults in that people with better mental and physical health are more likely to find new partners than are those with health problems (Booth & Amato, 1991; Murphy, Glaser, & Grundy, 1997).

EFFECTS ON CHILDREN OF STEPFAMILY LIVING

Over a third of the studies published—the most on any topic—dealt with the effects on children of living with a remarried or cohabiting stepparent. Many were national studies (e.g., National Study of Families and Households [NSFH]) or large representative samples (e.g., Avon Longitudinal Study of Parents and Children in the U.K.) conducted in North America, Europe, Asia, Australia, Israel, and New Zealand.

Research on young and adolescent stepchildren focused primarily on academic achievement (e.g., grades, school completion, achievement test scores), psychological adjustment and well being, and behavior problems. Typically, stepchildren and children living with one parent were compared on the outcome measures with children living with both parents. Demographic characteristics of children and families were usually included, as were various mediating variables related to such constructs as family relationships and peer characteristics.

Stepchildren and children with single parents did not achieve as well on average as children living with both parents in grades earned in school (e.g., Astone & McLanahan, 1991; Bogenscheider, 1997), grades completed (e.g., Teachman, Paasch, & Carver, 1996), and scores on achievement tests (e.g., Dronkers, 1994; Pong, 1997). However, the largest differences were in dropout rates, school attendance, and whether the student graduated or received a GED (regression coefficients of $-.36$, $-.38$, and $-.33$, respectively, for the differences between children in stepfamilies and first-marriage families) (Astone & McLanahan). The finding pertaining to dropout rates may be related to the fact that stepchildren tend to leave home to establish independent households at younger ages than do children living with both parents (e.g., Aquilino, 1991b; Kiernan, 1992). For example, stepdaughters were more likely to cohabit (Goldscheider & Goldscheider, 1998) or to marry than were women from first-marriage families (Aquilino) or from other family forms (Thornton, 1991), which may be related to leaving home and school early.

Compared with children in first-marriage families, stepchildren on average showed more internalizing behavior problems, such as depression (e.g., Zill et al., 1993), and were more at risk for having emotional problems (e.g., Dawson, 1991; Hanson, McLanahan, & Thomson, 1996). Some studies found that boys have more problems than girls (e.g., Coley, 1998; Dunn et al., 1998); others found that girls had more problems than boys (Needle, Su, & Doherty, 1990) or that girls had more adjustment problems than boys only when living with stepfathers (e.g., Lee, Burkam, Zimiles, & Ladewski, 1994). Still others found more problems for girls living with stepmothers (e.g., Suh, Schutz, & Johanson, 1996).

Adolescent stepchildren also generally showed more externalizing behavioral problems than children living with both parents, such as using drugs and alcohol (e.g., Hoffman & Johnson, 1998; Needle et al., 1990), engaging in sexual intercourse (Day, 1992), nonmarital childbearing (e.g., Astone & Washington, 1994), and being arrested (Coughlin & Vuchinich, 1996). African American children may benefit from, or are at least not harmed by, the involvement of stepfathers (e.g., Salem, Zimmerman, & Notaro, 1998; Wojtkiewicz, 1993).

Although the findings ranged widely, most researchers reported that stepchildren were similar to children living with single mothers on the preponderance of outcome measures and that stepchildren generally were at greater risk for problems than were children living with both of their parents. However, most researchers also found that the differences between stepchildren and children in first-marriage families were small, with effect sizes from Amato's (1994) meta-analysis ranging from $-.07$ for academic achievement to $-.32$ for problems in either or both conduct or behavior and $-.37$ for psychological adjustment (according to Cohen's (1969) commonly used convention, effect sizes of .20, .50, and .80 are considered small, moderate, and large, respectively). Most stepchildren do well in school (e.g., Pong, 1997) and do not have emotional or behavioral problems (e.g., Dorius, Heaton, & Steffen, 1993; Lissau & Sorenson, 1994).

Long-Term Effects on Stepchildren

In addition to the plethora of studies focusing on children and adolescents, a substantial number (*n* =39) of investigations examined the long-term effects of having a stepparent. The availability of several large, longitudinal data sets that extended data collection from birth or early childhood into adulthood or that followed adolescents into adulthood contributed to the number of studies on long-term effects.

Although the negative effects of having a stepparent were often reported to be long lasting (e.g., Biblarz, Raftery, & Bucur, 1997; Kiernan, 1992), parental remarriage during childhood was found not to be related to emotional problems during early (Chase-Lansdale, Cherlin, & Kiernan, 1995; Rodgers, Power, & Hope, 1997) and middle adulthood (Rodgers, 1994) in a British longitudinal study. Studies of local samples also reported no relation between parental remarriage and adjustment in early adulthood (e.g., Lissau & Sorenson, 1994). Long-term effects may be related to age at parental remarriage (Zill et al., 1993).

Theoretical Explanations for Stepparent Effects on Stepchildren

Although views vary widely in the scholarly community regarding the effects of stepfamily living (e.g., see Booth & Dunn, 1994), the prevailing perspective was that living with a stepparent was harmful to children and adolescents. Parental remarriage and cohabitation generally were viewed as family disruptions that negatively affected children, similarly to parental divorce or residing with a never-married mother (see Amato, 2000, for a discussion of the explanatory models used in divorce research). Although many explanations were proposed, based on systems theory (Hetherington & Clingempeel, 1992; Hetherington, Henderson, & Reiss, 1999), role theory (Skopin, Newman, & McKenry, 1993; Whitsett & Land, 1992), gender theory (MacDonald & DeMaris, 1996), exchange theory (Marsiglio, 1992), Bronfenbrenner's social ecology model (Bogenscheider, 1997; Fine & Kurdek, 1992), and the life course perspective (Aquilino, 1994), among others, most explanations for stepparent effects on stepchildren could be categorized as variants of

stress models, (step)parent involvement rationales, (step)parent style models, and selection.

Stress models. Many explanations centered on the idea that parental repartnering was stressful for children and adults (e.g., Henry & Lovelace, 1995). Parental remarriage and cohabitation involve many changes for adults and children, such as moving to a new residence, adapting to new household members, and learning new household routines and activities. These changes are thought to increase stress for children, which in turn leads to poorer performances in school and more internalizing and externalizing behavior problems (Menaghan, Kowaleski-Jones, & Mott, 1997).

A related stress model, the *cumulative effects hypothesis,* proposed that the more marital disruptions experienced by a parent, the more internalizing and externalizing problems children exhibit as a result of having to cope with these multiple transitions (Capaldi & Patterson, 1991). Support for this hypothesis was found; children whose parents had several partners over time had more problems than children who lived with a parent who had repartnered only once (e.g., Capaldi & Patterson; Kurdek & Fine, 1993a).

Another stress model proposed that *parental competencies are compromised* when beginning stepfamily relationships (e.g., Hoffman & Johnson, 1998). Stepchildren's problems are thus attributed to the diminished or poor-quality parenting they receive from stressed parents who do not have the personal resources to monitor children's behavior, participate in school activities, or interact with their children at the same levels that they did prior to remarriage or cohabiting (Dawson, 1991). A variation of this explanation proposed that the stepparent, as an added adult, would reduce familial stress related to economic burdens and the monitoring of children (e.g., Bulcroft et al., 1998; Hawkins & Eggebeen, 1991).

Conflicts between divorced parents and within stepparent households also were hypothesized as stress-related explanations for stepchildren generally faring worse on behavioral and psychological outcomes than children living with both parents (e.g., Downey, 1995; Hanson, McLanahan, & Thomson, 1996). Researchers attributed higher rates of early home leaving (e.g., Kiernan, 1992) and lower rates of coresidence of adult children in remarried families (e.g., Aquilino, 1991a) to the stressful atmosphere in step-households. Stepchildren may withdraw as a way to keep peace in the family and to try to maintain their own well-being

(Hanson et al.). Although not all researchers reported more conflict in stepfamilies than in nuclear families (Barber, 1994; Salem et al., 1998) and studies did not always find that intra- and interhousehold conflicts were related to stepchildren's outcomes (e.g., Hanson et al.), stepfamily conflict was a viable explanation for poorer children's outcomes in many investigations (Kurdek & Fine, 1993a).

The amount of conflict in stepfamilies may be related to the ages and sexes of the stepchildren. Adolescent stepchildren often reported more conflict with stepparents than did adolescents from first-marriage families (Barber & Lyons, 1994; Kurdek & Fine, 1993b). Adolescents may be more resistant to accepting authority from a stepparent than younger stepchildren. Sex also may be relevant in predicting how stepparents relate to stepchildren. For example, Vuchinich, Hetherington, Vuchinich, and Clingempeel (1991) found that adolescent girls had more difficulty than boys interacting with stepfathers and had more extended conflicts with and were more likely to withdraw from stepfathers and treat them like outsiders.

Another explanation for the greater risk of problems for stepchildren was the *economic deprivation hypothesis,* which postulated that stepchildren and children living with a single parent were at a disadvantage compared with children living with both parents because of economic hardships and the associated deficit conditions that accompany poverty, such as inadequate schools, dangerous neighborhoods, and adults working long hours (e.g., Pong). Evidence to support this hypothesis was mixed; when researchers controlled for differences in household income or socioeconomic status, effects were sometimes attenuated (e.g., Pong, 1997) but not always (e.g., Hoffman & Johnson, 1998).

The final explanatory model related to stress was the *incomplete institutionalization hypothesis.* Over two decades ago, Cherlin (1978) proposed that the absence of societal norms for remarried families regarding role performances; the dearth of established, socially acceptable methods of resolving problems; and the lack of institutionalized social support contributed to greater stress for remarried families. In this view, stepchildren fare worse than children in first-marriage families because, lacking culturally institutionalized support, stepparents are unsure about how to relate to stepchildren, and remarried adults lack appropriate solutions to family problems. Critics have argued that Cherlin's views overstate the degree to which

remarried families lack institutional support (Jacobson, 1995), and some researchers have not found support for all of his contentions (e.g., Coleman, Ganong, & Cable, 1997). However, there is support for the claim that expectations for stepparents are less clear than expectations for parents (e.g., Bulcroft et al., 1998; Fine, Coleman, & Ganong, 1998). There needs to be more research on this popular hypothesis.

(Step)parent involvement models. Many researchers sought to explain stepchildren's behaviors as the result of reduced involvement in their lives by either parents or stepparents. For example, stepparent households were hypothesized to lack social capital, defined as time and energy engaged in positive interactions with children. That is, remarriage disrupts parents' abilities to competently raise their children because they are investing time and energy in new partners rather than in childrearing (e.g., Downey, 1995; Pong, 1997). Similarly, stepparents do not invest as much social capital in stepchildren because they are expending resources on the adult relationship or on their children from prior unions (e.g., Bogenscheider, 1997; Teachman et al., 1996). Consequently, children in stepparent households have more problems than other children do because they are thought to be receiving inadequate parenting and adult support. Researchers often employed the *social capital model* to investigate stepparent effects on stepchildren's academic achievement; generally, stepparents and remarried parents were reported to spend less time working with stepchildren on schoolwork and being involved with school-related activities than were parents in nuclear families (e.g., Leung, 1995; Pong). Also, support for the social capital model was found in studies of behavior problems (e.g., Kim, Hetherington, & Reiss, 1999). However, cooperation between the parent and stepparent in raising children from prior relationships may be nearly as important as the level of stepparents' involvement with the stepchildren (Bronstein, Stoll, Clauson, Abrams, & Briones, 1994).

In general, stepparents interacted less with stepchildren than parents did. In addition to the social capital explanation, a number of other explanations for their lower involvement have been investigated. For instance, stepfathers may find it hard to break into tightly knit mother-child systems because of efforts by both mothers and children to keep them at a distance (Hetherington & Clingempeel, 1992). Social cognitive factors also may play a role—several studies showed that people generally expect stepparents to be less supportive and less close to stepchildren than parents (e.g., Ganong & Coleman, 1995). Moreover, the stepparent role has low salience for the identities of many stepparents, so they may find more satisfaction in work, marriage, or raising their own children than they do in relating to their stepchildren (Thoits, 1992).

Evolutionary scholars postulated that stepparents invest little of themselves in their stepchildren because they are not genetically related to them (Daly & Wilson, 1996). This theory proposes that stepparents who also are parents discriminate in favor of their genetic children and that stepfathers interact with stepchildren to impress their new partners rather than to foster stepchildren's growth and well-being. The parental investment-parental discrimination proposition was supported in some studies (e.g., Flinn, 1999; Mekos, Hetherington, & Reiss, 1996) but not in all (e.g., Bulcroft et al., 1998; Menaghan et al., 1997). For example, stepfathers who lived with their children spent more time with stepchildren than did stepfathers who just had stepchildren (Cooksey & Fondell, 1996).

Not only was the evolutionary theory used to explain relative emotional distances and disengaged parenting practices for stepparents, it was also the theory receiving the most attention in research on child abuse, although several other theories also were proposed to explain child abuse in stepfamilies (Giles-Sims, 1997). The more than two dozen studies on child abuse in stepfamilies were evenly divided between investigations of physical and sexual abuse. Most researchers reported that children in households with nonnatal adults, particularly stepfathers, mothers' boyfriends, and other nonnatal males, were at much greater risk for sexual abuse (Margolin, 1992) and physical abuse (Daly & Wilson, 1996). However, others argued that stepchildren were not more likely to be abused by stepparents (Gelles & Harrop, 1991; Malkin & Lamb, 1994). Unfortunately, given how abuse data are recorded, it is sometimes difficult to determine whether the perpetrator of child abuse is a stepparent or another adult. For example, mothers' boyfriends and legally remarried stepfathers are often categorized as one group. Children are more at risk for abuse if they live in a household with an adult who is not their genetic parent, but the extent to which stepchildren are at greater risk for being abused by a stepparent continues to be debated (Giles-Sims).

(Step)parental style. Some researchers examined differences between parenting styles of stepparents and parents that may have placed children at risk for problems (e.g., Fine & Kurdek, 1992; Salem et al., 1998). Most compared parenting styles in stepparent households with other types of households, but a few compared stepparents in various types of stepfamilies (e.g., Crosbie-Burnett & Giles-Sims, 1994). Unfortunately, most researchers developed their own measures of stepparenting styles, which makes comparisons across studies difficult.

Consistent with the research on stepparents' involvement with stepchildren, the parenting styles of stepparents were more disengaged than were those of parents. On average, stepfathers showed less affection toward stepchildren and engaged in less supervision of them (e.g., Hetherington & Clingempeel, 1992; Kurdek & Fine, 1995). Similar findings were reported for stepmothers (Kurdek & Fine, 1993b).

However, not all investigators found differences in parenting style between stepparent households and first-married–parent households. For example, stepfather households containing adolescents did not differ from nuclear families in permissiveness and in democratic decision making (Barber & Lyons, 1994); in support and monitoring of adolescents (Salem et al., 1998); or in permissive, authoritarian, or authoritative parenting styles (Shucksmith, Hendry, & Glendinning, 1995). Also, no major differences were found in adolescent independence-giving (i.e., staying home alone, household rules, and weekend curfews) between nuclear, single-parent, and stepparent households (Bulcroft et al., 1998).

Researchers generally found that authoritative parenting (high warmth and high control) was positively related and that authoritarian parenting (low warmth and high control) was negatively related to adolescent well-being, suggesting that the same family processes that influence adolescent well-being in first-marriage families are also associated with well-being in stepfamilies (e.g., Hetherington & Clingempeel, 1992; Fine & Kurdek, 1992). Stepparent support was a better predictor of stepchild adjustment than stepparents' monitoring behaviors (Crosbie-Burnett & Giles-Sims, 1994).

Although several studies identified sex differences in stepchildren's perceptions of stepparents' warmth and control, consistent patterns are difficult to discern (e.g., Kurdek & Fine, 1993a, 1993b). There are indications that stepmothers have a harder time raising stepchildren than stepfathers do (MacDonald & DeMaris, 1996). Additionally, Thomson, McLanahan, and Curtin (1992) found that parenting was less gendered in father-stepmother families than in mother-stepfather or first-marriage families, although the differences were considered to be "relatively small" (p. 376).

Selection. A few researchers examined the selection argument that differences between stepchildren and children living with both parents were due to factors that predated parental remarriage or cohabitation (see Amato, 2000). Because correlational data do not allow causal inferences, some researchers questioned whether differences between stepchildren and other children were due to pre-existing factors, such as parental psychopathology or poverty, that influenced both family transitions and child problems (Capaldi & Patterson, 1991). Findings regarding selection factors have been mixed, with some reporting that children's behavior problems predated parental remarriage (e.g., Capaldi & Patterson; Cherlin et al., 1991) and others finding that girls showed negative effects before parental separation but that boys showed more negative effects after separation (Doherty & Needle, 1991).

STEPFAMILY RELATIONSHIPS AND PROCESSES

Nearly one fourth of the studies in this decade dealt with stepfamily relationships or dynamics. Stepfathers' and fathers' relationships with children were studied much more often than stepmothers' and mothers' relationships with children, as was true during the 1980s. Relationships between siblings and stepsiblings and between children and grandparents or stepgrandparents were rarely studied.

Development of Stepparent-Stepchild Relationships

Few researchers considered the development of step-relationships, and findings were mixed among those who did. In three in-depth longitudinal studies of stepfathers, relationships with stepchildren generally became more negative over time (Bray & Kelly, 1998; Hetherington, 1993; Hetherington & Clingempeel, 1992). However, in another study, some relationships among stepparents and adolescent stepchildren became closer, some grew more distant, and some changed little

over a 5-year period (Ganong & Coleman, 1994a). Research is needed to determine why some relationships become closer and others grow more hostile or distant.

Some evidence suggests that stepchildren reject stepparents who engage in discipline and control early in the relationship (Bray & Kelly; Ganong, Coleman, Fine, & Martin, 1999). In contrast, affection more often characterized stepparent-stepchild relationships when stepfathers initially engaged in supportive behaviors with stepchildren than when no such efforts were made (Bray & Kelly, 1998; Hetherington & Clingempeel, 1992). Moreover, stepparents who intentionally tried to get their stepchildren to like them and who continued their affinity-seeking and -maintaining efforts had warmer, closer bonds with their stepchildren than did those who gradually reduced affinity-seeking efforts (Ganong et al., 1999). The most effective relationship-building strategies for stepparents were dyadic activities chosen by the stepchild.

However, stepchildren are not passive observers in the developing stepparent-stepchild relationship (Hetherington, 1993). How they treat stepparents also affects the relationship. For example, Hetherington and Clingempeel (1992) found that stepfathers withdrew from stepchildren who ignored their overtures early in the remarriage. We found that when stepchildren recognized that their stepparents were trying to do things with them that the stepchildren liked, they generally responded with their own affinity-seeking efforts (Ganong et al., 1999). Similarly, O'Connor, Hetherington, and Clingempeel (1997) found that the observed responses of adolescents to (step)parents was as strong a predictor of adolescent adjustment as was (step)parent-to-adolescent behavior. Nonetheless, even when positive stepparent-stepchild relationships are established when the child is a preadolescent, conflict may still arise when the child gets older (Hetherington, 1993). Additionally, adolescent stepchildren tend to see parents as more accepting of them than stepparents. Using vignettes as stimuli, Russell and Searcy (1997) found that adolescents responded to parents in a friendlier way than they did to stepparents in the same situations. This study suggests that adolescent stepchildren are primed to respond to stepparents in ways that create emotional distance and to attribute motives to stepparents that discourage warm feelings toward them.

Stepparents' Roles

Stepfamily members often do not agree on what role the stepparent should play (Fine et al., 1998). Beyond a general consensus that parents are expected to exhibit more warmth toward children and to more carefully monitor their behavior than are stepparents (Fine & Kurdek, 1994), there is little consistency in perceptions of the content of the stepparent role (Fine et al.). Stepparents are less certain about their role than are other family members. Some stepfathers deal with the issue of role confusion and stepparent identity by assuming a parent role (Berger, 1995; Erera-Weatherly, 1996), a role that contributes to their family life satisfaction (Marsiglio, 1992), although mothers and stepchildren may have different reactions. Stepmothers are much less likely to assume a parental role (Church, 1999). Instead, most stepmothers, and many stepfathers, especially nonresidential ones, see themselves as a friend to their stepchildren (Church) or in some role between a friend and a parent (Erera-Weatherly). A number of studies showed that role clarity and role agreement are related to adjustment in stepfamilies (e.g., Fine, Ganong, & Coleman, 1997; Fine et al.). For example, stepfathers' and adolescents' perceptions of stepfather-stepchild relationship quality were predicted best by the degree to which stepfathers and mothers agreed on how adolescents should be raised (Skopin et al., 1993).

Mothers and Children

Generally, mother-child relationships in stepfamilies received little attention from researchers. In a longitudinal study, Hetherington and Clingempeel (1992) found that mother-preadolescent child relationships deteriorated after remarriage but that after 2 years, they were similar to mother-child relationships in first-marriage families. In fact, children in all family types showed increasingly negative behavior as they entered adolescence, but they eventually behaved more positively toward their mothers as they were granted greater autonomy.

Fathers and Children

Most studies of fathers in stepfamilies were of nonresidential fathers. Results were mixed regarding whether remarriage affects nonresidential parental involvement. For example, the remarriage of either parent was not related to the frequency of contacts with nonresidential parents (Stephen, Freedman, & Hess, 1993) or the amount of time children spent in nonresidential fathers' households (Stephen et al.). Other researchers, however, found that contact diminished after either parent began residing with a new partner (McKenry, McKelvey, Leigh, & Wark, 1996).

Older Parents and Adult Children

In examinations of coresidence, emotional closeness, and intergenerational exchanges of resources and support, researchers found that adult children were less likely to live in a remarried parent's home than with a parent in a first marriage (Aquilino, 1991a). Adult children who grew up with a remarried father also were less likely to take older parents into their homes than were adults from first-marriage families, although adults with remarried mothers were as likely as adults from first-marriage families to share their residences (Szinovacz, 1998). Findings have been mixed on whether adult stepchildren help their stepparents and parents as much as adult children in nuclear families—some researchers found no differences (Aquilino, 1994; Spitze & Logan, 1992), and some found that stepchildren provide less support to parents (White, 1992) and stepparents (Amato, Rezac, & Booth, 1995). However, when help given to or received from the households of both parents was combined for adult children of divorced and remarried parents, there were no significant family structure differences in exchanges between parents and adult children (Amato et al., 1995).

Remarried parents (White, 1992) and stepparents (Spitze & Logan, 1992) in general provided less support to adult (step)children than did parents in first marriages, but remarried mothers gave some types of support as much as first-married mothers did (Marks, 1995; Spitze & Logan). Differences between remarried adults and those in first marriages in attitudes about their financial obligations to assist children (Marks), normative beliefs about intergenerational responsibilities after remarriage (Ganong & Coleman, 1999), and differences in family solidarity were offered to explain these findings (White).

Stepfamily Processes

There has been relatively little work examining family-level processes beyond parenting styles in stepfamilies. However, some investigators assessed the extent to which stepfamily processes are similar to those of first-marriage families.

Several investigators reported similar processes among stepfamilies and first-marriage families (Bogenscheider, 1997; O'Connor, Hetherington, & Reiss, 1998; Waldren, Bell, Peek, & Sorell, 1990). In fact, a substantial proportion of stable, long-term stepfamilies appear to function similarly to nuclear families (O'Connor et al.; Vuchinich et al., 1991). For example, stepfathers' involvement in supporting and monitoring stepchildren is related to better outcomes and more satisfaction with family life for stepchildren (Henry & Lovelace, 1995), a finding that suggests that the more a stepfather acts like a parent, the better it is for children. It may be that stepfamilies come to function more similarly to first-marriage families over time. For example, over a 2-year period, Vuchinich, Vuchinich, and Wood (1993) found that mother-stepfather–preadolescent stepson triads became similar to first-marriage family triads in problem-solving effectiveness. In both types of families, parental agreement facilitated problem solving, but parental coalitions did not. Marital conflict also was not related to problem-solving effectiveness in either type of family.

A few researchers reported differences in perceived family functioning between stepfamilies and first-marriage families, with remarried individuals viewing their families as more stressful and as less cohesive and adaptable and reporting less positive affect toward children than individuals in first marriages (e.g., Waldren et al., 1990). Moreover, remarried couples used different coping styles and were more likely to seek counseling than those in first marriages, and parents generally were perceived to be closer to children than were stepparents (Brown, Green, & Druckman, 1990; Waldren et al., 1990). Additionally, O'Connor et al. (1997) found that the patterns of relations among newly formed stepfamilies were less "coherent" than the pattern of relationships in first-marriage families. For example, mothers' marital positivity and positivity toward their adolescent children were closely related in first-marriage families but were unrelated in stepfamilies. Similarly, Fine and Kurdek (1995) found that the association between stepparents' marital quality and the quality of the stepparent-stepchild relationship was stronger than the relation between parents' marital quality and parent-child relationship quality, suggesting that the boundary between marital and stepparent-stepchild dyads is more permeable than the boundary between marital and parent-

child dyads. These findings suggest that perhaps unlike the case in first-marriage families, boundaries among subsystems in stepfamilies may be differentially permeable for different stepfamily members. In contrast, Rogers (1996a) found that marriage was less influential on mothers' parenting and children's outcomes in remarried families than in first-marriage families. Clearly, more research is needed on how stepfamily processes differ from those of first-marriage families.

Some researchers examined variations within stepfamilies. For example, legally remarried stepfather families did not differ from first-marriage families in cognitive stimulation for children, maternal warmth and responsiveness, and active structuring of the child's environment (e.g., monitoring behaviors, parental involvement in school activities), but cohabiting stepfather households differed from first-marriage families in these areas (Menaghan et al., 1997). Relationship problems of mothers and their partners were related to children's behavior problems, particularly when the partner and mother were not married.

In a comparison of family dynamics among stepfamilies and between different family structures, Banker and Gaertner (1998) found that college students who were members of first-marriage families or stepfamilies did not differ in perceived family harmony or in perceptions of being treated equally to other children in the family by adults, although stepchildren rated their families as less cooperative. The degree to which stepchildren perceived their stepfamily as one inclusive group was related to stepfamily harmony. Factors that facilitated perceiving stepfamilies as one unit instead of two included perceived cooperation, fair treatment of children by adults, and positive relationships among stepkin.

Differences in processes generally were found between clinical and nonclinical samples of stepfamilies. For example, compared with nonclinical stepfamilies, clinical stepfamilies were characterized by less involvement between stepfathers and their stepchildren, stronger tendencies toward relationship coalitions, more conflict, less emotional expressiveness, poorer problem solving, less spousal individuation, lower marital quality, and more negative and less positive parent-child interactions (Bray & Kelly, 1998). These characteristics were related to more behavior problems and less prosocial behavior for stepchildren. In another study, stepfamilies in therapy did not differ from other stepfamilies in the amount of stepparents' authority-related or nurturing behaviors and couples' ability to communicate and resolve conflicts. However, they differed in that stepchildren in non-clinical stepfamilies reciprocated appropriately rather than not reciprocating to stepparents' behaviors, as in clinical stepfamilies (Brown et al., 1990). Also, clinical stepfamilies reported more conflict and less expressiveness, and adults were less satisfied with stepparents' role performances than in nonclinical stepfamilies.

Stepfamilies develop as family units in several different ways (Baxter, Braithwaite, & Nicholson, 1999). They also configure themselves in disparate ways—as reconstituted nuclear families, as integrated but distinct cultures, as binuclear systems, and as separate units (Berger, 1995; Erera-Weatherly, 1996).

SOCIETAL VIEWS OF REMARRIAGE AND STEPFAMILIES

During the past decade, a body of work has emerged on societal views about stepfamilies. The prevailing perspective on stepfamilies, shared cross-culturally, is that they are deviant and harmful environments for children and adolescents (e.g., Ganong & Coleman, 1997; Levin, 1993). Stepfamilies are stigmatized through labels (Ganong, Coleman, & Kennedy, 1990), stereotypes (e.g., Ganong & Coleman, 1995) and cultural myths (Coleman & Ganong, 1995; Dainton, 1993). Also, the behaviors and attitudes of helping professionals are affected by negative stereotypes about stepparents (Ganong & Coleman, 1997).

When stepfamilies are not stigmatized, they are often invisible to social systems—the policies and practices of schools (Crosbie-Burnett, 1994) and youth organizations (Ganong, 1993) create barriers to participation by stepfamily members because they are based on models of first-marriage families. There is less consensus on the responsibilities that stepkin have to each other than there is about family obligations between genetic kin (e.g., Ganong & Coleman, 1999), indicating fewer norms about step-relationships. Given these findings, it is not surprising that outsiders have more favorable impressions of stepfamilies who present themselves to others as first-marriage families (Ganong et al., 1990), which could reduce stress for stepfamily members (Dainton, 1993). It has been hypothesized that stepfamilies are adversely affected by being viewed as inherently less functional than nuclear families (Ganong & Coleman, 1997), but there have been few investigations of

the effects of negative societal views on stepfamilies and stepfamily members.

Legal Issues

Both social scientists and attorneys wrote prodigiously about the absence of legal relationships between stepparents and stepchildren (e.g., Fine & Fine, 1992; Mason & Mauldon, 1996). Because the legal system in the United States has not codified stepfamily members' rights and responsibilities to each other, various solutions have been proposed, such as allowing a stepparent or a nonmarital partner who has lived with a child and the custodial parent for at least 3 years to obtain a residence order that gives him or her almost the same authority as the parent (Fine, 1997; Mason, 1998). The granting of a residence order to a stepparent does not remove parents' rights or responsibilities; rather, it means that children have legal relations with three adults. Whether such a law would work is unclear; changes in laws related to marital dissolution and reconstitution are seldom informed by research on the effects of such changes.

An Overview of Conceptual and Methodological Trends

There has been an exponential increase over the course of the 20th century in stepfamily research. The empirical knowledge base is broader, researchers from more disciplines and more countries are making contributions, investigations are more theoretically grounded and methodologically sophisticated, and more is known about stepfamilies apart from how they compare to other types of families.

In several large research projects, remarriages and stepfamilies are either the primary or among the main foci (e.g., the NEAD project, Kurdek's longitudinal project on marriages and remarriages, the Virginia Longitudinal Study of Divorce and Remarriage, Hetherington and Clingempeel's longitudinal study of stepfather households, Booth's longitudinal study of marriages, the ALSPAC study). Other longitudinal projects (e.g., the Oregon Social Learning Center study of at-risk youths) and national panel studies (e.g., NSFH) have allowed researchers to look at changes in stepfamilies and in stepfamily members over time. Both the large-scale national and regional data sets and the small-scale, intensive studies of whole households or families have enabled researchers to examine more variables and to use more sophisticated analytic strategies. In many of these studies, data have been gathered from multiple family members. There were a few more observational studies (e.g., Vuchinich et al., 1991) this decade, multiple methods of data collection were used more frequently than before, and there were more qualitative studies (e.g., Erera-Weatherly, 1996; Pyke, 1994) using a variety of approaches (e.g., ethnography, dialectics, grounded theory). The research on stepfamilies also was characterized by more frequent use of grand and midrange theories to explain phenomena and to test theoretical propositions (e.g., Banker & Gaertner, 1998; O'Connor et al., 1997). These developments in research and theory were facilitated by the increased number of researchers interested in remarriage and stepfamilies and by the maturing of several programs of research.

In contrast to earlier decades, more researchers attempted to reflect the complexity of stepfamilies in their work. Sex of the stepparent and stepchild, whether the household configuration is simple (one stepparent) or complex (both adults are stepparents), years residing together, socioeconomic status, and race were often included as control variables. Also, a few researchers distinguished between remarried stepparents and cohabiting, de facto stepparents (e.g., Bulcroft et al., 1998; Menaghan et al., 1997). However, despite the heightened sensitivity to the structural diversity of stepfamilies, researchers continued to be challenged to adequately describe the complicated dynamics and complex configurations of remarriages and stepfamilies. For instance, only a few researchers took note of the multiple pathways to creating stepfamilies, and samples did not always adequately reflect the diversity of step-relationships, either because some types of stepfamilies were excluded or because potentially important distinctions between types of stepfamilies were ignored. In addition, the interactions of stepfamily household members with nonresidential parents or former spouses and other nonresidential family members were usually ignored. Treating stepfamily households as if they were unaffected by family members not sharing a residence full time leads to distorted conclusions about stepfamily dynamics. Moreover, factors related to the larger social environments in which families reside were not included. This was true for small-scale, local samples and for many large-scale secondary data sets.

Some of the reasons why researchers disregarded stepfamily complexity are pragmatic. It is prohibitively expensive to recruit as many stepfamilies as are needed to examine or control for all relevant structural variables. Certain types of stepfamilies are hard to identify (i.e., members of father-stepmother households may share a last name; some stepfamilies are reluctant to identify themselves to researchers), so they end up being underinvestigated. Consequently, stepfather households were often the only stepfamilies studied.

The extraordinary emphasis (i.e., more than 200 studies) placed on the effects on children of living with a stepparent is probably only partially due to the importance of the issue. These studies were possible because of the availability of large data sets and the ease with which family structure and a variety of outcomes can be measured. Since at least the middle of the decade, it has been safe to conclude that stepchildren are at somewhat greater risk for educational difficulties and internalizing and for externalizing behavior problems than children living with two parents, although the vast majority of stepchildren do not exhibit these problems. Nonetheless, researchers continue to spend enormous efforts studying a similar set of child outcomes using between-group designs that compare stepchildren to children in other family structures. A typical approach is to examine the distribution of selected outcome variables by family structure, control for various demographic characteristics, and sometimes family process variables and then to see whether the relations between family structure and the outcome variables persist. Although a useful way to determine group differences, this design enlightens our understanding of family processes only incrementally. If data sets contain variables that fit with investigators' explanatory models, it can potentially be determined why one group of children differs from another based on certain predictor variables, but too often researchers are left trying to infer causal relations from correlational data. Even longitudinal data sets, which can help researchers make inferences about causality, may fall short because measures do not adequately assess constructs in researchers' explanatory models.

The emphasis of too many studies has been on identifying problems within stepfamilies; researchers focused heavily on only part of the findings (e.g., stepchildren were more likely than those living with both parents to be depressed), while barely mentioning the rest (e.g., three fourths of stepchildren were not clinically depressed). When small, but statistically significant, effects are treated by many researchers as if they were large and generalizable to all stepfamily members (Amato, 1994) or when extremist positions are taken (Cherlin, 1999), scholarship is not well served. We want to note that many researchers were careful in their reporting and interpreting of complicated findings, but to paraphrase Kuller's (1999) critique of circular epidemiology, family journals are filled with well-conducted studies that primarily repeat known findings or are variations on a theme. It is time for research on stepchildren to move on in ways we suggest in the final section of this paper.

The use of the deficit comparison approach (Coleman & Ganong, 1990) continued into this decade. Additionally, cultural values that depict the first-marriage family as the best or only acceptable family structure in which to raise children no doubt influenced social scientists (Clingempeel, Flescher, & Brand, 1987). Epistemic values that shape stepfamily research are as heavily influenced by cultural and personal beliefs as they are by the guidelines and rules for sound social science. For example, a between-group bias and deficit comparison approach taken by many researchers has been popular in part because it is congruent with a socially approved way of thinking about nonnuclear families as deficient and harmful to children. The functionalist framework is not dead; it just has gone underground. There are many examples—Popenoe (1994) recommends that the United States should discourage remarriage because stepchildren are at risk, researchers compare stepfamilies to "intact" families, and sociobiologists devote an issue of a major journal (Flinn, 1999) on studies of why stepfathers invest less in their stepchildren than parents invest in children (adoptive fathers apparently escape such scrutiny, despite lacking genetic connections to children).

Many areas of research suggested in the previous decade review remain relatively unexplored. For example, too few studies focused on stepfamily processes, we continue to be limited in our understanding of variables that contribute to positive stepfamily functioning, and we know little about factors that facilitate the formation of positive stepparent-stepchild bonds, stepsibling bonds, or remarried couple relationships. Knowledge of African American, Latino, and other ethnic stepfamilies remains woefully inadequate as well. Perhaps even more surprising is the small number of studies investigating mothers in stepfamilies. We know more about nonresidential fathers than we do about residential mothers in stepfamily households.

On a more encouraging note is the increased attention to the legal aspects of stepfamily living, although many questions about this have yet to be examined. Also encouraging is the increase in information being derived from well-designed longitudinal studies, the interest shown by researchers from communication (e.g., Baxter et al., 1999), and the application of theories and methods not previously associated with stepfamily research (e.g., Bogenscheider, 1997; O'Connor et al., 1997; Pyke, 1994).

CONCLUSIONS AND SUGGESTIONS FOR RESEARCH
IN THE NEXT MILLENNIUM

In this final section, we offer suggestions to build upon the advances made in the past decade. First, the clinical, empirical, and conceptual literatures on remarriage and stepfamilies have all suggested that change over time is both critical and constant in the life course of stepfamilies. Thus, we believe that longitudinal work is needed that assesses how stepfamily members' experiences, perceptions, interactions, and adjustment change over time, both long term (years) and shortterm (i.e., daily, weekly).

Second, we suggest that new insights on stepfamily dynamics will be gained by focusing more attention on nontraditional stepfamilies, particularly cohabiting couples and gay or lesbian couples with children. Because remarriage is the traditional gateway into a stepfamily, cohabiting couples with children generally have been overlooked in studies on stepfamilies. However, cohabiting couples with children are likely to have both similarities to (e.g., the presence of a nongenetically related adult) and differences from (e.g., marriage has legal rights and responsibilities that cohabiting arrangements do not) married couples. By investigating similarities and differences, we can add greatly to our understanding of stepfamily dynamics.

Third, although progress was made in this domain, there remains a need for within-group designs. We continue to need more studies of factors that contribute to healthy and adaptive functioning in stepfamilies. To design more effective interventions and educational programs, we need greater insights into the characteristics of well-functioning stepfamilies. Therefore, we encourage researchers to use a variety of quantitative and qualitative methods and to more frequently study a variety of processes in stepfamilies (e.g., parenting practices, marital conflict) and how they relate to the adjustment of individuals.

Fourth, research would be enhanced by studying bidirectional effects (i.e., how stepchildren are affected by their parents and stepparents and how parents and stepparents are affected by stepchildren) (e.g., see Hetherington et al., 1999). Researchers generally have narrowly conceptualized stepchildren as passive recipients of effects from parents and stepparents, but there is evidence that stepchildren's responses to stepparents may be critical in developing stepfamily relationships.

Fifth, because families are too often conceptualized as households, we call for more studies that include nonresidential parents and other nonresidential family members. Researchers cannot continue to assume that where a child lives is static rather than changing; there is ample evidence that many children who do not share a household with both parents nonetheless live at various times with both parents.

Sixth, we recommend more studies of how stepfamilies interface with other societal institutions. Stepfamily members are clearly affected by social policies and by cultural attitudes, and they affect change in social policies and cultural attitudes as well. Stepfamily members adopt roles from cultural norms, and they also create their own roles that influence cultural attitudes and, eventually, social policy.

Seventh, we strongly support theory-based research. Research increasingly has been grounded in conceptual frameworks, but there is room for improvement. Advances in knowledge will occur more rapidly if researchers both use and explicitly identify the theoretical considerations underlying their work. Theoretical grounding yields numerous benefits, including clearer definitions of key constructs, the potential for greater consensus in which measures might be used to assess particular constructs, and greater acknowledgment of how different methods can yield complimentary contributions to our understanding.

Finally, we encourage more qualitative work that examines the experiences, perceptions, and reflections of stepfamily members. Quantitative studies have yielded tremendous benefits, but we also need research that explores the mechanisms underlying some of the trends, patterns, and relations found in quantitative work. We need studies of the meanings of experiences for people. We could gain considerable insight from such qualitative approaches as in-depth interviewing and grounded theory approaches to data analysis. In addition, the triangulation of methods (qualitative and quantitative) can be used to better capture stepfamily processes. Future work should combine biological, psychological, interpersonal, and cultural influences on individuals and families. The increase in the volume of studies in the past decade has been phenomenal, the increase in quality has been steady, and yet there is much to know to enhance our understanding of stepfamilies.

REFERENCES

Amato, P. R. (1994). The implications of research findings on children in stepfamilies. In A. Booth & J. Dunn (Eds.), *Stepfamilies: Who benefits? Who does not?* (pp. 81–87). Hillsdale, NJ: Erlbaum.

Amato, P. R. (2000). The consequences of divorce for adults and children. *Journal of Marriage and the Family, 62* .

Amato, P. R., Rezac, S., & Booth, A. (1995). Helping between parents and young adult offspring: The role of parental marital quality, divorce, and remarriage. *Journal of Marriage and the Family, 57,* 363–374.

Aquilino, W. S. (1991a). Predicting parents' experiences with coresident adult children. *Journal of Family Issues, 12,* 323–342.

Aquilino, W. S. (1991b). Family structure and home-leaving: A further specification of the relationship. *Journal of Marriage and the Family, 53,* 999–1010.

Aquilino, W. S. (1994). Impact of childhood family disruption on young adults' relationships with parents. *Journal of Marriage and the Family, 56,* 295–313.

Astone, N. M., & McLanahan, S. S. (1991). Family structure, parental practices and high school completion. *American Sociological Review, 56,* 309–320.

Astone, N. M., & Washington, M. L. (1994). The association between grandparental coresidence and adolescent childbearing. *Journal of Family Issues, 15,* 574–589.

Banker, B. S., & Gaertner, S. L. (1998). Achieving stepfamily harmony: An intergroup-relations approach. *Journal of Family Psychology, 12,* 310–325.

Barber, B. (1994). Cultural, family, and personal contexts of parent-adolescent conflict. *Journal of Marriage and the Family, 56,* 375–386.

Barber, B. L., & Lyons, J. M. (1994). Family processes and adolescent adjustment in intact and remarried families. *Journal of Youth and Adolescence, 23,* 421–436.

Baxter, L., Braithwaite, D., & Nicholson, J. (1999). Turning points in the development of blended families. *Journal of Social and Personal Relationships, 16,* 291–313.

Berger, R. (1995). Three types of stepfamilies. *Journal of Divorce and Remarriage, 24,* 35–50.

Biblarz, T. J., Raftery, A. E., & Bucur, A. (1997). Family structure and social mobility. *Social Forces, 75,* 1319–1339.

Bogenscheider, K. (1997). Parental involvement in adolescent schooling: A proximal process with transcontextual validity. *Journal of Marriage and the Family, 59,* 718–733.

Booth, A., & Amato, P. R. (1991). Divorce and psychological stress. *Journal of Health and Social Behavior, 32,* 396–407.

Booth, A., & Dunn, J. (Eds.). (1994). *Stepfamilies: Who benefits? Who does not?* Hillsdale, NJ: Erlbaum.

Booth, A., & Edwards, J. N. (1992). Starting over: Why remarriages are more unstable. *Journal of Family Issues, 13,* 179–194.

Bray, J., & Kelly, J. (1998). *Stepfamilies.* New York: Broadway.

Bronstein, P., Stoll, M., Clauson, J., Abrams, C. L., & Briones, M. (1994). Fathering after separation or divorce: Factors predicting children's adjustment. *Family Relations, 43,* 469–479.

Brown, S. L., & Booth, A. (1996). Cohabitation versus marriage: A comparison of relationship quality. *Journal of Marriage and the Family, 58,* 668–678.

Brown, A. C., Green, R.-J., & Druckman, J. (1990). A comparison of stepfamilies with and without child-focused problems. *American Journal of Orthopsychiatry, 60,* 556–566.

Buckle, L., Gallup, G. G., & Rodd, Z. A. (1996). Marriage as a reproductive contract: Patterns of marriage, divorce, and remarriage. *Ethology and Sociobiology, 17,* 363–377.

Bulcroft, R., Carmody, D., & Bulcroft, K. (1998). Family structure and patterns of independence giving to adolescents. *Journal of Family Issues, 19,* 404–435.

Bumpass, L., Raley, R. K., & Sweet, J. (1995). The changing character of stepfamilies: Implications of cohabitation and nonmarital childbearing. *Demography, 32,* 425–436.

Bumpass, L., Sweet, J., & Castro Martin, T. (1990). Changing patterns of remarriage. *Journal of Marriage and the Family, 52,* 747–756.

Bumpass, L. L., Sweet, J. A., & Cherlin, A. (1991). The role of cohabitation in declining rates of marriage. *Journal of Marriage and the Family, 53,* 913–927.

Burgoyne, C. B., & Morison, V. (1997). Money in remarriage: Keeping things simple–and separate. *Sociological Review, 45,* 363–395.

Capaldi, D. M., & Patterson, G. R. (1991). Relation of parental transitions to boys' adjustment problems: I. A linear hypotheses. II. Mothers at risk for transitions and unskilled parenting. *Developmental Psychology, 27,* 489–504.

Chase-Lansdale, P. L., Cherlin, A. J., & Kiernan, K. E. (1995). The long-term effects of parental divorce on the mental health of young adults: A developmental perspective. *Child Development, 66,* 1614–1634.

Cherlin, A. (1978). Remarriage as an incomplete institution. *American Journal of Sociology, 84,* 634–650.

Cherlin, A. J. (1992). Marriage, divorce, remarriage. *Social trends in the United States.* Cambridge, MA: Harvard University Press.

Cherlin, A. J., & Furstenberg, F. F. (1994). Stepfamilies in the United States: A reconsideration. *Annual Review of Sociology, 20,* 359–381.

Cherlin, A. J. (1999). Going to extremes: Family structure, children's well-being, and social science. *Demography, 36,* 421–428.

Cherlin, A. J., & Furstenberg, F. F., Chase-Lansdale, P., Kiernan, K., Robins, P. K., Morrison, D. R., & Teitler, J. O. (1991). Longitudinal studies of the effects of divorce on children in Great Britain and the United States. *Science, 252,* 1386–1389.

Chevan, A. (1996). As cheaply as one: Cohabitation in the older population. *Journal of Marriage and the Family, 58,* 656–667.

Church, E. (1999). Who are the people in your family? Stepmothers' diverse notions of kinship. *Journal of Divorce and Remarriage, 31,* 83–105.

Clarke, S. C., & Wilson, B. F. (1994). The relative stability of remarriages: A cohort approach using vital statistics. *Family Relations, 43,* 305–310.

Clingempeel, G., Colyar, J., & Hetherington, E. M. (1994). Toward a cognitive dissonance conceptualization of stepchildren and biological children loyalty conflicts: A construct validity study. In K. Pasley & M. Ihinger-Tallman (Ed.), *Stepparenting: Issues in theory, research, and practice* (pp. 151–174). Westport, CT: Greenwood.

Clingempeel, G., Flescher, M., & Brand, E. (1987). Research on stepfamilies: Paradigmatic constraints and alternative proposals. In J. P. Vincent (Ed.), *Advances in family intervention: Assessment and theory* (pp. 229–251). Greenwich, CT: JAI.

Cohen, J. (1969). *Statistical power analysis for the behavioral sciences.* New York: Academic Press.

Coleman, M., & Ganong, L. (1990). Remarriage and stepfamily research in the 80s: New interest in an old family form. *Journal of Marriage and the Family, 52,* 925–940.

Coleman, M., & Ganong, L. (1995). Insiders' and outsiders' beliefs about stepfamilies: Assessments and implications for practice. In D. Huntley (Ed.), *Assessment of stepfamilies* (pp. 101–112). American Counseling Association Press.

Coleman, M., Ganong, L., & Cable, S. (1997). Perceptions of stepparents: An examination of the incomplete institutionalization and social stigma hypotheses. *Journal of Divorce and Remarriage, 26,* 25–48.

Coley, R. L. (1998). Children's socialization experiences and functioning in single-mother households: The importance of fathers and other men. *Child Development, 69,* 219–230.

Cooksey, E. C., & Fondell, M. M. (1996). Spending time with his kids: Effects of family structure on fathers' and children's lives. *Journal of Marriage and the Family, 58,* 693–707.

Cornman, J. M., & Kingson, E. R. (1996). Trends, issues, perspectives, and values for the aging of the baby boom cohorts. *Gerontologist, 36,* 15–26.

Coughlin, C., & Vuchinich, S. (1996). Family experience in preadolescent and the development of male delinquency. *Journal of Marriage and the Family, 58,* 491–501.

Crosbie-Burnett, M. (1994). The interface between stepparent families and schools: Research, theory, policy, and practice. In K. Pasley & M. Ihinger-Tallman (Eds.), *Stepparenting: Issues in theory, research, and practice* (pp. 199–216). Westport, CT: Greenwood.

Crosbie-Burnett, M., & Giles-Sims, J. (1991). Marital power in stepfather families: A test of normative-resource theory. *Journal of Family Psychology, 4,* 484–496.

Crosbie-Burnett, M., & Giles-Sims, J. (1994). Adolescent adjustment and stepparenting styles. *Family Relations, 43,* 394–399.

Dainton, M. (1993). The myths and misconceptions of the stepmother identity: Descriptions and prescriptions for identity management. *Family Relations, 42,* 93–98.

Daly, M., & Wilson, M. I. (1996). Violence against stepchildren. *Current Directions in Psychological Science, 5,* 77–80.

Day, R. D. (1992). The transition to first intercourse among racially and culturally diverse youth. *Journal of Marriage and the Family, 54,* 749–762.

Dawson, D. A. (1991). Family structure and children's health and well-being: Data from the 1988 National Health Interview Survey on Child Health. *Journal of Marriage and the Family, 53,* 573–584.

Deal, J. E., Stanley-Hagan, M., & Anderson, J. C. (1992). The marital relationships in remarried families. *Monographs of the Society for Research in Child Development, 57* (2–3), Serial No. 227.

Demo, D. H., & Acock, A. C. (1993). Family diversity and the division of domestic labor: How much have things really changed? *Family Relations, 42,* 323–331.

Doherty, W., & Needle, R. (1991). Psychological adjustment and substance use among adolescents before and after a parental divorce. *Child Development, 62,* 328–337.

Dorius, G. L., Heaton, T. B., & Steffen, P. (1993). Adolescent life events and their association with the onset of sexual intercourse. *Youth and Society, 25,* 3–23.

Downey, D. B. (1995). Understanding academic achievement among children in stephouseholds: The role of parental resources, sex of stepparent, and sex of child. *Social Forces, 73,* 875–894.

Dronkers, J. (1994). The changing effects of lone parent families on the educational attainment of their children in a European welfare state. *Sociology, 28,* 171–191.

Dunn, J., Deater-Deckard, K., Pickering, K., O'Connor, T. G., Golding, J., & the ALSPAC Study Team. (1998). Children's adjustment and prosocial behaviour in step-, single-parent, and non-stepfamily settings: Findings from a community study. *Journal of Child Psychology and Psychiatry, 39,* 1083–1095.

Erera-Weatherly, P. (1996). On becoming a stepparent: Factors associated with the adoption of alternative stepparenting styles. *Journal of Divorce and Remarriage, 25,* 155–174.

Fine, M. A. (1997). Stepfamilies from a policy perspective: Guidance from the empirical literature. *Marriage and Family Review, 26,* 249–264.

Fine, M. A., Coleman, M., & Ganong, L. (1998). Consistency in perceptions of the stepparent role among stepparents, parents, and stepchildren. *Journal of Social and Personal Relationships, 15,* 810–828.

Fine, M. A., & Fine, D. R. (1992). Recent changes in laws affecting stepfamilies: Suggestions for legal reform. *Family Relations, 41,* 334–340.

Fine, M., Ganong, L., & Coleman, M. (1997). The relation between role constructions and adjustment among stepparents. *Journal of Family Issues, 18,* 503–525.

Fine, M., & Kurdek, L. (1992). The adjustment of adolescents in stepfather and stepmother families. *Journal of Marriage and the Family, 54,* 725–736.

Fine, M., & Kurdek, L. (1994). A multidimensional cognitive-developmental of stepfamily adjustment. In K. Pasley & M. Ihinger-Tallman (Eds.), *Stepparent-*

ing: Issues in theory, research, and practice (pp. 15–32). Westport, CT: Greenwood.

Fine, M. A., & Kurdek, L. A. (1995). Relation between marital quality and (step)parent-child relationships quality for parents and stepparents in stepfamilies. *Journal of Family Psychology, 9,* 216–223.

Flinn, M. (1999). Growth and fluctuating asymmetry of stepchildren. *Evolution and Human Behavior, 20,* 465–479.

Furstenberg, F. F., Jr., & Cherlin, A. J. (1991). *Divided families: What happens to children when parents part.* Cambridge, MA: Harvard University Press.

Ganong, L. (1993). Family diversity in a youth organization: Involvement of single-parents families and stepfamilies in 4-H. *Family Relations, 42,* 286–292.

Ganong, L., & Coleman, M. (1994a). Adolescent stepchild-stepparent relationships: Changes over time. In K. Pasley & M. Ihinger-Tallman (Eds.), *Stepparenting: Issues in theory, research, and practice* (pp. 87–106). New York: Greenwood.

Ganong, L., & Coleman, M. (1994b). *Remarried family relationships.* Newbury Park, CA: Sage.

Ganong, L., & Coleman, M. (1995). The content of mother stereotypes. *Sex Roles, 32,* 495–512.

Ganong, L., & Coleman, M. (1997). How society views stepfamilies. *Marriage and Family Review, 26,* 85–106.

Ganong, L., & Coleman, M. (1999). *New families, new responsibilities: Intergenerational obligations following divorce and remarriage.* Hillsdale, NJ: Erlbaum.

Ganong, L., Coleman, M., Fine, M., & Martin, P. (1999). Stepparents' affinity-seeking and affinity-maintaining strategies with stepchildren. *Journal of Family Issues, 20,* 299–327.

Ganong, L., Coleman, M., & Kennedy, G. (1990). The effects of using alternate labels in denoting stepparent or stepfamily status. *Journal of Social Behavior and Personality, 5,* 453–463.

Gelles, R. J., & Harrop, J. W. (1991). The risk of abusive violence among children with nongenetic caretakers. *Family Relations, 40,* 78–83.

Giles-Sims, J. (1997). Current knowledge about child abuse in stepfamilies. In I. Levin & M. Sussman (Eds.), *Stepfamilies: History, research, and policy* (pp. 215–230). New York: Haworth.

Goldscheider, F., & Goldscheider, C. (1998). The effects of childhood family structure on leaving and returning home. *Journal of Marriage and the Family, 60,* 745–756.

Hanson, T. L., McLanahan, S. S., & Thomson, E. (1996). Double jeopardy; Parental conflict and stepfamily outcomes for children. *Journal of Marriage and the Family, 58,* 141–154.

Hawkins, A. J., & Eggebeen, D. J. (1991). Are fathers fungible? Patterns of coresident adult men in maritally disrupted families and young children's well-being. *Journal of Marriage and the Family, 53,* 958–72.

Henry, C. S., & Lovelace, S. G. (1995). Family resources and adolescent family life satisfaction in remarried family households. *Journal of Family Issues, 16,* 765–786.

Hetherington, M. (1993). An overview of the Virginia longitudinal study of divorce and remarriage with a focus on early adolescence. *Journal of Family Psychology, 7,* 39–56.

Hetherington, E. M., & Clingempeel, W. G. (1992). Coping with marital transitions: A family systems perspective. *Monographs of the Society for Research in Child Development, 57* (2–3, Serial No. 227).

Hetherington, E. M., & Henderson, S. H. (1997). Fathers in stepfamilies. In M. Lamb (Ed.), *The role of fathers in child development (3rd ed.)* (Pp. 212–226). Erlbaum.

Hetherington, E. M., Henderson, S., & Reiss, D., in collaboration with Anderson, E., Bridges, M., Chan, R., Insabella, G., Jodl, K., Kim, J., Mitchell, A., O'Connor, T., Skaggs, M., & Taylor, L. (1999). *Adolescent siblings in stepfamilies: Family functioning and adolescent adjustment.* Monographs of the Society for Research in Child Development, 64 (4, Serial No. 259). Malden, MA: Blackwell.

Hobart, C. (1991). Conflict in remarriages. *Journal of Divorce and Remarriage, 15,* 69–86.

Hoffmann, J. P., & Johnson, R. A. (1998). A national portrait of family structure and adolescent drug use. *Journal of Marriage and the Family, 60,* 633–645.

Holden, K. C., & Kuo, H.-H. D. (1996). Complex marital histories and economic well-being: The continuing legacy of divorce and widowhood as the HRS cohort approaches retirement. *Gerontologist, 36,* 383–390.

Ihinger-Tallman, M., & Pasley, K. (1997). Stepfamilies in 1984 and today—a scholarly perspective. In I. Levin & M. Sussman (Eds.), *Stepfamilies: History, research, and policy* (pp. 19–40). New York: Haworth.

Ishii-Kuntz, M., & Coltrane, S. (1992). Remarriage, stepparenting, and household labor. *Journal of Family Issues, 13,* 215–233.

Jacobson, D. (1993). What's fair: Concepts of financial management in stepfamily households. *Journal of Divorce and Remarriage, 19,* 221–238.

Jacobson, D. (1995). Incomplete institution or culture shock: Institutional and processual models of stepfamily instability. *Journal of Divorce and Remarriage, 24,* 3–18.

Kiernan, K. E. (1992). The impact of family disruption in childhood on transitions made in young adult life. *Population Studies, 46,* 213–234.

Kim, J. E., Hetherington, E. M., & Reiss, D. (1999). Associations among family relationships, antisocial peers, and adolescents' externalizing behaviors: Gender and family type differences. *Child Development, 70,* 1209–1230.

Kuller, L. (1999). Invited commentary: Circular epidemiology. *American Journal of Epidemiology, 150,* 897–903.

Kurdek, L. A. (1991). Predictors of increases in marital distress in newlywed couples: A 3-year prospective longitudinal study. *Developmental Psychology, 27,* 627–636.

Kurdek, L. (1999). The nature and predictors of the trajectory of change of marital quality for husbands and wives over the first 10 years of marriage. *Developmental Psychology, 35,* 1283–1296.

Kurdek, L., & Fine, M. (1993a). The relation between family structure and young adolescents' appraisals of family climate and parenting behavior. *Journal of Family Issues, 14,* 279–290.

Kurdek, L., & Fine, M. (1993b). Parent and nonparent residential family members as providers of warmth

and supervision to young adolescents. *Journal of Family Psychology, 7,* 245–249.

Kurdek, L. A., & Fine, M. A. (1995). Mothers, fathers, stepfathers, and siblings as providers of supervision, acceptance, and autonomy to young adolescents. *Journal of Family Psychology, 9,* 95–99.

Lee, V., Burkam, D., Zimiles, H., & Ladewski, B. (1994). Family structure and its effect on behavioral and emotional problems in young adolescents. *Journal of Research on Adolescence, 4,* 405–437.

Leung, J. J. (1995). Family configurations and students' perceptions of parental support for schoolwork. *Sociological Imagination, 32,* 185–196.

Levin, I. (1993). Family as mapped realities. *Journal of Family Issues, 14,* 82–91.

Lissau, I., & Sorensen, T. I. A. (1994). Parental neglect during childhood and increased risk of obesity in young adulthood. *Lancet, 343,* 324–327.

MacDonald, W., & DeMaris, A. (1996). Parenting stepchildren and biological children: The effects of stepparent's gender and new biological children. *Journal of Family Issues, 17,* 5–25.

Malkin, C. M., & Lamb, M. E. (1994). Child maltreatment: A test of sociobiological theory. *Journal of Comparative Family Studies, 25,* 121–133.

Margolin, L. (1992). Child abuse by mothers' boyfriends: Why the overrepresentation? *Child Abuse and Neglect, 16,* 541–551.

Marks, N. F. (1995). Midlife marital status differences in social support relationships with adult children and psychological well-being. *Journal of Family Issues 16,* 5–28.

Marsiglio, W. (1992). Stepfathers with minor children living at home: Parenting perceptions and relationship quality. *Journal of Family Issues, 13,* 195–214.

Mason, M. A. (1998). The modern American stepfamily: Problems and possibilities. In M. Mason & A. Skolnick (Eds.), *All our families: New policies for a new century* (pp. 95–116). New York: Oxford University Press.

Mason, M. A., & Mauldon, J. (1996). The new stepfamily requires a new public policy. *Journal of Social Issues, 52,* 11–27.

McKenry, P., McKelvey, M., Leigh, D., & Wark, L. (1996). Nonresidential father involvement: A comparison of divorced, separated, never married, and remarried fathers. *Journal of Divorce and Remarriage, 25,* 1–13.

Mekos, D., Hetherington, E. M., & Reiss, D. (1996). Sibling differences in problem behavior and parental treatment in nondivorced and remarried families. *Child Development, 67,* 2148–2165.

Menaghan, E. G., Kowaleski-Jones, L., & Mott, F. L. (1997). The intergenerational costs of parental social stressors: Academic and social difficulties in early adolescence for children of young mothers. *Journal of Health and Social Behavior, 38,* 72–86.

Montalto, C. P., & Gerner, J. L. (1998). The effect of expected changes in marital status on labor supply decisions of women and men. *Journal of Divorce and Remarriage, 28,* 25–51.

Montgomery, M. J., Anderson, E. R., Hetherington, E. M., & Clingempeel, W. G. (1992). Patterns of courtship for remarriage: Implications for child adjustment and parent-child relationships. *Journal of Marriage and the Family, 54,* 686–698.

Murphy, M., Glaser, K., & Grundy, E. (1997). Marital status and long-term illness in Great Britain. *Journal of Marriage and the Family, 59,* 156–164.

National Center for Health Statistics. (1993). *1988 marriages: Number of the marriage by of bride by groom* [Computer program]. Washington, DC: NCHS Computer Center.

Needle, R., Su, S., & Doherty, W. (1990). Divorce, remarriage, and adolescent substance use: A prospective longitudinal study. *Journal of Marriage and the Family, 52,* 157–169.

Neff, J. A., & Schluter, T. D. (1993). Marital status and depressive symptoms: The role of race/ethnicity and sex. *Journal of Divorce and Remarriage, 20,* 137–160.

Nielsen, L. (1999). Stepmothers: Why so much stress? A review of the research. *Journal of Divorce and Remarriage, 30,* 115–148.

O'Connor, T. G., Hetherington, E. M., & Clingempeel, W. G. (1997). Systems and bidirectional influences in families. *Journal of Social and Personal Relationships, 14,* 491–504.

O'Connor, T. G., Hetherington, E. M., & Reiss, D. (1998). Family systems and adolescent development: Shared and nonshared risk and protective factors in nondivorced and remarried families. *Development and Psychopathology, 10,* 353–375.

O'Connor, T. G., Pickering, K., Dunn, J., Golding, J., & the ALSPAC Study Team. (1999). Frequency and predictors of relationship dissolution in a community sample in England. *Journal of Family Psychology, 13,* 436–449.

Pasley, K., & Ihinger-Tallman, M. (1990). Remarriage in later adulthood: Correlates of perceptions of family adjustment. *Family Perspectives, 24,* 263–274.

Pasley, K., Koch, M., & Ihinger-Tallman, M. (1993). Problems in remarriage: An exploratory study of intact and terminated remarriages. *Journal of Divorce and Remarriage, 20,* 63–83.

Pasley, K., Sandras, E., & Edmondson, M. (1994). The effects of financial management strategies on the quality of family life in remarriage. *Journal of Family and Economic Issues, 15,* 53–70.

Phillips, R. (1997). Stepfamilies from a historical perspective. In I. Levin & M. Sussman (Eds.), *Stepfamilies: History, research, and policy* (pp. 5–18). New York: Haworth.

Pong, S.-L. (1997). Family structure, school context, and eighth grade math and reading achievement. *Journal of Marriage and the Family, 59,* 734–746.

Popenoe, D. (1994). The evolution of marriage and the problem of stepfamilies. In A. Booth & J. Dunn (Eds.), *Stepfamilies: Who benefits? Who does not?* (pp. 3–27). Hillsdale, NJ: Erlbaum.

Pyke, K. D. (1994). Women's employment as a gift or burden? Marital power across marriage, divorce, and remarriage. *Gender and Society, 8,* 73–91.

Pyke, K., & Coltrane, S. (1996). Entitlement, obligation, and gratitude in family work. *Journal of Family Issues, 17,* 60–82.

Richards, M., Hardy, R., & Wadsworth, M. (1997). The effects of divorce and separation on mental health in a national UK birth cohort. *Psychological Medicine, 27,* 1121–1128.

Rodgers, B. (1994). Pathways between parental divorce and adult depression. *Journal of Child Psychology and Psychiatry, 35,* 1289–1994.

Rodgers, B., Power, C., & Hope, S. (1997). Parental divorce and adult psychological distress: Evidence from a national birth cohort: A research note. *Journal of Child Psychology and Psychiatry, 38,* 867–872.

Rogers, S. (1996a). Marital quality, mothers' parenting and children's outcomes: A comparison of mother/father and mother/stepfather families. *Sociological Focus, 29,* 325–340.

Rogers, S. J. (1996b). Mothers' work hours and marital quality: Variations by family structure and family size. *Journal of Marriage and the Family, 58,* 606–617.

Russell, A., & Searcy, E. (1997). The contribution of affective reactions and relationship qualities to adolescents' reported responses to parents. *Journal of Social & Personal Relationships, 14,* 539–548.

Salem, D., Zimmerman, M., & Notaro, P. (1998). Effects of family structure, family process, and father involvement on psychosocial outcomes among African American adolescents. *Family Relations, 47,* 331–341.

Seltzer, J. A. (1994). Intergenerational ties in adulthood and childhood experience. In A. Booth & J. Dunn (Eds.), *Stepfamilies: Who benefits? Who does not?* (pp. 153–163). Hillsdale, NJ: Erlbaum.

Shapiro, A. D. (1996). Explaining psychological distress in a sample of remarried and divorced persons: The influence of economic distress. *Journal of Family Issues, 17,* 186–203.

Shucksmith, J., Hendry, L. B., & Glendinning, A. (1995). Models of parenting: Implications for adolescent well being within different types of family contexts. *Journal of Adolescence, 18,* 253–270.

Skopin, A. R., Newman, B. M., & McKenry, P. (1993). Influences on the quality of stepfather-adolescent relationships: View of both family members. *Journal of Divorce and Remarriage, 19,* 181–196.

South, S. J. (1991). Sociodemographic differentials in mate selection preferences. *Journal of Marriage and the Family, 53,* 928–940.

Spitze, G., & Logan, J. (1992). Helping as a component of parent-adult child relations. *Research on Aging, 14,* 291–312.

Stephen, E. H., Freedman, V. A., & Hess, J. (1993). Near and far: Contact of children with their non-residential fathers. *Journal of Divorce and Remarriage, 20,* 171–191.

Suh, T., Schutz, C. G., & Johanson, C. E. (1996). Family structure and initiating non-medical drug use among adolescents. *Journal of Child & Adolescent Substance Abuse, 5,* 21–36.

Szinovacz, M. E. (1998). Grandparents today: A demographic profile. *Gerontologist, 38,* 37–52.

Teachman, J. D., Paasch, K., & Carver, K. (1996). Social capital and dropping out of school early. *Journal of Marriage and the Family, 58,* 773–783.

Thoits, P. A. (1992). Identity structures and psychological well-being: Gender and marital status comparisons. *Social Psychology Quarterly, 55,* 236–256.

Thomson, E., McLanahan, S. S., & Curtin, R. B. (1992). Family structure, gender, and parental socialization. *Journal of Marriage and the Family, 54,* 368–378.

Thornton, A. (1991). Influence of the marital history of parents on the marital & cohabitational experiences of children. *American Journal of Sociology, 64,* 868–894.

U.S. Bureau of the Census. (1995). *Statistical abstract of the United States:* 1995. (115th ed.). Washington, DC: U.S. Government Printing Office.

Vuchinich, S., Hetherington, E. M., Vuchinich, R., & Clingempeel, G. (1991). Parent-child interaction and gender differences in early adolescents' adaptation to stepfamilies. *Developmental Psychology, 27,* 618–626.

Vuchinich, S., Vuchinich, R., & Wood, B. (1993). The interparental relationship and family problem-solving with preadolescent males. *Child Development, 64,* 1389–1400.

Waldren, T., Bell, N., Peek, C., & Sorell, G. (1990). Cohesion and adaptability in post-divorce remarried and first-married families: Relationships with family stress and coping styles. *Journal of Divorce and Remarriage, 14,* 13–28.

White, L. K. (1992). The effect of parental divorce and remarriage on parental support for adult children. *Journal of Family Issues, 13,* 234–250.

Whitsett, D., & Land, H. (1992). Role strain, coping, and marital satisfaction of stepparents. *Families in Society, 73,* 79–91.

Wilson, B., & Clarke, S. (1992). Remarriages: A demographic profile. *Journal of Family Issues, 13,* 123–141.

Wineberg, H. (1990). Childbearing after remarriage. *Journal of Marriage and the Family, 52,* 31–38.

Wineberg, H., & McCarthy, J. (1998). Living arrangements after divorce: Cohabitation versus remarriage. *Journal of Divorce and Remarriage, 29,* 131–146.

Wojtkewicz, R. A. (1993). Duration in parental structures and high school graduation. *Sociological Perspectives, 36,* 393–414.

Wojtkiewicz, R. A. (1994). Parental structure experiences of children: Exposure, transitions, and type at birth. *Population Research & Policy Review, 13,* 141–159.

Wu, Z. (1994). Remarriage in Canada: A social exchange perspective. *Journal of Divorce and Remarriage, 21,* 191–224.

Wu, Z., & Penning, M. (1997). Marital instability after midlife. *Journal of Family Issues, 18,* 459–478.

Zill, N., Morrison, D. R., & Cioro, M. J. (1993). Long-term effects of parental divorce on parent-child relationships, adjustment, and achievement in young adulthood. *Journal of Family Psychology, 7,* 91–103.